DATE DUE

		DISCARD	
GAYLORD			PRINTED IN U.S.A.

THE CAMBRIDGE GUIDE TO THE
MUSEUMS
OF EUROPE

KENNETH HUDSON
AND
ANN NICHOLLS

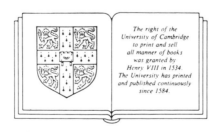

*The right of the
University of Cambridge
to print and sell
all manner of books
was granted by
Henry VIII in 1534.
The University has printed
and published continuously
since 1584.*

CAMBRIDGE UNIVERSITY PRESS

CAMBRIDGE

NEW YORK   PORT CHESTER

MELBOURNE   SYDNEY

Published by the Press Syndicate of the University of Cambridge
The Pitt Building, Trumpington Street, Cambridge CB2 1RP
40 West 20th Street, New York, NY 10011-4211, USA
10 Stamford Road, Oakleigh, Melbourne 3166, Australia

First published 1991

Printed in Great Britain by Ebenezer Baylis, Worcester

Designed by Chris McLeod

Maps by Jeff Edwards

British Library cataloguing in publication data

Hudson, Kenneth 1916–
The Cambridge guide to the museums of Europe.
1. Europe. Museums
I. Title II. Nicholls, Ann
069.094

Library of Congress cataloguing in publication data

Hudson, Kenneth,
The Cambridge guide to the museums of Europe/Kenneth Hudson and Ann Nicholls.
p.   cm.
Includes indexes.
ISBN 0–521–37175 9
1. Museums—Europe—Directories.
2. Europe—Description and travel—1991– —Guide-books.
I. Nicholls, Ann.
II. Title.
AM40.H83   1991
069'.025'4—dc20   90–27183 CIP

ISBN 0 521 37175 9 hardback

Frontispiece: **The Musée d'Orsay, Paris, transformed in 1986 from a railway station and hotel into a national museum of art.**

(Photo: Jim Purcell, Musée d'Orsay/Musées Nationaux)

CONTENTS

INTRODUCTION

This is the first-ever guide to the museums of western Europe. It reflects the new tendency to think of Europe as a whole, rather than as a collection of self-contained political, economic and cultural units, a tendency which is certain to grow stronger with the coming of the Single Europe Act in 1992.

As the Director and Administrator of the European Museum of the Year Award since its beginnings in 1976, and as constant travellers throughout the twenty countries which make up the membership of the Council of Europe under whose auspices the Award operates, we believe we can fairly claim to have an unequalled knowledge of the area's 15,000 museums. In making the selection contained in these pages, we have kept particularly in mind the needs of the more active and independent tourists, the people who like to plan itineraries themselves and make their own way around, discovering non-obvious and non-hackneyed places. We have therefore concentrated on locations away from capital cities and on museums which illustrate particular aspects of a country's character, history and culture – its natural environment, its handicrafts and industries, the life and work of its painters, scientists, statesmen and religious leaders.

The aim has been to provide a good balance of museums and to offer a satisfying variety, both to those who use the *Guide* as a source of travel information and to those who find pleasure in it as a book to dip into. What is contained here is, in museum terms, both a portrait of each country and a mirror of Europe. Nobody, we hope, could even skim the book without realising that, whatever national differences may exist within it, Europe has a flavour and a set of values and traditions of its own, a totality which unmistakably marks it off from other continents. This has been the rationale for grouping Europe's museums together between the same covers, to show what the Council of Europe's member-states have in common culturally and historically and, at the same time, to illustrate how they preserve the national identities which make travel worthwhile.

Museums reveal the bones, the blood and the priorities of a nation. It is no accident that France has so many museums devoted to its writers, generals and politicians, that Italy is so anxious to honour its painters and musicians, and that the majority of the museums in Greece are concerned in one way or another with archaeology. But, precisely because life in Italy contains many interesting ingredients besides art and music and because not everything of value in Greece is of an archaeological nature, we have taken particular pains to include museums in these countries which introduce visitors to other aspects of the national character and culture. As Greeks know all too well, humankind does not live by temples and statues alone.

Although this is a book primarily for foreign visitors – Britons planning travel in mainland Greece, Swedes in Portugal, Germans in Spain, Americans everywhere – we hope that locals will find pleasure in seeing their national and regional temples through the eyes of people born and reared elsewhere. Readers may occasionally be puzzled and perhaps annoyed to discover that certain cherished museums have been omitted. In response, we should explain that we could find room for rather less than one in seven of Europe's museums, and each of our chosen 2,000 had to fight hard for a place. Those which we felt obliged to lay aside included many local museums of a general nature, with no strongly marked specialisation, and a number, often excellent in themselves, which could be visited only by appointment or which were open very infrequently. In general, only local people are likely to be greatly attracted by a museum, however good, which is accessible no more frequently than the first Sunday afternoon of the month.

If a museum has an interesting history or if there is something special about the building, we have said so. We have also drawn attention, through the symbols in individual entries, to those museums which do more than display objects and which show evidence of concern for making visits as pleasant and comfortable as possible, providing a café or restaurant, a shop or bookstall, facilities for the disabled, and somewhere to park. All in all, we have tried to pack as much information as possible into a comparatively small space so that potential visitors can make their plans in the reasonably certain knowledge that they will find what they think they are going to find.

It may be useful to indicate certain general features of the European museum scene – that the further north one goes, the better the facilities for disabled people are likely to be; that museum cafés become rarer and rarer as one moves towards the Mediterranean, especially in Italy, where State and municipal museums are forbidden to undertake any kind of money-making enterprise; that car-parking facilities almost never exist at museums in large cities, and that a southern climate is no guarantee at all that a museum will be even tolerably warm in winter. On the whole, however, the standard of Europe's museums is steadily rising and today's visitors can expect a higher level of presentation and greater attempt to attract and please the public than ten years ago. In terms of visitor comfort, the 2,000 or so museums described in the present *Guide* are also, in most respects, above average.

We have certainly not favoured large museums at the expense of small ones. On the contrary, many of the museums featured, including a number of the best, employ fewer than ten people. We realise, however, that every country has a handful of museums which most travellers feel they should see once in a lifetime. These, the British Museum in London, the Louvre in Paris, the Uffizi in Florence, the Prado in Madrid, we call flagship museums. In their methods of presentation, their amenities, their attitude to the public, some of them do not try as hard as they might, but on lists of places to be visited, they are musts.

This is the first appearance of a publication which we hope will have many subsequent editions. Looking ahead no further than the second, one can be reasonably sure that coverage of what will need to be an enlarged *Guide* will extend into central and eastern Europe, once the dust has settled on recent political events, not least German unification, and the new pattern of Europe's museums has become clear. The future promises to lend new vigour to cultural interaction right across Europe.

Kenneth Hudson
Ann Nicholls
PO Box 610
Bath BA1 2ZY
England

LOCATION MAPS

Map 1

Map 2

NORWAY

Faroe Is.

Tórshavn

SKAGERAK

SWEDEN

Skagen

Frederikshavn

KATTEGAT

Hanstholm

Øsløs

Aalborg

Nykøbing Mors

Farsø

Rebild

Skive

Hobro

Hjerl Hede

Viborg

Holstebro

Randers

Auning

Herning

Silkeborg

Aarhus

Frederiksvaerk

Elsinore

Humlebaek

Hillerød

Hørsholm

Glud

Lyngby

Kalundborg

Valby

Copenhagen

D E N M A R K

Holbaek

Esbjerg

Roskilde

Odense

Tersløse

Nyborg

Højbjerg

Haderslev

Svendborg

Troense

Praestø

Padborg

Sønderborg

Rudkøbing

Maribo

Nykøbing

Rønne

Bornholm

GERMANY

Map 3

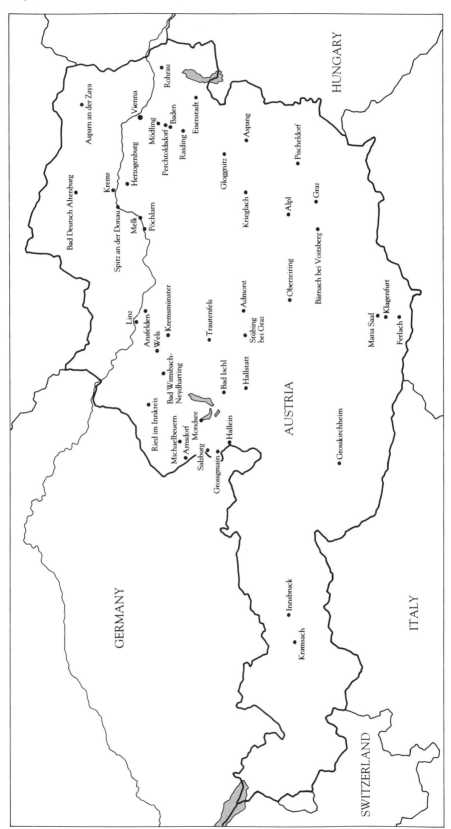

Map 4

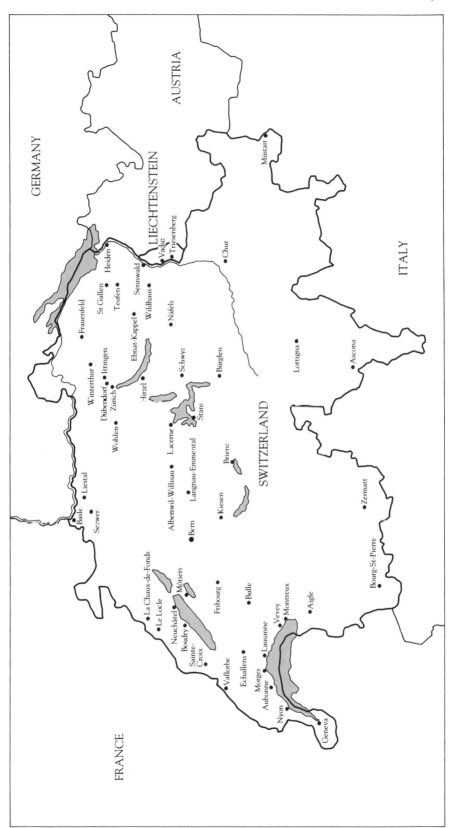

GERMANY

AUSTRIA

LIECHTENSTEIN

ITALY

FRANCE

SWITZERLAND

Müstair

Heiden
Vaduz
Triesenberg
Chur

St Gallen
Teufen
Sennwald
Wildhaus
Näfels

Frauenfeld
Ebnat-Kappel

Winterthur
Ittingen
Schwyz
Bürglen
Lottigna
Ascona

Dübendorf
Zürich
Hirzel

Wohlen
Stans

Alberswil-Willisau
Lucerne
Langnau-Emmental
Brienz

Liestal
Kiesen
Zermatt

Basle
Bern

Sewen

La Chaux-de-Fonds
Môtiers
Bourg-St-Pierre

Le Locle
Fribourg
Bulle
Montreux

Neuchâtel
Vevey
Aigle

Boudry
Lausanne

Sainte-
Croix
Echallens
Morges

Vallorbe
Aubonne

Nyon

Geneva

Map 5

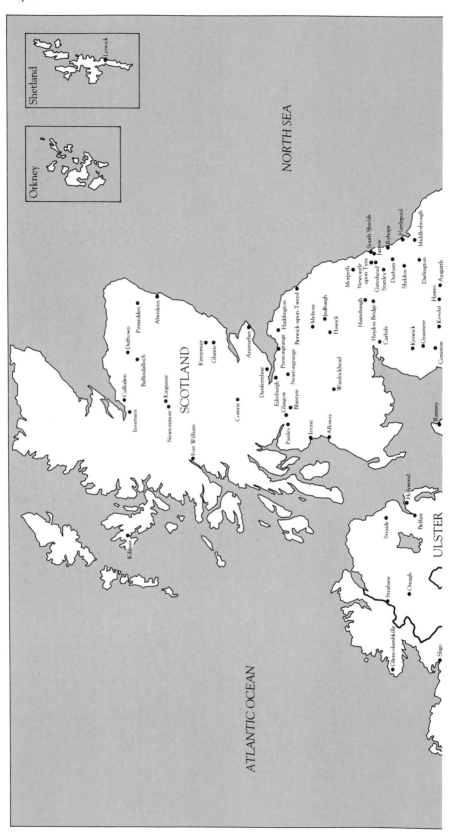

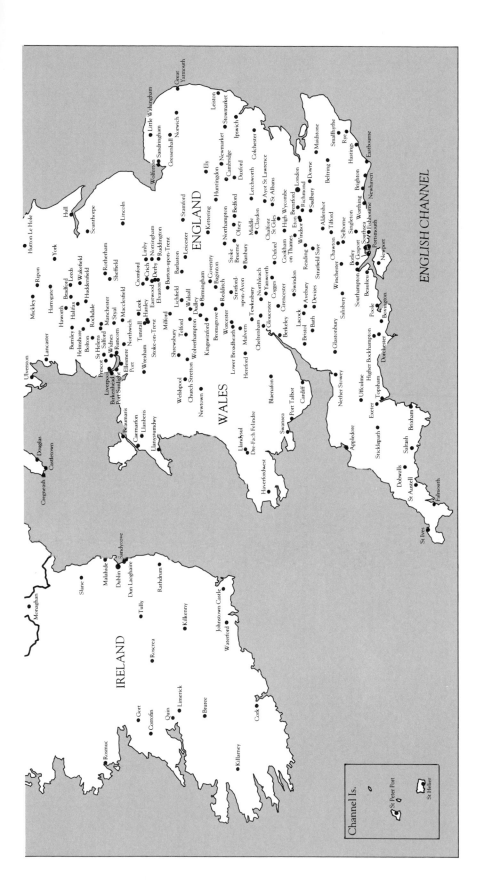

Map 6

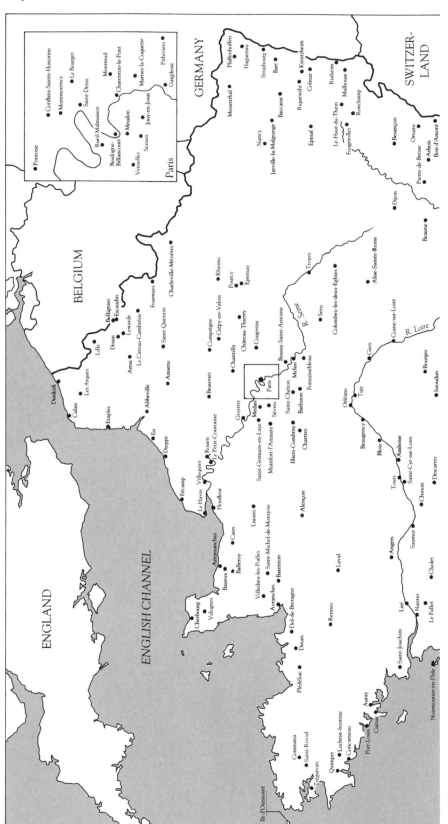

ENGLAND

ENGLISH CHANNEL

BELGIUM

GERMANY

SWITZER-
LAND

Paris

Île d'Ouessant

Dunkirk
Calais
Étaples
Les Arques
Lille
Douai
Arras
Le Cateau-Cambrésis
Bellignies
Escadin
Lewarde
Fournies
Saint-Quentin
Charleville-Mézières
Abbeville
Amiens
Beauvais
Rheims
Pourcy
Épernay
Compiègne
Crépy-en-Valois
Chantilly
Château-Thierry
Coupvray
Troyes
Sens
Colombey-les-deux-Églises
Alise-Sainte-Reine
Cosne-sur-Loire
R. Seine
R. Loire
Eu
Dieppe
Fécamp
Le Havre
Honfleur
Villequier
Le Petit-Couronne
Rouen
Giverny
Médan
Sèvres
Saint-Germain-en-Laye
Montfort-l'Amaury
Illiers-Combray
Chartres
Barbizon
Fontainebleau
Saint-Cheron
Melun
Boussy-Saint-Antoine
Paris
Orléans
Tigy
Gien
Bourges
Issoudun
Beaugency
Blois
Amboise
Saint-Cyr-sur-Loire
Descartes
Tours
Chinon
Saumur
Angers
Nantes
Liré
Le Pallet
Cholet
Saint-Joachim
Noirmoutier-en-l'Île
Cherbourg
Valognes
Bayeux
Arromanches
Balleroy
Caen
Lisores
Villedieu-les-Poêles
Saint-Michel-de-Montjoie
Barenton
Avranches
Alençon
Laval
Rennes
Dol-de-Bretagne
Dinan
Pleélélac
Commana
Saint-Rivoal
Trégarvan
Quimper
Concarneau
Lochrist-Inzinzac
Saint-Joachim
Auray
Carnac
Port-Louis

Meisenthal
Pfaffenhoffen
Haguenau
Strasbourg
Barr
Riquewihr
Kientzheim
Colmar
Rixheim
Mulhouse
Ronchamp
Le Haut-du-Them
Fougerolles
Épinal
Baccarat
Nancy
Jarville-la-Malgrange
Dijon
Beaune
Besançon
Ornans
Arbois
Bois d'Amont
Pierre-de-Bresse

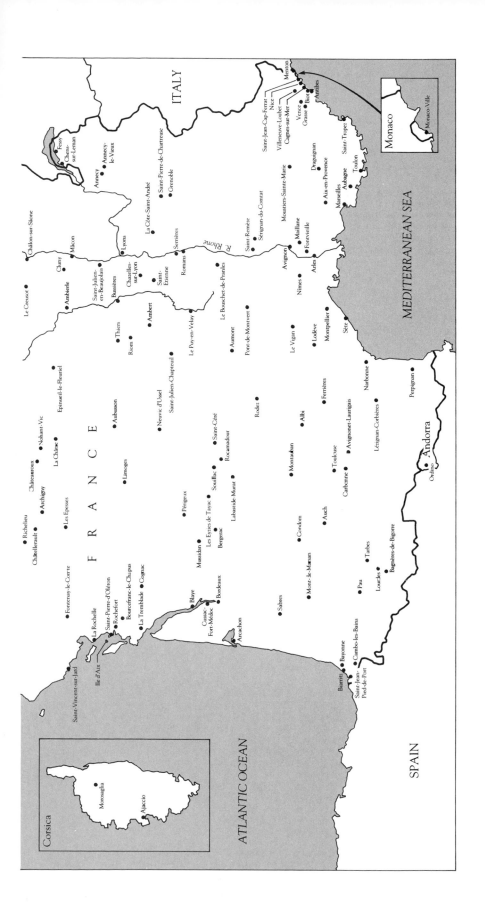

Map 7

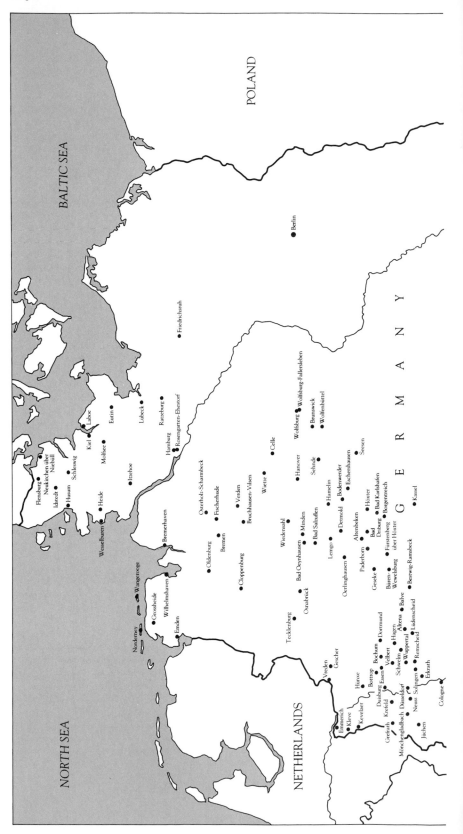

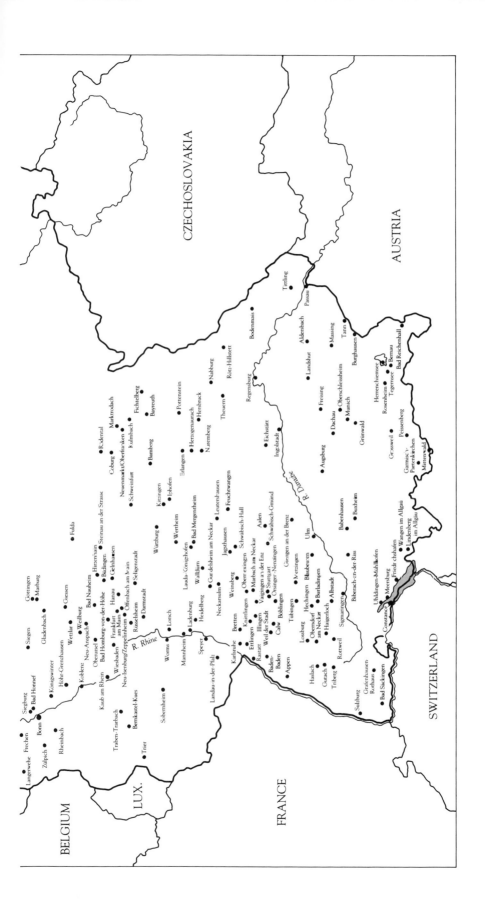

Map 8

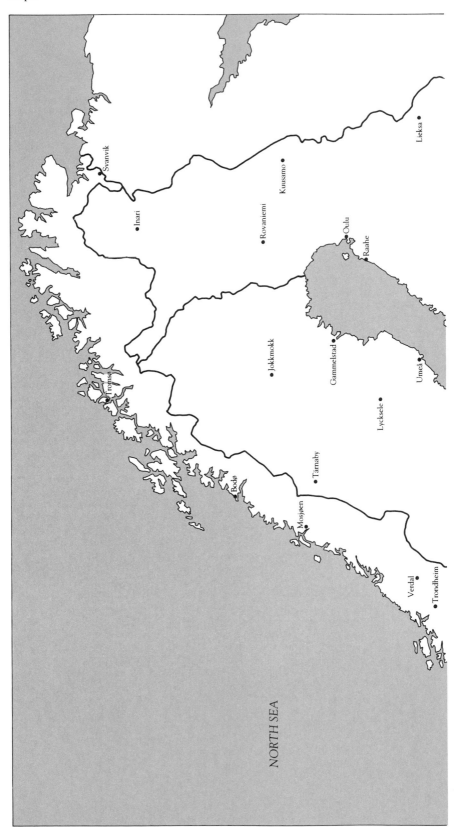

Lieksa •

Kuusamo •

Svanvik •

Inari •

Rovaniemi •

Oulu •
Raahe •

Jokkmokk •

Gammelstad •

Umeå •

Tromsø •

Lycksele •

Tärnaby •

Bodø •

Mosjøen •

Verdal •

Trondheim •

NORTH SEA

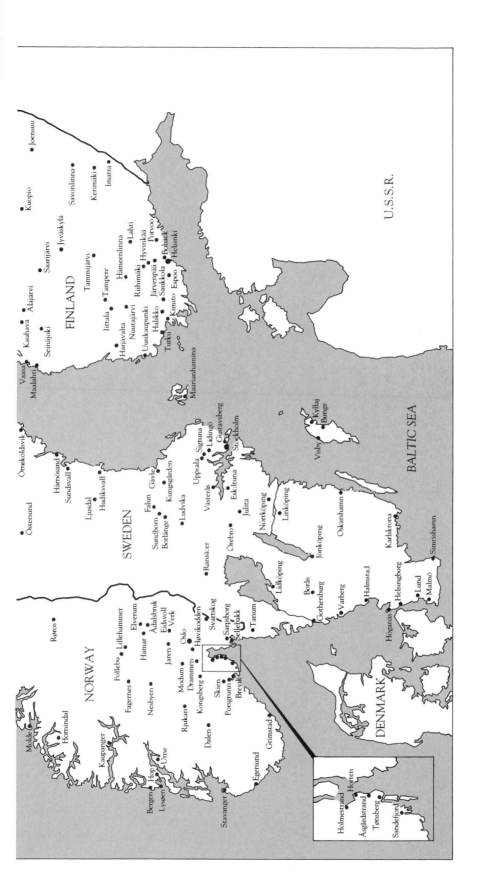

Map 9

Map 10

Map 11

Map 12

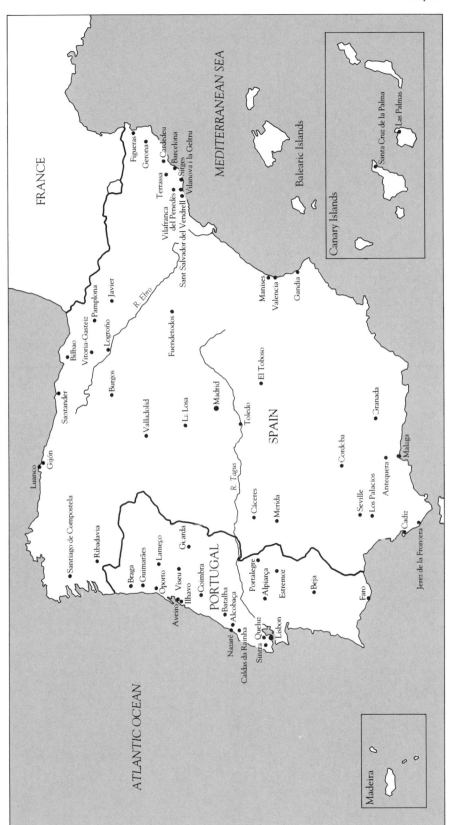

KEY TO SYMBOLS

C	Admission charge
F	Free admission
🚗	Visitors' car park
📖	Bookstall
🛍	Shop
☕	Refreshments
🌳	Picnic area
♿	Facilities for disabled people
■	Special exhibitions
☛	Guided tours

AUSTRIA

Admont

Art Museum of the Benedictine Monastery

Kunsthistorisches Museum des Benediktinerstiftes,
A-8911 Admont, Steiermark
☎ 03613 231235
Apr and Oct, daily 10–12, 2–4. May–Sept, daily
10–1, 2–5. Nov–Mar, by appt only.
ⓒ 🍺 ⚞

Admont, established in 1074, was the first
monastery in Styria to follow the Rule of St
Benedict. Its splendid buildings and their
contents reflect more than nine centuries of
monastic life here and a high proportion of the
treasures displayed in the museum have been
used for religious purposes. They include
embroidery of exceptional quality, carried out
during the 17th and 18th centuries by lay
brothers of the monastery, gold and silver
vessels and ornaments, pewter and brass.
Among other noteworthy items are sculpture by
J. T. Stammel (1695–1765), the Fathers of the
Church series of paintings by G. B. Goetz, and
landscapes by A. Kurtz (d. 1916). The superb
Baroque library, completed in 1776, is the
largest monastery library in the world.

Alpl

Peter Rosegger's Birthplace

Peter Roseggers Geburtshaus, Alpl 42, A-8671
Alpl bei Krieglach, Steiermark
☎ 03855 8230
Apr, daily 10–12.30, 1.30–5. May–Oct, daily
8–12.30, 1.30–5. Nov–Mar, Tues–Sun
11 4.
ⓒ 🍴 🍺

This is an Alpine farm and motor vehicles have
to stop a considerable distance from it. The
farmhouse, built in 1744, was the birthplace of
the novelist, Peter Rosegger (1843–1918). After
falling into decay, it was bought by the Province
of Styria in 1927 and partially restored. Two
rooms are furnished as they would have been
during the lifetime of Rosegger's parents, with
some original items, including paintings of
Rosegger himself. There are also a number of
memorabilia of the novelist. In the former
smoke-kitchen, visitors can see traditional
Styrian farming implements and equipment used
in flax processing.

Ansfelden

Bruckner Museum

Anton Bruckner Gedenkstätte des Landes
Oberösterreich, Augustiner Straße 3, A-4052
Ansfelden, Oberösterreich
☎ 07229 87128/879014
Apr–Oct, Wed 2–5; Sun 10–12, 2–5.
ⓒ 🍴 ⚞

The composer, Anton Bruckner, was born here
in 1824. His father was the schoolmaster in
Ansfelden and the school and the Bruckners'
house were in the same building. A schoolroom
has been furnished to show how it would have
looked c. 1830, when Anton Bruckner was a
pupil at the school. Elsewhere there are exhibits
illustrating the life and career of the composer,
including instruments on which Bruckner used
to play.

Arnsdorf

Franz Xavier Gruber Museum

Franz Xavier Gruber Museum, A-5112 Arnsdorf
46, Salzburgerland ☎ 06274 7443
Daily 10–5
ⓒ ⚞

The house was the home of Franz Xavier
Gruber, the composer in 1818 of the carol 'Stille
Nacht, Heilige Nacht', who was the church
organist in Arnsdorf for 21 years. It has its
original furnishings and memorabilia of Gruber.

Aspang

Automobile Museum

Automobil-Museum, A-2870 Aspang/Wechsel,
Niederösterreich
☎ 02642 2329 or 0222 931660
May–Oct, Sat, Sun and public holidays 7–5.
Groups of 20 people or more also Mon–Fri by
telephone appt.
ⓒ 🍺 ⚞

This is the largest automobile museum in
Austria. Its collections contain 120 items,
ranging in date from 1888 to 1970 and in type
from racing cars to fire-engines. A special
feature of the museum is its display of models
produced by the Austrian manufacturer, Steyr,
between 1920 and 1938.

Asparn an der Zaya

Museum of Lower Austrian Prehistory

Museum für Urgeschichte des Landes
Niederösterreich, A-2151 Asparn an der Zaya,
Niederösterreich ☎ 02577 239
Apr–Oct, Tues–Sun 7–5
ⓒ 🗪 🍺 ⚞

The museum illustrates the prehistoric cultures
of Lower Austria, with exhibits ranging from
60,000 to 100 BC. An open-air section contains
reconstructions of a number of prehistoric
buildings of different types and periods.
Schoolchildren are given an opportunity to
experiment with the handicraft skills of
prehistoric people, using the tools and
equipment which were available at the time.

Bad Deutsch Altenburg

Carnuntum Museum

*Freilichtmuseum Petronell-Carnuntum und
    Museum Carnuntinum, Badgasse 40-44,
    A-2405 Bad Deutsch Altenburg,
    Niederösterreich*   ☎ 02165 2480
Apr–Oct, daily 9–5
© ♦ ♠

Carnuntum was the capital of Upper Pannonia,
a province of the Roman Empire. The museum
illustrating its history is in two parts, a museum
containing finds from the excavations and an
open-air museum or archaeological park within
the area of the legionary camp and the civilian
settlement.

The museum has rich collections of
monuments, mosaics, statues, gold and silver
ornaments, pottery, glass, bronzes, coins, and
architectural fragments. The open-air museum
displays the largest excavated site in Austria,
and has partial reconstructions, using Roman
building techniques, of the Temple of Diana, a
pillared hall and the Amphitheatre.

**Head of the goddess Diana. Carnuntum
Museum, Bad Deutsch Altenburg.**

Baden

Baden Museum

*Städtische Sammlungen Archiv/Rollettmuseum der
    Stadtgemeinde Baden, Weikersdorferplatz 1,
    A-2500 Baden, Niederösterreich*
☎ 02252 48255
*Museum: May–Oct, Wed, Sat 3–6; Sun 9–12.
    Archive: By appt.*
© ♠

The museum originated with the private
collection of a local doctor, Anton Rollett
(1778–1842), to which further items were added
during the 19th century. In the closing stages of
the Second World War, the more valuable
items from the museum and the archives were
removed to safe storage elsewhere and between
1945 and 1955 the building was commandeered
by the Russians. It was reopened for its normal
purposes in 1957.

The museum contains sections devoted to
regional geology, palaeontology, mineralogy
and botany. There is important prehistoric and
Roman material from local sites, a collection of
weapons and targets, altars, paintings and ritual
objects from former churches in Baden and a
large collection of plans, paintings, portraits,
coins and medals relating to the history of
Baden.

Special features of the museum include death
masks of famous people, watercolours, fabrics
and handicrafts of the Biedermeier period and
memorabilia of Grillparzer, Beethoven and
Mozart. There are also a number of works by the
local sculptor Josef Müllner, and the herbarium
of Anton Rollett (1837).

Bad Ischl

The Emperor's Villa

*Kaiservilla, Jainzen 38, A-4820 Bad Ischl,
    Oberösterreich*   ☎ 06132 3241
May–mid Oct, daily 9–12, 1–4.45
© ♦

This was the summer residence of the Emperor,
Franz Josef II. It has its original furnishings and
contains memorabilia of the Imperial family,
including trophies of animals shot by the
Emperor. There are 19th-century paintings by
Austrian and other European artists, together
with sculpture and porcelain.

Franz Lehár's Villa

*Lehár Villa, Franz Lehár Kai 10, A-4820 Bad
    Ischl, Oberösterreich*
May–Sept, daily 10–12, 2–5
© ✐

The house, built in the 1830s, was bought by
Franz Lehár from Count Kalnoky. It contains
original furniture and personal possessions of the
composer, together with original scores and
paintings illustrating his life and career.

Museum of Photography

*Photomuseum des Landes Oberösterreich, Jainzen
    1, A-4820 Bad Ischl, Oberösterreich*
☎ 06132 4422
Apr–Oct, daily 9.30–5
© ✐

The marble-clad building housing the museum
formerly belonged to the Empress Elisabeth,
who called it her 'cottage'. The collections,
drawn mainly from the territories of the former
Austro-Hungarian Empire, illustrate the history

of photography from its beginnings to the present day. The exhibits include cameras, prints, dark room equipment and an original 19th-century photographer's studio, transferred to the present building.

Bad Wimsbach-Neydharting

Transport Museum

Neydhartinger Verkehrs-Museum, 'Moor-Hof', A-4654 Bad Wimsbach-Neydharting, Oberösterreich ☎ *07245 4131*
Wed from 3 pm onwards. At any other time by appt.
F 🖉 💺 🚿

The museum contains mementoes of local railways, including the earliest railway in Austria, the horse-drawn line from Budweis (České Budějovice) in what is now Czechoslovakia, to Linz and Gmunden in Austria. The exhibits include furnishings from the Emperor Franz Josef I's special coach, and models and parts of the signalling installation.

Bärnach bei Voitsberg

Alt Kainach Castle Museum

Burgenkundliches Museum Schloß Alt-Kainach, Hauptstraße 68, A-8572 Bärnach bei Voitsberg, Steiermark ☎ *03142 61386*
May–Oct, Tues–Sun 9–12, 2–5
C 🛇 🚿

Alt Kainach is a Renaissance castle, complete with its original wooden ceilings, stone floors and chapel. The museum is devoted mainly to the history of castles, especially in Styria. A feature of this exhibition is a collection of 30 models of Styrian castles, built to a 1:100 scale. There is also an international collection of postage stamps depicting castles, biographical material of Austrian noble families with castles in Styria, and exhibits of Stone Age and Roman objects from local excavations.

Eisenstadt

Haydn Museum

Haydn Museum, Joseph Haydngasse, A-7000 Eisenstadt, Burgenland ☎ *02682 2652*
Easter–Oct, daily 9–12, 1–5
C 🛇

The house was Haydn's home from 1766 to 1788. It contains memorabilia of Haydn and material illustrating Eisenstadt during his residence there. There are also musical instruments, portraits, paintings and autograph letters and musical manuscripts. A section of the museum is devoted to Franz Liszt and to the dancer, Fanny Eisler.

Museum of Austrian Culture

Museum Österreichischer Kultur, Haydngasse 1, A-7000 Eisenstadt, Burgenland ☎ *02682 5040*
Mid Mar–Oct, Tues–Sun 9.30–4.30
C 🛇 💺

Haydngasse 1 was originally a monastery, founded in 1678. The museum was established in Vienna in 1946 as part of the Kunsthistorisches Museum, with the aim of stimulating an interest in Austrian history and traditions, after the collapse of the National Socialist system. The collection was transferred to Eisenstadt in 1985 and the new museum opened in 1987.

In eight rooms, visitors are given an outline of human achievement since prehistoric times, within the territory of pre-1919 Austria. Particular attention is paid to political history, the Church, the aristocracy, the rôle of the peasants, the growth and organisation of the town, and to the relation between humans and their environment.

Sculptures of Woman and Man. Museum of Austrian Culture, Eisenstadt.

Ferlach

Gunsmiths' Museum

*Büchsenmachermuseum, Hauptplatz 5, A-9170
    Ferlach, Kärnten*   ☎ 04227 266031
Mid May–Sept, Mon–Fri 10–1, 3–6; Sat 9–12.
Ⓒ ▮ ♿ ⌖

The iron industry in Carinthia has existed for
3,000 years. Gunmaking here dates from the
mid 16th century and local craftsmen still enjoy
an international reputation for the quality of
their work. The museum tells the story of
gunmaking in Ferlach from its early years until
the present day and illustrates the processes
involved. The displays include tools and
machines, manufacturing techniques, and guns
produced in workshops in the area.

Gloggnitz

Karl Renner Museum

*Dr Karl Renner Museum, Rennergasse 4, A-2640
    Gloggnitz, Neiderösterreich*   ☎ 02662 2498
*Fri–Sun and public holidays, 9–5. Other times by
    appt.*
Ⓒ

The museum is in the former home of the
statesman and Austrian President, Karl Renner.
It presents his life and career against the
background of the history of Austria from 1918
to 1950.

Graz

Hunting Museum

*Steiermärkisches Landesmuseum Joanneum:
    Abteilung für Jagdkunde, Schloß Eggenberg,
    Eggenberger Allee 90, A-8020 Graz,
    Steiermark*   ☎ 0316 53264
Mar–Nov, daily 9–12, 1–5
Ⓕ ▮

The museum, a department of the Joanneum
Provincial Museum, is devoted to the history
and methods of hunting, especially in Austria.
It contains paintings, prints and sculpture with
hunting as their subject. Among the artists
represented are Johan Georg Hamilton (1672–
1737) and Veit Hauckh (1663–1746). There is
also a glass and porcelain collection of objects
with hunting motifs. The weapons collection
includes sporting guns from the 16th and 17th
centuries. Among these is a group of falconry
rifles.
    The dioramas showing animals and birds in
their natural habitats are celebrated, as is the
section of the museum which deals with the
diseases and abnormalities that afflict wild
creatures.
    The museum adjoins a park containing a herd
of deer.

**Ducal crown from the Styria region. Museum
of Applied Art, Graz.**

Museum of Applied Art

*Steiermärkisches Landesmuseum Joanneum:
    Abteilung für Kunstgewerbe, Neutorgasse 45,
    A-8010 Graz, Steiermark*
    ☎ 0316 7031 2393/2458
*Mon, Wed–Fri 10–5; Sat, Sun and public holidays
    10–1.*
Ⓒ ⌖

With 42,000 items in its collections, of which
five per cent are displayed at any one time, the
department is the second largest in Austria. The
arrangement is mostly by period and the
categories of material displayed include
furniture, glass, ceramics, clocks, textiles, gold
and silver, pewter and ivory. A separate section
is devoted to musical instruments. The museum
has the largest wrought-iron collection in
central Europe.
    Among the special features of the museum are
an 18th-century apothecary shop, two panelled
rooms dating from 1577 and 1607, the 1750
Maria Theresa Room from Murska Sobota and
the 1564 Renaissance Room from Schloss
Radmannsdorf, near Weiz.

Museum of Archaeology and Numismatics

*Steiermärkisches Landesmuseum Joanneum:
    Abteilung für Vor- und Frühgeschichte und
    Münzensammlung, Schloß Eggenberg,
    Eggenberger Allee 90, A-8020 Graz,
    Steiermark*   ☎ 0316 53264
Feb–Nov, daily 9–12, 1–5
Ⓒ ▮ ⌖

The museum collections illustrate the cultural
history of Styria from the Stone Age to the early
Middle Ages, with a particular emphasis on the
Hallstatt period and the Roman period. The
displays include the celebrated Strettweg bronze
carriage dating from *c.* 600 BC and bearing
symbolic figures of warriors and goddesses. The
numismatic collection, the second largest in
Austria, concentrates on coins and medals
illustrating the history of Styria but also includes
items from many other countries.

Museum of the Ethnology of Styria

Steiermärkisches Landesmuseum Joanneum:
  Abteilung für Volkskunde, Paulustorgasse
  11-13A, A-8010 Graz, Steiermark
  ☎ *0316 830416*
Apr–Oct, Mon–Fri 9–4; Sat, Sun and public
  holidays 9–12.
C

This department of the museum is concerned
with the popular culture of Styria. It contains
furnished rooms from peasant houses, painted
furniture, costumes, masks, scenes from
religious plays, and musical instruments.
Separate sections are devoted to wrought-iron
votive plaques and to agricultural implements,
special attention being given to the
development of the plough.

Museum of the History of Graz

Steiermärkisches Landesmuseum Joanneum:
  Historisches Museum, Schloß Eggenberg,
  Eggenberger Allee 90, A-8020 Graz,
  Steiermark ☎ *0316 53264*
Apr–Oct, daily guided tours at 10, 11, 12, 2, 3 and
  4
C 🛈 💺 ♿ ♨

The museum presents the history of Graz and of
early settlements in the area. 17th–19th-century
models, paintings and engravings illustrate the
development of the city. A special section is
devoted to the history of the theatre, opera and
music in Graz, with displays related to the life
and work of Joseph Marx, Hugo Wolf, Robert
Hamerling, Peter Rosegger and Bruno Ertler.

The Old Gallery

Steiermärkisches Landesmuseum Joanneum: Alte
  Galerie, Neutorgasse 45, A-8010 Graz,
  Steiermark ☎ *0316 7031 2457*
Tues–Fri 10–5; Sat, Sun 10–1. Closed Jan 1,
  Dec 25.
C 🛈

The gallery has collections of paintings and
sculpture dating from the 12th century to 1800,
together with an outstanding collection of
medieval stained glass. German, Dutch and
Italian artists are well represented and separate
sections are devoted to the work of 16th–18th-
century Austrian painters, especially those who
lived and worked in Styria.

The Provincial Armoury

Landeszeughaus Graz, Steiermärkisches
  Landesmuseum Joanneum, Herrengasse 16,
  A-8010 Graz, Steiermark. Office at
  Schmiedgasse 34/11. ☎ *0316 828796*
Day following Palm Sunday–Oct, Mon–Fri 9–5
  (last guided tour 4); Sat, Sun and public
  holidays 9–1 (last guided tour 12 noon).
C 🛈

The armoury is a department of the Joanneum.
It contains a huge collection of weapons and
other objects used in warfare from the 16th

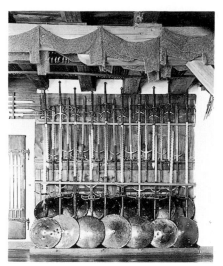

Display of swords and shields at The
Provincial Armoury, Graz.

century to the 18th. The building dates from
1642–4 and has always been used for this
purpose. Among the more remarkable parts of
the collection are richly decorated wheel-lock
pistols from the second half of the 16th century,
high quality armour for both field and
tournament use, made by various 16th-century
master craftsmen, and a complete set of horse
armour, made c. 1510, from the workshop of
Conrad Seusenhofer of Innsbruck.

Grossgmain

Salzburg Open-Air Museum

Salzburger Freilichtmuseum, Hasenweg, A-5084
  Grossgmain, Salzburgerland
  ☎ *0662 850011*
Apr–Oct, Tues–Sat 9 5
C 🛈 💺 ♨

The museum, on a 50-hectare site, in beautiful
countryside, has a collection of 18th- and 19th-
century buildings from different parts of the
region which have been moved to the present
site and which illustrate, with their contents,
the traditional way of life of this area of Austria.
They are arranged in groups, corresponding to
the different types of landscape to be found
within the province of Salzburg. In recent years
the museum has been a focal point for people
interested in the traditional crafts and in folk
dancing, art and handicrafts.

Grosskirchheim

Castle Museum

Schloß Museum, A-9843 Grosskirchheim, Döllach,
  Kärnten ☎ *04825 226*
Daily 9–6
C 🛈 ♨

The castle was built in 1561. After the Second
World War, it was restored and converted into a

museum by its present owner. It now contains exhibits of the flora and fauna of the Hohe Tauern National Park and of items illustrating the traditional rural way of life of the area. There is also an interesting collection of Renaissance and Baroque furniture. A special section of the museum is devoted to the history and techniques of goldmining in the area, which flourished from Celtic and Roman times until the present century.

Hallein

Celtic Museum

Keltenmuseum Hallein, Pfelegerplatz 5, A-5400 Hallein, Salzburgerland
☎ 06245 2783/4288
May Sept, daily 9–5. Oct, daily 12–5. Pre-booked parties at other times.
Ⓒ 🅰 💻 🔙

Dürrnberg, near Hallein, was one of the most important economic centres in central Europe in the pre-Roman Iron Age. Between 600 and 15 BC its prosperity was based on saltmining. The extensive trade resulting from this allowed the import of luxury goods from all over Europe, especially the Mediterranean south. The extremely rich grave equipment, displayed in the museum, indicates a standard of living found at no other Celtic site. Other exhibits include items from excavations at the settlement and tools and implements from the prehistoric saltmines. Log huts have been reconstructed on their original stone foundations. Salt extraction continued into modern times and the displays in the museum illustrate methods of saltmining, boiling, barrel production and transport, especially by river boat.

Other departments of the museum are devoted to local history, the guilds, religious art, wooden toys, handicrafts and traditional costumes. There are also memorabilia of Franz Xavier Gruber, the composer of the carol 'Stille Nacht, Heilige Nacht', who lived in Hallein and is buried there.

Hallstatt

Museum of Prehistory and Hallstatt Museum

Prähistorisches Museum und Heimatmuseum Hallstatt, Seestraße 56, A-4830 Hallstatt, Oberösterreich   ☎ 06134 208
Museum of Prehistory: Apr and Oct, daily 10–4. May–Sept, daily 9.30–6. Hallstatt Museum: daily 10–6.
Ⓒ

The Museum of Prehistory contains a wide range of material discovered during the excavations of local sites of the Hallstatt and La Tène periods, approximately the last eight centuries of the pre-Christian period.

The Hallstatt Museum is concerned with the history of Hallstatt and the surrounding district. There are displays relating to the local saltmining industry, to the area during the Roman period, to musical instruments, weapons and religious art, and to traditional costumes and handicrafts. The section devoted to the natural history of the region includes memorabilia of the naturalist Friedrich Simony (1813–96).

Herzogenburg

Herzogenburg Monastery Art Museum

Kunstschätze im Stift Herzogenburg, Stiftsgasse 3, A-3130 Herzogenburg, Niederösterreich
☎ 02782 3112
Apr–Oct, daily 9–11, 1–5. Guided tours available by arrangement at other times.
Ⓒ 🅰 💻 🔙

An Augustinian monastery was established at Herzogenburg in the 13th century. Most of the present buildings, however, date from the 18th century. The richly decorated rooms include the Grand Hall (1718), the Chapel (1757), the Library (1751), the Picture Gallery (1737) and the Church (1785).

Among the items in the exceptionally rich collections are gold and silver ornaments and liturgical objects, mostly 18th century, musical instruments, 14th–15th-century stained glass and 14th–16th-century panel paintings and sculpture from former monasteries and churches. The 17th–18th-century paintings in the Picture Gallery are still hung in the original, wallpaper-like way.

Death of Mary, wooden sculpture, c. 1490. Monastery Art Museum, Herzogenburg.

Innsbruck

Ambras Castle

Schloß Ambras, Schloß-Straße 20, A-6020 Innsbruck, Tirol   ☎ 05222 48446/41215
May–Sept, Wed–Mon 10–4
Ⓒ 🅰 💻 🔙

Doctor Jenner about to Vaccinate a Child.

Doctor Jenner was below the middle stature
his hair dark and a little inclining to curl
and it was observed at his death he was not the least
gray. He was rather near sighted but never made
use of Glasses. his dress was black, a large Collar to
the Coat and loose low trowsers. the dress of the day

**Historic print from the Jenner Museum,
Berkeley (Britain).**

The Day, 1899, by Ferdinand Hodler.
Art Museum, Bern (Switzerland).

Jealousy, 1895, by Munch. Edvard Munch Museum, Oslo (Norway).

Fantasy painting by Néstor Martin Fernandez de la Torre. Néstor Museum, Las Palmas (Spain).

The castle dates from the 16th century. It contains collections of 16th-century weapons and armour and displays illustrating the history of Tyrol regiments. There are also numerous Austrian portraits dating from the 15th to the early 19th century. Other exhibits include 16th–17th-century musical instruments, coins, gold- and silversmiths' work and minerals. One of the castle's most remarkable features is a 16th-century museum of art and natural curiosities.

Ferdinandeum Museum

Tiroler Landesmuseum Ferdinandeum,
Museumstraße 15, A-6020 Innsbruck, Tirol
  ☎ *05222 59489*
May–Sept, daily 10–5; Thurs also 7–9 pm. Oct–
Apr, Tues–Sat 10–12, 2–5; Sun 9–12.
[C]

The Ferdinandeum is a museum of art and archaeology. It contains archaeological material discovered during the excavation of prehistoric, Celtic and Roman sites in the Tyrol. There are also displays of local minerals, 14th–16th-century gravestones and memorials from the Tyrol, ivories, goldsmiths' work, glass and weapons. The collections of European art include paintings and sculpture by 12th–20th-century Tyrolean artists.

Hofburg

Hofburg Innsbruck, Rennweg 1, A-6020
Innsbruck, Tirol   ☎ *05222 587186*
May 15–Oct 15, daily 9–4. Oct 16–May 14,
Mon–Sat 9–4. Closed public holidays during
winter.
[C] ✐

A Habsburg palace was built on this site during the 15th century. It was rebuilt in its original form between 1754 and 1770, at the behest of

Carved wooden cupboard dating from 1864. Museum of Tyrolean Folk Art, Innsbruck.

the Empress Maria Theresa. Considerable remodelling of the façade took place at intervals between 1836 and 1962 and a thoroughgoing restoration of the interior was carried out in 1947–9, to repair war damage.

The Hofburg contains 17th–19th-century furniture, tapestries, portraits and paintings of historic scenes. The Silver Chapel and the Palace Church have statues of the Imperial family and other historic personages, together with tombs of the Emperors and their relatives and of the Tyrolean national hero, Andreas Hofer.

Museum of Tyrolean Folk Art

Tiroler Volkskunstmuseum, Universitätsstraße 2,
A-6020 Innsbruck, Tirol ☎ *05222 584302*
May–Sept, Mon–Sat 9–5; Sun and public holidays
9–12. Oct–Apr, Mon–Sat 9–12, 2–5; Sun
and public holidays 9–12. Closed Jan 1, Easter
Sun, May 1, Whitsun, Corpus Christi, Nov 1,
Dec 25.
[C] *(ex. children)* ▮

The museum building was originally a monastery, founded in 1553 and considerably altered in 1729. It has accommodated the internationally famous folk art collections since 1926. Among the objects displayed are agricultural implements, cow bells, carved and painted furniture, spinning and weaving equipment, costumes, masks and religious art.

Considerable use is made of models in order to show the different types of house and farm carts and waggons to be found in the Tyrol. The reproductions of farmhouse and town rooms provide an opportunity to show furniture, stoves, pottery, glass and domestic equipment in attractive and appropriate settings.

Paul Troger, self-portrait, c. 1730. Ferdinandeum Museum, Innsbruck.

Klagenfurt

Carinthia Museum

Landesmuseum für Kärnten, Museumgassse 2,
A-9021 Klagenfurt, Kärnten
☎ *0463 536 30552*
Tues–Sat 9–4; Sun 10–1
C ⓘ

The museum is concerned with the history and natural environment of Carinthia. There are sections devoted to geology, palaeontology, botany, zoology and entomology, with dioramas showing the wildlife of the province.

Prehistoric and Roman archaeology are strongly featured in the museum. Among the more important exhibits are the Hallstatt lead figures, the Roman marble sculpture from Virunum, frescoes from the settlement on the Magdalensberg and a Dionysos mosaic.

There are also displays relating to the history of mining in Carinthia and collections of costumes, furniture, tools and household equipment from the rural areas. The museum has two out-stations for which it is responsible, the group of archaeological museums on the Magdalensberg and at Teurnia, and the open-air museum at Maria Saal, which has farm buildings and rural houses from sites in Carinthia.

Kramsach

Museum of Tyrolean Farmsteads

Museum Tiroler Bauernhöfe, A-6233 Kramsach,
Mosen, Tirol   ☎ *05337 2636*
Easter–Oct, daily 10–6
C 🖭 ⚲

The Association of the Museum of Tyrolean Farmsteads was founded in 1974. Its aim was to discover, transport to and rebuild on the museum site, farmhouses and farm buildings typical of North and East Tyrol. So far, fifteen buildings have been installed at the museum. When the project is completed, probably in 1995, the total will be about 95, ranging in date from the 13th century to the early 19th.

Each building contains appropriate furniture and equipment, and buildings other than farmhouses are being steadily added to the collection. These include a chapel, a smithy, a sawmill, a shooting-range, a cornmill, a bath-house and a threshing mill.

Krems

Museum of Wine and of the History of Krems

Historisches Museum und Weinbaumuseum der
Stadt Krems, Dominikaner-platz 8-9, A-3500
Krems, Niederösterreich
☎ *02732 2511 339 or 02732 4927*
Apr–Oct, Tues–Sat 9–12, 2–5; Sun and public
holidays 9–12. Closed the Tues after public
holidays.
C ⚲ ⚲

The museum is housed in a former Dominican church and its associated monastery building. Its displays cover the history, art, crafts and ethnography of Krems and the surrounding region. A special section is devoted to the production of wine. There are collections of 13th–17th-century religious art, guild relics, pottery, stained glass, and peasant art and handicrafts.

A series of furnished interiors includes the furnishings of the early 16th-century Krems physician and apothecary, Wolfgang Kappler. The museum has a collection of the work of Martin Johann Schmidt, known as Kremser Schmidt (1718–1801), the last great Austrian Baroque painter.

Part of the 14th-century monastery building housing the Museum of Wine and of the History of Krems.

Kremsmünster

Monastery Collections

*Stiftsammlungen, Benediktinerstift, A-4550
Kremsmünster, Oberösterreich*
☎ 07583 2750
*Easter–Oct, daily 9.30–10.30, 2–5.30. Guided
tours only.*
C ▪

The Benedictine monastery was founded in 777.
It has outstanding collections of weapons,
armour, religious art and astronomical
instruments, displayed in a mid 18th century
observatory. Among the exhibits are 16th–
17th-century Dutch, Flemish, German and
Italian paintings, 14th–19th-century Austrian
paintings and sculpture, 8th–14th-century
religious art, snuffboxes, gold- and silversmiths'
work and church textiles. The 65m long library
contains 150,000 volumes and numerous
illuminated manuscripts and incunabula.

Krieglach

Peter Rosegger Museum

*Peter Rosegger Museum, Roseggerstraße 44,
A-8670 Krieglach, Steiermark*
☎ 03855 2375
Daily 9–5
C ▪ ✍

The museum is in the former home of the
short-story writer, novelist and poet, Peter
Rosegger (1843–1918). His workroom and the
room in which he died are preserved as they
were in his lifetime. Others contain portraits,
manuscripts and memorabilia of the writer.

Linz

Castle Museum

*Schloßmuseum Linz, Tummelplatz 10, A-4020
Linz, Oberösterreich*   ☎ 0732 274419
*Tues–Fri 9–5; Sat, Sun and public holidays 10–4.
Closed Jan 1, Dec 24, 25, 26.*
C ▪ ▄ ✍

Linz Castle was built in 1486–9 by Emperor
Friedrich III, and completely renovated early in
the 17th century by Rudolf II. Since 1963 it has
formed part of the Museum of the Province of
Upper Austria. The museum contains important
collections of Stone Age, Bronze Age and
Roman material from sites in the province, as
well as exhibits illustrating more recent history,
among which are a 17th-century castle
apothecary's equipment and the Museum
Physikum from an 18th-century Jesuit college.
There are important exhibits of peasant
furniture and crafts and of Austrian art of the
medieval and Renaissance periods and of the
19th and early 20th centuries.

Nordico Museum

*Stadtmuseum Linz-Nordico, Bethlehemstraße 7,
A-4020 Linz/Donau, Oberösterreich*
☎ 0732 2393
*Mon–Fri 9–6; Sat, Sun 3–5. Closed New Year,
Easter Day, May 1, Nov 1, Christmas.*
F ♿ ✍

The museum presents the archaeology and
history of Linz since prehistoric times. There are
collections of paintings, drawings and prints by
Linz artists, and of medieval and baroque
sculpture. Other exhibits are of furniture,
craftsmen's tools, costumes and material relating
to the local guilds.

Stifter Memorial Museum

*Stifter-Gedänkstätte, Adalbert-Stifter-Institut des
Landes Oberösterreich, Untere Donaulände 6,
A-4020 Linz/Donau, Oberösterreich*
☎ 0732 2720
*Mon, Tues, Thurs 7.30–1, 2–6; Wed 7.30–1.30;
Fri 7.30–1. Closed public holidays.*
F ✎

The museum forms part of the Adalbert Stifter
Institute. Untere Donaulände 6 is the house in
which the poet lived and where he died in 1868.
It contains Stifer's furniture and other personal
possessions, together with a collection of
portraits, drawings, manuscripts and documents
illustrating his life and work.

Maria Saal

Open-Air Museum of Carinthia

*Kärntner Frelichtmuseum, Museumweg 1, A-9063
Maria Saal, Kärnten*   ☎ 04223 2352/2812
*May–Sept, daily 10–6. Groups at other times by
appt.*
C ▪ ☕ ✍

**18th-century view of Linz Castle from the
river. Castle Museum, Linz.**

The museum, which was opened in 1968, occupies a four-acre site on the outskirts of Maria Saal. Its exhibits consist of wooden farmhouses and other farm buildings from different parts of Carinthia. The houses contain appropriate furniture and domestic equipment. Among the many other rural buildings which have been transferred to the museum site are a bath house, a covered bridge, a watermill, a sawmill and a salt store.

Melk

Monastery Museum

Museum des Stifts, Stift Melk, A-3390 Melk,
Kärnten   ☎ *02752 2312*
Daily 9–4
C ✎

The great Baroque Benedictine Abbey of Melk, which still functions as a monastery, dates from the 18th century. The Imperial Rooms have been converted into a museum. They contain important art collections, including Lucas Cranach's *Madonna in the Vine Arbour*, and exhibits illustrating the history of the Abbey and the Benedictine Order.

Michaelbeuern

Monastery Collection

Klostersammlung, Benediktinerabtei, A-5152
Michaelbeuern, Salzburger Land
   ☎ *06274 8116*
Easter Mon–Oct, Fri, Sat, Sun. Guided tour at 2.
Other days and times by arrangement.
C ✎

First established in the 8th century, the Benedictine Abbey at Michaelbeuern was refounded in 1072. After its destruction by Bavarian troops in 1266, it was rebuilt and rededicated in 1280. Further building and modification took place during the succeeding centuries, including considerable Baroque enrichment in the 18th.

The museum contains collections of both religious and folk art, including paintings and sculpture by Austrian Baroque artists, clocks, porcelain, glass and pewter. There are also displays of peasant furniture and tools and equipment used in traditional handicrafts and domestic industries.

Mödling

Schoenberg House Museum

Schönberg-Haus, Internationale Schönberg-
Gesellschaft, Bernhardgasse 6, A-2340
Mödling, Niederösterreich   ☎ *02236 82223*
Tues, Thurs 9–5; Fri 9–12. Other times by appt.
F ✎

The house, which is the headquarters of the International Schoenberg Society, contains the apartment occupied by the composer, Arnold Schoenberg, between 1918 and 1925. In it can

Cellars of the former Benedictine Abbey, Michaelbeuern, which contains the Monastery Collection.

be seen his furniture, musical instruments and other memorabilia, as well as a number of his original manuscripts.

Mondsee

Lake Dwellings Museum

Heimat- und Pfahlbaumuseum, Marschall-von-
Wrede-Platz, A-5310 Mondsee,
Oberösterreich   ☎ *06232 2270*
May–mid Oct, daily 9–6. Other times by appt.
C ♦ ✎

The museum occupies the library of the former Benedictine Abbey. Its collections illustrate the prehistory and history of the Mondsee area and include material discovered during excavations of the sites of the Mondsee lake dwellings. There are displays of peasant handicrafts, costumes and household equipment, and exhibits relating to charcoal-burning and fishing, once important industries in the district.

Mondsee Open-Air Museum

Freilichtmuseum Mondseer Rauchhaus,
Hilfbergstraße 7, A-5310 Mondsee,
Oberösterreich   ☎ *06232 2270*
May–mid Oct, daily 8–6. Other times by appt.
C ♦ ✎

The museum is centred on a one-roomed, chimneyless house, dating possibly from the early 15th century. Grouped around it are a number of subsidiary wooden buildings associated with the house, including a mill, granary and fruit store, with their tools and equipment.

Oberzeiring

Mining Museum

Schaubergwerk und Bergbaumuseum, A-8762
Oberzeiring, Steiermark   ☎ *01043 3571*
May–Oct, guided tours daily at 10, 11, 2, 3 and 4.
Nov–Apr, guided tours daily at 11 and 2. Other
times by appt.
C ✎

The celebrated silver mine at Oberzeiring was closed down in 1361 as a result of serious flooding, which destroyed the underground installations. Parts of the mine have now been restored as far as possible to their appearance before the flood and are easily accessible to visitors. A site museum contains tools and equipment found in the mine, together with certain other archaeological material and examples of local minerals.

The air in the mine has been shown to possess curative properties for people suffering from respiratory complaints, and facilities have been installed in the galleries for the purpose of treatment.

Perchtoldsdorf

Hugo Wolf Memorial Museum

Hugo Wolf-Museum, Brunner Gasse 26, A-2380 Perchtoldsdorf, Niederösterreich
☎ *0222 867634*
Apr–early Nov, Sat, Sun and public holidays 10–5. Other times by appt.
Ⓕ 🖉 🚗

Brunner Gasse 26 was the home of the composer, Hugo Wolf, from 1888 to 1891. The museum contains memorabilia and personal possessions, covering the whole of his life and career and illustrating his working methods and social circle.

Pischeldorf

Magdalensberg Open-Air Museum

Freilichtmuseum der Keltisch-Römischen Ausgrabungen auf dem Magdalensberg, A-9064 Pischeldorf, Kärnten
☎ *04224 2255*
May–Oct, daily 8–6
Ⓒ 🖊 🖳 🚗

Archaeological excavations. Magdalensberg Open-Air Museum, Pischeldorf.

Excavations on the site of the spectacular late Celtic–early Roman hill town on the Magdalensberg, near Pischeldorf, have been in progress for many years. Finds are displayed in a main museum and in a number of subsidiary museums distributed over the site. The exhibits include pottery, sculpture, frescoes and metal objects. The area so far excavated includes the praetorium, the temple precinct, houses, workshops and commercial premises.

Pöchlarn

Oskar Kokoschka Centre

Oskar Kokoschka-Dokumentation, Regensburger Straße 29, A-3380 Pöchlarn, Niederösterreich
☎ *02757 7816*
June–Sept, during special exhibitions. Tues–Sun 10–12, 2–5. Oct–May by appt only.
Ⓒ 🖉 🚗

The house now occupied by the Centre is the birthplace of the Austrian artist, Oskar Kokoschka (1886–1980). The extensive collections provide a comprehensive background to his life and art. There are no permanent displays, but an annual exhibition is organised in order to present a particular aspect of his work.

Raiding

Liszt Museum

Liszt Museum, Lisztstraße 42, A-7321 Raiding, Burgenland
Easter–Oct, daily 9–12, 1 5. Other months by appt.
Ⓒ

The museum, established in 1911, is in the house where Franz Liszt was born. The exhibits include portraits of Liszt and his friends, together with letters, manuscripts and other memorabilia of the composer.

Ried im Innkreis

Regional Folklore Museum and Gallery

Innviertler Volkskundehaus und Galerie der Stadt, Postfach 100, Kirchenplatz 13, A-4910 Ried im Innkreis, Oberösterreich
☎ *07752 5855 extn 244/245*
Tues–Fri 9–12, 2–5. May–Oct, also Sat 2–5. Closed public holidays.
Ⓒ

The local Protestant Minister, Johann Veichtlbauer, formed an outstanding collection of folklore material, which was bequeathed after his death in 1939 to the town of Ried and forms the core of the present museum. Considerable additions have been made from other sources.

The displays include costumes, painted furniture, pipes, toys, clocks and popular remedies. The museum also has exhibits of weapons, targets, 16th–19th-century engravings and woodcuts and paintings by the Ried artist,

Wilhelm Dachauer (d. 1951). An outstanding feature of the Art Gallery is the collection of Baroque sculptures by members of the Schwanthaler family, of which seven generations lived in Ried from 1633 onwards, and which produced 21 sculptors, of whom Thomas Schwanthaler (1634–1707) was among the best in Europe.

Rohrau

Haydn's Birthplace

Haydn-Geburtshaus, Hauptstraße, A-2471 Rohrau, Niederösterreich   ☎ *02164 2268 Tues–Sun 10–5. Closed Dec 24, 25.*

Ⓒ ♢ ♠

This small, thatched farmhouse in Rohrau was built by Haydn's father, the wheelwright Matthias Haydn, in 1728. The composer, Josef Haydn, was born here in 1732 and his brother, Michael, in 1737. The house was restored in 1958–9 and suitably furnished, partly with items which belonged to the Haydn family, including a piano played by Josef Haydn himself. Among the other exhibits are original scores and editions of Haydn's works and paintings, engravings and figurines with Haydn associations.

Salzburg

Carolino Augusteum Museum

Salzburger Museum Carolino Augusteum, Museumsplatz 1 and 6, A-5020 Salzburg   ☎ *0662 841134 Tues 9–8; Wed–Sun 9–5. Closed Nov 1.*

Ⓒ ♠ ☈

Having been the seat of a Prince Archbishop for hundreds of years, Salzburg was demoted in 1816 to the status of a rural district in the Archdukedom of Austria ob der Enns. The Carolino Augusteum Museum, founded in 1835 and named after its patroness, preserved much of the district's past glory and became a patriotic symbol. It was destroyed by bombing in 1944 and rebuilt in 1966.

The museum's collections illustrate the art and history of the Province of Salzburg. There are displays of prehistoric and Roman archaeology, memorabilia of local celebrities including Paul Hofhaymer, Hans Baumann and Georg Trakl; also to be seen are musical instruments, furniture, and household equipment, as well as portraits, religious art and paintings by 18th–20th-century Austrian artists.

Other sections of the museum are devoted to costumes, prints and drawings, weapons and coins and medals and to the Swiss alchemist and medical practitioner, Paracelsus.

Mozart's Birthplace

Mozarts Geburtshaus, Getreidegasse 9, A-5020 Salzburg   ☎ *0662 844313 Jan–Apr and mid Oct–Dec, daily 9–6. May–mid Oct, daily 9–7.*

Ⓒ ♠

Wolfgang Amadeus Mozart was born in this early 15th-century house in 1756 and wrote nearly all of his early works here. Since 1917, it has been the property of the International Foundation Mozarteum, having been open to the public as a museum since 1880. It contains portraits and memorabilia of Mozart and his family, a number of musical instruments, including Mozart's first violin and first clavichord, and a pianoforte, violin and viola used by him. There is also a collection of autograph letters and musical manuscripts relating to the composer and his family.

The Mozart Family by J. N. della Croce, c. 1780. Mozart's Birthplace, Salzburg.

Residence Gallery

Residenzgalerie, Postfach 527, Residenzplatz 1,
  A-5020 Salzburg   ☎ *0662 8042/2270*
Daily 10–5. Closed Dec 24, 31.
Ⓒ

The museum building, with its famous painted
ceilings, is the former residence of the
Archbishops of Salzburg. The present Gallery
continues the tradition of the episcopal art
collection, which was founded in 1789.
Through subsequent acquisitions, it has become
one of the most important art galleries in
Europe. The principal collections are French,
Italian, German, Dutch and Flemish paintings,
but 17th–20th-century Austrian artists are also
well represented.

Salzburg Baroque Museum

Salzburger Barockmuseum, Postfach 12,
  Mirabellgarten, A-5024 Salzburg
  ☎ *0662 77432*
Tues–Sat 9–12, 2–5; Sun and public holidays
  9–12.
Ⓒ ▮

The museum comprises the Rossacher
Collection of sketches, designs and models
prepared by 17th- and 18th-century European
architects, painters, sculptors and goldsmiths as
a preliminary to their finished works, a high
proportion of which are to be found in Austria.
These include the Mirabell Palace and its
celebrated garden in Salzburg and the Horse
Bath in the same area.

Spitz an der Donau

Museum of Navigation

Schiffahrtsmuseum, Auf der Wehr 21, A-3620
  Spitz an der Donau, Niederösterreich
  ☎ *02713 2246/2647/2114*
Apr–Oct, Mon–Sat 10–12, 2–4; Sun and public
  holidays 10–12, 1–5.
Ⓒ ↩

The museum building dates from the second half
of the 13th century. It was subsequently
remodelled a number of times and took on its
present form during the 18th century. Its
exhibits tell the story of navigation on the
Danube since Roman times, by means of
models, photographs, documents and
equipment. Special attention is given to the life
of the boatmen and their families and to the
skilled craft of log-floating.

Stübing bei Graz

Austrian Open-Air Museum

Österreichisches Freilichtmuseum, A-8114 Stübing
  bei Graz, Steiermark   ☎ *03124 22431*
Apr–Oct, Tues–Sun 9–4
Ⓒ ▮ ↩

This national museum contains rural buildings
brought from all parts of Austria, with
appropriate furnishings and equipment. An

Reconstructed rural house interior. Austrian
Open-Air Museum, Stübing bei Graz.

attempt has been made to harmonise the
individual buildings within the landscape and to
group them according to the province of Austria
from which they came.

The exhibits include farmhouses, mills,
barns, storehouses and workshops of all kinds.
The range of farm and domestic equipment is
remarkably comprehensive.

Trautenfels

Schloss Trautenfels

Steiermärkisches Landesmuseum Joaneum,
  Abteilung Schloß Trautenfels, A-8951
  Trautenfels 1   ☎ *03682 22233*
Palm Saturday–Oct, daily 9–5. Other months by
  appt.
Ⓒ ▮ ☕ ↩

This is a museum of the countryside. It presents
the region, natural and manmade, as a whole.
There are dioramas and mounted specimens of
wild creatures, exhibits of minerals and fossils,
and sections devoted to agriculture and forestry,
and to dairying and beekeeping. Other sections
deal with housing, popular art and traditions,
and handicrafts.

The castle, Schloss Trautenfels, has
interesting Baroque ceilings and paintings in its
more elaborate rooms, and the tower provides
splendid views over the surrounding
countryside.

Vienna

Austrian Folklore Museum

Österreichisches Museum für Volkskunde, Palais
  Schönborn, Laudongasse 15-18, A-1080
  Wien   ☎ *0222 4389050*
Tues–Fri 9–4; Sat 9–12; Sun and public holidays
  9–1. Closed Jan 1, Easter Sun, May 1,
  Whitsun, Corpus Christi, Nov 1, Dec 25.
Ⓒ ▮ ☕

Farmer's wife, pottery, second half of 18th century. Austrian Folklore Museum, Vienna.

The museum is in the former Garden Palace (1706–10) of the Imperial Vice-Chancellor, Friedrich Carl von Schönborn. It contains a wide range of material illustrating the traditional popular culture of Austria, in its European context. The exhibits include models of houses, furniture, household equipment, dolls, toys, costumes and ornaments. Also on display are handicrafts, wooden masks and other equipment for folk plays, musical instruments, cribs and popular religious art.

Beethoven Memorial

Beethoven-Gedenkstätte, Pasqualatihaus, Mölkerbastei 8, A-1010 Wien
☎ *0222 6370665*
Tues–Sun 10–12.15, 1–4.30. Closed Jan 1, May 1, Dec 25.
Ⓒ ▮

In the course of his 35 years in Vienna, Beethoven moved house 80 times, including short stays in the suburbs and in neighbouring small towns. Of his 27 apartments in the city

itself only one, the Pasqualatihaus, served him more than once and for long periods. He was here from 1804 to 1808 and again from 1810 to 1814 and during these two periods he wrote most of *Fidelio*, the Fourth piano concerto op. 58 in G major and part of the 4th, 5th, 6th and 7th symphonies.

The memorial contains a number of portraits and personal possessions, as well as Beethoven's 1821 Streicher piano and his death mask.

Belvedere Gallery

Österreichische Galerie im Schloß Belvedere, Prinz Eugen-Straße 27, A-1037 Wien
☎ *0222 784114/784121/784158*
Tues–Sun 10–4. Closed Jan 1, May 1, Nov 1, 2, Dec 24, 25.
Ⓒ ▮ ◼ ௬

The Lower and the Upper Belvedere were built in 1714–16 and 1721–3 as the summer residence of the Austrian Chancellor, Prince Eugen of Savoy. The two palaces and their park, designed by the Austrian architect, Johann Lucas von Hildebrandt, form an outstandingly beautiful Baroque ensemble.

The Gallery has paintings and sculpture by Austrian artists from the Middle Ages to the present day. In the Lower Belvedere there are works by the principal Austrian Baroque artists and 18th-century portraits of members of the Imperial family. The Orangery of the Lower Belvedere has 14th–16th-century wood and stone sculpture and altar paintings and carvings, and in the Upper Belvedere the exhibitions are of 19th- and 20th-century portraits, landscapes, historical scenes, frescoes and miniatures by Austrian artists.

Collection of Popular Religious Art

Sammlung Religiöse Volkskunst, Johannesgasse 8, A-1010 Wien   ☎ *0222 5121337*
Wed 9–4; Sun 9–1. Closed Jan 1, Easter Sun, May 1, Whit Sun, Corpus Christi, Nov 1, Dec 25.
Ⓒ ▮

The museum is in a former 18th-century Ursuline convent, which has an apothecary's shop of the same period, with its original furnishings and equipment and a painting representing Christ as an apothecary. The works exhibited represent popular devotions to Christ, the Virgin and the Saints, in the form of paintings, sculpture and reliefs.

Court Collection of Furniture

Ehemalige Hofmobiliendepot, Mariahilferstraße 88, A-1070 Wien   ☎ *0222 934240*
Tues–Fri 9–4; Sat 9–12. Hourly guided tours. Closed public holidays.
Ⓒ

In 1750 the Empress Maria Theresa founded the Hofmobiliendepot, which was responsible for the administration, maintenance and repair of the Court's furniture. After the end of the monarchy in 1918, the Depot was taken over by the Republic, to provide the furniture for those Imperial palaces which had been opened to the public, for Austrian embassies abroad, and for the most important Federal Government offices. During official state visits, the Depot also furnishes the rooms of foreign guests.

In 1924 showrooms were opened for the benefit of the general public. These contain both fine individual pieces and complete ensembles – furniture, carpets, tapestries, wallpaper, pictures and lamps – of different periods and styles.

Recently, attempts have been made to enlarge the collection and to give a comprehensive view of the development of the Austrians' attitudes towards furnishing their homes.

Court Collection of Tableware and Silverware

Ehemalige Hofsilber- und Tafelkammer, Hofburg-Michaelertor, A-1010 Wien
☎ *0222 5331044*
Tues–Fri, Sun and public holidays 9–1. Closed Jan 1, Good Fri, Easter Sun, May 1, Whit Sun, Corpus Christi, Nov 1, 2, Dec 24, 25.
[c]

All the utensils and equipment needed by the Court for its daily table service and for festive occasions were provided, stored and cared for in the Imperial Tableware and Silver Treasury. In 1918, after the end of the monarchy, the finest pieces were transferred to the Museum of Applied Arts. However, a considerable number of outstanding pieces of 18th–19th-century tableware remained in the Treasury and this was opened to the public as a museum in 1922.

The objects on display include items of very high quality from the Vienna Porcelain Factory, Bohemian glass, and the pure gold personal cutlery of the Empress, Maria Theresa and her grandson, Francis I.

Haydn's House

Haydn Wohnhaus, Haydngasse 19, A-1060 Wien
☎ *0222 561307*
Tues–Sun 10–12.15, 1–4.30. Closed Jan 1, May 1, Dec 25.
[c]

Josef Haydn lived here from 1797 to 1809 and during this time he composed 'The Seasons' and 'The Creation'. The exhibits include Haydn's death mask and portraits of his friends and contemporaries, as well as scores, autograph manuscripts and other memorabilia. A room in the same house is devoted to the life and work of Johannes Brahms, with items of furniture from his last home in Vienna, at Karlsgasse 4.

Johann Strauss's House

Johann-Strauss-Wohnung, Praterstraße 54, A-1020 Wien
☎ *0222 240121*
Tues–Sun 10–12.15, 1–4.30. Closed Jan 1, May 1, Dec 25.
[c] ⚲

The museum contains memorabilia of the composer in the house where he lived and where, in 1867, he wrote *The Blue Danube*. The exhibits include furniture, paintings and musical instruments which belonged to Johann Strauss and to members of his family.

Mozart's House

Mozart-Wohnung (Figaro-Haus), Domgasse 5, A-1010 Wien
☎ *0222 5136294*
Tues–Sun 10–12.15, 1–4.30. Closed Jan 1, May 1, Dec 25.
[c] ⚲

The apartment was the home of Wolfgang Amadeus Mozart in 1784–7. It has its original floor, shutters and wainscot, and contains memorabilia of the composer and material recalling Vienna as it was in the 1780s.

Museum of the Alsergrund District

Bezirks-Museum Alsergrund, Währinger Straße 43, A-1091 Wien
☎ *0222 423575 extn 229*
Wed 9–11, Sun 10–12. Closed public and Catholic holidays.
[F] ⬧

The museum presents the social and cultural history of the people who have lived in the Ninth, Alsergrund, District of Vienna. The story is told with the help of paintings, engravings and photographs, and includes memorabilia of notable residents, including Mozart, Beethoven, Johann Strauss and Anton Bruckner.

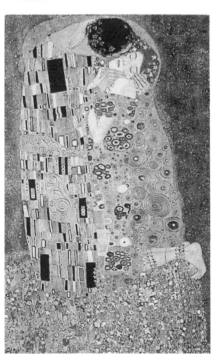

The Kiss, **c.1909, by Gustav Klimt. Belvedere Gallery, Vienna.**

Three rooms are a memorial to the Viennese poet, novelist, essayist and short–story writer, Heimito von Doderer (1896–1966). His works are, in effect, a dramatisation of European history from about 1880 to 1960, the main character being the City of Vienna and its society.

Museum of the History of Art

Kunsthistorisches Museum, Burgring 5, A-1010
*   Wien   ☎ 0222 934541/930620*
Tues, Fri 10–6, 7–9; Wed, Thurs 10–6; Sat, Sun
*   9–6*
C ▮ 🖾

The Kunsthistorisches Museum is one of the most important art museums in the world. Its possessions are largely due to the Habsburgs, who for centuries were enthusiastic patrons and collectors of art. In the 16th century, Archduke Ferdinand II and Emperor Rudolf II, and in the 18th, Archduke Leopold Wilhelm, created collections which form the core of the present museum and determine its character. The Kunsthistoriches Museum was built between 1871 and 1891 during the reign of Emperor Franz Josef I. It is divided into eight departments. Its collections range from Ancient Egypt through Greek and Roman Antiquities to the Middle Ages, the Renaissance and the Baroque, and are European in scale and scope, with works by all the principal masters.

The collection of arms and armour is one of the finest in the world and there are noteworthy displays of musical instruments, carriages, coins and medals and court uniforms.

Museum of Military History

Heeresgeschichtliches Museum, Arsenal, Obj. 1,
*   A-1030 Wien   ☎ 0222 782303*
Sat–Thurs 10–4. Closed Jan 1, Easter Sun,
*   May 1, Whit Sun, Corpus Christi, Nov 1, 2,*
*   Dec 24, 25, 31.*
C ▮ 🖾 ☕

The museum is housed in the oldest State museum building in Vienna, constructed in the Moorish-Byzantine style in 1850–6 as part of the Vienna Arsenal. Formerly the Imperial Military Museum, it was restored after wartime damage and reopened as the Museum of Military History in 1958.

It illustrates the history of the Austrian armed forces from the Thirty Years War to the present day. Visitors can see comprehenive collections of weapons, uniforms, decorations, flags and military musical instruments, together with models and dioramas, paintings of scenes from military history and portraits and memorabilia of Austrian military leaders.

A separate room commemorates the immediate cause of the First World War, the assassination of the Archduke Ferdinand in Sarajevo in June 1914. The exhibits include the uniform being worn by the Archduke and the motorcar in which the murder took place.

The Roggendorfer Altar, *c.* 1500. Museum of Lower Austria, Vienna.

Museum of Lower Austria

Niederösterreichisches Landesmuseum, Herrengasse
*   9, A-1014 Wien   ☎ 0222 635711*
Tues–Fri 9–5; Sat 9–2; Sun 9–12. Easter Sat,
*   Easter Mon, Whit Mon, Nov 2, 11, 9–12.*
*   Closed Jan 1, Good Fri, Easter Sun, Whit*
*   Sun, Dec 24, 25, 31.*
C ✑

The museum is in the former Palais Mollard, built in the 17th century. It presents the natural history, archaeology, industrial, social and religious history and art of Lower Austria. There are collections illustrating the production of timber, coal, minerals, petroleum and gold, and exhibits of wine-making equipment, craftsmen's tools, and models showing the different types of rural houses. The particular strengths of the art collections are medieval panel-paintings and sculpture, 19th-century paintings and prints and drawings. The museum has 12 branches in the province.

Museum of Vienna

Historisches Museum der Stadt Wien, Karlsplatz,
*   A-1040 Wien   ☎ 0222 5058747*
Tues–Sun 9–4.30. Closed Jan 1, May 1, Dec 25.
C ▮ ♿

The museum tells the story of Vienna, from prehistoric times to the present day. There is sculpture, pottery and household objects from excavations on the site of Roman Vienna and, for the later period, medieval sculpture, architectural features and paintings. The development of Vienna from the 15th century onwards is illustrated by means of plans, models and topographical paintings and prints. There are collections of armour and exhibits relating to the siege of Vienna by the Turks.

Other exhibits relate to costumes, coins and medals, Freemasonry in Vienna, furniture, and

Vienna porcelain and silver. Literature, music, painting and theatre all have sections devoted to them and there are three rooms from the house of the dramatist, Franz Grillparzer (1791–1872), who was born and died in Vienna.

Prater Museum

Pratermuseum, Oswald Thomas-Platz 1, A-1020 Wien
Sat, Sun and public holidays 2–6.30. Closed Aug and Dec 24, 31.
© ♿

The museum tells the story of the Prater amusement park, its activities and its institutions. There are paintings and drawings to show the celebrated area developed generation by generation from the 18th century onwards and memorabilia of the Basilio Calafatis family, which was influential in creating the Prater's international reputation.

Schönbrunn Palace

Schloß Schönbrunn, A-1130 Wien
   ☎ *0222 811 13238*
Apr–Oct, daily 8.30–5.30. Nov–Mar, daily 9–4. Closed Jan 1, Nov 1, Dec 24.
© ♿ 💺 ♿ ☕

In 1569 Emperor Maximilian II bought the Manor of Katerburg. Over the centuries, his descendants redesigned and added to the property. It was rebuilt in 1605, after its devastation by the Hungarians, and again in 1696, following its destruction by the Turks during the siege of Vienna. In 1743 it was enlarged by Empress Maria Theresa and since then its appearance has hardly changed. It was used by the Imperial family as a residence until 1918 and opened to the public as a museum in 1922.

The former Imperial Apartments contain 18th- and 19th-century furniture, including a Biedermeier billiard table, clocks and paintings. The portraits of the Emperors and Empresses and the members of their families are especially interesting.

Schubert Museum

Schubert-Museum, Nußdorfer Straße 54, A-1090 Wien   ☎ *0222 3459924*
Tues–Sun 10–12.15, 1–4.30. Closed Jan 1, May 1, Dec 25.
© ♿

Schönbrunn Palace, Vienna.

The museum is in the tiny first-floor apartment in which Franz Schubert was born in 1797. It has been restored to its appearance in the year of the composer's birth, and contains the marble bust of Schubert by Carl Kundmann, views of the western suburbs of Vienna and, among other memorabilia, Schubert's famous round spectacles.

Sigmund Freud Museum

Sigmund Freud Museum, Berggasse 19, A-1090 Wien   ☎ *0222 311396*
Daily 10–3
© ♿

The museum, financed and administered by the Sigmund Freud Society of Vienna, contains memorabilia of the founder of psychoanalysis, in his former consulting room. The waiting-room furniture of Freud's practice in London has been installed, and elsewhere there is part of Freud's collection of antiques. The other exhibits include original manuscripts and first editions of his books, and documents, photographs and letters illustrating his life and career.

Sigmund Freud Museum, Vienna.

Technical Museum of Industry and Crafts

Technisches Museum für Industrie und Gewerbe Wien, Mariahilferstraße 212, A-1140 Wien
   ☎ *0222 833618*
© ♿ 💺 ♿ ☕

The Technical Museum of Industry and Crafts was opened in 1918 and is one of the world's earliest museums of this kind. It was created in order to show the development of technology in all its fields and especially the Austrian contribution to this. There are reconstructions of historic laboratories and workshops and a replica of part of a coalmine. Among the exhibits of particular interest are Madersperger's sewing machine, Voigtländer's pioneering metal-cased camera, Thonet's bentwood furniture, Lilienthal's glider and the first Kaplan turbine.

Treasury of the Holy Roman Empire

*Kunsthistorisches Museum, Weltliche und
   Geistliche Schatzkammer, Hofburg,
   Schweizerhof, A-1010 Wien*
   ☎ *0222 934541/930620/5337931*
Mon, Wed–Fri 10–6; Sat, Sun 9–6
F 🔒 ♿

The museum contains the Crown Jewels of the
Holy Roman Empire, the Habsburg Crown, the
Treasure of Burgundy and the Imperial insignia
from the 9th century onwards, including the
Order of the Golden Fleece, together with the
Ecclesiastical Treasure of the Habsburg family.
The latter includes gold, silver and jewelled
religious ornaments and liturgical objects. Also
on display are a wide range of ceremonial
garments and paintings of coronations and other
ceremonies and of Emperors and members of
their families wearing the Imperial insignia. The
Treasury contains a memorial room to Marie-
Louise, Archduchess of Austria.

**Technical Museum of Industry and Crafts,
Vienna.**

Wels

Castle Museum

*Burgmuseum Wels, Kulturzentrum Burg Wels,
   Burggasse 13, A-4600 Wels, Oberösterreich*
   ☎ *07242 5311 or 07242 4147*
*Tues–Fri 10–5; Sat, Sun and public holidays
   10–12. Closed Jan 1, Good Fri, Dec 25, 31.*
F 🔒 🚻 ☕

Wels Castle existed as a fortified site in the 8th
century AD. The Castle Museum at Wels is
celebrated for its collections relating to
agriculture and rural life in the region. The
displays, arranged in ten galleries, deal with
implements and farm operations, fishing,
forestry, markets, crafts, farm livestock, cider,
building work, domestic activities and religious
beliefs and practices. A special section is
devoted to the Austrian Bread Museum. There
is an exhibition of Biedermeier objects,
including furniture, and a collection of rural
furniture from the 16th century onwards. The
Emperor Maximilian died here in 1519 and
there are memorabilia of him on show.

BELGIUM

Andenne

Museum of Ceramics

*Musée Communal de la Céramique d'Andenne, 29
rue Charles Lapierre, B-5220 Andenne,
Namur* ☎ *085 844181/841150/842186
May–Sept, Tues, Fri, Sat, Sun and public holidays,
2.30–5.30. Oct–Apr by appt.*

C ▮

The existence of excellent local clays has
allowed Andenne to flourish as an important
pottery centre from Roman times to the present
day. The museum's collections of pottery, pipes,
faïence and stoneware illustrate the history and
techniques of the industry. There is a
reconstruction of a 10th-century kiln, an
authentic 19th-century kiln and a pipe-maker's
workshop showing all the stages in the
manufacture of clay pipes.

Antwerp

Brewers' Hall

*Brouwerhuis, Adriaan Brouwersstraat 20, B-2000
Antwerpen* ☎ *03 2326511
Tues–Sun 10–4.30. Closed Jan 1, 2, May 1,
Ascension Day, Nov 1, 2, Dec 25, 26.*

C ▮ ◢

What is now known as Brewers' Hall was built
in 1553–4 as the Water House to distribute fresh
water to premises in this part of Antwerp,
including newly constructed breweries. The
brewers began to meet there in 1581, and
constructed a magnificent hall for the purpose.
Pumping was carried out by two horses until the
1870s. The pumping equipment and the
reservoir have been preserved, together with the
Brewers' Hall and its furnishings.

Butchers' Hall

*Museum Vleeshuis, Vleeshouwersstraat 40,
B-2000 Antwerpen* ☎ *03 2336404
Tues–Sun 10–5. Closed Jan 1, 2, May 1,
Ascension Day, Nov 1, 2, Dec 25, 26.*

C ▮

Butchers' Hall, in the middle of the old city of
Antwerp, dates from the early 16th century and
was built for the Butchers' Corporation. It
ceased to be used for its original purpose after
the French Revolution in 1789, when the guilds
and corporations were dissolved. At the end of
the 19th century it became the property of the
City of Antwerp, which restored it and, in
1913, opened it as a museum of antiquities. It is
now a museum of prehistory and history, with a
strong emphasis on the history of Antwerp.
There are departments of arms and armour,
sculpture, ceramics, musical instruments made
in Antwerp, religious art, coins, posters,
furniture and domestic equipment.

Folklore Museum

*Volkskundemuseum, Gildekamersstraat 2-6,
B-2000 Antwerpen* ☎ *03 2208211
Tues–Sun 10–5. Closed Jan 1, 2, May 1, Nov 1,
2, Dec 25, 26.*

C ▮ ♿

The museum occupies five 17th-century guild
houses. Its collections illustrate Flemish popular
arts and traditions. There are sections devoted
to furniture, household equipment, handicrafts
and trades, popular beliefs and superstitions,
magic, medicine, folk songs, folk literature and
puppet plays. Festivals, pageants and giants are
also well represented.

Maritime Museum

*Nationaal Scheepvaartmuseum, Steenplein 1,
B-2000 Antwerpen* ☎ *03 2320850
Daily 10–4.45. Closed Jan 1, 2, May 1,
Ascension Day, Nov 1, 2, Dec 25, 26.*

C ▮ ▬ ♿ ↩

The museum building is in what remains of an
old castle. It is concerned with maritime
history, with particular reference to Belgium.
There are ten galleries, devoted to the arts and
crafts of the waterfront; ship models; devotion
and magic; people of the waterfront; inland
navigation; fishing; yachting; shipbuilding; the
history of shipping until the end of the 18th
century; and the history of shipping from the
beginning of the 19th century.

The story is told with the help of ship models,
navigational instruments, charts, ships'
ornaments and decorations, photographs,
paintings and a wide range of equipment,
together with actual small vessels.

Brewers' Hall, Antwerp.

Museum of Flemish Culture

Archief en Museum voor het Vlaamse Cultuurleven (AMVC), Minderbroedersstraat 22, B-2000 Antwerpen ☎ *03 2325580*
Tues–Sun 10–5. Closed Jan 1, 2, May 1, Ascension Day, Nov 1, 2, Dec 25, 26.
[C] 🔒

The museum documents the development of Flemish culture and the Flemish movement from 1750 onwards. The collections consist of documents, books, posters, photographs, paintings and memorabilia relating to literature, music, the theatre and the fine arts. There is also an extensive body of material telling the story of the Flemish movement. The museum is the central cultural archive of Flanders.

Plantin-Moretus Museum

Museum Plantin-Moretus, Vrijdagmarkt 22, B-2000 Antwerpen
☎ *03 2330294/2322455*
Daily 10–5. Closed Jan 1, 2, May 1, Ascension Day, Nov 1, Dec 25, 26.
[C] 🔒

Christophe Plantin, the great printer, established himself in Antwerp in 1548 and, between then and 1589, the year of his death, he published more than 1,500 works. He left the printing house to his son-in-law, Jan Moretus. The business continued in the family until 1876, when it passed to the City of Antwerp, to become a museum. In 1945 the building was severely damaged during a rocket attack, but was re-opened after restoration in 1951.

The museum library contains copies of virtually all the books printed by Plantin and the Moretuses, about 30,000 volumes, together with a fine collection of other Antwerp publications. There are also the firm's business records, illustrated manuscripts, drawings for book illustrations, woodblocks, copperplates and a large quantity of punches and matrices for type-founding. Decorating the walls of the rooms are 150 paintings and family portraits by Flemish artists, including 18 by Rubens. The old printing room contains 16th–18th-century presses used by the firm, together with type, cast in the time of Plantin and the Moretuses, still in its original type-cases.

Rockox House

Rockoxhuis, Keizerstraat 12, B-2000 Antwerpen
☎ *03 2314710*
Tues–Sun 10–5
[F] 🔒

Nicolaas Rockox (1560–1640), Burgomaster of Antwerp and friend and patron of Peter Paul Rubens, played an important part in the life of Antwerp for over 50 years. His home was a cultural centre for scholars and artists from many countries. In 1971 a foundation was established to restore and open the house as a museum, with 16th and early 17th-century furnishings and pictures. Visitors can now get an impression of how the house looked during the lifetime of Rockox.

Jean Foucquet, *Madonna with Child.* Royal Museum of Fine Art, Antwerp.

Royal Museum of Fine Art

Koninklijk Museum voor Schone Kunsten, Leopold de Waelplein, B-2000 Antwerpen. Correspondence to: Plaatsnijdersstraat 2, B-2000 Antwerpen. ☎ *03 2387809*
Tues–Sun 10–5. Closed Jan 1, May 1, Ascension Day, Dec 25.
[F] 🔒 ☕ ♿

The museum was established in 1890, but its origins are much earlier. The core of its collections are works of art which belonged to the Guild of St Luke, an association of painters, sculptors and other artists, founded in 1442. The collection was greatly enlarged during the 19th century and in 1927 the municipal museum became a national institution.

The present museum is divided into two sections. The Department of Old Art provides a survey of Flemish painting from c. 1360 until the end of the 18th century. It includes many works by Rubens, and covers the most important aspects of Dutch, Italian, French and German art during the same period. The Department of Modern Art is devoted to Belgian art of the 19th and 20th centuries. The expressionist, abstract and surrealist movements are all well represented.

Rubens' House

Rubenshuis, Rubensstraat 9-11, B-2000 Antwerpen
Daily 10–5. Closed Jan 1, 2, May 1, Ascension Day, Nov 1, Dec 25, 26.
[C]

The museum is a reconstruction of the house and studio once occupied by Peter Paul Rubens and destroyed in Second World War bombing. It has the original 17th-century portico and garden pavilion. The house contains 17th-century Flemish furnishings and paintings by Rubens, his collaborators and his pupils.

Arlon

Luxembourg Museum

*Musée Luxembourgeois, 13 rue des Martyrs,
B-6700 Arlon, Hainaut-Luxembourg*
☎ 063 226192
*Jan 2–Dec 14, Mon–Sat 9–12, 2–5. Closed public
holidays and Dec 15, 31.*
© 🛈 ⌖

The museum at Arlon is particularly celebrated
for its splendid Gallo-Roman and Merovingian
collections of objects discovered during
excavations on the site of the ancient fort and
settlement and the associated cemeteries. The
sculptures relating to the Gallo-Roman period
are arranged in galleries, according to their
theme – military life, religion and, most
abundant of all, daily life. Other displays
present pottery, glass and metal objects.

Elsewhere in the museum are displays
illustrating life in the region during the 18th and
19th centuries, special attention being given to
furniture and household equipment. The
collection of firebacks (1570–1818), jacks, spits
and other domestic ironwork is particularly
interesting. A series of room interiors from
houses in the region shows the development of
style and comfort among the more prosperous
classes.

Bastogne

Bastogne Historical Centre

*Bastogne Historical Centre, Hill of the Mardasson,
B-6650 Bastogne, Hainaut-Luxembourg*
☎ 062 211413
*Feb–Apr, Sept–Nov, daily 10–5. May–Sept, daily
9–6.*
© 🛈 ⌑ ⌖

The location of Bastogne, where seven roads
meet and near the frontiers of Holland, France,
Luxembourg and Germany, explains why battles
have taken place there throughout history. The
Centre is concerned with events during the
Second World War and particularly with the
Battle of Bastogne, which took place during the
winter of 1944, as part of the campaign in the

Ardennes, and in which American troops were
heavily involved. The course of the battle is
documented with the help of both German and
American weapons, uniforms, vehicles,
dioramas and an audio-visual programme.

Binche

Museum of the Carnival and the Masque

*Musée international du Carnaval et du Masque, rue
de l'Eglise, B-7130 Binche, Hainaut-Mons*
☎ 064 335741
*Feb–Mar, Mon–Thurs 10–1, 2–6; Sun 2–6. Sun
of 'Percussion and Musical Performances',
Carnival Sun and Mon, 10–1, 2–6. Apr–
Nov 15, Mon–Thurs, Sat 10–12, 2–6. Sun
and public holidays 10–1, 2–6. Closed Carnival
Tues, Ash Wednesday, Nov 1. Groups of more
than 20 people by appt only.*
© 🛈 ⌑ ⌖ ⌖

Belgium is one of Europe's most important
centres of traditional carnival festivities. In an
18th-century building which was formerly the
College of the Augustinians, the museum
presents the winter and spring feasts and
carnivals in Europe, masked festivities and
carnivals in Latin America, the masques of
Africa, Amazonia and Latin America, masks
and theatre in Asia, and the Walloon carnivals
in Belgium, with particular attention being paid
to the extraordinary Binche carnival, with its
Trouilles de Nouilles, Mam'zelles, Pierrots,
Arlequins, Paysans and Gilles. The Binche
carnival has taken place, without interruption,
from the 14th century to the present day. The
finale lasts for three days, but the preliminaries
are spread over six weeks.

The museum has excellent and steadily
growing collections of costumes, masks and
other equipment and in its exhibitions and
audio-visual displays illustrates the traditions
surrounding carnivals and masques.

Bruges

The Béguine's House

*Begijnhuis, Monasterium de Wijngaard, Oud
Begijnhof 30, B-8000 Brugge, West-
Vlaanderen*   ☎ 050 330011
*Mar–Nov, Mon–Thurs, Sat 10.30–12, 1.45–5;
Fri 10.30–12; Sun and public holidays 10.45–
12, 1.45–6.*
© 🛈

The Béguines were a Netherlands order of nuns
who did not take vows. The Princely Béguinage
of the Vineyard was founded in 1245. The nuns
who occupy it today are no longer Béguines but
Benedictine sisters, who have kept the 15th-
century costume.

The church and the houses surrounding it
form an historic complex of great charm. The
house, which is open to the public, was
occupied by a single nun and, furnished in the
old way, gives a good idea of how the Béguines
lived.

**North American Indian dancer's mask.
Museum of the Carnival and the Masque,
Binche.**

Folklore Museum

*Museum voor Volkskunde, Rolweg 40, B-8000
    Brugge, West-Vlaanderen*   ☎ 050 330044
*Apr–Sept, daily 9.30–12, 2–6. Oct–Jan, Mar,
    Mon, Wed–Sun 9.30–12, 2–5. Closed Jan 1.*
ⓒ ⓪ ⬛

The museum occupies a row of small houses in
the old part of the city. Its collections illustrate
the traditional culture of the region. There are
exhibits showing popular art, folk customs,
handicrafts and domestic equipment. Among
the larger items are the interiors of a 19th-
century pharmacy and an inn of the same
period.

Gruuthuse Museum

*Gruuthusemuseum, Dijver 17, B-8000 Brugge,
    West-Vlaanderen*   ☎ 050 339911
*Apr–Sept, daily 9.30–12, 2–6. Oct–Mar, Mon,
    Wed–Sun 9.30–12, 2 5.*
ⓒ ⓪

This 15th-century building was the palace of the
Lords of Gruuthuse. It is now a museum showing
the work of Belgian craftsmen in the field of the
applied arts. The collections include goldsmiths'
work, guild insignia, musical instruments,
pottery, lace, tapestries and other textiles, and
coins and medals.

The museum also has sections devoted to
prehistoric and medieval archaeology.

Museum of Our Lady of the Pottery, Bruges.

Memling Museum

*Memlingmuseum, Sint-Janshospitaal, Mariastraat
    38, B-8000 Brugge, West-Vlaanderen*
    ☎ 050 332562
*Apr–Sept, daily 9–12.30, 2–6. Oct–Mar, Mon,
    Tues, Thurs–Sun 10–12, 2–5. Closed Jan 1.*
ⓒ ⓪

The museum is in the building of a medieval
hospital. It contains a completely equipped
pharmacy, dating from the 17th century, and
furniture and household utensils of the same
period. In the museum are a number of paintings
by Hans Memling (c. 1430–94), who spent
most of his life in Bruges, where he became a
citizen in 1465 and was one of the largest
taxpayers by 1480. Works by other Bruges artists
are also included in the collection.

Museum of Our Lady of the Pottery

*Museum Onze-Lieve-Vrouw ter Potterie,
    Potterierei 79, B-8000 Brugge, West-
    Vlaanderen. Correspondence to: Mariastraat
    38, B-8000 Brugge.*   ☎ 050 333898
*Apr–Sept, daily 9–12.30, 2–6. Oct–Mar, Mon,
    Tues, Thurs–Sun 10–12, 2–5. Closed Jan 1.*
ⓒ ⓪ ⬛

The museum is housed in a 14th-century
hospital building, linked to an 18th-century
church, which has all its original furnishings.
Despite the name, this is not a museum of
pottery. It contains ecclesiastical gold- and
silversmiths' work, furniture and 16th-century
tapestries and paintings.

Detail of Empress Eugénie's robe, Brussels
lace, c. 1867. Museum of Costume and Lace,
Brussels.

Brussels

The Béguinage at Anderlecht

Le Béguinage d'Anderlecht, 8 rue de Chapelain,
*   B-1070 Bruxelles*   ☎ *02 5211383*
Mon–Wed, Sat, Sun 10–12, 2–5
Ⓒ 🛏 ♨ ↝

Founded in 1252, the convent of Béguine nuns
has been restored to its original appearance.
Visitors are able to see the Mother Superior's
room, the kitchen, the oratory and other
buildings. There are exhibits illustrating the
daily life of the nuns in the 18th century. The
museum also has collections relating to the
archaeology and history of Anderlecht and to
the popular art, crafts and customs of the region.

Erasmus' House

La Maison d'Erasme, 31 rue du Chapitre, B-1070
*   Bruxelles*   ☎ *02 5211383*
Mon, Wed, Thurs, Sat, Sun 10–12, 2–5
Ⓒ 🛏 ↝

31 rue du Chapitre dates from 1515 and was at
one time lived in by Erasmus (1467–1536). It is
now a museum dedicated to him, with period
furniture and décor and collections of
documents, paintings, manuscripts and first
editions of books relating to Erasmus and other
humanists of the 16th century.

Museum of Brussels

Musée communal de la Ville de Bruxelles, 1 rue du
*   Poivre, B-1000 Bruxelles*   ☎ *02 5112742*
Apr–Sept, Mon–Wed, Fri 10–12.30, 1.30–5;
*   Thurs 10–5; Sat, Sun 10–1. Oct–Mar, Mon–*
*   Wed, Fri 10–12.30, 1.30–4; Thurs 10–4;*
*   Sat, Sun 10–1. Closed Jan 1, May 1, Nov 1,*
*   2, Dec 25.*
Ⓒ 🛏

The museum is in the Maison du Roi, entirely
rebuilt in the 19th century according to the
original 16th-century plans. Recently entirely

refurbished, it presents on the ground floor its
collections of Brussels-made sculpture and
decorative art – tapestries, retables, goldsmiths'
work, faïence, porcelain, lace and jewellery.
The exhibits on the first floor tell the story of
the development of Brussels as a city and the
second floor is devoted to particular aspects of
the city's past, its economic, political, social,
religious and cultural history. One gallery is
given over to the celebrated Manneken-Pis,
showing him in a large variety of costumes, from
the 18th century to the present day.

Museum of Costume and Lace

Musée du Costume et de la Dentelle de la Ville de
*   Bruxelles, 6 rue de la Violette, B-1000*
*   Bruxelles*   ☎ *02 5127709*
Apr–Sept, Mon–Fri 10–12.30, 1.30–5; Sat, Sun
*   2–4.30. Oct–Mar, Mon–Fri 10–12.30,*
*   1.30–4; Sat, Sun 2–4.30.*
Ⓒ 🛏

The museum occupies two 18th-century houses,
close to the Grand'Place. It has collections of
costumes with lace trimmings, dating from the
18th century to the 20th, and of modern and
traditional lace, including Brussels, Chantilly,
Valenciennes and Malines. There are also
exhibits showing the history and techniques of
lace-making.

Railway Museum

Musée du Chemin de fer, 76 rue du Progrès,
*   B-1210 Bruxelles*   ☎ *02 12186050*
Mon–Fri 9–4.30. 1st Sat in month 9–4.30. Closed
*   public holidays.*
Ⓕ 🛏

Belgium had the first railway on the Continent,
running from Brussels to Malines (1835). The
museum was set up in 1951 to tell the story of
railways in Belgium. It does this mainly by
means of models of locomotives and rolling
stock, documents and photographs, but there
are also exhibits of uniforms, items of signalling
and other operating equipment, as well as
sections of rail at different periods. A single
historic locomotive serves as a centrepiece. It is
the 'Pays de Waes' (1845), one of the oldest
surviving locomotives in the world.

Royal Museum of the Army

Musée Royal de l'Armée et d'Histoire Militaire,
   3 parc du Cinquantenaire, B-1040 Bruxelles
   ☎ *02 7339794/7345252*
Tues–Sun 9–12, 1–4.45 (4 in winter). Closed
   Jan 1, May 1, Nov 1, Dec 25.

F 🛈 ✈

The Royal Museum of the Army forms part of
the Cinquantenaire, the enormous architectural
complex begun in 1880 to mark the 50th
anniversary of Belgian independence, and
completed in 1905 with the construction of a
triumphal area. Founded in 1910, the museum
was transferred here in 1923. Its collections and
exhibitions present the military history of
Belgium from the 18th century to the present
day. The collections of weapons, transport,
pictures, documents, uniforms and other
militaria are very large, covering not only the
forces of Belgium, but those of her allies and
enemies as well. They include tanks, armoured
vehicles and aircraft.

Deurle

Dhondt-Dhaenens Museum

Museum Mevrouw Jules Dhondt-Dhaenens,
   Museumlaan 14, B-9831 Sint-Martens-Latem/
   Deurle, Oost-Vlaanderen   ☎ *091 825123*
Mar–Oct, Wed–Fri 2–5; Sat, Sun 10–12, 2–5.

C ♿ ☕

The museum's collections are of paintings and
sculpture from the period 1860–1960, with an
emphasis on works by Flemish artists. Among
the more important items are the sculptures by
George Minne, *The Passion of Jesus* by Albert
Servaes and paintings by members of the
Martens-Latem group.

Enghien

Tapestry Museum

Musée de la Tapisserie, Maison Jonathan, 7 rue
   Montgomery, B-1390 Enghien, Hainaut
   ☎ *02 3955906*
Mon–Fri 2–5; Sat 2–7; Sun 10–12, 2–7

F 🛈 ♿

The core of the museum consists of five locally-
made 16th-century tapestries. The exhibition
which surrounds them presents the history of
the tapestry industry in Enghien, the names of
famous makers and the location of Enghien
tapestries throughout the world today.

Genk

Bokrijk Open-Air Museum

Openluchtmuseum Bokrijk, Domein Bokrijk,
   B-3600 Genk, Limburg   ☎ *011 224575*
Apr–Sept, daily 10–6. Oct–Mar, Sat, Sun 10–6.

C 🛈 💼 ♿ ☕

Bokrijk Estate, one of the most frequented
recreation areas in Belgium, covers 1,400 acres

**Aircraft display. Royal Museum of the Army,
Brussels.**

and includes a large arboretum and a zoo, as well
as the open-air museum. It contains about 120
buildings brought from all parts of Belgium.
They are arranged in village groupings to
illustrate, with their contents, the daily life and
work of the people to whom they once
belonged. The buildings date from the 16th
century to the 19th and reflect both rural and
urban lifestyles.

Ghent

Byloke Museum of Antiquities

Oudheidkundig Museum van de Byloke,
   Godshuislaan 2, B-9000 Gent, Oost-
   Vlaanderen   ☎ *091 251106*
Tues–Sun 9–12.30, 1.30–5. Closed Jan 1, 2,
   Dec 24, 25.

C 🛈

The museum is housed in the former Cistercian
Abbey of the Byloke, founded in 1228. It
contains 14th-century frescoes, a Gothic room
with mementoes of the Ghent merchant and
craft guilds and rooms furnished in the styles of
the 17th, 18th and 19th centuries. Visitors can
also see the Insignia of the Corporation of the
City of Ghent, the City's weights and measures
of 1281 and the furniture of the Chamber of the
Governors of the Poor, originally in the Town
Hall. There are collections of 18th-century
tapestries and Brussels carpets, of weapons,
costumes and uniforms, and of Flemish pottery,
faïence, porcelain and crystal, as well as of
copper, brass, bronze and pewter.

Michel Thiery Botanical Garden

Hortus Museum Michel Thiery, Berouw 55,
  B-9000 Gent, Oost-Vlaanderen
  ☎ *091 250542*
Mon–Thurs, Sat, Sun 9–12.15, 1.30–5.15; Fri
  9–12.15. Closed public holidays.
F

In 1923 Michel Thiery, a Ghent teacher, created a botanical garden on ecological principles. The garden was arranged according to the habitats to be found in Belgium, a revolutionary system at the time. The botanical garden has now been replanted, following the original plans of the founder. A new beekeeping section has been created, with a transparent beehive inside the museum, which allows visitors to watch the bees at work.

The museum is run in conjunction with the Michel Thiery School Museum at Sint Pietersplein 14, which occupies two wings of a medieval abbey and houses worldwide collections of the natural sciences.

Museum of Folklore

Museum voor Volkskunde, Kraanlei 65, B-9000
  Gent, Oost-Vlaanderen   ☎ *091 231336*
Apr–Nov 2, daily 9–12.30, 1.30–5.30.
  Nov 3–Mar, Tues–Sun 10–12, 1.30–5.
  Closed Jan 1, Dec 25.
C 🛈

Since 1962, the museum's collections and the Library of the Royal Folklore Society of East Flanders have been housed in the buildings of the 14th-century Alijn Children's Hospice, which have been completely restored. The exhibits illustrate daily life in the city of Ghent, especially in the 19th century. There are exhibits showing the work of a grocer, cooper, cobbler, innkeeper, chandler, baker, hairdresser, pharmacist, woodturner, printer and tinsmith. Other displays include toys, fashion, tobacco pipes and distilling.

Many items relate to popular religion and domestic crafts, and the museum has its own puppet theatre, with performances on Wednesday and Saturday afternoons. Lace-making classes are also organised.

Museum of Science and Technology

Museum voor Wetenschap en Techniek,
  Rijksuniversiteit Gent, Korte Meer 9, B-9000
  Gent, Oost-Vlaanderen
  ☎ *091 257651 extn 296*
Mon, Wed 2–5; Tues, Thurs, Fri 9–12, 2–5 by
  appt. Closed public holidays.
F

The museum, which is financed and organised by the University of Ghent, was created to illustrate the evolution of science and technology. It has a fine collection of surgical equipment going back to antiquity which was formed by Victor Deneffe in the 19th century, and collections of scientific instruments and demonstration models relating to alchemy, chemistry, photography, electricity, light and sound, cinematography, telecommunications and holography.

Special exhibits document the pioneering work carried out by Ghent scientists, including Joseph Plateau, pioneer of cinematography; D. van Monckhoven, pioneer of the photographic industry; Kekulé van Stradonitz, who helped to define the molecule; and Leo Baekeland, inventor of bakelite.

Grimbergen

Museum of Technology

Museum voor de Oudere Technieken, Guldendal
  20, B-1850 Grimbergen, Brabant
  ☎ *02 2696771*
Apr–Sept, Mon–Fri 9–3; Sat, Sun 2–6. Oct–Mar,
  Mon–Fri 9–3. Closed Dec 23–Jan 2 inclusive.
C 🛈 ⬛ ⇲

The museum's collections illustrate, by means of Belgian examples, the history of technology before the age of steam. The displays are arranged according to the source of power – the muscles of men and animals, water or wind. The museum has the most comprehensive collection in Belgium of woodworking tools, pincers and tongs. It also possesses two working watermills.

Ittré

Forge Museum

Musée de la Forge, 11 rue Basse, B-1460 Ittré,
  Brabant   ☎ *067 646300/647372*
Easter–Nov 1, Sun 2–6.
C ⇲

The museum is located in Ittré's old blacksmith's shop, established in 1701, where the last blacksmith worked until 1956. Since 1963, in Gretna Green fashion, wedding ceremonies have taken place, on request, in front of the anvil, after the official ceremony.

The forge is in operating condition and retains all its tools and equipment. There is also a large collection of horseshoes. According to the ancient custom, the forge has been placed under the protection of Saint Eloi, the patron saint of blacksmiths, while its master is absent. A statue of the saint, placed in the forge, symbolises the fact.

Museum of Science and Technology, Ghent.

**Marionette of the Emperor Charlemagne.
Museum of Walloon Life, Liège**

Kortrijk

Flax and Linen Museum

*Nationaal Vlasmuseum, E. Sabbelaan 4, B-8500
Kortrijk, West-Vlaanderen* ☎ *056 210138
Mar–Nov, Mon, Wed, Thurs, Fri 9.30–12.30,
1.30–6; Tues 1.30–6; Sat, Sun 2–6. Closed
public holidays.*

Ⓒ 🖾

The museum is located on an old farm, where
flax once used to be grown. 38 dioramas show all
the stages involved in the cultivation and
processing of flax and the manufacture of linen
in the days before mechanisation. There is a
good collection of tools and equipment used in
the Belgian linen industry.

The former farmhouse has been converted
into an inn and café, its walls illustrating the
flax year with paintings by the Belgian artist,
Paul Haghemans.

La Gleize-Stoumont

December 1944 Historical Museum

*SC December 1944, 7 rue de l'Eglise, B-4981 La
Gleize-Stoumont, Liège* ☎ *041 785191
Mar 1–Oct 15, daily 10–6*

Ⓒ 🖼 ♿ 🖾

In December 1944 the Battle of the Bulge was in
progress in the Ardennes, the last desperate
German armoured counter-offensive to prevent
an Allied invasion of Germany. The museum
was built in 1987–8 on the exact site, in La
Gleize, where the battle ground to a halt in the
north of the offensive. Six weeks later, by the
end of January 1945, the Germans were in
retreat.

Dioramas and other exhibits present the
course of events and the armies taking part.
Among the items on show are tanks and other
vehicles, uniforms and a wide range of military
equipment, together with contemporary
photographs, newspapers, pamphlets and
posters.

Liège

Ansembourg Museum

*Musée d'Ansembourg, En Feronstrée 114, B-4000
Liège* ☎ *041 221600/232068
Mon, Thurs–Sat 10–12.30, 2–5; Wed 10–12,
2–5, 7–9; Sun and public holidays 10–1.
Closed Jan 1, May 1, Nov 1, Dec 25.*

Ⓒ 🖼

The museum is in the former Hôtel
d'Ansembourg, built for the banker Michel
Willens in 1735–41. It is devoted to the
decorative arts of Liège and contains
reconstructions of room interiors and collections
of tapestries, glass, wrought-iron, furniture and
woodcarving.

Liège Print Collection

*Cabinet des Estampes de la Ville de Liège, 3 Parc de
la Boverie, B-4020 Liège* ☎ *041 423923
Tues–Sat 1–6; Sun and public holidays 11–4.30.
Closed Jan 1, May 1, Nov 1, Dec 25.*

Ⓒ 🖾 🖼 🖾

The museum occupies a building constructed in
1905 for the World Exhibition. It contains an
important collection of 16th–20th-century
engravings and drawings, especially by Liège
and Flemish artists.

Museum of Architecture and Eugène Ysaye's Studio

Musée de l'Architecture de l'ancien Pays de Liège et Studio Eugène Ysaye, 14 impasse des Ursulines, B-4000 Liège   ☎ *041 235513*
Tues–Sun 1–6
C ♿

The museum, which is also a major architectural documentation centre, is in a former convent of Béguine nuns, dating from the 17th century. It contains Belgian architects' plans and decorative elements from buildings in Belgium. There is also a reconstruction of the Modern Style studio of the famous violinist, Eugène Ysaye (1858–1931), with his furniture and library and portraits and busts of him, together with an urn containing his embalmed heart. A further section of the museum, known as the Espace Leloup, displays memorabilia of the master glassmaker, Louis Leloup.

Museum of Firearms

Musée d'Armes de Liège, 8 quai de Maestricht, B-4000 Liège   ☎ *041 233178/231562*
Tues–Sat 10–12.30, 2–5; Sun and public holidays 10–2. Closed Jan 1, May 1, Nov 1 and Dec 25.
C ♿

The museum building was constructed c. 1775 in the classical style for the de Hayme de Bomal family. From 1795–1814, when Liège was under French rule, it was the house of the French Governor, and Napoleon stayed here in 1803 and 1811. The very large collections consist of sporting and military firearms from the 15th to the 20th century, armour and edged weapons, orders and decorations and Napoleonic medals.

Liège was an important centre of the gunmaking trade and one of the features of the museum is its comprehensive survey of Liège firearms production from the Middle Ages to the present day.

Museum of Architecture, Liège.

Museum of Walloon Life

Musée de la Vie Wallonne, Cour des Mineurs, B-4000 Liège   ☎ *041 236094*
Tues–Sat 10–12, 2–5; Sun 10–4. 1st Fri of month (except Aug), also open 7.30–9.30 pm. Closed Jan 1, May 1, Nov 1, Dec 25.
C ♿ 🍴 ✉

The museum occupies a 17th-century monastery. It has collections illustrating the history, daily life and traditional crafts of the French-speaking areas of Belgium. The themes covered include religion and festivals, magic and popular science, food and cooking, heating and lighting, justice and punishment, sports and pastimes, agriculture and rural crafts, dairying, weights and measures and the dialects of Wallonia.

There is a special display of Liège puppets and marionettes, an important collection of sundials and, in the basement, a coalmine gallery.

A feature of the museum is its series of reconstructions of craftsmen's workshops. These include the premises of a coppersmith, chandler, cooper, pewterer, gunstock maker, slate slitter, clay-pipe maker, stringed instrument maker, wheelwright, basket-maker and clog-maker.

Louvain

Vander Kelen Mertens Museum

Museum Vander Kelen-Mertens, Savoiestraat 6, B-3000 Leuven, Brabant
☎ *016 226906/232778*
Easter–Sept, Tues–Sat 10–12, 2–5; Sun 2–5. Oct–Easter, Tues–Sat 10–12, 2–5.
C ♿

In 1919 Senator Victor Vander Kelen gave to the city the old family house in Louvain, for use as a museum in memory of his father, Léopold Vander Kelen, who had been Mayor, his mother, Marie Mertens, and his brother, Léon. It is now used as a museum of the fine and decorative arts, with 15th–16th-century religious sculpture, porcelain, 16th–20th-century paintings by Louvain artists, stained glass and wrought-ironwork as outstanding features of the collections.

Malmédy

Paper Museum and Museum of the Malmédy Carnival

Musée National du Papier et Musée du Carnaval de Malmédy, 11 place du Rome, B-4890 Malmédy, Liège   ☎ *080 337058*
Paper Museum: July–Aug, daily 2–5. Other times by appt. Carnival Museum: daily 2–5 throughout the year. Closed during period of the Carnival (4 days preceding Ash Wed), Jan 1, Dec 24–26, 31.
F ♿

The Paper Museum, which is still in the course of development, occupies the first two floors of the Maison Cavens, and the Carnival Museum the third. The Paper Museum presents the history of paper-making and shows how the industry has developed in Belgium since the Industrial Revolution. Visitors can see how hand-made paper is produced and contrast this with the modern machines at the museum.

Malmédy has one of the strangest of the Walloon Carnivals, which still bears its original dialect name, the Cwarmê. The museum has created a permanent record of this local tradition, which dates back more than 500 years. There are displays of costumes, photography, documents and posters, together with some of the floats that have been used.

Mechelen

Hof Van Busleyden Museum

Stedelijk Museum 'Hof van Busleyden', Frederik de Merodestraat 65-7, B-2800 Mechelen, Antwerpen   ☎ *015 202004*
Mon, Wed–Sun 10–12, 2–5. Closed Jan 1.
ⓒ

The museum is in a house dating from 1507. It is concerned with local history and folklore. There are collections of guild objects, especially those relating to crossbow makers, Mechelen lace, and 15th–19th century paintings. The museum also has the collection of musical instruments formed by C. J. J. Tuerlincks, an instrument-maker active in Mechelen during the first half of the 18th century. The most celebrated object in the museum is the processional doll known as Op Signoorke (1644).

Mons

Puissant Museum

Musée Chanoine Edmond Puissant, 22 rue Notre-Dame Débonnaire, B-7000 Mons, Hainaut-Mons   ☎ *065 336670*
Tues–Sun 10–12.30, 2–6
ⓒ ▮

The museum occupies a 13th-century Romanesque chapel and a 16th-century house, the 'Vieux Logis'. It has collections of antiquities, and works of art relating to the area, including manuscripts, incunabula, 15th–18th-century books, paintings, drawings and engravings. There are also displays of furniture, lace, wooden sculpture, weapons and silver. The collection of 14th–18th-century textiles is particularly good. A separate section of the museum is devoted to modern ceramics by Sars-La-Bruyère.

Morlanwelz-Mariemont

Mariemont Royal Museum

Musée Royal de Mariemont, 100 chaussée de Mariemont, B-6510 Morlanwelz-Mariemont, Hainaut-Luxembourg
☎ *064 212193/221243/226563*
Tues–Sun 10–6. Closed Dec 25, 26, Jan 1.
Ⓕ ▮ ▰ ⅃ ↻

Mariemont owes its name to Marie of Austria, Queen of Hungary, who built a Renaissance palace here in 1545. It was burnt down in 1554 by Henri II of France, but immediately rebuilt. In the mid 18th century it was demolished and rebuilt on a much grander scale by Charles, Duke of Lorraine, only to be burnt down again in 1794 during the campaign between the French and the Austrians. In 1802, it passed into the hands of a wealthy coal-owner, Nicolas Warocqué. He built a house for himself which was to be the fourth Castle of Mariemont. This remained in the Warocqué family throughout the 19th century and eventually descended to Raoul Warocqué (1870–1915), who enlarged it and filled it with an enormous art collection, which he bequeathed to the State, on condition that it remained at Mariemont.

The collections are worldwide, but Belgium is well represented, with Neolithic, Gallo-Roman and Merovingian materials from excavations in the region and the world's most important collection of Tournai porcelain. There are also exhibitions about the successive royal castles of Mariemont and their most famous guests, about the Industrial Revolution in Belgium and about the development of the coalmines. Today's museum is a new building. The Warocqué castle was burnt down in 1960, but the collections were saved.

Iron door-knocker, 16th-century, Puissant Museum, Mons.

A Walloon burial, lithograph by Rops. Félicien Rops Museum, Namur.

Namur

Félicien Rops Museum

*Musée Félicien Rops de la Province de Namur, 13
rue Fumal, B-5000 Namur*   ☎ 081 220110
*Jan–June and Sept–Dec, Wed–Mon 10–5. July–
Aug, daily 10–6.*
Ⓒ î ↩

Félicien Rops, lithographer, cartoonist,
engraver and illustrator (1833–98), was born at
Namur, not far from the museum dedicated to
his memory. The museum came into being as a
result of the generosity of Count Visarte de
Bocarme, who in 1964 gave his collection of
works by Rops to the Province of Namur. Since
that time the Province has made further
purchases and the museum's collection of the
artist's work is now the most important in the
world.

Forest Museum

*Musée Provincial de la Forêt, 7 route Merveilleuse,
B-5000 Namur*   ☎ 081 224894
*Apr–Oct, Sat–Thurs 9–12, 2–5. June 15–Sept 15
and public holidays, daily 9–12, 2–5. Nov–
Mar by appt only. Closed 1st complete week in
Oct.*
Ⓒ î ⬛ ↩

The Palace of the Forest, which houses the
museum, was built for the National Agricultural
Congress in 1901 in the style of a hunting lodge.
Its highly technical nature, planned for
sylviculturalists and gamekeepers, was modified
at the time of its refurbishment in 1964. This
was the birth-date of the Forest Museum, which
is now oriented towards the protection of
nature, while not forgetting its original purpose.
It has collections of flora and fauna of the
Ardennes, together with exhibits showing the
formation and growth of the trees in the local
forests and the damage resulting from disease
and parasites, with the appropriate remedies.

Oelegem-Ranst

Vrieselhof Textile Museum

*Provinciaal Textielmuseum Vrieselhof,
Schildesteenweg 79, B-2231 Oelegem-Ranst,
Antwerpen*   ☎ 03 3834680
*Mar–Oct, Tues–Thurs, Sat, Sun 10–5. Groups at
other times by appt.*
Ⓒ î ⬛ ↩

The museum is housed in a neo-Renaissance
castle, built in 1920. It is concerned with
European woven, printed and embroidered
textiles and with the tools and equipment for
textile production. The emphasis is on lace and
the museum has a fine collection of Flemish lace
from the 16th to the 20th century. Costumes
and accessories are shown, as well as textiles
displayed as materials.

Oostduinkerke

Fishery Museum

*Nationaal Visserijmuseum, Pastoor Schmitzstraat
5, B-8458 Oostduinkerke/Koksijde, West-
Vlaanderen*   ☎ 058 512468
Daily 10–12, 2–6. Closed Jan 1, Nov 1, Dec 25.
Ⓒ î ⬛ ⅙ ↩

The museum tells the story of the Flemish
fishing industry. It contains a large collection of
models of fishing boats used along the Belgian
coast, from the 9th century to the present day;
paintings by artists who lived and worked in the
area and painted coastal and fishing scenes; and
photographs and examples of the equipment
used by fishermen. There are also shipbuilding
tools, porcelain bearing fishing scenes, and the
tombstones of fishermen drowned at sea.
Among the larger exhibits there is the interior
of a fisherman's house and an inn, 'The
Fisherman on Horseback', used by fishermen
and now serving beer and shrimps to visitors.

Ostend

Fine Art Museum

Museum voor Schone Kunsten, Wapenplein,
  B-8400 Oostende, West-Vlaanderen
  ☎ 059 805335
Wed–Mon 10–12, 2–5. Closed Jan 1, May 1,
  Dec 25.
C 🏛 🔊 ♿

The museum contains a collection of modern
European painting and sculpture, with a special
emphasis on Belgian art between 1800 and
1914, including works by Musin, Ensor, Finch,
Spillipert, de Clerck, Permeke and Bulcke.

James Ensor's House

J. Ensorhuis, Vlaanderenstraat 27, B-8400
  Oostende, West-Vlaanderen ☎ 059 805335
June–Sept, Wed–Mon 10–12, 2–5. Easter and
  Christmas holidays, 10–12, 2–5.
C 🏛 ♿

Vlaanderenstraat 27 was the last home of the
painter James Ensor (1860–1949), a native of
Ostend. The museum contains a selection of his
works, famous for their emphasis on masks and
the carnival, together with memorabilia of the
artist.

North Sea Aquarium

Noordzee Aquarium, Visserskaai, B-8400
  Oostende, West-Vlaanderen ☎ 059 500876
Apr–Sept, daily 10–12, 2–5. Oct–Mar, Sat, Sun
  10–12, 2–5. Parties and school groups by appt.
C

The Aquarium building was formerly an auction
hall for shrimps. It now contains a collection of
living specimens of the fish, crustaceans,
shellfish and seaweeds to be found in North Sea
waters.

Provincial Museum of Modern Art

Provinciaal Museum voor Moderne Kunst,
  Romestraat II, B-8400 Oostende, West-
  Vlaanderen ☎ 059 508118
Tues–Sun 10–5
C

Installed in the former buildings of the SEO
department store, dating from 1947–50, the
collections are concerned exclusively with
works by Belgian artists, from 1900 to the
present day. They include paintings, sculpture,
graphics, films and video recordings.

Oudenaarde

Oudenaarde Museum

Stedelijk Museum, Stadhuis Oudenaarde, Markt 1,
  B-9700 Oudenaarde, Oost-Vlaanderen
  ☎ 055 311491
Apr–Oct, daily 8.15–5.30
C ♿

**The Policemen, 1892, by James Ensor. Fine
Art Museum, Ostend.**

The museum, in the 16th-century town hall,
has collections illustrating the social history of
the town. These include guild material,
costumes, tapestries, domestic equipment and
craftsmen's tools. There is an interesting
selection of crossbows and twelve pewter jugs,
which the authorities used to present, filled with
wine, to important persons passing through the
town. The pictures include 15th–19th-century
Dutch paintings and 19th-century Flemish
paintings showing Oudenaarde as it was at that
time. Works by the Flemish artist Adriaan
Brouwer (1605–38) are among the museum's
most valuable possessions.

Poperinge

Hop Museum

Nationaal Hopmuseum, Gasthuisstraat 71,
  B-8970 Poperinge, West-Vlaanderen
  ☎ 057 334081 extn 230
May, June, Sept, Sun and public holidays 2.30–
  5.30. July–Aug, daily 2.30–5.30. Parties daily
  by reservation 10 days ahead through the
  Tourist Board.
C 🏛 🔊 ♿

The museum is in a former hop-store, which was
in use until 1967. The displays show the history
and techniques of hop-growing and hop-drying
in the area. A film, made in 1936, documents
work in the hop-gardens before the coming of
mechanisation. There are now about 90,000
hectares of hops in the world. Of these, Europe
has 60,000 hectares and Belgium 850, of which
70 per cent are in the Poperinge area.

North Sea Aquarium, Ostend.

Rance

Marble Museum

*Musée National du Marbre, Place Albert 1er,
B-6478 Rance, Hainaut-Luxembourg
☎ 060 412048/411334
Apr–Oct, Mon–Sat 9.30–6; Sun and public
holidays 2–6. Nov–Mar, Mon–Sat 8.30–5.
Closed public holidays in winter.*

C ⬛ ⬛

The red marble of Rance was well known abroad
in the early 17th century. It is to be seen at its
best in the Mirror Gallery at Versailles and in
the Rubens Room in the Louvre. The museum,
in the former town hall and in a purpose-built
extension, shows the geological, technical,
commercial and social aspects of this once
important local industry, by means of
machinery, tools, photographs and commercial
records. There is also a display of the main types
of marble quarried throughout the world.

The monuments in the church at Rance
themselves constitute a museum of the local
marble.

Ronse

Museum of Textile History

*Stedelijk Museum voor de Geschiedenis van de
Textiel, Bruulpark, B-9600 Ronse, Oost-
Vlaanderen. Correspondence to: Priesterstraat
11, B-9600 Ronse   ☎ 055 211730
Easter–mid Nov, Thurs–Sat 10–12, 2–5; Sun and
public holidays 10–12, 3–6. Other times by
appt.*

C ⬛

The textile industry of Ronse was at the centre
of the life of the town from the late 18th century
until 1950. The museum displays equipment
and machinery once used in the industry and
shows how industrialisation changed the
character of local society.

The large collection of machines illustrates
the development of the industry from its earliest
domestic days. There are also displays which, by
means of old photographs, diplomas and other
forms of documentation, emphasise the human
aspects of industry. Among the themes
considered in this way are child labour, housing,
the working environment and education. The
museum's important collection of pattern-books
allows visitors to see the range of products for
which Ronse was famous.

Saint-Hubert

St Michael's Furnace Museum

*Musées Provinciaux du Fourneau Saint-Michel,
B-6900 Saint-Hubert, Hainaut-Luxembourg
☎ 084 210830/210613
Iron Museum: Mar–Dec, daily 9–6. Walloon
Rural Life Open-Air Museum: Apr 1–Sept 15,
daily 9–6.*

C ⬛ ⬛ ⬛

St Michael's Furnace Museum, Saint-Hubert.

There are two museums on the site, a museum of
the local iron industry and an open-air museum
of Walloon rural life. The first contains the
remains of the 1771 ironworks, with
reconstructions of parts of the works. Displays
illustrate the history and techniques of iron-
smelting and there is a large collection of tools
and implements, the main parts of which are
made of cast-iron.

The Museum of Walloon Rural Life opened
in 1981. The buildings forming its collection
have been brought from other parts of the
Walloon area of Belgium and rebuilt on the
museum site, using traditional materials and
techniques. Most of the buildings – farmhouses
and their outbuildings, a chapel and a school –
date from the 18th and 19th centuries.

Saint-Idesbald

Paul Delvaux Museum

*Museum Paul Delvaux, Kabouterweg 42, B-8460
Saint-Idesbald, West-Vlaanderen
☎ 058 512971
Apr–June and Sept, Tues–Sun 10.30–6.30. July–
Aug, daily 10.30–6.30. Oct–Dec, Sat, Sun
and public holidays 10.30–4.30.*

C ⬛ ⬛ ⬛

In 1979 the Belgian painter, Paul Delvaux, gave
a large collection of his works to the newly-
formed Paul Delvaux Foundation and a museum
to display them was opened in 1982. The core of
the museum building is an old fisherman's
house. The paintings, drawings, etchings and
lithographs on view illustrate practically every
period of Delvaux's work.

Spa

Ville d'Eaux

*Musée de la Ville d'Eaux, 77B avenue Reine
    Astrid, B-4880 Spa, Liège   ☎ 087 771768*
*June 15–Sept 15, daily 2.30–5.30. Mar 16–
    June 14 & Sept 16–end of Christmas holiday,
    2.30–5.30. Open Christmas and Easter school
    holidays.*
C 🛈 ↩

Since 1970 the museum has occupied part of the
building which was the summer residence of
Queen Marie-Henrietta, the second Queen of
the Belgians. She died here in 1902. The
collections are of typical arts and crafts from
Spa, of the kind known as 'jolités'. The earliest
of these, in the 16th century, were walking-
sticks, designed to make it easier for those
taking the cure at Spa to walk to the mineral
springs. In the 17th century, there appeared
objects inlaid with mother-of-pearl, tin and
copper and later boxes and other items finished
in imitation of Chinese lacquerware.

In the 17th century, artists who also made
drawings on vellum, decorated objects of all
kinds with India ink. They found their
inspiration in mythology and in the landscape
around Spa.

Thieu

Living Museum of the Central Canal

*Musée vivant du Canal du Centre, Ecluse No. 1,
    69, rue des Peupliers, B-7058 Thieu, Hainaut-
    Mons   ☎ 064 662561*
Tues–Sun 10–5.
C 🛈 ↩

This ecomuseum includes a large section of the
19th-century Canal du Centre, now bypassed by
a large new canal. The exhibits include tunnels,
hydraulic boat-lifts, a pumping station and
several lock-keepers' houses. There are exhibits
showing the operation of the Canal and the life
of the people who worked on it.

Tournai

Museum of Fine Art

*Musée des Beaux-Arts, Cour de l'Hôtel-de-Ville,
    B-7500 Tournai, Hainaut-Mons
    ☎ 069 222043*
*Wed–Mon 10–12, 2–5.30. Closed Jan 1,
    Nov 11, Dec 25.*
C 🛈 ↩

The museum was opened in 1928, in a building
designed by the Belgian Art Nouveau architect,
Victor Horta, in order to display the large
collection of paintings bequeathed to the City
by the Brussels collector, Henri van Cutsem.
The collection has since been considerably
augmented by gifts and purchases and now
provides an interesting survey of European
painting from the 15th century to the present
day. Flemish artists are well represented and a
special section is reserved for works by Gallait,
Leroy, Grard and Pion, who were all natives of
Tournai.

Museum of History and Archaeology

*Musée d'Histoire et d'Archéologie, 7 rue des
    Carmes, B-7500 Tournai, Hainaut-Mons
    ☎ 069 221672*
Wed–Mon 10–12, 2–5.30. Closed Jan 1, Dec 25.
F 🛈

The museum was established in the Cloth Hall
in 1889. This historic building was destroyed in
1940 and in 1953 the museum was re-opened in
the former pawnbroker's shop (Mont de Piété),
which dates from 1622. The collections
illustrate the history and arts and crafts of
Tournai. There are sections devoted to
medieval and Renaissance sculpture and to
pottery, tombstones and carvings salvaged from
churches damaged in the 1940 bombing raids.
Other displays are of 15th–16th-century
Tournai tapestries, to the products of the
Tournai mint and to the famous Tournai
porcelain factory.

**Tournai porcelain, 1752–1850. Museum of
History and Archaeology, Tournai.**

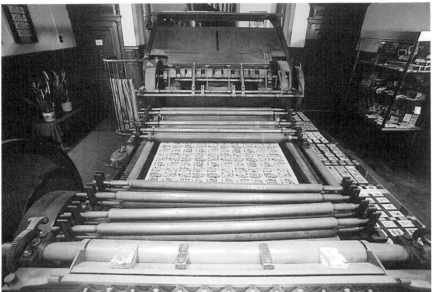

Playing Card Museum, Turnhout.

Turnhout

Playing Card Museum

Nationaal Museum van de Speelkaart,
Druivenstraat 18, B-2300 Turnhout,
Antwerpen   ☎ *014 415621*
Jan–May and Sept–Dec, Wed, Fri 2–5; Sun
10–12, 2–5. June, Tues–Fri 2–5; Sun 10–12,
2–5. July–Aug Tues–Sat 2–5; Sun 10–12,
2–5. Closed Jan 1, 2, Dec 25, 26.
ⓒ ▮ ⅋ ☜

During the 15th–16th centuries, the Low
Countries were important for the production
and export of playing cards, with Tournai,
Antwerp, Amsterdam, Dinant, Liège, Bruges
and Brussels as the main centres. From the mid
19th century onwards, Turnhout acquired a
monopoly of the trade and since 1970 the
industry has become concentrated in a single
large company.

The museum's exhibits tell the story of
playing cards, illustrated by items from its very
large historical collections, and explain the
printing processes involved. The collections
include printing presses and other technical
equipment.

Waimes

Botrange Nature Centre

Centre Nature Botrange, 131 route de Botrange,
B-4898 Waimes, Liège   ☎ *080 445781*
Daily 10–6. Closed Jan 1, Dec 25. Exhibition
closed Dec 15–Apr 1.
ⓒ ▮ 💷 ⅋ ☜

The centre is in the Hautes-Fagnes-Eifel nature
park. It was established in 1984 in order to
explain to visitors the evolution and

characteristics of an area which is of particular
interest to the geologist, naturalist and social
historian. The information in the permanent
exhibition is arranged under the headings of
history, geography, habitat, fauna, flora,
agriculture, forestry, methods of safeguarding
the natural environment, and tourism.
Temporary exhibitions are arranged on subjects
such as endangered birds, rabies, beekeeping
and pond life.

There is a giant relief-model of the park area,
on a scale of 1:15,000, with a computer-
controlled laser system which allows 60 points of
interest to be rapidly picked out. Visitors are
also introduced to the park by means of a
multi-vision projection system, which uses 450
slides.

Waterloo

Wellington Museum

Musée Wellington, 147 chaussée de Bruxelles,
B-1410 Waterloo, Brabant   ☎ *02 3547806/*
3545954
Apr 1–Nov 15, daily 9.30–6.30. Nov 16–
Mar 31, daily 10.30–5. Closed Jan 1, Dec 25.
ⓒ ▮

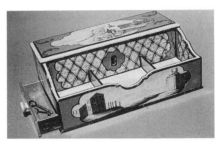

Writing cabinet, 18th-century. Ville d'Eaux
Museum, Spa.

The museum building, a former inn, was the Duke of Wellington's headquarters before and after the Battle of Waterloo, the most bloody of all Napoleon's battles. A large illuminated map explains the progress of the battle, hour by hour, and there are exhibits which illustrate the contribution made by each national contingent of the Allied army, with displays of uniforms, weapons and equipment. There are memorabilia of the Duke and his officers, including the wooden leg of Lord Uxbridge. The room in which Sir Alexander Gordon, ADC to the Duke, died of his wounds, has been preserved.

Willebroek

Fort Breendonk Memorial

Nationaal Gedenkteken van het Fort van Breendonk, B-2660 Willebroek, Antwerpen
☎ 03 8866209
Apr–Sept, daily 9–6. Oct–Mar, daily 10–5. Closed Jan 1, Dec 25.
C ⓘ 🎦 ♨

Fort Breendonk was constructed in 1906–14. During the Second World War it was a German concentration camp and is now preserved as a memorial to the 4,000 men and women who were imprisoned, tortured and murdered here.

Ypres

Ypres Salient Museum

Herinneringsmuseum Ypres Salient '14–'18, Lakenhalle, Grote Markt, B–8900 Ieper, West-Vlaanderen ☎ *057 202623 extn 263*
Apr 1–Nov 15, daily 9.30–12, 1.30–5.30. By appt other months.
C ⓘ & ♨

The collections consist of equipment, weapons, medals, documents and maps of British, American, Belgian, German and French forces who were involved in the First World War battles around Ypres. There is an extensive photographic collection and a number of noteworthy personal souvenirs of the battles belonging to leaders of the Allied and German armies involved, including especially Field-Marshal Earl Haig and Prince Mauritz von Battenberg.

The museum is in what was, until the First World War, one of Belgium's most beautiful medieval buildings, the 13th-century Cloth Hall. It was almost entirely destroyed by shellfire during the War, but rebuilt during the 1920s, with the original design meticulously reproduced.

Botrange Nature Centre, Waimes.

BRITAIN

Aberdeen

Aberdeen Art Gallery

Schoolhill, Aberdeen, AB9 1FQ
☎ 0224 646333
Mon–Wed, Fri, Sat 10–5; Thurs 10–8; Sun 2–5.
Ⓕ ⓘ ▣ ⓖ ↝

This important gallery was established in 1884.
The main strength of the collection is in 18th-,
19th- and 20th-century British art. Many of the
paintings came to the gallery as gifts from
prominent local people, who also bequeathed
funds for further purchases. Other works have
been donated by the Contemporary Art Society
and the War Artists' Advisory Committee, and
acquired with the help of grants from other
national bodies.

Scottish and local artists are well
represented and the gallery is especially rich in
landscapes by the French Impressionists.
Among the outstanding works on display are
Turner's *Ely Cathedral*, Sir John Lavery's *Tennis
Party*, Monet's *La Falaise à Fécamp*, Sisley's *La
Petite Place*, and Blake's *Raising of Lazarus*.

Aberdeen Maritime Museum

Provost Ross's House, Shiprow, Aberdeen
☎ 0224 585788
Mon–Sat 10–5
Ⓕ ⓘ ↝

For more than 200 years, Aberdeen has been
one of Britain's most interesting ports, adapting
itself successfully to far-reaching commercial
and technical change. The museum is housed in
the city's oldest surviving building, the house of
an 18th-century merchant with substantial
shipping interests. The first display illustrates
the development of Aberdeen Harbour over the
past two centuries while another section tells
the story of Aberdeen's involvement in the
Arctic whaling trade, which lasted from 1752 to
the early 1860s. The strong local shipbuilding
tradition is well documented in a number of
exhibits.

Shipowning also receives careful attention,
as does the local fishing industry in its various
branches: small line fishing for haddock, codling
and whiting; herring fishing; trawling, which
made Aberdeen a boom town; and great line
fishing, which used long lines to catch halibut,
turbot, skate, torsk, cod and ling. Other
exhibits present the history of local wrecks and
rescues, and of the London Boats, the
steamships which carried freight and passengers
between Aberdeen and the metropolis and
operated from 1835 until the early 1960s.

Aldershot

Aldershot Military Museum

Queens Avenue, Aldershot, Hampshire,
GU11 2LG   ☎ 0252 314598
Mar–Oct, daily 10–5. Nov–Feb, daily 10–4.30.
Closed Dec 18–26 and Jan 1.
Ⓒ ⓘ ⓖ ↝

Before the establishment of Aldershot nearly
150 years ago, Britain had no large military
base. The museum buildings are the only
surviving example of Aldershot's original
Victorian bungalow barrack blocks, which
replaced the original wooden huts. The museum
has been established to present the daily life of
the soldier, within the story of Aldershot, the
home of the British Army and the birthplace of
British military aviation, from its beginnings in
1854 to the present time. There is a
reconstruction of an original Victorian barrack
room, with period uniforms and equipment,
models of successive camps, and a sectional
model of the cavalry barracks, where the horses
were stabled below the men's living quarters,
described as warm but aromatic.

Alloway

Burns Cottage

Alloway, Ayrshire, KA7 4PY   ☎ 0292 41215
Spring, Autumn, Mon–Sat 10–5; Sun 2–5. June–
Aug, Mon–Sat 9–7; Sun 10–7. Winter, Mon–
Sat 10–4.
Ⓒ ⓘ ▣ ⓖ ↝

The thatched cottage was the birthplace of
Scotland's most famous poet, Robert Burns. It
has been restored to its original appearance, and
furnished in the style of the period, with the
help of a few items of furniture which belonged
to the poet or to his family. A separate museum
building has been constructed nearby, to display
the large collection of material relating to
Burns. These items include his duelling pistols,
pieces of furniture, his family Bible, a large
number of letters and many of the manuscripts
of his songs and poems, including those of *Tam
O'Shanter* and *Auld Lang Syne*.

Burns Cottage, Alloway.

Anstruther

Scottish Fisheries Museum

St Ayles, Harbourhead, Anstruther, Fife,
    KY10 3AB   ☎ 0333 310628
Apr–Oct, Mon–Sat 10–5.30; Sun 11–5. Nov–
    Mar, Mon–Sat (ex Tues) 10–4.30; Sun
    2–4.30.
Ⓒ ⓘ 🖾 ⌂

The museum is housed in a group of 16th–19th
century buildings grouped around a cobbled
courtyard where, in the past, a community of
fishermen, coopers and brewers carried on their
work. The displays cover nearly every aspect of
the fishing industry, including whaling and
industrial salmon fishing, as well as the ancillary
trades. Among the larger exhibits are
reproductions of the interior of a fisherman's
home as it would have looked c.1900 and of the
wheelhouse of a fishing boat. There are
excellent collections of model boats,
photographs and equipment, and visitors can
see actual vessels in the courtyard and in the
adjacent harbour. A marine aquarium contains
fish and shellfish found in Scottish waters.

One room is kept as a memorial to fishermen
and lifeboatmen lost at sea and other displays
relate to the superstitions and beliefs of the
Scottish fishing communities, such as never
turning a boat in harbour against the sun, and to
such words as pig, rat, minister and salmon
which, for superstitious reasons, fishermen were
forbidden to use.

Appledore

North Devon Maritime Museum

Odun House, Odun Road, Appledore, Devon,
    EX39 1PT   ☎ 02372 74852
Easter–Sept, Tues–Fri 11–1, daily 2–5.30
Ⓒ ⌀ ⌂

North Devon has a long and interesting
maritime history, of which the museum provides
a comprehensive picture. There are scale models
of ships using North Devon ports from the 17th
century onwards, together with paintings of
ships and maritime scenes, and old photographs
of the district and its people. The former
important trade with Prince Edward Island
receives attention, as does the story of local
lifeboats, wrecks and smuggling. Exhibits deal
with the industries of North Devon, including
shipbuilding, and scale models illustrate the
working of a shipyard, sail-loft and rope-works.
A special display presents the history and
techniques of the different types of fishing
carried out by boats from the area.

Avebury

Alexander Keiller Museum

Avebury, nr Marlborough, Wiltshire, SN8 1RF
    ☎ 06723 250
Summer, daily 10–6. Winter, Mon–Sat 10–4;
    Closed Jan 1, Dec 24–26.
Ⓒ ⌀

The museum houses Neoliothic finds from sites
in southern Britain which were mostly
excavated by the celebrated archaeologist,
Alexander Keiller, in the 1920s and 1930s –
Avebury, Windmill Hill, West Kennet Long
Barrow and Silbury Hill. The displays explain
the nature of the sites and illustrate the
archaeological material. Special attention is
devoted to the history of Avebury and to the
excavations carried out there, with
photographs, artefacts and reconstructions.

Great Barn Museum of Wiltshire Rural Life

Avebury, nr Marlborough, Wiltshire, SN8 1RF
    ☎ 06723 555
Mar–Nov, daily 10–5.30. Nov–Mar. weekends
    only, 1–4.30.
Ⓒ ⓘ 🖾 ⌂

The thatched Great Barn, 44 metres long and
11 metres wide, was built c.1690. It was used
mainly for storing and threshing corn and during
the summer, when it was almost empty, it may
also have provided covered space for the annual
sheep shearing. In the 1970s it was restored by
the Wiltshire Folk Life Society, to become the
centre of its activities.

The barn, with its magnificent roof
structure, is the oldest and largest of the
museum exhibits. The displays inside are
devoted to the life and agriculture of the
essentially rural county of Wiltshire from the
16th to the 20th centuries. They include
reconstructions of a blacksmith's forge,
wheelwright's shop, saddler's and cooper's
workshops. Other sections deal with thatching,
sheep and shepherding, and farm implements
and equipment. All the exhibits are open and
visitors are allowed to come into close contact
with them. There is a regular programme of craft
demonstrations and performances of folk
dancing.

Great Barn Museum, Avebury.

Ayot St Lawrence

Shaw's Corner

Ayot St Lawrence, Welwyn, Hertfordshire,
    AL6 9BX   ☎ *0438 820307*
Mar 30 – Oct, Mon–Thurs 2–6; Sun, Bank
    Holiday Mon 12–6.
Ⓒ ⌦ ⌖

The celebrated playwright, George Bernard
Shaw, took over this modest villa, formerly the
'Old Rectory', built in 1902, and lived in it from
1906 until his death in 1950. The rooms
downstairs, including Shaw's study, have been
preserved as they were during his lifetime, with
their furniture and personal possessions intact.
Visitors can also see the upstairs rooms on
weekdays.

Aysgarth

Yorkshire Carriage Museum

Aysgarth Falls, Aysgarth, Leyburn, North
    Yorkshire, DL8 3SR   ☎ *09693 652*
Easter–Oct, Mon–Fri 11–5; Sat, Sun, Bank
    Holiday 10.30–7.
Ⓒ ▮ ◨ ⌖

This is probably the most comprehensive
collection of both everyday and more lavish
horse-drawn vehicles in Britain today, ranging
from smart town coaches to bread vans,
butchers' carts and milk floats.

The collection is housed in Yore Mill, built as
a water-powered cotton mill in 1784, and
includes harness, bits, liveries and many other
articles, some of them rare, from the coaching
and driving age. The displays are changed
occasionally, since only 60 vehicles can be
shown at any one time.

Many of the vehicles in the collection are
used for film and television work, and for private
hire, so they are maintained in good condition
and are seen regularly on the road.

Baginton

The Lunt Roman Fort

Coventry Road, Baginton, nr Coventry, West
    Midlands   ☎ *0203 303567*
May 24–Sept 28, daily 12–6 ex. Mon, Thurs.
    Open every day Bank Holiday weeks.
Ⓒ ⌦ ◔ ⌖

The 1st-century Roman cavalry fort here has
been excavated and is being reconstructed *in
situ*, under the general direction of the Herbert
Art Gallery and Museum in Coventry. The
work so far carried out includes nearly 100
metres of turf and timber rampart, the two-
storey Eastern Gateway, the *Gyrus* – a training
ring for cavalry, unparalleled in the Roman
Empire – and a timber-built granary. The latter
now houses a display illustrating life in the fort,
with artefacts discovered on the site and full-
sized models of a legionary and a cavalryman of
the mid 1st century.

The Great Hall, Sulgrave Manor, Banbury.

Ballindalloch

Glenfarclas Distillery

Glenfarclas Distillery, Ballindalloch, Banffshire,
    AB3 9BD   ☎ *08072 257*
Mon–Fri 9–4.30. July–Sept, also Sat 10–4. Closed
    Jan 1, 2, Dec 25, 26.
Ⓕ ▮ ⌖

The commercial production of whisky has been
a speciality of the Highland region for more
than 150 years and continues to be one of
Scotland's principal industries. The distillery at
Ballindalloch is 17 miles from Grantown-on-
Spey and 18 miles from Elgin. The museum is
constructed around the equipment of an old
illicit still and illustrates the processes involved
in making whisky by traditional methods.

Banbury

Sulgrave Manor

Sulgrave, Banbury, Oxfordshire, OX17 2SD
    ☎ *029576 205*
Apr–Sept, Thurs–Tues 10.30–1, 2–5.30. Oct–
    Dec & Mar, Thurs–Tues 10.30–1, 2–4. Feb
    by appt only.
Ⓒ ▮ ◨ ☞

This mid-16th-century house, built by Lawrence
Washington, an ancestor of George
Washington, was lived in by members of the
family for 120 years. In 1914, when it was in
poor condition, it was bought by a body of
British subscribers, carefully restored and
furnished by joint British and American effort,
and opened to the public in 1921. The house
presents a good example of a small manor and
garden of Shakespeare's time, with fine period
furniture and an outstanding kitchen.

Two rooms, known as the Porch Room and
the Deed Room, are used as a museum. This
contains several portraits of George Washington
– others can be seen elsewhere in the house –
Washington memorabilia, including his
saddlebags, his oak wine and spirit chest, a
velvet coat belonging to him and a lock of his
hair.

Barlaston

The Wedgwood Museum

Josiah Wedgwood & Sons Limited, Barlaston,
Stoke-on-Trent, Staffordshire, ST12 9ES
☎ 0782 204141
Mon–Fri & Bank Holiday 9–5. Sat 10–4. Easter–
Oct Sun 10–4. Closed Jan 1 and Christmas
week.

Ⓒ ▯ ☕ ᶜᵃ ⚘

Wedgwood has been a famous name in the
pottery industry since the middle of the 18th
century. The museum, opened in 1975 and
re-designed in 1985, is located in Wedgwood's
modern factory. The collection contains more
than 20,000 pieces, a high percentage of which
are on display in the museum, considerable use
being made of period settings. The 18th-century
exhibits include an extensive range of trial
pieces produced by Josiah Wedgwood (1730–
95), in his search for improved ceramic bodies
and resulting in the introduction of Queen's
Ware, Black Basalt and Jasper.

The museum also includes an art gallery.
Among the artists represented are Reynolds,
Stubbs, Wright of Derby, Romney and Sargent.

Bath

Bath Industrial Heritage Centre

Camden Works, Julian Road, Bath, Avon,
BA1 2RH   ☎ 0225 318348
Feb–Nov, daily 1–5. Jan & Dec, weekends only,
2–5.

Ⓒ ⌯ ☕ ⚘

The museum building was constructed in 1777
as a Real Tennis court, but only traces of the
original interior remain. It now houses the
Bowler Collection which is presented as a
reconstruction of the works of J. B. Bowler, a

Victorian brass founder, general engineer and
aerated water manufacturer. During 97 years of
trading in Bath, the firm threw practically
nothing away. As a result, visitors can see a
remarkable collection of working machinery,
hand-tools, brasswork, patterns, bottles and
documents of all kinds displayed as realistically
as possible to convey an impression of the
working life of a small provincial family business
in Victorian times. The correspondence,
accounts and other documents relating to the
business are also extraordinarily complete.

A separate section of the museum tells the
story of Bath stone and looks at all aspects of
this important local industry. The 18th-century
development of the city, using the characteristic
local limestone, gave Bath much of its special
architectural quality. The displays include a
mine working face in the days before
mechanisation, explanations of the tools and
skills involved in working the stone, and a look
at how it was transported.

Holburne Museum

Great Pulteney Street, Bath, Avon, BA2 4DB
☎ 0225 466669
Mid Feb–mid Dec, weekdays 11–5; Sun 2.30–6.
Open on Mon from Easter–Nov.

Ⓒ ⌯ ☕ ᶜᵃ ⚘

This 1796–7 building designed to serve as a
hotel, was adapted to house the Holburne
collection in 1911–15. The exhibits include
Flemish, Dutch, Italian and English paintings,
especially works by Guardi, Zoffany,
Gainsborough and Stubbs; Italian majolica;
Renaissance bronzes; minatures; furniture and
glass.

An important and nationally celebrated
department of the museum is devoted to 20th-
century crafts. Among the items displayed here,
all of outstanding quality, are woven and
printed textiles, pottery by Bernard Leach,
furniture and calligraphy. A Crafts Study
Centre offers facilities for research in these and
allied fields.

Museum of Costume

Assembly Rooms, Bennett Street, Bath, Avon,
BA1 2QH   ☎ 0225 461111
Museum: Mar–Oct, Mon–Sat 9.30–6; Sun 10–6.
Nov–Feb, Mon–Sat 10–5; Sun 11–5.

Ⓒ ▯ ᶜᵃ

In its recently restored 18th-century Assembly
Rooms, Bath has one of the largest and most
comprehensive displays of costume in Britain.
The museum illustrates, with period room
settings and dioramas, the history of fashionable
dress for men, women and children from the late
16th century to the present day. There are
outstanding items of the 16th, 17th and 18th
centuries, and extensive 19th- and 20th-century
collections, including designer clothes, as well
as special displays of millinery, jewellery,
underwear, dolls and toys. A selection of Royal
clothes and ceremonial dress is also on view.

Two-handled cup and cover, 1736. Holburne
Museum, Bath.

Museum of Modern Art, Saint-Etienne (France).

The Mackintosh House, a reconstruction of the principal rooms of C.R. Mackintosh's Glasgow home. Hunterian Art Gallery, Glasgow (Britain).

Waterloo Warrior, 1875, by P.M. Slager,
Slager Museum, 's Hertogenbosch
(Netherlands).

Shoemakers At Work, 1839, by J.B. Pflug.
Biberach Museum, Biberach-an-der-Riss
(Germany).

A study collection and library on the history of costume and textiles is provided at the Fashion Research Centre, 4 The Circus (Mon–Fri 10–1, 2–5. Free admission. Closed public holidays). The library includes collections of books, periodicals, fashion plates, photographs, patterns and other archival material. Most notable are the Worth and Paquin archives (1902–56) and the *Sunday Times* Fashion Archive (1957–72).

Roman Baths

Pump Room, Stall Street, Bath, Avon, BA1 1LZ
  ☎ *0225 461111*
Mar–June and Sept–Oct, daily 9–6. July–Aug,
  daily 9–7. Nov–Feb, Mon–Sat 9–5; Sun
  10–5. Closed Dec 25–26.
C ♦ ☕

The Roman bathing establishment, with its magnificent Great Bath, flourished as an important feature of the town of *Aquae Sulis* between the 1st and 5th centuries AD. It was built around the natural hot spring which rises from the ground at 46.5°C. The survivals of the Baths are remarkably complete in layout and are amongst the best Roman remains in Britain.

The exhibits in the museum include mosaics and stone monuments from the Roman town and the surrounding area, along with many votive offerings thrown into the sacred spring. The finest of the exhibits is the gilt-bronze head of the goddess Minerva. The recently excavated Roman Temple Precinct underneath the Pump Room can also be viewed.

Beaulieu

Buckler's Hard Maritime Museum

Buckler's Hard, Beaulieu, Brockenhurst,
  Hampshire, SO42 7XB ☎ *0590 616203*
March–Spring Bank Holiday, daily 10–6. Spring
  Bank Holiday–Sept 1, daily 10–9. Oct–Easter,
  daily 10–4.30. Sept–Oct 10–6. Winter
  10–4.30. Closed Dec 25.
C ♦ ☕ ♠

Originally intended by the 2nd Duke of Montagu to be a major port, Buckler's Hard eventually developed, more realistically, into a shipbuilding village. Between 1745 and 1822 many wooden ships for the Navy were built here, including Nelson's favourite ship, HMS *Agamemnon*. The Maritime Museum reflects the shipbuilding history of the village, with displays on the shipwrights' techniques, and on Henry Adams, the site's most notable shipbuilder. Displays in the cottages re-create life at Buckler's Hard in the 18th century.

National Motor Museum

John Montagu Building, Beaulieu, Brockenhurst,
  Hampshire, SO42 7ZN ☎ *0590 612345*
Easter–Sept, daily 10–6. Oct–Easter, daily 10–5.
  Closed Dec 25.
C ♦ ☕ ♿ ♠

In 1970, the Montagu Motor Museum, established by Lord Montagu in 1952, became the National Motor Museum, owned and controlled by a charitable trust, in order to preserve the collections and the library for the nation. It is now one of the largest and most comprehensive automobile museums in the world, telling the story of motoring, particularly in Britain, from 1894 to the present day. Both private and commercial vehicles are on display, as well as celebrated racing cars.

To mark the centenary of the motorcar a permanent feature, 'Wheels – the Legend of the Motor Car', was opened in 1985. This gives visitors an automated trip in a moving 'pod' through a series of dioramas illustrating 100 years of motoring.

Beaumaris

Beaumaris Gaol

Steeple Lane, Beaumaris, Gwynedd
  ☎ *0248 810921/750262 extn 269*
Gaol: Late May – end Sept, daily 11–6.
  Courthouse: Late May–end Sept, daily 11.30–
  5.30 (except when court is in session).
C ⟁

The prison at Beaumaris, built in 1829, has remained unchanged since it was closed in 1878. Visitors can see the cells, including the punishment cell and the condemned cell, where prisoners were kept before execution, and the only treadwheel in Britain to survive on its original site. There is an exhibition of documents illustrating prison life in the 19th century.

The nearby courthouse, built in 1614 and renovated in the early 19th century, is still in use as a magistrates court and can be visited by the public. Prisoners sentenced here were taken to Beaumaris Gaol.

A 1966 Ford GT40 model. National Motor Museum, Beaulieu.

Bedford

Bunyan Museum

*Bunyan Meeting Free Church, 55 Mill Street,
    Bedford*   ☎ *0234 58075*
May–Oct, Tues–Sat 2–4. Other times by appt.
Ⓒ ✎

The church which contains the museum is on
the site of an earlier building where John
Bunyan, the author of one of England's most
celebrated books, *The Pilgrim's Progress*, was
Pastor from 1672 to 1688. The bronze doors,
presented by the 9th Duke of Bedford in 1876,
have 10 sculpted panels showing scenes from
Bunyan's book. Among the items on display are
Bunyan's iron anvil and violin, his vestry chair,
the flute he made out of a chairleg while he was
in prison, and the jug used by his blind
daughter, Mary, to take soup to him during this
period. The Church Minute Book for 1672, in
Bunyan's handwriting, is also shown. The
museum has the world's largest collection of
translations of *The Pilgrim's Progress*.

Cecil Higgins Museum and Art Gallery

Castle Close, Bedford, MK40 3NY
    ☎ *0234 211222*
*Tues–Fri 12.30–5; Sat 11–5; Sun 2–5. Closed
    Mon (ex Bank Holiday Mons), Good Fri, Dec
    25, 26.*
Ⓕ ♿

Cecil Higgins, a local brewer, was an
enthusiastic and discriminating collector of
porcelain and glass throughout his life. When
the family business was sold in 1928, he began
to extend his collections, with the aim of
establishing a museum in his home town,
and investing money to ensure that further
acquisitions would be made after his death. The
museum and gallery combine the original home
of the Higgins family with a new gallery, added
in 1976.

The house displays costumes, toys, lace and
an outstanding collection of English furniture,
mainly Victorian. One room is devoted to
furniture designed by the famous Victorian
architect, William Burges. The galleries in the
new wing contain exhibits of ceramics and glass,
mainly of the 17th to 19th centuries. The
picture collection is especially strong in English
watercolours, with nearly every major artist in
this field represented.

Belfast

Ulster Museum

*Botanic Gardens, Belfast, Northern Ireland,
    BT9 5AB*   ☎ *0232 381251*
*Mon–Fri 10–5; Sat 1–5; Sun 2–5. Closed Jan 1,
    July 12, Dec 25, 26.*
Ⓕ ♿ 🖭 ♿

The Ulster Museum is one of Britain's small
group of national museums. Its important
archaeological collections extend from the first

**Egyptian mummy of Takabuti. Ulster
Museum, Belfast.**

arrival of man in Ireland c. 7000 BC until the
late 17th century and include material
recovered from two Spanish Armada ships,
Girona and *La Trinidad Valencera*.

Sections are devoted to the animals and
plants of Ireland and the Local History Gallery
illustrates various aspects of Ulster history over
the past four centuries, with an emphasis on
political and military events. The collections
range from maps to police and secret society
badges, and from uniforms to the coins and
medals of Ireland. A special section is
concerned with the industrial history and
archaeology of Ulster and particularly with the
flax and linen industry, which was formerly of
very great importance in Ulster. The 'Made in
Belfast' Gallery deals with the history of Belfast
manufacturing during the past 200 years.

There are paintings, drawings, watercolours
and prints by Irish artists and the decorative art
collections include silver, glass, ceramics,
costume jewellery and furniture.

The Dinosaur Show is a popular display
introducing dinosaurs and their world using
murals, games and a small video theatre. The
highpoint is a real skeleton of Anatosaurus, one
of the last of the dinosaurs, with other favourites
Tyrannosaurus and Triceratops also on show.

Beltring

Whitbread Hop Farm

Beltring, Paddock Wood, Kent, TN12 6PY
    ☎ *0622 872408/872068*
*Easter–late Oct, Tues–Sun 10–5.30. Open Bank
    Holiday Mon.*
Ⓒ ♿ 🖭 ♿ ♿

This working farm supplies Whitbread's, one of the major English brewing concerns, with a quarter of the hops used in their breweries. A group of six Victorian oasts has been preserved. Three of them are now used as museums, containing exhibits of rural crafts, hop-growing and processing, agricultural tools and implements, and horse harness and equipment.

The celebrated Whitbread Shire horses are kept here, when not working. Their duties include pulling the coaches of the Lord Mayor of London and the Speaker of the House of Commons.

Berkeley

Jenner Museum

The Chantry, Church Lane, Berkeley, Gloucestershire, GL13 9BH ☎ *0453 810631 Apr–Sept, Tues–Sun & Bank Holiday Mons 12.30–5.30. Oct, Sun 1–5.30. Parties by appt.*

Ⓒ 🛈 🚗

Edward Jenner, doctor, naturalist and Fellow of the Royal Society, was born in 1749. He was the son of the Vicar of Berkeley and spent most of his life practising medicine in this small Gloucestershire market town. He was the discoverer of vaccination against small-pox and at his home, The Chantry, he vaccinated the poor free of charge, in a thatched hut which he called the Temple of Vaccinia. The Chantry later became the Vicarage, and was bought in 1980 by the Jenner Appeal with the help of a generous gift from a Japanese philanthropist and by 1985 it had been restored and converted into a Jenner Museum and immunology conference centre.

The museum displays illustrate the characteristics and effects of smallpox, as well as the life and career of Jenner, and contain a large collection of memorabilia and personal possessions. The Temple of Vaccinia, also restored, can be seen by visitors.

Reconstruction of 1862 lecture room. Ravensdowne Barracks, Berwick-upon-Tweed.

Berwick-upon-Tweed

Ravensdowne Barracks

The Parade, Berwick-upon-Tweed, Northumberland, TD15 1DF ☎ *0289 304493 Mar 28–Oct, daily 10–6. Winter, Tues–Sun 10–4.*

Ⓒ 🛈 🚗

Ravensdowne Barracks, built 1717–21, was one of the earliest purpose-built barracks in Britain. The buildings have recently been restored and now contain an exhibition on the history of the British infantry, from Tudor times to 1881. The displays include a reconstructed barrack-room of the 1750s, an army schoolroom of the 1860s with period figures, and other tableaux.

Birkenhead

Willamson Art Gallery

Slatey Road, Birkenhead, Merseyside, L43 4UE ☎ *051 652 4177 Mon–Sat 10–5 (Thurs until 9); Sun 2–5.*

🅕 🗌 🚻 🚗

Victorian oil paintings and 18th- and 19th-century British watercolours are well represented in the gallery's fine art collections, which include important works by Philip Wilson Steer and artists of the Liverpool School. There is a growing collection of contemporary works. Prominent in the decorative arts section is a range of ceramics produced on Merseyside – Liverpool porcelain, Seacombe pottery and Della Robbia ware. The displays in the museum reflect the maritime past of Birkenhead and the Wirral, and illustrate the history of the region in general.

Birmingham

Aston Hall

Aston Park, Trinity Road, Aston, Birmingham, B6 6JD ☎ *021 327 0062 Easter–Oct, daily 2–5*

Ⓒ 🛈 🚗

Aston Hall was built by Sir Thomas Holte, the 1st Baronet, between 1618 and 1635 and the family continued to live in the house until 1817. It was eventually bought by Birmingham Corporation in 1864. It contains Jacobean decorative plaster and woodwork, together with sculptured fireplaces.

It is now organised as the country house branch museum of Birmingham Museum and Art Gallery. Nearly 30 rooms have been recently redecorated and rearranged in order to give a clearer impression of what it was like to live in them, either in the 1760s or when the house was last substantially altered. Very little furniture remains from the days when the house was lived in, but it now contains many fine paintings, pieces of furniture, textiles, silver and ceramics from the museum's collections, as well as portraits and heirlooms of the Holte family.

Birmingham Museum of Science and Industry

Newhall Street, Birmingham, B3 1RZ
  ☎ 021 236 1022
*Mon–Sat 9.30–5; Sun 2–5. Closed Jan 1, Dec
24–26.*
Ⓕ ◿ 💺 & ✍

Founded in 1950, surprisingly late, considering
Birmingham's long-standing international
importance as a manufacturing centre, the
museum was established in a group of Victorian
factory buildings, with modern additions. The
James Watt Building, a new extension opened
in 1983, is built round the 1779 Boulton and
Watt beam engine, which pumped water back
to the canal locks at Smethwick. This is by far
the oldest working steam engine in the world.

The collections include locomotives,
stationary steam engines, gas, oil and hot-air
engines, veteran cars – John Cobb's world
record-holder is among them – motorcycles and
bicycles, and the only surviving Birmingham
tramcar. The aircraft gallery includes two
Second World War fighter aircraft, and a
number of aircraft engines. There are sections
devoted to science, mechanical music, machine
tools, clocks, weapons and writing instruments.

Regular Steam Days are held on the first and
third Wednesday of each month, in addition to
Steam Weekends in March and October. There
is an annual Traction Engine Rally round the
city streets in May and a Stationary Steam
Engine Rally in September.

City Museum and Art Gallery

Chamberlain Square, Birmingham, B3 3DH
  ☎ 021 235 3890
Mon–Sat 9.30–5; Sun 2–5.
Ⓕ 🛈 💺 & ✍

This is one of Britain's largest provincial
museums. It was founded in 1867 and opened in
its present building in 1885. Extensions were
built in 1912 and 1919 and a Local History
Gallery was opened in the former Commercial
and Patents Library in 1981.

Birmingham has been a rich and powerful
city and the collections are now enormous. The
local history section is concerned with the
origins and growth of Birmingham and its
suburbs.

There are strong natural history,
archaeological and ethnographical sections and
an outstanding feature of the Fine Arts Galleries
is a collection, the finest in the world, of works
by the English Pre-Raphaelites. Also well
represented are 18th- and 19th-century English
drawings and watercolours.

National Motorcycle Museum

Coventry Road, Bickenhill, Birmingham, B92 0EJ
  ☎ 06755 3311
Daily 10–6. Closed Dec 25.
Ⓒ 🛈 💺 & ✍

The National Motorcycle Museum is
strategically placed at the junction of the M42
and A45. It has a collection of 600 British
motorcycles – foreign makes are excluded –

dating from 1898 to the present day. There are
rare and famous racing and competition
machines, as well as everyday road models. All
the exhibits have been painstakingly restored to
their original specification, using, wherever
possible, authentic materials. The aim is to
provide a social as well as an engineering history
of this once great industry.

Blaenafon

Big Pit Mining Museum

Blaenafon, Gwent, NP4 9XP ☎ 0495 790311
Mar–Nov, daily 10–3.30 (last tour)
Ⓒ 🛈 💺 ✍

Big Pit is just off the A4248 between Blaenafon
and Brynmawr. Mining came to an end here in
1980 and the installations at Big Pit are the last
to survive in this once important centre of the
coal and iron industries. Visitors can see the
pithead bath, an exhibition which shows the
history of the pit and the conditions under
which the miners lived and worked, the winding
engine house, the blacksmith's forge, and a
reconstruction of the interior of a miner's
cottage.

Before going 100 m underground visitors put
on a helmet and cap lamp. Once down the pit,
they are given a guided tour by one of a team of
ex-miners. In the course of this they are able to
observe the pit-pony stables, haulage engines
and coal faces, and hear about the methods of
extracting and transporting the coal.

Regrettably, small children cannot be taken
underground, and visitors are reminded to wear
practical shoes and warm clothing for their
underground tour.

Blantyre

The David Livingstone Centre

Station Road, Blantyre, Lanarkshire, G72 9BT
  ☎ 0698 823140
*Mon–Sat 10–6; Sun 2–6. Closed Jan 1, 2, Dec
25, 26.*
Ⓒ 🛈 💺 ♿ ✍

David Livingstone, the Scottish missionary and
explorer, was born at Blantyre in 1813. The
tenement building which contained his
birthplace is now the David Livingstone
Memorial. Using several of the original items,
the single-room dwelling has been furnished and
decorated to resemble Livingstone's home
during his boyhood, and in other rooms of the
same building, which once accommodated 24
families, there are displays to tell the story of the
explorer's life.

The Livingstone Gallery contains eight
tableaux, in concrete, which illustrate aspects of
Livingstone's life. The Africa Pavilion, built in
the shape of a cluster of African huts,
concentrates attention on African life today.
The Social History Gallery, in the former
Works School of the cotton mill, shows the
impact which the Industrial Revolution made.

Bolton

Bolton Steam Museum

*Northern Mill Engine Society, The Engine House,
Atlas No. 3 Mill, Chorley Old Road, Bolton,
Greater Manchester, BL1 4LB*
☎ *0204 74557*
*Every Sun: static viewing only. Steam Days: 5 per
year (Apr, May, Aug, Oct, Dec). Please check
locally for exact dates.*

© ⚙

Atlas No. 3 Mill is a mile and a half north-west
of the centre of Bolton, once an important
centre of the Lancashire cotton industry. The
museum displays the Society's collection of
stationary steam engines, mainly from textile
mills in the North West, which have been
rescued from destruction and fully restored to
run in steam again. They include an 1840 beam
engine; an 1893 non-dead-centre vertical
engine; a 1902 tandem-coupled horizontal
engine; and an 1860 'A-frame' vertical engine.

Tonge Moor Textile Museum

*Tonge Moor Library, Tonge Moor Road, Bolton,
Greater Manchester, BL2 2LE*
☎ *0204 21394*
*Mon, Thurs 9.30–7.30; Tues, Fri 9.30-5.30; Sat
9.30–12.30. Closed Wed, Sun, Bank
Holidays.*

Ⓕ ✐

Bolton occupied a prominent position in
Britain's 19th- and early 20th-century cotton
industry.

The museum, two miles north of the town
centre, on the Burnley road, is devoted entirely
to the conservation and display of early textile
machinery, including Crompton's mule,
Hargreaves' spinning jenny and Arkwright's
water-frame – key inventions which made it
possible to develop the industry on a factory
basis. There are few surviving examples of these
pioneering machines and the museum offers a
rare opportunity of seeing them and to
understand their function and significance.

Botley

Manor Farm

*Upper Hamble Country Park, Brook Lane, Botley,
Hampshire, SO3 2ER* ☎ *04892 87055*
*Easter – end Oct, daily 10–5.30. Nov – Easter,
Sun only.*

© ⚱ 🖥 ♿ ⚙

The museum is signposted from Exit 8 on the
M27. It has been set up to show, explain and
demonstrate agricultural change in Hampshire
between 1850 and 1950. Three buildings, a
forge, wheelwright's workshop and staddle
barn, have been rescued from demolition and
re-erected at Manor Farm. They form part of the
historical survey.

This working farm makes use of a wide range
of tools, implements and machinery. The
livestock kept on the farm also illustrates the

Tank Museum, Bovington.

changes which have taken place in farming
during the past century. The Dairy Shorthorn
cow, for instance, and the Wessex Saddleback
pig, were once common in the area, but are
rarely seen there today.

The farmhouse, dating from the early 15th
century, is arranged as a farm worker's cottage of
about 1900. There is also a 13th century church
on the site.

Bovington

Tank Museum

Bovington Camp, Wareham, Dorset, BH20 6JG
☎ *0929 462721 extn 3463/3329*
Daily 10–5. Closed Christmas and New Year.

© ⚱ 🖥 ♿ ⚙

Founded in 1923 as the Royal Tank Corps
Museum, the present Tank Museum illustrates
the history of all Regiments of the Royal
Armoured Corps, past and present. Its
collection of more than 200 armoured fighting
vehicles is one of the largest in the world. The
majority originate from the United Kingdom,
but 16 other countries are represented. The
earliest exhibit, a Hornsby Chain Track
Tractor, dates from 1909 and the earliest tank
from 1915.

There are separate exhibitions of
armaments, engines, uniforms, medals,
equipment, memorabilia and campaign relics.
The explanatory material includes video
displays, working models, simulators and a
section of a Centurion tank. The museum
maintains a large library and photographic
archive.

Bradford

Bradford Industrial Museum

*Moorside Mills, Moorside Road, Bradford, West
Yorkshire, BD2 3HP* ☎ *0274 631756*
*Tues–Sun 10–5. Open Bank Holiday Mon. Closed
Good Fri, Dec 25, 26.*

Ⓕ ✐ 🖥 ♿ ⚙

The original Moorside Mill was built for worsted
spinning in 1875. A second mill was added in

1916 and production continued until 1970, after which the premises were converted into Bradford's Industrial Museum.

The museum specialises in the history of the wool manufacturing industry, and has an important collection of worsted textile machinery, with many working exhibits. There are in addition a motive power gallery, with live steam demonstrations every Wednesday afternoon and on the first Saturday in each month, and a transport collection, which includes a range of Bradford-built Jowett cars and the only surviving Bradford tram. Moorside House, the former mill-owner's residence, has been furnished in Victorian style with partial gas lighting, to reflect the life-style of a comfortably-off middle-class family in the late 19th century.

National Museum of Photography, Film and Television

*Prince's View, Bradford, West Yorkshire,
    BD5 0TR   ☎ 0274 727488
Tues–Sun 10.30–6 (special exhibitions, box office ,
    shop and coffee bar open until 7.30). Open
    Good Fri, Easter Mon, Spring and Summer
    Bank Holidays. Closed Jan 1, May Day, Dec.
    25, 26.*
F ⓘ ⬛ ⑁ ⌨

During the post-war redevelopment of Bradford, a new theatre was constructed in the city centre. It was, however, never used for its original purpose and now houses the museum, which presents and explores the past, present and future of photography, film and television, especially in Britain. Working models, original equipment and dramatic reconstructions allow visitors to experience the full range of photographic possibilities, from the camera obscura to satellites, from galaxy to microbe and from photojournalism to portraiture. Special galleries illustrate the history and practice of television and an important section based on the former Kodak collections, covers the development of popular photography from its beginnings. The museum possesses Britain's only IMAX theatre. Its 19 m by 16 m cinema screen is the largest in the country.

Brentford

Kew Bridge Steam Museum

*Green Dragon Lane, Brentford, Middlesex,
    TW8 0EN   ☎ 081 568 4757
Daily 11–5. In steam Sat, Sun, Bank Holiday Mon
    throughout year, except weekend preceding Dec
    25.*
C ⓘ ⬛ ⌨

The museum is housed in a restored Victorian pumping station, which once supplied water to the whole of West London, in the magnificent building which is an important monument of 19th century industrial architecture. The original four Cornish beam engines have been preserved and three of them are in operating condition. The collection also includes steam

engines from other parts of the country, all restored to working order, diesel engines and miscellaneous exhibits associated with the history of steam power and water supply.

Brighton

Art Gallery and Museum

*Church Street, Brighton, East Sussex BN1 1UE
    ☎ 0273 603005
Tues–Sat 10–5.45; Sun 2–5. Closed Jan 1, Good
    Fri, Dec 25, 26.*
F ⓘ ⬛ ⌨

The museum building was remodelled from stabling and coach-houses which formed part of the Royal Stables built by the Prince of Wales in the early 1870s. There are sections devoted to Art Nouveau and Art Deco, Sussex archaeology and folk life, ceramics, ethnography and Brighton history. There are some Old Master paintings and watercolours, and an unconventional costume gallery, deliberately planned to provoke thought about the wearing of clothes.

The Royal Pavilion

*Brighton, East Sussex, BN1 1UE
    ☎ 0273 603005
June–Sept, daily 10–6. Oct–May, daily 10–5.
    Closed Dec 25, 26.*
C ⓘ ⬛

The Royal Pavilion was designed by John Nash and built between 1815 and 1822 for George, Prince of Wales, later George IV. The picturesque exterior recalls Moghul India while the so-called Chinese taste prevails in the sumptuous furnished interiors, which include the recently restored Music Room, severely damaged by fire in 1975, and by a storm in 1987. The displays include much of the original furniture lent by HM The Queen and a magnificent collection of Regency silver and silver-gilt. The fully-equipped kitchens are a notable feature of the exhibits in the Royal Pavilion.

The Royal Pavilion, Brighton.

Bristol

Bristol Industrial Museum

Princes Wharf, City Docks, Bristol, BS1 4RN
☎ 0272 251470
Sat–Wed 10–1, 2–5. Closed Thurs, Fri, Jan 1,
Good Fri, Dec 25–27.
F ▮ ⛏ ⚭

The museum is in a dockside transit shed of the 1950s, with cranes of the same period preserved outside, together with a surviving section of the docks' railway network, now used for the museum's steam train operation.

The collections cover the manufacturing and transport history of Bristol and the surrounding area. Local railway material is strongly represented, including gauge 0 and 1 models, especially a working layout of gauge 1 historic models. The museum has the world's earliest purpose-built motor caravan, the *Wanderer*, 1885, and the oldest working self-propelled road-vehicle, the 1875 Grenville Steam Carriage. The definitive collection of Bristol-built Rolls-Royce aero-engines is here, and the aeronautical section also includes the development mock-up of the nose section and cockpit of Concorde, a replica of the 1910 Bristol Boxkite, and a Bristol Sycamore helicopter.

The important maritime collection illustrates the history of the Port of Bristol, and many other local industries especially tobacco, glass, and wagon and carriage building, are represented by comprehensive collections.

City of Bristol Museum and Art Gallery

Queen's Road, Bristol, BS8 1RL
☎ 0272 223601
Daily 10–5. Closed Jan 1, Good Fri, May Day,
Late Spring Bank Holiday Mon & Tues, Dec
25–27.
F ▮ ⛴ ⛏

The listed 1905 museum, building, with an extension added in 1928, is of considerable architectural importance. The collections cover a wide field: paintings – the works by artists of the Bristol School are particularly important – drawings, watercolours, prints; sculpture; ceramics, especially of local manufacture; exceptional 18th–19th-century glass, including many important Bristol pieces. There are galleries of British and foreign natural history, special attention being paid to plants, insects, birds and animals of South-West England, and good collections of rocks, minerals and fossils. The museum has both local and worldwide collections of archaeology and ethnography.

John Wesley's Chapel: The New Room

36 The Horsefair, Bristol, BS1 3JE
☎ 0272 264740
Summer: Mon–Sat, 10–4. Closed Sun, Bank
Holidays and Weds in winter.
F ⚭ ⚭

Timber roof with decorative wind-braces.
Avoncroft Museum of Building, Bromsgrove.

This is the oldest Methodist building in the world. The foundation stone was laid by John Wesley in 1739 and the Chapel was extended in 1748. Above it are rooms where both John and Charles Wesley once lived. There are a number of items associated with the Wesleys and with the early days of the New Room. They include furniture, a 1761 organ, letters and membership lists in John Wesley's handwriting. An equestrian statue of John Wesley and a statue of Charles Wesley stand in the courtyards of the Chapel.

Brixham

British Fisheries Museum

Old Market House, The Quay, Brixham, South
Devon, TQ5 8AW   ☎ 08045 2861
June–Sept, Mon–Sat 9–1, 2–6; Sun 10–1, 2–5.
Oct–May, Mon 2–5; Tues–Fri 9–1, 2–5; Sat
9–1.
C *(ex. children)* ⚭ ⛏ ⚭

The museum shares Brixham's original Market House with the Tourist Information Centre. It illustrates the history of the British fishing industry from the Middle Ages to the present day. There are exhibits devoted to early fishing methods, the Icelandic and Newfoundland cod fisheries, and the evolution of the fishing smack and its replacement by the steam drifter. Other sections of the museum are concerned with EC policy towards the industry and with the reorganisation of deep-sea fishing since 1945.

Bromsgrove

Avoncroft Museum of Building

Stoke Heath, Bromsgrove, Hereford and
Worcester, B60 4JR   ☎ 0527 31363
Mar and Nov, Tues–Thurs, Sat, Sun, Bank
Holiday, 11–4.30, Apr–May and Sept–Oct,
Tues–Sun, Bank Holiday 11–5.30. June–Aug
daily 11–5.30.
C ▮ ⛴ ⛏ ⚭

The museum is two miles south of Bromsgrove, off the A38 Bromsgrove bypass and 400 metres north of its junction with the B4091. Its primary aim has been to rescue historic buildings from destruction, rather than to illustrate the social history of a community.

Among the buildings already on the site are

a 15th-century merchant's house from Bromsgrove, a thatched barn from Cholstrey in Herefordshire, and an 18th-century forge cottage. A Warwickshire windmill grinds corn for flour and a Bromsgrove nailshop is now used by the museum's blacksmith.

Among the rarer attractions are the Counting House from Bromsgrove cattle market, an ice house from Tong in Shropshire, and a three-seater earth closet from Herefordshire. Visitors may also now see the great 14th-century roof originally from the monastic Guesten Hall at Worcester.

Burnley

Queen Street Mill

Harle Syke, Burnley, Lancashire, BB10 2HX
   ☎ *0282 59996*
Mar 20–Sept 28, daily 10.30–4.30 ex Tues, Wed.
Ⓒ 🛈 💺 ♿ ♠

Harle Syke is three miles from the centre of Burnley on the Briercliffe Road. Queen Street Mill, built in 1894, is a fully operational steam-powered cotton-weaving mill, the last of its kind and now preserved as a museum by Pennine Heritage Ltd. Visitors can experience the noisy working atmosphere of hundreds of Lancashire looms crammed tightly together and driven by the steam-engine, *Peace*.

Cloth is woven at the mill today, just as it was 100 years ago. The traditional skills are being preserved by employing experienced mill workers. In addition to opportunities for watching the production of cloth, there are displays illustrating the history of the textile industry, especially in Lancashire, and the lives of the workers and their families.

Weavers' Triangle Visitor Centre

85 Manchester Road, Burnley, Lancashire,
   BB11 1JZ
Apr–Sept, Tues, Wed, Sat, Sun 2–4. Oct, Sun,
   Bank Holiday Mon. Parties at other times by
   appt.
Ⓕ ✐ 💺 ♠

The building housing the Centre is the former Wharfmaster's House and Canal Toll Office at Burnley Wharf on the Leeds and Liverpool Canal. The museum is concerned mainly with

Victorian Parlour. Weavers' Triangle Visitor Centre, Burnley.

Burnley's traditions and archaeology as a leading cotton-weaving town. By means of photographs, drawings, maps, models and objects, the displays explain the techniques of cotton-manufacturing and introduce the Weavers' Triangle, a well-preserved Victorian area on both sides of the Leeds and Liverpool Canal. The Triangle contains a complete cross-section of 19th-century buildings dating from the days when Burnley could claim to be the cotton-weaving capital of the world – weaving sheds, spinning mills, warehouses, foundries, domestic buildings and a school.

The Visitor Centre also has a weaver's dwelling, a Victorian parlour, a 'Burnley Fair Room' with a working model fairground, and a small Victorian-style classroom.

Burton-upon-Trent

Bass Museum of Brewing History

Horninglow Street, Burton-upon-Trent,
   Staffordshire DE14 1JZ   ☎ *0283 45301*
Mon–Fri 10–4; Sat, Sun 10.30–4.
Ⓒ 🛈 💺 ♿ ♠

The former brewery carpenters' workshop, which houses the museum, was built in 1866. The displays illlustrate the history and development of brewing in Britain from the 18th century to the present day, with an emphasis on the Bass Company and on brewing in Burton-upon-Trent. Among the special themes are the influence of the public house on social life, and Bass advertising over the years. There are interesting collections of ale glassware and brewery transport, a model of Burton-upon-Trent in 1921, and a reconstruction of an Edwardian taproom.

The brewery Shire horses can be seen in the stable area, and brewery tours are available, by appointment only.

Caernarfon

Segontium Roman Fort

Beddgelert Road, Caernarfon, Gwynedd
   ☎ *0286 5625*
Mar–Apr, Oct, Mon–Sat 9.30–5.30; Sun 2–5.
   May–Sept, Mon–Sat 9.30–6; Sun 2–6. Nov–
   Feb, Mon–Sat 9.30–4; Sun 2–4. Closed Jan 1,
   Good Fri, May Day, Dec 24–26.
Ⓕ ✐ ♠

The Roman auxiliary fort of *Segontium*, overlooking the town of Caernarfon, is one of the most famous in Britain. The museum, which is on the site of the fort, tells the story of the conquest and occupation of what is now Wales by the Romans and describes the military organisation of the day, the garrisons of *Segontium*, and the history of the fort as illustrated by its remains. It also displays finds from the excavations at *Segontium* which throw light on daily life in this remote Roman outpost. A model of a fully equipped Roman auxiliary infantryman of the early 2nd century AD forms the centrepiece of the exhibition.

Cambridge

Cambridge and County Folk Museum

2–3 Castle Street, Cambridge, CB3 0AQ
☎ *0223 355159*
*Mon–Sat 10.30–5; Sun 2–5. Oct–Easter, closed
Mon except for school holidays.*

C 🏛 ■

The former White Horse Inn, which houses the
museum, was built in the 16th century. The
collections cover the everyday life of people in
the city of Cambridge and the county of
Cambridgeshire from c. 1650 to the present day.
Ten exhibition rooms are devoted to trades and
occupations: Room 2 contains the original bar
of the White Horse, which was used as such
until 1934, and other rooms are devoted to
cooking and lighting; the kitchen; domestic
crafts; the city and university; dolls' houses,
miniature furniture, dolls, toys and games; the
farm, the Fens and folklore; and costume and
dress. There are regularly changing temporary
exhibitions.

Fitzwilliam Museum

Trumpington Street, Cambridge, CB2 1RB
☎ *0223 332900*
*Tues–Sat 10–5; Sun 2.15–5. Open Easter Mon,
Spring & Summer Bank Holidays. Closed
Good Fri, May Day, Dec 24–Jan 1.*

F 🏛 💻 ♿ ☕

The impressive first block of the museum
buildings was opened in 1848. Major extensions
were carried out between 1924 and 1975. The
Fitzwilliam, one of Britain's most prestigious
museums, contains the University's fine art
collections, most of which have been acquired
through private benefactions, and which
comprise Egyptian, Greek, Near Eastern and
Roman antiquities; coins and medals; medieval
manuscripts; paintings, including works by
masters such as Titian and Veronese, and
drawings; prints; Oriental and Occidental
pottery and porcelain; textiles; arms and
armour; and medieval and Renaissance objects
of art. There is also a notable library.

Kettle's Yard

Castle Street, Cambridge, CB3 0AQ
☎ *0223 352124*
*House: Tues–Sun 2–4. Gallery: Tues–Sat 12.30–
5.30; Sun 2–5.30.*

F 🖌 ■

Kettle's Yard has been created from a conversion
of four 17th-century buildings, with a modern
extension. It has been conceived as a home,
rather than a museum, and every attempt is
made to preserve an intimate atmosphere. It
houses a substantial collection of British art of
the early 20th century, collected by the late Jim
Ede and placed in domestic settings, with books,
furniture and other objects.

The adjacent gallery shows changing
exhibitions of 20th-century and contemporary
art, with an accompanying programme of
activities and events for all age groups.

Fitzwilliam Museum, Cambridge. The ornate
High Victorian entrance hall by E.M. Barry,
1870–5.

Cardiff

National Museum of Wales

*Cathays Park, Cardiff, South Glamorgan,
CF1 3NP* ☎ *0222 397951*
*Tues–Sat 10–5; Sun 2.30–5. Closed Jan 1, Good
Fri, May Day, Dec 24–26.*

F 🏛 ♿ ☕

The emphasis of the permanent collections is on
the story of Wales from the earliest times. The
galleries illustrate Welsh geology, plants and
animals, as well as the story of man, his work
and his art. The art collection is of international
standing and is particularly strong on French
Impressionist and Post-Impressionist painters
including Monet, Renoir, Cézanne and Pissarro.

The industrial section has original objects
and machines relating to the older industries,
together with dioramas and models. There is a
mining gallery and other displays tell the story of
iron, steel and tinplate manufacture in Wales.
The modern industries featured include
electricity and oil-refining.

Welsh Folk Museum

St Fagans, Cardiff, South Glamorgan, CF5 6XB
☎ *0222 569441*
*Apr–Oct, daily 10–5. Nov–Mar, Mon–Sat 10–5.
Closed Good Fri, Dec 24–26.*

C 🏛 💻 ⚄ ♿ ☕

The museum, which illustrates the traditional
life and culture of Wales, is four miles west of
Cardiff, near Junction 33 on the M4 motorway.
The open-air section covering a site of about
40 hectares, contains a number of historic
buildings moved from other parts of Wales.
These include farmhouses, cottages, a tannery,
forge, tollhouse, cockpit, chapel and working
woollen and flour mills. Among the craftsmen

who give regular demonstrations are a cooper and woodturner.

In St Fagans, an Elizabethan mansion with formal gardens within the curtain wall of a Norman castle, are the Galleries of Material Culture, which have displays of costumes, transport, agricultural implements, furniture and domestic equipment.

Welsh Industrial and Maritime Museum

Bute Street, Cardiff, South Glamorgan, CF1 5AN
   ☎ *0222 481919*
Tues–Sat 10–5; Sun 2.30–5. Open Bank Holiday
   Mon. Closed Jan 1, Good Fri, May Day, Dec
   24–26.
F ▮ ₺ ☞

Situated in the dock area of Cardiff, the museum, which is still in the course of development, has been set up in order to interpret the industrial and maritime heritage of Wales. There are at present two galleries which trace the history of motive power in Wales and an open-air section which displays a wide range of machines, vehicles and shops. A railway exhibition is housed nearby at Bute Railway Station.

Carlisle

Carlisle Museum and Art Gallery

Tullie House, Castle Street, Carlisle, Cumbria,
   CA3 8TP   ☎ *0228 34781*
Apr–Sept, Mon–Fri 9–6.45; Sat 9–5; Sun (June–
   Aug only) 2.30–5. Oct–Mar, Mon–Sat 9–5.
F ✍ ☞

The museum building, a Jacobean house with Victorian extensions, is named after the Tullie family, who occupied it from the early 17th century until 1817. There are important collections relating to the prehistoric and Roman periods in Cumbria, the Roman items coming mainly from excavations in the Cumbrian section of Hadrian's Wall and the Roman city of Carlisle, *Luguvalium*. The natural history and geological collections are mainly local in origin and are particularly strong in birds and minerals. The art collections emphasise 19th- and 20th-century British

paintings and 18th- and 19th-century English porcelain, with excellent examples from all the major factories. Toys and dolls, costumes and musical instruments are also well represented.

The social history collections include a wide range of objects from 1600 to the present day. There are displays on farming, weaving, firearms, the fire service, law and order, photography, pharmacy and the State-managed public houses.

Castletown (Isle of Man)

Nautical Museum

Bridge Street, Castletown, Isle of Man
   ☎ *0624 75522*
May 5–Sept 27, Mon–Sat 10–1, 2–5; Sun 2–5.
C ✍ ☞

The Nautical Museum presents a picture of the maritime life of the Isle of Man in the days of sail. The displays centre on the armed schooner-rigged yacht, *Peggy*, built in Castletown in 1791 and still housed in her original boat-cellar. The exhibit also contains papers and personal possessions of the Quayle family who built the yachts. The collections also include a wide range of nautical equipment and relics, ship models, and photographs of Manx sailing vessels. There is a reconstruction of a sailmaker's loft. Part of the original building is designed to resemble a cabin of the Nelson period.

Chalfont St Giles

Milton's Cottage

21 Deanway, Chalfont St Giles, Buckinghamshire,
   HP8 4JH   ☎ *02407 2313*
Feb–Oct, Tues–Sat 10–1, 2–6; Sun 2–6. Open
   Spring, Summer Bank Holiday 10–1, 2–6.
C ✍ ☞

The cottage, a 16th-century building, contains collections illustrating the life and times of the poet, John Milton, and of the history of the cottage, the village and the surrounding area. There are portraits of Milton and first editions of his famous long poems, *Paradise Lost* and *Paradise Regained*.

Chawton

Jane Austen's House

Chawton, Alton, Hampshire, GU34 1SD
   ☎ *0420 83262*
Apr–Oct, daily 11–4.30. Nov–Dec and Mar,
   Wed–Sun 11–4.30. Jan–Feb, Sat, Sun
   11–4.30. Closed Dec 25, 26.
C ✍ ⚘ ☞

The house was built in 1690 as a posting inn. It was altered in 1809, when Mrs Austen came to live here with her daughters, and looks substantially the same now as in the Austens' time. There are many items associated with the novelist, Jane Austen, and her family, including

Jane Austen's House, Chawton.

the topaz crosses given to Jane and Cassandra by their brother, Charles, the patchwork quilt made by Jane and her mother and sister, and a large number of letters and documents. The table on which Jane Austen wrote *Mansfield Park*, *Emma* and *Persuasion* is in the dining-parlour, as is part of the Wedgwood dinner service bought by her brother, Edward.

Cheltenham

Cheltenham Art Gallery and Museum

Clarence Street, Cheltenham, Gloucestershire,
GL50 3JT   ☎ *0242 237431*
Mon–Sat 10–5.20. May 1–Sept 30, Sun 2–5.20.
Closed Bank Holidays.

F 🛈 🖾

The Arts and Crafts Movement collections at Cheltenham are of national importance, with furniture by Gimson, the Barnsleys, Voysey, Ashbee and Gordon Russell and others. A section is devoted to Arts and Crafts metalwork and jewellery.

There are also collections of 17th- and 19th-century Dutch and Belgian paintings, 17th–20th-century British paintings, English furniture, ceramics, glass and pewter, together with local archaeology displays and exhibits relating to the Regency town of Cheltenham. A special section is devoted to Edward Wilson, the Antarctic explorer.

Gustav Holst's Birthplace

4 Clarence Road, Cheltenham, Gloucestershire,
GL52 2AY   ☎ *0242 524846*
Tues–Fri 12–5.20; Sat 11–5.20. Closed Bank
Holidays.

F 🖉

The composer, Gustav Holst, was born at 4 Clarence Road, a typical Cheltenham Regency house, in 1874. The museum illustrates Holst's working life and his music and reflects domestic life in the 19th century. The displays include Holst's grand piano, made c.1850, a selection of his published music which illustrates his development as a composer, and a chronological survey of his career, with photographs, pictures, concert programmes and other documents.

There is a working Victorian kitchen and laundry, where school parties can dress up in order to re-enact life below stairs in Victorian and Edwardian England. Other period rooms are a Regency drawing room, a Victorian bedroom and an Edwardian children's nursery.

Church Stretton

Acton Scott Working Farm Museum

Wenlock Lodge, Acton Scott, nr Church Stretton,
Shropshire, SY6 6QN   ☎ *06946 306/307*
Apr–Oct, Tues–Sat 10–5; Sun, Bank Holiday
10–6.

C 🛈 🖾 ♿ 🐾

Traditional butter-making at Acton Scott Working Farm Museum, Church Stretton.

The museum occupies a range of late-18th-century farm buildings, formerly part of the Home Farm of the nearby Acton Scott Hall, together with a 4-bay cart shed and a horse-gin house which have been brought to the site and re-erected. Acton Scott Hall dates from 1580–85 and is one of the earliest brick buildings in the area.

The Working Farm Museum demonstrates life on a Shropshire upland farm before the coming of the petrol engine. Its 9 hectares are worked with Shire horses, allowing visitors to watch 19th-century arable techniques in action. The farm is stocked with horses, cows, pigs and poultry of breeds rarely seen today.

Cirencester

Corinium Museum

Park Street, Cirencester, Gloucestershire,
GL7 2BX   ☎ *0285 655611*
Apr–Oct, Mon–Sat 10–5.30; Sun 2–5.30. Nov–
Mar, Tues–Sat 10–5; Sun 2–5. Open Bank
Holidays.

C 🛈 ♿ ■ 🐾

The museum takes its name from *Corinium*, the Roman name for Cirencester, which was the second largest town of Roman Britain. The displays are arranged in chronological order, beginning with a newly-designed Cotswold prehistory gallery and progressing through the Roman period to Saxon and medieval times. The exhibits include mosaics of high quality, full-scale reproductions of a Roman kitchen, dining-room and stonemason's workshop, personal possessions, jewellery, pottery and coins. A reconstructed Roman garden in Pompeian style has recently been opened.

There is a small Anglo-Saxon display with a medieval section illustrating religious and secular life. One of the great medieval abbeys was at Cirencester, and its story is told in the museum. Other exhibits relate to the Cotswold wool trade, and to the history of Cirencester from Tudor times onwards.

Cogges

Cogges Farm Museum

Cogges, nr Witney, Oxfordshire, OX8 6LA
☎ *0993 72602*
*Apr 9–Nov 4, Tues–Sun 10.30–5,30 (until 4.30
   in Oct). Open Bank Holiday Mon.*
C ♿ 🖼 ⓰ 🐾

The museum site contains the moated area of
the first manor house on the site built in the
12th century. The existing manor house dates
from the 13th century, with many subsequent
modifications and additions. The farm buildings
were constructed at various times during the
17th to 20th centuries.

The aim of Cogges is to show changes in the
landscape, the village and its rural community.
There are displays of historic and rare breeds of
animals and demonstrations of farm and
domestic activities.

Colchester

Colchester and Essex Museum

The Castle, Colchester, Essex, CO1 1TJ
☎ *0206 712931/2*
*Apr–Sept, Mon–Sat 10–5; Sun 2.30–5. Oct–
   Mar, Mon–Fri 10–5; Sat 10–4. Closed Good
   Fri, Dec 25, 26.*
C ♿

Colchester Castle, *c.*1076, is one of the earliest
stone castles to be built in Britain. It was
constructed on the foundations of the Roman
Temple of Claudius. Now converted into a
museum, it presents displays of archaeological
material discovered during the excavation of
sites in the county of Essex. The collections
from the Roman city at Colchester are of
exceptional quality and interest.

Sir Alfred Munnings Art Museum

*Castle House, Dedham, Colchester, Essex,
   CO7 6AZ*   ☎ *0206 322127*
*Early May–early Oct, Sun, Wed, Bank Holiday
   Mon 2–5. Aug also Thurs, Sat 2–5.*
C 🐾

Castle House, part Tudor, part Georgian, was
the home of the artist, Sir Alfred Munnings,

**Study of Jockeys and Horses by Munnings. Sir
Alfred Munnings Art Museum, Colchester.**

from 1919 until his death in 1959. It now
contains a large collection of his paintings,
sketches and other work, in the setting of the
house in which he lived and had his studios.
There are many studies of racehorses and of
racing, equestrian portraits and hunting scenes.
Several large early canvases are displayed in the
Courtyard Gallery and examples of his early
poster work in the studios. The exhibitions are
changed from time to time and augmented by
paintings by Munnings borrowed from other
galleries and from private sources.

Comrie

Scottish Tartans Museum

Drummond Street, Comrie, Perthshire, PH6 2DW
☎ *0764 70779*
*Mar–Apr and Oct, Mon–Fri 10–5; Sat 10–1.
   May–Sept, Mon–Sat 10–5; Sun 11–3.*
C ♿

The museum houses a comprehensive collection
of objects and pictures illustrating the origins
and development of tartans and Highland dress.
There is a dye garden, containing plants which
have been used for the dyeing of the woollen
thread used in making tartan cloth, and a
weaver's cottage.

Coniston

Brantwood

Coniston, Cumbria, LA21 8AD
☎ *05394 41396*
*Mid Mar–mid Nov, daily 11–5.30. Mid Nov–mid
   Mar, Wed–Sun 11–4.*
C ♿ 🖼 ⓰ 🐾

Brantwood, the home of John Ruskin from 1872
until his death in 1900, lies on the eastern shore
of Coniston Water, two and a half miles from
Coniston village. The original Lakeland cottage
was extended by Ruskin into a rambling
30-room mansion with many interesting
architectural features. It contains a large
collection of Ruskin's paintings and drawings,
together with works by some of his friends,
including T. M. Rooke, Sir Edward Burne-Jones
and William Holman Hunt. Some of his
furniture and a number of his personal
possessions are also on display, and his coach
and his boat, *Jumping Jenny*, are to be seen in
the coach house.

Further Ruskin material, including
paintings, drawings, letters and other personal
relics, is to be seen in the Ruskin Museum at
Yewdale Road, Coniston (☎ 05394 41387).

Cookham on Thames

Stanley Spencer Gallery

*Kings Hall, Cookham on Thames, nr Maidenhead,
   Berkshire*   ☎ *06285 20890/20043*
*Easter–Oct, daily 10.30–5.30. Nov–Easter, Sat,
   Sun, public holidays 11–5.*
C ⬙ ⓰ 🐾

The gallery is in the former Wesleyan Chapel which Spencer attended as a child. It contains a permanent collection of the artist's works, together with letters, documents and memorabilia. Each summer, in a special exhibition, it also displays important works by Spencer which are on loan from private and public collections.

Coventry

Herbert Art Gallery and Museum

Jordan Well, Coventry, West Midlands,
    CV1 5RW   ☎ *0203 25555 extn 2315*
Mon–Sat 10–5.30; Sun 2–5.30. Closed Jan 1,
    Good Fri, Dec 25, 26.
F ▪ ♿ ⚓

The collections in the Art Gallery concentrate on works by British artists. They include watercolours, paintings and sculpture and 20th-century figure drawings, together with local topography and portraits, and paintings on the theme of Lady Godiva. Graham Sutherland's studies for the tapestry in Coventry Cathedral are on display and the gallery has the Poke Collection of English furniture, silver and paintings on long-term loan.

A special display, Phoenix, tells the story of the rebuilding of Coventry after the destruction caused by the air raids during the Second World War.

Cregneash (Isle of Man)

Cregneash Folk Museum

Cregneash, Isle of Man   ☎ *0624 75522*
May 5–Sept 27, Mon–Sat 10–1, 2–5; Sun 2–5.
C ⚲ ▰ ⚓

The village of Cregneash is near Port St Mary and Port Erin. The museum illustrates life in a typical Manx crofting and fishing community at the turn of the century. Most of the buildings are thatched, and include a crofter-fisherman's cottage; a weaver's shed, with its handloom; a turner's shed, with a treadle lathe; a farmstead; and a smithy.

Spinning demonstrations are given on Wednesdays and Thursdays and a blacksmith works in the smithy on two days each week, carrying out tasks which illustrate various aspects of the craft.

Crich

Tramway Museum

Crich, Matlock, Derbyshire, DE4 5DP
    ☎ *0773 852565*
Mar 31–end Oct, Sat, Sun 10–6.30. May 5–July,
    Mon–Thurs 10–5.30. July 20–end Aug, Mon–
    Fri 10–5.30. Please check for additional
    opening at Easter and late Oct.
C ▪ ▰ ⚃ ♿ ⚓

The Tramway Museum was established in order to preserve and display an important collection

London tram, built 1903. Tramway Museum, Crich.

of tramcars, built between 1873 and 1953, from Britain and abroad. As a setting for the trams a street scene has been created, with items brought from a number of cities, and including the façade of the Derby Assembly Rooms (1765). The upper floors of this building now house the museum's library and archive, and the ground floor has the video theatre and the Tramways exhibition, which shows the social effects of the tram in the late 19th and early 20th centuries.

There is a regular electric tram service on the scenic, mile-long track, much of which is built on the site of a narrow-gauge mineral line originally developed by George Stephenson.

Cromford

Arkwright's Mill

Mill Lane, Cromford, Derbyshire, DE4 3RQ
    ☎ *0629 824297*
Easter–Oct, Mon–Fri 10–4.30; Sat, Sun and
    Bank Holidays 11–5. Oct–Easter, Mon–Fri
    10–4; Sat, Sun 11–4.
C ▪ ▰ ⚓

In 1771 Richard Arkwright established the world's first successful water-powered cotton-spinning mill at Cromford. After 200 years of industrial use, the Cromford Mills were bought by the Arkwright Society, which is engaged in a major restoration programme.

The museum is housed in a mill building (c.1790), adjacent to Arkwright's 1771 cotton mill. It contains two exhibitions. The first relates to the life of Sir Richard Arkwright and to the development of the British cotton industry, and the second, 'Cromford Village', to the social implications of Arkwright's vision of the Factory Settlement.

Culloden

Culloden Visitor Centre

Culloden, nr Inverness   ☎ 0463 790607
Easter–May, Oct, daily 9.30–5.30. June–Sept,
    daily 9–7.30.

C � 🅰

The 1745 Jacobite Rising ended when Prince
Charles Edward's army was disastrously defeated
at Culloden on 16 April 1746. The National
Trust for Scotland now owns the Grave of the
Clans, the Well of the Dead, the Memorial
Cairn, the Cumberland Stone, Old Leanach
farmhouse, and a large part of the battlefield.

The Visitor Centre at the site includes an
historical display and an audio-visual
programme which interprets the Battle of
Culloden and its background.

Darlington

Darlington Railway Centre

North Road Station, Darlington, Co Durham,
    DL3 6ST   ☎ 0325 460532
Daily 9.30–5 (last admission 4.30). Closed at
    Christmas and New Year (check actual dates).

C 📀 💻 ᬗ 🅰

North Road Station was built in 1842 for
George Stephenson's pioneering Stockton and
Darlington Railway. The museum collection
includes locomotives, rolling stock, models,
photographs, documents and other items
relating to railways in North-East England, with
particular reference to the Stockton and
Darlington Railway. The principal large
exhibits are the Stockton and Darlington
locomotives No 1, *Locomotion* (1825) and
No 25, *Derwent* (1845). Working locomotives
run on the adjoining Hopetown Sidings area on
selected dates.

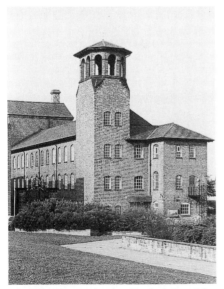

**The Silk Mill, now housing Derby Industrial
Museum.**

Derby

Derby Industrial Museum

The Silk Mill, off Full Street, Derby, DE1 3AR
    ☎ 0332 255308
Tues–Sat 10–5; Mon 11–5; Sun and Bank
    Holidays 2–5.

C 📀 ᬗ 🅰

The Silk Mill, in which the museum is located,
was built between 1717 and 1721. It was the
prototype for subsequent factory development.
After a fire in 1910, it had to be substantially
rebuilt. Its displays provide an introduction to
the industrial history of Derby and Derbyshire.
There are sections on mining and quarrying,
general and railway engineering, and the
manufacture of bricks and stoneware. The
museum also has a famous and growing
collection of Rolls-Royce aero engines, ranging
from an Eagle of 1915 to an RB211 from the first
TriStar airliner.

Derby Museum and Art Gallery

The Strand, Derby, DE1 1BS
    ☎ 0332 255586/255578
Tues–Sat 10–5; Sun and Bank Holidays 2–5.

F 🍴 ■

Most of the displays in the museum are closely
related to the region. They include exhibits on
local prehistory, life in Derby during the period
of the Roman occupation, and medieval Derby.
Sections are devoted to the geology and wildlife
of the district, and to objects made from Blue
John and Ashford Black Marble. Outstanding
exhibitions include works by the late-18th-
century painter, Joseph Wright of Derby, who
specialised in industrial subjects, and Derby
porcelain from 1750 to the present day.

Royal Crown Derby Museum

194 Osmaston Road, Derby, DE3 8JZ
    ☎ 0332 47051
Mon–Fri 9–12.30, 1.30–4. Closed Good Fri,
    Easter Mon, one week at May Bank Holiday,
    Christmas.

F 🍴 🅰

The displays illustrate the history of Derby
china, from c.1750 to the present day, and
cover the Nottingham Road, King Street and
Osmaston Road manufactories. The exhibits
include some of the early patch mark figures,
topographical pieces and a selection of rare blue
and white ware. There is also a fine biscuit
group, dated 1775 and, for the period 1811–48,
finely gilded vases, teapots and figures and some
of the earliest of the Japanese patterns for which
Derby is celebrated.

For the Osmaston Road factory there is
outstanding work by Désiré Leroy, with
elaborately gilded and jewelled patterns. Among
the more modern products there are
commemorative items and pieces made for
Royalty.

Devizes

Devizes Museum

Wiltshire Archaeological and Natural History
Society, Long Street, Devizes, Wiltshire,
SN10 1NS   ☎ *0380 727369*
Mon–Sat 10–5
© ≜

The museum is the headquarters of the
Wiltshire Archaeological and Natural History
Society, formed in 1853. The prehistoric
collections are of international standing and
include weapons, exotic ornaments and
personal finery. The new Bronze Age Gallery
contains the richest and most comprehensive
collection of Bronze Age artefacts in Britain.
There is a Henge Monument Room and galleries
devoted to the archaeology of the Roman,
Saxon and Medieval periods. The exhibits in
the Natural History Gallery have been
completely reorganised and redisplayed, and
there is a new Local History Gallery. The
Picture Gallery has a window by John Piper.

Dobwalls

Thorburn Gallery

Dobwalls, Liskeard, Cornwall, PL14 6HD
    ☎ *0579 20325/21129*
Easter–Oct, daily 10–6. Nov–Easter, daily 11–5.
Closed Jan 1, Dec 25, 26.
© ≜ 🖳 ਠ ⚓

The exhibitions in the museum portray the life
and times of the celebrated wildlife painter,
Archibald Thorburn (1860–1935). The 200
paintings on view represent the largest display of
his work which can be seen by the public. There
are also exhibits of sketches, books, letters,
photographs, proofs, prints and memorabilia,
together with reconstructions of his house and
studio, and environmental scenes similar to
those to be found in his paintings, brought alive
by audio-visual techniques.

Dorchester

Dorset County Museum

High Street West, Dorchester, Dorset, DT1 1XA
    ☎ *0305 62735*
Mon–Sat 10–5. Closed Good Fri, Dec 25, 26.
© ⌀ ■ ⚓

The 1884 museum building is one of
Dorchester's most prominent architectural
features. The collections, which have been built
up continuously by the Dorset Natural History
and Archaeological Society since 1846, cover
anything to do with Dorset, below, on or above
the ground. The natural history gallery
concentrates on the conservation of the variety
of Dorset habitats. The geological gallery
illustrates the rock types and fossils which can
be found in the county, and the archaeology
gallery stresses the need to preserve sites in the
region.

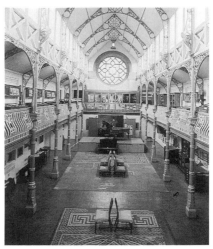

Dorset County Museum, Dorchester.

A special section is devoted to the rural and
industrial past of Dorset, and the large
collections of photographs, drawings, paintings
and costume may be seen if a prior booking is
made. The reconstruction of Thomas Hardy's
study from his home at Max Gate forms the
heart of the museum's large and important
Hardy collection. Other famous Dorset people
and local history in general are also well
represented.

Douglas (Isle of Man)

The Manx Museum

Crellin's Hill, Douglas, Isle of Man
    ☎ *0624 75522*
Mon–Sat 10–5. Closed Good Fri, morning of
Tynwald Day (usually July 5), Dec 25, 26.
🄵 ≜ ⚓

This is the Island's principal museum. It
contains a reconstructed 19th-century
farmhouse, a barn and dairy and collections of
Manx archaeology, social history and natural
history. There are paintings of Manx subjects
and works by Manx artists, and a memorial
room to T. E. Brown, the Manx poet.

Downe

Down House

Luxted Road, Downe, Orpington, Kent, BR6 7JT
    ☎ *0689 59119*
Mar–Jan, Tues–Thurs, Sat, Sun 1–6. Open Bank
Holiday Mon. Closed Dec 24–26. Groups by
appt.
© ≜ ਠ ⚓

Down House was the home by Charles Darwin
for 40 years. Visitors can see his study, where he
wrote *The Origin of Species*, and the drawing-
room, with its original furnishings. There is an
exhibition explaining the principles of Darwin's
theory of evolution and the researches which
provided the evidence on which it was based.

Dre-Fach Felindre

Museum of the Welsh Woollen Industry

Dre-fach Felindre, Llandysul, Dyfed, SA44 5UP
☎ 0559 370929
*Apr–Sept, Mon–Sat 10–5. Oct–Mar, Mon–Fri
10–5. Closed Jan 1, Good Fri, May Day, Dec
24–26.*

F 🛈 ⬛ ⌕ ♿ 🚗

The museum is situated three and a half miles
east of Newcastle Emlyn and half a mile south of
the A484 Carmarthen to Newcastle Emlyn
road. It occupies the former Cambrian Mills,
the largest of the 23 mills and 19 weaving shops
which were in production in the area at the turn
of the century. Melin Teifi, a mill which is still
working, occupies part of the museum buildings
and forms part of the exhibition.

The interpretive exhibition traces the
manufacture of woollen cloth from fleece to
fabric and shows the development of Wales'
most important rural industry from its domestic
beginnings to the 19th- and early-20th-century
factory units. There are large collections of
textile machinery and tools, a working
waterwheel and a number of gas, oil and steam
engines. Visitors can see regular demonstrations
of manufacturing processes and a display of the
products of contemporary woollen mills in
Wales.

Dudley

The Black Country Museum

Tipton Road, Dudley, West Midlands, DY1 4SQ
☎ 021 557 9643
*Daily 10–5 (earlier closing in winter). Closed
Dec 25.*

C 🛈 ⬛ ♿ 🚗

All the historic buildings which form part of the
museum have been moved from elsewhere in the
district and carefully reconstructed on the 10-
hectare site. The Museum illustrates the social
and industrial history of the Black Country,

Black Country Museum, Dudley.

through open-air exhibits, working
demonstrations, transport systems and
interpretive displays. Special features include
ironworking displays, an electric tramway, a
replica of a coal-pit and early fairground items.

The museum adjoins the Dudley Canal
Tunnel and a group of former lime-kilns. There
are regular boat trips into the man-made
limestone caves.

Dufftown

The Glenfiddich Distillery Museum

*The Glenfiddich Distillery, Dufftown, Moray,
AB5 4DH*   ☎ 0340 20373
*Mon–Fri 9.30–4.30. Easter to Oct, Sat 9.30–
4.30; Sun 12–4.30. Closed Jan 1, Dec 25–26.*

F 🛈 ♿ 🚗

The celebrated Glenfiddich Distillery, half a
mile north of Dufftown on the A941, is itself a
living museum, with regular guided tours for
visitors. The Malt Barn, which forms part of the
tour, contains items relating to the history of
the Distillery and to the Grant family which
founded it. These include late 19th-century
furniture, which belonged to William Grant,
many of the distillery ledgers, coopers' tools,
and distillery equipment used in the past.

Dunfermline

Andrew Carnegie's Birthplace

Moodie Street, Dunfermline, Fife, KY12 7PL
☎ 0383 724302
*Apr–Oct, Mon–Sat 11–5 (Wed until 8); Sun 2–5.
Nov–Mar, daily 2–4.*

F ⊘ ♿ 🚗

The museum consists of two linked buildings,
the original weaver's cottage in which the
industrialist and philanthropist, Andrew
Carnegie, was born in 1835 in an upstairs room
above his father's loom shop, and the Memorial
Hall, where the displays tell the story of
Carnegie's life and achievements in Britain and
America. The cottage is furnished to show it as
it was during Andrew Carnegie's boyhood.
Among the exhibits in the Memorial Hall is a
re-creation of Carnegie's study and the original
draft for one and a half million dollars given by
Carnegie to build the Peace Palace at The
Hague, together with a silver model of the
building.

Durham

Durham Cathedral Treasury

Cathedral Green, Durham, DH1 3EH
☎ 091 386 2489
Mon–Sat 10.30–4.30; Sun 2–4.

C 🛈 ⬛

The treasury is situated in the undercroft of the
cathedral's 14th-century dormitory. The relics
from the coffin of St Cuthbert (d.687) are at the
hub of the exhibition: they include the cross,

Battle of Britain Operations Room. Imperial War Museum, Duxford.

the small altar, the embroidery and the incised wood fragments of the 7th-century coffin itself. There are also 8th–15th-century illuminated manuscripts from the Saxon monastic houses in Northumbria and from the Benedictine monastery at Durham. Other displays include archival seals, 15th- and 17th-century copes, 18th-century silver-gilt church plate, manuscript music books, and the grotesque, lively 12th-century lion's head Sanctuary knocker from the north door of the cathedral.

Duxford

Duxford Airfield

Duxford, Cambridge, CB2 4QR
   ☎ *0223 835000/833963*
Daily 10–5.30. Closed Jan 1, Dec 24–26.
Ⓒ 🍴 🖃 ♿ 🚗

Duxford is 8 miles south of Cambridge, on Junction 10 of the M11. Duxford Airfield, an outstation of the Imperial War Museum, preserves all the main features of a Battle of Britain fighter station and incorporates hangars which date from the First World War. The impressive series of civil aircraft, including Concorde, is maintained by members of the Duxford Aviation Society. Duxford was an American base from 1943 to 1945 and the museum has a collection of American military aircraft which is unique in Europe. Most of the 100 or so aircraft on show belong to the museum's own collection, permanently preserved and displayed at Duxford together with the civil airliners collected and cared for by the Duxford Aviation Society. There are also a number of privately owned aircraft, many of them in flying condition, which are on loan to the museum. A full programme of air displays and other special events is mounted each year.

Duxford is the home not only of the finest collection of military and civil aircraft in Britain, but also of a wide variety of other military exhibits, ranging from tanks, trucks and artillery to radar equipment, missiles and midget submarines.

A giant superhangar was opened in 1986, while other developments include the renovation of the former station cinema and of the original Battle of Britain Operations Room, which has been restored to its 1940 appearance.

Eastbourne

Towner Art Gallery and Eastbourne Museum

*High Street/Manor Gardens, Old Town,
   Eastbourne, East Sussex, BN20 8BB*
   ☎ *0323 411688/25112*
Tues–Sat 10–5; Sun 2–5.
Ⓕ 🍴 ■

The gallery and museum occupy an 18th-century mansion, formerly Eastbourne Manor House. The gallery has an important collection of over 3,000 works of art, mostly 19th- and 20th-century British paintings, watercolours and prints. Especially noteworthy are a group of Georgian caricatures by George Cruikshank; watercolours of Sussex scenes; and the largest collection of works by the Eastbourne artist, Eric Ravilious (1903–42).

The Local History Museum traces the history of human occupation in the Eastbourne area from Neolithic times to the Edwardian period. The exhibits include artefacts, models and photographs, and the original cast iron kitchen ranges of the Manor House form part of a reconstructed Victorian kitchen.

Eastwood

D. H. Lawrence's Birthplace

8a Victoria Street, Eastwood, Nottingham
   ☎ *0773 763312*
*Apr–Oct, daily 10–5. Nov–March, daily 10–4.
   Closed Dec 24–Jan 1.*
Ⓒ 🍴 🚗

Eastwood, where the novelist D. H. Lawrence was born, is seven miles form Nottingham and three miles from Junction 26 on the M1. The house at 8a Victoria Street has been restored and furnished in the style of a miner's home of 1885, when the Lawrence family lived there. A video presentation in the exhibition room tells the story of Lawrence's early years in the district.

Edinburgh

City Art Centre

1–4 Market Street, Edinburgh, EH1 1DE
   ☎ *031 225 2424 extn 6650*
*June–Sept, Mon–Sat 10–6. Oct–May, Mon–Sat
   10–5. During Edinburgh Festival, also Sun
   2–5. Closed Christmas and New Year.*
Ⓕ 🍴 🖃 ♿ ■

This late-19th-century listed building was erected as a warehouse for *The Scotsman* and was later used as a market. It now houses the city's large permanent collection of paintings, drawings, prints and sculpture, mostly by Scottish artists. The works range in date from the 17th century to the present day and include topographical views of Edinburgh and portraits of eminent citizens. Late-19th- and early-20th-century artists are well represented and the number of more recent works continues to grow.

Huntly House Museum

142 Canongate, Edinburgh, EH8 8DD
   ☎ *031 225 2424 extn 6689*
June–Sept, Mon–Sat 10–6. Oct–May, Mon–Sat
10–5. During Edinburgh Festival also Sun 2–5.
Closed Christmas and New Year.
F ▮

Huntly House is Edinburgh's main museum of
local history. The museum building, dating from
the 16th century, is one of the finest early
houses in the Royal Mile. It includes period
rooms and reconstructions relating to traditional
industries and aspects of the city's history. It also
has important collections of Edinburgh silver
and glass, Scottish pottery, shop signs, and
memorabilia and personal possessions of Field
Marshal Earl Haig, Commander-in-Chief of the
British forces during the later stages of the First
World War.

The small rooms of Huntly House have been
preserved, giving the museum an intimate
atmosphere and allowing natural transitions
from one theme to another.

Lady Stair's House

Lady Stair's Close, Lawnmarket, Edinburgh,
   EH1 2PA   ☎ *031 225 2424 extn 6593*
June–Sept, Mon–Sat 10–6. Oct–May, Mon–Sat
10–5. Closed Jan 1–3, Dec 25, 26.
F ✑

Built in 1622, Lady Stair's House was
remodelled between 1893 and 1897 for the Earl
of Roseberry, to be used as his town house. Now
a museum, it contains displays relating to the
life and work of Scotland's three great literary
figures of the late 18th and 19th centuries,
Robert Burns, Sir Walter Scott and Robert
Louis Stevenson. A number of Scottish
museums pay tribute to one or other of these
writers, but Lady Stair's House is the only place
where they are commemorated together.

National Gallery of Scotland

The Mound, Edinburgh, EH2 2EL
   ☎ *031 556 8921*
Mon–Sat 10–5; Sun 2–5. Extended opening hours
during Edinburgh Festival. Closed Jan 1, 2,
May Day, Dec 25, 26.
F ▮ & ✿

The gallery, Scotland's art-flagship, occupies an
early-19th-century neo-classical building
designed by William Playfair. Its collection of
paintings contains works dating from the 14th
century to 1900. Among the artists represented
are Gainsborough, Constable, Van Dyck,
Gauguin, El Greco, Monet, Rembrandt, Titian,
Velázquez, Degas and Cézanne. Scottish
painters are also much in evidence.

There are important collections of prints,
drawings and watercolours, including the
Vaughan bequest of Turner watercolours and
works by Dürer, Goya and Rembrandt.

Royal Museum of Scotland (1)

Chambers Street, Edinburgh, EH1 1JF
   ☎ *031 225 7534*
Mon–Sat 10–5; Sun 2–5. Closed Jan 1, 2, May
Day, Dec 25, 26, 31.
F ▮ ✑ & ✿

Formerly known as the Royal Scottish Museum,
this is one of the most comprehensive museums
in Europe. Its building, an outstanding example
of Victorian architecture, has been described as
'a huge elegant bird-cage of glass and iron'. The
principal displays cover the decorative arts of
the world, geology, natural history, and science
and technology.

This huge collection, which is housed in one
building, includes European and Oriental
ceramics and metalwork, Egyptian art and
archaeology, arms and armour and primitive art.

The collections of natural history and of
fossils and minerals are of international
importance. The technology displays include
'Wylam Dilly', one of the oldest locomotives in
existence, and there is an excellent collection of
scientific instruments.

Royal Museum of Scotland (2)

1 Queen Street, Edinburgh, EH2 1JD
   ☎ *031 557 3550*
Mon–Sat 10–5; Sun 2–5. Closed Jan 1, 2, May
Day, Dec 25, 26, 31.
F ▮ & ✿

Until 1985 this section of the Royal Museum of
Scotland was called the National Museum of
Antiquities of Scotland. Its late Victorian
building has been justly labelled a Venetian
Gothic Palace. The collections include
prehistoric and Roman archaeology, coins and
medals, carved stones, as well as Stuart relics,
Highland weapons, domestic equipment,
costumes and textiles. The museum shares its
premises with the National Portrait Gallery.

Local History Museum, Eastbourne.

Scottish National Gallery of Modern Art

Bedford Road, Edinburgh, EH4 3DR
☎ 031 556 8921
*Mon–Sat 10–5; Sun 2–5. Extended opening during
Edinburgh Festival. Closed Jan 1, 2, May Day,
Dec 25, 26, 31.*
🄵 🛈 💻 ♿ ♨

The gallery occupies the building of the former
John Watson's School, designed by William
Burn in the neo-classical style in 1828. It
contains the national collection of 20th-century
paintings, sculpture and graphic art, including
works by Derain, Matisse, Braque, Giacometti,
Picasso, Hockney and Hepworth. Artists of the
Scottish School are also well represented.

Scottish National Portrait Gallery

1 Queen Street, Edinburgh, EH2 1JD
☎ 031 556 8921
*Mon–Sat 10–5; Sun 2–5. Extended opening during
Edinburgh Festival. Closed Jan 1, 2, May Day,
Dec 25, 26, 31.*
🄵 🛈 ♿ ♨

The striking red sandstone building in which
the gallery is housed was completed in 1889. It
is decorated internally with a painted frieze and
murals by William Hole. The collection consists
of portraits of people who have been influential
in Scottish life from the 16th century to the
present day, including Prince Charles Edward
Stewart, Flora MacDonald, David Hume,
Robert Burns, Sir Walter Scott, Ramsay
MacDonald and Hugh MacDiarmid. Among the
artists whose work is represented are Epstein,
Gainsborough, Kokoschka, Lely and Raeburn.

The gallery also has an important print
collection and holds Scotland's national
collection of photography, which includes
5,000 photographs by Hill and Adamson.

Ellesmere Port

The Boat Museum

*Dockyard Road, Ellesmere Port, South Wirral,
L65 4EF*   ☎ 051 355 5017
*Apr–Oct, daily 10–5. Nov–Mar, Mon–Thurs,
Sat, Sun 11–4. Closed Dec 24–26.*
🄲 🛈 💻 🄰 ♿ ♨

Ellesmere Port is at the northern end of the
Shropshire Union Canal, at its junction with
the Manchester Ship Canal. The whole
museum area was once a major trans-shipment
port, enabling cargoes to be transferred between
ocean-going craft and the smaller canal boats.

The museum buildings are the old
warehouses and workshops of the Shropshire
Union trans-shipment dock. The core of the
museum's collection consists of over 50 canal
and river craft, ranging from both narrow and
wide canal boats to tugs and ice-breakers.
Restoration work takes place at the museum and
visitors are often able to see the traditional
boat-building techniques in progress. There are
exhibitions tracing the development of the Port
of Manchester and of Ellesmere Port as an
industrial town and telling the story of canal
building, carrying on the canals and the life of
the boat people. The Pump House contains
engines which worked the hydraulic lifting gear
in the docks. These have been restored and are
regularly in steam. A row of cottages built in
1833 have been furnished to show how dock
workers lived.

The new Archive and Resource Centre
houses Britain's foremost collection of canal
artefacts and documents.

Elvaston

Elvaston Castle Working Estate Museum

Burrowash Lane, Elvaston, nr Derby, DE7 3EP
☎ 0332 71342
*Easter–Oct, Wed–Sat 1–5, Sun and Bank Holiday
10–6.*
🄲 🛈 💻 ♿ ♨

The buildings which comprise the museum are
the original estate workshops, contemporary
with Elvaston Castle, which is an early-19th-
century rebuild of an earlier castle. The
Elvaston estate was a close-knit, self-sufficient
community, with its own craftsmen, tradesmen,
labourers and their families. The workshops
have been restored and illustrate the work of the
sawyer, blacksmith, wheelwright, carpenter,
plumber, saddler and cobbler, while old breeds
of livestock and vintage implements and
machinery reflect the agricultural basis of the
estate economy. Aspects of domestic life are
shown in the cottage, wash-house and dairy,
and visitors have the opportunity of involving
themselves in the company of staff in period
costume, with life and work as it was at
Elvaston in 1910.

Ely

The Stained Glass Museum

*North Triforium, Ely Cathedral, Ely,
Cambridgeshire*   ☎ 0353 5103/60148
*Mar–Oct, Mon–Fri 10.30–4.30; Sat, Bank
Holiday 10.30–4.30; Sun 12–3.*
🄲 🛈 💻 ♨

The museum is the only one in the country
which is devoted to stained glass. It was
established in 1972, with the object of rescuing
fine glass from redundant churches, and opened
to the public in 1975 in the magnificent setting
of the nave gallery, which offers spectacular
views of the Cathedral from a level not
otherwise accessible to visitors. Access is by
spiral staircase.

The exhibits include more than 60 windows
from medieval to modern times, a photographic
display of the styles and techniques of medieval
glass, and models of a modern stained glass
workshop. The collection is strongest in 19th-
century glass, with examples of work from all
the leading studios and designers. Also displayed
are selected entries from an annual competition
organised by the British Society of Master Glass-
Painters.

Eton

Museum of Eton Life

Eton College, Eton, Windsor, Berkshire, SL4 6DB
☎ *0753 863593*
Mar 28–Oct 5, daily 10.30–5 during term time
Ⓒ ⬷

Eton College was founded by Henry VI in 1440. The museum, in the vaulted College Hall Undercroft, tells its story. There are memorabilia of former masters and head masters, and displays devoted to daily life and duties, food and living conditions, punishments, uniforms, and school books and equipment. Other sections include the history of rowing at the College and of the Officer Training Corps.

A reconstruction of a typical study and an audio-visual presentation supplement the other items in the museum.

Exeter

Rougemont House Museum of Costume

Castle Street, Exeter   ☎ *0392 265858*
Mon–Sat 10–5.30. Open Bank Holidays & Suns in summer. Free admission Fri.
Ⓒ ⬩ ⬛ ⬥ ■

Rougemont House is a Regency building in the grounds of Exeter Castle. It has outstanding collections of costume and lace, which together with furniture, paintings and decorative objects are displayed in period rooms to illustrate changing fashion from the 1740s to the 1960s. There are regular demonstrations of lace-making and new exhibitions are arranged every year.

Falmouth

Maritime Museum

2 Bell's Court, Falmouth, Cornwall
☎ *0326 250507*
Museum: daily 10–4, Tug: Apr–Oct, daily 10–4.
Ⓒ ⬷ ⬷

The museum was founded in 1981 to specialise in the maritime history of Cornwall and of South-West Cornwall in particular. It is in two

Mosaic panel showing Cupid riding a dolphin. Roman Palace, Fishbourne.

parts, the first at 2 Bell's Court, where the Riot Act was read to mutinous Packet Men in 1810, and the second part on the steam tug *St Denys*, which has interesting engineering features and which worked in Falmouth between 1929 and 1980. The displays cover the themes of ship and boatbuilding, trade, ports, communications – especially the Falmouth Packet Service – safety and rescue, wrecks and war.

Fishbourne

Roman Palace

Salthill Road, Fishbourne, Chichester, West Sussex, PO19 3QR   ☎ *0243 785859*
Mar–Apr and Oct, daily 11–5. May–Sept, daily 10–6. Nov, daily 10–4. Dec–Feb, Sun 10–4.
Ⓒ ⬩ ⬛ ⬥ ⬷

The museum presents the remains of the north wing of a 1st-century palace of Italianate style, protected by a modern cover-building. Visitors can see Britain's largest group of 1st-century mosaics, as well as several floors of the 2nd and 3rd centuries. Parts of the underfloor heating systems have also survived. Two 4th-century polychrome mosaic floors from elsewhere in the area, where they were threatened with destruction, are also on display.

The most important finds from the excavations are shown in a separate part of the museum, supplemented by photographs, plans and models. A reconstruction of a dining-room suggests what one room in the Palace may have looked like c100 AD. An audio-visual programme gives the story of the site through the voices of people who may have lived there. The northern half of the formal garden attached to the Palace has been restored to its original plan.

Fort William

West Highland Museum

Cameron Square, Fort William, Inverness-shire, PH33 6AJ   ☎ *0397 2169*
June and Sept, Mon–Sat 9.30–5.30. July–Aug, Mon–Sat 9.30–9. Oct–May, Mon–Sat 10–1, 2–5. Closed Jan 1, 2, Dec 25, 26.
Ⓒ ⬷ ⬷

The museum occupies one of the oldest buildings in Fort William, formerly a branch of the British Linen Bank. The exhibits illustrate many aspects of the district and its history, including geology, wildlife, Fort William as a garrison town, and the Ben Nevis weather observatory. There is a reconstruction of the interior of a crofter's house, together with displays of tartans and maps and a collection of items connected with the 1745 Jacobite rising, including the anamorphic painting of Prince Charles Edward Stewart, known as the Secret Portrait. When first seen, it appears to be a meaningless blur of paint but the panel reveals a perfect likeness when reflected in a polished cylinder.

Gateshead

Bowes Railway Centre

Springwell Village, Gateshead, Tyne and Wear,
NE9 7QJ ☎ *091 416 1847*
Static exhibits: Sat 12–5. Operating dates: Easter–
Sept, first Sun of each month and Bank Hols.
Please telephone for further details.

C 🛈 💻 🚗

The Bowes Railway, called the Pontop and
Jarrow Railway until 1932, was one of a number
of colliery railways developed in North-East
England to carry coal to the rivers for shipment.
Its oldest section was designed by George
Stephenson and opened in 1826. By 1855 the
line was 15 miles long and during its lifetime it
served 13 collieries. It had seven rope-worked
and three locomotive sections and for a time it
ran its own passenger service. In 1976 Tyne and
Wear District Council bought the one-and-a-
quarter miles between Blackfell Bank Head and
Springwell Bank Head, together with the link to
the Pelaw Main Railway, the engine houses,
line-side cabins and well over 40 of the
Railway's historic wagons. It later acquired the
19th-century engineering and wagon shops,
together with much of their machinery. Now a
scheduled monument, the Bowes Railway, the
world's only standard-gauge rope-hauled
railway, has been restored to its original
condition.

A number of diesel and steam locomotives
and a range of rolling stock can be seen. On
operating days passenger trains and the rope
haulage system are in use.

Glamis

Angus Folk Museum

Kirkwynd, Glamis, Angus, DD8 1RT
☎ *030784 288*
Easter weekend, then May–Sept, daily 12–5.

C 🖉 🚗

The Angus Folk Collection, one of the finest in
Scotland, is housed in a row of six early-19th-
century cottages with stone-slabbed roofs,
restored and adapted to museum purposes by the
National Trust for Scotland. The collection
illustrates many aspects of country life in the
past and includes a Victorian parlour and a
cottar house kitchen with box beds. The local
craft of linen weaving is represented by a handloom and spinning-wheel and their accessories,
and by many examples of the cloth produced.

Glasgow

Art Gallery and Museum

Kelvingrove, Glasgow, G3 8AG
☎ *041 357 3929*
Mon–Sat 10–5; Sun 2–5. Closed Jan 1, Dec 25.

F 🛈 💻 👤 🚗

The museum was opened in 1902. The
geological gallery contains a stratigraphic

**Dresser from the Whistler display at the
Hunterian Art Gallery, Glasgow.**

treatment of fossils, with an emphasis on the era
of greatest significance in Scotland, as well as a
selection of minerals and rocks. An entire room
is devoted to birds, some of them, such as the
Moa, Huia, Quetzal and Great Auk, now very
rare or extinct.

There are important collections relating to
Scottish prehistory and of arms and armour and
ethnography. The department of decorative art
contains exhibits of silver, metalwork,
jewellery, ceramics, glass, furniture, costumes
and textiles, covering the period from the
Renaissance to the present day. Kelvingrove has
the finest civic collection of European paintings
in Britain, the main strengths being in Dutch
17th-century and French 19th–early-20th-
century paintings, and in Scottish art in all
media from the 17th to the 20th centuries.

The Burrell Collection

Pollok Country Park, 2060 Pollokshaws Road,
Glasgow, G43 1AT ☎ *041 649 7151*
Mon–Sat 10–5; Sun 2–5. Closed Jan 1, Dec 25.

F 🛈 💻 👤 🚗

The Burrell Collection was presented to the
City of Glasgow in 1944 by Sir William and
Lady Burrell. Sir William was a wealthy
Glasgow shipowner with a longstanding passion
for art collecting, and his collection, eclectic
and worldwide and never displayed or even
unpacked during his lifetime, is an essential part
of his biography. It contains more than 8,000
items and covers a remarkable range – ceramics,
jades, bronzes, prints, carpets, metalwork,
paintings. The tapestries and stained glass are
world-famous. The distinguished new building
which houses the collection incorporates
medieval architectural stonework in the
structure.

Glasgow School of Art

167 Renfrew Street, Glasgow, G3 6RQ
☎ *041 332 9797*
Mon–Fri 10–12, 2–5. Closed Easter week,
Christmas week & Bank Holidays. Parties must
book in advance.
C ⬤

The School of Art is the most important
building designed by the celebrated Glasgow
architect, Charles Rennie Mackintosh. It
contains a substantial collection of furniture,
watercolours and architectural designs and
drawings by Mackintosh. All the principal
rooms are open to the public.

Hunterian Art Gallery

University of Glasgow, 82 Hillhead Street,
Glasgow, G12 8QQ   ☎ *041 330 5431*
Main Gallery: Mon–Fri 9,30–5; Sat 9.30–1. The
Mackintosh House: Mon–Fri 9.30–12.30,
1.30–5; Sat 9.30–1. Admission charge
weekday afternoons and Sat. Closed public
holidays.
F ✑

This purpose-built gallery, opened in 1980, has
the largest permanent exhibition anywhere of
the works of J.M. Whistler, including paintings,
prints and drawings, together with a collection
of the artist's furniture, silver and porcelain.
The gallery's paintings include works by
Rembrandt, Chardin, Reynolds and Pissarro,
with a strong representation of 19th- and 20th-
century Scottish artists. The print collection,
the largest in Scotland, contains over 20,000
items, by artists ranging from Dürer to Hockney.
Contemporary sculpture is shown in the
Sculpture Courtyard.

A separate section of the gallery displays
furniture and designs by Charles Rennie
Mackintosh and includes The Mackintosh
House, a reconstruction of the principal rooms
from the architect's Glasgow home, now
demolished, at 78 Southpark Avenue,
containing his furniture and re-created
decorative schemes.

Studio-drawing room, The Mackintosh House,
Hunterian Art Gallery, Glasgow.

People's Palace

Glasgow Green, Glasgow, G40 1AT
☎ *041 554 0223*
Mon–Sat 10–5; Sun 2–5. Closed Jan 1, Dec 25.
F ⬤ 🍴 ♿

The museum is housed in an impressive red
sandstone building in the French Renaissance
style, with large cast iron and glass winter
gardens attached. The People's Palace was
designed and built as part of a Victorian plan to
provide pleasant educational and leisure
facilities for working-class people. The displays
in the museum cover the history of Glasgow
from 1175 to the present day. The collections
are arranged by theme and include the history of
the tobacco trade; social and domestic life in
Glasgow; politics and religion; the trade unions;
the suffragettes and the women's movement.
Other themes are the rise of socialism,
temperance and drunkenness, Freemasonry, the
history of photography, life in two World Wars,
the peace movement and entertainments,
including music hall, cinema, football and
boxing.

The emphasis is on people as well as places
and the museum has portraits of famous
Glaswegians, from St Mungo to Billy Connolly.
There are special collections of Glasgow stained
glass and ceramic tiles.

Tenement House

145 Buccleuch Street, Garnethill, Glasgow,
G3 6QN   ☎ *041 333 0183*
Easter–Oct, daily 2–5. Nov–Easter, Sat, Sun 2–4.
C ✑

Now the property of the National Trust for
Scotland, the Tenement House was built in
1892, when Garnethill was a superior residential
district in Glasgow's West End. In 1911 the
first-floor flat became the home of Agnes Reid
Toward, a shorthand-typist with a local
shipping firm who lived here for 54 years, part of
the time with her widowed mother. The flat,
consisting of a kitchen, parlour, bedroom, hall
and bathroom, has changed very little since the
1890s, and visitors are able to see not only the
furniture and fittings of this late Victorian
home, but also many of Miss Toward's personal
papers – letters, postcards, calendars, recipes,
receipted bills and photographs – which give a
remarkably complete picture of her life and
times.

Glastonbury

Somerset Rural Life Museum

Abbey Farm, Chilkwell Street, Glastonbury,
Somerset, BA6 8DB   ☎ *0458 31197*
Easter–Oct, Mon–Fri 10–5; Sat, Sun 2–6. Nov–
Easter, Mon–Fri 10–5; Sat, Sun 2–4.30.
Closed Jan 1, Good Fri, Dec 25, 26.
C ⬤ 🍴

The principal buildings of the museum are the
farmhouse, built in 1896, and the magnificent
14th-century barn of Glastonbury Abbey, which

is close to the farmhouse and has been restored. The displays in the barn and the farmbuildings surrounding the courtyard illustrate the tools and techniques of farming in Victorian Somerset. Other exhibits relate to such local specialities as willow-growing, mud-horse fishing, peat-digging and cider-making.

The Abbey Farmhouse is devoted to the social and domestic life of Victorian Somerset. A special feature is a carefully researched and documented exhibition which tells the story of a local farmworker John Hodges, from the cradle to the grave. In the cellar there is a reconstruction of a traditional farmhouse cheese room.

Gloucester

Gloucester Folk Museum

99–103 *Westgate Street, Gloucester, GL1 2PG*
☎ 0452 26467
Mon–Sat 10–5; Sun (July–Sept only) 10–4.
Ⓕ ◿ ■

The museum is in three adjoining timber-framed buildings. No. 99–101 Westgate Street is a late 15th-century merchant's house and 103 is early 17th century. An annealing forge used in making brass pins by hand, can still be seen on the second floor of 99–101. The exhibits illustrate the social history, crafts, industries customs and traditions of the City and County of Gloucester. On the ground floor there are displays on the horn industry, Bishop Hooper, laundry equipment, a kitchen range and equipment, glass, ceramics, pewter, toys, games and some working models. A cow byre, Double Gloucester dairy, ironmonger's shop and wheelwright and carpenter workshops may also be seen.

The first floor offers weights, measures and balances, fishing on the River Severn, the Port of Gloucester from 1580 onwards, the Civil War in Gloucester, and the customs and traditions of the County. The top floor features the manufacture of brass pins in Gloucester, a cobbler's workshop, Victorian agriculture in Gloucestershire and a Victorian classroom in which period lessons are held.

There is a regular programme of special exhibitions each year, along with special events, activities and demonstrations.

Gloucester Museum and Art Gallery

Brunswick Road, Gloucester, GL1 1HP
☎ 0452 24131
Mon–Sat 10–5
Ⓕ ◿ ⬅

The museum's collections are divided into three main parts. The natural history section shows the rocks, minerals and fossils of Gloucestershire, together with the birds, mammals, fish, moths, butterflies and beetles of the region, displayed with the help of many dioramas and a freshwater aquarium. Archaeology is represented by prehistoric, Roman and medieval finds from Gloucester and

Old photograph illustrating the working lives of canal-boat women. National Waterways Museum, Gloucester.

Gloucestershire, by Celtic metalwork, including the famous Birdlip mirror, by Anglo-Saxon sculptured cross-shafts and wooden bowls, and by a unique Norman backgammon set.

The Art Gallery has paintings by Gainsborough, Lawrence, Turner, Sickert and Wilson Steer. There are also collections of 18th-century walnut furniture, barometers, long-case clocks, domestic silver, Staffordshire porcelain and Bristol blue glass.

National Waterways Museum

Llanthony Warehouse, Gloucester Docks, Gloucester, GL1 2EH   ☎ 0452 307009
Summer: daily 10–6. Winter: daily 10–5.
Ⓒ ♙ ⬛ ⬅

The museum is housed in and around Llanthony Warehouse, a dockside building dating from 1873. It has been created to tell the story of Britain's canals and of the people who built and worked on them. There are sections devoted to the construction of the canals, to boatbuilding, to the operation of the narrowboats, to the living conditions of those on board, and to the cargoes carried. In a replica of a canal maintenance yard, visitors can watch craftsmen demonstrating their skills in the workshops. There is also an engine house, and a Shire horse bus providing trips around the Docks. Throughout the museum, the exhibits are supplemented by working models, sound recordings and archive film.

Outside, in the former Docks, is a growing collection of vessels once used on inland waterways. These include a steam-dredger, which operates at weekends.

Gosport

Royal Navy Submarine Museum and HMS Alliance

Haslar Jetty Road, Gosport, Hampshire, PO12 2AS   ☎ 0705 529217
Apr–Oct, daily 10 to last tour 4.30. Nov–Mar, daily 10 to last tour 3.30. Closed Jan 1, Dec 24, 25.
Ⓒ ♙ ⬛ ⬅

The museum tells the story of submarines from the earliest experiments to the present nuclear-powered vessels. A special display explains how a nuclear power-plant functions. HMS *Alliance* is an interesting blend of old and new, with her living space still providing reminders of wartime austerity, but with more modern torpedo fire-control, sensors and navigational equipment. An introductory audio-visual presentation explains how a submarine works and visitors then tour the ship with retired submariner guides.

Alliance provides a strong contrast to Britain's first submarine, *Holland 1*, which was salvaged in 1982 and is now on view.

Grasmere

Dove Cottage

Town End, Grasmere, Ambleside, Cumbria,
*   LA22 9SH   ☎ 09665 544/547*
Apr–Sept, Mon–Sat 9.30–5.30; Sun 11–5.30.
*   Oct–Mar, Mon–Sat 10–4.30; Sun 11–4.30.*
*   Closed Jan 1, Nov, Grasmere Sports Day.*
Ⓒ 🚻 🖼 ■ 🍴

Dove Cottage was the home of the poet, William Wordsworth and his sister, Dorothy, from 1799 to 1808. After the Wordsworths left, the essayist, Thomas De Quincey and his family lived there for more than 20 years. The cottage has been restored, but is little changed, and is furnished with Wordsworth's possessions. It has been open to the public since 1891. Visitors are offered guided tours.

Associated with it, the nearby Wordsworth Museum illustrates the poet's life and the development of his poetry within the context of the scenery and people of the Lake District. The exhibits include manuscripts, books, paintings, drawings, photographs and memorabilia. A programme of special exhibitions complements the permanent displays.

Great Yarmouth

Maritime Museum

Marine Parade, Great Yarmouth, Norfolk,
*   NR30 2EN   ☎ 0493 842267*
June–Sept, Sun–Fri 10–5.30. Oct–May, Mon–Fri
*   10–1, 2–5.30. Closed Bank Holidays between*
*   Oct and May.*
Ⓒ 🍴

Model of underwater turtle. Royal Navy Submarine Museum, Gosport.

The museum building, dating from 1860, was formerly a home for shipwrecked sailors. The displays illustrate the maritime history of Norfolk and the surrounding area, including the Broads, and cover shipbuilding, merchant and naval shipping, sailors' crafts, life-saving, Lord Nelson – Nelson was a Norfolk man – and inland waterways. There is a good collection of small marine engines. The local vessels preserved at the museum include the unique Broadland racing lateener, *Maria*, built in 1827.

Gressenhall

Norfolk Rural Life Museum

Beech House, Gressenhall, Dereham, Norfolk,
*   NR20 4DR   ☎ 0362 860563*
Easter Sun–Oct, Tues–Sat 10–5; Sun 2–5.30.
*   Open Bank Holiday Mon 10–5.*
Ⓒ 🚻 ♿ 🍴

The museum is in the former House of Industry, or workhouse, of the Mitford and Launditch Union, a large and handsome brick building, completed in 1777. The displays cover rural life in Norfolk over the past 200 years, with an emphasis on agriculture. The collection of farm tools and implements, many of them made locally, is one of the best in the country. There are reconstructions of a saddler's, baker's, wheelwright's and blacksmith's premises, and of an old-fashioned general store and seed merchant's shop. There is also a typical farmworker's cottage of about 1910–20.

Other displays feature dairying, ironfounding, education, shoemaking, tailoring, the building trades and other rural crafts and industries. An engine room contains steam and oil engines, together with items of machinery.

Union Farm is a working farm of the 1920s with traditional breeds of livestock. There is a nature trail around the farm.

Haddington

Jane Welsh Carlyle Museum

Lodge Street, Haddington, East Lothian,
*   EH41 3EE   ☎ 062082 3738*
Apr–Sept, Wed–Sat 2–5
Ⓒ 🍴

The house, which dates from *c.*1800, was the family home of Jane Welsh Carlyle (1801–66), the wife of the celebrated historian, Thomas Carlyle, who described the drawing-room, the background to his courtship, as 'the finest apartment I ever stood or sat in, bearing the stamp of its late owner's solid temper'. The room is furnished to reflect the personality and tastes of Jane's father, a local doctor, and his wife. In the dressing-room, where Carlyle slept on his visits, are portraits of the famous people Thomas and Jane Carlyle attracted to themselves, and of the luminaries of the literary world.

Halifax

Calderdale Industrial Museum

Winding Road, Halifax, West Yorkshire, HX1 1PR
☎ *0422 59031*
*Tues–Sat 10–5; Sun 2–5. Open Bank Holiday
Mon.*
Ⓒ ✑ ⓰ ⌖

The museum occupies a 19th-century woollen
mill, adjoining the historic Piece Hall. It reflects
the wide range of the local industries, from
toffee to reflecting road studs, and from carpets
to washing machines and the Halifax Building
Society, and concentrates particularly on the
textile and engineering trades, with good
collections of original machinery, much of it,
including steam engines, operational. There is
also a reconstruction of a corner of Victorian
Halifax.

Throughout the museum care has been
taken to present the different industries within
their social context and to avoid the creation of
purely technological displays. The same policy
has been followed in the adjoining Piece Hall
Pre-Industrial Museum.

Piece Hall Pre-Industrial Museum

Piece Hall, Halifax, West Yorkshire, HX1 1PR
☎ *0422 59031*
*Apr–Sept, Mon–Sat 10–6; Sun 10–5. Oct–Mar,
daily 10–5.*
Ⓕ ✑ ⌖

Piece Hall was built by private subscription in
1779 for the sale of lengths of cloth 'pieces',
manufactured on hand looms in the valleys and
on the moors around Halifax. The museum
illustrates the production of cloth from fleece to
piece before the Industrial Revolution. There is
a spinner's cottage and a weaver's loom
chamber, as well as workshops for preparing the
wool and finishing the cloth. A merchant can
be seen selling his wares in an original Piece
Hall room setting.

Shibden Hall, Folk Museum of West Yorkshire

Halifax, West Yorkshire, HX3 6XG
☎ *0422 52246*
*Apr–Sept, Mon–Sat 10–6; Sun 2–5. Mar, Oct–
Nov, Mon–Sat 10–5; Sun 2–5. Feb, Sun 2–5.
Closed Dec–Jan.*
Ⓒ ✑ ▣ ⌖

This fine half-timbered house dates from c. 1520,
with some later additions. It contains
furnishings, mainly of the 17th and 18th
centuries, displayed in period room settings in
order to give the house the appearance of being
lived in.

In a 17th-century Pennine barn there are
collections of horse-drawn vehicles, harness and
other accessories and of agricultural tools and
implements, as well as a brewhouse and a dairy.
Around an open courtyard are reconstructions
of the workshops of 19th-century craftsmen,
including those of a clogger, cooper and
wheelwright, as well as a public-house and an
estate worker's cottage.

Hanley

Stoke-on-Trent City Museum and Art Gallery

*Bethesda Street, Hanley, Stoke-on-Trent,
Staffordshire, ST1 3DE*   ☎ *0782 273173*
*Mon–Sat 10.30–5; Sun 2–5. Closed Good Fri and
Dec 25–Jan 1.*
Ⓕ ⓘ ▣ ⓰ ⌖

The museum, in a modern building designed for
the purpose, has departments of fine art,
decorative arts, natural history, archaeology and
social history, and its collections of ceramics are
among the finest in the world, with a strong
emphasis on pottery and porcelain made in
Staffordshire. The art gallery is concerned
almost entirely with British art of the 18th, 19th
and 20th centuries.

Harrogate

Royal Pump Room Museum

Royal Parade, Harrogate, North Yorkshire
☎ *0423 503340*
*Mon–Sat 10.30–5; Sun 2–5. Closed Jan 1, Dec
25, 26.*
Ⓒ ✑

The museum is in Harrogate's historic Pump
Room which includes the old Sulphur Well in
the basement where the water can be tasted.
Visitors can also see the octagonal Pump Room,
built in 1842, and the larger annexe, which
dates from 1913. This contains displays relating
to the history of Harrogate and the surrounding
district, including exhibits of pottery, costumes
and Victoriana.

**Portrait of William Wordsworth, 1806, by
Henry Edridge. Dove Cottage, Grasmere.**

Hartlepool

Hartlepool Maritime Museum

Northgate, Hartlepool, Cleveland, TS24 0LT
   ☎ *0429 272814*
Mon–Sat 10–5. Closed Jan 1, Good Fri, Dec 25, 26.
F 🖉 ⌕

An important port in the Middle Ages, Hartlepool declined during the following centuries into a small fishing village. The construction of a railway from the East Durham coalfields and the excavation of the docks in the 1830s renewed the town's prosperity. West Hartlepool was founded in 1860; a Victorian new town built around a rival dock complex to the south of the original town. By the 1890s the 'Hartlepools' had become the third busiest English port and a major shipbuilding centre.

The museum illustrates the Hartlepool industries of shipbuilding, marine engineering, shipping and fishing. The exhibits include an important collection of ship models, a simulated ship's bridge, one of the earliest gas-lit lighthouse lanterns and a reconstruction of a fisherman's cottage. The Fish Quay and working port can be viewed from the museum windows.

Hastings

Old Town Hall Museum

High Street, Hastings, East Sussex, TN34 3EW
   ☎ *0424 721209*
Easter–Sept, Mon–Sat 10–1, 2–5. Oct–Easter, Sun 3–5.
F 🖉

The former town hall was built in 1823. The downstairs arches originally formed an open market area, but were later enclosed to form Hastings' first police station. The section dealing with the history of Hastings includes exhibits on the growth of tourism and on famous people who have lived in the area, including Logie Baird, Grey Owl, Titus Oates, Teilhard de Chardin and Robert Tressell. Special displays are devoted to the Battle of Hastings, the Cinque Ports, and maritime history – smuggling, shipwrecks, fishing.

Haverfordwest

Graham Sutherland Gallery

Picton Castle, The Rhos, Haverfordwest, Dyfed, SA62 4AS
   ☎ *043786 296*
Apr–Sept, Tues–Sun 10.30–12.30, 1.30–5. Open Bank Holiday Apr–Sept.
C 🖉 ♿ ■ ⌕

The gallery possesses the largest collection of works by the celebrated mid–20th-century artist, Graham Sutherland, many of them inspired by the surrounding countryside. The exhibits are changed from time to time and there is also a programme of temporary exhibitions by other well-known artists.

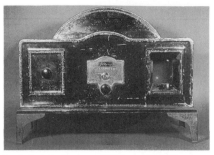

Logie Baird televisor. Old Town Hall Museum, Hastings.

Hawes

Upper Dales Folk Museum

Station Yard, Hawes, Wensleydale, North Yorkshire, DL8 3NT   ☎ *09697 494*
Easter or April 1–Sept, Mon–Sat 11–5; Sun 2–5. Oct, Tues, Sat, Sun 2–5. Half-term holidays, open all week.
C 🖉 ♿ ⌕

The museum occupies what was the goods warehouse at Hawes Station, built in 1883 in the Victorian Gothic style. The collections illustrate the traditional rural life of Wensleydale and Swaledale. The exhibits cover domestic equipment and the household crafts and a wide range of rural skills and occupations including hand-knitting and the making of Wensleydale cheese.

Hawick

Hawick Museum and the Scott Gallery

Wilton Lodge Park, Hawick, Roxburghshire, TD9 7JL   ☎ *0450 73457*
Apr–Sept, Mon–Sat 10–12, 1–5; Sun 2–5. Oct–Mar, Mon–Fri 1–4; Sun 2–4.
C 🖉 ■ ⌕

The museum's exhibits are devoted to the history and natural environment of Hawick and the Border region. There are good geological, archaeological and natural history displays, and social history collections which concentrate mainly on domestic life in and around Hawick in the 19th and early 20th centuries. The knitwear and hosiery industry, which made Hawick internationally important, is well represented in the museum, by exhibits of machinery, photographs and other material.

Haworth

Brontë Parsonage

Haworth, Keighley, West Yorkshire, BD22 8DR
   ☎ *0535 42323*
Apr–Sept, daily 11–5.30. Oct–Mar, daily 11–4.30. Closed for 3 weeks commencing on Mon of the last full week in Jan, Dec 24–26.
C ♦ ■ ⌕

The parsonage was once the home of the Rev. Brontë and his family, which included the celebrated novelists, Emily and Charlotte. It is now the property of the Brontë Society and has its main rooms decorated in early-19th-century style and arranged as they were in the Brontës' day, with original furnishings and paintings. A large number of books, manuscripts, drawings and personal possessions relating to the family are also on display, together with a permanent exhibition, 'The Brontës: a family history', as well as temporary exhibitions.

Haydon Bridge

Housesteads Roman Fort

Haydon Bridge, Hexham, Northumberland, NE47 6NN ☎ *04984 363*
Apr 1–Sept 30, daily 10–6; Oct 1–Maundy Thurs, 10–4. Closed Jan 1, Dec 24–26.

The site-museum outlines the history of the fort, an important and well-preserved site on Hadrian's Wall, and illustrates it with finds from the long series of excavations of both the fort and the surrounding settlement. Models include a life-sized replica of a Roman auxiliary soldier, complete with equipment.

Helmshore

Textile Museum

Higher Mill, Holcombe Road, Helmshore, Rossendale, Lancashire, BB4 4NP ☎ *0706 226459/218838*
Mar, Mon–Fri 2–5. Apr–June, Mon–Fri, Sun 2–5. July–Aug, Mon–Fri 10–5; Sat, Sun 2–5. Sept, Mon–Fri 10–5; Sun 2–5. Oct, Mon–Fri, Sun 2–5.

Housed in two former textile mills, Helmshore Textile Museum aims to give a picture of the development of Lancashire's textile industry. The earlier mill, a water powered fulling mill, was built in 1789. The restored 18-foot diameter waterwheel and fulling stocks are demonstrated daily.

The other part of the museum complex consists of a 3-storey mill, originally constructed in the early 19th century and largely rebuilt in 1859–60, after a fire. This contains a complete set of condenser cotton preparation and spinning machinery. The main spinning room remains in its original condition, with much of the machinery restored to running order and demonstrated regularly.

Brontë Parsonage, Haworth.

Hereford

Cider Museum and King Offa Distillery

Pomona Place, Whitecross Road, Hereford, HR4 0LW ☎ *0432 354207*
Apr–Oct, daily 10–5.30. Nov–Mar, Mon–Sat, 1–5. Pre-booked parties at any time.

The Cider Museum tells the story of cider-making, from traditional farmhouse methods right through to mechanical production in factories. The exhibits include a farm cider house, with all its equipment, together with a complete set of travelling cidermaker's equipment which used to be taken from farm to farm. The original champagne cider cellars, where the champagne method was first applied to cidermaking, have been restored and can be seen with their tiers of bottles. Another cellar display illustrates cider production in the late 1920s, with the hydraulic presses and machinery for washing, filling, bottling and corking. Other exhibits include an enormous 17th-century French beam press and a travelling still.

The King Offa Distillery produces cider brandy, using copper stills brought from Normandy. Cider brandy was common in England in the 16th and 17th centuries, but was gradually taxed out of existence. The museum has a licence to distil and is the first producer for over 200 years of cider brandy, which is sold in the museum shop.

City Museum and Art Gallery

Broad Street, Hereford, HR4 9AU ☎ *0432 268121 extn 207/334*
Apr–Sept, Tues, Wed, Fri 10–6; Thurs 10–5; Sat 10–5. Oct–Mar, Tues, Wed, Fri 10–6; Thurs 10–5; Sat 10–4. Closed Good Fri, Dec 25, 26. Open Bank Holidays.

The museum displays illustrate the natural history, early history and traditional culture of Hereford and the area surrounding it. The natural history collections include an observation hive and beekeeping displays, and among the archaeology exhibits are finds from Iron Age hillforts and from the Roman town of *Magnis* (Kenchester).

The art gallery, which changes exhibitions each month, has an important collection of early English watercolours. The works of modern artists and local painters are also well represented.

Higher Bockhampton

Hardy's Cottage

Higher Bockhampton, nr Dorchester, Dorset,
*   DT2 8QJ*   ☎ *0305 62366*
Good Fri–late Oct, daily except Tues morning 11–6
*   or dusk if earlier.*
Ⓒ ✍

The thatched cottage, built by Thomas Hardy's
great-grandfather in 1800, lies three miles
north-east of Dorchester, half a mile south of
the A35. It contains the room where Hardy was
born in 1840 and the room where, in the 1870s,
he wrote *Under the Greenwood Tree* and *Far
From the Madding Crowd*, after giving up his
career as an architect in order to devote all his
time to writing. It has been very little altered
since Hardy's death, and is now owned by the
National Trust.

High Wycombe

Hughenden Manor

High Wycombe, Buckinghamshire HP14 4LA
*   ☎ 0494 32580*
Mar, Sat, Sun 2–6. Apr–Oct, Wed–Sat 2–6; Sun,
*   Bank Holiday Mon 12–6. Closed Good Friday.*
Ⓒ 🍴 ♿ ✍

Hughenden Manor is a mile and a half north of
High Wycombe on the A4128 road to Great
Missenden. The Victorian Prime Minister,
Benjamin Disraeli, bought it in 1848, and
remodelled the outside of the house. He and his
wife are buried in the churchyard in the park.
    Hughenden, now a National Trust property,
contains much of Disraeli's furniture, portraits
of his family, friends and political associates,
and much of his library. The Disraeli Room, the
Politician's Room and the Berlin Congress
Room provide clues to different aspects of his
character. In his study, visitors can see portraits
of his father and mother, the black-edged
notepaper that he always used after his wife's
death, his school books, some of the novels he
wrote in this room, and his wife's diaries.

Holywood

Ulster Folk and Transport Museum

Cultra Manor, Holywood, Co. Down, Northern
*   Ireland, BT18 0EU*   ☎ *02317 5411*
May–Sept, Mon–Sat 11–6; Sun 2–6. Oct–Apr,
*   Mon–Sat 11–5; Sun 2–5. Closed Christmas*
*   period.*
Ⓒ 🍴 🖥 ♿ ✍

The museum is on the A2 Belfast to Bangor
road, seven miles from Belfast. With both
indoor and open-air sections, it illustrates the
way of life, past and present, of the people of
Northern Ireland. Examples of vernacular
buildings, including houses, workshops, a
church and school, have been brought from all
over Ulster and erected in settings which re-
create the original environment. Both in the old

buildings and in specially designed galleries,
there are displays of furnishings and of domestic
and craftsmen's equipment, presented in a way
which allows visitors to understand its use and
purpose.
    The extensive transport collections illustrate
the history of land, water and sea transport in
Ireland and its influence on the social life of the
community.

Huddersfield

Huddersfield Art Gallery

Princess Alexandra Walk, Huddersfield, West
*   Yorkshire HD1 2SU*
*   ☎ 0484 513808 extn 216*
Mon–Fri 10–6; Sat 10–4. Closed Bank Holiday.
Ⓕ ♿ ■ ✍

The gallery's collections reflect national
developments in 20th-century British painting,
sculpture and graphics, as well as the work of
artists living in the Kirklees area. Of particular
importance are works by members of the
Camden Town Group. British art of the 1940s
and 1950s is also well represented with
important works by Francis Bacon, L. S. Lowry,
Augustus John, Edward Burra, David Bomberg
and Henry Moore.

Hull

University of Hull Art Collection

The Middleton Hall, University of Hull,
*   Cottingham Road, Hull, North Humberside,*
*   HU6 7RX*   ☎ *0482 465035*
During term-time, Mon, Tues, Thurs, Fri 2–4;
*   Wed 12.30–4.*
Ⓕ ✍ ♿ ✍

Scarecrows, 1949, by Edward Burra.
Huddersfield Art Gallery.

Still-Life with Bust of Vanessa Bell, by Duncan Grant. University of Hull Art Collection.

The University Art Collection specialises in British art of the period 1890–1940 and covers paintings, sculpture, drawings and prints. It includes works by Beardsley, Sickert, Steer, Lucien Pissarro, Augustus John, Stanley Spencer, Wyndham Lewis and Ben Nicholson. Artists of the Camden Town Group and the Bloomsbury Circle are particularly well represented.

Wilberforce House

23–25 High Street, Hull, North Humberside
    ☎ 0482 222737
Mon–Sat 10–5; Sun 1.30–4.30. Closed Good Fri, Dec 25, 26.
F ⊘ ⊷

Of this group of three 17th- and 18th-century merchants' houses, No. 25 was the birthplace of William Wilberforce, the slave emancipator. The museum contains displays relating to Wilberforce and to slavery and there are also period rooms, an early-20th-century chemist's shop and exhibits of dolls, costumes, militaria and Hull silver.

Humshaugh

Chesters Roman Fort Museum

Humshaugh, nr Hexham, Northumberland
    ☎ 0434 681379
Good Fri–Sept 30, daily 10–6; Oct 1–Maundy Thurs, daily 10–4.
C ⊘ ⬛ ♿ ⊷

The museum, built c.1895, is thought to have been designed by the noted Victorian architect, Richard Norman Shaw. It is a fine example of a period museum, with many of its original fittings still intact. The collection comprises almost entirely Roman material recovered from excavations carried out along the line of Hadrian's Wall by John Clayton (1792–1890), a former owner of the Chesters Estate and a noted local antiquary. It is particularly rich in sculpture and inscriptions, but also includes a wide variety of objects from everyday Romano-British life.

Huntingdon

Cromwell Museum

Grammar School Walk, Huntingdon, Cambridgeshire   ☎ 0480 425830
Apr–Oct, Tues–Fri 11–1, 2–5; Sat, Sun 11–1, 2–4. Nov–Mar, Tues–Fri 2–5; Sat 11–1, 2–4, Sun 2–4. Open Good Fri.
F ⊘

The building which houses the museum is the remaining western end of the Hall of the Hospital of St John the Baptist, founded in the reign of Henry II. Following the Dissolution it was converted into a town grammar school, of which both Oliver Cromwell and Samuel Pepys were subsequently pupils.

The museum illustrates the history and activities of the Parliamentary-Commonwealth side of the Puritan Revolution, 1640–60, but in the case of material relating to the Cromwell family, the period begins earlier and ends later. Among the Cromwell memorabilia are his apothecary's chest, a death mask, some of his swords, and his despatch box, as well as a large number of autograph letters, pamphlets and ordinances illustrating his career and period of rule. There is also an extensive collection of Cromwell family portraits.

Hutton le Hole

Ryedale Folk Museum

Hutton le Hole, North Yorkshire, YO6 6UA
    ☎ 07515 367
Last Sun in Mar–Oct, daily 11–6
C ⊘ ⊷

The museum, in the North York Moors National Park, is housed in a group of 18th-century farm buildings, with an open-air section in the ground behind the museum. The displays illustrate the daily life of the people who inhabited the Ryedale area from prehistoric times onwards. There are exhibits of material relating to rural and agricultural crafts, including a complete iron foundry and an Elizabethan glass furnace. The open-air section contains a medieval longhouse, a 15th-century manor house, an 18th-century crofter's cottage, an operational blacksmith's forge, and an important collection of farm wagons, implements and machinery.

Inverness

Inverness Museum

Castle Wynd, Inverness, Inverness-shire, IV2 3ED
☎ 0463 237114
Mon–Sat 9–5. Closed public holidays in winter.
F ⓘ ⬛

The museum illustrates the social and natural history, archaeology and geology of the Highlands. Dioramas form an important part of the displays and there are reconstructions of a taxidermist's shop and an Inverness cottage as it looked in the 1930s. There is an important collection of Highland silver. Other features of the museum are a display on the Clans and a number of paintings by Scottish artists.

Ipswich

Christchurch Museum

Christchurch Park, Soane Street, Ipswich, Suffolk,
IP4 2BE   ☎ 0473 213761/2
Mon–Sat 10–5; Sun 2.30–4.30. Closes at dusk in winter. Closed Jan 1, Good Fri, Dec 25.
F ⚬ ⌁

The house which is now the museum was built in 1548. Additions and modifications were made to it at various times up to the 1920s. The large collections of furniture and the decorative arts include 18th-century Chinoiserie lacquerwork, 16th-century tapestries, lantern and longcase clocks, pottery, porcelain, glass – especially 18th-century wineglasses – and pewter. There are also interesting 17th–19th-century portraits. The Servants' Wing contains the kitchen, with its copper pans, moulds and roastings spits, and the servants' hall. The 18th-century State Rooms on the first floor provide a striking contrast to conditions below stairs. Some of the rooms still contain the original wallpaper of the 1730s.

In the Wolsey Gallery Suffolk artists are well represented, with paintings by Gainsborough, Constable, John Moore, the Smyths, Alfred Munnings and Wilson Steer. There are also displays of 20th-century prints and sculpture, of costumes and of material illustrating the history of Ipswich and the surrounding area.

Irvine

Scottish Maritime Museum

Harbourside, Irvine, Ayrshire, KA12 8QE
☎ 0294 78283
Easter–end Oct, daily 10–5
C ⓘ ⬛ ⌁

This new and expanding museum, housed in the Laird Forge, famous as makers of block pulleys for the Royal Navy, is devoted to the maritime history of Scotland. It possesses a number of sea-going craft, which visitors can board in the harbour, ranging from an early-19th-century barge to an experimental wind turbine boat and including a tug, yachts, lifeboats and fishing vessels. On summer weekends there are trips on

the Seamew, the tender for Sir Thomas Lipton's yacht, Shamrock.

The 1872 Linthouse Engine Shop is under reconstruction to house a large collection of 19th- and 20th-century machinery and historic vessels.

Jarrow

Bede Monastery Museum

Jarrow Hall, Church Bank, Jarrow, Tyne and
Wear, NE32 3DY   ☎ 091 4892106
Apr–Oct, Tues–Sat 10–5.30; Sun 2.30–5.30.
Nov–Mar, Tues–Sat 11–4.30; Sun 2.30–
5.30. Open Bank Holiday Mon. Closed
Christmas and New Year.
C ⓘ ⬛ ⌁

The museum contains an interpretive display of archaeological material from the excavations at the adjacent Saxon Monastery of St Paul. The exhibits contain a model of the monastery during its years of activity. There is also an introductory audio-visual presentation explaining the building of the monastery and the life of the monks, and a herb garden where visitors can see many of the culinary and medicinal plants grown by the monks.

Jedburgh

Jedburgh Castle Jail

Castle Gate, Jedburgh, Roxburghshire, TD8 6QD
☎ 0835 63254
Easter–Sept, Mon–Sat 10–12, 1–5; Sun 2–5.
C

This is the only remaining Scottish example of a 19th-century Howard Reform Prison. The outstanding features of the museum are the cells and the prison blocks, which remain much as they were in 1823. The interpretive displays include reconstructed rooms illustrating prison life and the development of the town of Jedburgh as a Royal Burgh.

Kendal

Abbot Hall Art Gallery

Kirkland, Kendal, Cumbria, LA9 5AL
☎ 0539 722464
Mon–Fri 10.30–5.30; Sat, Sun 2–5. Spring Bank
Holiday–Oct 31, Sat 10.30–5. Closed Jan 1,
Dec 25–26.
C ⓘ ⅋ ⌁

Abbot Hall was built in 1759, reputedly to the design of Carr of York, the leading Northern architect of the period. The ground-floor rooms have been restored to their original splendour. The collection contains a number of portraits by George Romney, among them his masterpiece, The Gower Family. The gallery has a fine collection of watercolours, those by John Ruskin being particularly noteworthy.

Period cabinets display 18th-century porcelain, silver and glass. The famous

Kendal Museum.

furniture-makers, Gillow of Lancaster are well represented. The collection of contemporary British art includes works by Ben Nicholson, John Piper and Barbara Hepworth.

Kendal Museum

Station Road, Kendal, Cumbria, LA9 6BT
☎ 0539 721374
Mon–Fri 10.30–5; Sat 2–5. Closed Jan 1, Dec 25–26.
Ⓒ ✐ ᕤ ♿

The museum displays and interprets the natural history and human story of the Lake District. It is housed in a former wool warehouse, built c.1850. The Natural History Gallery shows how the rocks have been formed and the landscape shaped and contains a series of reconstructions of typical Lake District habitats, closely based on actual localities, providing a realistic setting for the specimens of plants and animals. The World Wildlife Gallery displays the trophies shot by a local big-game hunter, Colonel Edgar Harrison, and his friends. These have now been restored and are presented to illustrate the hunting passions and habits of a past age.

The Kendal and Westmorland Gallery tells the story of Kendal and the surrounding area back to prehistoric times. A section of the museum recently re-created shows Alfred Wainwright's 'Cabinet of Curiosities'. The famous fellwalker was unpaid curator here for nearly 30 years.

Vintage delivery van of the Cumberland Pencil Company. Pencil Museum, Keswick.

Museum of Lakeland Life

Kirkland, Kendal, Cumbria, LA9 5AL
☎ 0539 722464
Mon–Fri 10.30–5; Sat, Sun 2–5. Spring Bank Holiday–Oct 31, Sat 10.30–5. Closed Jan 1, Dec 25, 26.
Ⓒ ✐ ♿

The museum building was converted from Abbot Hall's stable block. Its displays are concerned with the social and economic history of the area. A wide range of trades and occupations are represented in the exhibits, including farming and the Kendal woollen industry, and there are reconstructions of a smithy, a wheelwright's shop and a printer's workshop, together with a 17th-century parlour and bedroom.

Recent additions to the museum include a reconstruction of a Victorian street scene, with a chemist's shop, a tailor's, a penny bazaar and a pawnbroker's premises, the Arthur Ransome Room containing many personal possessions of the famous children's author, a mine gallery and a display, 'The Arts and Crafts Movement in Cumbria'.

Keswick

Keswick Museum

Fitz Park, Keswick, Cumbria, CA12 4NF
☎ 0596 73263
Apr–Oct, Mon–Sat 10–12, 2–5.30.
Ⓒ ✐ ♿

This is a late Victorian general museum with literary and geological leanings. The collections are very broad and range from butterflies and moths to dolls, fossils and stone axes. The museum's main strength, however, lies in geology and in its world-famous collection of manuscripts of the English Romantic poets, especially Wordsworth and Southey. It also possesses manuscripts by Sir Hugh Walpole, including those of the Rogue Herries novels.

One of the museum's special attractions is Flintoft's 1867 model of the Lake District, made on a scale of three inches to the mile and accurate both horizontally and vertically. It is much used by visitors planning walking tours and other excursions. The famous Musical Stones are a popular feature.

Pencil Museum

The Cumberland Pencil Company, Greta Bridge, Keswick, Cumbria, CA12 5NG
☎ 07687 73626/72116
Daily 9.30–4.30 (last admission 4). Closed Jan 1, Dec 25, 26.
Ⓒ ✐ ᕤ ♿

The first graphite pencils ever produced came from Keswick in the mid 16th century, using Borrowdale graphite, which was ideally suited to the purpose. The Cumberland Pencil Company was formed in the early 1800s. Its museum, which includes carefully restored equipment and machinery, traces the development of the pencil from its cottage industry origins to the writing instrument we know today. The exhibits include many examples of early pencils together with some interesting curios.

Kettering

Alfred East Art Gallery

Sheep Street, Kettering, Northamptonshire
        ☎ 0536 85211
Mon–Wed, Fri, Sat 10–5
Ⓕ 🚗

The gallery displays a collection of oil paintings, watercolours and etchings by Sir Alfred East RA (1849–1913), presented to his native town by the artist. The gallery, which also contains a general collection of paintings, watercolours and prints was built to house Sir Alfred's gift.

Kilmuir (Isle of Skye)

Skye Museum of Island Life

Kilmuir, Isle of Skye   ☎ 047052 279
Apr–Oct, Mon–Sat 9–6
Ⓒ 🛏 ♿ 🚗

The museum occupies a group of thatched cottages, typical of the croft houses of Skye a century ago, and the displays illustrate the way of life of the community at that time. Each building concentrates on a particular theme, such as the work of the blacksmith and weaver and the domestic life and equipment of the islanders.

Kingswinford

Broadfield House Glass Museum

Barnett Lane, Kingswinford, West Midlands,
        DY6 9QA   ☎ 0384 273011
Tues–Fri 2–5; Sat 10–1, 2–5; Sun 2–5. Closed
        Jan 1, Dec 25, 26.
Ⓕ 🛏 🚗

Glass-making in the area dates back to the early 17th century, when glass-makers from Normandy and Lorraine settled in the district. To begin with, window glass and bottles were the main products, but in the 18th century the

glass-houses began producing the tableware and ornamental glass for which the district became renowned.

The museum's displays illustrate the history of glass-making from the Roman period to the present day, with an emphasis on the range of coloured glass and crystal produced by the Stourbridge industry during the 19th century. There are exhibits of old glass-making equipment and, at the rear of the museum, studios for designing and making glass.

Kingussie

Highland Folk Museum

Duke Street, Kingussie, Inverness-shire,
        PH21 1JG   ☎ 05402 307
Apr–Oct, Mon–Sat 10–6; Sun 2–6, Nov–Mar,
        Mon–Fri 10–3. Closed Jan 1, Dec 25, 26, and
        public holidays Nov–Mar.
Ⓒ 🛒 ♿ 🚗

Opened in 1935, this is probably the oldest folk museum in Britain. The reception building is an 18th-century shooting lodge. The indoor displays, most of which are interpretive in nature, deal with the clans, costume, handicrafts and social life of the Scottish Highlands. There are important collections of vernacular furniture and textiles.

Kirriemuir

Barrie's Birthplace

9 Brechin Road, Kirriemuir, Angus, DD8 4BX
        ☎ 0575 72646
May–Sept, Mon–Sat 11–5.30; Sun 2–5.30. Open
        Easter weekend, Fri–Mon.
Ⓒ 🛒 🚗

The two-storey house, now a property of the National Trust for Scotland, was the birthplace, in May 1860, of the author and playwright, Sir James Barrie. The museum contains many of Barrie's personal possessions, including his desk, together with original manuscripts of his works. There are also two original Peter Pan costumes. The outside wash house, said to have been his first theatre and his inspiration for the Wendy House in *Peter Pan*, houses a Peter Pan exhibition.

Lacock

Fox Talbot Museum of Photography

Lacock, nr Chippenham, Wiltshire, SN15 2LG
        ☎ 024973 459
Mar–Oct, daily 11–5.30. Closed Good Fri.
Ⓒ 🛒 ♿ ■ 🚗

The museum is in a converted 16th-century barn, at the gates of Lacock Abbey. It contains collections commemorating the pioneering photographic achievements of William Henry Fox Talbot (1800–77), whose home was at the abbey. The exhibits include cameras and other apparatus used by Fox Talbot and examples of

Croft house. Skye Museum of Island Life, Kilmuir.

his pictures (Calotypes). The museum also organises temporary exhibitions related to the history of photography and to the work of contemporary photographers.

The museum forms part of the National Trust complex of Lacock Abbey, which has been inhabited continuously since the 13th century and is still lived in by the Talbot family, and the village of Lacock, where the carefully preserved 13th–19th-century houses present a remarkable panorama of English domestic architecture.

Lancaster

Judges' Lodgings

Church Street, Lancaster, LA1 1YS
☎ *0524 32808*
Good Fri–Apr and Oct, Mon–Fri 2–5. May–June, Mon–Sat 2–5. July–Sept, Mon–Fri 10–1, 2–5; Sat 2–5.
C 🛈 ☕ ♿

The former Judges' Lodgings, a distinguished and impressively sited 18th-century town house, contains two distinct museums, the Gillow and Town House Museum and the Museum of Childhood. The first has exhibits illustrating the history and products of the famous Lancaster cabinet-making firm of Gillows, together with period room settings containing furniture by Gillows and other local makers. These include a parlour of c.1750, a dining-room and servants' hall of c.1820 and a bedroom of c.1850.

In the Museum of Childhood visitors can see displays of dolls from the Barry Elder Collection, showing the variety and types of dolls produced over the last three centuries, together with toys and games and reconstructions of a Victorian schoolroom, and Edwardian day and night nurseries.

Lancaster Maritime Museum

Custom House, St George's Quay, Lancaster, LA1 1RB   ☎ *0524 64637*
Easter–Oct, daily 11–5. Nov–Easter, daily 2–5. Closed Jan 1, Dec 25–27. Free admission in winter.
C ✎ ☕ ♿

The museum is in Lancaster's former Custom House, built in 1764 by Richard Gillow, during the Golden Age of the town's overseas trade. The collections illustrate this trade during the 18th and early 19th centuries, especially with the West Indies, together with the development of shipbuilding and allied activities. Other displays show the former importance of fishing and shellfish gathering in Morecambe Bay and the Lune estuary. The exhibits include fishing equipment, the *Hannah*, a 5-metre boat used for salmon fishing on the Lune, and a reconstruction of an early-20th-century fisherman's cottage.

Further sections of the museum contain ship models, examples of raw materials transported via the smaller ports and the Lancaster Canal, and a reconstruction of the room used by the

Old photograph of Sunderland Point fishermen. **Lancaster Maritime Museum.**

Collector of Customs in Lancaster, as it looked in about the year 1780.

An extension to the museum, opened in 1987, includes exhibits on the Lancaster Canal, Morecambe Bay and its ecology, and other topics. At the rear of the museum are a number of local vessels, including *Sir William Priestley*, the former Morecambe fishermen's lifeboat.

Leeds

City Art Gallery

Calverley Street, Leeds, West Yorkshire, LS1 3AA
☎ *0532 462495*
Mon, Tues, Thurs, Fri 10–6; Wed 10–9; Sat 10–4; Sun 2–5.
F 🛈 ♿

The gallery's collections are held in common with those of two other Leeds museums, Temple Newsam House and Lotherton Hall. The Art Gallery houses the prints and drawings, including a fine collection of British Romantic watercolours, most of the paintings after 1800 and the modern sculpture. There are important collections of 20th-century British paintings, particularly work by members of the Camden Town Group. The sculpture collection is strong in works by Jacob Epstein and Henry Moore.

Leeds Industrial Museum

Armley Mills, Canal Road, Leeds, West Yorkshire LS12 2QF   ☎ *0532 637861*
Apr–Sept, Tues–Sat 10–6; Sun 2–6 (last admission 5), Oct–Mar, Tues–Sat 10–5; Sun 2–5 (last admission 4). Open Bank Holiday Mon. Closed Dec 25.
C 🛈 ♿

Armley Mills, which dates from 1806, was at one time the world's largest woollen mill. The four-storey stone building, with its unique fireproof construction, is one of Britain's most impressive industrial monuments. Originally water-powered, it was converted to steam in the late 19th century. Its galleries show the development of the principal Leeds industries, including textiles, clothing, optics and heavy engineering. The textile exhibits cover the complete production of woollen cloth, using both static displays and working machinery.

The local tailoring and garment-making industry is realistically illustrated by reconstructions of early sweatshops and fully equipped workrooms and showrooms. Engineering is represented by machine tools and workshops. As Leeds was a major world centre of locomotive construction, a collection of engines made by local companies has been established. Restored narrow-gauge locomotives are driven around the museum site on open days. The Armley Palace Picture Hall, a reconstructed cinema of the 1920s, shows early films on original projectors of the period, commemorating the important part played by Leeds in the optical and cinematographic industries. A newly opened gallery tells the story of underground haulage systems in the coal mines.

Leek

The Brindley Mill

Mill Street, Leek, Staffordshire. ☎ *0538 381446 Easter–June, Sept–Oct, Sat, Sun, Bank Holiday Mon 2–5. July–Aug, Sat–Wed 2–5.*
C ⊘ ♠

The great 18th-century millwright and engineer, James Brindley, spent part of his childhood at Leek and set up his millwright's business in the town in 1742. The water-powered cornmill which he designed in 1752 is fully operational. After being abandoned in 1940, it has been fully restored and illustrates

Brindley Mill, Leek.

the evolution of milling practice over a period of 225 years.

The museum set up within the Mill is a centre of information on the life and work of James Brindley (1716–72). The exhibits include two of his personal possessions: a surveyor's level and a notebook containing accounts of visits to mills.

Leicester

Jewry Wall Museum

St Nicholas Circle, Leicester
☎ *0533 544766/554100 extn 3021*
Mon–Sat 10–5.30; Sun 2–5.30. Open Bank Holiday Mon. Closed Dec 25, 26.
F ⊘

The Jewry Wall, 9 metres high and 45 metres long, is one of the largest sections of Roman masonry still standing in Britain. The site adjacent to it is that of the 2nd-century baths of Roman Leicester.

The museum's collections and displays are concerned with the history of human settlement in Leicester from the earliest times to the present day. Among the more important exhibits are the Bronze Age Welby hoard, a Roman milestone, Roman wall-plaster, Romano-British mosaics and an Anglo-Saxon burial. There is also late medieval painted glass formerly in Wygston's House.

Newarke Houses Museum

The Newarke, Leicester, LE2 7BY
☎ *0553 554100 extn 3222*
Mon–Sat 10–5.30; Sun 2–5.30. Open Bank Holiday Mon. Closed Good Fri, Dec 25, 26.
F ▮

The buildings comprise a 16th-century chantry house and a 17th-century dwelling house, with some 19th-century additions. The museum's collections and displays concentrate on the history of Leicestershire from c.1500 onwards. The displays include a panelled room, with 17th-century furniture, a 19th-century street scene, showing local domestic industries, a clockmaker's workshop and an early-20th-century village shop. Among the other exhibits are locally made clocks, toys and games, furniture by Ernest Gimson and the Cotswold group of craftsmen, and clothes and furniture which belonged to Daniel Lambert (1770–1809), claimed to be England's heaviest man.

Leiston

The Long Shop Museum

Main Street, Leiston, Suffolk, IP16 4ES
☎ *0728 832189*
Apr–Sept, daily 10–4
C ▮ ♠

The firm of Richard Garrett was established at Leiston in 1778. In the 19th century it made steam engines, threshing machines and agricultural implements. In the 1920s and 1930s it added tractors, machine-tools and a range of electrically powered vehicles to its products. In 1932 it was taken over by Beyer Peacock and during the Second World War it produced shells and naval guns. After further changes of ownership, it finally closed in 1980.

The museum buildings are grouped around the Long Shop, built in 1853 for the flow-line production of portable steam engines. 24m long and one of the 19th century's most impressive industrial structures, it is now a listed building. It contains a range of Garrett products and exhibits illustrating the history of the firm.

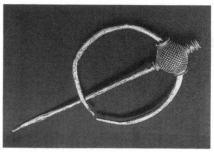

Silver thistle brooch of the Viking period from Gulberwick. Shetland Museum, Lerwick.

Lerwick (Shetland)

Shetland Museum

Lower Hillhead, Lerwick, Shetland Islands,
ZE1 0EL   ☎ 0595 5057
Mon, Wed, Fri 10–7; Tues, Thurs, Sat 10–5.
Closed public holidays.
Ⓕ ⬲ ㅺ ⬅

This is a regional museum, created to illustrate the theme, 'Life in Shetland through the Ages'. The collections include archaeology, farming and rural crafts, seafaring and fishing, and Shetland textiles. There are growing study collections of Shetland natural history, including a registered herbarium. The collections of textiles, items salvaged from wreck sites, ship models and natural history are of international importance.

Letchworth

First Garden City Heritage Museum

296 Norton Way South, Letchworth,
Hertfordshire, SG6 1SU   ☎ 0462 683149
Mon–Fri 2–4.30; Sat 10–1, 2–4.
Ⓕ ⬲

No. 296 Norton Way South was built in 1907 as offices for the architects of Letchworth Garden City, Parker and Unwin, and was later lived in by Barry Parker. It is in a typical Parker style with a thatched roof. The museum's displays illustrate the birth and development of the Garden City movement and the personalities involved. Additional material relates to the social and economic history of Letchworth. There are extensive collections of architectural drawings and photographs, referring especially to the work of Barry Parker.

Lichfield

Samuel Johnson's Birthplace

Breadmarket Street, Lichfield, Staffordshire,
WS13 6LG   ☎ 0543 264972
Daily 10–5. Closed Jan 1, Spring Bank Holiday,
Dec 25, 26.
Ⓒ ▮ ⬅

The house where the celebrated biographer, essayist and critic, Samuel Johnson was born in

September 1709 had been completed in the previous year. The collections now displayed in it illustrate Johnson's life, work and personality, and set him against the background of his friends and contemporaries. The wide range of exhibits shown to visitors include books manuscripts, furniture, pictures and personal possessions.

The museum includes two newly created period rooms. A bookshop is housed in the room where Johnson's father sold books, and visitors can watch a short film on Samuel Johnson's associations with the Midlands.

Linby

Newstead Abbey

Linby, Nottinghamshire, NG15 8GE
    ☎ 0623 793557
Good Fri–Sept, daily 1.45–5
Ⓒ ▮ ⬛ ⬅

Newstead Abbey is 12 miles north of Nottingham on the A60. An Augustinian house, it was founded in 1170 by Henry II as the Priory of St Mary. In 1540, after the Dissolution of the Monasteries, it was bought, together with 300 hectares of land, by Sir John Byron and remained in the family until 1817 when Lord Byron, the poet, sold it to help meet his debts. In 1931 it became the property of the City of Nottingham.

It now houses a series of collections in period settings. The Byron Museum displays an important collection of the poet's manuscripts and letters, first editions of his works, portraits, his dog's inscribed brass collar, personal possessions, including the shoe lasts made to correct his deformed right foot, a lock of his hair and much of his furniture. There is a collection of Crimean War relics, formed by General Gerald Goodlake, brother-in-law of William Frederick Webb, who owned Newstead from 1859 to 1899. General Goodlake was one of the first people to be awarded a Victoria Cross, in 1854.

There are pictures and plans illustrating the evolution of Newstead's architecture since the 17th century and displays of 14th- and 15th-century manuscripts and relics of the medieval priory.

Lincoln

Lincoln Cathedral Treasury

The Cathedral, Lincoln, LN2 1PZ
☎ *0522 544544*
Mon–Sat, 11–3.
Ⓕ ⬥ ■ ⚓

The treasury contains gold and silver plate from churches in the diocese of Lincoln. Most of this is on permanent display, but some items are changed each year. Among the more important permanent exhibits are the medieval chalices and patens taken from the graves of Bishops Grosseteste, Sutton and Gravesend. The collection also includes the bronze Anglo-Saxon hanging bowl, made *c.*700, which was discovered in 1978 on the site of the Church of St Paul-in-the-Bail, Lincoln.

Cathedral treasuries have existed for a long time on the Continent, but Lincoln, where the treasury was established in 1960, was the pioneer in England.

Museum of Lincolnshire Life

Burton Road, Lincoln, LN1 3LY ☎ *0522 28448*
*Mon–Sat 10–5.30; Sun 2–5.30. Evening parties
    by appt.*
Ⓒ ⚫ ⚞ ⚓

The museum is housed is buildings known as the Old Barracks, erected in 1856 as the headquarters of the Royal North Lincoln Militia. When the museum was established the aim was to present a picture of the agricultural, industrial and social history of Lincolnshire from Elizabeth I to Elizabeth II, but at the present time the emphasis is on the 19th and early 20th centuries.

There is a large collection of locally made agricultural and industrial machinery, together with horse-drawn vehicles and displays devoted to domestic, community and commercial life within the county, and to crafts and trades.

Usher Gallery

Lindum Road, Lincoln, LN2 1NN
☎ *0522 27980*
*Mon–Sat 10–5.30; Sun 2.30–5. Closed Good Fri,
    Dec 25, 26.*
Ⓒ ⬥ ⚓

The gallery, opened in 1927, was designed to house the decorative art collections of the Lincoln jeweller, James Ward Usher. Additions were made in 1959 and 1972. One of the strong points of the gallery is its coin collections, which present a comprehensive history of English coins and tokens from pre-Roman times to the present day, with a special emphasis on items connected with Lincolnshire.

There are Italian, Dutch and Flemish paintings, and since the 1930s a large number of English 20th-century paintings have been presented by the Contemporary Art Society. The Usher Gallery has the largest public collection of oils and watercolours by the

**The Brayford Pool and Lincoln Cathedral, by
J.W. Carmichael (1800–68). Usher Gallery,
Lincoln.**

Staffordshire-born artist, Peter de Wint (1784–1849), who came to live in Lincoln. A number of other Lincolnshire artists are represented in the gallery, which also possesses a large collection of oils, watercolours and drawings of Lincolnshire scenes.

A section of the gallery is devoted to portraits and personal effects of Alfred Lord Tennyson, the Poet Laureate, who was born at Somersby Rectory in Lincolnshire.

Little Walsingham

Shirehall Museum

*Common Place, Little Walsingham, Norfolk,
    NR22 6BP* ☎ *0328 820510*
*Maundy Thursday–Sept, Mon 10–1, 2–5; Tues–
    Sat 10–5; Sun 2–5. Oct, Sat 10–5; Sun 2–5.*
Ⓒ ⬥ ⚓

The museum occupies a Georgian courthouse with its original fittings and prisoners' lock-up, which was constructed within the shell of a medieval building with a 15th-century roof. At its peak Walsingham was second only to Canterbury as a place of pilgrimage. An exhibition in the museum tells the story of the medieval pilgrimage and the Shrine of Our Lady, which was suppressed by Henry VIII, but was revived in the present century.

Liverpool

Croxteth Hall and Country Park

Croxteth Hall Lane, Liverpool, L12 0HB
☎ *051 228 5311*
*Good Fri–end Sept, Hall, Farm, Walled Garden &
    Cafeteria, 11–5. Farm 11–4 on Craft Fair
    Suns, 1–4 on other days.*
Ⓒ ⚫ ⬛ ⚓

Croxteth, given to the City of Liverpool in 1974, was formerly the home of the Earls of Sefton. The original building dates from about 1575 and further wings were built in 1702 and 1902. An audio-visual show tells the story of this historic sporting estate and, throughout the house, life at Croxteth as it was in 1905 is re-created by means of costume groups and rooms furnished in the style of the period. There are Sefton family portraits, equestrian portraits, mainly by Towne, and two examples of the more sumptuous kind of Edwardian bathroom. More of the servants' areas have recently been opened, including the confectionery kitchen which contains a unique 19th-century dual function coal/gas cooking range.

The walled kitchen garden and glasshouses have been carefully maintained and the Home Farm has been developed as a centre for rare breeds of farm animals. There is also a carriage collection.

Merseyside Maritime Museum

Albert Dock, Liverpool, L3 4AA
   ☎ *051 207 0001*
Daily 10.30–5.30 (Last admission 4.30)
🄲 🄸 ▬ 🄳 ᚷ ᴀ

The buildings of this dockside museum include the former headquarters (1883) of the Liverpool pilotage service, the 1765 dry docks, with the original cast-iron dock furniture, the Albert Dock warehouse – an 1846 Grade I listed building – and the 1852 Piermaster's house. There is a growing collection of full-size craft, including the pilot boat, *Edmund Gardner* (1953) and an important collection of models, paintings and marine equipment. Special exhibits illustrate the history of cargo-handling in the Port of Liverpool and the development and operation of the enclosed dock system. A special section of the museum tells the story of the seven million emigrants who passed through Liverpool between 1830 and 1930.

Museum of Labour History

Islington, Liverpool, L3 8EE   ☎ *051 207 0001*
Mon–Sat 10–5; Sun 2–5. Closed Jan 1, Good Fri, Dec 24–26.
🄵 🄸 ᚷ

Opened in March 1986, in the former County Sessions House erected in 1884, the museum tells the story of working-class life on Merseyside from 1840 to the present day. There is an introductory audio-visual programme, 'Merseyside – the People's Story', and displays on employment, housing – including a reconstructed street and scullery – education, with a part-reconstruction of an Edwardian classroom, leisure and trade unionism. A display of trade union banners can be seen in the main Court Room.

Sudley Art Gallery

Mossley Hill Road, Liverpool, L18 8BX
   ☎ *051 724 3245*
Mon–Sat 10–5; Sun 2–5. Closed Jan 1, Good Fri, Dec 24–26.
🄵 🗘 ᴀ

Sudley is an early-19th-century neo-classical building, with additions made in the 1880s by the Liverpool shipowner, George Holt, when he bought the property. It contains Holt's collection of paintings, composed chiefly of 18th- and 19th-century works by British artists,

including Gainsborough, Romney, Turner, Bonington and the Pre-Raphaelites. The most important items are Gainsborough's *Viscountess Folkestone*, a sympathetic study of old age, and Turner's *Rosenau*, the German home of the Prince Consort.

The gallery also has displays of late-19th-century 'New Sculpture' from the Walker Art Gallery and ship models and children's toys from the Merseyside Museums.

University of Liverpool Art Gallery

3 Abercromby Square, PO Box 146, Liverpool, L69 3BX   ☎ *051 794 2347/8*
Mon, Tues, Thurs 12–2; Wed, Fri 12–4. Closed Bank Holiday and Aug.
🄵 🗘 ᴀ

The building is a typical early-19th-century Liverpool merchant's house in a square of such houses. The gallery displays sculpture, paintings, drawings, prints, furniture, ceramics, silver and glass selected from the University's collections. The English watercolours are outstanding, including works by Turner, Girtin, Cozens and Cotman, among others. The English porcelain is also of good quality, with examples from nearly all the main factories, including Chelsea, Worcester, Derby and Bow.

There are original paintings by John James Audubon, and also oil paintings by Turner, Joseph Wright of Derby and Augustus John. Contemporary work includes sculpture by Elisabeth Frink, paintings by Adrian Berg, Lucian Freud and Bridget Reiley, and prints by Howard Hodgkin and David Hockney.

The Sluggard, by Frederick Leighton. University of Liverpool Art Gallery.

'And When Did You Last See Your Father?', by William Frederick Yeames. Walker Art Gallery, Liverpool.

Walker Art Gallery

William Brown Street, Liverpool, L3 8EL
   ☎ 051 227 5234 extn 2064
*Mon–Sat 10–5; Sun 2–5. Closed Jan 1, Good Fri,
   Dec 24–26.*
[F] 🐾 🍵

The gallery's collections are of European painting and sculpture from the 14th to the 20th centuries. British paintings range from the portrait of Henry VIII after Holbein to Gainsborough's *Countess of Sefton*. Among the other 18th-century English painters represented are Stubbs, Wilson and Wright of Derby.

The 19th-century paintings are dominated by Turner, Millais, Watts and the Pre-Raphaelites, with many narrative paintings, including the celebrated *And when did you last see your father?* by W. F. Yeames. The 20th-century exhibits range from Sickert and Gilman to Hockney, with many works from recent John Moore exhibitions. The gallery's sculpture collection is notable for the works by Gibson and the 'New Sculpture' of the 1890s and is displayed in a new sculpture gallery, which won a National Art-Collections Award in 1989.

Llanberis

Welsh Slate Museum

Gilfach Ddu, Llanberis, Gwynedd, LL55 4TY
   ☎ 0286 870630
*Easter Sat–Apr, daily 9.30–5.30. May–Sept, daily
   9.30–6.30. Closed May Bank Holiday. Oct–
   Easter, by appt.*
[C] 🐾 🍵 🐾

The museum is located within what were, until the closure of the great Dinorwic slate quarry in 1969, the quarry's main repair and maintenance workshops and the place where the rough blocks were converted into roofing slates. The buildings were reputedly designed on the pattern of a British army fort in India. The machinery in the workshops was powered by a waterwheel 15 metres in diameter, which is now restored and working again.

Most of the tools and machines have been kept in their original location and condition, and many are still demonstrated by members of the Museum staff. The fitting and blacksmiths' shops, foundry, Pelton wheel, timber sawing sheds and pattern lofts can all be seen.

Llandysul

Maesllyn Woollen Mill

Maesllyn, Llandysul, Dyfed, SA44 5LO
   ☎ 023975 251
*Easter–Oct, Mon–Sat 10–6; Sun 2–6. Nov–
   Easter, Mon–Sat 10–5. Closed Dec 25. Other
   times by appt.*
[C] 🚻 🍵 🐾 🐾

The mill, built in 1881 to carry out all the processes of woollen manufacture, lies between Croeslanon on the A486 and Penrhiwpal on the B4571. It was never a commercial success, but the quality of its buildings and machinery were such that it has functioned to this day with very little modification.

It is now a privately run museum, which preserves the atmosphere of a Victorian mill and where the changes from hand spinning and weaving to powered machinery are explained and demonstrated. Some of the machinery is driven from the restored waterwheel.

Llanystumdwy

Lloyd George Museum

Llanystumdwy, Criccieth, Gwynedd, LL52 0SH
   ☎ 0766 522071 or 0286 4121 extn 2098
*Easter, May–Sept, daily 10–5. Other times by
   appt.*
[C] 🚻 🐾

The museum's collection illustrates the life and career of Earl Lloyd George of Dwyfor. The exhibits include caskets, deeds of freedom, scrolls and other mementoes of the Liberal leader and Prime Minister. There is also a talking head of the statesman.

An extension to the museum opened at the end of 1990, to commemorate the centenary of Lloyd George's entry into Parliament.

London

Bank of England Museum

Bartholomew Lane, London EC2R 8AH
 ☎ *071 601 5792*
Good Fri–Sept, Mon–Fri 10–5; Sat, Sun 11–5.
 Oct–Maundy Thurs, Mon–Fri 10–5. Open on
 day of Lord Mayor's Show.
F ♟ ♿

The museum illustrates the history of the Bank from its foundation by Royal Charter in 1694 to its position today as Britain's central bank. Visitors enter through the reconstructed Bank Stock Office, which houses a display on the architectural history of the Bank's premises. Three rooms then deal with the Bank's early years and the chronological history of the Bank is completed in the Rotunda. The Bank Note Gallery houses one of the most important collections of English banknotes. The route then leads back to the Bank Stock Office through 'The Bank Today'. The up-to-date equipment here includes interactive videos and an operational dealing desk.

The British Museum

Great Russell Street, London WC1B 3DG
 ☎ *071 636 1555*
Recorded information: ☎ *071 580 1788*
Mon–Sat 10–5; Sun 2.30–6. Closed Jan 1, Good
 Fri, 1st Mon in May, Dec 24–26.
F ♟ 🖳 ♿ ■

The present museum buildings were designed by Robert Smirke and completed by his younger brother, Sydney. Work began in 1824 and took over 30 years. Extensions were added in 1884, 1914, 1938 and 1978. The celebrated domed Reading Room was built in 1857.

The British Museum, which is a major research institution, is encyclopaedic. It houses the national collections of archaeology and art, representing human achievement from prehistoric times to the 20th century. The collections and displays in the galleries are in the care of nine departments – Egyptian, Greek and Roman, Western Asiatic, Prehistoric and Romano-British, Medieval and Later, Coins and Medals, Oriental, Prints and Drawings, and Ethnography. The ethnographical collections are displayed at the Museum of Mankind in Burlington Gardens.

Cabinet War Rooms

Clive Steps, King Charles Street, London
 SW1A 2AQ ☎ *071 930 6961*
Daily 10–6. Last admission 5.25. Closed Jan 1,
 Dec 24–26. May be closed at short notice on
 State occasions.
C ♟ ♿

The Cabinet War Rooms are the most important surviving part of the underground emergency accommodation which was constructed to protect the Prime Minister, the War Cabinet and the Chiefs of Staff against air attacks during the Second World War. The suite of 21 historic rooms includes the Cabinet Room; the Transatlantic Telephone Room, from which Churchill would speak directly to President Roosevelt in the White House; the Map Room, where information about operations on all fronts was collected; and the Prime Minister's Room, which served as Churchill's emergency office and bedroom throughout the war.

Carlyle's House

24 Cheyne Row, London SW3 5HL
 ☎ *071 352 7087*
End Mar–end Oct, Wed–Sun, Bank Holiday Mon
 11–5 (last admission 4.30). Closed Good Fri.
C

Thomas Carlyle and his wife, Jane, lived in this early 18th-century terrace house in Chelsea from 1834 until their respective deaths in 1866 and 1881. In 1881 it was bought for the nation by public subscription, and furniture and personal possessions were returned to the house. In 1936 it passed to the National Trust.

Visitors now see it much as it was in the Carlyle's day. Apart from the furnishings and the trivia of everyday life, the house contains portraits, manuscripts, prints, books and relics of many eminent 19th-century figures, including Goethe and Mazzini.

Court Dress Collection

Kensington Palace, London W8 4PX
 ☎ *071 937 9561*
Mon–Sat 9–5; Sun 1–5 (last admission 4.15).
 Closed Jan 1, Good Fri, Dec 24–26.
C ✎

Kensington Palace, originally built in 1607, was known for more than a hundred years as

Bank of England Museum, London.

Dickens's Dream by Robert William Buss.
Dickens House, London.

Nottingham House. It was altered for
William III by Sir Christopher Wren and
decorated for George I by William Kent. The
collection of court dress and uniform is of items
worn at the British Court from c.1750 onwards,
displayed in the context of rooms restored to
their original 19th-century appearance. The
exhibits now include the wedding dress worn by
HRH the Princess of Wales.

Dickens House

48 Doughty Street, London WC1N 2LF
☎ *071 405 2127*
Mon–Sat 10–5. Closed Bank Holidays.
Ⓒ 🛈 ♨

Charles Dickens lived at 48 Doughty Street
between April 1837 and December 1839. It was
here that he consolidated his reputation,
completing *Pickwick Papers*, writing all of
Nicholas Nickleby and most of *Oliver Twist*, and
beginning *Barnaby Rudge*. The museum collects
and displays books, letters, manuscripts,
pictures, furniture and personalia relating to
Dickens. Some of the rooms have been restored
to present the appearance they are judged to
have had during Dickens' residence in the
house.

Dr Johnson's House

17 Gough Square, London EC4A 3DE
☎ *071 353 3745*
May–Sept, Mon–Sat 11–5.30. Oct–Apr, Mon–
Sat 11–5. Closed Good Fri, Dec 24, 25 and
public holidays.
Ⓒ ♨

Of the many houses in London in which Samuel
Johnson lived, 17 Gough Square is the only one
that survives. Built c.1700, it has seven rooms.
It has been preserved and restored as a memorial
to the compiler of the first definitive English
dictionary and the subject of James Boswell's
celebrated biography.

There is a good collection of portrait-prints
of Johnson and the members of his circle. Of
particular interest among the original portraits
are those of Elizabeth Carter, the noted classical
scholar by Catherine Read, and of Anna
Williams, Johnson's blind, adopted sister, by
Frances Reynolds, Sir Joshua's sister. The other

exhibits include holograph letters from Johnson
and Boswell, a number of personal relics and the
probate copy of Johnson's will.

Dulwich College Picture Gallery

College Road, London SE2 7AD
☎ *081 693 5254*
Tues–Sat 10–1, 2–5; Sun 2–5. Closed Jan 1,
Good Fri, Dec 25, 26 and Bank Holidays.
Ⓒ *(ex children)* ♨ ♨

This pioneering building, the first in England to
be designed specifically to house an art gallery,
dates from 1811, ten years before the
establishment of the National Gallery. The
architect was Sir John Soane. With its 13 rooms
and about 300 pictures in view, the gallery is on
a pleasantly small scale and can easily be seen in
half a day.

The collections include both familiar works
and interesting lesser known paintings, mostly
17th-century – Poussin, Claude, Rubens, Van
Dyck, Teniers, Murillo, Rembrandt, Ruysdael,
Hobbema and many other Dutch artists. The
18th century is represented by major English
portraitists, including Hogarth, Reynolds,
Gainsborough and Lawrence and works by
Watteau, Tiepolo and Canaletto.

Florence Nightingale Museum

2 Lambeth Palace Road, London SE1 7EW
☎ *071 620 0374*
Tues–Sun 10–4
Ⓒ 🛈 ♿

The museum is in a new building on the site of
St Thomas's Hospital, the home of Britain's first
school of nursing. It contains important
material relating to the career of the great
Victorian nursing pioneer, Florence Nightingale
and to the Nursing School at St Thomas's.
Included are Florence Nightingale's medicine
chest, childhood books and items of her
clothing. Period settings are used and there is a
reconstruction of one of the wards at Scutari in
the Crimea.

Geffrye Museum

Kingsland Road, London E2 8AE
☎ *071 739 8368/9893*
Tues–Sat 10–5; Sun 2–5. Bank Holiday 10–5.
Closed Mon (unless a Bank Holiday), Jan 1,
Good Fri, Dec 24–26.
Ⓕ 🍴 ♿

The museum occupies the former almshouses of
the Ironmongers' Company, built in 1713. The
exhibits, illustrating the development of
domestic design, are arranged in a series of room
settings covering the period 1600–1939. Other
features include a reconstruction of an 18th-
century woodworker's shop, an open-hearth
kitchen and John Evelyn's *Closet of Curiosities*.
The paintings have been chosen principally to
illustrate costume and social life. A separate
gallery displays costumes and accessories from
the museum's collection.

HMS Belfast

*Symons Wharf, Vine Lane, Tooley Street, London
SE1 2JH*   ☎ *071 407 6434*
*Mar 20–Oct, daily 11–5.50. Nov–Mar 19, daily
11–4.30. Closed Jan 1, Dec 24–26.*
Ⓒ 👤 💻

The cruiser, HMS *Belfast*, launched in 1938, is
the last of the Royal Navy's big ships whose
main armament was guns. She is now
permanently moored in the Thames, opposite
the Tower of London, as a floating naval
museum. Visitors may tour most of the ship,
which has been preserved as far as possible in
her original condition.

Among the areas open to visitors are the
operations room, messdecks, which are fitted
out in the traditional and in a more modern
style, sick bay, boiler room, engine room,
Captain's and Admiral's bridges, galley,
punishment cells and two 6-inch gun turrets.

Hogarth's House

*Hogarth Lane, Great West Road, London
W4 2QN*   ☎ *081 994 6757*
*Apr–Sept, Mon, Wed–Sat 11–6; Sun 2–6. Oct–
Mar, Mon, Wed–Sat 11–4; Sun 2–4. Closed
first two weeks in Sept and last three weeks in
Dec.*
Ⓕ 👤 🚗

This Georgian house, close to the River
Thames, was the country home of William
Hogarth (1697–1764) for 15 years. It contains
memorabilia of the artist, copies of his paintings
and many of his most famous engravings.

Imperial War Museum

Lambeth Road, London SE1 6HZ
☎ *071 735 8922*
*Daily 10–6. Closed Jan 1, Dec 24–26. Free
admission Fri.*
Ⓒ 👤 💻

The museum building was originally the central
portion of the Bethlem Royal Hospital (or
Bedlam) for the insane, completed in 1815. In
1846 the dome, designed by Sydney Smirke, was
added. It now accommodates the museum's
reading room. The collections are devoted to all
aspects of the armed conflicts which have
involved Britain and the Commonwealth since
1914. The Large Exhibits Gallery houses tanks,
fighter aircraft, and artillery pieces. Among the
historical displays are uniforms, photographs,
documents, medals and posters. The museum's
collection of British 20th-century art related to
war is outstanding.

Jewish Museum

*Woburn House, Upper Woburn Place, London
WC1H 0EP*   ☎ *071 388 4525*
*Tues–Thurs 10–4; Fri, Sun 10–12.45 (summer
only, Fri until 4). Closed Mon, Sat, public &
Jewish holidays.*
Ⓕ ✍ ♿ 🚗

The aim of the museum is to illustrate Jewish
life, history and religion, particularly in Britain,
by means of objects of historical interest and
artistic merit. The collection includes ritual
objects from early City of London synagogues,
1st- and 2nd-century coins, 18th- and 19th-
century ceramic figures of Jewish pedlars, and
Sabbath lamps and candlesticks. There are also
decorated scroll-cases and, as the centrepiece of
the museum, a large 16th-century Ark, in which
the Scrolls of the Law were kept in the
synagogue.

John Wesley's House

47–49 City Road, London EC1Y 1AU
☎ *071 253 2262*
*Mon–Sat 10–4; Sun after 11 am service. Other
times by appt. Closed Dec 25, 26.*
Ⓒ 👤

John Wesley laid the foundation stone of the
New Chapel, in what is now City Road, in
1778. He himself lived and died in a house,
47 City Road, beside the front courtyard of the
chapel and is buried in the adjacent graveyard.
The Museum of Methodism is in the crypt of the
chapel, which has been restored. Its collections
tell the story of Methodism from its 18th-
century beginnings to the present day. John
Wesley's house contains items of his furniture,
in addition to books, letters and other
possessions, including his hat, travelling cloak,
shoes and buckles. There is also the celebrated
electrical machine which he used in his clinic
for the treatment of mental illness and the pen
with which he wrote his last letter a week before
he died, to Wilberforce, urging him to carry on
with his campaign against 'that execrable
villainy', the slave trade. Visitors can also see
the prayer closet off his bedroom, in which he
prayed every morning at 4 am.

HMS Belfast, London.

Keats House

Wentworth Place, Keats Grove, London
*   NW3 2RR*   ☎ *071 435 2062*
April–Oct, Mon–Fri 2–6; Sat 10–1, 2–5; Sun &
*   Bank Holiday 2–5. Nov–Mar, Mon–Fri 1–5;*
*   Sat 10–1, 2–5; Sun 2–5. Closed Jan 1, Good*
*   Fri, Easter Sat, May Day Bank Holiday, Dec*
*   24–26.*
F 🔔

Once a pair of semi-detached villas, built in
1815–16 and later made into a single house,
Keats House, located in Hampstead, has been
restored and redecorated in the style of the
period of the poet's residence here, 1818–20.
Care has been taken to give it the atmosphere of
a house rather than a museum, and the rooms
are furnished accordingly. They contain relics,
books, letters and portraits of John Keats, who
spent the most creative years of his life here.
The exhibits range from his student medical
notebook to the engagement ring he gave to
Fanny Brawne.

Library and Museum of the United Grand Lodge of England

Freemason's Hall, Great Queen Street, London
*   WC2B 5AZ*   ☎ *071 831 9811*
Mon–Fri 10–5; Sat by appt. Closed public holidays
*   and preceding Sat.*
F ✐

The museum is concerned with the history of
Freemasonry, mainly in England and Wales. A
large part of its holding consists of mid-18th- to
20th-century regalia and medals, but there are
also good collections of glass, porcelain –
including rare Masonic Chien Lung –
silverware, enamels and snuffboxes. The
portraits include several of Royal Freemasons.

London Cab Company Museum

1–3 Brixton Road, London SW9 6DJ
*   ☎ 071 735 7777*
Mon–Fri 9–5; Sat 9–2. Closed Bank Holiday.
F

The museum contains examples of London taxi-
cabs, from 1907 to the present day. The UNIC,
of which the museum has a 1907 model, was
manufactured from 1904 until 1921 and worked
on the London streets until 1931. It is still
operational and is much in demand for film,
television and special functions. The collection
also includes the first London taxi to have
front-wheel brakes, the first to be fitted with a
driver's door, the first to carry an illuminated
roof sign, and the first to have an adjustable
driver's seat and a fully enclosed driving cabin.

London Transport Museum

Covent Garden Piazza, London WC2E 7BB
*   ☎ 071 379 6344*
Daily 10–6 (last admission 5.15). Closed Dec
*   24–26.*
C 🔔 🚌 ♿ ♨

The museum building in Covent Garden
formerly housed London's main flower market
and dates from 1871–2. The collections include
horse- and motorbuses, trams, trolleybuses and
Underground rolling stock, and illustrate the
development of London's public transport
system and the influence it had on life in the
capital.

The story is told with the help of
contemporary illustrations, photographs,
tickets, uniforms, signs, video programmes
showing transport in action, and working
models. Posters from London Transport's
celebrated collection are on display.

MCC Museum

Lord's Cricket Ground, St John's Wood Road,
*   London NW8 8QN*   ☎ *071 289 1611*
Cricket match days: Mon–Sat 10.30–5. Sun
*   afternoons when cricket is being played. Other*
*   times by appt.*
C 🔔 🚌 ♨

The Marylebone Cricket Club began forming a
collection of cricket bygones in 1865. Until
1953 it was housed in the Members' Pavilion,
but in that year a public museum and gallery, in
a converted racquets court, was opened as an
international memorial to cricketers killed in
the two World Wars. This now houses about
half of the MCC's collection of paintings and
cricketana, and exhibits are exchanged from
time to time between the gallery and the
pavilion. The displays in the gallery include
paintings, ceramics, objets d'art, trophies and
personalia illustrating the history of cricket. The
most famous exhibit is probably The Ashes, the
trophy awarded to the victor in the series of Test
Matches between England and Australia.

The Ashes trophy. MCC Museum, London.

Reconstruction of a late 19th-century barber's shop. Museum of London.

Michael Faraday's Laboratory

The Royal Institution, 21 Albemarle Street, London WIX 4BS ☎ *071 409 2992*
Tues, Thurs 1–4
Ⓒ ✍

The Royal Institution, which houses the museum, is an historic building in its own right. Founded in 1799, its premises are a conversion of two early-18th-century houses, with considerable alterations, including the addition of the present imposing façade, undertaken during the 19th century.

Michael Faraday's laboratory, where many of his most important discoveries were made, was restored in 1972 to the form it was known to have had in 1845. The recently created museum adjoining the laboratory contains a collection of original apparatus which illustrates the more important aspects of Faraday's immense contribution to the advancement of science during his fifty years at the Institution.

Museum of London

London Wall, London EC2Y 5HN
☎ *071 600 3699*
Tues–Sat 10–6; Sun 2–6. Closed Mon, except Bank Holiday Mon, and Dec 24–26.
Ⓕ 🍴 🖥 ♿ ☕

The Museum of London illustrates the history of London and its people from prehistoric times to the present day. The galleries are arranged in chronological order and all the exhibits are set in their social context. The items on display include everyday domestic equipment, shop fronts, bank and pub interiors, vehicles, costumes, photographs, the fine and decorative arts, industrial relics and archaeological finds.

Especially popular features are the Lord Mayor's coach, 'The Great Fire Experience' – an audio-visual display – the model of a Roman waterfront, the full-size reconstruction of a 17th-century room from Poyle Park, and the newly re-designed 18th-century gallery.

Museum of the Moving Image

South Bank, Waterloo, London SE1 8XT
☎ *071 401 2636*
Tues–Sat 10–8; Sun & Bank Holidays 10–6.
Ⓒ 🍴 ♿ ■

The museum traces the history of moving images from the early Chinese shadow theatre to the latest film and television technology. There are 72 laser players for video pictures, allowing images to be shown continuously throughout the exhibition areas. The collections range from early optical toys such as the Zoetrope, to props from modern science fiction films. Among the exhibits are Charlie Chaplin's hat and cane, Fred Astaire's tail coat, and the IBA collection of period television sets.

The museum houses a cinema with the world's first four-screen unit. The screens for rear, flat, Perlux and 3-D projection are mounted on a travelling gantry, allowing perfect projection of different film image ratios and light intensities. Many of the exhibits can be operated by visitors themselves, an activity which is encouraged by the museum's eight actor-guides.

National Army Museum

Royal Hospital Road, London SW3 4IIT
☎ *071 730 0717*
Mon–Sat 10–5.30; Sun 2–5.30. Closed Jan 1, Good Fri, May Day Bank Holiday, Dec 24–26.
Ⓕ 🍴 ♿ ☕

The museum was established in 1960 in Chelsea, to collect, preserve and exhibit objects and records relating to the regular and auxiliary forces of the British Army and to encourage research into their history and traditions. It is the only museum in Great Britain dealing with the Army as a whole during the five centuries of its existence and includes the story of the colonial forces and of the Indian Army up to the time of Independence in 1947.

Two galleries are devoted to a chronological survey of the development, organisation and achievements of the Army from 1485 to 1982. The uniform gallery contains a selection of the 20,000 items in the collection, and there are also displays of weapons, badges, medals and insignia, including the decorations of HRH the Duke of Windsor and the batons of five Field Marshals. The art gallery contains the best of the museum's collection of 17th-, 18th- and 19th-century portraits and paintings of military subjects.

The weapon gallery traces the development of hand-held weapons used by British soldiers from medieval times to the present.

National Gallery

Trafalgar Square, London WC2N 5DN
☎ 071 839 3321
Mon–Sat 10–6; Sun 2–6. Closed Jan 1, Good Fri,
    May Day Bank Holiday, Dec 24–26.
Ⓕ 🛈 ♨ ♿

The gallery building, housing Britain's principal
art collection, was designed by William Wilkins
and completed in 1838. There are more than
2,000 pictures in the collection, which covers
the major European schools up to 1900 and has
the reputation of being the most representative
and best-balanced collection in the world.
Among the artists represented are Leonardo,
Raphael, Titian, Rembrandt, Vermeer, Rubens,
Poussin, Velázquez, Hogarth, Constable,
Turner, Cézanne and Renoir.

National Maritime Museum

Romney Road, London SE10 9NF
☎ 081 858 4422
Late Mar–late Oct, Mon–Sat 10–6; Sun 2–6. Late
    Oct–late Mar, Mon–Sat 10–5; Sun 2–5.
Ⓒ 🛈 ♨ ♿ ⌂

The central feature of the main museum
buildings (located in Greenwich, south
London) is Inigo Jones' 17th-century Queen's
House, recently refurbished. The museum
displays illustrate the rôle the sea has played in
British history. Ship design forms an important
part of the exhibits with many actual boats and
hundreds of detailed models. There are large
collections of compasses, telescopes, sextants,
maps and charts and interesting examples of
ships' logs. Among the weapons exhibited are
ships' guns, muskets, pistols, swords and
cutlasses. Visitors can also see ships' furniture
and fittings, uniforms and many personal items
associated with famous figures in Britain's
maritime history, such as the bullet-holed coat
in which Nelson died.
    The museum has extensive collections of
historic paintings, prints, drawings and
photographs relating to maritime scenes and
personalities. Included in the site is the old
Royal Observatory.

National Portrait Gallery

St Martin's Place, London WC2H 0HE
☎ 071 930 1552
Mon–Fri 10–5; Sat 10–6; Sun 2–6. Closed Jan 1,
    Good Fri, May Day Bank Holiday, Dec
    24–26.
Ⓕ 🛈 ■ ⌂

The gallery, in the style of an Italian palazzo,
opened in 1896. Round the exterior is a frieze of
busts of Hogarth, Lawrence and other
celebrated British portrait artists. The aim of the
gallery is to collect likenesses of famous British
men and women, in media which include
paintings, drawings, sculpture, photographs and
videos. The criteria for admission are the
importance of the subject and the authenticity
of the portrait, which must have been taken
from life.

The National Portrait Gallery, London, by Sir
Hugh Casson.

The portraits date from Tudor times to the
present day and include kings and queens,
scholars, statesmen, soldiers, poets, sportsmen
and scientists.

Natural History Museum

Cromwell Road, London SW7 5BD
☎ 071 938 9123
Mon–Sat 10–6; Sun 2.30–6. Closed Jan 1, Good
    Fri, May Day Bank Holiday, Dec 24–26.
Ⓒ 🛈 ■ ■ ⌂

The Natural History Museum in South
Kensington, designed by Alfred Waterhouse, is
among the greatest of Victorian buildings.
Internally, it is richly decorated with terracotta
mouldings of plants and animals. One of the
small group of State museums, it holds one of
the most extensive collections in the world of
natural history specimens of all kinds – living
and fossil plants and animals, minerals, rocks
and meteorites. Most of the display galleries
have been completely modernised in recent
years and a number of theme exhibitions
introduced. These include Human Biology,
Man's Place in Evolution, Origin of Species,
Introducing Ecology, Dinosaurs and their Living
Relatives, and Discovering Mammals.

Operating Theatre Museum

9A St Thomas' Street, London SE1 9RT
☎ 071 407 7600 extn 2739
Mon, Wed, Fri 12.30–4. Closed public holidays.
Ⓒ 🛈

In 1821 St Thomas's Hospital moved its
operating theatre for women to the attic of what
used to be the Parish Church of St Thomas and
is now the chapter house of Southwark
Cathedral. In 1862 the theatre ceased to be used
and was sealed off. Discovered by chance after

the Second World War and since fully restored with the addition of contemporary equipment and instruments, it now gives a good impression of conditions during the first half of the 19th century, when many patients understandably preferred death to surgery.

Pollock's Toy Museum

1 Scala Street, London W1P 1LT
☎ *071 636 3452*
Mon–Sat 10–5. Closed Good Fri, Easter Mon, Dec 25, 26.
Ⓒ ▮

The museum is in two small 18th-century houses. The small rooms and narrow winding staircases give it a certain dolls' house quality. It adjoins Pollock's Theatrical Print Warehouse, where Pollock's Toy Theatres and their associated plays are sold, preserving the tradition of the Victorian Juvenile Drama. The collections include dolls of china, wood, fabric, celluloid, wax and composition; dolls' houses; rocking horses; tin and lead toys; teddy bears; folk toys from many countries; puppets; toy theatres; board games; and optical, mechanical and constructional toys.

Royal Air Force Museum

Grahame Park Way, London NW9 5LL
☎ *081 205 2266*
Daily 10–6. Closed Jan 1, Dec 24–26.
Ⓒ ▮ ⬛ ♿ ⚲

The museum buildings, situated on part of the historic former airfield at Hendon, north London, incorporate two hangars constructed in 1915. The displays cover the history of the Royal Air Force and its predecessors and of aviation generally. The collections include about 150 aircraft, of which over 60 are on display. Among the other exhibits are aero-engines, propellers, instruments, navigation aids, armament, uniforms, decorations, trophies and paintings.

Within the museum complex are two special exhibitions, the Battle of Britain Experience, with British and German aircraft and other relics of the air attack of 1940, and the Bomber Command Hall, which presents aircraft and a wide range of mementoes of the Allied bombing offensive.

All three sections of the museum contain realistic reconstructions of historic settings connected with RAF history, from a Royal Flying Corps workshop of the First World War to a Battle of Britain Operations Room.

The Royal Armouries

Tower of London, Tower Hill, London EC3N 4AB
☎ *071 480 6358*
Mar–Oct, Mon–Sat 9.30–5; Sun 2–5; Mar–Feb, Mon–Sat 9.30–4.30. Closed Jan 1, Good Fri, Dec 24–26.
Ⓒ ▮

The Royal Armouries is the national museum of arms and armour. Located within the Tower of London, it is also Britain's oldest public museum. The collection has its origins in the great arsenal at the Tower which supplied the armed forces of the Crown from the 13th to the 19th century, as well as in the royal armoury begun by Henry VIII and continued by the early Stuarts, which was brought to the Tower from Greenwich Palace during the English Civil War. As early as the reign of Charles II the Armouries, on show to privileged visitors since Tudor times, were open to the general public. At present, the collections displayed in the White Tower and New Armouries comprise European arms and armour from the Dark Ages to the 20th century, including not only military equipment but weapons and armour for sport and for display. The centrepiece remains the royal armours of Henry VIII (four personal armours and three horse armours) and of the early Stuarts. There is also a substantial Oriental Armoury, in the Waterloo Barracks, drawn from all parts of Asia, which includes the only surviving Mughal elephant armour in the world and a major collection of Samurai armours.

Other parts of the museum's collections are at Fort Nelson near Portsmouth, the Royal Armouries museum of artillery, at Littlecote House, Berkshire, where the great hall contains a unique Civil War armoury, and on loan to museums and sites throughout the country.

Science Museum

Exhibition Road, London SW7 2DD
☎ *071 938 8111*
Mon–Sat 10–6; Sun 11–6. Closed Jan 1, Good Fri, May Day Bank Holiday, Dec 24–26.
Ⓒ ▮ ⬛ ♿ ■

Properly called the National Museum of Science and Industry but better known simply as the Science Museum, this important State museum had its origin in the scientific and educational collections of the South Kensington Museum (now the Victoria and Albert Museum), opened in 1857. The construction of the present building in South Kensington took place by stages from 1913 onwards. The collections cover a wide range of subjects from the pure sciences to engineering, and from transport to space technology, illustrating the ways in which

Aeronautics Gallery, Science Museum, London.

science and industry have influenced our lives.
The exhibits include working models and
historic machinery, instruments and equipment.

Two floors devoted to the Wellcome
Museum of the History of Medicine tell the
story of medicine from Neolithic times to the
present day.

Sir John Soane's Museum

13 Lincoln's Inn Fields, London WC2A 3BP
☎ *071 405 2107*
Tues–Sat 10–5. Closed Bank Holiday and Dec 24.
Ⓕ 𝒞

Nos. 12, 13 and 14 Lincoln's Inn Fields were
designed by Sir John Soane, and built 1812–14.
Nos. 12 and 13, together with the back part of
14, now form the museum. The interior of 13,
Soane's own house and museum, is one of his
finest architectural achievements and illustrates
both his tastes and his collecting habits – Greek
and Roman antiquities and architectural
fragments; Renaissance sculpture and casts; and
18th-century paintings, drawings, engravings
and sculpture. Among the particular treasures
are two series of paintings by Hogarth, *The
Rake's Progress* and *The Election*; paintings by
Turner, Canaletto, Watteau, Piranesi and Sir
Thomas Lawrence; the Egyptian sarcophagus of
Seti I; and a fragment from the frieze of the
Erectheum in Athens.

The Tate Gallery

Millbank, London SW1P 4RG ☎ *071 821 1313*
Recorded information: ☎ *071 821 7128*
Mon–Sat 10–5.50; Sun 2–5.50. Closed Jan 1,
*   Good Fri, May Day Bank Holiday, Dec*
*   24–26.*
Ⓕ 💻 ♿ ■

The gallery opened in 1897, the building being
paid for by Sir Henry Tate – of Tate and Lyle,
the sugar refiners – whose gift of 70 recent
British paintings and sculptures formed the
nucleus of the collection. Extensions were built
in 1899–1906, also at Sir Henry's expense, and
in 1910, 1926, 1937 and 1979. The Clore
Gallery, to house the Turner collection, opened
in the Spring of 1987.

The Tate Gallery houses two national
collections. The British Collection covers the
period *c.*1500–1900 and consists of
watercolours, drawings, engravings, sculpture
and paintings. Hogarth, Blake, Stubbs,
Constable and the Pre-Raphaelites are
particularly strongly represented. The Modern
Collection includes paintings and sculpture by
British artists born after 1860 and by foreign
artists from the Impressionists onwards. There is
also a large collection of prints, dating from the
mid-1960s to the present day. A complete
re-arrangement of the Collection opened in
January 1990, providing a chronological
sequence of galleries for visitors to follow. The
gallery now pursues a policy of rotating its
displays on a regular 9–12 months basis, to allow
a larger proportion of its collections to be seen
over a two-year period.

Tate Gallery, London.

Theatre Museum

Russell Street, London WC2E 7PA
☎ *071 836 7891*
Tues–Sun 11–7
Ⓒ 🛈 💻 ♿ ■

The Theatre Museum, in the former Flower
Market, at Covent Garden, is a branch of the
Victoria and Albert Museum. It illustrates major
British developments, events and personalities
in all the performing arts. The story is told with
the help of stage models, costumes, pottery,
prints, drawings, puppets, props and
memorabilia. There are also galleries for
temporary exhibitions, named in honour of Sir
John Gielgud and Sir Henry Irving. Paintings
are displayed in the Lower Foyer.

Among the museum's particular treasures are
the Spirit of Gaiety, a gilded angel rescued from
the top of the Gaiety Theatre; the elephant-
decorated boxes from the Palace Theatre,
Glasgow; and the Duke of York's Theatre box
office, from which entrance tickets to the
museum are sold.

Tower of London

Tower Hill, London EC3N 4AB
☎ *071 709 0765*
Mar–Oct, Mon–Sat 9.30–5; Sun 2–5. Nov–Feb,
*   Mon–Sat 9.30–4. Closed Jan 1, Good Fri, Dec*
*   24–26. Jewel House usually closed Jan.*
Ⓒ 🛈 💻

The Tower of London was begun by William the
Conqueror in 1078, as a royal palace and
fortress, on the site of a garrison fort constructed
soon after the Normans occupied London in
1066. During the next two centuries William's
great tower, the White Tower, was encircled by
two lines of walls and towers and a moat, the
work being completed in the 1280s, in the reign
of Edward I. As well as being a garrisoned
fortress and occasional royal residence the
Tower also housed the national arsenal, part of

the royal treasury including public records and Crown Jewels, and the royal mint. There was also a royal menagerie, as an adjunct of the palace. In the Tudor period the palace went out of use, and the Tower became increasingly employed as a state prison. In the 19th century, the arsenal, mint, public records and menagerie moved elsewhere.

The Tower is the most complete example of castle architecture in Britain, comprising one of the earliest Norman keeps in the country within a classic concentric fortress. Most of the castle buildings and defences remain, as well as relics of the Tower's use as a prison (notably, more than a hundred prisoners' graffiti as well as the instruments of torture and punishment); the Crown Jewels (displayed in the Waterloo Barracks); the Yeoman Warders who were established at the Tower in Henry VIII's reign; and the ravens, the origin of whose presence is one of the Tower's many mysteries.

Victoria and Albert Museum

Cromwell Road, London SW7 2RL
☎ 071 938 8500
Mon–Sat 10–5.50; Sun 2.30–5.50. Closed Jan 1, May Day Bank Holiday, Dec 24–27.
Ⓒ 🍴 🎧 ♿ ■

Created during the second half of the 19th century and partly as a consequence of the Great Exhibition of 1851, the Victoria and Albert Museum, located in South Kensington, contains the world's greatest collection of the decorative arts, brought together from five continents.

In several miles of galleries there are displays of paintings, jewellery, sculpture, costume, furniture, ceramics and armour. Prints, drawings, photographs and paintings are to be seen in a new wing, named after Sir Henry Cole, the museum's first Director.

Among the special attractions are the Victorian Cast Courts, the Fakes Gallery and the Constable Collection. The museum also houses the National Art Library.

The Wallace Collection

Hertford House, Manchester Square, London W1M 6BN ☎ 071 935 0687
Mon–Sat 10–5; Sun 2–5. Closed Jan 1, Good Fri, May Day Bank Holiday, Dec 24–26.
Ⓒ 🎧 ♿

Hertford House was built in the late 1770s for the 4th Duke of Manchester, as the family's town house. It was bought by the 2nd Marquess of Hertford in 1797. In the early 1870s Sir Richard Wallace, the illegitimate son of the 4th Marquess, made alterations to the building and arranged the Hertford family art collection in furnished rooms and in purpose-built galleries. His widow, Lady Wallace, bequeathed the house and the collection to the nation in 1897. Today it is displayed in 25 galleries on the ground and first floors of Hertford House.

The paintings, of the Italian, Dutch, Flemish, Spanish, French and English Schools,

include Rembrandt's *Titus, The Laughing Cavalier* by Frans Hals, and *Lady with a Fan* by Velázquez. There is French 18th-century furniture of high quality, and Sèvres porcelain, together with 16th-century Italian maiolica, Venetian glass, Limoges enamels, silver and silver-gilt and other medieval and Renaissance works of art. Among other important parts of the museum's collection are English and Continental miniatures and the paintings of Richard Parkes Bonington.

Westminster Abbey Treasury Exhibition

Westminster Abbey, London SW1P 3PA
☎ 071 222 5152
Daily 10.30–4.30 (last admission 4). Closed Good Fri and Dec 25 and when special services are in progress.
Ⓒ 🎧

The Exhibition, which has recently been completely re-designed, is in the Norman undercroft of the abbey, probably used by the monks as a common room. The displays are related to the history and architecture of Westminster Abbey. There is a remarkable collection of realistic wooden and wax funeral effigies, dating from the 14th to the early 19th centuries, the earliest being that of Edward III (d. 1377). Other exhibits include replica Coronation regalia and furniture, and copes and plate from the abbey and St Margaret's, Westminster.

An early tennis racquet workshop. Wimbledon Lawn Tennis Museum.

William Morris Gallery

*Water House, Lloyd Park, Forest Road, London
    E17 4PP   ☎ 081 527 5544 extn 4390
Tues–Sat 10–1, 2–5. Also 1st Sun of each month,
    10–12, 2–5. Closed public holidays.*

F ⬙ ᴀ

William Morris was born in Walthamstow, east
London in 1834. From 1848 to 1856 the Morris
family home was the Water House, an 18th-
century building in the same London district.
Since 1950 it has housed the William Morris
Gallery, with a collection illustrating the
achievements of the designer, craftsman, poet
and socialist.

The gallery's displays include wallpapers,
printed and woven textiles, embroideries, rugs
and carpets, furniture, stained glass and
ceramics designed by Morris and his associates.

Wimbledon Lawn Tennis Museum

*The All England Club, Church Road, London
    SW19 5AE   ☎ 081 946 6131
Tues–Sat 11–5; Sun 2–5. Closed public & Bank
    Holidays and Fri–Sun preceding Championships.*

C ⬙ ◼ ᴀ

In a building adjoining the centre court at
Wimbledon the museum illustrates the history
of lawn tennis, a British invention, first played
in 1870, and the games which preceded it.
Among the exhibits are trophies, clothing, an
early tennis racquet workshop, a Victorian
parlour furnished with tennis items, and an
1877 dressing room.

Recent acquisitions include a bronze figure
of a Victorian lady tennis player by François
Carot and a poster 2 metres high and 3 metres
wide by the Italian artist, Leopoldo Metlicovitz,
printed by G. Ricurdi and Co of Milan c.1900.

A new special exhibitions gallery is devoted
to temporary exhibitions. The first was 'Love
All – The Romance of Tennis' and the second
featured the museum's growing collection of
Continental tennis posters, 1900–39.

Longton

Gladstone Pottery

*Uttoxeter Road, Longton, Stoke-on-Trent,
    Staffordshire, ST3 1PQ   ☎ 0782 319232
Mar–Oct, Mon–Sat 10–5; Sun 2–5. Nov–Feb,
    Tues–Sat 10–5. Closed Dec 25.*

C ⬙ ▆ ᴀ

The museum is set in a Victorian potbank or
pottery factory. The buildings consist of four
bottle ovens surrounded by workshops and an
engine house. The central courtyard is cobbled.
The bottle ovens are among the very few still
remaining of what was once a characteristic
feature of the Potteries.

Gladstone tells the story of the British
pottery industry, by means of both displays and
workshop demonstrations. Specialised galleries
illustrate the history of the industry in
Staffordshire, social history, tiles and tile-
making, sanitary ware, colour and decoration.

Gladstone Pottery, Longton.

Lower Broadheath

Elgar's Birthplace

*Crown East Lane, Lower Broadheath, Worcester,
    Hereford and Worcester, WR2 6RH
    ☎ 090566 334
Mid Feb–Apr & Oct–mid Jan, Thurs–Tues 1.30–
    4.30. May–Sept, Thurs–Tues 10.30–6.*

C ⬙ ᴀ

The early 19th-century cottage in which Edward
Elgar was born in 1857 now contains a
collection of material illustrating the life and
work of the composer, including manuscripts,
scores, concert programmes, ceremonial robes
and press-cuttings. The photographs range from
family snapshot albums to records of formal and
ceremonial occasions. Elgar's desk has been
arranged by his daughter in the way her mother
prepared it when her father was composing.

Macclesfield

Paradise Mill

*Old Park Lane, Macclesfield, Cheshire, SK11 6TJ
    ☎ 0625 618228
Tues–Sun 1–5. Open Bank Holiday Mon. Closed
    Jan 1, Good Fri, Dec 24–26. Parties mornings
    and evenings by appt.*

C ⬙ ⬙

Silk handloom weaving began in Macclesfield in
the 1750s. Paradise Mill, a typical Victorian silk
mill, houses the last handloom business in the
town. It closed in 1981. Twenty-six of the
Jacquard looms remain in their original setting
and have been restored to allow the skills of a
dying craft to be demonstrated to visitors. There
are supporting exhibitions illustrating working
conditions and telling the story of the family
firm, Cartwright & Sheldon which ran the mill.
Yarn preparation machinery and a design and

card-cutting room have been assembled, and the
Manager's Office has been reconstructed as it
was in the 1930s. Guides conduct parties on the
Silk Trail and Town Trails by arrangement.

The Silk Museum

Macclesfield Heritage Centre, Roe Street,
Macclesfield, Cheshire, SK11 6UT
☎ *0625 613210*
Tues–Sat 11–5; Sun 1–5. Open Bank Holidays.
Closed Jan 1, Good Fri, Dec 24–26.
Ⓒ ▮ ☕ ♿

The Silk Museum is housed in the Heritage
Centre, the former Macclesfield Sunday School,
built in 1813 by public subscription. At the peak
of its activity it registered 2,500 pupils.

The museum describes the history of the silk
industry in Macclesfield from its origins to the
present day. An audio-visual programme
introduces the visitor to the social and
economic conditions in the town over two
centuries. There are also displays illustrating the
technology, design and fashion related to silk. A
separate exhibition describes the history of the
Sunday School building in relation to the
National Sunday School movement.

Maidstone

Tyrwhitt-Drake Museum of Carriages

Mill Street, Maidstone, Kent, ME15 6YE
☎ *0622 54497*
Jan–Dec, Mon–Sat 10–1, 2–5; April–Sept, Sun
2–5; Bank Holiday 11–5.
Ⓕ ⊘

The collection, formed by Sir Garrard Tyrwhitt-
Drake, 12 times Mayor of Maidstone, is housed
in the old stables of the Archbishop's Palace.
The stables are 45 metres long and were built
c.1390 to provide accommodaton for the
numerous carts, horses and retainers required by
the Archbishops of Canterbury on their
journeys between Canterbury and Lambeth.

The 50 vehicles in the collection date from
1675, but most of them were made during the
19th-century. All are in their original,
unrestored condition. There are also sedan
chairs, sleighs and handcarts. Exhibits of
particular interest include a dress landau built by
Hooper for Queen Victoria c.1870, George III's
travelling chariot of c.1780, and a hansom cab
owned by Sir H. M. Stanley. The museum also
has the carriage made in 1840 for the Earl of
Moray to use on his honeymoon. The marriage
did not take place and the carriage was
consequently never used.

Sir Garrard Tyrwhitt-Drake was a horse
enthusiast and drove his own gig for local
transport until 1926. Brought up in the days
when British carriages, horses and general
equipment were the finest in the world, he was
afraid that the younger generation would grow
up knowing nothing of this form of transport.
'In a very few years,' he said, 'the only examples
in existence will be in a museum such as this.'

Malvern

Malvern Museum

Abbey Gateway, Abbey Road, Malvern, Hereford
and Worcester   ☎ *0684 567811*
Easter–Oct, daily 10.30–5 ex Wed. Open Wed
during school summer holidays.
Ⓒ ⊘

The museum is housed in one of the two
surviving buildings of Malvern's Benedictine
monastery, founded in 1085, the other being
the priory church. Parts of the gatehouse date
from the late 15th century, since when it has
been enlarged and restored several times.

The collections reflect the history of the
town from medieval times to the present day. Of
particular interest are the exhibits relating to
the monastery, the Malvern Water cure, the
Malvern Festival, and the development of radar
at the Royal Signals and Radar Establishment.

Manchester

Gallery of English Costume

Platt Hall, Platt Fields, Rusholme, Manchester,
M14 5LL   ☎ *061 224 5217*
Mon, Wed–Sat 10–6; Sun 2–6. Nov–Feb closes 4.
Ⓕ ⊘ 🍴

Platt Hall is two miles south of Manchester. It
was built in 1762–4 as the home of a textile
manufacturer and is surrounded by a large park.
The gallery was opened in 1947, to house the
collection formed by Dr C. Willett
Cunnington, and has since been developed into
one of the largest costume museums in Britain,
reflecting the dress of the 17th to 20th
centuries. From the beginning, the aim has been
to include items which illustrate the clothing of
society as a whole.

The library of some 180,000 items contains
not only modern costume books, but also rare
works from the 18th and 19th centuries, such as
magazines and etiquette books, as well as a large
number of fashion plates and photographs.

18th-century gentleman's waistcoat,
embroidered with silk threads and spangles.
Gallery of English Costume, Manchester.

Manchester City Art Gallery

Mosley Street, Manchester, M2 3JL
☎ 061 236 9422
Mon–Sat 10–6; Sun 2–6. Closed Jan 1, Good Fri, Dec 25, 26.
F ⓘ ⌖

The gallery, designed by Charles Barry, was opened in 1823. It has recently been re-decorated and stencilled in neo-classical and Victorian styles. The entrance hall contains casts of the Parthenon frieze. The important collections of British and European paintings, drawings and prints include works by Stubbs, Gainsborough, Turner, Duccio and Canaletto. The gallery has a celebrated collection of Pre-Raphaelite and high Victorian paintings. The decorative arts are represented by collections of ceramics, glass, silver and furniture.

Manchester Jewish Museum

190 Cheetham Hill Road, Manchester, M8 8LW
☎ 061 834 8979 and 061 832 7353
Mon–Thurs 10.30–4; Sun 10.30–5. Closed Jewish Holidays.
C ⓘ ■ ⌖

The museum is in a former Spanish and Portuguese synagogue, a Grade II listed building, dating from 1874. Since the movement of the Jewish population away from this area of earliest settlement made the synagogue redundant, it has been completely restored and opened as a museum in 1984. The central part of the synagogue has been retained intact, to provide an introduction to Jewish religious customs. The former succah provides a location for temporary exhibitions, which change at approximately three-monthly intervals.

The exhibition in the former Ladies Gallery shows the evolution of Manchester Jewry against the background of major developments in Anglo-Jewish history. It re-creates the experience of the Jewish community by means of objects, photographs and tape-recorded interviews. The display is enhanced by detailed reconstructions of the home life, work, worship and leisure of Jews drawn to Manchester from every part of the world.

Museum of Science and Industry

Liverpool Road Station, Liverpool Road, Castlefield, Manchester, M3 4JP
☎ 061 832 2244
Daily 10–5 (last admission 4.30). Closed Dec 23–25.
C ⓘ ⌹ ⓭ ■ ⌖

The museum occupies five historic buildings: the world's oldest passenger railway station; the oldest railway warehouse in the world; a railway freight shed of the 1850s; a fireproof warehouse of c.1880; and an iron-framed Victorian market-hall. The aim of the museum is to portray the rôle played by North-West England in the development of science and industry and to present the story of Greater Manchester itself,

the world's first industrial conurbation.

A strong emphasis is placed on restoring exhibits to fully operating condition and on regularly demonstrating them. The Power Hall contains an extensive display of mill engines, all demonstrated with steam every afternoon. Internal combustion engines, road vehicles and railway locomotives also illustrate the importance of Manchester in the production of power plant. The Warehouse Exhibition presents exhibits of textile machinery and printing. The Electricity Gallery tells the story of the generation, distribution and use of electricity from its beginnings to the present day. It also contains two special exhibitions, one on computers, the other 'Energy for the Future'. There is also a special display, 'Microscopes in Manchester', and an exhibition and audio-visual presentation on the Liverpool and Manchester Railway. The Air and Space Gallery shows the history of manned flight and space exploration, and contains historic aircraft.

The museum's restoration workshop is open to visitors and contains a display of machine tools, regularly demonstrated. Working locomotives, including the replica 1830 'Planet' class Stephenson locomotive, operate on tracks within the museum site.

Whitworth Art Gallery

The University, Oxford Road, Manchester, M15 6ER   ☎ 061 273 4865
Mon–Wed, Fri, Sat 10–5; Thurs 10–9. Closed Good Friday and Christmas period.
F ⓘ ⌹ ⓭ ■ ⌖

The gallery, founded in 1889, resulted from a legacy by the Manchester engineer and machine-tool manufacturer Sir Joseph Whitworth. It now contains one of the world's greatest collections of English watercolours, as well as the finest collection of European drawings, prints and engravings in the north of England. There are important sections devoted to British, European and Oriental textiles, historic wallpapers, and 20th-century British art.

Floral dado paper, *c.* 1880. Whitworth Art Gallery, Manchester.

Sir Walter Scott's study, Abbotsford House, Melrose.

Melrose

Abbotsford House

Melrose, Roxburghshire, TD6 8BQ
☎ *0896 2043*
Apr–Oct, Mon–Sat 10–5; Sun 2–5.
Ⓒ ✎ 🍽 ♿ ♠

Abbotsford, three miles from Melrose on the B6360, was the home of the novelist, Sir Walter Scott, from 1812 until his death in 1832. It is still lived in by his descendants. Visitors can see his study, library, drawing room and entrance hall and the dining room in which he died, together with his collection of historic relics, especially armour and weapons. The exhibits include Rob Roy's gun, a lock of Bonnie Prince Charlie's hair, and what are claimed to be the keys of Lochleven Castle, thrown into the loch after Queen Mary's escape. An item of special interest is the toadstone amulet, set in silver, which belonged to Sir Walter's mother. Toadstone was supposed to be a sovereign charm against fairies and, on this account, mothers used to hang pieces of it around the necks of their new-born babies.

Many interesting people came to stay at Abbotsford as guests of Sir Walter, among whom were Maria Edgeworth, William Wordsworth, Thomas Moore and Washington Irving.

Mickley

Cherryburn

Mickley, Stocksfield, Northumberland, NE43 7DB
☎ *0661 843276*
Easter–Christmas, Tues–Sun 10–5; Christmas–Easter, Fri–Sun 10–4.
Ⓒ 🏺 🍽 ♿ ♠

The engraver and naturalist, Thomas Bewick, was born in the cottage at Cherryburn, overlooking the Tyne valley, in 1753. He was apprenticed to an engraver in Newcastle and later set up his own business in the city. The larger house at Cherryburn was built by the family of Bewick's brother, William. The whole complex now forms the Bewick Museum, with an exhibition of his work including engravings made for 18th-century children's books and copies of his own famous publications such as *British Birds* and *Quadrupeds*. There is a printing house where demonstrations are given to show how books were printed in Bewick's time using his wood engravings. The farmyard is stocked with animals and poultry representative of the breeds which were here during Thomas Bewick's childhood.

Middle Claydon

Florence Nightingale Museum

Claydon House, Middle Claydon, nr Aylesbury, Buckinghamshire, MK18 2EY
☎ *029673 349/693*
Late Mar–Oct, Sat–Wed 2–6. Bank Holiday Mon 1–6. Closed Thurs, Fri.
Ⓒ 🍽 ♠

Claydon House, formerly the home of the Verney family, now belongs to the National Trust. An 18th-century house, it contains splendid state rooms with elaborate rococo decorations. The nursing pioneer, Florence Nightingale, frequently visited Claydon to stay with her sister, Lady Verney, and the bedroom she used can be seen, with its Victorian furnishings and woodwork grained to resemble bamboo. In the museum room, one case contains objects associated with her and with the Crimean War, during which she became a celebrated public figure. Photographs taken after her return from Scutari show how thin and frail she had become as a result of the strain of organising the hospital there.

Middlesbrough

Captain Cook's Birthplace

Stewart Park, Marton, Middlesbrough, Cleveland
☎ *0642 311211*
Daily 10–6 (summer); 10–4 (winter). Closed Jan 1, Dec 25, 26.
Ⓒ 🏺 🍽 ♿ ♠

The museum is in a modern building in the grounds of Stewart Park, close to the granite vase which marks the site of the cottage where James Cook was born in 1728. The displays follow the life of Cook from the time of his birth at Marton to the streets of Staithes, where he worked as a shop apprentice and to the quayside at Whitby. There is a reconstruction of the below-deck accommodation in his famous ship, the *Endeavour*, and galleries illustrating each place he visited until his death in Hawaii in 1779. The exhibits include ethnographical material from the countries he explored during his voyages.

Milford

Shugborough

Milford, nr Stafford, ST17 0BX ☎ *0889 881388*
End Mar–end Oct, daily 11–5; end Oct–late Dec,
daily 11–4 (Booked parties from 10.30 on
weekdays) Jan 2–end Mar, Mon–Fri 10.30–4
(Phone for weekend arrangements. Booked
parties only). Closed Christmas–Jan 1.
Ⓒ ♿ 🖵 ♨ ⌂

Shugborough has been the home of the Anson
family since 1624. The central block of the
present house was built in 1693 and extensions
and remodelling were carried out in 1745–58
and between 1790 and 1806. Most of the
original contents were sold in 1842 to meet the
debts of the 1st Earl of Lichfield. The house was
given by the Treasury to the National Trust in
1960 in lieu of death duties.

Shugborough contains a fine collection of
18th-century English and French furniture,
ceramics, paintings and silver, much of which
was acquired during the 19th century by the 2nd
Earl. Among the special features are furniture by
Gillow of Lancaster, animal studies by Sir Edwin
Landseer, who was a friend of the Ansons,
watercolours of the house and park, a large
collection of paintings of horses and foxhounds,
and many family portraits.

The Anson Room contains a large number
of relics and mementoes of Admiral Lord Anson
(1697–1762), the circumnavigator, together
with prints of shops and naval engagements
associated with his long career.

Shugborough Farm

Shugborough Estate, Milford nr Stafford,
ST17 0XB ☎ *0889 881388*
Mid Mar–mid Oct, Tues–Fri & Bank Holiday
Mon 10.30–5.30; Sat, Sun 2–5.30. Open
Good Fri. Mid Oct–mid Mar, Tues–Fri
10.30–4.30; 1st & 3rd Sun of each month
2–4.30.
Ⓒ ♿ 🖵 ♿ ⌂

The complex of farm buildings, completed in
1805, was originally designed as the home farm
of the Shugborough estate, but was tenanted
since the mid 19th century. In 1975 it was taken
over by the Staffordshire Museum Service as the
home of its agricultural collection and its
developing herds of local breeds of farm
livestock.

The displays illustrate the agricultural
history of Staffordshire and the Shugborough
estate, with special features on the story of
ploughing and cultivation, barn machinery, the
transition from horses to tractors, and food
production by cottagers. The restored Mill
Block has been developed as a working corn
mill, driven by a waterwheel, and also contains
displays on milling and agriculture. The
farmhouse is being restored as a 19th-century
farm steward's house. The living conditions of
the cottagers and tenant farmers of the 18th and
19th centuries are also illustrated.

The 'crowd scene' from the Rothbury Cross,
early 9th-century. Museum of Antiquities,
Newcastle upon Tyne.

Staffordshire County Museum

Shugborough Estate, Milford, nr Stafford,
ST17 0XB ☎ *0889 881388*
Mid Mar–mid Oct, Tues–Fri & Bank Holiday
Mon 10.30–5.30; Sat, Sun 2–5.30. Open
Good Fri. Mid Oct–mid Mar, Tues–Fri
10.30–4.30; 1st & 3rd Sun of each month
2–4.30.
Ⓒ ♿ 🖵

Shugborough is six miles east of Stafford. The
museum, in the 18th-century service block of
the Hall, has displays covering the social and
agricultural history of rural Staffordshire. The
stables, laundry, ironing room, brewhouse and
coachhouse have been restored almost to their
18th-century condition, with their original
equipment. The collection of horse-drawn
vehicles ranges from family coaches and
carriages to farm carts. The smithy and living-
room of a Mayfield blacksmith, Charles
Woodward, who died in 1974, have been
reconstructed in two rooms of the stable yard.
There are also reconstructions of a tailor's shop
and a village general stores.

There is a costume gallery, where the items
date from the late 18th to the mid 19th
centuries. A reconstructed schoolroom uses
furniture and fittings from a number of
Staffordshire schools to re-create the
atmosphere of a classroom early this century.
The toy gallery displays 18th–early-20th-
century children's toys, games and amusements.

Morpeth

Morpeth Chantry Bagpipe Museum

Bridge Street, Morpeth, Northumberland,
NE61 1PJ ☎ *0670 519466*
Jan–Feb, Mon–Sat 10–4. Mar–Dec, Mon–Sat
9.30–5.30. Open Bank Holidays.
Ⓒ ♿ ♿

The chantry was built in the 13th century to
serve both as a religious building and a Grammar
School. It was later used as a mineral water
factory and a ladies' lavatory. In 1965 Morpeth
Antiquarian Society began using part of it as a

museum and subsequently the ground floor was occupied by the Northumbrian Craft Centre and the local Tourist Information Centre, while the Bagpipe Museum was installed upstairs.

The extensive collection includes Northumbrian small-pipes, Scottish bagpipes, Border half-long bagpipes, Irish Union pipes and many types of foreign bagpipe as well as replica models of historical instruments.

Nether Stowey

Coleridge Cottage

*35 Lime Street, Nether Stowey, Bridgwater,
   Somerset, TA5 1NQ*   ☎ *0278 732662*
Apr–Sept, Tues–Thurs, Sun 2–5.
Ⓒ ✎ ⌨

The poet and essayist, Samuel Taylor Coleridge (1772–1834) and his wife, with their infant son, Hartley, moved to the cottage in December 1796 and stayed for three years. During part of this time, the poet, William Wordsworth and his sister, Dorothy, were living nearby at Alfoxden and the two families saw each other nearly every day. The building was much altered during the 19th century. It passed into the possession of the National Trust in 1909, as one of the Trust's first properties, and great efforts have been made to reproduce something of the atmosphere of the cottage as it was during the Coleridges' tenancy.

Newcastle upon Tyne

Laing Art Gallery

Higham Place, Newcastle upon Tyne, NE1 8AG
   ☎ *091 232 7734/6989*
*Mon–Fri 10–5.30; Sat 10–4.30; Sun 2.30–5.30.
   Closed Jan 1, Good Fri, Dec 25, 26.*
Ⓕ ✎ ♿ ■ ⌨

One of the special features of the gallery is its collection of paintings by the early-19th-century Northumberland artist, John Martin. There are also displays of British and Tyneside silver, pottery and glass, including 18th-century enamelled glass by William Beilby of Newcastle, and changing exhibitions of items from the large collection of costumes and accessories and of British watercolours. Two stained glass windows by Edward Burne-Jones are also on show.

The four first floor galleries devoted to British paintings and sculpture include works by Reynolds, Landseer and Burne-Jones and, from the present century, Stanley Spencer and Henry Moore.

Museum of Antiquities

*The Quadrangle, The University, Newcastle upon
   Tyne, NE1 7RU*   ☎ *091 222 7844*
*Mon–Sat 10–5. Closed Jan 1, Good Fri, Dec
   24–26.*
Ⓕ ▮ ⌨

This is the principal museum for Hadrian's Wall. It contains scale models, life-size figures of

Germania (To the Brothel), 1987, by R.B. Kitaj. Laing Art Gallery, Newcastle upon Tyne.

Roman soldiers and a reconstruction of a Temple of Mithras. The collections of archaeological finds from sites in the region cover the prehistoric, Roman, Anglo-Saxon and medieval periods, from about 6000 BC to AD 1600.

Museum of Science and Engineering

*Blandford House, West Blandford Street,
   Newcastle upon Tyne, NE1 4JA*
   ☎ *091 232 6789*
*Mon–Fri 10–5.30; Sat 10–4.30. Closed Jan 1,
   Good Fri, Dec 25, 26.*
Ⓕ ▮ 💻 ♿ ⌨

The magnificent early-19th-century building which houses the museum was formerly the headquarters of the Co-operative Wholesale Society. The displays relate to mechanical and electrical engineering, mining, shipbuilding, science and a wide range of manufacturing industries, with special reference to North-East England. There is also a maritime collection and a large gallery with exhibits illustrating the history and development of motive power. The recently opened section, Pioneers of Tyneside Industry, presents the achievements of Parsons, Stephenson, Swan and other notable figures of the 19th and early 20th centuries.

Newhaven

Newhaven Military Museum

The Fort, Newhaven, East Sussex, BN9 9DL
   ☎ *0273 517622*
*Easter–Oct, Wed–Sun and Bank Holiday 10.30–6
   (last admission 5). Open daily during school
   summer holidays.*
Ⓒ ▮ 💻 ♿ ⌨

Constructed in 1862, the fort, set deep in the headland, commands a wide field of fire over Seaford Bay and the approaches to Newhaven Harbour. It comprises a complex of magazines, barrack rooms, underground passageways, tunnels and galleries around a central parade ground. Since 1981, it has been restored to its 1870 condition. Graphic display panels and an audio-visual presentation, in part of the former officers' quarters, tell the story of the fort from the time of its construction to the present day. The museum, in the former underground magazine for the Eastern Battery, illustrates the rôle of Newhaven Fort in coastal defence, with special reference to the 1942 Dieppe raid and to both military and civilian life in two World Wars.

Newmarket

National Horseracing Museum

99 High Street, Newmarket, Suffolk, CB8 8JL
    ☎ 0638 667333
Easter–early Dec, Tues–Sat 10–5; Sun 2–5.
    Closed Mon, ex Aug, and Bank Holiday Mon.
ⓒ ♿ 🖥 ♿ ♨

The museum, established in 1983 in Newmarket's elegant early-19th-century Subscription Rooms, illustrates the history of racing in Britain since the time of Charles II. The displays cover racehorse breeding, outstanding horses, great jockeys and famous owners and trainers, with a special section devoted to bookmakers and betting. Other parts of the collection include trophies, saddles, whips, racing colours, and sporting paintings and prints.

Reconstruction of a jockeys' weighing-room. National Horseracing Museum, Newmarket.

Newport (Isle of Wight)

Carisbrooke Castle Museum

Carisbrooke Castle, Newport, Isle of Wight,
    PO30 1XY   ☎ 0983 523112
Good Fri–Sept, daily 10–6; Oct–Maundy Thurs,
    daily 10–4. Closed Jan 1, Dec 24–26.
ⓒ ♿ 🖥 ♨

The museum is in the castle's former Governor's Lodge, the home of Queen Victoria's youngest daughter, Beatrice, until her death in 1944. The main displays relate to various aspects of the history of the Isle of Wight and to the history of the castle. The upper gallery contains a fine 1602 chamber organ and in the lower gallery there is a collection of Stuart relics, especially material connected with Charles I, who was imprisoned here in 1647–8 before his execution. Another section of the museum is devoted to memorabilia of Alfred, Lord Tennyson, including items used by him when he lived on the Isle of Wight. A favourite exhibit in the castle is a well-preserved donkey-wheel which the resident donkeys still tread to raise water from the castle's 700-year-old well.

Newtongrange

Scottish Mining Museum

Lady Victoria Colliery, Newtongrange, Midlothian,
    EH22 7QN   ☎ 031 663 7519
Tues–Fri 10–4; Sat, Sun 12–5.
ⓒ ♿ 🖥 ♿ ♨

The museum is at the end of the Coal Heritage Trail, which begins at Prestongrange, the Scottish Mining Museum's other site. Along the Trail are information boards, which tell the story of 800 years of coalmining in Scotland.

At Newtongrange, the museum is housed in a Victorian colliery building, where a series of tableaux re-create the atmosphere of the village and describe the construction and operation of the Lady Victoria Colliery. At the pithead visitors can see the Grant Ritchie steam winding engine, erected in 1895.

Newtonmore

Clan Macpherson House

Newtonmore, Inverness-shire   ☎ 05403 332
May–Sept, Mon–Sat 10–5.30; Sun 2.30–5.30.
Ⓕ ♿ ♨

The house displays historical relics of the Clan Macpherson and its relations with neighbouring clans. These include mementoes of the 'Forty-five' and other Highland battles; the Black Chanter which is reputed to have fallen from heaven at the Battle of North Inch of Perth; and the Green Banner, which ensured that the Clan never lost a battle when it was present on the battlefield. Among other interesting exhibits is the fiddle on which James Macpherson played the Rant before he was illegally hanged at Banff.

Newtown

Newtown Textile Museum

5–7 Commercial Street, Newtown, Powys,
SY16 2BL ☎ *0686 26243*
Apr–Oct, Tues–Sat 2–4.30. Other times by appt.
F ⚓

At the end of the 18th century Newtown began to develop as an important centre of the woollen industry, producing high-quality flannel on hand-looms. After a period of decline in the previous two decades, the introduction of steam-driven machinery brought about a temporary revival in the 1860s, but the local manufacturers failed to meet the competition from other areas of Britain, especially Yorkshire, and the mills gradually shut down, the last in 1935.

In 1967 a museum illustrating the story of the local woollen industry was opened in the top floors of an 18th-century building which, in the days of the handloom weavers, was half dwelling-house, half workshop. There are also exhibits relating to the history of the local railways and canal.

Northampton

Northampton Museum and Art Gallery

Guildhall Road, Northampton, NN1 1DP
☎ *0604 39415*
Mon–Sat 10–5. Late night Thurs until 8.
F ▮

The museum is particularly distinguished by possessing the largest historical collection of boots and shoes and shoe-making machinery in the world, with items ranging from Cromwellian boots to Queen Victoria's wedding shoes. There are also displays of shoemaker's tools and a reconstruction of a mid 19th-century cobbler's shop. The Northamptonshire Room displays selections from the museum's collections of glass and pottery and archaeological material from sites in the county, including a bust thought to be of the Roman emperor, Lucius Verus, found during ironstone quarrying at Duston, and Saxon jewellery from cemeteries at Brixworth and Holdenby.

The art gallery contains 15th–18th-century Italian paintings, a collection of works by 18th–20th-century British artists, including Crome, Morland, Sickert and John Nash, and Chinese and English ceramics.

Northleach

Cotswold Countryside Collection

Northleach, Gloucestershire, GL54 3JH
☎ *0451 60715*
Apr–Oct, Mon–Sat 10–5.30; Sun 2–5.30.
C ▮ ⬛ ♨ ⚅ ■ ⚓

The museum is in buildings of the 1791 House of Correction, one of a series of country prisons which led the field in prison reform. The former prison atmosphere is re-created in the surviving cell block and court room.

The Countryside Collection illustrates the social and agricultural history of the Gloucestershre countryside in the days of horses. There is an exceptionally good collection of farm wagons, together with horse-drawn implements and hand-tools. Panel displays illustrate and explain the farming seasons and the processes involved in farm work. The tasks of the carter, shepherd and wheelwright are shown, together with the domestic skills of the laundry and dairymaid.

Northwich

Salt Museum

162 London Road, Northwich, Cheshire,
CW9 8AB ☎ *0606 41331*
Easter–June & Sept, Tues–Sun & Bank Holiday
Mon 2–5. July–Aug, Tues–Sat 10–5; Sun
2–5. Oct–Easter, Tues–Sun 2–5. Closed Good
Fri, Dec 24–26.
C ✐ ⚓

The Salt Museum is housed in the district's former workhouse, a listed building which dates from 1837.

The displays tell the story of salt-making in Cheshire from Roman times to the present day. Models, photographs, maps, diagrams and objects are used to show where salt is found and how it is extracted, transported and used. There are explanations of the vacuum process of salt production as well as Cheshire's traditional open-pan method, which evaporates brine. The displays provide information on the working environment in the saltworks, living conditions in the salt towns, Trade Unions, Friendly Societies, and the leading 19th-century saltworks proprietors.

Norwich

Bridewell Museum

Bridewell Alley, St Andrew's Street, Norwich,
NR2 1AQ ☎ *0606 611277 extn 298*
Mon–Sat 10–5. Closed Good Fri, Dec 23–26.
C ✐ ⚓

The museum building was formerly a prison. Its knapped flint side wall is said to be the best in the country. The last room on the visitor's route through the museum features Norfolk-made clocks, and other displays illustrate local markets, the food industries, ironfounding and engineering, brewing and printing. Sections are devoted to the once-important Norwich textile industry and to shoe manufacturing. There is a well-stocked period pharmacist's shop.

Castle Museum

Norwich, NR1 3JU ☎ *0603 222222*
Mon–Sat 10–5; Sun 2–5. Closed Jan 1, Good Fri,
Christmas period.
C ▮ ⬛

The castle keep, constructed between 1100 and 1130, is the oldest part of the museum building. It contains displays of medieval material and an exhibition illustrating the links between Norfolk and Europe, which have existed since prehistoric times. The themes covered in the exhibition range from trade and commerce to tourism, agriculture and horticulture.

The exhibits elsewhere in the museum cover the ecology and natural history of Norfolk, archaeology and social history. There are also collections of paintings and watercolours, especially by artists of the Norwich School, Norwich silver and ceramics. The museum has the finest public collection of Lowestoft porcelain in the world, and houses a highly important collection of over 2,600 British ceramic teapots of the 18th and 19th centuries.

Sainsbury Centre for Visual Arts

University of East Anglia, Norwich NR4 7TJ
☎ 0603 56060/56161 extn 2470
Daily 12–5 (ex Mon)
C ⓘ ⚏ ⓗ ■

The Sainsbury Centre was opened in 1978, and houses the Robert and Lisa Sainsbury Collection and the University of East Anglia Art History Sector. The collection comprises objects and paintings from many cultures, with strong holdings of Oceanic, African, native North American and Pre-Columbian Art, as well as works by 20th-century artists. Moore, Epstein, Giacometti and John Davies are each represented by a number of pieces.

The building, designed by Foster Associates, is of considerable technical interest.

Strangers Hall

Charing Cross, Norwich, NR2 4AL
☎ 0603 667229
Mon–Sat 10–5. Closed Jan 1, Good Fri, Dec 23–26.
C ⚏

Strangers Hall is a medieval merchant's house, with a 14th-century vaulted undercroft and a 16th-century great hall, with a minstrel's gallery. It now houses a museum of urban life,

Regency music room, Strangers Hall, Norwich.

containing rooms furnished in the style of various periods form the 16th century onwards. Among the exhibits are a set of 15th-century tapestries, a chandelier of 18th-century Irish glass, Norwich shop signs, costumes and toys. The Lord Mayor's coach is also kept here.

Nottingham

Canal Museum

Canal Street, Nottingham, NG1 7ET
☎ 0602 598835
Apr–Sept, Wed–Sat 10–12, 1–5.45; Sun 1–5.45. Oct–Mar, Wed, Thurs, Sat 10–12, 1–5; Sun 1–5.
F ⚏ ⚓

The museum is in a canal warehouse, built in the 1890s. Inside the building is the former canal basin. The displays show the history of the River Trent and its local tributaries and the associated canal system. Among the themes illustrated are the natural environment, archaeological evidence, transport on the waterways, bridges, ferries and floods. Two narrow-boats are maintained in working order.

Castle Museum

Nottingham, NG1 6EL   ☎ 0602 483504
Apr–Sept, daily 10–5.45. Oct–Mar, daily 10–4.45. Closed Dec 25. Admission charge Sun, Bank Holidays.
F ⓘ ⚏ ⓗ ■ ⚓

The castle is a 17th-century mansion built for the Dukes of Newcastle on the site of a medieval royal castle. Fragments of the old castle survive in the grounds, the most important being the outer bailey gatehouse, dating from 1251–5. There are collections of ceramics, silver, glass and medieval Nottingham alabaster carvings. The paintings in the art gallery include works by the Nottingham-born artists, R. P. Bonington and Thomas and Paul Sandby.

The History of Nottingham Gallery shows a selection of the museum's extensive collections of archaeological and historical material relating to the area.

Museum of Costume and Textiles

43–51 Castle Gate, Nottingham, NG1 6AF
☎ 0602 483504
Daily 10–5. Closed Dec 25.
F ⚏ ⚓

The museum is in a row of elegant terrace houses, built in 1788. It contains the Lord Middleton collection of 17th-century costume, the 1632 Eyre map tapestries of Nottinghamshire, and period rooms displaying costume from the mid-18th-century to 1960. The very fine lace collections trace the development of local lace from the earliest hand-made pieces to the important rôle played by Nottingham in the history of machine-made lace. There are also collections of printed, woven and knitted textiles.

Nottingham Industrial Museum

Courtyard Buildings, Wollaton Park, Nottingham,
*   NG8 2AE*   ☎ *0602 284602*
Apr–Sept, Mon–Sat 10–6; Sun 2–6. Oct–Mar,
*   Thurs, Sat 10–4.30; Sun 1.30–4.30. Closed*
*   Dec 25. Admission charge Sun, Bank Holidays.*
Ⓕ 🎫 ♿ ♨

The museum is in the 18th-century stables,
carriage house and service buildings of the
Wollaton estate. It presents the history of
Nottingham's industries, including machine
lace, hosiery, pharmaceuticals, printing,
engineering, tobacco and bicycles. There is a
beam pumping engine and a collection of other
prime movers. One of the most popular exhibits
is a pair of working steam ploughing-engines.
The transport collection includes horse-drawn
carriages, motorcycles and cars.

Olney

Cowper and Newton Museum

Orchard Side, Market Place, Olney,
*   Buckinghamshire, MK46 4AJ*
*   ☎ 0234 711516*
Easter–May & Oct, Tues–Sat 10–12, 2–5. June–
*   Sept, Tues–Sat 10–12, 2–5; Sun 2.30–5.*
*   Nov–Easter, Tues–Sat 2–4. Open Bank*
*   Holiday Mon.*
Ⓒ 🗢 ♨

Orchard Side is the house in which William
Cowper, the poet and hymn-writer, lived and
entertained between 1768 and 1786, in order to
be near his friend, the Rev. John Newton,
author of *Amazing Grace* and other well-known
hymns. The museum contains memorabilia of
both Cowper and Newton, together with a
specialist Cowper library and manuscript
collection. There is also a local collection, the
contents of which range from geological
specimens to material relating to the trades of
the town. Lace-making, once an important
cottage industry here, is particularly featured.

Omagh

Ulster-American Folk Park

Camphill, Omagh, Co Tyrone, Northern Ireland,
*   BT78 5QY*   ☎ *0662 243292/243293*
Easter–early Sept, Mon–Sat 11–6.30; Sun and
*   public holidays 11.30–7. Mid Sept–Easter,*
*   Mon–Fri ex public holidays 10.30–5.*
Ⓒ 🎫 🖴 ♿ ♨

The Folk Park is an outdoor museum of
emigration, situated four miles north of Omagh,
on the A5 to Newtownstewart and
Londonderry.

It contains traditional buildings, displaying
examples of Ulster and American vernacular
buildings. It is laid out in an Old World Area
and a New World Area, illustrating the history
of 18th- and 19th-century emigration from
Ulster to North America. Each area contains
examples of the traditional dwelling houses,
farm buildings and workshops that the emigrants

**Blacksmith's forge. Ulster-American Folk
Park, Omagh.**

would have been familiar with on both sides of
the Atlantic. The Folk Park's collection of
furniture, kitchen equipment, farm implements
and craftsmen's tools are displayed in the
buildings.

A new emigration complex contains a street
of 19th-century shops and a dockside section of
an Ulster port with reconstructed buildings from
Belfast and Derry and a full-scale replica of an
early-19th-century emigrant ship. In a large
indoor gallery there are displays illustrating
emigrant life. Traditional crafts are demonstated
regularly in the outdoor museum and special
displays of seasonal festivals and customs such as
Hallowe'en, Harvest Home and Christmas
Mumming are also organised.

Oxford

Ashmolean Museum

Beaumont Street, Oxford, OX1 2PH
*   ☎ 0865 278000*
Tues–Sat 10–4; Sun 2–4; most Bank Holiday Mon
*   2–5. Closed Good Fri–Easter Sun, St Giles'*
*   Fair (Mon/Tues following 1st Sun in Sept) &*
*   Christmas/New Year period*
Ⓕ 🗢 ♨

The Ashmolean was designed by C.R.
Cockerell and completed in 1845. The southern
front is one of the finest neo-Grecian buildings
in Britain. It is the private museum of the
University of Oxford, but has been open to the
public since 1683. The surviving nucleus of the
17th-century Founding (Tradescant) Collection
is at the heart of the four present Departments –
Antiquities, Western Art, Coins and Eastern
Art. Among the exhibits are the Alfred Jewel
and a collection of Old Master paintings,
particularly Uccello's *Hunt in the Forest* and
works by Samuel Palmer and the Pre-
Raphaelites. There is an important collection of
drawings, notably by Raphael, Michelangelo
and Rembrandt, together with bronzes, silver,
ceramics and musical intruments.

The Heberden coin room is second in
Britain only to that of the British Museum. The
department of Eastern art has major collections
of Chinese and Japanese porcelain, sculpture
and lacquerwork, Chinese bronzes, Tibetan art,
Indian sculpture and paintings, and Islamic
pottery and metalwork.

Museum of Oxford

St Aldates, Oxford, OX1 1DZ ☎ *0865 815559*
Tues–Sat 10–5. Closed Good Fri, Dec 25, 26.
F ▮

The museum is housed on two floors of the
south-west corner of Oxford's 1893 Town Hall.
It tells the story of the growth of Oxford from
the earliest times to the present day. The
exhibits are complemented by a series of
reconstructed furnished period rooms, including
an Elizabethan inn parlour, an 18th-century
student's room, a 19th-century working-class
kitchen and a corner of Cape's Cash Drapery.

Individual exhibits of note include the
complete base of a Roman pottery kiln, the
oldest surviving English town seal (1191), Jan
de Wyck's remarkable painting of the Siege of
Oxford in 1645 and an 18th-century fire-engine.
An electrically operated car-engine and working
fairground models add movement to the
displays.

Pitt-Rivers Museum

South Parks Road, Oxford, OX1 3PP
☎ *0865 512541*
Mon–Sat 2–4. Closed Easter & Christmas weeks.
F ✏

The museum, which forms part of a University
teaching department, possesses one of the six
most important ethnographic collections in the
world, a major collection of prehistoric
archaeology, and a fine British and European
folk life section. The musical instrument
collection, which represents many cultures
throughout the world, is one of the three largest
in existence.

The Alfred Jewel, gold and cloisonné enamel,
9th century. Ashmolean Museum, Oxford.

In accordance with the deed of gift, the
displays are arranged typologically, to illustrate
technical and evolutionary principles. In a
building nearly a century old, this has resulted
in gross overcrowding. A new building, opened
in 1986, has exhibitions of pre-agricultural
archaeology and of musical instruments,
supplemented, in the case of the latter, by
sophisticated audio-visual equipment, which
makes it possible to appreciate the instruments
in a realistic context.

Paisley

Paisley Museum and Art Gallery

High Street, Paisley, Renfrewshire, PA1 2BA
☎ *041 889 3151*
Mon–Sat 10–5. Closed public holidays.
F ▮ ↩

Paisley shawls are a major feature of the
museum. The collection includes over 700
shawls of different types and styles, and
examples are always on show. The displays in
this purpose-built gallery trace the history of the
Paisley patterns and illustrate the development
of weaving techniques and the social aspects of
the industry. The Local History Gallery presents
the social and economic history of Paisley, with
exhibits relating both to work and to leisure.
The Natural History Gallery, in addition to its
general displays, shows the geology and wildlife
of the area.

There are approximately 1,500 sculptures,
drawings, prints and paintings in the fine arts
collection, the emphasis being on works by
Scottish and French artists. Within the
decorative arts section, the ceramics are
particularly notable. The studio pottery
collection is considered to be the best in
Scotland.

Pitmedden

Museum of Farming Life

*Pitmedden Garden, Ellon, Aberdeenshire,
AB4 0PD*
☎ *06513 2352*
May–Sept, daily 10–6 (last admission 5.15)
C ▮ 🗮 ⅙ ↩

Pitmedden, now the property of the National
Trust for Scotland, is best known for its Great
Garden, a remarkable late-17th-century formal
garden in the French style, now fully restored
and carefully maintained. The museum is based
on a group of 18th- and 19th-century farm
buildings. It displays the large collection of farm
tools and domestic equipment given to the Trust
in 1978 by William Cook, who farmed at Little
Meldrum, near Pitmedden. These items,
augmented by other gifts, are shown in a
furnished farmhouse and bothy, and in the
restored outbuildings, with interpretive panels
telling the history of Scottish farming. The
hayloft over the stable is used for teaching
school parties.

Domestic items recovered from the *Mary Rose.* HM Naval Base, Portsmouth.

Poole

Royal National Lifeboat Institution Museum

West Quay Road, Poole, Dorset, BH15 1HZ
  ☎ 0202 671133
Mon–Fri 9.30–4.30. Closed Bank Holidays.
F ⬦ ⛭ ⌂

Situated within the headquarters of the RNLI, which provides the back-up service for 200 lifeboat stations throughout the country, the museum traces the Institution's history since its establishment in the early 19th century by means of models, paintings, photographs, medals, memorabilia and commemorative items. Among the celebrities featured are Sir William Hillary, founder of the RNLI, and Henry Blogg of Cromer, the most decorated of all lifeboatmen.

Waterfront Museum

4 High Street, Poole, Dorset, BH15 1BW
  ☎ 0202 683188
Mon–Sat 10–5; Sun 2–5.
C ⬦ ⛭

The museum, just off Poole Quay, is housed in part of a 15th-century quayside woolhouse, known as the Town Cellars, and in the adjoining Oakleys Mill, an 18th–19th-century grain and feed mill. The displays trace the history of Poole's maritime community – the merchants and seamen, the fishermen, the shipwrights and allied craftsmen, and the tradesmen of the port. The exhibits include boats, ship-models, shipbuilding tools, navigational instruments and objects associated with naval celebrities, and a Victorian street scene, incorporating items from now-demolished shops in Poole.

Portsmouth

Charles Dickens' Birthplace

393 Old Commercial Road, Portsmouth,
  Hampshire, PO1 2JS   ☎ 0705 827261
Mar–Oct, daily 10.30–5.30
C ⬦ ⌂

Charles Dickens was born at 393 Old Commercial Road in 1812. The house was restored in 1970 and furnished to illustrate the kind of home which John and Elizabeth Dickens would have created for themselves. An exhibition room shows items which once belonged to the novelist. They include a set of his waistcoat buttons, a signed cheque, a lock of his hair and the couch on which he died in 1870.

HMS Victory

HM Naval Base, Portsmouth, Hampshire,
  PO1 3PZ   ☎ 0705 819604
Mar–Oct, Mon–Sat 10.30–5.30; Sun 1–5.30.
Nov–Feb, Mon–Sat 10.30–5; Sun 1–5.30.
Closed Dec 25. (Last tour 40 mins before
  closing time)
C ⬦ ⛭ ⌂

The keel of HMS *Victory* was laid at Chatham in 1729. She was the flagship of Admiral Lord Nelson at the Battle of Trafalgar in 1805 and she still serves as the flagship of the Commander in Chief Naval Home Command. Discreetly, but substantially, restored over the years, she is preserved in dry dock and is manned by serving members of the Royal Navy and Royal Marines, who conduct visitors on tours between decks. Each tour lasts approximately 40 minutes.

Mary Rose

HM Naval Base, Portsmouth, Hampshire,
  PO1 3LR   ☎ 0705 839766
Mar–Oct, daily 10–5.30. Nov–Feb, daily
  10.30–5. Closed Dec 25.
C ⬦ ⛭ ⌂

The Ship Hall is based on an old dry dock, itself a historic monument, while the exhibition is housed in an early 19th-century timber building, which was originally a masthouse. In the Ship Hall is displayed what remains of Henry VIII's warship, the *Mary Rose*, which sank off Portsmouth in 1545 and was raised in 1982. Visitors can see the reconstruction and conservation of the surviving starboard hull structure.

The exhibition shows more than a thousand of the 14,000 objects recovered by divers from the wreck. These include weapons – especially longbows – personal possessions and clothing of the crew, cooking and eating utensils, and fittings from the ship.

Royal Naval Museum

HM Naval Base, Portsmouth, Hampshire,
  PO1 3LR   ☎ 0705 733060
Daily 10.30–5, with some seasonal variations.
  Closed Dec 25, 26.
C ⬦ ⛭ ⌂

Part of the museum is housed in three Georgian storehouses which form part of the original 18th-century Royal Dockyard. The displays illustrate the history of the Royal Navy from Tudor times to the South Atlantic campaign of

1982, with special emphasis on the social development of the Navy and on the Nelson and Victorian periods. Among the exhibits are personal items relating to Lord Nelson and his officers and men, ships' figureheads, ship models, naval campaign medals and a fine collection of paintings.

Port Sunlight

Lady Lever Art Gallery

Port Sunlight, Wirral, Merseyside, L62 5EQ
☎ 051 645 3623
Mon–Sat 10.5; Sun 2–5. Closed Jan 1, Good Fri, Dec 24–26.
F

The Beaux-Arts classical building dates from 1914–22. The collections, mainly of British art, were formed by the gallery's founder, William Lever, Viscount Leverhulme (1851–1925), who also established the soap firm, Lever Brothers, and the model village of Port Sunlight. The principal collections are of British 18th–19th-century paintings; 19th-century British watercolours; British and Continental sculpture, especially of the late 19th-century; 16th- to early-19th-century furniture, mainly English and including an outstanding collection of late-18th-century marquetry commodes; 17th–19th-century tapestry and needlework; Wedgwood pottery; Chinese ceramics, jades and hardstones; and antique sculpture and Greek vases.

***Fatidica*, 1894, by Frederick Leighton. Lady Lever Art Gallery, Port Sunlight.**

Port Talbot

Welsh Miners' Museum

Afan Argoed Country Park, Cynonville, Port Talbot, West Glamorgan
Apr–Sept, daily 10.30–6. Oct–Mar, Sat, Sun 10.30–5.
C

The museum, in a now abandoned coal-mining area, was created as a community enterprise in order to tell the story of the Welsh miner from the earliest days of mining in the Welsh Coalfield. The exhibits include a replica of a coal mine, equipment, clothing and personal possessions of miners, and photographs and documents illustrating different aspects of coal-mining and the society of which it formed a part.

Prescot

Prescot Museum of Clock and Watchmaking

34 Church Street, Prescot, Merseyside, L34 3LA
☎ 051 430 7787
Tues–Sat & Bank Holiday Mon 10–5; Sun 2–5. Closed Jan 1, Good Fri, Dec 24–26.
F

Prescot is 10 miles from Liverpool. The museum occupies a late-18th-century house on a corner site in the Town Centre Conservation Area.

The displays tell the story of the South-West Lancashire watch and watch toolmaking trades, which existed from c.1600 to the 1960s. An introductory section is devoted to the history of time measurement and other exhibits illustrate the products of the industry, the watch and toolmakers and the tool merchants, against the social and industrial background of the area.

There is a reconstruction of a traditional workshop, equipped with a range of hand tools and machinery. This is contrasted with a reconstruction of part of the Lancashire Watch Company's steam-powered factory, established in 1899. An accompanying display gives the history of the factory and the reasons for its closure in 1910.

The museum also presents modern developments in watch and clockmaking, including the application of electronics to horology, and contrasts hand and steam-powered manufacturing methods with those in use today.

Prestongrange

Scottish Mining Museum

Prestongrange, Prestonpans, East Lothian
☎ 031 665 9904
Tues–Fri 10–4.30; Sat, Sun 12–5.
F

The museum at Prestongrange is the starting point of the Coal Heritage Trail, which takes visitors by way of Tranent and Fa'side to the Lady Victoria Colliery, the Scottish Mining Museum's second site at Newtongrange.

At Prestongrange, there is a Visitor Centre; substantial remains of a Hoffman brick kiln; an exhibition hall containing relics of the mining industry; and, dominating the site, the Cornish beam pumping engine built by Harveys of Hayle in 1874.

Ramsey (Isle of Man)

'The Grove'

Andreas Road, Ramsey, Isle of Man
☎ *0624 75522*
Easter–Sept, Mon–Fri 10–5; Sun 2–5.
Ⓒ ⬤ ▆ ▟

This early Victorian house, with its outbuildings, illustrates the living style of a comfortably-off family of the time. There is a series of Victorian period rooms, a display of 19th-century costumes, and collections of dolls, toys and Victorian greetings cards. The outbuildings contain early beekeeping equipment, agricultural implements and horse-drawn vehicles, together with a horse-driven threshing mill.

Reading

Blake's Lock Museum

Gas Works Road, off Kenavon Drive, Reading,
*   RG1 3DH*
Wed–Fri 10–5; Sat, Sun 2–5. Closed Bank
*   Holidays.*
Ⓕ ⬤ ▟ ▟

The museum occupies a brick-built Victorian sewage pumping station by the side of the River Kennet, close to its junction with the Thames. The displays, based mainly on 19th- and early-20th-century material, concentrate on the trades and industries of Reading, other than the traditional Three Bs – biscuits, beer and bulbs. There are reconstructions, using original material, of a printer's workshop, a bakery, and a barber's, and more general displays include brickmaking ironfounding, dairying, pharmacies, tailors, sweetmakers, toy shops, Cock's sauce, shoes and mineral water manufacture.

The waterways section includes the wharves, the Kennet and Avon Canal, bridges, mills and the natural history of the rivers and the canal. Boatbuilding, once an important local industry, is represented and so is the recreational use of the Thames, fishing and the Reading Regatta being specially featured.

Redditch

National Needle Museum

Forge Mill, Needle Mill Lane, Redditch, Hereford
*   and Worcester, B97 6RR   ☎ 0527 62509*
Apr–Oct, Mon–Fri 11–4.30; Sat 1–5; Sun
*   11.30–5.*
Ⓒ ⬤ ▆ ▟

Forge Mill is the world's only surviving water-powered needle mill. The 18th-century building contains a working waterwheel and original needle-making machinery. There is also a series of displays illustrating the technology of the industry and the social conditions of the workers in Redditch during the period when the town was the world centre of the needle industry.

Richmond

The Georgian Theatre Royal

Victoria Road, Richmond, North Yorkshire,
*   DL10 4DW   ☎ 0748 3021*
Easter Sat–Oct, Mon–Sat 11–4.45; Sun 2.30–
*   4.45. Other times by appt.*
Ⓒ ⬤

The Theatre, seating 200 people, was built by the actor-manager, Samuel Butler, in 1788. It continued as a theatre until 1848 and then, over a century, served successively as wine vaults, an auction room, a corn-chandler's and a salvage depot. Restoration work began in 1960 and the building reopened as a theatre in 1963.

The Theatre Museum contains a collection of original playbills from 1792 to the 1840s and the oldest and largest complete set of painted scenery in Britain, dating from 1836. There are also displays of model theatres, star photographs and photographs of visits paid to the Theatre by members of the Royal Family since its reopening.

Ripon

Ripon Prison and Police Museum

St Marysgate, Ripon, North Yorkshire, HG4 1LX
*   ☎ 0765 3706*
May–Sept, Tues–Sun 1.30–4.30
Ⓒ ⬤ ▟

The prison complex includes a House of Correction, built in 1686 and now a private house, and the Liberty Prison, which dates from 1815 and which still has its original iron doors and windows.

The old gaol building was used as a prison for felons between 1816 and 1887, then until 1956 as Ripon Police Station. The ground floor has displays of police mementoes and equipment from the 17th century to the present day. In the nine cells on the first floor are exhibits illustrating 17th–19th-century methods of confinement and punishment.

Rochdale

Rochdale Pioneers Memorial Museum

31 Toad Lane, Rochdale, Greater Manchester
*   ☎ 061 832 4300*
Tues–Sat 10–12, 2–4
Ⓒ ⬤ ▟

No. 31 Toad Lane is regarded as the home of the worldwide Co-operative Movement, because it contains the room in which the Rochdale Equitable Pioneers Society opened their grocery store in 1844. The building has been restored and the front room furnished, arranged and stocked as it was in the 1840s. The museum has displays of documents and mementoes which tell the story of the Rochdale Pioneers Society from 1844 up to the 1944 centenary celebrations.

Rotherham

Art Gallery

Walker Place, Rotherham, South Yorkshire,
S65 1JH   ☎ 0709 382121
Mon, Wed–Fri 10–6; Sat 10–5. Closed Bank
Holiday.
C ⓘ 💻 ⓹ ⌂

The Art Gallery houses Rotherham's permanent
collections of ceramics and pictures. There is a
collection of Rockingham pottery and porcelain
numbering over 1,000 pieces, together with
items from other Yorkshire potteries, and a
selection of 18th- and 19th-century English and
Continental pottery and porcelain.

The Fine Art collection includes paintings,
watercolours and sculpture, and a large number
of prints and drawings, mostly topographical.
Many of the works in the collection have local
associations and most are by 19th-century
British artists.

Ruddington

Ruddington Framework Knitters' Museum

Chapel Street, Ruddington, Nottinghamshire,
NG11 6HE   ☎ 0602 846914
Apr–Oct, Tues–Fri and Bank Holiday 10–4. July–
Sept also Sun 2–4.
C ⓘ ⌂

The museum, four miles south of Nottingham,
illustrates the living and working conditions of
19th-century framework knitters, in a group of
purpose-built houses and workshops, which
have been restored by a Trust and equipped with
original machinery, much of it now in working
condition. There is an audio-visual description
of the industry in the East Midlands and two
exhibitions, one showing the general
development of framework knitting and the
other telling the story of handframe knitting in
Ruddington.

The museum contains a workshop of
restoration and framesmithing and, with an
apprentice learning frame-knitting from the
Technical Director, the Trust is now working
for the preservation of the craft itself.

Two of the houses have now been restored
and furnished as they would have been in 1850
and 1900 respectively. One was formerly
occupied by a framework knitter, the other by a
hosier.

Runcorn

Norton Priory

Tudor Road, Runcorn, Cheshire, WA7 1SX
☎ 0928 569895
Mar–Oct, Mon–Fri 12–5; Sat, Sun 12–6. Nov–
Feb, daily 12–4. Closed Dec 24–26.
C ⌔ 💻 ⓹ ⌂

Norton Priory, an Augustinian house, was
established in the 12th century. In 1545 the
buildings and lands were bought by the Brooke

12th-century undercroft, Norton Priory,
Runcorn.

family who made Norton their residence. They
converted some of the priory buildings to a
Tudor mansion there, later replaced by a
Georgian country house, which was demolished
in 1928. The site then became an abandoned
and overgrown wilderness. The extensive site of
the priory was excavated during the 1970s and
the large and wide-ranging finds discovered then
are displayed now in a modern museum.

The exhibition tells the story of the priory
and of monastic life and of the medieval crafts
employed there such as a tile-making, bell-
founding and stonemasonry. There are fine
collections of carved stonework and medieval
floor-tiles. The foundations of the priory
buildings can now be clearly followed and
visitors can also see the undercroft building, of
c.1200, with its fine Norman doorway, the only
substantial part of the priory to survive.

Rye

Lamb House

West Street, Rye, East Sussex, TN31 7ES
Late Mar–Oct, Wed, Sat 2–6
C

Lamb House was built in 1723 by James Lamb,
13 times Mayor of Rye, an office held by his son
for 20 terms. In 1899 it was bought by Henry
James, who spent much of the last 18 years of his
life here. The house was visited by most of
James's distinguished literary contemporaries. It
was presented to the National Trust in 1950 and
is now tenanted, with three rooms on the
ground floor open to the public and containing
some of the novelist's furniture and part of his
library, together with a number of portraits of
him.

Ryhope

Ryhope Engines Museum

Ryhope Pumping Station, Ryhope, Sunderland,
Tyne and Wear, SR2 0ND ☎ 0783 210235
Easter–Dec, Sat, Sun 2–5. Steam Days include
Bank Holiday weekends and two other days as
advertised.
C ⌔ 💻 ⌂

The museum is about three miles south of Sunderland. Ryhope Pumping Station was constructed by the Sunderland and South Shields Water Company. Its two steam-powered beam engines, built by R. and W. Hawthorn of Newcastle upon Tyne, were in use from 1869 until 1967. Subsequently, a Trust was formed to preserve the Pumping Station as near as possible to its 1869 condition. The engines are kept in working order and periodically steamed. There is also an exhibition of items associated with the supply and use of water.

St Albans

Verulamium Museum

St Michael's, St Albans, Hertfordshire, AL3 4SW
☎ 0727 66100 extn 2912
Mar–Oct, Mon–Sat 10–5.30; Sun 2–5.30. Nov–Feb, Mon–Sat 10–4; Sun 2–4. Closed Dec 25, 26.
Ⓒ ⚐ ✈

The museum is in St Michael's village, signposted from the A414 to Hemel Hempstead. It is on the site of the important Roman city of *Verulamium* and displays material discovered during the excavations there, forming one of the best late Iron Age and Roman collections outside London. The exhibits include fine mosaics, reconstructions of painted wall-plasters and the celebrated *Verulamium Venus* statuette.

St Austell

Wheal Martyn

Carthew, nr St Austell, Cornwall
☎ 0726 850362
Apr–Oct, daily 10–6. Open Bank Holiday. Other months by appt.
Ⓒ ⚐ 📷 ✈

Wheal Martyn, which is partly an indoor and partly an outdoor museum, tells the story of the Cornish china-clay industry. The museum includes two old clay works and illustrates china-clay extracting and processing as they were carried out up to the Second World War, together with the social and domestic life of the works in the industry.

Equipment has also been moved to Wheal Martyn from elsewhere in the china-clay area.

Reconstruction of Roman Forum. Verulamium Museum, St Albans.

Stained glass panel. Pilkington Glass Museum, St Helens.

St Helens

Pilkington Glass Museum

Prescot Road, St Helens, Merseyside, WA10 3TT
☎ 0744 692499/692104
Mon–Fri 10–5; Sat, Sun & Bank Holiday 2–4.30. Evenings for groups by appt. Closed Dec 25–Jan 1.
Ⓕ ⚐ ♿ ✈

The museum occupies part of the headquarters building of Britain's largest glass-making concern. It was created to illustrate the history of glass-making techniques and glass products, from prehistoric times to the present day. The development of the Pilkington Company itself also forms part of the displays.

St Helier (Channel Islands)

Jersey Museum

9 Pier Road, St Helier, Jersey, Channel Islands
☎ 0534 75940
Mon–Sat 10–5. Closed Jan 1, Good Fri, Dec 25, 26.
Ⓒ ♿ ✈

Since 1893, the Jersey Museum has occupied what was formerly a private house, built in 1817. The museum, which is at present being enlarged, has collections covering many aspects of the island's history and natural environment. These include a wide range of domestic equipment, furnishings, natural history, shipping and shipbuilding, commerce, postal services, coins and banknotes. There are several period rooms and a reconstruction of a pharmacy of the 1880s.

Special sections of the museum are devoted to silver, pewter, musical instruments, the German Occupation (1940–45) and to the celebrated Victorian beauty, Lillie Langtry, born in Jersey in 1853.

St Ives

Barbara Hepworth Museum

Trewyn Studio, Barnoon Hill, St Ives, Cornwall,
*   TR26 1AD   ☎ 0736 796226*
Apr–June, Sept, Mon–Sat 10–5.30. July–Aug,
*   Mon–Sat 10–6.30; Sun 2–6, Oct–Mar, Mon–*
*   Sat 10–4.30 Closed Good Fri, Dec 25, 26.*
Ⓒ ⌖

The early-19th-century granite house was the
home of the sculptor, Dame Barbara Hepworth,
from 1949 to 1975. The studio was damaged in
the fire that caused the artist's death, and
although no works of art were destroyed, much
of the furniture and many books cannot be
exhibited. Instead, an attempt has been made to
reconstruct something of the feeling the Trewyn
Studio had in the 1950s, when Barbara
Hepworth was working there.

St Peter Port (Channel Islands)

Guernsey Museum and Art Gallery

Candie Gardens, St Peter Port, Guernsey, Channel
*   Islands   ☎ 0481 26518*
Apr–Oct, daily 10.30–5.30. Nov–Mar, daily
*   10.30–4.30. Closed 5 days at Christmas.*
Ⓒ ⌖ ▣ ♿ ▪ ☞

The museum's octagonal galleries repeat the
shape of an original Victorian bandstand, which
is incorporated in the building and is now used
as the museum tea room. The collections are
based on those formed by the Lukis family
during the 19th century, which consisted
mainly of local archaeology. The displays
present a portrait and pedigree of Guernsey,
through exhibitions on natural history and
geology, archaeology and history.
    The art gallery contains paintings, mainly
watercolours, of local scenes, and is also used for
the museum's frequent special exhibitions.

**Victorian mineworkings. Salford Mining
Museum.**

Salford

Salford Mining Museum

Buile Hill Park, Eccles Old Road, Salford, Greater
*   Manchester, M6 8GL   ☎ 061 736 1832*
Mon–Fri 10–12.30, 1.30–5; Sun 2–5. Closed Jan
*   1, Good Fri, Dec 25, 26.*
Ⓕ ▪ ▣ ☞

Buile Hill was built between 1825 and 1827 to
the design of Sir Charles Barry. It is his only
known attempt at the Greek neo-classical style.
The top floor and porte-cochère were added in
the 1860s. Since the late 1950s, the house and
its basement have been developed as a realistic
mining museum. Buile Hill No. 1 Pit has a series
of underground scenes showing coal-mining
techniques at different periods. Buile Hill No. 1
Drift re-creates the atmosphere of a working
drift mine in the 1930s. The other underground
and surface displays include a coalface, a
pityard, a lamp-room, pithead baths and a
blacksmith's shop. Temporary exhibitions on
mining themes are mounted in the Gallery of
Mining Art.

Salford Museum and Art Gallery

Peel Park, The Crescent, Salford, Greater
*   Manchester, M5 4WU   ☎ 061 736 2649*
Mon–Fri 10–5; Sun 2–5. Closed Jan 1, Good Fri,
*   Dec 25, 26.*
Ⓕ ⌖ ▪ ☞

The museum has a large collection of social
history material, much of which is displayed in
Lark Hill Place, a reconstruction of a 19th-
century street, which includes items rescued
from now-demolished houses and shops in the
Salford area. Among the exhibits here are a
pawnbroker's, a clogmaker's, a public house, a
chemist's and a typical corner shop. There is
also a series of period rooms, illustrating living
styles from the 17th century to Victorian times.
    One room in the Art Gallery contains
Victorian paintings, sculpture and decorative
arts, and another is devoted to paintings and
drawings by L. S. Lowry, together with
memorabilia of the artist.

Salisbury

Salisbury Museum

The King's House, 65 The Close, Salisbury,
*   Wiltshire, SP1 2EN   ☎ 0722 332151*
Mon–Sat 10–5; July–Aug, also Sun 2–5; Closed
*   Christmas.*
Ⓒ ▪ ▣ ♿ ▪ ☞

The museum building, known since the early
17th century as the King's House, was originally
the Salisbury residence of the Abbots of
Sherborne. Between 1851 and 1978 it was the
Diocesan Training College. On the closure of
the college, it was bought by the museum,
established elsewhere in Salisbury in 1860, and
the museum opened in its new premises in 1981.
    It contains very important archaeological

collections, illustrating human settlement in Wiltshire from Palaeolithic times to the Saxon period. Special exhibits are devoted to Stonehenge and to the pioneering work of Lt. Gen. Pitt-Rivers, which established archaeology as a scientific discipline. The Hugh Shortt Galleries tell the story of Old Sarum and the city of Salisbury, with an emphasis on life during the medieval period. It includes the Drainage Collection, a large group of everyday objects discovered in the drainage channels which once flowed through the streets.

The museum has an important post-medieval ceramics collection, displayed in its own gallery, and the Print Room houses regularly changing exhibitions of the museum's extensive collection of paintings, including 5 Turner watercolours, prints, drawings and photographs of Salisbury and the historic sites of South Wiltshire. The recently opened gallery, 'Stitches in Time – Historical Costume of Wiltshire', also includes embroidery, accessories and Downton lace.

Saltash

Cotehele Quay

St Dominick, nr Saltash, Cornwall, PL12 6TA
☎ *0579 50830*
Apr–Oct, daily 11–6
C ♿

Cotehele Quay is an outstation of the National Maritime Museum. The museum tells the story of the Tamar sailing barge, *Shamrock*, and of the local shipping, shipbuilding and related industries. *Shamrock*, built in 1899 at Stonehouse, Plymouth, is the principal exhibit in the museum. She worked until 1970 and then, beached and in a semi-derelict condition, she was rescued from breaking up and between 1974 and 1979 restored to her 1921 condition by means of a project organised by the National Trust, which has also restored Cotehele Quay to its 19th-century appearance. The *Shamrock* is now owned jointly by the Trust and by the National Maritime Museum, and is available for day charter in the summer.

Sandringham

Sandringham House

Sandringham, nr King's Lynn, Norfolk,
PE85 6EN ☎ *0553 772675*
April 29–Sept 30, House: Mon–Thurs 11–4.45;
Sun 12–4.45. Grounds: Mon–Thurs 10.30–5;
Sun 11.30–5. House closed July 16–Aug 4;
grounds July 20–Aug 1; also at other times
when HM The Queen or any member of the
Royal Family is in residence.
C ♿ 🅿 ♿ ♿

Sandringham is eight miles from King's Lynn. A late-18th-century house, it was bought for the Prince of Wales in 1862 and completley rebuilt in 1870. Extensive repairs were carried out after a serious fire in 1891. It is still in the possession

Vintage royal motorcar. Sandringham House.

of the Royal Family and horses from the Queen's thoroughbred stud are housed here and at nearby Wolferton.

The Ranger's Room contains an interpretive display of birds, trees, and animals which can be seen in the Country Park, and a museum houses vintage Royal motorcars, big game trophies and gifts presented to the Royal Family. There are also collections of dolls and of archaeological finds from the area.

Scunthorpe

Scunthorpe Museum and Art Gallery

Oswald Road, Scunthorpe, South Humberside,
DN15 7BD ☎ *0724 843533*
Mon–Sat 10–5; Sun 2–5. Closed Dec 25, 26.
F ♿ ■ ♿

The displays include a countryside gallery, showing the geology and natural history of the area and the uses of the countryside, especially the exploitation of the local ironstone. The local history gallery illustrates the history of the iron and steel industry and of the 'industrial island' of Scunthorpe, as well as the agricultural history of the town's rural surroundings. The archaeology gallery has collections relating to the earlier occupation of the area from prehistoric to post-medieval times. There are also Jacobean, Georgian and Victorian period rooms and a reconstruction of an ironworker's cottage.

The art gallery presents temporary exhibitions from the main collections, together with works by local artists and craft-workers.

Selborne

The Oates Museum and Gilbert White Museum

The Wakes, Selborne, nr Alton, Hampshire,
GU34 3JH ☎ *042050 275*
Mar–Oct, Wed–Sun 11–5.30 (last admission 5).
Open Bank Holiday Mon, and on Tues in
July–Aug.
C ♿ ♿

'The Wakes' dates from the early 16th century, but it has been altered and enlarged several

'The Wakes'. Gilbert White Museum, Selborne.

times since then. It was the home of the Rev. Gilbert White, the naturalist, until his death in 1793 and his book, *The Natural History of Selborne*, was written here.

The ground floor now contains two rooms furnished in the style of the 18th century, and also displays relating to Gilbert White and to the natural history and antiquities of Selborne. Money to save 'The Wakes' and to preserve it as a museum was provided by Robert Washington Oates, in memory of two members of his family, Frank Oates, the 19th-century African explorer, and Captain Lawrence Oates, who was a member of Captain Scott's Antarctic expedition, and who walked out to his death in the snow. The museum on the first floor illustrates their lives and achievements.

Sheffield

Abbeydale Industrial Hamlet

Abbeydale Road South, Sheffield, S7 2QW
☎ 0742 367731
Mon–Sat 10–5; Sun 11–5. Closed Dec 24–26.
Ⓒ 🛈 💷 ⌨

Abbeydale is five miles south-west of Sheffield. It consists of an 18th–19th-century water-powered scythe-works, restored to full operational condition, and shows all the processes involved, from making the steel in the crucible steel furnace to forging, grinding and finishing the blades in the workshops surrounding the courtyard. Every aspect of the work is represented, including packing, storing and preparing for market, the clerical work involved (in the Counting House), the living conditions of the workmen (the Workman's Cottage) and of the manager or site foreman (the Manager's House).

Graves Art Gallery

Surrey Street, Sheffield S1 1XZ ☎ 0742 734781
Mon–Sat 10–8; Sun 2–5. Closed Dec 24–26.
Ⓕ 🖉 💷 ■ ⌨

The principal collections in this gallery of fine and applied art are of 20th-century British paintings and watercolours. Other sections are devoted to Chinese ivories, to 16th–19th-century European paintings and to non-European fine and applied art.

Kelham Island Industrial Museum

Kelham Island, off Alma Street, Sheffield S3 8RY
☎ 0742 22106
Wed–Sat 10–5; Sun 11–5. Open 10–5 Easter Mon, May Day Bank Holiday, and Spring and Late Summer Bank Holiday Mon.
Ⓒ 🛈 💷 ⌨ ⌨

The museum building was formerly a generating station which provided power for the City's trams. The displays tell the story of Sheffield's industrial development and of the wide range of its products. The machines on show include the 12,000 hp River Don steam engine and the 150 hp Crossley gas engine, both of which can be seen working. Much attention is given to the living conditions of Sheffield's workers and two of the self-employed craftsmen on whom the cutlery trade depended, the Little Mesters, work full-time in specialist workshops within the museum. Visitors are able to watch the processes involved and talk to the experts about their work.

Mappin Art Gallery

Weston Park, Sheffield, S10 2TP
☎ 0742 726281
Tues–Sat 10–5; Sun 2–5. Open Bank Holiday Mon. Closed Dec 25, 26.
Ⓒ 🖉 💷 ⌨ ■

The gallery occupies an 1887 neo-classical building. Its main strength is in 18th–20th-century British art, but there are also collections of 20th-century European and American works. The exhibits are regularly changed and the collections of the Graves Art Gallery and Mappin Art Gallery are shared. As exhibitions change frequently, check in advance if you are interested in specific artists, works or themes.

Ruskin Gallery

101 Norfolk Street, Sheffield, S1 2JE
☎ 0742 734781
Mon–Fri 10–6; Sat 10–5. Closed Dec 24–26.
Ⓕ 🖉 ⌨

The gallery was opened in 1985 in a building in the centre of the city, which had formerly been a wine shop. The collection, previously exhibited elsewhere in Sheffield, belongs to the Guild of St George, founded by John Ruskin in the 1870s. One of the most successful aspects of the guild's work was its museum, established in Sheffield in 1875 for the liberal education of the artisans of Sheffield. It was broad in its conception and included minerals, selected especially for their colours, watercolours, a library, illuminated manuscripts, plaster casts of architectural details, photographs, paintings and prints. It has now been redisplayed in a way which shows how it developed naturally from Ruskin's philosophy and which makes it easier to experience its overall impact.

In 1988 the Ruskin Craft Gallery opened adjoining the Ruskin Gallery and houses changing exhibitions of contemporary crafts.

Shildon

Timothy Hackworth Museum

Soho Cottages, Shildon, Co Durham, DL4 1LX
    ☎ *0388 772036 & 777340*
Apr–Sept, Wed–Sun & Bank Holiday, 10–12,
    1–6. Other times by appt.
Ⓒ ✏ 🍴 ♿

Timothy Hackworth (1786–1850), the great
locomotive designer, had a contract for running
the Stockton and Darlington Railway and built
locomotives for British and foreign railways at
his works at New Shildon. Soho House, where
he lived, has been restored, together with the
Paint Shop at the Works, as a memorial to him.
One part of the house is furnished as it would
have been in his lifetime, the other contains an
exhibition illustrating his life and times. There
are displays relating to pioneering railway
engineers and inventions, and coalmining. A
full-size replica of his famous locomotive, *Sans
Pareil*, can be seen in the paintshop.

Shrewsbury

Rowley's House

Barker Street, Shrewsbury, SY1 1QT
    ☎ *0743 61196*
Mon–Sat 10–5. Easter–late Sept, also Sun 12–5.
Ⓒ 🍴

The museum building is in two parts: Rowley's
House, which is timber-framed and dates from
the late 16th century, and an adjoining brick
and stone mansion, built in 1618. There are
displays illustrating the geology, natural history,
local history and archaeology of Shropshire,
with an interesting collection of material from
the Roman city of *Viroconium*, the modern
Wroxeter, incuding the original Forum
inscription. A recently opened gallery explores
the development of medieval Shrewsbury by
means of exhibits and interpretive displays.

Singleton

Weald and Downland Open Air Museum

Singleton, nr Chichester, West Sussex, PO18 0EU
    ☎ *024363 348*
Apr–Oct, daily 11–5. Nov–Mar, Wed, Sun 11–4.
Ⓒ 🍴 ✏ ♿

The museum consists of a collection of historic
buildings from the region which have been
rescued from destruction and re-erected on an
extensive downland site. It illustrates the
development of traditional building from
medieval times to the 19th-century in the
Weald and Downland area of south-east
England. The museum is continually expanding
and its present exhibits include timber-framed
medieval houses, farm buildings, a Tudor
market hall, a blacksmith's forge, a village
school, a 19th-century toll cottage, a charcoal-
burner's camp, and a working watermill,
producing stone-ground flour.

Smallhythe

Ellen Terry Museum

Smallhythe Place, Smallhythe, Tenterden, Kent,
    TN30 7NG   ☎ 05806 2334
Apr–Oct, Sat–Wed 2–6 or dusk if earlier (last
    admission 5.30). Open Good Fri.
Ⓒ ♿

Smallhythe is two and a half miles south of
Tenterden. The early-16th-century yeoman's
house, now the property of the National Trust,
was owned by the celebrated actress, Dame
Ellen Terry, from 1899 until her death in 1928.
It remains much as it was when she lived in it
and contains many of her personal possessions
and theatrical mementos, including
photographs, paintings and costumes. Her
collection of mementoes of Henry Irving, Sarah
Siddons, David Garrick and other notabilities of
the English theatre is also on display.

Southampton

Southampton Art Gallery

Civic Centre, Southampton, SO9 4XF
    ☎ *0703 832769*
Tues–Fri 10–5; Sat 10–4; Sun 2–5. Thurs late
    opening till 8. Closed Jan 1, Dec 25.
Ⓕ 🍴 ♿ ■ ♿

The gallery's present collecting policy
concentrates on contemporary British paintings
and sculpture. There are also works by British
Surrealists and by members of the Camden
Town Group. There is an important collection
of 20th-century portraits, especially of
significant figures in the art world. The large
Old Master collection includes *The Holy Family*
by Jordaens and *Lord Vernon* by Gainsborough.
    The 19th-century in England and France is
represented by Turner, John Martin and the
Pre-Raphaelites, and by works by the French
Impressionists.

**The Juvenile Lead, by Walter Sickert.
Southampton Art Gallery.**

Southampton Maritime Museum

The Wool House, Town Quay, Southampton
   ☎ *0703 223941*
Tues–Fri 10–1, 2–5; Sat 10–1, 2–4; Sun 2–5.
   Closed Good Fri, Dec 25, 26, & Bank
   Holiday.
F ▮ ⋒

The museum occupies a 14th-century wool warehouse, later used to house French prisoners-of-war, whose initials can be seen carved in the roof timbers. The collections include ship models and paintings recalling Southampton in the days of sail, pioneer steamships, steam yachts, paddle steamers, and the great liners.

Special exhibits include *Miss Britain III*, the record-breaking power boat built by Hubert Scott-Paine and the British Power Boat Company at Hythe in 1933, the only surviving oscillating steam engine, from the paddle steamer *Empress* (1879), and the vertical compound engine from the local ferry, *Venus* (1947), There is also an exhibition devoted to the ill-fated maiden voyage of the *Titanic* from Southampton to New York in 1912.

Southsea

D-Day Museum

Clarence Esplanade, Southsea, Hampshire,
   PO5 3PA
Daily 10.30–5.30 (last admission 4.30). Closed
   Dec 24–26.
C ▮ � ⋒

The displays in the museum tell the story of the Normandy landings in 1944. The military equipment and vehicles include field guns, jeeps and a Sherman tank. There are also uniforms worn by the Allied forces taking part in the invasion. The planning and carrying out of the operation is explained by means of models, maps, photographs, uniforms and war-time objects.

The celebrated Overlord Embroidery, 80 metres long, illustrates the progress of the operation, in much the same way as the Bayeux Tapestry did for the invasion of Britain by William of Normandy in 1066.

The equipment on display includes a DUKW, jeep, scout car, Sherman and Churchill Crocodile tanks, field guns and a rare Beach Armoured Recovery Vehicle.

South Shields

Arbeia Roman Fort

Baring Street, South Shields, Tyne and Wear,
   NE33 2BD   ☎ *091 456 1369*
Tues–Fri 10–5.30; Sat 10–4.30; Sun 2–5 (Closed
   Sun, Oct–Easter). Open Bank Holiday Mon,
   10–5.30.
F ⟳ ⅟ ⋒

The Roman Fort at South Shields is at the eastern end of the Hadrianic frontier. It was built in the late 1st or early 2nd century to guard the mouth of the River Tyne and was enlarged c. AD 207–8. Excavations have revealed the foundations of the headquarters building, granaries, barracks and fort defences, including gateways and ditches. The West gate of the fort has been reconstructed to full size. The museum contains displays of objects discovered during excavations at the Fort. Exhibits include tombstones, building inscriptions and sculpture. There are also swords, enamelled belt-mountings, sling-stones, fragments of armour, lead baggage seals, tools, surveying instruments and a wide range of household and personal items.

The continuing excavations are open to visitors, and Event days are held with special activities and displays.

South Shields Museum and Art Gallery

Ocean Road, South Shields, Tyne and Wear,
   NE33 2AU   ☎ *091 456 8740*
Mon–Fri 10–5.30; Sat 10–4.30; Sun 2–5. Closed
   Jan 1, Good Fri, Dec 25, 26.
F ▮ ⅟ ■

The museum's collections relate to the natural history, archaeology and history of South Shields. The maritime section includes displays on local shipbuilding, for many years an important industry in the area and a major source of employment. South Shields is also identified with the invention of the lifeboat and the museum's section devoted to this contains a model of W. Wouldhave's pioneering lifeboat (1789).

The art gallery is organised on the basis of temporary exhibitions.

Panel of the Overlord Embroidery. D-Day Museum, Portsmouth.

Stamford

Stamford Steam Brewery

All Saints Street, Stamford, Lincolnshire, PE9 2PA
    ☎ *0780 52186*
Apr (or Good Fri if earlier)–Sept, Wed–Sun &
    Bank Holiday 10–4. Closed Tues & Wed in
    Bank Holiday weeks. Evening parties by appt.
Ⓒ 🅰 🖳 🚗

The museum has been created from a small
Victorian steam brewery, one of 22 which
existed in Stamford in the late 19th century.
Though not now suitable for brewing, the steam
engine and original plant remain intact. A rare
survival, Melbourn Brothers' All Saints Brewery
gives a good impression of the 16,798 small
breweries which in 1870 existed all over the
British Isles and which have now nearly all
disappeared, as the brewing industry has become
increasingly centralised.

Stanley

Beamish: North of England Open Air Museum

Beamish, Stanley, Co. Durham, DH9 0RG
    ☎ *0207 231811*
March–Oct, daily 10–6 (last admission 4). Nov–
    March, Tues–Sun 10–5 (last admission 4).
Ⓒ 🅰 🖳 🍴 ♿ 🚗

This steadily developing museum, on a 120-
hectare site has been planned to illustrate life in
the North-East as it was immediately prior to
the First World War. A recent feature is the
Town Street, comprising houses; the Sun Inn,
with stables; a printing works; the Co-operative
stores; and a Victorian park with its bandstand.
All these buildings have been carefully
dismantled, moved from their original sites to
the museum, rebuilt and furnished as they would
have been in the 1920s.

Other parts of Beamish include a Primitive
Methodist Chapel, a railway station, with
footbridge, signal-box and operational track, a
tramway providing services to different points of
the site, a row of miners' cottages, pit-head
installations and a drift mine. The Home Farm
and Pockerley Farm have collections of
agricultural implements and equipment and
displays showing changes in farming methods
over the past 150 years. Around the farm are
Saddleback pigs and poultry, and in the fields
Teeswater sheep, and a herd of Durham
Shorthorn cattle, which are being bred at
Beamish, as they are rapidly disappearing
elsewhere.

Sticklepath

Finch Foundry Museum

Sticklepath, Okehampton, Devon, EX20 2NW
    ☎ *0837 840286*
Daily 11–6
Ⓒ 🅰 🚗

Sticklepath is four miles east of Okehampton.
The 'Foundry' is, in fact, a 19th-century water-

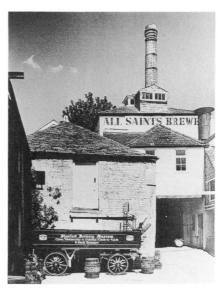

Stamford Steam Brewery.

powered edge tool factory. Its three waterwheels
and machinery, including a pair of tilt-
hammers, a fan or blower for the forges,
grindstone, emery-wheel and bandsaw, are all in
working order. Visitors can see all these
operating.

Two of the museum galleries contain
exhibitions of tools made or used at the
Foundry, together with photographs,
documents, catalogues and other items
illustrating the history of the business. The third
gallery is devoted to the history of the industrial
use of water-power. The forge area was once a
three-storey woollen mill and some of the floor
beams of this building can still be seen. The
present grinding house was originally a grist
mill, the thatched roof of which still exists.

Stoke Bruerne

Canal Museum

Stoke Bruerne, Towcester, Northamptonshire
    NN12 7SE   ☎ 0604 862229
Easter–Oct, daily 10–6. Oct–Easter, Tues–Sun
    10–4. Last admission 30 mins before closing.
    Closed Dec 25, 26.
Ⓒ 🅰 🖳 🚗

The museum is on three floors of what was
formerly a canalside cornmill. The exhibits
illustrate the way of life of canal boatmen and
their families over a period of two centuries, and
include costumes, traditional painted ware,
tools, tokens and Measham Ware teapots, as
well as a large collection of prints, plans and
photographs. A special feature of the museum is
a full-size replica of a canal boat cabin, complete
with kitchen range, brassware and lace curtains.

The entrance to Blisworth Tunnel, the
longest still in service on the waterways system
is only a short walk from the museum along the
towpath.

Doulton figures from the 1920s to the 1950s:
The Mirror, The Bather, Circe, Sweet Sixteen.
Sir Henry Doulton Gallery, Stoke-on-Trent.

Stoke-on-Trent

Minton Museum

Minton House, London Road, Stoke-on-Trent,
*   Staffordshire, ST4 7QD   ☎ 0782 744766*
Mon–Fri 9–12.30, 2–4.30. Closed Pottery
*   Holidays.*
F 🛈 🚗

The Minton Museum is situated within the
Minton factory. It contains chronological
displays of Minton wares from the factory's
foundation in 1793 to the present day. Special
features include early tableware with
corresponding pattern books and Thomas
Minton's original copper-plate engraving of the
celebrated willow pattern. Also on show are
ornamental wares and figures exhibited at the
Great Exhibition of 1851, together with life-size
maiolica-glazed birds and animals, examples of
decoration by the acid-gold process, tiles, studio
art pottery, Art Nouveau and Art Deco
influenced wares.

The outstanding items in the Minton
collection are the Pâte-sur-Pâte decorated
ornamental wares by Louis Solon, in which
layer upon layer of liquid clay was gradually built
up to form three-dimensional semi-clad maidens
or cherubs on to a tinted parian body in its
unfired state. The first firing was critical and
would prove whether or not the relief figure had
achieved the desired translucent effect.

Sir Henry Doulton Gallery

Royal Doulton Ltd., Nile Street, Burslem, Stoke-
*   on-Trent, Staffordshire, ST6 2AJ*
*   ☎ 0782 575454*
Mon–Fri 9–12.30, 1.30–4.30. Closed Bank
*   Holiday & Pottery Holidays.*
F 🛈 🖭 🚗

The exhibits in the gallery trace the story of the
Royal Doulton pottery since its foundation in
1815. They include wares from both the
Lambeth and the Burslem factories. Stoneware
jugs and vases by well-known designers, such as
the Barlows, George Tinworth and Mark
Marshall, are also on show, together with the
large bone china Raby Vase, the celebrated
Danté Vase and a selection of flambé and
experimental glazes.

A section of the gallery is devoted to the
Royal Doulton figure collection, which includes
a number of rare items, especially 'Boy on a
Crocodile' and 'Marquise Sylvestre'. Visitors
can aso see medals awarded to Royal Doulton at
international exhibitions held during the 19th
and 20th centuries.

Spode Museum

Spode Limited, Church Street, Stoke-on-Trent,
*   Staffordshire, ST4 1BX   ☎ 0782 744011*
Mon–Thurs 9–12.30, 1.30–4.30; Fri 9–12.
*   Closed Bank Holiday & Pottery Holidays.*
F 🛈 🚗

The Spode factory, which contains the
museum, was founded in 1770 and still occupies
its original site. There are displays of its earliest
wares – drabware, caneware, black basalt,
jasper, fine white stoneware, pearl and
creamwares – and a collection of Spode's
celebrated blue printed wares.

The introduction of fine bone china by
Spode c.1800 allowed further technical
improvements to be made. In 1845 the factory
developed a very fine porcelain known as
Parian, from which the drawing-room statuary
beloved of the Victorians was made. There is
also a display of recent commemorative wares.

Stowmarket

Museum of East Anglian Life

Abbots Hall, Stowmarket, Suffolk, IP14 1DL
*   ☎ 0449 612229*
Easter–Oct, Mon–Sat 11–5; Sun 12–5.
C 🛈 🖭 ♿ 🚗

The museum is being developed on a 30-hectare
open-air site, to reflect the agricultural, social
and industrial history of the counties of Essex,
Cambridgeshire, Norfolk and Suffolk. A
number of historic buildings have already been
moved to the site. They include a 14th-century
farmhouse, an 18th-century timber-framed
smithy, a mid-19th-century drainage windmill
and an 18th-century watermill.

The largest building at the museum formed
the engineering workshops of Robert Boby Ltd
of Bury St Edmunds, and dates from the 1870s.
The oldest is the great Abbot's Hall barn which
contains 13th-century roof timbers and is on its
original site. The museum buildings house
historic carts and wagons, industrial and
domestic displays, craft demonstrations and an
exhibition, *The Farming Year*, which illustrates
the sequence of tasks which farmers carry out on
the land. Among the special exhibits are a pair
of steam ploughing engines of 1912, built by
Charles Burrell and Sons of Thetford.

An exhibition, *Travellers and Sporting Men*,
is concerned with gypsies, travelling showmen,
sporting men and poachers. Its exhibits include
a small gypsy encampment, a showman's van,
part of a fairground site and large horse-drawn
game vans, for carrying away the day's bag,
which often amounted to several hundred
pheasants or partridges.

Strabane

Gray's Printing Press

*49 Main Street, Strabane, Co. Tyrone, Northern
Ireland, BT82 8AU   ☎ 0504 884094
Apr–Sept, Mon–Wed, Fri, Sat 2–6.*
Ⓒ ♠ ⌂

The print shop at 49 Main Street was in
existence in the 18th century and it may have
been here that John Dunlap, the printer of the
American Declaration of Independence, and
James Wilson, the grandfather of President
Woodrow Wilson, learned their trade. Now the
property of the National Trust, the building
contains a range of printing presses, survivals
from the 18th and 19th centuries, when
Strabane was an important publishing centre.

Stratfield Saye

Dairy Museum

*Wellington Country Park, Stratfield Saye, Reading,
RG7 2BT   ☎ 0256 882882
Mar–Oct, daily 11.30–5. Nov, Sat, Sun 10–5.30
or dusk if earlier.*
Ⓒ ♿ ⌂

The museum illustrates the history of the dairy
industry over the past 150 years. Among the
themes of the displays are milk transport, the
development of the milk churn and the glass
bottle, cheese-making, science and the dairy
industry, the milk round, and milk processing.
There are collections of chocolate moulds and
infant feeding bottles, and reconstructions of a
Victorian dairy and of a pre-1919 dairy shop
window. An audio-visual display presents the
main features of the history of the dairy industry
in Britain.

Stratfield Saye House

*Stratfield Saye, Reading, RG7 2BT
☎ 0256 882882
May–late Sept, Sat–Thurs 11.30–5.*
Ⓒ ♠ ♨ ♿ ⌂

After the defeat of Napoleon at Waterloo in
1815, the 1st Duke of Wellington was voted
£600,000 by a grateful nation to buy himself a
suitable house and estate. He chose Stratfield
Saye, and his descendants have lived in it ever
since. The main part of the house and the stable
blocks were built c. 1630. Extensions and
modifications were made during the 18th and
19th centuries.

The house contains memorabilia of the
Duke and relics of his military achievements,
family portraits, busts and a magnificent
collection of porcelain. Among the special
items are paintings of horses, many books from
Napoleon's personal library, and an 1837
billiards table. The grave of Copenhagen, the
charger ridden by the Duke at Waterloo, is in
the grounds.

Part of the stable block and an adjoining
barn have been converted to house the
Wellington Exhibition, which illustrates the life

and times of Arthur, 1st Duke of Wellington.
Among the exhibits are mementoes of his long
life as a statesman and a soldier, personal
possessions, and a fine collection of clothes,
including the original Wellington boots. There
are examples of the stable books, which include
records referring to Copenhagen in retirement.

Also on display is Wellington's great funeral
carriage, which weighs 18 tonnes. It has six
wheels and was made of bronze cast from
melted-down French cannon captured at
Waterloo.

Stratford-upon-Avon

Hall's Croft

*Old Town, Stratford-upon-Avon, Warwickshire,
CV37 6PG   ☎ 0789 292107
Apr–Sept, Mon–Sat 9–6; Sun 10–6. Oct, Mon–
Sat 9–5; Sun 10–5. Nov–Mar, Mon–Sat
9–4.30.*
Ⓒ ♧ ♨

Hall's Croft, a 16th–17th-century half-timbered
house, was the home of Dr John Hall, who
married Susanna Shakespeare, the poet's
daughter. The rooms are now furnished in the
style of a middle-class Elizabethan home, with a
garden which attempts to portray some of the
formality of Shakespeare's day and at the same
time to create the atmosphere of a more homely
garden, with familiar trees, flowers and shrubs.

The house contains an exhibition
illustrating the theory and practice of medicine
in the late 16th and early 17th centuries.

Royal Shakespeare Company Collection

*Royal Shakespeare Theatre, Stratford-upon-Avon,
Warwickshire, CV37 6BB   ☎ 0789 296655
Mon–Sat 9.15–8; Sun 12–5 (11–4, Nov–Mar)*
Ⓒ ♠ ♨ ▪ ⌂

The RSC at Stratford possesses a large
collection of designs for sets and costumes, and
photographs of productions dating back to the

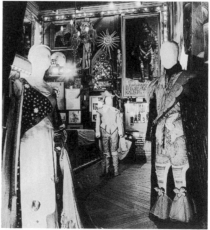

**Stage costumes and memorabilia. Royal
Shakespeare Company Collection, Stratford-
upon-Avon.**

founding of the Theatre in Stratford over 100 years ago, together with costumes, theatre properties and paintings spanning nearly two centuries of Shakespearean performances.

Each year, the theatre mounts a major exhibition relating to the current season's plays and illustrating the changing styles of production and lighting. The exhibitions are built up with sound tracks, theatre lighting and material selected from all the elements of the theatre's collections.

Shakespeare's Birthplace

Henley Street, Stratford-upon-Avon,
*   Warwickshire, CV37 6QW* ☎ *0789 204016*
Late Mar–late Oct, Mon–Sat 9–6; Sun 10–6.
Nov–Mar, Mon–Sat 9–4.30; Sun 1.30–4.30.
C̄ ▲

One section of this half-timbered building is the house in which William Shakespeare was born and the other forms part of the premises which his father used for his business as a glover and a dealer in wool. The rooms of the house are furnished in the style of the period and in the former commercial area of the building there is a museum, with exhibits illustrating the history of the property and the life, work and times of the dramatist.

Styal

Quarry Bank Mill

Styal, Cheshire, SK9 4LA   ☎ *0625 527468*
Oct–Mar, Tues–Sun 11–4; April–Sept, daily
*   11–5.*
C̄ ▲ 🖼 ⤶

Founded in 1784, Quarry Bank is the finest surviving example of a Georgian cotton mill. It has been preserved and restored by the National Trust and is leased to the Quarry Bank Mill Trust, together with the Apprentice House and the unaltered village of Styal, with cottages, school, two chapels and a shop built to serve the mill workers. The buildings, archives and exhibits at Quarry Bank tell the story of the origins and growth of the Factory System. The techniques of textile manufacturing, from hand

The parlour in the Apprentice House, Quarry Bank Mill, Styal.

processes to mechanisation, are demonstrated daily by skilled workers. The section devoted to mill workers illustrates both the working environment, with a full-scale working weaving shed and mule spinning room, and living conditions. An 1850 Fairbairn iron waterwheel, 7 metres in diameter, has been restored as a working exhibit.

Sudbury

Gainsborough's House

46 Gainsborough Street, Sudbury, Suffolk,
*   CO10 6EU*   ☎ *0787 72958*
Easter Sat–Oct, Tues–Sat 10–5; Sun and Bank
*   Holiday Mon 2–5. Nov–Maundy Thurs,*
*   Tues–Sat 10–4; Sun 2–4. Closed Good Fri,*
*   Dec 24–Jan 2.*
C̄ ⌀ ▪ ⤶

The birthplace of Thomas Gainsborough is a half-timbered house dating from the 14th century. It was altered *c.* 1520 and Georgianised in 1722 and *c.* 1790. The exhibition space is equally divided between permanent and temporary exhibitions. The temporary exhibitions are of 18th–20th-century crafts and fine art. The Gainsborough collection of portraits, landscapes and drawings, with loans from public and private sources, illustrates the artist's complete career. Works by Heins, Frost, Dupont, Bunbury and other contemporaries of Gainsborough with Suffolk connections are also shown.

Swansea

Swansea Maritime and Industrial Museum

Museum Square, Maritime Quarter, Swansea,
*   SA1 1SN*   ☎ *0792 50351/470371*
Daily 10.30–5.30
F̄ ▲ ⤶

The museum building is an early-20th-century dock warehouse. The maritime section consists both of indoor displays and of boats moored to a pontoon outside. The floating exhibits are a lightship, steam tug, Bristol Channel pilot cutter and fishing trawler, and the former Mumbles lifeboat, *The William Gammon*. The inside displays illustrate the development of Swansea Docks, cargo handling, navigation and the vessels which used the port of Swansea.

The industrial exhibits refer especially to marine and stationary engines, railway locomotives and local agriculture. There is a working woollen mill, where visitors can watch wool being carded, spun and woven into finished cloth.

Swansea Museum

Victoria Road, Swansea, SA1 1SN
*   ☎ 0792 653763*
Tues–Sat 10–4.30
C̄ ⌀ ⤶

This is the oldest museum in Wales, founded in 1835. Its collections are concerned mainly with West Glamorgan, the ceramics section being particularly noteworthy, with a large display of Swansea pottery. There is a new exhibition of natural history, arranged in habitat settings. The archaeological displays tell the story of the area over a period of 20,000 years and a chronological exhibition illustrates the history and rehabilitation of the Lower Swansea Valley, once one of the worst areas of industrial dereliction in Britain.

There is a display of Welsh domestic equipment and handicrafts, together with a reconstruction of a 19th-century kitchen.

Swindon

Great Western Railway Museum

Faringdon Road, Swindon, Wiltshire, SN1 5BJ
☎ *0793 526161 Extn 3189/4552*
Mon–Sat 10–5; Sun 2–5. Closed Good Fri, Dec 25, 26.
Ⓒ ✏

The museum building was originally a lodging-house for men working in the nearby Great Western works. It subsequently became a Wesleyan Chapel. Its collections illustrate the history of the Great Western Railway and of the leading personalities associated with it, especially Brunel, Churchward and Gooch. Five locomotives are on display, covering practically the whole period of Great Western steam locomotives. Among the wide range of exhibits are early tickets and passes, uniforms and badges, fittings from Queen Victoria's royal saloon, posters, maps and a fine collection of early railway prints by J. C. Bourne and others.

A new exhibition chronicles the history of the works and the associated facilities provided for the Company's employees – the Railway Village, the Mechanics Institute and the GWR Medical Fund. Next door, at 34 Faringdon Road, a workman's cottage has been restored to look as it would have done c. 1900.

Telford

Ironbridge Gorge Museum

The Wharfage, Ironbridge, Telford, Shropshire, TF8 7AW
☎ *095245 3522/2751(Weekends)*
Mar–Oct, daily 10–6. Nov–Feb, daily 10–5. Closed Dec 24, 25.
Ⓒ ⓘ ☕ ♿ ♠

The museum complex, based on the industrial monuments of the Ironbridge Gorge, covers an area of six square miles. In the 18th century the valley was the most important centre of ironmaking in the workd. At Coalbrookdale there is Abraham Darby's original furnace where, in 1709, he pioneered the technique of smelting iron ore with coke. The Museum of Iron, also at Coalbrookdale, illustrates the history of ironmaking and of the Coalbrookdale Company.

Further along the valley is the celebrated Iron Bridge and its tollhouse. Built in 1779, this was the first cast-iron bridge in the world. The town of Ironbridge developed at its northern end in the 1780s. Jackfield in the 1880s had two of the largest decorative tileworks in the world. In the original Cravan Dunnill Works is a museum of decorative wall and floor tiles produced in the area.

Blists Hill is a 20-hectare open-air museum, with shops, workshops, ironworks, a candle factory, a coalmine and a printing-shop. The Hay Inclined Plane runs down to the Severn from the Blists Hill site. Also nearby is the Coalport China Works, which has been restored as a museum to illustrate the techniques of china manufacture.

Tewkesbury

John Moore Countryside Museum

41 Church Street, Tewkesbury, Gloucestershire, GL20 5SN
☎ *0684 297174*
Easter–Oct, Tues–Sat and Bank Holiday 10–1, 2–5.
Ⓒ ✏ ■ ♠

The museum is in part of a row of half-timbered cottages, built c. 1450, in the precincts of Tewkesbury Abbey.

John Moore was born in Tewkesbury and wrote more than 40 books before his death in 1967. All had countryside settings and themes, and the museum has aimed at reflecting the author's love of nature.

The galleries house countryside collections of the past and present, the displays including The Farming Year, The Willow, Where the Severn and Avon Meet, and Sounds of the Seasons, with recordings of Gloucestershire wildlife. The displays are changed on a seasonal basis.

Blists Hill open-air museum, one of the sites making up the Ironbridge Gorge Museum complex, Telford.

Horse-drawn bread van. Old Kiln Rural Life Centre, Tilford.

Tilford

Old Kiln Rural Life Centre

Reeds Road, Tilford, Farnham, Surrey,
* GU10 2DL*   ☎ *025125 2300*
Apr–Sept, Wed–Sun and Bank Holidays 11–6.
Ⓒ ♿ 🦽 ⛲ 🅰

The museum's collections illustrate life in the district before the coming of the internal combustion engine. There is a wide range of hand tools used for all aspects of farm work and for forestry. The large collection of horse-drawn vehicles includes a Surrey wagon from the workshop of the celebrated George Sturt, of Farnham, and a timber-wagon. A wheelwright's shop and a blacksmith's shop have been reconstructed at the museum, and among the items illustrating the local hop-growing industry are stilts used to enable workers to reach the top wires when tying up the hops, wicker baskets for measuring the hops, a hop-press and a hessian hop-pocket.

The forestry display includes a timber nib – a horse-drawn vehicle used to tow logs from the forest – early motorised chain-saws, pit saws, and machines for de-winging and cleaning seed before it was sown in the forest nursery.

Topsham

Topsham Museum

Holman House, 25 The Strand, Topsham, Exeter,
* Devon, EX3 0AX*   ☎ *039287 3244*
Mon, Wed, Sat 2–5
Ⓒ 🧷 ⛲ 🅰

Holman House dates from *c.* 1690. It is one of a series of Dutch-style houses built along The Strand at Topsham at a time when the town was prospering by exporting Devon-manufactured

serge to European ports, principally Amsterdam and Rotterdam. A further room contains memorabilia of the founder of the museum, Dorothy Holman (d. 1983), whose 19th-century ancestors were shipowners and shipbuilders in Topsham.

Local history items are displayed in a former sail-loft, built behind the house in 1858. Here, special attention is given to Topsham's trading days and shipbuilding industry. There are exhibits of half-models and shipbuilding tools, and a model of Topsham as it was in 1900. The displays in the Estuary Room illustrate the wildlife of the estuary.

Tunstall

Chatterley Whitfield Mining Museum

Tunstall, Stoke-on-Trent, Staffordshire, ST6 8UN
*   ☎ 0782 813337*
Daily 10–4. Last pit tour 3.30. Evening tours by
*   special arrangement.*
Ⓒ ♿ ⛲ ⛟ 🅰

Chatterley Whitfield Colliery was worked from 1860 to 1976. It was the first colliery to produce a million tons of coal in a year. A number of the surface installations have been preserved, including the lamp-room, canteen, and the steam winding engine, which raised coal up the 600-metre deep Hesketh shaft. Visitors descend the 200-metre Winstanley shaft, where they are guided around the workings by former miners and shown reconstructed scenes of miners at work, illustrating the different methods of extraction used over the past 150 years.

Chatterley Whitfield now houses the National Mining Collection, brought from Lound Hall in Nottinghamshire.

Uffculme

Coldharbour Mill

Uffculme, Cullompton, Devon, EX15 3EE
*   ☎ 0884 40960/40858*
Easter–Oct, daily 11–5. Last admission 4. Oct–
*   Easter, Mon–Fri 11–5 (Please telephone to*
*   confirm).*
Ⓒ ♿ ⛲ 🅰

During the 18th century Coldharbour Mill was used first as a paper mill and then, after damage from a flood, was rebuilt as a grist mill. In 1797 it was bought by Thomas Fox, a Wellington woollen manufacturer, who needed a new source of water power for the expansion of his business. His new factory, by the side of the River Culm, continued in production until 1981.

The factory has now been converted into a working museum, with the original machinery. Visitors can watch the whole process of woollen manufacture from fleece to woven cloth and combed tops to knitting wool. The 5-metre breast-shot waterwheel, used until 1978, can still be seen, as can the 300 horse-power steam engine, which powered the machinery from 1910 to 1981.

Ulverston

Stott Park Bobbin Mill

Finsthwaite, Newby Bridge, Via Ulverston,
Cumbria, LA12 8AX   ☎ 0448 31087
Apr–Oct 13, daily 10–6. Oct 14–31, daily 10–4.
Pre-booked parties during winter months.
Ⓒ *(ex children)* ♥ ♠

Stott Park is on the road between Newby Bridge
and Hawkshead, along the western shore of
Lake Windermere. It was built as a bobbin mill
in 1835 and was in use until 1971. Now
operated as a working museum, it illustrates not
only all the processes involved in the
manufacture of bobbins, but also the woodland-
based economy of the Furness Fells. Bobbin-
turning was one skilled woodland industry it
proved possible to mechanise. The steam-driven
machinery at the mill, regularly demonstrated,
includes a turbine, steam engine, line shafting
and lathes. Visitors are made aware of the cold,
dirty, noisy and dangerous working conditions
which existed at the mill before the Factory
Acts and the Health and Safety at Work
regulations came into force.

Wakefield

Wakefield Art Gallery

Wentworth Terrace, Wakefield, West Yorkshire,
WF1 3QW   ☎ 0924 375402
Mon–Sat 10.30–5. Open all public and local
government holidays, in the spring and summer.
Ⓕ ♥ ♠

The building, which dates from 1885, was
formerly a vicarage. It has good plasterwork and
fine decorative glass panels on the main
staircase. It became an art gallery in 1934. The
emphasis of the collections is on British 20th-
century paintings and sculpture, but Edwardian,
Victorian and earlier artists are well
represented. Special rooms are devoted to
Barbara Hepworth, born and brought up in
Wakefield, and to Henry Moore, a native of
nearby Castleford. The gallery holds some
outstanding works by both these artists.

Some of the Barbara Hepworth sculptures
are placed in the garden around the gallery,
where there are also works by Austin Wright
and Kim Lim.

Yorkshire Mining Museum

Caphouse Colliery, New Road, Overton,
Wakefield, WF4 4RH   ☎ 0924 848806
Daily 10–5.
Ⓒ ♦ ▬ ♿ ☞ ♠

Caphouse Colliery produced coal from 1790
until 1985. Its wooden headstock, the last to
survive in Yorkshire, and its stone engine house
both date from 1876. The original twin-cylinder
steam winding engine has survived and the main
shaft, sunk in 1795, may be the oldest usable
shaft in Europe. The other buildings show the
pit's gradual modernisation, and nearby are
bell-pits illustrating the earliest days of coal

extraction. A horse-gin shows how coal and
men were brought up and down the shaft before
the arrival of steam-engines.

There is a tour of the underground workings,
with exhibits showing technical developments
during the life of the colliery. Above ground,
there are outdoor machinery exhibits and a
gallery with displays showing the history of the
Yorkshire coalfield and the life of the mining
communities. The museum also has a reference
library and a photographic collection relating to
Yorkshire coalmining.

Walsall

Jerome K. Jerome's Birthplace

Belsize Houe, Bradford Street, Walsall, West
Midlands, WS1 1PN
     ☎ 0922 21244 extn 3124/3115
Tues–Sat 10–5
Ⓕ ▪

The author of the very popular novel, *Three
Men in a Boat* (1889) was born here in 1859.
The house has been recently renovated and two
rooms arranged as a Jerome museum. One of
these contains displays about the writer's life
and achievements and the other has been
reconstructed as a parlour of the 1850s, to give
the impression of what the interior of a middle-
class Walsall town house of the period looked
like. Among the Jerome memorabilia on show
are his pens, inkwell, cigarette case and walking
stick.

Walsall Museum and Art Gallery

Lichfield Street, Walsall, West Midlands,
WS1 1TR   ☎ 0922 21244 extn 3124/3115
Mon–Fri 10–6; Sat 10–4.45. Closed Bank
Holiday.
Ⓕ ♥ ♿ ♠

Walsall Art Gallery contains a collection
donated by Lady Kathleen Epstein, the nucleus
of which is composed of important works by her
husband, the sculptor, Sir Jacob Epstein.
Among the remainder of the collection are
pieces by Epstein's friends, relations, colleagues
and acquaintances, including Picasso, Braque,

**On the Thames (*How Happy I Could Be with
Either*), 1876, by J.J. Tissot. Wakefield Art
Gallery.**

Matthew Smith and Lucian Freud. Most of the items date from the late 19th to early 20th centuries, but there are a number of earlier works, notably Dürer woodcuts and Rembrandt drawings.

The museum uses a selection of its extensive local history collection to illustrate the origins and development of Walsall and to show what it was like to live in the town in the past. There is good coverage of Walsall's major trades, saddlery and leatherworking and lorinery (saddlers' ironmongery) and, at the branch museum at Willenhall, locks.

Wanlockhead

Museum of Scottish Lead Mining

Goldscaur Row, Wanlockhead, By Biggar, Lanarkshire, ML12 6UP   ☎ 06594 387
Easter–Sept, daily 11–4 (last mine tour 3.30).
Ⓒ ♨ ♿

Wanlockhead, in the Lowther Hills, is Scotland's highest village. The Mining Museum contains relics of 250 years of lead mining in the area, including machinery, tools and equipment. There are also displays of maps, documents, photographs and models, and of gold, silver and minerals mined locally. Reconstructions of a miner's kitchen and miner's library (1756) illustrate social and family life in the mining community.

The open-air section of the museum includes Loch Nell, a drift mine worked from the early 1700s to 1860, the Wanlockhead beam engine, Pates Knowes, a smelt-mill which operated from 1764 to 1842, and the workshops and forge at the Bay Mine, where William Symington assembled his first atmospheric steamboat engine in 1788.

Welshpool

Powis Castle

Welshpool, Powys, SY21 8RF   ☎ 0938 4336
Easter–June, Sept–Oct, Wed–Sun 12–5. July–Aug, Tues–Sun 11–6.
Ⓒ ♦ 🍴 ♿ ♨

Powis Castle, with its famous gardens, is one mile south of Welshpool on the Newtown road. Built in the 13th century, it was remodelled during the 16th, late 17th and late 19th centuries to meet the changing requirements of the Herbert family, who have lived here since 1587. The castle is now a National Trust property. It contains fine furniture, paintings and tapestries from a variety of periods. Among the series of family portraits are works by Kneller, Gainsborough, Reynolds and Romney. The castle includes the Clive Museum, which displays the remarkable collection of Indian treasures started by the 18th-century colonial governor, Robert, Lord Clive, and continued by his son, Edward, 2nd Lord Clive and 1st Earl of Powis.

Widnes

Catalyst: The Museum of the Chemical Industry

Mersey Road, Widnes, Cheshire, WA8 0DF
☎ 051 420 1121
Tues–Sun and Bank Holidays 10–5. Closed Jan 1, Good Fri, Dec 24–26.
Ⓒ ♦ ♿ ♨

Catalyst is housed in a complex of mid-19th-century listed buildings which have a long association with the chemical industry.

The exhibition, 'Industry in View', is in a specially designed observation gallery thirty metres up, which gives visitors an excellent view over the surrounding district. It concentrates on the rôle of the chemical industry in everyday life and is the first in a series of developments. It has a number of exhibits which visitors can operate themselves.

Winchester

Winchester Museum

The Square, Winchester, Hampshire.
☎ 0962 840269
Apr–Sept, Mon–Sat 10–5; Sun 2–5. Oct–Mar, Tues–Sat 10–5; Sun 2–4.
Ⓕ ♨

The museum's displays reflect the archaeology and history of Winchester, where excavations have produced a rich collection of Roman, Anglo-Saxon and medieval material. Among the exhibits are Anglo-Saxon jewellery and metalwork, including a reliquary, a late Anglo-Saxon wall painting, Anglo-Saxon and Romanesque sculpture, and Roman glass, metalwork and ceramics from the Lankhills cemetery.

The historical collections include reconstructions of an Edwardian bathroom and of a chemist's and a tobacconist's shop formerly in the High Street.

Anglo-Saxon reliquary with acanthus-leaf decoration, early 10th-century. Winchester Museum.

Windsor

Madame Tussaud's *Royalty and Empire* exhibition, Windsor.

Royal Borough Collection

Windsor and Eton Central Station, Windsor, Berkshire, SL4 1PJ   ☎ *0753 857837*
Daily 9.30–5.30. Closed Dec 25.
ⓒ 🔒 ♿ 🅿

The Royal Borough Collection, formerly displayed in the Guildhall, illustrates the history of the town in Victorian times. The items on display form a section of Madame Tussaud's *Royalty and Empire* exhibition. They illustrate the strong connections between Windsor and the Royal Family, living conditions in Victorian Windsor, which was notorious for its poverty and slums during the earlier years of the Queen's reign, local shops and trades, and the social activities of the town.

Wolferton

Wolferton Station Museum

Wolferton, Sandringham Estate, King's Lynn, Norfolk, PE31 6HA   ☎ *0485 40674*
Apr–Sept, Mon–Fri 11–1, 2–6; Sun 2–6.
ⓒ 🔒 🅿

The mock-Tudor station building at Wolferton was designed by the Great Eastern Railway's architect, W.N. Ashbee, to meet the requirements of the Royal Family and their guests when visiting Sandringham. The interior is panelled throughout in oak, with decorative ceilings and all the windows in leaded opaque lights, to prevent the public looking through.

Between 1898 and its closure in 1965, all the kings and queens of Europe passed through its doors. Preserved as it was in its heyday, it now forms part of the home of its present owner. The Equerries' Corridor contains relics of the golden years of steam travel. The Centre Hall displays personal letters, photographs and documents connected with various sovereigns who used it. Queen Alexandra's Room has Queen Victoria's travelling bed, together with

some of her clothes and memorabilia of Alexandra and her children.

There is a collection of furniture and other items from Royal trains, and among the exhibits are the personal lavatories of the King and Queen, complete with their unique fittings which have been restored to full working order.

Wolverhampton

Wolverhampton Art Gallery and Museum

Lichfield Street, Wolverhampton, West Midlands, WV1 1DU   ☎ *0902 24549*
Mon–Sat 9–6. Closed Bank Holiday.
Ⓕ 🔒 💻 ♿ 🅿

The fine art collection comprises 18th–20th-century paintings, prints, drawings and sculpture, mainly British. Among the earlier artists represented are Gainsborough, Wilson, Zoffany, Fuseli, Turner, Sandby, Cox and Landseer, with special sections devoted to Edward Bird and the Cranbrook Colony, including F. D. Hardy. The Modern collection includes Pop Art by British and American artists. The earlier 20th-century part of the collection has paintings by Spencer, Paul Nash, Wadsworth, Hillier, Grant and Armstrong.

There is also a good collection of Oriental applied art, including weapons, ivories, ceramics and woodcarvings, originating from China, Japan and the Indian sub-continent.

Worcester

The Dyson Perrins Museum

Severn Street, Worcester, WR1 2NE
☎ *0905 23221*
Mon–Fri 9.30–5; Sat 10–5. Closed Dec 25, 26.
Ⓕ 🔒 💻 ♿ 🅿

The museum is housed in a former Victorian school and contains the world's largest

Royal Worcester decorative tea-pot. Dyson Perrins Museum, Worcester.

collection of Royal Worcester porcelain. The exhibits include the Wigornia Creamboat, which dates from 1751 and was the first piece made by the Company, and the giant vase made for the Chicago Exhibition in 1893. There are also items from a number of the services made for British and Continental monarchs and many examples of the decorative porcelain produced over the past 240 years.

Tours of the modern factory give visitors an opportunity to see how Royal Worcester is made.

Worthing

Worthing Museum and Art Gallery

Chapel Road, Worthing, West Sussex, BN11 1HD
   ☎ *0903 39999 extn 121*
Apr–Sept, Mon–Sat 10–6. Oct–Mar, Mon–Sat
   10–5. Closed Jan 1, Good Fri, Dec 25, 26.
F 🛈 ♿

The museum's collections are wide-ranging but with an emphasis on local themes. There is good coverage of local archaeology and social history, an excellent costume section and paintings and watercolours of the 19th and 20th centuries, as well as interesting collections of English glass and ceramics.

The museum has recently been reorganised. Particularly noteworthy now are the Costume Gallery, the Downland section and the new Archaeology Gallery, which displays the fine Anglo-Saxon glass and jewellery from Highdown Hill. The newly refurbished art gallery is one of the most attractive in the South-East.

Wrexham

Bersham Industrial Heritage Centre

Bersham, Wrexham, Clwyd, LL14 4HT
   ☎ *0978 261529*
Easter–Oct, Tues–Sat and Bank Holiday Mon
   10–12.30, 1.30–4; Sun 2–4. Nov–Easter,
   Tues–Fri 10–12.30, 1.30–4; Sat 12.30–3.30.
F 🖉 ♿ ♿

The centre is two miles west of Wrexham. It was established in 1983 to interpret the history of local industries, on the site of the celebrated 18th-century Bersham ironworks. It was here that John 'Iron Mad' Wilkinson made cannons which were used in the American War of Independence, and developed a method of boring cylinders which made the Boulton and Watt steam engine a practical possibility. There is a special exhibition, with an authentically reconstructed forge, on the Davies Brothers, the gatesmiths who made the famous Chirk Castle gates.

Yanworth

Chedworth Roman Villa

Yanworth, Cheltenham, Gloucestershire,
   GL54 3LJ   ☎ *024 289256*
March–Oct, daily 10–5.30 (Last admission 5).
   Nov–mid Dec, Wed–Sun 11–4. Feb, booked
   parties.
F 🛈 ♿ ♿

This is the most thoroughly exposed Romano-British villa in the west of Britain and is a National Trust property. There is a site museum with an introductory audio-visual display.

The villa was occupied from about AD 120 to about AD 400: in the fourth century it was a large and wealthy establishment. There are two bath suites, a water shrine built over the spring which still supplies the site, and at least two *triclinia*, or dining rooms. There are fine fourth-century Corinian mosaics. The three ranges of buildings are set in the head of an attractive wooded valley and were first examined in 1864. Further excavation is in progress.

The villa is three miles west of the A429 Fosse Way from Stow to Cirencester. Approach from Northleach or, from Cheltenham, through Withington (cars only). Do not go to Chedworth village itself.

York

Castle Howard

Castle Howard, York, YO6 7DA
   ☎ *065384 333*
Late Mar–Oct, daily 11–5 (last admission 4.30).
   Grounds and Gardens, 10–6.30.
C 🛈 ♿ ♿ ♿ ♿

Castle Howard is 6 miles south-west of Malton, off the A64.

It has the unusual distinction of having been open to the public since it was built in the 18th century. The later Stable Court, by John Carr of York, contains the largest private collection of period costumes in Britain. Each year a different selection is displayed, in settings which reflect the atmosphere of the period. The collection contains domestic, occupational, ceremonial, ecclesiastical, theatrical and children's items.

Jorvik Viking Centre

Coppergate, York, YO1 1NT   ☎ *0904 643211*
Apr–Oct, daily 9–7. Nov–Mar, daily 10–5.30.
  Closed Dec 25.
Ⓒ 🃏 ♿ ⇨

The centre is on the site of the Viking
settlement discovered by archaeologists at
Coppergate. Visitors are taken by electrically
operated train through a reconstruction of a
Viking street, with a recorded commentary on
the early history of the city, and on living and
working conditions in Viking York. The
Skipper Gallery contains examples of the wide
range of objects found during the excavations
and shows techniques employed by the
archaeologists.

National Railway Museum

Leeman Road, York, YO2 4XJ   ☎ *0904 621261*
Mon–Sat 10–6; Sun 11–6. Closed Jan 1, Dec
  24–26.
Ⓒ 🃏 ♿ ⇨

The museum occupies a former steam
locomotive maintenance depot and operates as
part of the National Museum of Science and
Industry. It was created to tell the story of
railways and railway engineering in Britain. Its
large collections include locomotives, rolling
stock, signalling equipment, sections of rail used
at different periods, and uniforms. There are
also working models, posters, paintings,
photographs, drawings, films and a wide range of
smaller railway relics.

York Castle Museum

York, YO1 1RY   ☎ *0904 653611*
Apr–Oct, Mon–Sat 9.30–6.30; Sun 10–6.30.
  Nov–Mar, Mon–Sat 9.30–5; Sun 10–5. Last
  admission one hour before closing time. Closed
  Jan 1, Dec 25, 26.
Ⓒ 🃏 🖼 ♿

The museum is in two 18th-century prisons,
built on the site of York Castle. There are period
rooms, reconstructed workshops and displays of
armour, weapons, especially swords, musical
instruments, toys and dolls, and craftsmen's
tools. The collection of costumes and
accessories is one of the best in Britain. Kirkgate
is a reconstruction of a York street, with its
courts and alleys, and contains a number of old
shop fronts and other buildings from York and
elsewhere in Yorkshire, rescued from
destruction during the 1930s. Horse-drawn
vehicles, including the Sheriff of York's State
Coach, are to be seen in Half Moon Court, the
museum's Edwardian street scene.
  Some of the debtors' cells, which formed the
late 18th-century prison, have been converted
into reconstructions of the workshops of a
comb-maker, wheelwright, clay pipe-maker,
brush-maker, blacksmith and printer. One of
the former cells is arranged as a visiting cell,
with late-18th-century fixtures brought from
Northallerton Gaol. The former condemned
cell in which, according to tradition, Dick
Turpin, the highwayman, was imprisoned
before his execution, has also been preserved in
its original form.
  The Military Gallery houses an exhibition
called 'Great Yorkshire Battles', which
concentrates on the English Civil War, 1642–
48.

York City Art Gallery

Exhibition Square, York, YO1 2EW
  ☎ *0904 23839*
Mon–Sat 10–5; Sun 2.30–5. Closed Jan 1, Dec
  25, 26.
Ⓒ 🃏

The gallery's collections consist of European and
British paintings from the 14th century to the
present day; watercolours and prints, mainly of
Yorkshire subjects; works by Yorkshire artists,
especially William Etty, whose sketchbooks are
also preserved and exhibited here; and modern
stoneware pottery.

Yorkshire Museum

Museum Gardens, York, YO1 2DR
  ☎ *0904 629745*
Mon–Sat 10–5; Sun 1–5. Closed Jan 1, Dec 25,
  26.
Ⓒ 🃏 ⇨

The Museum building was designed in the Doric
style by William Wilkins, the architect of the
National Gallery in London. There are
exceptionally rich collections of Roman, Anglo-
Saxon, Viking and medieval antiquities,
including Viking weapons and everyday objects
from Coppergate and other sites in York. The
museum also has Roman mosaics and a fine
display of Yorkshire pottery. The Roman Life
Gallery uses archaeological evidence to present
a picture of Roman civilisation in Britain, with
a special emphasis on *Eboracum* (York), the
most important town in the North of England
during the Roman period.

**Time tunnel tableau. Jorvik Viking Centre,
York.**

Reconstructed street facade. York Castle Museum.

DENMARK

Aalborg

North Jutland Museum of Art

*Nordjyllands Kunstmuseum, Kong Christians Allé
50, DK-9000 Aalborg, N. Jylland*
☎ 98 138088
*Tues–Sun 10–5. June 15–Sept 15, also open Mon.
Closed Dec 24, 25, 31.*
Ⓒ ⓘ 💻 ⚹ ♿

The museum, opened in 1972, is in a building
designed by Elissa and Alvar Aalto and Jean-
Jacques Baruël. Its basic collection, still
growing, is of Danish and foreign 20th-century
art, with the emphasis on contemporary works.
Among the more important items in its
collections are early Danish Modernist
paintings, paintings from the international
Cobra group, and paintings and objects
representing the Fluxus movement.

Aarhus

Aarhus Art Museum

*Aarhus Kunstmuseum, Vennelystparken,
DK-8000 Aarhus C, S. Jylland*
☎ 86 135255
Tues–Sun 10–5
Ⓒ ⓘ 💻 ♿

The museum, founded in 1859, was Denmark's
first public art collection outside the capital. Its
present building was opened in 1967. It contains
paintings, drawings and sculptures by Danish
artists from 1750 to the present day. In recent
years, it has built up a considerable collection of
Danish contemporary art, supplemented by
international material, especially from Germany
and the United States.

**Fibre art exhibits. North Jutland Museum of
Art, Aalborg.**

'The Old Town'

*'Den Gamle By', Viborgvej, DK-8000 Aarhus C,
S. Jylland*   ☎ 86 123188
*Jan–Feb, reduced opening hours. Mar and Nov,
daily 11–3. Apr and Oct, Mon–Sat 10–4; Sun
10–5. May and Sept, daily 10–5. June–Aug,
daily 9–5. Dec, Mon–Sat 11–3; Sun 10–3.*
Ⓒ ⓘ 💻 ⚹ ♿

'The Old Town' is a museum of urban life,
containing 65 buildings from the late 16th
century to the present day, which have been
brought from all over Denmark and rebuilt on
the museum site. They are all suitably furnished
and equipped and include workshops, a
chemist's shop, a school, a post office, a customs
house and an early-19th-century theatre. There
are also collections of toys, china, silver,
textiles, musical instruments, clocks and
watches.

Auning

Danish Agricultural Museum

*Dansk Landbrugsmuseum, Gammel-Estrup,
DK-8963 Auning, S. Jylland* ☎ 86 483444
Daily 10–5. Closed Dec 24, 25, 31.
Ⓒ ⓘ 💻 ⚹ ♿

The museum occupies farm buildings in the
grounds of a large manor house, with a history
going back to 1300. This is open as a separate
museum and illustrates the style of life of two
noble families, Brok and Schell, who
successively occupied the manor until 1936.
    The Agricultural Museum illustrates the
development of Danish agriculture from the late
18th century until c. 1960. The displays cover
life in the farmhouse as well as on the farm and
there are comprehensive collections of tools,
machinery, vehicles and household equipment.

Copenhagen

Copenhagen City Museum

*Københavns Bymuseum, Vesterbrogade 59,
DK-1620 København V* ☎ 31 210772
*Correspondence to: Absalonsgade 3, Postbox 3004,
DK-1507 København V.*
*May–Sept, Tues–Sun 10–4. Oct–Apr, Tues–Sun
1–4.*
Ⓕ ⓘ ♿

The Copenhagen City Museum was founded in
1901. In 1956 it was moved from the attics of
the town hall to the former Royal Shooting
Society building, which dates from 1787. It
documents the history of Copenhagen from the
Middle Ages until c. 1900, by means of
paintings, engravings and models.
    Sections of demolished houses, trade signs
and other survivals give an impression of the
Copenhagen street scene in the 18th and 19th

centuries. An outdoor museum street, with cobblestones, gas lamps, benches, a telephone kiosk and other street furniture from *c.* 1860–1940 has been constructed in Absalonsgade, next to the museum. The exhibition also illustrates firefighting in earlier times.

There is a section devoted to the Danish philosopher and essayist, Søren Kierkegaard (1813–55), who was born and died in Copenhagen.

Freedom Museum

Frihedsmuseet, Churchillparken, DK-1263 København K   ☎ *33 137714*
May–Sept 15, Tues–Sat 10–4; Sun and public holidays 10–5. Sept 16–Apr, Tues–Sat 11–3; Sun and public holidays 11–4. Closed Whit Sun, June 5, Dec 24, 25, 31.

Ｆ 🅰 💻 ﹠

The museum, which is a branch of the National Museum, contains historic collections which tell the story of the years of German occupation between 1940 and 1945, and especially of the Danish resistance movement and its anti-German activities, such as illegal printing, receiving supplies dropped by parachute, sabotage and the rescue of Danish Jews.

Hirschsprung Collection

Den Hirschsprungske Samling, Stockholmsgade 20, DK-2100 København Ø   ☎ *31 420336*
Wed–Sun 1–4. Oct–Apr, also Wed 7–10 pm. Closed Easter Sun, Whit Sun, June 5, Dec 24, 25.

Ｆ 🅰 🚗

Heinrich Hirschsprung (1836–1909), a tobacco merchant, left to the nation his art collection which is the core of this still growing museum. It comprises Danish art of the 19th and early 20th centuries, displayed in room interiors, with furnishings from the homes of the artists. The emphasis is on works from the so-called Golden Age of Danish painting, 1780–1850, as well as on Hirschsprung's younger contemporaries, and above all on painters of the Skagen school, particularly P.S. Kirøyer.

National Museum

Nationalmuseet, Frederikholms Kanal 12, DK-1220 København K   ☎ *31 134411*
June 16 – Sept 15, Fri–Wed 10–4. Sept 16 – June 15, Fri–Wed 11–3; Sun 1–5.

Ｆ 🅰 💻 ﹠

The major part of the museum's collections relate to the prehistory and history of Denmark. There are period rooms, illustrating the living styles of different social levels of the Danish people. Other important sections of the museum illustrate the history and archaeology of Europe during the classical period. There are large collections of European coins and medals, from Greek and Roman times onwards, with an emphasis on those found and produced in Denmark.

Painting by Anna Ancher. Hirschsprung Collection, Copenhagen.

Rosenborg Castle

Rosenborg Slot, Øster Voldgade 4 A, DK-1350 København K   ☎ *33 153286*
Castle: Jan–Apr and Oct 23–Dec 31, Tues, Fri 11–1; Sun 11–2. May and Sept–Oct 22, daily 11–3. June–Aug, daily 10–3. Treasury: Jan–May and Oct 23–Dec, Tues–Sun 11–3. June–Aug, daily 10–3. Sept–Oct 22, daily 11–3.

Ｃ 🅰 ﹠

Rosenborg was built in 1606–34 as a Royal Garden House, in the Dutch Renaissance style. It contains the Crown Jewels and memorabilia and treasures of the Royal Family, from the 15th to the 19th century. There are notable collections of furniture, porcelain, silver and paintings.

Rundetårn

Rundetårn, Købmagergade 52A, DK-1150 København K   ☎ *33 936660*
Apr–May and Sept–Oct, Mon–Sat 10–5; Sun and public holidays 12–4. June–Aug, Mon–Sat 10–8; Sun and public holidays 12–8. Nov–Mar, Mon–Sat 10–4; Sun and public holidays 12–4. Closed Jan 1, Dec 24, 25. Observatory: Oct–Mar, Tues, Wed 7–10 pm.

Ｃ 🅰 ﹠

Rundetårn (the Round Tower) was built in 1637–42 on the initiative of King Christian IV. It contains a spiral walk which is unique in European architecture. The 209-metre ramp winds 7.5 turns round the hollow core of the Tower, forming the only connection between the three parts of the building complex it was designed to serve, a university library, a students' church and an astronomical observatory.

Rundetårn is the oldest functioning observatory in Europe. Until 1861 it was still used by the University of Copenhagen, but now anyone can observe the night sky through its fine telescope.

The old University Library contains an exhibition of the Round Tower's collection of instruments and explains the Tower's connection with the great Danish astronomers, Tycho Brahe, Ole Rømer and Thomas Bugge. In another room of the Library the Oldnordisk Museum was to be found from 1807 to 1832. This was the beginning of the present National Museum.

St Ansgar's Church Museum

Sankt Ansgars Kirkes Museum, Bredgade 64, DK-1260 København K ☎ *33 133762* *Tues–Sat 11–4; Sun 11–4. Please telephone before visit.*
F

After the Reformation of 1536, the practice of the Catholic faith was not allowed, except to foreign diplomats. In Copenhagen, local Catholics went, illegally, to the Embassy chapel, and in the mid 17th century a register of Catholic baptisms, marriages and deaths and of the names of priests was begun, under the aegis of the Spanish Ambassador. In 1764, the community received a permanent chapel at what is now Bredgade 64, personally paid for by the Austrian Empress, Maria Theresa. A new building, the present St Ansgar's, was opened in 1840 and officially consecrated in 1865, the millennium of the death of Ansgar, the Apostle of the North. It became a cathedral in 1958.

The museum in the church tells the story of the Catholic Church in Denmark from the Reformation to the present day. The exhibits include vestments, church silver, documents, paintings and portraits.

State Museum of Art

Statens Museum for Kunst, Sølvgade, DK-1307 København K ☎ *31 122126* *Tues, Thurs–Sun 10–5; Wed 10–10.*
F 👤 💼 👤

Night with her children, sleep and death, 1815, by Bertel Thorvaldsen. Thorvaldsen Museum, Copenhagen.

The museum has collections of Danish paintings and sculpture from the 18th to the 20th century. 19th- and 20th-century paintings from the other Scandinavian countries and 16th–20th-century Italian, Flemish, Dutch, German and French paintings are also represented.

Theatre Museum

Teatermuseet, Christiansborg Ridebane 18, DK-1218 København K ☎ *33 115176* *June–Sept, Wed, Fri, Sun 2–4. Oct–May, Wed, Sun 2–4.*
C 👤

The Court Theatre at the Royal Palace of Christiansborg was a conversion of the Armoury above the Royal Stables. It was opened in 1767 and was ingeniously designed , so that the floor could be raised to the level of the stage, to make a huge ballroom. On these occasions, the scenery was concealed by large movable walls, while the boxes were transformed into private gambling cabinets. The theatre was very much used for ballet and for concerts during the 19th century, but was closed for all performances in 1881 after the fire at the Ring Theatre in Vienna in which hundreds of people died. It was re-opened in 1923 as a museum of the history of the Danish theatre from the time of the dramatist Baron Ludvig Holberg (1684–1754) to the present day. The exhibits include costumes, models of scenery and stage sets, paintings, drawings and photographs.

Thorvaldsen Museum

Thorvaldsens Museum, Posthusgade 2, DK-1213 København K ☎ *33 321532* *Tues–Sun 10–5. Closed Jan 1, May 1, June 5, Dec 24, 25, 31.*
F 👤 💼 👤

In 1838 the Danish sculptor Bertel Thorvaldsen (1770–1844) returned to Copenhagen in triumph, after working very successfully in Rome for 40 years. He devoted his art collection, his library and his fortune to the creation of a museum for his own sculpture and paintings. It was built between 1839 and 1848 to a very unconventional design. Thorvaldsen did not live to see its completion. He died during a performance at the Royal Court Theatre and was buried in the courtyard of his museum.

Elsinore

Danish Maritime Museum

Handels- og Søfartsmuseet på Kronborg, Kronborg Slot, DK-3000 Helsingør, Sjaelland ☎ *49 210685* *May–Sept, daily 10.30–5. Apr and Oct, daily 11–4. Nov–Mar, Tues–Sun 11–3. Closed Mon in winter except at Christmas, Easter and the autumn holiday.*
C 👤 👤

The fortified Royal Castle, Kronborg, dates from the late 16th century. The Royal apartments are open to the public and the castle also contains the Danish Maritime Museum, with collections illustrating the history of Danish merchant shipping and trade with foreign countries, especially the former Danish colonies. The exhibits include ship models, navigational equipment, paintings, prints and charts.

Danish Technical Museum

Danmarks Tekniske Museum, Ole Rømersvej,
*   DK-3000 Helsingør, Sjaelland*   ☎ *03 22261*
Daily 10–5
Ⓒ ⓘ 🖳 ⓧ ⓪

The museum's collections illustrate the development and significance of the natural sciences, technology, transport, industry and means of communication in Denmark from the 17th century onwards. There are examples of early aeroplanes, motor cars, bicycles, tram cars and an entire railway train of 1868.

Esbjerg

Esbjerg Museum

Esbjerg Museum, Nørregade 25, DK-6700
*   Esbjerg, S. Jylland*   ☎ *75 127811*
Tues–Sun and public holidays 10–4
Ⓒ ⓘ 🖳 ⓧ ⓪

The main feature of the museum is a series of scenes showing the town as it was during the period 1890–1940, with house-fronts, shops and harbour scenes, including the quayside, a fish-processing factory and a machine shop. The exhibition gives a general impression of the development of Esbjerg and its special characteristics.

There are also displays of domestic equipment, costumes, embroidery and other traditional crafts, together with prehistoric and Viking material from local excavations.

Bangsbo Museum, Frederikshavn.

Fishing and Maritime Museum

Fiskeri-og Søfartsmuseet, Tarphagevej, DK-6710
*   Esbjerg, S. Jylland*   ☎ *75 150666*
Sept–May, daily 10–4. June, daily 10–5. July–
*   Aug, daily 10–8. Closed Jan 1, Dec 24, 25,*
*   31.*
Ⓒ ⓘ 🖳 ⓧ ⓪

The museum's collections illustrate the history and techniques of the Danish fishing industry, together with the maritime history of Esbjerg and Fanø. There are displays of boats and fishing equipment and of shipbuilding. The salt-water aquarium shows the fish to be found in the North Sea, and there is a sealarium.

Farsø

Hessel Agricultural Museum

Hessel Landbrugsmuseum, Hesselvej 40,
*   Hvalpsund, DK-9640 Farsø, N. Jylland*
*   ☎ 98 638125*
Apr–Oct, daily 10–5.30
Ⓒ ⓘ ⓪

Hessel is Denmark's last surviving thatched manor house. The house, farm buildings and estate were bought and restored by the North Jutland County Authority in 1966 and converted into a museum.

The main building was rebuilt *c.* 1700 after a fire and alterations and extensions were made during the first part of the 19th century. The various rooms contain their original mid-19th-century furnishings. The large barn, which survived the fire, is dated 1655 and now contains a large collection of horse-drawn vehicles and agricultural implements.

Frederikshavn

Bangsbo Museum

Bangsbomuseet, Dronning Margrethesvej 6,
*   DK-9900 Frederikshavn, N. Jylland*
*   ☎ 98 423111*
Apr–Oct, daily 10–5. Nov–Mar, Tues–Sun 10–5.
Ⓒ ⓘ 🖳 ⓧ ⓪

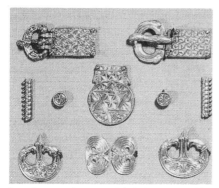

Late Roman 'chip-carved' belt fittings in gilded silver. Haderslev Museum.

The present manor house of Bangsbo was built in 1660, on the foundations of an earlier house. Additions were made in the 19th and early 20th centuries. The house was bought by the municipality in 1944 and converted into a museum showing the history of Frederikshavn, especially the development of its fishing and shipping industries. There are collections of ship models and half-models, especially of ships built in the local yards, and of figureheads and ornaments from vessels wrecked along the local coast. The museum also has a 12th-century Viking cargo ship, discovered at Ellingå, near Frederikshavn.

Other exhibits include a collection of vehicles covering the period from the 17th century to the Second World War, and two furnished room interiors, one from the mid 19th century and the other c. 1900. Displays of domestic equipment, glass and china are presented in smaller rooms. There is also a large collection of 19th-century jewellery and other ornaments made from human hair. The Second World War room is divided into five sections, each showing one of the five years, 1940–1945, of the German occupation of Denmark.

Frederiksvaerk

Frederiksvaerk Museum

Frederiksvaerkegnens Museum og Frederiksvaerk Bymuseum, Torvet 3, DK-3300 Frederiksvaerk, Sjaelland ☎ 42 125493
June 15 – Aug 15, Tues–Sun 11–3. Aug 16 – June 14, Sat, Sun 1–4.
© ⚓

The town of Frederiksvaerk grew up around its important armament works, which supplied cannons and ammunition to the Danish Army from 1750 onwards, as well as to the former Danish colonies in Africa, Asia and the West Indies. The museum, in the former Arsenal, illustrates the history of the Works and there are also exhibits from Dronningholm Castle, now a ruin, which dates from c. 1200, and a fine textile collection from the North Zealand region, as well as paintings and drawings related to the development of the town.

Glud

Glud Museum

Glud Museum, Museumsvej 44, Glud, DK-8700 Horsens, S. Jylland ☎ 75 683082
Apr–Sept, daily 10–5. Oct, Sun and autumn school holiday, 12–3.
© ⬧ ⚓

This was Denmark's first village museum, established in 1912 by the folklorist Søren Knudsen (1878–1955). The buildings include a threshing barn (1688), a fisherman's house (1725), three farmhouses, including Denmark's earliest dated farmhouse (1662), part of a vicarage, and a smithy (1758). All the buildings contain appropriate furniture and equipment. A new gallery, built in 1960, explains round-the-year operations on the farm and shows rural craftsmen going about their work.

Haderslev

Haderslev Museum

Haderslev Museum, Dalgade 7, DK-6100 Haderslev, S. Jylland ☎ 74 527566
June 16–Aug 31, Tues–Fri 10–5; Sat–Mon 12–5. Sept 1–June 15, Tues–Sat 1–4; Sun 12–4.
© ⬧ 🖼 ⚓

This regional museum is concerned with the archaeology and history of Haderslev and South Jutland. It is the principal archaeological museum in South Jutland and has good collections of Stone, Bronze and Iron Age tools, weapons, household equipment and burial objects, including two Bronze Age sacrificial bowls.

Exhibits in the local history section cover the development of the town of Haderslev, traditional crafts, the guilds, housing, domestic equipment, furniture, costumes, and the Danish–German wars of the 19th and 20th centuries. There is a series of furnished rooms, c. 1900, together with collections of faïence and silver.

Adjoining the museum is an open-air section, with houses, workshops and a post-mill from South Jutland.

The Schleswig Collection of Carriages

Slesvigske Vognsamling, Sejlstensgyde, DK-6100 Haderslev, S. Jylland ☎ 74 527566
June 15 – Aug 15, daily 2–5. Groups at other times by prior arrangement.
© ⚓

The Carriage Collection is 10 minutes' walk from the main museum at Haderslev. It includes the Schleswig Collection, one of Denmark's largest collections of horse-drawn vehicles. A representative selection from the collection is displayed in the former Holstein Lancers' riding school, near the harbour. The exhibits include a variety of carriages and carts, as well as sleighs, and a horse-drawn ambulance and fire-engine. There is also a coach-building section.

Herning Art Museum.

Hanstholm

Hanstholm Museums

*Museerne i Hanstholm, Tårnvej, Hanstholm,
DK-7700 Thisted, N. Jylland. Correspondence
to: Museet for Thy og Vester Hanherred,
Munkevej 20, 2 sal., DK-7700 Thisted*
☎ 97 920577
*Jan–Mar, Mon–Fri 8–3. Mar–June 14 and Sept–
Nov, Mon–Fri 8–3, Sat, Sun 11–4. June
15–Aug, daily 10–5. Closed Jan 1, June 5,
Dec 25, 31.*
C 🛈 📷 🚗

The museums are in a group of historic buildings
around the lighthouse. There are exhibits
relating to the building of the harbour, the
development of the local fishing industry and
the geology and natural history of the area. In
the old lifeboat house, there is an exhibition on
the history of the rescue service along the Thy
coast. In a former bunker on Molevej there is a
museum of the German occupation of the
district in 1940–5.

Herning

Carl-Henning Pedersen and Else Alfelt
Museum

*Carl-Henning Pedersen og Else Alfelts Museum,
Anglig̊arden, Birk, DK-7400 Herning,
S. Jylland*   ☎ 97 221079
Tues–Sun 10–5
C 🛈 📷 🚗

Part of the complex which includes the Herning
Art Museum, the Carl-Henning Pedersen and
Else Alfelt Museum, designed by C. F. Møller,
is an architectural and artistic attraction in
itself. It houses 4,000 paintings by the married
couple, Carl-Henning Pedersen and Else Alfelt,
two Danish artists linked to the international
Cobra Group. A frieze of ceramic slabs, by
Pedersen, covers the outside of the building, a
length of 90 metres.

Herning Art Museum

*Herning Kunstmuseum, Anglig̊arden, Birk,
DK-7400 Herning, S. Jylland* ☎ 97 121033
Tues–Sun 10–5.
C 🛈 📷 🚗

The museum, opened in 1976–7, consists of
three separate circular constructions, an open-
air sculpture park, with its Geometrical Garden,
the Herning Art Museum, which is ring-shaped
around an open courtyard, and the Carl-
Henning Pedersen and Else Alfelt Museum.

The Herning Art Museum and the Sculpture
Park contain an international collection of
paintings and sculpture from 1930 to the present
day, with an emphasis on works by Danish
artists. The Italian artist, Piero Manzoni, is also
well represented.

Hillerød

Frederiksborg Museum

*Det Nationalhistoriske Museum på Frederiksborg,
Frederiksborg Slot, DK-3400 Hillerød,
Sjaelland*   ☎ 42 260439
*May–Sept, daily 10–5. Oct, daily 10–4. Nov–
Mar, daily 11–3. Apr, daily 11–4.*
C 🛈 📷 🚗

Frederiksborg Castle, which houses the
museum, was built in 1600–20, as a palace of
the Danish Kings. After the mid-18th century it
was seldom used and in 1859 it suffered serious
damage from a fire. A national collection
allowed it to be restored and then, as a result of
pressure and financial help from J.C. Jacobsen,
owner of the Carlsberg Breweries, it was
converted into a museum of Danish national
history, organised as an independent
department of the Carlsberg Foundation, which
Jacobsen had set up in 1876. The museum was
established in 1878.

The building contains many notable
features, including the Coronation Chapel of
the Danish Kings, the Baroque Audience
Chamber and the Great Hall. There are
collections of historical paintings, specially
commissioned for the Museum, portraits,
furniture and objects of art from the Middle
Ages to modern times.

Hjerl Hede

Open-Air Museum

*Frilandsmuseet, Hjerl Hede, DK-7830 Vinderup,
N. Jylland*   ☎ 07 548380
Apr–Oct, daily 9–5
C 🛈 📷 ♿ 🚗

This important open-air museum contains old
farmhouses, mills and a dairy. There are
reconstructions of an Iron Age settlement and
craftsmen's workshops. The forestry section
contains a tree nursery and steam and diesel-
driven sawmills. An exhibit not often found in
an open-air museum shows the techniques of the
peat industry.

Hobro

Hobro Museum

Sydhimmerlands Museum, Vestergade 23,
*   DK-9500 Hobro, N. Jylland*   ☎ 98 523898
Apr–Oct, Tues–Sun 10–4
Ⓒ ✑ ☞

The museum, a branch of the South
Himmerland Museum, is in Hobro's oldest
house, a merchant's house, erected in 1821. It
formerly stood in Adelgade, but was moved to
the present site in 1930, for the purpose of
accommodating the museum. The displays,
which show how Hobro has developed over the
centuries, are arranged in three sections:
prehistory, the Viking period, and the historical
period. There are collections of domestic
equipment, coins, watches and tools for flax-
processing and peat-digging. The museum's fine
collection of copper kitchen ware is shown in a
reconstructed kitchen. A special exhibition
deals with industrialisation in Hobro and
particularly with the town's brewery,
engineering works, tobacco factory and
distillery.

Højbjerg

Møsgård Museum of Prehistory

Forhistorisk Museum Møsgård, Møsgård,
*   DK-8270 Højbjerg, S. Jylland*   ☎ 86 272433
Apr–Sept 9, daily 10–5. Sept 10–Mar, Tues–Sun
*   10–4.*
Ⓒ ♟ ▣ ⓖ ☞

The museum has been in the manor house of
Møsgård since 1970. The history of the house
goes back to the 16th century, but in its present
form it dates from the 1770s. The collection
illustrates Danish prehistory and early history,
especially in the Iron Age and Viking periods.
There are also ethnographical exhibitions from
Greenland and Nuristan. Among the more
important exhibits are Grauballe Man, a
completely preserved body from the Iron Age,
discovered in a bog, and a large collection of
runic stones from the old Viking town of
Aarhus. A 'prehistoric trackway', leading
through fields and woods down to Møsgård
beach, has reconstructions of prehistoric houses
and graves on either side.

Holbaek

Holbaek Museum

Museet for Holbaek og Omegn, Klosterstraede
*   14–16, DK-4300 Holbaek, Sjaelland*
*   ☎ 53 432353*
May–Oct, Tues–Sun 10–4. Nov–Apr, Tues–Sun
*   1–4. Closed Jan 1, Easter Sun, Dec 24, 25,*
*   31.*
Ⓒ ♟ ☞

The museum collections illustrate the cultural
history of the Holbaek area and include period
rooms, shops and workshops showing different
aspects of life in the town within the period
1600–1900. Other sections contain agricultural
implements and the pottery products for which
Holbaek was celebrated. The museum is housed
in nine adjacent buildings, mostly half-
timbered, from the period 1660–1867.

Holstebro

Holstebro Museum of Art

Holstebro Kunstmuseum, Sønderbrogade 2,
*   DK-7500 Holstebro, N. Jylland*
*   ☎ 97 424518*
Tues–Fri 12–4; Sat, Sun 11–5.
Ⓒ ♟ ▣ ☞

In 1967 the museum was opened in a large villa,
which had formerly been the home of a local
tobacco manufacturer. Extensions were made in
1981. The collections of Danish contemporary
art concentrate on a small number of artists, five
painters and two sculptors. A collection of the
work of young Danish artists is in the process of
formation and, to provide an international
context for the Danish collections, there are
exhibits of African, Balinese and Tibetan art
and Peruvian pottery.

Hørsholm

Danish Hunting and Forestry Museum

Jagt- og Skovbrugsmuseet, Folehavevej 15,
*   DK-2970 Hørsholm, Sjaelland*   ☎ 42 860572
Feb–Nov, Tues–Sun 10–4
Ⓒ ♟ ☞

The museum was opened in 1942 and is housed
in the early-18th-century stables and barn
belonging to the former palace of Hirschholm,
demolished in 1810–12. The exhibits are
concerned with the history of hunting and
forestry, with Danish game birds and animals,
with the timber industry and with the
cultivation of heath and moorland. There are
collections of hunting weapons ranging from
Stone Age bows to modern rifles, hunting
trophies and forestry tools and equipment.

Grauballe Man, an Iron Age bog burial of
***c.* 300 BC discovered during peat-cutting in**
1952. Møsgård Museum of Prehistory,
Højbjerg.

Humlebaek

Louisiana Museum of Modern Art

Louisiana Museum for moderne Kunst, G1.
  Strandvej 13, DK-3050 Humlebaek, Sjaelland
  ☎ *42 190719*
Daily 10–5. Wed open until 10 pm. Closed Dec
  24, 25, 31.
Ⓒ 🛉 💺 ⑇ ↪

The Louisiana Museum of Modern Art was
founded in 1958 by the industrialist and art
collector, Knud Jensen. It is situated in a large
park in which many of the sculptures have been
placed. The exhibition rooms are in buildings
which are considered to be among the best
achievements of modern Danish architecture.
The collections represent the main trends in
international art from 1950 to the present.

Kalundborg

Kalundborg Museum

Kalundborg og Omegns Museum, Adelgade 23,
  DK-4400 Kalundborg, Sjaelland
  ☎ *53 512141*
May–Aug, Tues–Sun and autumn and winter
  school holidays, 11–4. Sept–Mar, Sat, Sun and
  Bank Holidays 11–4. Closed Jan 1, Dec 24,
  25, 31. Groups and school parties by appt.
Ⓒ ↪

The museum is in a former merchant's house,
parts of which date from the mid 17th century.
Sections of the house were used for grain storage
until the early years of the present century when
the property was presented to the Danish
National Museum to be preserved as a
monument. The displays illustrate the
prehistory and history of Kalundborg and the
surrounding region. The prehistoric section
contains finds dating from the early Stone Age
to Viking times. For the historical period, there
are reconstructions of craftsmen's workshops,
two furnished rooms from the mid 18th century
and collections of silver, domestic equipment,
porcelain, and the contents of an apothecary's
shop.

Lyngby

Open-Air Museum

Frilandsmuseet, Kongevejen 100, DK-2800
  Lyngby, Storkøbenhavn   ☎ *42 850292*
Apr 15–Sept, daily 10–5. Oct 1–14, daily 10–3.
  Oct 15–Apr 14, Sun and public holidays 10–3.
Ⓒ 🛉 💺 ⑇ ↪

The museum, on the outskirts of Copenhagen,
contains rural buildings, mostly from the 18th
and 19th centuries, which have been brought
from their original sites in different parts of
Denmark and the former Danish provinces of
Southern Sweden and South Schleswig. These
have been re-erected in a countryside setting
and equipped with traditional furniture,
equipment and tools.

**Re-erected rural house. Open-Air Museum,
Lyngby.**

Maribo

Open-Air Museum

Frilandsmuseet i Maribo, Meinckesvej, DK-4930
  Maribo, Sjaelland. Correspondence to:
  Museumsgade 1, DK-4930 Maribo.
  ☎ *53 881101*
May–Sept, daily 10–5.
Ⓒ 🛉 💺 ↪

The museum, opened in 1927, consists of rural
buildings, the earliest dating from c. 1800, from
Lolland–Falster. There are houses, illustrating
different methods of construction, a rope-walk,
a malt-kiln, a school and a fire-station, together
with an example of the Village Tree, the
assembly place of the village, where matters of
common interest were discussed.

The growing of sugar-beet became important
in the district in the 19th century and the
museum has a steam ploughing-engine, used for
preparing the ground for this crop. It dates from
1872.

Nyborg

Nyborg Castle

Nyborg Slot, DK-5800 Nyborg, Fyn
  ☎ *65 310207*
Mar–May and Sept–Oct, Tues–Sun 10–3. June–
  Aug, daily 10–5.
Ⓒ ↪

Nyborg is reputed to have been founded in 1170
as a link in the chain of fortresses guarding the
Great Belt. The oldest surviving part, however,
dates from the early 13th century. Extensions
were made c. 1500 and in 1549. It was at
Nyborg that the Danish Kings held the famous
'danehof', national assemblies attended by the
spiritual and temporal leaders of the country.
Until the final gathering in 1413, 25 of them
took place and some of the most important
decisions in the history of Denmark were made
here. In 1917, the Danish State began a full
restoration of the castle and opened it to the
public in 1923. It is now furnished in the style of
the 17th century, with collections of armour,
weapons and paintings.

Nykøbing

Museum of the History of Falster

*Museet Falsters Minder, Langgade 2, DK-4800
Nykøbing, Falster, Sjaelland*   ☎ *54 852671*
*May–Sept 15, Tues–Sat 10–4; Sun and public
holidays 2–4. Sept 16–Apr, Tues–Sat 2–4;
Sun and public holidays 2–4.*
Ⓒ 🏛 🖭

The museum is housed partly in two 18th-
century granaries and one of the mid 19th
century, and also in The Czar's House (Czarens
Hus), built *c.* 1690, which acquired its present
name after a visit by the Czar, Peter the Great,
in 1716. It has collections of regional costumes
and of household articles from farmsteads and
provincial towns on Falster, including pottery,
pewter, copperware and faïence. There is a
model and some relics of the former Nykøbing
Castle and among other interesting items on
display are a 15th-century oak dugout boat, the
oldest surviving Danish cembalo, or dulcimer,
(*c.* 1770) and a complete 19th-century
goldsmith's shop.

Nykøbing Mors

Morsland Historical Museum

*Morslands Historiske Museum, Dueholm Kloster,
DK-7900 Nykøbing Mors, N. Jylland*
☎ *97 723421*
Daily 10–4
Ⓒ 🏛 🚗

The museum is housed in the former Monastery
of the Order of St John of Jerusalem, established
c. 1370. After the Reformation in 1536, it
became a Royal property and considerably later
a private estate, owned in its time by various
local families.

The collections of the museum cover the
prehistory and history of the island of Mors,
with displays of religious art, furniture, and
craftsmen's tools and equipment. There are also
sections dealing with fishing and the maritime
history of Mors, and with agriculture. The
island's geology and fossils are exceptionally
interesting and both are illustrated by means of
special displays.

Odense

Carl Nielsen Museum

*Carl Nielsen Museet, Claus Bergs Gade 11,
DK-5000 Odense C, Fyn*   ☎ *66 131372*
*Daily 10–4. Sept–May, also Thurs 4–8 pm. Free
admission Thurs.*
Ⓒ 🏛 ♿ 🚗

The museum, in a new building, presents a
detailed picture of the life and work of the
composer Carl Nielsen (1865–1931), and of his
wife, the sculptress Anne Marie Carl-Nielsen.
A house at Odensevej 2A, at Årslev, close to
Odense, was the birthplace and childhood home
of Nielsen. Exhibits in two commemorative
rooms illustrate the composer's early years (Carl
Nielsens Barndomshjem, May–Aug, daily 11–3).

Columbia printing press. Danish Museum of
Graphic Art, Odense.

Danish Museum of Graphic Art

*Danmarks Grafiske Museum, Brandts
Klaedefabrik, Brandts Passage 37, 3. sal,
DK-5000 Odense C, Fyn*   ☎ *66 121020*
*Mon–Fri 10–5; Sat, Sun 11–5. Closed Jan 1, Dec
25. Free admission Sun and holidays.*
Ⓒ 🏛 🖭 ♿ ♿ 🚗

The museum forms part of Brandts Klaedefabrik,
an international art and cultural centre. It
presents a survey of the production of graphic
art in Denmark from the Middle Ages to the
present day, with exhibits of tools and
equipment, materials and products.
Demonstrations are held regularly.

DSB Railway Museum

*DSB Jernbanemuseum, Dannebrogsgade 24,
DK-5000 Odense C, Fyn*
☎ *66 120148 extn 238*
*May –Sept, daily 10–4. Oct–Apr, Sun 10–3.
Autumn and Winter Holidays, daily 10–4.
Closed Easter and Christmas periods.*
Ⓒ 🏛 🖭 ♿ ♿ 🚗

The museum was enlarged and modernised in
1988, tripling the exhibition area, and now
ranks as one of Europe's leading railway
museums. The displays illustrate more than a
century of Danish railway history and include
locomotives, coaches, operating equipment and
a reconstruction of a 19th-century station.
There is also a model track and a collection of
models of the train ferries which have played an
important part in the transport system of
Denmark.

Horse-drawn plough. Funen Village, Odense.

Funen Village

*Den fynske Landsby, Sejerskovvej 20, DK-5260
    Odense S, Fyn   ☎ 66 131372
Apr–May and Sept–Oct, daily 9–4. June–Aug,
    daily 9–6.30. Nov–Mar, Sun and public
    holidays 10–4. Free admission Sun.*
C ⓘ ☞ ⓠ ⓖ ⊶

The village, on the outskirts of Odense, is an
open-air museum with about 20 rural buildings
dating from the 19th and 20th centuries. In
addition to farmhouses, there is a smithy, a
windmill, a watermill, a vicarage, a school and
an almshouse. Agriculture and cattle-raising are
carried on in the village, using traditional
methods.

There are occasional craft demonstrations,
especially during the summer months.

Hans Christian Andersen's House

*H.C. Andersens Hus, Hans Jensens Straede
    37–45. DK-5000 Odense C, Fyn
    ☎ 66 131372
Apr–May and Sept, daily 10–5. June–Aug, daily
    9–6. Oct–Mar, daily 10–3. Autumn holiday,
    daily 10–5. Free admission Sun.*
C ⓘ ☞ ⓖ ⊶

The poet, playwright, novelist, travel writer
and, above all, writer of fairy stories, Hans
Christian Andersen (1805–75), was born in this
house, which is now a memorial to him, with
collections illustrating his life and his career as a
writer.

There are portraits, letters, orders conferred
on him, and editions of the *Fairy Tales*,
translated into 50 languages, as well as furniture
and a wide range of personal belongings,
including his travelling equipment – trunks,
hat-case, umbrella, walking stick and the length
of rope he always carried with him for use in the
event of a fire at his hotel. There is also a
reconstruction of his study at Nyhavn 18,
Copenhagen.

The house at Munke Møllestraede 3–5,
where Hans Christian Andersen lived as a child,
from 1807 to 1819, is now a branch of the
museum (Apr–Sept, daily 10–5; Oct–Mar, daily
12–3).

Hollufgård Prehistoric Museum

*Fyns Stiftsmuseum – Hollufgård, Hestehaven 201,
    DK-5220 Odense SØ, Fyn   ☎ 66 131372
Apr–Sept, Tues–Sun 11–4. Oct–Mar, Tues–
    Thurs, Sat, Sun 12–4.*
C ⓘ ⓠ ⓖ ⊶

Hollufgård is a manor, with farm buildings
attached. The main building dates from 1577.
The first stage of a new museum of prehistory
was opened here in 1988. In the former farm
buildings there are now exhibitions illustrating
the prehistory of the region. Outside, a Bronze
Age farm has been created, providing the
setting for a range of activities involving
members of the general public.

Møntergården Museum

*Kulturhistorisk, byhistorisk Museum,
    Møntergården, Overgade 48–50, DK-5000
    Odense C, Fyn   ☎ 66 131372
Daily 10–4. Closed Jan 1, Dec 24, 25, 31. Free
    admission Sun and holidays.*
C ⓘ ⓠ

Møntergården is a museum complex, with a
collection of town buildings from earlier periods
of Odense's history, from the 16th century
onwards. They are used to display collections of
costumes, glass, ceramics, silver, clocks,
furniture and craftsmen's tools. The
reconstructed rooms include an impression of a
19th-century photographer's studio. A special
section is devoted to medieval Odense. The
museum has one of Denmark's finest collections
of coins and medals.

Øsløs

Skjoldborg House

*Skjoldborgs Hus, Skippergade 6, Øsløs, DK-7742
    Vestløs, N. Jylland   ☎ 97 920577
Daily in school holidays, 10–5*
C ⊶

The novelist, Johan Martinus Skjoldborg
(1861–1936), was the son of a smallholder and
shoemaker in North Jutland. For some years he
was a village schoolmaster and then devoted all
his time to writing. In 1961 his childhood home
was opened as a museum. The arrangements
inside the house are based on his autobiography,
published in 1934. The museum contains
memorabilia of the writer and his family,
including the shoemaking workshop.

Padborg

Frøslev Camp Museum

*Frøslevlejrens Museum, Lejrvejen 97, DK-6330
    Padborg, S. Jylland   ☎ 74 676557
May–Sept, daily 10–5. Oct–Apr, during autumn
    and Easter holidays only. 10–5. Closed Easter
    Sun. Other times by appt.*
C ⓘ ☞ ⊶

This was a camp in which Danes imprisoned for resistance activities were held during the Second World War before deportation to German concentration camps. The museum is situated in a former barrack hut and in the camp's main watch-tower. Most of the buildings are still intact, so that visitors can get an overall impression of the camp.

The exhibitions deal with daily life in the camp, with the tragic fate of those who were deported to Germany, and with events and resistance activities in the southern part of Jutland during the 1940–5 German occupation.

Praestø

Thorvaldsen Collection

Thorvaldsen Samlingen på Nysø, Nysøvej 5,
DK-4200 Praestø, Sjaelland ☎ *53 791403*
May–June and Aug, Wed, Sat 2–5; Sun 11–5.
July, Mon–Sat 2–5; Sun 11–5. Other times by
appt.
C 🛈 ⌂

Nysø manor house was built in 1673. In 1839 its owner, Baron Henrik Stampe and his wife, Christine, provided a studio in the house for the famous sculptor, Bertel Thorvaldsen (1770–1844), who had recently returned from Rome and was unable to find a place to work in his official apartment at the Royal Academy of Fine Arts in Copenhagen. A second studio, which is still standing, was built for him in the garden at Nysø.

The museum at Nysø contains memorabilia of Thorvaldsen and statues, reliefs and busts by him, as well as drawings and clay models, including a group which Christine Stampe rescued from destruction when the moulds were being removed and which she had fired at the estate brickworks.

Mask in baked clay from self-portrait statue by Bertel Thorvaldsen, 1839. Thorvaldsen Collection, Praestø.

Randers

Randers Art Museum

Randers Kunstmuseum, Stemannsgade 2,
DK-8900 Randers, N. Jylland ☎ *86 422738*
Tues–Sun 11–5. Closed Good Fri, Dec 24.
F 🛈 ⌷ ♿ ⌂

The museum was established in 1887. The collections grew steadily and by the 1950s a new building had become essential. The present building was opened in 1959. The museum's collections fall into two sections: Danish painting and sculpture from the late 18th century to the present day, and international art from 1880 to the contemporary period. Works by Danish artists form the bulk of the collections.

Rebild

Spillemand Museum

Spillemands- Jagt- og Skovbrugsmuseet, Cimbrervej
2, Rebild, DK-9520 Skørping, N. Jylland
☎ 98 391604
Jan–May and Sept–Dec, Tues, Thurs 10–4. June–
Aug, Tues–Sat 10–4; Sun 2–5
C 🛈 ⌷ ⌂

The museum's collections cover the traditional culture of the district. A section is devoted to forestry and hunting, with exhibits of weapons, forestry tools and poaching, including a reconstruction of a forestry ranger's office. There are displays of craftsmen's tools and craft products, the principal trades dealt with being those of the coach-builder, shoemaker, blacksmith, clog-maker, charcoal burner, rope-maker, thatcher and potter. There are also reconstructions of a handweaver's workshop and of a farmhouse living-room and kitchen.

Folk music forms an important part of the museum, with exhibits of music books, instruments and items relating to the wandering fiddlers ('spillemand'), formerly to be seen all over Denmark.

Rønne

Bornholm Museum

Bornholms Museum, Sct. Mortensgade 28,
DK-3700 Rønne, Bornholm, Sjaelland
☎ 03 950735
May–Sept, daily 10–4. Oct–Apr, Tues, Thurs,
Sun 2–5
C

The museum contains paintings, drawings and sculptures by artists who were either born on the island of Bornholm or who worked there. There are also exhibits illustrating the island's history as a centre of shipping and navigation and its natural history, especially the sea-birds to be seen there. A special section has ethnographical material from all over the world brought back by Bornholm sailors from their voyages.

The Girl with the Sunflowers, 1893, by
Michael Ancher. Michael and Anna Ancher's
House, Skagen.

Roskilde

Viking Ship Museum

*Vikingeskibshallen i Roskilde, Strandengen, Postbox
298, DK-4000 Roskilde, Sjaelland*
   ☎ *42 356555*
*Apr–Oct, daily 9–5. Nov–Mar, daily 10–4.
   Closed Dec 24, 31.*
Ⓒ 🛈 🖭 🏠

The museum has been designed and built to
exhibit five Viking ships, which were discovered
in Roskilde Fjord and excavated in 1962. At the
end of the Viking period, at some time between
AD 1000 and AD 1050, the navigation channel
in Roskilde Fjord was blocked by a series of
barriers, in order to protect the important
trading town of Roskilde from attacks by enemy
fleets. The ships in the museum formed part of a
barrier of this kind. The ships were sunk across
the channel and heaped with boulders.

The ships are of different types, a deep-sea
trader, a small merchant ship, a warship, a ferry,
and a Viking longship, used for long-range
raiding. An exhibition associated with the ships
illustrates the history of the Viking period,
shipbuilding, and the techniques and
achievements of underwater archaeology.

Rudkøbing

Langeland Museum

*Langelands Museum, Jens Winthersvej 12,
   DK-5900 Rudkøbing, Fyn   ☎ 62 511347*
*Mon–Fri 10–4; Sat, Sun 2–4. June–Aug, also Sun
   10–4. Closed Jan 1, Dec 24, 25, 31.*
Ⓒ 🛈 🏠

The museum was formed and developed by a
local shopkeeper, Jens Winther (1863–1955),
who was born in Rudkøbing. He became
interested in antiquities early in his life and built
up a considerable collection of archaeological

material. In 1905 he put his collections on
public display in a building paid for by himself.
He continued working in the museum until his
92nd year and in his will left Langeland
Museum, which had by then acquired an
international reputation, to the Municipality.

The archaeological exhibits are of items
discovered during the excavations at local sites,
especially those of the Stone Age and Viking
periods. The more modern material includes
18th–19th-century furniture, domestic
equipment, handicrafts and silver. There is also
a display of finds from the site of the 16th-
century fishing hamlet at Sandhagen.

Silkeborg

Silkeborg Museum of Cultural History

*Silkeborg Kulturhistoriske Museum, Hovedgården,
   DK-8600 Silkeborg, N. Jylland ☎ 86 821578*
*May–Oct, daily 10–5. Nov–Apr, Wed, Sat, Sun
   12–4. Other times by appt.*
Ⓒ 🛈 🖭 🔥 🏠

The museum is in a manor house dating from
1767. The collections illustrate local history and
prehistory and include what has become known
as Tollund Man, the now famous and well-
preserved remains of a man who died 2,000
years ago, found in a nearby bog.

Skagen

Michael and Anna Ancher's House

*Michael og Anna Anchers Hus, Markvej 2,
   DK-9990 Skagen, N. Jylland   ☎ 98 443009*
*Apr and Oct, daily 11–3. May–June 20 and Aug
   16–Sept. daily 10–5. June 21–Aug 15, daily
   10–6. Nov–Mar, Sat, Sun and public holidays,
   11–3. Other times by appt.*
Ⓒ 🛈 🏠

Helga Ancher (1883–1964) was the daughter of
the painters, Michael (1849–1927) and Anna
Ancher (1859–1935). Like her parents, Helga
Ancher painted most of her pictures in the
Skagen area. In her will, Helga Ancher left the
house and all its contents to a foundation
established for the purpose, as a memorial to her
father and mother, and it was opened as a
museum in 1967. It contains many paintings
and drawings by the three Anchers and by their
friends.

Skive

Annine Michelsen Memorial Room

*Frk. Annine Michelsens Mindestuer, Østergade
   4A, DK-7800 Skive, N. Jylland*
   ☎ *97 520746*
*Mon–Fri 2–4. At Easter and at weekends
   throughout year, by appt. Closed Christmas
   period.*
Ⓒ

In 1903 Annine Michelsen (1885–1969) was apprenticed to Anna Topp, a confectioner in Skive. When Topp married in 1909, Michelsen took over the business. In 1927 she opened a café, baker's and confectioner's in a new building and developed it into a nationally celebrated concern. She travelled a great deal, both inside and outside Europe and brought back many souvenirs. She also had visits from writers who came to Skive. They presented her with their books and she accumulated a considerable library as a result.

In making her will, she decided that her home should be converted into a memorial to her. The confectionery business continued until 1965. It is now a restaurant.

Skive Museum

*Skive Museum, Havnevej 14, DK-7800 Skive,
N. Jylland*   ☎ 97 521093
Mon–Fri 11–5; Sat, Sun and public holidays 2–5.
Ⓒ 🍴 ♿

The museum's displays cover local archaeology and life in the region in the 19th and 20th centuries. The archaeological material includes the biggest collection of amber to have been discovered in Denmark. There is also an exhibition of 20th-century Danish paintings and sculpture, in which Expressionist and Neo-Realist artists are particularly well represented.

Sønderborg

Castle Museum

*Museet på Sønderborg Slot, DK-6400 Sønderborg,
S. Jylland*   ☎ 74 422539
*Apr and Oct, daily 10–4. May–Sept, daily 10–5.
Nov–Mar, daily 1–4. Closed Jan 1, Dec 23–6,
31.*
Ⓒ 🍴 💺 ♿ 🚻

The first castle was built c. 1170 as part of Denmark's coastal defences against the Wends. Additions were made during the 13th and 14th centuries and in the 1550s it was rebuilt, transforming a medieval castle into a Renaissance palace. Its church, Queen Dorothea's Chapel, was Denmark's first princely Protestant church and the earliest Renaissance room in the Nordic countries. It was badly damaged by fire during the 1657–8 war with Sweden and during 19th-century wars. Each time, repairs were carried out, but when the Danish Government bought it in 1921 to house the regional museum, it was in poor condition. A thorough restoration was carried out in 1964–73, re-creating the Baroque palace, but retaining some rooms from the Middle Ages and the Renaissance.

The rooms now contain displays illustrating many aspects of life in the region from prehistoric times onwards. These include military, naval and political history, paintings and portraits, traditional crafts and the style of living of the different social classes.

Svendborg

Svendborg Museum

*Svendborg og Omegns Museum, Grubbemøllevej
13, DK-5700 Svendborg, Fyn*   ☎ 62 210261
*The museum is in four sections, three in Svendborg
and one in Troense. Opening times of the
sections in Svendborg are as follows:
Viebaeltegård: May–Oct, daily 10–4. Nov–
Apr, daily 1–4; Langes Ovnmuseum: May–
Oct, daily 10–4. Nov–Apr, daily 1–4; Anne
Hvides Gård: May–Oct, daily 10–4.*
Ⓒ 🍴 💺 ♿ 🚻

Viebaeltegård is Svendborg's former poorhouse and workhouse, built in 1872. This complex of buildings now houses the museum offices as well as its stores and part of the exhibitions. On the ground floor, all the rooms of the workhouse have been preserved unchanged, with their original fittings and equipment. On the other floors, there are archaeological exhibits, including finds from the Franciscan monastery and cemetery. The former mortuary contains part of an old printing house and there is also a complete goldsmith's workshop. A working potter is installed in what was once the chapel. There is a special exhibition telling the story of the social services in Svendborg from 1870 to 1970.

Anne Hvide's House (Anne Hvides Gård) is located at Fruestraede 3. This house, the oldest in Svendborg, dates from the 1550s. For 200 years it continued to be a private house and was then successively a club, an inn, offices for the town's tax department, the mayor's office and the town and county library. It became part of the County Museum in 1916 and was carefully restored in 1978. Visitors today can see reconstructions of 18th- and 19th-century rooms, with paintings and portraits, as well as Svendborg glass, silver, copper and brass. In the attic there is a reconstruction of a lumber room.

Lange Stove Museum (Langes Ovnmuseum) is located at Vestergade 45. In 1986 a large collection of stoves, produced from 1850 until 1984 in the Svendborg factory of L. Lange and Co. was donated to the County Museum. It is now displayed in the firm's former office building. The collection consists of stoves, fire-plates, kitchen ranges and models, as well as the Lange archives, with designs, accounts and correspondence. The manager's office has been kept as it was c. 1900.

Svendborg Museum.

Tersløse

Tersløse Manor

Den Holbergske Stiftelse Tersløsegård, Holbergvej
    101, Tersløse, DK-4293 Dianalund, Sjaelland
    ☎ 53 563384
Apr–Oct, Mon, Wed–Sat 10–11, 2–4; Sun and
    public holidays 10–11, 2–5.

C ⚓

The great Danish playwright, satirist, essayist
and historian, Baron Ludvig Holberg (1684–
1754) in 1745 bought Tersløse Manor, built in
1727, and lived there until his death. In his
will, he left his large fortune for the re-
establishment of the college at Sorø, and for this
he was made a baron. The manor contains
memorial rooms to him, with memorabilia of
the writer and Danish and foreign editions of his
works.

Tórshavn

Faroes Historical Museum

Føroya Fornminnissavn, Hoyvík, Postbox 1155,
    110 Tórshavn, Faeøerne   ☎ 298 10700
May 15 – Sept 15, Mon–Fri 10–4; Sat, Sun 3–5.
    Sept 16 – May 14, Sun 3–5.

F ♀ ⚓

The museum at Tórshavn illustrates the
archaeology and social history of the Faroes.
There are exhibits of archaeological material
from the Viking period and the Middle Ages
and collections of objects relating to seafaring
and fishing, including a number of Faroese boats
of different types and sizes. Other sections of the
museum illustrate religious life, handicrafts and
agriculture on the islands.

Troense

Maritime Museum

Søfartsmuseet, Strandgade 1, Troense, DK-5700
    Svendborg, Fyn   ☎ 62 210261
May–Oct, daily 9–5. Nov–Apr, Mon–Fri 9–5; Sat
    9–12.

C ♀ ⛴ ⚓

The museum is housed in a former school
building and contains collections illustrating the
maritime history of the Troense area. There are
models of the principal types of local vessel and
exhibits of shipbuilding, souvenirs brought
home by sailors from their voyages abroad.
Modern shipping is represented by exhibits
relating to A.E. Sørensen, for many years the
biggest Danish coastal shipping company, and
A.P. Møller, one of the most important
shipping companies in the world, which began
in Svendborg.
    The museum also has an extensive
collection of ships' portraits, in which many
well-known artists are represented, and a
collection of drawings and half-models from the
shipbuilding firm of Abeking and Rasmuller.

Valby

Carlsberg Museum

Carlsberg Museum, Valby Langgade 1, DK-2500
    Valby, Storkøbenhavn   ☎ 01 210112
Mon, Tues, Thurs–Sat 10–3.

F ☞ ⚓

Carlsberg is the most famous name in Danish
beer. The museum tells the story of the
breweries and of the Jacobsen family which
established them. There are also technical
exhibits illustrating the brewing processes and
the marketing and distribution of the beer.
    The building, which dates from 1882–95
and has some curious architectural features, was
originally constructed to house the large
European art collections of Carl and Ottilia
Jacobsen. After their death, the collection was
moved to a new building, the Carlsberg
Glyptothek, on Dantes Plads.

Viborg

Viborg Museum

Viborg Stiftsmuseum, Hjultorvej 4, DK-8800
    Viborg, N. Jylland   ☎ 86 623066
June–Aug, daily 11–5. Sept–May, Tues–Fri 2–5;
    Sat, Sun 11–5.

F ♀ ⚓

The museum building was erected in 1858 for
the first credit institution in Jutland. The
collections illustrate the history of the area from
the Stone Age to the present day. There is a
large prehistoric department, with exhibits of
tools, pottery and personal adornments and with
a special emphasis on the Viking period.
Another section is devoted to the equipment
and products of traditional occupations,
including hunting, fishing, agriculture, pottery
and tool-making. For each of these, the museum
shows implements from the oldest to the
newest, to make visitors aware of the continuity
of skill, knowledge and usefulness. The same
method is applied to the exhibition on the
necessities of everyday life, Making and Serving
Food, Leisure, Light and Warmth, Sleep,
Cleanliness and Clothes, where the themes are
presented historically, with a concentration on
the last 100 years.
    There are also exhibitions on the public
services, the workers' movement, social classes,
the Church and the Military.

**Early editions of works by Ludvig Holberg.
Tersløse Manor.**

FINLAND

Alajärvi

The Nelimarkka Museum

Nelimarkka museo, KP 3, SF-62900 Alajärvi,
Vaasa　　　　　　　　☎ 966 2129
May–Aug, Tues–Fri 11–7; Sat 11–4; Sun 12–6.
Sept–Apr, Tues–Fri, Sun 12–6; Sat 12–4.

C ⓘ 💻 🔗

The museum, opened in 1964, was established
by the Finnish artist, Eero Nelimarkka (1891–
1977), on the site of his father's family home.
The building was designed by his friend, Hilding
Ekelund. Half the works in the museum's
collections are paintings by Nelimarkka,
executed between 1910 and 1975. Most of the
other exhibits are of Finnish art from the late
19th century to the present day. The graphics
section is outstanding and includes some items
by foreign artists.

Bobäck

Hvitträsk

Hvitträsk, SF-02440 Bobäck, Uusimaa
　　　　　　　　☎ 90 2975779
June–Aug, Mon–Fri 10–8; Sat, Sun 10–7. Sept–
May, Mon–Fri 11 7; Sat, Sun 11–6. Closed
Christmas period.

C ⓘ 💻 🔗

The building complex at Hvitträsk was designed
by the architectural partnership of Eliel
Saarinen, Herman Gesellius and Armas
Lindgren, and built in 1902. Their office,
established in 1896, already possessed an
international reputation, especially for the
Finnish pavilion at the 1900 Paris World Fair.
The partners and their staff lived at Hvitträsk
and it was here that the plans were worked out
for a number of Finland's great 20th-century
buildings, including Helsinki Railway Station
and the National Museum of Finland.
　　The main building is now a museum. It
contains Saarinen's studio and furniture, and a
collection of memorabilia of the architect.

Espoo

Gallen-Kallela Museum

Gallen-Kallelan museo, Gallen-Kallelantie 27,
SF-02600 Espoo, Uusimaa　　☎ 90 513388
May–Aug, Tues–Thurs 10–8; Fri–Sun 10–5.
Sept–May, Tues–Sat 10–4; Sun 10–5.

C ⓘ 💻 🔗

Akseli Gallen-Kallela (1865–1931) is the
national artist of Finland. He painted in oils and
watercolours, introduced the fresco technique to
Finland, carved in wood and stone, worked
metal and was the first Finnish artist to
experiment with stained glass, graphic art and

posters. He designed fabrics, flags, insignia,
decorations and uniforms for the Army and
trade marks for industrial firms.
　　The museum building was Gallen-Kallela's
studio-house, built according to the artist's own
design in 1911–13. It contains paintings,
graphics, sculpture, posters and designs by him.

Glims Farmstead Museum

Glims talonmuseo, Glimsintie 1, SF-02740 Espoo,
Uusimaa. Correspondence to: Espoon
kaupunginmuseo, Thurmaninpuistotie 10, SF-
02700 Kauniainen.　　　　☎ 90 862979
May–Aug, Tues–Sun 12–6. Sept–Apr, Tues–Sun
12–4.

C ⓘ 💻 🔗

The farmstead at Glims, on the old road from
Turku to Viipuri, is mentioned in documents
from 1540 onwards, but the present buildings
date mostly from the 19th century. They
include, in addition to the main farmhouse, an
inn, a granary and foodstore, a carriage-shed, a
stable, a dairy, a poultry house, a sauna, a
threshing shed, and a shop. The objects
displayed have been collected from different
places in the region. Among them are furniture,
craftsmen's tools, and sledges and carriages.

Halikko

Halikko Museum

Halikon museo, Kirkkorinne 7, SF-24800 Halikko,
Turku ja Pori　　　　　　☎ 924 623320
Sun and public holidays 11–5. Closed Good Fri,
Dec 25.

C ✎ 💻 🔗

There has been a river trading-post at Halikko
since the 10th century. The museum, opened in
1987 in a stone building of 1849 which was
originally a public granary, contains collections
illustrating the traditional life of the area. There
are reconstructions of the workshops of a
tanner, shoemaker and carpenter.

Hämeenlinna

Sibelius's Birthplace

Sibeliuksen syntymäkoti, Hallituskatu 11, SF-
13210 Hämeenlinna, Häme　　☎ 917 25698
May–Aug, daily 10–4. Sept–Apr, Mon–Fri, Sun
12–4. Closed Jan 1, Easter, Midsummer, Dec
24, 25.

C ⓘ

The composer, Jean (Johan Julius Christian)
Sibelius (1865–1957), was born in this wooden
house of 1834 and spent his childhood in the
town. It became a museum in 1965 and contains
photographs and other material illustrating
Sibelius's early years.

Harjavalta

Emil Cedercreutz Museum

Emil Cedercreutzin museo, Museotie, SF-29200
Harjavalta, Turku ja Pori   ☎ 939 740356
Daily 11–5; Tues and Thurs also 5–8 pm. In the
case of two successive holidays, the museum is
closed on the first day.

C 🎗 💻 🏛

The museum is in 'Harjula', the former house
and studio of the sculptor and collector, Baron
Emil Cedercreutz (1879–1949). 'Harjula' was
his home from 1914 until his death. Extensions
were made to the original house from time to
time, in order to house the museum's growing
collections. In addition to his work as a
sculptor, Cedercreutz was an internationally
famous silhouette artist, a collector of carriages
and sledges and of folk art, and a pioneer of the
appreciation and preservation of old Finnish
rugs. He was also active in his support of animal
welfare movements.

The museum's collections illustrate the
various aspects of Cedercreutz's life and work.
There are important displays of popular arts and
crafts, especially rugs, and of agricultural
implements and domestic equipment.

Helsinki

Alko Shop Museum

Alkon myymälämuseo, Tallberginkatu 2 B,
SF-00180 Helsinki   ☎ 90 13311
By appt.

F

In 1932, following the repeal of the Prohibition
Act, the Finnish Alcohol Monopoly (Oy
Alkoholiliike Ab) began the legal sale of
alcohol through 58 retail outlets. Over the years
the operations of this State monopoly were
diversified, the number of retail outlets was
increased and the company name was shortened
to Oy Alko Ab. The Alko shops now have an
established place in Finnish society. The
museum tells the story of Alko, within the wider
context of the history of the sale of alcohol from
the Middle Ages to the present day.

Amos Anderson Art Museum

Amos Andersonin taidemuseo, PO Box 14,
Yrjönkatu 27, SF-00100 Helsinki
☎ 90 604782
Mon–Fri 11–6; Sat, Sun 11–4. Closed public
holidays.

C 🎗 💻

Amos Anderson (1878–1961) was a leading
publisher, newspaper-owner and patron of the
arts. Yrjönkatu 27 was constructed for business
and residential purposes in 1912–13. After
Anderson's death, the upper floors were
converted into a museum and the first floor,
originally used for offices, became an exhibition
gallery. A gallery annexe was opened in 1985,
together with the Café Amos.

The museum is owned by a foundation,
established in 1940, to which Amos Anderson
bequeathed all his belongings. The collections
consist of 20th-century Finnish art and 15th–
16th-century European paintings, graphics and
medals.

Arabia Museum

Arabian museo, Hämeentie 135, SF-00560
Helsinki   ☎ 90 668132
June 12 – Aug 31, daily 11–5.30.

F 🎗 🏛

The museum is at the important Arabia
Porcelain Works, which has operated since the
18th century. There are historical collections of
its products, especially those in the Art
Nouveau and Finnish National Romantic styles.

Helsinki City Museum

Helsingin kaupunginmuseo, Villa Kakasalmi,
Karanzininkatu 2, SF-00100 Helsinki
☎ 90 1691
Wed–Sun 11–6.30

C 🎗 💻

The museum presents the social, economic,
cultural and political history of Helsinki. There
are 18th–20th century period rooms and
collections of costumes, porcelain, glass, textiles
and coins and medals. Special sections are
devoted to pharmacy and to the city's trade
guilds.

Maritime Museum of Finland

Suomen merimuseo, Hallituskatu 2, SF-00170
Helsinki   ☎ 90 1355379
May 2 – Oct 9, daily 11–5. Oct 10 – Apr 30, Sat,
Sun 10–3.

C

The museum was established to tell the story of
the naval and maritime history of Finland. The
collections include paintings, prints, documents
and a wide range of relics. The lightship Kemi
also belongs to the museum.

**Decanter and glasses. Alko Shop Museum,
Helsinki.**

Santa Joana Princesa, 15th-century, attributed to Nuno Gonçalves.
Aveiro Museum, Aveiro (Portugal).

**A writing machine, built by Friedrich von Knaus in 1760 for the Empress Maria Theresa.
Technical Museum of Industry and Crafts, Vienna (Austria).**

Military Museum

Sotamuseo, Maurinkatu 1, SF-00170 Helsinki
☎ *90 177791*
Sun–Fri 11–3
Ⓒ 🔒 ⟲

The Military Museum is the national museum of the history of the Finnish defence forces. It is housed in a former barrack block designed in Renaissance style and built in 1882. The museum was first located on the island of Suomenlinna, but was transferred to its present site in 1948. The collections illustrate the history and campaigns of the Finnish armed services. There is an extensive archive and exhibits of uniforms, weapons, equipment and flags.

Museum of Applied Arts

Taideteollisuusmuseo, Korkeavuorenkatu 23,
SF-00130 Helsinki   ☎ *90 174455*
Tues–Fri 11–5; Sat, Sun 11–4.
Ⓒ 🔒 ▣

The museum of Applied Arts in Helsinki, founded in 1873, is the oldest in the Nordic countries. It is now housed in an 1876 building which was formerly a school and which is an outstanding example of the architecture of the period. It was re-opened in 1979, after a long period of inactivity.

The permanent exhibition illustrates the history and special character of Finnish design and pays special attention to the most creative period, Art Nouveau – known in Scandinavia as Jugendstil – and the 1950s and 1960s. There is a large collection of Marimekko textile designs.

Museum of Finnish Architecture

Suomen rakennustaiteen museo, Kasarmikatu 24,
SF-00130 Helsinki   ☎ *90 661918*
Exhibition, Library, Bookshop: Tues, Thurs–Sun
10–4; Wed 10–7. Closed public holidays.
Archives: Tues, Thurs, Fri 10–4; Wed 10–7.
Closed public holidays.
Ⓕ 🔒 ▪

The museum's permanent collections comprise original drawings, photographs and models

Display of contemporary tableware. Museum of Applied Arts, Helsinki.

illustrating the history of architecture in Finland, with an emphasis on the 20th century. Several exhibitions are organised each year on Finnish and foreign architecture.

The museum library's comprehensive collection of books on architecture and related fields has a special section, Fennica, containing books on architecture published in Finland and foreign books on Finnish architecture.

Museum of Technology

Tekniikan museo, Viikintie 1, SF-00560 Helsinki
☎ *90 797066*
May–Sept, Tues–Sun 11–5. Oct–Apr, Wed–Sun
12–4. Closed Jan 1, Easter, May 1,
Midsummer Day, Dec 6, 24, 25.
Ⓒ ▣ ⟲

The museum, founded in 1969, is in the former City Waterworks buildings. Its exhibitions illustrate the history of technology in Finland, in two galleries, with a total floor area of 5,000 square metres. The first gallery contains printing, the production of coins and banknotes, surveying, meteorology, power and the chemical and sugar industries. In the second gallery there are sections devoted to communications, industries using wood as a raw material, building construction, mining and the metal industries. The history of milling is presented in an operational water-powered mill.

Photographic Museum of Finland

Suomen valokuvataiteen museo, Keskuskatu 6,
7th floor, Box 10596, SF-00101 Helsinki
☎ *90 658544*
Mon–Fri 11–5; Sat, Sun 11–4.
Ⓒ 🔒 ⟲

The museum's displays illustrate the history of Finnish photography. There are 360,000 negatives and prints, and collections of photographic equipment. Among the more interesting items are Lumière Autochrome slides made in 1907–12 and stereoslides from 1908 to 1914.

Seurasaari Open-Air Museum

Seurasaaren ulkomuseo, Seurasaari, SF-00250
  Helsinki   ☎ 90 984712
Mon–Fri 9.30–3; Sat, Sun 11.30–5.

ⓒ 🛈 💻 ♠

Finland has a great many open-air museums of
which this is the largest. It contains farm
buildings and rural houses from all regions of
Finland. The exhibits include the Church of
Karuna (1680), windmills, fishermen's houses,
with fishing equipment, and craftsmen's
workshops. There are also collections of
agricultural implements and craftsmen's tools.

Sports Museum of Finland

Suomen Urheilumuseo, Olympiastadion, SF-00250
  Helsinki   ☎ 90 407011
Mon–Wed, Fri 11–5; Thurs 11–7; Sat, Sun 12–4.
  Closed Midsummer Day, May 1, Dec 24, 25.

ⓒ 🛈 ♠

The museum is in the Olympic Stadium, built
for the 1952 Games, and one of the most famous
functional buildings in the world. It is devoted
to the history of sport and physical training in
Finland. There are displays of sports equipment,
especially skis, photographs of historic sporting
events and trophies and memorabilia of
outstanding Finnish athletes and sportsmen.
Among the exhibits are one of Paavo Nurmi's
running shoes, covered in gold leaf for the New
York World Fair, and Hannes Kolehmainen's
spiked shoes and the withered laurel crown,
awarded to him after his triumph in the 1912
5,000 metres and 10,000 metres events.

Stockmann Museum

Stockmann museo, Keskuskatu 1, SF-00101
  Helsinki   ☎ 90 1213546
Mon–Thurs 12–1

🅕 🛈 💻

Stockmann's is one of the great European
department stores and a favourite with those
members of the Soviet élite who are in a
position to shop there, and with members of
foreign embassies in Moscow. The museum tells
the story of Stockmann's from 1862 to the
present day.

Theatre Museum

Teatterimuseo, Aleksanterinkatu 12 A, SF-00170
  Helsinki. Correspondence to: Snellmaninkatu
  17 A 6, SF-00170 Helsinki
  ☎ 90 636750/605047
Tues, Thurs–Sun 12–4; Wed 12–6. Closed
  Midsummer Day weekend, Dec 6, 24, 25.

ⓒ ✑

The museum's collections relate to the history of
the stage in Finland and include paintings and
photographs illustrating theatres, performances
and performers. There are also exhibits of
programmes, posters and costumes, mostly from
the National Theatre.

Glassware, Iittala Glass Museum.

Hyvinkää

Railway Museum

Rautatiemuseo, Hyvinkäänkatu 9, SF-05800
  Hyvinkää, Uusimaa   ☎ 914 18351
May 2–Aug, Tues, Thurs, Fri 11–3; Wed 11–7;
  Sat 11–4; Sun 11–5. Sept–Apr, Tues–Fri
  12–3; Sat, Sun 12–4.

ⓒ 🛈 💻 ♿ ♠

The development of Hyvinkää started with the
railway. The building of the rail line, first from
Helsinki to Hämeenlinna between 1850 and
1870 and then from Hyvinkää to Hanko, led to
the growth of a small community in the
borderland between Häme and Uusimaa
provinces.
  The museum, founded in 1898 and
originally in Helsinki, is now housed in the
original railway buildings dating from the 1870s
and in a specially-built exhibition hall of 1987.
It tells the story of Finland's railways. The
building complex includes three 19th-century
railwaymen's houses, an engine house and
stores. The collections include a wide range of
historic railway material. Among the many
exhibits are the oldest locomotive to be
preserved in Finland, 'Pässi' (1868), the three-
carriage Russian Imperial train, in use between
1870 and 1879, and Finland's oldest rail car, a
Fiat (1914). There are also models of railway
station buildings and an operational miniature-
gauge track.

Iittala

Iittala Glass Museum

Iittalan lasimuseo, SF-14500 Iittala, Häme
  ☎ 17 721230
May–Aug, daily 9–8. Sept–Apr, daily 9–6. Closed
  Dec 24, 25.

🅕 🛈 💻 ♠

The Iittala Glassworks was established in 1881 and in the 1930s decided to identify itself with the new functional style which was interesting both designers and the public throughout Europe, and in which Finland was playing a leading rôle. The museum illustrates the history of the firm from the beginning, and presents the work of the prominent designers who have been involved in the company's development.

Imatra

Industrial Workers' Museum

Teollisuustyövaen a suntomuseo, Ritikanranta, SF-55120 Imatra, Kymi ☎ *954 22584 May–Aug, Tues–Sun 10–6. Other times by appt.*
ⓒ ✐

Industrialisation began in Imatra in the 1890s. The companies accepted the responsibility of housing their employees, and the wooden buildings in the museum area illustrate how the workers lived at the beginning of the present century, and in the 1920s, 1940s and 1960s. The rooms are furnished in every detail as they would have been during the period in question.

Inari

Inari Lapp Museum

Inarin saamelaismuseo, SF-99870 Inari, Lappi ☎ *9697 51107 June–Aug 10, daily 8 am–10 pm; Aug 11–31, daily 8–8. Sept 1–20, daily 9–3.30.*
ⓒ ✐

This open-air museum was set up in 1962, in response to the situation following the Second World War, in which the dwellings in the central areas of Finnish Lapland had been destroyed and old houses left intact only in the most remote regions. It was necessary to try to preserve the material evidence of a culture which was rapidly dying out, and with this in mind a number of buildings were moved to the museum site from different types of Lapp villages and settlements. They are displayed together with equipment used by their former inhabitants and with an exhibition of Lapp handicrafts.

Järvenpää

Sibelius's House

'Ainola', SF-04400 Järvenpää, Uusimaa ☎ *90 287322 May–Sept, Tues, Wed, Sat, Sun 11–5*
ⓒ ♠ ▉ ✐

'Ainola' was the home of the composer Jean Sibelius (1865–1957), from 1904 until his death. It was designed by the architect, Lars Sonck, who was also responsible for 'Kultaranta', the summer residence of the President of the Republic, and for the cathedral in Tampere. 'Ainola' is derived from Aino, the name of the composer's wife. The grave of Jean and Aino Sibelius is in the garden of their home. The house has been a museum since 1974. It contains many of its original furnishings, together with memorabilia and personal possessions of the family.

Joensuu

Art Museum

Joensuun taidemuseo, Kirkkokatu 23, SF-80100 Joensuu, Pohjois-Karjala ☎ *973 201697 Tues, Thurs, Fri 12–4; Wed 12–8; Sat 10–4; Sun 10–6.*
ⓒ ✐ ♿ ✐

The museum was established in 1962. Its collection of Finnish art has been formed as a result of six major donations which, with the addition of subsequent purchases by the museum, make it possible to cover the full development of art in Finland from 1850 to the present day. Other bequests have included collections of Persian bowls, Oriental carpets and silver, Russian icons, Chinese porcelain and Greek, Etruscan and Roman antiquities.

Museum of North Karelia

Pohjois-Karjalan museo, Karjalan Talo, Siltakatu 1, SF-80110 Joensuu, Pohjois-Karjala ☎ *973 201634 Tues, Thurs, Fri 12–4; Wed 12–8; Sat 10–4; Sun 10–6.*
ⓒ ✐

The museum, set up in 1917, is concerned mainly with the prehistory, history and folk culture of North Karelia. For historical reasons, exhibits from the former Ladoga Karelia region, ceded to the Russians during the Second World War, are also included.

The displays comprise sections on hunting, fishing, farming, folk costumes and textiles, healing and magic, handicrafts, folk poetry, musical instruments, vernacular architecture and furniture. There is also a collection of icons from the Old Believers' monastery of Megri, in Ilomantsi.

Art Museum, Joensuu.

Jyväskylä

Alvar Aalto Museum

Alvar Aalto museo, Alvar Aallton katu 7, PO Box 461, SF-40101 Jyväskylä, Keski-Suomi
☎ 941 624809
Tues–Sun 12–6
ⓒ 🏛 ⛴ 🚗

The celebrated architect, Alvar Aalto (1898–1976) attended school in Jyväskylä and established his first office there. From the 1950s onwards he carried out a number of projects for the town, including the Museum of Central Finland (1959–61) and the Alvar Aalto Museum (1971–3). There is a permanent exhibition illustrating Aalto's work, including sketches, drawings, designs, furniture and experiments with bent wood. The museum also has a large international collection of paintings, graphics and drawings executed between 1910 and 1960. The works from outside Finland are mainly by French and Italian artists. Most of the Finnish art in this collection is from the 1950s.

The museum arranges an international graphic arts triennial and also, as a separate venture, an Alvar Aalto symposium, and has a regular programme of visual arts exhibitions, with a broad scope that includes industrial design and photography.

Museum of Central Finland

Keski-Suomen museo, Ruusupuisto, SF-40600 Jyväskylä, Keski-Suomi   ☎ 941 294421
Tues–Sun 11–6
ⓒ 🏛 🚗

The museum building, completed in 1961, was designed by Alvar Aalto. It has displays illustrating the history, art and traditional occupations of the region. There are good collections of handicrafts, especially rugs, domestic equipment, popular art and modern Finnish art.

Kauhava

Knife and Textile Museum

Puukko ja tekstiilimuseo, SF-62210 Kauhava, Vaasa
June 1 – Aug 14, Mon–Fri 10–4; Sat, Sun 12–6. Other times by appt.
ⓒ 🗒 🚗

The Knife Museum was established in 1978 and the Textile Museum in 1982. The collections of the two museums were combined in 1988, when accommodation was provided in a new library building. There are exhibits showing the production of knives, with a display of knives made both in Kauhava and in other parts of Finland, and of birch knife-handles, decorated with thin strips of metal. The textile section of the museum is in two parts, the first of which shows traditional peasant woven fabrics before 1900 and the second products of the industrial period, from 1900 until the 1950s.

Kerimäki

Finnish Museum of Lake Fishing

Suomen järvikalastusmuseo, Puruvedentie 65, SF-58200 Kerimäki, Mikkeli   ☎ 957 541401
May 11–June 6 and Aug 3–30, daily 12–3. June 15–Aug 2, daily 11–6. Other times by appt.
ⓒ 🏛 🚗

Finland has an abundance of lakes, and fishing in them has been an important activity since prehistoric times. The museum's displays illustrate the historical development of fishing techniques in Finland, with collections of nets, line tackle and hooks, as well as boats and fishermen's clothing. In association with the museum, there is also a village museum, with exhibits relating to local history, handicrafts and domestic equipment.

Historic photograph in the Finnish Museum of Lake Fishing, Kerimäki.

Kimito

Sagalund Museum

*Sagalunds hembygdsmuseum, Vreta, SF-25700
   Kimito, Turku ja Pori* ☎ 925 1738
*Jan–May, Sept–Dec, Mon–Fri 10–3. June–Aug,
   Tues–Sun 12–5. Other times by appt. Closed
   Easter, Midsummer Day, Dec 24, 25.*
ⓒ ℹ 🖼 🚶

Opened in 1900, Sagalund, is one of the largest
open-air museums in Finland. Among the
eighteen 18th- and 19th-century rural buildings
moved to the museum are the Engelsby
Courthouse and a school, Tjuda Pedagogi
(1649). There are exhibits illustrating the social
and educational history of the district and the
site also contains the Villa Sagalund (1911),
which was formerly the home of two local
teachers, Nils-Oskar Jansson (1862–1927), who
established the Museum, and Adèle Weman
(1844–1936), who wrote poems under the name
of Parus Aters.
   Kobböli Watermill (1880) also belongs to
the Museum. It is on its original site, in the
village of Västanfjörd, 12 km from Sagalund,
and from time to time corn is still ground there.

Kuopio

Kuopio Museum

*Kuopion museo, Kauppakatu 23, SF-70100
   Kuopio* ☎ 971 182603
*Sept–Apr, Mon–Fri 9–4; Wed also 4–8; Sun
   11–6. May–Aug, also Sat 9–4. Closed some
   public holidays.*
Ⓕ ℹ 🚶

The museum contains two separate collections,
those of the Kuopio Museum of Cultural History
and of the Kuopio Museum of Natural History.
The cultural history collections date from 1883,
when the Kuopio Patriotic Society was founded,
and the natural history section from 1897, with
the foundation of the Kuopio Naturalists'
Society. The Jugendstil building dates from
1905–7.
   Prior to the establishment of the Kuopio
Museum, there were very few Finnish museums
of any kind outside Helsinki and in 1905 there
was no other building in the country which had
been designed specifically for museum purposes,
except for the Athenaeum in Helsinki and
Turku Art Gallery.
   The Natural History Department, on the
first floor, has displays illustrating the mammals,
birds, freshwater fish, amphibians, reptiles and
insects of the region, together with some exotic
specimens. There are also aquaria and rock and
mineral collections. The second and third floor
are devoted to the cultural history of Northern
Savo. The second-floor exhibits are concerned
with life and work in the 19th century, while
the third floor features urban culture of the
present century.

Kuopio Open-Air Museum

*Kuopion ulkomuseo, Kirkkokatu 22, SF-70100
   Kuopio* ☎ 971 182625
*May 15–Sept 15, daily 10–5 (until 7 Wed). Sept
   16–May 14, Tues–Sun 10–3.*
ⓒ ℹ 🖼

In 1972, when the decision was taken to restore
and preserve a group of five traditional wooden
buildings in the centre of Kuopio as the core of
an open-air museum, modern buildings were
rapidly changing the face of the town. Five
additional wooden buildings, from elsewhere in
the town centre, were dismantled and re-erected
on the museum site to complete the block.
   The interiors of the houses have been
restored and completely furnished in order to
show how people lived from the late 18th
century until the 1930s. One building contains
the workshops of a tailor and a weaver and
another that of a cobbler. A room in a third
house has been arranged to reproduce the room
of Minna Canth (1844–97), the novelist and
dramatist, who lived in Kuopio from 1880 until
her death in 1897.

Museum of the Orthodox Church

*Ortodoksinen kirkkomuseo, Karjalankatu 1,
   SF-70300 Kuopio* ☎ 971 122611
*May–Aug, Tues–Sun 10–4, Sept–Apr, Mon–Fri
   10–2; Sat, Sun 12–5.*
ⓒ ℹ 🚋 🚶

The museum is housed in part of a complex of
buildings which also includes the Archbishop's
residence, a seminary and the offices of the
Finnish Orthodox Church. The displays
illustrate the history of the Church in Finland.
There are special exhibits of liturgical objects,
vestments and icons.
   Most of the items are from the monasteries
of Valamo and Konevitsa, but there are also
some from Petsamo. As regards paintings, only
Viipuri and Kökisalmi are well represented.
During the Second World War campaigns
between the Finns and the Russians, most of the
treasures belonging to other parishes were lost or
destroyed.

Kuusamo

Kuusamo Museum

*Kuusamon kotiseutumuseo, Porkkatie 4, SF-93600
   Kuusamo, Lappi* ☎ 989 2046027
June–Aug, daily 12–6
Ⓕ 🚶

During the 1950s, a local history society in
Kuusamo formed plans to create a museum from
a traditional Kuusamo farmstead, a courtyard
with its main buildings along all four sides, and
wide spaces between the buildings as a fire
precaution. During the 1960s and 1970s, a
collection of suitable wooden buildings was
assembled and the buildings were gradually
dismantled and transferred to the museum site.
There are now 15 of them. They include, in
addition to the farmhouse, a cowshed, stable,

bear trap, windmill, water mill, granary, sauna, smithy, boat and net shed, hay barn and threshing shed.

Within the buildings, there is a large collection of objects relating to various occupations – fishing, dairying, farming and hunting – illustrating the life and activities of a fairly prosperous peasant farm in Kuusamo during the 19th and 20th centuries.

Lahti

Art and Poster Museum

*Taidemuseo ja julistemuseo, Vesi järvenkatu 11,
SF-15140 Lahti, Häme*   ☎ *918 102353
Daily 10–6*
C ♠ ☞

The museum is devoted to works by Finnish artists, with collections of paintings, graphics and sculpture, including items from the former Art Museum at Viipuri, in territory acquired by the Soviet Union during the Second World War. There is also an important collection of Finnish and international poster art from *c.* 1900 to the present day.

Historical Museum

Lahden historiallinen museo, Lahdenkatu 4, SF-15110 Lahti, Häme. Correspondence to: Box 115, SF-15111 Lahti.   ☎ *918 8182228
Tues 12–4, 6–8; Wed–Sun 12–4. Closed public holidays.*
C ✍

The museum is concerned with the history of Lahti and the surrounding region. It was founded in 1914, but the original collections were mostly destroyed during a fire at the town hall in 1914. The museum is now housed in the main building of Lahti Manor (1897). The collections include archaeological material from local sites, and peasant furniture, rugs, kitchen equipment, handicrafts, costumes and accessories.

There are also displays illustrating hunting, fishing, agriculture, dairying, brewing and home distilling and exhibits of locks and keys, woodworking – including a turner's workshop – and weapons. A private collection, given to the city in 1953, includes European faience, silver, furniture and paintings. Visitors can also see a display of coins and medals, illustrating the history of coinage in Finland, and part of the collections, especially paintings, from the former Historical Museum in Viipuri.

Ski Museum

Urheilukeskus, PL 115, SF-15111 Lahti, Häme
☎ *918 8182017
Daily 10–6 (closed at 4 on day preceding public holidays). Closed Jan 1, Good Fri, Easter Mon, May 1, Midsummer Eve, Midsummer Day, Dec 6, 24–6.*
C ♠ ☕ ☞

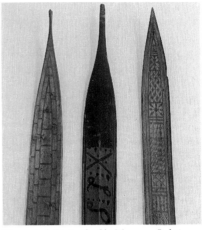

Decorated skis in the Ski Museum, Lahti.

The museum is at Lahti Sports Stadium. It is concerned with the history of skiing in Finland since prehistoric times. The collections include examples of skis proved by radiocarbon-dating to be 5,000 years old. The displays illustrate skiing for useful purposes and skiing for sport and contain a wide-ranging historical collection of skis. There is also a trophy collection and a film and photographic archive.

Lieksa

Pielinen Museum

*Pielisen museo, Pappilantie 2, SF-81720 Lieksa,
Pohjois-Karjala*   ☎ *975 20490
Mid May–mid Aug, daily 9–6. Mid Aug–mid Sept, daily 10–6. Mid-Sept–mid-May, Tues–Fri 10–2; Sat, Sun 11–3. Other times by appt. Closed Easter, Midsummer Eve, Christmas.*
C ♠ 🍴 ♿ ☞

There was a Karelian village named Lieksa in the early 16th century. In the 19th century the small village began to grow into a busy trading centre as a result of the development of the woodworking industry and timber trade, and in 1936 it became a borough, incorporating the municipality of Pielisjärvi in 1973.

The museum presents the life of Lieksa/ Pielisjärvi in the 19th and 20th centuries, with exhibits of domestic equipment, handicrafts and tools illustrating the period of subsistence economy, the clothing and furniture of middle-class families and a collection relating to the Second World War in the region. The open-air part of the museum is extensive and comprehensive, depicting life from the 17th century onwards, with sections devoted to farmhouses and their outbuildings, wind and watermills, forestry and logging, farming and fire-fighting.

The exhibits and the buildings of the museum have mostly been collected and transferred from the region between Lake Pielinen and Soviet Karelia, a district which has received cultural influences from both the West and the East.

Maalahti (Malax)

Kvarken Boat Museum

Kvarkens båtmuseum, SF-66100 Maalahti, Vaasa
☎ *961 651123*
June–July (5 weeks after Midsummer Day), Tues–
Sun 10–4. Other times by appt.
🅕 ⏴ ⌂

The museum, owned and run by the Maalahti
Museum Association, is one of the largest of its
type in Northern Europe. The collection
contains more than 50 traditional clinker-built
boats, together with shipbuilding tools and
equipment used in the region for fishing and
hunting. There is a special section dealing with
the boats and equipment used for seal-hunting
during the winter months.

Maarianhamina (Mariehamn)

Åland Historical Museum

Ahvenanmaan museo, Öhbergsvägen 1, PO Box
60, SF-22101 Maarianhamina, Ahvenanmaa
☎ *928 15000*
May–Aug, daily 10–4; Tues also 4–8. Sept-Apr,
Tues–Sun 11–4; Tues also 6–8. Closed Jan 1,
Apr 1, 3, May 1, June 9, 24, 25, Dec 6, 24,
25, 26, 31.
🅒 ⏴ ⯍ ⚅ ⌂

The museum's collections illustrate the natural
history, archaeology – Neolithic, Bronze Age,
Early Iron Age and Medieval – and history of
the Åland islands. There are displays of
furniture, domestic equipment, handicrafts and
costumes and among the exhibits is a complete
pharmacy. In the same building, but
independently managed, there is a museum of
Finnish art.

Maritime Museum of the Åland Islands

Ahvenanmaan museo, Hamngatan 2, SF-22100
Maarianhamina, Ahvenanmaa ☎ *28 11930*
Daily 8–4. Closed some public holidays.
🅒 ⏴ ⌂

The museum presents the maritime history of
the Åland islands, the base of the last big fleet of
long-distance sailing ships in the world, the
property of the Erikson Company. The
collections include the *Pommern*, which carried
grain from Australia to England, and the saloon
of the *Herzogin Cecilien*. There are displays of
ship models, photographs, paintings, log books,
ships' documents and navigational instruments.

Nuutajärvi

Prykäri Glass Museum

Prykäri-lasimuseo, SF-31160 Nuutajärvi, Häme
☎ *37 60460*
May–Aug, daily 10–7. Sept–Apr, daily 10–6.
Closed Dec 24–Jan 15.
🅒 ⏴ ⯍ ⌂

The glassworks at Nuutajärvi was established in
1793. In 1977 a museum was opened in a former
brewery building of *c.* 1850, to tell the story of
the works and to present an historical collection
of its products which, over the years, have
ranged from window-glass to cut-glass decanters
and from demi-johns to tumblers. There are
exhibits illustrating the equipment and
techniques involved, the development of
mechanical systems of production, the designers
employed and the relations with customers.

Oulu

Museum of Northern Ostrobothnia

Pohjois-Pohjanmaan museo, Ainola, PL 17,
SF-90101 Oulu ☎ *981 225200*
May–Sept 15, Mon, Tues, Thurs 11–6; Wed
11–8; Sat 11–3; Sun 12–6. Sept 16–Apr,
Mon, Tues, Thurs 11–4; Wed 11–7; Sat
11–3, Sun 12–6.
🅒

The museum, founded in 1896, is concerned
with the history of the City of Oulu,
Ostrobothnia and Lappland. Special exhibits
are devoted to important local industries,
especially charcoal-burning and wood-tar
production, and to maritime history. There are
collections illustrating rural handicrafts,
hunting, sealing, agriculture, dairy farming, the
craft trades, the archaeology of northern
Finland and the traditions of the Lapps.

Porvoo (Borgå)

Johan Runeberg House

J. L. Runebergin koti, Runeberginkatu 20, SF-
06100 Porvoo, Uusimaa ☎ *915 171330*
June–Aug, Mon–Sat 9.30–4; Sun 10.30–5. Sept–
May, Mon–Fri 10–4; Sat, Sun 11–5.
🅒 ⏴

The celebrated and much-loved Finnish poet,
Johan Ludwig Runeberg (1804–77), acquired
the house in 1853. After his death and, soon
afterwards, that of his wife, the Finnish State
bought Runeberg's house, together with his
library and household effects. It was opened to

Porvoo Museum.

the public in 1882 and has, more recently, been restored to its appearance during the last years of the poet's life. The rooms contain many memorabilia of Runeberg and his family, as well as material illustrating life in his time.

Porvoo Museum

Porvoon museo, Välikatu 11, SF-06100 Porvoo, Uusimaa   ☎ 915 170589
May–Aug, daily 11–4. Sept–Apr, Tues–Sat 12–3; Sun 12–5. Closed Jan 1, Good Fri, Easter Sun, May 1, Midsummer Eve, Midsummer Day, Nov 1, Dec 6, 24, 25 and some other public holidays.
Ⓒ ▮

The museum, which is concerned with the cultural history of Porvoo, is in the old town hall of 1764, and in the adjacent building (1761–2), formerly a merchant's residence. The museum and its collections are owned by the Porvoo Museum Society, which was founded in 1896 to save the town hall from destruction. Special exhibitions are devoted to furniture, textiles, glass, porcelain, pewter, weapons and handicrafts.

Two great Finnish artists, the painter, Albert Edelfelt (1854–1905) and the sculptor, Ville Vallgren (1855–1940) were born in Porvoo and always maintained close contact with the town. In addition to works by them, the museum has an excellent collection of 19th- and 20th-century Finnish and Swedish art.

One of the most remarkable sections of the museum is devoted to the Iris factory, which operated in Porvoo from 1897 until 1902. It was set up by the Jugendstil artists, Count Louis Sparre (1863–1964), a Swede, and Alfred William Finch (1854–1930), an Anglo-Belgian. The partners had no business sense and the factory soon went bankrupt, but its products – furniture and ceramics – were of the highest quality and they are collectors' items today.

Early diving suit. Raahe Museum.

Walter Runeberg Sculpture Collection

Walter Runebergin veistoskokoelma, Aleksanterinkatu 5, SF-06100 Porvoo, Uusimaa   ☎ 915 172186
June–Aug, Mon, Wed–Sat 9.30–4; Sun 10.30–5. Sept–May, Mon, Wed–Fri 10–4; Sat, Sun 11–5.
Ⓒ ▮

Walter Runeberg (1838–1920), was the son of the poet, Johan Runeberg. After many years abroad, in Rome and in Paris, where he became famous for his portrait busts and public sculptures, he returned to the north, first to Copenhagen and then in 1896, to Finland. In 1921, his children gave the town of Porvoo all the studies, sketches and casts of their father's works which were in his possession at the time of his death. The collection has since been considerably augmented and gives a good impression of the range of Runeberg's work.

Raahe

Raahe Museum

Raahen museo, Rantatori, SF-92100 Raahe, Oulu   ☎ 982 37003
June–Aug, Mon–Fri 12–6; Sat, Sun 12–5. Sept–May, Tues, Thurs–Sun 1–5; Wed 1–7.
Ⓒ ▮ ↝

Raahe has been a prosperous port since the end of the 18th century. The museum occupies a former customs warehouse (1848). Established in 1862, it claims to be the oldest museum of cultural history in Finland. Its collections illustrate the social, maritime, industrial and natural history of the town and the region. There are displays of handicrafts and of 17th-century sculptures from the old church in Raahe, which was destroyed by fire in 1908. Among the exhibits of particular interest is an 18th-century diving suit and a large and very varied collection of objects brought back by Raahe seamen from their travels around the world.

Riihimäki

The Finnish Glass Museum

Suomen lasimuseo, Tehtaankatu 23, SF-11910 Riihimäki, Häme   ☎ 914 741494
Feb–Mar and Oct–Dec, Tues–Sun 10–6. Apr–Sept, daily 10–6.
Ⓒ ▮ ▣ ♿ ↝

Glassmaking has been an important industry for more than 300 years. In the 18th century, during the years of Swedish rule, more than half the glass produced in the kingdom of Sweden was made in Finland. The museum, established in 1961, is in an old glassworks. It presents an historical survey of the techniques of glassmaking and tells the story of the industry in Finland. There are displays of the products of the Finnish glass industry since its early days, with an emphasis on the period since 1950, during which Finland became recognised as a world leader in glass design.

Rovaniemi

Art Museum

Rovaniemen taidemuseo, Lapinkävijäntie 4, SF-96100 Rovaniemi, Lappi ☎ *960 3222821*
Tues–Fri, Sun 12–6; Sat 10–4.

The museum occupies part of a former bus-garage, one of the few buildings in the town to survive the German destruction of 1944. After restoration and adaptation, it was opened as a museum in 1986. It houses the Wihuri Foundation collection of contemporary Finnish art, which provides a good impression of what has been achieved in Finland during the modern period.

Saarijärvi

Saarijärvi Museum

Saarijärvi museo, PL 13, SF-43101 Saarijärvi, Keski-Suomi ☎ *944 2911*
Tues–Sun 11–7

The museum, now in a new building, illustrates the traditional life and occupations of the region. There are collections, mainly from the 19th century, of handicrafts, folk art, domestic equipment and costumes. There are also large archives of photographs and printed material.

Squire's House Museum

Säätyläiskotimuseo, Saarijärven museo, PL 13, SF-43101 Saarijärvi, Keski-Suomi ☎ *944 2911*
May 15–Aug, Tues–Sun 10–6

Captain E. G. af Enehjelm farmed the Kolkanlahti estate at Saarijärvi in the early 19th century. The main residential building, the present museum, dates from the 1780s. From 1823 to 1825, Finland's national poet, J.F. Runeberg (1804–77), worked as a tutor in the house and wrote poems about the life of the people in the region. The museum contains an exhibition about Runeberg's years in Saarijärvi and about the influences of Saarijärvi on these poems.

The house itself was restored in 1976, and contains period furnishings and household equipment. It illustrates the style of living of a well-to-do family in the early 19th century.

The Stone Age Village

Kivikauden kylä, Saarijärven museo, PL 13, SF-43101 Saarijärvi, Keski-Suomi ☎ *944 2911*
May 15–Aug, Tues–Sun 10–7

The reconstruction of the village, close to Lake Summasjärvi, has been carried out by the Saarijärvi Museum. It represents a settlement site as it would probably have looked between 4,200 and 2,000 BC. The purpose of the village

The reconstructed Stone Age Village, Saarijärvi.

is to show the different kinds of dwellings that were probably used in Finland during the later Stone Age.

The Exhibition Room contains a display of genuine Stone Age artefacts and copies of artefacts from the Stone, Bronze and Iron Age. In the Demonstration Room, visitors can try out Stone Age working methods for themselves.

Saukkola

The Dairy Museum

Meijerimuseo, SF-09430 Saukkola, Uusimaa ☎ *912 71176*
May–Sept, Tues–Sun 10–5. Oct–Apr, Tues–Fri, Sun 10–5. Closed public holidays.

Saukkola is 66 km west of Helsinki, near the E3 Helsinki-Turku road. The museum is financed and administered by the Valio Finnish Cooperative Dairies Association and occupies an old granite-built creamery of 1904, which was in use up to 1980. The building is a fine example of Finnish Jugendstil architecture.

The exhibits illustrate the history of dairying in Finland from 1850 to 1960. There is a comprehensive collection of dairy and cheese-making machinery and equipment covering the period, with explanations of the processes involved.

Savonlinna

Savonlinna Museum

Savonlinnan maakuntamuseo, Riihisaari, SF-57130 Savonlinna, Mikkeli ☎ *957 22194*
June–Aug, daily 10–8. Oct–May, Tues–Sun 12–6.

The museum is situated on Riihisaari Island, near Olavinlinna Castle (1475). The museum building (1852) was originally a Crown granary. The displays cover the archaeology, history and traditional activities of the Etelä-Savo (South Savo) region. The history of navigation on Saimaa, the largest of the lake districts, has been developed as a special section.

By the lakeside there is a jetty for the

museum's three ships, the passenger steamship, *Savonlinna* (1903), the steam freighter, *Mikko* (1914) and the steam schooner, *Salama* (1874), which was built in Viipuri and carried passengers between Savonlinna, Lübeck and St Petersburg. The *Salama* sank in a collision on Lake Saimaa in 1898 and was raised and restored in 1971.

In this area crofters formed the main body of the agricultural workers. They owned practically nothing and lived in simple wooden buildings for which the rent was a certain number of working days in the fields and the woods. The open-air museum illustrates the life of the crofters and consists of a number of cottages and farm buildings on their original sites, grouped in the form of a village.

Seinäjoki

Museum of Southern Ostrobothnia

Etelä-Pohjanmaan maakuntamuseo, Törnävä,
SF-60200 Seinäjoki, Vaasa ☎ *964 120735*
May 15–Aug, Tues–Sun 11–7. Sept–May 14,
Mon–Fri 9–2.30; Sun 12–4. Other times by
appt.
C ♦ ⚘

This is an open-air museum of 17th–19th-century rural buildings, illustrating the social history of the region. Among the exhibits are a farmhouse, with its outbuildings – granaries, haybarns, cowhouses, stable and windmill, a blacksmith's forge, a village shop, a sauna, a watermill and an ironworks. The museum also has collections illustrating the history and technology of the local gunpowder industry.

Tammijärvi

Peltola Cotters Museum

Peltolan mäkitupalaismuseo, SF-19910
Tammijärvi, Luhanka, Keski-Suomi
☎ *947 63108*
June–Aug 15, daily 10–7.
C ♦ ⚘

Moomin House, based on Tove Jansson's children's books. Moomin Valley, a branch of Tampere Art Museum.

Tampere

Sara Hildén Art Museum

Sara Hildénin taidemuseo, Särkänniemi, SF-33230
Tampere, Häme ☎ *931 113134*
Daily 11–6
C ▣ ⚓ ■ ⚘

The Sara Hildén Foundation was established in 1962, when Mrs Hildén, art collector and well-known figure in the Tampere business community, gave her collection of modern Finnish art to the Foundation. The collection has since been greatly augmented and includes, in addition to contemporary works, paintings and sculpture by influential Finnish artists from the first half of the 20th century. The non-Finnish works in the collection reflect the international art styles in vogue during the 20th century.

Tampere Art Museum

Tampereen taidemuseo, Puutarhakatu 34,
SF-33230 Tampere, Häme ☎ *931 121244*
Daily 11–7. Closed Good Fri, Midsummer Day,
Dec 24, 25. Moomin Valley: May–Aug, daily
12–6. Sept–Apr, Wed–Sun 12–6.
C ♦ ▣ ⚓ ⚘

The museum occupies a former public granary, built in 1838, the collections comprising paintings, drawings, graphics and sculpture by 19th–20th-century Finnish artists.

The museum is also responsible for Moomin Valley (Muumilaakso), a children's museum at Hämeenpuisto 20, based on the fantasy world created by Tove Jansson in his popular books for children. The displays include Jansson's original illustrations, three-dimensional tableaux of adventures in the Moomin books, and a large, fully-furnished Moomin House, with its balconies and secret passages.

Turku (Åbo)

Biological Museum

Biologinen museo, Neitsytpolku 1, SF-20800
Turku, Turku ja Pori. Correspondence to:
Turun maakuntamuseo, Kalastajankatu 4,
SF-20100 Turku. ☎ *921 356491*
May–Sept, daily 10–6. Oct–Apr, daily 10–3.
Closed Good Fri, May 1, Midsummer Eve and
Day, Dec 6, 24, 25.
C ✍

After visiting the new Biological Museum in Stockholm in 1902, Alfred Jacobsson and his wife, Hélène, decided to give a large sum of money to create a similar museum in Turku. Following the Swedish example, the new museum contained a wide range of Finland's flora and fauna, presented in habitat-dioramas, an exciting novelty at the time. Three of the original dioramas remain almost unaltered, but most of the others were restored or rebuilt between 1960 and 1990. Minimum changes have been made but today the birds and animals are displayed not just sitting or standing, but engaged in some activity, and are named in several languages, including Latin.

Goldsmith's workbench. Luostarinmäki Handicrafts Museum, Turku.

Luostarinmäki Handicrafts Museum

Luostarinmäen käsityöläismuseo, SF-20700 Turku, Turku ja Pori. Correspondence to: Turun maakuntamuseo, Kalastajankatu 4, SF-20100 Turku. ☎ 921 337150
May 2–Sept, daily 10–6. Sept–Apr, daily 10–3. Closed Good Fri, May 1, Midsummer Eve and Day, Dec 6, 24, 25.
ⓒ ♿ ☕

As with most towns composed of wooden buildings, Turku – the oldest town in Finland and its former capital – was often ravaged by fire. The destruction caused by the fire of 1827 was so complete that Turku was rebuilt on a new street plan. But the fire did not reach Luostarinmäki, which was on a hill on the outskirts of the town and inhabited by poor people. It survived virtually unchanged until 1937, when it was decided that ten of the seventeen courtyard houses on the hill should be preserved, to accommodate a museum of traditional crafts, forming part of Turku Historical Museum.

Workshops have been reconstructed in these buildings and among the trades represented are those of a goldsmith, potter, watchmaker, rope-maker, saddler, violin-maker, bookbinder, wig-maker, glove-maker, comb-maker and printer. There is also a small-scale tobacco factory.

Maritime and Astronomical Museum

Merenkulkumuseo ja tähtitieteelliset kokoelmat, Vartiovuori, SF-20700 Turku, Turku ja Pori. Correspondence to: Turun maakuntamuseo, Kalastajankatu 4, SF-20100 Turku.
☎ 921 337140
May–Sept, daily 10–6. Oct–Apr, daily 10–3. Closed Good Fri, May 1, Midsummer Eve and Day, Dec 6, 24, 25.
ⓒ ♿

The museum building was originally an observatory, built in 1817–19 for the Royal Academy in Turku. It later became a naval school. Since 1986 it has housed the Academy's astronomical and maritime collections, which were previously in temporary premises.

When the Maritime Museum was founded in 1936, it was the first of its kind in Finland. Thanks to its early start, before the age of sail was over, it was able to save many valuable objects which would otherwise have been lost.

The collections include portraits, paintings of ships, navigational instruments, ship models, carpenters' and sailmakers' tools, souvenirs made by sailors and a number of boats. In the archives, the museum has large collections of photographs, ships' logbooks, charts, shipowners' records and architects' drawings. The museum's most treasured possession is the barque, *Sigyn*, built in Gothenburg in 1887.

Sibelius Museum

Sibelius-museo, Piispankatu 17, SF-20500 Turku, Turku ja Pori ☎ 921 654494
Tues–Sun 11–3
ⓒ ♿

The Sibelius Museum, the only music museum in Finland, is the collective name of the different sections of the Institute of Musicology at Åbo Akademi, the Swedish university of Turku. The museum is divided into two parts of equal standing, an exhibition section and a teaching section. It contains an important collection of manuscripts of Sibelius, as well as concert programmes from different countries and newspaper articles and photographs relating to the composer. There is also an important collection of musical instruments. Concerts are held regularly in the museum's auditorium.

Turku Art Gallery

Turun taidemuseo, Puolalanpuisto, SF-20100 Turku, Turku ja Pori ☎ 921 330954
Mon–Sat 10–4; Sun 10–6. Thurs, also 6–8 pm.
ⓒ ♿

The museum, a monumental red granite building in the Jugendstil style, was designed by Gustaf Nyström (1856–1917), one of whose pupils was Eliel Saarinen. It was opened in 1904. The collections are the second largest in Finland and belong to the Art Society of Turku, founded in 1891. They give a good impression of the development of Finnish art from the beginning of the 19th century to the present day. There are also good examples of works by Scandinavian artists and an international graphics collection. The ground floor of the museum originally housed an art school, the first in Finland. Since 1933 it has been used for temporary exhibitions.

Turku Historical Museum

*Turun kaupungin historiallinen museo, Turun
linna, SF-20100 Turku, Turku ja Pori.
Correspondence to: Turun maakuntamuseo,
Kalastajankatu 4, SF-20100 Turku.*
☎ 921 303300
*Jan–Apr and Oct–Dec, daily 10–3. May 2–Sept,
daily 10–6. Closed Good Fri, May 1,
Midsummer Eve and Day, Dec 24, 25.*

Ⓒ ⓘ ⬛

The museum is in Finland's largest medieval
castle. The fortress dates from the late 13th
century and the bailey, which houses the
museum, from the 10th. The museum presents
the history of the castle and of Turku, with
exhibits of costumes, domestic equipment and
craftsmen's tools. In the period rooms there are
displays of Finnish, Scandinavian and European
furniture, porcelain, glass, pewter and gold- and
silversmiths' works. There are also many
portraits.

Wäinö Aaltonen Museum

*Wäinö Aaltonen museo, Itäinen Rantakatu 38,
SF-20810 Turku, Turku ja Pori*
☎ 921 355690
*Mon–Fri 10–4, 6–8; Sat 10–4; Sun 10–6. Closed
Good Fri, May 1, Midsummer Eve and Day,
Dec 6, 24, 25.*

Ⓒ ⓘ ⬛ ↩

Wäinö Aaltonen (1894–1966) was the youngest
of a famous trio of Nordic sculptors, the other
two being the Norwegian, Gustaf Vigeland
(1869–1943) and the Swede, Carl Milles
(1875–1955). Few artists have dominated their
own generation as Aaltonen did in Finland in
the 1920s and 1930s, and his style continued to
have influence, even after the Second World
War. Like the architect Alvar Aalto, he was a
national symbol.
  Aaltonen studied painting at Turku Art
School, but was self-taught as a sculptor. The
museum, designed by his son and daughter-in-
law, was opened in 1967. In addition to its
library and archives, it contains a large
collection of paintings, drawings, sculpture and
graphics by Aaltonen, plus a number of works by
modern Finnish artists.

Uusikaupunki

Museum of Cultural History

*Uudenkaupungin kulttuurihistoriallinen museo,
Ylinenkatu 11, SF-23500 Uusikaupunki,
Turku ja Pori*   ☎ 922 155399
*June–Aug 15, Tues–Fri 10–5; Sat, Sun 12–3.
Aug 16–May, Tues–Sun 12–3.*

Ⓒ ↩

Founded in 1895, the museum was for many
years in the town's Old Church. In 1967 the
collections were transferred to a wooden house
built in 1870 by the tobacco manufacturer,
F. W. Wahlberg, and this building is a good
example of 19th-century upper-middle-class
architecture.

The rooms have period furnishings and
contain exhibitions of local and maritime
history – at the end of the 19th century the
town's sailing fleet was the third biggest in
Finland – shipbuilding, textiles and
navigational instruments. As early as the
Middle Ages, Uusikaupunki was the centre of
an industry for manufacturing different types of
wooden container (Vakkas), which were
exported, especially to Denmark and Germany.
The museum contains an exhibition of these.

Vaasa

Bragegården

*Sandviken, SF-65350 Vaasa   ☎ 961 127161
June–Aug, Tues–Fri 2–7; Sat, Sun 12–4.*

Ⓒ

In 1906 the first Brage Association was
established in Helsinki, with the aim of
preserving and promoting the Swedish folk
culture of Finland. It was followed two years
later by a similar association in Vaasa. In 1933
the Vaasa Association set up an open-air
museum, to show what the life of a farmer in the
Swedish part of Ostrobothnia was like at the end
of the 19th century.
  The buildings were brought to the museum
site from Harf in Närpio. They include the main
dwelling house (1810) – 'the big house' – and
'the small house', for the former owner and his
wife, who were entitled to free board and
lodging on the farm after they had handed it
over to their heirs. Other buildings enclosing
the farmyard were the stable, the cowhouse, the
sheep-house, the pigsty, the lavatory, the sauna,
the grain store and the cart-shed. Outside the
farmyard there was a threshing building, a
windmill, another grain store, a smithy, the
seal-hunters' house and the fishermen's
building. The rooms in the main farmhouse
have been given appropriate period furniture
and equipment.

Inner courtyard, Turku Historical Museum.

FRANCE

Abbeville

Boucher de Perthes Museum

*Musée Boucher de Perthes, rue Gontier Patin,
F-80000 Abbeville, Somme* ☎ *22 21 08 49*
May 2–Sept, Mon, Wed–Sun 2–6. Oct–Apr,
Wed, Sun 2–6. Also open school holidays at
Whitsun, Christmas and Spring.

F 🔍

Jacques Boucher de Perthes (1788–1868) was a
pioneering writer on prehistory. His work is
commemorated in the name of the museum,
which itself has important collections of worked
flints and other prehistoric material, as well as
exhibits illustrating Gallo-Roman sites in the
neighbourhood. There are also displays of
Brussels tapestries, of 15th–18th-century French
and Flemish paintings, and furniture, pewter
and religious sculpture, and ceramics from
northern France. Sections of the museum are
devoted to the natural history, especially birds,
of the Somme valley and to the industries of the
region.

Aix-en-Provence

Granet Museum

*Musée Granet, Palais de Malte, place Saint-Jean-
de-Malte, F-13100 Aix-en-Provence, Bouches-
du-Rhône* ☎ *42 38 14 70*
July–Aug, daily 10–12, 2–6. Sept–June, Wed–
Mon 10–12, 2–6.

C 🔍

The painter, François-Marius Granet (1775–
1849), was a pupil of J. L. David. In 1826 he
became curator of the Louvre and in 1830 he
became keeper of pictures at Versailles. During
the Revolution of 1848 he retired to his native
Aix-en-Provence, where he founded the
museum which bears his name. It contains a
celebrated portrait of him by Ingres. The
museum's possessions grew rapidly and between
1856 and 1930 four extensions to the original
building, the former Priory of the Order of St
John of Malta, were required.

The museum has remarkable 3rd–2nd-century
BC Celtic-Ligurian sculptures, as well as
Egyptian, Roman, Greek, Gallo-Roman and
early Christian material from excavations in the
town and the surrounding area. There are also
interesting collections of 16th–19th-century
French, Flemish and Dutch paintings, a room
being devoted to the 19th-century School of
Provence and another to the works of Cézanne
and his friends. The sculpture section contains
works by, among other celebrated French
artists, Pierre Puget (1824–98), Jean–Antoine
Houdon (1741–1828) and Pierre-Jean David –
'David d'Angers' – (1788–1856).

Museum of Old Aix

*Musée du Vieil Aix, Hôtel d'Estienne de St Jean,
17 rue Gaston de Saporta, F-13100 Aix-en-
Provence, Bouches du Rhône*
☎ *42 41 43 55*
May–Sept, Tues–Sun 10–12, 2.30–6. Nov–Apr,
Tues–Sun 10–12, 2–5. Closed Oct and public
holidays.

C 🔍

The museum occupies the Hôtel d'Estienne de
St Jean, a splendid late-17th-century house.
Some of the original wall and ceiling paintings
are still visible. The museum was built up during
1930–6 by Marie d'Estienne de St Jean, who
donated her family mansion and most of its
contents to the State on condition that the
Museum of Old Aix should be established here,
and that the administration should be in the
hands of a private voluntary association.

Since the museum opened in 1930, the
collection has been greatly enriched by other
gifts. It includes a wide range of items –
furniture, pictures, prints, pottery, dolls,
miniatures, costumes, musical instruments,
documents and drawings relating to Aix-en-
Provence, and other objects illustrating the life
and traditions of the region.

The museum possesses two remarkable early-
19th-century rod puppet shows, the Talking
Crib (Crèche Parlante), which reproduces in 20
scenes the mystery play and legends of the
Nativity, and the Fête-Dieu celebrations, held
every year in June.

**19th-century rod puppets. Museum of Old
Aix, Aix-en-Provence.**

Paul Cézanne's Studio

Musée de l'Atelier de Paul Cézanne, 9 avenue Paul Cézanne, F-13100 Aix-en-Provence, Bouches-du-Rhône   ☎ 42 21 06 53
May–Oct, Wed–Sun 10–12, 2.30–6. Nov–Apr, Wed–Sun, 10–12, 2–5.

C

The studio is on the first floor of the house which Cézanne had built in 1900–02. It has been preserved intact, thanks to the generosity and public spirit of a group of Americans who raised the money to buy the property in order that it should become a museum. The museum contains some of Cézanne's watercolours and drawings and a number of his personal possessions, including his easel and palettes and the models he used for his still-life paintings.

Ajaccio (Corsica)

House of the Bonapartes

Musée National de la Maison Bonaparte, rue Saint-Charles, F-20000 Ajaccio, Corse
☎ 95 21 43 89
June 22–Sept 30, Mon 2–6; Tues–Sat 9–12, 2–6; Sun 9–12. Oct 1–June 21, Mon 2–5; Tues–Sat 10–12, 2–5; Sun 10–12. Free admission Wed.

C 🛈

This small house, in the historic centre of Ajaccio, became the property of the Bonaparte family in 1743 and Napoleon was born here in 1769. After 1799 he never revisited the house, which was given to the nation by Prince Napoleon in 1923. The rooms on the second floor were formerly the private apartments of the family and now contain portraits, documents and personal possessions relating to the Bonapartes. The drawing-room and reception room reserved for Napoleon's mother, Laetitia, are on the first floor and have Louis XV, Louis XVI or Directoire furniture. The room where the future Emperor was born contains a trapdoor, through which he escaped when he was obliged to flee from Corsica in 1799. On the ground floor there is a reconstruction of a traditional Corsican oil-mill and stable, old agricultural implements and photographs showing the properties which at one time belonged to the Bonaparte family.

Albi

Toulouse-Lautrec Museum

Musée Toulouse-Lautrec, Palais de la Berbie, BP 100, F-81003 Albi, Tarn   ☎ 63 54 14 09
Apr–May, daily 10–12, 2–6. June–Sept, daily 9–12, 2–6. Oct–Mar, Wed–Mon 10–12, 2–5. Closed Jan 1, Mar 1, 10–30, May 1, Nov 1, Dec 25.

C 🛈 🚃

Henri de Toulouse-Lautrec (1864–1901) was born in Albi. The museum in the former Archbishops' Palace, a fortified brick building dating from the 13th century, contains the

Seated woman by Henri de Toulouse-Lautrec. Toulouse-Lautrec Museum, Albi.

largest collection of paintings and graphics by Toulouse-Lautrec in the world, illustrating the development of his art from his earliest works to his last canvas, and demonstrating the various themes which brought him fame – horses, the theatre, the café-concert, brothels, women. An important part of the exhibition is devoted to his work as a lithographer and as one of the creators of the modern poster.

There are also paintings by his friends and contemporaries, such as Bonnard, Vuillard, Valadon and Serusier. Their work and experiments anticipate the evolution of art during the first half of the 20th century, represented in the museum by Rouault, Utrillo, Vlaminck and Dufy.

Alençon

Alençon Point Lace Museum

Musée du Point d'Alençon, Association de la Dentelle, 31 rue du Pont-Neuf, F-61000 Alençon, Orne   ☎ 33 26 27 26
Apr–Sept, Tues–Sat 2–6. Closed public holidays. Oct–Mar, by appt.

C 🛈 ♿ 🚃

Alençon is traditionally famous for its point lace, known as 'the queen of lace and the lace of queens'. The museum has historical collections of lace, showing the way in which techniques and designs have gradually changed and developed since the 17th century, and paying particular attention to the local industry. A lace-making school at the museum preserves the old tradition.

Alise-Sainte-Reine

Alésia Museum

Musée Alésia, rue de l'Hôpital, Alise-Sainte-Reine,
    F-21150 Les Laumes, Côte-d'Or
    ☎ 80 96 10 95/30 54 60
Late Mar–June, daily 10–6. July–Sept 10, daily
    9–7. Sep 11–Nov 5, daily 10–6.
C ▌ ✍

In 52 BC Julius Caesar laid siege to the hill
fortress of Alésia, which was defended by native
Celtic troops under the command of
Vercingetorix. Caesar's victory here decided not
only the future of Gaul, but also that of Rome
and its empire. The siege was one of the turning
points in European history.

Over the next three centuries a substantial
Gallo-Roman town grew up on the site. It has
been excavated during the present century and
visitors can now see the ruins of many of the
buildings and the street plan. The museum, in
the 17th-century Hôtel du Croissant, illustrates
the siege of Alésia and everyday life in the town
afterwards, by means of objects discovered in
the course of the excavations.

Ambert

Museum of Papermaking

Musée Historique du Papier, Moulin Richard-de-
    Bas, F-63600 Ambert, Puy-de-Dôme
    ☎ 73 82 03 11
July–Aug, daily 9–8. Sept–June, daily 9–12, 2–6.
    Closed Jan 1, Dec 25. Guided tours only.
C ▌ ✍

An example of 'the lace of queens' from the
Point Lace Museum, Alençon.

There has been a paper-mill at Ambert since the
14th century. The present mill, with its well-
preserved water-driven machinery, dates from
the 18th century and is in working order. Since
1943 it has been a museum of paper-making,
illustrating the various processes involved.
There is a collection of 2,000 watermarks,
classified according to type, and the first paper-
making machine, invented by Robert in 1798.
The house of the master-papermaker has also
been preserved and can be visited.

Ambierle

Alice Taverne Museum

Musée Alice Taverne, F-42820 Ambierle, Loire
    ☎ 77 65 60 99
Mar–Sept, daily 10–12, 2–6. Oct–Nov, daily
    10–12, 2–5. Dec–Mar, by appt only.
C ▌

From the 1930s until the time of her death,
Alice Taverne (1904–69) collected material
which illustrated the traditional life of the
département of the Loire. The objects were
arranged in an 18th-century house, mostly in
reconstructions of room interiors, workshops
and shops. In recent years, the collections have
been augmented and the presentation has been
refurbished.

Special sections and reconstructed rooms are
devoted to peasant furniture and domestic
equipment, an inn and posting station, a village
grocer's, a nursery, a quack doctor, popular
religion, costumes and accessories, agriculture
and the traditional crafts of the region. There is
an excellent collection of 16th–19th-century
furniture.

Amboise

Postal Museum

Musée de la Poste et des Voyages, 6 rue Joyeuse,
    F-37400 Amboise, Indre-et-Loire
    ☎ 47 57 02 21
Apr–Sept, Tues–Sun 9.30–12, 2–6.30. Oct–Dec
    & Feb–Mar, Tues–Sun 10–12, 2–5.
C ▌

The museum building was originally the Hôtel
de Joyeuse, built in the 16th century to the
design of a Franciscan friar, Giovanni
Giocondo, brought from Italy by Charles VIII,
together with his friend, the gardener Pacello di
Mercogliano. These two Italians brought the
first orange trees to France. The house was
restored in the early 20th century and became a
museum in 1971.

The displays tell the story of the postal service
in France. The exhibits include models of
vehicles used to transport the mail, posters,
route-maps, old letters, the first stamp printed in
France, and items relating to Chappe's
semaphore system. Special sections are devoted
to the development of air mail delivery, to
communications during the siege of Paris in
1870–1, to the telegraph and to military postal
systems.

**Statue of the Gaulish leader, Vercingetorix.
The head is based on a likeness of Napoleon
III. Alésia Museum, Alise-Sainte-Reine.**

Amiens

Museum of Art and Regional History

*Musée d'Art Local et d'Histoire Régionale, Hôtel de
    Berny, 36 rue Victor Hugo, F-80000 Amiens,
    Somme*   ☎ *22 91 81 12*
Tues–Sast 10–12.30, 2–6; Sun 10–12, 2–6
Ⓒ ▮

The museum is located in a 17th-century
building, the former Hôtel des Trésoriers de
France. In the arrangements of the collections
of furniture, musical instruments, tapestries,
porcelain and other objects, considerable use is
made of period rooms. The Flemish, Aubusson
and Maincy tapestries include designs by Le
Brun and Lurçat. There are portraits and
memorabilia of local celebrities, including
Marshal Leclerc, Choderlos de Laclos and Jules
Verne.

Picardy Museum

*Musée de Picardie, 48 rue de la République,
    F-8000 Amiens, Somme*   ☎ *22 91 36 44*
*Tues–Sat 10–12.30, 2–6; Sun 10–12, 2–6.
    Closed public holidays.*
Ⓒ ▮ ▆ 占

The museum building, constructed in 1855–67,
is one of the 19th-century monumental type,
complete with grand staircase. It houses one of
the six largest provincial museums in France.
The collections fall into three categories –
archaeological, medieval, and paintings and
sculpture. The archaeological material is mainly
regional, but also includes Greek and Roman
antiquities. The medieval section includes
ivories, enamels and objets d'art of exceptional
range and quality, as well as a large collection of
sculptures representing religious art and

architecture in Picardy from the 12th century to
the end of the Gothic period.
   Most of the items in the sculpture collection
consist of 19th-century French works. The main
strength of the collection of paintings is in
works by 18th–20th-century French artists,
especially of the Barbizon school, but Flemish,
Dutch and Italian painters are also well
represented. The museum has recently
undergone a thoroughgoing programme of
restoration and rearrangement.

Angers

Gallery of the Apocalypse

*Galerie de l'Apocalypse, Château d'Angers,
    F-49000 Angers, Maine-et-Loire*
            ☎ *41 87 43 47*
*Day following Palm Sun–June 30, daily 9.30–12,
    2–6. July–Sept, daily 9.30–6.30. Oct 1–Palm
    Sun, daily 9.30–12, 2.30–5.*
Ⓒ

'The Apocalypse' tapestry was woven in Bruges
in 1373–80 by Jean de Bruges and Nicolas
Bataille for Angers Cathedral. It is the greatest
tapestry of the medieval period, measuring 100
metres in length and 5.50 metres in width.
Together with other tapestries, mainly French,
dating from the 15th to the 18th centuries, it
has been displayed at the Château since 1952.
These works constitute one of Europe's most
important tapestry collections.

The Jean Lurçat Tapestry Museum

*Musée Jean Lurçat et de la Tapisserie
    Contemporaine, 4 quai Arago, F-49000
    Angers, Maine-et-Loire*   ☎ *41 87 41 06*
*June 15–Sept 15, daily 10–12, 2–6. Sept 16–
    June 14, Tues–Sun 10–12, 2–6.*
Ⓒ

In 1874 the former Hospital of St Jean, built in
1188, and preserving its chapel, cloister and
splendid infirmary, was used to house the town's
archaeological collections. In 1968, these were
put into store, except for the lapidarium and the
pharmacy of the hospital, with its 17th–19th-
century equipment. The space freed was then
used to display an important tapestry series by
Jean Lurçat (1892–1966), *The Song of the World.*
It is in ten sections and was woven in 1957–65.
An extension to the Lurçat museum has
subsequently been opened and contains other
works by the artist given by his widow,
consisting of paintings, ceramics, jewellery,
illustrated books and further tapestries.

Annecy

Castle Museum

*Musée-Château d'Annecy, place du Château,
    F-74000 Annecy, Haute-Savoie*
            ☎ *50 45 29 66*
May–Sept, daily 10–12, 2–6. Free admission Wed.
Ⓒ ◛

The impressively situated castle was built at different periods from the 12th to the 17th centuries. In 1954 the municipal archaeological and natural history collections were transferred here from the town hall and completely reorganised in the process. The exhibits now cover the natural history of the Alps, with particularly important collections of geology and minerals from the mountains of Savoy, and archaeological material from the early historical period, including finds from the lake villages in the region.

Annecy-le-Vieux

Museum of Bells

Musée de la Cloche, 3 chemin de l'Abbaye, F-74000 Annecy-le-Vieux, Haute-Savoie
☎ *50 27 98 74*
June 15–Sept 15, Mon–Sat 10–12, 2.30–6.30; Sun and public holidays 2.30–5. Sept 16– June 14, Tues–Sat 10–12, 2.30–5.30; Sun and public holidays 2.30–6.30.
C

The museum was created in 1984 in the Paccard bell foundry. It contains a range of tools and equipment used in founding and tuning bells, as well as documents, engravings and photographs illustrating the processes involved. There is a gallery devoted to old bells and another to carillons. A special section tells the story of the two largest bells made in France, the 19-tonne 'Savoyarde' for the Sacré-Coeur in Montmartre and the 'Jeanne d'Arc', which weighed 16 tonnes and which was destroyed in the bombardment of Rouen in 1944. There is also a series of American Liberty Bells, made in 1956.

Antibes

Picasso Museum

Musée Picasso, Château Grimaldi, place Mariéjol, F-06600 Antibes, Alpes-Maritimes
☎ *93 33 67 67*
July–Sept, Wed–Mon 10–12, 3–7. Oct, Dec– June, Wed–Mon 10–12, 3–6. Closed Nov.
C

A Roman fortified camp was on the site of the present château. Later the residence of the Bishops of Antibes was here and the building was subsequently acquired and modified by the Grimaldi family. The town of Antibes bought it in 1925 and opened it three years later as a museum of art and history, with local Greek and Roman antiquities and inscriptions and collections of pictures and objects illustrating the development and traditions of Antibes.

Pablo Picasso worked in the museum for six months in 1946 and left it most of the paintings and drawings executed during this time. Further substantial bequests of his works followed later, together with a large number of paintings, sculptures and drawings by his contemporaries, including Modigliani's drawing, *Portrait of Picasso*.

Outside, there is a Garden of Sculpture and Perfume, which brings together a large number of perfumed plants and flowers around items of sculpture from the museum's collections.

Arbois

The Pasteur Family Home

Musée de la Maison Paternelle de Pasteur, 83 rue de Courcelles, F-39600 Arbois, Jura
☎ *84 66 11 72*
Easter–Nov, Wed–Sat, Mon 10–12, 2–6; Sun 10–12, 2–5. During Apr, May & June, closed 2nd Sun in month. Guided tours only, every 30 min.
C

The father of the scientist Louis Pasteur (1822– 95) came to live at 83 rue de Courcelles in 1827, and operated his tanning business from here. Louis Pasteur himself lived and worked in the house every summer throughout his life and extended it in order to make it more suitable for his researches. Close by is the vineyard where he carried out experiments. The premises have been left as they were at the time of his death, with his bedroom, laboratory and equipment, study and library.

Arcachon

Arcachon Museum and Aquarium

Musée-Aquarium, 2 rue du Professeur-Jolyet, F-33120 Arcachon, Gironde ☎ *56 90 91 60*
Mon–Fri 2–6. Closed public holidays.
C

The institution was established in 1863 by the Arcachon Scientific Society as a marine biological society. Since then it has developed in two directions. The museum has collections of local geology, archaeology, palaeontology, zoology, rocks, marine fauna, shells and oysters, as well as maps. The aquarium has the invertebrates and fish to be found in the Arcachon basin and the adjoining ocean, including some very large specimens, presented in a modern and lively way.

Kitchen interior. Alice Taverne Museum, Ambierle.

Archigny

Acadian Farm Museum

Ferme Musée Acadienne, Les Huit Maisons,
  Archigny, F-86210 Bonneuil-Matours,
  Vienne ☎ 49 85 31 26
Thurs, Sat, Sun 3–7. Other times by appt.
F ▯ 🚗

The museum building is one of the 54 farmhouses constructed in 1773 to accommodate the
French settlers who had been driven out of
Canada ten years earlier. It contains
contemporary furniture together with
agricultural tools and implements. There is also
an exhibition telling the story of the Acadians.

Arles

Museum of Arles

Muséon Arlaten, 42 rue de la République, F-13200
  Arles, Bouches-du-Rhône ☎ 90 97 10 82
Apr–May, Tues–Sun 9–12, 2–6. June–Aug,
  Tues–Sun 10–12, 2–7. Sept–Oct, Tues–Sun
  9–12, 2–5. Nov–Mar, Tues–Sun 10–12, 2–5.
  July–Sept, also open Mon. Closed May 1,
  Dec 25.
C ▯

The museum was founded in 1896 by the
Provençal poet, Frédéric Mistral (1820–1914).
In 1906 it was installed in an early-16th-century
town mansion, with its collection devoted to
the popular arts and traditions of Provence. In
Mistral's time, the exhibits were arranged in
three sections: costumes, furniture and domestic
equipment. Since then, new themes have been
introduced – the history of Arles, Provençal
paintings, Rhône navigation, the rural activities
of the Crau and the Camargue, popular
Provençal festivals, and amulets and talismans.

**Sculpture exhibit from the Museum of Art,
Arras.**

Museum of the Camargue

Musée Camarguais, Mas du Pont de Rousty, route
  des Saintes Maries de la Mer, F-13200 Arles,
  Bouches-du-Rhône ☎ 90 97 10 82
Apr–June & Sept, daily 9–6. July–Aug, daily 9–7.
  Oct–Mar, Wed–Mon 10–5. Closed Jan 1,
  May 1, Dec 25.
C ▯ 🖼 🚗

The museum, winner of the European Museum
of the Year Award in 1979, is in the Camargue
Regional Natural Park. Situated in the disused
buildings of a former sheep farm, it shows how
the area has developed since the earliest times
and interprets the natural history and
agriculture of the region. Its collections include
many objects contributed by old people locally.

Arras

Museum of Art

Musée des Beaux-Arts d'Arras, 22 rue Paul
  Doumer, F-62000 Arras, Pas-de-Calais
  ☎ 21 71 26 43
Mon, Wed–Sat 10–12, 2–5; Sun 10–12, 3–5.
  Closed public holidays.
C ▯ 🚗

The museum is in the former Benedictine
Abbey of Saint Vaast. The collections cover a
wide range – 12th–15th-century religious
sculptures, Arras tapestries, archaeological
material from local sites, 15th-century Arras
pewter, and gold- and silversmith's work. There
are notable displays of Tournai and Arras
porcelain and of 17th–19th-century French
paintings. The 19th-century works are centred
round the pre-Impressionists and the Arras
School, especially Corot. The official art of the
same period, often of great size, is also
exhibited. Flemish and Dutch paintings occupy
a large gallery on the first floor.

Arromanches

Museum of the Normandy Landings

Musée du Débarquement, F-14117 Arromanches,
  Calvados ☎ 31 22 34 21
Easter, daily 9–6.30. Mid Apr–mid May & Sept
  3–16, daily 9–11.30, 2–6.30. Mid-May–
  Sept 2, daily 9–6.30. Sept 17–Easter, daily
  9–11.30, 2–5.30. Mon mornings open at 10,
  except June–Aug, when open at 9.
C ▯ 🚗

On 6 June 1944, the Allied landings along the
Normandy beaches began the liberation of
France and then the rest of Europe from the
German occupation. The events are
commemorated in a network of 15 museums and
exhibitions throughout the area, of which those
at Caen and Arromanches are the most
important. The museum at Arromanches faces
the remains of the Mulberry Harbour, the
artificial port which was towed across the
Channel from England in sections. Visitors can
see photographs, film, documents and dioramas
illustrating the landings, and battle relics.

Aubagne

The Foreign Legion Museum

Musée de la Légion Etrangère, Quartier Viénot,
   F-13400 Aubagne, Bouches-du-Rhône
   ☎ 42 03 03 20
May–Sept, Tues–Sun 10–12, 3–7. Oct–Apr,
   Wed, Sat, Sun 10–12, 2–6.
F ⓘ ♨

Between 1892 and 1962, the French Foreign
Legion developed its Hall of Honour at Sidi-bel-
Abbès, in Algeria. In 1964 a new Hall of
Honour and Museum were established at
Aubagne. Its exhibits illustrate the history and
campaigns of the Legion since its establishment
in the early 19th century. There are collections
of uniforms, weapons, flags, decorations,
trophies, paintings, engravings and documents.

Foreign Legion Museum, Aubagne.

Aubusson

Museum of Tapestry

Musée Départemental de la Tapisserie, Centre
   Culturel et Artistique Jean-Lurçat, avenue des
   Lissiers, F-23200 Aubusson, Creuse
   ☎ 55 66 33 06
June–Sept, Mon 2–7; Tues–Sun 9–12, 2–7. Oct–
   May, Wed–Mon 9.30–12, 2–6.
C

The painter and designer, Jean Lurçat (1892–
1966) is chiefly known for his achievements in
reviving and popularising the art of tapestry,
especially at Aubusson. The museum was
established in 1981 and consists of works by
Lurçat and other designers who have worked at
Aubusson. The tapestries by Lurçat which are
on display include two designed by him for the
transatlantic liner, *France*. Associated with the
museum is a large library and documentation
centre relating to tapestry. Regular
demonstrations of tapestry weaving take place
during the summer months.

Auch

Jacobin Museum

Musée des Jacobins, 4 place Louis Blanc, F-32000
   Auch, Gers   ☎ 62 05 74 79
May 2–Oct, Tues–Sun 10–12, 2–6. Nov 2–Apr,
   Tues–Sat 10–12, 2–4. Closed Jan 1, May 1,
   Nov 1, Dec 25.
C ⓘ

What are now the museum buildings were
formerly a Dominican or Jacobin monastery.
Founded in 1409, it was closed during the
Revolution. A museum was installed in 1793 in
what has been the town's Jesuit College and,
after a number of moves during the 19th century
and greatly enriched, it eventually found a
permanent home in the Jacobin Museum in
1979.

   It has collections of Gallo-Roman
archaeology, medieval sculpture and paintings,
18th-century Auch faïence and 18th-century

French paintings and decorative arts. There are
also exhibits of the popular art and ethnography
of Gascony, including domestic equipment,
popular religious art, regional costumes and
headdresses, and agricultural tools.

   In 1911 Guillaume Pujos (1852–1921) left his
remarkable collection of Latin American art to
the museum. A native of Auch, Pujos had
emigrated to Chile, where he worked as a tailor.
After the earthquake in Santiago in 1906, he
returned to Auch, where he became Spanish
Vice-Consul and afterwards, in 1911, curator of
the museum.

Aumont

Henri Barbusse Museum

Musée Henri-Barbusse, Villa Sylvie, Aumont,
   F-60300 Senlis, Oise   ☎ 44 53 21 41
Wed–Mon 2–6
F

The writer and pacifist, Henri Barbusse (1873–
1935), became famous as a result of his anti-war
novel, *Le Feu* (1916). He died in 1935 while
visiting the USSR. The house which he
occupied from 1910 until 1935 has been
restored. It contains his furniture, red flags
presented to him by branches of ex-servicemen's
associations, personal possessions, photographs,
manuscripts and copies of his books, documents
relating to his life and career and items of
correspondence with his friends, including
Edmond Rostand, Maxim Gorki and Lenin.

Auray

Breton Costume Gallery

La Galerie du Costume Breton, Basilique Sainte-
   Anne d'Auray, F-56400 Auray, Bretagne
   ☎ 97 57 68 80
May–Sept, daily 10–12, 2–6
C ⓘ

The museum is in the Basilica of Sainte-Anne
d'Auray, built in 1865–72. It has notable
collections of traditional Breton costumes, both
for women and for men, together with exhibits
of headdresses.

Avignon

Théodore Aubanel Museum

Musée Théodore Aubanel, 7 place Saint Pierre,
F-84057 Avignon, Vaucluse
☎ *90 82 46 26*
Jan–July & Sept–Dec, Mon–Fri 9–12. Closed
public holidays and Dec 25–Jan 1. Groups by
appt.
Ⓕ 🛉

In 1744 Antoine Aubanel founded what was to
become one of Europe's great printing houses.
His *Courrier d'Avignon*, with correspondents at
all the European courts, was one of the most
important 18th-century newspapers. For some
time before and after the Revolution he was
'only printer to the Pope', a title which became
hereditary. Ownership of the firm has continued
from father to son without interruption down to
the present day.

One of Antoine Aubanel's sons, the
Provençal poet Théodore Aubanel (1829–86),
was one of the founders of the Félibrige, the
society formed to preserve the Provençal
language. He was in correspondence with most
of the great literary figures of his time. The
museum dedicated to him is in the 14th-century
house which once belonged to Cardinal de
Praeneste. The printing house and the family
residence were transferred there in 1865, when
the original centre of the business in the Rue
Saint-Marc was demolished to make way for a
new road. The house in the Place Saint Pierre is
still occupied by the family.

The museum is in two sections. The first is
concerned with the life and work of Théodore
Aubanel, and contains his correspondence,
manuscripts and published works. The second
illustrates the history of printing and publishing
in Avignon and displays books, portraits,
Provençal furniture and old printing machinery
and equipment, with a reconstruction of a
19th-century printing shop.

Portrait of the Provençal poet, Théodore
Aubanel. Aubanel Museum, Avignon.

Avignonet-Laurigais

Pierre Paul de Riquet Centre

Centre Pierre-Paul-de-Riquet, Port-Laurigais,
Avignonet-Laurigais, F-31290 Villefranche-de-
Laurigais, Haute-Garonne ☎ *61 27 14 61*
May–Sept, daily 9–8. Oct–Apr, daily 9–6.30.
Ⓒ ⚓

France was a pioneer in the construction of
canals. The Briare Canal, connecting the Loire
with the Seine, and the Burgundy Canal were
both completed in the first half of the 17th
century, but the great achievement of that
century was the Canal du Midi, joining the
Atlantic to the Mediterranean, by way of the
Garonne. Designed by Pierre Paul de Riquet
(1604–80), it is 290 km long and took 15 years
to build. It begins at Toulouse and ends near
Agde, at the Etang de Thau. It crosses the Col
de Naraize by means of 65 locks and a tunnel.
The museum illustrates the history and the
character of the Briare Canal and
commemorates the life of its creator.

Avranches

Avranches Museum

Musée d'Avranches, Palais Episcopal, place Jean de
Saint-Avit, F-50300 Avranches, Manche
☎ *33 58 25 15*
Mar–Nov, Mon, Wed–Sun 9.30–12, 2–6
Ⓒ 🛉 ⚓

The museum is in the former Bishop's Palace
where, according to tradition, St Michael
appeared to St Hubert. During the French
Revolution, the building served as a prison.
Now, as a museum, it contains exhibits
illustrating the traditions of Lower Normandy.
It has collections of costumes, objects in
everyday use, and handicrafts, with
reconstructions of craftsmen's workshops, relics
of St Thomas à Becket, and Anglo-Saxon and
other manuscripts from the Abbey of Mont St
Michel. There are also collections of paintings
and sculpture by Normandy artists.

Treasury of Saint Gervais

Trésor de Saint-Gervais, place Saint-Gervais,
F-50300 Avranches, Manche
☎ *33 58 25 15*
June–Sept, Mon, Wed–Sat 10–12.30, 1.30–6;
Sun 1.30–6
Ⓒ 🛉 ⚓

The Basilica of Avranches is reputed to have
been visited by Charlemagne. Its treasury
displays 14th–15th-century reliquaries,
including one containing the head of St Aubert,
church plate and religious ornaments from the
Abbey of Mont St Michel, and medieval
sculptures and church furnishings.

Baccarat

Museum of Crystal

Musée du Cristal, Compagnie des Cristalleries de Baccarat, F-54120 Baccarat, Meurthe-et-Moselle ☎ 83 75 10 01
Easter weekend, May 1, Ascension, Whit weekend 2–6. Apr & Oct 1–15, Sun 2–6.
May 1–June 15, Sat, Sun 2–6. June 16–July 15, daily 2–6.30. July 16–Sept 15, Mon, Wed–Sat 10–12, 2–6.30; Tues, Sun 2–6.30. Sept 16–30, daily 2–6. Closed October 15–Easter.
C 🏛 🚗

The famous Sainte Anne glassworks was established in the early 19th century. The museum is in the 18th-century home of its founder. It contains exhibits illustrating the techniques used in the manufacture of crystal, and collections of plain, cut and engraved crystal made at Baccarat from 1816 to the present day. These items include table services made specially for sovereigns and heads of state all over the world.

Bagnères-de-Bigorre

Bigorre Museum

Musée Bigorre, rue du Hount-Blanque, F-65200 Bagnères-de-Bigorre, Hautes-Pyrénées ☎ 62 95 01 62
Mon, Wed–Sat 10–1, 3–7
C

Opened in 1983, the museum occupies the former town mill. It contains two private collections of material illustrating the traditional life of the Campan valley, including furniture, costumes and the workshops of a clogmaker, sandal-maker, slater, woollen weaver and linen weaver. There is also equipment used in the agricultural and dairying industries and the reconstruction of a Bigorre kitchen.

Balleroy

Balloon Museum

Musée de Ballons, Château de Balleroy, F-14490 Balleroy, Calvados ☎ 31 21 60 61
Thurs–Tues 9–12, 2–6
C 🏛 🚗

The balloon is very much a child of France, pioneered by the Montgolfier brothers, Joseph (1740–1810) and Etienne (1745–99). It is therefore appropriate that the only museum wholly devoted to balloons should be in France, in the stables of the early-17th-century Château de Balleroy.

Its collections illustrate the history of balloons and ballooning from the 18th century to the present day, with collections showing the use of balloons for scientific, military and sporting purposes.

Barbizon

Museum of the Barbizon School

Musée Municipal de l'Ecole de Barbizon, 55 Grande Rue, F-77630 Barbizon, Seine-et-Marne ☎ 60 66 22 38
Apr–Sept, Wed–Mon and public holidays 10–12.30, 2–6. Oct–Mar, Wed–Mon and public holidays 10–12.30, 2–5.
C 🏛

The Barbizon School was influential in French landscape painting between 1825 and 1875. In 1975 a museum dedicated to the artists concerned was set up in the house and studio of one of the School's principal representatives, Théodore Rousseau (1812–67), who settled at Barbizon in 1844. The museum tells the story of Barbizon and its artists and illustrates their aims, their life and their work.

Barenton

Apple and Pear Museum

Maison de la Pomme et de la Poire, La Logerais, Château Briquebec, F-50720 Barenton, Manche ☎ 33 59 56 22
June 15–Sept 30, daily 10.30–12.30, 2.30–7. March 29–June 14, Sat, Sun, public holidays 10.30–12.30, 2.30–7. Rest of year, groups by appt.
C 🚗

The area around Barenton is celebrated for its cider and perry orchards. In 1979 a complex of buildings on the estate of the Château Briquebec was acquired by the regional natural park of Normandy-Maine and converted into an outdoor and indoor museum explaining the traditional and modern methods of cider and perry production and of orchard cultivation. There are also displays illustrating the economic basis of the industry.

Tall-stemmed glasses made in 1896 for Tsar Nicholas II. Museum of Crystal, Baccarat.

Barr

Marco's Folly

Musée de la Folie Marco, 30 rue Dr Sultzer,
  F-67140 Barr, Bas-Rhin   ☎ 88 08 94 72
July–Sept, Wed–Mon 10–12, 2–6. June & Oct,
  Sat, Sun 10–12, 2–6. Groups by appt
  throughout year.
Ⓒ

Louis Félix Marco was a barrister. In 1760–3 he
built himself a splendid mansion on the edge of
the town, which soon became known as Marco's
Folly. After his death, it passed through several
hands, eventually becoming the property of the
brothers, Henri and Gustave Schwartz, who
refurnished it and bequeathed it, together with
its contents, to the town. A museum since
1964, it contains a collection of 17th–19th-
century furniture from Alsace, together with
French, especially Strasbourg, faïence,
porcelain and pewter. There is also a section
devoted to the history and techniques of timber-
sledging.

Bayeux

The Bayeux Tapestry Museum

Musée de la Tapisserie de Bayeux, Centre
  Guillaume le Conquérant, rue de Nesmond,
  F-14400 Bayeux, Calvados   ☎ 31 92 05 48
Mar 16–May 15, Sept 17–Oct 15 daily 9–12.30,
  2–6.30. Easter weekend, May 1, 8, 16–
  Sept 16, daily 9–7. Oct 16–Mar 15, daily
  9.30–12.30, 2–6. Closed Jan 1, 2 (am),
  Dec 25, 26 (am).
Ⓒ ▮

The museum contains the embroidery which
was woven in England after the Battle of
Hastings (1066), on the order of Odo, Bishop of
Bayeux and half-brother of William the
Conqueror, to decorate the nave of his
cathedral. It depicts the principal events leading
up to the Norman conquest of England. There is
an interpretive exhibition, with displays,
models and films, which precedes the visit to the
tapestry itself.

Museum of the Battle of Normandy, 1944

Musée Mémorial de la Bataille de Normandie,
  boulevard Fabian Ware, F-14400 Bayeux,
  Calvados   ☎ 31 92 93 41
Mar 16–May, Sept–Oct 15, daily 9.30–12.30,
  2–6.30. June–Aug, daily 9–7.
  Oct 16–Mar 15, daily 10–12.30, 2–6.
Ⓒ ▮ 🖾 🖎 ㄥ 🖚

Between 6 June and 25 August 1944, two
million Allied soldiers landed on the beaches of
Normandy. They brought with them 500,000
vehicles and eight million tons of supplies. The
museum, opened in 1981, presents the story of
the battle and of its consequences for the
civilian population, illustrated by dioramas,
uniforms, military vehicles and equipment,
models, films and photographs.

Bayonne

Bonnat Museum

Musée Bonnat, 5 rue Jacques-Laffitte, F-64100
  Bayonne, Pyrénées-Atlantiques
  ☎ 59 59 08 52
June 11–Sept 10, Wed–Mon 10–12, 4–6 (until 10
  Fri). Sept 11–June 10, Mon, Wed, Thurs
  1–7; Fri 4–10; Sat, Sun 10–12, 3–7. Closed
  public holidays.
Ⓒ ▮

Léon Bonnat (1833–1922) was a prolific and
renowned painter of portraits, especially of the
official variety. He was also a great and eclectic
collector, and left all his 400 paintings, 2,000
drawings and a quantity of sculpture to his
native town. A new building to contain them
was completed in 1923. The exhibits range from
Greek and Roman sculpture and Phoenician
glass to Dutch and Spanish paintings. A special
section of the museum is devoted to paintings by
Bonnat himself.

**A small section of the celebrated work of
embroidery known as the Bayeux Tapestry;
11th-century, coloured wool on linen, *c.* 50
centimetres by 68 metres. The Bayeux
Tapestry Museum, Bayeux.**

The Basque Country Museum

*Musée Basque et de la Tradition Bayonnaise, 1 rue
Marengo, F-64100 Bayonne, Pyrénées-
Atlantiques* ☎ 59 59 08 98
Enquire locally for opening times
C

The museum's collections range over the whole
of Basque culture. The displays illustrate
handicrafts, popular beliefs and superstitions,
dancing, costumes, music and literature. There
are models of Basque homesteads, period rooms
and reconstructions of craftsmen's workshops.
Special sections are devoted to pelota and to the
memorabilia of Basque writers.

Beaugency

Museum of the Orléans Region

*Musée de l'Orléanais, Château Dunois, 2 place
Dunois, F-45190 Beaugency, Loiret*
☎ 38 44 55 23
*Apr–Sept, Wed–Mon 10–12, 2–6.30. Oct–Mar,
Wed–Mon 10–12, 2–5.*
C 🏛 🎨

Jean Dunois (1403–68), 'Le bâtard d'Orléans',
was the natural son of Louis I, Duke of Orléans.
He was created Count of Dunois in 1439 and
built the present castle on the site of an earlier
one, of which some parts still remain. By his
marriage to Marie d'Harcourt, he had acquired
the Lordship of Beaugency. The castle remained
in his family until 1789, when it was confiscated
and sold by the Revolutionary government. For
most of the 19th century, it served as a
workhouse for beggars (Dépôt de Mendicité).
   A museum since 1928, it has collections
illustrating the history of the Orléans region
and the Loire. There is prehistoric and Gallo-
Roman material from local excavations,
costumes, furniture and domestic equipment,
together with medieval and Renaissance
sculpture and special sections relating to
vineyard cultivation and wine production and
to local personalities, including the novelist,
Eugène Sue (1804–57).

Beaune

Museum of the Wines of Burgundy

*Musée du Vin, Hôtel des Ducs de Bourgogne,
F-21200 Beaune, Côte-d'Or*
☎ 80 22 08 19
*Apr–Nov 20, daily 9–12.30, 1.30–6.
Nov 21–Mar, daily 10–12, 2–5.30. Closed
Tues Dec–Feb, also Jan 1, Dec 25. Guided
tours.*
C 🏛 🖼 🎨

The museum tells the story of vineyards and
wine production in Burgundy since Gallo-
Roman times. There are collections of wine-
presses and of pottery and figurines relating to
wine. Other exhibits are concerned with
coopering, with traditions connected with wine,
with wine-tasting and with the history and

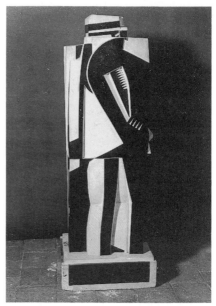

Le gendarme, 1919, by John Storrs. Museum
of the Orléans Region, Beaugency.

organisation of the wine trade. Visitors can see
the reconstruction of a vineyard proprietor's
house in Savigny as it was c.1870. Tapestries by
Michel Dufour, Jean Lurçat and Michel
Tourlière, one of Lurçat's pupils, have wine and
the vine as a theme. The large work by Lurçat
was created specially for the room in which it is
shown.

Beauvais

Cathedral Treasury

*Trésor de la Cathédrale, Cathédrale Saint-Pierre,
F-60000 Beauvais, Oise* ☎ 44 45 06 46
Daily, guided tours at 12, 2, 3, 4, 5
C

The ancient treasury of the cathedral was
reorganised in the 1920s and opened in 1929. It
was enlarged and rearranged in 1933 and again
in 1950. It contains an important collection of
15th–18th-century goldsmiths' and silversmiths'
work, monstrances and reliquaries, 17th–18th-
century liturgical ornaments, 15th–17th-
century Limoges enamels, 17th-century
tapestries and 18th-century furniture.

Museum of the Oise Region

*Musée Départemental de l'Oise, Ancien Palais
Episcopal, F-60000 Beauvais, Oise*
☎ 44 84 37 37
Wed–Mon 10–12, 2–6. Closed public holidays.
C 🏛

The museum was established in 1841 and since
1908 had been housed in a building adjoining
the cathedral, which was totally destroyed in an
air-raid in 1940. Such of the collections as could
be saved were stored in rooms of the former

Palace of the Bishops and Counts of Beauvais. Later, the museum acquired the whole of this 14th–16th-century building, which has been carefully restored, and the new museum opened in 1981.

Its collections are wide-ranging, consisting of prehistoric, Gallo-Roman and Merovingian archaeology, stone and wooden sculptures from the churches of Beauvais, 16th–20th-century Beauvais ceramics, 16th–20th-century French paintings, including the immense and celebrated *Enrolment of the Volunteers, 1792*, painted in 1848–51 by Thomas Couture, surrounded by studies for the work. There is also a natural history collection.

The National Tapestry Gallery

Galerie Nationale de la Tapisserie, rue Saint-Pierre, F-60000 Beauvais, Oise   ☎ 44 48 24 53
Wed–Mon 10–12, 2–6
ⓒ

The famous Tapestry Manufactory at Beauvais was established by Colbert in 1664. On the outbreak of war in September 1939 it was evacuated to Aubusson and transferred finally to the Gobelins precinct of Paris in October 1940, after the bombing of Beauvais. In 1964 it was decided by André Malraux to create a new Tapestry Gallery at Beauvais in order to allow the town to rebuild its links with the past and the new building, adjoining the Cathedral, was opened in 1976. Exhibitions of both historic and contemporary tapestries are held here and weavers come from the Beauvais workshops in Paris to demonstrate their craft.

Display of memorabilia at the Museum of the Resistance, Besançon.

Bellignies

Marble Museum

Musée du Marbre, Bellignies, F-59570 Bavay, Nord   ☎ 27 63 16 01
Daily 2–6 or by appt.
ⓒ 🚗

The museum is in a former marble works, established in 1830. It contains a collection of historic tools and equipment used locally in the industry, together with exhibits showing the working and living conditions of the workers and their families. There are also examples of objects made of marble, including chimney-pieces from the Renaissance to the present day.

Bergerac

Tobacco Museum

Musée du Tabac, Maison Peyrarède, place du Feu, F-24100 Bergerac, Dordogne
☎ 53 57 60 22
Tues–Fri 10–12, 2–6; Sat 10–12, 2–5; Sun 2.30–6.30. Closed public holidays.
ⓒ

The museum, opened in 1983, presents the history of growing, manufacturing and using tobacco. There are collections of carved and decorated tobacco pipes, some with representations of Napoleon, Louis XVIII and other famous people, of smoking accessories and of the trade marks and labels of 17th–18th-century brands of tobacco. Other sections are devoted to smoking in art and literature, with examples from the works of, among others, Cézanne, Daumier, Corneille, Molière, Baudelaire, Rimbaud and Rostand, and two 1951 Aubusson tapestries, *The Cigarette* and *The Pipe*.

Besançon

Museum of the Resistance

*Musée de la Résistance et de la Déportation, La
    Citadelle, F-25000 Besançon, Doubs*
☎ *81 83 37 14*
*Apr–Sept, Mon, Wed–Sun 9.15–6.15. Oct–Mar,
    Mon, Wed–Sun 9.45–4.45. Closed Jan 1,
    Dec 25.*

The museum illustrates the rise of the Nazi
régime and its eventual defeat, together with
the German occupation of France and the
organisation and activities of the Resistance
movement.

There is a collection of drawings, paintings
and sculptures made in the prison camps to
which French people were deported.

Museum of Time

*Musée de Temps, Palais Granvelle, 96 Grande
    Rue, F-25000 Besançon, Doubs*
☎ *81 81 45 14*
*Wed–Mon 9.30–12, 2–6. Closed Jan 1, May 1,
    Nov 1, Dec 25. Free entry Wed, Sun.*

The Palais Granvelle, a fine 16th-century
mansion, has recently been completely restored,
in order to accommodate a major new museum,
produced by merging the collections of the
Museum of History and the Museum of Clocks
and Watches, which used to form part of the
Museum of Fine Art.

The title, Museum of Time, consequently has
a double meaning. It is both the museum of the
passage of time and the museum of devices by
which time has been measured. The devices
include 17th–19th-century clocks and watches,
of which the collection of 17th-century watches
in particular is very fine. The historical section
presents Besançon as the capital of Franche-
Comté. Special exhibits relate to Victor Hugo,
to the 19th-century sociologists of Franche-
Comté, especially Proudhon, Fourier and
Considérant, and to local inventors, notably
Chardonnet, the discoverer of a process for
making artificial silk.

Biarritz

Museum of the Sea

*Musée de la Mer, Centre d'Etudes et de Recherches
    Scientifiques, Plateau de l'Atalaye, F-64202
    Biarritz, Pyrénées-Atlantiques*
☎ *59 24 02 59*
*Jan–June & Sept–Dec, daily 9–12, 2–6. July–Aug,
    daily 9–7.*

The museum, opened in 1936, and in a building
typical of the period, forms part of a Research
and Study Centre. Its aim is to show visitors the
ocean in all its forms, the sea-bed, the role of
the sea in the formation of continents, the
plants and living creatures which inhabit it, and

Museum of the Sea, Biarritz.

its coasts. The large aquarium, with its 40 tanks,
is devoted to the fauna of the Gulf of Gascony.
There is also a sea-water pool, with seals, and an
aviary containing about 300 species of birds
found locally.

The museum galleries contain exhibits
relating to local palaeontology and geology and
to the fishing industry. A viewing platform
provides an opportunity to put the ocean in its
local land context, from the beginnings of the
Pyrenees at Cap Saint Martin to the flat
landscape of the Landes.

Biot

Fernand Léger Museum

*Musée National Fernand Léger, chemin du Val-de-
    Pome, F-06410 Biot, Alpes-Maritimes*
☎ *93 33 42 14*
Jan–Oct, Dec, Thurs, Sat, Sun 2.30–6

Léger (1881–1955) was a Norman and disliked
the South of France. Even so, his widow built a
splendid museum dedicated to him on a site at
Biot which he had bought a few months before
his death. The architecture is conditioned by
two immense works by him, a huge mosaic, 500
square metres in all, which covers the façade,
and which was originally intended for the
Olympic Stadium at Hanover, and the stained
glass window, of a similar size, which adorns the
entrance hall.

The museum, opened in 1960, contains 360
of Léger's works, illustrating the development of
his work from 1904 until his death and
including drawings, gouaches, paintings,
ceramics and tapestries.

Blaye

Museum of the Blaye Region

*Musée d'Art et d'Histoire du Pays Blayais, Société
    des Amis du Vieux Blaye, Pavillon de la Place,
    Citadelle de Blaye, F-33390 Blaye, Gironde*
☎ *57 42 13 70*
Apr–Oct, daily 2.30–7

The Duchess of Berry, captive at the Blaye Citadel. Museum of the Blaye Region.

The rocky promontory on which the Citadel of Blaye stands has been fortified since Roman times. The present citadel was built between 1685 and 1689 by the great military engineer, Field-Marshal Vauban. With its streets, public squares and gardens, the citadel is a small town, covering 22 hectares. Although designed to withstand a siege, its principal use, in fact, has been to house political prisoners and prisoners of war.

In the Pavillon de la Place, the Duchess of Berry, daughter-in-law of Charles X, was imprisoned in 1832–3, after attempting to put her son, the Duke of Bordeaux, on the throne. The Pavillon now houses a museum, with collections of prehistoric archaeology and 18th–20th-century paintings by local artists. There are displays showing the history of the citadel and the life of the Duchess of Berry during her captivity. The museum also has memorabilia of the Blaye writers, André Lamandé and André Lafon, and of the Montmartre chansonnier, Roger Toziny.

Blois

Château de Blois

Château de Blois, F-41000 Blois, Indre-et-Loire
☎ *54 74 16 06*
Mar 15–31 & Sept, daily 9–12, 2–6.30. Apr–Aug, daily 9–6.30. Oct 1–Mar 14, daily 9–12, 2–5.
C 🛈 💺

The Château de Blois was constructed at different periods between the 13th and 17th centuries. Both the exterior and the interior of the buildings were restored in 1845–69. The château contains three separate museums, the Royal apartments, the Museum of Fine Art, and the Archaeological Museum.

The former Royal apartments contain 16th–17th-century furniture, tapestries and portraits and 19th-century paintings. The Museum of Fine Art has 16th–19th-century French, Flemish and Dutch paintings and portraits, including works by Boucher, David and Ingres, together with French faïence. The Archaeological Museum, opened in 1980, displays prehistoric, Gallo-Roman and medieval material, mostly from excavations in the region.

Bois d'Amont

Museum of Wooden Objects

Musée de la Boissellerie, Mairie, Bois d'Amont,
F-39220 Les Rousses, Jura ☎ *84 60 30 51*
Sat, Sun 3–6; Wed 2–6 during school holidays.
Groups at any time by appt.
F

This small but interesting and significant museum illustrates the history since the 18th century of the use of wood as the material for a range of products, especially combs and small boxes, and including cheese boxes, postboxes and clock cases. The displays show tools and simple machines and explain the techniques and processes involved.

Bordeaux

Jean Moulin Centre

Centre National Jean Moulin, place Jean Moulin,
F-33000 Bordeaux, Gironde
☎ *56 90 91 60*
Mon–Fri 2–6. Closed public holidays.
F

The centre has large collections of material relating to the Resistance, the deportation and the Free French Forces during the Second World War. They include documents, posters, pamphlets, correspondence, weapons, photographs and equipment. There is also a reconstruction of the important secret office and communications centre run by Jean Moulin and a number of contemporary paintings and drawings relevant to the theme of the centre.

Museum of Aquitaine

Musée d'Aquitaine, 20 cours Pasteur, F-33000
Bordeaux, Gironde ☎ *56 90 91 60*
Wed–Mon 10–6. Closed May 1.
C 🛈 💺 ♿ ☕

In 1880–5 the city of Bordeaux pulled down the remains of an old convent in order to construct a new and grand University Faculty building on the site. The university moved in the late 1950s and, after considerable work on the interior, the Museum of Aquitaine moved in. The museum had its origins in the Lapidary Museum, established in 1784 to accommodate a collection of Gallo-Roman remains which had resulted from excavations in the area. After the Second World War, the collections were considerably enlarged and diversified. The museum is now able to show, over a wide field, how the region has developed.

The prehistoric collections now have an international reputation and a systematic collecting policy has made it possible to present the history of the rural, maritime and urban activities of the region in attractive detail. There are exhibits of 15th–16th-century Bordeaux statues, 16th–18th-century sculpture and 17th–18th-century furniture, and of domestic equipment and craftsmen's tools. Special displays are devoted to wine production and to the wine trade, to oyster cultivation and to fishing. The important part played by Bordeaux in the former French colonial empire is illustrated by a splendid collection of ship models and by a collection of exotic objects brought back by Bordeaux sailors and travellers.

Museum of Decorative Arts

*Musée des Arts décoratifs de la Ville de Bordeaux,
    39 rue Bouffard, F-33000 Bordeaux, Gironde*
☎ 56 90 91 60
Mon, Wed–Sun 2–6
C ⓲ 🖳

The museum is in a fine 18th-century mansion. Its collections help to give an impression of elegant life in Bordeaux in the 18th and 19th centuries. They include 17th–18th-century European ceramics, 16th–18th-century French glass, 18th–19th-century French furniture and faïence, goldsmiths' work and 18th-century locks made in Bordeaux. There is also a 19th-century royalist collection, centred on the last kings of France.

Museum of Fine Art

*Musée des Beaux-Arts, 20 cours d'Albret,
    F-33000 Bordeaux, Gironde*
☎ 56 90 91 60
Wed–Sun 10–12, 2–6. Free admission Wed, Sun.
C ⓲

The museum was created by a Consular Decree of the 14 Fructidor of the year IX in the Revolutionary Calendar (1 September 1801), which founded 15 departmental museums. After several changes of premises, it was finally established in 1875–81 in a specially built wing of the town hall and has since taken over the parallel wing vacated by the Museum of Aquitaine.

It has important collections of 15th–20th-century European and French paintings and sculpture, including works by Titian, Murillo, Brueghel, Rubens, Delacroix, Boudin, Reynolds and Rodin. There is a growing section of works by 19th- and 20th-century artists, among them Matisse, Lhoty, Dufy and Zadkine.

Boulogne-Billancourt

Boulogne Museum

*Musée Municipal, Hôtel de Ville, 26 avenue
    André-Mouzel, F-92100 Boulogne-
    Billancourt, Hauts-de-Seine* ☎ 46 84 77 39
Mon–Fri 9–12, 2–5; Sat 9–12. Closed public
    holidays.
F

The museum, on the fourth floor of the town's imposing modern town hall, was opened in 1958. Its collections illustrate old Boulogne and its transformation into an urban community, the history of the Seine islands, and of the pre-industrial and industrial enterprises of the area. Prominent among the first are its laundry undertakings, and among the second its aeronautical concerns (Blériot, Voisin, Farman), its automobile factories (Renault) and its film studios.

There is a photographic exhibition of buildings by distinguished artists in Boulogne-Billancourt and documents and paintings relating to artists, including Juan Gris and Paul Landowski, who have lived in the area.

Bourcefranc-le-Chapus

Oyster Museum

*Musée de l'Huître, Fort-Louvois, Bourcefranc-le-
    Chapus, Charente-Maritime*
☎ 46 85 07 59
May 15–June 30 & Sept 1–15, when high tide is
    between 9 and 6. July–Aug, daily 10–6. Boat
    service whenever the tide covers the causeway.
C

Fort Louvois was built in the reign of Louis XIV. In the first room of the keep is a large animated model, with a commentary, representing the whole oyster-bearing region of Marennis-Oléron. The second room has displays illustrating the cultivation of oysters and the different stages in their development.

**Bust of the goddess Diana. Museum of
Decorative Arts, Bordeaux.**

Bourges

Hotel Lallemand

*Musée de l'Hôtel Lallemand, 6 rue Bourbonnoux,
F-18000 Bourges, Cher*   ☎ 48 70 19 32
*Tues–Sun 10–12, 2–6. Closed Jan 1, May 1,
Nov 1, Dec 25. No charge Wed.*
© C

The Hôtel Lallemand was built c. 1487 for Jean
Lallemand, a wealthy merchant and Receiver-
General of Taxes for Normandy. It was
improved and embellished by his son in the
early 16th century and remodelled in the 17th,
when changes were made to the roof. The
recent restoration of the interior has allowed the
museum collections to be reorganised. The
exhibits are now presented in room settings,
showing furniture, paintings, ceramics, enamels
and clocks from the Renaissance to the 19th
century. Among the outstanding items are a
carved marquetry ebony cabinet c. 1650 and the
very large Flanders tapestry depicting
'Maximilian Hunting'.

The museum also has an important collection
of dolls and toys from the period 1830–1914.
They include miniature furniture, games and
optical toys.

Museum of Berry

*Musée du Berry, 4–6 rue des Arènes, F-18000
Bourges, Cher*   ☎ 48 70 41 92
*Mon, Wed–Sun 10–12, 2–6; Tues 2–6. Closed
public holidays. No charge Wed.*
© C

The Hôtel Cujas, which contains the museum,
dates from 1515. The collections cover the
history, art and popular traditions of Berry,
including the Iron Age and Gallo-Roman
history of the region. Notable among the
sculptures are the figures of the prophets and the
mourners from the tomb of the Duke of Berry,
by Jean de Cambrai. There are also 16th–19th-
century French and European paintings,
drawings and prints and an important collection
of coins and medals. A section of the museum is
devoted to a remarkable series of popular
ceramics made in the 19th century by the
Talbot family and including jugs, writing-tables,
fountains and crosses for placing at crossroads.
The museum has large displays of costumes,
craftsmen's tools, domestic equipment,
agricultural implements and popular religious
objects.

Boussy-Saint-Antoine

Dunoyer de Segonzac Museum

*Musée Dunoyer de Segonzac, Mairie de Boussy-
Saint-Antoine, F-91800 Brunoy, Essonne*
☎ 69 60 81 59
*July–Aug, Tues–Sat 8.30–12, 3–6. Sept–June,
Tues–Sat 3–6.*
© C

**Detail of carving on a wedding wardrobe,
1820–30. Normandy Museum, Caen.**

The museum has been established in the
birthplace of the painter, designer and graphic
artist, André Dunoyer de Segonzac (1884–
1974). The collections, a large part of which
were bequeathed by the artist himself, illustrate
his life and career. They include documents
relating to him and to his family, engravings,
especially for the *Georgias*, posters, illustrated
books and engraved portraits.

Bussières

Museum of Weaving

*Musée du Tissage, rue Jacquard, Bussières,
F-42510 Balbigny, Loire*   ☎ 77 27 33 95
*Mar–Oct, 2nd Sun in month, 3–7. Open public
holidays. Groups by appt.*
© C

The history of the textile industry in and around
Bussières goes back at least 1,000 years. The
museum has an extensive collection of hand and
powered looms and of other 18th-, 19th- and
20th-century machinery and equipment
illustrating the development of textile
technology. The machines are in working
condition and are regularly demonstrated.

Caen

Battle of Normandy Memorial

*Monument à la Bataille de la Normandie, F-14000
Caen, Calvados*   ☎ 31 86 27 05
*May–Sept, daily 9–6 (Fri 9–8). Oct–Apr, Tues–
Sun 10–5.*
© C

Caen, which suffered severe damage during the
battles which followed the Normandy landings
in June 1944, has recently established what it
calls 'a museum dedicated to peace'. It puts the
events of 1944 into their historical context by
providing 'a journey through our century's
history, from 1918 to the present day'. A
research and documentation centre is included
in the museum's facilities.

Normandy Museum

*Musée de Normandie, Logis des Gouverneurs,
    Château, F-14000 Caen, Calvados*
    ☎ *31 86 06 24*
Wed–Mon 10–12, 2–6
Ⓒ 🛈 ♿

The museum, which presents the archaeology
and social history of Normandy, occupies the
former lodging of the governor of the castle.
Established in 1963, it was completely
rearranged in 1985–6 and is now based on three
principal themes – settlements, techniques and
religious beliefs. The three sections of the
museum are 'From Prehistory to 911' – 911 was
the year in which the Vikings first arrived in the
region – 'Man and the Soil' and 'Man and
Materials'.

There are collections of furniture, rural
pottery, costumes, domestic equipment,
craftsmen's tools and agricultural implements.
Models are used extensively in the exhibitions,
to show archaeological sites, landscapes and
rural houses.

**'Arnaga', the poet's former home, now the
Edmond Rostand Museum, Cambo-les-Bains.**

Cagnes-sur-Mer

Renoir Museum

*Musée Renoir, chemin des Collettes, F-06800
    Cagnes-sur-Mer, Alpes-Maritimes*
    ☎ *93 20 61 07*
*June–Nov 14, Wed–Mon 10–12, 2–6.
    Nov 16–May, Wed–Mon 2–5.*
Ⓒ 🛈 ♿

The Impressionist painter, Auguste Renoir
(1841–1919), lived in Cagnes from 1908 until
his death. His former home is now a museum.
Both the house and its furnishings have
remained as they were when the artist lived
there. Visitors can see Renoir's studio, and his
easel, armchair, brushes and frames, and the
small studio, facing north, east and west, which
could be shaded from the sun.

From the terrace of Madame Renoir's
bedroom, there is a magnificent view of the
Mediterranean, Cap d'Antibes, the old village
of Cagnes and the Renoir estate with its 140
ancient olive trees, among which visitors are
free to wander, sit or paint.

The museum contains works from Renoir's
Cagnes period and objects belonging to the
family are exhibited in the 9 rooms of the house
open to the public. A selection of works by his
painter and sculptor friends, including Bonnard,
Dufy and Maillol, is also on display.

Calais

Museum of Fine Art and Lace

*Musée des Beaux-Arts et de la Dentelle, 25 rue
    Richelieu, F-62100 Calais, Pas-de-Calais*
    ☎ *21 97 99 00*
Wed–Mon 10–12, 2–5.30. Closed public holidays.
Ⓒ ☎

The original museum, established in 1836, was
destroyed by wartime bombing in 1940. The
new museum was opened in 1965 in a modern
building. It has exhibits illustrating the history
of the town and port, with an emphasis on the
local industries. Calais has a long tradition of
lace-making and a complete section of the
museum is devoted to this, with examples of
both hand-made and machine-made lace. There
are collections of 19th-century French and
English watercolours, drawings and engravings,
and of European Old Master paintings,
especially by Dutch and Flemish artists. For
some years the museum has been building up an
international collection of contemporary art.

An interesting feature of the museum is its
series of 19th- and 20th-century French
sculptures, arranged around studies and models
of the celebrated monument by Auguste Rodin,
The Burghers of Calais (1884–6).

Cambo-les-Bains

Edmond Rostand Museum

*Musée Edmond Rostand, route de Bayonne,
    F-64250 Cambo-les-Bains, Pyrénées-
    Atlantiques*   ☎ *59 29 70 57*
*Easter–Apr & Oct, daily 2–5. May–Sept, daily
    10–5.*
Ⓒ 🛈 ♿

In 1900, the poet and dramatist, Edmond
Rostand (1868–1918), came to Cambo to
convalesce after an attack of pneumonia.
Enchanted by the area, he built a sumptuous
house, 'Arnaga', here in 1903–6. After his
death, it was sold and re-sold three times and
finally, in 1962, it was bought by the
municipality of Cambo and restored, together
with its extensive gardens, as a memorial to the
writer. It now contains many memorabilia of
Rostand, including decorations, paintings,
portraits and autograph letters and manuscripts.
A reconstruction of his drawing room gives an
impression of the style in which he lived.

Carbonne

Abbal Museum

Musée Abbal, rue du Sculpteur Abbal, Carbonne,
  Haute-Garonne   ☎ 61 87 96 50
Daily 9–12, 2–7. Workshop Sat, Sun.
ⓒ

The monumental sculptor, André Abbal, died
in 1953. On the site where he used to work, a
museum paying tribute to him has been
established. It contains studies for his *Centaur*,
Reaper and *Sculpture*, a low-relief of the façade of
the Chaillot Palace in Paris, the metopes of the
Theatre in Montauban, the models of the war
memorials in Toulouse and Moissac and a
number of busts, including one of President
Vincent Auriol.

Carnac

Museum of Prehistory

Musée de Préhistoire J. Miln-Z. Le Rouzic, 10
  place de la Chapelle, F-56340 Carnac,
  Morbihan   ☎ 97 52 22 04
Jan–May & Oct–Dec, Wed–Mon 10–12, 2–5.
  June & Sept, Wed–Mon 10–12, 2–6. July–
  Aug, daily 10–12, 2–6.30. Closed Jan 1,
  May 1, Dec 25.
ⓒ 🍴 ♿ ✍

The original museum at Carnac was opened in
1882. It was the gift and creation of a rich Scot,
James Miln, a self-taught and talented
archaeologist who had carried out many
excavations in the area and who gave his finds
to the town of Carnac. His work was continued
by Zacharie Le Rouzic, who had been his pupil
as a boy and who eventually became curator of
the museum.

**A burial from the Stone Age cemetery at
Hoëdic, St Pierre de Quiberon, mid 6th-
century. Museum of Prehistory, Carnac.**

In 1982, when the old museum was bursting
at the seams, the municipality decided to
convert an old presbytery (1877) and boarding
house for pupils of religious schools into a new
museum. This was opened in 1985. It is the
third most important museum in Europe for
prehistory and the most important in the world
for the megalithic period. It has remarkable
collections of objects discovered in dolmens,
polished axes in high-quality stone, pottery, and
jewellery in gold and precious stones. The total
number of items in the museum's collections
exceeds half a million. A selection of them has
been arranged to illustrate, in chronological
order, the different civilisations which have
existed in the region of Carnac.

Châlon-sur-Sâone

Denon Museum

Musée Denon, place de l'Hôtel-de-Ville, F-71100
  Châlon-sur-Sâone, Sâone-et-Loire
          ☎ 85 48 01 70
Wed–Mon 9.30–12, 2–5.30. Closed public
  holidays.
ⓒ

The engraver, Baron Dominique-Vivant Denon
(1747–1825), was the first Director-General of
the Museums of France. He was born at Denon
and his name was given to the museum in 1905.
The museum has an exceptionally strong
archaeology section, including what is held to
be the most beautiful flint object ever made,
together with good collections of Flemish,
Dutch, Italian and French paintings. Apart
from a youthful self-portrait, the pictures in the
Denon Room are by his contemporaries, not by
himself.

The recently arranged department of popular
arts and traditions contains local handicrafts
and craftsmen's tools, domestic equipment,
costumes and country furniture.

Photograph by the avant-garde photographer, Alexander Rodchenko (1891-1956). Nicéphore Niépce Museum, Chalon-sur-Sâone.

Nicéphore Niépce Museum

Musée Nicéphore Niépce, 28 quai des Messageries, F-71100 Châlon-sur-Sâone, Sâone-et-Loire
☎ *85 48 41 98*
Wed–Mon 9.30–11.30, 2.30–5.30
C ▮

The museum was established in 1972 to commemorate the life and work of the photographic pioneer, Nicéphore Niépce (1765–1833), who was born at Châlon. Niépce has a good claim to have invented photography, in 1816, and the museum has his original equipment, which is displayed in a position of honour. The collections also include a wide range of items illustrating the history of photography and photographic processes. Among the museum's most cherished possessions is a copy of a very rare work by William Henry Fox Talbot, *The Pencil of Nature* (1844),which has photographic illustrations.

Chantilly

Living Museum of the Horse

Musée Vivant du Cheval, Les Grandes Ecuries, F-60500 Chantilly, Oise
☎ *44 57 40 40*
Apr–Oct, Wed–Mon 10.30–5.30. Nov–Mar, Mon, Wed, Thurs, Fri 2–4.30; Sat, Sun 10.30–5.30. Riding demonstrations at 11.30, 3.30, 5.15 in summer and at 3 and 4 in winter. Open Tues 2–5 during school holidays.
C ▮ � ▮

The magnificent stables in which the museum is located were built in 1719–35 for Prince Louis-Henri de Bourbon. They contain several different breeds of horse, with commentaries to

explain the various movements. These are further shown in full-size models. There are reconstructions of a shoeing-smith's forge, a veterinary surgeon's premises and a room for attending to injured and sick horses. Visitors can also see a remarkable array of harness.

Charenton-le-Pont

The Bread Museum

Musée Français du Pain, 25 bis, rue Victor Hugo, F-94221 Charenton-le-Pont, Val-de-Marne
☎ *43 68 43 60*
Jan–June & Sept–Dec, Tues, Thurs 2.30–4.30. Closed July & Aug.
F

In 1988 the newspaper, *Le Figaro*, conducted a survey to discover what its readers would miss most, if they could no longer get it. In first place, and by a considerable distance, was bread. The museum at Charenton takes note of the special place which bread has in French life and announces that it has attempted to create 'surroundings worthy of bread'. Visitors are welcomed by a wooden sculpture of Saint Honoré, the patron saint of bakers, and the great variety of objects, mostly French, in the collections all have some connection with bread. They range from a document issued by Marie-Antoinette, announcing the appointment of a new Royal baker, to a 17th-century bread mould for Communion bread.

Charleville-Mézières

Rimbaud Museum

Musée Rimbaud, BP 490, F-08109 Charleville-Mézières, Ardennes
☎ *24 56 24 09/24 33 31 64*
Wed–Mon 10–12, 2–6. Closed Jan 1, Dec 25.
F ▮

The museum is in the town's old mill, which dates from 1626. It commemorates the life and work of the poet, Arthur Rimbaud (1854–91), who was born in Charleville. Rimbaud abandoned literature for ever when he was 20 and spent the rest of his life wandering about the world, finally settling in Abyssinia, where he earned a living in the coffee business, gun-running and in the slave trade. The museum has mementoes of his time in Africa and among the other exhibits are portraits and original manuscripts of his poems.

Chartres

Cathedral Treasury

Trésor de la Cathédrale, BP 131, F-28003 Chartres, Eure-et-Loire ☎ *37 21 32 33*
Feb–Mar & Oct–Dec, Mon–Sat 10–12, 2.30–4.30; Sun 2.30–4.30. Apr–Sept, Mon–Sat 10–12, 2–6; Sun & Ascension Day, Aug 15, 2–6.
F ▮

The treasury is in the cathedral's former Chapter House, dating from the 16th century. It contains 11th–17th-century liturgical objects, items of religious art and remains of the cathedral rood screen. There is also a collection of Royal arms, given as ex-votos.

One of the cathedral's most precious relics, Our Lady's Veil, is also displayed in the treasury.

Museum of Fine Art

Musée des Beaux-Arts de Chartres, 29 Cloître Notre Dame, F-28000 Chartres, Eure-et-Loire   ☎ 37 36 41 39
Easter–Sept, Tues–Sun 10–12, 2–6. Special exhibitions, 10–6. Oct–Easter, Tues–Sun 10–12, 2–5.
© ♟

The museum occupies the former Bishop's Palace, a large and splendid building constructed in stages between the 15th and 18th centuries. It has collections of medieval art, especially polychrome wooden sculptures, 16th- and 18th-century Beauvais, Gobelins and Brussels tapestries, 16th-century enamels, and 17th–18th-century clavichords and spinets. The paintings, from the 16th to the 19th centuries, are mainly French, but there are also works by Flemish, Dutch, Italian and Spanish artists.

Other sections of the museum are devoted to Rouen and Nevers faïence, arms and armour, popular art, agriculture, and porcelain, and to the art and ethnography of Africa and Oceania. Henri Navarre (1885–1971) left his collection of modern glass to the museum and in the 1960s a large collection of objects and archives relating to Overseas France came as a legacy from a former colonial governor.

Châteauroux

Bertrand Museum

Musée Bertrand, 2 rue Descente-des-Cordeliers, F-36000 Châteauroux, Indre
☎ 54 27 36 31
June–Oct, Wed–Mon 9.30–12, 2–6. Nov–May, Wed–Mon 2–5.
🅵

General Count Henri-Graiten Bertrand (1773–1844) was born at Châteauroux. He is remembered chiefly for his extreme devotion to Napoleon Bonaparte, whom he accompanied into exile on Elba and on St Helena, and whose ashes he brought back to France. The house which is now the museum belonged to him and he died here. It contains portraits and memorabilia of both Napoleon and Bertrand, together with other 18th–20th-century French paintings, as well as enamels and furniture, some of which are 16th century.

There is a large archaeological section, with Gallo-Roman material from the region, and 12th–13th-century architectural fragments from local churches. Another section is devoted to regional furniture, handicrafts, craftsmen's tools and equipment, including looms, and costumes.

The antiquary monkey. **Museum of Fine Art, Chartres.**

Château-Thierry

Jean de la Fontaine Museum

Musée Jean de la Fontaine, 12 rue Jean-de-la-Fontaine, F-02400 Château-Thierry, Aisne
☎ 23 69 05 60
Apr–June, Wed–Mon 10–12, 2–6. July–Sept, Wed–Mon 10–12, 2.30–6.30. Oct–Mar, Mon, Wed–Sat 2–5; Sun 10–12, 2–5.
🅲

Best known for his version of Aesop's *Fables*, Jean de la Fontaine (1621–95) was born in the house, built in 1559, which now contains the museum to him. The exhibits include his birth certificate and other memorabilia, busts, portraits and topographical paintings showing the town in the 17th century. There are also 17th–20th-century editions of his works and illustrations to subjects in them by a wide range of artists, including Delacroix.

Châtellerault

Descartes' House

Maison de Descartes, 162 rue Bourbon, F-86100 Châtellerault, Vienne   ☎ 49 21 05 47
Wed–Sat 10–12, 2–6. Closed public holidays.
🅲

The philosopher and mathematician, René Descartes (1596–1650), spent several years of his life in this house, his family home, although he was not born here. The museum contains portraits of him and of members of his family, together with documents relating to property they owned in the district.

Votive relief of 'Pensive Athena', 460 BC.
Acropolis Museum, Athens (Greece).

The Grobet-Labadié Museum, Marseilles (France).

Chazelles-sur-Lyon

Hat Museum

*Musée du Chapeau, 16 route de Saint-Galmier,
  F-42140 Chazelles-sur-Lyon, Loire*
☎ *77 94 23 29*
Wed–Mon 2–6. Closed Jan 1, Dec 25.
C 🛈 ♿ 🚗

Chazelles has been a centre for the manufacture
of felt hats since the 15th century. At its peak,
the industry employed 2,000 people. Today,
only one factory survives, with 25 workers. The
museum, in a former hat factory, has displays
showing the complete manufacturing process
and the changes in fashion over the centuries.
A section is devoted to the social and industrial
history of Chazelles.

Chens-sur-Leman

Milouti Museum

*Musée de Milouti, Granges de Servette, Chens-sur-
  Leman, F-74140 Douvaine, Haute-Savoie*
☎ *50 94 00 12*
1st Sun in July–Aug 31, daily 3–7
F

The museum is in a large barn, characteristic of
the 17th–19th-century architecture of rural
Savoy, isolated in the middle of a large plain. It
displays, in four galleries, more than 1,000 tools
and items of equipment belonging to the
traditional trades of the Lower Chablais region.
These include two old presses, a loom, a baker's
van and a delivery sledge used by a grocer.

**Felt-hat factory, c. 1930. Hat Museum,
Chazelles-sur-Lyon.**

Cherbourg

Museum of the Liberation

*Musée de la Libération, Fort du Roule, F-50100
  Cherbourg, Manche*   ☎ *33 20 14 12*
*Apr–Sept, daily 9–12, 2–6. Oct–Mar, Wed–Sun
  9.30–12, 2–5.30.*
C 🛈

The museum is housed in a fort built in 1857, in
the time of Napoleon III. It is concerned with
the history of the German occupation of France
during the Second World War, and with the
military activities which eventually liberated
the Cotentin Peninsula. There are collections of
weapons, equipment and uniforms used by the
armies which took part in the campaign, scale
models of German and Allied aeroplanes, ships
and fighting vehicles, and maps, posters and
leaflets.

Chinon

Jeanne d'Arc Museum

*Musée Jeanne d'Arc, Château de Chinon, F-37500
  Chinon, Indre-et-Loire*   ☎ *47 93 13 45*
*May–Sept, daily 9–12, 2–6. Oct–Nov & Feb–
  Apr, daily 9–12, 2–5.*
C

Jeanne d'Arc, the Maid of Orléans, was born at
Domrémy in 1412 and burnt alive as a heretic in
the market place in Rouen in 1431. The
museum, in the castle's clock tower, tells her
story and traces her journeys with the help of
documents, models, photographs and facsimiles.
There are also a number of views of the Château
de Chinon through the ages. Of the Throne
Room in which Jeanne 'recognised' Charles VII,
there remains only its western gable and its
enormous chimney.

Frankish bronze belt-buckle. Cognac Museum, Cognac.

Cholet

Cholet Museum

*Musée d'Histoire et des Guerres de Vendée, place
    Travot, F-49300 Cholet, Maine-et-Loire*
    ☎ 41 62 21 46
Wed–Mon 10–12, 2–5. Closed public holidays.
Ⓕ 🛇

The museum is in the former mairie (1820–30).
There are paintings, drawings and prints of the
town at different stages of its development and
exhibits illustrating local industries, especially
textiles. A section is devoted to the counter-
revolutionary civil war in the Vendée, which
continued from 1793 to 1796. It includes maps,
flags, weapons, portraits of the military
commanders and paintings showing different
episodes in the war.

Museum of the Peasantry

*Musée de la Paysannerie, Ferme de la
    Goubaudière, Parc de Loisirs de Ribou,
    F-49300 Cholet, Maine-et-Loire*
    ☎ 41 58 00 83
Wed–Mon 3–6
Ⓕ 🚜

The museum, opened in 1984, is based on a
group of 18th–19th-century farm buildings,
which have been restored to their late-19th-
century appearance. The rooms in the
farmhouse contain collections of regional
furniture, costumes and headdresses. Displays
illustrating agricultural techniques and rural
traditions and activities have been installed in
the former stables of the farm.

Cluny

Ochier Museum

*Musée Ochier, Palais-Jean-de-Bourbon, F-71250
    Cluny, Sâone-et-Loire*   ☎ 85 39 05 87
*Mar 15–Oct 31, daily 9.30–12, 2–6.30.
    Nov 1–Dec 19 & Jan 16–Mar 14, Wed–Mon
    9.30–12, 2–6. Closed May 1.*
Ⓒ 🛇

The famous Benedictine abbey at Cluny was
founded in 910. The Abbot's palace was built by

Jean de Bourbon at the end of the 15th century.
In 1864 it was given to the town by the Ochier
family, on the condition that a museum should
be installed in it. Among the exhibits are 1:200
scale models of Cluny in the 10th, 10th–11th
and 11th–12th centuries, together with plans,
maps, engravings and drawings of the town and
abbey, and architectural fragments. There are
also 18th-century French paintings, drawings,
engravings and paintings by Pierre-Paul
Prud'hon (1758–1823), the portrait and
historical painter, born at Cluny, and 15th–
18th-century furniture, ivories and ceramics, as
well as 18th-century Limoges enamels.

Cognac

Cognac Museum

*Musée Municipal, 48 boulevard Denfert-
    Rochereau, F-16100 Cognac, Charente*
    ☎ 45 32 07 25
*June–Sept, Wed–Mon 10–12, 2–6. Oct–May,
    Wed–Mon 2–5.30. Closed Jan 1, May 1, 8,
    July 14, Aug 15, Nov 1, 11, Dec 25.*
Ⓕ 🛇

The museum, opened in 1892, is in the former
mansion of the Dupuy d'Angeac family, dating
from 1838. It presents the prehistory and history
of the town and region, with exhibits of
archaeology, topographical paintings, drawings
and prints. A section is devoted to the history,
production and marketing of cognac. There are
exhibits of craftsmen's tools, and agricultural
and vineyard implements, including those of the
cooper, an important person in the economy of
the town. Other rooms contain traditional
costumes and headdresses, and displays of
pottery, faïence and glass from factories in the
region. Until the end of the 19th century,
bottles still had to be blown by the glassmaker,
but between 1893 and 1898 a local man, Claude
Boucher (1842–1913) perfected a machine
which made it possible to manufacture bottles
by a moulding process. The wine industry in
particular gave a warm welcome to the
invention.

Colmar

Bartholdi Museum

*Musée Bartholdi, 30 rue des Marchands, F-68000
    Colmar, Haut-Rhin*   ☎ 89 41 90 60
*Apr–Oct, daily 10–12, 2–6. Nov–Mar, Sat, Sun
    10–12, 2–6.*
Ⓒ 🛇

The sculptor, Auguste Bartholdi (1834–1904),
was born in Colmar. He made his name with
two major works, the Lion of Belfort (1880) and
the colossal statue of Liberty Enlightening the
World in New York harbour (1884), which had
an internal iron structure designed by Gustave
Eiffel.
    The 17th-century house in Colmar where the
museum is located was the Bartholdi family
home for three generations and the birthplace of
Auguste Bartholdi. In 1907, Bartholdi's widow

bequeathed the property, together with the contents of her Paris house, to the town of Colmar, on condition that it became a museum. The museum was opened in 1922 and restored and refurbished in 1976–9. It is now divided into two sections. The first is devoted to the history of the house and the Bartholdi family, and to the life and work of Auguste Bartholdi, with a reconstruction of his Paris studio and collections of his paintings and graphic works and models and sketches of his statues. The second section is concerned with the history of Colmar.

Unterlinden Museum

Musée d'Unterlinden, 1 rue des Unterlinden,
*   F-68000 Colmar, Haut-Rhin*
*   ☎ 89 41 89 23*
Apr–Oct, daily 9–12, 2–6. Nov–Mar, Wed–Mon
*   9–12, 2–5. Closed Jan 1, Nov 1, Dec 25.*
*   Guided tours in several languages by appt.*
C ▮

The museum is in the basement of the former Dominican convent. It has displays of prehistoric archaeology, Romanesque and Renaissance sculpture, and regional history from the 15th century until the Industrial Revolution. There are collections of popular arts and traditions, furniture, porcelain, arms and armour, and 15th–16th-century German paintings. Of particular interest is the Issenheim altarpiece, composed of sculptures by Nicolas Haguenau (c. 1490) and paintings by Grunewald (c. 1512–16). The local industry of Alsace is represented by a reconstruction of an Alsatian wine cellar and by a display of wine presses and casks.

Colombey-les-deux-Eglises

La Boisserie

La Boisserie, F-52330 Colombey-les-deux-Eglises,
*   Haute-Marne   ☎ 25 01 52 52*
Wed–Mon 10–12, 2–5. Closed Jan 1, Dec 25.
C ▮ ⚑

General, later President, Charles de Gaulle (1880–1970) bought 'La Boisserie' in 1934 and, apart from absence abroad during the Second World War, lived there until his death. The house, containing his furniture and personal possessions, has been left much as it was in his lifetime. It still belongs to the family and the ground floor was opened as a museum in 1979.

Commana

Kerouat Mills

Moulins de Kerouat, Ecomusée des Monts d'Arrée,
*   Commana, F-29237 Sizun, Finistère*
*   ☎ 98 68 87 76*
Mar 15–May 15 & Sept–Oct, Sun–Fri 2–6.
*   May 16–June 30, daily 2–6. July–Aug, daily*
*   11–7. Nov–Mar 14, closed except for pre-*
*   booked groups.*
C ▮ ⚑

The village of Commana developed in the 17th–19th centuries. It now forms part of the Armorique Regional Natural Park. Among its preserved buildings are two overshot watermills, built and operated originally by monks. After the Revolution, the mills were sold and the Fagot family occupied and ran them until 1967. They are in working condition. The site also includes two bread ovens, a dwelling house (1831), with its original furniture, a tannery transferred from its original location, and a variety of agricultural buildings. The complex is presented as an illustration of the traditional pattern of living in the area.

Compiègne

Château de Compiègne

Musée National du Château de Compiègne, place
*   du Général-de-Gaulle, F-60200 Compiègne,*
*   Oise   ☎ 44 44 02 02*
Wed–Mon 9.30–12, 1.30–5
C ▮ ⚑

The Château de Compiègne has three museums: the State Apartments, the Museum of the Second Empire, and the Museum of Carriages and Travelling. In the first and third of these, visitors have to be accompanied by a guide.

The present château dates from the reigns of Louis XV and Louis XVI. After the Revolution, the State Apartments were entirely refurnished by Napoleon, who also made important changes to the decorations. The present furnishings are 18th and 19th century. The Museum of the Second Empire is in the apartments formerly occupied by Marshals and distinguished guests. The 20 rooms contain furniture, paintings, sculpture, objets d'art and memorabilia of the life, manners and taste of the reign of Napoleon III. Among the paintings is that of *The Empress Eugénie and her Ladies in Waiting*, by

Unterlinden Museum, Colmar.

Winterhalter. There is also a reconstruction of the saloon of the Imperial train and a number of the pieces of French furniture shown at the World Exhibitions of 1855 and 1867.

The Museum of Carriages and Travelling is in the former kitchen area of the château. It illustrates the history of road travel in France through the ages, with horse-drawn vehicles from the mid 18th century onwards, steam cars and early petrol-driven cars by Panhard, Levassor, Citroen and Peugeot. The bicycle collection also includes early models by Peugeot.

Concarneau

Museum of Fishing

Musée de la Pêche, Ville Close, BP 118, F-29181 Concarneau, Finistère   ☎ *98 97 10 20*
Jan–June & Sept–Dec, daily 10–12.30, 2.30–6. July–Aug, daily 9.30–8.30.
F █

The museum is inside the Closed Town (Ville Close), an island fortress in the fishing port of Concarneau. Its collections and displays present all aspects of the industry. There are exhibits of fishing techniques, methods of preserving fish, shipbuilding and sailmaking, aquaria and mounted specimens of fish, together with models illustrating different types of fishing boat and 10 real boats, including the 32-metre Hémerica.

The museum also contains a collection of paintings and engravings with maritime and fishing themes and an exhibition on the history of the town.

Condom

Armagnac Museum

Musée de l'Armagnac, 2 rue Jules Ferry, F-32100 Condom, Gers   ☎ *62 28 31 41*
May–Sept, Mon–Sat 10–12, 2.30–6.30. Oct–Apr, by appt. Sun visits by appt.
C █ ↩

The museum is in the outbuildings of the former Bishop's Palace. It is primarily concerned with the history and production of Armagnac brandy, but also has more general collections illustrating the traditional life and customs of the region. The exhibits include vineyard and distillery equipment, jars, bottles and glasses, and a reconstruction of a cooper's workshop.

Conflans-Sainte-Honorine

Inland Waterways Museum

Musée de la Batellerie de la Ville de Conflans-Sainte-Honorine, Château du Prieuré, place Jules Gévelot, F-78700 Conflans-Sainte-Honorine, Yvelines   ☎ *39 72 58 05*
Mon, Wed–Fri 9–12, 1.30–6; Sat, Sun & public holidays 3–6 (3–5 in winter). Closed May 1. Groups by appt Mon–Fri.
F █ ↩

Miller's pocket-knife. Cosne Museum, Cosne-sur-Loire.

Conflans, situated at the point where the Oise meets the Seine, has a claim to be the capital of France's inland waterways. The museum was created in 1967 to tell the story of navigation on French rivers and canals and to show the economic importance of this method of transport. There are exhibits relating to technical developments in boatbuilding and propulsion, to the life of bargemen and to the waterways of France. There are numerous models and dioramas to illustrate the various themes and the museum's documentation is the best research centre in the country for specialists in this field.

Cosne-sur-Loire

Cosne Museum

Musée de Cosne, place de la Résistance, F-58200 Cosne-sur-Loire, Nievre   ☎ *86 26 71 62*
C █ ↩

The museum occupies a former Augustinian monastery, dating from the 17th century. It has two sections, one devoted to 20th-century French art, including works by Dufy, Chagall, Derain and Vlaminck, and the other to the Loire. The exhibits illustrate the importance of the river as a means of transport and as a centre of the fishing industry and of other commercial activities.

The museum owns a number of barges, fishing boats and other vessels used locally. They are moored in front of the museum.

Coupvray

Louis Braille Museum

Musée Louis Braille, rue Louis-Braille, Coupvray, F-77450 Esbly, Seine-et-Marne   ☎ *60 04 22 85*
Apr–Sept, Wed–Mon 10–12, 2–6. Oct–Mar, Wed–Mon 2–5.
C

Louis Braille (1809–52) was born at Coupvray. Blind from the age of three, he invented the system of touch-reading which allowed blind people to read and which is in general use, bearing his name, throughout the world. The house in which he was born has been preserved as a museum, with exhibits illustrating his life and work and the history of the development and techniques of Braille. His father was a harness-maker and saddler and, in the cellar which he used as a workshop, visitors can see where the accident took place which deprived Louis Braille of his sight.

Crépy-en-Valois

Archery Museum

*Musée du Valois et de l'Archerie, rue Gustave
    Chopinet, F-60800 Crépy-en-Valoise, Oise*
    ☎ *44 59 21 97*
3rd Sun in Mar–Nov 11, Wed–Mon 10–12, 2–6
C 🔒 🔓

The museum is in the keep of the former castle of the Dukes of Valois. The castle was the residence of Henri IV and Marguerite de Valois, Blanche de Castille, St Louis, Philippe IV Le Bel, Louise de Savoie and Francis I. The keep dates from the 9th century and was redesigned in the 14th and 15th centuries. The museum is divided into two parts. The first is devoted to archery and to the traditions of the archery companies in France. Its collections include 15th-century bows and crossbows. The second contains a collection of 150 wooden and polychromed stone statues from churches throughout the Oise region. These include four equestrian statues of St Martin and an early 16th-century statue of the Virgin of Luat.

Virgin and child, wooden sculpture. Archery Museum, Crépy-en-Valois.

Cussac-Fort-Médoc

Museum of the Horse

*Musée du Cheval, F-33460 Cussac-Fort-Médoc,
    Gironde*   ☎ *56 58 94 80*
Mar 20–Nov 12, daily 9–12, 2–6.
    *Nov 13–Mar 19, Mon–Sat 9–12, 2–6. Closed
    public holidays in winter.*
C 🔒

The museum is in buildings belonging to the Château Lanessan and houses the equestrian collections formed by the owners of the property, the Bouteiller family. The 1880s stable-block in which the displays are arranged is remarkably luxurious. The mangers are made of marble and the drinking bowls of copper, there is mechanically-controlled ventilation and the staff quarters are unusually comfortable. The pine-panelled harness room contains a wide range of saddles and other equipment, all perfectly maintained, with heating to preserve the condition of the leather in winter time. The carriage collection contains ten vehicles, all by the best makers and dating from 1844 to 1904. All are fully equipped.

Descartes

Descartes Museum

*Musée Descartes, 29 rue Descartes, F-37160
    Descartes, Indre-et-Loire*   ☎ *48 59 79 19*
Wed–Mon 2–6.30
C

The philosopher, René Descartes (1596–1650), was possibly born in the house which is now the museum. The building has certainly changed greatly since the 16th century. The small museum on the first floor contains documents, portraits, a parish register with a record of Descartes' birth, family archives, a cast of his skull and ancient and modern editions of his works. In the same building is a memorial exhibition to the novelist, René Boylesoe, who was born in 1867 in a house nearby.

Dieppe

Dieppe Museum

*Musée Municipal, Château, rue de Chastes,
    F-76200 Dieppe, Seine-Maritime*
    ☎ *35 84 19 76*
Mon 10–12, 2–5; Wed–Sun 10–12, 2–6.
C 🔒

The museum was founded in 1864. The 15th-century château, to which it moved in 1923, was its third home. It was reopened to the public in 1948, after the damage caused by wartime bombing had been repaired. The section devoted to the sea contains 16th–17th-century models of sailing ships, paintings of ships and maritime scenes, sea-chests, navigational instruments and details of voyages. There are documents relating to 16th–17th-century Dieppe navigators and hydrographers and an important collection of 17th–20th-century

Saddlery exhibition. Museum of the Horse, Cussac-Fort-Médoc.

Dieppe ivories, a local speciality, with an exhibit showing the tools and the techniques used for ivory carving.

There are displays of local furniture and of paintings of Normandy scenes and landscapes executed during their stay in the area by, among others, Sickert, Sisley, Boudin and Pissarro. Other special exhibitions are of regional archaeology and ethnology, sculpture by Jean-Baptiste Carpeaux (1827–75), and Dutch and Flemish paintings. A gallery is devoted to the life and work of Camille Saint-Saëns (1835–1921).

Dijon

Archaeological Museum

Musée Archéologique, 5 rue Docteur Maret,
F-21033 Dijon, Côte-d'Or
☎ 80 30 86 23/80 30 88 54
Jan–May & Sept–Dec, Wed–Mon 9–12, 2–6.
June–Aug, Wed–Mon 9.30–6.
C (*ex children*) ▮

The museum occupies the former dormitory of the 11th-century Benedictine Abbey of Saint Bénigne. It contains important archaeological and historical collections from the region, dating from prehistoric times to the 17th century. There is a wide range of sculpture from the Gallo-Roman period and a remarkable collection of naïve wooden heads and figures, preserved in excellent condition by the marshy ground in which they were discovered.

The museum also has interesting collections of Merovingian, Romanesque, Gothic and Renaissance religious sculptures.

Museum of Fine Art

Musée des Beaux-Arts, place de la Sainte-Chapelle,
F-21000 Dijon, Côte-d'Or ☎ 80 30 31 11
Wed–Sat 10–6 (the sections on modern and
contemporary art, and the temporary exhibitions
area close between 12.15 and 2.15); Sun
10–12.30, 2–6. Closed Jan 1, May 1, 8,
July 14, Nov 1, 11, Dec 25.
C ▮

Dijon has had an art museum, open to the public, since before the Revolution, but the paintings were limited to historical works glorifying the military achievements of the Grand Conté and the sculptures to copies of the antique. During the Revolution, the possessions of the Church and of people who had left the country were confiscated. In Dijon, they greatly enriched the collections of the museum, which was installed in the former palace of the Dukes of Valois and re-opened to the public in 1790. Its premises were later extended to include part of the Palace of the States of Burgundy. Subsequent gifts and purchases have further enlarged the collections, which now include Italian, Flemish, German and Swiss primitives, and works by 17th–19th-century French artists, as well as contemporary paintings.

Other sections of the museum are devoted to ceramics, objets d'art, Egyptian archaeology, 16th-century Flemish tapestries, Renaissance sculpture and furniture, arms and armour, 14th-century ivories and an historical collection relating to the Dukes of Burgundy. The tombs of the Dukes of Burgundy are also within the museum building.

Puycousin Museum of Burgundian Life

Musée de la Vie Bourguignonne Perrin de
Puycousin, Cloître des Bernardines, 17 rue
Sainte-Anne, F-21000 Dijon, Côte-d'Or
☎ 80 30 65 91
Wed–Mon 9–12, 2–6
C ▮ ꜛ

In 1935, Maurice Bonnefond Perrin de Puycousin gave to the city of Dijon his large collection of objects illustrating the traditional life of Burgundy. In 1985 they were transferred to a former Cistercian convent, built in 1623, which had served after the Revolution as a barracks, an orphanage, a training school for nurses and, finally, a nursery. Extensive restoration was needed before the museum could be installed there.

The displays now cover both rural and urban life in Dijon and the surrounding area during the 19th century. They are mostly arranged in room or workshop settings, and contain costumes, furniture, agricultural implements, domestic equipment, musical instruments and a wide range of craftsmen's tools.

Dinan

Castle Museum

Musée du Château, F-22100 Dinan, Côtes-du-
Nord   ☎ 96 39 45 20
Apr–May & Oct–Nov, Wed–Mon 10–12, 2–6.
June–Aug, daily 10–6.30. Dec–Mar 14,
Wed–Mon 1.30–5.
C ▮ ꜛ

The museum, founded in 1845, occupies the keep of the castle. Its collections illustrate principally the history and art of this well-preserved medieval town and its region. There are examples of 12th–17th-century wooden and stone sculpture, Breton furniture, headdresses and costumes, and regional handicrafts, especially weaving, woodwork, pottery and basketmaking.

Dol-de-Bretagne

Dol Museum

Musée, 4 place de la Cathédrale, F-35120 Dol-de-Bretagne, Ile-et-Vilaine ☎ *99 48 04 84 Easter–Sept, daily 10–12, 2–6*
C 🔒 ⏣

This privately owned and run museum is devoted to the archaeology and history of Dol and its region. It occupies a house which formerly served as the Cathedral Treasury. Its collection of 13th–18th-century polychrome and waxed wooden statues is one of the finest in France. There are also displays of 18th–19th-century French and Jersey faïence, and 17th–19th-century weapons. The museum has memorabilia of the writer, François-René de Chateaubriand (1768–1848), who was at school in Dol, and of the Chouans leader, Saigne-Paulout.

Douai

The Charterhouse Museum

Musée de la Chartreuse, Section Beaux-Arts, 4 rue des Chartreux, F-59500 Douai, Nord ☎ *27 87 26 63 Wed–Mon 10–12, 2–5. Closed public holidays.*
C 🔒

The museum was founded c. 1800, the basis of the original collections being material stolen from the Church and aristocratic families by the Revolutionary authorities. Installed in the former Residence of the Jesuits, the museum's building was seriously damaged during the First World War and completely destroyed in 1944, when the natural history and ethnographical collections were annihilated. The paintings, sculpture and objets d'art had been previously moved to safety elsewhere and from 1958 onwards were progressively redisplayed in the

Gold Iron Age bracelet. Archaeological Museum, Dijon.

16th–18th-century buildings of the former Charterhouse.

There are sculptures from the Middle Ages to the modern period, including works by Rodin and Constantin Meunier and important collections of Flemish, Dutch, Italian and French paintings. The French artists represented include Chardin, Corot, Combet, Sisley, Renard and Pissarro.

Draguignan

Museum of the Popular Arts and Traditions of Central Provence

Musée des Arts et Traditions Populaires de Moyenne-Provence, 15 rue de la Motte, F-83300 Draguignan, Var ☎ *94 47 05 72 Apr–Sept, daily 9–12, 3–6. Oct–Mar, Wed–Sat 9–12, 3–6. Closed public holidays.*
C 🔒

The museum, opened in 1985, is concerned with the traditional life and occupations of Central Provence. There are exhibits relating to the growing and processing of wheat, olives, and grapes and to the rearing and use of sheep, horses, mules, donkeys and oxen. Other material on display illustrates the trades of the blacksmith, shoeing-smith, wheelwright, saddler, cooper and potter. Sections are devoted to silk manufacture and cork production, both important industries in the area – there is a reconstruction of a cork-maker's workshop – to Provençal music, and to furniture, domestic equipment and local costumes.

Dunkirk

Museum of Contemporary Art

Musée d'Art Contemporain de Dunkerque, Jardin des Sculptures, avenue des Bains, F-59240 Dunkerque, Nord ☎ *28 59 21 65 Apr–Sept, Wed–Mon 10–7. Oct–Mar, Wed–Mon 10–6. Closed Jan 1, Dec 25.*
C ⏣ ♿ ⏣ ■

The distinguished building of the museum, opened in 1982, has transformed a previously bombed, derelict area into one of the town's main amenities. The core of the permanent collection was assembled previously by an Association of Friends, under the inspired leadership of a regional factory inspector and art enthusiast, Gilbert Delaine, who exploited the admirable French system, by which industrial and commercial concerns may save tax by giving 1 per cent of their profits to an approved cultural undertaking, and bought works of art on the international market.

The paintings, drawings and sculptures which have been acquired as a result of this remarkable enterprise illustrate the principal trends in international art during the past 50 years. Many of the sculptures are displayed outside, in the park which forms an integral part of the museum. Five or six temporary exhibitions are arranged each year, in addition to the permanent displays.

Museum of Fine Art

Musée des Beaux-Arts, place du Général de
  Gaulle, F-59240 Dunkerque, Nord
  ☎ 28 66 21 57
Wed–Mon 10–12, 2–6. Closed Jan 1, May 1,
  Sun following Shrove Tues, Nov 1, Dec 25.
Ⓒ ▮ ♿ ✍

The museum, in a modern building designed for
the purpose, is not exactly what the title
suggests. It has, in fact, five sections, devoted to
naval construction; paintings; sculpture,
ceramics and goldsmiths' work; natural history;
and the Second World War. The first gallery
shows, by means of models, plans and drawings,
the evolution of naval construction from the
17th century onwards. The 18th-century ship
models from the Arsenal at Dunkirk are
particularly noteworthy. The art gallery has
European works from the 16th to the 20th
century and is distinguished by its collection of
17th-century French paintings and of drawings
and engravings of Dunkirk.

The emphasis of the third section of the
museum is on 17th and 18th-century sculpture,
porcelain and pottery, and work by 17th–18th-
century silversmiths and goldsmiths. The
natural history gallery contains collections of
minerals, shells, insects and birds and the
gallery dedicated to the Second World War
presents the history of Dunkirk during this
period, especially the sufferings of the town and
its inhabitants in May–June 1944.

18th-century statue gallery, Museum of Fine
Art, Dijon.

Epernay

Epernay Museum

Musée Municipal, 13 avenue de Champagne,
  F-51200 Epernay, Marne   ☎ 26 51 49 91
Mon, Wed–Sat and public holidays 9–12, 2–6; Sun
  10–12, 2–5
Ⓒ ▮

The museum, which is in the former Château
Perrier, a 19th-century building, is in three
parts. The Museum of Art has collections of
17th–19th-century French faïence and
porcelain, 18th-century furniture, sculpture and
17th–18th-century statues of saints. The
Museum of Champagne illustrates vineyard
cultivation and the production of champagne,
with the help of documents, engravings, tools
and equipment and collections of bottles,
glasses, labels and posters. The Museum of
Regional Prehistory and Archaeology shows the
activities of the civilisations which once
peopled the Marne, particularly the south of the
Département.

Epinal

Museum of the Vosges

Musée Départemental des Vosges, 1 place Lagarde,
  F-88000 Epinal, Vosges   ☎ 29 82 20 33
Apr–Sept, Wed–Mon 10–12, 2–6. Oct–Mar,
  Wed–Mon 10–12, 2–5. Closed Jan 1, May 1,
  Nov 1, Dec 25.
Ⓒ ▮

Founded in 1822, the museum was established
from the beginning in a former workhouse, with
funds provided by the Duc de Choiseul. The
Gallo–Roman material is of particular interest
and there are also important collections of
medieval and Renaissance sculpture, French
and Italian paintings (Rembrandt, Bellot,
Claude Lorrain, Georges de la Tour) and 18th-
century drawings, gouaches and watercolours
(Boucher, Fragonard, Tiepolo, Canaletto,
Watteau). In recent years, particular attention
has been given to building up an international
collection of contemporary art.

Since 1951 the museum has created a
remarkable international collection of popular
prints on religious, patriotic, historical,
narrative, political, satirical and humorous
themes. Selections from the 30,000 items in the
museum's possession are regularly presented.

Epinueil-le-Fleuriel

Le Grand Meaulnes Museum

Musée du Grand Meaulnes, Ecole d'Epinueil-le-
  Fleuriel, F-18360 Saulzais, Cher
  ☎ 48 63 02 23
Telephone before visit
Ⓕ

The poet and novelist, Alain Fournier (1886–
1914), was killed in action during the First
World War. His Le Grand Meaulnes (1913), set
in his native Sologne country, has been one of
the most popular and influential novels of the

present century. The museum dedicated to him is in the school where he was a pupil for several years. It is described in *Le Grand Meaulnes* under the pseudonym of Sainte Agethe. Visitors see it as it was in 1890, with its classrooms, kitchen, staircase to the attics and corn loft. There is an exhibition describing the life and work of the novelist. A meticulously organised guided tour of the area is related to 31 chapters of *Le Grand Meaulnes*.

Escaudin

Escaudin Museum

Musée Municipal, 6 rue Paul-Bert, F-59124
Escaudin, Nord ☎ *27 44 07 38*
Sun 10–12. Other times by appt.
Ⓒ

Escaudin was formerly an important coal-mining centre. The museum, opened in 1977, is concerned with the history of the area and especially with its mining activities. The exhibits illustrating the life of the miners include reconstructions of a coal-miner's living-room at the beginning of the present century and of a local tavern of about the same period.

Etaples

Museum of the Sea

Musée de la Marine, boulevard de l'Impératrice,
F-62630 Etaples, Pas-de-Calais
☎ *21 94 66 27*
July–Aug, Tues–Sun 3–7
Ⓒ 🏛

The museum occupies a former fish market, dating from the mid 19th century. It presents a number of aspects of the maritime history of Etaples, with documents, photographs, ship models, costumes, drawings and paintings illustrating the history and occupations of the town. An important section is devoted to the fishing industry, with exhibitions showing its techniques and an aquarium containing the fish to be found along the local coasts. Visitors can also see an armed shrimp-fishing trawler, the bridge of a fishing-boat with all its instrumentation, and the hull of the last wooden trawler to operate from Etaples.

Eu

Louis-Philippe Museum

Musée Louis-Philippe, Château d'Eu, F-76260 Eu,
Seine-Maritime ☎ *35 86 44 00*
Sat preceding Palm Sunday–Sun following Nov 1,
Wed–Mon 10–12, 2–6
Ⓒ 🏛 ♿ 🚌

In 1050 William of Normandy married Mathilde of Flanders in the original castle at Eu. The castle and the town were destroyed by fire in 1475. The present Château d'Eu was begun in 1578 by Henri de Guise and completed in 1665 by the Grande Mademoiselle, cousin of

Louis XIV. Subsequently altered and extended, it became, in the 19th century, the summer residence of King Louis-Philippe, who received Queen Victoria in his palace on two occasions.

The estate was owned by the Princess of Orléans until it became the property of the town of Eu and now houses both the museum and the town hall. In the wing of the château which is open to the public, visitors can see the apartment decorated by Viollet Le Duc in 1874–9 for Louis-Philippe's grandson, the Comte de Paris. Other apartments and rooms, including the Servants' Hall, have been restored to their original appearance, with Louis-Philippe's own furniture.

In the King's private apartment, destroyed by fire in 1902 and afterwards restored, there is a section of the museum illustrating the history of the Bresle Valley, with exhibits devoted to Le Tréport, the local glassworks; traditions, customs and handicrafts; and 19th-century paintings, prints and drawings of local scenes.

Fécamp

Fécamp Museum

Musée Municipal, 21 rue Alexandre Legros,
F-76400 Fécamp, Seine-Maritime
☎ *35 28 31 99*
Wed–Mon 10–12, 2–5.30. Closed Jan 1, May 1,
Dec 25.
Ⓒ *(ex children)* 🏛

The museum has been in existence since 1879. It has a park or 'English garden', in which the trees and shrubs are labelled for study purposes. The park contains a monument to Dr Dufour, a pioneer of modern child-welfare, and an interesting ceramic monument, made in 1904 by Alexandre Bigot, which is dedicated to sailors lost at sea.

The museum has displays illustrating the art, history and traditional life of the area, with collections of furniture, especially chests and Norman marriage-wardrobes, 19th-century landscape paintings, costumes, Rouen and Delft earthenware, religious art, and 16th–19th-century drawings. There are also exhibits of toys and of paintings, drawings and sculpture on subjects related to childhood.

Babies' feeding-bottles: French, 17th- and 18th-centuries, and pre-Colombian Inca, in terracotta. Fécamp Museum, Fécamp.

Museum of Fishing

Musée des Terre-Nuevas et de la Pêche, 27
  boulevard Albert 1er, F-76400 Fécamp, Seine-
  Maritime   ☎ 35 29 76 22
Jan–June & Sept–Dec, Wed–Mon 10–12, 2–5.30.
  July–Aug, daily 10–12, 2–5.30. Closed Jan 1,
  May 1, Dec 25.
Ⓒ *(ex children)* 🅰 🖾 ♿

This museum, opened in 1988, is in a
building overlooking the sea. It has displays
illustrating the life of fishermen from Fécamp
who were away from home for months fishing for
cod on the Newfoundland Banks. Other
exhibits present, with the help of model boats,
fishing and navigational equipment and ex-
votos, the history of the port's fishing industry
and of the community which earned its living
from it. The collections include original fishing
vessels and there are reconstructions of
workshops used for building and equipping the
boats.

Ferrières

Languedoc Museum of Protestantism

Musée de Protestantisme en Haut-Languedoc,
  Château de Ferrières, F-81263 Brassac, Tarn
  ☎ 63 50 03 53
June 15–Sept 15, daily 3–6
Ⓒ 🖾

In 1598 Henri IV issued the Edict of Nantes,
granting limited tolerance to French
Protestants. In 1685, during the minority of
Louis XIV, the Edict was revoked and as a result
many of the most skilled workers in France left
the country. Before 1685, the Château de
Ferrières, under Guillot, Baron de Ferrières, had
been a centre for the defence of Protestant
rights. Afterwards, it became a notorious state
prison for Protestants. The museum, opened in
1968, contains collections illustrating the
history of Protestantism in France, especially in
the Ferrières region. The exhibits include
furniture used in Protestant meeting places,
communion vessels, baptismal goblets,
headdresses worn at communion services,
paintings, engravings, documents and 17th–
19th-century Protestant parish registers.

The Stringed Instrument Maker's House

Maison de Luttier, Château de Ferrières, F-81263
  Brassac, Tarn   ☎ 63 74 03 53
June 15–Sept 15, daily 3–6.30
Ⓒ 🖾

Claude Tournier, who belonged to a long line of
stringed instrument makers in Paris, gave his
collection of instruments to a society in
Ferrières. They were displayed first in a 16th-
century house and then, in 1987, they were
transferred to the château, which is of the same
period and served as a state prison for
Protestants in the 18th century. The exhibition
includes the traditional tools and equipment of
the craft, displayed in a reconstructed workshop
dating from 1783, which comes from the
Tourniers' premises in Paris. There is also a
collection of documents, books and illustrations
concerning the making of stringed instruments.

**Royal elephant, 16th-century fresco by
Giovanni Rosso, in the François I Gallery at
the Royal Palace of Fontainebleau.**

Fessy

Museum of Art and Folklore

Musée d'Art et de Folklore Régional, Fessy,
F-74140 Douvaine, Haute-Savoie
  ☎ 50 95 01 93
May–Sept, daily 2.30–4.30. Other months by
appt.
C &

The 10,000 items in the museum have been
assembled by the painter, poet and musician,
Bernard Lacroix, over 40 years. They recall the
traditional life of the Bas-Chablais region, with
reconstructions of the village grocer's shop, the
farmhouse living-room, the forge, the Alpine
farmhouse, the weaver's and carpenter's
workshops and the flax mill. There are
collections of farm implements, equipment for
spinning and weaving wool and flax and for
making butter and cheese. The collection of
signed tiles is unique in France.

Fontainebleau

The Royal Palace of Fontainebleau

F-77300 Fontainebleau, Seine-et-Marne
  ☎ 1 64 22 27 40
Wed–Mon 9.30–12.30, 2–5 (last visits 11.45 and
4.15). Closed Jan 1.
C & ☖ ☛ ☕

This former royal palace dates from the 12th
century. It was reconstructed by François 1 in
1528–47 and further changes were made during
the 18th century. The principal rooms were
decorated by French and Italian artists, and
there are some particularly good Renaissance
frescoes. The furnishings, scattered after the
Revolution, have subsequently been restored as
far as possible to their original settings. The
Louis XVI furniture includes a bureau encrusted
with mother-of-pearl, which belonged to Marie
Antoinette. There are tapestries by Jean-
Baptiste Oudry (1686–1755), Court Painter to
Louis XV, who worked for the Beauvais factory
from 1726 onwards.
    The palace has a theatre dating from the
Second Empire and there is also a Bonheur
Museum, with works by Rosa Bonheur (1822–
99), who was, after Landseer, the most famous
animal painter of the 19th century.

Fontenay-le-Comte

Vendée Museum

Musée Vendéen, place du 137e Régiment
d'Infanterie, F-85200 Fontenay-le-Comte,
Vendée   ☎ 51 69 31 31
June 15–Sept 15, Tues–Fri 10–12, 2–6; Sat, Sun
2–6. Sept 16–June 14, Wed–Sun 2–6.
C ☕

In the twelve galleries of the museum are
displays of prehistoric and Gallo-Roman
archaeology, which include one of the best
collections of Gallo-Roman glass, and of
material illustrating the traditional life and

**Ethnography exhibition. Vendée Museum,
Fontenay-le-Comte.**

occupations of the region. The museum has a
particularly important collection of regional
furniture. Other exhibits explain the history of
the town, with the help of a model which allows
visitors to discover points of interest, and shows
the birds to be seen locally. The art section of
the museum contains 17th–19th-century
paintings, especially by French artists.

Fontvieille

Alphonse Daudet Museum

Musée Alphonse Daudet, avenue des Moulins,
F-13990 Fontvieille, Bouches-du-Rhône
  ☎ 90 97 60 78
May–Sept, Wed–Mon 9–12, 2–7. Oct–Apr,
Wed–Mon 9–12, 2–6.
C &

The novelist, Alphonse Daudet (1840–97),
became famous with his collection of stories
published as *Lettres de Mon Moulin* (Letters from
my Mill) in 1869. The Moulin Saint-Pierre, in
which the museum has been located since 1935,
is not the mill referred to in the book. It is,
however, the only one in the region to have
preserved its machinery. In the bolting room
there are exhibits relating to Daudet and his
work, including his desk, manuscripts, first
editions of his books, portraits, photographs and
caricatures.

Fougerolles

Le Petit Fahys Ecomuseum

Ecomusée du Petit-Fahys, Le Petit-Fahys, F-70220
Fougerolles, Haute-Saône   ☎ 84 49 12 53
May 15–Sept 30, Wed–Mon 2–6
C ☕

The museum comprises six buildings, of which
the largest, the dwelling house, dates from

1829. Together, they form a complex which, from the beginning, has been used to distill kirsch. There are six old stills and around them there are exhibits explaining the processes involved. The surrounding orchards show the different varieties of cherries which have been traditionally used for distillation.

Fourmies

Ecomuseum of the Fourmies-Trélon Region

Ecomusée de la Région Fourmies-Trélon, Centre Ville, F-59610 Fourmies, Nord
   ☎ 27 60 66 11
Mar–Nov, Mon–Fri 9–12, 2–6; Sat, Sun & public holidays, 2.30–6.30. Atelier Musée du Verre: Apr–Oct, Mon–Fri 2–6; Sat, Sun & public holidays 2.30–6.30.
C ▮ ⚒ ✏

The museum is a complex of six separate museums, administered centrally, which together present a picture of the industrial and social history of the area. The mother-museum, the Museum of Textile History and Social Life (Musée du Textile et de la Vie Sociale) in Fourmies, is in a former textile mill. It offers its visitors a survey of the history of the Fourmies region during the 19th and 20th centuries. It contains the largest collection of working textile machinery in Europe, together with machinery used in other industries. The displays also include reconstructions of domestic, shop and factory interiors, as well as objects recalling the past social and economic life of the area.

A second museum (Atelier Musée du Verre) at Trélon, is in the former Parant glassworks, founded in 1823. Its furnaces and equipment show, with demonstrations, the whole production cycle for hand-made and machine-made glass. There are displays of the products of the local industry and exhibits illustrating the life of the works.

Gargilesse

George Sand's House

Maison de George Sand, F-36190 Gargilesse, Indre   ☎ 54 47 84 14
Apr–Oct, daily 9.30–12.30, 2.30–7
C ▮ ✏

George Sand was the pseudonym of the French novelist, Amandine Aurore Lucie Dupin (1804–76), who became notorious for her many stormy love-affairs with, among others, Musset and Chopin. When she was 18, she married Baron Casimir Dudevant, and by him had a son, Maurice. Her little country retreat at Gargilesse, where she frequently stayed during the last years of her life, was restored in 1960 under the direction of her granddaughter, Aurore Sand, and is still a family property. It contains furniture, personal possessions and memorabilia of George Sand and her son, together with manuscripts, drawings and paintings and early editions of the novelist's work.

Gien

Gien Faïence Factory

Musée de la Faïencerie de Gien, 78 place de la Victoire, F-45500 Gien, Loiret
   ☎ 38 67 00 05
Daily 9–11.45, 2–5.45. Closed Jan 1, Nov 1, 11, Dec 25.
C ▮ ✏

The factory at Gien was set up in 1820 by an Englishman, Thomas Hulm, also known as Hall, who had previously operated, unsuccessfully, pottery and porcelain works in the Paris region. During the 19th and 20th centuries the business changed hands several times, constantly experimenting with new techniques and styles.

The museum, which is within the factory complex in a former ceramic paste cellar, illustrates production at Gien since 1820. Visitors can also take tours of the factory.

Hunting Museum

Musée International de la Chasse, place du Château, F-45500 Gien, Loiret
   ☎ 38 67 00 01
Daily 9.15–12.15, 2.15–7 (Nov–Mar until 6)
C ▮ ✏

The museum is in the Château de Gien, which overlooks the Loire and was built by Anne de Beaujeu in 1484. The collections include trophies, hunting horns and hunting weapons, including sporting guns used by Louis XIV and Napoleon Bonaparte. There are also paintings, engravings, sculpture and tapestries showing hunting scenes, including works by François Desportes (1661–1743), court painter to Louis XIV.

Trophy room at the Hunting Museum, Gien.

The cat's dinner by Marguerite Gérard.
Fragonard Museum, Grasse.

Giverny

Claude Monet Museum

*Fondation Claude Monet, Giverny, F-27620
    Gasny, Eure*   ☎ *32 51 28 21*
*Apr–Oct, Tues–Sun. House: 10–12, 2–6.
    Garden: 10–6.*
🅲 🛈 💻 ♿

The painter, Claude Monet (1840–1926), came
to live in this house and remained here until his
death. He was responsible for planting the
beautiful gardens, which surround the house and
in which he painted regularly. The house
contains all his possessions, including furniture,
ceramics, books and his collection of Japanese
prints. The paintings that were in the house in
1926 have since been removed to the Orangerie
in Paris, for security reasons.

Grasse

Fragonard Museum

*Musée Villa Fragonard, 23 boulevard Fragonard,
    F-06130 Grasse, Alpes-Maritimes.
    Correspondence to: 2 rue Mirabeau, F-06130
    Grasse.*   ☎ *93 36 01 61*
*June–Sept, Mon–Fri 10–12, 2–6. Open 1st & last
    Sun in month. Oct, Dec–May, Mon–Fri
    10–12, 2–5. Open 1st & last Sun in month.*
🅲 🛈

Jean-Honoré Fragonard (1732–1806), a native
of Grasse, made his name as a painter of gallant
and sentimental subjects in the reigns of Louis
XV, during the period when Madame du Barry
was influential, and of Louis XVI. The French
Revolution put an end to his patrons and to the
demand for his kind of art. The museum
contains paintings, drawings, engravings and
memorabilia of Fragonard and his family,
including his son, Alexandre (1780–1850), his
grandson, Théophile (1809–76) and his sister-
in-law, Marguerite Gerard (1761–1837). There

are also collections of art, costumes and pottery
of lower Provence.
    The staircase walls in the house containing
the museum are decorated with murals painted
in 1792 by Alexandre Fragonard, when he was
only 12.

Museum of Perfume

*Musée International de la Parfumerie, 8 place du
    Cours, F-06130 Grasse, Alpes-Maritimes*
    ☎ *93 36 80 20*
May–Sept, daily 10–6. Oct–Apr, daily 10–5.
🅲 🛈 ♿

Grasse is a traditional centre for the production
of perfumes. The museum occupies two 19th-
century buildings linked by a modern addition.
It contains displays showing the preparation of
perfume, soap and cosmetics, from the raw
materials to the finished product, with
reconstructions of part of a factory and a
research laboratory. There are important
historical collections of objects associated with
perfumes from antiquity to our own times and of
publicity material. Glasshouses contain
Mediterranean and non-European plants used in
the perfumery industry.

Grenoble

Grenoble Museum

*Musée de Grenoble, place de Verdun, F-38000
    Grenoble, Isère*   ☎ *76 54 09 82*
Wed–Mon 10–12, 2–6
🅲 🛈 ♿

The Art Museum at Grenoble is one of the most
prestigious provincial galleries in France, both
for its Old Master and its modern and
contemporary collections. The rooms on the
ground floor contain 16th–18th-century Italian,
Flemish and French paintings, while on the first
floor there are works by 19th-century artists,
mainly French – Fantin-Latour, Gérard, Ingres,
Delacroix, Rousseau and Monet are all
represented. The 20th-century section includes
paintings by Matisse, Léger, Bonnard, Picasso,
Chagall and Klee, as well as the major Surrealist
names. The museum's holdings of French and
foreign contemporary art are presented on an
alternating basis with temporary exhibitions.
The museum also possesses an important
collection of Egyptian works of art, mostly from
the Ptolemaic period (4th century BC).

Museum of the Dauphiné

*Musée Dauphinois, 30 rue Maurice-Gignoux,
    F-38000 Grenoble, Isère*   ☎ *76 87 66 77*
*Wed–Mon 9–12, 2–6. Closed Jan 1, May 1,
    Dec 25.*
🅲 🛈 ♿

The Dauphiné is the old province between the
Rhône and Italy. Its museum is in the former
convent of Sainte-Marie-d'en-Haut, built in
1619. The baroque chapel, cloister and terraced
gardens are open to visitors. The collections

18th-century lantern. Museum of the Dauphiné, Grenoble.

illustrate the history of the region, with archaeological material from prehistoric, Gallo-Roman and Merovingian sites in the area. There are displays of furniture, pottery, Grenoble faïence, costumes and headdresses. Sections are also devoted to religious art, 20th-century paintings by Grenoble artists and portraits of local celebrities.

Museum of Painting and Sculpture

Musée du Peinture et de la Sculpture, place de Verdun, F-38000 Grenoble, Isère
☎ 76 54 09 82
Wed–Mon 12.30–7. Closed public holidays. Free admission Wed.
C ▮

This has some of the most important collections of any art museum in the provinces. It was opened to the public in 1800, to display works of art stolen from the Church and aristocratic families by the Revolutionary government. It was the first museum in France, in 1923, to acquire the so-called 'modern' art, and since then a carefully planned collection policy has made it a pilot institution in this field. All the main movements and the great names are represented from the Impressionists to the present day.

The museum also has important works by artists belonging to the principal European schools of the 17th–18th centuries, especially French, Spanish, Italian and Flemish. There are sections devoted to Egyptian archaeology and to Greek and Roman sculpture.

Haguenau

Museum of Alsace

Musée Alsacien, place Joseph-Thierry, F-67500 Haguenau, Bas-Rhin ☎ 88 93 12 50
Tues–Fri 8–12, 2–6; Sat, Sun 2–5.
C

The 16th-century building which houses the museum served until 1790 as the chancery of the ancient Free Town of Haguenau, after which it

was used for a variety of municipal purposes until 1968, when it was restored and converted into a museum. Displays of 17th–18th-century locally-made furniture occupy the ground floor and on the first floor there are exhibits showing the wide range of objects made by craftsmen working in wood, traditional costumes and headdresses from the region, and locks and other metal objects made by local specialists. The second floor is devoted to a reconstruction of a potter's house, with its workshop, living room and kitchen, and to a gallery of popular art.

Honfleur

Eugène Boudin Museum

Musée Eugène Boudin, place Erik Satie, F-14600 Honfleur, Calvados ☎ 31 89 16 47
Mar 15–Sept, Wed–Mon 2–6. Oct–Dec & Feb 21–Mar 15, Mon, Wed–Fri 2.30–5; Sat, Sun 10–12, 2.30–5. Closed Jan 1, May 1, July 14, Dec 25.
C ▮ ▰

The museum was founded in 1868 by the painter, Louis-Alexandre Dubourg, who was a friend of Eugène Boudin (1824–98), a precursor of Impressionism. In his will, Boudin left to the museum a large collection of his own paintings and drawings, together with a number of works by his friends. In 1924 the museum was transferred from the town hall to a former Augustinian monastery. In 1971, the accommodation was extended and modernised.

The collections include 17th-century French and Dutch paintings, and 19th–20th-century works by painters of the Honfleur school, especially Boudin. There are also 18th–19th-century regional costumes and headdresses, and furniture.

Maritime Museum

Musée de la Marine, Eglise Saint-Etienne, F-14600 Honfleur, Calvados ☎ 31 89 14 12
June 15–Sept 15, daily 10.30–12, 2.30–6. Sept 15–Dec & Feb–June 14, Sat, Sun 2.30–6; weekdays by appt.
C ▮

The Church of Saint-Etienne, which houses the museum, was built in 1369 on the orders of Charles V and enlarged by Henry VI of England in 1432, during the period of English occupation in the Hundred Years War. Closed at the Revolution, it subsequently served as a shop, a theatre and an exchange. Between 1802 and 1809 it functioned as the town's herring market. In 1897 it became the property of the Old Honfleur Society, which restored it.

The museum contains a collection of models of locally-built fishing boats, paintings of ships commissioned by their captains, portraits of shipowners, shipbuilders and famous captains, and documents relating to privateers and slave ships. There are also exhibits telling the story of the port of Honfleur.

Museum of Old Honfleur

*Musée du Vieux Honfleur, rue de la Prison,
F-14600 Honfleur, Calvados*
☎ 31 89 14 12
*June 15–Sept 15, daily 10.30–12, 2.30–6.
Sept 15–Dec & Feb–June 14, Sat, Sun
2.30–6; weekdays by appt.*
C &

The museum, established in 1899 by the Old
Honfleur Society, is in a 16th-century house and
in the town's former prison. It contains
reconstructions of domestic interiors and
workshops, 14th–18th-century sculpture,
topographical paintings, prints and drawings,
and portraits of Honfleur celebrities. There are
also collections of traditional Norman costumes,
headdresses and accessories, and of popular
religious art. A section is devoted to an
exceptional collection of costumes from the
period of Louis XV and Louis XVI.

Ile d'Aix

Napoleonic Museum

*Musée National Napoléonien, Maison de
l'Empéreur, rue Napoléon, F-17123 Ile d'Aix,
Charente-Maritime*   ☎ 46 88 66 40
*May–Sept, Wed–Mon 10–12, 2–6. Oct–Apr,
Wed–Mon 10–12, 2–4.*
C &

The commandant's Residence, which today
houses the museum, was built in 1808 on the
orders of Napoleon and it was where he spent
his last night in France before leaving for exile
on St Helena. The five rooms on the ground
floor contain furniture, paintings and other
objects associated with Napoleon, together with
portraits of the Emperor, his family and his
marshals and generals. There are also personal
possessions of General Gourgaud, who
accompanied Napoleon to St Helena
   The Emperor's own room is on the first floor.
Most of the furnishings have been preserved and
there is a portrait of him in the robes of the king
of Italy, by Appiani. One room is devoted to St
Helena and to the return of the Emperor's ashes
to France, another to the Napoleonic legend.

Ile d'Ouessant

Lighthouse Museum

*Centre d'Interpretation des Phares et Balises, Ile
d'Ouessant, Phare du Creach, F-29242
Ouessant, Finistère*   ☎ 98 48 80 70
*Apr–June, Wed–Sun 2–6. July–Sept, daily
11–6.30. Other times by appt.*
C & ⌂

The museum is in the Creach lighthouse, one of
several on this rocky and dangerous part of the
coast of Brittany. The exhibits include 18th-
and early-19th-century lighthouse signalling
equipment, brought from other sites, and
models and dioramas showing the siting and
functioning of lighthouses. The museum forms
part of the Parc Naturel Régional d'Armorique.

Ouessant Ecomuseum

*Ecomusée de l'Ile d'Ouessant, Maison du Niou
Huella, F-29242 Ouessant, Finistère*
☎ 98 68 81 71
*Apr–June, Wed–Sun 2–6. July–Aug, daily
11–6.30. Sept, Wed–Sun 11–6.30.*
C &

The headquarters of this ecomuseum, which
forms part of the Parc Naturel Régional
d'Armorique, is an 18th-century house in the
village of Niou Huella. The house, together
with a second of the same type, both in
traditional settings, is evidence of a society
based on the work of men at sea and that of
women on the land. The design of the interior
of the house, which has its original painted
furniture, appears rooted in the spatial
organisation of a vessel and is, so to speak,
a boat on dry land. On display is furniture,
domestic equipment, paintings by sailors,
religious images, maps and photographs.

Illiers-Combray

Marcel Proust Museum

*Musée Marcel Proust, 4 rue du Docteur Proust,
F-28120 Illiers-Combray, Eure-et-Loire*
☎ 37 24 30 97
Wed–Mon, open for visits at 3 pm and 4 pm only.
C &

The house, the headquarters of the Society of
the Friends of Marcel Proust, is in the Maison de
Tante Léonie of Proust's novels. Proust (1871–
1922), spent childhood holidays here. The
museum contains personal possessions and
memorabilia of the writer and his family,
together with portraits of people who served as
models for his characters.

Issoudun

Saint Roch Museum

*Musée Saint-Roch, rue de l'Hospice Saint-Roch,
F-36100 Issoudun, Indre*   ☎ 54 21 01 76
*Apr 15–Oct 15, Wed–Mon 10–12, 2–7.
   Oct 16–Jan 14 & Feb 16–Apr 14, Mon,
   Wed, Thurs 2–6; Fri–Sun 10–12, 2–3.*
F & ⌂

Saint Roch Museum, Issoudun.

The museum is in the former Hospice of Saint Roch, founded in the 12th century and enlarged and modified in the 16th, 17th, 18th and 20th centuries. It was restored beween 1960 and 1984. The museum, opened in 1968, contains collections of Gallo-Roman and Merovingian archaeology, Romanesque and Gothic sculpture, medieval religious art and 16th-century Limoges enamels. There are also displays relating to the history of the town and exhibits of 17th–19th-century furniture, paintings and tapestries. A section of the museum is devoted to memorabilia of the novelist, Honoré de Balzac (1799–1850). Another major attraction is a complete 17th-century pharmacy.

Jarville-la-Malgrange

Museum of the History of Iron

Musée de l'Histoire du Fer, Avenue du Général de Gaulle, F-54140 Jarville-la-Malgrange, Meurthe-et-Moselle   ☎ 83 56 01 42
Mon, Wed–Sat 2–5; Sun & public holidays, 2–6. July–Sept, open until 6. Groups by appt.
Ⓒ ⋔ ⇌

The museum, opened in 1986, presents the history of iron-smelting and ironworking, in economic, social and cultural context, from its prehistoric beginnings to the 'Eiffel Tower Age'. It contains 18th–19th-century tilt-hammers and other machinery, scale models of plant and machinery, and a collection of everyday objects made of wrought and cast iron and steel.

Jouy-en-Josas

Oberkampf Museum

Musée Oberkampf, Château de Montebello, Les Metz, F-78350 Jouy-en-Josas, Yvelines   ☎ 1 39 46 80 48
Tues, Thurs, Sat, Sun and public holidays 2–5. Closed Sat, Sun in July and the month of Aug. Groups every day by appt.
Ⓒ ⋔ ⇌

The patterned calicos which began to arrive in Europe from India at the end of the 16th century met with such an enthusiastic reception that Louis XIV eventually banned their importation and imitation in France, in order to protect the traditional manufacture of woollen and silk fabrics. In 1759, 73 years later, it became legal to produce printed fabrics in France and in 1760 Christoph-Philippe Oberkampf (1738–1815) left his native Württemberg and set up in business at Jouy. By the beginning of the 19th century the factory was the most important in Europe, employing 1,322 people. It ceased production in 1843.

The museum tells the story of the factory and the industry and explains the technical processes involved. There are displays of 18th- and 19th-century printed cottons, showing the designs available at different periods. These ranged from floral patterns to fabrics depicting pastoral, theatrical and mythological scenes and

political events. A scale model of the factory indicates the size of the enterprise and letters and commercial documents provide evidence of the market for the firm's products.

Kientzheim

The Vineyard Museum

Musée du Vignoble et des Vins d'Alsace, 1B Grande Rue, F-68240 Kientzheim, Haut-Rhin   ☎ 89 78 21 36
June 15–Oct 31, daily 10–12, 2–6
Ⓒ ⋔ ⇌

The museum, in outbuildings of the Château de la Confrèrie Saint-Etienne, presents the history of vineyard cultivation and wine production over the centuries. There are exhibits showing the life of the wine-producing community and of the tools and implements used in the vineyard. Special sections deal with the diseases of vines, wine in art, wine glasses and traditions linked to wine.

Labastide-Murat

Murat Museum

Musée Murat, place de l'Eglise, F-46240 Labastide-Murat, Lot   ☎ 65 31 12 45
July 1–Sept 14, Wed–Mon 10–12, 2–6. Other months, groups by appt.
Ⓒ

General Joachim Murat (1767–1815), born at Labastide-Murat where his father kept the village inn, was the brother-in-law of Napoleon Bonaparte, He was king of Naples from 1808 to 1814, but condemned to death and shot in

Transport exhibition, with a 1908 Renault in the foreground. Museum of the History of Iron, Jarville-la-Malgrange.

1815. His birthplace became a museum in 1959, after restoration. It contains personal possessions and memorabilia of Murat, including his cradle, together with documents, prints and portraits illustrating his life and career.

La Châtre

Museum of George Sand and the Vallée Noire

Musée George Sand et de la Vallée Noire, rue Venôse, F-36400 La Châtre, Indre
☎ 54 48 36 79
Apr–Sept, daily 9–12, 2–7. Oct–Mar, daily 2–5.
C 🛈 &

The castle which houses the museum was built in the 15th century by Guy de Chauvigny, who was the Lord of La Châtre. There are exhibits of costumes, headdresses and embroidery from Lower Berry and a worldwide collection of birds, containing more than 3,000 specimens. The museum also has manuscripts and memorabilia of George Sand (1804–76), and of other writers and artists who stayed at her house at Nohant.

La Côte-Saint-André

Berlioz Museum

Musée Hector-Berlioz, 69 rue de la République, F-38200 La Côte-Saint-André, Isère
☎ 74 20 24 88
Mar–Dec, Tues–Sun 9–12, 3–6. Feb, Mon–Sat 2–5; Sun 10–12, 2–5.
C ✍

The composer, Hector Berlioz (1803–69) was born in La Côte-Saint-André, where his father was a doctor. His birthplace, where he lived until he was 18, dates from 1680 and was converted into a museum in 1935. It contains portraits and busts of the musician, scores, programmes, correspondence, letters and other memorabilia. Visitors can also see the consulting room of Dr Berlioz, the dining-room, the room in which Hector Berlioz was born, and the rooms of his sisters. There is a listening room in which recordings of works by Berlioz can be heard on request, on Wednesday, Saturday and Sunday afternoons.

La Rochelle

Museum of Fine Art

Musée des Beaux-Arts, 28 rue Gargoulleau, F-17000 La Rochelle, Charente-Maritime
☎ 46 41 64 65
Wed–Mon 2–5
C 🛈

The museum occupies the second floor of the Hôtel Crussol d'Uzès, the former Bishops' Palace, built in 1733–77. The original collections were formed by the town's Society of the Friends of Art and opened to the public in 1844. There are paintings by German, Dutch, Flemish, Spanish and Italian artists, but most of

Wine press. The Vineyard Museum, Kientzheim.

the works on display are French, many of them by artists working in La Rochelle. Two rooms are devoted to the 58 engravings of the Miserere, by Rouault.

Natural History Museum

Musée d'Histoire Naturelle et d'Ethnographie, 28 rue Albert 1er, F-17000 La Rochelle, Charente-Maritime ☎ 46 45 17 87
June 15–Sept 15, Tues–Sun 10–12, 2–6. Sept 16–June 14, Tues–Sun 10–12, 2–5.
C 🛈

La Rochelle's Natural History Museum occupies two buildings facing one another at the entrance to the Jardin des Plantes. One houses the Fleuriau Museum and the other the Lafaille Museum.

The 18th-century La Rochelle naturalist, Clément de Lafaille, bequeathed his Cabinet of Curiosities to the town. It was opened to the public in 1782 and formed the core of a museum of the natural sciences which grew steadily during the 19th century, when it was transferred to the present building, then known as the Hôtel du Gouvernement. Lafaille's collection has been preserved intact. It is the only 18th-century naturalist's cabinet to have survived in its original form.

The Lafaille Museum contains worldwide collections of mammals, birds and reptiles, including specimens of now-extinct species. Among the exhibits are the first giraffe to be seen in France, presented to Charles X by the Pasha of Egypt in 1826, and the first orangutan to be kept alive in France, at the court of the Empress Josephine at Malmaison, in 1808. The museum also has collections of mineralogy, palaeontology and prehistory. These include the complete skeleton of a cave bear.

The most important part of the museum is, however, the Department of Ethnography, which is mainly concerned with the arts and crafts of tribal peoples. Its collections are worldwide, with an emphasis on Oceania and Africa. They include the large amount of material brought back by Dumont d'Urville from the voyages he undertook in 1826–40.

The Fleuriau Regional Museum was founded in 1836 by the Société des Sciences Naturelles de la Charente-Maritime, with the aim of creating a comprehensive study collection of the natural history of the Department. It contains important sections devoted to the geology, palaeontology, prehistory and fauna of the region.

La Tremblade

Maritime Museum

Musée Maritime, 17 boulevard Roger-Létélié, F-17390 La Tremblade, Charente-Maritime
☎ 46 36 02 35
July 1–Sept 15, daily 3–7. Other months, groups by appt.
C

The museum is mainly concerned with the cultivation of oysters, an important industry in the district. There are displays of fossil oysters, oysters at different stages of development, ancient and modern tools and equipment and scientific equipment used in early laboratories, as well as postcards and photographs from the beginning of this century.

Laval

Museum of the Old Castle

Musée du Vieux Château, place de la Trémoille, F-53018 Laval, Mayenne   ☎ 43 53 39 89
Tues–Sun 10–12, 2–6. Closed public holidays.
C 🛈

The museum has sections devoted to Gallo-Roman, Merovingian and medieval antiquities, medieval sculpture and Oriental, Egyptian, Greek and Etruscan antiquities. There are also drawings and watercolours of old Laval by J.-B. Messager. The particular strength of the museum, however, is in its international collection of modern naïve paintings, especially by Henri (Le Douanier) Rousseau (1844–1910), who was a native of Laval. The museum has a number of his paintings, including Le Pont de Grenelle, a reconstruction of his studio and an archive of his notes, letters and other manuscript material.

18th-century cabinet. Museum of Fine Art, La Rochelle.

Le Bourget

Air and Space Museum

Musée de l'Air et de l'Espace, Aérogare du Bourget, F-93350 Le Bourget, Seine-Saint-Denis
☎ 1 48 35 99 99
May–Sept, daily 10–6. Oct–Apr, daily 10–5.
C 🛈 🖬 🚗

Le Bourget was the civilian airport for Paris between the two World Wars and continued in service for a considerable time after 1945. It is now used to display the aviation collections which were kept between 1921 and 1981 at the military aerodrome at Chalais-Meudon and which have since been considerably expanded.

The development of aviation from its beginnings to the present day and the conquest of space are presented in four exhibition halls, in chronological order – Hall A 1912–39; Hall B 1939–45; Hall C, re-establishment of the French aircraft industry after 1945; and Hall D 1945 to the present day. Hall F is devoted to Space and the beginnings of aviation until 1914, and the events of 1914–18 are presented in the former air terminal building. The largest aircraft, including Concorde 001, the first prototype, are displayed outside.

Le Bouschet-de-Pranles

Museum of the Protestant Vivarais

Musée du Vivarais Protestant, Le Bouschet-de-Pranles, F-07000 Privas, Ardèche
☎ 75 64 22 74
Palm Sun–June 15 & Sept 16–Nov 1, Sat, Sun 2.30–6.30. June 16–Sept 15, Mon–Sat 10–12, 2.30–6; Sun 2.30–6. Closed from Nov 1–Palm Sun.
C

This fortified house, built in the 15th and 16th centuries, was the birthplace of the Protestant pastor, Pierre Durand, hanged at Montpellier in 1732, and of his sister, Marie, who was held prisoner at Aigues-Mortes for 38 years. It has been converted into a museum of the Reformed Church in the Vivarais. The exhibits include letters from Pierre and Marie Durand, Royal edicts and other documents, Bibles, Psalters, weapons and other objects dating from the time of the persecution. The original kitchen remains, with its secret entrance to the hiding place used by Protestants avoiding the authorities.

Le Cateau-Cambrésis

Matisse Museum

Musée Matisse, Palais Fénélon, place Ed. Richez, F-59360 Le Cateau-Cambrésis, Nord
☎ 27 84 13 15
Apr–Sept, Wed–Sat 10–12, 2–6; Sun 10–12, 2.30–6. Oct–Mar, Wed–Sat 10–12, 2–5; Sun 10–12.30, 2.30–6.
C 🛈 🚗

Morning, 1952, by Auguste Herbin. Matisse Museum, Le Cateau-Cambrésis.

The painter, Henri Matisse (1869–1954), was born in Le Cateau-Cambrésis and in 1952 he decided to give the town a large collection of his works, including paintings, engravings, drawings, sculpture and illustrated books. The Matisse Museum was established in 1972 and in 1982, when the collection had greatly expanded as a result of the donation and purchase of other works by Matisse and his contemporaries, it was transferred to the 18th-century Palais Fénélon.

The first floor of the museum displays works by Matisse and on the ground floor there are paintings, drawings and sculpture by two local artists, Auguste Herbin (1882–1960) and his great-niece, Geneviève Claisse (b. 1935), both of whom were born at Quélvy, near Le Cateau-Cambrésis.

Le Creusot

Ecomuseum of Le Creusot

Ecomusée de la Communauté Le Creusot/ Montceau-les-Mines, Château de la Verrerie, F-71720 Le Creusot, Sâone-et-Loire
☎ *85 55 01 11*
Tues–Fri 10–12, 2–6; Sat, Sun 2–6.
Ⓒ 🏛 ♿

The Royal Crystal Manufactory at Le Creusot functioned from 1786 until 1833, after which it and the château to which it was attached became the property of the Schneider family of ironmasters. With the closure of this important heavy engineering and armament works after the Second World War, the district became semi-derelict and has only recently been revived as the result of a second industrial revolution. In the 1970s, an area of 382 square km containing Le Creusot and Montceau-les-Mines was designated an 'exploded museum' (musée éclaté)

and became the centre of a famous international experiment, whereby a whole district became an industrial museum and focal centre of research. The château contains exhibitions illustrating the industrial and social history of the district and there are five smaller museums at specialised sites.

Le-Haut-du-Them

Mountain Museum

Musée de Montagne, Château-Lambert, F-70480 Le-Haut-du-Them, Haute-Sâone
☎ *84 20 42 24*
Easter–Nov 1, Mon, Wed–Sat 9–12, 2–6. Groups Sun morning by appt.
Ⓒ ♿

The museum, created in 1975–77, is in the buildings of a mountain farm. The kitchen, living-room and farmer's bedroom on the ground floor are appropriately furnished and equipped, and on the first floor one bedroom contains a loom and the granary has an exhibition of farm tools and equipment. Three plots of land are sown with rye, buckwheat and millet. Mountain huts have been reconstructed in order to present exhibits illustrating the different forest skills – woodcutter, clogmaker, pit-sawyer, timber-sledger, bark-stripper. A watermill and a mountain sawmill have been re-erected on the museum site and restored to working order.

Le Havre

André Malraux Museum of Fine Art

Musée des Beaux-Arts André Malraux, boulevard J. F. Kennedy, F-76600 Le Havre, Seine-Maritime   ☎ *35 42 33 97*
Wed Mon 10 12, 2 6. Closed Jan 1, May 1, 8, July 14, Nov 11, Dec 25.
Ⓕ 🏛

The Museum of Fine Art in Le Havre was established in 1845. It developed considerably during the 19th century and was one of the first museums in France to buy Impressionist paintings. The museum was entirely destroyed by bombing in 1944, but the collections had fortunately been removed to safety elsewhere. The new aluminium, steel and glass building, opened in 1961, opens on to the sea and was conceived as a pilot-museum by André Malraux, who was Minister of Culture at the time. It has remarkable collections of Italian, Flemish, Dutch, Spanish and French paintings from the 16th century to the present day. There are nearly 300 paintings, drawings and watercolours by Boudin, and other artists represented are Corot, Monet, Sisley, Pissarro, Braque, Dubuffet and Dufy.

There are also important collections of glass, crystal, ceramics, engravings, sculpture and pre-Columbian art. One of the museum's most treasured possessions is an Etruscan vase of the 6th century BC.

Corneille's 16th-century 'Maison des Champs', Le Petit-Couronne.

Museum of Medieval Sculpture and Archaeology

Musée de Sculpture Médiévale et d'Archéologie, rue Elisée Rechis, F-76600 Le Havre, Seine-Maritime ☎ 35 47 14 01
Wed–Sun 10–12, 2–6. Closed Jan 1, May 1, 8, July 14, Nov 11, Dec 25.
F

The museum is in the church and monastic buildings of the former priory of Graville-Sainte-Honorine, which date from the 12th–18th centuries. The exhibits consist of architectural fragments, 12th–18th-century statues and statuettes, low-reliefs, polychrome wooden statues, 15th–17th-century chests, documents relating to the priory and a collection of 150 models of 12th–18th-century houses. In the church there is a remarkable series of Romanesque capitals of c. 1090.

Museum of Old Le Havre

Musée de l'Ancien Havre, 1 rue Jérôme Bellarmato, F-76600 Le Havre, Seine-Maritime ☎ 35 42 27 90
Wed–Sun 10–12, 2–6
F ▮

Known as 'the Widow's House', the flint and stone building which is now the museum was built in the late 17th and early 18th centuries for the navigator, Michel-Joseph du Bocage de Bléville, born in Le Havre in 1676. It was damaged by wartime bombing in 1944, but subsequently fully restored. Its collections illustrate the history of the port and town of Le Havre from 1517 to the present day, concentrating especially on the naval shipyards and on the Second World War bombing and reconstruction. The exhibits include engravings showing Le Havre at different stages in its history, ship models, ships' figureheads, Ingouville faïence, porcelain belonging to the Compagnie des Indes, glass and ironwork. A room is devoted to street music in Le Havre at the time of the Third Republic.

Le Pallet

Peter Abelard Museum

Musée Pierre Abelard, Chapelle Saint-Michel, rue Saint-Michel, Le Pallet, F-44330 Vallet, Loire-Atlantique ☎ 40 80 40 24
Apr–Oct, Sat, Sun and public holidays 2.30–6.30. Groups at other times by appt.
C ▮ ♿ ☕

The philosopher and theologian, Peter Abelard (1079–1142) was born at Le Pallet and the museum tells his story and that of Héloise, against the background of his times. There is also a section devoted to the history of Le Pallet and its region from the Gallo-Roman period to the 19th century, with particular attention being paid to the Wars of the Vendée and the Revolutionary period. Other exhibits relate to Admiral Roland-Michel de la Galissonière (1693–1756), Administrator of Canada from 1747 to 1749 and an enthusiastic botanist, who brought back rare species to his native country, and to the history, traditions and economic importance of wine production in the region.

Le Petit-Couronne

Corneille's Maison des Champs

Maison des Champs de Pierre-Corneille, 502 rue Pierre-Corneille, F-76650 Le Petit-Couronne, Seine-Maritime ☎ 35 68 13 89
Fri–Wed 10–12, 2–5 (6 in summer months). Closed 1st week in Sept, month of Nov, and public holidays.
C ▮

This 16th-century house was bought by the father of the dramatist, Pierre Corneille (1606–84) and remained the property of the family throughout the 17th century. Pierre and his brother Thomas spent their school holidays here and subsequently lived in the house with their wives, the Lempérière sisters, and their numerous children. It was bought and restored by the Department in 1874 and opened as a museum in 1878.

The house has been equipped with period furnishings in order to provide an impression of a middle-class country home of the time of Henri IV to Louis XIV. It contains 17th–18th-century engravings and sculptures, archive material, and rare editions of books, including one annotated by Corneille in his own hand.

Le Puy-en-Velay

Crozatier Museum

Musée Crozatier, Jardin Henri Vinay, F-43000 Le Puy-en-Velay, Haute-Loire ☎ 71 09 38 90
May–Sept, Wed–Mon 10–12, 2–6; Oct–Jan & Mar–Apr, Mon, Wed–Sat 10–12, 2–4; Sun 2–4.
C ▮ ☕

Founded in 1820 by Charles Crozatier, the museum moved in 1868 from its original location in an old chapel to a new building, constructed for the purpose. The collections were reorganised and re-displayed after the Second World War. There are displays of regional mineralogy, petrography and palaeontology, and of prehistoric Gallo-Roman, Carolingian, Romanesque and Gothic archaeology, medieval sculpture and furniture and French and Italian faïence. The handicrafts section includes gold- and silversmith's work and the finest lace collection in France. There are also 16th–17th-century Aubusson tapestries and 15th–19th-century European paintings.

Other galleries in the museum contain exhibits of regional natural history and 19th-century models of machines, many of which are now electrically driven. Special attention is given to Emile Reynaud, inventor of the praxinoscope (1888), and a pioneer of moving pictures.

Pillow-Lace Teaching centre

Centre d'Enseignement de la Dentelle au Fuseau, 2 rue Duguesclin, F-43000 Le Puy-en-Velay, Haute-Loire ☎ 71 02 01 68 *Mon–Fri 8.30–12, 2–5.30. Sat, Sun by appt only.*
Ⓒ 🔌 💻 🔌

Pillow-lace, as a domestic industry, prospered in Le Puy during the 16th century. It suffered a setback in the 17th century, following a decree of the Parliament of Toulouse, which forbade the manufacture and sale of lace, but began to flourish again after Jean-Baptiste Colbert (1619–83) became Controller-General of Finance. Its recovery was greatly assisted by the foundation at Le Puy of the Béates, a teaching order of nuns, who brought the lace-makers together in working groups and taught girls to make lace. The industry suffered another blow when the Revolution caused most luxury trades to disappear, but there was a revival later in the 19th century.

The Pillow-Lace Teaching Centre, established in 1974, has set itself the task of maintaining the tradition of lace-making and of safeguarding historic lace. It has collections of European and Oriental lace and of the tools and equipment used in lace-making.

Les Arques

Zadkine Museum

Musée Zadkine, Les Arques, F-46250 Cazals, Lot ☎ 65 22 83 77/65 22 84 81 *July–Sept & Easter holiday, daily 10.30–7. Other months, Sat, Sun 2–6.*
Ⓒ 🔌

The sculptor, Ossip Zadkine (1890–1967) was born in Russia and lived there until he was 17. He studied in Paris and spent the greater part of his life in France. From the 1920s onwards, he lived in a large house in the village of Les Arques and did much of his most important work there. The museum, opened in 1988, contains a representative collection of his sculptures in stone and wood, as well as

engravings and tapestries. There is also an archive of photographs, letters and documents. Zadkine presented a number of his religious works to the church in Les Arques.

Les Epesses

Ecomuseum of the Vendée

Château du Puy du Fou, F-85590 Les Epesses, Vendée ☎ 51 57 60 60 *June–Sept, Wed–Mon 10–12, 3–7. Oct–May, Thurs, Fri 10–12, 2–6; Sat, Sun 2–6. Closed Dec 25–Jan 1.*
Ⓒ 🔌 🔌

The headquarters of the museum is in the 15th–16th-century Castle of Le Puy du Fou, which was acquired and restored by the Department in 1977. It now contains an exhibition illustrating the history of the Vendée from prehistoric times to the present day. Having received his general orientation in this way, the visitor is then directed to five other sites within the ecomuseum area. These include the Museum of the Railways of the Vendée at Les Epesses railway station, and the Museum of Mining and Mines at Faymoreau-les-Mines.

Les Eyzies de Tayac

Museum of Prehistory

Musée National de Préhistoire, Château, F-24620 Les Eyzies de Tayac, Dordogne ☎ 53 06 97 03 *Mar–Nov, Wed–Mon, 9.30–12, 2–6. Dec–Feb, Wed–Mon 9.30–12, 2–5.*
Ⓕ 🔌

The museum is in a 13th-century castle. It has collections of flint and bone objects recovered from the area, carvings in stone and bone, and prehistoric weapons. There are also Magdalenian tombs, mammoth skeletons and copies of the low-reliefs of human figures at Laussel.

Ecomuseum of the Vendée, Les Epesses.

Liré

Joachim du Bellay Museum

Musée Joachim du Bellay, 18 rue du Grand-Logis,
F-49530 Liré, Maine-et-Loire
☎ 40 83 24 13
July–Aug, Tues–Sun 10–12, 2–5.30. Rest of year,
Tues–Thurs, Sat, Sun 10–12, 2–5.30. Closed
Jan 15–Feb 15.
C

The poet, Joachim du Bellay (1522–60), was
born near Liré and the 16th-century house in
the rue du Grand-Logis, now the home of the
museum, belonged to his family, which was
influential in the region. The exhibitions are
devoted half to du Bellay, his family and his
friends, and half to the history, folklore and
ethnography of Liré and the surrounding
district.

Lisores

Fernand Léger Farm Museum

Ferme-Musée Fernand-Léger, Lisores, F-14140
Livarot, Calvados   ☎ 31 63 53 13
Apr–Sept, daily 10–12, 2–7. Oct–Mar, Sat, Sun
10–12, 2–6. Other times by appt.
C ✿

The Léger family farm has always been preserved
much as it is today, Fernand Léger (1881–1955)
having come to work here from time to time.
After his death, his widow transformed the barn
into a museum of his work. It was opened to the
public in 1970 and in it visitors can see bronzes,
ceramics, mosaics, stained glass, lithographs,
one painting, The Cow, and reproductions of
some of his paintings. A large mosaic, The
Farmer's Wife and the Cow, decorates one of the
gables of the building. Several monumental
ceramics are arranged in a nearby meadow.

Lochrist-Inzinzac

Industrial Ecomuseum

Ecomusée Industriel, Zone Industrielle, F-56650
Lochrist-Inzinzac, Morbihan
☎ 97 36 98 21/36 84 43
July–Aug, Mon 2–6; Tues–Sun 9–12, 2–6. Sept–
June, Tues–Fri 9–12, 2–6; Sun, Mon 2–6.
C ♦ ✿

The museum, which has recently been enlarged
and refurbished, is in two parts. The first, in the
former laboratory building of Hennebout
Ironworks, tells the story of the works and has
exhibits illustrating the family and social life of
the workers. The second, the Maison de l'Eau,
in a former works security office at Kerglaw, is
concerned with the history of the local water
supply, with the Blavet Canal, with fishing and
with maritime history. The ecomuseum has
extensive collections relating to both sites.
They include blacksmiths' and other craftsmen's
tools, sculptures, paintings, Breton costumes
and navigational and fishing equipment. There
are also aquaria displaying the fish to be found in
the Blavet Canal.

Medieval circular memorial stones. Fleury
Museum, Lodève.

Lodève

Fleury Museum

Musée Fleury, Square Georges Auric, rue de la
République, F-34700 Lodève, Hérault
☎ 67 44 08 63
Tues–Sun 9–12, 2–6. Closed public holidays.
C ♦

André-Hercule Fleury (1653–1746), Cardinal-
Bishop of Fréjus and Prime Minister of Louis
XV, was born at Lodève. The museum occupies
his former residence, a listed monument, which
was built in the 16th–17th centuries and
extended in the 18th. Lodève is in a region of
exceptional geological and palaeontological
interest. In 1864 the novelist, George Sand,
wrote to the Mayor of Lodève to thank him for
the fossil prints he had sent her and to say how
impressed she had been by the natural heritage
of the area. The museum exhibits illustrate this
heritage and also include prehistoric and Gallo-
Roman material from sites in the region and
elsewhere in France. Other sections are devoted
to medieval archaeology and to traditional rural
life.

Lourdes

Museum of Our Lady

Musée Notre-Dame, Pavillon de Notre-Dame,
Domaine de la Grotte, F-65100 Lourdes,
Hautes-Pyrénées   ☎ 62 94 72 26
Palm Sun–Oct 31, Wed–Mon 9–12, 2.30–6.30.
Nov 1–Palm Sun, Wed–Mon 9.30–12,
2.30–6.
F ♦ ✿

Bernadette Soubirous, later to be beatified as
Saint Bernadette, was born at Lourdes in
miserable circumstances in 1844. In 1858 she
had visions of Our Lady which caused Lourdes
to become an immensely frequented place of
pilgrimage. The Bernadette Museum was
founded in 1932 and in 1974 moved to another
building designed for the purpose. It tells her
story in chronological order – her family life, the
visions, the pilgrimages, the building of the
sanctuaries, the cures effected. There are large
collections of mementoes, models, statues,
banners and decorated candles.

Museum of the Pyrenees

*Musée Pyrénéen, Château Fort de Lourdes,
    F-65100 Lourdes, Hautes-Pyrénées*
    ☎ 62 94 02 04
*Apr–Sept, daily 9–12, 2–7. Oct–Mar, Wed–Mon
    9–12, 2–6. Closed Jan 1, Nov 1, 11, Dec 25.*
Ⓒ ▮ ⚫

The museum, in Lourdes Castle, presents the
natural environment, social history, art and
handicrafts of the Pyrenees. There are
collections of furniture, costumes, craftsmen's
tools, Samadet faïence, popular musical
instruments and ox-bells. Visitors can also see
reconstructions of typical room interiors and
exhibits showing the history of local mountain-
climbing, with mementoes of notable climbs.
Special sections are devoted to prehistoric and
Gallo-Roman archaeology and to the flora and
fauna of the region.

Lyons

Lyons Museum and the Marionette Museum

*Musée Historique et Musée International de la
    Marionnette, 14 rue de Gadagne, F-69005
    Lyon, Rhône   ☎ 78 42 03 61
Wed–Mon 10.45–6*
Ⓕ ▮ ⚫

The Hôtel Gadagne, in which the two museums
are located, dates from the early 16th century. It
was bought and restored by the city of Lyons in
1901, for conversion to an historical museum.
Among its contents are Romanesque sculptures
from churches and abbeys in the Lyons region,

**Puppet from the Lyons Museum and
Marionette Museum, Lyons.**

16th–18th-century Lyons pottery and furniture,
and documents relating to the Revolution and
to the siege of Lyons in 1793. There are also
collections of pewter, Nevers faïence, plans and
maps, portraits of Lyons celebrities, and views of
the city at different periods.

The Marionette Museum, established in
1950, now possesses one of the most celebrated
collections of puppets in the world, which
includes the oldest English puppet, Old Mother
Shipton (c. 1700), complete series of 18th-
century Venetian puppets, and other puppets
from Cambodia, Java, Belgium, Sicily, Russia
and Turkey. A large number of puppets have
been deposited by the Museum of Popular Arts
and Traditions in Paris.

Marius Berliet Automobile Museum

*Fondation de l'Automobile Marius Berliet, 39
    avenue Esquirol, F-69003 Lyon, Rhône
        ☎ 78 54 15 34
Mon–Fri 8.30–12, 1.30–4.30*
Ⓕ ⚫

The foundation was established in 1982. Its
headquarters, documentation centre and
reading room are in the former home of Marius
Berliet, an Art Nouveau building of 1911–12.
Since the late 19th century, Lyons has been a
major centre of the French automobile industry
and the Foundation was created in order to
preserve its automobile heritage and to form a
reference archive. It has a warehouse at Le
Montellier, where it keeps a large collection of
historic vehicles, all of them French and all in
working order, including an almost complete
collection of cars built by Berliet between 1895
and 1940. Items from the collection can be seen
at nine automobile museums in France, and
often appear at motoring events in France and
overseas. Vehicles awaiting restoration are
stored in a building at Saint-Priest.

Museum of Decorative Arts

*Musée des Arts Décoratifs de Lyon, 30 rue de la
    Charité, F-69002 Lyon, Rhône
        ☎ 78 37 15 05
Tues–Sun 10–12, 2–5.30. Closed public holidays.*
Ⓒ ▮

The hôtel, built in 1739, which contains the
museum, adjoins the Museum of the History of
Textiles. Both museums are run by the Lyons
Chamber of Commerce and Industry, which
displays its collections in 18th-century room
settings. The exhibits include 18th-century
furniture by the best Paris makers, clocks,
carpets, Aubusson and Flemish tapestries, 16th–
17th-century Lyons faïence and French
porcelain and silver. There are also Limoges
enamels, ivories, liturgical objects and one of
the best collections in France of 15th–16th-
century Italian majolica.

The museum has a large collection of 16th–
19th-century French, Italian, German, Flemish
and Dutch drawings, some of which are on
display.

Museum of Fine Art

*Musée des Beaux-Arts, Palais Saint-Pierre, 20
    place des Terreaux, F-69001 Lyon, Rhône*
    ☎ 78 28 07 66
Wed–Mon 10.45–6. Closed public holidays.
F ▮ ▬

One of the 15 museums created in 1801 by
Consular Decree, the museum in Lyons was
installed from the beginning in a Benedictine
convent, built in 1659–87. There are
collections of Greek, Etruscan and Roman
archaeology, primitive Christian sculptures and
medieval and Renaissance sculpture. The
paintings represent one of the largest and finest
collections in France – primitives, 18th-century
Italian, 15th–17th-century Flemish, German,
Spanish and, above all, 16th–20th-century
French, with all the great masters of
Impressionism represented and several galleries
devoted to the important School of Lyons,
especially in the 19th century. Sections of the
museum specialise in Renaissance bronzes,
particularly Italian, enamels, ivories, ceramics,
Venetian glass, Islamic art and weapons.

Museum of Gallo-Roman Civilisation

*Musée de la Civilisation Gallo-Romaine, 17 rue
    Cléberg, F-69005 Lyon, Rhône*
    ☎ 78 25 94 68
Wed–Sun 9.30–12, 2–6
F ▮ ⌂

The museum, opened in 1976, was constructed
on the site of the Roman settlement of *Colonia
Copia Lugdunum*. The city was the capital of
Gaul. Excavations carried out during the 19th
and 20th centuries produced an astonishing
range of statues, vases, tombstones, mosaics,
coins and other objects, including the most
remarkable collection of Roman inscriptions in
France. To house these finds a museum was built
on the hillside overlooking the Odeon and
Hadrian's Theatre. The displays include Bronze
Age, Iron Age and Gallo–Roman material from
other sites in France, especially in the Lyons and
Vienne areas.

Museum of the Resistance

*Musée de la Résistance et de la Déportation, 5 rue
    Boileau, F-69006 Lyon, Rhône*
    ☎ 78 93 27 83
Wed–Mon 10.45–1, 2–6. Closed public holidays.
F

Lyons was the capital of the French Resistance
during the Second World War and the museum
established here recalls the activity of the
Resistance network and life in the camps to
which the deportees were taken. Among the
exhibits are the prison register from Montluc,
the gallows from Eysses, a machine which
printed illegal newspapers throughout the
occupation, furniture from the room in which
the Resistance organiser Jean Moulin was
arrested, and a number of mementoes brought
back by the deportees.

Silk-Weavers' Museum

*La Maison des Canuts, 10 rue d'Ivry, F-69004
    Lyon, Rhône*   ☎ 78 28 62 04
*Mon–Fri 8.30–12, 2–6.30; Sat 9–12, 2–6.
    Closed public holidays.*
C ▮

The 'canuts' were the silk-weavers, whose work
once made an important contribution to the
economy of Lyons. The museum tells the story
of silk manufacturing and silk-worm breeding in
the city. The exhibits include hand looms,
historic fabrics, embroidery, patterns and
documents relating to the industry.

Textile History Museum

*Musée Historique des Tissus, 34 rue de la Charité,
    F-69002 Lyon, Rhône*   ☎ 78 37 15 05
Tues–Sun 10–12, 2–5.30. Closed public holidays.
C ▮

Since the 17th century, Lyons has been a major
textile-producing area, especially for silk fabrics.
The museum, opened in 1864, is run by the
Lyons Chamber of Commerce and Industry. It
has large collections of textiles from the
principal centres of production, in both Europe
and the Orient. These include Lyons textiles
from the 17th century onwards, 18th-century
costumes, ecclesiastical vestments and 16th–
17th-century Oriental carpets. There are also
collections of lace, embroidery and tapestries. A
room is devoted to Philippe de la Salle, the
18th-century silk fabric designer.

The mansion in which the museum is
located, the Hôtel Villeroy, is one of the finest
houses in Lyon. Until the Revolution, it was the
seat of government of the Lyons, Beaujolais and
Forez regions. The international centre for the
study of ancient textiles also has its offices in the
building.

**Weaving demonstration. Silk-Weavers'
Museum, Lyons.**

Mâcon

Lamartine Museum

Musée Lamartine, Hôtel Senecé, 41 rue Sigorgne,
F-71000 Mâcon, Saône-et-Loire
☎ *85 38 81 18*
May–Sept, Wed–Mon 2–5. Palm Sun–Apr 30, by
appt.
C

The poet, diplomat and politician, Alphonse de
Lamartine (1790–1869), was born at Mâcon.
The museum occupies a fine town house built in
the early 18th century. Both the collections and
the building belong to the Academy of Mâcon,
which developed a section devoted to Lamartine
in 1960–9. Lamartine was an illustrious member
of this Academy and the museum has
documents relating to him, together with a
number of his personal possessions. The
woodwork, furniture, paintings, tapestries and
objets d'art give the Hôtel Senecé the
atmosphere of a provincial aristocratic
household.

Maillane

Frédéric Mistral Museum

Museon Frédéric Mistral, 11 avenue Lamartine,
F-13910 Maillane, Bouches-du-Rhône
☎ *90 95 74 06*
Apr, May & Oct, Tues–Sun 10–12, 2–5. June–
Sept, Tues–Sun 9–12, 2 6. Nov–Mar, Tues–
Sun 10–12, 2–3. Closed Jan 1, Ascension
Thurs, May 1, July 14, Aug 15, Nov 1, 11,
Dec 25.
F

The Provençal poet, Frédéric Mistral (1830–
1914), was born in Maillane and died there. He
wrote entirely in Provençal and was a leading
figure in the Provençal Renaissance movement.
He received the Nobel Prize in 1905. His widow
continued to live in the house until her death in
1943 and it became a museum in the following
year. It contains the Mistral family furniture,
together with memorabilia and a selection of
Mistral's correspondence.

Marnes-la-Coquette

Pasteur Institute Museum

Musée des Applications de la Recherche, 3
boulevard Raymond Poincaré, F-92430
Marnes-la-Coquette, Hauts-de-Seine
☎ *47 01 15 97*
Mon–Fri 2–6. Closed public holidays and Aug.
C

The building housing the museum is known as
the Pavillon des Cent Gardes and was used as a
barracks by Napoleon III's soldiers. In 1878,
after the collapse of the Napoleonic Empire, it
became public property and in 1844, after
restoration and conversion, it was put at the
disposal of Louis Pasteur (1822–95), to allow
him to continue his experimental work on
rabies. Laboratories and quarters for animals

**Italian velvet, 17th-century. Textile History
Museum, Lyons.**

were installed here, together with a pied-à-terre
for Pasteur himself. He died in the Pavillon des
Cent Gardes in 1895 and his room has been
preserved as a memorial to him. The museum
tells the story of the struggle against infectious
diseases and of the research on which preventive
measures have been based.

Marquèze

Ecomuseum of the Grande Lande

Ecomusée de la Grande-Lande, Marquèze,
F-40630 Sabres, Landes ☎ *58 07 52 70*
Apr 1–June 14 & Sept 16–Oct 31, Sat, Sun,
public holidays 3–5. June 15–Sept 15, daily
9–5.
C

The centre of the ecomuseum, which is in the
Natural Park of the Landes de Gascogne, is a
group of 16th–18th-century wooden buildings in
a clearing in the pine wood. It includes the mid
19th century 'master's' house, with furniture and
household equipment of the period, other
houses, barns, a pigsty, sheep folds, a poultry
house and a mill. These, together with the
associated gardens, vineyards, cultivated fields
and beehives, give an impression of the living
and working conditions of the local people, who
earned much of their living from extracting and
distilling the resin from the pine trees.

Marseilles

Cantini Museum

Musée Cantini, 19 rue Grignan, F-13006
Marseille, Bouches-du-Rhône
☎ *91 54 77 75*
Daily 12–7
C

The museum occupies an 18th-century
mansion, built for the Montgrand family. Its last
owner, Jules Cantini, left it to the city of
Marseilles in 1936, together with his large art
collections, which have since been considerably
augmented. The ground-floor galleries contain
the most important collection, more than 500
items of Marseilles and Provençal faïence. Most
of the rest of the building is devoted to the
museum's collection of contemporary paintings
and sculpture, chiefly by French artists, which is
one of the finest in France.

Grobet-Labadié Museum

Musée Grobet-Labadié, 140 boulevard Longchamp,
F-13001 Marseille, Bouches-du-Rhône
☎ *91 62 21 82*
Mon, Thurs–Sun 10–12, 2–6.30; Wed 2–6.30.
Closed public holidays.
Ⓒ ⓘ

In 1873 the Marseilles industrialist, Alexandre
Labadié (1814–92), built himself a mansion in
the boulevard Longchamp. On his death, his
daughter, Marie, who was at that time married
to Bruno Vayson, inherited the house and its
contents. Widowed in 1896, she later married
her second husband, Louis Grobet, a talented
painter, musician and art collector. They built
up a large art collection which augmented that
of Alexandre Labadié. Being without heirs, the
Grobets gave the house and the collections to
the city of Marseilles, which opened it as a
museum in 1926.

The collection consists of Flemish, German
and Italian primitives, medieval and
Renaissance sculptures, 16th–18th-century
Flemish and French tapestries, and French
paintings and drawings of the 17th, 18th and
19th centuries. There are also collections of
Oriental rugs and carpets, furniture, faïence,
wrought-ironwork and musical instruments.
The exhibits are shown in room settings.

Museum of Fine Art

Musée des Beaux-Arts, Palais Longchamp, 142
boulevard Longchamp, F-13004 Marseille,
Bouches-du-Rhône   ☎ *91 62 21 17*
Wed 2–6.30; Thurs–Mon 10–12, 2–6.30
Ⓒ ⓘ

The museum was one of the 15 Departmental
museums created by Consular Decree in 1801.
In 1869 it was installed in a wing of the Palais
Longchamp, built in 1862 and completely
renovated in 1977–80. A children's museum
was created in 1967.

The main staircase is decorated with two large
paintings by Puvis de Chavannes, *The Greek
Colony of Marseilles* and *Marseilles, Port for the
East*. On the ground floor there are 15th–17th-
century Italian, Flemish, German and French
works, including paintings and sculptures by
Pierre Puget (1620–94), the greatest French
sculptor of the 17th century, who was born in
Marseilles.

The first floor is devoted to 18th and 19th-
century Italian and French paintings, including
works by 19th-century Provençal artists. There
are also some naturalistic sculptures and a few
early 20th-century paintings.

Museum of the History of Marseilles

Musée d'Histoire de Marseille, Centre Bourse,
Square Belsunce, F-13001 Marseille, Bouches-
du-Rhône   ☎ *91 90 42 22*
Tues–Sat 10–7. Closed Jan 1, May 1, July 14,
Dec 25.
Ⓒ ⓘ

**Reconstruction of a Roman quay with wine
amphorae and windlass. Museum of the
History of Marseilles.**

Marseilles was founded as Massilia in 600 BC by
Greeks from Asia Minor. They established their
city and trading centre on a site of about 50
hectares, on the north side of the old harbour.
Excavations carried out in 1967 revealed the
foundations of ancient buildings. A garden
containing these remains has been created on
the site, together with a museum containing the
finds. The exhibition illustrates the history of
Marseilles from 600 BC to the 4th century AD.
Most of the items are concerned with the city's
maritime and trading history and include the
wreck of a Roman ship from the 3rd century
AD.

Museum of Old Marseilles

Musée du Vieux Marseille, 2 rue de la Prison,
F-13002 Marseille, Bouches-du-Rhône
☎ *91 55 10 19*
Wed 2–6.30; Thurs–Mon 10–12, 2–6.30.
Ⓒ ⓘ

The Maison Diamantée, in which the museum
is located, was built *c.* 1570 for a rich Marseilles
merchant. The ground floor is devoted to 18th-
century Provençal furniture, the first floor to life
in Marseilles in the 18th and 19th centuries,
and on the third floor there are paintings and
engravings of Marseilles, including a late 15th-
century view of the old port, painted on wood.
There is also a gallery of traditional 18th- and
19th-century Marseilles costumes.

Museum of Popular Arts and Traditions

Musée des Arts et Traditions Populaires du Terroir
Marseillais, 5 place des Héros, F-13003
Marseille, Bouches-du-Rhône
☎ *91 68 14 38*
Apr–Sept, Sat–Mon 3–7. Oct–Mar, Sat–Mon
2–6. Other times by appt.
Ⓒ ⓘ ⚘

In 1925 the Château Gombert, a Renaissance-
style building with battlements and turrets, was
constructed to house the museum, a private
foundation run by volunteers. The museum is
concerned with the history of the rural areas
close to Marseilles. It has reconstructions of
domestic interiors and collections of costumes

and accessories, agricultural implements, Provençal musical instruments and traditional figures used in Christmas cribs. There is a special display of religious objects used by country people.

Natural History Museum

Musée d'Histoire Naturelle, Palais Longchamp, 142 boulevard Longchamp, F-13004 Marseille, Bouches-du-Rhône
☎ 91 62 30 78
Mon, Thurs–Sun 10–12, 2–6; Wed 2–6
C

The museum occupies part of the Palais Longchamp, an elaborate water tower, built in the mid 19th century when the water from the Durance was brought to Marseilles. Its collections illustrate the natural history of Provence and include exhibits of palaeontology, birds, mammals, shells and prehistoric archaeology. There is also an aquarium, containing fish found in the region.

The Roman Docks

Musée des Docks Romains, 28 place Vivaux, F-13002 Marseille, Bouches-du-Rhône
☎ 91 91 24 62
Wed 2–6.30, Thurs–Mon 10–12, 2–6.30
C 🛈

The existence of the docks was revealed in 1947, during excavations at the Old Port. The remains include those of a storehouse for 30 large jars and of a granary, parts of 2nd–3rd-century ships and collections of amphorae and coins. An introductory exhibition shows, with the help of plans, models and documents, the extent of the ancient town and the network of roads and sea-routes which served it.

Medan

Emile Zola Museum

Musée Emile Zola, 26 rue Pasteur, Medan, Yvelines
☎ 39 75 35 65
June–Sept, daily 2–7. Oct–May, daily 2–6.
C 🖉

The novelist, Emile Zola (1840–1902) bought this house in 1878 and enlarged it in stages between 1879 and 1886. He referred to it as his 'rabbit hutch on the banks of the Seine' and its furnishings and decorations bear witness to his strange and eclectic taste. Reorganised as a museum, it contains a wide range of objects illustrating his life and career. A section is devoted to the Dreyfus affair.

Meisenthal

Glass and Crystal Museum

Maison du Verre et du Cristal, place Robert Schuman, F-57960 Meisenthal, Moselle
☎ 87 96 91 51
Easter–June & Oct, Mon–Fri 2–4; Sat, Sun 2–6. July–Sept, daily 2–6. Other times by appt.
C 🛈 ⚲

There was a glassmaking industry in the Northern Vosges from 1704 until 1969. The museum, opened in 1983 and run by the Association of Friends of the Museum, has been installed in some of the earliest buildings of the Meisenthal glassworks. There are reconstructions of a kiln and the manufacturing hall and displays showing the techniques involved. The exhibits include tools and equipment used in the manufacture and decoration of glass and crystal and a large number of examples of Meisenthal products. A section of the museum is devoted to the life of glassworkers and their families in the early part of the present century.

Melun

Gendarmerie Museum

Musée de la Gendarmerie Nationale, Quartier Augereau, Ecole des Officiers de la Gendarmerie Nationale, F-77010 Melun, Seine-et-Marne   ☎ 64 52 22 90
Jan–July & Sept–Dec, Mon–Fri 8–12, 2–6 by appt. Closed public holidays.
F 🛈 ⚲

The museum is on the premises of the Officers' School of the Gendarmerie. It presents the history of the Gendarmerie and its predecessor, the Maréchaussée, from its 13th-century beginnings to the present day. The modern name dates from 1791. The exhibits include documents, paintings, uniforms and weapons and illustrate the organisation of the Gendarmerie in both France and her colonial empire.

Glass wall-vase decorated with enamel, c. 1900. Glass and Crystal Museum, Meisenthal.

Menton

Jean Cocteau Museum

Musée Jean Cocteau, Le Bastion, Vieux Port,
F-06500 Menton, Alpes-Maritimes
☎ 93 57 72 30
June 15–Sept 15, Wed–Mon 10–12, 3–7.
Sept 16–June 14, Wed–Mon 10–12, 2–6.
Closed public holidays.
F ▮ ⌂

Jean Cocteau (1889–1963) was distinguished as
a poet, dramatist and artist. The museum, in a
17th-century fortress, contains pastels,
ceramics, sculpture, paintings and tapestries by
him, together with memorabilia and
correspondence. There are also works by his
friends, given to the museum in memory of
Cocteau.

Museum of Prehistory

Musée Préhistoire Régionale, rue Lorédan Larchey,
F-06500 Menton, Alpes-Maritimes
☎ 93 35 84 64
June 15–Sept 15, Wed–Mon 10–12, 3–7.
Sept 16–June 14, Wed–Mon 10–12, 2–6.
Closed public holidays.
F ▮

The museum reopened in 1988 after
reorganisation and presents a million years of
prehistory on the Cote d'Azur, with collections
from sites at Rochers-Rouges, the Lazaret grotto
at Nice, and elsewhere in the region.
    There are also displays of 14th–17th-century
Italian, Flemish, Spanish and Dutch paintings
and of 19th–20th-century works by French
artists. Other sections of the museum are
devoted to the history and folklore of Menton
and the surrounding area.

Palais Carnoles

Musée Palais Carnoles, 3 avenue de la Madone,
F-06500 Menton, Alpes-Maritimes
☎ 93 35 49 71
June 15–Sept 15, Wed–Mon 10–12, 3–7.
Sept 16–June 14, Wed–Mon 10–12, 2–6.
Closed public holidays.
F ▮ ⌂

The museum is in the former palace of the
princes of Monaco. Its collections are mainly of
paintings – Italian and French primitives, works
by 16th-century Spanish, Italian and Flemish
painters, 17th–18th-century paintings by artists
of the School of Nice, and 18th–20th-century
French and English paintings.

Meudon

Museum of Art and History

Musée d'Art et d'Histoire, 11 rue des Pierres,
F-92190 Meudon, Hauts-de-Seine
☎ 1 45 34 75 19
Wed–Sun 2–6. Closed Jan 1, May 1, July 14,
Aug 15.
F ▮ ⌂

Hercules the Archer by Emile-Antoine
Bourdelle (1861–1929), a native of
Montauban. Ingres Museum, Montauban.

Part of the building in which the museum is
situated dates from the 16th century. Additions
were made during the 17th and 18th centuries.
In 1676 the house was bought by Armande
Béjart, the widow of Molière, the assumed name
of Jean-Baptiste Poquelin (1622–73). Since
1973, it has been a museum, with collections of
16th–20th-century paintings and drawings,
Rodin sculptures, ceramics and glass. There are
sections dealing with the Meudon observatory,
aircraft manufacturing at Meudon and the
history of the Château-Vieux and Château-
Neuf, their owners and their guests.

Rodin Museum

Musée Rodin, 19 avenue Auguste-Rodin, F-92190
*   Meudon, Hauts-de-Seine   ☎ 1 45 34 13 09*
Apr–Oct, Sat, Sun, Mon 1–7
C ⌀

The sculptor, Auguste Rodin (1841–1917),
occupied the Villa des Brillants, a Victorian
house in the Louis XIII-suburban style, from
1895 until his death. The museum was installed
in it and a large annexe was built in 1929–32,
having as its entrance the 1681 portico from the
Château d'Issy, which Rodin had bought. The
annexe contains the plaster models of Rodin's
principal monuments. There are also sketches,
studies and models showing the stages by which
Rodin developed his work. Auguste Rodin and
his wife are buried in the garden beneath a
replica of his statute, *The Thinker.*

Montauban

Ingres Museum

Musée Ingres, 19 rue de l'Hôtel-de-Ville, F-82013
Montauban, Tarn-et-Garonne
☎ 63 63 18 04
July–Aug, daily 9.30–12, 1.30–6. Sept–June,
Tues–Sat 10–12, 2–6; Sun 2–6.
C ▮ ⌂

The painter, Jean Auguste Dominique Ingres (1780–1867), was born in Montauban. The museum dedicated to him occupies the former Bishop's Palace, which was built during the 17th century on the site of a 14th-century fortress. After the Revolution, it was converted first into a town hall and then into a museum.

The collections include 30 paintings by Ingres and more than 1,000 drawings left by Ingres to his native town, as well as paintings by his pupils. There are also more general collections of 15th–20th-century French and foreign art, French faïence, medieval and Renaissance religious sculpture and of Gallo-Roman, Merovingian and Carolingian archaeology from local sites.

Mont-de-Marsan

Despiau-Wlerick Museum

Musée Despiau-Wlerick, place Pujolin, F-40000 Mont-de-Marsan, Landes   ☎ 58 75 00 45
Tues–Sat 9.30–12, 2–6; Sun 2–6.
F ▌ ⌂

The museum is in the keep of a 13th–14th-century castle, which was built on Roman foundations, and in an adjacent Romanesque house, restored for museum purposes in 1970. It is the only museum in France which specialises in sculpture of the 1920s and 1930s, with an emphasis on the work of two local artists, Charles Despiau (1874–1946) and Robert Wlerick (1881–1944). There are also works by the sculptor and potter, Edouard Cazoux (1889–1974), and a collection of 18th-century faïence from the factory at Samadet.

Other sections of the museum have collections of paintings, glass, and of archaeology and natural history of the region. A sculpture garden contains 20th-century French works.

A visit to Rousseau's house, Mont Louis, by the Marshal of Luxembourg. Jean-Jacques Rousseau Museum, Montmorency.

Montfort-l'Amaury

Maurice Ravel Museum

Musée Maurice Ravel, 5 rue Maurice-Ravel, F-78490 Montfort-l'Amaury, Yvelines
☎ 34 86 00 89
Mon, Wed, Thurs 2.30–6; Sat, Sun 9–11.30, 2–6.
C

The composer, Maurice Ravel (1875–1937), lived here from 1921 until his death, the most productive period of his life. The interior of this neo-Baroque house, built in 1900, was altered by Ravel, but has been little changed since then. The furnishings and arrangement are much as he left them, including the baby-grand piano at which he composed many of his works.

Montmorency

Jean-Jacques Rousseau Museum

Musée Jean-Jacques Rousseau, 4 rue du Mont-Louis, F-95160 Montmorency, Val d'Oise
☎ 39 64 80 13
Tues–Sun 2–6. Closed Jan 1, May 1, Dec 25.
C ▌ ⌂

The Montmorency family is one of the most illustrious in France. Originally the Bouchards, they came to the village of Montmorency in the 11th century and adopted its name. The writer and philosopher, Jean-Jacques Rousseau (1712–78) lived in a house here, 'Le Mont Louis', from 1757 to 1762. During this period he wrote Le Contrat Social, Emile and La Nouvelle Héloïse. 'Le Mont Louis' is now a museum dedicated to him. It contains his furniture, autograph letters, manuscripts, and early editions of his works, some annotated by him.

Montpellier

Fabre Museum

Musée Fabre, 13 rue Montpellieret, F-34000 Montpellier, Hérault   ☎ 67 66 06 34
Tues–Fri 9–12, 2–5.30; Sat, Sun 9–12, 2–5.
C ▌

The museum has one of the most important art collections in the provinces. It existed in embryo in 1798, as a result of the confiscation of the property of aristocratic families and the Church by the Revolutionary government. It was transformed in 1925 as a result of the gift to his native town by the painter, François-Xavier Fabre (1766–1837) of the collection of Italian paintings he had formed during his residence in Italy. Other major donations followed during the second half of the 19th century. The Bruyas Gallery commemorates the curious resident of Montpellier who was equally famous for his fondness for paintings and for his vanity. There are 17 portraits of him.

French painting of the 18th and 19th centuries is strongly represented. Among the exhibits is a remarkable group of works by Houdon.

Montreuil

Museum of Living History

*Musée de l'Histoire Vivante, Parc de Montreau,
31 boulevard Théophile-Sueur, F-93100
Montreuil, Seine-Saint-Denis*
☎ 18 54 85 66
Tues–Sun 10–5
© C

The museum was founded in 1937 by the
Communist deputy, Jacques Duclos. It is
concerned with the history of political and
social struggle in France, mainly by the political
left and with the history of Montreuil, which is
a mainly working-class district of Paris. The
principal events, from the Revolution of 1789 to
the Commune and the Popular Front, are
illustrated by documents (7,000 for the
Commune alone), paintings, manuscripts,
prints, caricatures, medals, photographs and a
wide range of objects. The documents
concerning Marx and Engels are particularly
important.

Morosaglia (Corsica)

Pascal Paoli Museum

*Musée Pascal Paoli, Morosaglia, F-20218 Ponte
Leccia, Haute-Corse*   ☎ 95 31 09 12
Daily 9–12, 3–6
© C

The museum is in the birthplace of Pascal Paoli
(1725–1807), the hero of the Corsican War of
Independence. The collections, which include a
number of historical documents, illustrate his
life and career. His ashes were brought back
from England in 1889 and placed in a marble
tomb in one of the ground-floor rooms which
has been converted into a chapel.

**Equipment for hand-blocking textiles. Museum
of Printed Textiles, Mulhouse.**

Moustiers-Sainte-Marie

Faïence Museum

*Musée de la Faïence, Presbytère, F-04360
Moustiers-Sainte-Marie, Alpes-de-Haute-
Provence*   ☎ 92 74 66 19
*Apr 1–June 3 & Sept–Oct, daily 10–12, 2–6.
July–Aug, daily 9–12, 2–7.*
© C ▯

Moustiers is traditionally one of the most
important French centres for the manufacture of
faïence. The museum, which since 1978 has
been in the crypt below the Presbytery, presents
examples of Moustiers faïence, grouped by
factory. There are also displays of tools, moulds
and other equipment.

Mulhouse

French Railway Museum

*Musée Français du Chemin de Fer, 2 rue Alfred de
Glehn, F-68200 Mulhouse, Haut-Rhin*
☎ 89 42 25 67
*Apr–Sept, daily 9–6. Oct–Mar, daily 9–5. Closed
Jan 1, Dec 25, 26.*
© C ▯ ▭ ▱

In 1969 the French Ministry of Transport made
it possible for SNCF, the Société Nationale des
Chemins de Fer Français, to house its historic
collections in Mulhouse. The museum was
temporarily located in the disused depot of
Mulhouse-Nord and in 1976 it was opened on
its permanent site, where there is a large hall
containing 1,350 metres of track in 12 parallel
bays and an enclosed yard, which is used to
display signalling and other fixed equipment.

The collections illustrate the technical and
social history of railways in France. There is a
wide range of locomotives and rolling stock,
including pullman and sleeping cars and the
trains of French heads of state.

Museum of Printed Textiles

*Musée de l'Impression sur Etoffes, 3 rue des
Bonnes-Gens, F-68100 Mulhouse, Haut-
Rhin* ☎ 89 45 51 20
*Wed–Mon 10–12, 2–6. Closed Jan 1, Easter Sun,
May 1, Whit Sun, July 14, Nov 1, 11,
Dec 25, 26.*

C 🛉

Alsace has been an important centre of textile
printing for many years. The building housing
the museum was designed in 1884 for the Fine
Arts collection belonging to the Industrial
Society of Mulhouse. Since 1955 it has been
occupied by the Museum of Printed Textiles.
The main collection consists of textiles from all
five continents. There are also displays which
illustrate the evolution of textile printing
machinery, and which explain the various
processes of engraving and printing.
Demonstrations of printing take place on
Monday, Wednesday and Friday afternoons
during the summer months.

Mussidan

Voulgre Museum of Popular Arts

*Musée des Arts et Traditions Populaires du Périgord
du Docteur André Voulgre, 1 rue Raoul
Grassin, F-24400 Mussidan, Dordogne*
☎ 53 81 23 55
*June 15–Sept 15, Wed–Mon 9.30–12, 2–6. Oct–
Nov & Mar–June 14, Sat, Sun and public
holidays 2–6. Groups throughout the year
Wed–Mon by appt. Closed Sept 16–30 and
Dec–Feb.*

C 🛖

The museum is in an 18th-century
Charterhouse, furnished in period style. There
are reconstructions of the interior of a 19th-
century Périgord middle-class house and of
craftsmen's workshops and displays of costumes,
furniture, domestic equipment and agricultural
tools and equipment, including a threshing
machine driven by a steam engine. Audio-visual
displays allow visitors to see traditional
craftsmen at their work.

Nancy

Cordeliers Chapel

*Eglise des Cordeliers, 66 Grande rue, F-54000
Nancy, Meurthe-et-Moselle* ☎ 83 32 18 74
*July–Aug, Mon, Wed–Sat 10–12, 2–5; Sun and
public holidays 10–12, 2–6. Remainder of year,
Wed–Mon 10–12, 2–5.*

C

This chapel was built in 1482–6 and decorated
in the late 15th and the early 16th centuries. It
was restored in 1938 in order to receive some of
the religious sculptures, especially from
memorials, which belonged to the museum.
Outstanding among these are the family tombs
of the princes and dukes of Lorraine.

In the adjoining Cordeliers Convent are
exhibits illustrating life in Lorraine before the

coming of industrialisation. There are
reconstructions of room interiors and religious
paintings from churches in Nancy.

Museum of Fine Art

*Musée des Beaux Arts, 3 place Stanislas, F-54000
Nancy, Meurthe-et-Moselle*
☎ 83 35 55 53
*Mon 2–6; Wed–Sun 10–12, 2–6. Closed Jan 1,
May 1, July 14, Nov 1, Dec 25.*

C 🛉

The museum was created in 1793, its first
collections coming from the possessions of the
Church and aristocratic families seized by the
Revolutionary government. In 1801 it became
one of the 15 Departmental museums designated
by Consular Decree. It contains 15th–19th-
century paintings, especially Italian, but the
bulk of its collection is composed of works by
16th–19th-century French artists. The Cabinet
of Graphic Art has 800 drawings, mostly
French. In 1982 the museum acquired 115 items
of glassware, made by the Daum crystal works at
Nancy and dating from the end of the 19th
century to the present day.

Museum of Lorraine

*Musée Historique Lorrain, Palais Ducal, 64
Grande Rue, F-5400 Nancy, Meurthe-et-
Moselle*
☎ 83 32 18 74
*July–Aug, Mon, Wed–Sat 10–12, 2–5; Sun and
public holidays 10–12, 2–6. Remainder of year,
Wed–Mon 10–12, 2–5.*

C

This museum is concerned with the
archaeology, history and art of Lorraine. Special
features include 16th-century Tournai
tapestries, the works of 17th-century Lorraine
painters and engravers and Lorraine faïence.

**The kitchen sink. Voulgre Museum of Popular
Arts, Mussidan.**

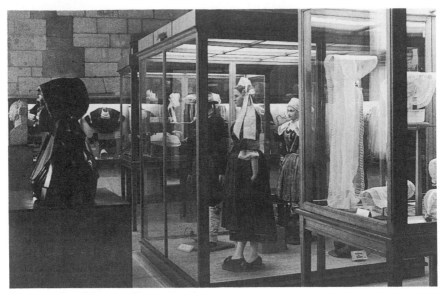

Costume gallery. Museum of Breton Popular
Art, Nantes.

Nantes

Jules Verne Museum

*Musée Jules Verne, 3 rue de l'Hermitage, F-44100
    Nantes, Loire-Atlantique*   ☎ 40 69 72 52
Mon, Wed–Sat 10–12, 2–5; Sun 2–5. Closed
    public holidays.
Ⓒ (ex children) ⚘

The popular writer of adventure stories, Jules
Verne (1828–1905), was born in Nantes. The
museum dedicated to him is run by the Public
Library of Nantes, and is located in a
picturesque villa. Its collections illustrate the
writer's life and his career as a writer. There are
memorabilia of Jules Verne, manuscript letters
to members of his family and books by and about
Verne in the original French and in foreign
languages. Among the special exhibits are a
reconstruction of his sitting room in Amiens
and models of the inventions described in his
books. Visitors can also see his yacht, *Nautilus*,
and the globe which he used when planning the
routes to be followed by his heroes in their
travels around the world.

Museum of Breton Popular Art

*Musée d'Art Populaire Régional, Château des Ducs
    de Bretagne, 1 place Marc Elder, F-44000
    Nantes, Loire-Atlantique*   ☎ 40 47 18 15
July–Aug, daily 10–12, 2–6. Sept–June, Wed–
    Mon 10–12, 2–6. Closed public holidays.
Ⓒ 🅰 ♿

The collections illustrate the traditional arts and
crafts of Brittany from the 16th century to the
early 20th. They include costumes and
headdresses, 17th–19th-century furniture and
ironwork made in Nantes between 1600 and
1900. There is also a notable collection of
17th-century pottery from western France, with

pieces from the Le Croisic factory. The
museum, in the late-15th-century castle of the
Dukes of Brittany, has two reconstructions of
room interiors from the marchlands and from
the Saille in the salt-panning region.

Museum of Fine Art

*Musée des Beaux-Arts, 10 rue Georges-
    Clemenceau, F-44000 Nantes, Loire-
    Atlantique*   ☎ 40 74 53 24
Mon, Wed–Sat 10–12, 1–5.45; Sun 11–5. Free
    admission Sat, Sun.
Ⓒ

This was one of the 15 Departmental museums
created by Consular Decree in 1801. Its real
development, however, began with the
acquisition of a very magnificent private
collection in 1810. The 19th-century buildings
are very large and arranged around a central
courtyard. A major reorganisation of the
collections has recently taken place. The
foreign paintings, mostly Italian, Flemish and
Dutch, are of high quality. The majority of the
pictures in the museum are French, ranging
from the 17th century to the 20th, and
including important works by Georges de la
Tour, Ingres and the Impressionists and Post-
Impressionists. There is also a department of
19th- and 20th-century prints and drawings.

Salorges Museum

*Musée des Salorges, Château des Ducs de Bretagne,
    1 place Marc Elder, F-44000 Nantes, Loire-
    Atlantique*   ☎ 40 47 18 15
July–Aug, daily 10–12, 2–6. Sept–June, Wed–
    Mon 10–12, 2–6. Closed public holidays.
Ⓒ 🅰 ♿

The museum, founded in 1928, was transferred
to the castle of the dukes of Brittany in 1955. It
was created by two Nantes industrialists, Louis
and Maurice Amieux, to show the commercial,
colonial and industrial history of Nantes since

the 18th century. There are sections illustrating the triangular slave trade between France, Africa and America and the general maritime history of Nantes, with displays of ship-models and ships' figureheads. A diorama shows Nantes as it was in the late 19th century.

Narbonne

Archaeological Museum

*Musée Archéologique, Hôtel-de-Ville, BP 823,
    F-11108 Narbonne, Aude*   ☎ *68 32 31 60*
*May–Sept, Mon, Sat, Sun 10–11.50, 2–6; Tues–
    Fri 10–11.50, 2–6, 9–11. Oct–Apr, Tues–
    Sun 10–11.50, 2–5. Closed Jan 1, May 1,
    July 14, Nov 1, Dec 25.*
C 🏛

The museum, housed in the former Archbishop's Palace, contains important collections from prehistoric and Roman sites in the district. *Narbo Martius*, established in 118 BC, was the first Roman colony ouside Italy and the first provincial capital. Among the exhibits discovered during excavations are a milestone (120 BC), contemporary with the construction of the Domitian Way, bearing the oldest Latin inscription of the Gauls; a splendid statue of the drunken Silenus; portraits of the dead and illustrations of their occupations, as in the famous Column of the Miller; sculptures showing ships; and inscriptions relating to the shipowners of Narbonne.

Art Museum

*Musée d'Art et d'Histoire, BP 823, F-11108
    Narbonne, Aude*   ☎ *68 32 31 60*
*May–Sept, daily 10–11.50, 2–6. Oct–Apr, Tues–
    Sun 10–11.50, 2–5. Closed Jan 1, May 1,
    July 14, Nov 1, Dec 25.*
C 🏛

The museum is on the first floor, the Apartments, of the Archbishop's Palace. The decorations date from the 17th century. There are several portraits and a large collection of French and foreign paintings. Other exhibits are of French porcelain, pharmacy jars in Montpellier faïence, English alabasters, medieval paintings on wood, jewellery and French furniture. The museum also displays the library of Le Goux de la Berchère, who was Archbishop from 1703 to 1719. A number of the volumes bear his coat of arms.

The Roman Warehouse

*Horreum Romain, BP 823, F-11108 Narbonne,
    Aude*   ☎ *68 32 31 60*
*May–Sept, daily 10–11.50, 2–6. Oct–Apr, Tues–
    Sun 10–11.50, 2–5.15. Closed Jan 1, May 1,
    July 14, Nov 1, Dec 25.*
C 🏛

The Horreum Romain, completed at the end of the 1st century BC, was a very large public warehouse, forming the basement of a market. It consisted of small cells opening off galleries.

This arrangement made it possible to classify goods into categories for storage purposes.

Part of the building is now used as a lapidarium, to display carved fragments of Roman buildings which no longer exist – the Amphitheatre, the Circus, the Theatre, the Public Baths and Cybele's Temple. There are also two models of the now-vanished Capitol, a magnificent monument, comparable to the Capitol in Rome.

Neuvic d'Ussel

Henri Queuille Museum of the Resistance

*Musée de la Résistance Henri Queuille, rue du
    Commerce, F-19160 Neuvic d'Ussel,
    Corrèze*   ☎ *55 95 96 87*
*May–June 14 & Sept 15–Oct, Sun 10–12, 3–6.
    June 15–Sept 15, daily 10–12, 3–6.*
C 🏛

The politician, Henri Queuille (1884–1960), was responsible for the reorganisation of French railways in 1937 and was known as 'the father of the SNCF'. He spent the war years in London and returned after the war to reorganise the radical Left and, between 1947 and 1951, the finances of the country. He also played an important part in the electrification of rural France.

The museum, established in 1982 in the former family home, illustrates the life and career of Henri Queuille, against the background of the political history of the time. There are also displays showing the German occupation and the activities of the Resistance in the region during the war years.

Nice

Anatole Jakovsky Museum of Naïve Art

*Musée International d'Art Naif Anatole Jakovsky,
    Château Sainte Hélène, avenue Val Marie,
    F-06200 Nice, Alpes-Maritimes*
    ☎ *93 71 78 33*
*May–Sept, Wed–Mon 10–12, 2–6. Oct–Apr,
    Wed–Mon 10–12, 2–5. Closed Jan 1, Easter
    Mon, May 1, Dec 25.*
F 🏛 ♿ 🚌

The Pantheon by Louis Vivin (1861–1936).
Anatole Jakovsky Museum of Naïve Art.

In 1978 the writer and art critic, Anatole Jakovsky, gave his library and his remarkable collection of naïve art to the city of Nice. The museum containing them was opened in 1982. Jakovsky, an international authority on the subject, was anxious that this form of art should be taken seriously, describing it as 'the realisation of the paradise and dreams of childhood'. The collection, ranging from the 18th century to the present day, contains 600 paintings from 27 countries. To display it and to provide research facilities, the municipality of Nice bought the Château Sainte Hélène which, with its hillside site and its surrounding park, encourages the dream-like atmosphere which Jakovsky believed to be necessary for the proper appreciation of naïve art.

Chagall Museum of the Message of the Bible

Musée National Message Biblique Marc Chagall, avenue Docteur Ménard, Angle Boulevard de Cimiez, F-06000 Nice, Alpes-Maritimes
☎ 93 81 75 75
July–Sept, Wed–Mon 10–7. Oct–June, Wed–Mon 10–12.30, 2–5.30.
Ⓒ 🛈 💻

The Russian painter, Marc Chagall (1887–1985) spent much of his life in France and became a French citizen. The museum in Nice was built during the artist's lifetime and opened to the public in 1973. It contains a large collection of his work, including paintings, drawings, engravings, lithographs, sculpture, stained glass, tapestries and mosaics. The central feature of the museum consists of 17 large paintings, illustrating the Message of the Bible, together with his 205 preparatory sketches for the series.

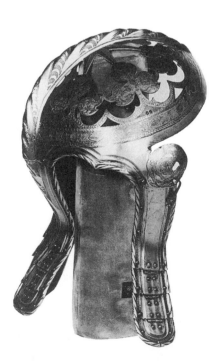

Matisse Museum

Musée Matisse, 164 avenue des Arènes, F-06000 Nice, Alpes-Maritimes   ☎ 93 53 17 70
Please enquire locally for opening times
Ⓕ 🛈 💻 🚗 ■

Henri Matisse (1869–1954) went to Nice for the winter in 1914 and spent most of the rest of his life on the Riviera. The museum in Nice dedicated to him was opened in 1963 and has very recently been reconstructed and enlarged. The site includes an olive grove, a former Franciscan monastery, Roman remains and an Italian-style garden, and lies not far from the Chagall Museum.

The permanent collections include paintings, drawings, engravings, models and sculptures by Matisse, together with furniture and personal possessions. There are temporary exhibitions relating to Matisse, his contemporaries and his times.

Museum of Fine Art

Musée des Beaux-Arts, 33 avenue des Baumettes, F-06000 Nice, Alpes-Maritimes
☎ 93 44 50 72
May 2–Sept, Tues–Sun 10–12, 3–6. Oct–Apr, Tues–Sun 10–12, 2–5. Closed Jan 1, Easter Sun, May 1, Dec 25.
Ⓕ 🛈

The museum building was formerly the Residence of the Ukrainian Princess Kotschuberg. Its construction began in 1878 and was completed by a later owner, the American, James Thomas. It is an important example of the architecture of the Belle Epoque. The collections of paintings and sculpture illustrate the development of French art during the 19th century and include works by Fragonard, Jean-Baptiste and Carlo Vanloo, Ziem and Dufy. There are also Italian primitive paintings, Japanese and Chinese sculpture and Gobelins tapestries. A special section is devoted to the history of the Nice carnival.

Palais Masséna

Musée d'Art et d'Histoire, 65 rue de France, F-06000 Nice, Alpes-Maritimes
☎ 93 88 11 34/93 88 06 22
Apr–Sept, Tues–Sun 10–12, 3–6. Dec–Mar, Tues–Sun 10–12, 2–5.
Ⓕ 🛈 ♿

The mansion containing the museum was built in 1900 for Victor Masséna, prince of Essling. It contains memorabilia of Masséna and exhibitions illustrating the history of Nice. There are also collections of 15th–18th-century religious art, 15th–16th-century paintings, 16th–19th-century faïence from factories in the region, furniture, arms and armour and jewellery. Among the more modern works of art in the possession of the museum are primitives by Nice artists and Impressionist paintings.

Helmet made for the Emperor Charles V, 16th-century. Palais Masséna, Nice.

Gallo-Roman tombstone. Archaeological Museum, Nîmes.

Terra Amata Museum

*Musée de Paléontologie Humaine de Terra Amata,
    25 boulevard Carnot, F-06300 Nice, Alpes-
    Maritimes* ☎ 93 55 59 93
*Tues–Sat 9–12, 2–6. Closed Jan 1, Easter Sun,
    May 1, Dec 25.*
F ⚲

In 1958, foundation work for a new block of flats revealed the existence of a habitation site of Stone Age hunters: huts made of stakes bent over to form a roof, the ridge supported by posts and the base of the stakes supported by heavy stones. Inside each hut was a hearth. Subsequent excavation and scientific research on the fossil material showed the date to have been c. 400,000 BC.

   With the agreement of the contractors, the site was preserved as an underground museum, in a basement originally intended for use as a car park. The museum provides an interpretation of the site and of the material discovered in the course of the excavations.

Nîmes

Archaeological Museum

*Musée Archéologique, 13 boulevard Amiral
    Courbet, F-30000 Nîmes, Gard*
☎ 66 67 25 57
*June 15–Sept 15, Mon–Sat 9–7; Sun 2–7.
    Sept 16–June 14, Mon–Sat 9–12, 2–6;
    Sun 2–6.*
F

The museum is in the town's former Jesuit College, the chapel of which is an excellent example of 17th-century Jesuit architecture. It contains displays of Roman, Gallo-Roman, Gallo-Grecian and Celtic archaeological material from local sites. Sections of the museum are devoted to Roman and pre-Roman sculptures and inscriptions, to daily life in the Roman period, to Roman glass and coins, and to Greek, Etruscan and Punic ceramics. There are also Roman portrait busts and mosaics.

Museum of Contemporary Art

*Musée d'Art Contemporain, Carré d'Art, 3B rue
    Saint-Yon, F-30000 Nîmes, Gard*
☎ 66 76 70 76
Daily 9–12, 1.30–6.30
C ⚲

The museum was opened at the end of 1990, in a new building which embodies the neo-classical façade of a theatre which was constructed in 1807 and burnt down in 1952. Acquisition began in 1985 and the collections now consist of about 200 works, two-thirds of which are by French artists. About a quarter of them either work on the Côte-d'Azur or in Languedoc Roussillon or were born there. 'Contemporary' is defined as 'since 1960' and in building up the collections preference has been given to the Mediterranean region, especially France, Spain and Italy.

Nohant-Vic

George Sand's House

*Maison de George Sand, Château de Nohant,
    F-36400 La Châtre, Indre* ☎ 54 31 06 04
*May–Sept, daily 9–12, 2–6. Oct–Apr, daily
    10–12, 2–4.*
C

Built c. 1775, Nohant was bought by Madame Dupin de Franceuil in 1793 and was inherited by her granddaughter, Armandine Lucile Aurore Dupin, Baronne Dudevant (1804–76), better known as the writer, George Sand, who spent much time here and wrote many of her books in the house. Writers, musicians and artists continually visited her here. They included Chopin, Delacroix, Flaubert, Turgenev, Liszt and Balzac. Visitors can see the piano on which Chopin played, the small theatre for pantomime and the room in which George Sand died.

Noirmoutier-en-l'Isle

Museum of Boatbuilding

*Musée de Construction Navale, rue de l'Ecluse,
    F-85330 Noirmoutier-en-l'Isle, Vendée*
☎ 51 39 24 00
*Apr–June & Sept–Nov 15, Tues–Sun 10–12,
    2.30–6. July–Aug, daily 10–7.*
C ⚓

Salt, obtained by the evaporation of seawater, was once an important industry on Noirmoutier and the wooden building now housing the museum was originally constructed as a salt warehouse. It is surrounded by salt marshes, and was used as a boatbuilding yard from 1930 to 1979.

   The museum's exhibitions show the different stages in the building of the traditional wooden boats used in the area, with sections devoted to the plans and half-models, the machines and tools, two hulls under construction, and caulking. There is also a model of the saltworks, with an explanation of the saltmaking process, and a presentation of the maritime history of Noirmoutier.

Noyon

Calvin Museum

Musée Calvin, 6 place Aristide Briand, F-60400
*   Noyon, Oise*   ☎ *44 44 03 59*
Apr–Oct, Wed–Mon 10–12, 2.30–5. Groups by
*   appt at other times.*
Ⓒ ▮ ⌂

The old cathedral town of Noyon was the
birthplace of the religious reformer, Jean Calvin
(1509–64), famous for the theocracy he founded
in Geneva in 1541. This both directed the
affairs of the city and controlled the social and
private life of its citizens.

The house in Noyon in which Calvin was
born was destroyed at the end of the 16th
century during the religious wars. There is no
record of its appearance. During the 17th
century it was replaced by another house which,
like the rest of the town, was completely
destroyed in 1918. This was rebuilt and a
museum was opened in it in 1930. Damaged
during the Second World War, the house was
restored in 1954. It now belongs to the Society
for the History of French Protestantism.

The museum contains portraits of Calvin,
engravings, documents and books relating to
him, 16th-century editions of his works and an
important collection of Bibles. There are also
sections devoted to the Revocation of the Edict
of Nantes in 1685 – the Edict (1598) had
granted French Protestants civil rights – and to
the spread of Calvinism during the 17th
century.

Ordino (Andorra)

Areny de Plandolit House

Casa d'Areny de Plandolit, Ordino, Principat
*   d'Andorra*   ☎ *078 36 9 08*
Tues–Sat 10–1, 3–6; Sun 10–1.
Ⓒ

Sovereignty of the Principality of Andorra,
which has fewer than 50,000 people, is
exercised jointly by the President of the French
Republic and the Bishop of Urgel in Catalonia.
Its main industry is tourism and it attracts
around 7 million visitors a year.

Now a State museum, the Areny de Plandolit
House was for more than three centuries the
home of one of the most celebrated families in
Andorra. It contains original furnishings,
paintings and domestic equipment and provides
a microcosm of the history of Andorra. The
building dates from 1633 and visitors can tour
the whole of the interior, including the family
dining-room, the banqueting hall, the
bedrooms, the chapel, the oil and wine cellars,
the kitchen, the library, the music room and the
attics, which were used to store vegetables and
dried fruits and to house pigeons, chickens and
rabbits.

Among the exhibits are iron ingots produced
by the family forges, a large collection of Papal
bulls and indulgences, and the original score of
the Andorran national anthem.

Calvin Museum, Noyon.

Orléans

Charles Péguy Centre

Centre Charles Péguy, 11 rue de Tabour, F-45000
*   Orléans, Loiret*   ☎ *38 53 20 23*
Mon–Thurs 2–6; Fri 2–5. Closed Aug.
Ⓕ ▮

The poet, essayist and pamphleteer, Charles
Péguy (1873–1914) was born in Orléans and
killed in the Battle of the Marne. At the age of
25 he founded the Cahiers de la Quinzaine, in
which many now-famous writers, including
himself, first became known to the public. The
museum dedicated to him is in a Renaissance
mansion, known as the House of Agnes Sorel. It
illustrates the life and career of Péguy and the
political and cultural movements at the turn of
the century, with portraits, manuscripts,
newspaper articles and other mementoes.

Museum of Fine Art

Musée des Beaux-Arts, 1 rue Fernand Rabier,
*   F-45000 Orléans, Loiret*   ☎ *38 53 39 22*
Wed–Mon 10–12, 2–6. Closed Jan 1, May 1, 8,
*   Nov 1, Dec 25.*
Ⓒ ▮

The museum was established in 1825 and
transferred to a new building in 1984. It has
collections of 15th–20th-century European
paintings, sculpture, porcelain, faïence, ivories
and enamels, as well as drawings and prints with
the emphasis on works by French artists. Among
its especially prized exhibits are an important
series of pastel portraits by Jean-Baptiste
Perroneau (1715–83) and *Saint Thomas* by
Velasquez. There is a gallery devoted to the
works of two Orléans-born sculptors, Charles
Malfray (1887–1940), and Henri Gaudier-
Brzeska (1891–1915) who was killed in the First
World War.

Orléans Museum

*Musée Historique et Archéologique de l'Orléanais,
square Abbé Desnoyers, F-45000 Orléans,
Loiret* ☎ *38 53 39 22*
*Apr–Sept, Wed–Mon 10–12, 2–6. Oct–Mar,
Wed–Mon 10–12, 2–5. Closed Jan 1, May 1,
8, Nov 1, Dec 25.*
C ⌂

The museum occupies an attractive Renaissance
mansion, the Hôtel Cabu. Its collections
include religious images from the Orléans
region, wooden ex-voto carvings from
Montbouy, medieval religious sculptures, and
Gallo-Roman bronzes from excavations at
Neuvy-en-Sullias. There are also displays of
clocks and watches, goldsmiths' work and
tapestries. The museum has the oldest known
example of Orléans porcelain, 'Bacchus on a
Barrel', and some outstanding glass items,
including a glass medal, with a profile portrait of
Louis XIV, made by Bernard Perrot, who was
one of the pioneers of Venetian-style glass in
France in the 17th century.

Ornans

Gustave Courbet Museum

*Musée Départemental Maison Natale G. Courbet,
1 place Robert Fernier, F-25290 Ornans,
Doubs* ☎ *81 62 23 30*
Easter–Oct, Wed–Mon 2–6
C ⌂ ⚓

The painter, Gustave Courbet (1819–77), was
born at Ornans. The house where he was born

Gustave Courbet Museum, Ornans.

was opened as a museum to him in 1971. It is on
the banks of the Loue and overlooks La Roche
du Mont, which figures in several of his
paintings and sculpture. The museum contains a
number of works by Courbet and his
contemporaries as well as memorabilia and
letters. The room in which he was born is
furnished as it would have been at the time.

Paris

Army Museum

*Musée de l'Armée, Hôtel des Invalides, F-75007
Paris* ☎ *1 45 55 30 11*
*Apr–Sept, daily 10–6. Oct–Mar, daily 10–5.
Napoleon's tomb open until 7 pm June–Aug.
Closed Jan 1, May 1, Nov 1, Dec 25.*
C ⌂ ⚑

The museum was established in 1905, by
merging the Artillery Museum (1871) and the
Museum of the History of the Army (1895). It
occupies part of the buildings of the Hôtel Royal
des Invalides, built in 1674 as a home for
disabled soldiers. The Dome Chapel, completed
in 1706, contains the tomb of Napoleon
Bonaparte.

The museum contains mainly military relics
from the time of Henri IV (1553–1610)
onwards, although there are some earlier
exhibits. There are collections of uniforms,
trophies and plaques. Napoleon Bonaparte is
strongly represented, by exhibits which include
his campaign tent, his horse, 'Vizir', a
reconstruction of his bedroom at Longwood
House on St Helena, his greatcoat and the
sword which he carried at Austerlitz.

Auguste Rodin Museum

Musée National Auguste Rodin, Hôtel Biron,
*   77 rue de Varenne, F-75007 Paris*
    ☎ *1 47 05 01 34*
Apr–Sept, Tues–Sun 10–5.45. Oct–Mar, Tues–
*   Sun 10–5.*
C ▮ ▆

Auguste Rodin (1840–1917) was the most
celebrated sculptor of the late 19th century. The
museum bearing his name was established in
1915 in the Hôtel Biron, constructed in 1729–
31. It contains works by Rodin in marble, stone,
bronze and wax, including *The Burghers of*
Calais, *The Cathedral* and *The Thinker*. There are
also engravings and watercolours by him,
together with his personal collection of Greek,
Roman and medieval sculpture and of paintings
by Van Gogh, Monet and Renoir.

Balzac's House

Maison de Balzac, 47 rue Raynouard, F-75016
*   Paris*
    ☎ *1 42 24 56 38*
Tues–Sun 10–5.40. Closed public holidays.
C ▮

The novelist, Honoré de Balzac (1799–1850),
lived in a number of houses in Paris. This is the
only one to have survived. He lived in it
between 1840 and 1867, during which time he
wrote a number of his best novels, including *La*
Cousine Bette and *Le Cousin Pons*. It was also
where he corrected the whole of *La Comédie*
Humaine. The museum contains collections
illustrating his life and career as a writer,
including a number of his personal possessions –
his coffee-pot, his walking stick with turquoise
ornaments, his worktable and a number of
letters and manuscripts.

There is a specialised library relating to Balzac
and his work and, on the ground floor, a large
genealogical table containing the names of all
the characters in the Comédie Humaine, more
than 1,000 altogether.

Bourdelle Museum

Musée Bourdelle, 16 rue Antoine-Bourdelle,
*   F-75015 Paris*
    ☎ *1 45 48 67 27*
Tues–Sun 10–5.45. Closed public holidays.
C

Emile-Antoine Bourdelle (1861–1929) was at
one time Rodin's chief assistant. He was
particularly interested in the relationship of
sculpture to architecture and some of his finest
work is to be seen in the reliefs for the Théâtre
des Champs-Elysees (1912). He lived in the
house which is now the museum from 1884 until
his death and executed most of these works
here. Visitors can see the studios – the main one
is 40 m long – and the small apartment which
he shared with his parents.

The museum contains 876 sculptures and
plaster models, 100 paintings and frescoes and
many portraits, sketches, drawings and models.
There is a sculpture garden, 50 m long.

Préville, a player of the Comédie Française.
Comédie Française Library and Museum,
Paris.

Branly Museum

Musée Branly, Institut Supérieur d'Electronique,
*   21 rue d'Assas, F-75006 Paris*
    ☎ *1 45 48 24 87*
Mon–Fri 9–12, 2–5. Closed Aug.
C

The physicist, Edouard Branly (1846–1940),
was one of the pioneers and probably the
inventor of radio-telephony. The room which
constitutes the museum contains the
instruments which he used in the course of his
experiments. The equipment is as he left it.
Nothing has been rearranged or specially
presented to make it more intelligible to the
public. The most remarkable item is the Branly
receiver (1890), and the most curious the
transmitter which sends out 'Vive la France' in
morse code.

Carnavalet Museum

Musée Carnavalet, 23 rue de Sévigné, F-75003
*   Paris*   ☎ *1 42 72 21 13*
Tues–Sun 10–5.40
C ▮

Opened in 1888, the museum was housed until
1988 in the mid-16th-century Hôtel
Carnavalet, which had been enlarged in the
19th and 20th centuries. The collections had,
however, outgrown the space available and to
solve the problem, the late-17th-century Hôtel
Le Peletier de Saint-Fargeau, at 29 rue de
Sévigné, was acquired. A passage constructed
through the Lycée Victor Hugo allows the two
parts of the museum to be linked.

The exhibits illustrate the history of Paris
from the 16th century onwards. There are
paintings, drawings and engravings of the city,
portraits of famous Parisians, inn and shop signs,
17th–18th-century period rooms and a

collection of coins and medals. There are also memorabilia of Napoleon Bonaparte, Madame de Sévigné, who lived in the Hôtel Carnavalet for 20 years, and George Sand.

Fourteen rooms in the museum are devoted to the most important collection in the world of material relating to the Revolution of 1789.

Clemenceau Museum

Musée Clemenceau, 8 rue Franklin, F-75116 Paris ☎ *1 45 20 53 41 Tues, Thurs, Sat, Sun and public holidays 2–5. Closed April, also Jan 1, Dec 25.*
C 🛉

During the First World War, Georges Clemenceau (1841–1929), known as The Tiger, was Minister of War and President of the Council. He lived in this four-roomed ground-floor apartment for nearly 35 years, from 1895 until his death. Nothing has been changed since then. On the first floor there is a museum illustrating his life and career. It contains portraits, documents, photographs, manuscripts and personal possessions, including his overcoat and the gaiters which he invariably wore during his visits to the Front.

The museum has a complete file of all the newspapers which he founded and for which he wrote – *La Justice, L'Aurore, Le Bloc, L'Homme Libre* and *L'Homme Enchaîné.*

Comédie Française Library and Museum

Bibliothèque-Musée de la Comédie-Française, place Colette, F-75001 Paris ☎ *1 42 96 10 24 Mon–Fri 2–6. Closed Aug 1–Sept 15. By appt only: guided tours. Visitor must be a member of the theatrical profession, a university student, or a specialist in theatre history.*
C 🛉

The museum contains portraits, paintings and engravings, stage scenes, busts and statues illustrating the history of the Theatre. Among the objects on display is the armchair used in *Le Malade Imaginaire* in which Molière sat when he felt the first signs of the illness which was to cause his death a few hours later.

The archives of printed and pictorial material are kept in the Library. They include the complete business records of the Theatre, 20,000 letters, 4,000 posters, 30,000 programmes, 12,000 models and sketches of scenery and costumes, and photographs of the stage set for every presentation since the beginning of the present century.

Delacroix Museum

Musée Eugène Delacroix, 6 place de Fürstenberg, F-75006 Paris ☎ *1 43 54 04 87 Wed–Mon 9.45–5.*
C

Eugène Delacroix (1798–1863) was the greatest French painter of the Romantic movement and in his later career one of the most distinguished painters of monumental murals in the history of

French art. He worked very fast and his output was enormous. After his death, more than 9,000 paintings, pastels and drawings were found in his studio. He lived at the Place de Fürstenberg with its pleasant garden from 1857 until his death and his three-roomed apartment is little changed. It contains original furniture, personal possessions, letters, drawings, lithographs and a few paintings, which are frequently changed. The huge studio is reached by means of an outside staircase. It contains, evocatively, only his easel and the table on which he kept his painting requisites.

Edith Piaf Museum

Musée Edith Piaf, 5 rue Crespin du Gast, F-75011 Paris ☎ *1 43 55 52 72 Mon–Thurs 1–6, by telephone appt only. Closed public holidays.*
F

The celebrated popular singer, Edith Piaf, died in 1963. The exhibits illustrate her life and career from her birth in 1915 and include paintings, sculptures, posters, letters, photographs and recordings of her songs. There are also collections of posters publicising her performances and clothes which she wore on the stage.

The Hôtel Cluny

Musée des Thermes et de l'Hôtel de Cluny, 6 place Paul-Painlevé, F-75005 Paris ☎ *1 43 25 62 00 Wed–Mon and public holidays 9.45–12.30, 2–5.15*
C

The 15th-century residence of the priests of Cluny was built at the end of the century near the remains of the 2nd–3rd-century baths of Lutetius, making use of their foundations. The medieval collections formed in the mid 19th century by Alexandre du Sommerard (1779–1842) and placed in the Hôtel Cluny were acquired in 1843 and the ruins of the baths added to the museum complex. After the Second World War, it was decided that Cluny Museum should be reserved for medieval material, and that the Renaissance objects

The celebrated subject of the Edith Piaf Museum, Paris.

should be kept for another museum to be constructed in the future.

The collections are concerned with all the artistic activities, mostly French, of the Middle Ages. The exhibits include sculpture in stone and wood, tapestries, goldsmiths' and silversmiths' work, enamels, textiles, stained glass and wrought-ironwork. There are notable collections of sculpture, liturgical objects and religious ornaments, and of Jewish religious art.

Jean-Jacques Henner Museum

Musée National Jean-Jacques Henner, 43 avenue de Villiers, F-75017 Paris   ☎ *1 47 63 42 73*
Tues–Sun 10–12, 2–5
C̄ 🔒

Henner (1829–1905) was born in Alsace and achieved a great reputation in his lifetime, especially for his portraits and his nudes. The museum, established in 1923 in a former privately owned mansion, has a collection of 700 of his works, including paintings, sketches, studies and drawings.

Le Corbusier Foundation

Musée de la Fondation Le Corbusier, 8 square du Docteur Blanche, F-75016 Paris
Mon–Thurs 10–12, 1.30–6; Fri 10–12, 1.30–5. Closed Aug and Dec 23–Jan 2.
C̄ 🔒

The museum is in a building designed by the French architect, C. E. Jeanneret, known as Le Corbusier (1887–1965). It contains drawings, plans and photographs of buildings for which he was responsible, together with an exhibition of his paintings and sculpture. The Foundation also has an important archive of material relating to Le Corbusier.

The Louvre

Musée du Louvre, Palais du Louvre, F-75041 Paris   ☎ *1 42 60 39 26*
Wed–Mon 9.45–5.45. Free admission Sun.
C̄ *(ex children)* 🔒 💻 ♿

The Museum of the Louvre occupies the former Royal Palace, extended both by Napoleon I and Napoleon III. In 1791, after the Revolution, the Museum of the Palace of the Louvre was created, which became the Central Museum of the Arts in 1793 and then, under the Empire, the Napoleon Museum. During the Revolutionary and Napoleonic periods, the collections were enormously swollen by the works of art stolen from the occupied countries of Europe by the Napoleonic armies and from the Church and aristocratic families. After Waterloo, much of the foreign booty was returned to its rightful owners, but what had originated in France remained. With the additions of nearly two centuries, the Louvre is now one of the largest scholarly museums in the world, with two of the greatest visitor-attractions to be found anywhere, the Venus de Milo and the Mona Lisa.

The collections, each constituting a major museum in itself, are divided into the following sections – Roman antiquities; Greek antiquities; Oriental antiquities; Islamic art and antiquities; Egyptian antiquities; medieval, Renaissance and modern sculpture, paintings and drawings; and medieval, Renaissance and modern objets d'art, which include the Royal jewels. There are also princely collections of furniture, tapestries and religious art.

The museum is at present engaged in considerable reorganisation, taking advantage of the opportunities provided by the removal of the Ministry of Finance to other premises and of the new entrance area, surrounded by I. M. Pei's celebrated glass pyramid.

Musée d'Orsay

Musée d'Orsay, 62 rue de Lille, F-75007 Paris
    ☎ *1 40 49 48 14*
Tues, Wed, Fri, Sat 10–6; Thurs 10–9.45; Sun 9–6. Last admission 5.15 (9 on Thurs). Closed May 1.
C̄ 🔒 💻 ♿

Built in 1900, the Gare d'Orsay, known as the Diplomats' Station, was one of Europe's grandest termini. An equally distinguished hotel formed part of the complex of buildings. After its closure in the 1970s, the decision was eventually taken to transform the station and the hotel into France's national museum of 19th- and early-20th-century art, the emphasis being on works produced in France. The new museum opened in 1986.

The general arrangement is chronological and there are sections devoted to paintings, sculpture, the decorative arts, architecture, photography and film. Audio-visual presentations are shown continuously.

The Musée d'Orsay, Paris.

Museum of Decorative Arts

Musée des Arts Décoratifs, 107 rue de Rivoli,
F-75001 Paris   ☎ 1 42 60 32 14
Wed–Sat 12.30–6; Sun 11–6.
Ⓒ ▮

The museum possesses nearly 100,000 objects,
dating from the Middle Ages to the present day.
They are displayed chronologically and grouped
by manufacturing techniques, by materials –
tapestry, textiles, furniture, metal, gold and
silver, glass, ceramics – or in room settings of
the 18th, 19th and 20th centuries.

There are also collections of 15th–16th-
century Spanish and Italian paintings and of
17th–20th-century French paintings.

Museum of Modern Art at the Pompidou Centre

Musée National d'Art Moderne (MNAM), Centre
Georges Pompidou, F-75191 Paris
☎ 1 42 77 12 33
Mon, Wed–Fri 12–10; Sat, Sun 10–10.
Ⓒ ▮ 💻 🚐

The formation of the collections began in 1937.
In 1947 they were installed in the Palais de
Tokyo and in 1976 in the newly-constructed
Centre Georges Pompidou.

Covering the period from 1905 to the
present day, they constitute one of the most
important collections of modern art in the
world, with 20,000 works created by 3,000
artists. French artists, including Matisse, Braque
and Léger are strongly represented.

The museum has four sections, historical
(1905–65), contemporary (1965–today),
graphics, and temporary exhibitions of
contemporary art. There is also a large
documentation centre.

Museum of Modern Art at the Pompidou
Centre, Paris.

Museum of Popular Arts and Traditions

Musée National des Arts et Traditions Populaires,
6 avenue du Mahatma-Gandhi, F-75116
Paris   ☎ 1 40 67 90 00
Wed–Mon 9.45–5
Ⓒ *(ex children)* ▮ 💻 ♿ 🚐

The museum presents French rural society from
the middle of the 18th century to the middle of
the 20th. It is in two parts, one primarily for the
general public and the other for specialists. Both
sections contain exhibits of homes, costumes,
tools, trades, pastimes, religion and
superstitions, farming, literature, music, sports,
games and dancing. There is also a large
documentation and research centre.

Museum of Technology

Musée National des Techniques, 292 rue Saint-
Martin, F-75003 Paris   ☎ 1 42 71 24 14
Tues–Sat 1–5.30; Sun 11–5
Ⓕ

The museum was established by decree in 1794,
in order to act as a depository for the originals of
patented machines. The buildings of the former
priory of Saint Martin were allocated for the
purpose. As the collections grew, they were
enlarged in 1848, 1870 and 1889. The museum
is now one of the greatest treasure-houses of old
machines and scientific equipment in the world,
with more than 80,000 objects, dating from the
16th century onwards. Restrictions of space,
however, prevent all but a very small proportion
of these from being shown, although a
programme of complete reorganisation and representation is now under way.

Naval Museum

Musée de la Marine, Palais de Chaillot, place du
*   Trocadéro, F-75116 Paris* ☎ *1 45 53 31 70*
Wed–Mon 10–6. Closed public holidays.
C 🛢

The museum was created in 1827 by Charles X,
under the name of the Dauphin Museum. It was
housed in the Louvre where, since 1748, there
had been a collection of models of ships and port
installations. It was transferred to the Palais de
Chaillot in 1943. Since 1971 the museum has
had overall responsibility for all aspects of
French maritime history, including that of the
Navy, Merchant Service and fishing fleets. This
includes the collections not only of the Naval
Museum itself, but of 12 provincial museums.
    The central museum in Paris has displays of
models of 17th–19th-century warships, carvings
from wooden warships and navigational
instruments. There arc also drawings and
engravings of ships, charts and portrait busts of
famous sailors and sections devoted to five
voyages of exploration, trading voyages,
lighthouses, lifesaving and fishing.

Notre-Dame Cathedral Treasury

Trésor de la Cathédrale Notre-Dame, 6 parvis
*   Notre-Dame, F-75004 Paris*
    ☎ *1 43 26 07 39*
Mon–Sat 10–6; Sun 1–6.
C 🛢

The Cathedral of Notre-Dame dates from 1163.
It was much restored in the mid 19th century
under the direction of Eugène Viollet Le Duc
(1814–79), when the Treasury and Chapter
House were built.
    It contains remarkable collections of liturgical
objects, reliquaries, chalices, crucifixes,
illuminated manuscripts, religious sculptures
and vestments, together with mementoes of the
Coronation of Napoleon 1 and gifts from Popes
and Cardinals.

Museum of the Opera

Musée de l'Opéra, 1 place Charles-Garnier,
F-75009 Paris   ☎ *1 47 42 07 02*
Mon–Sat 10–5. Closed Easter fortnight.
C 🛢

The museum, founded in 1878, occupies the
circular building originally intended for
Napoleon III. On the ground floor is the model
of 'The Mystery of Valenciennes', performed in
1547, and a reconstruction of the theatre at
Orange. Upstairs, there are busts of Lully,
Rameau, Gluck, Wagner and Debussy and
documents, paintings, stage designs, costumes,
caricatures, photographs, sculptures and
statuettes evoking performances at the Opera
and its leading personalities. Among the
mementoes on display are Massenet's table
piano, Nijinsky's sandals, diadems and ballet
shoes worn by Anna Pavlova and some of
Diaghilev's personal possessions. There are also
collections of posters and programmes.

Naval Museum, Paris.

Pasteur Museum

Musée Pasteur, 25 rue Docteur Roux, F-75015
Paris
    ☎ *1 45 68 82 82*
Mon–Fri 2–5.30. Closed public holidays and Aug.
C 🛢

Louis Pasteur (1822–95) was internationally
celebrated for his researches into the diseases of
silk-worms, rabies, fermentation and contagious
human diseases. Since 1935 his former
apartment has been a museum dedicated to his
memory. It contains his furniture and a number
of memorabilia and personal possessions, as well
as displays of scientific instruments and
apparatus which he used, papers and historical
photographs.

Victor Hugo's House

Maison de Victor Hugo, 6 place des Vosges,
F-75004 Paris
    ☎ *1 42 72 10 16*
Tues–Sun 10–5.40. Closed public holidays.
C 🛢

The poet, novelist and playwright, Victor-
Marie Hugo (1802–85), lived in this house,
which was formerly the Hôtel de Rohan-
Guénénée. Now a museum, it contains
collections of memorabilia and personal
possessions of the writer and his family. There
are portraits of him, including busts by Rodin
and David d'Angers, furniture which he
designed for Juliette Drouet's Chinese drawing
room in Guernsey, and illustrations for books by
contemporary artists. The museum also has
manuscripts and first editions of his works.

Pau

The Château de Pau

Musée National du Château de Pau, Château de
*   Pau, F-64000 Pau, Pyrénées-Atlantiques*
    ☎ *59 27 36 22*
Apr 16–Oct 15, daily 9.30–11.45, 2–5.45.
*   Oct 16–Apr 15, 9.30–11.45, 2–4.45. Closed*
*   Jan 1, May 1, Dec 25.*
C 🛢

The Château de Pau was constructed in stages between the beginning of the 12th and the end of the 16th century. It was the birthplace of Henri IV (1553–1610), the founder of the Bourbon dynasty. During the Revolution it was severely damaged. Restoration and redecoration began in 1838 and it was refurnished both as a royal residence, being occupied by Louis-Philippe's sons, and by Napoleon III and the Empress Eugénie, and as an historic castle memorable for being the birthplace of Henri IV. This policy has continued, so that the interior has now regained its early-19th-century splendour and at the same time contains an outstanding collection of paintings, prints, objets d'art, documents and literature relating to Henri IV and his period.

The castle has one of France's finest tapestry collections and among other outstanding exhibits are an 1817 Sèvres breakfast set representing the apotheosis of Henry IV and a painting (1819) by Ingrès showing Don Pedro of Toledo kissing Henri IV's sword. The most celebrated exhibit, however, is the tortoise shell, reputed to have been the King's cradle.

Périgueux

Périgord Museum

Musée du Périgord, 22 cours Tourny, F-24000 Périgueux, Dordogne ☎ 53 53 16 42
July–Sept, Wed–Mon 10 12, 2–6. Oct–June, Wed–Mon 10–12, 2–5. Closed public holidays.
C ⌀ ↩

The museum building was constructed at the beginning of the present century on the site of an Augustinian monastery, of which the 17th-century chapel still exists. It has one of the most important prehistoric collections in France, with both flint and bone tools. The archaeological exhibits cover the Neolithic, Palaeolithic, Bronze Age, Iron Age, Gallo-Roman and Merovingian periods. There are also interesting anthropological collections which include both Neanderthal and Magdalenian skeletons.

Other sections of the museum display Romanesque sculpture, Renaissance furniture and statuettes, enamels, ironwork, faïence and 19th-century French and European paintings. There are also natural history collections relating to the region.

Perpignan

Joseph Puig Museum of Coins and Medals

Musée Numismatique Joseph Puig, 42 avenue de Grande-Bretagne, F-66000 Perpignan, Pyrénées-Orientales ☎ 68 34 11 70
June 15–Sept 15, Mon, Wed–Sat 9.15–12, 2.15–7; Sun 2.15–7. Sept 16–June 14, Mon, Wed–Sat 8.45–12, 1.45–6; Sun 1.45–6.
F ▯

The museum occupies an early-20th-century house which was bequeathed to the town of Perpignan, together with his large numismatic collections, by a wealthy local collector, Joseph Puig. There are approximately 350,000 items in the collections, which are international and cover all periods. There is an exceptionally fine series of Roussillon and Catalan coins, some of which are extremely rare.

Pfaffenhoffen

Museum of Popular Painted Imagery

Musée de l'Imagerie Peinte et Populaire Alsacienne, 38 rue du Docteur-Albert-Schweitzer, F-67350 Pfaffenhoffen, Bas-Rhin ☎ 88 07 70 23
Wed, Sat, Sun 2–5
C

The collections in this remarkable museum complex comprise every kind of popular message which at one time was painted by hand in Alsace, associated with every type of event, religious and secular. They include professional diplomas, marriage, confirmation and death certificates and decorated legal documents. One room is devoted to souvenirs of military conscription and another has the most important collection of christening cards in Europe.

Pierre-de-Bresse

Bresse Ecomuseum

Ecomusée de la Bresse Bourguignonne, Château, F-71279 Pierre-de-Bresse, Sâone-et-Loire ☎ 85 76 27 16
Daily 2–6. Closed last week of Dec.
C ▯ ↩

The Château de Bresse was completed in 1670 and was known because of its grandeur as 'the little Versailles'. It has contained the headquarters of the museum since 1981. Following the usual ecomuseum pattern, the mother-museum at Pierre-de-Bresse forms the

Chairmaking exhibition at the Bresse Ecomuseum, Pierre-de-Bresse.

centre of a cluster of smaller museums in the area, each illustrating a particular theme.

The collections in the Château provide an introduction to the landscape, natural history, traditional customs and occupations, and speech of Burgundian Bresse. The seven branch museums (*antennes*) are located as follows:
Cuiseaux Museum of Wine and the Vineyard (May–Sept, daily 3–7).
Louhans Newspaper Office Museum (May–Sept, daily 3–7 or by appt).
Rancy Chairmaking Museum (May–Sept, Sun 3–7 or by appt).
Sagy Watermill Museum (details from Ecomuseum at Pierre-de-Bresse).
Saint-German-du-Bois Museum of Agricultural Machinery (May–Sept, Sun 3–7 or by appt).
Saint-Martin-de-Bresse Museum of Forestry and Wood (May–Sept, Sun 3–7 or by appt).
Verdun-sur-le-Doubs Museum of Wheat and Bread (July–Sept, daily 2–5 or by appt).

Pithiviers

Transport Museum

Musée des Transports, Rue Carnot, F-45300 Pithiviers, Loiret   ☎ 46 28 23 47
May–June & Sept–Oct 15, Sun & public holidays 2–6. July–Aug, Sat, Sun 2–6.
Ⓒ ⓘ ▣

The museum, which opened in 1965, was created and run by an association of volunteers. Pithiviers is at the junction of the SNCF main line and the 32 km narrow-gauge tramway which linked Pithiviers and Toury between 1892 and 1964. The association has preserved 3.5 km of track, over which it runs steam-hauled trains for the benefit of visitors. It also maintains a collection of steam, petrol-electric and diesel locomotives, and goods and passenger rolling stock.

Plédéliac

Historic Farm Museum

Ferme d'Antan, Le Saint-Esprit-des-Bois, Plédéliac, F-22270 Jugon-les-Lacs, Côtes-du-Nord   ☎ 98 84 44 99/96 34 14 67
May–June & Sept–Oct 15, Sun 2–7. July–Aug, Mon–Sat 10–12, 2–7; Sun 2–7. Other times by appt.
Ⓒ ⌂

The museum is in an 1810 farmhouse and its outbuildings. Some of the late 19th and early-20th-century furniture is original to the house. There are collections of domestic equipment, agricultural tools and implements and displays illustrating flax-processing, dairying, grain-cleaning and the care of livestock.

On the first Sunday in August there is a Bread Festival, showing village life at the beginning of the present century. The main theme of the Festival is the making and baking of bread. Many people wear traditional costumes for the occasion.

Transport Museum, Pithiviers.

Pont-de-Montvert

Mont Lozère Ecomuseum

Ecomusée du Mont Lozère, F-48220 Pont-de-Montvert, Lozère   ☎ 66 45 80 73
June–Sept, daily 10.30–12.30, 2.30–6.30. Open during school holidays, and by appt for groups at other times.
Ⓒ ⌂

The ecomuseum was established in 1984 by the Cevennes National Park and the town of Pont-de-Montvert in order to draw the attention of visitors to the natural features of this mountainous area and to the settlements and occupations which have developed there. The central museum at Pont-de-Montvert has exhibits relating to the history of the region and to the way in which man has adapted himself to the somewhat hostile environment, characterised by granite boulders and peat bogs. From there visitors are introduced to a series of routes which they can follow to see farms, watermills, reservoirs, houses, bridges and other features, the history of which has already been described at the interpretation centre.

Pontoise

Pissarro Museum

Musée Pissarro, 17 rue du Château, F-95300 Pontoise, Val d'Oise   ☎ 30 38 02 40
Wed–Sun 2–6. Closed public holidays.
Ⓕ ⓘ

From 1866 to 1869 the painter, Camille Pissarro (1831–1903), worked on landscapes at Pontoise, painting entirely in the open. In 1870 he fled before the German invasion, first to Brittany and then to London. In 1872, after his return to Pontoise, he was joined by Cézanne, who worked with him there.

The museum which bears his name is an annexe of the Tavet Museum. It was established in 1980 and is devoted to the works of artists who lived in the Pontoise region during the 19th century.

Port-Louis

Museum of the India Company

*Musée de la Compagnie des Indes, Citadelle de
Port-Louis, F-56290 Port-Louis, Morbihan*
☎ 97 82 19 13
*June–Sept, Wed–Mon 10–7. Oct, Dec 16–May,
Wed–Mon 10–12, 2–5. Closed some public
holidays.*
C ▯ ↩

During the 17th and 18th centuries, a number
of India Companies were established in France
to trade with Africa, India, China and the New
World. The museum, in a 17th-century barrack
block which formed part of the fortress, tells the
story of the French trading voyages to and from
these regions, with details of the ships involved
and their cargoes. There are collections of India
Company porcelain, ship models, engravings,
maps and charts, and of 18th-century Chinese,
Japanese and Indian art brought back from
voyages.

Pourcy

Ecomuseum of the Montagne de Reims

*Ecomusée de la Montagne de Reims, Maison du
Parc, Pourcy, F-51160 Ay, Marne*
☎ 26 59 44 44
*Mon–Fri 9–5; Sat, Sun and public holidays 2.30–
6.30.*
C ▯ ↩

The central building of the ecomuseum received
a special architectural award in 1984. The
exhibits within this building illustrate different
aspects of the area of the park – its geology, flora
and fauna, its traditions and customs,
handicrafts and art, agriculture, wine
production, forestry and trades, and its
commercial contacts with the outside world.
There are also displays showing the landscape
and architecture of the district and the
industries which have been established there in
recent years. The sites to which special
attention is drawn in the introductory
exhibition include a forestry museum, a quarry,
a Neolithic stone-polisher's workshop and a
group of Romanesque churches.

Quimper

Museum of Brittany

*Musée Départemental Breton, 1 rue du Roi
Gradlon, F-29000 Quimper, Finistère*
☎ 98 95 21 60
*June–Sept, daily 10–7. Oct–May, Wed–Sun
9–12, 2–5.*
C ▯

Founded in 1846, the museum moved to its
present home in the former Bishop's Palace in
1911. It presents the traditional culture of
Brittany, with exceptionally good collections of
costumes, furniture, domestic equipment and
craftsmen's tools. There are also displays of

Late 19th-century chinaware from Quimper.
Museum of Brittany, Quimper.

statues of Breton saints, Quimper ceramics,
drawings and engravings depicting everyday life
in Brittany, 16th–18th-century chests and the
carved wooden façade of a 15th-century
Quimper house. The museum's archaeological
collections are of both Gallo-Roman and
prehistoric material and include an engraved
menhir.

Rennes

Rennes Ecomuseum

*Ecomusée du Pays de Rennes, Ferme de la
Bintinais, route de Chatillon, F-35200 Rennes-
Sud, Ille-et-Vilaine*   ☎ 99 51 38 15
*Apr–Oct 15, Wed–Mon 2–7. Oct 16–Mar, Wed–
Mon 2–6. Closed public holidays and
Jan 1–15.*
C ▯ ▦ ↩

The museum is based on a group of restored farm
buildings, La Ferme de la Bintinais,
representative of the area's architecture. The
surrounding fields are cultivated and have been
planted in a way which illustrates the crops and
the varieties grown both yesterday and today.
Inside the museum, there are displays, computer
databases and audio-visual presentations which
help visitors to understand life in the Rennes
area as it was in former times and as it is now.
The multi-disciplinary approach covers history,
natural history, architecture, urban history and
agriculture, and the exhibits include farm
machinery, tools and vehicles, domestic
equipment, and masonry, carpentry and roofing
tools, as well as equipment for cider and milk
production.

Rheims

Cathedral Treasury and Museum

*Trésor et Musée de l'Oeuvre de la Cathédrale,
Palais de Tau, 2 place du Cardinal-Luçon,
F-51100 Reims, Marne*   ☎ 26 47 74 39
Wed–Mon 10–12, 2–6
C

The building containing the museum is at the former Palace of the Archbishops of Rheims, constructed at different periods in the 13th–18th centuries. It was badly damaged by fire during the First World War and restored in the 1950s. The museum preserves a number of original sculptures from the Cathedral which were in bad condition and had to be replaced by copies, including 'The Coronation of the Virgin' from the central portico and 'Goliath', the largest sculpture in the cathedral. The cathedral tapestries are also displayed in the museum. They include the hangings woven for the coronation of Charles V. Other items associated with coronations include the mantles of the King and the Dauphin worn at the coronation of Charles V, and the golden symbolic ornaments used for the same occasion. Among the other particularly interesting items are the 9th-century Talisman of Charlemagne and the Reliquary of St Ursula, made for the marriage of Louis XII and Anne of Brittany in 1499.

The Hôtel le Vergeur, which houses the Museum of Old Rheims.

Hôtel le Vergeur

Musée-Hôtel le Vergeur, Musée du Vieux Reims, 36 place du Forum, F-51100 Reims, Marne
☎ 26 47 20 75
Tues–Sun 2–6. Closed Jan 1, May 1, July 14, Nov 1, Dec 25.

C ✎

The mansion is the headquarters of the Society of the Friends of Old Rheims, who own the building. Constructed in stages during the 13th, 15th and 16th centuries, it was converted into a museum after the death of the last private owner in 1935. Restored after damage during the First World War, it now has displays illustrating the history of Rheims. The exhibits include fine 18th–19th-century furniture, paintings, sculpture, porcelain and documents, shown in room settings. Among the especially interesting items are a complete set of original woodcuts of the Apocalypse and the Passion by Albrecht Dürer (1471–1529), together with 10 of his best-known engravings. The museum also has a collection of engravings showing the coronation of kings in Rheims Cathedral.

Saint Denis Museum

Musée Saint Denis, 8 rue Chanzy, F-51100 Reims, Marne   ☎ 26 47 28 44
Mon, Wed–Fri 10.30–12, 2–6; Sat, Sun 10–12, 2–6. Closed Jan 1, May 1, July 14, Nov 1, 11, Dec 25.

C

During the Revolution, the Abbey of Saint Denis, where Talleyrand had been a priest, was destroyed. The only building to survive was an 18th-century mansion belonging to the Abbey. After being used as a college, a military hospital and a seminary, it was converted to museum purposes in 1913. The formation of the collections goes back to 1794, when the Revolutionary government brought together works of art which had belonged to religious communities and to people who had left France. During the 19th century, the collections were considerably augmented, and were very unsatisfactorily accommodated.

Between 1960 and 1967, the museums of Rheims were reorganised. The Saint Denis Museum was then allocated the collections of art from the Renaissance onwards, natural history, coins, 19th–20th-century caricatures, religious art, iron firebacks and French ethnography. The Director decided to put his coins, engravings, caricatures, ethnography and religious art into store and to display the rest, although items from the reserve collections are constantly drawn on for special exhibitions.

Among the particularly interesting items shown in this large and important museum are 13 drawings by Lucas Cranach and his son, the painting, *Vulcan's Forge* by Le Nain, the second largest collection of Corots in France – the Louvre has the largest – and David's famous painting, *The Assassination of Marat*.

War Room

Salle de Guerre, 12 rue Franklin Roosevelt, F-51100 Reims, Marne   ☎ 26 47 84 19
Wed–Mon 10–12, 2–6. Closed Jan 1, May 1, July 14, Nov 1, 11, Dec 25.

C ⓖ

The room is in the former Collège Moderne et Technique, now the Lycée Roosevelt, which General Eisenhower used as his advance headquarters in 1945 while the war was being carried further towards Germany. The room, which is much as it was in 1945, is papered with operational maps, and was used for the German surrender on 7th May 1945. In preparation for the signature ceremony, a large table used for teachers' meetings was brought into the room, together with a few chairs and ashtrays. Two carpets were added to produce a more comfortable and cheerful atmosphere. In July 1945, the room was officially handed over to the City of Rheims by the American military authorities.

Richelieu

Richelieu Museum

Musée, place du Marché, F-37120 Richelieu, Indre-et-Loire   ☎ *47 58 10 13*
Apr–Sept, Wed–Mon 10–12, 2–6. Oct–Mar, Mon, Wed–Fri 10–12, 2–4.

F 🔊

The museum is in the town's former Law Courts, a building dating from the 17th century. It has collections illustrating the history of the town and the life and career of Armand-Jean du Plessis (1585–1642), Cardinal de Richelieu, enemy of the Protestants, Minister of Louis XIII and founder of the French Academy. The museum contains woodwork from the Château de Richelieu, demolished in 1809, and portraits and paintings formerly at the Château.

Riom

Museum of the Auvergne

Musée Régional d'Auvergne, 10 bis, rue Delille, F-63200 Riom, Puy-de-Dôme
☎ *73 38 17 31*
Apr–Sept, Wed–Mon 10–12, 2–5.30. Oct–Mar, Wed–Sun 10–12, 2–4.30. Closed public holidays.

C 🔒

On the ground floor of the museum the exhibits are related to rural life. There is a reconstruction of the interior of an Auvergne farmhouse, with its enclosed bed and other traditional furnishings and its domestic equipment. In this section there are also models of rural houses, displays of vineyard and wine-making tools and equipment and explanations of dairying and cheese-making methods. A painting, *The Virgin with the Grapes*, forms the centrepiece of an exhibit concerning St Verny, the patron saint of winemakers. The first floor is given over to domestic life, weaving, with an 18th-century loom, and the different trades and industries of the region – mining, pottery, pit-sawing, the woodland crafts and cutlery. There are exhibitions showing the Ages of Man, from the cradle to the grave, games and traditional festivals.

On the second floor there are costumes from Puy-de-Dôme and Cantal, headdresses and shawls, jewellery, popular religious art and musical instruments, with a representation of an Auvergne dance known as the 'bourrée'.

Early 17th-century message-box or escutcheon from the Haut-Rhine. Postal Museum, Riquewihr.

Riquewihr

Postal Museum

Musée Historique des PTT d'Alsace, F-68340 Riquewihr, Haut-Rhin   ☎ *89 47 93 80*
2 weeks before Easter–June & Sept–Nov 11, Wed–Mon 10–12, 2–6. July–Aug, daily 10–12, 2–6.

C 🔒

The museum, in the 16th-century castle of the Princes of Württemberg-Montbéliard, tells the story of the postal services and communications in north-eastern France from Gallo-Roman times to the present day. There are collections of uniforms, postage stamps, photographs and documents and of telegraph and telephone equipment. Attention is also given to the Montgolfier balloon, the effects of the railways on mail deliveries and to the postal service during the two World Wars. There is a celebrated collection of mail coaches, both originals and replicas.

Rixheim

Wallpaper Museum

Musée du Papier Peint, 28 rue Zuber, F-68170 Rixheim, Bas-Rhin   ☎ *89 64 24 56*
Wed–Mon 10–12, 2–6. Closed Jan 1, Good Fri, Easter Day, May 1, Whit Sun, July 14, Nov 1, 11, Dec 25, 26.

C 🔒 🔊

The Commanderie, which has housed the museum since 1983, was built in 1735–8 for the Teutonic Knights. In 1797 it became a wallpaper factory. The museum retains much of the old machinery and many of the printing-blocks which were made in the factory. The collection of wallpapers dates from the late 18th century and contains 130,000 different designs. These include eight scenic papers, in which a panorama runs continuously around the walls of a room, and a number of hand-printed papers.

Roller printing-machine. Wallpaper Museum, Rixheim.

Rocamadour

François Poulenc Museum

*Musée d'Art Sacré François Poulenc, Pèlerinage,
    Notre-Dame de Rocamadour, F-46500
    Rocamadour, Lot*   ☎ 65 33 63 29
Easter–Nov 1, daily 10–12, 2–6
Ⓒ

The composer, François Poulenc (1899–1963),
gave a number of objects, and his name, to the
museum as a token of gratitude for having
rediscovered his religious faith in the Sanctuary
of the Church of Saint-Amadour, which has
been a place of pilgrimage since the Middle
Ages. The collections in the museum consist of
religious art from churches in Lot. They include
12th–19th-century church plate, 15th–18th-
century sculpture and 16th–18th-century votive
paintings.

Rochefort

Naval Museum

*Musée Naval, Hôtel des Cheusses, Place de la
    Galissonière, F-17300 Rochefort, Charente-
    Maritime*   ☎ 46 87 11 22
Wed–Mon 10–12, 2–6. Closed public holidays.
Ⓒ

The 17th-century Hôtel des Cheusses was
originally the residence of the Commanders of
the naval squadrons, then the headquarters of
the Commissariat, until the closure of the
Arsenal in 1927. The museum, opened in 1930,
inherited the Arsenal's remarkable collection of
models of the warships which had been built
there from the 17th century until the reign of
Louis XV and then from the Restoration until
our own times. There are also many models and

actual examples of machinery used by the Navy
on ships and in the dockyards, including rope-
making machinery, capstans and a floating
crane in service at Rochefort for stepping and
unstepping masts. The Sculptors' Hall contains
ships' figureheads, wooden trophies and
allegorical figures in wood and marble. There
are also memorabilia of Rochefort sailors and
examples of objects made by prisoners held in
the hulks at Rochefort.

Pierre Loti's House

*Maison de Pierre Loti, 141 rue Pierre Loti,
    F-17300 Rochefort, Charente-Maritime*
        ☎ 46 99 16 88
*Mon, Wed–Sat, guided tours at 10, 11, 2, 3 and 4.
    Sun, guided tours at 2, 3 and 4. Closed
    Dec 20–Jan 20.*
Ⓒ ▮

The novelist, Louis Marie Julien Viand (1850–
1923), who wrote under the name of Pierre
Loti, was born in Rochefort. He transformed the
family home into a fairytale dwelling, in which
he reconstructed with the help of original
material, some of the exotic surroundings he
had encountered during his travels. These
interiors have been carefully preserved by the
municipality. The house also contains a number
of Loti family portraits.

Rodez

Denys Puech Museum of Fine Art

*Musée des Beaux-Arts Denys Puech, place Georges
    Clemenceau, F-12000 Rodez, Aveyron*
        ☎ 65 42 70 64
Mon, Wed–Sat 10–12, 3–7; Sun 3–7.
Ⓒ ▮ ↩

The distinguished sculptor, Denys Puech
(1854–1942) was born at Gavernac, in
Aveyron, and is buried in Rodez. The museum
dedicated to him contains 15th–17th-century
Italian, Flemish and Dutch paintings, 18th-
century French portraits and 19th–20th-century
French engravings. There are also 19th- and
20th-century paintings and sculpture by local
artists and an international collection of
contemporary paintings.

Romans

Shoemaking Museum

*Musée de la Chaussure et d'Ethnographie
    Régionale, 2 rue Sainte-Marie, F-26100
    Romans, Isère*   ☎ 75 02 44 85
*Mon 2–5.45; Wed–Sat 10–11.45, 2–5.45; Sun
    and public holidays 2.30–6. Closed Jan 1,
    May 1, Dec 25.*
Ⓒ ✐

The town of Romans has a long shoemaking
tradition. Its museum devoted to the subject is
housed in the former Convent of the Visitation,
built in stages between the 17th and 18th

centuries. The collection in this part of the
museum illustrates the history of footwear and
tanning from classical times to the present day.
The displays explain the processes involved and
include tools used in shoemaking and
clogmaking.

The second part of the museum contains
exhibits relating to life in the district during the
19th century and the earlier part of the 20th.
They include costumes, furniture and
reconstructions of a Roman market and a typical
regional kitchen.

A separate section deals with the Resistance
movement in the region during the Second
World War.

Ronchamp

Mining Museum

*Musée de la Mine, 33 place de la Mairie,
    Ronchamp, Haute-Sâone*   ☎ 084 206065
*May–June, Sun and public holidays 3–6. July–
    Aug, daily 3–6. Groups by appt May–Aug.*
[C]

The museum tells the story of the coalmine at
Ronchamp, which operated from 1750 to 1958.
Among the themes followed are the growth of a
major commercial enterprise, the growth of the
workers' movement, the development of social
legislation and changes in technology. One
gallery is devoted to technical matters, to
mining documents and to the flora and fauna to
be found in the local coal fossils. The second
gallery aims to recapture the life of the miners
and their families – their social, municipal and
sporting activities, their living conditions and
their occupational diseases. There are also
collections of paintings of mining subjects and
of tools and equipment.

Rouen

Ceramics Museum

*Musée de la Céramique, Hôtel d'Hocqueville, 1 rue
    Faucon, F-76000 Rouen, Seine-Maritime*
    ☎ 35 71 28 40
Thurs–Mon 10–12, 2–6. Closed public holidays.
[C]

The museum building dates from 1657. It
presents, in its 18 galleries, the ceramics which
were formerly in the Museum of Fine Art, and
which are especially notable for the collection of
16th–19th-century Rouen faïence. There are
also pieces from other factories in France and
abroad which were inspired by the Rouen style,
and from Asia Minor, Rhodes, China and
Japan.

Corneille Museum

*Musée Corneille, 4 rue de la Pie, F-76000 Rouen,
    Seine-Maritime*   ☎ 35 71 63 92
Thurs–Mon 10–12, 2–6. Free admission Sun.
[C]

**15th-century *Christ* in wood. François
Poulenc Museum, Rocamadour.**

The 16th-century house in which the dramatist,
Pierre Corneille (1606–84), was born is now a
museum. It contains an ebony-veneered cabinet
which belonged to Corneille, together with
prints, engravings, medals, autograph letters,
his baptismal certificate and other items
illustrating his life and career.

There is also an important library of editions
of the works of Pierre Corneille and his younger
brother Thomas, who was also a dramatist.

Flaubert and Medical History Museum

*Musée Flaubert et d'Histoire de la Médicine, Hôtel-
    Dieu, 51 rue de Lecat, F-76000 Rouen, Seine-
    Maritime*   ☎ 35 89 81 30
Tues–Sat 10–12, 2–6. Closed public holidays.
[F]

The house in which the museum has been
located since 1945 was built in 1755 to
accommodate the surgeon of Rouen Hospital. It
was occupied by Achille Cléophas Flaubert from
1816 until 1846 and by his son, Achille
Flaubert, from 1846 to 1882. The writer,
Gustave Flaubert (1821–80), was born here.

The museum has a collection of surgical and
medical instruments and of portraits,
memorabilia and manuscripts of the Flaubert
family, as well as a library of medical works,
mainly assembled by Dr Achille Flaubert. One
of the more treasured exhibits is a coloured
anatomical study in wax by the surgeon,
Laumonier, who was appointed by Napoleon I
in 1806 to establish and run a 'school of artificial
anatomy', the task of which was to reproduce
human organs in wax for the benefit of medical
students.

Museum of Fine Art

*Musée des Beaux-Arts, square Verdrel, F-76000
Rouen, Seine-Maritime*   ☎ *35 71 28 40*
*Wed 2–6; Thurs–Mon 10–12, 2–6. Closed public
holidays.*
C 🛈

The museum is one of the most richly endowed
of the French provincial art museums. It was
one of the 15 set up by Consular Decree in 1801
and, like the 14 others, received its original
stock from the works of art seized by the
Revolutionary government from the Church
and aristocratic families. It has excellent
collections of works by Flemish, Spanish Italian
and Dutch artists, but its principal strength is in
French paintings of the 17th and 19th centuries.
For the 18th and 20th centuries, its holdings are
less notable. An exception is its collection of
portraits of 20th-century literary figures,
including Gide, Valéry, Montherlant, Mauriac
and Cocteau. The museum was severely
damaged by bombing in 1944, but has been
completely restored and reorganised.

National Museum of Education

*Musée National de l'Education, 185 rue Eau-de-
Robec, F-76000 Rouen, Seine-Maritime*
☎ *35 75 49 70*
Tues–Sat 1–6. Closed public holidays.
C 🛈

The museum is located in a 15th-century half-
timbered house. Financed and administered by
the Ministry of Education, it presents the
history of education in France, illustrated by
prints, photographs, school furniture, teaching
material, books and manuscripts. Topic-
exhibitions are organised annually and in every
exhibition visitors can go back to school as it
was a century ago.

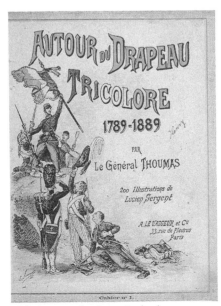

**19th-century school exercise-book cover.
National Museum of Education, Rouen.**

Rueil Malmaison

Château de Bois-Préau

*Musée National du Château Bois-Préau, 1 avenue
de l'Impératrice Joséphine, F-92500 Rueil
Malmaison, Hauts-de-Seine*
☎ *1 47 49 20 07*
*Apr–Sept, Wed–Mon 10.30–1, 2–6 (last visits
12.30 and 5.30). Oct–Mar, Wed–Mon
10.30–1, 2–5.30 (last visits 12.30 and 5).*
C 🛈 ⟳

This was the estate acquired in 1810 by the
Empress Joséphine in order to enlarge her
adjoining property at Malmaison. The owner
did not wish to sell and, after being put under
immense pressure, drowned herself in the lake.
Her heir subsequently decided to part with the
property. After the death of the Empress, Bois-
Préau passed from hand to hand and in 1853 was
substantially rebuilt. It was bought by an
American, Edward Tuck, in 1920 and presented
to the State.
    It now contains collections illustrating
Napoleon's captivity and death, the return of
his ashes in 1840 and the Imperial legend.

Château de Malmaison

*Musée National du Château de Malmaison, avenue
du Château, F-92500 Rueil Malmaison,
Hauts-de-Seine*   ☎ *1 47 49 20 07*
*Apr–Sept, Wed–Mon 10–12.30, 1.30–5.30 (last
visits 12 and 5). Oct–Mar, Wed–Mon 10–
12.30, 1.30–5 (last visits 12 and 4.30).*
C 🛈 ⟳

From 1390 to 1763 the agricultural estate of
Malmaison belonged to the same family. A
house flanked by pavilions was built here early
in the 17th century. It was extended in 1690
and again in 1770, when the gardens were laid
out. In 1799 it was bought by Marie-Joséphine-
Rose Bonaparte, whom Napoleon Bonaparte
had married in 1796. As Empress after 1804, she
improved both the house and the gardens and
spent most of her time there until her death in
1814. Napoleon repudiated her after she had
failed to give him a son, seldom visited her and
divorced her in 1809. After several changes of
ownership, the property passed to the State and
was opened as a museum in 1907.
    Apart from its furnishings and paintings, it
contains collections illustrating the history of
Napoleon I and his family and of the Emperor's
exile on St Helena. There are also exhibitions of
weapons and of court and military uniforms.

Sabres

Ecomuseum of the Grande Lande

*Ecomusée de la Grande Lande, Marquèze,
F-40630 Sabres, Landes*   ☎ *58 07 52 70*
*Apr–May, Sat 2.25–6; Sun and public holidays
10.15–7. June–Sept 15, daily 10.15–7.
Sept 16–Oct, Sat 2.25–6; Sun and public
holidays 10.15–7.*
C 🛈 🖥 ♿ ⟳

Reconstructed 19th-century farm buildings.
Ecomuseum of the Grande Lande, Sabres.

The Grande Lande is a great stretch of what was once heathland in the Leyre basin. Until the mid 19th century it was mostly grazed by sheep, but then extensive planting of pine forests began to be carried out and today these forests cover a million hectares. Within the Grande Lande, the inhabitants and their holdings were divided into Quartiers. The ecomuseum concentrates on the Quartier de Marquèze and tries to show it, in every detail, as it was at the end of the 19th century. Some of the buildings have been restored on their original sites, others have been brought from elsewhere.

The fields, vineyards and gardens are cultivated in the old way and the domestic equipment, furniture and agricultural implements are authentic for the period. A resin-distillation plant and a weaver's workshop nearby at Luxey form part of the museum. The equipment was in use from 1859 until 1954.

Saint-Céré

Jean Lurçat's Studio

Atelier-Musée Jean Lurçat, Saint-Laurent-Le-Tours, F-46400 Saint-Céré, Lot
☎ *65 38 28 21/65 38 11 85*
Palm Sun–Sun following Easter, also July 14–Sept 30, daily 9–12, 2.30–6.30
Ⓒ 🚗

The Castle of Saint-Laurent-Le-Tours dates partly from the 12th and partly from the 14th century. In 1945 it was bought by the artist, Jean Lurçat (1892–1966), who came from the region. Lurçat began as a painter, but he started

The Château du Marais, which now houses the Talleyrand Museum, Saint-Chéron.

working on tapestries in 1917. From 1937 he worked as a designer for the Aubusson factory and was the only great tapestry designer for generations, doing much to revive the art. The displays in his former studio illustrate the range and quality of his work as a painter and as a designer of ceramics, fabrics and furniture.

Saint-Chéron

Talleyrand Museum

Musée Talleyrand, Château du Marais, F-91530 Saint-Chéron, Essonne ☎ *64 91 91 26*
Mar–Nov 15, Sun and public holidays, 2–6.30. Groups at other times by appt.
Ⓒ 🚗

The Château de Marais was built in 1788, close to the remains of the medieval castle. In 1899 the American, Anna Gould, the daughter of the New York financier, Jay Gould, bought the Château from the Duchesse de Noailles, who later married the Duc de Talleyrand. Their daughter, the present owner, married the diplomat and politician, Gaston Palewski.

The house, now open to the public, contains portraits and memorabilia of Prince Charles-Maurice de Talleyrand (1754–1838), who successfully survived all the Revolutionary upheavals, as Bishop of Autun, President of the National Assembly and Foreign Minister for the Directorate, the Consulate and the Emperor. There are also souvenirs of the Talleyrand family and a more general collection of furniture, objets d'art and portraits, including two of Louis XVIII and Charles X in coronation robes, given by the kings to Talleyrand.

Saint-Cyr-sur-Loire

Anatole France's House

Maison d'Anatole France, 'La Béchellerie', Saint-Cyr-sur-Loire, F-37100 Tours, Indre-et-Loire
May–Sept, Tues–Sat 10–12, 2–5
Ⓒ

The celebrated novelist and short-story writer, Jacques-Anatole Thibaut (1844–1924), always known as Anatole France, bought this house in 1914. He enlarged and remodelled it, and decorated the interior in a variety of eclectic tastes which have not always met with approval, but which provide interesting clues to his personality. The room in which he died has been preserved exactly as it was at that time.

Sheet-bronze figure of a god, Celtic, 1st century BC. Museum of National Antiquities, Saint-Germain-en-Laye.

Saint-Denis

Museum of Art and History

Musée d'Art et d'Histoire, 22 bis, rue Gabriel Péri, F-93200 Saint-Denis, Seine ☎ *42 43 05 10 Mon, Wed–Sat 10–5.30; Sun 2–6.30. Closed public holidays.*

C &

The museum, winner of the European Museum of the Year Award in 1982, occupies a former Carmelite convent, built in the 17th century. It has exhibits telling the story of the convent and of the town of Saint-Denis. Other sections of the museum are devoted to the 19th-century industries of Saint-Denis and to the Commune, the revolutionary government set up in Paris in 1871, after the end of the siege of the city by the Prussians. The museum also has the reconstructed 18th-century pharmacy of the Hôtel-Dieu and a collection of 19th–20th-century French paintings.

Saint-Etienne

Museum of Art and Industry

Musée d'Art et d'Industrie, 8 place Louis-Comte, F-42000 Saint-Etienne, Loire ☎ *77 33 04 85 Wed–Mon 10–12, 2–5*

F

In the 19th century, Saint-Etienne depended mainly on the manufacture of textiles, especially ribbons, and weapons for its livelihood. Its first museum collections, built up from 1833 onwards, reflected this. Its art collections were created later. The museum now has sections devoted to arms, including firearms, and

armour, the production of ribbons and trimmings, looms, and coalmining. There are also displays of Gallo-Roman archaeology from local sites, of late 19th–early 20th century posters and of 18th–19th-century French and Italian paintings.

Museum of Modern Art

Musée d'Art Moderne, La Terrasse, F-42000 Saint-Etienne, Loire ☎ *77 93 59 58 Mon, Thurs–Sun 10–7; Wed 10–8*

C & 💻 ⌂

This local museum has one of the best collections of modern and contemporary art in France. Established in 1947 and installed in a new building since 1987, both the collections and the large library have been greatly enriched by donations from the Casino and a leading local bank. The selection of works displayed is international, but French artists are very strongly represented.

Saint-Germain-en-Laye

Museum of National Antiquities

Musée des Antiquités Nationales, BP 30, F-78103 Saint-Germain-en-Laye, Yvelines ☎ *34 51 53 65 Wed–Mon 9–5*

C & 💻 ♿ ⌂

The Château de Saint-Germain, which houses the museum, dates from the 16th century. Its important archaeological collections illustrate the history of France from prehistoric times to 800 AD, with stone and bone tools, weapons and jewellery. There are tombs of the Gallo-Roman, Barbarian and Merovingian periods.

Saint-Jean-Cap-Ferrat

Ephrussi de Rothschild Museum

Musée Ephrussi de Rothschild, Villa Ile-de-France, F-06230 Saint-Jean-Cap-Ferrat, Alpes-Maritimes ☎ *93 01 33 09 Museum: Tues–Sun 2–6 (July–Aug 3–7). Gardens: Tues–Sun 9–12, 2–6 (July–Aug 3–7).*

C & ⌂

In 1905 Baroness Ephrussi de Rothschild bought seven hectares of land at Cap Ferrat and built a mansion, the Villa Ile-de-France, in the Italian style, as a home for herself and her art collections. She died in 1934, leaving her property to the Institut de France for use as a museum. The house and gardens suffered severely from neglect during the Second World War, but have now been restored.

The collections displayed in the Villa include Beauvais and Aubusson tapestries, Siennese and Florentine primitives, paintings by Boucher and Fragonard, and Vincennes, Sèvres and Saxe porcelain. There are also Oriental objets d'art, wrought ironwork, and Impressionist paintings, including some by Monet, Renoir and Sisley.

Saint-Jean-Pied-de-Port

Museum of Pelote

*Musée de la Pelote, rue de l'Eglise, F-64220
Saint-Jean-Pied-de-Port, Pyrénées-
Atlantiques* ☎ *59 37 00 92
June 15–Sept 15, daily 10–12, 3–6*
Ⓕ

The museum was created in 1970 and occupies a
room in the former mairie. It displays the
equipment used in the Basques' favourite
pastime and includes costumes and equipment
which form part of the ritual. There is also a
collection of photographs showing play in
action at different periods and commemorating
celebrated practitioners.

Saint-Joachim

Bridal Museum

*Maison de la Mariée, 130–132 Ile de Fédrun,
F-44720 Saint-Joachim, Loire-Atlantique*
☎ *40 88 42 04
Mar–May, daily 9–12.30, 1.30–7.30. June–Sept,
daily 9–7.30.*
Ⓕ

During the second half of the 19th century,
from the Second Empire to the Belle Epoque,
the Romantic period, two factories flourished in
Saint-Joachim making orange blossom in wax
for weddings. The museum's collections
illustrate the product and the practice and
contain bridal bouquets and garlands, together
with designs, photographs and lithographs.

**Villa Ile-de-France, home of the Ephrussi de
Rothschild Museum, Saint-Jean-Cap-Ferrat.**

Saint-Julien-Chapteuil

Jules Romains Museum

*Musée Jules-Romains, Mairie, Saint-Julien-
Chapteuil, Haute-Loire*
☎ *71 08 70 14
July–Aug, Mon–Wed, Fri, Sat 10–12, 2–6*
Ⓕ

The poet, dramatist and novelist, Jules Romains
(1885–1972) – the pen-name of Louis Farigoule
– was born near Saint-Julien-Chapteuil. A
memorial museum to him has been established
in a room at the mairie. It contains furniture,
paintings, books, manuscripts and photographs
from his Paris apartment and from his estate at
Grandcour-en-Tomaine, as a bequest from his
wife.

Saint-Julien-en-Beaujolais

Claude Bernard Museum

*Musée Claude Bernard, Saint-Julien-en-Beaujolais,
F-69640 Denicé, Rhône*
☎ *74 67 51 44
Apr–Sept, Tues–Sun 9–12, 2–6. Oct–Feb, Tues–
Sun 9–12, 2–5. Closed Mar and Aug 15.*
Ⓒ

The great physiologist, Claude Bernard (1813–
78) was born in the vine-grower's house which is
now the museum. The exhibits include
memorabilia of Dr Bernard and his friends and
contemporaries. There are original manuscripts,
diplomas, portraits, letters and items of
scientific equipment used by Bernard in the
course of his researches.

Saint-Michel-de-Montjoie

Granite Museum

*Musée du Granit, Le Bourg, Saint-Michel-de-
  Montjoie, F-50670 Saint-Pois, Manche*
  ☎ *33 59 84 94*
*Easter–June 14 & Oct 16–31, Sat 2–6.30, Sun
  2–6. June 15–Oct 15, daily 10–12, 2–6.*
Ⓒ

The Cotentin peninsula's granite quarries are an
important local industry. This open-air museum
presents their history and shows how the granite
is extracted and worked. Visitors can see
examples, past and present, of the final product,
as feeding and watering troughs, millstones,
paving stones, kitchen sinks and as pillars,
lintels and balustrades. There is also an
exhibition of granite sculpture.

Saint-Pierre-de-Chartreuse

Carthusian Museum

*Musée de la Correrie de la Grande-Chartreuse,
  Grande-Chartreuse, Saint-Pierre-de-
  Chartreuse, F-38380 Saint-Laurent-du-Pont,
  Isère*   ☎ *76 88 60 45*
*Apr & Oct, Mon–Sat 9–12, 2–6; Sun 9.30–12,
  2–6. May–Sept, Mon–Sat 9–12, 2–6.30; Sun
  9.30–12, 2–6.30.*
Ⓒ 🔨

The museum was opened in 1957. The
Chartreuse or Charterhouse, the great
monastery in a valley in the Alps, was founded
by St Bruno (1035–1110) in 1084. It was the
headquarters of the Carthusian order and
functioned as a monastery until 1903. In 17
rooms, the museum tells the story of the order

and the Grande-Chartreuse and gives a picture
of the religious life here. The layout of the
monastery can be studied with the help of a
model and visitors can see a cell furnished as it
was in the active days of the monastery. Among
the paintings are eight from the studio of
Eustach Le Sueur (1616–55), which show some
of the principal events in the life of St Bruno.
Among the other exhibits are habits worn by
the monks, liturgical books and a still used to
make the celebrated Chartreuse liqueur.

Saint-Pierre-d'Oléron

Eleanor of Aquitaine Museum

*Musée Oléronais Aliénor d'Aquitaine, 31 rue
  Pierre Loti, F-17310 Saint-Pierre-d'Oléron,
  Charente-Maritime   ☎ 46 47 39 88*
*Easter period, then June 15–Sept 15, Mon–Sat
  10–12, 3–7. Other times by appt.*
Ⓒ 🔗

In 1154 Eleanor of Aquitaine, the divorced wife
of Louis VII, married Henry Plantagenet, Duke
of Normandy, afterwards Henry II. She brought
him as a dowry the island of Oléron, which
remained a possession of the English Crown for
more than two centuries.

The museum, opened in 1963, is devoted to
the social history of the island, with displays
illustrating its costumes and headdresses,
agriculture, wine production, domestic life,
customs and traditions, and handicrafts.
Sections are devoted to the salt industry, with a
model showing the operation of a salt marsh,
and to the writer, Pierre Loti (1850–1923),
whose family came from Oléron.

Saint-Quentin

Antoine Lécuyer Museum

*Musée Antoine Lécuyer, 28 rue Antoine Lécuyer,
  F-02100 Saint-Quentin, Aisne*
  ☎ *23 64 06 66*
*Mon, Wed–Fri 10–12, 2–5; Sun 2–6. Closed
  Jan 1, May 1, July 14, Nov 1, Dec 25, 26.*
Ⓒ 🏛

In 1877 the banker, Antoine Lécuyer,
bequeathed his mansion to the town, with the
intention of displaying there a remarkable
collection of 80 pastel portraits by Maurice-
Quentin Delatour (1704–88), who was born at
Saint-Quentin. Delatour was official portrait
painter to Louis XV and the collection now in
the museum includes many of the leading
personalities of the age. The building was
destroyed in 1917 and rebuilt in 1928–32 on the
original site. It contains, in addition to the
Delatour portraits, paintings and drawings by
artists associated with his studio. There are also
18th–20th-century French paintings, especially
by the Impressionists and by members of the
Barbizon School, together with European and
Oriental ceramics, ivories, enamels, faïence and
tapestries.

Femme se coiffant **by Aristide Maillol; bronze,
1919. Museum of the Annunciation, Saint-
Tropez.**

Saint-Remèze

Museum of the World Underground

L'Aven-Grotte de Marzal, Musée du Monde
Souterrain, Saint-Remèze, F-07700 Bourg-
Saint-Andeol, Ardèche   ☎ *75 55 14 82*
Mar & Nov, Sun 10–6. Apr–Oct, daily 9–6.
C ⓘ 💻 ↩

The spectacular Aven Cave at Marzal, near
Saint-Remèze, was found in 1892. The entrance
was then closed and the cave was lost until
1949, when it was rediscovered and adapted for
visits by the general public. Outside, there is
now a Prehistoric Zoo, with life-size models
based on scientific evidence, of prehistoric
animals and early man. There is also a museum,
presenting the history of speleology from its
earliest days, containing early photographs and
equipment.

Saint-Rivoal

Cornec House

Ecomusée des Monts d'Arrée, Maison Cornec,
F-29190 Saint-Rivoal, Pleyben, Finistère
☎ *98 68 87 76*
June & Sept 1–15, daily 2–6. July–Aug, daily 1–7.
Groups at other times by appt.
C

Built in 1702, this house is a good example of
the style which developed in Léon and Monts
d'Arrée between the 17th and 19th centuries. It
is characterised by a protruding wing, called the
Apoteis, where the table was placed, and by an
outdoor staircase, protected by a porch. The
living quarters inside were shared with
livestock. The house is partly furnished and
contains exhibitions on the history of the house
and on the surrounding countryside. The
museum forms part of the Parc Naturel Régional
d'Armorique.

Saint-Tropez

Museum of the Annunciation

Musée de l'Annonciade, F-83990 Saint-Tropez,
Var   ☎ *94 97 04 01*
June–Sept, Wed–Mon 10–12, 3–7. Oct, Dec–
May, Wed–Mon 10–12, 2–6.
C ⓘ

The Chapel of Our Lady of the Annunciation
was built c. 1510, as the headquarters of a
brotherhood of White Penitents. It became
disused as a result of the Revolution and in 1973
the upper part of the church was converted to
house the Musée Tropelen. Between 1950 and
1955 the whole building was fitted out for
museum purposes at the expense of Georges
Grammont, who endowed the new museum
with 56 items from his own celebrated
collection.
   The exhibits are of 20th-century art and
include works by Bonnard, Braque, Dufy,
Maillol, Matisse, Rouault, Sera, Utrillo,
Vuillard, Derain and Seurat.

Russian 18th-century sledge. Museum of the
Horse, Saumur.

Saint-Vincent-sur-Jard

Georges Clemenceau Museum

Musée Georges-Clemenceau, Saint-Vincent-sur-
Jard, F-85520 Jard-sur-Mer, Vendée
May–Sept, Wed–Mon 9–12, 2–6. Oct–Apr,
Wed–Mon 9–12, 2–5.
C ↩

Georges Clemenceau (1841–1929), Minister of
War and President of the Council during the
First World War, compelled the Germans to
capitulate unconditionally and negotiated the
Treaty of Versailles. He spent the last ten years
of his life in this late 19th-century fisherman's
house, 'La Bicoque', facing the sea, where he
gardened assiduously. It remains much as it was
when he lived here, with a nondescript
assortment of furniture. His personal possessions
and the presents given to him by foreign
personalities bear witness to his long and
remarkable career.

Saumur

Museum of Decorative Arts and Museum of
the Horse

Musée des Arts Décoratifs et Musée du Cheval,
Château de Saumur, F-49400 Saumur, Maine-
et-Loire   ☎ *41 51 30 46*
Apr–June 14 & Sept 16–Oct, daily 9–11.30, 2–6.
June 15–Sept 15, daily 9–6.30. Oct–Mar,
Wed–Mon 9.30–11.30, 2–5. July–Aug, also
8.30–10.30 pm. Closed Jan 1, Dec 25.
C ⓘ 💻 ↩

The first fortress at Saumur dates from c. 1230.
In the second half of the 14th century, it was
transformed by Louis I of Anjou into a graceful
residence. During the 18th and 19th centuries,
the buildings slowly decayed and the west wing
eventually collapsed. The remainder of the
castle was bought by the municipality in 1906
and restored. In 1912 the two restored wings

were converted into museums, the Town Museum on the ground floor and the Museum of the Horse on the first floor.

What was the Town Museum is now the Museum of Decorative Arts. It has collections of French furniture, tapestries, small sculptures, Limoges enamels, faïence and porcelain. The Museum of the Horse contains displays illustrating the history of harness and horsemanship from classical times to the present day, with collections of saddles, spurs, bits and stirrups.

Sceaux

Ile-de-France Museum

Musée de l'Ile-de-France, Château de Sceaux, F-92330 Sceaux, Hauts-de-Seine
☎ 46 61 06 71
Apr–Oct, Mon, Fri 2–6; Wed, Thurs 10–12, 2–6; Sat, Sun 10–12, 2–7. Nov–Mar, Mon, Fri 2–5; Wed, Thurs 10–12, 2–5; Sat, Sun 10–12, 2–5. Closed public holidays.
C ▮

The museum, opened in 1936, occupies the Louis XIII château, built in 1857 for the Duc de Trévise on the site of one designed by Colbert which was destroyed during the Revolution. It was closed during the war years and reopened in 1949. Its aim is to present the history of the Paris region, with its seven Departments and 2,000 Communes. The collections are displayed on a Departmental basis. There is an audio-visual introduction lasting eleven minutes. Considerable use is made of contemporary paintings, engravings and watercolours in order to recapture the appearance of the region in the past and there is a large documentation centre.

Sèvres porcelain vase, *c.* 1785. Museum of Ceramics, Sèvres.

Sens

Museum of Sens

Musée de Sens, Palais Synodal, place de la Cathédrale, F-89100 Sens, Yonne
☎ 86 64 15 27
June–Sept, Wed–Mon 10–12, 2–6. Oct–May, Mon, Thurs, Fri 2–6; Sat, Sun 10–12, 2–6. Free admission Wed.
C ▮ ⬛

The museum has recently been transferred to the former Archbishops' Palace, built in the early 13th century. One section is devoted to the archaeology of Sens and to architectural sculptures, the other to the cathedral treasury. The treasury contains reliquaries, liturgical objects and religious ornaments from the 5th century onwards and textiles from the 5th to the 14th centuries, including an 18th-century chasuble said to have been worn by Saint Ebbon.

Sérignan-du-Comtat

J. H. Fabre's House

Harmas de J. H. Fabre, Musée National d'Histoire Naturelle, F-84830 Sérignan-du-Comtat, Vaucluse   ☎ 90 70 00 44
Apr–Sept, Wed–Mon 9–11.30, 2–6. Nov–Mar, Wed–Mon 9–11.30, 2–4. Closed Oct.
C ▮ ⬛

The great entomologist, Jean-Henri Fabre (1823–1915), bought 'Harmas' in 1879 and lived there until his death. At 'Harmas' he wrote nine of the ten volumes of his *Souvenirs Entomologiques*, which earned him a recommendation for the Nobel Prize for Literature in 1904. The museum dedicated to him was established in his former home in 1922. It contains displays illustrating his life and work. The exhibits include Fabre's herbaria and his collections of superb molluscs, fossils, minerals and prehistoric material, as well as his 300 watercolours of the mushrooms to be found in the region.

There are 600 species of plants in the park adjoining the house. Each is labelled with its name in Latin, French, Provençal, German, Spanish, English, Italian and Dutch.

Serrières

Museum of Rhône Shipping

Musée de la Batellerie du Rhône, Ancienne Eglise Saint-Sornin, F-07340 Serrières, Ardèche
☎ 75 34 05 03
Easter–Nov 1, Sat, Sun, public holidays 3–6 or by appt
C

The museum is in a 14th-century church, which has its roof timbers in the shape of the hull of an upturned boat. There are collections of local ethnography, including costumes, furniture, pottery, spinning and weaving equipment, and exhibits devoted to basketmaking and glassmaking. A special section contains iron crosses, of different sizes, which were carried by bargemen on their journeys. The crosses, masterpieces of popular art, are ornamented with the instruments used during the Passion. There are also documents and pictures relating to the history of Rhône shipping.

Sète

Paul Valéry Museum

Musée Paul Valéry, rue François-Desnoyers, F-34200 Sète, Hérault ☎ 67 46 20 98
May–Sept, Wed–Mon 10–12, 2–7. Oct–Apr, Wed–Mon 10–12, 2–6. Closed public holidays. Free admission Wed.
C

The poet, essayist and critic, Paul Valéry (1871–1945) was born at Sète and is buried in the celebrated 'cimetière marin' overlooking the sea and the town. A room in the museum is devoted to him. It contains manuscripts of his works and portraits of him at different stages of his life. Other sections are devoted to local archaeology and to the history of Sète and the Canal du Midi, which joins the Mediterranean at Sète. There are also paintings by, among others, Gustave Doré, Lhoty, Sarthon and Dufy, together with 14 drawings by Marquet, made at Sète.

Sèvres

Museum of Ceramics

Musée National de Céramique, place de la Manufacture, F-92310 Sèvres, Seine-et-Oise ☎ 45 34 99 05
Wed–Mon 10–12, 1.30–5.15. Groups by appt only.
C *(ex children)* 🛈 🚶

The museum was created in the early 19th century by Alexandre Brongniart, then director of the Sèvres porcelain factory, to show all types of ceramics, from all periods and from all parts of the world. In this very varied collection, the Sèvres porcelain plays a prominent part, with exhibits of the products of the factory since its foundation in 1756.

Souillac

Museum of Automata

Musée d'Automate, Place de l'Abbaye, F-46200 Souillac, Lot ☎ 65 37 07 07
Jan–Mar & Nov–Dec, Wed–Sun 2–6. Apr–June & Sept–Oct, Tues–Sun 10–12, 3–6. July–Aug, daily 10–1, 3–7.
C 🛈 🚶

Jean Roullet, born in 1829, was trained as a machine-tool maker in Paris. In 1865 he established a business to make performing clockwork figures of exceptional quality. It still continues, under the direction of his descendants, the Decamps family. The Decamps' collection of more than 3,000 items,

Decorated pottery from the 4th millennium BC. Archaeological Museum, Strasbourg.

all but two made by the firm, was acquired by the State in the 1970s and constitutes the National Collection.

The pieces, all in operating condition, include a woman powdering herself in front of a mirror, a toy theatre with a scene representing Christ's passion, a snake-charmer, a jazz band and a rickshaw with its passenger.

Strasbourg

Alsace Museum

Musée Alsacien, 23 quai Saint-Nicolas, F–67000 Strasbourg, Bas-Rhin ☎ 88 35 55 36
Wed–Mon 10–12, 2–6. Closed Jan 1, Good Fri, May 1, Dec 25.
C 🛈

The museum is devoted to the social history and traditional customs and occupations of Alsace. The displays include reconstructions of Alsace domestic interiors and collections of painted furniture, household equipment, costumes, pottery, craftsmen's tools, wooden sculpture and military coloured prints. Sections are also devoted to tools and equipment used in vineyard cultivation and architecture, and to objects from synagogues in Alsace.

Archaeological Museum

Musée Archéologique, Palais Rohan, 2 place du Château, F-67000 Strasbourg, Bas-Rhin ☎ 88 32 48 95
Apr–Sept, Wed–Mon 10–12, 2–6. Oct–Mar, Mon, Wed–Sat 2–6; Sun 10–12, 2–6. Closed Jan 1, Good Fri, May 1, Nov 1, Dec 25.
C 🛈 ♿ 🚶

The Archaeological Museum, one of the most important in France, occupies the basement of the Rohan Palace, built in 1735–42, which was the residence of the four Prince-Bishops of Strasbourg, Cardinals de Rohan. Its collections cover the history of the region from 100,000 BC to 800 AD. Among the exhibits are objects illustrating the daily life of mammoth hunters in the Palaeolithic Age and of the first Neolithic farmers, jewellery, weapons and pottery from Bronze and Iron Age graves, and material showing Strasbourg and Alsace in the Gallo-Roman period, including Gallo-Roman glassware and religious and funeral sculpture. There are also notable displays of Merovingian jewellery and weapons.

Museum of Decorative Art

*Musée des Arts Decoratifs, Palais Rohan, 2 place
du Château, F-67000 Strasbourg, Bas-Rhin*
☎ 88 32 48 95
*Apr–Sept, Wed–Mon 10–12, 2–6. Oct–Mar,
Wed–Sat 2–6; Sun 10–12, 2–6. Closed Jan 1,
Good Fri, May 1, Nov 1, Dec 25.*

F â

The museum occupies the State Apartments of
the Rohan Palace, sumptuously decorated for
the Prince-Bishops of Strasbourg in 1735–42.
The collections include the 17th–19th-century
furniture, some of it made for the Cardinals de
Rohan and some for Napoleon I, Gobelins
tapestries, and faïence and porcelain made in
eastern France, some of it at the celebrated
Hannong factory in Strasbourg. There is also
18th–19th-century pewter, mostly Strasbourg,
18th–19th-century Strasbourg goldsmiths' and
silversmiths' work, and a range of historic
musical instruments.

Museum of Modern Art

*Musée d'Art Moderne, 5 place du Château,
F-67000 Strasbourg, Bas-Rhin*
☎ 88 32 48 95
*Wed–Mon 10–12, 2–6. Closed Jan 1, Good Fri,
May 1, Nov 1, Dec 25.*

C â &

The period covered by the museum is from the
Impressionists to the present day (1870–1990).
The collections include paintings, sculpture,
decorative art objects and stained glass. The
artists represented are mainly French and the
aim has been to give an overall view of the main
movements in modern art – Impressionism,
Post-Impressionism, Art Nouveau, Fauvism,
Expressionism and Surrealism.
  The annexe of the museum, the Gallery of
Alsatian Art, has recently been opened, in the
same building. It illustrates the main trends in
the art of Alsace since 1850.

Museum of Notre-Dame

*Musée de l'Oeuvre de Notre-Dame, 3 place du
Château, F-67000 Strasbourg, Bas-Rhin*
☎ 88 32 06 39
*Apr–Sept, Wed–Mon 10–12, 2–6. Oct–Mar,
Wed–Sat 2–6; Sun 10–12, 2–6. Closed Jan 1,
Good Fri, May 1, Nov 1, Dec 25.*

F â

The museum occupies a group of 14th–17th-
century buildings. Its collections illustrate the
development of art in Alsace during the Middle
Ages and the Renaissance. The exhibits include
sculptures, many of them from the cathedral,
from where they have been removed on account
of the threat of further damage from the weather
and from atmospheric pollution. There are also
collections of stained glass, furniture, paintings,
woodwork, objets d'art and tapestries.

**Fulfilment, 1909, by Gustav Klimt.
Museum of Modern Art, Strasbourg.**

Tarbes

Marshal Foch's Birthplace

*Maison Natale du Maréchal Foch, 2 rue de la
Victoire, F-65000 Tarbes, Hautes-Pyrénées*
☎ 62 93 19 02
*July–Sept 15, Mon, Thurs–Sun 8–12, 2.30–5.45.
Sept 16–June, Mon, Thurs–Sun 8–12,
2–5.15. Closed Jan 1, May 1, Nov 1,
Dec 25.*

C â

The Marshal of France, Ferdinand Foch (1851–
1929) was a native of Tarbes, his father being
Bernard Jules Napoleon Foch, Secretary of the
Prefecture. The museum, established in 1951 in
the house where he was born, contains furniture
which belonged to the Marshal, together with a
number of his personal possessions and a
collection of paintings, posters and photographs
relating to him and to the First World War.
There are also trophies and decorations given to
him by the Allied powers.

Thiers

Cutlery Museum

*Musée de la Coutellerie, Maison des Couteliers, 58
rue de la Coutellerie, F-63300 Thiers, Puy-de-
Dôme*   ☎ 73 80 58 86
*June–Sept, daily 10–12, 2–6.30. Oct–May, Tues–
Sun 10–12, 2–6.*

C â

18th-century French knife. Cutlery Museum, Thiers.

Thiers is traditionally the centre of the French cutlery industry. The main part of the museum is in a 15th-century magistrate's house. It contains an historical collection of locally-made cutlery – knives, scissors and razors – together with tools and equipment and exhibits showing the working, domestic and social life of the cutlers and their families. Demonstrations of craftsmen at work take place in the museum workshop, with a forge and grinding shop in a separate building, 21 rue de la Coutellerie.

Tigy

Museum of Old Rural Handicrafts

Musée de l'Artisanat Rural Ancien, Clos Rolland
du Roscoat, 60 rue de Sully, F-45510 Tigy,
Loiret
Easter–Nov 1, Sun and public holidays 2.30–6.30.
Also open Sat, July–Aug.
C

The museum was created in order to preserve the memory of the traditional trades and crafts which have either disappeared or which are in the process of being transformed almost out of recognition. The large collection of tools and equipment is accompanied by relevant photographs, old postcards, invoices and workmen's pay and record books. The displays are completed by early agricultural implements and by equipment introduced before the days of mechanisation in order to facilitate the making of bread, butter, cheese, honey and the processing of flax. There are reconstructions of the interior of a country cottage, a grocer's shop, a village forge and a clogmaker's workshop.

Toulon

Naval Museum

Musée de la Marine, Place Ingénieur-Monsenergue,
F-83100 Toulon, Var   ☎ 94 02 02 01
Jan–June & Sept–Dec, Wed–Mon 10–12, 1.30–6.
July–Aug, daily 10–12, 2–6. Open Easter Sun
and Whit Sun, but closed other public holidays.
C 🔱

The decision to establish a naval museum in Toulon was taken under Louix XIV, but it was only realised in 1814. Since 1981 it has occupied a new building by the side of the 1738 gateway to the Arsenal. There are large collections of ships' figureheads and of models of warships from the 18th century onwards. A section is devoted to the great military engineer, Marshal Sebastien la Prestre de Vauban (1633–1707), the creator of the Arsenal at Toulon, to notable Toulon navigators and naval officers, and to the local convict hulks.

Toulouse

Museum of the Augustinians

Musée des Augustins, 21 rue de Metz, F-31000
Toulouse, Haute-Garonne   ☎ 61 22 21 82
Mon, Thur–Sat 10–12, 2–6; Wed 10–12, 2–10.
Closed public holidays.
C

The museum's original collections were composed of works of art seized by the Revolutionary government from the Church and from aristocratic families, and were opened to public view in 1795. The museum was one of the 15 constituted by Consular Decree in 1801. It was allocated the buildings of the Augustinian monastery, to which a new building was added in 1880. The collections of 6th–19th-century sculpture come almost entirely from the region. The large and important collection of paintings is European, but particularly strong in works by Toulouse artists of the 17th–19th centuries, the great period of painting in the region.

Museum of Old Toulouse

Musée du Vieux Toulouse, 7 rue Dumas, F-31000
Toulouse, Haute-Garonne   ☎ 61 80 23 10
June–Sept, Mon–Sat 3–6. Mar–May & Oct,
Thurs 2.30–5.30.
C

The Hôtel Dumas, which houses the museum, dates from the late 16th century. Its collections aim to recapture something of life in the city in past centuries. There are collections of costumes and accessories, craftsmen's tools, portraits, views, models and displays devoted to festivals, processions, the theatre, popular art, painting, and sculpture. The museum also has a remarkable collection of 18th–19th-century Toulouise faïence, signed by the makers.

Tours

Museum of Fine Art

Musée des Beaux-Arts, 18 place François Sicard,
F-37000 Tours, Indre-et-Loire
   ☎ 47 05 68 72
Wed–Mon 9–12.45, 2–6. Closed Jan 1, May 1,
July 14, Nov 1, 11, Dec 25.
C

The museum was created after the Revolution in 1794. It occupies the former Archbishops' Palace, built in the 17th–18th centuries. The furniture, pictures and objets d'art are shown in a series of period rooms. There are collections of 16th–19th-century French, Dutch, Flemish and Italian paintings and of contemporary French paintings. Among the artists represented are Mantegna, Rembrandt, Rubens, Delacroix, Degas and Monet.

Trégarvan

Breton Rural School Museum

Musée de l'Ecole Rurale, Trégarvan, F-29127
Plomodiern, Finistère   ☎ 98 68 87 76
June–Sept 9, daily 1.30–7. Other times by appt.
C ⌨

The history of schooling in rural Brittany is presented in a school built at the beginning of the present century, with its large single classroom for pupils of all ages. An exhibition links the school at Trégarvan with the movement which, as early as 1881, ensured that even those children living in rural areas received some instruction. The classroom contains original school furniture and equipment of the period. The museum forms part of the Parc Naturel Régional d'Armorique.

Troyes

Cathedral Treasury

Trésor de la Cathédrale, 2 place du Préau, F-10000
Troyes, Aube   ☎ 25 80 58 46
June–Sept, Tues–Sun 2–6. Oct–May, Sat, Sun
2–6.
F ⌨

The cathedral at Troyes dates from the 13th–17th centuries. It has had a treasury since the 16th century. Over the centuries, the collection became steadily larger and more rich, but it was looted and much of it destroyed on the outbreak of the Revolution. During the 19th century a new treasury was gradually assembled and in recent years its collections have been greatly augmented by valuable items brought from the comparative insecurity of churches in the diocese. The treasury now contains 16th–19th-century church plate, reliquaries and religious ornaments, vestments, 16th-century tapestries and medieval enamels, statues and illuminated manuscripts.

Museums of the Abbey of Saint-Loup

Musées de l'Abbaye Saint-Loup, 1 rue Chrétien de
Troyes, F-10000 Troyes, Aube
☎ 25 73 49 49
Wed–Mon 10–12, 2–6. Closed public holidays.
C ▮ ⌨

The abbey, close to the cathedral, was built in the 17th century. At the Revolution, it ceased to be used for religious purposes, and since 1831 it has been a museum. Three museums are now housed in it, the Archaeological Museum, the Museum of Fine Art and the Museum of Natural History.

Archaeology is in the basement, the former cellars of the Abbey. The Stone Age, Bronze Age, Iron Age and Gallo-Roman periods are all strongly represented and there are a number of items from Egypt, Greece and Etruria. The natural history collections are concerned mainly with the geology, fauna and flora of the region, although there are some exotic specimens, particularly fish and butterflies.

The Fine Art Museum has an impressive collection of 13th–15th-century religious sculpture from the southern part of Champagne and of 15th–19th-century French and European paintings. French 18th-century painting is particularly well represented. Tapestries, furniture, medieval enamels and 16th-century furniture are displayed in the picture galleries.

Museum of Modern Art

Musée d'Art Moderne de Troyes, place Saint-
Pierre, F-10000 Troyes, Aube
☎ 25 80 57 30
Wed–Mon 11–6. Closed public holidays.
C ▮ ⌨

In 1976 a Troyes businessman and his wife, Pierre and Denise Lévy, gave part of their art collection to the French government. The bequest consisted of about 2,000 works by French artists from the period 1850–1950, mostly paintings and drawings, but with some sculpture, glassware and ceramics, and tapestries. Among the artists represented are Bonnard, Cézanne, Dufy, Rouault, Vuillard, Degas, Derain, Matisse, Maillol and Rodin.

The collection is displayed in the former Bishop's Palace, a 16th–17th-century building, which was fully restored by the municipality.

Portrait of Jeanne Hébuterne, the artist's mistress, by Amedeo Modigliani. Museum of Modern Art, Troyes.

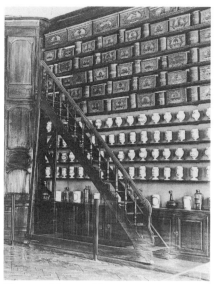

Pharmacy Museum, Troyes.

Museum of Troyes and the Champagne Region

*Musée Historique de Troyes et de la Champagne,
Hôtel de Vauluisant, 4 rue de Vauluisant,
F-10000 Troyes, Aube*   ☎ *25 73 49 49
extn 482*
Wed–Sun 10–12, 2–6. Closed public holidays.
© ⛭

The Hôtel de Vauluisant was built in the 16th
and 17th centuries. In 1954 it was converted to
museum use and now houses two museums, one
dealing with paintings and sculpture and with
the history of the town and the region, the other
with the local knitwear industry.

There was a remarkable flowering of religious
art in Troyes during the 16th century. The
museum has a large and important collection of
paintings and sculpture produced locally during
this period which indicates both the quantity
and quality of what was achieved. Other
displays within this section of the museum give
an impression of the changing scene in Troyes
during the 18th–20th centuries, with the help of
paintings, drawings, engravings, old
photographs, costumes and craftsmen's tools.

Troyes has for a long time been the capital of
the French knitwear industry. The part of the
museum which deals with this illustrates the
history and techniques of the industry. There is
an excellent collection of looms of various
types, including one in use in the 18th century.
Visitors can also see a hosier's workshop and a
display of stockings, socks, bonnets, gloves,
bathing suits, underclothing and other knitted
products.

Pharmacy Museum

*Musée de la Pharmacie, Hôtel-Dieu-Le-Comte,
quai des Comtes de Champagne, F-10000
Troyes, Aube*   ☎ *25 80 98 97*
Wed–Mon 10–12, 2–6. Closed public holidays.
Ⓕ ⛭

The Hôtel-Dieu-Le-Comte is a vast early 18th-
century hospital. The pharmacy, one of the
finest in France, looks almost exactly as it did
when it was first opened. It has 320 wooden
storage boxes and 240 faïence jars, a wide range
of pestles and mortars and other equipment of
the period. The pharmacy's former laboratory
now contains the hospital's museum, with its
records and a fine collection of works of art
relating to healing, including a number of 16th-
century reliquary busts.

Valognes

Cider Museum

*Musée Régional du Cidre, rue du Petit Versailles,
F-50700 Valognes, Manche*
    ☎ *33 40 22 73/33 40 18 87*
*Easter period, then June 15–Sept 15, Mon–Tues,
Thurs–Sat 10–12, 2–6; Sun 2–6. Groups at
other times by appt.*
© ⛭ ⚙

The building in which the Cider Museum was
established in 1979 dates from the 15th century.
It was originally used as a dyer's workshop. The
exhibits tell the story of cider-making from
antiquity to modern times and of the customs
and traditions associated with it. There are
collections of old presses, stone vats and other
equipment, together with traditional furniture
and tableaux of rural life.

Vence

Museum of Perfume and Liqueurs

*Musée du Parfum et de la Liqueur, Château
Notre-Dame-des-Fleurs, 2618 route de Grasse,
F-06140 Vence, Alpes-Maritimes*
    ☎ *93 58 06 00*
*May–Sept, Mon–Sat 10–12.30, 2–6; Sun 2–6.
Oct–Apr, Mon–Sat 10–12.30, 2–5.30; Sun
2–5.30.*
© ⛭ 📖 ⚙

In the 11th century, a Benedictine priory was
built here. In the course of time it was acquired
by the Chapter of Vence, which transformed it
into a residence for the Bishops of Vence. It was
taken over by the town of Vence in 1788, but in
1812 it was bought by a wealthy Grasse
perfumier, Bruno Court, who changed its name
from Notre-Dame-des-Crottons to Notre-Dame-
des-Fleurs, which was the name of his company
in Grasse. In 1977, the property was bought and
restored by M. Lavoillotte, who established a
Museum of Perfume here.

Versailles

Château de Versailles

F-78000 Versailles, Yvelines   ☎ *30 84 74 00*
Tues–Sun 9.45–5.30
© ⛭ 📖 ♿

Louis XIV transformed his father's country seat
into a Baroque palace. Further improvements

were made during the 18th century, when it continued to be the main centre of the Court. Visitors today can see the Chapel, the Opera, the Hall of Mirrors and the Royal Apartments, as well as the celebrated gardens, laid out by André le Nôtre (1613–1700). Among the particular attractions are the painted ceilings by Charles Le Brun (1619–90) and his pupils and the 17th–18th-century mural decorations. There are also collections of French furniture, Gobelins tapestres, portraits, Savonnerie carpets and paintings illustrating scenes from French history.

Lambinet Museum

*Musée Lambinet, 54 boulevard de la Reine,
    F-78000 Versailles, Yvelines* ☎ 39 50 30 32
Tues–Sun 2–6. Closed public holidays.
F ▲

The museum is in a mid-18th-century mansion, owned by the Lambinet family and their heirs from 1852 until 1929, when it was given to the municipality, but without most of its contents. It opened as a museum of regional history in 1932. The rooms are furnished in 18th-century style. Among the exhibits are rooms devoted to Charlotte Corday (1768–93) and Jean-Paul Marat (1743–93), whom she murdered in his bath; material relating to General Lazare Hoche (1768–97), who was born at Versailles; and the National Arms Factory at Versailles, run by Nicholas-Noël Boutet (1761–1833).

Among the 18th- and 19th-century paintings, portraits and sculptures, there are several busts by Jean-Antoine Houdon (1741–1828), including his portraits of Voltaire and Rousseau. Houdon was a native of Versailles.

Villedieu-les-Poêles

Copperware Museum and Lacemaker's House

*Musée du Cuivre et Maison de la Dentellière, Cour
    du Foyer, 25 rue du Général Huard, F-50800
    Villedieu-les-Poêles, Manche*
    ☎ 33 61 00 16
June–Sept, daily 9–12, 2–6. Other times by appt.
C

'Poêle' means 'frying-pan', and the museum concentrates on the history, techniques and products of the copper kitchen-ware industry which flourished in Villedieu from the 14th century onwards. There are demonstrations of the traditional manufacturing methods. There are also displays of the decorative lace which was made in the area.

Villeneuve-Loubet

Museum of Culinary Art

*Musée de l'Art Culinaire, Fondation Auguste
    Escoffier, 3 rue Auguste Escoffier, F-06270
    Villeneuve-Loubet, Alpes–Maritimes*
    ☎ 93 20 80 51/93 73 93 79
*Tues–Sun 2–6. Closed Nov and public holidays,
    including Christmas.*
C ▲ 🞄

**Reconstruction of a Provençal kitchen.
Museum of Culinary Art, Villeneuve-Loubet.**

The great chef, restaurateur and hotelier, Auguste Escoffier (1846–1935), was closely associated with César Ritz in his development of the Ritz in Paris and the Savoy and Carlton in London. The house in which he was born has been converted into a museum in his memory. It contains memorabilia of Escoffier, including a signed portrait of the singer, Dame Nellie Melba, given to him as an acknowledgement of his creation of the Peach Melba. Among other exhibits are sugar works of art, provided by the Association of Pastry Chefs, a reconstruction of a Provençal kitchen, portraits of 18th–19th-century chefs and gastronomes, and menus for which Escoffier had been responsible. There are also first editions of his books in many languages, including *The Book of Menus, Rice and Cod.*

Villequier

Victor Hugo Museum

*Musée Victor-Hugo, rue Ernest Binet, Villequier,
    F-76490 Caudebec-en-Caux, Seine-Maritime*
    ☎ 35 56 78 31
*Mar 16–Sept 30, Wed–Mon 10–12, 2–7.
    Oct 1–31 and Feb 1–May 15, Wed–Mon
    10–12, 2–5. Closed Nov–Jan.*
C

The house now occupied by the museum belonged to the Vacquerie family, who were friends of the Hugos and whose son, Charles, married their daughter, Léopoldine. Charles and Léopoldine Vacquerie were drowned at sea off Villequier in 1843. In 1985, the centenary of Victor Hugo's death, the house was renovated and converted into a museum to him and to his daughter. The exhibits include his portrait bust by David d'Angers, a collection of his wash-drawings, and many other family memorabilia, including Marie Hugo's drawings of her daughter and childhood letters from Léopoldine.

GERMANY

Aalen

Limes Museum

*Limesmuseum, St-Johann Straße 5, D-7080
Aalen, Baden-Württemberg*
☎ *07361 500230*
Tues–Sun 10–12, 1–5
© ♦

Opened in 1964, the museum was reconstructed
and extended in 1979–81. Its collections
illustrate the Roman occupation of what is now
Baden-Württemberg and include portrait busts,
household equipment, pottery, gravestones,
statues of the gods, inscriptions, weapons, tools,
armour, coins and medals. There are also
dioramas illustrating the life of Roman soldiers
in the Limes.

The museum building is a reconstruction, on
its original site, of the Roman cavalry camp, the
largest north of the Alps, which was in use from
138 to 260 AD and accommodated the Ala II
Flavia Militaria Regiment, which contained
1,000 cavalry soldiers.

Museum of Local Life and Schubart Museum

*Heimat- und Schubartmuseum, Marktplatz 2,
D-7080 Aalen, Baden-Württemberg*
☎ *07361 500219*
Tues–Sun 10–12, 2–5
© ♦

Established in 1907 and reorganised in 1978–9
and 1982, the museum occupies a half-timbered
house on the market place. Its important
ceramics collections illustrate German faïence
production in the 18th century, especially at
Schrezheim, Crailsheim and Ansbach, as well as
porcelain from Ludwigsburg. There is also a
section devoted to the life of the poet and
composer, Christian Friedrich Daniel Schubart
(1739–91), who was imprisoned at Ohenasperg
for ten years without trial for an alleged libel on
the Duke of Württemberg.

Other displays in the museum are of Greek,
Roman and medieval archaeology, craftsmen's
tools, costumes for festive occasions,
agricultural implements and furniture.

Albstadt

Jehle Collection of the History of Music

*Musikhistorische Sammlung Jehle, Schloß
Lautlingen, D-7470 Albstadt 15, Baden-
Württemberg*
☎ *07431 162122*
Wed, Sat 2–5; Sun 10–12, 2–5.
Ⓕ ♠

This large and important collection belonged
until 1970 to the Schenk von Stauffenberg
family. Since then it has been in the possession
of Martin Jehle, who opened it to the public in

1978. It includes portraits, 18th–19th-century
musical instruments, mostly by German and
Austrian makers, and manuscripts and printed
music from the 16th to the 19th century. The
collection is arranged thematically and
illustrates the history of European music and
musical performance from the Middle Ages
onwards.

There is a workshop for the manufacture and
restoration of keyboard and stringed
instruments.

Aldersbach

Brewery Museum

*Brauereimuseum, Freiherr-von-Aretin-Platz 1,
D-8359 Aldersbach, Bayern*
☎ *08543 1642*
*Mon–Fri 3–5.30; Sat 10–11.30. Enquire locally
for guided tours.*
© ♦ ♨ ♠

Beer is known to have been brewed in Bavaria
in the early 9th century and brewing was always
an important activity at the Cistercian
monastery in Aldersbach, which was founded in
1146. After the monastery was secularised in
1803, the brewery was sold and subsequently
changed hands several times. It continues in
operation, now on a much greater scale than in
monastic times.

The museum, opened in 1979, contains a
wide range of 19th- and 20th-century brewing,
malting and coopering equipment and explains
the various processes involved. Visitors are also
able to tour the modern brewery and bottling
plant.

Brewery Museum, Aldersbach.

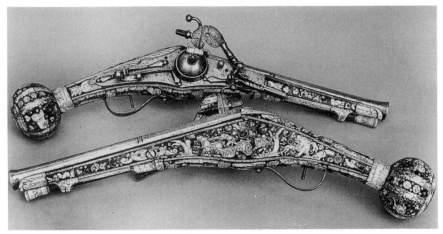

Pistols *c.* 1580. Museum of the County of
Mark, Altena.

Altena

Museum of the County of Mark
with the German Blacksmiths' Museum, the German
Wire Museum and the German Museum of Walking
for Pleasure

*Museum der Grafschaft Mark: Märkisches
    Schmiedemuseum; Deutsches Drahtmuseum;
    Deutsches Wandermuseum; Fritz-Thomée-
    Straße 80, D-5990 Altena, Nordrhein-
    Westfalen*   ☎ 02352 200151
Tues–Sun 9.30–5. Closed Jan 1, Dec 25.
Ⓒ ⓘ ☕ ⌂

All four museums are in the Castle of Altena,
parts of which date from the first half of the
twelfth century. Together, they contain displays
of local geology, natural history, prehistory and
cultural history. There are collections of
furniture, paintings, faïence, porcelain, and firebacks, and special sections are devoted to 15th–
18th-century weapons and armour, blacksmiths'
tools and wrought iron and the wire-drawing
trade – at one time Altena was the wire-drawing
capital of Europe.
    The first youth hostel in the world (1912) was
established within the Castle precinct at
Altena. Its rooms are now used as a museum of
the history of the Youth Hostel Movement and
of walking for pleasure.

Altenbeken

Egge Museum
*Egge-Museum, Alter Kirckweg, D-4791
    Altenbeken, Nordrhein-Westfalen*
        ☎ 05255 387/388
Tues, Thurs, Sat 2–5; Sun 3–6
Ⓒ ⓘ ⌂

The museum, opened in 1976, occupies a house
dating from 1583 and enlarged in 1789. It is
mainly devoted to the history of the local iron
industry, which flourished in the region from
1392 until the last blast-furnace closed down in

1926. There are collections of 16th–19th-
century stoves, ranges, fire-backs and kitchen
equipment made locally, together with
furniture, craftsmen's tools, agricultural
implements and household equipment from the
Altenbeken district. Altenbeken was formerly
an important railway centre and a section of the
museum is devoted to this aspect of the town's
history.

Appen

Luftwaffe Museum
*Luftwaffenmuseum, Hauptstraße 141, D-2081
    Appen, Schleswig-Holstein*   ☎ 04122 8067
Tues–Sun 9–5
Ⓕ ⓘ ⛴ ⌂

The museum, opened in 1957, is owned and
organised by the Armed Forces of the Federal
Republic. It is at the Hans Joachim Marseille air
base, built in 1936. The collections are
displayed in the original hangars. They present
the history of military aviation in Germany
since 1884 and include aircraft, uniforms,
equipment, documents, photographs and
medals. There are also displays of weapons,
anti-aircraft guns and rockets.

Augsburg

Berthold Brecht Memorial Museum
*Bert-Brecht-Gedenkstätte, Auf dem Rain 7,
    D-8900 Augsburg, Bayern*
        ☎ 0821 3242779
*May–Oct, Tues–Sun 10–5. Nov–Apr, Tues–Sun
    10–4.*
Ⓒ

The dramatist, Berthold Brecht (1898–1956),
the author of *Mother Courage*, was born and
educated in Augsburg. His work was banned by
the Nazis and he spent the war years in exile.
The museum, established in 1985 in the house
where he was born, tells the story of his life and
work, with an emphasis on his Augsburg days
and on his later connections with the city.

MAN Museum

MAN Museum Augsburg, Heinrich-von-Buz-
  Straße 28, Postfach 1000 80, D-8900
  Augsburg, Bayern   ☎ *0821 3223791*
Mon–Fri 8–4. Closed public holidays.

F

MAN is an abbreviation of Maschinenfabrik
Augsburg-Nürnberg, formed after the First
World War after a merger of the
Maschinenfabrik Augsburg and the
Maschinenfabrik Nürnberg. The company now
forms part of the larger Gutehoffnungshütte
steel and engineering group.

   The museum presents the story of MAN,
illustrating its varied development, especially in
machine-building and the manufacture of diesel
engines and printing presses. The development
work for Rudolf Diesel's pioneering engine was
carried out at the Augsburg factory between
1893 and 1895 and the first engine is displayed
in the museum, together with a series of later
models. Other exhibits include a very early
flatbed printing press, built in Augsburg in
1846, and an 1877 single-reel rotary press.

State Gallery

Staatsgalerie, Maximilianstraße 46, D-8900
  Augsburg, Bayern   ☎ *0821 510350*
May–Sept, Tues–Sun 10–5. Oct–Apr, Tues–Sun
  10–4.

C

The gallery forms part of the art museum
complex in the former Dominican church. It
contains 15th–16th-century German paintings,
including works by Augsburg artists. Among
those represented are Albrecht Dürer (1471–
1528), with his portrait of Jakob Fugger, Hans
Holbein the Elder (1465–1524), who had a
large workshop in Augsburg, and Hans
Burgkmair (1473–1531).

**Hans Fugger and his two wives, from the
16th-century book in honour of the family.
Fugger Museum, Babenhausen.**

State Gallery in the Kunsthalle

Staatsgalerie in der Kunsthalle Augsburg,
  Imhofstraße 7-13, D-8900 Augsburg, Bayern
  ☎ *0821 3242178*
May–Sept, Tues, Thurs–Sun 10–5; Wed 10–9.
  Oct–Apr, Tues, Thurs–Sun 10–4; Wed 10–9.

C 🛋

The Bavarian State art collections consist of
about 20,000 items. They are distributed
between the principal cities of Bavaria. The
works displayed here in the Kunsthalle illustrate
the development of art in Germany from the
late 19th century. Among the artists
represented are Max Liebermann, Louis
Corinth, Franz Marc, Max Beckmann and Paul
Klee. There is also a good collection of works by
members of the Expressionist group, Die
Brücke, especially Nolde, Schmidt-Rottluff,
Kirchner and Müller.

Babenhausen

Fugger Museum

Fugger Museum, Schloß Babenhausen, D-8943
  Babenhausen, Bayern   ☎ *08333 8078/2931*
Apr–Nov, Tues–Sat 10–12, 2–5; Sun 10–12,
  2–6.

C 🚹 📷 🛋

The Fuggers first became prominent as weavers
in Augsburg in the mid 14th century. By the
15th they were involved in finance on an
international scale, with a network of offices
throughout Europe and greatly helped by
Imperial patronage, which they obtained in
exchange for enormous loans to the Habsburgs.
In 1534 the Emperor, Charles V, granted Anton
Fugger (1493–1560) the right to mint coins and
in 1539 Anton Fugger bought the estate of
Babenhausen and built a castle, Schloss
Babenhausen, there. Later generations of the
family made modifications to the interior and
greatly enriched its contents.

   In the 1880s Prince Leopold Fugger
established a museum in Augsburg which was
dedicated to the history of the family and
contained a number of its possessions. In 1955
this was reopened in Schloss Babenhausen. The
exhibition in the present museum illustrates the
powerful influence of the Fuggers on the
political and cultural life of Europe over a long
period and presents a selection of their large
collections of paintings, porcelain, glass,
ivories, religious art and gold and silverware.
The Ancestors' Room contains 16th- and 17th-
century Fugger family portraits.

Bad Driburg

Weber's House

Weberhaus, Alhausen, Weberplatz, D-3490 Bad
  Driburg-Alhausen, Nordrhein-Westfalen
  ☎ *05253 2572*
Daily 10–12, 3–6

C

The physician and poet, Friedrich Wilhelm
Weber (1813–94) was born in Alhausen. He

translated Tennyson, who had a considerable
influence on him. His epic poem,
Dreizehnlinden, on the conversion of the Saxons
to Christianity, was immensely popular and
went through 60 editions between 1878 and
1893. The museum contains memorabilia of
Weber and collections illustrating the life and
career of the poet against the background of the
period in which he lived.

Baden-Baden

Brahms's House

Brahms-Haus, Maximilianstraße 85, D-7570
  Baden-Baden, Baden-Württemberg.
  Correspondence to: Brahmsgesellschaft Baden-
  Baden e.V., Goethestraße 56, D-7560
  Gaggenau   ☎ *07221 71172*
Mon, Wed, Fri 3–5; Sun and public holidays 10–1.
  Other times by appt.
Ⓒ 🛆 ↩

Johannes Brahms (1833–97) occupied two
rooms at 85 Maximilianstrasse during the
summer months of 1865–74. This is his only
home to survive in Germany. The rooms are
furnished in the style of the period and contain
memorabilia of Brahms, Clara Schumann
(1810–56) and the violinist, Joseph Joachim
(1831–1907). The exhibits include
photographs, letters and a plaster-cast of Clara
Schumann's hand.

The house contains a flat in which
composers, musicians and musicologists can stay
free of charge. There have been over 300 such
guests since the opening of the museum in 1966.

Bad Homburg-von-der-Höhe

Castle Museum

Schloßmuseum, Schloß Homburg, D-6380 Bad
  Homburg-von-der-Höhe, Hessen
  ☎ *06172 26091*
Mar–Oct, Tues–Sun 10–5. Nov–Feb, Tues–Sun
  10–4. Guided tours only.
Ⓒ 🛆 ▬ ⅙ ↩

Building of the castle began in the 14th century.
Additions and modifications were made in
1680–95 and during the first half of the 19th
century. Between 1622 and 1866 it was the
residence of the Counts of Hessen-Homburg and
from 1866 until 1918 the summer residence of
the Prussian Kings and German Emperors.
Visitors can see the living quarters and state
rooms of Wilhelm I and II and collections of
18th-century portrait busts, 17th–18th-century
paintings and 19th-century furniture. The
English-style garden was laid out in the 19th
century.

Gothic House Museum

Museum Gotisches Haus, Tannenwaldweg 102,
  D-6380 Bad Homburg-von-der-Höhe, Hessen
  ☎ *06172 37618*
Tues, Thurs–Sat 2–5; Wed 2–7; Sun 10–6.
Ⓒ 🛆 ▬ ⅙ ↩

A nineteenth-century game of roulette. Gothic
House Museum, Bad Homburg-von-der-Höhe.

What is now the museum was built in 1823 as a
hunting lodge for Count Friedrich VI Josef of
Homburg (1769–1829). The family never used
it, however, and it gradually fell into decay. In
1968 a group of public-spirited people succeeded
in getting it saved from demolition and listed as
a historical monument. It was restored and
opened as a museum in 1985.

The museum tells the story of Bad Homburg
and Marienbad and of their joint development
as a fashionable spa and gambling centre during
the 19th century. Among its exhibits is what is
claimed to be the oldest surviving roulette table.
A special section is devoted to the history of the
Homburg hat, reputed to have been invented by
Edward, Prince of Wales, in 1890.

Bad Honnef

Chancellor Adenauer's House

Stiftung Bundeskanzler-Adenauer-Haus, Rhöndorf,
  Konrad-Adenauer-Straße 8c, D-5340 Bad
  Honnef 1, Nordrhein-Westfalen
  ☎ *02224 6731/6340*
Tues–Sun 10–4.30. Last guided tour begins at 4.
Ⓕ 🛆 ↩

Konrad Adenauer (1875–1967) became
Chancellor in 1948 and continued to hold this
office until 1963. He built the house in
Rhöndorf in 1937 and lived there until his death
in 1967. It is now used as a memorial museum to
him.

Adenauer's study and the bedroom in which
he died have been preserved as they were in his
lifetime. Visitors may look into them, but not
enter. The entrance hall, music room, living
room and garden pavilion are, however,
accessible and contain family possessions and
memorabilia of the Chancellor's political career.

His grave is in Rhöndorf cemetery, 15
minutes' walk from the house. A separate
exhibition building presents the story of his life,
against the background of four periods of
German history.

Pin-cushion for lace-making. Huguenot Museum, Bad Karlshafen.

Bad Karlshafen

German Huguenot Museum

Deutsches Hugenotten-Museum, Hafenplatz 9a,
D-3522 Bad Karlshafen, Hessen
☎ 05672 1410
Tues–Sat 2–6; Sun 11–1, 2–6. Closed
Dec 31–Feb 16.
Ⓒ ⓘ 💼 ⚓

In 1699 Count Carl von Hessen-Cassel founded a river-port at the point where the Diemel meets the Weser. Originally called Sieburg, it was renamed Carlshaven in 1717, at the request of the Huguenots who had been allowed to settle there by the Count. 'Bad' was added in 1977 to commemorate the medicinal springs discovered in the town by the Huguenot doctor and apothecary, Jacques Galland, in 1730.

The museum's displays are in two parts. The first illustrates the Reformation in France, the persecution of the Huguenots and their flight from France to neighbouring countries and the New World. The second part tells the story of 44,000 Huguenots who found refuge in Germany. The museum building, dating from the mid-19th century, was formerly a tobacco factory. An exhibit in the museum explains the processes involved in converting the raw tobacco leaf into a saleable product.

Bad Mergentheim

Museum of the Teutonic Order

Deutschordensmuseum, Schloß, D-6990 Bad
Mergentheim, Baden-Württemberg
☎ 07931 57209
Mar–Oct, Tues–Fri 2.30–5.30; Sat, Sun and
public holidays 10–12, 2.30–5.30. Nov–4th
Sun in Advent & Jan 6–Feb, Sat, Sun &
public holidays 10–12, 2.30–5.30.
Ⓒ ⓘ 💼 ⚓

The earliest parts of the castle date from the 12th century. Considerable additions were made in the 14th, 15th and 16th centuries, and in the 18th century the chapel was decorated in the Baroque style. The castle served as the headquarters of the Teutonic Order from 1525 until 1809, when Napoleon's intervention compelled a move to Vienna.

Displays in the castle present the history of the Order from the time of the Crusades to the present day. There are also collections of 18th–19th-century paintings, religious art, Baroque and Rococo furniture, 19th-century dolls' houses and popular art.

Bad Nauheim

Rose Museum

Rosenmuseum, Raiffeisenplatz, D-6350 Bad
Nauheim-Steinfurth, Hessen. Correspondence
to: Sabine Kübler, Friedrichstraße 3, D-6350
Bad Nauheim.   ☎ 06032 343284
Wed–Sat 2–5; Sun 10–5.
Ⓕ ⚓

The museum occupies an 18th-century half-timbered house, which was moved in 1830 from the saltworks at Wisselsheim to its present site. Bad Nauheim is a traditional centre of the rose-growing industry, with 100 businesses producing 30 per cent of all the roses marketed in Germany. The museum tells the story of the industry and has collections of porcelain, paintings, books and other objects which have representations of roses. There are also exhibits of tools used in rose-growing and of containers used for pot pourri, rose-oil and rose-scented perfumes. Other sections of the museum are concerned with the history of Bad Nauheim and its region.

Personified impression of the Eglantine rose, 1867. Rose Museum, Bad Nauheim.

Salt Museum

*Salzmuseum des Hessischen Staatsbades,
    Teichhaus-Schlößchen, Nördlicher Park 17,
    D-6350 Bad Nauheim 1, Hessen
    ☎ 06032 344220/32929
Tues, Thurs, Sat 3.30–5.30; Sun 9.30–11.30.
    Groups at other times by appt. Closed
    Dec 21–Jan 2.*

C 🔒 🔊

In 1780 Prince Wilhelm von Hessen-Kassel
built a Lustschloss (pleasure castle) for his
mistress. The museum was moved there in 1977
from cramped quarters in the Spa, where it had
been established in 1960. Nauheim was noted
for its salt production in prehistoric times and
the museum's displays show how techniques
developed over a period of more then 2,500
years, until the industry finally came to an end
in 1959. There is a section devoted to the
history of the Spa during the 19th and 20th
centuries, when many famous people came to
Nauheim to take advantage of its healing
springs, which are reputed to be of particular
benefit to sufferers from heart complaints. The
Jugendstil spa buildings, erected in 1905–11,
were commissioned by Grand Duke Ernst
Ludwig of Hessen, at a cost of 10 million gold
marks.

Bad Oeynhausen

Museum of Fairytales and Weser Legends

*Märchen- und Wesersagen-Museum, Am Kurpark
    3, D-4970 Bad Oeynhausen, Nordrhein-
    Westfalen   ☎ 05731 22428
Tues–Sun 10–12, 3–5.30. Closed Jan 15–Feb 15.*

C

This is the only museum in Germany and one of
the very few in the world to be devoted solely to
folk-tales. It contains approximately 4,000
objects relating to German fairytales and local
legends. They include paintings, sculpture,
broadsheets, books, posters and folk art of all
kinds.

Bad Reichenhall

Salt Springs Museum

*Bad Reichenhaller Quellenbau, Saline Bad
    Reichenhall, Reichenbachstraße 4, D-8230 Bad
    Reichenhall, Bayern   ☎ 08651 70020
Apr–Oct, daily 10–11.30, 2–4. Nov–Mar, Tues,
    Thurs 2–4.*

C 🔒 🔊

With a mineral content of 26 per cent, the
springs at Reichenhall are the richest in Europe.
They have been exploited since prehistoric
times and now produce 200,000 tons of salt a
year. Since 1850 two large waterwheels have
been used to pump the brine to the surface, and
constitute a major tourist attraction, alongside
modern equipment which pumps from a greater
depth.
    The saltworks dates from 1834, when it
replaced an earlier building which had been

destroyed by fire. There are displays showing the
history of the techniques of salt-extraction and
processing. The chapel, rebuilt in 1849, is
distinguished by a fine series of mural paintings
and Stations of the Cross, and by three stained-
glass windows in the choir, representing Christ,
St Rupertus and St Virgilius.

Bad Säckingen

Trumpet Museum

*Trompetenmuseum, Trompetenschloß, Postfach
    1143, D-7880 Bad Säckingen, Baden-
    Württemberg   ☎ 07761 51311
Tues, Thurs, Sun 2–5. During summer months,
    also open Wed.*

C 🔒 🔊

The castle at Säckingen was built c. 1300, but
considerable modifications were carried out in
the 17th century. It formerly belonged to the
Schönau family and was consequently known as
Schönau Castle, but the name has now been
changed to Trumpet Castle.
    In 1854 Josef Viktor von Scheffel (1826–86)
published his narrative poem, *The Trumpeter of
Säckingen*. It was immensely popular and
reached its 332nd edition by 1921. It was
followed in 1884 by an opera of the same name
and in 1918 by a film. After this, it was natural
that a trumpeter should be chosen as the town's
marketing image, and that it should have a
trumpet museum, which opened in 1985.

**An Arban cornet. Trumpet Museum, Bad
Säckingen.**

Its director is the American trumpeter and musicologist, Dr Edward H. Tarr.

It has a notable historical collection of trumpets, cornets and flügelhorns, the oldest of which was made in Nuremberg in 1664. There is also an archive of woodcuts, watercolours, drawings, engravings, lithographs, postcards and posters showing trumpets and trumpet players.

Bad Salzuflen

Museum of German Spas and of Bad Salzuflen

Stadt- und Bädermuseum, Lange Straße 41,
D-4902 Bad Salzuflen, Nordrhein-Westfalen
☎ 05222 59766
Mar–Nov, Tues–Sun 10–12.30, 2.30–6. Dec–
Feb, Tues–Sun 3–6.
Ⓒ 🛈 🍴 🚗

The 1618 gabled building has fine carved woodwork on the façade. A museum of local history occupies the first floor and on the second there are displays illustrating the history of spas and sea-bathing establishments in the German-speaking countries. Among the subjects covered are the social life of the spa towns, spa architecture, spa souvenirs and equipment, glasses for taking the waters, and the history of the local salt industry from 1048 onwards. There are exhibits of handicrafts, traditional furniture and domestic equipment, Fürstenberg porcelain, 16th-century paintings, embroidery, guild material, coins, medals and orders. The museum also has a complete pharmacy, presented by the Brandes family, who ran the pharmacy over a long period.

Balve

Luise Ironworks at Wocklum

Luisenhütte Wocklum, D-5983 Balve, Nordrhein-
Westfalen   ☎ 02375 3134
May–Oct, Tues–Sat 10–6; Sun and public holidays
11.30–6. Nov–Apr, by telephone appt.
Ⓒ 🛈 🍴 🚗

The Luise ironworks was established in 1748, on the site of earlier installations. It ceased operating in 1865 and is the oldest blast furnace with its complete equipment to survive in the Federal Republic. It is an industrial monument of the first importance. The works include the blast furnace, the melting furnace, the machine hall with its waterwheel, bellows and steam-engine, the reservoir, and the office and counting-house. There is also an exhibition illustrating the life of the men and their families.

Bamberg

Diocesan Museum

Diözesanmuseum Bamberg, Domplatz 5, D-8600
Bamberg, Bayern   ☎ 0951 502316
Apr–Oct, Tues–Sun 10–5. Dec 26–Jan 6, Tues–
Sun 1–4.
Ⓒ 🛈

E.T.A. Hoffmann. Hoffmann's House, Bamberg.

The museum is in the Cathedral Chapter House, built in 1731–3. Most of the exhibits were formerly in the Cathedral Treasury. They include 11th–19th-century European and Byzantine vestments and religious art, altar-hangings and liturgical objects. Among the items on display are the vestments of Pope Clement II (1046–7), the shroud of Bishop Gunther (d. 1065), cloaks worn by the Emperor Heinrich II (1002–24) and sculptures from the Adam doorway of the Cathedral.

E. T. A. Hoffman's House

E. T. A. Hoffman-Haus, Schillerplatz 26,
D-8600 Bamberg, Bayern   ☎ 0951 23889
May–Oct, Tues–Fri 5–6; Sat, Sun and public
holidays 11–12
Ⓒ 🚗

The writer, composer and caricaturist, Ernst Theodor Wilhelm Hoffman (1776–1822) changed Wilhelm to Amadeus in honour of Mozart. In 1808–13, he was musical director at the theatre in Bamberg. The house in which he lived has been converted into a museum dedicated to him, his birthplace in Rönigsberg and the house in Berlin where he died having been destroyed during the Second World War. The museum contains portraits, manuscripts, first editions and memorabilia of the writer, illustrating his years in Bamberg.

Karl May Museum

Karl-May Museum, E. T. A. Hoffmanstraße 2,
D-8600 Bamberg, Bayern   ☎ 0951 22262
Wed–Sun 9–1
Ⓒ 🛈

Karl May (1842–1912) was an extremely successful writer of adventure stories. More than 61 million copies of his works have been sold in

the German language alone. He wrote vividly of
countries and peoples he had never seen,
especially the American Wild West, the Near
East and the Balkans. After his death, the
contents of his house, 'Shatterhand', at
Radebeul, near Dresden, were moved to
Bamberg, where visitors can see his large library,
his workroom and his extensive collections of
Orientalia and of material relating to the
opening up of the American West, including
lassoes, bows and arrows, cowboy outfits and
saddles, and Winchester and Kentucky rifles.

Bayreuth

Jean Paul Museum

Jean Paul Museum der Stadt Bayreuth,
  Wahnfriedstraße 1, D-8580 Bayreuth,
  Bayern   ☎ 0921 25399
July–Sept, daily 9–12, 2–5. Oct–June, Mon–Fri
  9–12, 2–5; Sat and public holidays 10–1.
  Closed Jan 1, Easter Sun, Whit Sun, Dec 24,
  25

Ⓒ

Jean Paul was the pen-name of the writer,
Johann Paul Friedrich Richter (1763–1825),
who spent the last 17 years of his life in
Bayreuth. Between 1804 and 1813 he changed
homes seven times. The museum, opened in
1980, is furnished in period style and contains
portraits of Jean Paul and his friends,
memorabilia of the writer, manuscripts and first
editions of his works.

New Palace Museum

Stadtmuseum, Neues Schloß, Ludwigstraße,
  D-8580 Bayreuth, Bayern   ☎ 0921 65313
May–Sept, Mon, Thurs–Sat 9–12, Tues, Wed
  9–12, 2–5

Ⓕ 🛈 ♿

The Neues Schloss or New Palace in Bayreuth,
constructed in 1753–8, was the last Residence of
the Margraves of Bayreuth. Its 38 splendid
Rococo rooms are open to the public. The
museum forms a separate unit within the palace
and is partly within the Rococo section. It
contains some of of the finest examples of
18th-century Bayreuth porcelain, together with
collections of furniture, faïence, paintings,
clocks and glass, as well as portraits of the
Margraves.
  Other sections of the museum are devoted to
weapons and militaria, 19th-century furniture,
paintings, toys and objets d'art, and to displays
illustrating the lifestyles of both peasant and
middle-class families in the region.

Wagner Museum

Richard-Wagner-Museum, Haus Wahnfried,
  Richard-Wagner-Straße 48, D-8580 Bayreuth,
  Bayern   ☎ 0921 25404
Daily 9–5. Closed Jan 1, Easter Sun, Whit Sun,
  Dec 24, 25.

Ⓒ

**Table-lamp from 1923. The Bauhaus Archives
and Museum of Design, Berlin.**

The composer, Richard Wagner (1813–83)
designed Haus Wahnfried for himself. He
moved into it in 1874 and remained here until
his death. The house was seriously damaged
during the Second World War and completely
restored in 1974–6. It now contains collections
illustrating the life and work of Wagner and the
history of the Bayreuth Festival.

Berlin

The Bauhaus Archives and Museum of Design

Bauhaus-Archiv, Museum für Gestaltung,
  Klingelhöfer Straße 14, D-1000 Berlin 30
  ☎ 030 2611618
Wed–Mon 11–5. Closed May 1, Dec 24, 31.
Ⓒ 🛈 ▣ ♿

The Bauhaus existed in Weimar from 1919 to
1925, in Dessau until 1932 and finally in Berlin
from 1932 to 1933, when it was suppressed by
the Nazis, forcing its leading architects, artists
and designers to emigrate. Among them was the
moving spirit of the Bauhaus, the architect
Walter Gropius (1883–1969), whose last task
was to design the Bauhaus Museum. The
museum was established in order to collect all
kinds of material related to the activities and
cultural ideas of the Bauhaus and the
institutions which succeeded it, especially those
in the United States – Chicago, Black
Mountain College, Harvard – and the Ulm
Institute of Design.

Berlin Museum

Berlin Museum, Lindenstraße 14, D-1000 Berlin
  61   ☎ 030 25861
Tues–Sun 10–10
Ⓒ 🛈 ▣ ♿

The museum was founded in 1962, following
the division of the city. It was to provide, in
addition to the Märkisches Museum in East

Berlin, a museum in the western part of the city which would present the history of Berlin. After several moves, permanent accommodation was found in the former Court of Appeal, a Baroque building dating from 1734–5.

The collections illustrate the history of Berlin since *c*. 1650. The exhibits include paintings, drawings, prints, sculpture and portraits. Special sections are devoted to industrial development of the city, the story of its theatres, cartoons and satires of Berlin life, fashion, artistic ironwork, the products of the Imperial Porcelain Factory, and the Jewish community in Berlin. There are a number of period rooms, illustrating the living style of Berliners between 1800 and 1920.

Brücke Museum

Brücke Museum, Bussardsteig 9, D-1000 Berlin
*   33*   ☎ *030 8312029*
Wed–Mon 11–5
C ⬧

The museum was opened in 1967 in a building designed for the purpose on the edge of the Grünewald. It is devoted to works by the four artists – Ernst Ludwig Kirchner, Fritz Bleyl, Erich Heckel and Karl Schmidt-Rottluff – who were members of the Brücke movement of Expressionist artists which was established in Dresden in 1905 and which later transferred itself to Berlin. The museum owes its existence to comprehensive collections of works by members of the Brücke and artists associated with it, presented by Schmidt-Rottluff and Heckel.

Emil Fischer District Museum

Emil-Fischer-Heimatmuseum, Ganghoferstraße
*   3-5, D-1000 Berlin 44*   ☎ *030 68092535*
Wed 12–8; Thurs–Sun 10–5. Archive only open
*   Mon, Tues and can be used during working*
*   hours, 9–5.*
F ⬧

Neukölln is a traditionally working-class district of Berlin. It has a dormitory character, since most of its inhabitants have worked in other parts of the city, and its varied social life has been characterised by a number of important experimental institutions, especially in the field of education. In 1961 a museum was established in the former public library, built in 1912. It has only temporary exhibitions, which usually last for nine months. After each exhibition, the items displayed in it are added to the permanent collection, so that the museum now has excellent material relating to sports history, especially the pioneer gymnastic instructor, Turnvater Jahn; the training of circus performers, for which Neukölln was one of the leading European centres; the Bohemian immigration; daily life in 1910; and the occupations and activities of Neukölln's Jewish population.

Georg Kolbe Museum

Georg-Kolbe-Museum, Sensburger Allee 25,
*   D-1000 Berlin 19*   ☎ *030 3042144*
Tues–Sun 10–5. Closed Dec 24, 25, 31.
C ⬧

The sculptor, Georg Kolbe (1877–1947), built a house and a studio in Berlin in 1928. The building now contains a museum to him. Its collection comprises works by Kolbe himself and sculptures, drawings and paintings by his contemporaries, left to the Kolbe Foundation in his will. The museum also possesses more than 200 of Kolbe's original plaster models and an extensive archive relating to his life and work.

Kolbe was a prolific artist, but fate has not been kind to him. Of over a thousand sculptures that he is known to have produced, a large number were destroyed during the Second World War or have simply vanished.

Reconstructed period room of *c*. 1900. Berlin Museum.

Display of plant and machinery at the Museum of Transport and Technology, Berlin.

Memorial Museum of the German Resistance

Gedenkstätte Deutscher Widerstand,
Stauffenbergstraße 13-14, D-1000 Berlin 30
☎ *030 26042202*
Mon–Fri 9–6; Sat, Sun and public holidays 9–1.
Closed Jan 1, Dec 24, 25, 31.
F

Opened in 1986, the memorial documents the German resistance to National Socialism and the fate of those who refused to conform. Among the many victims commemorated are Hans and Sophie Scholl and Christoph Probst (d. 1942) and Count Stauffenberg and his fellow officers, who made an unsuccessful attempt on Hitler's life in 1944. Sections of the museum are devoted to the story of the growth of National Socialism and of the progressive destruction of the forces of liberalism and democracy in Germany, to anti-semitism and to resistance by particular sections of Germans, including the trade unions, the churches, scientists, writers and artists, and to the distinguished exiles who were forced to seek refuge abroad.

Museum of German Ethnology

Museum für Deutsche Volkskunde SMPK Berlin,
Im Winkel 6-8, D-1000 Berlin 33
☎ *030 832031*
Tues–Sun 9–5. Closed Jan 1, May !, Dec 24, 25,
31.
F

The museum is devoted to the popular culture, both urban and rural, of German-speaking Central Europe from the 16th century to the present day. It was established in 1889. During the Second World War, the collection suffered serious losses, but it has subsequently been possible to fill many of the gaps. Popular culture of earlier periods still remains a focus, but recent collecting policy has concentrated increasingly on the records and artefacts of everyday life during the last 100 years. The museum was reopened in 1976 in a former storage building of the Secret State Archive.

The displays cover popular religion, costumes and accessories, household equipment, peasant jewellery, glassware, pottery, handicrafts, furniture, guild material, toys and craftsmen's tools.

Museum of Transport and Technology

Museum für Verkehr und Technik, Trebbiner
Straße 9, D-1000 Berlin 61 ☎ *030 254840*
Tues, Wed 9–6; Thurs, Fri 9–9; Sat, Sun 10–6.
C

The museum has been created on and around the site formerly occupied by the Anhalter Goods Station. The first section was opened in 1983. The policy has been to arrange historical exhibits which illustrate the conveyance of people and goods and the transmission of energy and information in a way which makes clear their cultural and social links. There are sections devoted to motive power, road, rail and air transport, automation and computing, research methods, domestic technology, printing, paper technology, textiles and navigation. The museum archive includes records from both private and public sources and covers the whole field of technology.

Questions about German History

Historische Ausstellung 'Fragen an die deutsche
Geschichte', Reichstagsgebäude, D-1000
Berlin 21 ☎ *030 3977141*
Tues–Sun 10–5
F

The political history of the united German state began in 1871, when Wilhelm I was proclaimed Kaiser in the Hall of Mirrors at Versailles. A few weeks later, the newly-elected Reichstag established itself in Berlin, but for a long time had to meet in the remodelled Royal Prussian Porcelain Factory. The present Reichstag building was ready for use in 1894. It was severely damaged by Nazi-inspired arson in 1933, marking the temporary end of Parliamentary democracy in Germany, and suffered further destruction during street fighting in the last stages of the Second World War.

The permanent exhibition, 'Questions about German History', was opened in part of the restored Reichstag building in 1974. Organised and financed by the Bundestag, it presents the political history of Germany from 1800 to the present day.

Bernau

Hans Thoma Museum

*Hans-Thoma-Museum, Rathaus, D-7821 Bernau,
    Baden-Württemberg*
*Mon–Fri 9–12.30, 2–6; Sat, Sun and public
    holidays 10–12, 2–6.*

C &

The naturalistic painter, Hans Thoma (1839–
1924) was born in Bernau and the museum,
opened in 1949, is in the town hall. It contains
80 works by him, illustrating the range of his
activities and including paintings, watercolours,
drawings, woodcarvings and ceramics. There are
also memorabilia of Thoma and paintings,
graphics and sculpture by winners of the Hans
Thoma Prize.

Bernkastel-Kues

Museum of Moselle Wine

*Mosel-Weinmuseum, Cuscanußstraße 2, D-5550
    Bernkastel-Kues, Rheinland-Pfalz*
    ☎ 06531 4141
*Apr 16–Oct 31, Tues–Sun 10–12, 2.30–5.
    Nov 1–Apr 15, Tues–Sun 2.30–5.*

C

The museum, established in 1981, is in one of
Germany's principal wine-producing areas. It
contains a wine-tasting room where visitors can
taste some of the choicest local wines for
themselves. The collections and displays
illustrate the history and techniques of vineyard
cultivation and the production of wine. There is
a separate historical collection of wine glasses.

Bestwig-Ramsbeck

Mining Museum and Demonstration Mine

*Bergbaumuseum and Besucherbergwerk Ramsbeck,
    Postfach 1163, D-5780 Bestwig-Ramsbeck,
    Nordrhein-Westfalen*
    ☎ 02905 250 or 02904 81275
*Mar 16–Oct 14, daily 9–5. Oct 15–Mar 15,
    Tues–Sun 9–5. Closed from 1st Sun in Advent
    to Dec 26.*

C 🎧 💺 ⚓

The silver, zinc and lead deposits at Ramsbeck
were known in prehistoric times. Exploitation
on a modern scale began in the mid 16th
century and continued until 1974, when the last
pit closed. A peak was reached in 1854, when
2,000 people were employed in the industry. A
museum was established after closure, in the
former pithead baths. It shows the history of the
local mines and the techniques employed, with
machines and tools dating from the Middle Ages
to the present day. There are also exhibits of the
minerals found in the area. Visitors are taken on
underground tours of the mine galleries.

Biberach-an-der-Riss

Biberach Museum

*Städtische Sammlungen (Braith-Mali-Museum),
    Museumsstraße 6, D-7950 Biberach-an-der-
    Riss, Baden-Württemberg*
    ☎ 07351 51331
*Tues–Sun 10–12, 2–5. Open Easter Mon &
    Whit Mon. Closed Jan 1, Carnival Tues
    (pm), Maundy Thurs (pm), Good Fri, Easter
    Sat, May 1, Nov 1, Dec 24, 25, 31.*

F 🎧

The museum is housed in a 16th-century
building. Its displays illustrate the archaeology,
history, art and handicrafts of the area. There
are collections of 15th–20th-century paintings
and sculpture, but the particular strength of
the museum is in 19th-century works by
German artists. Visitors can see the studios of
Anton Braith (1836–1905) and Christian Mali
(1833–1906). Both Braith and Mali specialised
in animal paintings and landscapes and left
large collections of their work to the town of
Biberach. The museum also has many
examples of works by Munich artists,
especially the Expressionist painter, Ernst
Ludwig Kirchner (1880–1938), who was an
original member of Die Brücke.

Wieland Museum

*Wieland-Schauraum, Stadtbücherei, Martkplatz
    17, D-7950 Biberach-an-der-Riss, Baden-
    Württemberg*
    ☎ 07351 51307/51459
*Apr–Sept, Wed 10–12, 2–6; Sat, Sun 10–12.
    Oct–Mar, Wed 10–12, 2–6; Sat, Sun
    10–12, 2–5. Other times by appt.*

F 🎧

The museum is in the town's public library
building, a former granary, dating from the
15th century. It contains exhibits illustrating
the life and work of the poet and novelist,
Christoph Martin Wieland (1733–1813),
during his years in Biberach. Visitors can see a
slide presentation of the places where he
lived, together with portraits of him and a
number of his personal possessions.

**Underground at the Mining Museum and
Demonstration Mine, Bestwig-Ramsbeck.**

Blaubeuren

Historic Forge Museum

Historische Hammerschmiede, Bürgermeisteramt
Blaubeuren, Karlstraße 2, D-7902
Blaubeuren, Baden-Württemberg
☎ 07344 1358
Mar 11–May, daily 10–6. June–Oct, daily 9–6.
Nov–Mar 10, Sat, Sun 11–4.
C ⌘ ⌂

In 1744 Johannes Friedrich, a shoeing smith and
armourer, built a grinding mill next to the
town's former waterworks on the river Blau. In
1804, his grandson, Abraham Friedrich, was
given permission to extend the mill and to add a
water-powered hammer to it. The hammer-
works continued to operate until 1948 and then
in 1966, after restoration, it was opened to the
public as a museum.

Museum of Prehistory

Urgeschichtliches Museum, Bürgermeisteramt
Blaubeuren, Karlstraße 2, D-7902
Blaubeuren, Baden-Württemberg
☎ 07344 1357
Apr–Oct, Tues–Sun 10–5. Nov–Mar, Sun 10–4
and groups by appt only at other times.
C ⌘ ⌂

The valleys in the Swabian Alps were carved
out 5 million years ago by the Danube, which
now runs several kilometres east of its original
course. The caves formed by the river along the
valleys were occupied first by animals and then
by Stone Age people. These caves were above
the reach of the alpine ice sheets and have
preserved an exceptionally good range of
prehistoric material, a selection of which is to be
found in the museum.

The 33–30,000-year-old figurines carved from
mammoth ivory are among the oldest works of
art in the world. One, a half-relic plaque, is the
earliest known representation of a human figure.
It predates the preoccupation with animals
which seems to have characterised Iron Age
artists.

Böblingen

German Butchers' Museum

Deutsches Fleischermuseum, Am Marktplatz,
D-7030 Böblingen, Baden-Württemberg
☎ 07031 669473/669278
Tues–Sun 11–5. Guided tours by appt.
F ⌘ ⌂

The museum occupies a 3-storey half-timbered
house, which dates from the 15th century and
which has been restored after bomb damage
during the Second World War. The displays
illustrate the history of the butchery trade in
Germany and the slaughtering and processing
techniques used at different periods. Much
attention is given to the production of sausage,
an important feature of the meat industry in
Germany. Other sections relate to the retail side
of the business and to the butchers' guilds and
trade associations. The top floor of the museum
is devoted to an exhibition of works of art with
meat and the butcher's trade as the subject.

Bochum

German Mining Museum

Deutsches Bergbau-Museum, Am Bergbaumuseum
28, D-4630 Bochum, Nordrhein-Westfalen
☎ 0234 51881/2
Tues–Fri 8.30–5.30; Sat, Sun and public holidays
9–1.
C ⌘ ⊟ ⌂

In 1930 the Ruhr mineowners and the
municipality of Bochum decided to establish a
museum which would present, both to the
layman and the expert, an account of the past
and present of mining in Germany. The
museum, covering all types of mining, has since
become very large and includes 2.6 km of
demonstration mine galleries beneath the
museum building. The displays of models, tools
and equipment, plans, paintings, portraits and
photographs show how the techniques of mining
have developed, how miners and their families
have been housed and how mining communities
have developed customs and traditions peculiar
to themselves.

The museum maintains two out-stations, the
1823 prayer-house at Witten-Bommern, in the
Muttental, and the Art Nouveau engine hall
and administration building of the Zollern II
colliery at Dortmund-Bövinghausen.

**17th-century cup of welcome. German
Butchers' Museum, Böblingen.**

Bodenmais

Historic Ore Mine

Historisches Erzbergwerk, Erzbergwerk Bodenmais,
D-8373 Bodenmais, Bayern
☎ 09924 304
Apr–May & Oct, daily 10–4. June–Sept, daily
9–5. Dec 25–Jan 8 & Easter 10–4.
Jan 8–Mar 31, Tues, Fri 1–3.
C ♠

The mine contains 60 different minerals. It has
been worked, chiefly for silver, since the 14th
century. There are collections of historic tools
and machinery and demonstration galleries, in
which mining techniques are illustrated.

Bodenwerder

Baron Münchhausen Museum

Baron-Münchhausen-Museum, Rathaus, D-3452
Bodenwerder, Niedersachsen
☎ 05533 2560
May–Sept, daily 10–12, 2–5. Other times by appt.
C ♠

The museum, in the town hall, is devoted to the
achievements of Karl Friedrich Hieronymus,
Freiherr von Münchhausen (1720–97), the
soldier whose exaggerated accounts of his
achievements passed into legend. They were the
subject of a series of adventures, *The Adventures*
of Baron Münchhausen (1793), written by
R. E. Raspe (1737–94) while he was was
working in England as a mining engineer. The
collections include memorabilia and personal
possessions of the Baron and editions of his
Adventures in foreign languages.

Bonn

Beethoven's House

Beethoven-Haus, Bonngasse 20, Postfach 2463,
D-5300 Bonn 1, Nordrhein-Westfalen
☎ 0228 635188
Apr–Sept, Mon–Sat 10–5; Sun 10–1. Oct–Mar,
Mon–Sat 10.30–4; Sun 10–1.
C ▮

Ludwig van Beethoven (1770–1827) was born
in Bonn, in the house dating from 1715 which is
now part of the museum. It was the composer's
home until 1792. The exhibits in the museum
illustrate Beethoven's life and career and the
history of his family. They include portraits, a
life-mask at the age of 42 and a death-mask, his
will and a number of personal possessions,
among them the viola which he played as a
child, articles which he kept on his desk in
Vienna, his quartet instruments, his last piano
with six and a quarter octaves, built for him in
1823, and four early trumpets, made in 1812–14
by Mätzel, the inventor of the metronome.

Ernst Moritz Arndt House

Ernst-Moritz-Arndt-Haus, Adenauerallee 79,
D-5300 Bonn, Nordrhein-Westfalen
☎ 0228 773686
Tues–Sun 10–5
F

What is now Adenauerallee 79 was formerly the
home of Ernst Moritz Arndt (1779–1860). Now
a museum dedicated to him, it contains books,
manuscripts and personal possessions of the
writer and politician. There are also exhibits
illustrating the history of Bonn, including 16th–
19th-century views of the town and the
surrounding region.

Museum of Art

Städtisches Kunstmuseum, Rathausgasse 7,
D-5300 Bonn 1, Nordrhein-Westfalen
☎ 0228 773686
Wed, Fri–Sun 10–5; Tues, Thurs 10–9.
C ▮

The museum dates back to 1884. Between then
and the Second World War, during which the
museum building was destroyed, the collections
consisted mostly of 16th–19th-century works by
Bonn and Rhineland artists. with the
development of Bonn as the Federal capital, the
decision was taken to put the emphasis of the
museum on German art in the 20th century.
There are particularly good collections of works
by August Macke (1887–1914).

**Figure-studies by Heinrich Nauen. Museum of
Art, Bonn.**

Borgentreich

Organ Museum

*Orgelmuseum, Marktstraße 6, Postfach 4, D-3532
Borgentreich, Nordrhein-Westfalen*
☎ 05643 1212
*Thurs, Sat, Sun 2.30–5.30; Fri 9.30–11.30,
2.30–5.30. Groups at other times by appt.*
C ♦ ☐ ♿ ♠

The eastern part of the former bishopic of
Paderborn is famous for its historic church
organs, built during the 17th and 18th
centuries. One of the finest examples is the
parish church of Borgentreich. It was built by
Johann Patroclus Möller of Lippstadt in 1730.
Opposite the church, in the former town hall,
the municipality has created a museum which
tells the story of the organ and explains its
technicalities and construction. There are
working models which allow visitors to discover
for themselves the way in which the different
kinds of timbre, sonority, tone, pitch and
intonation are produced. There is a special
exhibition of photographs of Spanish and
Portuguese organs.

Bottrop

Quadrat: Josef Albers Museum

*Josef-Albers-Museum, Im Stadtgarten 20, D-4250
Bottrop, Nordrhein-Westfalen*
☎ 02041 29716
Tues–Sun 10–6
F ♦ ☐ ♠

The painter Josef Albers (1888–1976) was born
in Bottrop and taught in the area from 1908
until 1919. In 1920 he went to the Bauhaus,
where he became recognised as a pioneer
abstract artist. He and his wife emigrated to
America in 1933 and eventually became
American citizens. After his death, the city of
Bottrop agreed to build a museum, linked to the
existing Quadrat, which would be devoted
entirely to Albers' work. His widow and the
Josef Albers Foundation gave 90 paintings and a
complete collection of Albers' 250 prints to the
new museum.

Bremen

Art Gallery

Kunsthalle, Am Wall 207, D-2800 Bremen
☎ 0421 324785
Tues–Sun 10–4; Tues & Fri also 7–9 pm
C ♦ ☐

The Kunsthalle in Bremen is one of Germany's
largest and most important art galleries. It is still
owned and run by the Society which founded it
in 1849. It owes much to the vigorous collecting
policy of its first professional Director, Gustav
Pauli, between 1899 and 1913 and to the
generous gifts made by citizens of Bremen since
its early years.
    German and French painters of the 19th

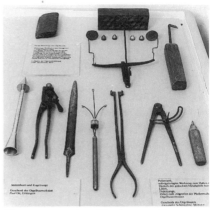

Organ parts, tools and implements. Organ
Museum, Borgentreich.

century are particularly strongly represented in
the Kunsthalle and the 19th- and 20th-century
sculpture collection is one of the finest in the
world. There are also large departments of prints
and drawings and of illustrated books, from
incunabula to the present day. The gallery is
celebrated for its collections of the work of the
German impressionists, especially Max
Lieberman (1847–1935) and Louis Corinth
(1858–1925), and of Paula Modersohn-Becker
(1876–1907).

Bremen Museum of Art and Cultural History
– Focke Museum

*Bremer Landesmuseum für Kunst- und
Kulturgeschichte – Focke Museum,
Schwachhauser Heerstraße 240, D-2800
Bremen 1, Niedersachsen* ☎ 0421 4963575
Tues–Sun 10–6
C ♦ ♿ ♠

In the 19th century Dr Johann Focke (1848–
1922) formed a private collection illustrating
the artistic and cultural history of Bremen.
During the succeeding years the museum,
steadily increasing in size, had several changes
of name and location and during the Second
World War its exhibits were put into safe
storage away from the city. A small Focke
Museum was opened in 1953 in the manor
house of the Riensberg estate and in 1960–8 a
new building was added next to it, in order to
house the rural life collection. In 1970 the
museum acquired a Dutch-type windmill
(1848), 8 km away, which now contains a
permanent exhibition called 'From Grain to
Bread'. In 1973–4 an 1803 barn was transferred
to the museum site and the collection of
agricultural implements is now displayed in it.
    In these four buildings the museum presents
exhibitions illustrating the social and cultural
history of Bremen from the 14th to the 20th
centuries. There are special sections relating to
Bremen silversmiths, the sculptors Ludwig
Münstermann (1579–1637) and Theophil
Wilhelm Freese (1696–1763), furniture, the
tobacco trade, weapons, faïence and porcelain,
agriculture and maritime history.

Roselius House

Roselius-Haus, Böttcherstraße 6, D-2800 Bremen
☎ *0421 321911*
Mon–Thurs 10–4; Sat, Sun 11–4.
C 🔒

Ludwig Roselius, who invented the celebrated caffeine-free Kaffee Hag, was a notable patron of the arts in Bremen and in 1928 he opened the Roselius House, which was not only a museum of 600 years of North German art and craftsmanship, but which formed part of his project for a street, the Böttcherstrasse, in the old quarter of Bremen, in which the traditional architecture of the city was presented and where the lifestyle of Bremen's patrician years could be displayed to the present generation. The area was severely damaged by bombing in 1944, but has since been fully restored by the Roselius Foundation.

Bremerhaven

German Maritime Museum

Deutsches Schiffahrtsmuseum, van-Ronzelen-Straße, D-2850 Bremerhaven (Mitte),
Niedersachsen   ☎ *0471 44048*
Tues–Sun 10–6. Guided tours by appt.
C 🔒 🖼 🚻

The museum, situated near the docks, aims to present the history of shipping and navigation from German ports since prehistoric times. There are 60 full-size ships, the largest collection in Europe, exceeded only by two museums in the USA. The general arrangement of the museum is chronological, but three themes – the control of shipping routes, the German Navy from 1848 to the present day, and boating and yachts – are treated separately. Much use is made of models and reconstructions of cabins and other parts of ships, in an attempt to convey the atmosphere of life on board.

Special sections of the museum are devoted to European expansion overseas, whaling, emigration, shipbuilding, inland shipping, the German Lifeboat Institution, big passenger liners 1919–45, and control from the bridge.

The Biedermeier Room in Riensberg manor. Focke Museum of Art and Cultural History, Bremen.

Bretten

Melanchthon Memorial

Melanchthon Gedächtnishaus, Promenadenweg 27,
D-7518 Bretten, Baden-Württemberg
☎ *07252 2557*
Sun 11–5. Other times by appt.
C 🕮

The religious reformer and friend of Martin Luther, Philipp Melanchthon (1497–1560), was born in Bretten. The building which forms the memorial to him was constructed in 1897–1903 on the site of his birthplace. It contains exhibitions which illustrate the history of the Reformation and the prominent people associated with it, including manuscripts, letters, books, paintings and portraits. The Room of the Town contains the coats of arms of the 121 towns, mostly in Germany, with which Melanchthon was regularly in correspondence, the Room of the Theologians commemorates a number of Melanchthon's friends, and the Room of the Princes displays the portraits of 11 noblemen who played a leading part in the Reformation and who were important in Melanchthon's life.

Bruchhausen-Vilsen

'The First Museum-Railway in Germany'

Erste Museums-Eisenbahn Deutschlands,
Deutscher Eisenbahn Verein e.V., Postfach
1106, D-2814 Bruchhausen-Vilsen,
Niedersachsen   ☎ *04252 2626*
May–Sept, Sat, Sun and public holidays 9–6.
Oct–Apr, museum only. Closed Jan 1, Dec 25.
C 🔒 🖼 🚻

The 8 km narrow-gauge track from Bruchhausen-Vilsen to Asendorf was built in 1899 as part of the local railway network. It is now operated by a private association, which has assembled a collection of more than 50 steam locomotives and diesel cars, passenger coaches and freight waggons, all restored to running order. With three stations on the line, the railway functions as a museum of rural transport.

Brunswick

Friedrich Gerstäcker Memorial Museum

Friedrich-Gerstäcker-Gedächtnisstätte,
Cavaliershaus von Schloß Richmond,
Wolfenbütteler Straße 230, D-3300
Braunschweig, Niedersachsen
☎ *0531 342124*
Sun 10–12. Other times by appt.
F

The novelist Friedrich Gerstäcker (1816–72) was born in Hamburg and died in Brunswick. Between 1837 and 1852 he roamed all over America doing whatever work turned up and afterwards he travelled to Central and South America, Australia, the Dutch East Indies,

Egypt and Ethiopia. His 44 novels are based on his experiences as a world traveller. The museum, created and maintained by the Gerstäcker Society, contains material relating to his life and his career as a writer.

Museum of Brunswick

Städtisches Museum, Am Löwenwall, D-3300 Braunschweig, Niedersachsen ☎ 0531 43446/4702450
Tues, Wed, Fri–Sun 10–5; Thurs 10–8.
F

The museum was established in 1861 and transferred to its present building, with its inner courtyard covered with a glass dome, in 1906. Its collections illustrate the history of Brunswick and its region. The exhibits include guild material, religious art, popular art, traditional costume, handicrafts, coins, industrial products and Brunswick silver. There is also an historical collection of hollow-ware, accumulated by the School of Industrial Design.

The sections devoted to painting and sculpture contain especially works by 18th–20th-century Brunswick artists or by those who have had some connection with the city.

Museum of Lower Saxony

Landesmuseum für Geschichte und Volkstum, Mönchstraße 1, D-3300 Braunschweig, Niedersachsen
Tues–Sat 10–5; Sun 10–1.
F

The museum was established in 1891. It is the main museum for the prehistory and history of Lower Saxony. Brunswick was at one time the principal centre in North Germany for the manufacture of weapons and armour, reflected in the museum's collections from the former Provincial Armoury. There is also a display of

The Room of the Town at the Melanchthon Memorial, Bretten.

18th–early-20th-century uniforms. Other major exhibits include pewter, copper and brass, household objects, stove plates, costumes, furniture, craftsmen's tools and the complete contents of an 18th-century convent pharmacy.

At its outstation at Bortfeld, the museum preserves a large farmhouse, in which it presents exhibits illustrating agricultural history and techniques and the way of life of the rural community.

Wilhelm Raabe Memorial Museum

Wilhelm-Raabe-Gedächtnisstätte, Leonhardstraße 29a, D-3300 Braunschweig, Niedersachsen ☎ 0531 75225
Wed, Fri, Sun 11–1
F

The novelist Wilhelm Raabe (1831–1910) spent his last years in Brunswick. The house in which he died is now a museum and study centre. His workroom has been preserved as it was during his lifetime, with his library and some of his collection of drawings, watercolours, manuscripts and family photographs. The museum is the headquarters of the Raabe Society and contains a reference collection of Raabe's books and of writings about him, as well as works by his contemporaries.

Büdingen

Schloss Museum

Fürstlich Ysenburgisches Schloßmuseum, Schloß, D-6470 Büdingen, Hessen ☎ 06042 6622
Mar–Oct, daily, tours at 2, 3 & 4. Groups at other times by appt.
C

The castle at Büdingen has belonged for 700 years to the Princes of Ysenburg and Büdingen, who are responsible for the museum. Visitors can see the State rooms, with their collections of furniture, weapons, porcelain and hunting trophies, and the 15th-century chapel, with its fine oak choir stalls, and the grand sandstone pulpit, made in 1610 after Count Wolfgang Ernst had introduced Calvinism, a pulpit-centred religion, into his territories. The castle has its 'alchemist's kitchen' where, until the 18th century, the court apothecary worked.

Büren-Wewelsburg

District Museum and Niederhagen Concentration Camp Memorial

Kreismuseum Wewelsburg mit Gedenkstätte KZ Niederhagen, Wewelsburg, D-4793 Büren-Wewelsburg, Nordrhein-Westfalen
☎ 02955 6108
Tues–Fri 10–12, 1–5; Sat 1–6; Sun 10–12, 1–6.
C 🖾 🖚

The Wewelsburg was a Renaissance castle, built in 1604–7. Until 1802 it was a secondary residence of the Prince Bishops of Paderborn. A museum was established here in 1925, but from 1934 until 1945, when it was destroyed, the castle was taken over by Heinrich Himmler and used as a cult centre for the SS. Part of it was destroyed by the SS in 1945, but then rebuilt.

The museum was reopened in 1967. Its collections include locally-made oak furniture from the 16th century onwards, 18th-century religious sculpture, 19th-century agricultural implements, craftsmen's tools and the products of rural domestic industries, especially wooden shoes and linen and material relating to

Early 18th-century chapel, part of the German Carthusian Museum, Buxheim.

industries once important in the area, especially iron-founding and glassmaking.

Special sections of the museum are devoted to the SS and to its ideological centre in the Wewelsburg and to the concentration camp in which 1,285 people died.

Burghausen

Castle Museum

Burgmuseum, Burg, D-8263 Burghausen, Bayern
☎ 08677 4659
Apr–Sept, daily 9–12, 1–5. Oct–Mar, daily 9–12, 1–4.
C 🛉 🖾 🖚

The castle, a masterpiece of military engineering, was built in the late 15th century, as the Turks were fighting their way across central Europe. It was later extended by the addition of a Renaissance palace, which contains 15th- and 16th-century furniture and works of art. On the second floor of the palace, the Bavarian State Gallery has installed an exhibition of 15th–18th-century paintings by Bavarian and Austrian artists.

Burladingen

Burladingen-Melchingen Village Museum and Alpine Path

Dorf-Museum und Albpfad, Maichle-Hof, D-7453 Burladingen-Melchingen, Baden-Württemberg
☎ 07475 1071
Mon–Fri 9–5
C 🖚

The museum, opened in 1973, occupies a large group of farm buildings which once belonged to Kaspar Maichle, who later became a weaver. The displays illustrate the living and working conditions of an Alpine farm in the mid 19th century. The living and sleeping rooms and the kitchen have their original furniture and equipment and in the outbuildings are the implements and tools used to work the farm and to carry out the forestry work connected with it.

An 'Alpine teaching path' leading from the farm introduces visitors to the natural history of the area and includes visits to 13 villages, a Baroque church and an agricultural, educational and research institute.

Buxheim

German Carthusian Museum

Deutsches Kartausen Museum, Rathaus, c/o Heimatdienst, D-8941 Buxheim, Bayern
☎ 08331 71028/71926
Apr–Oct, Mon–Fri 10–12, 2–4; Sat and public holidays 2–4. Groups at other times by appt.
C 🛉 🖚

The charterhouse at Buxheim was established in 1402 in the buildings of an old Collegiate Foundation. In 1802, after secularisation, it became private property and the contents, including the library, were sold off. Buxheim had been an exceptionally well-endowed house and the loss of its treasures at this time was a disaster. It was eventually restored by the Bavarian State and opened as a museum in 1975.

There are exhibitions presenting the history of the Carthusian Order and of the monastery at Buxheim. The monks' cells have been restored and show the commodious quarters which were provided for them. The superb 17th-century choir-stalls, among the finest in Europe, are back in position, after a romantic history. Put up for sale in 1883, they found no market and in 1886 the Director of the Bank of England bought them for a trifling sum and gave them to the Convent of the Presentation in London. In 1962, the Sisters moved their Convent to Hythe and the choir-stalls returned to Buxheim.

Calw

Calw Museum

Museum der Stadt Calw, Bischofstraße 48, D-7260 Calw, Baden-Württemberg
☎ *07051 167260*
Mar–Oct, Tues–Sat 2–4; Sun 10–12.
Ⓕ ⌂

The museum is really three museums. Calw Museum itself is at 48 Bischofstrasse, the Herman Hesse Museum and the Art Gallery at 30 Marktplatz. Calw Museum contains the town's archaeological collections and has early- and mid-19th-century furniture, popular art and handicrafts, and agricultural implements. A section is given over to small sculptures by Fritz Grosshaus (1884–1963). The Art Gallery, opened in 1987, concentrates on works by modern German artists, especially Richard Ziegler.

The novelist, poet and essayist, Herman Hesse (1877–1962), was born in Calw. The museum which has been created in his memory contains drawings and watercolours by Hesse, together with manuscripts and early editions of his works. There are photographs of the places where he lived and sketches made by Günther Böhmer to illustrate Hesse's life and work.

Celle

Bomann Museum

Bomann-Museum, Schloßplatz 7, D-3100 Celle, Niedersachsen ☎ *05141 12372*
Apr–Oct, daily 10–5. Nov–Mar, Mon–Sat 10–5; Sun and public holidays 10–1.
Ⓒ ⌂

The Association of the Museum of the Fatherland was founded in Celle in 1892 on the occasion of the 600th anniversary of the town of Celle. Among its members was the industrialist, Wilhelm Bomann. The museum, built between 1903 and 1907, was named after him. The collections follow Bomann's guidelines and concentrate on the history and folklore of the region surrounding Celle, especially the former

Display of soldiers' uniforms and equipment. Bomann Museum, Celle.

kingdom of Hanover, the boundaries of which correspond approximately to those of Lower Saxony today. The exhibits include farmhouse interiors, including a reconstructed farmhouse from the Fallingbostel district, regional handicrafts and craftsmen's tools, 18th–20th-century furniture, costumes and domestic equipment, Hanoverian military uniforms and portraits of the Dukes of Braunschweig-Lüneberg and members of their families.

Cloppenburg

Museum Village

Museumsdorf, Museumstraße, Burg Arkenstede, D-4590 Cloppenburg, Niedersachsen
☎ *04471 2504*
Apr–Sept, Mon–Sat 8–6; Sun 9–6. Oct–Mar, Mon–Sat 9–5; Sun 10–5.
Ⓒ ⌂ ⌂ ⌂

Established in 1922, this is now the largest open-air museum in Germany. There are more than 50 traditional buildings, brought from different parts of Lower Saxony and dating from the 16th to the 19th century. Among them are houses, different types of wind-, water- and horse-powered mill and completely equipped workplaces of a potter, turner, indigo-dyer, blacksmith, clog-maker, brewer and baker. Exhibits illustrating particular themes are arranged in some of the buildings. Among the items grouped in this way are carts and waggons, sledges and butter-making equipment.

Coburg

Coburg Fortress Art Collections

Kunstsammlungen der Veste Coburg, D-8630 Coburg, Bayern ☎ *09561 95055*
Apr–Oct, daily 9.30–1, 2–5. Nov–Mar, Tues–Sun 2–5. Dept of Prints & Drawings: Tues, Thurs 2–5; Wed 9–12. Closed local holidays in Nov and Dec 24, 25, 31.
Ⓒ ⌂

The fortress and the hill on which it stands dominate the former Duchy of Saxe-Coburg-Gotha. It is one of the most extensive fortified strongholds in Germany. Building probably began in the 11th century. Johann Casimir became the first Duke in 1596 and much of what one sees today was commimssioned by him. The last Duke abdicated in 1918, and the fortress was taken over in 1920 by the State of Bavaria. The works of art now belong to a foundation.

Martin Luther did much of his most important work here, and consequently the fortress is one of his most important memorials. Visitors see the Luther Chapel, where Luther prayed and attended services during his stay in 1530, in the course of their guided tour. The Cranach Room has paintings by Lucas Cranach the Elder.

The art collections contain European works of all periods, but are especially strong in 15th–16th-century paintings, drawings and graphics, and in 14th–16th-century religious sculpture. There are also notable collections of furniture, textiles, weapons, armour, glass and ceramics. The gallery devoted to sledges and carriages has a number of exceptionally rare and elegant items, including the two oldest ceremonial carriages in Europe, dated 1560 and 1586, and 13 richly decorated sledges from the 17th and 18th centuries.

Cologne

Cathedral Treasury

Domschatzkammer, Dom, D-5000 Köln,
 Nordrhein-Westfalen ☎ *0221 244546*
Mon–Sat 9–4; Sun and public holidays 12.30–4.
 May–Sept, open until 5.
Ⓒ ▮

Cologne is among the oldest Christian communities in Germany. The history of the City is closely linked to that of the Episcopal See and the Cathedral. The rich collections of the Treasury have been accumulated since early medieval times. They include vestments, altar frontals, liturgical objects, bishops' croziers from the 14th century to the present day, and illuminated manuscripts. The Treasury also has a staff and chain said to have belonged to St Peter.

Diocesan Museum

Erzbischöfliches Diözesan-Museum, Roncalliplatz
 2, D-5000 Köln 1, Nordrhein-Westfalen
 ☎ *0221 244546*
Mon–Wed, Fri, Sat 10–5; Sun 10–1.
Ⓒ ▮

The museum, one of the richest collections of religious art in Germany, contains items from the Romanesque period to the present century. They include shrines and reliquaries, sculptures from the cathedral, 9th–16th-century gospels, missals and Books of Hours, 15th–20th-century rosaries, church ornaments, vestments and altar-frontals.

In 1959 excavations under the cathedral revealed a group of 6th-century graves of members of the Franconian ruling family. The objects found in the graves represent one of the most important collections of artefacts ever assembled from this period. They include jewellery, weapons, armour, coins, beakers, drinking horns and fragments of textiles, wood and leather which allow reconstruction of the original objects to be made.

KHD Engine Museum

KHD Motorenmuseum, Deutz-Mülheimer Straße
 111, D-5000 Köln 80, Nordrhein-Westfalen
 ☎ *0221 8222915*
Mon–Fri 9–4. Groups by appt at other times.
Ⓕ ⚙

In 1864 Nicolaus August Otto, together with Eugen Langen, founded in Cologne the first factory in the world for building internal combustion engines. It is now run by the Klockner-Humboldt-Deutz Company. Otto made his first experiments in 1861, but did not succeed in producing a practicable four-stroke engine until 1876. His first four-stroke engine has a place of honour in the museum, which is devoted to the history of the internal combustion engine from its earliest days.

There are original engines, drawings, photographs and personal possessions of people important in the development of engine technology, from the four-stroke gas engine to the petrol engine, including the diesel engine with and without compressor, with pre-combustion chamber and with air-cooling.

16th-century half-armour. Coburg Fortress Art Collections.

Museum of the City of Cologne

*Kölnisches Stadtmuseum, Zeughausstraße 1-3,
    D-5000 Köln 1, Nordrhein-Westfalen*
    ☎ 0221 2212352
Tues, Wed, Fri–Sun 10–5; Thurs 10–8.
Ⓒ 🛢 💺 ♿

The museum reopened in 1984 after several
years of renovation. Its collections present a
comprehensive picture of the history of the city.
Among the themes illustrated are local trade
and commerce, coins, weights and measures,
weapons and armour, furniture, costumes and
musical instruments. There are other sections
devoted to prints, drawings and engravings
illustrating the development of Cologne and the
history of the Jewish community.

Roman-Germanic Museum

*Römisch-Germanisches Museum, Roncalliplatz 4,
    D-5000 Köln, Nordrhein-Westfalen*
    ☎ 0221 2214438
Tues, Fri–Sun 10–5; Wed, Thurs 10–8.
Ⓒ 🛢 💺 ♿ 🚗

Opened in 1974, in a new building next to the
cathedral, the museum's collections consist of
Roman and Germanic material found during the
excavation of sites in and around the city of
Cologne, which was an important military and
commercial centre in Roman times. Part of a
Roman road which carried traffic to and from
the Rhine can be seen by visitors to the
museum.

The displays illustrate life in Cologne during
the Roman and Germanic periods, with
particularly interesting and important
collections of monuments and other sculpture,
mosaics, glass, lamps and jewellery.

**Roman cut glass diatretum, or cage-cup, with
Greek inscription below the rim. Roman-
Germanic Museum, Cologne.**

Schnütgen Museum

*Schnütgen-Museum, Cäcilienstraße 29, D-5000
    Köln, Nordrhein-Westfalen*
    ☎ 0221 2212310
Thurs–Tues 10–5; Wed 10–8.
Ⓒ

The museum occupies the former Basilica of St
Cecilia, which dates from the 12th century. The
core of its remarkable collection of religious art
from the Middle Ages to the 18th century was
formed in the 1860s by a canon of the cathedral,
Johann Wilhelm Alexander Schnütgen, who
discovered these objects in secondhand shops,
in churches and presbyteries, at auction sales
and on art-dealers' premises, at a time when the
value of such things was not well understood or
appreciated.

The exhibits include sculpture, ivories, 11th–
18th-century bronze objects, liturgical items,
and medieval enamels and goldsmiths' work,
especially from Limoges, the Rhineland and the
Maas area. There are also examples of Coptic
and Byzantine textiles and medieval stained
glass.

Wallraf Richartz Museum

*Wallraf-Richartz-Museum, An der Rechtsschule,
    D-5000 Köln, Nordrhein-Westfalen*
    ☎ 0221 2212379
Daily 10–5; Tues, Thurs open until 8.
Ⓒ 🛢 💺

This is one of the most important art museums
in Germany. It owes its origins to a 19th-
century canon of the cathedral, Ferdinand Fraut
Wallraf, who rescued great quantities of church
property in Cologne from dispersal after the
secularisation of 1803. This collection became
the property of the city in 1824. In 1861 it was
greatly enriched by a bequest made by a Cologne
merchant, Johann Heinrich Richartz, a process
which has continued into modern times. Hardly
any losses were suffered as a result of wartime
bombing, the collections having been removed
to safety in good time.

The museum has particularly strong sections
devoted to Stefan Lochner (d. 1451) and the
artists of the Cologne School, to Dürer and
Cranach and the artists of the 15th-century
German Renaissance to the 14th–16th-century
Italian painters, to Rembrandt and Rubens and
their contemporaries, to the 19th century in
Germany and France, and to Kandinsky, Klee
and other German representatives of the early-
19th-century Avant-Garde movement.

Constance

House of Jan Hus

*Johannes-Hus-Haus, Hussenstraße 64, D-7550
    Konstanz, Baden-Württemberg*
    ☎ 07531 29042
Tues–Sat 10–12, 2–4; Sun 10–12.
Ⓕ

The followers of the Bohemian heretic, Jan Hus
(1372–1415) demanded a reformed national

church with a vernacular liturgy. In 1414 Hus lived at the house which is now Hussenstrasse 64 at the beginning of the Council of Constance, when he was arrested and afterwards burnt as a heretic. In 1980 the house was restored and a museum, designed by Czech artists, created in it. It contains collections illustrating the life and work of Hus and of other important figures in the Reformation, especially John Wycliffe.

Natural History Museum of Lake Constance

Bodensee-Naturmuseum, Katzgasse 5-7, D-7750 Konstanz, Baden-Württemberg ☎ *07735 284245 Apr–Oct, Tues–Fri 10–5; Sat, Sun 10–4. Nov– Mar, Tues–Fri 11 5; Sat, Sun 11–4.* **F** **⌾**

The museum is housed in a 15th-century building, the birthplace of the religious reformer Ambrosius Blarer (1492–1564), which was restored in 1968 for use as a museum. It is the only natural history museum around the shores of Lake Constance and has collections illustrating the geology, mineralogy, palaeontology, botany and zoology of the region. A section is devoted to explaining the threats to the natural environment and to methods of protecting local wildlife. There are special displays illustrating the fishing industry of Lake Constance and its lake and river shipping and navigation.

Dachau

Dachau Concentration Camp Memorial

KZ-Gedenkstätte Dachau, Alte Römerstraße 75, D-8060 Dachau, Bayern ☎ *08131 1741 Tues–Sun 9–5. Closed Dec 24, 31.* **F** **⌾** **♿**

The memorial, which includes a museum, reflects an attempt to show objectively what happened in Dachau and other Nazi concentration camps between 1933 and 1945. In Dachau alone, 31,591 prisoners died during this period, as a result of disease, malnutrition,

Monument by Glid Nandor at the Dachau Concentration Camp Memorial.

ill-treatment or execution. Dachau was the first camp to be established and during its years of operation housed a total of nearly a quarter of a million prisoners, drawn from every country in Europe.

Darmstadt

Artists' Colony Museum

Museum der Künstler-Kolonie, Europaplatz 1, D-6100 Darmstadt, Hessen ☎ *06151 132778 Tues–Sun 10–12, 2–4* **C** **⌾** **♿**

Between 1900 and 1914, Darmstadt, with its artists' colony on the Mathildenhöhe, was an important centre of the international Art Nouveau movement. In 1899–1900 the Austrian architect, Joseph M. Olbrich, designed a museum to display the work of artists belonging to the colony, of which he himself was a member. Within the museum building are studios for the artists. The building was damaged during the Second World War but has been completely restored. It contains displays of the applied and decorative arts, including furniture, glass, pottery made by Joseph Olbrich, Peter Behrens, Hans Christiansen, Albin Müller and others.

In a separate section there are paintings by 19th- and 20th-century artists who have worked in Darmstadt.

Castle Museum

Schloßmuseum, Residenzschloß, D-6100 Darmstadt, Hessen ☎ *06151 24035 Mon–Thurs 10–1, 2–5; Sat, Sun 10–1.* **C**

The Castle Museum was established in 1924 by the Grand Duke Ernst Ludwig of Hesse. It was severely damaged by bombing in 1944 and reopened in 1965. The collections illustrate the history of the Grand Duchy of Hesse and include pre-1914 uniforms of the Hesse-Darmstadt regiments, decorations and medals and uniform jackets which belonged to famous people – the Emperor Franz Joseph Bismarck, Moltke and others. There are fine collections of court costumes and of carriages, sedan chairs, sleighs and harness, one in the possession of the House of Hesse.

Most of the paintings in the museum are the work of 18th–19th-century Hesse-Darmstadt artists. The museum also has, as one of its greatest treasures, the *Madonna of the Bürgermeister of Basel, Jacob Meyer*, painted by Hans Holbein the Younger in 1526.

Museum of Hesse

Hessisches Landesmuseum Darmstadt,
Friedensplatz 1, D-6100 Darmstadt, Hessen
☎ *06151 125434*
Tues, Thurs–Sun 10–5; Wed 10–5, 7–9. Dec 24,
31 & Carnival Tues 10–12. Closed Jan 1,
Good Fri, Easter Sun, May 1, Assumption,
Whit Sun, Corpus Christi, June 17, Thurs
before Lent, Dec 25.
F ⌂ ☛

The museum in Darmstadt had its origins in the collections of art and natural history formed by the Counts of Hesse-Darmstadt during the 17th and 18th centuries. These were transferred to the Province of Hesse in 1820, an exceptionally early instance of public access to a former court collection. The present building was constructed in 1897–1906 with the exterior in the Art Déco style, and the interior in styles considered to be appropriate to the contents – a Roman atrium, a Romanesque hall, a Gothic chapel, a Baroque hall. Extensions were constructed in 1980–4.

Iphégénie, 1862, by Anselm Feuerbach.
Museum of Hesse, Darmstadt.

The art galleries include paintings by Stephan Lochner, Lucas Cranach, Rubens, Breughel, Rembrandt, Maillol, Corinth and Beuys, sculptures from 800 to 1930 and important collections of drawings, watercolours, graphics and posters, as well as ivories, enamels, glass, ceramics, silver and tapestries. There are also sections devoted to the geology, minerals, fossils and natural history of the region and to material discovered during the excavation of prehistoric, Roman and Merovingian sites.

Detmold

The Prince's Residence

Fürstliches Residenzschloß, D-4930 Detmold,
Nordrhein-Westfalen   ☎ 05231 22507
Guided tours daily, 9.30–5. Closed Dec 24, 25,
31.
C ⌂ ☛

The castle at Detmold was built in the 13th century and rebuilt in the 16th–18th centuries. The architecture is a particular local Renaissance style, which became celebrated as 'Weser Renaissance'. The museum, which forms part of the castle, has been open to the public since 1900. It consists of a group of rooms, furnished and decorated in the taste of the 18th century, with a world-famous series of Brussels tapestries showing the life of Alexander the Great. There are also collections of family portraits, early Meissen and Oriental porcelain, weapons, Venetian and Bohemian glass.

Westphalian Open-Air Museum

Westfälisches Freilichtmuseum Detmold,
Landesmuseum für Volkskunde, Krummes
Haus, Postfach 3032, D-4930 Detmold,
Nordrhein-Westfalen   ☎ 05231 23964
Apr–Oct, Tues–Sun 9–6 (last admission 5). Open
public holidays.
C ⌂ ☛

Arranged on an 80-hectare site, this is the largest open-air museum in Germany. It contains rural houses, farm buildings, workshops and other structures from different parts of Westphalia, grouped according to the area from which they came. Among the exhibits are windmills, barns and storehouses, an early 19th-century school, bakehouse, boundary stones and a fire-engine house. There are regular craft demonstrations and visitors can see examples of traditional breeds of farm animals. The various buildings contain appropriate furniture and equipment, together with a collection of popular art.

Dortmund

Dortmund Brewery Museum

Dortmunder Brauereimuseum, Märkische Straße
85, D-4600 Dortmund, Nordrhein-Westfalen
☎ 0231 54132
Tues–Sun 10–6
F ⌂ ☛ ⌂

With its 700-year history of brewing, Dortmund is one of the world's largest beer-producing centres. The museum was set up in 1980 by the Dortmund Kronen Brewery in restored buildings on its own premises and passed under the control of the municipality as a foundation two years later. Its displays show the changes in the brewing and distribution of beer in Westphalia from the mid 19th century onwards.

German Cookery Book Museum

Deutsches Kochbuchmuseum, Westfalen Park,
D-4600 Dortmund, Nordrhein-Westfalen.
Correspondence to: Museum für Kunst- und
Kulturgeschichte, Hansastraße 3, D-4600
Dortmund ☎ *0231 543 25741/25525*
Daily 10–6
Ⓒ ▮ ☕ ↩

The museum is a branch of the Museum of Art and Cultural History, and draws on the excellent collections of this museum for its exhibitions, which are regularly changed, in order to make further use of its small display area.

The aim of the museum is to present what it describes as 'the cultural history of eating and drinking'. In order to achieve this, it uses cookery books, especially those of Henrietta Davidson, the German Mrs Beeton, as important clues to the problems of women in 19th-century society and as an introduction to social history in general. The museum has established close connections with two institutions which are established nearby in the same attractive park which surrounds the museum: the Cookery Studio, run by the local electricity company, and a popular restaurant for which a Dortmund brewery is responsible. Both of these make parts of their premises available to the museum from time to time.

Museum of Art and Cultural History

Museum für Kunst- und Kulturgeschichte,
Hansastraße 3, D-4600 Dortmund,
Nordrhein-Westfalen
☎ *0231 542215*
Apr–Sept, Sat–Thurs 10–6
Ⓕ ▮

The museum has the largest display of the decorative arts in Westphalia. The exhibits include furniture from the late Middle Ages until the Jugendstil period, including three groups from the years 1903, 1907 and 1908, of which two were made in Glückert's Court Furniture Factory in Darmstadt. There is also the celebrated set of tiles depicting hunting scenes, made from copper engravings by Johann Elias Ridinger, a 1790 apothecary's shop, which has been embellished with contemporary tiles from another collection, and sections devoted to faïence, porcelain, especially Meissen, glass, silver, ironwork, coins, weapons and textiles.

Among the medieval items in the museum is the oldest known likeness of a German emperor, a gilded copper portrait bust of Frederick Barbarossa, dating from the 12th century. The

18th-century room furnished in the taste of the period. The Prince's Residence, Detmold.

many modern painters represented in the collections include Carl Spitzweg (1808–85), Anselm Feuerbach (1829–80) and Max Liebermann (1847–1935).

Museum on the East Wall

Museum am Ostwall, Ostwall 7, D-4600
Dortmund, Nordrhein-Westfalen
☎ *0231 542232*
Tues–Sat 9.30–6; Sun 10–2.
Ⓕ ▮

The museum was opened in 1949. Its collections are of late 19th–20th century sculpture, paintings and graphics, especially by the German Expressionists and by artists from the 1960s onwards. A special section of the museum provides painting facilities for children.

Natural History Museum

Museum für Naturkunde, Münsterstraße 271,
D-4600 Dortmund, Nordrhein-Westfalen
☎ *0231 54224850*
Tues 10–6; Thurs open until 8.30
Ⓕ ▮ ☕

The museum was founded in 1910, with the collections which had been formed from 1887 onwards by the Dortmund Natural History Society. It was transferred to large new buildings on a parkland site in 1980, where it has been possible to create a Geological Garden of the rocks and fossils found in the slate, schist and brown-coal beds of the Rhineland. Some of these specimens weigh as much as 16 tons. The outdoor section of the museum also includes a petrified forest, where survivals of the plants and trees which originally formed the coal-measures are also being grown. Other exhibits include fossilised animal remains, including the skeleton of a 55-million-year-old primitive horse, discovered in the Messel oil shale near Darmstadt in 1975–8, and a wide range of minerals.

There are also a 73,000 litre fresh-water aquarium, one of the largest tropical aquaria in Germany, living colonies of bees and ants, dioramas of saurians and a demonstration coalmine.

Duisburg

Wilhelm Lehmbruck Museum

*Wilhelm-Lehmbruck-Museum, Düsseldorfer-Straße
51, D-4100 Duisburg 1, Nordrhein-
Westfalen*   ☎ 0203 2833294
Tues 11–8; Wed–Sun 11–5.

Ⓒ ⬛ ᶑ

The sculptor Wilhelm Lehmbruck (1881–1919)
was born in Duisburg. The museum which bears
his name was built by his son, Manfred
Lehmbruck, and opened in 1964. It contains
works by Lehmbruck and collections of 20th-
century German paintings, prints, engravings
and sculpture.

Düsseldorf

Art Museum

*Kunstmuseum Düsseldorf, Ehrenhof 5, D-4000
Düsseldorf 30, Nordrhein-Westfalen*
☎ 0211 8992460
*Tues–Sun 11–6. Closed Thurs & Sun before Lent,
May 1, Dec 24, 25, 31.*

Ⓒ ⬛ ᶑ

The Ehrenhof, built in the 1920s, is Düsseldorf's
cultural centre. It includes, as well as the
Kunstmuseum, the Kunstpalast, for changing
exhibitions of contemporary art, the
Landesmuseum Volk- und Wirtschaft, which
concentrates on social and economic history,
and the Tonhalle, or Concert Hall. The
Ehrenhof complex is also important for its
decoration. Many of the artists commissioned
for this belonged to the avant-garde and in
particular to the Junges Rheinland group.

The collections include 16th–17th-century
Dutch paintings, 18th-century French and
Italian paintings, 19th-century paintings by
artists of the Düsseldorf School and 20th-
century German paintings. The museum also
has an exhibition of glass, especially of the
Jugendstil period, and an international
collection of engravings.

Plaster relief of Goethe, dated 1775. Goethe
Museum, Düsseldorf.

Goethe Museum

*Goethe-Museum, Anton-und-Katharina-
Kippenberg-Stiftung, Schloß Jägerhof,
Jacobistraße 2, D-4000 Düsseldorf 1,
Nordrhein-Westfalen*
☎ 0211 8996262
Tues–Fri, Sun 11–5; Sat 1–5.

Ⓒ ⬿

Anton Kippenberg (1874–1950) became famous
as the owner and managing director of the Insel
publishing house in Leipzig. The second great
achievement of his life was his collection of
Goetheana, the creation of which took him half
a century. After his death the Anton and
Katharina Kippenberg Foundation and the
collection were housed in the Schloss Jägerhof,
completed in 1774 and extended in 1828. The
1828 side-wings were demolished in 1910.

The 35,000 items in the collection, of which
about 1,000 are exhibited at any one time, were
chosen to illustrate the life and work of Johann
Wolfgang von Goethe (1749–1832) and the
spirit of his age. They consist of manuscripts,
paintings, graphics, busts, medals and coins.
There is, in addition, a library of 17,000 books
and 3,000 pieces of music of the Goethe era.

Heinrich Heine Institute

*Heinrich-Heine-Institut, Bilker Straße 14, Postfach
1120, D-4000 Düsseldorf 1, Nordrhein-
Westfalen*   ☎ 0211 5571 (Museum);
0211 5574 (Secretary)
Tues–Sun 11–5

Ⓒ ▮

The poet Heinrich Heine (1797–1856) was
born in Düsseldorf. The Institute, which
occupies two houses built in about 1800, has a
large collection of documents and manuscripts –
these include many in Heine's own hand – the
poet's library, many portraits and views of the
town, as well as personal possessions and
memorabilia. Among the museum's best-known
possessions is the original manuscript of *Die
Lorelei.*

Museum of Düsseldorf

*Stadtmuseum Düsseldorf, Bäckerstraße 7-9,
D-4000 Düsseldorf 1, Nordrhein-Westfalen*
☎ 0211 8996170
Tues, Thurs, Fri, Sun 11–5; Wed 11–8; Sat 1–5.

Ⓒ ⬿ ᶑ

The museum occupies the former Graf Spee
Palace, to which a modern extension was added
in 1990. The collections cover local prehistory
and history, paintings, the decorative arts,
sculpture, coins, textiles and photographs.
Among the paintings are works by members of
the 19th-century Düsseldorf School. There are
also paintings and drawings by the Young
Rhineland Group of the 1920s.

A special section is devoted to Düsseldorf
during the National Socialist period. This
includes works by artists persecuted by the Nazis
and drawings by Jewish children.

The Nordrhein-Westfalen Art Collection

*Kunstsammlung Nordrhein-Westfalen, Grabbeplatz
   5, D-4000 Düsseldorf 1, Nordrhein-
   Westfalen* ☎ *0211 133961*
Tues–Sun 10–6
C 👤 🖼 ♿ 🚃

In 1961 the Province of Nordrhein-Westfalen
established a foundation to collect
contemporary art, following its acquisition in
1960 of 88 works by Paul Klee. Over a period of
20 years, substantial funds were made available
for building up the collection – 15 million DM
came from German television – and in 1986 it
was moved into a new building designed by
Danish architects.

Today the collection has about 200 works,
in addition to paintings and drawings by Paul
Klee (1879–1940) and numerous paintings and
drawings by Julius Bissier (1893–1965), all
bequeathed by the artist.

Theatre Museum

*Theatermuseum, Jägerhofstraße 1, D-4000
   Düsseldorf 30, Nordrhein-Westfalen*
   ☎ *0211 8994660*
Tues–Sun 11–5
C 👤

The museum forms part of the collection of
material relating to the history of the theatre in
Düsseldorf made by the founders of the theatre,
Louise Dumont and Gustav Lindemann. It
includes costumes, stage designs, posters,
programmes, manuscripts and photographs.
There are also objects relating to the life and
work of Gustaf Gründgens, Louise Dumont and
Gustav Lindemann.

Eichstätt

Diocesan Museum

*Diözesan-Museum Eichstätt, Residenzplatz 7,
   D-8078 Eichstätt, Bayern*
   ☎ *08421 50248/50279*
*Apr–Oct, Tues–Sat 9.30–1, 2–5; Sun and public
   holidays 11–5.*
C 👤

In 1982 Eichstätt opened its new diocesan
museum adjoining the cathedral, in a building
skilfully and elegantly converted from a
medieval granary and a group of 18th-century
rooms. The exhibits include 15th–18th-century
wooden and stone sculptures from churches in
the diocese, vestments and other medieval
textiles, chalices and other liturgical items, and
paintings of religious subjects.

Emden

Museum of Ostfriesland

*Ostfriesisches Landesmuseum, Rathaus am Delft,
   2970 Emden, Niedersachsen*
   ☎ *04921 22855*
*May–Sept, Mon–Fri 10–1, 3–5; Sat, Sun 11–1.
   Oct–Apr, Tues–Fri 10–1, 3–5; Sat, Sun
   11–1.*
C 👤

Founded in 1833, this is one of the oldest
museums in Germany. Its collections illustrate
the history of Ostfriesland. There are exhibits of
13th–16th-century sculpture, 16th–19th-
century paintings, portraits of regional
celebrities, furniture, household equipment,
18th–19th-century Delftware and costumes
from Westphalia and the Lower Rhine. The
collection of weapons is outstanding and there
are also interesting sections devoted to
Ostfriesian silver and to 16th- and 17th-century
Emden municipal silver, including pieces made
in Augsburg, Antwerp, Strasbourg and Emden,
as well as to historical maps and 18th–20th-
century prints and engravings.

Emmerich

Rhine Museum

*Rheinmuseum Emmerich, Martinikirchgang 2,
   D-4240 Emmerich, Nordrhein-Westfalen*
   ☎ *02822 74320*
*Mon–Wed 9–12.30, 2–5; Thurs 9–12.30, 2–6;
   Fri, Sun 9–12.30. Closed Jan 1, Easter Sun,
   Whit Sun, Dec 25.*
F 👤 🚃

Opened in 1964 to replace an earlier museum
destroyed in a 1944 bombing raid, the Rhine
Museum tells the story of shipping and
navigation on the Rhine, with the help of ship
and shipyard models and equipment used on
land and on ships and barges. There is also a
section devoted to the history of Emmerich.

**Mid 18th-century Passion cross. Diocesan
Museum, Eichstätt.**

Neanderthal Museum, Erkrath.

The models include one of a Dutch timber-raft used *c.* 1800, which was propelled by oars and had a crew of 500 men. There is also the bridge from a motor-driven cargo ship, with an operational radar installation which allows visitors to watch traffic passing along the Rhine.

A section is devoted to the fish to be found in the river and to the fishing industry. Among the museum's particular treasures are a 15th-century stone sculpture of St Christopher, which formerly stood on one of the town gates, and a full-sized Roman representation in stone of a river boat carrying four large casks of wine.

Erkrath

Neanderthal Museum

*Neandertal-Museum, Thekhauser Quall, D-4006
    Erkrath, Nordrhein-Westfalen*
    ☎ *02104 31149*
Tues–Sun 10–5.
C 🛈 🐾

Near its junction with the Rhine, the River Düssel runs between chalk cliffs – the Neanderthal – which contain a number of deep caves. In one of these, in 1856, a 60,000-year-old skeleton was discovered. It was, not unnaturally, decided to refer to it as a representative of Neanderthal Man, who existed from 200,000 to 40,000 BC, who had to accustom himself to a considerable change of climate and who was the first to bury his dead.

The museum tells the story of the 1856 discovery and, from the evidence provided by this and other sites in the area, reconstructs the way in which Neanderthal Man lived.

Erlangen

Erlangen Museum

*Stadtmuseum, Martin-Luther-Platz 9, D-8520
    Erlangen, Bayern*
*Mon 8–12, 1.30–6; Tues–Thurs 8–12, 1.30–5;
    Fri 8–12; Sun 10–1.*
F

Established in 1913, the museum was reorganised in 1964. It has exhibits of the Hallstatt period and early Iron Age pottery, material illustrating the history of the town and views and models showing the growth of Erlangen. Other sections relate to traditional local industries, especially the manufacture of leather gloves and stockings, with looms belonging to the Huguenot refugees. There are also tapestries made in 1701–79 at the Dechasseau factory and works by the sculptor Karl May (d. 1961) and the painter Hans Barthelmes (d. 1916).

Tennenlohe Woodland Museum

*Waldmuseum Tennenlohe, Franzosenweg 60,
    D-8520 Erlangen, Bayern   ☎ 09131 26042*
Apr–Oct, Mon–Fri 9–12; Sun 10–4.
F 🐾

The Woodland Museum is at the same time a museum, and an exhibition and information centre, created and run by the Bavarian State Forestry Service. It occupies a group of log huts and open-fronted sheds and sets out to tell the story of the Forestry Service and of forestry methods, explaining the methods of timber extraction and processing. There are collections of tools, vehicles and other equipment and of photographs and documents connected with the development of the Forestry Service. A special section is devoted to the natural history and ecology of woodlands.

Eschershausen

Wilhelm Raabe Memorial Museum

*Wilhelm-Raabe-Gedenkstätte, Raabestraße 5,
    D-3456 Eschershausen, Niedersachsen*
    ☎ *05534 533/3313*
Wed, Fri 3–5; Sat 2–4; Sun 11–1.
F 🐾

The novelist Wilhelm Raabe (1831–1910) was born in Eschershausen. In 1957, the Raabe Society, in collaboration with the municipality, opened a museum to him in the house where he was born. It contains portraits, editions of his works and other memorabilia.

Essen

Cathedral Treasury

*Domschatzkammer Essen, Burgplatz 2, D-4300
    Essen 1, Nordrhein-Westfalen*
    ☎ *0201 2204206*
Tues–Sun 10–4.30
C 🛈 🐾

In the year 852 St Altfrid, the fourth Bishop of Hildesheim, founded a church on his property in Essen and in 870 linked it to a convent for well-born ladies, in charge of an abbess. The early abbesses were always members of the royal family. In due course, the church became a cathedral and the collections which accumulated in its Treasury are among the finest in Germany. They include 10th–11th-century goldsmiths' work, including the celebrated Golden Madonna, which dates from 973–82 and is of wood covered with gold-leaf. Of the same period is the equally famous Seven-Armed Candelabra. The Treasury also has important collections of reliquaries, medieval manuscripts, processional crosses, vestments and Burgundian brooches.

Folkwang Museum

Museum Folkwang, Goethestraße 41, D-4300
　Essen 1, Nordrhein-Westfalen ☎ *0201 8484*
Tues, Wed, Fri–Sun 10–6; Thurs 10–9.
Ⓒ ⓘ 📺 ♿ ☕

The museum, which was established in 1921, is financed and administered jointly by the municipality and by industry. Its collections cover the fields of fine and decorative arts and include medieval–18th-century religious art, ceramics, porcelain, glass, 19th-century drawings and engravings, and 19th–20th-century paintings and sculpture, especially French and German, Impressionism, German Expressionism and post-1945 art.

The Old Synagogue

Alte Synagoge, Steeler Straße 29, D-4300 Essen 1,
　Nordrhein-Westfalen ☎ *0201 1814643*
Tues–Sun 10–6. Closed Dec 24, 25.
Ⓕ ♿

In 1933, at the beginning of the Nazi period, the Jewish community in Essen had 4,500 members. In 1950 there were about 200. The great synagogue, of cathedral-like size and proportions, was opened in 1913. Its activities came to an end with the November pogroms of 1938, when it was seriously damaged by Nazi-inspired arson. The basic structure, however, survived both that fire and the later bombing raids, which destroyed most of the centre of Essen.

In 1959 the ruined synagogue became the property of the City of Essen, which restored it and, despite protests from the international Jewish community, converted in into a Centre of Industrial Design. This was burnt out in 1979 and the synagogue then became a memorial museum to 'Resistance and Persecution in Essen, 1933–45'. Further restoration and modification of the building took place in 1986–8. The new, permanent exhibition is called 'Stages in Jewish Life, from the Emancipation to the present day'.

Ruhrland Museum

Ruhrlandmuseum, Goethestraße 41, D-4300 Essen
　1, Nordrhein-Westfalen ☎ *0201 888411*
Tues, Wed, Fri–Sun 10–6; Thurs 10–9. Closed
　Good Fri, Easter, May 1, Whit Sun, Dec 24,
　25, 31.
Ⓒ ⓘ 📺 ♿ ☕

The Ruhrland Museum and the Folkwang Museum occupy different sections of the same building and share certain services. The Ruhrland Museum is subtitled 'From Ruhrland to Ruhrgebiet – the Geology, Industrial History and Social History of an Area'. These three aspects of the Ruhr are closely linked in the museum's presentation, as the development of the region from a relatively unimportant agricultural area to a heavily populated industrial area would not have been possible without the mineral resources formed over millions of years.

The geological section on the ground floor emphasises the industrial use of the raw materials and a spiral staircase surrounding a mine-cage provides a link with the exhibits on the first floor, which illustrate the social and industrial history of the Ruhr and cover three main topics, work in heavy industry, the life of the workers outside the factory gates, and the bourgeoisie of the Ruhr in Prussian society. Everything is shown as it was in about 1900.

Villa Hügel

Villa Hügel, Postfach 268, D-4300 Essen,
　Nordrhein-Westfalen ☎ *0201 1884821*
Tues–Sun 10–6
Ⓒ ✎

Villa Hügel is the former family home of the Krupp family. The museum, opened in 1961 to commemorate the 150th anniversary of the Krupp industrial and armaments firm, contains a museum in two parts. The first tells the story of the family and the firm, with original furniture, portraits of members of the family, German emperors, and the Krupp collection of paintings. The second section is devoted to an exhibition illustrating the wide-ranging activities of the Krupp concern today.

**Jewelled and enamelled crucifix, c. 1000 AD.
Cathedral Treasury, Essen.**

Reconstructed farmhouse room. Franconian Museum, Feuchtwangen.

Ettlingen

Ettlingen Museum

Museum Ettlingen, Schloß, D-7505 Ettlingen, Baden-Württemberg   ☎ 07243 101273
Tues–Sun 10–5. Closed Jan 1, Dec 24, 25, 31.
Ⓒ ▮ ♿

The first castle at Ettingen was built in the 13th century. Most of this, with the exception of the keep, was demolished in the mid 16th century and a new castle was constructed. This was burnt down in 1689 by French troops during the War of the Palatine Succession. It remained a ruin until 1727, when Sibylla Augusta, the widow of Ludwig Wilhelm, Margrave of Baden, decided to rebuild it and to use it as her home. It was sumptuously decorated for her in the Baroque style.

After her death in 1733 it was used for miscellaneous purposes until 1924, when it became a museum. It was completely restored in the 1970s. The State rooms and the Chapel are open to visitors and there are exhibits illustrating the history of the area around Ettlingen from Neolithic times until the present century. The collections include guild material, popular religious art, handicrafts, especially flax-processing, spinning and weaving, and mechanical musical instruments. The museum has a special section devoted to the art of East Asia, which the Margravine Sibylla Augusta greatly admired, and also to the work of the painter Karl Hofer (1878–1955) and the sculptor Karl Abiker (1878–1961).

Eutin

Palace Museum

Schloß Museum, Schloß, D-2420 Eutin, Schleswig-Holstein   ☎ 04521 2312
May 15–Sept 30, daily, guided tours at 11, 3 and 4 and by arrangement.
Ⓒ ♿

The medieval castle at Eutin was remodelled as the palace of the Grand Dukes of Oldenburg during the 17th and 18th centuries. Still owned by the Oldenburg family, it presents an excellent picture of life at a minor North German court in the 17th–19th centuries and of the relationships between the various noble families. It contains 17th–early-19th-century furniture, Brussels tapestries, portraits, landscapes and historical paintings and a large porcelain collection.

One of the most interesting exhibits consists of a group of five large early-18th-century ship models which belonged to Tsar Peter III of Russia (1728–62), who was assassinated at the instigation of his wife in the same year in which he was crowned.

Feuchtwangen

Franconian Museum

Fränkisches Museum, Museumstraße 19, D-8805 Feuchtwangen, Bayern   ☎ 09852 575
Mar–Dec, daily 10–12, 2–5. Groups by appt.
Ⓒ ▮

Since 1926 the museum has occupied a 17th-century bourgeois house, with some exhibits in its garden. The annexe, containing reconstructions of craftsmen's workshops, has been installed in the cloisters of the former Benedictine abbey. The trades represented are those of a confectioner, indigo-dyer, pewterer, shoemaker, potter and weaver. Within the main museum building there are displays of costumes, popular art, craftsmen's tools, domestic equipment, pottery and porcelain. The collection of faïence is one of the best in south Germany. There is also a series of reconstructions of rooms from the 18th to the early-20th centuries.

Fichtelberg

Fichtelberg Demonstration Mine

Besucher Bergwerk Fichtelberg, Panorama Straße, D-8591 Fichtelberg, Bayern   ☎ 09272 848
Sat, Sun and public holidays 10–5
Ⓒ ▮ ♿

This 500-year-old silver mine is the only one in North Bavaria which is still operating and which can be visited by the public. Apart from demonstrations in the underground workings, there are displays illustrating the history of the mine.

Fischerhude

Otto Modersohn Museum

*Otto-Modersohn-Museum, In der Bredenau 88,
D-2802 Fischerhude-Ottersberg 2,
Niedersachsen*   ☎ 04293 328
*Apr–Oct, daily 10–1, 2.30–6. Nov–Mar, Sat,
Sun 10–5.*
C ⓘ ⌂

Otto Modersohn (1865–1943) was the husband
of Paula Modersohn-Becker (1876–1907), the
most important German woman artist of her day
and one of the main precursors of
Expressionism. He, however, was a considerable
artist in his own right and, like his wife, one of
the founders of the celebrated artists' colony at
Worpswede. The museum dedicated to him at
Fischerhude contains only his early works, from
between 1884 and 1889, when his time was
spent painting scenes from the flat North
German landscape. The collection includes
about 100 oil paintings and watercolours, 50
drawings and 35 of his sketchbooks.

Flensburg

Flensburg Museum

*Städtisches Museum, Lutherplatz 1, D-2390
Flensburg, Schleswig-Holstein*
        ☎ 0461 852956
Tues–Sat 10–5; Sun 10–1.
C ⓘ ⌂

The museum was founded in 1876 by the local
furniture manufacturer, Heinrich Sauermann.
The present building in the Dutch Renaissance
style dates from 1901–3. The collections
illustrate the cultural history of Schleswig-
Holstein. The fine art section, which has mostly
works by artists connected with the region,
includes an important group of paintings and
watercolours by the Expressionist painter Emil
Nolde (1867–1956), who was persecuted by the
Nazis, although many of his ideas were similar to
theirs. The pottery, porcelain and glass exhibits
also have regional connections, as do the
collections of 16th–19th-century furniture,
faïence and popular art. A series of rooms from
peasant houses in Schleswig-Holstein forms a
major attraction in the museum.

Frankfurt am Main

Albert Schweitzer Archive and Museum

*Deutches Albert Schweitzer-Archiv und Zentrum,
Neue Schlesingergasse 22-24, D-6000
Frankfurt am Main 1, Hessen*
        ☎ 069 284951
Mon–Fri 10–4. Other times by appt.
F ⓘ ⍰

The displays in the museum illustrate the life
and achievements of the philosopher, writer,
organist, theologian and doctor, Albert
Schweitzer (1875–1965), who was awarded the
Nobel Peace Prize in 1952 and became an

**Reconstructed late 17th-century interior.
Flensburg Museum.**

Honorary Citizen of Frankfurt in 1959. The
museum has many of his letters, manuscripts
and personal possessions, including his tin
trunk.

Friedrich Stoltze Memorial Museum

*Gedenkstätte für Friedrich Stoltze, im Haus
Stadtsparkasse Frankfurt, Töngesgasse 34-6,
D-6000 Frankfurt am Main, Hessen*
        ☎ 069 2170266
Mon, Tues, Thurs, Fri 10–5; Wed 10–8.
F

The museum was opened in 1978 as a memorial
to one of Frankfurt's most remarkable citizens,
the folk-poet, local patriot, journalist,
publisher, satirist and bitter enemy of Bismarck,
Friedrich Stoltze (1816–91). The exhibits
include Stoltze's furniture and a wide selection
of memorabilia, and the aim is to keep his
memory alive by means of temporary exhibitions
which illustrate different aspects of his life and
achievements.

German Postal Museum

*Deutsches Postmuseum, Schaumainkai 53, D-6000
Frankfurt am Main 70, Hessen*
        ☎ 069 60600
Tues–Sun 10–5
F ⍰ ⌂

From 1872 onwards the German Post Office
began systematically collecting items related to
its history. A museum was established in Berlin
and remained open until 1940, when the
collections were dispersed in order to protect
them against air raids. A new museum was
opened in 1958, in Frankfurt, and this has
recently been reorganised and extended into a
new building, a large part of which is
underground.

    In its new form, the museum presents the
history of postal, telephone and radio
communications in Germany over a period of

500 years. There are collections of uniforms, horse-drawn and motor vehicles used by the Post Office, letter-boxes and telegraph, telephone and radio equipment. The museum has a large archive of paintings, drawings, prints and photographs, a number of which are on display.

Goethe Museum

Freies Deutsches Hochstift, Frankfurter Goethe-Museum, Goethe-Haus, Großer Hirschgraben 23-25, D-6000 Frankfurt am Main 1, Hessen
☎ *069 282824*
Apr–Sept, Mon–Sat 9–6; Sun and public holidays 10–1. Oct–Mar, Mon–Sat 9–4; Sun and public holidays 10–1. Closed Jan 1, Fasching Tues (after 12), Good Fri, Tues following Whit Sun (after 12), Dec 24, 25, 31.
Ⓒ 🔒

A telephone of 1905. German Postal Museum, Frankfurt am Main.

The house in which Johann Wolfgang von Goethe (1749–1832) was born was one of a pair, built in 1590 and made into a single house in 1754. The poet lived here until 1775, when he went to live in Weimar. It was almost totally destroyed on 22 March 1944, during an air raid which obliterated the old part of the city of Frankfurt. The house was rebuilt after the war, using as much of the original material as possible. Furnished in the style of the late 18th century, the house has collections illustrating the life and work of Goethe and the period in which he lived. There are late-18th- and early-19th-century German furniture, paintings, drawings, engravings and sculpture, manuscripts and first editions of Goethe's works, and a number of memorabilia and personal possessions. The museum also contains a collection of German literary manuscripts, dating from 1750 to 1850.

Heinrich Hoffmann Museum

Heinrich-Hoffmann-Museum, Schubertstraße 20, D-6000 Frankfurt am Main 1, Hessen
☎ *069 1747969*
Tues–Sun 10–5
Ⓒ 🔒 💺 🚗

The museum's collections illustrate the life and work of Dr Heinrich Hoffmann (1809–94), physician, psychiatrist and author of the celebrated Struwwelpeter children's books. The exhibits include early editions and parodies of the books, objects relating to Struwwelpeter, and memorabilia of Heinrich Hoffmann.

Historical Museum

Historisches Museum, Saalgasse 19, D-6000 Frankfurt am Main 1, Hessen
☎ *069 2125599*
Tues, Thurs–Sun 10–5; Wed 10–8.
Ⓕ 🔒 💺 ♿ 🚗

The museum was established in 1878. During the Second World War its buildings were destroyed in bombing raids, but the collections, which were stored elsewhere for safety, mostly survived. In 1972 it was reopened in a complex of five 12th–19th-century buildings. The displays follow certain general themes, but are mostly concerned with the history of Frankfurt from the 8th to the 19th centuries. Particular sections are devoted to German coins, discoveries made during the excavation of graves in the old city, Frankfurt furniture – mostly shown in period rooms – Frankfurt faïence, and silver belonging to the town council. There is a reproduction of a local goldsmith's workshop.

Jewish Museum

Jüdisches Museum, Untermainkai 14-15, D-6000 Frankfurt am Main, Hessen
☎ *069 2125000*
Tues–Sun 10–5; Wed also 5–8.
Ⓕ 🔒 💺

From the Middle Ages until the Nazi period, Frankfurt had a large Jewish population, which was almost annihilated between 1934 and 1945. The new museum, created by the municipality, occupies a building which formerly belonged to the Rothschild family and illustrates Jewish history and customs, especially in Frankfurt. A notable feature is a large and detailed model of the main street in the former Jewish quarter of Frankfurt, from which the inhabitants were taken away to the concentration camps. Each house is thoroughly documented. Video programmes are available throughout the museum, at points where they relate to particular displays.

Schopenhauer Archive

Schopenhauer Archiv, Bockenheimer Landstraße 134-8, D-6000 Frankfurt am Main, Hessen
☎ *069 7907249*
Mon–Fri 9–4.30. Other times by appt.
Ⓕ

The philosopher Arthur Schopenhauer (1788–1860) lived in seclusion in Frankfurt from 1831 until his death. The museum contains memorabilia of him, including his flutes, the prisms that he used for his optical experiments, his watch and his walking stick, as well as portraits of him. The centre of the collection is his library, with notes and commentaries on his books.

Frechen

Keramion

Museum für zeitgenössische keramische Kunst, Bonnstraße 12, D-5020 Frechen, Nordrhein-Westfalen ☎ *02234 505286*
Tues, Thurs 10–12, 2–5; Sat 2–5; Sun 10–4. Groups by appt.
C 🔒

Opened in 1971, Keramion is devoted to ceramic ware, especially from the German-speaking countries. Special exhibitions give the public an opportunity to gain a detailed appreciation of the work of particular artists. Frechen has been a major centre of German ceramic production since the 18th century. Its famous bearded-man stoneware jugs, often known as Bellarmines, were exported all over north-west Europe.

Freising

Diocesan Museum

Diözesanmuseum, Domberg 21, D-8050 Freising, Bayern ☎ *08161 2432*
Tues Fri 10 4; Sat, Sun 10 6.
C

For centuries, Freising was the centre of a diocese which embraced most of Upper Bavaria. It was also the seat of the Prince Bishops whose territory extended to Lower Austria, Styria and the South Tyrol. With its 8th-century cathedral, the Palace of the Prince Bishops, the secondary churches and its ecclesiastical Residence, it conveys an unforgettable impression of the wealth and grandeur of the Church in Bavaria in medieval times. The collections of 8th–19th-century religious art, drawn from churches and monasteries in Upper Bavaria, Munich, Landshut and Salzburg, make it one of the world's greatest religious museums.

Friedrichshafen

Museum of Lake Constance

Städtliches Bodensee Museum, Adenauerplatz 1, D-7990 Friedrichshafen 1, Baden-Württemberg ☎ *07541 203/230*
Tues–Sun 10–12, 2–5
C 🔒

Friedrichshafen is the birthplace of Zeppelins, which carried passengers in great comfort between German cities in 1910–14 and across the Atlantic in the 1920s and 1930s. The museum tells the story of their development and their years in service, with models, components, photographs, and mementoes of the flights. There are also collections of archaeological material from local sites and of medieval–20th-century paintings by local artists.

Friedrichsruh

Bismarck Museum

Bismarck-Museum, D-2055 Friedrichsruh, Schleswig-Holstein ☎ *04104 2419*
Apr–Sept, Mon 2–6; Tues–Sun 9–6. Oct–Mar, Tues–Sat 9–4; Sun 10–4.
C 🚗

Friedrichsruh was the home of Prince Otto von Bismarck (1815–98). In 1927 a large number of paintings, photographs and other memorabilia were transferred to Friedrichsruh from another Bismarck property at Schönhausen and until 1945 the collections where shown to the public. The castle was damaged by bombing in April 1945 and the museum was closed for repairs until 1951.

It contains, in addition to the furnishings, paintings and photographs of Bismarck and his family and of European royalty who were prominent during his lifetime, letters and documents relating to his political career.

There is a model of the cruiser, *Bismarck*, built in 1872 and paintings and photographs of other warships bearing the same name.

Fulda

German Museum of Firefighting

Deutsches Feuerwehr-Museum e.V., St-Laurentius-Straße 3, D-6400 Fulda, Hessen ☎ *0661 75017*
Tues, Wed, Fri–Sun 10–5; Thurs 2–9
C ☕ ♿ 🚗

The museum tells the story of firefighting in Germany from the 15th century onwards. It has large collections of fire-engines and other equipment, including a 1624 hose and nozzle,

19th-century dish. Keramion, Frechen.

Street hydrant of cast iron. German Museum of Firefighting, Fulda.

an 1808 revolving ladder, magnificently decorated Baroque equipment and two steam-driven pumps. There are also also displays of uniforms, helmets and badges, and information about the recruitment, organisation and training of firefighting personnel at different periods.

Fürstenberg über Höxter

Museum of the Fürstenberg Porcelain Factory

Museum des Porzellanmanufaktur Fürstenberg, Schloß, D-3476 Fürstenberg über Höxter, Niedersachsen   ☎ 05271 5081/3
Apr–Sept, Mon–Sat 9–11, 1–4; Sun 10–12. Oct–Mar, Mon–Fri 9–11, 1–4; Sat 9–12.
C i ⚐

The celebrated Fürstenberg factory was founded in 1747 and is still in operation. The museum tells the story of its development and its products in the 18th and early-19th centuries and illustrates the technical processes involved. There is also an exhibition of the company's more recent products.

Garmisch-Partenkirchen

Werdenfelser Museum

Werdenfelser Museum, Ludwigstraße 47, D-8100 Garmisch–Partenkirchen, Bayern
☎ 08821 3522 and 2134
Tues–Fri 10–1, 3–6; Sat 10–1.
C i ⚐

Opened in 1973 in a large and attractive 17th-century house, the museum has rooms furnished to illustrate different styles of traditional town and country life in the region. Other sections are devoted to particular themes, including

wrought-ironwork, carnival and religious art. There is also an important collection of 16th–18th-century sculpture.

Gelnhausen

Ruins of the Imperial Palace

Kaiserpfalzruine, Burgstraße 14, D-6460 Gelnhausen, Hessen   ☎ 06051 3805
Apr–Sept, Tues–Sun 10–4 (guided tours only). Oct–Mar, Tues–Sun 10–3 (guided tours only).
C i ⚐ ⚐

In 1180–92 the Emperor Frederick Barbarossa built himself a moated palace in Gelnhausen. Its ruins are a rare survival of the non-religious architecture of the period and illustrate the character and organisation of the Imperial court and the scale and standard of its building projects.

Gescher

Museum of Bells

Glockenmuseum, Lindenstraße 4, D-4423 Gescher, Nordrhein-Westfalen
☎ 02542 60017
Apr–Oct, Tues–Sat 3–6; Sun 10–12. Nov–Mar, Tues–Sat 3–5; Sun 10–12.
C ⚐

The tradition of bell-founding in Gescher goes back to the 17th century. The techniques involved are illustrated by means of a replica of a bell-pit, with its associated moulds and equipment. There is also a display of historic bells, ranging in date from the 12th century to the 20th.

Geseke

Hellweg Museum

Hellweg-Museum, Hellweg 13, D-4787 Geseke, Nordrhein-Westfalen   ☎ 02942 50056
Wed, Sat 4–6; Sun 11–12, 4–6.
F ⚐

During the Middle Ages Geseke developed into a small trading town, situated on the Hellweg, the road of merchants and inns. In 1664, on this road, Friedrich Dickmann, a prosperous merchant, built himself a splendid house and office. It was substantially rebuilt in the early 19th century and today is protected as an historic monument. The Local History Society installed its museum and headquarters here in 1954. Its collections include prehistoric and palaeontological material from the area, religious art, furniture, domestic equipment and coins. There are five workshop reconstructions, containing the tools and equipment of a clogmaker, saddler, cooper, basket-maker and blacksmith. There are also exhibits showing the history and techniques of flax-growing, sheep-breeding and beekeeping and the processing of agricultural products.

The Prince's Residence, Detmold (Germany).   Iittala Glass Museum, Iittala (Finland).

A painting advocating support for William Wilberforce's campaign against slavery, finally victorious in 1807. Wilberforce House, Hull (Britain).

The Palazzo Arringo, part of which now houses the Art Gallery at Ascoli Piceno (Italy).

Giengen an der Brenz

Museum of the Margarete Steiff Company

Museum der Firma Margarete Steiff, Margarete Steiff GmbH, Postfach 1560, D-7298 Giengen an der Brenz, Baden-Württemberg
☎ 07322 5432
Mon–Fri 10–5
F 🛈 ♿

The famous toy-making company was established in 1880. The museum contains examples of wooden toys, children's racing cars, kites and dolls, as well as the legendary Teddy Bear, created by Margarete Steiff's nephew, Richard Steiff, and its many subsequent variants. Visitors to the museum can also see the complete production process for a modern soft toy.

Giessen

Art Museum of Upper Hesse

Oberhessisches Museum: Abteilung Gemäldegalerie und Kunsthandwerk, Altes Schloß, Brandplatz 2, D-6300 Giessen, Hessen
☎ 0641 3062477
Tues–Sun 10–4
F 🛈

The Old Castle in Giessen was built in the 14th century. It was substantially altered in 1900, destroyed by bombing in 1944 and subsequently rebuilt in the early-20th-century style, the internal arrangement being much changed at the time.

Justus Liebig's laboratory. Liebig Museum, Giessen.

The museum has a large coin and note collection, ranging from Celtic and Roman items to the emergency currency of the 1920s and including money issued in Hesse. There are also sections devoted to 17th–19th century faïence and majolica, with examples from Hanau and Frankfurt, 16th-century sculpture and 16th–18th-century paintings, drawings, engravings and furniture by German artists and designers.

Liebig Museum

Liebig-Museum, Liebigstraße 12, Postfach 11 03 52, D-6300 Giessen, Hessen
☎ 0641 76392
Tues–Sun 10–12, 2–4
C 🛈 ♿

Justus Liebig (1803–73), the greatest chemist of his time, was professor of chemistry at the University of Giessen from 1824 to 1852. It was at the Chemical Institute here that he made his most important discoveries and where the real development of the teaching, research and technology of modern chemistry began. The Institute was restored after the First World War and, converted to a museum, was dedicated to the memory of Liebig.

Visitors can see the room where Liebig taught and carried out his research. The laboratories are equipped as they would have been in Liebig's time. There are exhibits showing the development of chemistry during the 19th century and Liebig's contribution to it. Special sections are devoted to the careers of Liebig's pupils, to his inventions, including silvered mirrors, meat extract, baking powder, a corrosion-resistant nickel-iron alloy, and superphosphate, and to the exceptionally accurate balances used in his laboratories.

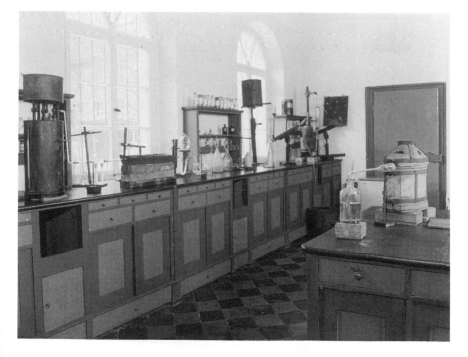

Gladenbach

Karl Lenz's House

Künstlerhaus Lenz, Blaumühlenweg 10, D-3569
   Gladenbach, Hessen   ☎ 06462 8484
Wed–Mon 10–7
Ⓕ ⚊

Karl Lenz (1898–1949) was celebrated as a
painter of people wearing the regional costumes
of Hesse. In 1950 his house was opened as a
museum. It contains a representative selection
of 50 of his paintings, together with a collection
of country furniture from the area and examples
of contemporary ceramics from Hesse.

Göttingen

Göttingen Museum

Städtisches Museum, Ritterplan 7/8, D-3400
   Göttingen, Hessen   ☎ 0551 4002843
Tues–Fri 10–5; Sat, Sun 10–1
Ⓕ ⚊

The Hardenberger Hof, which houses the
museum, has had a remarkable history. It was
built in 1592 as the residence of the Chancellor
of Brunswick, Johann von Jagemann. In 1620 it
passed into the possession of the Counts of
Hardenberg. In 1812 it became the headquarters
of the 'Augusta of the Golden Circle' masonic
lodge, and from 1832 it served as a piano
factory. The town of Göttingen acquired it in
1896 and converted it into a museum,
presenting the prehistory and history of the area
and the history of the University.

There are collections of medieval–18th-
century religious sculpture, furniture, musical
instruments, faïence, Göttingen silver and
pewter, prints and drawings, and Fürstenberg
porcelain. A special section is devoted to the
history of the Jewish community in Göttingen.

Grafenhausen-Rothaus

Hüsli Museum of Local Life

Heimatmuseum 'Hüsli', D-7821 Grafenhausen-
   Rothaus, Baden-Württemberg   ☎ 07748 212
May–Sept, Tues–Sat 9.30–12, 1.30–5.30; Sun
   1.30–5.30. Oct & Dec 16–Apr, Tues–Sat
   10–12, 1.30–5; Sun 1.30–5. Closed
   Nov 1–Dec 15.
Ⓒ ⚊ ⚊

The concert singer Helene Siegfried (1867–
1966) spent most of her life in Berlin. In 1912
she built the 'Hüsli' as a summer residence.
During the Second World War she lost
everything she possessed in Berlin and moved
permanently to her 'Hüsli', where she died in
her 100th year. She was a devoted collector of
objects which illustrated the traditional crafts
and skills of the people in the Black Forest.
These includes stoves, painted furniture,
decorated ceilings, utensils, votive pictures,
crucifixes and painted glass. The house and its
collections, augmented since Helene Siegfried's
death, became a museum in 1969.

The Hardenberger Hof, home of the Göttingen
Museum.

Grefrath

Open-Air Museum of the Lower Rhine

Niederrheinisches Freilichtmuseum, D-4155
   Grefrath 1, Nordrhein-Westfalen
   ☎ 02158 3840
Apr–Oct, Tues–Sun 10–6. Nov–Mar, Tues–Sun
   10–4.30.
Ⓒ ⚊ ⚊ ⚊

The museum consists of rural buildings from the
Lower Rhine area moved to the site and re-
erected in village settings, with hedges,
footpaths, gardens and fields. There are theme-
exhibitions in the Dorenburg, a 17th-century
moated castle, which was destroyed during the
Second World War and subsequently rebuilt
and furnished in the style of c. 1800. There are
displays of traditional handicrafts and
agricultural techniques.

Grossheide

Berumfehn Forest Museum

Waldmuseum Berumfehn, Dorfstraße, D-2987
   Grossheide, Niedersachsen
   ☎ 04963 526/7104
Apr–Oct, Wed, Sat, Sun 10–6
Ⓒ ⚊

The museum's exhibits illustrate the ecology of
the woodland areas of the region. There are
displays of the animals, birds and insects which
live in the forest, together with specimens of the
bark and timber of the trees growing locally.
Associated with the museum there is a garden
and a forest path which supplement the
information provided in the displays within the
building. Relief maps show the historical
development of Berumfehn and the colonisation
and enclosure of the moorland.

Grossweil

Open-Air Museum of Upper Bavaria

Freilichtmuseum des Bezirks Oberbayern, An der
*   Glentleiten, D-8119 Grossweil, Bayern*
*   ☎ 08841 1095*
Apr–Oct, Tues–Sun 9–6. Nov, Sat, Sun, 10–5.
🄲 ⓘ ⬛ ⛄ 🔔

Established in 1976, the museum contains a
large collection of rural buildings from Upper
Bavaria which have been moved to the present
site. They include different types of farmhouse,
granaries, barns, mills, flax-kilns, a wooden
chapel, an apiary and a fisherman's hut. The
houses are suitably furnished and the workshops
have their original equipment. Demonstrations
of handicrafts, trades and agricultural processes
are regularly held and there is a garden where
visitors are shown the plants traditionally grown
in monasteries in the region.

Grünwald

Castle Museum

Burgmuseum Grünwald, Zeillerstraße 3, D-8022
*   Grünwald, Bayern   ☎ 089 6413218*
Mar 15–Nov, Wed–Sun 10–4.30
🄲 🔔

This is a branch museum of the State Prehistoric
Collection in Munich and is one of eight such
museums recently established in Bavaria. The
castle dates from the 12th century and from the
13th to the 15th centuries it was a hunting-
lodge of the Dukes of Bavaria. In 1486–7 it was
rebuilt and subsequently served as a prison and a
powder magazine. In 1879 it was sold at auction
to the Munich sculptor and wax-figure maker,
Paul Zeiller, who prepared here 'curiosities' for
museums and exhibitions, such as the head of a
girl with one eye in the middle of her forehead.
An exhibition in the museum tells the story of
the castle.
   The collections of the present museum
illustrate the history of the Munich area during
the prehistoric and Roman periods, with Roman
tombstones, milestones and other stone objects
from throughout Bavaria and other Roman
provinces. There are exhibits illustrating life in
the region during the Roman occupation. These
include reconstructions of a Roman pottery kiln
and a Roman kitchen and heating system.

Gundelsheim am Neckar

Siebenburg Museum

Siebenbürgisches Museum und Museum der Stadt
*   Gundelsheim, Schloß Horneck, D-6953*
*   Gundelsheim am Neckar, Baden-*
*   Württemberg   ☎ 06269 373*
Apr–Nov, Tues–Fri 3–5; Sat, Sun and public
*   holidays 10–12, 2–5. Dec–Mar, Sat, Sun and*
*   public holidays 10–12, 2–5.*
🄲 🔔

Castle Horneck at Gundelsheim played a
prominent part in the history of the Teutonic
Order and in 1430 it was the seat of the Master
of the Order. The museum tells the story of the
Order and has collections illustrating the
traditional culture of the Siebenburg Saxons.
There are displays of regional costumes,
embroidery, ceramics, pewter, goldsmiths' work
and country furniture, all of exceptional quality.
A section of the museum is devoted to Roman
archaeology.

Gutach

Vogtsbauernhof – The Black Forest Open-Air Museum

Schwarzwälder Freilichtmuseum 'Vogtsbauernhof',
*   D-7625 Gutach/Schwarzwaldbahn, Baden-*
*   Württemberg   ☎ 07831 230*
Apr–Nov 1, daily 8.30–6
🄲 ⛄ 🔔

The museum consists of 16th- and 17th-century
Black Forest farmhouses and other rural
buildings moved to the museum site. Among
the exhibits are a smithy, an oil mill, a hemp
crusher and a drying room, an apiary, a water-
powered sawmill, and a bakehouse. All the
houses contain appropriate furnishings and
domestic equipment and in the farm buildings
there are agricultural implements and vehicles.

Hagen

Karl Ernst Osthaus Museum

Karl Ernst Osthaus Museum, Hochstraße 73,
*   D-5800 Hagen 1, Nordrhein-Westfalen*
*   ☎ 02331 207576*
Tues, Wed, Fri, Sat 11–6; Thurs 11–10; Sun
*   11–4.*
🄵 ⓘ ⬛

In 1898–1902, Karl Ernst Osthaus, the son of a
Hagen banker, created his Folkwang Museum of
the Visual Arts, in a Victorian building which
had been given a Jugendstil interior by the
architect, Henry van der Velde. After the death

**Farmhouse at Vogtsbauernhof – The Black
Forest Open-Air Museum, Gutach.**

Karl Ernst Osthaus Museum, Hagen.

of Osthaus in 1921, his heirs sold the world-famous contents of the museum to the City of Essen, which appropriated the name Folkwang. The museum still exists.

A few years later the city authorities in Hagen began to form a new collection of 20th-century German art. This was practically recreated after the Second World War and is now installed in two buildings by Henry van der Velde, one constructed in 1902 and the other in 1906–8. It contains German paintings, graphics, sculpture and furniture from 1900 to the present day.

Westphalian Open-Air Museum of Technology

Westfälisches Freilichtmuseum, Landesmuseum für Handwerk und Technik, Mäckingerbach, D-5800 Hagen 1, Nordrhein–Westfalen
☎ 02331 78070
Apr–Oct, Tues–Sun 9–6
Ⓒ 👤 💼 ⅋ ✉

Since 1963, workshops and small factory buildings from other areas have been transferred to a two-and-a-half km stretch of valley to show how work was carried on in the region in pre-industrial and early industrial times. What has been created is in effect a leisure park of technology, covering the period from about 1780 to 1870. There are more than 70 exhibits and all are in working order. They are grouped according to their raw materials – iron and steel, non-ferrous metals, wire, paper and printing, wood, food and drink, textiles, hides, skin and fur, and gold and silver. Other sections are devoted to agriculture and to domestic handicrafts. There are regular demonstrations in, for example, a scythe mill, a rope-walk, different forges, a printing shop, a paper mill and a sawmill.

The museum also houses, as an additional activity, the German Blacksmiths' Museum.

Haigerloch

Atomic Energy Cellar

Atomkeller-Museum, Oberstadtstraße 11, D-7452 Haigerloch, Baden-Württemberg
☎ 07474 6061/1800
May–Sept, daily 10–12, 2–5. Oct–Nov & Mar–Apr, Sat, Sun 10–12, 2–5.
Ⓒ 💼 ✉

In 1944, the team working at the Kaiser Wilhelm Institut in Berlin on nuclear fission transferred its activities to a former beer cellar belonging to the Swan Inn, carved out of the rock, directly under the parish church. The museum tells the story of German research in this field during the war years and the personalities associated with it, especially Heisenberg, von Weizsächer and Wirtz. A section of the museum describes how members of the team were moved to the United States at the end of the war in order to continue their researches there on behalf of the American Government.

Hamburg

Altona Museum

Altonaer Museum im Hamburg, Norddeutsches Landesmuseum, Museumstraße 23, Postfach 50 01 25, D-2000 Hamburg 50
☎ 040 3807483
Tues–Sun 10–5. Closed Jan 1, Easter Sun, May 1, Whit Sun, Dec 25.
Ⓒ 👤 💼 ⅋

Established in 1863 and moved to its present site in 1901, this is one of the Federal Republic's most important museums. It was badly damaged during the Second World War, but has since been fully restored to its former glory. The range of its collections, covering the natural environment and culture of North Germany, is very wide. Hamburg's maritime history inevitably plays an important part, with exhibits relating to shipping and navigation, shipbuilding, the fishing industry, and the geology and characteristics of the North German coastal area, as well as collections of ship models, ships' figureheads and portraits of ships' captains.

Other sections of the museum are devoted to regional natural history and ecology, folk art, costumes and toys. Inside the museum there are a number of original farmhouses, moved from their sites. The art department displays 18th–20th-century paintings of the North German landscape, drawings and prints, 18th–19th-century English ceramics and porcelain bearing scenes of North German life.

Ernst Barlach House

Ernst Barlach Haus, Stiftung Hermann F. Reemtsma, Baron-Voght-Straße 50a, Jenischpark, D-2000 Hamburg 52
☎ 040 826085
Tues–Sun 11–5
Ⓒ 👤

The sculptor and graphic artist, Ernst Barlach (1870–1938), died in Rostock, after many years of persecution by the Nazis. In 1960 Hermann Reemtsma's Barlach Collection was converted, according to his wishes, into an endowed foundation and two years later it was opened to the public in the new Ernst Barlach House, which had been specially designed for the purpose. Since Reemtsma's death in 1961, further works have been added to the collection, which includes sculptures – the 24 wooden sculptures form the largest collection in the Federal Republic – drawings and graphics.

The museum has recently begun to acquire works by contemporaries of Barlach, which help to provide a context within which his work can be better understood.

Ernst Thälmann Memorial Museum

Gedenkstätte Ernst Thälmann, Ernst Thälmann-
  Platz, D-2000 Hamburg 20 ☎ *040 474184*
Tues–Fri 10–5; Sat, Sun 10–1.
Ⓒ ♿ ⬛ 🔄

Ernst Thälmann was a member of the Reichstag during the Weimar Republic and a leading figure in German and international workers' movements, as well as President of the German Communist Party. He was arrested as soon as the Nazis came to power in 1933 and spent the remainder of his life under particularly harsh conditions in concentration camps. He was murdered in Buchenwald in 1944.

The Memorial Museum, opened in 1969, contains exhibits relating to the life and career of Thälmann, and collections illustrating the history of the labour movement, the struggle against fascism in Germany, and the concentration camps.

Hamburg Art Gallery

Hamburger Kunsthalle, Glockengießerwall,
  D-2000 Hamburg 1 ☎ *040 248251*
Tues–Sun 10–5
Ⓒ ♿ ⬛

Opened in 1869, the gallery is celebrated particularly for its collection of works by 19th- and 20th-century German painters. Among the artists represented are Corinth, Barlach, Nolde, Dix, Beckmann, Kokoschka, Klee and Arp. There are also world-renowned international collections of engravings and of Greek and Roman coins and of medals from Renaissance times to the present day.

Museum of Wilhelmsburg, and Milk Museum

Museum der Elbinsel Wilhelmsburg mit
  Milchmuseum, Kirchdorferstraße 163, D-2102
  Hamburg 93 (Wilhelmsburg)
  ☎ *040 7543982*
May–Oct, Sun 4–6
Ⓕ

The museum, first opened in 1907, illustrates country life and farming in the Wilhelmsburg area during the 18th–early-19th centuries.

There are reconstructions of an 18th-century farmhouse living-room and kitchen and a comprehensive collection of 19th-century tools and implements used in farming and vegetable growing in the area.

Over a long period Wilhelmsburg supplied Hamburg with a large part of its milk and milk products. The Milk Museum has a comprehensive collection of the equipment used in the industry between 1600 and 1950, including the boats, barrows and carts and the costumes worn by people who worked in the dairy.

Museum of the History of Hamburg

Museum für Hamburgische Geschichte,
  Holstenwall 24, D-2000 Hamburg 36
  ☎ *040 34912 2360*
Tues–Sun 10–5
Ⓒ ♿ ⬛

The museum was originally opened in 1839 on behalf of the Society for the History of Hamburg. In 1972 the then Director redefined the aim of the museum as being to illustrate the development of Hamburg in terms of its political history, its trade and its shipping. Among the many remarkable exhibits in this large and important museum are the contemporary model of the convoy ship, *Wappen von Hamburg III*, 'a floating Baroque palace', built to protect merchant ships against pirates; the superstructure, with the bridge and saloon, of the merchant ship, *Werner*, built in 1909, which completely fills a large gallery in the museum, and a model of the complete Hamburg railway system, built to the scale of 1:32.

The collections cover a wide range, from 17th–20th-century ship models and drawings, paintings and engravings of the city and the port installations to the skulls of two pirates, beheaded for their crimes against shipping.

The Altona Museum, Hamburg.

Museum Village

Museumsdorf, Im Alten Dorfe 48, D-2000
Hamburg 67   ☎ *040 6039098*
Buildings: Wed, Sat, tours at 3; Sun tours at 10
and 3. Grounds: Mon, Wed, Fri–Sun 9–12,
2–dusk or 6 if earlier.
Ⓒ ⬙ ⚓

The museum consists of a reconstruction of a
Holstein village, with 17th–18th-century rural
buildings transferred to the museum site. They
include a village inn, smithy, drive-through
barn, mill and farmhouse. Within the buildings
there are displays of furniture, handicrafts,
agricultural implements and horse-drawn
vehicles.

Neuengamme Concentration Camp Memorial

KZ-Gedenkstätte Neuengamme, Jean-Dolidier-
Weg, D-2050 Hamburg 80 ☎ *040 7231031*
Tues–Sun 10–5
Ⓕ ⌂ ⅃ ⚓

The concentration camp at Neuengamme was
established in 1938 as a satellite of
Sachsenhausen. It achieved full concentration
camp status in 1940. Its original purpose had
been to use prisoners in the SS brickworks near
the camp, but by 1942–3 it had become an
importance source of slave labour for the
German war industry. During the war, the
Gestapo deported tens of thousands of people
from occupied countries throughout Europe to
Neuengamme. Of the total of 106,000 inmates,
55,000 died as a result of their treatment.

The specially-created museum, within the
area of the former camp, tells the story of
Neuengamme between 1938 and 1945, and of
Europe under German occupation. There is a
model of the camp, showing its layout and the
purpose of each building.

Skeleton clock, from 1820. Hamelin Museum.

Rieck House

Rieck-Haus, Curslacker Deich 284, D-2050
Hamburg 80   ☎ *040 7231223*
Apr–Sept, Tues–Sun 10–5. Oct–Mar, Tues–Sun
10–4. Closed Jan 1, May 1, Easter Sun, Whit
Sun, Dec 24, 25.
Ⓒ ⌂ ⚓

The Rieck House and its adjoining barn, built in
1533, is the oldest surviving complex of farm
buildings in the Vierlande region. It forms the
core of the open-air museum which has been
created around it since the Second World War.
The exhibits consist of 16th–19th-century
houses and other rural buildings from the area,
re-erected on the museum site. They are
equipped with appropriate furniture, domestic
equipment and agricultural implements and
tools.

Hamelin

Hamelin Museum

Museum Hameln, Osterstraße 8-9, D-3250
Hameln, Niedersachsen   ☎ *05151 202215*
Tues–Sun 10–5. Closed public holidays.
Ⓒ ⌂ ▣

The museum's collections, installed in two
adjoining Renaissance houses, document the
history of the town and its region. There are
displays of gold- and silversmiths' work,
including items by Hamelin craftsmen, weapons
and militaria, pewter and religious art. One of
the features of the museum is a diorama of the
Battle of Langensalza (1866), with 11,000 tin
figures.

In 1984 Hamelin celebrated the 700th
anniversary of the Pied Piper legend, and special
displays illustrate the origins and development
of the story.

Hanau

Philippsruhe Palace

Schloß Philippsruhe, Museum Hanau, Philippsruher
Allee 45, Postfach 1852, D-6450 Hanau 1,
Hessen   ☎ *06181 295510*
Tues–Sun 10–5. Closed Easter Mon, May 1, Whit
Mon, Dec 25.
Ⓕ ⌂ ▣ ⚓

The Baroque palace was built in 1701–12 for
Count Philipp Reinhard of Hanau, who died a
few weeks after its completion. In 1743, during
the Battle of Dettingen, the English army used
the buildings as a barracks and a hospital. The
palace and its gardens were modified in the 19th
century. After several changes of ownership, it
became the property of the City of Hanau in
1950 and the Historical Museum was eventually
transferred there and enlarged. The new
museum was destroyed by fire in 1984, shortly
after it had been opened. It was reconstructed
and in 1988 reopened to the public.

The exhibits are divided into four sections,
the Middle Ages to the 18th century; the early
19th century; the period of industrialisation;

'Hanomag' car of 1928. Historical Museum, Hanover.

Hanover

Historical Museum

*Historisches Museum, Pferdestraße 6, D-3000
    Hannover 1, Niedersachsen
    ☎ 0511 1682352
Tues 10–8; Wed–Fri 10–4; Sat, Sun 10–6. Easter
    Mon, Whit Mon, Dec 26, 10–6. Easter Sat,
    Whit Sat, Feast of the Assumption, Day of
    Prayer and Repentance, 10–1. Closed Jan 1,
    Good Fri, Easter Sun, May 1, Whit Sun,
    Dec 24, 25, 31.*

F ▌ ▆

The museum building dates from 1906 and
incorporates the last surviving tower (1357) on
the medieval town wall and the 1643–9
Arsenal. It presents the social and cultural
history of Hanover and Lower Saxony. Sections
are devoted to traditional costumes, furniture,
handicrafts and domestic equipment, to
paintings and engravings, to fashion in the
17th–20th centuries, and to 19th–20th-century
toys. Among the exhibits is a Hanomag car, a
reminder of Hanover's once flourishing
automobile industry and the 1782 Golden
Coach of the Prince of Wales, on loan from the
Princes of Hanover.

Wilhelm Busch Museum

*Wilhelm-Busch-Museum, Georgengarten 1,
    D-3000 Hannover, Niedersachsen
    ☎ 0511 714076
Apr–Sept, Tues–Sun 10–5. Oct–Mar, Tues–Sun
    10–4.*

C

The poet, painter and caricaturist, Wilhelm
Busch (1832–1908), was born at Wiedensahl,
near Hanover. Much of his influence came from
the ferocious satire which he directed against
the Roman Catholic clergy, which formed part
of Bismarck's 'Kulturkampf'. The museum to the
'Father of the Comics' contains 300 paintings
and 1500 drawings, which represent two-thirds
of his original work. There are also manuscripts
of his work and memorabilia, documents and
other objects illustrating his life and career.
   The museum is linked to an international
'Collection of Critical Graphics', which has
works by such artists as Hogarth, Daumier and
Ronald Searle.

Haslach

Hansjakob Museum

*Hansjakob-Museum im Freihof, Hansjakobstraße
    17, D-7612 Haslach i.K., Baden-
    Württemberg   ☎ 07832 4715/8080
Apr–Oct, Wed 10–12, 3–5; Fri 3–5; Sun and
    public holidays 10–5. Nov–Mar, Wed 10–12,
    3–5; Fri 3–5.*

C ▌ ✿

Heinrich Hansjakob (1837–1916) was a Roman
Catholic priest and a popular writer. He
published 70 books about the life of people in
the rural areas of the Black Forest. In the
present century, he had a house, Freihof, built
for himself in the typical style of a Black Forest
farmhouse, with a private chapel. The house is
now the museum. It has much of its original
contents, including Hansjakob's library,
together with an account of his life and career.
   There are also paintings by regional artists,
including Carl Sandhaas (1801–59), Louis Blum
(1822–54) and Otto Laible (1898–1962).

Museum of Black Forest Costumes

Schwarzwälder Trachtenmuseum, Im Alten
Kapuzinerkloster, D-7612 Haslach i. K.,
Baden-Württemberg   ☎ 07832 8080
Apr–Oct, Tues–Sat 9–5; Sun and public holidays
10–5. Nov–Mar, Tues–Fri 9–12, 1–5. Open
in January only on request.

C ▌ ✿

The Black Forest and the districts adjoining it
are well known for their colourful costumes. At
the end of the 19th century the writer and
priest, Dr Heinrich Hansjakob, who was born in
Haslach, initiated a revival of interest in the
wearing of these costumes and in 1980 a
museum was opened to collect and preserve
them. There are special collections of carnival
costumes, militia uniforms, bridal gowns and
gold and silver bonnets.

The museum has been installed in a restored
early-17th-century Capuchin monastery, where
visitors can see the cells, the refectory and the
church.

Hechingen

Hohenzollern Castle

Burg Hohenzollern, D-7450 Hechingen, Baden-
Württemberg   ☎ 07471 2428
Apr–Oct, daily 9–5.30. Nov–Mar, daily 9–4.30.
Closed Dec 24.

C ▌ ☕ ⅋ ✿

This late medieval castle, the seat of the
Hohenzollerns, was reconstructed by Frederick
William IV of Prussia between 1850 and 1867.
Frederick the Great and Frederick William I are
buried in the Protestant Chapel of the Castle.
The museum is financed and administered by
Prince Louis Ferdinand of Prussia and Prince
Friedrich Wilhelm of Hohenzollern. It contains
18th–19th-century paintings and portraits,
orders and decorations, silver, and costumes and
uniforms. Among the exhibits are the Royal
crown of Prussia, and diamond snuff-boxes
which belonged to Frederick the Great.

Hohenzollern Museum

Hohenzollernische Landessammlung und Hechinger
Heimatmuseum, Schloßplatz 5, D-7460
Hechingen, Baden-Württemberg
☎ 07471 5051
Sun 10–12. Other times by appt.

C ✿

The museum, in the Old Palace, was opened in
1922, shortly after the collapse of the
Hohenzollern Empire. Its collections illustrate
the prehistory and early history of the former
Hohenzollern territories. There are medieval–
18th-century religious paintings and portraits,
tombs and memorabilia of the Hohenzollern
Royal House.

Other sections of the museum are devoted to
costumes, country furniture and the history of
the town of Hechingen.

Museum of Black Forest Costumes, Haslach.

Heide

Klaus Groth Museum

Klaus-Groth-Museum, Lüttenheid 48, D-2240
Heide, Schleswig-Holstein   ☎ 0481 63742
Mon–Sat 9.30–12; Mon, Tues, Thurs, Fri also
2–4.30.

C ✿

The poet, Klaus Groth (1819–99) was born in
Heide. He came from a farming family, wrote in
Low German and ended as an honorary
professor of Low German literature at the
University of Kiel. Together with Fritz Reuter,
with whom he quarrelled, he rehabilitated Low
German as a literary language. His poems have
often been set to music, by Brahms and other
composers.

The museum, established in 1914, contains a
comprehensive collection of manuscripts of
works by him, as well as personal possessions
and memorabilia, his library and portraits of his
family and friends.

Heidelberg

German Apothecaries' Museum

Deutsches Apotheken-Museum, Heidelberger
Schloß, D-6900 Heidelberg, Baden-
Württemberg   ☎ 06221 25880
Apr–Oct, daily 10–5. Nov–Mar, Sat, Sun and
public holidays 11–5.

C

The museum is in the Ottheinrich living
quarters of Heidelberg Castle, one of the most
impressive Renaissance buildings in Germany.

Arranged in 14 rooms, the collections illustrate the history of pharmacy and medicaments in Germany from the alchemist's kitchen to the modern pharmaceutical library. There are important 17th- and 18th-century pharmacies, historical equipment of all kinds, apothecary jars, glassware, porcelain and furnishings from old apothecaries' premises, as well as paintings and books on pharmaceutical subjects.

Museum of the Palatinate

Kurpfälzisches Museum, Hauptstraße 97, D-6900 Heidelberg, Baden-Württemberg
☎ 06221 58206
Tues–Sun 10–1, 2–5
C ▮

The museum is in the Palais Morass, which dates from 1712. On the ground floor there is the collection of 'Palatine Antiquities', formed by Count von Graimberg, who came to live in Heidelberg in 1810. The archaeological department of the museum today contains collections dating from the Palaeolithic to the Merovingian period. Other sections are devoted to the history of the Palatinate and the University and to 14th–20th-century European paintings, sculpture and drawings. The 19th- and 20th-century works emphasise the achievements of German artists. There are also important collections of topographical paintings and prints, coins and medals.

Herrenchiemsee

New Palace and Ludwig II Museum

Neues Schloß und König Ludwig II-Museum, Staatliche Verwaltung Herrenchiemsee, D-8210 Herrenchiemsee, Bayern
☎ 08051 3069
Apr–Sept, daily 9–5. Oct–Mar, daily 10–4. Closed Jan 1, Shrove Tues, Nov 1, Dec 24, 25, 31.
C ⬙

The museum is in the palace built in 1876–86 for King Ludwig II of Bavaria on the model of Versailles. It contains paintings, furniture, porcelain and silver from the royal collections, together with an exhibition describing the history of the palace and pictures illustrating performances of Wagner's operas.

Hersbruck

German Shepherds' Museum

Deutsches Hirtenmuseum, Eisenhüttlein 7, D-8562 Hersbruck, Bayern   ☎ 09151 2161
Tues–Sun 10–12, 2–4. Jan 6, 9–5.
C ▮

The museum occupies a group of half-timbered buildings, including a large barn and a 16th-century house with a galleried courtyard. Its collections illustrate the life and duties of shepherds and cowboys from all over the world, but especially Germany, together with the traditional life of rural Franconia. There are

displays of costumes, cow- and sheep-bells, and musical instruments used by shepherds. Other sections of the museum are devoted to handicrafts – more than 40 craftsmen are represented – country furniture and domestic equipment, popular art, hop-growing and carved pipes.

Herzogenaurach

Adidas Sports Shoe Museum

adidas Sportschuh Museum, Adi Dassler Straße 1-2, D-8522 Herzogenaurach, Bayern
☎ 09132 840
Guided tours by appt with the PR Department
F ▰ ▰

Adi Dassler was born in Herzogenaurach in 1900 and trained at the college of footwear technology at Pirmasens. After the Second World War, he developed the largest sports shoe business in the world. The museum illustrates the technology of shoemaking and documents the history of the firm and its products. Among the celebrities whose adidas shoes are displayed are Jesse Owens, who won four gold medals at the Olympic Games in 1936, Muhammad Ali, Ivan Lendl and the Spanish basketball player, Fernando Romey, who required a size 22 shoe.

Hirzenhain

Museum of Decorative Cast-Iron

Eisenkunstgußmuseum, Buderus Aktiengesellschaft, D-6476 Hirzenhain, Hessen   ☎ 06045 68235
Mon–Fri 9–12, 1–4. On Thurs at 10 there is a free guided tour. Closed public holidays.
F ▰

In 1950, the firm of Buderus opened its iron foundry in Hirzenhain, to make decorative products. It was under the direction of Peter Lipps, who had previously been in charge of a similar enterprise in Gleiwitz, now part of Poland. In establishing a new tradition in Hirzenhain, Lipps believed that it would be helpful to have a collection of similar objects made elsewhere, particularly in Germany, during the 18th, 19th and early 20th centuries. The museum, which is attached to the present

A shepherds' caravan. German Shepherds' Museum, Hersbruck.

Iron openwork ornaments of the early 19th century. Museum of Decorative Cast-Iron, Hirzenhain.

foundry, displays a wide range of such items and explains the techniques involved. Among the exhibits are iron jewellery, a wide range of domestic ornaments, 16th–18th- century firebacks and the largest collection of wooden patterns in the world.

Höhr-Grenzhausen

Westerwald Museum of Ceramics

Keramikmuseum Westerwald, Lindenstraße, D-5410 Höhr-Grenzhausen, Rheinland-Pfalz
☎ 02624 3666
Tues–Sun 10–5
C 🛈 💻 ⛄ 🚗

The Westerwald region has been famous for its grey-blue, salt-glazed stoneware since the 15th century. There is a modern ceramics industry at Höhr-Grenzhausen and a technical college which specialises in the subject. The museum was established in 1976 and took over its new building in 1982. The displays illustrate the history and techniques of the local stoneware industry, together with the work of celebrated contemporary ceramic artists. There are regular demonstrations of stoneware techniques.

Höxter

Höxter-Corvey Museum

Museum Höxter-Corvey, Schloß Corvey, D-3470 Höxter, Nordrhein-Westfalen
☎ 05271 68139
Apr–Oct, daily 9–6
C 🛈 💻 🚗

Corvey was a royal abbey, founded in 822 by Ludwig the Pious. New convent buildings were added after the Thirty Years War. The community was dissolved in 1803, following the secularisation of church property and the proeprty came into the hands of the Prussians. In 1820 ownership passed to Count Viktor Amadäus von Hessen-Rotenburg, as a result of an exchange of estates, and was substantially rebuilt. It later passed to his nephew, Viktor von Hohenlohe-Schillingfürst, Duke of Ratibor and Prince of Corvey, whose family still lives in Corvey today.

The museum occupies two floors of the house. Its displays illustrate the geology and development of the area, the history of the town of Höxter and of Corvey and the traditional culture of the region. There is also a collection of modern graphic art.

The library contains 80,000 volumes. From 1860 until his death in 1874, it was in the care of the scholar and poet, August Heinrich Hoffmann von Fallersleben, who wrote the words of the Deutschlandslied, and who is buried at Corvey.

Hünxe

Otto Pankok Museum

Otto-Pankok-Museum, Haus Esselt, Otto-Pankok-Weg 4, D-4224 Hünxe/Drevenack, Nordrhein-Westfalen   ☎ 02856 754
Fri–Sun 10–1, 3–7
F 🚗

The painter, sculptor and woodcarver, Otto Pankok (1893–1966), lived at Haus Esselt, which dates from the 17th century. The adjoining building, which he used as his studio, is now a museum. It contains collections of his work and documents, photographs and other memorabilia relating to his life and career. The house is still in the occupation of his family.

Husum

Nissen's House

*Nissenhaus, Nordfriesisches Museum, Herzog-
    Adolf-Straße 25, D-2250 Husum, Schleswig-
    Holstein*   ☎ 04841 2545
*Apr–Oct, Mon–Sat 10–12, 2–5; Sun and public
    holidays 10–5. Nov–Mar, Mon–Fri 10–12,
    2–4; Sun and public holidays 10–4.*
[C] 🔔 ♨

Ludwig Nissen (1855–1924) was born in Husum
and emigrated to the United States when he was
17, where he made a fortune. In later life he
planned to build a museum, an art gallery and a
library for his native town. Construction began
in 1920, but the museum was not opened until
after his death, in 1937. Its exhibits show the
landscape and natural history of Nordfriesland,
the methods of coastal protection employed
from the Middle Ages onwards, and the history
of the town of Husum. There are also important
collections of German art from the 16th to the
20th centuries, and of American art *c.* 1900.

Storm's House

*Storm-Haus, Theodor-Storm-Gesellschaft,
    Wasserreihe 31, D-2250 Husum, Schleswig-
    Holstein*   ☎ 04841 666270
*Apr–Oct, Tues–Fri 10–12, 2–5; Sat–Mon 2–5.
    Nov–Mar, Tues, Thurs, Sat 3–5.*
[C] 🔔

The poet and short-story writer, Theodor Storm
(1817–88), was born in Husum and later
returned there as provincial governor. The
museum in his honour was opened in 1972, in
his former home. It contains some of Storm's
furniture and other possessions, together with
material illustrating his life and work.

Idstedt

Idstedt Memorial Hall

*Idstedt-Gedächtnishalle, Idstedtkirche Nr. 1,
    D-2381 Idstedt, Schleswig-Holstein*
    ☎ 04625 402
*Apr–Sept, Tues–Sun 8–6. Oct–Mar, Sun–Fri
    9–5.*
[C] 🔔 📽 ♨

The Battle of Idstedt, on 25 July 1850, between
the armies of Denmark and Schleswig-Holstein,
was an important event during the years
following 1848, the Year of Revolutions in
Europe. It formed part of the struggle to set up a
German federation which would be
independent of foreign power and was the sequel
to a Schleswig-Holstein revolt against the Danes
which had grown in strength since 1848. The
Battle was exceptionally ferocious and one man
in ten of both armies died. It is of particular
symbolic importance in German history.
    The museum shows the significance of the
Battle of Idstedt in the development of
Germany and of Europe and traces the course of
the Schleswig-Holstein revolt.

Illingen

VSE Elektro Museum

*VSE-Elektromuseum, Gymnasialstraße 720,
    D-6688 Illingen, Saarland*   ☎ 06825 44011
Mon–Fri 7.30–4. Closed public holidays.
[F] ♨

VSE stands for Vereinigte Saar-Elektrizitäts-
AG, and this company museum, opened in
1981, has an historical collection of more than
2,000 objects, mostly German, illustrating the
applications of electricity from its earliest days.
There are particularly comprehensive sections
dealing with radio and recording machines.
Among the items of particular interest is a
replica of Werner von Siemens 1866 dynamo,
an electrically-heated cooking pot of 1900, an
early domestic refrigerator (1933), a washing
machine (1929) and an electric iron (1928).
    The star of the collection, however, is a Lems
electrically-driven locomotive, built in 1903,
which reached a speed of 20 km per hour.

Ingolstadt

Ingolstadt Museum

*Stadtmuseum, Auf der Schanz 45, D-8070
    Ingolstadt, Bayern*   ☎ 0841 3058430
Tues–Sun 9.30–5
[C] 🔔

From 1392 to 1447 Ingolstadt was the capital of
the Duchy of Bavaria-Ingolstadt and from 1447
to 1800 it was the home of the first University of
the Province of Bavaria. In 1981 the museum
was reopened in a building known as the
Kavalier Hepp, a fortress built in 1828. It has
been created in order to show the history of the
town and the region since prehistoric times. Its
collections contain prehistoric and early
historical material from local excavations,
especially at the site of the Celtic town of
Manching. Sections are also devoted to 15th–
18th-century sculpture and printed books, views
of Ingolstadt and the history of the Ingolstadt
guilds and of the University. The museum is
richly endowed with portraits of local celebrities
and of professors of the University.

**Display of early televisions, gramophones and
wirelesses. VSE Elektro Museum, Illingen.**

Museum of the Bavarian Army

Bayerisches Armeemuseum, Neues Schloß,
Paradeplatz 4, D-8070 Ingolstadt, Bayern
☎ 0841 2838
Tues–Sun 9.30–4.30

The museum is in the 15th-century Palace of
the Dukes of Bavaria. It presents the history of
the Bavarian Army, which was disbanded at the
end of the First World War. There are excellent
collections of weapons, uniforms and military
equipment, together with military band
instruments, correctly attired model soldiers
and 16th–19th-century paintings, prints and
drawings of soldiers and battle and parade
scenes. Special features include a diorama of the
Battle of Leuthen in 1757, at which the
Austrians were defeated by troops under the
command of Frederick of Prussia, and a
collection of booty from the 17th–18th-century
wars against the Turks.

Iphofen

Franconian Museum of Farming and Handicrafts

Fränkisches Bauern- und Handwerkermuseum,
Kirchenburg Mönchsondheim e.V., Kirchstraße
7, D-8715 Iphofen-Mönchsondheim, Bayern
☎ 09326 1224
Apr–Nov, Tues–Sat 1.30–6; Sun 11–6.

'Kirchenburg' is a cluster of medieval buildings
forming a square around the church, with its
own entrance from the street. This allowed the
whole area to be closed off and defended. At
Iphofen, the Kirchenburg was restored during
the 1970s and now houses a museum illustrating
the traditional life of the town and the district,
with 17 craftsmen's workshops, 12 galleries
showing farm implements and 6 for vineyard
cultivation and wine production.

Itzehoe

Prinzesshof Museum

Kreismuseum Prinzeßhof, Kirchenstraße 20,
D-2210 Itzehoe, Schleswig-Holstein
☎ 04821 69520/69260
Tues, Thurs–Sun 10–12, 3–6; Wed 10–12, 3–8.
Closed Dec 24, 31.

Founded in 1938, the museum has recently
reopened after refurbishment and
reorganisation. The building which it occupies,
the Prinzeshof, is a small palace, dating from
1580. Three abbesses of the local convent lived
here, all Princesses of Schleswig-Holstein-
Sonderburg-Glücksburg, the Danish royal line.
    In the museum there are exhibits illustrating
the history and culture of the area, with displays
of locally-made silver and glass, costumes,
furniture, handicrafts and domestic equipment.
Other sections are devoted to the local Portland
cement industry and to the military history of
the area during the period of Prussian rule.

Castle Museum, Jagsthausen.

Jagsthausen

Castle Museum

Schloßmuseum, Rotes Schloß, D-7109
Jagsthausen, Baden-Württemberg
☎ 07943 2335
Mar 15–Oct 30, daily 9–12, 1–5

The castle has been in the possession of the
Berlichingen family for more than 600 years. Its
most celebrated representative, Götz
(Gottfried) von Berlichingen (1480–1562) was
the hero of Goethe's drama of that name. Since
the 19th century visitors have been admitted to
the castle, especially to see the Roman material
displayed there. Götz had his right hand shot off
in 1504 during the War of the Bavarian
Succession and its ingenious iron replacement is
preserved in the castle, where visitors can also
see exhibits of weapons and armour and displays
illustrating the history of the town and the
castle.

Jüchen

Shloss Dyck

Waffensammlung der Fürsten zu Salm-
Reifferscheidt, Schloß Dyck, D-4053 Jüchen 5,
Baden-Württemberg ☎ 02182 4061
Apr–Oct, Tues–Sun 10–5

Schloss Dyck is a medieval castle, substantially
rebuilt and modified in the 17th and 18th
centuries by the Salm-Reifferscheidt family,
which still owns it. The park, laid out in the
18th century by Thomas Blaikie, is celebrated
for its trees and plants.
    The castle contains leather and silk wall
hangings, tapestries and furniture, and domestic
equipment used by the family. There is also an
important collection of 16th–20th-century
weapons and hunting items. The collection of
sporting guns is the largest in Germany.

Karlsruhe

Baden Museum

Badisches Landesmuseum Karlsruhe, Schloß,
D-7500 Karlsruhe 1, Baden-Württemberg
☎ *0721 1356542*
Tues, Wed, Fri–Sun 10–5.30; Thurs 10–9. Some
parts of the exhibitions are closed between 1 and
2.

The 18th-century palace was formerly the
residence of first the Margraves and then the
Grand Dukes of Baden-Durlach. After the
abdication of Grand Duke Friedrich II in 1918
the former family art collections were absorbed
into those of the museum and installed in the
palace. Severe damage to the building was
caused by bombing during the Second World
War, but between 1955 and 1966 the façade was
restored to its original appearance and the
interior remodelled in order to make it more
suitable for museum purposes.

The collections include trophies brought back
by Margrave William von Baden from wars with
the Turks, weapons, and medieval–20th-
century sculpture, furniture, gold- and
silversmiths' work, textiles, porcelain and
faïence. There are also displays of traditional
costumes, jewellery and Black Forest clocks.
Sections are devoted to the prehistory and early
history of Baden and to Greek, Roman,
Etruscan, Phoenician and Egyptian art.

Historical Museum

Stadtgeschichte im Prinz-Max-Palais, Karlstraße
10, D-7500 Karlsruhe 1, Baden-Württemberg.
Correspondence to: Zähringerstraße 96-98,
D-7500 Karlsruhe 1.
☎ *0721 1332010/1332048*
Tues, Thurs–Sun 10–1, 2–6; Wed 10–1, 2–6,
7–9.

The Prince Max Palace which houses the
museum was built in 1881–4 as the residence of
Prince Max von Baden, who lived here until
1918. The interior was destroyed by incendiary
bombs in 1944, but restoration took place
quickly after the war and between 1951 and
1969 it accommodated the Federal Constitution
Court. From 1969 to 1975 it was occupied by a

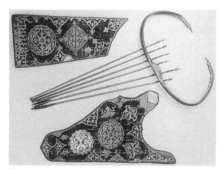

**Turkish quivers and arrows, early 17th-
century. Baden Museum, Karlsruhe.**

teachers' training college, and in 1981, after
considerable rebuilding, it was opened as the
museum. The collections illustrate the history of
Karlsruhe and of Baden from the 18th century to
the present day. Sections are devoted to town
planning and architectural history, municipal
organisation and local and regional
personalities, the theatre and associations,
social life and handicrafts.

Karlsruhe Art Gallery

Städtische Galerie im Prinz-Max-Palais, Karlstraße
10, D-7500 Karlsruhe 1, Baden-Württemberg
☎ *0721 1333670*
Tues–Sun 10–1, 2–6; Wed also 7–9 pm.

The strong points of the gallery's collections are
paintings and sculpture since 1854 by artists
from Baden, and German art since 1945 with an
emphasis on what has been produced in Baden-
Württemberg. There is, in addition, a large
collection of 15th–19th-century European
graphics, with works by German, French,
Italian and Dutch artists, including Dürer,
Piranesi, Canaletto and Rembrandt.

State Art Gallery

Staatliche Kunsthalle, Hans-Thoma-Straße 2,
D-7500 Karlsruhe 1, Baden-Württemberg
☎ *0721 1353355*
Main building: Tues–Sun 10–1, 2–5. Orangery:
Tues–Sun 10–5.

Established in 1837, this is one of the largest
and most important art museums in Germany.
A large part of the collections were formerly in
the possession of the Princes of Baden and
especially the Margravine Karoline Luise (1723–
83). The exhibits are divided into five sections –
German and Dutch Old Masters, French
Baroque paintings, 19th-century paintings, and
modern paintings and sculpture. The early
German paintings are particularly distinguished,
with works by Matthias Grünewald, Hans
Baldung Grien, Dürer, Cranach and Holbein.

Kassel

Kassel Museum

Hessisches Landesmuseum, Brüder-Grimm-Platz
5, D-3500 Kassel, Hessen   ☎ *0561 12787*
Tues–Sun 10–5

The museum's collections relating to the
prehistoric and early history periods come
mostly from the excavations carried out in the
time of Landgrave Carl, who gave orders for a
number of barrows to be opened. At the Celtic
town of Altenburg, near Niederstein, the soil
conditions have preserved wooden objects
which are extremely rare survivals in Europe.

The folklore collections are the best in Hesse.
They are particularly strong in the fields of
country furniture, ceramics, costumes,

beekeeping and basketmaking. From the Middle
Ages onwards, the Landgraves of Hesse were
notable collectors of all forms of art and the
results are to be seen in the museum's
departments. Kassel also has Europe's finest
collection of scientific instruments, some of
them from the first institutional, as distinct from
private observatory in Europe, set up in 1560 by
the Landgrave Wilhelm IV of Hessen-Kassel in
the then Palace of Kassel.

Louis Spohr Museum and Research Institute

Louis-Spohr-Gedenk-und-Forschungstätte, Schloß
   Bellevue, Schöne Aussicht 2, D-3500 Kassel,
   Hessen   ☎ *0561 15209*
Fri 3–5 and by appt.
[F]

Louis Spohr (1784–1859) was a gifted violinist,
conductor and composer. He was also the
founder of the last great German violin-school,
known to historians as 'the Kassel School'. The
Institute, established in 1954, is the only one in
the world to be concerned solely with violinists,
violins, violin-makers and compositions for the
violin. Part of its premises, the 18th-century
Palais Bellevue, is occupied by a museum
devoted to the life, work and worldwide
influence of Spohr.
   The exhibits include a wide range of Spohr's
personal possessions and manuscripts. Among
the particularly valued items are one of his
pianos, on which Liszt played, and a wax-relief
of Paganini by David d'Angers.

Museum of the Brothers Grimm

Brüder Grimm-Musum, Schöne Aussicht 2,
   D-3500 Kassel, Hessen. Correspondence to:
   Brüder-Grimm-Platz 4A, D-3500 Kassel.
   ☎ *0561 774866*
Daily 10–5. Archives: Mon–Fri 10–4. Closed
   public holidays which fall on a weekday.
[F] 🏛

There were three Brothers Grimm. Jakob
(1785–1863) and his inseparable brother,
Wilhelm (1786–1859) founded the study of
scientific philosophy and, as a result of their
interest in folklore, collaborated to write their
famous volumes of fairy-tales and legends. The
third brother, Ludwig Emil (1790–1863), was a
successful artist.
   The museum and archive contain their
manuscripts and printed works, personal
possessions, furniture, domestic equipment,
paintings, prints and drawings, and books and
articles about the three brothers.

New Gallery: State and Municipal Art Collections

Neue Galerie, Staatliche und Städtische
   Kunstsammlungen, Schöne Aussicht 1, D-3500
   Kassel, Hessen   ☎ *0561 15266*
Tues–Sun 10–5. Closed May 1, Dec 24, 25, 31.
[F] 🏛 ♿

**Wooden sculpture of the shepherds
worshipping Christ, c. 1525. Folklore and
Cultural History Museum of the Lower Rhine,
Kevelaer.**

The original City Art Gallery, opened in 1877,
was destroyed by bombing during the Second
World War. It was subsequently rebuilt and
opened as the New Gallery in 1976, with
collections of European painting and sculpture
from 1750 to the present day. Among the
special features of the museum is a collection of
paintings by members of the celebrated
Tischbein family, especially Johann Heinrich
Wilhelm (1751–1829), who became Director of
the Naples Academy in 1789 and supervised the
engraving of the Greek vases belonging to Sir
William Hamilton, which were of great
importance in the spread of neo-classicism.

Provincial Museum of Hesse and the Gatehouse Museum

Staatliche Kunstsammlungen Kassel, Hessische
   Landesmuseum und Torwache am Hessischen
   Landesmuseum, Brüder-Grimm-Platz 5,
   D-3500 Kassel, Hessen   ☎ *0561 780036*
Tues–Sun 10–5. Closed May 1, Dec 24, 25, 31.
[F] 🏛

The main museum building dates from 1913. Its
displays illustrate the prehistory and history of
the province. There are collections of
prehistoric material from Palaeolithic,
Neolithic, Bronze Age, Celtic and Carolingian
graves, Hesse pottery from medieval times
onwards, gold- and silversmiths' work, glass and
German and Chinese porcelain. Other sections
of the museum are devoted to country furniture,
18th–20th-century regional costumes,
handicrafts, domestic equipment and scientific,
especially astronomical, instruments.
   The Gatehouse, which forms an annexe to
the main building, contains the museum's
collections of applied art and design from 1840
to the present day.

Wilhelmshöhe Castle

Schloß Wilhelmshöhe, D-3500 Kassel, Hessen
   ☎ *0561 36011*
Tues–Sun 10–5. Closed May 1, Dec 24, 25, 31.
[F] 🏛 🍴 ♿

Schloss Wilhelmshöhe was built at the end of the 18th century as the seat of the Counts and Electoral Princes of Hessen-Kassel. It was badly damaged by bombing during the Second World War and has since been restored. It has important collections of Dutch, German and Italian paintings of the 16th–18th centuries, including 11 works by Rembrandt, together with Greek and Roman sculpture, vases, glass and jewellery.

Kaub am Rhein

Blücher Museum

*Blüchermuseum, Metzgergasse 6, D-5425 Kaub
am Rhein, Rheinland-Pfalz*
☎ 06774 400/222
*Wed–Mon 10–12, 2–4. Nov–Mar, Wed–Fri,
Mon 10–12.*
F ✿

In December 1813, Field-Marshal Blücher, the Prussian Commander of the Silesian army, established his headquarters in the 1790 house which is now the museum, during the course of the Allied campaign which finally ousted Napoleon from Germany.

The interior of the house has been little altered since Blücher lived here. The exhibits include painted canvas wall hangings, a grand piano of 1790 – one of the first ever made in Germany – a number of the Field-Marshal's personal belongings and collections of portraits, uniforms, weapons, drums, decorations and Orders of the Day.

Kevelaer

Folklore and Cultural History Museum of the Lower Rhine

*Niederrheinisches Museum für Volkskunde und
Kulturgeschichte, Hauptstraße 18, D-4178
Kevelaer 1, Nordrhein-Westfalen*
☎ 02832 6066
Apr–Oct, daily 10–5. Nov–Mar, Tues–Sun 10–5.
C ♟ 🖩 ✿

The *Bussard*, a 1906 steamship. City and Maritime Museum, Kiel.

The museum was established in 1910. The new building into which it was transferred in 1938 was destroyed during the Second World War. The museum reopened in other premises in 1960 and extensions were added in 1979. The collections include religious art, domestic equipment, costumes, popular religious items, 18th–20th-century toys and children's books, locally-made stoneware and earthenware, handicrafts and 19th-century portraits. There are also reconstructions of a hairdressing salon of 1927, a grocer's shop, a bakery and period rooms from an 18th-century house.

Kiel

City and Maritime Museum

*Kieler Stadt- und Schiffahrtsmuseum, Dänische
Straße 19 (Warleberger Hof) und Wall 65
(Fischhalle), D-2300 Kiel 1, Schleswig-
Holstein*   ☎ 0431 9013425/9013428
Apr–Sept, daily 10–6. Oct–Mar, Tues–Sun 10–5.
C ♟

Both museum buildings are protected as historic monuments. The Warleberger Hof dates from 1615 and was substantially rebuilt in 1765. It was subsequently used by the University. The Maritime Museum, built in 1909–10, was formerly the *Fischhalle* or Fish Market. Together, the two groups of collections present the history of the town and the port of Kiel, with special reference to the shipping, shipbuilding and fishing industries.

The museum has a good range of ship models and three original ships, the *Bussard* (1906), the *Kiel* (1941) and the *Hindenburg* (1944).

Schleswig-Holstein Open-Air Museum

*Schleswig-Holsteinisches Freilichtmuseum, D-2300
Kiel-Rammsee, Schleswig-Holstein*
☎ 0431 65555
Apr 1–Nov 15, Tues–Sun 9–5
C ♟ ✿

Established in 1958 on a 60-hectare site and exended in 1965, the museum contains buildings from all parts of Schleswig-Holstein. They include rural houses, mills, barns and workshops, all with the appropriate furniture and equipment. There are regular demonstrations of basket-making, weaving and blacksmith's work. The museum also has a good collection of horse-drawn vehicles.

Kitzingen

German Carnival Museum

*Deutches Fastnachtmuseum, Alemannenstraße 76,
D-8710 Kitzingen, Bayern* ☎ 09321 23355
Sat, Sun 2–5. Groups at other times by appt.
C ♟

The steepled tower which houses the museum dates from the 15th century. The collections tell the story of carnival in Germany and include costumes, masks, paintings and literature relating to the subject.

Kleve

Haus Koekkoek Museum

Städtisches Museum Haus Koekkoek,
    Kavarinerstraße 33, D-4190 Kleve, Nordrhein-
    Westfalen   ☎ *02821 84302*
Tues–Sun 10–1, 2–5
Ⓕ ♟ ♨

Kleve was much painted by Dutch artists. One
of Rembrandt's best-known pupils, Govaert
Flink, was born here and the mansion now
containing the museum was built in 1847 by the
Dutch landscape painter, Barend Cornelis
Koekkoek (1803–62). The museum has a
number of paintings by him and by members of
his family, together with works by medieval–
19th-century artists and gold- and silversmiths
from the region.

Knittlingen

Faust Museum

Faust-Museum, Kirchplatz 2, D-7134 Knittlingen,
    Baden-Württemberg   ☎ *07043 31212*
Tues–Fri 9.30–12, 1–5; Sat, Sun 10–6
Ⓒ ♨

Johann Georg Faust, master of the black arts,
was born in Knittlingen, near the half-timbered
house which accommodates the museum. The
exhibits show the origins of the Faust legend and
trace its development in plays, music, films,
ballet and Faust marionettes. The displays
include paintings, drawings and prints
illustrating the Faust story. There is a special
collection of postage stamps of ships named
Faust and the name has been marketed
commercially.

Koblenz

Museum of Industry

Landesmuseum Koblenz: Staatliche Sammlung
    technischer Kulturdenkmäler, Festung
    Ehrenbreitstein, D-5400 Koblenz, Rheinland-
    Pfalz   ☎ *0261 71012/3*
Mar–Nov, daily 9–5
Ⓕ ♟ ♨ ⅙ ♨

Ehrenbreitstein, the Prussian fortress which
houses the museum, was built between 1816 and
1828. The collections illustrate the industrial
history of the Middle Rhine area. The industries
include pumice production, stone-quarrying,
tobacco-processing, steel-rolling and wine and
schnapps production. Special sections are
devoted to celebrated local industrialists, among
them N. A. Otto (internal combustion
engines), August Horch (cars), and Carl
Clemens Bücker (aeroplanes).

Rhine Museum

Rhein-Museum, Festung Ehrenbreitstein, Hohe
    Ostfront, D-5400 Koblenz, Rheinland-Pfalz.
    Correspondence to: Postfach 1627, D-5400
    Koblenz 1.   ☎ *0261 71715*
Easter–Nov, daily 9–5
Ⓕ ♨ ♨

This museum was established in 1912 and is
concerned with the uses which have been made
of the river Rhine. There are displays
illustrating goods and passenger traffic, with
models of ships and boats from the Bronze Age
to the present day, fish and fishing, hydrography
and methods of water-control and water-
extraction. There are also paintings and
engravings of the Rhineland landscape and of
fishing scenes.

Museum of Industry, Koblenz.

Königswinter

Museum of the Seven Mountains

Siebengebirgsmuseum der Stadt Königswinter,
Kellerstraße 16, D-5330 Königswinter 1,
Niedersachsen   ☎ *02223 3703*
Apr–Oct 15, Tues, Thurs–Sat 2–5; Wed 2–7;
Sun 11–5. Oct 16–Mar, Wed 2–7; Sat, Sun
2–5. Groups at other times by appt.
F

Königswinter lies on one of the most picturesque
sections of the Rhine, beloved by tourists for
nearly 200 years. The museum was installed in
its present building, a 1732 house, in 1934. It
reopened in 1984, after being closed for
reorganisation. The collections cover the
geology and history of the region, its castles,
monasteries and historic personages, tourism,
and traditional occupations, including the
production of wine. Changes in the local
landscape are conveyed by means of paintings,
drawings and prints.

Krefeld

Burg Linn Museum

Museum Burg Linn, Rheinbabenstraße 85, D-5140
Krefeld 12, Nordrhein-Westfalen
    ☎ *02151 570036*
Apr–Oct, Tues–Sun 10–6. Nov–Mar, Tues–Sun
10 1, 2–5.
C ▯ ▵

The castle and town of Linn were incorporated
into the urban district of Krefeld in 1901. The
little medieval town has remained almost
untouched by the modern industrial city which
surrounds it. The 14th-century castle was rebuilt
in the 17th century and the museum premises
also include a hunting lodge, which dates from
c. 1730. The collections illustrate the
prehistory, history and ethnography of Krefeld
and the Lower Rhine. Among the particularly
interesting exhibits are Roman and Franconian
finds from the cemetery at Krefeld-Gellep, a
large collection of Roman glassware, objects
from the 6th-century tomb of a Franconian
prince, including a gilt helmet and a collection
of 18th–19th-century Lower Rhenish
earthenware.

There is also a series of period rooms,
illustrating the living style of the castle's
inhabitants during the 16th–19th centuries.

German Textile Museum

Deutsches Textilmuseum, Andreasmarkt 8,
D-4150 Krefeld 12 (Linn), Nordrhein-
Westfalen   ☎ *02151 572046*
Apr–Oct, Tues–Sun and public holidays 10–6.
Nov–Mar, Tues–Sun and public holidays
10–1, 2–5.
C ▯ ♿

During the 18th century Krefeld began to
produce silk textiles and throughout the 19th
century this was the basis of the local economy.

German Textile Museum, Krefeld.

A school was established to train designers and
technicians for the textile industry and in 1880
the school opened a museum which provided an
international collection which could be used for
training and inspirational purposes. In 1936 the
municipality took over the collection, which by
that time amounted to 18,000 items, and in
1981 installed it in two buildings away from the
school. The first, dating from the 18th century,
now contains the library, archives and research
rooms, and the second is new, designed to house
the exhibition rooms, restoration workshops
and photographic studio.

The collections, which are worldwide and
include cotton, as well as silk fabrics, are
displayed in regularly changed special
exhibitions.

Kulmbach

German Museum of Tin Figures

Deutsches Zinnfigurenmuseum, Plassenburg,
D-8650 Kulmbach, Bayern   ☎ *09221 5550*
Apr–Sept, Tues–Sun 10–4.40. Oct–Mar, Tues–
Sun 10–3.30. Closed Jan 1, Carnival Tues,
Nov 1, Dec 24, 25.
C ▯ ▱ ▵

Plassenburg, the castle which houses the
museum, is first mentioned in 1135. In its
present form it dates from the 16th–18th
centuries. The museum contains a collection of
300,000 miniature tin figures, many of which
are arranged in dioramas of historical scenes.

Kulmbach is an internationally famous centre
for collectors of tin figures. A market is held
here every two years.

Laboe

Naval Memorial

Technisches Museum des Deutschen Marinebundes
e.V. – U 995, Verwaltung Marine-Ehrenmal,
Strandstraße 92, D-2304 Laboe, Schleswig-
Holstein   ☎ *04343 8755*
Apr–Oct, daily 9–6. Nov–Mar, daily 9–4.
C ▯ ▵

Opened in 1972, the memorial is dedicated to
the memory of those who served in the German
Navy during the two World Wars. It contains

paintings, drawings and models illustrating the development of merchant and naval ships and navigational techniques, together with other objects relating to maritime history.

A major exhibit is the submarine U 995, which was built in 1943 at the yards of Blohm and Voss in Hamburg. In 1945 it was transferred to the Norwegian Navy, for use in patrols in the Polar regions, and subsequently returned to Germany for display at Laboe.

Ladenburg

Lobdengau Museum

Lobdengau-Museum, Bischofshof, D-6802
Ladenburg, Baden-Württemberg
Sat 2.30–5.30; Sun 11–12.30, 2.30–5.30.
C ♿

Ladenburg, the Roman *Lopodunum*, is the oldest German town on the right bank of the Rhine. It was the Roman administrative centre for the Lower Neckar valley and continued its importance into the Middle Ages. Some of the most interesting of the finds from local excavations are displayed in the Museum. They include the remarkable stone heads of the sun-gods, Sol and Mithras.

Among the museum's large collection of country furniture and popular art is what has become known as the Town Hall Madonna (Rathausmadonna). Made in 1510 to the commission of Bishop von Dalberg, it is a wooden sculpture of exceptional quality.

Landau-in-der-Pfalz

Landau Museum

Städtisches Heimatmuseum, 'Haus Mahla',
Marienring 8, D-8640 Landau-in-der-Pfalz,
Rheinland-Pfalz   ☎ 06341 13297
Tues–Fri 9–12, 2–4; Sun 10–12
F ♿

In 1892 the Landau lawyer, Ludwig Norbert Mahla, built himself a mansion on the Kaiserring. He was mayor of Landau from 1904 to 1920 and after his daughter's death in 1974 the house was bequeathed to the town for use as a museum. Landau's Museum, founded in 1895 in a former Augustinian monastery, suffered severe damage and losses during the Second World War and had to be moved to temporary accommodation before opening its doors in Mahla's former house in 1978.

The centrepiece of the museum is a 6×4 m model, made in 1742, of the fortifications of Landau, designed by Vauban in 1688–91 as 'one of the strongest fortresses in Christendom'. There are collections of weapons and uniforms and portraits of 18th-century French and Bavarian commanders of the fortress. The museum also has a section devoted to Landau writers and artists, and to wine production, local furniture, pottery and handicrafts and to regional prehistory.

Museum of Tin Figures, Kulmbach.

Landshut

Landshut Museum

Stadt- und Kreismuseum, Altstadt 79
(Stadtresidenz), D-8300 Landshut, Bayern
        ☎ 0871 88218
Apr–Sept, Tues–Sun 9–12, 1–5. Oct–Mar, Tues–
Sun 9–12, 1–4.
F ♿

Dating from 1536–43, the Residence of Ludwig X of Bavaria in Landshut was the first Renaissance palace to be built north of the Alps. The museum illustrates the history and art of Lower Bavaria, with prehistoric and Roman material from local sites, 13th–19th-century weapons and metalwork, 15th–18th-century religious sculpture, ornaments and metalwork, and 16th–19th-century textiles, faïence and pottery. There are also collections of furniture, domestic equipment and costumes, and of 17th–19th-century paintings and sculpture.

A section of the museum is devoted to Ludwig Maximilian University, which was established in Landshut in 1800 and transferred to Munich in 1826.

Langerwehe

Pottery Museum

Töpfereimuseum, Pastoratsweg 1, D-5163
Langerwehe, Nordrhein-Westfalen
        ☎ 02423 4446
Tues–Fri 10–12, 2–5; Sat, Sun 10–5. Closed
Good Fri, Nov 1, and from the Sun before
Dec 24 until Jan 6.
F ♿ ♿

Langerwehe was on the important medieval road between Flanders and Brabant and South Germany, which was much used by soldiers, merchants and pilgrims, and by Emperors travelling to their coronation in Aachen. A pottery industry developed here in the early 11th century, helped by excellent supplies of clay and wood for the kilns. The industry prospered until it was nearly killed by machine production elsewhere in the late 19th century. Only two potteries survived, but they continued in operation until they were given a new lease of life after the Second World War by turning to the production of garden ornaments and crib figures. Hand-made pottery has also enjoyed a recent revival.

The museum illustrates the history, techniques and products of the local pottery industry, by means of displays and demonstrations. There are also exhibits of paintings and furniture.

Lauda-Königshofen

Lauda-Königshofen Museum

Heimatmuseum, Rathausstraße 25, D-6970 Lauda-Königshofen, Baden-Württemberg
☎ *09343 4517*
Apr–Oct, Sun and public holidays 3–5. Groups by appt.
F ▪ ↻

The house containing the museum dates from 1551 and was the birthplace of the agricultural pioneer, Philipp Adam Ulrich. It contains a wine-press which is as old as the house, together with exhibits illustrating the history and techniques of wine-production in the region. There are reconstructions of a farmhouse kitchen and living room, a number of middle-class rooms and several craftsmen's workshops. Other sections of the museum are devoted to the history of local railways, carnival, silver, porcelain, faïence, furniture, weapons and armour. There is also a collection of portraits and coats of arms, especially of members of the House of Hohenlohe.

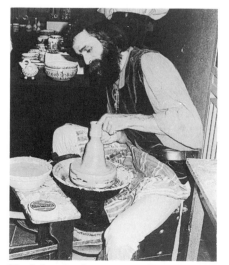

Hand-throwing demonstration. Pottery Museum, Langerwehe.

Lemgo

House of the Witches' Mayor

Hexenbürgermeisterhaus, Breitestraße 19, D-4920 Lemgo, Nordrhein-Westfalen
☎ *05261 213275*
Tues–Fri, Sun 10–12.30, 1.30–5; Sat 10–1
C ▪

The museum is in a 16th-century building and contains exhibits relating to 16th–17th-century witchcraft trials in the town, including instruments of torture used to extract confessions. There are also local history collections, with material relating to the guilds and to handicrafts, including the manufacture of meerschaum pipes. Other exhibits are of 18th–19th-century maps, coins, incunabula and oriental antiquities.

Leutershausen

Gustav Weisskopf-Museum

Gustav-Weisskopf Museum, Plan 6, D-8811 Leutershausen, Bayern. Correspondence to: Historical Flight Research Committee, c/o Herrn Hermann Betscher, Bahnhofstraße 10, D-8811 Leutershausen.
☎ *09823 8923*
Easter–Oct, Mon, Tues, Thurs, Fri 10–12; Wed 10–12, 2–4; Sun 10–12. Other times by appt.
C ▪ ↻

The museum building was originally a small castle, rebuilt in 1624 to serve as a grain store and subsequently used as a court house. It is now a museum dedicated to Gustav Weisskopf (1874–1927). Born in Leutershausen, he settled in the United States in 1894 and changed his name to Whitehead. There is strong evidence that he succeeded in making a powered flight in 1901, four years before the Wright Brothers. The museum, established in 1987, contains details of Weisskopf's life and career, including contemporary photographs of his flying machine and a model of an aircraft engine made by him.

Lindenberg im Allgäu

Hat Museum

Hutmuseum, Hirschstraße 6a, D-8998 Lindenberg im Allgäu, Bayern   ☎ *08381 3011*
Wed 3–5.30; Sun 10–12
F ↻

At the end of the 17th century, country people in the western part of the Allgäu began to make straw hats as a way of relieving their severe poverty. The industry was greatly encouraged by Kaiser Wilhelm II, who decided to equip the crew of his ocean-going yacht *Hohenzollern*, with broad-brimmed straw hats, which were bought from Lindenberg, an order which was repeated on behalf of the battleships, *Möve* and *Freya*. As a result of this, the straw hat workers of Lindenberg came to regard themselves as the leaders of the industry in Germany.

Lorsch

Benedictine Abbey

Ehemaliges Benediktinerkloster, Nibelungenstraße
32, D-6143 Lorsch, Hessen
☎ 06251 51446
Apr–Sept, Tues–Sun 10–4. Oct–Mar, Tues–Sun
10–3 (last admission).
© ♦ ◻ ☙

The abbey at Lorsch is first mentioned in 764.
In the early Middle Ages it was one of the
richest and most prestigious religious houses in
Europe and its ruins indicate its size at the peak
of its power. In 1700 the Electoral Prince,
Lother Franz von Schörnborn, built a hunting
lodge here. It now contains exhibits giving the
history of the abbey, with items of sculpture and
Carolingian architecture. In other rooms,
visitors can see furniture, tapestries and other
possessions of the Electoral Prince.

Tobacco Museum

Tabak-Museum, Altes Rathaus im Marktplatz,
D-6143 Lorsch, Hessen   ☎ 06521 5041
May–Sept, Mon–Fri 9–12.30, 1.30–4; Sat
10.30–12.30; Sun 10.30–12.30, 1.30–4.
Oct–Apr, Mon–Thurs 9–12, 2–4; Fri 9–12.
Other times by appt.
Ⓕ ◒ ◻ ☙

Tobacco-growing and processing was an
important industry in Hessen in the 18th and
19th centuries. The museum, which was
installed in the Old Town Hall in 1984, shows
how the tobacco was cultivated and prepared for
manufacturing, especially for cigars. There are
exhibits of the tools and machinery used and
prints and photographs of the factories and their
works and collections of pipes and other
smoking requisites.

Lossburg

Black Forest Museum

Schwarzwaldmuseum, Hauptstraße, D-7289
Loßburg, Baden-Württemberg
May–Oct, Tues–Sun 9–12, 1–6. Winter months
by appt.
©

Cigar-makers' workshop. Tobacco Museum,
Lorsch.

The museum was opened in 1969, in a 19th-
century building originally used as a granary. Its
centrepiece is a giant cask, holding 7,000 litres
with a complete cooper's workshop. There are
also collections of agricultural implements and
peasant costumes, and a large group of Black
Forest clocks, which shows how the technology
developed from wooden to metal mechanisms.
Among the examples shown is a clock with the
figure of a slaughterman, who hits an ox on the
head every time the clock strikes, and another
with an executioner, who raises his sword as the
clock strikes the hour.

Lübeck

Behn House Museum

Behnhaus, Königstraße 9-11, D-2400 Lübeck,
Schleswig-Holstein ☎ 0451 1224148
Apr–Sept, Tues–Sun 10–5. Oct–Mar, Tues–Sun
10–4.
© ♦

The museum building dates from *c.* 1780 and
was formerly occupied by a Lübeck merchant. It
contains period rooms and collections of 19th–
20th-century German paintings, sculpture and
the applied arts. Among the artists represented
are Johann Friedrich Overbeck (1789–1869),
Edvard Munch (1863–1944), Caspar David
Friedrich (1774–1840), Max Liebermann
(1847–1939) and Louis Corinth (1858–1925).

Dräger House Museum

Drägerhaus, Museum für Kunst- und
Kulturgeschichte der Hansestadt Lübeck,
Königstraße 9-11, D-2400 Lübeck, Schleswig-
Holstein   ☎ 0451 1224148
Apr–Sept, Tues–Sun 10–5. Oct–Mar, Tues–Sun
10–4.
© ♦

The museum occupies the Dräger House, the
former mansion of an 18th-century Lübeck
merchant. Its collections document the social
and cultural history of Lübeck, with exhibitions
of paintings, graphics, handicrafts, furniture and
costumes. There are also memorial collections
to the novelists, Thomas Mann (1875–1955)
and Heinrich Mann (1871–1950), both of
whom were born in Lübeck.

Holstentor Museum

Museum Holstentor, Holstentorplatz, D-2400
Lübeck, Schleswig-Holstein
☎ 0451 1224129
Apr–Sept, Tues–Sun 10–5. Oct–Mar, Tues–Sun
10–4.
© ♦

Constructed in 1470, the Holstentor is one of
the most famous city gates in Germany. The
museum's collections illustrate the history of
Lübeck and contain views and models of the
Hanseatic town at different periods, and objects
related to occupations and domestic life. There
is also a display of ship models and exhibits
documenting the maritime history of Lübeck.

Lüdenscheid

Lüdenscheid Museum

Stadtmuseum, Liebigstraße 11, D-5880
Lüdenscheid, Nordrhein-Westfalen
☎ 02351 17445
Tues–Sat 9–12.30, 3.30–6; Sun 10.30–1.
[F]

Lüdenscheid's button industry began in the late 16th century, when the local blacksmiths began to cast metal buttons. By the 19th century, workshops and factories making buttons had become a major source of employment. The museum, opened in 1959, illustrates the rise of the industry and its fall under competition from the zip-fastener. It also has comparative exhibits from other countries. The museum also displays agricultural implements and items illustrating the history and development of the town, including an engine, made locally, which was used in the first dirigible.

As an outstation, the museum also looks after an important technical monument, the 'Bremeker Hammer', at Brüninghausen. It is shown in the context of the history of ironworking and can be seen between May and the middle of October on Mondays, and on other days by arrangement.

Ludwigshafen am Rhein

Schiller's House

Schillerhaus, Schillerstraße 6, D-6700
Ludwigshafen-Oggersheim, Rheinland-Pfalz
☎ 0621 675943
Mon, Tues, Thurs, Fri 2–5; Sat, Sun 10–12.
Closed public holidays.
[F]

This is the house in which the poet and dramatist, Johann Christoph Friedrich Schiller, lived in 1782, and in which he wrote *Don Carlos*. The museum contains portraits, letters and memorabilia of the poet and first editions of his works, as well as material relating to the history of Oggersheim and a collection of Frankenthal porcelain.

Wilhelm Hack Museum

Wilhelm-Hack-Museum, Berliner Straße 23,
D-6700 Ludwigshafen am Rhein, Rheinland-
Pfalz   ☎ 0621 5043411
Tues, Wed, Fri–Sun 9.30–5; Thurs 9.30–9.
[F] 🏛

The museum, opened in 1979, is named after Wilhelm Hack, of Cologne, who gave his private collection to the town of Ludwigshafen in 1971. The building is designed in the open style of the 1970s, with almost no interior walls. On the south side of the outside of the museum there is a mural by Joan Miró, 55 m long and 10 m high, composed of 7,010 ceramic tiles.

The collections include examples of Roman, Franconian and medieval art and works by 20th-century painters. Among the artists

Circular Forms, 1912, by Robert Delaunay. Wilhelm Hack Museum, Ludwigshafen am Rhein.

represented are Paula Modersohn-Becker (1876–1907), Karl Hofer (1878–1955), Wassily Kandinsky (1866–1944), Robert Delaunay (1885–1941), Kasimir Malévitch (1878–1935), Piet Mondrian (1872–1944), Kurt Schwitters (1887–1948), Piero Dorazio (b. 1927) and Jackson Pollock (1912–56).

Mainz

Cathedral Museum

Bischöfliche Dom- und Diözesanmuseum,
Domstraße 3, D-6500 Mainz, Rheinland-
Pfalz   ☎ 06131 253343
Mon–Wed, Fri 2–5; Thurs, Sat 9–12. Closed
public holidays.
[C] 🏛

The cathedral was severely damaged by wartime bombing. The museum, in the restored south wing, was the first to be opened in Mainz after the War. It contains religious art from the cathedral and from churches in the diocese of Mainz. Among the items on display are medieval wall-hangings, 18th-century paintings and coloured engravings, reliquaries, and gold and silver liturgical items. There are also many monuments and other items of sculpture, vestments, illuminated manuscripts and items of furniture.

Gutenberg Museum

Gutenberg-Museum, Liebfrauenplatz 5, D-6500
Mainz, Rheinland-Pfalz   ☎ 06131 122644
Feb–Dec, Tues–Sat 10–6; Sun 10–1. Closed
public holidays. Carnival: closed Sat–Shrove
Tues.
[F] 🏛

The 17th-century house containing the museum became an inn, known as 'Zum Römischer Kaiser', in 1742. It became a museum in memory of the great printer, Johannes Gutenberg (1397–1468), who was born in Mainz. It was burnt out during the Second World War, but rebuilt and extended into a new building. The exhibits illustrate the history of writing, printing and paper-making. There are examples of 15th–20th-century book printing and binding and graphic techniques, 19th–20th-century posters, prints and engravings and an important collection of incunabula. Printing demonstrations are held in a reconstruction of Gutenberg's workshop and there are German and English versions of a film on Gutenberg's life and work.

Roman Germanic Central Museum

Römisch-Germanisches Zentralmuseum, Ernst-Ludwig-Platz 2, D-6500 Mainz, Rheinland-Pfalz
Tues–Sun 10–6
F ▮

Founded in 1852, the museum is a major international research centre into the links between Europe, the Mediterranean world and the East during the Bronze and Iron Age and into the military and cultural history of Rome and the fringe cultures of the ancient world. The public exhibitions reflect these special interests, with an emphasis on Roman and Frankish archaeology and the prehistory of the Middle Rhine area. There are, in addition, collections of medieval German paintings and sculpture, Flemish, Dutch and French paintings, 19th–20th-century German porcelain and Jugendstil glass.

Mannheim

Mannheim Art Gallery

Städtische Kunsthalle Mannheim, Moltkestraße 9, D-6800 Mannheim 1, Baden-Württemberg
☎ 0621 2936412
Tues, Wed, Fri–Sun 10–5; Thurs 10–8.
F ▰

The city's Jugendstil art gallery was built in 1906–7 and enlarged in 1983. It contains 19th–20th-century French and German paintings and 20th-century sculpture, especially by Wilhelm Lehmbruck. Among the artists represented are Manet, Monet, Franz Marc, Paul Klee, George Crosz, Louis Corinth and Anselm Feuerbach.

Reiss Museum

Städtisches Reiß-Museum, Zeughaus C5, D-6800 Mannheim, Baden-Württemberg
☎ 0621 2932421
Tues–Thurs, Sat 10–1, 2–5; Fri 2–8; Sun and public holidays 10–5.
F ▮ ▱

The museum is in the former arsenal. Dating from 1777–9, it is the last monumental building in Mannheim to be commissioned by the Electoral Prince. Its collections illustrate mainly prehistory and the history of Mannheim and its

region. There are sections devoted to medieval and baroque sculpture, 17th–19th-century German paintings, popular art, Central European porcelain and glass, 17th–18th-century furniture and silver and the history of the theatre in Mannheim. The museum also has celebrated worldwide ethnographical collections.

Marbach am Neckar

National Schiller Museum

Schiller-Nationalmuseum, Schillerhöhe 8-10, D-7142 Marbach am Neckar, Baden-Württemberg   ☎ 07144 6061
Daily 9–5. Closed Dec 24 (pm), 25, 26, 31 (pm).
C ▮ ▰

The dramatist, Johann Christoph Friedrich Schiller (1759–1805), was born in Marbach. The museum named after him was opened in 1903. It was created by the Swabian Schiller Society, which later became the German Schiller Society. The original collections illustrated the development of Swabian literature from Schiller's time onwards, but have since been extended to cover German literature as a whole, with displays of early and luxury editions, portraits and manuscripts. Among the writers represented are Schiller, Goethe, Hölderlin, Mörike, Thomas Mann, Hermann Hesse and Franz Kafka.

Movement in Space, 1913, by Umberto Boccioni. Art Gallery, Mannheim.

following century. After the death of Ludwig IV of Hesse-Marburg in 1604, it served as a granary, a prison, a repository for the State archives and, later, as a temporary home for the Prussian State Library. It was opened by the University as a museum in 1981, on the basis of collections formed much earlier by the Marburg lawyer, Ludwig Bickell (1838–1901), who had been inspired by the Musée de Cluny in Paris and the South Kensington Museum in London.

The present displays illustrate the prehistory and history of Hesse until the end of the monarchy. The exhibits include religious art, furniture, stoves, household equipment, handicrafts and costumes. Works by local cabinet-makers are a special feature of the displays.

Carved wooden organ. University Museum of Art, Marburg.

Marburg

University Museum of Art

Museum für Bildende Kunst, Biegenstraße 11,
D-3550 Marburg, Hessen ☎ 06421 282355
Apr–Sept, Wed–Mon 10–1, 3–5. Oct–Mar,
Wed–Mon 11–1, 3–5.
[F] 🛉 ⚓

The museum building, in the Art Déco style, was erected in 1926–7 to commemorate the 400th anniversary of the founding of the University. It contains collections of paintings, sculpture and graphics by 18th–20th-century German artists, including a number from Hesse. Carl Spitzweg, Paul Klee, Georg Kolbe and Hans Thoma are among those represented.

University Museum of Cultural History

Marburger Universitätsmuseum für Kunst- und
Kulturgeschichte, Biegenstraße 11, D-3550
Marburg, Hessen ☎ 06421 282355
Apr–Sept, Wed–Mon 10–1, 3–5. Oct–Mar,
Wed–Mon 11–1, 3–5.
[F] 🛉 ⚓

The castle at Marburg, formerly the seat of the Counts and Princes of Hesse, was built in 1492 and modified at various times during the

Marktrodach

Unterrodach Raftsmen's Museum

Flössermuseum Unterrodach, D-8641
Marktrodach, Bayern ☎ 09261 885
Sat, Sun 2–4. Other times by appt.
[C]

The museum's exhibits illustrate the history and techniques of log-floating in the Frankenwald region, together with the life of the men who earn their living by it. This method of moving timber from the forest areas has a tradition which goes back 800 years.

Massing

Massing Open-Air Museum

Freilichtmuseum Massing, Spirknerstraße 13,
D-8332 Massing, Bayern ☎ 08724 1661
Mar–Dec, Tues–Fri 10–12, 1–5; Sat, Sun and
public holidays 1–5.
[C] 🛉 🖤 ⚓

The museum was inaugurated in 1969 in order to preserve and display farm and other buildings from Lower Bavaria south of the Danube, giving an impression of rural life in the 19th century. The exhibits include two large farmhouses, with appropriate furniture and equipment, reconstructions of rural craftsmen's workshops and agricultural implements and vehicles.

Meersburg

Dornier Museum

Dornier Museum, Neues Scholß, D-7758
Meersburg, Baden-Württemberg
☎ 07532 82382
Mar 16–Oct, daily 10–1, 2–6
[C] 🛉

The museum is in the historic castle of Meersburg, overlooking Lake Constance. It tells the story of the Dornier concern, with models of aircraft built by the company, original parts of Dornier planes and examples of Dornier flying boats, which were important in building up the reputation of the firm.

Meersburg Old Castle

*Altes Schloß Meersburg, D-7758 Meersburg,
    Baden-Württemberg*   ☎ *07532 6441*
Mar–Oct, daily 9–6. Nov–Feb, daily 10–5.

The castle at Meersburg, from which the
adjacent town received its name, was built in
the early 7th century and claimed to be the
oldest in Germany, although it was subsequently
greatly extended and modified, especially during
the 18th century.

The museum contains medieval–18th-
century furniture, paintings, sculpture,
weapons, armour and hunting trophies. The
poetess, Annette von Droste-Hülshoff (1797–
1848) spent the last years of her life in the castle
and died here. Visitors can see her study and the
room where she died.

**Tailor's workshop. Museum of History and
Folklore, Minden.**

Metzingen

Wine Museum

*Weinbaumuseum, Postfach 1646, D-7430
    Metzingen, Baden-Württemberg*
    ☎ *07123 161217*
Apr–Oct, Sun 10–5

When wine production was flourishing at the
beginning of the 17th century, the vineyard area
in and around Metzingen covered 315 hectares.
Today it consists of only 35, but as a result of
new varieties and techniques, more grapes are
harvested than 400 years ago.

The museum tells the story of local vineyard
cultivation and wine production since the 17th
century. The exhibits include vineyard
implements and equipment, wine-presses and
casks and vats. A special section illustrates the
skills of cellar management.

Minden

Museum of History and Folklore

*Mindener Museum für Geschichte, Landes- und
    Volkskunde, Ritterstraße 23-33, D-4950
    Minden, Nordrhein-Westfalen*
    ☎ *0571 89331/89316/89437*
*Tues, Wed, Fri 10–1, 2.30–5; Thurs 10–1,
    2.30–6.30; Sat 2.30–5; Sun 11–6. Enquire
    locally for opening times during public holidays.*

The group of six houses which contains the
museum dates from the 15th and 16th centuries.
The collections relate to the history of Minden
and its region.

There is a section devoted to geology,
palaeontology and prehistory, and there are also
exhibits of 17th–18th-century furniture,
domestic equipment and costumes, 17th–19th-
century weapons and paintings by local artists.
Among the special features of the museum are a
series of reconstructed craftsmen's workshops
and a panorama of the Battle of Minden (1761)
with 1,500 model figures.

Mittenwald

Mittenwald Museum and Museum of Violin-
Making

*Geigenbau- und Heimatmuseum, Ballenhausgasse
    3, D-8102 Mittenwald, Bayern*
    ☎ *08823 2511*
*Jan–Oct & Dec 22–31, Mon–Fri 10–12, 2–5;
    Sat, Sun 10–12.*

The museum is in the former home and
workshop of the celebrated violin-maker,
Mathias Klotz, who was taken to Italy at the age
of 10 and learnt his craft in Cremona with
Guarneri and Stradivarius. It contains stringed
instruments made by members of the Klotz
family and by other makers in the district, who
were attracted by the excellent wood to be
found in the local forests. At the peak of the
industry, violin-making was a cottage industry
here and nearly every house had its workshop.
The State School for Violin-Makers is
established here.

The museum contains exhibitions showing
how violins are made, as well as rural furniture
and household equipment.

Molfsee

Schleswig-Holstein Open-Air Museum

*Schleswig-Holsteinisches Freilichtmuseum,
    Hamburger Landstraße, D-2300 Molfsee/Kiel,
    Schleswig-Holstein*   ☎ *0431 65555*
*Apr 1–Nov 15, Tues–Sat 9–5; Sun and public
    holidays 10–6. July 1–Sept 15, also open Mon
    9–5. Nov 16–Mar 31, Sun and public holidays
    in good weather only, 10–dusk.*

In 1961 the museum began to build up its
collections of traditional buildings and their
contents from different parts of Schleswig-
Holstein and in 1965 the first part of the
museum was opened to the public. Considerably
developed since that time, it now contains
16th–19th-century buildings, with their

associated furniture, domestic equipment and agricultural implements. Among the exhibits are farmhouses, windmills, a dairy and an apothecary's shop.

Mönchengladbach

Schloss Rheydt Museum

Städtisches Museum Schloß Rheydt, D-4050 Mönchengladbach 2, Nordrhein-Westfalen
☎ 02166 20101
Mar–Oct, Tues–Sun 10–6. Nov–Feb, Tues–Sun 11–5.
Ⓒ ⓘ 🖳 & ⚘

As its name, Mönchengladbach – Gladbach of the Monks – suggests, the town was built around a Benedictine abbey, founded in 974. The moated Renaissance castle of Schloss Rheydt was built between 1560 and 1590. It suffered no damage during the Second World War and was opened as a museum of the prehistory and history of the area in 1953, with displays of 16th–18th-century weapons and armour, gold- and silversmiths' work, furniture, clocks, portraits, and weights and measures. A special section of the museum is devoted to the history of the local textile industry, from hand weaving to the mechanised production of the 20th century.

At present the Renaissance-Baroque section of this important museum, winner of the European Museum of the Year Award in 1978, is closed, to permit the building to be extensively restored, but parts of the collection are displayed in the outer bailey section of the building and in other museums in the area. The textile departments are unaffected by this.

Schloss Rheydt Museum, Mönchengladbach.

Munich

Bavarian National Museum

Bayerisches Nationalmuseum, Prinzregentenstraße 3, D-8000 München 22, Bayern
☎ 089 21681
Tues–Sun 9.30–5
Ⓒ ⓘ 🖳 & ⚘

One of Europe's major museums, the National Museum was established in 1859 in a building which today contains the Folklore Museum. The new building, opened in 1910 and restored after damage in the Second World War, was one of the most original and important museum buildings of its day. The collections had their origin in those which had been formed by the Bavarian royal house of Wittelsbach.

The extensive exhibition galleries cover, broadly speaking, 9th–20th-century European arts and crafts, with a strong emphasis on items produced in Germany. Sections are devoted to paintings on glass, ivories, miniatures, early German sculpture, woodcarvings, Bavarian pottery, 16th-century armour, clocks and tapestries. There are also exhibits of scientific instruments, porcelain and popular religious art.

The National Museum has one of the finest collections of Christmas cribs in Europe.

BMW Museum

BMW Museum – Zeitmotor, Petuelring 130, D-8000 München 40, Bayern
☎ 089 38953307
Daily, including public holidays, 9–5. Last admission 4.
Ⓒ ⓘ 🖳 ⚘

BMW stands for Bayerische Motor Werke, although today the firm is known only by its initials. The museum presents the history of the BMW company and of its manufacturing techniques. It is the starting point for tours of the adjacent production plant. The exhibits include a representative selection of motorcycles, passenger cars, sports cars and racing cars made by the company, together with a number of its aero-engines. Films, videos and other audio-visual material contribute to the understanding of BMW's historical and technical development.

City Museum

Münchner Stadtmuseum, St-Jakobs-Platz 1, D-8000 München 2, Bayern
☎ 089 2332370
Tues–Sat 9–4.30; Sun and public holidays 10–6.
Ⓒ ⚏ 🖳

The museum, which sets out to present the cultural history of Munich, occupies a group of buildings, the oldest of which dates from the 15th century and was formerly an arsenal. Substantial rebuilding and restoration was carried out after the Second World War. The collections include approximately 2,250 weapons and pieces of armour, dating from the

**The first automobile, 1886, by Benz.
Deutsches Museum, Munich.**

15th to the 17th century, and originally in the
arsenal. There are portraits, views of Munich,
paintings, sculpture, furniture, costumes,
musical instruments, toys, posters and
handicrafts. Some of the exhibits are set out in
period rooms.

As part of the City Museum, and in the same
building, there are separate Puppet and
Photography Museums. The Puppet Theatre
collection is the largest in the world.

Deutsches Museum

*Deutsches Museum, Museuminsel 1, Postfach 26
01 02, D-8000 München 22, Bayern*
☎ *089 21791*
*Daily 9–5. Closed Jan 1, Shrove Tues, Good Fri,
Easter Sun, May 1, Whit Sun, Corpus Christi,
June 17, Nov 1, Dec 24, 25, 31.*
C 🚹 ⛴ ♿

The Deutsches Museum, devoted to the history
of science and technology, is one of the world's
largest museums. Opened in 1925, as the result
of the energy and determination of a Munich
engineer, Oskar von Müller, the museum had to
endure the destruction of 80 per cent of its
buildings and 20 per cent of its exhibits in air
raids during the Second World War, but it is
now considerably larger than before. It includes
an important library and research institutes.

The sections range from telecommunications
to musical instruments, from aeronautics to
technical toys and from mineral oil and natural
gas to carriages and bicycles. Nothing is missing.
No other museum in the world, even the
Smithsonian in Washington DC, is as
comprehensive. There is also a Hall of Fame,
where great German scientists and inventors are
honoured by means of portraits and busts. Not
surprisingly, the Deutsches Museum also has a
number of firsts: the first Diesel engine (1897),

the first electric locomotive (1879) by Werner
Siemens, the first automobile, by Benz (1886),
the bench on which Otto Hahn discovered the
nuclear fission of uranium (1938), and many
others.

Residence Museum

*Residenzmuseum, Residenzstraße 1, D-8000
München 1, Bayern (entrance Max-Joseph-
Platz)*   ☎ *089 224641*
*Tues–Sat 10–4.30; Sun and public holidays 10–1.
Closed Good Fri, Easter Sun, Whit Sun,
May 1.*
C

In 1385 the Duke of Bavaria began building a
citadel, the Neue Veste, in Munich. Between
1470 and 1500 this was expanded into a large
moated castle. During the 16th–18th centuries
it was transformed into a residence of a more
modern type and continued to be used for this
purpose until the end of the First World War. In
1920 it was opened as a museum and, after
severe damage in 1944, was rebuilt and restored
to allow it to continue this function. It contains
17th–19th-century silver, furnishings, oriental
and 18th–19th-century European porcelain,
majolica and paintings. There are also
reliquaries and liturgical items, and Greek and
Roman sculpture.

Residence Treasury

*Residenz Schatzkammer, Residenzstraße 1, D-8000
München 1, Bayern (entrance Max-Joseph-
Platz)*   ☎ *089 224641*
*Tues–Sat 10–4.30; Sun and public holidays 10–1.
Closed Good Fri, Easter Sun, Whit Sun,
May 1.*
C

In 1565 Duke Albert V of Bavaria began to form
a collection of jewellery and of gold and silver
objects. This was greatly added to by his

descendants and as it expanded it was progressively moved to new quarters. At the end of the Bavarian monarchy in 1918, the Crown Jewels, including the Crown, were added to the Treasury. Its contents include 11th–19th-century European goldsmiths' work and jewellery, carved ivory and artistic objects from Turkey, Sri Lanka, East Africa and Central America.

Siemens Museum

*Siemens-Museum, Prannerstraße 10, D-8000
    München 2, Bayern* ☎ *089 2342660
Mon–Fri 9–4; Sat, Sun 10–2. Closed public
    holidays.*
F ⬛ ♿

In 1847 Werner von Siemens and Johann Georg Halske founded the Siemens and Halske Telegraph Construction Company in Berlin. Between then and 1939, the Siemens group of companies acquired a worldwide reputation for its inventions and developments in electrical engineering and electronics and, after difficult years following the Second World War, continued to prosper. The museum in Munich tells the story of the firm and illustrates new trends and possibilities.

State Collection of Minerals

*Mineralogische Staatssammlung, Theresienstraße
    41, D-8000 München 2, Bayern*
    ☎ *089 23944312
Tues–Fri 1–5; Sat, Sun and public holidays 1–6.*
C ◀

During the 18th and 19th centuries the kingdom of Bavaria, which took the education of its citizens very seriously, developed a number of specialised museum collections, including one devoted to minerals. It was established in 1883 and was reorganised in 1974. Its large and

Bridegroom. A figure from the City Museum, Munich.

splendid collections illustrate the minerals of the world and include many remarkable examples, including a 4 carat South African diamond still in the lode, and an exceptionally large emerald from the Urals. The exhibits are selected both for their scientific value and for their beauty. Their properties and their formation are explained by means of models and diagrams.

Villa Stück

*Villa Stück, Prinzregentenstraße 60, D-8000
    München 80, Bayern* ☎ *089 4708074
Daily 10–5; Thurs until 7. Closed Dec 24, 31.*
C ⓘ ⬛

The sumptuous Villa Stück, built in 1897–8, was the home and studio of the painter and sculptor, Franz von Stück (1863–1928), known in his lifetime, on account of his wealth and influence, as 'the Artist-Prince'. Opened as a museum in 1968, it contains memorabilia of the artist in the place where he lived and worked, together with a collection of his work and of Jugendstil objects. Eleven special exhibitions a year, each of international standard, are arranged in the Villa.

Münster

Mühlenhof Open-Air Museum

*Mühlenhof-Freilichtmuseum, Sentruper Straße
    223, D-4400 Münster, Nordrhein-Westfalen*
    ☎ *0251 82074
Mar 15–Nov 30, daily 9.30–5.30. Dec–Mar 14,
    Mon–Sat 1.30–4.30; Sun and public holidays
    11–4.30.*
C

The museum, established in 1960, contains rural buildings brought to the site from other parts of the region. They include windmills, a farmhouse and a millhouse, both with period furnishings and household equipment. In the centre of the museum is the last survivor of the 23 post-mills which once enlivened the landscape of the Münster district. It bears the date 1748 on one of the beams that carry the weight of the stones.

Museum of Münster

*Stadtmuseum Münster, Salzstraße 28, D-4400
    Münster, Nordrhein-Westfalen*
    ☎ *0251 4922945
Tues–Sun 10–6. Closed Jan 1, Good Fri, Dec 24,
    25, 31.*
F ⓘ ⬛

This is a new museum, opened in 1989, in a building designed for the purpose. The collections illustrate the political, cultural and social history of the city of Münster from 800 AD to the present day. They include paintings and portraits, documents of all kinds, civic and guild material, and religious items, as well as models, plans and views showing the development of the city.

Palaeontology exhibition at the Westphalian Museum of Natural History, Münster.

Westphalian Museum of Natural History

Westfälisches Museum für Naturkunde, Planetarium, Sentruper Straße 285, D-4400 Münster, Nordrhein-Westfalen   ☎ *0251 82084*
Tues–Sun 9–6
F ♦ ▣ ↬

This is the museum which claims that it has 'the largest ammonite on earth'. Apart from this, it has collections of fossils, mammals, birds, insects, snails and plants, together with dioramas showing the wild creatures to be found in Westphalia. There is also a planetarium and exhibits illustrating the aims and methods of natural conservation.

Nabburg

Neusath-Perschen Open-Air Museum

Oberpfälzer Freilandmuseum Neusath-Perschen, Oberriechtacherstraße 20, D-8470 Nabburg, Bayern   ☎ *09433 6884*
Apr–Oct, Tues–Sun 9–6
C ↬

The museum consists of 18th–20th-century farmhouses and other rural buildings from the region, transferred to the museum site and equipped with original and contemporary furniture and domestic equipment. There are also agricultural tools and implements, especially ploughs, and models illustrating the different types of farmhouses to be found in the district. Within the museum area, visitors can see the traditional methods of working the fields and woodland areas.

Neckarsulm

German Bicycle and NSU Museum

Deutsches Zweirad-Museum and NSU-Museum, Urbaustraße 11, Postfach 1361, D-7170 Neckarsulm, Baden-Württemberg
☎ *07132 35341*
Daily, including public holidays, 9–12, 1.30–5
C ♦ ὣ ↬

The 4-storey building which now houses the museum dates from the 16th century and was formerly a castle belonging to the Teutonic

Order. The displays cover the history of the bicycle and motorcycle and of the Neckarsulm firm, NSU, which made two-wheeler vehicles and motorcars from 1880 onwards, and which in the 1950s was the world's most important motorcycle manufacturer. The tradition continued, since Audi, the result of a merger between NSU and Auto-Union, now has its factory here, employing 12,000 people.

Among the exhibits is the 1817 hobbyhorse bicycle belonging to Baron von Drais and the first motorcycle made by Daimler in 1885.

Neu-Anspach

Hessenpark Open-Air Museum

Frelichtmuseum 'Hessenpark', D-6392 Neu-Anspach, Hessen   ☎ *06081 9704*
Mar, Apr & Oct, daily 9–5. May–Sept, daily 9–6. Nov–Feb, Tues–Sun 9–4.
C ♦ ↬

Transferred here from different sites in Hessen, the wide range of traditional rural buildings has been arranged according to their area of origin and their period of construction. An attempt has also been made to create a natural environment appropriate to each group of buildings and to cultivate old varieties of cereals in small plots.

A market place, surrounded by old buildings, has been designed to be a centre of activity, even in the evening when the museum is closed. It contains restaurants, dwellings, shops in which regional handicrafts are on sale, and exhibition rooms.

Neuenmarkt/Oberfranken

German Steam Locomotive Museum

Deutsches Dampflokomotiv-Museum, Birkenstraße 5, D-8651 Neuenmarkt/Oberfranken, Bayern
☎ *09227 5700*
May–Oct, Tues–Fri 9–12, 1–5; Sat, Sun 10–5. Nov–Apr, Tues, Fri–Sun 10–12, 1–4. Groups at other times by appt.
C ♦ ▣ ↬

The museum contains 20 locomotives rescued from destruction after the German Federal Railways ceased to use steam in 1977. There is also some coaching stock. The museum buildings, which include a locomotive round-house, were formerly the depot at Neuenmarkt. They adjoin the main line, which is still operational.

Neu-Isenburg/Zeppelinheim

Zeppelin Museum

Zeppelin-Museum, Kapitän Lehmann-Straße 2, D-6078 Neu-Isenburg/Zeppelinheim, Hessen
☎ *069 694390/692214*
Fri, Sat, Sun 9–5. Tues–Thurs by telephone appt. Closed Dec 23–Jan 3.
F ♦ ↬

Count von Zeppelin flew his first big airship over Lake Constance in 1908. Between 1910 and 1914, five Zeppelins operated regular passenger flights between German cities, carrying 35,000 people without injury. Flights were resumed in the 1920s and 1930s with the much larger *Graf Zeppelin* and *Hindenburg*, which undertook transatlantic crossings long before aeroplanes did, allowing passengers to travel between Europe and America in liner-like comfort.

The museum at Neu-Isenburg, opened in 1988, tells the story of the Zeppelins and the services they provided. The other parts of the building, with a curved room reaching to the ground, are a full-scale reproduction of a quarter section of a Zeppelin, giving visitors an impression of the size of the airship.

Neukirchen über Niebüll

Nolde Museum

Nolde-Museum, D-2268 Neukirchen über Niebüll, Schleswig-Holstein ☎ 04664 364
Mar–Oct, daily 10–6. Nov, daily 10–5.
C ⓘ ⯏ 🅰

Emil Nolde (1867–1956) was a German Expressionist painter of landscapes, Biblical scenes and figure subjects based on a private mythology. A farmer's son, he was born Emil Nanser, in Nolde, which was ceded to Denmark in 1920, making him a Danish citizen. Between 1927 and 1937 he built a house to his own design on the German side of the border and called it 'Seebüll'. He was persecuted by the Nazis, although many of his ideas were similar to theirs, and between 1941 and 1945 the exhibition of his work was forbidden.

'Seebüll', which contained both his home and his studio, has more than 200 of his works – paintings, watercolours, drawings, graphics and craftwork – a selection of which are displayed each year.

Neuss

Clemens Sels Museum

Städtisches Clemens-Sels-Museum, Am Obertor, D-4040 Neuss, Baden-Württemberg ☎ 02101 25955
Tues–Sun 10–5
C ⓘ ⯏ 🅰

The original museum building, which dated from 1912, was severely damaged by bombing during the Second World War and the contents had to be temporarily stored in the adjacent 13th-century town gatehouse. In 1975 a new museum was built, linked to the gatehouse by a bridge. It contains collections illustrating the archaeology and history of Neuss, together with sections devoted to 19th–20th-century German art, naive art and popular art, the last of which extends into the popular art of the present time.

Norderney

Norderney Fisherman's House Museum

Norderneyer Fischerhausmuseum, Im Wäldchen am Weststrand, D-2982 Norderney, Niedersachsen ☎ 04932 2687
May–Sept, Mon–Sat 3–5; Sun 10–12. At other times, see local announcements.
C

The museum, opened in 1937, is in a replica of a traditional fisherman's house. Its exhibits illustrate the history of Norderney and the other Frisian islands and of the local fishing industry. There is a fisherman's workshop, with fishing tackle. Also in the museum is a display of the molluscs found along the Norderney coast and a collection of paintings of 9th–19th-century ships.

Interment, 1915, by Emil Nolde. Nolde Museum, Neukirchen über Niebüll.

Nuremberg

Albrecht Dürer's House

Albrecht-Dürer-Haus, Albrecht-Dürer-Straße 39,
  D-8500 Nürnberg, Bayern ☎ *0911 162271*
Mar–Oct, Tues–Fri, Sun 10–5; Sat 10–9. Nov–
  Feb, Mon–Fri 1–5; Sat, Sun 10–5.
C

The artist Albrecht Dürer (1471–1528) lived in
this house for the last 19 years of his life. It has
belonged to the city of Nuremberg since 1826
and in 1875 and 1928 restoration work was
undertaken. Visitors can see the original title-
deeds to the house and certain of the carved
woodwork is original. The items of furniture,
however, are period reproductions and the
printing press displayed has been made in
accordance with drawings by Dürer. There are
paintings and stained-glass window pictures
with scenes from Dürer's life by Joseph
Sauterleute, Wilhelm Keller and Karl Jäger.
Temporary art exhibitions are held in a modern
annexe to the house.

Museum of Transport

Verkehrsmuseum Nürnberg, Lessingstraße 6,
  D-8500 Nürnberg 70, Bayern
  ☎ *0911 2195428*
Apr–Sept, Tues–Fri 10–5; Sat, Sun 10–6. Oct–
  Mar, Tues–Fri 10–4; Sat, Sun 10–5. Closed
  Jan 1, Shrove Tues, Good Fri, Easter Mon,
  Whit Mon, May 1, June 17, Day of Prayer
  and Repentance, Dec 24, 31.
C ⓘ 🚊 🚗

The museum is run jointly by German Federal
Railways and the Post Office. Originally
established in 1899, the railway section is the
oldest technical museum in the German-
speaking world. The present museum tells the
story of railways in Germany and of the postal
services in Bavaria. In the railway collections
there are a number of original steam
locomotives and the saloon coaches used by
Ludwig II of Bavaria and Prince Bismarck,
together with a wide range of models, built to a
scale of 1:10. The postal section also has a
gallery which illustrates the development of
telephones in Germany, from the beginnings to
the present day.

National Museum of German Culture

Germanisches Nationalmuseum, Kornmarkt 1,
  D-8500 Nürnberg 1, Bayern. Correspondence
  to: Postfach 95 10, D-8500 Nürnberg 11.
  ☎ *0911 13310*
Tues–Sun 9–5; Thurs also 8–9.30 pm. Closed
  Jan 1, Shrove Tues, Good Fri, Easter Mon,
  May 1, Whit Mon, June 17, Dec 24, 25, 31.
C ⓘ 🚊 🚗

The architectural core of the museum consists of
the buildings of a former Carthusian monastery,
dating from the late 14th century. The
collections illustrate the art and culture of the
German-speaking regions of Europe from

Oil container, 1520. National Museum of
German Culture, Nuremberg.

30,000 BC to the present day and include
paintings and sculpture, coins and medals,
16th–18th-century goldsmiths' work, costumes,
scientific instruments, weapons and hunting
equipment, and musical instruments. There are
reconstructions of farmhouse rooms with their
associated domestic equipment and a section
devoted to the history of medicine and
pharmacology.

Among the museum's more remarkable
exhibits are a crucifix and a bracelet from the
time of Frederick Barbarossa, c. 1180, drawings
and paintings by Albrecht Dürer (1471–1528)
who was, with Tilman Riemenschneider (1460–
1531), the leading German sculptor in the Late
Gothic style. The museum also contains an
important crafts department.

Oberndorf am Neckar

Weaponry Museum

Heimat- und Waffenmuseum, Klosterstraße 14,
  D-7238 Oberndorf am Neckar, Baden-
  Württemberg ☎ *07423 77126/77182*
Wed, Sat 2–4; Sun 10–12.
F ⓘ 🚗

The building which houses the museum is
known as the 'Sweden Building'. It was
originally a factory constructed by Mauser in
1899 for the production of firearms ordered by
Sweden. The brothers Wilhelm and Paul
Mauser and their descendants worked at the

Royal Arms Factory here from 1872 until 1945 and were responsible for many important weapon developments during this period. The tradition is continued today by the firm of Heckler and Koch, established in its present form in 1949.

The museum collections include hand guns, machine guns and field guns, together with calculating machines and measuring instruments made by Mauser during the years of German disarmament, 1919–33.

Other sections of the museum contain important archaeological material from local sites, ranging from the Neolithic period to the Middle Ages. Further collections illustrate the more recent history of Oberndorf, with special exhibitions devoted to transport, social life, the fire brigade, the carnival and life in the town during the Nazi period and the Second World War.

Oberriexingen

Roman Wine Cellar

*Römischer Weinkeller, Ursula Geiger, Weilerstraße
14, D-7141 Oberriexingen, Baden-
Württemberg*   ☎ 07042 4570
Apr–Oct, sun 2–4.30. Weekdays by appt.
Ⓕ 🚗

In 1957–8, during excavations for a new housing estate, workmen discovered the cellar and foundations of a group of Roman farm buildings which had apparently been destroyed by fire. The cellar has been restored and now contains pictures and documents illustrating Roman methods of wine production. There are also objects found during the excavation of Roman graves in the area.

Oberschleissheim

Meissen Porcelain Collection

*Meißener Porzellan-Sammlung, Stiftung Ernst
Schneider, Schloß Lustheim im Park von Schloß
Schleißheim, D-8042 Obserschleißheim,
Bayern*   ☎ 089 3150212
*Apr–Oct, Tues–Sun 10–12.30, 1.30–5. Nov–
Mar, Tues–Sun 10–12.30, 1.30–4.*
Ⓒ ♿ 💻

Since 1968, the Ernst Schneider collection of early Meissen porcelain, the finest in the world, has belonged to the Bavarian National Museum. There are more than 2,000 pieces, covering the period from the beginnings until the Seven Years' War, when the Royal Factory was setting a new standard for Europe. The porcelain is displayed against a background of contemporary frescoes, paintings and furniture.

Oberursel

Hans Thoma Museum

*Hans-Thoma-Gedächtnisstätte, Marktplatz 1/
Schulstraße 22a, D-6370 Oberursel (Taunus),
Hessen*
Sat 3–5; Sun 10–12.
Ⓕ 🚗

The painter and ceramics and graphic artist, Hans Thoma (1839–1924), lived and worked in Oberursel for many years during the summer in order to escape from the bustle of Frankfurt. This museum to him was established in 1956. It is mainly concerned with his work as a ceramicist, which led in 1901 to the foundation of the majolica factory in Karlsruhe. There is also a large collection of his correspondence, together with drawings and sketches and examples of ceramics by him.

Oerlinghausen

Archaeological Open-Air Museum

*Archäologisches Freilichtmuseum, Triftweg,
D-4811 Oerlinghausen, Nordrhein-Westfalen*
☎ 05202 2220
*Apr–Sept, Tues–Sun 9–5. Nov–Mar, Tues–Sun
10–4. Closed Dec 24, 25, 31.*
Ⓒ ♿ 💻 🚗

The museum site contains 27 reconstructions of buildings dating from about 10,000 BC to 1,000 AD, showing how people lived at these times. There are also demonstrations of early farming methods, crafts and food preparation. The reconstructions are based on information gathered from the excavation of archaeological sites and there is an exhibition showing the building work in progress.

**Reconstruction of a Bronze Age house,
1500 BC, the cooking area below, sleeping
quarters on the platform above. Archaeological
Open-Air Museum, Oerlinghausen.**

Offenbach am Main

Leather Museum and Shoe Museum

*Deutsches Ledermuseum und Deutsches
    Schuhmuseum, Frankfurter Straße 86, D-6050
    Offenbach am Main, Hessen* ☎ 069 813021
Daily 10–5
Ⓒ 🍶 🖥 🚾 🚗

Offenbach is an important centre of the German
leather industry and for more than 150 years it
was the site of an international Leather Fair.
The Leather Museum was founded in 1917, with
the aim of forming an international collection
which would show the different ways of
producing and working leather and the different
uses to which it can be put.

In 1951 the Shoe Museum was established as
a separate unit within the Leather Museum.
Over the years, its international collection of
footwear had grown so large as to justify a
separate name, particularly since the items in it
are made of silk, bark, straw and wood, as well
as leather. The collection is one of the most
important in Europe.

Offenbach Museum

*Stadtmuseum, Parkstraße 60, D-6050 Offenbach
    am Main, Hessen* ☎ 0611 80652446
Tues, Thurs–Sun 10–5; Wed 2–8.
Ⓕ

The museum's exhibits illustrate the prehistory
and history of the area. Sections are devoted to
the arrival of the Huguenots, *c.* 1700 and their
influence on the establishment of industries in
Offenbach, to the Offenbach porcelain
manufactory (1739–1829) and to the artistic
cast-iron and carved ivory trades. There is also
material relating to Alois Senefelder, the
inventor of lithography, who lived in Offenbach

**Chinese leatherwork puppet. Leather
Museum, Offenbach am Main.**

c. 1800. The painter Leopold Bode (1831–
1906) is represented by a number of his most
important works.

Oldenburg

Oldenburg Art Collections

*Städtische Kunstsammlungen, Raiffeisenstraße
    32-33, D-2900 Oldenburg (Oldb.),
    Niedersachsen* ☎ 0441 14538
*Tues, Fri, Sat 10–1, 3–5; Wed 3–7.30; Thurs
    3–5; Sun and public holidays 10–6.*
Ⓕ

The museum occupies the 1877 Francksen
Villa. There are collections of 18th–19th-
century German furniture, 18th–20th-century
European graphics, German ceramics and
paintings by 19th-century Oldenburg artists.

Provincial Art Museum

*Landesmuseum für Kunst- und Kulturgeschichte,
    Schloßplatz 1, D-2900 Oldenburg (Oldb.),
    Niedersachsen* ☎ 0441 25097
Tues–Fri 9–5; Sat, Sun 9–1.
Ⓕ

The museum, founded in 1923, occupies the
former Residence of the Counts of Oldenburg.
Its collections cover German art and
ethnography from the Middle Ages to the
present day, with an emphasis on the Oldenburg
region. A complete room is devoted to the work
of the Hamburg woodcarver, Ludwig
Münstermann (1570–1637). Other important
sections of the museum illustrate the work of
German painters of the 19th and 20th centuries,
including Louis Corinth, Paula Modersohn-
Becker, Max Beckmann, and members of the
Brücke Group, as well as Franz Radziwills, who
lived from 1921 onwards in Dangast.

Orsingen-Nenzingen

Carnival Museum

*Fasnachtmuseum Langenstein, Schloß Langenstein,
    Schwarzwaldstraße 10, D-7769 Orsingen-
    Nenzingen, Baden-Württemberg*
    ☎ 07774 7788 or 07771 2175
*May–Oct, Mon–Sat 1–5; Sun and public holidays
    10–5. Nov–Apr, Wed, Sat, Sun 1–5. Groups
    at other times by appt.*
Ⓒ 🍶 🚗

Langenstein Castle, which houses the museum,
dates from the 15th–16th centuries. In 1872 it
passed by inheritance to the Douglas family,
who originally came from Scotland and had
lived in Sweden since 1631. Count Axel
Douglas lives here and for this reason the main
part of the castle is not accessible to the public.

The museum collections illustrate the history
and practices of the carnival in the Hegau and
Lake Constance region. Exhibits include 275
carnival figures, masks, paintings and
documents illustrating carnival in this part of
Germany.

A 1940s-style cinema usherette at the ticket booth. Museum of the Moving Image, London.

The Parvillie plate, from the Théodore Aubanel Museum, Avignon (France).

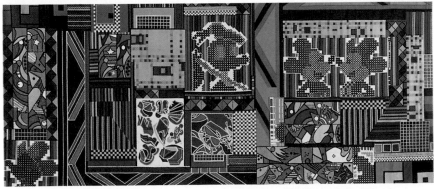

Industry by Paul Robert. Museum of Art and History, Neuchâtel (Switzerland).

The Whitworth Tapestry, by Eduardo Paolozzi. Whitworth Art Gallery, Manchester (Britain).

Carnival Museum, Orsingen-Nenzingen.

Osnabrück

Museum of Cultural History

Kulturgeschichtliches Museum, Heger-Tor-Wall,
D-4500 Osnabrück, Niedersachsen
☎ *0541 3234435*
Tues–Fri 9–5; Sat 10–1; Sun 10–5.
C ▯ ▯

The museum has important collections of 17th–
18th-century Dutch and German drawings,
prints and engravings, 16th–20th-century
paintings by Osnabrück artists and Osnabrück
silver and faïence. There are also sections
devoted to Greek, Roman and German
antiquities, coins and medals, militaria, glass,
porcelain and portraits.

Osterholz-Scharmbeck

Osterholz Museum

Kreisheimatmuseum, Bördestraße 42, D-2860
Osterholz-Scharmbeck, Niedersachsen
☎ *04791 16351*
Tues–Sun 10–6
C ▯ ▯

Osterholz lies between the sandy coastal plain
and an area of peat bogs. Until the Middle Ages
very few people lived in this infertile and
inhospitable region, but the situation began to
change at the end of the 12th century, when a
Benedictine monastery was founded here. It
eventually became the centre of the town's
economy. The museum occupies the former
Steward's House of the monastery, known as the
Findorff House, after Jürgen Christian Findorff,
who owned and enlarged it in 1753. A number
of traditional rural buildings from the region
have been transferred to the garden of the
Findorff House.

The museum has displays of Stone Age–
medieval archaeology from local excavations,

agricultural and domestic equipment and tools,
furniture, machinery and equipment illustrating
the textile, dyeing and ironfounding industries
of the district. There are also paintings by local
artists and a complete collection of the birds of
North Germany.

Paderborn

Diocesan Museum

Erzbischöfliches Diözesan-Museum, Markt 17,
D-4790 Paderborn, Nordrhein-Westfalen
☎ *05251 207216*
Tues–Sun 10–5
C ▯

Paderborn has one of the finest diocesan
museums in Germany, containing religious art
from the 11th to the 19th century. The exhibits
come from churches and monasteries in the
diocese and include vestments and other
textiles, liturgical items, religious sculpture and
paintings, reliquaries, altars and crucifixes.

Passau

Glass Museum

Passauer Glasmuseum, Rathausplatz, D-8390
Passau, Bayern   ☎ *0851 35071*
Daily 10–5
C ▯ ▯ ▯

The many famous people who have stayed at the
Hotel zum Wilden Mann overlooking the
Danube include the Empress Elisabeth II of
Austria, Goethe, Tolstoy, Alfred Krupp and
Justus von Liebig. One of the attractions of the
hotel is its large collection of 19th-century
glassware. This contains more than 10,000
individual pieces and includes the products of
glassworks in Bavaria, Bohemia and Austria.

Peissenberg

Mining Museum

Bergbaumuseum Peißenberg, An Tiefstollen 2,
*   D-8123 Peißenberg, Bayern* ☎ *08803 5102*
1st & 3rd Sun in month, 2–4 throughout year.
June–Sept, also Wed–Fri 9–11. Groups of
more than 10 people at other times by appt.
C ▮ ☞

The museum illustrates the history and
techniques of the mining of bituminous coal in
Upper Bavaria from 1837 to 1979. A section is
devoted to the geology of the region, showing
how the coal-seams originated, and there are
collections of mining tools and equipment and
mine plans. Visitors are taken 200 metres into a
19th-century mine gallery, where they can see
how the mine was worked.

Pottenstein

Fränkische-Schweiz Museum

Fränkische-Schweiz-Museum, Tüchersfeld,
*   D-8573 Pottenstein, Bayern* ☎ *09242 1640*
Apr–Oct, Tues–Sun 10–5. Nov–Mar, Tues,
*   Thurs 1.30–3.30; Sun 1.30–5. Groups at*
*   other times by appt.*
C ▮ ☞

In the early 18th century the local Jewish
community established itself in the ruins of the
former Lower Castle at Pottenstein. After a fire
in 1758 which destroyed many of the medieval
houses, the Jewish quarter was rebuilt and
remained in use until the community was
dissolved in 1872. In 1978 restoration and
conversion work began in order to form the new
Fränkische-Schweiz Museum, which was
opened in 1985.
    The museum's collections illustrate the
geology, natural history and history of this very

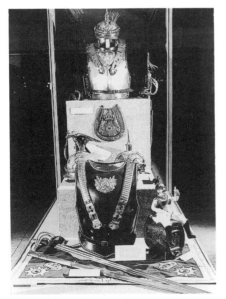

National Army Museum, Rastatt.

beautiful area, which was greatly beloved by
German Romantic writers of the 19th century.
The archaeological displays cover the period
from the Old Stone Age to Merovingian times.
There are reconstructions of farmhouse rooms,
collections of domestic equipment, costumes,
musical instruments, popular religious art,
handicrafts and objects relating to the
Pottenstein guilds. The synagogue, rebuilt after
the 1758 fire, forms part of the museum.

Rastatt

Museum of German Freedom Movements

Erinnerungsstätte für die Freiheitsbewegungen in der
*   deutschen Geschichte, Schloß, Herrenstraße*
*   18, Postfach 1235, D-7550 Rastatt 1, Baden-*
*   Württemberg* ☎ *07222 39475*
Tues–Sun 9.30–5
F ▮ ▉ ☞

The castle which houses the museum was built
in 1697–1905. Between 1956 and 1969 it
contained the Historical Museum of the Army
of Baden and in 1974 a new section was opened
by President Gustav Heinemann as a Museum of
German Freedom Movements from the Middle
Ages to modern times, with an emphasis on the
events of 1848–9. The exhibits include
documents, paintings, models, medals, flags and
orders.

National Army Museum

Wehrgeschichtliches Museum, Karlstraße 1,
*   Postfach 1663, D-7550 Rastatt, Baden-*
*   Württemberg*
Tues–Sun and public holidays 9.30–5. Closed
*   Jan 1, Dec 24, 25, 31.*
F ▮ ☞

The Castle of Rastatt was built in 1700 as the
Residence of the Margraves of Baden. The
museum, located here since 1956, is based on
the military collection of Baden State Museum
and on parts of the collection of the
Württemberg Army Museum. Recent
acquistions have widened the scope of the
collection, so that today's exhibits include
material relating to the military history of all the
former German states. The museum, which has
been controlled by the Ministry of Defence
since 1969, and is now the National Army
Museum, is responsible for the collection,
preservation and display of German military
artefacts from the Middle Ages to the present
day.

Ratzeburg

Ernst Barlach Museum

Ernst Barlach Museum, Barlachplatz 3, D-2418
*   Ratzeburg, Schleswig-Holstein*
*   ☎ 04541 3789*
Mar–Nov, Tues–Sun 10–12, 3–6. Guided tours
*   for blind visitors.*
C ▮ ☞

Ernst Barlach Museum, Ratzeburg.

The father of the great sculptor and illustrator, Ernst Barlach (1870–1938), moved to Ratzeburg when Ernst was seven. He trained as an artist in Hamburg and Dresden and spent a short time in the Ukraine. During the 1930s, his anti-militaristic and pessimistic work was condemned by the Nazis. Many items were removed from public exhibition and others destroyed.

In the museum, opened in 1956, there are collections illustrating his life and the development of his work. There are drawings, portrait busts, woodcuts, sculptures and notebook sketches.

Regensburg

City Museum

Museum der Stadt, Dachauplatz 2-4, D-8400 Regensburg, Bayern ☎ *0941 5072940 May–Sept, Tues–Sat 10–1, 2–5; Sun 10–1. Oct–Apr, Tues–Sat 10–1, 2–4; Sun 10–1.*
C 🐾

The museum occupies the former Minorite Convent of St Salvator, built in 1226–1460. It contains archaeological material from prehistoric and Roman sites in the district, views and models showing the development of Regensburg, costumes, furniture, popular religious art and household equipment. There are also collections of 14th–19th-century paintings and graphics, 11th–19th-century sculpture, musical instruments and medieval–19th-century ceramics, glass, wrought-iron, bronze, copper, brass and pewter.

Diocesan Museum

Diözesanmuseum St Ulrich, Domplatz 2, D-8400 Regensburg, Bayern. Correspondence to: Kunstsammlungen des Bistums Regensburg, Emmeramsplatz 1, Postfach 11 02 28, D-8400 Regensburg. ☎ *0941 51068/54677 Apr–Oct, Tues–Sun 10–4*
C 🏺

The museum building was built, probably in 1220–40, as the court chapel of the Bavarian duke, Ludwig I. After his death, it became a parish church, dedicated to St Ulrich. In 1824 it was secularised. Since 1986, this outstanding early Gothic building has been used as a

museum and church for the Chapter of the Cathedral of Regensburg.

It contains objects from the treasuries of the Regensburg churches of St Emmeram and St Johann and from the Niedermünster, ranging from the 12th to the 20th centuries. The exhibits include paintings, sculpture, ornaments and liturgical items. The medieval sculptures are of particular interest. Regensburg also has a Cathedral Treasury, which has been open to the public as a museum since 1974.

Kepler Memorial Museum

Kepler-Gedächtnishaus, Keplerstraße 5, D-8400 Regensburg, Bayern ☎ *0941 5072411 Tues–Sat 10–12, 2.30–4.30; Sun 10–12.*
C

This is the house, built c. 1500, in which the astronomer, Johann Kepler, died in 1630. It has been restored to its early-16th-century appearance and furnished appropriately. Its displays illustrate Kepler's life and his researches and scientific achievements.

Museum in the Stables of the Princes of Thurn and Taxis

Fürst Thurn und Taxis Marstallmuseum, Emmeramsplatz 6, D-8400 Regensburg, Bayern ☎ *0941 5048181 Mon–Fri, tours at 2.40 and 3.15; Sun, tours at 10.40 and 11.15. Closed Dec 24, 31.*
C

The building, constructed in 1832, was designed to accommodate an indoor riding-school, a coach-house and stables. It contains a large collection of 18th–20th-century coaches, carriages and sleighs, together with harness and saddles. Among the items on display is an 1890 wedding coach and a sedan chair of c. 1720. The museum occupies the former riding school.

Shipping Museum

Shiffahrtsmuseum, Liegeplatz Werftstraße (Unterer Wöhrd), Postfach 110510, D-8400 Regensburg, Bayern ☎ *0941 52510 Apr–Oct, daily 10–5*
C 🐾

The Danube is one of Europe's most important transport routes and Regensburg is one of its largest ports. To explain the history of navigation on the Bavarian part of the river, a museum has been created on the last Bavarian steamship to travel on the Danube, the *Ruthof*, built at Regensburg in 1922–3. In 1944 she hit a mine near Érsekcsanád in Hungary and sank. Raised 12 hours later, she was immediately rebuilt and put into service again by a Hungarian company, under the name Érsekcsanád, and remained in service until 1979, when she was returned to Germany.

The museum contains models, dioramas and displays illustrating the development of ships and shipbuilding on the Danube from the earliest times. Short trips on the river in small boats are arranged in connection with the visit to the *Ruthof*.

Remscheid

German X-Ray Museum

Deutsches Röntgen-Museum, Schwelmer Straße
41, D-5630 Remscheid 11 (Lennep),
Nordrhein-Westfalen   ☎ *02191 62759*
Mon–Thurs 10–5; Fri 10–2; Sun 2–5.
F

The discovery of X-rays in 1895 by Wilhelm
Röntgen changed the history of medicine and
surgery. Röntgen was born in Remscheid and in
1930 the town opened a museum in his memory.
Its displays cover the history, applications and
techniques of X-rays, as well as the life and
career of Röntgen.

Rheinbach

Glass Museum

Glasmuseum, Himmeroder Wall/Polligstraße,
D-5308 Rheinbach, Nordrhein-Westfalen
    ☎ *02226 14224/14231*
Tues–Fri 10–12, 2–5; Sat, Sun 2–5.
C ⬛ ♿ 🅿

The museum building forms part of a complex
once used by the Frankish court and which is
known to have existed in 1222. The collections
illustrate the production of glassware in
northern Bohemia from the 18th to the 20th
century. The museum has the largest display
collection of glass from this area.

Rödental

Goebel Porcelain Museum

Goebel Porzellanmuseum, W. Goebel
Porzellanfabrik, Coburger Straße 7, D-8633
Rödental, Bayern   ☎ *09563 920*
Mon–Fri 9–5; Sat 9–12. Closed public holidays
and Dec 24–Jan 10.
F 🅿

The porcelain factory in Rödental was
established in 1871. The museum at the factory
was opened in 1973 and contains examples of
18th–20th-century porcelain from the principal
manufacturers, including Meissen, Berlin,
Fürstenberg, Rosenthal and Vienna, as well as
Rödental. It has the largest collection in Europe
of 18th–19th-century porcelain from factories in
Thuringia.

Rosengarten-Ehestorf

Kiekeberg Open-Air Museum

Freilichtmuseum am Kiekeberg, Am Kiekeberg 1,
D-2107 Rosengarten-Ehestorf, Hamburg
    ☎ *040 7907662*
Mar–Oct, Tues–Fri 9–5; Sat, Sun 10–6. Nov–
Feb, Tues–Sun 10–4.
C 🍴 🅿

The museum was established in 1953 and it is
being continuously enlarged. The aim is to
illustrate changes in agriculture and rural life

since *c.* 1800. More than 20 buildings have
already been moved to the site from the
surrounding region. They include mills,
farmhouses, barns and storehouses, and
craftsmen's workshops, with appropriate
furniture and equipment. Special attention is
given to the development of farming methods
during the 19th and early 20th centuries and to
changes in the lifestyle of the rural population.

Rosenheim

Museum of the Inn

Innmuseum, Wasserbau- und Schiffahrtstechnische
Sammlung des Wasserwirtschaftsamtes
Rosenheim, Innstraße 74, D-8200 Rosenheim,
Bayern   ☎ *08031 17081*
Apr–Oct, Fri 9–12; Sat 9–4.
F 🅿

The museum occupies a 17th-century house,
near the bridge over the Inn. Its collections
cover the history and techiques of navigation
and shipbuilding on the Inn, the geology, flora
and fauna of the river and its basin, fishing and
the life of the boatmen and their families.
Among the exhibits is a flat-bottomed boat
(Innplatte), of the type used on the Inn for
centuries, and there are models of the wooden
river-bridges and of the boats which once
carried goods on the Chiemsee and Königsee,
on the Main and on the Ludwig–Danube–Main
canal.

Other displays are devoted to the uniforms
worn by members of the Royal Bavarian
Waterways Service, to ropemaking and to dike-
building and the management of watercourses.

Lorenzkapelle Art Collection, Rottweil.

The grand staircase of the Schloss Gottorf, now the Schleswig-Holstein Museum.

Rottweil

Lorenzkapelle Art Collection

Kunstsammlung Lorenzkapelle, Postfach 108, D-7210 Rottweil, Baden-Württemberg ☎ *0741 494255/494298* *Tues–Sat 10–12, 2–5; Sun 2–5. Closed public holidays.*

C 📖 🖼

The Lorenzkapelle, dedicated to the Roman deacon Laurentius, who was martyred in 251 AD, was built in 1580 as a cemetery chapel. The cemetery was transferred to a site outside the town in 1832. Until 1851, the chapel served first as a storage depot for archives and then as a market building. It has since been used to house an important collection of 13th–16th-century Swabian wood and stone sculptures. Since 1891, the 14th-century sculptures from an old church in Rottweil, the Kapellenturm, have been added to the collection.

Rötz-Hillstett

Museum of Trades and Crafts

Oberpfälzer Handwerksmuseum, D-8463 Rötz-Hillstett, Bayern ☎ *09976 1482* *Apr–Oct 15, Tues–Sun 10–12, 1.30–5. Groups by appt.*

C 📖 🖼 🖼

The museum was opened in 1974 in order to display workshops and tools dating from the pre-industrial period. The exhibits include a water-driven sawmill, a smithy, a forge and the workshops of a cutler, locksmith, saddler and shoemaker, as well as a baker's and a butcher's shop. Outside the main body of museum objects is a 1934 steam-engine, formerly used on the Wald-Rötz line, now used as a footpath.

Rüsselsheim

Rüsselsheim Museum

Museum der Stadt Rüsselsheim, Hauptmann-Scheuermann-Weg 4, D-6090 Rüsselsheim, Hessen ☎ *06142 42620* *Tues–Fri 9–12, 2–5; Sat, Sun 10–12, 1–5.*

F

Rüsselsheim is the centre of Opel car-production, and this pioneering museum shows the town as it was before and after Adam Opel arrived to manufacture first sewing-machines in the 1870s, then motorcycles and finally motorcars. There is a special emphasis on the effects of industrialisation on the social, political and economic life of the district, with the implication that what happened in Rüsselsheim took place throughout the industrialised areas of Germany.

Schleswig

Günderothscher Hof Museum

Städtisches Museum, Friedrichstraße 9, D-2380 Schleswig, Schleswig-Holstein ☎ *04621 814280* *Tues–Sun 10–5.*

C 🖼

Established in 1879, the museum is one of the oldest in Schleswig-Holstein. Since 1932 it has occupied the Günderothscher Hof, built in 1633–4 to provide accommodation for the ambassadors to the Gottorf court. The museum's collections illustrate the history of the town of Schleswig, with exhibits of furniture, paintings by local artists, Schleswig silver, faïence – Schleswig had the first faïence factory in Schleswig-Holstein (1755) – and pewter, and the weapons and equipment of regiments stationed in Schleswig.

There are exhibitions of works by celebrated Schleswig artists, including H. W. Bissen (1798–1868) and Niko Wöhlk (1887–1950). A special section is devoted to the history of book-printing in Schleswig and the museum also contains the famous library presented to the town by Peter Hoë (1772–1846), which has 17,000 volumes, most from the 17th–19th centuries.

Schleswig-Holstein Museum

Schleswig-Holsteinisches Landesmuseum, Schloß Gottorf, D-2380 Schleswig, Schleswig-Holstein ☎ *04621 8130* *Apr–Oct, Tues–Sun 9–5. Nov–Mar, Tues–Sun 9.30–4. Closed Jan 1, Good Fri, 3rd Wed in Nov, Dec 25. Closes at noon Dec 24, 31.*

C 📖 🖼 ♿ 🖼

The Renaissance palace which contains the museum is the most important secular building in Schleswig-Holstein. It was formerly the Residence of the Dukes of Schleswig-Holstein-Gottorf. The museum galleries are at the same time the historic rooms of the palace and include the Gothic Hall, the Church with its celebrated Prayer Room, and the Trophies Room.

The exhibits give a comprehensive picture of the art, social history and traditional life of the province from the 12th century to the present day. Sections of the museum are devoted to medieval sculpture, 15th–19th-century furniture and domestic equipment, weapons, the history of the guilds, court life at Gottorf, portraits of Schleswig-Holstein personalities and regional faïence. Other displays present middle-class life in the 19th century, traditional costumes, reconstructions of rooms in farmhouses, agricultural implements and handicrafts. There are also collections of 19th- and 20th-century German art.

Schwäbisch-Gmünd

Schwäbisch-Gmünd Musuem

*Städtisches Museum, Johannisplatz 3, D-7070
Schwäbisch-Gmünd, Baden-Württemberg*
☎ *07171 5737*
*Tues–Fri 2–5; Sat, Sun and public holidays 10–12,
2–5. Closed Fasching Tues and Dec 24.*
F

The present museum has its origins in a collection of artistic metalwork, opened to the public in 1876. In 1890 it was enlarged by the addition of two other local collections, one of folk objects and the other of natural history. In 1973 the museum was moved to a building known as the Prediger, which formed part of a 13th-century Dominican monastery.

It presents the history and natural history of the Schwäbish-Gmünd area. Among the exhibits are 13th–18th-century paintings and sculpture, examples of books printed locally, decorative metal objects, popular religious items and products of the cottage industries of the region. There is also a water-powered forge-hammer and reconstructions of a needle-maker's and gold-beater's workshop.

The natural history displays illustrate the geology, botany and wildlife of the district and the way in which the landscape has developed.

Schwäbisch Hall

Schwäbisch Hall Museum

*Hällisch-Fränkisches Museum, Keckenhof, D-7170
Schwäbisch Hall, Baden-Württemberg*
☎ *0791 751289*
Tues, Thurs–Sun 10–5; Wed 10–8.
C 🛉 💻

Reorganised during the 1980s, the museum now occupies seven historic buildings, including the castle known as the Keckenburg, which dates from 1238. Its collections include Stone Age, Bronze Age, Hallstatt, Roman and Merovingian archaeological material and objects illustrating the history of the town and the region. There are exhibits of costumes, medieval paintings and sculpture, painted furniture and sections devoted to popular religion and to the history of municipal government and justice in Schwäbisch Hall.

The museum has laid out a garden containing the useful plants of the late Middle Ages. These include cereals, vegetables, fruits and herbs.

Schweinfurt

Schweinfurt Museums

*Städtische Sammlungen, Obere Straße 11/13,
D-8720 Schweinfurt, Bayern*
☎ *09721 51479*
*Gallery: Tues–Sat 2–5; Sat, Sun 10–1. Cultural
History Collection and Local History
Collection: Wed, Fri, Sat 2–5; Sat, Sun 10–1.
Natural History: Wed 2–5 and by appt.*
F 🛉

The collections are now reorganised in four buildings. Local history occupies the Old Grammar School (Martin-Luther-Platz 12), built in 1582 as the Latin School; the Art Gallery is in the former Imperial Steward's office, which dates from 1576–7; the Natural History Museum the Harmony Building (Harmonie-Gebäude, Brückenstrasse 39), built in 1833 as the headquarters of the Harmony Society, and the Cultural History Collections the Gunnar Wester House (Martin-Luther-Platz 5). The headquarters is in the Old Grammar School.

In the Old Grammar School there are collections illustrating the history of this former Imperial City, with sections devoted to domestic life; the Guilds; popular religious beliefs and practices; the beginnings of industrialisation, including the history of Schweinfurt's celebrated ballbearing industry; the founding of the First Academy of Natural Sciences in Germany, the Leopoldina (1652);

**Natural History Museum, Schweinfurt
Museums.**

Hanover Tramway Museum, Sehnde.

and the poet and scholar, Friedrich Rückert (1786–1866).

The Art Gallery concentrates on 19th-century painters from South Germany, including Spitzweg, Thoma and Corinth and on contemporary artists from the Schweinfurt area. The Cultural History section of the museum contains Count Luxburg's collection of lamps and apparatus for producing fire, from classical times onwards, and the Natural History Museum is concerned entirely with the birds of the region.

Schwelm

Haus Martfeld Museum

Museum Haus Martfeld, Haus Martfeld 1,
D-5830 Schwelm, Nordrhein-Westfalen
☎ 02336 6990
Tues–Sun 10–12, 3–5. Closed public holidays.
F ✐ ⊶

Haus Martfeld is a former moated castle, built in the late Middle Ages, and extended and modified in the late 17th century. The museum, founded in 1890 and reopened in 1985 after modernisation and reorganisation, is devoted to the history of Schwelm and the surrounding area. The development of the town is shown by means of views and models and there are special exhibits of 16th–19th-century furniture and domestic equipment, coins and 18th–20th-century textile machinery – Schwelm has a long history as a textile centre.

Seesen

Municipal Museum

Städtisches Heimatmuseum, Wilhemsplatz 4,
D-3370 Seesen, Niedersachsen
☎ 05381 75247
Tues–Sun 3–5. Closed public holidays.
F ⊶

The museum occupies the former hunting lodge of Anton Ulrich, Duke of Brunswick, rebuilt in 1707. Its collections illustrate the history and character of the region and include minerals from mines in the Harz Mountains, closed in the 19th century. A section is devoted to memorabilia of the Steinway family, founders of the Steinway piano firm in New York, who emigrated from Seesen, where Heinrich Engelhard Steinweg built his first piano in 1836. Seesen was also a pioneer in the can-making industry and the museum has a reconstruction of the sheet-metal workshop which was making cans for preserving foodstuffs in 1830. An exhibit shows the development of this important local industry since that time.

Sehnde

Hanover Tramway Museum

Hannoversches Straßenbahn Museum,
Hohenfelserstraße 16, D-3163 Sehnde
(Wehmingen), Niedersachsen
☎ 05138 4575
Apr–Oct, Sun 11–5. Groups by appt at other
times.
C ♿ 🅿 ⊶

The museum is located in a former salt factory, which was built in 1890 and provides 15 hectares of floor space. With 300 exhibits from 44 towns, it claims to have the largest collection of electric-powered vehicles in Europe. These include items from electric railways, as well as tramways. Among them is a coach from the first underground railway on the Continent, in Budapest. A special exhibition is devoted to the history of tramways in Hanover.

Seligenstadt

Benedictine Abbey

Ehemaliges Benediktinerkloster, Klosterhof 1,
D-6453 Seligenstadt, Hessen
☎ 06182 22640
Apr–Sept, Tues–Sun 10–4. Oct–Mar, Tues–Sun
10–3 (last tour).
C ♿ 🅿 ⊶

This large abbey, which dates from the late 17th century, has its original 18th-century decorations and was for many years the centre of the economy of Seligenstadt. Visitors are given an impression of the organisation of the monastery and of the life of the monks. A special feature is the kitchen, with its wide range of equipment. There is also an impressive collection of paintings.

Siegburg

Treasury of the Church of St Servatius

Schatzkammer St Servatius, Kathedral,
Mühlenstraße 6, D-5200 Siegburg, Nordrhein-
Westfalen   ☎ 02241 63146
Daily 9–12, 1.30–5.30
C

With objects both from St Servatius and from
Michaelsberg Abbey, this is one of the most
important church treasuries in Europe. It has
outstanding collections of 12th–14th-century
reliquaries, shrines, altars, religious ornaments
and liturgical items.

Siegen

Siegerland Museum

Siegerland-Museum in Oberen Schloß, D-5900
Siegen 1, Nordrhein-Westfalen
          ☎ 0271 52228
Tues–Sun 10–12.30, 2–5
C

The museum is in a 15th-century castle. Its
collections illustrate the history of the
Siegerland region, with topographical
watercolours, memorabilia of Siegerland
personalities and portraits of members of the
House of Orange-Nassau. There are also
paintings, drawings and engravings by Rubens,
who was born here. The iron industry has been
important here and the museum has a
demonstration mine and examples of 19th-
century decorative cast-iron.

The Armoury, part of the Collections of the
Hohenzollern Princes, Sigmaringen.

Sigmaringen

Collections of the Hohenzollern Princes

Fürstliches Hohenzollern Sammlungen, Schloß,
D-7480 Sigmaringen, Baden-Württemberg
          ☎ 07571 7290
Feb–Nov, daily 8.30–12, 1–5. Dec–Jan, Mon–Fri
for pre-booked groups.
C ▮ ⇙

The earliest parts of the Hohenzollern Castle at
Sigmaringen date from the 12th century.
Extensions and modifications were made in the
16th century and the eastern wing was rebuilt in
1893, after a serious fire. Visitors can see the
enormous State Rooms, the Armoury with its
3,000 weapons and pieces of armour, family
portraits, 15th–16th-century paintings by
Swabian artists, tapestries and collections of
14th-century painted glass and prehistoric and
Alemannic archaeology. The stables contain a
number of coaches, carriages and sledges used by
the family.

Sobernheim

Open-Air Museum of the Rhineland Palatinate

Rheinland-Pfälzisches Freilichtmuseum,
Nachtigallental, Postfach 18, D-6553
Sobernheim, Rheinland-Pfalz ☎ 06751 3840
Apr–Oct, Tues–Sun 9–6
C *(ex. children)* ▮ 🖾 ⇙

The museum comprises a number of artificial
villages, each relating to a different area of the
Rhineland Palatinate and consisting of rural
buildings moved to the museum site. They
include houses, farm buildings and workshops,
each with the appropriate furnishings and
equipment.

drinking vessels and a display showing the production of wine in Germany over a period of more than 2,000 years.

The museum also contains the cathedral and diocesan museums and objects from the graves of kings, bishops and emperors in the cathedral.

Portrait of Liselotte von der Pfalz (1652–1722). Museum of the History of the Palatinate, Speyer.

Solingen

Museum of Edged Weapons and Cutlery

Deutsches Klingenmuseum, Klosterhof 4, D-5650 Solingen 1, Nordrhein-Westfalen
☎ 0212 59822
Tues–Sun 10–1, 3–5
© ⓘ ▇ ⌖

Solingen has long been famous for its production of swords, daggers and sabres, which reached its highest point of activity during the 17th century, up to the Thirty Years War. As the military demand fell away, the production of domestic cutlery took its place, an important technical school for the different specialities being set up in the town in 1901.

The large collections of this important museum, established in 1954, are centred on the history of the industry in Germany, but contain edged weapons and cutlery of all periods from all over the world. The museum is now housed in an 18th-century monastery.

Speyer

Museum of the History of the Palatinate

Historisches Museum der Pfalz, Große Pfaffengasse 7, Postfach 1429, D-6720 Speyer, Rheinland-Pfalz   ☎ 06232 77131
Daily 10–5. Closed Jan 1, Dec 24, 25, 31.
© ⓘ ▇

The museum has collections of exceptional quality, illustrating the prehistory and history of the region. There are exhibits of Roman sculpture, glass, and metalwork, Frankish jewellery, medieval tiles, sculpture, paintings and silver, 18th–19th-century furniture and Frankenthal porcelain, and religious art. Speyer is an important wine-making area and the museum has an historical collection of wine-

Steinau an der Strasse

Steinau Castle and Memorial to the Brothers Grimm

Museum Schloß Steinau mit Brüder-Grimm Gedenkstätte, Schloß, D-6497 Steinau an der Straße, Hessen   ☎ 06663 6843
Apr–Sept, Tues–Sun 10–4. Oct–Mar, Tues–Sun 10–3 (last admission).
© ⓘ ▇ ⌖

Building of the castle began in the 16th century and continued in the 17th and 18th. A number of the rooms have been restored and appropriately furnished to show the living style of a German Renaissance princeling.

At the end of the 18th century the three Grimm brothers grew up in Steinau. The museum has an exhibition of family portraits, memorabilia and a selection of their most important works to commemorate this.

Stuttgart

Daimler-Benz Museum

Mercedesstraße 136, D-7000 Stuttgart-Untertürkheim, Baden-Württemberg
☎ 0711 1722578
Tues–Sun 9–5. Closed public holidays.
Ⓕ ⓘ ▇ ⅙ ⌖

In 1886 Karl Benz (1844–1929) was issued a patent, the world's first, for 'a vehicle with gas-engine drive'. At the same time, Gottlieb Daimler (1834–1900) was experimenting with a 'motor carriage'. Benz and Daimler were, jointly, the fathers of the automobile and their enterprises later came together to form a single company.

The museum, with more than 70 models on display, illustrates the history of the two companies, separately and together and, in the process, the development of the automobile from its earliest beginnings to the present day.

German Agricultural Museum

Deutsches Landwirtschaftsmuseum, Garbenstraße 9A-15, Postfach 700562, D-7000 Stuttgart 70, Baden-Württemberg
☎ 0711 4592146/4592797
Apr–Oct, Wed–Sat 2–5; Sun 10–5. Nov–Mar, Sun 10–5.
© ⌔ ⌖

Until the 1940s, the German Agricultural Museum was in Berlin. It was totally destroyed during wartime bombing and in 1965 a new museum, dealing with the same subject, was opened at the University of Hohenheim, outside Stuttgart. Its aim is to illustrate how yesterday's farming methods developed into today's and it has collections of tools, implements and equipment dating from the 18th century to the present day. An important feature of the museum is the internationally famous collection of exact scale models of agricultural machinery made at the Hohenheim Implement Factory between 1819 and 1914.

Gottlieb Daimler Memorial

Gottlieb-Daimler-Gedächtnisstätte, Kurpark bad-Cannstatt, c/o Daimler-Benz AG, Daimler-Benz-Museum, Mercedesstraße 136, D-7000 Stuttgart-Untertürkheim, Baden-Württemberg
☎ *0711 1722578*
Apr–Oct, daily 11–4.
F

Gottlieb Daimler (1834–1900), the automobile pioneer, developed his high-speed engine in a lean-to greenhouse in the garden of his house in the Taubenheimstrasse. The building has been preserved and converted to a museum, containing original and replica tools. The house in Schorndorf, in the Höllgasse near the market square, where he was born, is open to visitors on Tuesdays and Thursdays from 2 pm to 4.30 pm.

Stuttgart City Gallery

Galerie der Stadt Stuttgart, Schloßplatz 2, D-7000 Stuttgart 1, Baden-Württemberg
☎ *0711 2162188*
Tues–Fri 10–6; Sat, Sun 11–5.
F ♿ 🖼 ♨

The gallery is at present in the building constructed for the purpose in 1913. Work will shortly begin on a new gallery, by I. M. Pei – celebrated for his Pyramid at the Louvre in Paris. The gallery's collections consist of paintings by 19th–20th-century artists in South-West Germany. There is also an important group of paintings and graphics by Otto Dix (1891–1969).

Württemberg Museum

Württembergisches Landesmuseum Stuttgart, Altes Schloß, Schillerplatz 6, D-7000 Stuttgart 1, Baden-Württemberg   ☎ *0711 21931*
Tues, Thurs–Sun 10–4; Wed 10–8.
F ♿ 🖼

Building of the Old Palace began c. 950. It was extended in the 11th–14th centuries and converted into a Renaissance palace in 1553–60. After the New Palace had been completed in 1746, what was now the Old Palace ceased to be used by the Dukes of Württemberg as a Residence. Much destruction was caused to it by a fire in 1931 and by air-raids in 1944. It was fully restored in 1947–69.

It contains very rich collections of Greek and Roman antiquities and of weapons, scientific instruments, musical instruments, textiles and costumes, Renaissance sculpture, porcelain, glass and 16th–19th-century clocks.

Big City, 1928, by Otto Dix. City Art Gallery, Stuttgart.

Sulzburg

Mining Museum

Landesbergbaumuseum Baden-Württemberg, Hauptstraße 56, D-7811 Sulzburg, Baden-Württemberg   ☎ *07634 702*
Tues–Sun 2–5.
C ♨

The old-established local mining industry has produced a range of minerals and metals in its time, ranging from jasper to iron. The museum, established in 1982 and at present accommodated in the town's Evangelical church, contains displays of mining tools and machinery and minerals, as well as exhibits illustrating the social and domestic life of miners and their families.

Tann

Rhön Museum Village

Freilichtmuseum 'Rhöpner Museumsdorf', Tann, Postfach 1127, D-6413 Tann (Rhön), Hessen   ☎ *06682 8011*
Apr–Oct, daily including public holidays 10–12, 2–5. Nov–Mar, by appt only for groups.
C 🖼 ♨

This open-air museum was created in the 1970s in order to preserve the evidence of a vanishing age. It is planned around a farmhouse and other buildings moved to the site to illustrate the way of life of a well-to-do rural family c. 1800 and its methods of operating the farm.

Tecklenburg

Doll Museum

Puppenmuseum, Am Markt, Postfach 12 20, D-4542 Tecklenberg, Nordrhein-Westfalen
☎ *05482 70701*
Apr–Oct, Tues–Sun 10–12, 2–5. Nov–Mar, Sun 10–12, 2–5.
C ♿

Tecklenberg's Gatehouse, in which the museum is situated, dates from 1577. Until the mid 19th century, it contained the official centre for certifying the quality of linen, an important local industry. The collection now installed in it was formed during the 1960s by Ute Botsch, who travelled all over Germany looking for old dolls, toys and puppets. Most are of German make, but some come from other countries.

Tegernsee

Olaf Gulbransson Museum

Olaf-Gulbransson-Museum, Im Kurgarten,
*   D-8180 Tegernsee, Bayern*   ☎ 08022 3338
Jan–Oct, Dec, Tues–Sun 11–5
C

A Norwegian, Olaf Gulbransson (1873–1958) settled in Germany and became very successful as a caricaturist. The museum displays examples of his paintings, drawings and graphics and tells the story of his life.

Theuern

East Bavarian Museum of Mining and Industry

Bergbau- und Industriemuseum Ostbayern,
*   Portnerstraße 1, Theuern, D-8451*
*   Kümmersbruck, Bayern*   ☎ 09624 832
Feb–Dec, Tues–Sat 9–5; Sun and public holidays
*   10–5. Closed Dec 20 Jan 31.*
C 🛈 🖙

The Amberg region, which includes Theuern, has been called 'the Ruhr of the Middle Ages', on account of its rich deposits of iron ore and the number and importance of the ironworks which used them. The museum occupies the former residence, built in 1781, of one of the district's leading ironmasters. A group of old

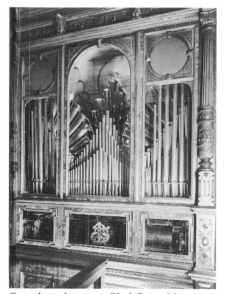

Carved wooden organ. Black Forest Museum, Triberg.

industrial buildings, including a water-powered forge hammer, a glass-grinding and polishing works, and the surface installations of a mine, have been re-erected in the grounds.

The collections in the museum illustrate the industrial development of the Upper Palatinate. In addition to ironworking, there are special sections on local minerals and on porcelain and glass made in the region.

Tittling

Bavarian Forest Open-Air Museum

Museumsdorf Bayerischer Wald, Am
*   Dreiburgensee, D-8391 Tittling, Bayern*
*   ☎ 08504 8482/4040*
Daily 9–5
C 🛈 🖙 🖙

This is one of the largest open-air museums in Europe. It was created during the 1970s by Georg and Centa Höltl, whose family have lived in the area since 1640. Their aim was to rescue historic wooden buildings, characteristic of the region, from destruction and to form them into an artificial village. They bought over 100 farmhouses and other rural structures, some of them very large, and re-erected them as a museum, with appropriate furniture and equipment, where they can serve as a tourist attraction.

Traben-Trarbach

Museum of the Central Mosel Region

Mittelmosel-Museum, Moselstraße, D-5580
*   Traben-Trarbach, Rheinland-Pfalz*
Tues–Fri 11–1, 3–5
C

The museum is in a house built in 1750. Its collections illustrate the prehistory and history of the region. There is, not unnaturally, a special concentration on the history of vineyard cultivation and wine production in this traditional and celebrated wine area, but there are also collections of 17th–18th-century furniture, paintings, prints, drawings, coins and weapons.

Triberg

Black Forest Museum

Schwarzwald-Museum, Wallfahrtstraße 4, D-7740
*   Triberg, Baden-Württemberg*
*   ☎ 07722 4434*
May–Sept, daily 9–6. Oct–Apr, daily 10–12, 2–5.
*   Closed Jan 1 (am), Dec 24 (pm), 25.*
C 🖉 🖙

The museum is concerned mainly with the traditional handicrafts of the Black Forest. There are exhibits of woodcarving, glass and Black Forest clocks, with a reconstruction of a clockmaker's workshop. The museum also has collections of costumes, minerals and mechanical musical instruments.

Trier

Cathedral Treasury

Domschatz, Hohe Domkirche, Hinter dem Dom 6, D-5500 Trier, Rheinland-Pfalz
☎ 0651 7105233
Easter–Oct, Mon–Sat 10–12, 2–5; Sun 2–5. Nov–Easter, Mon–Sat 10–12, 2–4; Sun 2–4.
C 🔒

The treasury is in a 15th-century room, with a central column supporting the roof. It contains a rich collection of medieval religious ornaments and liturgical objects in gold and silver, carved ivory and illuminated manuscripts.

Karl Marx House

Karl-Marx-Haus, Brückenstraße 10, D-5500 Trier/Mosel, Rheinland-Pfalz
☎ 0651 43011
Apr–Oct, Mon 1–6; Tues–Sun 10–6. Nov–Mar, Mon 3–6; Tues–Sun 10–1, 3–6, Closed Dec 24–Jan 1.
C 🔒

Karl Marx (1818–83) was born in Trier in the early 18th-century house which is now the museum. In 1928 the Social Democratic Party bought the house and restored it, with the intention of converting it into a museum to Marx and Engels. The opening had to be postponed, owing to the tense economic and political situation, and in 1933 it was appropriated by the Nazis and used as the editorial offices of their newspaper, *Nationalblatt*. After the War, the SDP got its property back and the museum opened in 1947.

It contains original manuscripts and letters by Marx and Engels, first and early editions of their works, together with a number of photographs. There are exhibitions on the life and work of Marx and Engels and on the international working-class movement. A special section is devoted to the history of the house.

Trier Museum

Städtisches Museum, Simeonstift, Simeonstiftplatz, D-5500 Trier, Rheinland-Pfalz
☎ 0651 7182440
Tues–Fri 9–5; Sat, Sun 10–1.
C 🔒 ☕ 🚗

The Simeonstift, which houses the museum, is a Romanesque monastery constructed in the 11th century against the Roman Porta Nigra, which at that time had been converted into a church. The collections cover the fields of archaeology, ethnology and art and cultural history since the 14th century. There are special sections devoted to regional crafts, oriental ivories and Coptic textiles.

Among the particularly interesting features of the museum are Trier's 958 AD market cross and a large-scale model of the city as it was in 1800.

Karl Marx. Marx House, Trier.

Tübingen

Hölderlin Museum

Hölderlinturm, Bursagasse 6, D-7400 Tübingen, Baden-Württemberg ☎ 07071 22040
Tues–Fri 10–12, 3–5; Sat, Sun and public holidays 2–5.
C 🔒

The poet Friedrich Hölderlin (1770–1843) died in Tübingen where, after becoming insane, he had spent the last 37 years of his life being looked after by a local carpenter. The museum is in the building where Hölderlin lived during this period. The exhibits illustrate his life as a divinity student in Tübingen, his later period in the town, and his literary achievements. There is also material relating to his family and friends and to Tübingen as it was in his lifetime.

Tübingen Museum

Städtische Sammlungen, Theodor-Haering-Haus, Neckarhalde 31, D-7400 Tübingen, Baden-Württemberg ☎ 07071 204242
Tues–Sun 2.30–5.30
C 🔒

What is now the museum was built in 1866–8 as an apartment house for professors at the University. It has sections dealing with the history of Tübingen and the University and with the printing, publishing and selling of books. There are also collections of furniture and domestic equipment, and memorabilia of writers, philosophers and musicians associated with the city, together with paintings, drawings and engravings, especially views of Tübingen.

Uhldingen-Mühlhofen

Open-Air Museum of German Prehistory

*Pfahlbaumuseum Deutscher Vorzeit, Seepromenade
6, D-7772 Uhldingen-Mühlhofen, Baden-
Württemberg*   ☎ *07556 8543*
Apr–Oct, daily 8–6
C

The museum consists of the reconstruction of a
lake village, giving an impression of the life of a
hunting and fishing community during the
period 2200–1100 BC. Prehistoric material from
local sites is on display at the museum.

Ulm

German Bread Museum

*Deutsches Brotmuseum, Fuersteneckerstraße 17,
D-7900 Ulm, Baden-Württemberg*
☎ *0731 30561*
Mon–Fri 10–5; Sun 10–1, 2–5.
C ⓘ ↩

The museum contains paintings, engravings and
objects of all kinds which are related to the
history of bread and breadmaking and to its
importance. The collections include a wide
range of baking equipment, some of which is
shown in dioramas. There is a special exhibition
illustrating the history of hunger in the 18th–
20th centuries.

Ulm Museum

*Ulmer Museum, Marktplatz 9, D-7900 Ulm,
Baden-Württemberg*   ☎ *0731 1614300*
Tues, Wed, Fri–Sun 10–5; Thurs 10–8.
F ⓘ ↪

Part of the museum's collection is displayed in
the Kiechel House, built in 1600. It is the last
surviving patrician house in Ulm. The principal
sections of the museum are devoted to the late
medieval art of Upper Swabia, modern and
contemporary drawings, watercolours, collages
and prints, and 16th–19th-century crafts. There
is also an exhibition of books printed in Ulm
and a prehistoric department.

Vaigingen an der Enz

Wine Museum

*Weinmuseum im Stadtteil Horrheim, Rathaus,
D-7143 Vaigingen an der Enz, Baden-
Württemberg*   ☎ *07042 18276/18259*
By appt
C ↩

The museum has been installed in an 18th-
century building originally used for pressing
grapes. Its displays illustrate vineyard
cultivation and wine-production in the area
since the mid 18th century, with a collection of
historic equipment, including a wine-press
dating from 1698. There is also a traditional
type of wine-tasting room.

Velbert

Museum of Locks and Hardware

*Deutsches Schloß- und Beschlägemuseum, Forum
Niederberg, Oststraße 20, D-5620 Velbert 1,
Nordrhein-Westfalen*   ☎ *2051 313285*
*Tues–Fri 10–5; Sat 10–1; Sun 10–1, 2–4. Closed
Jan 1, Easter, Whitsun, Dec 24, 25, 31.*
C ⓘ ☕ ↩

The museum, opened in 1936, shows the
development of locks, keys and bolts since early
times. There are examples of doors, windows
and furniture, explaining the fitting and
operation of different types of fastening, and
catalogues illustrating them. An important
section of the museum draws attention to the
social implications of security devices.

Verden

Museum of the Horse

*Deutsches Pferdemuseum, Andreasstraße 17,
D-2810 Verden (Aller), Niedersachsen*
☎ *04231 3901*
Tues–Sun 9–4
C ⓘ ↩

Verden has long been famous as a horse-
breeding centre and from the late 19th century
onwards cavalry units stationed in the district
used to compete in the prestigious riding
competitions which took place there. During
the 1930s these events became major occasions,
with motor-racing and air-shows added to the
attractions. A Museum of the Horse was
established in 1927, but had to be closed during
the Second World War, when the competitions
were also suspended.
The museum was reopened in 1965. It has
collections and displays illustrating the
development of the horse and its rôle in the

**Painted wooden relief of a baker, Austrian,
1700–50. German Bread Museum, Ulm.**

Museum of the Horse, Verden.

history of mankind. There are separate sections dealing with breeds of horses, the horse in agriculture, racehorses, military horses, hunting, horse-drawn vehicles, harness and horseshoes. The museum also has collections of coins and postage stamps bearing representations of horses.

Verden Museum

Verdener Heimatmuseum, Untere Straße 13, D-2810 Verden (Aller), Niedersachsen
☎ *04231 2169*
Tues, Wed, Fri, Sat 10–1, 3–5; Sun 2–5. Closed public holidays.
C

The museum occupies a half-timbered house, built in 1708. The archaeological sections cover the Stone Age, Bronze Age, Iron Age and Saxon periods, including what is claimed to be the oldest spear in the world, used 100,000 years ago and capable of killing a forest elephant four metres high. There are also collections of 18th- and 19th-century furniture and household equipment, religious images and ornaments, and uniforms of the soldiers who belonged to the Verden garrison in 1803–1985. There are also reproductions of a potter's, clog-maker's, tailor's, spinner's, weaver's, locksmith's, baker's, and cigar-maker's workshops and the complete shop and laboratory of an early-19th-century pharmacy.

Vreden

Hamaland Farmhouse Museum

Hamaland-Museum, Bauernhaus-Museum und KreismuseumBorken, D-4426 Vreden, Nordrhein-Westfalen   ☎ *02564 1036*
Tues–Sun 9–12.30, 2.30–6
C 🛈 🛏

The 16th-century building which houses part of the museum complex was originally an inn, the Inn of the Holy Ghost. A group of 18th-century farm buildings forms an annexe. Extensive rebuilding took place after damage from bombing during the Second World War. The collections illustrate the geology, flora and fauna, archaeology and history of the region and include views and plans of Vreden at different periods, 11th-century coins from the local mint, and sculptural fragments and liturgical items from local churches. There are also exhibits of costumes, furniture, domestic equipment, locally-made pottery and craftsmen's tools, displayed in workshop settings. Other sections are devoted to agricultural implements and horse-drawn vehicles.

Walldürn

Pilgrimage Museum

Heimat- und Wallfahrtsmuseum, Hauptstraße 39, D-6968 Walldürn, Baden-Württemberg
☎ *06282 8672*
May–Sept, Tues, Thurs Sun 2–4
C 🛈 🛏

The stone-built house at the Sign of the Golden Angel, which has been the home of the museum since 1912, dates from 1582. It contains contemporary murals and wall-inscriptions consisting of poems in the old German language. The collections include 17th–19th-century furniture from the region, craftsmen's tools, traditional costumes, pottery, folk art and 18th–19th-century paintings by the local artists, Michael and Sebastian Eckhardt.

During the Middle Ages, Walldürn was the centre of an important pilgrimage, based on the veneration of the Miracle of the Holy Blood, which is reputed to have occurred in 1330. A separate section of the museum contains documents and objects relating to the Miracle and to the pilgrimage.

Wangen im Allgäu

Cheesemaking Museum

Heimatmuseum und Käsereimuseum, Eselberg 1, D-7988 Wangen im Allgäu 1, Baden-Württemberg   ☎ *07522 74240*
Apr–Oct, Tues, Fri 3–6; Wed 10–12, 3–6; Sun 10–12.
C

The museum is in a 1568 mill, which continued to work until 1937. It is concerned with local archaeology and history, with exhibits showing the history of milling, linen-manufacturing, blacksmiths' work and cheesemaking, which has been for a long time a speciality of the area. There are also collections of pewter, faïence, weapons, targets, ironwork and religious and popular art, together with a number of works by the Court painter, Anton von Gegenbaur.

Early coffee-grinder. Verden Museum.

Eichendorff Museum and Archive

Deutsches Eichendorff-Museum und Archiv, Lange Gasse 1, D-7988 Wangen im Allgäu 1, Baden-Württemberg
☎ 07522 3840/74240-2
Apr–Oct, Tues 3–5; Wed, Sun 10–12.
C

The museum commemorates the lyric poet, Joseph Freiherr von Eichendorff (1788–1857). There are exhibits, including original manuscripts, illustrating his life and work, and manuscripts of composers who set Eichendorff's words to music. A separate section contains works of writers and artists from Silesia.

Gustav Freytag Museum and Archive

Gustav Freytag-Museum und Archiv, Lange Gasse 1, D-7988 Wangen im Allgäu, Baden-Württemberg   ☎ 07522 1369
Apr–Oct, Tues 3–5; Wed, Sun 10–12.
C

The poet and novelist, Gustav Freytag (1816–95) was one of the best-known writers in 19th-century Germany. The museum, opened in 1988, is in the same building as the Eichendorff Museum. It contains letters, books, photographs and other material relating to the life and work of Freytag.

Wangerooge

Island Museum in the Old Lighthouse

Inselmuseum Alter Leuchtturm, Zedeliusstraße 3, D-2946 Wangerooge, Niedersachsen
☎ 04469 8964
Mar–Oct, daily 10–12, 3–5. Nov–Feb, Sat 2–4.
C

The lighthouse was in operation from 1855 until 1969. It now serves as a lookout tower and as a museum. The exhibits cover the natural history and life of the Wangerooge district. There are examples of birds, shells, strange things found

on the beach and objects salvaged from the village when it was submerged by the tide in 1854. Other items in the collection include books, maps and photographs relating to the district, navigational equipment and household articles used on the island.

Weilburg

Castle Museum

Museum Schloß Weilburg, D-6290 Weilburg, Hessen   ☎ 06471 2236
Apr–Sept, Tues–Sun 10–4. Oct–Mar, Tues–Sun 10–3 (last admission).
C ♦ ■ ♠

The castle, built in the 16th century and enlarged and modified in the 17th–19th, was the Residence of the Counts of Nassau and Grand Dukes of Luxembourg. It has been excellently preserved and gives a good idea of the lifestyle enjoyed by this aristocratic family. There are handblocked French wallpapers, Baroque and Biedermeier furniture, and collections of portraits, paintings and porcelain.

Mining Museum

Heimat- und Bergbaumuseum, Schloßplatz 1, D-6290 Weilburg, Hessen   ☎ 06471 31459
Apr–Oct, Tues–Sun 10–12, 2–5. Nov–Mar, Mon–Fri 10–12, 2–5.
L ♠

For more than a century, iron-mining was the principal industry in the Weilburg area. In the 1930s 50 pits were working, but all except one are now closed. There is a reproduction of a mine gallery in the museum, and here and elsewhere in the museum visitors can see the processes involved in iron-mining and oil-processing and learn about the lives of the miners and their families.
There are also exhibits of local archaeology, furniture, domestic equipment, handicrafts, weapons, tools, and the pottery of Weilburg and the Westerwald. The transport section includes information about the part played by Weilburg in the development of airships.

Weil der Stadt

Kepler Museum

Kepler-Museum, Keplergasse 2, D-7252 Weil der Stadt, Baden-Württemberg   ☎ 07033 2197
Apr–Oct, Mon–Fri 9–12, 2–4; Sat 10–12; Sun 11–12, 2–5. Nov–Mar, Mon–Fri 9–12, 2–4; Sun 11–12, 2–5.
C

The astronomer, Johannes Kepler, was born in this house in 1571. The museum presents a comprehensive view of the personality, life and achievements of the man who, as Court Astronomer to Rudolf II, first explained and described the movement of the planets, by the laws that bear his name.

Weinsberg

Museum of the Devoted Wives

Weibertreu-Museum, Rathaus, D-7102
Weinsberg, Baden-Württemberg
☎ 07134 8051
Thurs 2–6; Sun 2–5. Other times by appt.
F 🛈 🖼

In 1140 the town of Weinsberg was besieged by
the army of the newly-elected Holy Roman
Emperor, Duke Konrad of Swabia. After his
success, the Emperor announced that he
intended to execute the men, but allow the
women to leave the town unharmed, together
with whatever possessions they could carry on
their shoulders. They chose to carry their
husbands, who in this way escaped.

Much of Weinsberg was destroyed by
American bombing in 1945, but in 1987 a new
museum was opened in the rebuilt town hall. It
contains 16th–20th-century German, French
and Dutch paintings and engravings depicting
the Devoted Wives episode – the subject
attracted artists over a long period – together
with exhibits illustrating the history of
Weinberg, especially during the 16th-century
Peasants' War.

A special section of the museum is devoted to
the life and work of Professor Heinrich
Seufferheld (1866–1940), who was a native of
Weinsberg and celebrated for his etchings.

Wertheim

Glass Museum

Glasmuseum, Mühlenstraße 22, D-6980
Wertheim, Baden-Württemberg
☎ 09342 6866
Apr–Oct, Tues–Sun 10–12, 2–4. Closed
Nov 1–1st day of Advent and from
Jan 7–Mar 31.
C 🛈

Hamaland Farmhouse Museum, Vreden.

The museum, opened in 1976, was created by a
group of enthusiasts and is believed to be the
only privately-run glass museum in the Federal
Republic. It occupies a half-timbered building of
1577, with its original wooden columns and
ceilings. It was fully restored in 1973–6.

The collections illustrate the history of glass
and glass-making techniques from the earliest
times. Special features of the displays include
the history and range of technical and
laboratory glassware, studio glass and the
travelling glassworks of the Spessart region of
Germany during the Middle Ages.

Each year between the first day of Advent and
6 January, there is a special exhibition of old
and new glass Christmas decorations.

Wesselburen

Hebbel Museum

Hebbel-Museum, Österstraße 6, D-2244
Wesselburen, Schleswig-Holstein
☎ 04833 2079
May–Oct, Tues–Fri 10–12, 2–5; Sat, Sun 10–12,
3–5. Nov–Apr, Tues, Thurs 2–5.
C 🛈 🖼

The dramatist, poet, short-story writer and
critic, Christian Friedrich Hebbel (1813–63),
was born at Wesselburen. The museum,
established in 1911, illustrates his life and career
against the background of his times. The
collections include manuscripts and first
editions of his works, documents, portraits and
photographs. The museum occupies a 1737
house, in which Hebbel lived from 1827 until
1835.

Wetzlar

Leitz Collection of Historic Microscopes

Sammlung Historischer Mikroscope der Ernst Leitz
Wetzlar GmbH, Ernst Leitz Straße, D-6330
Wetzlar, Hessen   ☎ 06441 292343
Mon–Fri 8–5. Closed public holidays.
F 🖼

The Leitz works at Wetzlar began to produce
microscopes in 1852 and quickly established
itself as one of the world's leading
manufacturers. The collection, opened to the
public in 1975, shows microscopes and their
associated equipment from 1730 onwards and
pays particular attention to examples which
represent milestones in their development. A
high proportion of its instruments on display
were made by Leitz.

Wiedensahl

Wilhelm Busch Birthplace Museum

Wilhelm-Busch-Gebburtshaus, D-3061 Wiedensahl
Nr. 89 bei Stadhagen, Niedersachsen
☎ 05726 388
Apr–Sept, daily 10–12, 2–5
C

The writer and artist, Wilhelm Busch (1832–1908), was born in this house in Wiedensahl and often returned here to live and write. The museum established in the house in 1968 contains a number of his personal possessions and items of furniture, as well as some of his parents' personal possessions. There are also manuscripts and editions of his works.

Wiesbaden

Wiesbaden Museum

Museum Wiesbaden, Friedrich-Ebert-Allee 2,
    D-6200 Wiesbaden, Hessen
    ☎ 06121 368670
Tues–Sun 10–4; Tues also 5–9.
F

In 1825 Johann Isaak von Gerning made over what he called his 'remunerative collection' of paintings, drawings, watercolours, engravings, coins, jewels, sculpture, vases, glass, insects and rocks to the State of Nassau, in exchange for a large annual rent. This forms the basis of the present museum, which has subsequently been greatly expanded by the addition of material from all the fields which were of interest to von Gerning. The present collections include important Roman discoveries from the region, medieval–Baroque sculpture, Westerwald stoneware, faïence and porcelain, and 16th–20th-century German paintings.

Wietze

Petroleum Museum

Erdölmuseum, Schwarzer Weg 7-9, D-3109
    Wietze, Niedersachsen   ☎ 05146 2888
Apr–Oct, Tues–Sun 10–12, 2–5
C ℹ 🖼 ✎

Prospectors struck oil in Wietze in 1858, the first time this had been achieved in Germany. The open-air museum which has been established on the site reproduces the original derricks, pumping, storage and other equipment and has displays which tell the story of the industry and its technology. Many of the exhibits can be demonstrated.

Wilhelmshaven

Heinrich Gätke Museum

Heinrich-Gätke-Halle, Institut für Vogelforschung
    'Vogelwarte Helgoland', An der Vogelwarte 21,
    D-2940 Wilhelmshaven, Niedersachsen
    ☎ 04421 61800
Tues 8–1; Thurs 1–5
F ✎

The core of the museum's collection is Heinrich Gätke's collection of rare birds found on Heligoland between 1840 and 1898. To this has been added other collections of birds of the North Sea coast. There are also exhibits illustrating and explaining methods of bird protection and the work of the Institute of Ornithological Research.

Museum of the Coast

Küsten-Museum der Stadt Wilhelmshaven, City-
    Haus, Rathausplatz 10, Postfach 1180,
    D-2940 Wilhelmshaven, Niedersachsen
    ☎ 04421 297460
Tues–Fri, Sun 10–1, 3–6; Sat 10–1.
F 🖼

The museum illustrates the principal features of the German North Sea coastal region and describes its geology, archaeology and economic history. Attention is drawn to its important jade industry and there are also sections dealing with shipping and navigation, with special reference to the German Navy.

Wolfenbüttel

Lessing's House

Lessing-Haus, Lessingplatz 1, Postfach 13 64,
    D-3340 Wolfenbüttel, Niedersachsen
    ☎ 05331 8080
Daily 10–5. Closed Good Fri, Dec 24, 26, 31.
C ℹ 🖼 ✎

The critic and dramatist, Gotthold Ephraim Lessing (1729–81), was the first German writer of European stature. He had no early connection with Wolfenbüttel, but spent the last three years of his life in a 1735 building here, which is now known as Lessing's house and used as a memorial museum to him. It contains collections illustrating his life and work, against the background of his time.

Lessing's House forms part of the complex of the Duke August Library (Herzog August Bibliothek), now a major European research institute.

Wolfsburg

Volkswagen Museum

Auto Museum Wolfsburg, Dieselstraße 35,
    D-3180 Wolfsburg 1, Niedersachsen
    ☎ 05374 52071
Daily 10–5. Closed Dec 24–Jan 1.
C ℹ ♿ ✎

The main Volkswagen plant is at Wolfsburg and the museum, established in 1985, has more than 100 cars, illustrating the firm's production from the 1930s onwards. There are also displays showing the technical and commercial library of the Volkswagen Group, together with prototypes which were never seen on the roads, but which were important for research purposes.

Wolfsburg-Fallersleben

Hoffmann von Fallersleben Museum

Hoffmann-von-Fallersleben-Museum, Schloßplatz,
    D-3180 Wolfsburg 12/Fallersleben,
    Niedersachsen   ☎ 05362 52623
Tues, Thurs 9–12, 4–6. Other times by appt.
C ℹ ✎

Volkswagen Museum, Wolfsburg.

The poet and scholar, Heinrich Hoffmann (1798–1874), composer of the *Deutschlandlied* and later known as Hoffman von Fallersleben, was born in the small town of Fallersleben, which now forms part of Wolfsburg. In 1928 a memorial to him was established and in 1974 was transferred to the mid-16th-century half-timbered house where he was born, sometimes referred to as Fallersleben Castle. Part of the building is also used for special exhibitions, concerts and other functions.

The museum contains important collections relating to Hoffmann's life and career, including books, manuscripts and a range of memorabilia.

Worms

Worms Museum

Museum der Stadt Worms, Weckerlingplatz 7, D-6520 Worms, Rheinland-Pfalz
☎ 06241 853336
Tues–Sun 10–12, 2–5. Closed May 1, Dec 24–31.
Ⓒ ▮

The museum is in the Andreasstift, a late Romanesque church dating from 1020. It has extensive archaeological material, especially Roman, Frankish and medieval, including a large collection of Roman glass. There are also collections of 15th–19th-century drinking glasses, furniture, paintings, portraits, drawings, coins and 18th–19th-century clocks. One room is devoted to Martin Luther and his associations with the city, the site in 1521 of the Emperor Charles V's Imperial Diet which ordered the destruction of all Luther's books.

Wuppertal

Engels House Museum

Historisches Zentrum, Engelsstraße 10, D-5600 Wuppertal 2, Nordrhein-Westfalen
☎ 0202 5636498
Tues–Sun 10–1, 3–5
Ⓕ ▮ ⦿

The 19th-century sociologist, Friedrich Engels (1820–95), came from a family of Wuppertal industrialists. Their house, built in 1775, was acquired by the municipality in 1962 and is now known as the Engels House. It contains exhibits illustrating the life and work of Friedrich Engels. It is not, however, the house in which Engels was born. This was 100 metres away and was destroyed by bombing in 1943.

Behind the Engels House, the Museum of Early Industrialisation (Museum für Frühindustrialisierung) has been installed in the former Engels factory building, which later became a warehouse. Its displays tell the story of the industrialisation of the Wupper Valley between the mid 18th and mid 19th centuries, including its technical, economic, social and political aspects.

Würzburg

Würzburg Art Gallery

Städtische Galerie, Hofstraße 3, D-8700 Würzburg, Bayern   ☎ 0931 37375
Tues–Fri 10–5; Sat, Sun 10–1.
Ⓕ ▮

The gallery contains 19th–20th-century paintings, graphics and sculpture by artists living in the Würzburg region, or with local associations, and includes works by Wilhelm Leibl and Max Slevogt as well as sculpture and drawings by Emy Roeder and her contemporaries.

Among other items on display are tapestries and the oldest known clock (1380). A special section is devoted to 20th-century autograph letters from artists.

Zülpich

Zülpich Museum

Heimatmuseum, Mühlenberg 7, D-5352 Zülpich, Nordrhein-Westfalen   ☎ 02252 2770
Mon–Fri 9–12, 2–4.20; Sat 9–12; Sun 10–12. Closed public holidays.
Ⓒ ▮ ⦿

The museum building was originally a priory, dating from 1124. A well-preserved group of Roman baths of *c.* 300 AD was discovered on the site in 1931 and there are also collections of prehistoric and Franconian material and of medieval sculpture.

In the section relating to the modern period, there are displays showing the development of Zülpich since medieval times, Biedermeier furniture and paintings by the local artist, Hubert Saalentin (d. 1910).

GREECE

Athens

Acropolis Museum

Mouseio Akropoleos, Lofos Akropoleos,
GR–117 42 Athina ☎ 01 3236665
Apr 1 – Oct 10, Mon–Fri 8–7; St, Sun 8.30–5.
Oct 11 – Mar 31, Mon–Fri 8–5; Sat, Sun
8.30–5. Closed Jan 1, Mar 25, Easter, May 1,
Dec 25, 26.
🅲 ⓘ

'Acropolis' means the highest point of the city.
In ancient times each of the many Greek city
states had its own acropolis, a fortified hill
which could be used as a place of refuge for the
inhabitants in emergencies. Eventually, the
Acropolis in Athens came to monopolise the
meaning of the word and from being a political
and military centre it became an exclusively cult
site, a sacred hill, with many temples on its
slopes.

The museum on the Acropolis was built in
1865 and restored and refurbished in 1955–9. It
contains mainly sculpture from the Archaic and
Classical periods (6th and 5th centuries BC),
which formed the architectural decorations of
the temples. These include temple pediments,
mostly depicting ancient myths and still painted
in their original colours. There are also slabs
from the frieze of the Parthenon (447 BC) and
metopes and sculptures from its pediment.
Other important exhibits are frieze slabs
depicting Victories from the parapet around the
temple of Athena Niké, dating from 410 BC,
and figures from the frieze of the Erechtheion
(409–405 BC). There are also Hellenistic and
Roman sculptures and vases and terracotta
plaques from the Geometric to the Classical
period.

Benakis Museum

Mouseio Benaki, Koumbari 1, GR–106 74
Athina ☎ 01 3611617
Wed–Mon 8.30–2. Closed Jan 1, 6, Lent Mon,
Mar 25, Good Fri–Easter Mon, May 1, Aug
15, Oct 28, Dec 25, 26.
🅲 ⓘ 🖅

The Benakis Museum was founded in 1930 by
Antonios Benakis (1873–1954), who was born
in Alexandria and lived there until 1926, when
he settled permanently in Greece. He began his
collection while he was in Egypt and continued
to enrich it throughout his life. The present
museum building was at one time the Benakis
family home in Athens. It was enlarged to make
it suitable for a museum.

The collections are wide-ranging within the
general fields of the decorative and applied arts.
They contain ancient Greek art, with a special
emphasis on jewellery, Byzantine and post-
Byzantine icons and ecclesiastical vestments,
woodcarvings, Greek folk art and costumes,

Coptic and Islamic art, textiles and embroidery
from the Far East and Western Europe, and
Chinese porcelain. There is also a section
devoted to the statesman, Eleftherios Venizelos
(1864–1936).

Byzantine Museum

Vyzantino Mouseio, Vassilisis Sophias 22,
GR–106 75 Athina ☎ 01 7211027
Tues–Sun 8.30–3. Closed Jan 1, Mar 25, Easter
Sun, May 1, Dec 25, 26.
🅲 ⓘ

The museum building, constructed in 1840, was
designed as the country home – it was then
outside the Athens conurbation – of the
Duchesse de Plaisance. The Greek architect
provided his client with a simple and elegant
mansion in the Florentine Renaissance style. It
was converted into a museum in the late 1920s
and opened in 1930.

The museum is entirely devoted to the art
which flourished in the extensive areas
constituting the Byzantine Empire from the
foundation of Constantinople in AD 330 until
its fall in 1453, and during the post-Byzantine
period. The collections include icons, frescoes,
mosaics, illuminated manuscripts, sculpture,
pottery, textiles, goldsmiths' work and
jewellery, embroidery, metalwork, glass and
seals.

Centre for Acropolis Studies

Kentro Meleton Akropoleos, Makrigianni 2–4,
GR–117 42 Athina ☎ 01 9239381
Daily 9–2
🅵 ♿

In antiquity, the Makrigiannis area of Athens
was the site of important sanctuaries. The
building now occupied by the centre was built in

Marble horse, 490 BC. Acropolis Museum,
Athens.

Pendant from Patmos, 18th-century. Benakis Museum, Athens.

1836 for use as a military hospital. In 1920 it was taken over by the Gendarmerie and it remained in their possession until 1975. Restoration began in 1985, with the intention of housing copies of the so-called Elgin Marbles here.

On the ground floor, there are plaster casts of almost all the Parthenon sculptures that survive today. On the first floor, an exhibition has been arranged presenting the history of the destruction and erosion of the Acropolis monuments and giving an impression of the restoration work which the State has been undertaking since the first years of Greek independence. There are also models showing the Acropolis and its monuments at every historical period. Outside the building, visitors can see tools and machines which were used in early restoration of the Acropolis monuments.

The Centre for Acropolis Studies will be an annexe of the new Acropolis Museum, which the Ministry of Culture is building in the area.

Goulandris Natural History Museum

Mouseio Goulandri Physikis Istorias, Levidou 13, Kifissia, GR–145 62 Athina   ☎ *01 8015870*
Tues–Sun 9–2. Closed Jan 1, Mar 25, Good Fri am, Easter Sun, Dec 25.
Ⓒ ▌ ➽

This large museum is devoted to the study of the Greek natural environment. It is the only museum of its kind in Greece, and although it is a private foundation, it functions effectively as the State Museum of Natural History. It presents the full range of plant and animal life, past and present, in Greece, with sections devoted to minerals, rocks, palaeontology, insects, birds, reptiles, fish, crustaceans and molluscs. It has a large library, herbaria and documentation centre and a carefully planned education programme for children. It is also responsible for important nature conservation and environmental projects throughout Greece.

Kerameikos Museum

Mouseio Keramikou, Ermou 38, GR–105 63 Athina   ☎ *01 3463552*
Tues–Sun 8.30–3
Ⓒ ▌

The exhibits in the museum, opened just before the Second World War, consist mostly of objects discovered during the excavations carried out by the German Archaeological Institute in the Kerameikos cemetery. They include Archaic-Classical grave sculptures, Sub-Mycenaean and Roman pottery and bronzes.

Museum of the Athenian Agora

Mouseio Archaias Agoras – Stoa Attalou II, Adrianou 24, GR–105 50 Athina   ☎ *01 3210185*
Tues–Sun 8.30–3
Ⓒ ▌

In Athens, as in other city-states of ancient Greece, the Agora was the focal point of community life. It was the seat of the administration and judiciary, the chief place for marketing and business, in early days the scene of drama competitions and athletic displays and always a favourite place for meeting and talking.

During the 19th and 20th centuries, extensive excavations have taken place on the site of the Agora in Athens and in 1953–6 a museum for the finds was built on the ruins of the Stoa of Attalos II (159–138 BC), one of the most used buildings around the Agora. The plan of the Stoa was followed exactly, and as much of the old material as possible was used in the construction of the new building. The exhibits in the museum range from the Neolithic right through to the Byzantine period.

Museum of the City of Athens

Mouseio tis Poleos ton Athinon, Paparrigopoulou 7, GR–105 61 Athina   ☎ *01 3231397*
July–Aug, Mon, Wed, Fri 9–1.30. Other times by appt.
Ⓒ ▌

The museum was opened in 1980 in the Stamatios Dekozis-Vouros house, also known as the Old Palace, since it served as a provisional palace for King Otto during the years 1836–43, after the declaration of independence from Turkey. It contains furniture, costumes, domestic equipment, paintings, watercolours and engravings, chosen and arranged to give as complete a picture as possible of the history of the city of Athens.

Museum of Cycladic Art

Mouseio Kykladikis ke Archeas Ellinikis Technis, Neophytou Douka 4, GR–106 74 Athina   ☎ *01 7228321*
Mon, Wed, Thurs, Fri 10–4; Sat 10–3. Closed Jan 1, 6, Epiphany, Mar 25, 1st Mon of Lent, Good Fri, Easter Sun, Easter Mon, May 1, Trinity Sun, Aug 15, Oct 28, Dec 25, 26.
Ⓒ ▌ ➽

During the 3rd millennium BC, the Early Bronze Age, the small islands of the central Aegean, the Cyclades, had a flourishing culture, which produced art objects, mostly in marble, of a distinct type and remarkable quality. A notable collection of these, together with a subsidiary collection of pots and animal and human figures, made of clay and dating from the 2nd millennium, was formed by the late N. P. Goulandris and the two collections are now housed in a modern marble building designed for the purpose and opened in 1986. They are complemented by a section devoted to works of Greek minor art and sculpture, made of clay, metal, glass and marble and dating from the 11th century BC to the 5th century AD. The museum's collections of early Greek art are among the most important in the world.

National Archaeological Museum

Ethniko Archeologiko Mouseio, Tositsa 1, GR–106 82 Athina ☎ *01 8217717*
Apr–Oct, Mon 12.30–7; Tues–Fri 8–7; Sat, Sun and public holidays 8.30–3. Nov–Mar, Mon 11–5, Tues–Fri 8–5; Sat, Sun and public holidays 8.30–3. Closed Jan 1, Mar 25, Easter Sun, May 1, Dec 25, 26.
© ♿ ▪

The National Archaeological Museum differs from apparently similar institutions in other countries in that the objects in its collections were all discovered within the Greek world. None of them represents foreign cultures. Building suitable premises began in 1866 and extensions were opened in 1939 and 1964. During the Second World War, many of the most precious objects were buried in sand in order to protect them.

The collections in this very large museum are, in general, arranged according to themes and occupy 60 rooms, covering the whole period of Greek culture, from the Neolithic to the Byzantine period. Among so much wonderful material, one can do no more than make an arbitrary selection of exhibits, among which might be the Cycladic figures, the Mycenean goldsmiths' work and frescoes, the early Classical stelae, the kraters and vases of various periods, and the bronzes from the Acropolis.

Celebration in the ruins of the Temple of Jupiter, Athens, after the War of Independence. National Historical Museum, Athens.

National Gallery and Alexandros Soutzos Museum

Ethniki Pinakothiki ke Mouseio Alexandrou Soutzou, Vassileos Konstantinou 50, GR–116 34 Athina ☎ *01 7235937*
Tues–Sat 9–3; Sun 10–2.
© ♿ ▪ ♨

The gallery's collections include 17th–20th century Greek paintings, sculpture and prints and 14th–20th century European paintings, with works by, among others, El Greco, Caravaggio, Jordaens, Poussin, Tiepolo, Delacroix and Picasso. There are also collections of engravings, drawings and icons.

National Historical Museum

Ethniko Istoriko Mouseio, Megaro Paleas Voulis, Odos Stadiou, GR–105 61 Athina ☎ *01 3237617*
Tues–Fri 9–2; Sat, Sun 9–1. Closed month of August.
© ♿

The Historical and Ethnological Society of Greece was founded in 1882, with the aim of collecting and safeguarding the nation's historical records, documents and historical relics and setting up a museum of modern Greek history. Since 1960 the material collected by the Society has been housed in the building which was the seat of the Greek Parliament from 1858 until 1934. The displays illustrate the development of Greece from the fall of Constantinople in 1453 to the present day.

The exhibits include paintings, portraits, uniforms, weapons and memorabilia of leading personalities, including Lord Byron and other philhellenes, the first Governor of Greece, Ioannis Capodistrias, and King Otto and King George I. There are also documents, seals and personal possessions of people prominent in the struggle for independence, from the 1821 Revolution to the First World War and military relics from the periods of the Byzantine Empire and the Turkish occupation.

The ethnological collections, which have always been of great importance to the Society, include costumes, embroideries, woodcarvings, pottery, metalwork and popular art.

Numismatic Museum

Nomismatiko Mouseio, Tositsa 1, GR–106 82 Athina ☎ *01 8217769*
Summer: Tues–Sun 7.30–1.15. Winter: Tues–Sun 8.30–3. Closed Jan 1, Good Fri, Easter Sun and Mon, Dec 25.
© ♿

Since 1946, the museum has been housed on the first floor of the National Archaeological Museum. Its collections include Ancient Greek, Roman, Byzantine, and medieval and modern Greek coins. There are also displays of tokens and modern medals, Byzantine lead seals, Ancient Greek and Byzantine weights and gems.

Among the particularly important exhibits are the prehistoric copper ingots, the iron spits (*oboloi*) from the Argive Heraeon find and the collection of Ptolemaic tetradrachms.

Paul and Alexandra Kanellopoulos Museum

Mouseio Pavlou ke Alexandras Kanellopoulou,
Panos & Theorias 14, GR–105 55 Athina
☎ 01 3212313
Tues–Sun 9–3
C ▮

The museum, opened in 1976, occupies a late-
19th-century mansion, which has ceilings
painted in the Pompeian manner in the 2nd-
floor rooms. The important collections include
ancient Greek, Byzantine and later jewellery,
Byzantine and post-Byzantine icons, coins, and
ancient Greek vases and terracotta figurines.

Ayios Nikolaos (Crete)

Archaeological Museum

Archeologiko Mouseio, Konstantinou Palaiologou
68–74, GR–721 00 Ayios Nikolaos, Kriti
☎ 0841 24943
Tues–Sun 8.30–3. Closed Jan 1, Mar 25, Easter
Sun, May 1, Dec 25, 26.
C ▮

The museum contains archaeological material
from sites in the area. This includes Archaic,
Classical, Geometric, Hellenistic and Roman
vases and other pottery, figurines, and coins.

It is second only to Heraklion for its
collection of Minoan treasures.

Chania (Crete)

Museum of Crete

Istoriko Archio Kritis, Sfakianaki 20, GR–731 34
Chania, Kriti   ☎ 0821 22606
Mon–Fri 9–1. Closed public holidays.
F ⚓

The museum contains exhibits relating to the
history and traditions of Crete. The historical
materials includes relics of the Cretan
revolutions, weapons, flags, coats of arms, coins
and seals, and in the ethnographical section
there are textiles, embroidery, furniture,
handicrafts and items of domestic equipment.

A room is dedicated to Eleftherios Venizelos
(1864–1936), the great Cretan politician and
Prime Minister of Greece.

Corinth

Archaeological Museum

Archeologiko Mouseio, GR–165 00 Korinthos
☎ 0741 31207
Summer: Mon–Sat 8–7; Sun 8–6. Winter: Mon–
Sat 9–3; Sun 10–2. Times may vary. Closed
Jan 1, Mar 25, Easter Sun, Dec 25.
C ⚲ ⚓

The excavations of Corinth have been almost
entirely the responsibility of the American
School of Classical Studies at Corinth. The
museum, opened in 1931, had an American
benefactor and an American architect. The
exhibits come from the site of the ancient city of

Mosaic panel. Delos Museum.

Corinth, with prehistoric material from
Korakou and Zygouies. They show the rise of
Corinth from a small settlement to an important
city state and include Neolithic pottery.
Geometric and Corinthian vases, figurines,
Classical Hellenistic and Roman pottery, lamps,
gold jewellery and household articles, together
with early Christian and Byzantine sculpture
and Byzantine pottery.

Delos

Delos Museum

Mouseio Dilou, GR–846 00 Mykonos
☎ 0279 22259
Tues–Sun 8.30–3. Closed public holidays.
C ⚲ ▬

In Greek mythology, Delos was the birthplace of
Apollo, the son of Leto by Zeus. This made the
sanctuary of Apollo here one of the most
respected and revered in the Greek world, a
position it retained throughout antiquity. The
boats which brought pilgrims to the sanctuary
also carried merchandise, so that the
development of Delos as a commercial port was
assured.

The museum, opened in 1910, is situated
among the extensive ruins of the ancient city
and contains archaeological material from the
excavations carried out here during the 19th
and 20th centuries. This includes Archaic,
Classical, Hellenistic and Roman sculptures,
architectural fragments and pottery, terracotta
and bronze statuettes and figurines of various
periods, ivory reliefs, gold and bronze jewellery,
and household utensils. There are also remains
of frescoes of the 2nd–1st century BC.

Delphi

Delphi Museum

Mouseio Delphon, GR–330 54 Delphi
☎ 0265 82313
Mon 11–5; Tue–Fri 8–5; Sat, Sun 8.30–3. Times
may vary during the summer season. Closed Jan
1, Mar 25, Easter Sun, May 1, Dec 25, 26.
C ▮ ▬

Delphi was the spiritual and religious centre of Hellenism in antiquity, the focal point of the worship of Apollo, a cult common to all the Greek people. Settlement here dates back to c. 5000 BC. The worship of Apollo probably began at Delphi c. 800 BC. The temple was subsequently rebuilt on a grander scale. It was partially destroyed by fire in 83 BC, but rites were apparently still being performed in the sanctuary as late as the 3rd century AD.

The French Archaeological School in Athens excavated the site between 1892 and 1903, when the first part of the museum was built to display the finds. It was extended and brought up-to-date in 1936–9 and further changes were made in the post-war period. The museum contains many of the outstanding examples of Greek sculpture, including the late Archaic sculptures from the Sicyonian, Siphnian and Athenian treasures and, from the Temple of Apollo, the Naxian Sphinx and the Bronze Charioteer. There are also Classical, Hellenistic and Roman sculptures and inscriptions, one with musical notation.

The small objects include pottery, statuettes, bronze weapons, tools and votive tripods. There is also an early Christian mosaic floor.

Eleusis

Archaeological Museum

Archeologiko Mouseio, GR 192 00 Elefsis
    ☎ 0554 6019
Mon 11–5; Tues–Fri 8–5; Sat, Sun, public
    holidays 8.30–3. Closed Jan 1, Mar 25, Good
    Fri am, Easter Sun, Dec 25.
Ⓒ ▮

Eleusis was one of the most important shrines of ancient Greece. It was devoted to the cult of Demeter, the Goddess of Fertility, which centred on the Eleusinian Mysteries. The museum is within the former sanctuary and contains archaeological material from the Archaic, Classical, Hellenistic and Roman periods, including vases, weapons, bronze and gold jewellery, vases and votive offerings and marble funeral monuments. Many of the architectural fragments and statues to be seen here are copies, the originals being in the National Archaeological Museum in Athens.

Epidauros

Archaeological Museum

Archeologiko Mouseio, GR–210 52 Epidavros
    ☎ Epidavros 22009
Mon 11–5; Tues–Fri 8–5; Sat, Sun, public
    holidays 8.30–3. Closed Jan 1, Mar 25, Good
    Fri am, Easter Sun, Dec 25.
Ⓒ ▮

For 1000 years, from the 6th century BC onwards, Epidauros functioned as a sanctuary dedicated to Asklepios, the god of healing. The theatre, the most famous and the best preserved in Greece, played a part in the cures effected here. Watching a performance of a tragedy or a comedy was considered therapeutic, elevating the spirit and purging it of evil passions. Sophocles was a priest at Epidauros. The collection of stone plaques in the museum, which is between the sanctuary and the theatre, list some of the more remarkable cures effected by Asklepios. There are models reconstructing buildings in the sanctuary, and statuettes, bronze articles and surgical instruments, mainly of the Roman period.

Gastouri (Corfu)

Achilleon Museum

Mouseion Achilleion, GR–491 00 Gastouri,
    Kerkyra   ☎ 0661 56210
Mar–Oct, daily 8–7. Nov–Feb, daily 8 6.
Ⓒ ▮ ▮

The museum is housed in the Achilleon Palace, built between 1889 and 1891 for the Empress Elizabeth of Austria. After her assassination in Geneva in 1898, the palace was sold to the German Emperor, Wilhelm II, who had the habit of visiting Corfu (Kerkyra) every March and drove round the island in one of the first cars to be seen there. At the end of the First World War, the palace became the property of the Greek State. During the Second World War, it was occupied by Italian and German troops and suffered a good deal of damage and looting. Between 1962 and 1982 the upper floors were used as a casino by a German company, which restored and refurbished the building, while continuing to run a museum on the ground floor. Once more state-controlled, the building is still divided in the same way.

The museum contains memorabilia of the Empress and the Kaiser, including furniture, paintings and photographs. There are portraits of the Empress Elizabeth by Winterhalter and the saddle-throne from which Wilhelm II dictated despatches.

Relief decorated pillar. Delphi Museum.

Gautsa (Corfu)

Archaeological Museum

*Archeologiko Mouseio, Vraila 5, GR–491 00
    Gautsa, Kerkyra*   ☎ *0661 38313
Tues–Sat 8.30–2. Closed Jan 1, Mar 25, Good Fri
    am, Easter Sun, Dec 25.*

C

Corfu, locally Kerkyra, has the distinction of
being one of the most important tourist
destinations in Greece. The contents of the
museum consist mainly of archaeological
material – terracottas, architectural fragments,
vases, statuettes, bronzes and coins – from the
site of the ancient city, now occupied by the
airport. Among the exhibits are two
exceptionally interesting pediments from the
6th-century BC Temple of Artemis, one
showing a bearded Dionysos and a young boy
reclining at a feast and the other a Gorgon.

Heraklion (Crete)

Archaeological Museum

*Archeologiko Mouseio, Odos Xanthoudidou,
    GR–712 02 Iraklion, Kriti*   ☎ *081 226092
Mar 17 – Oct 15, Tues–Fri 8–7; Sat, Sun 8.30–3.
    Oct 16 – Mar 16, Tues–Fri 8–5; Sat, Sun
    8.30–3.*

C ✐ ☕

The first museum was built in 1904–12. In 1937
work began on the present earthquake-resistant
building. During the Second World War the
museum suffered considerable damage, but the
collection survived, thanks to the precautions
taken by the authorities. The collections
illustrate the development of Minoan
civilisation between 2500 and 1400 BC, as
shown by finds from excavations at the palaces
and villas of Knossos, Phaistos, Malia, Tylissos
and Kato Zakro, and at the tombs and centres of
worship of prehistoric Crete. The exhibits
include tablets and fragments bearing the
Mycenean A and Mycenean B scripts, coins,
and Archaic, Classical, Hellenistic and Roman
sculpture, pottery and bronzes.

Museum of Crete

*Istoriko Mouseio Kritis, Megaro A. ke L.
    Kalokerinou, Odos Kalokerinou, GR–712 02
    Iraklion, Kriti*   ☎ *081 283219
Mar 15 – Nov 15, Mon–Sat 9–5. Nov 16 – Mar
    14, Mon–Sat 9–3. Closed public holidays.*

C ✐ ⚓

The museum, established in 1953 in the former
mansion of A. and L. Kalokerinos, tells the
story of Crete from the early Christian period to
the present day. There are Byzantine, Venetian
and Turkish sculptures and inscriptions, 13th–
16th-century frescoes, 15th–18th-century
Cretan icons, ecclesiastical vestments, liturgical
items and religious ornaments. The
ethnographical collections include costumes,
textiles, embroideries, lace, jewellery and
musical instruments.

**Minoan pottery, Archaeological Museum,
Heraklion.**

The historical section contains mementoes
of the 18th-century Cretan insurrections and of
the Cretan state which lasted from 1898 to
1913. Among the items are banners, weapons
and portraits of the insurgents. A section of the
museum is devoted to the Cretan novelist and
poet, Nikos Kazantzakis (1883–1957), with his
desk and library, together with personal
possessions and manuscripts of his works.

Ioannina

Archaeological Museum

*Archeologiko Mouseio, Odos Averoff, GR–445 00
    Ioannina, Ipiros*   ☎ *25490/33313
Tues–Sun 8.30–3. Closed Jan 1, Mar 25, Good
    Fri am, Easter Sun, Dec 25.*

C ▮

Ioannina was the 19th-century capital of
Southern Albania, celebrated during the early
part of the century for the ruler installed by the
Turks, the ruthless tyrant, Ali Pasha, whose
barbarous cruelties were remarked on by Lord
Byron. The museum occupies a modern building
and has texts in both Greek and English. Its
collections include archaeological material from
Palaeolithic–Roman sites, early Christian and
Byzantine sculpture, icons, metalwork and
silverware. There is also an art gallery
containing 19th–20th century Greek paintings
and 20th-century sculpture.

Kavala

Archaeological Museum

*Archeologiko Mouseio, Erythrou Stavrou 17,
    GR–651 10 Kavala*   ☎ *01 5546019
Tues–Sun 8.30–3*

C

The museum contains Neolithic and Bronze
Age pottery and figurines, architectural
fragments from the Parthenon at Neapolis (5th
century BC) and Classical, Hellenistic and
Roman sculpture and pottery, together with
statuettes from the Archaic to the Roman
periods, gilded and painted terracotta
ornaments, gold jewellery, coins and Hellenistic
and Roman vases and bronze utensils. A feature
of the exhibitions is part of a 3rd-century BC
tomb from Amphipolis.

Messolonghi

House of Kostis Palamas

*Ikia Ethnikou Piiti Kosti Palama, Triantafillou
Spondi 10, GR–302 00 Messolonghi*
*Mon–Fri 9–1, Sat, Sun 10–1. Closed Jan 1,
Easter, Dec 25.*
F 🛈 ♿

Kostis Palamas (1859–1943) was a scholar,
national poet and ardent patriot. The museum,
established in 1988, contains some of his
personal belongings and collections illustrating
his life and work, together with material relating
to other writers who were born or lived in
Messolonghi.

Museum of History and Art

*Mouseio Storias kai Tèchnes, Markou Botsari,
GR–302 00 Messolonghi* ☎ 0631 22134
*Daily 9–1.30, 4–6 (6–8 during summer months).
Closed Jan 1, Easter, Dec 25.*
F ♿

In 1824 Lord Byron arrived in Messolonghi to
give help to the insurgent Greeks there. He
formed the Byron Brigade and gave considerable
sums of money to support the struggle against
the Turks, but died of fever before he could
become involved in any serious action.
Memorial services for him were held all over
Greece, and the museum at Messolonghi has a
section devoted to him and to his life in Greece,
including a number of his personal possessions
and the original manuscript of his declaration as
a citizen of Messolonghi.

The museum's other collections include
paintings, maps and engravings illustrating the
history of the town.

Miliès

Miliès Museum

Topiko Mouseio, GR–370 10 Miliès
☎ 0423 86204
*June 15 – Sept 15, Tues–Sun 10–1, 5–7. Open at
these times at weekends throughout year, on all
public holidays and for 15 days at Easter and
Christmas. Other times by appt.*
C ✎ ♿

The village of Miliès, one of the most important
on Mount Pelion, was burnt by German troops
in 1943 and then, rebuilt, seriously damaged by
earthquakes in 1955. As a result of these two
disasters, the population dropped from 3,500 to
850. The museum, opened in 1987, was created
in order to help the village people of all ages to
be proud of their past and to put Miliès, with its
rich heritage and wide range of traditional
crafts, back on the tourist map. Close and
enthusiastic co-operation has been achieved
with the village people and the museum is now
installed on the ground floor of the new
municipal building, which is in the traditional
local style. The exhibits illustrate the traditional
life of the district and include costumes,
handicrafts, domestic equipment and
craftsmen's tools.

Mykonos

Museum of Rural Life

Agrotiko Mouseio, GR–846 00 Mykonos
☎ 0289 22591
June–Sept, daily 4–sunset
F

This open-air museum, which is a branch of the
Mykonos Folklore Museum, was established in
1987 in order to illustrate and demonstrate the
development of agricultural products during the
pre-industrial period. It is constructed around an
existing windmill and miller's house and
includes a wine-press, threshing-floor and
dovecote. In the miller's house there is an
exhibition of old farming tools and manually-
operated machines.

Folklore Museum

Laographiko Mouseio, GR–846 00 Mykonos
☎ 0289 22591
Apr–Oct, daily 5.30–8.30
F 🛈

During the period of Venetian rule, the two-
storeyed building now occupied by the museum
formed part of the walls of Mykonos Castle. The
displays illustrate the history and ethnography of
Mykonos and especially its maritime
importance. They include hand-made textiles,
costumes, embroidery, lamps and folk sculpture.
There are reconstructions of a 19th-century
bedroom and kitchen.

The Kyriazopoulos collection of Greek
pictorial commemoratives forms an important
part of the museum. It consists of dinner plates,
dishes, lamps and other domestic items bearing
portraits of members of the Greek Royal Family,
classical motifs, historical events or political
figures. The collection is believed to be the most
complete of its kind.

'Lena's House', in the Tria Pighadia area of
Mykonos, is a department of the museum. In
the 19th century it was the home of a sea-
captain and it has been preserved together with
its original furnishings.

**Windmill with twelve sails. Museum of Rural
Life, Mykonos.**

Papantonios Museum of Folklore, Nafplion.

Nafplion

Papantonios Museum of Folklore

Peloponnisiako Laographiko Idryma V.
Papantoniou, Vassileos Alexandrou 1,
GR–211 00 Nafplion ☎ *0752 2837927*
Wed–Mon 9–2.30. Closed month of February and
also Jan 1, 6, May 1, Dec 25.
C ▮ ⬤

The Museum, winner of the European Museum
of the Year Award in 1981, was established in
1974 in a restored traditional courtyard house. It
contains costumes and textiles from all regions
of Greece together with exhibits illustrating the
production and processing of natural fibres in
Greece by the traditional methods and their use
in the manufacture of costumes and household
textiles during the period 1835–1945.

The displays include a wide range of the
tools and equipment used in spinning, weaving,
knitting, embroidery, dyeing, fabric printing,
lacemaking and dressmaking.

Olympia

Museum of Ancient Olympia

Mouseio Archeas Olympias, GR–270 65 Archea
Olympia ☎ *0624 22529*
Apr–Oct 14, Tue–Sun 8–5. Oct 15–Mar, Tues–
Sun 11–5. Closed Jan 1, Mar 25, Good Fri,
Easter Mon, May 1, Dec 25, 26.
C ▮ ⬤ ⌂

Olympia was the most ancient and most famous
sanctuary in Greece. The area of the sanctuary
and its surroundings was inhabited continuously
from 2800 to 1100 BC, after which it was
gradually transformed into a centre for religious
cults and for the Games.

The first museum was erected in 1888. It was
severely damaged in the 1954 earthquake and a
new museum was opened in 1972. Its rich
collections make it one of the most important in
Greece. Its sculptural remains, especially the
statues from the Temple of Zeus, are of
exceptional quality. There are also Mycenean
objects, Geometric and Archaic bronzes, Pre-
Classical terracottas, bronze votive offerings,
weapons and armour.

The most famous exhibit in the museum is
the marble statue of Hermes, by Praxilites,
carved c. 330 BC. It was discovered by German
archaeologists in 1877.

Piraeus

Maritime Museum of Greece

Naftiko Mouseio tis Ellados, Akti Themistokleous,
GR–185 37 Pireas ☎ *01 4516264*
Tues–Sat 9–1. Closed public holidays and month of
August.
C ▮ ⌂

Opened in 1949 in buildings designed for the
purpose, the museum collects, preserves and
displays material which illustrates the history of
Greek seafaring since ancient times. It is
concerned with all forms of shipping, including
the navy, the merchant marine and fishing. The
13,000 exhibits cover a period of 5,000 years
and include models, charts, flags, portraits,
uniforms, memorabilia of naval personalities,
and paintings and engravings of ships and naval
scenes.

Among the many historic relics are the
periscope of the submarine *Delfino*, the first
submarine in the world to launch torpedoes, a
section of the poop of the royal launch used by
King Otto of Greece, remains of ships sunk at
the Battle of Navarino, and a large collection of
ships' figureheads.

Piskopiano (Crete)

Museum of Rural Life

*Agrotiko Mouseio, Piskopiano, GR–712 04
Hersonisos, Kriti*
Daily 11–1, 4–8
C

The museum, opened in 1988, contains
material relating to the Cretan farmers' way of
life before the changes brought about by modern
technology. Visitors can see an olive mill,
smithy, workshops of a carpenter and a cooper,
and a still for making the Cretan drink, raki.
The exhibits are shown together with their tools
and equipment.

Rhodes

Archaeological Museum

Archeologiko Mouseio Rodou, GR–851 00 Rodos
    ☎ *0241 27657*
*Apr–Oct, Tues–Sun 8–7. Nov–Mar, Tues–Sun
    8.30–3.*
C ✏

The most important archaeological material
found in Rhodes and other islands of the
Dodecanese is displayed in the impressive
building which was formerly the Grand Hospital
of the Knights of St John of Rhodes, built in
1440–1489. During the Italian occupation of
the Dodecanese, 1919–47, the building was
restored and converted to a museum.

It contains coats of arms and tombstones of
the knights, and weapons and other objects
from the medieval period. The collections also
include Neolithic pottery and tools, ceramics of
the Geometric to the late Classical periods,
votive and sepulchral altars, coins and an early

**The Venus of Rhodes, 1st century BC.
Archaeological Museum, Rhodes.**

Christian mosaic floor. The museum has a
particularly fine collection of sculpted
gravestones, including the remarkable 5th-
century BC 'Timarista and Krito'. There are also
some outstanding examples of Archaic Rhodian
ware.

Salonica (Thessaloniki)

Archaeological Museum

*Archeologiko Mouseio, Plateia HAN, GR–546 21
    Thessaloniki* ☎ *031 831037*
*Mon 11–5; Tues–Fri 8–5; Sat, Sun and public
    holidays 8–3.*
C 🗼 🚗

The museum, opened in 1961, contains
archaeological material from Central
Macedonia, ranging in date from the prehistoric
to the late Roman period. The collections
include Neolithic – Iron Age pottery, weapons
and jewellery, Classical, Hellenistic and Roman
sculpture, architectural fragments, vases,
bronzes and statuettes. There are also bronze
kraters and gold jewellery from Derveni, Roman
mosaic floors and glass utensils, mosaics from
the cathedral of Serres, and Byzantine jewellery.
Particularly rich material has come from the
excavations at the ancient city of Thessaloniki
and the Archaic cemetery at Sindos. The
central exhibits focus on the finds from the tomb
of Philip II of Macedon at Vergina.

Macedonian Folk Art Museum

*Mouseio Ethnologiko Laografiko Makedonias,
    Vassi lissis Olgas 68, GR–546 42 Thessaloniki*
    ☎ *031 830591*
*Daily 9.30–2. Closed Jan 1, Mar 25, Good Fri
    am, Easter Sun, Dec 25.*
C 🗼

The museum was established in 1970 as a
successor to the Folk Art Museum of Northern
Greece. It occupies a scheduled building,
known as Old Government House. Its large
collections illustrate the material culture of
Northern Greece and include folk costumes,
embroidery, weaving, woodcarvings, metalwork
and silver. There are also sections devoted to
craftsmen's tools, agricultural implements, and
domestic equipment.

Skyros

Faltaits Historical Museum

*Istoriko ke Laographiko Mouseio Faltaits,
    GR–340 07 Skyros* ☎ *0222 91232*
*Apr 1– Oct 15, daily 10–1, 5.30–8. Oct 16 –
    Mar 30, by appt.*
F 🗼 🖼 🚗

The museum building was erected in the late
19th century as the Faltaits family mansion, on
the site of a former temple of Astarte. The house
was opened as a museum in 1964. One room has
been reconstructed as a traditional Skyros
home, as it would have been in the 16th
century. The collections elsewhere in the

Reconstruction of traditional 16th-century Skyros home. Faltaits Historical Museum, Skyros.

museum illustrate the history, customs and traditions of Skyros, with costumes, domestic equipment, ceramics, embroideries and woodcarvings.

Old plates and vases from across the world are displayed around the walls. They are here as a result of Skyros having been a notorious centre of piracy.

Thebes

Archaeological Museum

Archeologiko Mouseio Thivon, Threpsiadi 1,
    GR–322 00 Thiva   ☎ 0262 23559
Mon 11–5; Tues–Fri 8–5; Sat, Sun, public
    holidays 8.30–3. Closed Jan 1, Mar 25, Good
    Fri am, Easter Sun, Dec 25.
C 🛇

There are few visible remains of the city which played such an important part in Greek mythology and early history, and where Oedipus and his family lived out their tragedy of incest and patricide. The museum, however, preserves a wide range of archaeological material from ancient Thebes, including huge stone lions which surmounted the tombs of prominent citizens, terracotta figurines performing everyday tasks, and an early Christian mosaic calendar, in which each month is represented by a figure carrying out labour appropriate to the time of year.

The most important feature of the museum, however, is its collection of painted Mycenean sarcophagi, known as larnaxes. These clay boxes, dating from the 13th–14th century BC come from burial chambers at Tanagra, east of Thebes. They are less than a metre long and bodies were folded up in order to fit into them. They are painted with impressionistic scenes of mourning and sacrifice and of games organised in honour of the dead.

Tripolis

Archaeological Museum

Archeologiko Mouseio, Evangelistrias 8,
    GR–221 00 Tripolis   ☎ 071 232397
Summer: Tues–Sun 7–2.30. Winter: Tues–Sun
    7.30–3.
F

The museum opened in 1986 in a late-19th-century building. Its collections consist of material dating from 3000 BC onwards, discovered during the 19th- and 20th-century excavations in the area. The Mycenean finds are particularly interesting and there are also sections devoted to the prehistoric periods, to sculpture and pottery, to coins and to lamps.

The excavated ruins of the theatre of ancient Tripolis and of houses and temples have been left exposed and allow the plan of the town to be easily followed.

Volos

Archaeological Museum

Archeologiko Mouseio, Odos Athanassaki,
    GR–380 01 Volos   ☎ 0421 25285
Tues–Sun 8.30–3
C 🛇

The museum was established in 1909, under the patronage of Alexios Athanassakis, to house the great collection of painted gravestones of the Hellenistic period from the cemetery of the ancient city of Demetriàs, together with Neolithic and later prehistoric material discovered during excavations elsewhere in Thessaly. There are also displays of Archaic, Classical, Hellenistic and Roman sculpture, Geometric and Classical pottery, glass vases and gold jewellery and weapons from graves of the Geometric and Classical periods.

IRELAND

Bruree

De Valera Cottage

Knockmore, Bruree, Co. Limerick
   On request to Mrs Nora O'Gorman, who lives
   100 metres north of the cottage
🅕 ♿

In 1885 the two-year-old Éamon de Valera, the future President of Ireland, was brought here from the United States to be placed in the care of his maternal grandmother. The cottage in which he was reared, 20 miles south of Limerick, had just been completed by the Kilmallock Board of Guardians. A neat, well-built stone house, it contains a kitchen-cum-living room and two small bedrooms downstairs, and another bedroom upstairs in the loft. Now a National Monument, it has been restored to its original appearance, and furnished with period items or, in some instances, replicas of originals.

De Valera Museum

Bruree, Co. Limerick
Sun, Thurs 2.30–5.30. Other times by appt with
   Mainchín Seoighe, Curator, Tankardstown,
   Kilmallock   ☎ Kilmallock 97
🅒 ♿ ♿

Bruree, one mile east of the main Cork to Limerick road, was the home of Éamon de Valera, later President of Ireland. He attended school there in the building which is now the museum. It contains the largest collection of de Valera memorabilia on display in Ireland. The exhibits include school books; a lock of his hair cut by his grandmother when he was a small boy; letters; photographs; a jacket, hat and walking stick; prayer books; rosaries; and his 1916 Rising and Irish War of Independence service medals.

The museum also has some important archaeological material, including stone and bronze axes, and a good collection of items illustrating rural life in the area, especially farm implements, craftsmen's tools and domestic equipment.

Cork

Cork Public Museum

Fitzgerald Park, Mardyke, Cork ☎ 021 290679
Mon–Fri 11–1, 2.15–5 (until 6 June–Aug); Sun
   3–5. Closed public holidays and Bank Holiday
   weekends. Admission charge Sun.
🅕 ♿ ♿ ♿

Housed in a Georgian mansion, the museum deals mainly with the history of the city of Cork from earliest times. The archaeology section includes material from the Stone Age to the early Christian period. There are also items found during the excavation of medieval sites in the city.

The historical section illustrates national political developments from the 18th to the 20th century. Several rooms are devoted to the municipal history of Cork, with exhibits of banners, guildhall furniture, glass and lace. The section devoted to the 1916–21 period concentrates on the patriot Lord Mayors, Terence MacSwiney and Tomás MacCurtain.

Special attention is paid to the Cork Butter Market, which exported to many parts of the world between 1770 and 1800. The museum's outstanding exhibits include the Glass Grace Cup of Cork Corporation, the silver collar presented by Queen Elizabeth I to Maurice Roche, Mayor of Cork in 1571, the municipal silver oar of c. 1690 and a number of silver Freedom Boxes. There are also examples of Cork Republican silver, cut and engraved glass representing Cork's short-lived glass industry and some fine pieces of Youghal needlepoint.

Crawford Art Galley

Emmet Place, Cork   ☎ 021 965033
Mon–Fri 10–5; Sat 10–1. Closed Bank Holidays
   and several days at Christmas
🅕 ♿ ♿ ♿

The northern wing of the gallery is the original Cork Customs House, built in 1724. The remainder of the building dates from 1884. There is an excellent collection of Irish 20th-century paintings and works by artists of the Newlyn School. The print collection is mainly of 20th-century woodcuts. The Harry Clarke Room includes three stained glass windows and the designs for his Eve of St Agnes window.

The nucleus of the sculpture on display in the gallery is the collection of classical statues made by Canova in 1819, but there are also works by modern Irish and British artists.

The Georgian Mansion which houses the Cork Public Museum.

***The Village School*, by Jan Steen. National
Gallery of Ireland, Dublin.**

Corofin

Clare Heritage Centre

Church Street, Corofin, Ennis, Co. Clare
☎ *065 27955*
*Daily 10–6. Closed weekends Nov–Mar. Other
times by appt.*
C

The Centre occupies a former church (Church
of Ireland), which dates back to c. 1717. During
the work of restoration and conversion, it was
discovered that the building had originally been
a barn. An extension, the George Macnamara
Gallery, was added in 1980. The exhibits in the
main building are concerned with conditions in
County Clare during the 19th century and with
the emigration which resulted from them. The
gallery houses a comprehensive genealogical
research service for people with Clare ancestry.

Dublin

Bewley's Cafe Museum

Bewley's Oriental Café, Grafton Street, Dublin 2
☎ *01 776761*
Daily 11–5
F

Bewley's large Oriental Café has been a feature
of Dublin life for more than 150 years. As a
social institution, it is comparable to the great
cafés of Vienna and Paris. A museum has now
been established upstairs in the Café, in the
former bakery. It presents a wide range of
objects, documents and photographs recalling
the history of the Café and its development from
the original tea and coffee business established
by the Bewley family in the 18th century. A
small number of café tables within the museum
allow visitors to eat and drink before, after or
during their tour.

Dublin Civic Museum

South William Street, Dublin 2
Tues–Sat 10–6; Sun 11–2.
F

The museum, in the former City Assembly
House, is the headquarters of the Old Dublin
Society. The displays tell the story of the City
and County of Dublin from medieval times to
the present century. The exhibits include early
maps and prints and a wide variety of historic
objects, ranging from Viking artefacts to
wooden watermains and from a model of Jacob's
biscuit factory to the head of the statue of Lord
Nelson, which stood in O'Connell Street until
1965.

There are frequent temporary exhibitions of
material drawn from the museum's collections
and archives.

Guinness Museum

*The Hop Store, Arthur Guinness Son & Company,
St James's Gate, Dublin 8*
☎ *01 756701 extn 5358*
Mon–Fri 10–4.30
F

The Guinness Museum, opened in 1986, is in
the former Hop Store of the St James's Gate
Brewery. The displays relate to brewing,
distribution and sale of the Company's products
over a period of more than two centuries, and to
the Guinness involvement in the life and
economy of Dublin since 1759. The sections
devoted to coopering and to advertising are
particularly interesting.

The Irish Jewish Museum

Walworth Road, South Circular Road, Dublin 8
☎ *01 760737*
*May–Sept, Tues, Thurs, Sun 11–3.30. Oct–Apr,
Sun 10.30–2.30. Other times by appt.*
F

Dublin has a long-established Jewish
community. The museum, in a former
synagogue, contains displays relating to all
aspects of the cultural, commercial and social
life of the Jewish people in Ireland, with
exhibits illustrating the full cycle of the Jewish
year. The synagogue, dating from the early part
of the present century, has been restored and
comprises part of the museum. In another room
the scene at the Sabbath table in a Jewish
household in Dublin has been re-created.

National Gallery of Ireland

Merrion Square West, Dublin 2   ☎ *01 615133*
Mon–Sat 10–6; Sun 2–5. Open until 9 on Thurs.
F

The National Gallery has the largest and most
important art collection in Ireland, with over
2,500 oil paintings spanning European art from
the early Renaissance to the beginning of the
20th century. There are also extensive holdings
of drawings, watercolours and engravings,

together with a considerable sculpture collection. The early Italian and 19th-century French works are particularly noteworthy and the Gallery possesses one of the finest and most extensive Dutch collections outside the Netherlands. Irish art is also well represented. The Gallery holds an annual exhibition of its collection of over 30 works by Turner during the month of January.

The National Portrait Collection is also housed here.

National Museum of Ireland

Kildare Street, Merrion Street and Merrion Row,
*   Dublin 2*   ☎ *01 618811*
Tues–Sat 10–5; Sun 2–5. Closed Good Fri,
*   Dec 25.*
Ⓕ ⬬

The collections of the museum cover archaeology, history and art, folklife, zoology and geology. The archaeological section is particularly noteworthy for its extensive collections of Bronze Age and Celtic gold ornaments and early Christian metalwork, and for the special exhibitions of Viking material and medieval metalwork.

The display of decorative arts covers glass, silver, ceramics, coins and medals, and textiles. The emphasis is on Irish craftsmanship, but there is also material from other European countries and from the Far East.

The historical section of the museum illustrates the political history of Ireland from 1700 until the achievement of independence.

National Transport Museum

Howth Castle, Co. Dublin
*   ☎ 01 475623/326295*
Sat, Sun, Bank Holiday 2–6, June–Aug, daily
*   2–6.*
Ⓒ ⬬

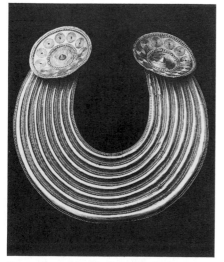

Bronze Age gold collar from Gleninsheen, County Clare. National Museum of Ireland, Dublin.

The museum is in recently opened premises in the grounds of Howth Castle. The collections include trams, buses and lorries, as well as steam-driven and horse-drawn vehicles. Nearly all the items have an Irish connection. Among the more noteworthy exhibits are an 1889 Merryweather fire engine and a tram built in 1883, from the Giant's Causeway electric tramway, which is believed to be the oldest tram in existence today.

Pearse Museum

St Enda's Park, Rathfarnham, Dublin 16
*   ☎ 01 934208*
Daily 10–12.30, 2–6 (closed at 4 in winter)
Ⓕ ⬬ ⬬

The museum, five miles from the centre of Dublin, occupies an 18th-century house set in 10 hectares of parkland. Through its collections of documents, photographs and memorabilia, as well as through a biographical audio-visual presentation, the museum provides a comprehensive view of the life of Patrick Pearse, a key figure in the Irish republican tradition, and in the events leading to the 1916 Rising. It also illustrates the ideals which inspired Pearse's school, St Enda's, now the location of the museum.

Dun Laoghaire

National Maritime Museum of Ireland

Haigh Terrace, Dun Laoghaire, Co. Dublin
*   ☎ 01 800969*
May–Sept, Tues–Sun 2.30–5.30
Ⓒ ⬬ ⬬

The museum is in the former Mariners' Church, which served the local Church of Ireland congregation, including Royal Navy guardships in the harbour. The Church includes two prisoners' docks in the gallery, from which prisoners under escort could participate in Sunday services. The museum has retained the excellent Victorian stained glass, which includes windows modelled on the Five Sisters windows in York Minster.

The collections cover most aspects of Irish maritime history. Of particular interest is the Bantry Longboat, a French ship's boat of 1796, believed to be the oldest of its kind in the world. The lighthouse display contains the optic from the Baily lighthouse at Howth and many other exhibits illustrate the history of lighthouse engineering. The history of Irish lifeboats and Ireland's indigenous small craft have separate display areas. A wide range of material relating to the SS *Great Eastern* is on view, bequeathed by the family of her Captain, Robert Charles Halpin. The museum houses a fine collection of maps, charts, nautical instruments and marine paintings and prints. There is also a library of books and pamphlets relating to the maritime history of Ireland.

Glencolumbkille

Folk Museum

Glencolumbkille, Co. Donegal   ☎ *073 30017*
Mon–Sat 10–5; Sun 12–6.

© ♦ 💺 ♿ ⚓

The museum takes the form of a group of four
thatched cottages, each furnished to illustrate a
distinct period during the past 200 years. They
present a picture of the domestic and social life
of a village in this very rural part of Ireland, at a
time when the traditional pattern of society was
being weakened by emigration and by influences
from the town.

Gort

Thoor Ballylee

Gort, Co. Galway   ☎ *091 31436/63081*
May–Sept, daily 10–6

© ♫ 💺 ⚓

Thoor Ballylee is 4 miles north-east of Gort, off
the Gort to Loughrea and Gort to Galway roads.
A 16th-century tower house, with cottage
attached, it was at one time the property of the
poet, W.B. Yeats, who used it as his summer
home during the 1920s. It was restored and
converted into a Yeats museum in 1965 and
contains some of Yeat's furniture, china and
other memorabilia, together with first and other
early editions of his work.

Johnstown Castle

Irish Agricultural Museum

Castle Farmyard, Johnstown Castle, Wexford
    ☎ *053 42888*
April–May & Sept–Nov 11, Mon–Fri 9–12.30,
    1.30–5; Sun 2–5. June–Aug, Mon–Fri 9–5;
    Sat, Sun 2–5. Nov 12–Mar, Mon–Fri
    9–12.30, 1.30–5.

© ♦ 💺 ⊕ ♿ ⚓

The museum is in early 19th-century restored
farm buildings in the grounds of Johnstown
Castle, four miles south-west of Wexford on the
road to Murrintown. The main sections of the

Irish Agricultural Museum, Johnstown Castle.

farmyard, including the harness room, stables
and cow-byre, have been restored and converted
to museum use.

The exhibits illustrate the history of Irish
agriculture and rural life. There are displays on
rural transport and the activities of the farmyard
and the rural household, together with a large
dairying section and a major collection of Irish
country furniture. Reconstructions of the
workshops of rural craftsmen show the tools and
techniques used.

Kilkenny

Kilkenny Castle

Kilkenny, Co. Kilkenny   ☎ *056 21450*
Easter–June 1, daily 10–5. June 2–Sept, daily
    10–7. Oct–Easter, Tues–Sun 10.30–1, 2–5.

© ♫ 💺 ■ ⚓

The Castle dates from the 13th century and was
extensively rebuilt in the 1830s. From the 14th
century it was the principal seat of the Butlers,
the Earls and Dukes of Ormonde. It now houses
the Butler collection of paintings and tapestries,
together with other possessions and memorabilia
of the family. Also on display is a large
permanent collection of modern – especially
Irish – art.

Rothe House

16 Parliament Street, Kilkenny   ☎ *056 22893*
Apr–Oct, Mon–Sat 10.30–5; Sun 3–5. Nov–
    Mar, Sat, Sun 3–5.

© ♫ ⚓

Built in the 16th century, this typical middle-
class house of the Tudor period, is named after
its original owner, the merchant, John Rothe.
He and his wife lived in this great stone house
from 1594 to 1610 and had twelve children
here. In 1960 it was bought by the Kilkenny
Archaeological Society and, after restoration,
opened to the public in 1966 as a museum
illustrating the history of the City and County of
Kilkenny. The collections contain geological,
archaeological, historical and ethnographical
material, as well as some fine oak furniture.

The Gaelic League, a movement to promote
the use of the Irish language, and to support the
cause of Irish independence, was established in
Rothe House, under the cover of a sports
organisation.

Killarney

Muckross House

National Park, Killarney, Co. Kerry
    ☎ *064 31440*
Easter–June and Oct, daily 10–7. July–Aug, daily
    9–9. Nov–Mar 16, Tues–Sun 11–5. Closed
    Dec 24, 25.

© ♦ 💺 ⚓

Muckross House was built in 1843 for Henry
Arthur Herbert. It remained in the possession of
the Herbert family until the end of the century

Oak Room, Malahide Castle, Malahide.

and in 1929 became the property of the Irish nation. Stripped of its furnishings, it remained empty until 1964, when it was opened as a museum of the life and social history of the people of County Kerry. A number of rooms have been appropriately furnished, to give an impression of the house as it was in its days as a private residence on the grand scale.

The displays illustrate life in Kerry between c. 1800 and 1950, with sections devoted to dairying, housing, fuel, lighting and crafts. The collections range from household equipment to farm implements and craftsmen's tools. An important feature of the museum is its programme of craft demonstrations. A weaver, blacksmith, basketmaker, potter and bookbinder are regularly to be seen at work.

Limerick

City Art Gallery

Pery Square, Limerick　　☎ *061 310633*
Mon–Fri 10–1, 2–6 (2–7 on Thurs); Sat 10–1.
Closed Bank Holidays and public holidays.
Ⓕ ▯ 💺 🚗

The interesting neo-Romanesque building which now contains the gallery dates from 1903. It was built as the City Library, an art gallery section being added in 1948. The library has now been relocated and the gallery occupies the whole of the premises. Most of the paintings in the permanent collection are by Irish artists or by artists with Irish connections. They range in date from the 18th to the 20th century and include good examples of the work of Jervas, Carver, Barrett, Mulcahy, Hone, Osbourne, Yeats, Orpen, Keating and Henry.

Limerick Museum

1 John's Square North, Limerick　　☎ *061 47826*
Tues–Sat 10–1, 2.15–5. Closed public holidays.
Ⓕ ◿ 🚗

The main part of the museum's collection consists of objects illustrating the history of the city of Limerick and the surrounding area. These include archaeological material ranging in date from the Stone Age to the medieval period, the City insignia, Limerick silver, lace and furniture, and 19th-century trade guild regalia.

Among other exhibits are coins, dating from the Viking period to the present time, including local tokens, 17th–19th-century local private banknotes, 16th–19th-century maps of Limerick, topographical paintings, prints and photographs, and Limerick-printed books and newspapers. There are also natural history and ethnographical collections.

Malahide

Malahide Castle

Malahide, Co. Dublin　　☎ *01 452655/542371*
Apr–Oct, Mon–Fri 10–5; Sat 11–6; Sun and
Bank Holidays 2–6. Nov–Mar, Mon–Fri
10–5; Sat, Sun and Bank Holidays 2–5.
Closed Christmas Week.
Ⓒ ▯ 💺 🚗

The Talbot family lived at Malahide Castle for nearly 800 years, from 1185 to 1976. The oldest part of the present building dates from the 14th century. When the last Lord Talbot de Malahide died, the property was bought by Dublin County Council. It now contains 16th- to 19th-century Irish furniture, early-18th-century painted leather wall hangings, and a collection of portraits on loan from the National Gallery in Dublin, including 31 of members of the Talbot family. To the portraits, the National Gallery has added battle, sporting and other pictures, to create a panorama of Irish life over the last few centuries.

Monaghan

Monaghan County Museum

The Hill, Monaghan　　☎ *047 82928*
Tues–Sat 11–1, 2–5. June–Aug, also Sun 2–5.
Closed public holidays.
Ⓕ ◿ 💺 🚗

The museum's displays deal with the prehistory, history, traditional life and natural history of County Monaghan. The prehistory displays include the Lisdrumturk cauldron and a new exhibit on the museum's own excavation at the Black Pig's Dyke. Within the historic period, after the coming of Christianity to Ireland c. 450 AD, there is a wide range of objects of everyday use excavated at the sites of the crannogs (lake-dwellings), and interesting examples of Christian metalwork, including the celebrated 14th-century Cross of Clogher.

Other sections of the museum are devoted to the 19th-century lace industry at Carrickmacross and Clones, and to the local flora and fauna. Smaller displays deal with canals, railways, forestry, costumes and coins. The Art Gallery extension houses a collection of paintings and textiles.

Processional cross. Monaghan County Museum.

St Louis Convent Heritage Centre

St Louis Convent, Monaghan   ☎ *047 83529*
Mon, Tues, Thurs, Fri 10–12, 2–5; Sat, Sun 2–5.
C & ♿

The St Louis Institute was founded in 1842 by Father Louis Bautain at Juilly, in France. Soon afterwards, the first St Louis Sisters began their teaching work and a group of them arrived at Monaghan in 1859. They were able to buy the Old Brewery as their headquarters, much of the money being contributed by Charles Bianconi, proprietor of Bianconi's Travelling Cars, the first public transport system in Ireland. The original buildings were subsequently much extended.

The Heritage Centre tells the story of the Institute and the Order and pays particular attention to the work at Monaghan and elsewhere in Ireland, against a background of Irish history. There are pointers to the wretched social and economic plight of Ireland in the 19th century and especially to the lack of educational facilities, which the Sisters did much to remedy.

The Centre highlights the European links which existed for centuries between Ireland and mainland Europe, and records the great contribution made by the St Louis Sisters to the social and cultural life of France, Ireland, England, Africa and America.

Quin

Craggaunowen Project

Craggaunowen, Quin, Co. Clare   ☎ *061 72178*
Apr–Sept, daily 10–6. Oct–Mar, daily 10–4.
C ♦ ♿

The Project is situated in wooded country two miles east of Quin. The site consists of a medieval tower house, which contains a display of furniture and objets d'art, including some rare Irish pieces. There are also reconstructions of Iron Age settlements, a lake dwelling and a ring fort, and a cooking site. A portion of an Iron Age road excavated in the Midlands has been installed at Craggaunowen, and cereal crops of the types available in Celtic times are cultivated. The leather boat, *Brendan*, sailed by Tim Severin from Ireland to Newfoundland, re-enacting a voyage believed to have been made by St Brendan the Navigator in the 6th century can also be seen.

Rathdrum

Parnell Museum

Avondale House, Rathdrum, Co. Wicklow
May–Sept, daily 2–6
F ♿

Avondale was the birthplace and family home of the Irish patriot and political leader, Charles Stewart Parnell (1846–91). The house has been restored as a memorial to Parnell, with furnishings of the period and many of his papers and personal possessions.

Roscrea

Roscrea Heritage Centre

Castle Complex, Roscrea, Co. Tipperary
    ☎ *505 21850*
June–Sept, Mon–Fri 10–5; Sat, Sun 2–5.
    Oct–May, Mon–Fri 10–5.
C ♦ ☕ ♿

The Centre occupies a distinguished 18th-century house, Damer House, and its annexe, which are within the courtyard of the 13th-century Roscrea Castle, an irregular polygonal structure with gatetower and corner turrets linked by a curtain wall.

The collections include displays relating to the Midland region in the prehistoric and early Christian periods as well as late-19th-century household items of a traditional type and 16th- to 19th-century archival material relating to the area.

Rosmuc

Patrick Pearse's Cottage

Rosmuc, Co. Galway
Mid June–mid Sept, daily 10–6. Other times by
    appt with the Office of Public Works, Athenry,
    Co. Galway   ☎ *091 44084*
F ♿

This is a restoration of the cottage used by Patrick Pearse (1879–1916), leader of the 1916 Rising, as a summer residence. The interior, although burned by the Black and Tans during the War of Independence, has been reconstructed and contains a number of mementoes of Pearse.

Sandycove

James Joyce Museum

Joyce Tower, Sandycove, Co. Dublin
    ☎ *01 809265/808571*
May–Sept, Mon–Sat 10–1, 2–5; Sun 2.30–6.
    Other times by appt.
Ⓒ ◔ ➹

The museum, in a Martello Tower, is on the seafront, a mile east of Dun Laoghaire. The Tower, which still has many of its original fittings, was the setting for the first chapter of Joyce's *Ulysses*. The exhibits relate to Joyce's life and career and include personal possessions, such as his guitar, waistcoat, travelling trunk and piano; letters and autographs; rare and signed editions of his works; photographs of the writer, his family, friends and residences; paintings and drawings; a bust of Joyce by Milton Hebald, and one of the two original death-masks made in 1941. There are also items relating to the Dublin of *Ulysses* and to the history of the Tower and Joyce's connection with it.

Slane

Francis Ledwidge Cottage

Jeanville, Slane, Co. Meath   ☎ *041 24336*
Apr–Sept, Mon–Sat 10–12.30, 2–5; Sun 2–6.
Ⓒ ও ➹

The poet, Francis Ledwidge (1887–1917), was killed in Flanders, during the First World War. The Community Council at Slane has bought his former home, a labourer's cottage, and furnished it as far as possible as it was in Ledwidge's lifetime. One room is devoted to an exhibition illustrating his life and work, with recordings of some of his poems.

Sligo

County Museum and Art Gallery

Stephen Street, Sligo   ☎ *071 42212*
Mar–May and Oct–Nov, Tues–Sat 10.30–12.30.
June–Sept, Tues–Sat 10.30–12.30, 2.30–4.30.
Ⓕ ➹

The museum has collections relating to the archaeology and history of Sligo, to the traditional life of the area, and the contribution of W.B. Yeats and his contemporaries to the Irish literary renaissance. The Art Gallery has paintings by Jack B. Yeats and contemporary Irish artists.

Straide

Michael Davitt National Memorial Museum

'Land League Place', Straide, Foxford, Co. Mayo
June–Aug, Tues–Sat 10–1, 2–6.30; Sun 2–7.
Ⓒ ◔ ও ➹

Straide is four miles from Foxford, on the Ballina to Castlebar road. The museum commemorates the Irish patriot, Labour Leader, writer and journalist, Michael Davitt (1846–1906), who was born here. Davitt was the founder of the Irish National Land League and the Irish Trade Union Congress and the founding patron of the Gaelic Athletic Association. There is an extensive collection of photographs and documents illustrating the many aspects of Davitt's life. Other exhibits are concerned with rural life in Ireland during the second half of the 19th century.

Tully

The Irish Horse Museum

Irish National Stud, Tully, Co. Kildare
    ☎ *045 21251*
Easter–Oct, Mon–Fri 10.30–5; Sat 10.30–5.30;
    Sun 2–5.30.
Ⓒ ♙ 🍽 ➹

The museum is in the grounds of the Irish National Stud and occupies a building converted from a groom's house and some old stallion boxes, in which Tulyar and Royal Charger, two of the Stud's most famous stallions, once lived. The displays illustrate the history of the horse and its uses in Ireland since prehistoric times. The exhibits include an old weighing-in chair from the Curragh racecourse, racing trophies, and the skeleton of the famous and much-loved steeplechaser, Arkle.

Chandelier, German, 16th-century.
Craggaunowen Project, Quin.

Waterford

Brother Rice Museum

Mount Sion, Barrack Street, Waterford
☎ *051 74390*
Daily on request, 9–12.30, 2.30–5.30
🄵 🢒 🢒

The museum building dates from 1802 and is furnished in period style. The purpose of the museum is to promote a knowledge of the Waterford merchant, Edmund Ignatius Rice (1762–1844), founder of the Presentation Brothers and the Christian Brothers, two congregations of laymen dedicated to the education of young people throughout the world. The displays in the museum illustrate the life and work of Brother Rice and include the room in which he died.

The 'Rice Trail', organised by the museum, provides a guide to the places in Waterford which were of significance in Brother Rice's life.

Garter Lane Arts Centre

5 and 22a O'Connell Street, Waterford
☎ *051 55038/77153*
Tues–Sat 12–6.
🄵 🢒 ■ 🢒

Garter Lane Arts Centre is based in two prominent Waterford buildings – one, at 5 O'Connell Street was the former home of the Waterford Library and the other, at 22a O'Connell Street, dating from the late 17th century, was formerly the Friends' Meeting House. Garter Lane has two galleries for temporary exhibitions and a permanent display of works by prominent 20th-century Irish artists.

Reginald's Tower

City Hall, The Mall, Waterford
☎ *051 73501 extn 408*
Apr–Oct, Mon–Fri 10–12.30, 2–5.30; Sat 10–12.30.
🄲 *(ex children)* 🢒 🢒

The circular building known as Reginald's Tower was erected by the Viking Governor of Waterford, Reginald Mclvor, in 1003 AD. It has played a significant part in the history of Waterford ever since, as a fortress, mint, prison, military stores depot and lock-up. Now used as a museum, its exhibits include the Waterford Charters, items from the City archives and regalia, and the *Liber Antiquissimus*, an oak-bound folio volume containing Acts and Ordinances of the Corporation from 1365 to 1659, together with other municipal documents.

The Charter Roll of Richard II is one of the Museum's most treasured possessions. Dating from the end of the 14th century, it is the only document of its age and type known to be in existence in connection with Ireland. The illustrations and drawings which accompany the text are a most valuable documentation of the period.

There is also a display illustrating Waterford's maritime history and a section devoted to the Young Ireland leader, Thomas Francis Meagher, who was condemned to death in 1848, but escaped to America, where he fought at Fort Sumter and Fredericksburg and became Governor of Montana.

Patrick Pearse's Cottage, Rosmuc.

ITALY

Adria

Archaeological Museum

*Museo Archeologico Nazionale, Via Badini 59,
I–45011 Adria, Rovigo* ☎ *0426 21612
Apr–Sept, daily 9–1, 3–7. Oct–Mar, daily 9–1,
3–6.*
Ⓕ ♟ ♿

This important museum was opened in 1961 in
order to conserve and display archaeological
material from local excavations, covering the
Palaeovenetian, Greek, Etruscan and Roman
periods. The exhibits include Greek vases,
Etruscan tombs, Roman glass and pottery of
exceptional quality, and pottery and bronzes
from prehistoric settlements.

Agrigento (Sicily)

Pirandello's House

*Casa di Pirandello, 115 Strada Porto Empedocle,
Contrada Caos, I–92100 Agrigento, Sicilia
Mon–Sat 10–5; Sun and public holidays 10–1.*
Ⓒ

The Greek poet Pindar called Agrigento 'man's
finest town'. The playwright, Luigi Pirandello
(1867–1936), who won the Nobel Prize for
Literature in 1934, was born here. After writing
many powerful and realistic novels and short
stories, he turned in his fifties to the theatre and
became a leading exponent of the 'grotesque'
school of contemporary drama. He established a
theatre of his own in Rome in 1925.

Pirandello's birthplace is preserved today as
a museum. It contains many of his personal
possessions, including items from his library and
manuscripts, as well as portraits and details of
performances of his plays.

Greek vase. Archaeological Museum, Adria.

Alba

Federico Eusebio Museum of Archaeology and
Natural Science

*Civico Museo Archeologico e di Scienze Naturali
Federico Eusebio, Via Paruzza 1a, I–12051
Alba, Cuneo* ☎ *0173 30092
Tues, Thurs, Sat 9–12, 3–6; Fri 9–12. Closed
public holidays.*
Ⓕ ♟ ♿

Established in 1897, the museum is dedicated to
the Latin scholar, Professor Federico Eusebio
(1852–1913), who was a native of Alba. At the
beginning, the collections were restricted to
archaeology. The Natural Science sections have
been added recently. *Alba Pompeii* was an
important town in Roman times and its museum
has a wide range of exhibits dating from this
period, together with material from prehistoric
sites in the area. The extension of the museum
is devoted to the geology, botany and zoology of
the region.

Ancona

Francesco Podesti Art Gallery

*Pinacoteca Civica F. Podesti e Galleria d'Arte
Moderna, Via Pizzecolli 17, I–60121 Ancona*
☎ *071 204262/56342
Tues–Sat 10–7; Sun 9–1. Closed public holidays.*
Ⓒ ♟ ♿

The gallery was opened in 1884 as a result of the
initiative of a group of local citizens and
especially of the Ancona painter, Francesco
Podesti (1800–95), who gave a number of his
own works to the new venture. Its first home
was a former monastery, but when this was
severely damaged during the Second World
War, the galleries were moved to the 16th-
century Palazzo degli Anziani.

The collections consist of 15th–17th-
century paintings by artists of the Schools of
Venice and the Marches and 18th–20th-century
works by local painters.

Aquileia

Archaeological Museum

*Museo Archeologico Nazionale, Via Roma 1,
I–33051 Aquileia, Udine* ☎ *0431 91016
Daily 10–1*
Ⓒ

Aquileia is so named, according to legend,
because an eagle ('aquila') flew overhead while,
according to Roman custom, the outline of the
town was being drawn with a plough. It
flourished under the Roman empire and was
used by Augustus as his general headquarters
during his conquest of the Germanic tribes.

Then, in 554–751, it became an important patriarchate, ruled by bishops.

The museum was founded in 1807, the exhibits being based on the collections formed by Bertoli during the 18th century. In 1882 the museum was transferred to its present building and reorganised. Further reorganisation took place in 1954–55. The displays are of prehistoric and Roman archaeological material discovered in and near Aquileia and include grave finds, sculptures, mosaics, inscriptions and statues. There is a remarkable series of portrait busts, including ones of Tiberius and of Augustus.

Early Christian Museum

Museo Paleocristiano Nazionale, Piazza
Monastero, I–33051 Aquileia, Udine
    ☎ *0431 91131*
Daily 10–1
[C]

The 11th-century basilica was built on the foundations of a 4th-century building. It was restored in the 14th century and again in 1895 and 1949–50. The 9th-century crypt is decorated with Romanesque frescoes. The museum is in another crypt, below the north aisle. It contains material from the early days of Christianity in Aquileia and from later periods, including sarcophagi, inscriptions and mosaics. The 4th-century mosaic paving, depicting religious scenes, is among the finest and most extensive in western Christendom.

Arezzo

Archaeological Museum

Museo Archeologico, Via Margaritone 10, I–52100
Arezzo   ☎ *0575 20882*
Tues–Sun 10–1
[C]

The museum overlooks the 1st–2nd-century Roman amphitheatre. Arezzo was an important Etruscan and Roman town, and the museum has remarkable collections of 6th–5th-century BC Etruscan statuettes and of Arezzo pottery made during the first two centuries of the Roman period. Among the museum's other strong points are coins and Roman bronzes and marble portrait busts.

Vasari's House

Casa del Vasari, Via XX Settembre 55, I–52100
Arezzo   ☎ *0575 20295*
Mon–Sat 10–5; Sun and public holidays 10–1.
[C]

The architect, painter and sculptor, Giorgio Vasari (1511–74) was the first real art historian. He bought this house in 1540 and decorated and slightly remodelled it. Acquired by the State in 1911, it was restored and converted into a Vasari museum and archive. It contains Vasari's sumptuous frescoes and paintings by him and by other 16th-century Tuscan painters.

17th-century ceramic miniature. Ascoli Piceno Art Gallery.

Ascoli Piceno

Ascoli Piceno Art Gallery

Pinacoteca Civica, Piazza Arringo 1, I–63100
Ascoli Piceno   ☎ *0736 558213/558282*
June 15 – Sept 15, Tues–Fri 10–12.30, 4.30–7;
Sat 10–12.30; Sun and public holidays 4–7.
Sept 16 – June 14, Tues–Sat 9–1; Sun and
mid-week holidays, 10–1. Closed Jan 1, Easter,
Apr 25, May 1, Aug 15, Nov 1, Dec 25.
[F] [i] [≡]

The gallery was established in 1861 after the suppression of the religious orders allowing the municipality to acquire paintings which were formerly the property of local churches and monasteries. Other important collections have subsequently been received as gifts. The gallery occupies part of the recently restored Palazzo Arringo, which dates from the 13th century, but was substantially rebuilt in the 17th and early 18th centuries.

The main body of the collection consists of 15th–20th-century Italian paintings, but there are some by foreign artists, including Van Dyck and Turner. There are also exhibits of 17th- and 18th-century lacquered and gilt furniture.

Bassano del Grappa

Bassano Museum

Museo Civico, Via Museo 12, I–36061 Bassano
del Grappa, Vicenza   ☎ *0424 22235/23336*
Tues–Sat 10–12.30, 2.30–6.30; Sun 10–12.30.
[F] [i] [≡] [↩]

The museum occupies the buildings of a former Franciscan monastery, which became the town's hospital in the 17th century and then, in 1828, its museum. The museum is larger and has more important collections than one might expect from a community of this size. The collections include Roman sculpture and inscriptions, 17th–20th-century Bassano ceramics, 17–19th-century printed works, and paintings and drawings by 12th–19th-century Italian artists, including Antonio Canova (1757–1822). There are also works by French, Flemish and Dutch painters.

There is an outstanding print section, including the remarkable collection of Italian and foreign works formed by the local printers, Giuseppe and Antonio Remondini in the second half of the 18th century. Other departments of the museum cover coins, sculpture and natural history. The museum has an exceptionally carefully organised educational programme.

Bentivoglio

Museum of Rural Life

Museo della Civiltà Contadina, Via San Marina
   35, I–40010 Bentivoglio   ☎ *051 891050*
Tues–Sun 9.30–12.30, 2.30–5.30
🅵 🛈 ⬛ 🚗

The Villa Smeraldi, which has housed the museum since its foundation in 1974, was formerly the summer residence of a well-to-do Bologna family. The outbuildings of the estate have been preserved and form part of the museum, which, when it was established, was of a type new to Italy and based on the pioneering work of the Ecomuseum at Le Creusot in France. Its collections, arranged thematically, illustrate the traditional pattern of life and work in the local countryside, which revolve around the cultivation of wheat, rice and flax.

Bologna

Aldrovandi Museum

Museo Aldrovandiano, Università di Bologna, Via
   Zamboni 35, I–40126 Bologna
   ☎ *051 243420*
Mon–Fri 9–7; Sat 9–1. Aug, Mon–Fri 9–2; Sat
   9–1. Closed week preceding Easter and Aug
   16–31.
🅵

The physician, naturalist, philosopher and encyclopaedist, Ulisse Aldrovandi (1522–1605), was born and died in Bologna. He founded botanical gardens in Padua, Pisa and Bologna and bequeathed his natural history museum, books and manuscripts to his native city. In 1617 they were transferred to the Institute of Science, from where they were looted by Napoleon Bonaparte and taken to Paris. On their return, they were distributed among the various specialist institutes of the University.

To celebrate the tercentenary of Aldrovandi's death, the objects which had constituted his museum were brought together again and now form a section of the University Library. They range from an elephant's tooth to two ostrich eggs.

Archaeological Museum

Museo Civico Archeologico, Via dell'Archiginnasio
   2, I–40124 Bologna   ☎ *051 233849*
Tues–Sat 9–2; Sun 9–1. Closed mid-week
   holidays.
🅒 🛈

The museum was established in 1881 by combining the university and the city of Bologna's collections. It is one of the most important archaeological museums in Italy, containing a wide range of Stone Age, Bronze Age, Iron Age, Etruscan and Roman material from excavations in Bologna and the surrounding region, and collections of Egyptian antiquities, mostly discovered in the tomb of Horemheb. There is also a large section devoted to Greek ceramics.

City Art Collections

Collezioni Comunali d'Arte, Piazza Maggiore 6,
   I–40121 Bologna. Correspondence to: Via
   Manzoni 4, I–40121 Bologna.
   ☎ *051 290526*
Mon, Wed–Sat 9–2; Sun 9–1. Closed mid-week
   holidays.
🅵 🛈

The City Art Collections occupy 20 rooms on the second floor of the Palazzo d'Accursio, which is now the City Hall. From 1508 until the unification of Italy, the palazzo was used as the residence of the cardinal representing the Pope. Afterwards, it served as the prefect's offices. It contains 18th–19th-century frescoes, restored at the same time as the palazzo itself, in 1934–5.

What are now known as the Rusconi Rooms – they contain the furniture and objets d'art bequeathed to the museum by the Marquis Pier Ignazio Rusconi – are an attempt to reconstruct a grand apartment of the kind which could have existed at the time of the Cardinal Legates. The remaining rooms display a collection of 14th–early-20th-century paintings. Those by artists of the Bologna School are especially important.

Coloured drawing of a lobster by Ulisse Aldrovandi. Aldrovandi Museum, Bologna.

Museum of Astronomy

*Museo di Astronomia, Università di Bologna, Via
    Zamboni 33, I-40126 Bologna*
    ☎ 051 259301
Mon–Fri 9–4; Sat 9–1.
F

The museum is in the Tower of the Specula,
erected in the early 17th century above the
Palazzo Poggi, formerly occupied by the Institute
of Science and now by the University of
Bologna. The tower was originally designed to
house the astronomical instruments given to the
Institute by General Luigi Ferdinando Marsili.
The instruments, which illustrate the history of
astronomy, especially in the 17th century, have
been restored and are placed in the Sundial
Room, the Top Tower Room and the Globes
Room. They include a 13th-century Arabian
astrolabe, an 18th-century wooden telescope,
17th–18th-century celestial and terrestrial
globes and a series of 18th-century astronomic
instruments by Lusverg, Sisson and Dollond.

Museum of the First and Second Risorgimento

*Museo Civico del I° e II° Risorgimento, Casa
    Carducci, Piazza Carducci 5, I-40125 Bologna*
    ☎ 051 225583
*Tues–Sat 9–2; Sun 9.30–12.30. Closed mid-week
    holidays, Easter, Aug 15, Christmas.*
C ♟ ☞ ☎

The 17th-century building into which the
museum has recently moved was originally the
church of Santa Maria del Piombo. In the 19th
century it was converted into a house for the
poet, Giosue Carolucci (1835–1907) and, after
his death, it was given to the city by Queen
Margherita of Savoy. The collections illustrate
Italy's struggle for independence from 1796 to
1945, and the part played by Bologna in this.
The First Risorgimento was concerned with the
19th-century unification of Italy, the Second
with the Resistance movement against the
Germans, 1939–45.

Museum of Industrial Art and Davia Bargellini Gallery

*Museo Civico d'Arte Industriale e Galleria Davia
    Bargellini, Strada Maggiore 44, I-40125
    Bologna. Correspondence to: Via Manzoni 4,
    I-40121 Bologna.*   ☎ 051 236708
*Tues–Sat 9–2; Sun 9–1. Closed mid-week
    holidays.*
F ☞ ☎

The museum is on the ground floor of the
17th-century Palazzo Bargellini, which has a
magnificent 18th-century staircase. Its
collections are in two parts. The first consists of
wrought-ironwork, ceramics, furniture, locks
and door-handles, terracotta statuettes and
other types of decorative art objects. The second
is a gallery of 14th–19th-century Italian
paintings, many of them by artists who were
born in Bologna or who worked there. Among
the special exhibits are a 17th-century coach
and a marionette theatre.

**Effigy of Domenico Garganelli (d. 1678) by
Francesco del Corsa. Museum of the Middle
Ages and Renaissance, Bologna.**

Museum of the Middle Ages and Renaissance

*Museo Civico Medievale e del Rinascimento, Via
    Manzoni 4, I-40121 Bologna* ☎ 051 228912
*Mon, Wed–Sat 9–2; Sun 9–1. Closed mid-week
    holidays.*
F ☞ ☎

The museum, one of the most important in
Italy, was opened in 1985 in the 15th-century
Palazzo Ghisilardi Fava. In the courtyard visitors
can see the tower erected in the 13th century by
the Conoscenti family and in some of the rooms
substantial sections of Bologna's first city wall.
In the galleries devoted to ceramics and musical
instruments, there is a celebrated series of
frescoes, painted in 1584 by the Bologna artists,
Annibale (1540–1609), Ludovico (1555–1619)
and Agostino (1557–1602) Carraci and other
members of their School.

There are sections devoted to sculpture,
weapons and armour, bronzes, glass and ivory,
from the Romanesque period to the 16th
century. Among the outstanding exhibits are
the statue of Pope Boniface VIII (1301), an
early-14th-century English cope, the 14th–
16th-century monuments of the Doctors of the
University (Dottori dello Studio), and the
model of the Neptune fountain by Giovanni
Bologna (1524–1608), the most famous sculptor
in Florence after the death of Michelangelo.

National Art Gallery

Pinacoteca Nazionale, Via della Belle Arti 56,
I-40126 Bologna ☎ 051 243249
Tues–Sat 9–2; Sun and public holidays 9–1. Closed
Easter Day, Aug 15, Dec 25.
Ⓒ ♠

The gallery, one of the most important in Italy,
was established in 1882 in the former building of
the Academy of Fine Arts. Its collections
illustrate the development of Italian and
especially Bolognese painting from the 15th
century to the 18th. Among the artists
represented are Giotto, Raphael, Perugino,
Parmigiano, Titian, Francesco Francia, the
Carracci brothers, Reni, Guercino,
Domenichino and Crespi.

Brescia

Marzoli Museum of Weapons

Civico Museo delle Armi Luigi Marzoli, Via
Castello, I-25121 Brescia ☎ 030 293292
June–Sept, Tues–Fri 10–12.45, 2–6. Oct–May,
Tues–Fri 9–12.45, 2–5. Closed Jan 1, 6, Feb
15, Easter, Apr 25, May 1, Aug 15, Nov 1,
Dec 8, 25, 26.
Ⓕ 🖾

Opened in 1988, the museum is dedicated to the
local industrialist and collector, Luigi Marzoli
(1883–1965), who played a considerable part in
establishing it. The collections are displayed in
the keep of the castle, built during the period of
Visconti rule in Brescia from 1337 to 1420.
Within the keep are the remains of the steps
leading up to a 1st century AD Roman temple.

The museum's collections contain 1,400
items, which are shown in rotation. They
include 15th–17th-century armour, helmets and
weapons, and 16th–18th-century arquebuses,
pistols and cannons.

Museum of the Risorgimento

Civico Museo del Risorgimento, Via Castello,
I-25121 Brescia ☎ 030 293292
June–Sept, Tues–Fri 10–12.45, 2–6. Oct–May,
Tues–Fri 9–12.45, 2–5. Closed Jan 1, 6, Feb
15, Easter, Apr 25, May 1, Aug 15, Nov 1,
Dec 8, 25, 26.
Ⓕ ♠ 🖾

The museum was established in 1887 in a part of
the castle which was built in 1597–8 during the
Venetian occupation of Brescia and used as a
granary by the troops quartered there. It tells the
story of Brescia from the second half of the 18th
century to the end of the 19th, including the
events of the Napoleonic period and the
changes which led to unification.

The exhibits include paintings, busts and
portraits of personalities, documents, books,
proclamations, weapons, uniforms and medals.
Among the most treasured objects on display are
a travelling carriage, poncho and saddle
belonging to Garibaldi and documents relating
to 'Brescia's Ten Days', the revolt against the
Austrians on March 23 – April 1, 1849.

Museum of Roman Archaeology

Civico Museo Romano, Via Musei 57A, I-25121
Brescia ☎ 030 46031
June–Sept, Tues–Fri 10–12.45, 2–6. Oct–May,
Tues–Fri 9–12.45, 2–5. Closed Jan 1, 6, Feb
15, Easter, Apr 25, May 1, Aug 15, Nov 1,
Dec 8, 25, 26.
Ⓕ 🖾 ♠

Brescia was the Roman town of *Brixa*, developed
on the site of a Bronze Age settlement. The
museum, opened in 1830, was created inside the
Capitoline Temple, erected in AD 73–74 by the
Emperor Vespasian on the site of a previous
sanctuary dating from the Republican period.
The temple is famous for its frescoes and
mosaics.

The collections consist of material found
during the excavation of prehistoric, Roman
and Gallic sites in Brescia and the neighbouring
region. Among the finds are inscriptions,
mosaics, coins and household objects as well as
vases from Etruria and *Magna Graecia*. There is
an important section devoted to Roman bronzes
of the Imperial period.

Tosio-Martinengo Art Gallery

Civica Pinacoteca Tosio-Martinengo, Piazza
Moretto 1, I-25121 Brescia ☎ 030 59120
June–Sept, Tues–Fri 10–12.45, 2–6. Oct–May,
Tues–Fri 9–12.45, 2–5. Closed Jan 1, 6, Feb
15, Easter, Apr 25, May 1, Aug 15, Nov 1,
Dec 8, 25, 26.
Ⓕ 🖾 ♠

In 1843 Count Paolo Tosio bequeathed his
notable art collection to the city of Brescia and
three years later his widow did the same with the
family home, Palazzo Tosio, in which the
collection was housed. Further bequests
followed and the gallery was subsequently
transferred to the 14th-century Palazzo
Martinengo, given to the city in 1884.

The principal collection consists of 13th–
18th-century Italian paintings, Brescia artists of
the Renaissance period being particularly well
represented. There are also collections of
goldsmiths' work, drawings and illuminated
manuscripts.

The Washerwoman by Ceruti. Tosio-
Martinengo Art Gallery, Brescia.

Brindisi

Francesco Ribezzo Archaeological Museum

Museo Archeologico Provinciale Francesco Ribezzo,
Palazzo Duomo, I–72100 Brindisi
☎ 0831 23418
Mon–Sat 10–1. Closed public holidays.
Ⓒ

Brindisi, the southern terminal of the *Via Traiana*, has been an important trading port since classical times. It was a port of embarkation for the Crusaders making for the Holy Land. The museum has important collections relating to the Roman and other cultures which have featured in the past of the town and the region.

Among the exhibits are commemorative inscriptions, bronze and marble statues, coins, vases, and terracottas.

Buonconvento

Val d'Arbia Museum of Religious Art

Museo d'Arte Sacra della Val d'Arbia, Via Soccini
17, I–53022 Buonconvento, Siena
☎ 0577 806012
Tues, Thurs 10–12; Sat 10–12, 4–6; Sun 9–1.
Ⓒ ⚲ ⚘

The museum was opened in 1979. The exhibits are drawn from the churches, monasteries and other religious foundations in the area and provide a good impression of the development of what is known as the Sienese School between the 13th and 17th centuries. There are two collections, one of paintings and the other of chalices, monstrances, crucifixes and other liturgical items.

Cagliari (Sardinia)

Sardinian Museum of Ethnology

Museo Sardo di Antropologia e Ethnografia, Via G.
T. Porcell 2, I–09100 Cagliari, Sardegna
☎ 070 659294
Mon–Fri 10–2
Ⓒ

This is a university museum, open to the general public. It was founded in 1953 and is well worth visiting for the sake of two remarkable collections, one of 800 carefully studied and documented Sardinian skulls, from the Neolithic period to modern times, and the other of traditional Sardinian costumes.

Caldarno sulla Strada del Vino

Trentino Wine Museum

Museo del Vino, I–39052 Caldarno sulla Strada del
Vino, Bolzano   ☎ 0471 963168
Easter Mon – Nov 30, Tues–Sat 9.30–12, 2–6;
Sun 2–6.
Ⓒ ⚲

Garibaldi's death-bed, enclosed by a balustrade erected in 1882 to protect it from the thousands who came in pilgrimage following the patriot's death. Garibaldi Museum, Caprera.

The museum illustrates the history of wine and wine production in the former South Tirol region since Roman times. There are collections of tools, implements and equipment used in vineyard cultivation and winemaking, information concerning pests and diseases which attack the vines and the grape, and details of the market for local wines at different periods and of the organisation of the trade. There are also sections devoted to coopering and to the transport of wine.

Caprera (Sardinia)

Garibaldi Museum

Compendio Garibaldino, I–07024 Caprera (La
Maddalena), Sardegna   ☎ 0789 727162
Tues–Fri 9–1.30; Sat, Sun 9–1. Closed Jan 1, Apr
25, May 1, 1st Sun in June, Aug 15, Dec 25.
Ⓒ ⚲ ⚘

Giuseppe Maria Garibaldi (1807–82) was born in Nice and died at Caprera, where he is buried. The museum consists of a complex of buildings, 'La Casa Bianca', which he began to build in the 1850s and where he spent the last 26 years of his life. 'La Casa Bianca' is now a State property and, after restoration, was opened as a national museum in 1978. It now appears much as it did in Garibaldi's day, with his furniture, including the orthopaedic bed on which he was compelled to spend much of his time, his paintings, guns, sabres, decorations, watches and other memorabilia.

Caprese Michelangelo

Michelangelo Museum

Museo Michelangeolesco, Castello, I–52033
Caprese Michelangelo, Arezzo
☎ 0575 793912
Tues–Sun 10–5
Ⓒ

Michelangelo (1475–1564) was born in the house which is now the museum. The room in which he is believed to have been born contains contemporary furniture and other exhibits in the museum include casts and photographs of his works. In 1969 an open-air museum was established, containing sculptures by contemporaries of Michelangelo. The castle, in which the museum is situated, dates from the 14th century. It has been restored several times.

Carpi

Giulio Ferrari Museum

Museo Civico Giulio Ferrari, Castello dei Pio de Savoia, Piazza dei Martiri 68, I–41012 Carpi, Modena ☎ 059 693096
May–Oct, Mon–Fri 4–7; Sat, Sun 10.30–12.30, 4–7. Nov–Apr, by appt only.
F ▮

The building which houses the museum was the Palace of the Princes of Savoy in the 14th–16th centuries and, with its frescoes and decorated ceilings, is of great historic and artistic interest. The collections include 16th–20th-century paintings, especially by local artists, medieval wooden sculptures, 17th–18th-century furniture, scagliola and inlaid work by local craftsmen, and Carpi terracottas.

Memorial Museum to the Deportees to Nazi Extermination Camps

Museo Monumento al Deportato Politico e Razziale nei Campi di Sterminio Nazisti, Castello dei Pio di Savoia, Piazza dei Martiri 68, I–41012 Carpi, Modena ☎ 059 690368
Thurs, Sat, Sun 9–12.30, 3–6.30
F ▮

The museum, in the former castle of the Princes of Savoy, is close to the concentration camp at Fossoli, where tens of thousands of Italian prisoners were held before being moved on to the death camps in central and eastern Europe. The Memorial Museum, designed by Italian architects and artists, is intended as a monument to all those, of whatever nationality, who suffered so severely in the Nazi camps.

The exhibits include clothing, sections of barbed wire, letters, ashes from crematory ovens, photographs, official announcements, objects made by prisoners and ropes used to hang deportees. Many works of art were created specially for the museum.

Giulio Ferrari Museum, Carpi.

Carrara

National Museum of Marble

Mostra Nazionale del Marmo, Via 20 Settembre, Stallio, I–54033 Carrara, Massa Carrara ☎ 0585 840561
May–Sept, daily 10–1, 3–6. Closed public holidays.
C ▲

Italian history, it has been well said, is made of marble. The museum contains examples of every kind of marble to be found in Italy, together with examples of what is produced from it. The Carrara quarries themselves have been celebrated since classical times for the exceptional quality and whiteness of their marble, and Michelangelo used to visit them in person to select blocks. The museum illustrates the history and techniques of the industry from its earliest days and shows the methods used to transport the marble from the quarries.

Casale Monferrato

Exhibition of Jewish Art and History

Mostra Permanente d'Arte e Storia Ebraica, Vicolo S. Olper 44, I–15033 Casale Monferrato, Alessandria ☎ 0142 71807
Mar 15 – Nov 15, Sun 10–12, 3–5. Nov 16 – Mar 14, on request. Closed Jewish religious holidays.
C

The synagogue of Casale Monferrato, one of the most beautiful in Italy, was built in 1595 and enlarged in 1866. Its size and splendour are evidence of the important rôle once played by the Jewish community in this city. The museum, opened in 1969, is in the former women's section of the synagogue. It contains documents and ceremonial objects from the 16th century onwards assembled from a number of Jewish communities in western Italy.

Caserta

Palazzo Reale and Vanvitelli Museum

Appartamenti Storici et Museo Vanvitelliano, Palazzo Reale, I–81100 Caserta ☎ 0823 321127
Tues–Sun 10–1
C

This very large palace, begun in 1752, was designed by the noted Neapolitan architect, Luigi Vanvitelli (1700–73) for the Bourbon King, Charles III, who had thoughts of building another Versailles. Constructed on a rectangular plan, it is 249 metres long and 190 metres wide and has 250 windows. The state apartments are sumptuously decorated and have 18th- and early-19th-century French furniture. There are also early-18th-century Dutch and Italian still life paintings.

The section devoted to Vanvitelli contains designs, sketches and wooden models of 18th-century architectural projects.

Castelfranco Veneto

Giorgione's House

Casa di Giorgione, Piazzetta Duomo, I–31033
   Castelfranco Veneto, Treviso
   ☎ 0423 491240
May–Sept, Tues–Sun 9–12.30, 3–6.30. Oct–Apr,
   Tues–Sun 9–12.30, 2.30–5.30.
C 🖼 🚃

The Venetian painter, Giorgione (c. 1478-
1511), was born in Castelfranco in a 14th-
century house which was modified in the 17th
century and restored in 1973–4. The principal
room has a painted frieze which is believed to
have been painted by Giorgione himself.
Another room has 16th-century frescoes by an
unknown artist. There are exhibits illustrating
Giorgione's life and work and a number of
radiographs of his paintings.

Castellamare di Stabia

Stabia Museum of Antiquities

Antiquarium Stabiano Statale, Via Marco Mario 2,
   I–80053 Castellamare di Stabia, Napoli
   ☎ 081 8707228
Daily 9–2. Closed Easter Mon.
F

The Roman town of Stabiae was destroyed,
together with Herculaneum and Pompeii, by the
eruption of Vesuvius in AD 79. The museum
contains a wide range of material discovered
during the excavation of the site, including
wall-paintings, stucco decorations, household
objects, tools and ornaments. There are also
items from Iron Age sites and medieval
sculptures from the cathedral.

Castiglione delle Stiviere

International Museum of the Red Cross

Museo Internazionale della Croce Rossa, Via
   Garibaldi, I–46043 Castiglione delle Stiviere,
   Mantova   ☎ 0376 638505
Mar–Oct, Tues–Sun 9–12, 3–7. Nov–Feb, Tues–
   Sun 9–12, 2–5.30. Closed Jan 1, Easter Sun,
   Aug 15, Dec 25.
F 🛈 🚃

In 1859 Piedmontese and French troops
defeated an Austrian army at the Battle of
Solferino and drove the Austrians out of
Lombardy. 40,000 men were left dead and
wounded, and the slaughter was witnessed by
the Swiss, Jean Henri Dunant, who helped local
people to look after the wounded in the Chiesa
Maggiore (The Great Church) in Castiglione. It
was here that Dunant conceived the idea of the
International Red Cross.
   The museum was opened in 1959, the
centenary of the Battle of Solferino. It contains
relics of the battle, including ambulances,
paintings, a photographic exhibition telling the
story of the Red Cross, and an international
exhibition of Red Cross postage stamps.

Section of frieze depicting the liberal and
mechanical arts, perhaps by Giorgione.
Giorgione's House, Castelfranco Veneto.

Catania (Sicily)

Bellini Museum

Museo Belliniano, Piazza S. Francesco d'Assisi 3,
   I–95124 Catania, Sicilia   ☎ 095 341523
Tues–Sun 10–1
C

The opera composer, Vincenzo Bellini (1801–
35) was born in Catania. His birthplace is now a
museum, founded in 1930 by Vittorio Emanuele
III. Its collections illustrate Bellini's short but
fruitful life. The exhibits include letters,
paintings, miniatures, documents, scores and
musical manuscripts by musicians from Catania.

Chieri

Martini Museum of the History of Wine

Museo Martini di Storia dell'Enologia, Piazza L.
   Rossi, I–10023 Chieri, Torino
   ☎ 011 947 0345
Daily 10–5
F 🛈

Chieri is one of Italy's most celebrated wine-
producing areas. The Museum, opened in 1961,
is organised by the firm of Martini & Rossi. It
tells the story of winemaking through the ages
and has exhibits of vineyard tools, vessels for
storing wine and equipment used in the
production of wine.

Chieti

Archaeological Museum of the Abruzzi

Museo Archeologico degli Abruzzi, Villa
   Comunale, I–66100 Chieti
   ☎ 0871 657041
Daily 10–1. Closed Jan 1, Apr 25, May 1, 1st Sun
   in June, Aug 15, Dec 25.
C

The museum is in the former Villa Frigeri and
an adjoining mansion, set in splendid gardens.
It contains notable archaeological material,
especially sculptures, dating from the 6th

century BC to the 4th century AD. Particularly interesting exhibits are the giant marble statue of Hercules, discovered in the ruins of the Roman colony of *Alba Fucens*, a portrait bust of Scylla, and the 6th-century BC limestone statue known as the Warrior of Capestrano. There are also several examples of the art of the Piceni, who occupied the central part of Italy before the Romans.

Chiusi

Etruscan Museum

*Museo Nazionale Etrusco, Via Porsenna, 1–53043
    Chiusi, Siena*   ☎ *0578 20177
Daily 10–1. Closed Jan 1, Easter Mon, May 1,
    Aug 15, Dec 25.*
[C]

The museum has outstanding collections of objects from the Etruscan cemeteries in the area, objects characterised by the strange Etruscan blend of fantasy and realism. The exhibits include tombstones, sarcophagi, burial urns in the shape of human heads, clay ex-votos, vases, jewellery and lamps. The museum provides guided tours of Etruscan tombs in the Chiusi area.

Cividale del Friuli

Archaeological Museum

*Museo Archaeologico Nazionale, Piazza del
    Duomo, 1–33043 Cividale del Friuli, Udine*
    ☎ *0432 731119
Daily 10–1*
[C]

The town was the Roman *Forum Julio*. From 554 until the 15th century it formed part of the independent patriarchate of Aquileia and became the residence of the Patriarchs. After the 15th century it belonged to Venice. It was severely damaged in the 1976 earthquake, but has since been rebuilt. The museum, established in 1817, was transferred in 1886–1904 to its present home, the Palazzo Nordis. Its collections illustrate the history of the town from the time of the Lombards and the Patriarchate. Among the exhibits are gold and silversmiths' work, weapons and sculptures from 7th-century Lombard tombs and an important collection of medieval manuscripts.

Como

Giovio Archaeological Museum

*Civico Museo Archeologico P. Giovio, Piazza
    Medaglie d'Oro 1, 1–20100 Como*
    ☎ *031 271343
Apr-Sept, Tues–Sat 9.30–12, 2.30–5.30; Sun
    9.15–12.15. Oct–Mar, Tues–Sat 9.30–12,
    2–5; Sun 9.15–12.15. Closed public holidays*
[C] 🔥

Paolo Giovio (1483–1552) belonged to an old and noble family and was born in Como. After

**Portrait of Paolo Giovio.
Giovio Archaeological Museum, Como.**

qualifying as a doctor, he embarked on an ecclesiastical career and served at the court of four popes. He later became celebrated as an historian and at some time between 1537 and 1543 he founded his own museum, 'my most happy museum' (*iucundissimo museo*) at Borgovico.

The museum at Como, which is named after him, occupies a mansion which once belonged to the Giovio family. It contains archaeological material from the Como region and from northern Italy and from prehistoric times to the Middle Ages.

Cortina d'Ampezzo

Ra Regoles Museum

*Museo de Ra Regoles, Via del Parco 1, 1–32043
    Cortina d'Ampezzo, Belluna* ☎ *0436 866222
July 1–31 & Sept 1–20, Mon–Sat 4–7.30. Aug,
    daily 10.30–12.30, 4–7.30. Dec 20–Jan 7,
    Mon–Sat 10.30–12.30, 4–7.30. Jan 8–Mar
    31, Mon–Sat 4–7.*
[C] 🔥

The Ra Regoles Museum was opened in 1975. It brings together four types of collection – paintings, sculpture and drawings by contemporary Italian artists; ethnographical items from the Ampezzo valley; religious art from local churches; and the fossils found in the Dolomites. The ethnographical material has been given or lent by local people and comprises particularly costumes, weapons, agricultural implements, craftsmen's tools, copperware, wrought-ironwork, articles made of wood and musical instruments.

The remarkable collection of fossils was given to the museum by Renaldo Zardini (1902–88). Zardini was self-taught and made major contributions to the study of the palaeontology of the Dolomite region. He received an honorary doctorate from the University of Modena in acknowledgement of his work.

Ile des Charmes, 1928, by A. Savinio. Rimoldi Gallery of Modern Art, Cortina d'Ampezzo.

Rimoldi Gallery of Modern Art

Galleria d'Arte Moderna Mario Rimoldi, Via del Parco 1, I–32043 Cortina d'Ampezzo, Belluno ☎ *0436 866222*
Dec 20 – Jan 7, Mon–Sat 10.30–12, 4–7. Jan 8 – Mar 31, Mon–Sat 4–7. July & Sept, Mon–Sat 4–7.30. Aug, daily 10.30–12.30, 4–7.30.
C ▮

Opened in 1974, the gallery contains the collection of modern Italian art formed by Mario Rimoldi during the 1920s and 1940s and subsequently bequeathed to the town. It contains nearly 400 works by the most important Italian artists of the 20th century, including Giorgio de Chirico (1888–1978), Filippo de Pisis (1896–1956), Mario Sironi (1885–1961) and Anton Zoran Music (b.1909).

Cortona

Museum of the Etruscan Academy

Museo dell'Accademia Etrusca, Piazza Signorelli 9, I–52044 Cortona, Arezzo ☎ *0575 62767*
Apr–Sept, Tues–Sun 10–1, 4–7. Oct–Mar, Tues–Sun 9–1, 3–5.
F ▮ 🖿 ⬗

The museum is of remarkable age. Established in 1727, it is accommodated in the Palazzo Casali, which was built in the 13th century and considerably altered in the 16th and 17th. It contains 14th–17th-century paintings by artists from Tuscany and 18th-century Venetian painting. A separate gallery is devoted to the work of the Cortona artist, Gino Severini (d.1966). There are also collections of 13th–14th-century illuminated song-books, costumes, coins and Egyptian, Etruscan and Greco-Roman antiquities.

Courmayeur

Duke of the Abruzzi Alpine Museum

Museo Alpino Duca degli Abruzzi, Piazza Henry 2, C.P. 45, I–11013 Courmayeur, Aosta ☎ *0165 842064*
July–Sept, daily 9–8. Oct–June, Tues–Sun 9–12.30, 3.30–6.30.
C

The museum was established in 1925. It contains collections formed by the Association of Alpine Guides since its foundation in the mid 18th century. The exhibits include minerals and animals of the Alpine region, photographs and mementoes of Alpine climbs and examples of climbing equipment used at different periods.

Cremona

'Il Cambonino' Museum of Peasant Life

Museo della Civiltà Contadina di Valpadana 'Il Cambonino', Via Castelleone 51, I–26100 Cremona ☎ *0372 21411*
Jan–July, Sept–Dec, Tues–Sat 9.30–12.30, 3–6; Sun and public holidays, 9.30–12.30
C ▮ ⬗

'Il Cambonino' is a large 19th-century cheese-making farm, on the outskirts of Cremona, typical of the region. Some of the milk was produced on the farm, the rest was bought in. The museum explains how the farm and the factory were run and illustrates the life and work of peasant communities in the region in the 19th and early 20th centuries. There are collections of agricultural implements, tools, vehicles and equipment, showing developments up to the coming of the first tractors. A section of the museum is devoted to rural craftsmen, including the cabinet-maker, waggon-builder and cooper.

Stradivarius Museum

Museo Stradivariano, Via Palestro 17, I–26100 Cremona ☎ *0372 29349*
Tues–Sat 8.30–12.15, 3–5.45; Sun 9.30–12.15.
C ▮ ⬗

Antonio Stradivari (c. 1644–1737) was the most prominent of the stringed-instrument makers who worked in Cremona during the 17th and 18th centuries. The museum pays tribute to them and illustrates the history and techniques of violin-making. The emphasis is, of course, on Stradivari himself and there is an important collection of tools and wooden and cardboard patterns which belonged to him. The museum also has an interesting series of bowed-instruments, dating from the 17th century to the 20th.

Crotone

Archaeological Museum

Museo Archeologico Nazionale, Via Risorgimento, I–88074 Crotone, Catanzaro ☎ *0962 23082*
May–Sept, Tues–Sat 10–1, 3–5; Sun, Mon 10–1. Oct–Apr, Tues–Sat 10–1, 2–5; Sun, Mon 10–1.
C

This rich Achaean colony of *Magna Graecia* was founded in 710 BC. Pythagoras established religious communities here *c.* 532 BC which were devoted to the study of mathematics. The museum, opened in 1964, has archaeological material, especially ceramics, coins and terracotta votive tablets, from Crotone and from other colonies of Magna Graecia, and a good collection of Greek and Roman coins.

Dozza

Dozza Fortress

La Rocca di Dozza, Piazza della Rocca 5, I–40050 Dozza, Bologna ☎ 0542 678089
Apr–Sept, Tues–Sun 10–12, 3–6; Oct–Mar, Tues–Sun 10–12, 2–5.
F

The brick-built medieval castle, the 'Rock of Dozza', was much involved in the quarrel between the Guelphs and the Ghibellines and was several times conquered and reconquered by both sides. Afterwards it belonged in turn to the Sforza, Campeggi and Malvezzi families, until it was finally bought by the municipality in 1960.

The State Rooms can be visited and in the basement there is a museum of rural life, with collections of furniture and domestic equipment, arranged in room settings. There is also an exhibition of the originals of the frescoes painted on the walls of Dozza during the annual Frescoed Wall Biennale, which has operated since 1960.

Faenza

International Museum of Ceramics

Museo Internazionale delle Ceramiche, Via Baccarini 19, I–48018 Faenza, Ravenna. Correspondence to: Via Campidori 2, I–48018 Faenza. ☎ 0546 21240
May–Sept, Tues–Sun 9.30–7; public holidays 9.30–1. Oct–Apr, Tues–Sun 9.30–1, 3–6; public holidays 9.30–1. Closed Jan 1, Easter, Apr 25, May 1, Dec 25.
C ⓘ ♠

Faenza has been famous for its pottery since the 12th century and has given its name to the glazed earthenware known as 'faience'. Its museum was founded in 1908 and has been systematically developed since then, in association with the training courses which the town organises for ceramic designers.

The collections include Roman pottery from excavations made in Faenza area and in central Romagna, majolica and earthenware made in Faenza in the 15th and 16th centuries, and Italian ceramics from the Renaissance to the present day. There are also items from South and Central America and the Middle East and contemporary international ceramics.

Torricelli Museum

Museo Torricelliano, Corso Garibaldi 2, CP 179, I–48018 Faenza, Ravenna
Tues 9–12
F

The physicist, Evangelista Torricelli (1608–47), was a pupil of Galileo and the discoverer of the principle of barometric pressure. He was born in Faenza and the museum, opened in 1947, contains collections which illustrate his life and work. The exhibits include memorabilia, documents and scientific instruments, especially barometers.

Feltre

Feltre Museum

Museo Civico, Via Lorenzo Luzo 23, I–32032 Feltre, Belluno ☎ 0439 80264
Tues–Fri 10–1; Sat, Sun 10–1, 4–6.
C ⓘ

The museum is in the 16th-century Palazzo Villabruna, where the ground-floor rooms still have their original furnishings. The exhibits include archaeological material from Palaeovenetian and Roman sites, furniture by local craftsmen, Renaissance goldsmiths' work, Italian ceramics, coins and medals and lace. There are also collections relating to the Risorgimento and to the history of the district in the period of the Venetian republic.

In the art gallery there are works by Gentile Bellini, Luzzo, Cima, Longhi and by 16th-century Venetian, Flemish and German artists.

Rizzarda Gallery of Modern Art

Galleria d'Arte Moderna 'Carlo Rizzarda', Via del Paradiso 8, I–32032 Feltre, Belluno
☎ 0439 89736
June–Sept, Tues–Sun 10–1, 4–7
C ⓘ

The 20th-century artist, Carlo Rizzarda, bought and restored the 16th-century Palazzo Cumano, primarily in order to display a large collection of his works in wrought iron. Some of the rooms are furnished in Renaissance style and there are also displays of contemporary paintings, ceramics and majolica, which Rizzarda bought as part of his policy of encouraging young Italian artists.

Dozza Fortress from the air.

Fenis

Museum of Furniture

Museo dell'Arredamento, Castello di Fenis,
*   I–11020 Fenis, Aosta*   ☎ *0165 764263*
Wed–Mon 10–1, 2–5. Closed Jan 1, Dec 25.
Ⓒ

The 14th-century castle which houses the
museum has a collection of fine carved furniture
in the local Valle d'Aosta style. Some items
were originally made for the castle itself and the
remainder is from other houses in the region.
The exhibits also include a wide range of
traditional domestic equipment. The walls of
many of the rooms in the Castle are decorated
with frescoes of saints, philosophers and other
figures.

Ferrara

Ariosto's House

Casa dell'Ariosto, Via Ariosto 67, I–44100
*   Ferrara*   ☎ *0532 32303*
Mon–Sat 10–1, 2–5. Closed public holidays.
Ⓒ

The poet, Lodovico Ariosto (1475–1533) spent
his lifetime in the service of the court of the Este
family at Ferrara and wrote his great epic poem,
Orlando Furioso, in his spare time. His house has
been preserved and the interior looks much as it
did when he lived here. Several rooms are
furnished and equipped in the style of the
period.

Museum of the Risorgimento and the Resistance

Museo del Risorgimento e della Resistenza, Corso
*   Ercole I d'Este 19, I–44100 Ferrara*
*   Correspondence to: Piazzetta Santa Anna*
*   3/11, I–44100 Ferrara*
*   ☎ 0532 37307/37161*
Mon–Sat 9–12.30, 3–6; Sun 9–12.30. Closed
*   Jan 1, Easter, May 1, Aug 15, Dec 25.*
Ⓒ 🖼 🚗

The museum was opened in 1958 and has
collections illustrating the history of Ferrara
during the past 150 years and particularly the
activities of local patriots during the 19th-
century Risorgimento and in the Second World
War Resistance movement against the German
occupying forces. There are also collections of
household objects, tools and costumes relating
to the traditional peasant culture of the area.

Filottrano

Museum of Carts

Museo del Bioccio Marchigiano, Via Beltrami 2,
*   I–60024 Filottrano, Ancona*
*   ☎ 071 33037/7221314*
Wed–Fri (check locally for times)
Ⓕ

The Archangel Michael and the Dragon by
Antonio Pollaiuolo (1432–98). Bardini
Museum, Florence.

The museum is in the 17th-century Palazzo
Beltrami and has a section devoted to the most
remarkable member of the family, Giacomo
Constantino Beltrami (1779–1855), who served
Napoleon I as both a soldier and a judge and
subsequently, in the course of a one-man
expedition, discovered the source of the
Mississippi. The main purpose of the museum,
however, is to display a collection of 19th–20th-
century brightly coloured farm carts, typical of
Italy, and ornamented with religious images,
rural scenes, female figures and floral
decorations.

Fiumicino

Museum of Ships

Museo delle Navi, Via Alessandro Guidoni 35,
*   I–00054 Fiumicino, Roma*   ☎ *06 6011089*
April–Sept, Mon–Sat 9–1, 2–6; Sun and public
*   holidays 9–1. Oct–Mar, Mon–Sat 9–1, 2–5;*
*   Sun and public holidays 9–1.*
Ⓕ 🚗

The port of Rome, built by the Emperor
Claudius in AD 41–54 at the mouth of the
Tiber, silted up rapidly and had become useless
by the 5th century. Its site is now 3 km from the
sea. The museum, opened in 1979, contains six
Roman cargo ships and a Roman fishing vessel,
with their contents, which had been buried by
sand in the port.

Florence

Accademia Gallery

Galleria dell'Accademia, Via Ricasoli 60, I–50122
*   Firenze*   ☎ *055 214375*
Tues–Sat 9–2; Sun 9–1.
Ⓕ 🛈 🖼 ♿ 🚗

This important state gallery was established in 1784. It contains 13th–16th-century Florentine paintings and sculpture by Michelangelo and 19th-century Italian artists. The collection of works by Michelangelo is particularly notable. It includes his *David*, the four *Prisoners* and the *St Matthew*. The gallery also has the *Madonna of the Sea* by Botticelli and *The Annunciation* by Lorenzo Monaco.

Bardini Museum

Museo Bardini, Piazza dei Mozzi 1, I–50125 Firenze   ☎ 055 2342427
Mon, Tues, Thurs, Fri 9–2; Sat, Sun 8–1. Closed Jan 1, Easter, May 1, Aug 15, Dec 25.
ⓒ 👤 💼 🔄

The Palazzo Bardini is one of the most important in Florence. It was built at the end of the 19th century by the antiquarian and collector, Stefano Bardini, and was intended from the beginning to be used for museum purposes. It has been a public museum since 1924 and contains the Bardini collection of paintings, sculpture, furniture, porcelain, tapestries and weapons and the Corsi collection of Italian paintings and sculpture.

Bargello Museum

Museo Nazionale del Bargello, Via dell'Acqua 5, I–50122 Firenze   ☎ 055 210801
Tues–Sat 9–2; Sun 9–1. Closed Jan 1, Apr 25, May 1, Aug 15, Dec 25.
ⓒ

The palace which has housed the museum since the 19th century is one of the oldest in Florence, built c. 1260 by Fra Sisto and Fra Ristoro. It was formerly the residence of the governing magistrate of Florence (*podestà*) and then became the police headquarters (*bargello*) and a prison. It was converted into a magnificent museum of sculpture and the decorative arts in 1857–65. The collections are of Italian art of the Renaissance and include sculptures by Michelangelo, Cellini, Donatello and Luca della Robbia, enamelled terracottas by Giovanni and Andrea della Robbia, bronzes, medals and seals, a large and important collection of weapons and armour as well as textiles, ceramics and furniture.

Buonarroti House

Casa Buonarroti, Via Ghibellina 70, I–50122 Firenze   ☎ 055 241752
Wed–Mon 9.30–1.30
ⓒ 👤

In 1508 Michelangelo bought a plot of land in the Via Ghibellina and built a house on it. He lived here from 1516 to 1525 and it was afterwards owned by the Buonarroti family until the death of Cosimo Buonarroti, when it became a museum. It contains drawings and sculpture by Michelangelo and memorabilia, art and archaeology collections of the Buonarrotis.

Cathedral Museum

Museo dell' Opera di Santa Maria del Fiore, Piazza del Duomo 9, I–50122 Firenze
        ☎ 055 213229
Mar–Oct, Mon–Sat 9–8; Sun 10–1. Nov–Feb, Mon–Sat 9–6; Sun 10–1. Closed Jan 1, Easter, Christmas. Free admission Sun.
ⓒ 👤

The museum contains works of art, especially sculpture, removed from the cathedral, Giotto's Tower and the baptistry in order to preserve them against atmospheric pollution and other forms of damage. They include Michelangelo's *Pietà*, the *Mary Magdalene* by Donatello and panels by Ghiberti from the Paradise Door of the Baptistry. There are also statues of the prophets, Jeremiah and Habakkuk by Donatello and two sculptures of Choirs by Donatello and Luca della Robbia.

Meridiana Costume Gallery

Galleria del Costume, Palazzina della Meridiana, Piazza Pitti 1, I–50125 Firenze
        ☎ 055 294279
Tues–Sat 9–2; Sun 9–1. Closed Jan 1, Apr 25, May 1, Dec 25.
ⓒ

The gallery occupies 15 rooms of the Meridiana Pavilion, which dates from 1776 and adjoins the Palazzo Pitti. It was the favourite residence of Vittorio Emanuele II of Savoy, in the days when Florence was a capital city (1865–71). The exhibits consist of 18th–20th-century Italian costumes for both men and women. They are displayed on modern figures, each one specially made for the costume in question, against a background of furniture, lamps, tapestries, mirrors and carpets appropriate to them.

Museum of the History of Science

Istituto e Museo di Storia della Scienza, Piazza dei Giudici 1, I–50122 Firenze
        ☎ 055 293493/298876
Mon–Sat 9.30–1. Closed mid-week holidays.
ⓒ

The Palazzo Castellani, which houses the museum, is one of the oldest buildings in Florence. It is built into the city walls and dates from the mid 12th century. Its last private owners were the Castellani family. In 1574 it became a law court, and the museum was established here in 1929.

The museum has one of the most important scientific collections in the world. It includes the instruments of Galileo Galilei (1564–1642), among them two of his telescopes and the objective lens with which he discovered the four satellites of Jupiter. There is also the Medici collection of quadrants, astrolabes, solar and nocturnal dials, compasses and armillary spheres, the magnificent instruments in blown glass which belonged to the Academie del Cimento, and the Lorena collection of chemical and pharmaceutical apparatus, surgical instruments, anatomical models in wax and terracotta, pneumatic and electrostatic machines and machines for mechanical and electromagnetic experiments.

Museum of Silver

Museo degli Argenti, Palazzo Pitti, Piazzi Pitti 1, I–50125 Firenze   ☎ 055 212557
Tues–Sat 9–2; Sun 9-1. Closed Jan 1, Apr 25, May 1, Dec 25.
C

Established in 1921 and reorganised in 1973–5, the museum contains the treasures of Lorenzo the Magnificent and the Prince Bishops of Salzburg, the Uffizi Cabinet of Gems, which includes cameo portraits of famous Florentines, and the jewels of the Electress Palatine. Among the exhibits are ivories, Limoges enamels, amber, painted glass and silversmiths' work.

Palatine Gallery

Galleria Palatina, Palazzo Pitti, I–50125 Firenze
☎ 055 201323
Tues–Sun 10–1. Closed Jan 1, 6, 7, May 1, Aug 13, 14, Dec 25.
C

The gallery reflects the taste and choice of the Medici family and the members of their court. The present random arrangement is much as it was at the end of the 18th century. The gallery was opened to the public in 1823. The paintings are mostly from the 16th, 17th and 18th centuries. There are portraits by Van Dyck and Titian and among the other artists represented are Raphael, Rubens, Andrea del Sarto, Veronese, Velasquez and Fra Bartolomeo.

Francesco I gallery, Palazzo Vecchio, Florence.

Palazzo Vecchio

Museo di Palazzo Vecchio, Piazza della Signoria, I–50100 Firenze   ☎ 055 27861
Mon–Fri 9–7; Sat, Sun 8–1.
C ⓘ 🖳 🖴

The Palazzo Vecchio was built in 1299 as the residence of the governors of the city. Over the centuries, and especially in the 15th, it was modified and enlarged. The museum consists of the state rooms, which have frescoes by Domenico Ghirlandaio (1449–94), Agnolo Bronzino (1513–72), Francesco Salviati (1510–63) and Giorgio Vasari (1511–74) and, on the mezzanine floor, the Loeser collection of 12th–16th-century Italian paintings and sculpture.

St Mark's Monastery

Convento e Museo di San Marco, Piazza San Marco, I–50121 Firenze   ☎ 055 210741
Tues–Sun 10–1. Closed some public holidays.
C

The former Dominican monastery was rebuilt *c.* 1436. Fra Angelico (1387–1435) took orders in Fiesole before coming to St Mark's, where he decorated the walls of the monks' cells with religious scenes. What used to be the guest quarters contain a number of his paintings on wood, including the triptych of the *Descent from the Cross* and the *Last Judgement*. The staircase is dominated by his *Annunciation*. Visitors can also see the cells of the fanatical and ascetic monk, Savonarola, who became prior of the Monastery of St Mark and who preached against the arts and the pleasures of the senses and who, in 1497, organised 'a bonfire of vanities' – musical instruments, paintings, books of poetry – in the Piazza della Signoria. He himself was burnt at the stake in the same place in 1498.

Uffizi Gallery

Galleria degli Uffizi, Loggiato degli Uffizi 6, I–50122 Firenze   ☎ 055 218341/2
Tues–Sat 9–7; Sun 9–1. Closed Jan 1, Easter, Apr 25, May 1, 1st Sun in June, Aug 15, Dec 25.
C 🖳

The gallery was created by the Medici, Grand Duke Francesco, in 1581, on the top floor of the building which housed the administrative offices of the Florentine state. The collections formed by the Medici family in the 15th and 16th centuries were greatly increased during the 17th and 18th and again after the suppression of convents and monasteries in Napoleonic times. In the present century acquisitions have been mostly confined to self-portraits.

The Uffizi is one of the world's major art galleries, with collections of 13th–18th-century Italian and foreign paintings, Greek sculpture, including the Medici Venus, tapestries, ceramics, furniture and objets d'art. Some artists, including Botticelli, Leonardo, Titian, Raphael, Michelangelo, Veronese and Rubens, have complete rooms devoted to them.

Foggia

Foggia Museum and Art Gallery

Museo e Pinacoteca Comunale, Piazza Nigri 1,
I–71100 Foggia   ☎ 0881 26245
Daily 9–1. Wed and Fri also 5–7. Closed Jan 1, 6,
Easter, Aug 15, Dec 25, 26.

C 🖥 🖉

The museum is in the former town hall. It
contains prehistoric and Roman archaeology –
the pottery is particularly notable – architectural
fragments from the early Christian period to the
present century, and ethnological material from
the region. There are also displays of paintings
by 18th-century artists of the Naples School and
by 19th-century artists from Foggia.

The museum has memorabilia, manuscripts
and documents relating to the composer,
Umberto Giordano (1867–1948), who was born
in Foggia, and whose work was performed by,
among others, Caruso, Gigli and Maria Callas.
The park in Foggia is dedicated to Giordano and
contains a statue of him by the Venetian artist,
Romano Vio (1913–84).

Forlì

Forlì Museums

Musei, Istituti Culturali ed Artistici, Corso della
Repubblica 72, I–47100 Forlì ☎ 543 32771
Tues–Sat 9–2; Sun 9–1. Closed Jan 1, Feb 4,
Easter, Apr 25, May 1, Aug 15, Nov 1,
Dec 8, 25.

F 🛈

The interesting museum complex at Corso della
Repubblica 72 has four constituent parts.

The Archaeological Museum displays
archaeological material found during the
excavations of Bronze Age and Roman sites in
the Forlì area.

The Pergoli Museum has collections
illustrating rural life in Romagna up to the
beginnings of the period of mechanisation and
industrialisation. There are sections devoted to
agricultural tools and implements, craftsmen's
tools and workshops, domestic equipment,
furniture, costumes and folk art.

The Saffi Art Gallery contains 15th–16th-
century paintings by local artists, ceramics,
Flemish tapestries, weapons and armour. There
are also collections of archaeological material.

Finally, the Museum of Ceramics has fine
collections of 15th–19th-century pottery and
porcelain made in the Romagna and Faenza
districts.

Genoa

Gallery of Modern Art

Civica Galleria d'Arte Moderna, Villa Serra, Via
Capolungo 3, I–16167 Genova
☎ 010 326025
June–Sept, Tues–Sat 9–1.15, 3–6. Oct–May,
Tues–Sat 9–1.15, 2–5. Closed public holidays.

C

**Flemish tapestry. The Saffi Art Gallery, Forlì
Museums.**

The villa which contains the museum was built
at the end of the 18th century by the Marchese
Saluzzo. In 1927 it was given to the city of
Genoa by the local shipbuilder, Carlo Barabino,
who had bought it, together with its fine gardens
and park (which can be visited), from the
Marchese Serra. The gardens have 18th-century
statues on the terrace.

The gallery contains paintings, sculpture
and graphics by 19th- and 20th-century Italian
artists, especially from Genoa and the Ligurian
coastal region.

Maritime Museum

Civico Museo Navale, Villa Doria, Piazza
Bonavino Cristoforo 7, Pegli, I–16156 Genova
☎ 010 480022
Tues–Sun 10–1, 2–5. Closed public holidays.

C

From the 11th century to the 16th, Genoa had a
large trading fleet and its dockyards were
famous. It became a mercantile republic in the
16th century, but its importance declined with
the development of ports on the Atlantic coast.
With the unification of Italy, its strength
returned and it is now once again the greatest
seaport in Italy. The museum, in a 16th-century
mansion, contains collections illustrating the
history of the port, including paintings, prints,
drawings and ship models.

Mazzini's House

Casa di Mazzini, Via San Luca 13, I–16124
Genova
Tues–Sun 10–1. Closed public holidays.

C

Genoa was the cradle of the Italian revolt
against Austrian rule, the Risorgimento. The
Young Italy movement was founded here by
Giuseppe Mazzini. The museum, in his former
home, tells the story of Mazzini's life and of the
revolts in Genoa.

Palazzo Bianco

*Galleria di Palazzo Bianco, Via Garibaldi 11,
    I–16124 Genova*   ☎ *010 291803*
*Mon 10–12.15, 3–5.45; Tues–Sat 9–7; Sun,
    guided tours only. Closed public holidays.*
C

The palazzo was built in the 1530s by Gerolamo
Grimaldi and reconstructed in the 18th century
by the Brignole Sale family. It was given to the
City of Genoa in 1889 by Maria Brignole Sale
de Ferrari, Duchess of Galliera and became a
public museum in 1892.

The collections on display are mostly
paintings, 13th-century Byzantine, 15th–18th-
century Genoese, 15th–17th-century Flemish
and Dutch – Genoa had strong trading links
with Flanders – 17th-century Spanish and 13th–
17th-century Italian. There are also displays of
Genoese furniture, Flemish tapestries and
Chinese porcelain.

Palazzo Rosso

*Galleria di Palazzo Rosso, Via Garibaldi 18,
    I–16124 Genova*   ☎ *010 589052*
*Mon 10–12.15, 3–5.45; Tues–Sat 9–7; Sun,
    guided tours only. Closed public holidays.*
C

The Palazzo Rosso was built by Ridolfo and Gio
Francesco Brignole Sale in 1671–9. It was given
to the City of Genoa in 1874, together with its
collections of paintings and sculpture, by Maria
Brignole Sale de Ferrari, Duchess of Galliera.

The works on display consist mainly of
paintings, graphics and sculpture by 16th–18th-
century Italian artists, including Veronese,
Caravaggio and Guercino, but there are also
paintings by Rubens and Van Dyck, both of
whom worked in Genoa – Van Dyck laid the
foundations of his career in the city. There are
also exhibits of ceramics, coins and medals.

***Judith* by Paolo Veronese (c. 1528–88).
Palazzo Rosso, Genoa.**

Gignese

Museum of Umbrellas and Parasols

*Museo dell'Ombrello e del Parasole, Viale Golf
    Panorama 4, I–28040 Gignese, Novara*
    ☎ *0323 90067*
Apr–Sept, Tues–Sun 10–12, 3–6
C ☂

Gignese has been a centre of umbrella-making
since the 18th century. The museum, opened in
1939, is built in the shape of an umbrella. On
the first floor there is an historical collection of
umbrellas and on the second, information about
personalities and firms in the industry during the
18th–20th centuries and about styles, materials
and manufacturing techniques.

Grinzane Cavour

Museum of the Wines of Piedmont

*Museo dell'Enoteca Regionale Piemontese Cavour,
    Via Castello 5, I–12060 Grinzane Cavour,
    Cuneo*   ☎ *0173 62159*
*May–Sept, Wed–Mon, tours at 9, 10, 11, 2.30,
    3.30, 4.30, 5.30. Oct–Dec & Feb–Apr,
    Wed–Mon, tours at 9, 10, 11, 2, 3, 4, 5.*
C ✎ ■ ☛

The castle of Grinzane Cavour dates from the
11th century. At one time it belonged to the
Cavour family, of which the statesman, Count
Camillo Cavour (1810–61), was a member. It
was restored during the 1960s, since when it has
become a centre for publicising the wines and
traditional cuisine of Alba.

In 1975 a museum was opened in the castle.
Its exhibits include memorabilia of Count
Cavour, reconstructions of Alba kitchens of the
early 16th and early 19th centuries, an 18th-
century distillery and a cooper's workshop.
There are also collections of farming
implements, wine-glasses and grape-decorated
plates from Mondové.

Grosseto

Maremma Museum of Art and Archaeology

*Museo Archeologico e d'Arte delle Maremma,
    Piazza Baccarini, I–58100 Grosseto*
    ☎ *0564 21151*
*Mon, Tues, Thurs–Sat 10–1, 3–5; Sun and public
    holidays 10–1. Closed Jan 1, Dec 25.*
C

The principal attraction of the museum is its
splendid collection of Etruscan and Roman
sculpture from local excavations. Among the
other exhibits are Bronze Age jewellery and
pottery. Greek and Etruscan ceramics and
Roman bronzes. There is also a large collection
of coins.

Gurro

Museum of Local Customs

Museo dei Costumi e Tradizioni Locali, I–28052
  Gurro, Novara   ☎ *0323 76100*
Fri–Wed 10–4
F 🛈 🚗

This local museum, established in 1975,
documents the pre-industrial way of life in an
area which is still largely dependent on
agriculture. There are displays of costumes,
domestic equipment, country furniture, popular
art, lace, agricultural implements and
craftsmen's tools. A special feature of the
museum is its collection of equipment for the
processing of hemp and wool, which are
important products of the region.

Ivrea

Garda Museum

Museo P. A. Garda, Piazza Ottinetti 18, I–10015
  Ivrea, Torino   ☎ *0125 48189*
Tues–Fri 10–12, 3–5.30; Sat 10–12, 3–4.30.
C 🛈 🖾 🚗

Ivrea is the principal town of the part of
Piedmont known as the Canavese. The museum
was established in 1876 in the former convent of
the Poor Clares. Its exhibits illustrate the
traditional crafts and industries of the region,
especially shoemaking, joinery and tinsmiths'
work. There is also Roman archaeological
material from local excavations, including a
very rare survival of a 'groma', a sighting
instrument used by Roman surveyors.

A separate section of the museum is devoted
to Japanese and Chinese art. This includes a
large collection of lacquer objects from the
Tokugawa family and Japanese Sho-gun of the
Edo period.

La Spezia

Museum of the Navy

Museo Tecnico Navale, Viale Amendola 1,
  I–19100 La Spezia   ☎ *0187 717600*
Tues, Wed, Thurs, Sat 9–12, 2–6; Mon, Fri 2–6.
  Closed public holidays.
C

La Spezia, on the Gulf of Genoa, has for many
years been the principal base of the Italian
Navy. The museum is opposite the main gate of
the Navy Yard. It contains models, maps,
photographs, figureheads, relics and documents
illustrating the history of the Navy. Among the
exhibits are mementoes of Guglielmo Marconi's
success in achieving radio contact over a
distance of 16 kilometres from a point near the
museum in 1897. There is also a cannon with
the initials of George III, which the British
placed on Mount Castellana in 1815, during an
unsuccessful attempt to occupy the Gulf, and
the tender which, in 1862, landed Garibaldi at

**Model of Egyptian boat, 1500 BC. Museum of
the Navy, La Spezia.**

Varignano, where he was held prisoner after
being injured at Aspromonti.

Among the models is one of the screw-
propelled corvette, *S. Giovanni*, built in 1849
for the Sardinian Navy. It was the first Italian
warship to have mechanical propulsion.

Lipari (Lipari Islands)

Aeolian Museum

Museo Eoliano, Castello, I–98055 Lipari,
  ☎ *090 9811031*
Mon– Sat 9–2; Sun and public holidays 9–1.
F

The Lipari Islands are also called the Aeolian
Islands because in classical times it was thought
that Aeolus, the god of the winds, lived there.
Lipari's large museum is in the middle of the
historic rock, the castle, that was the site of the
prehistoric settlements, the acropolis of the
Greek and Roman town and, until the 18th
century, the site of medieval and Renaissance
Lipari, with its Baroque churches and
fortifications of the Greek, Roman and Spanish
periods. The museum buildings, dating from the
15th, 17th, and 18th centuries, contain the
remains of an 11th–12th century abbey.

The collections cover the geology and
vulcanology of the Aeolian islands, the
prehistory of the islands and of Milazzo, and
Greek and Roman Lipari from its foundation in
580 BC to the Arab conquest in the 11th
century AD. A special section is devoted to
archaeological material found in the Aeolian
Sea. An exceptionally interesting feature of the
museum is its collection of 5th–3rd century BC
theatrical terracottas, including tragic and
comic masks.

Lucca

Lucca National Art Gallery

Pinacoteca Nazionale, Palazzo Mansi, Via Galli
  Tassi 43, I–55100 Lucca   ☎ *0583 55570*
Mon 2–5; Tues–Sun 10–5. Closed Mon if public
  holiday, also Jan 1, May 1, Dec 25.
C

Since 1978 the museum has occupied a 17th-century mansion, elaborately decorated in 18th-century style. The core of the collection consists of 15th–18th century paintings which were given to Lucca in 1847 by Leopoldo II and which had been taken from monasteries which had been closed. Both Italian and foreign artists are represented. Among the later additions is a portrait of Princess Elisa Bonaparte, by Marie Benoist, who ruled Lucca from 1805 to 1813. After Napoleon's Italian campaigns, he bestowed the title of Princess of Lucca and Piombino on his sister, who showed a remarkable aptitude for public affairs.

Puccini's House

Casa Museo Puccini, Corte San Lorenzo 9,
*   I–55100 Lucca*   ☎ 0583 584028
Apr-Sept, Tues–Sun 10–6. Oct-Mar, Tues–Sun
*   10–4. Closed Jan 1, Dec 25.*
F 🛈

The operatic composer, Giacomo Puccini (1858–1924), was born in Lucca and in 1978 a museum to him was established in the family home. The exhibits include furniture and other family possessions and memorabilia of the composer, including musical scores, letters and photographs.

Manfredonia

Manfredonia Museum

Museo Nazionale di Manfredonia, Via Nazario
*   Sauro, I–71043 Manfredonia, Foggia*
*   ☎ 0884 27838*
April–Sept, Tues–Sat 9–1.30, 4–7.30; Sun
*   9–1.30. Oct–Mar, Tues–Sat 9–1, 4–7;*
*   Sun 9–1.*
C ✐

This museum contains archaeological material of exceptional importance and is maintained by the State for this reason. It is concerned with the prehistoric settlement and the history of the Sipontum lagoon, lying between Candelaro and Ofanto. The inhabitants of these Neolithic villages concerned themselves with agriculture and animal husbandry and later, in Bronze Age and Iron Age times, had contacts with the Aegean world and produced strange stelae, the symbolism of whose designs is still not properly understood.

    The museum is in two parts, one on the Neolithic villages and the other on the stelae. The massive castle in which it is housed was founded by Manfred, King of Sicily, in 1263 and re-fortified at the end of the 15th century.

Mantua

Ducal Palace

Palazzo Ducale, Piazza Sordello 39, I–46100
*   Mantova*
*   ☎ 0376 320283*
Apr–Oct, Tues–Sat 9–6; Sun, Mon 9–1. Nov–
*   Mar, Tues–Sat 9–4; Sun, Mon 9–1.*
C

The 13th-century fortress was rebuilt in the 17th–18th centuries by the Gonzaga family, Dukes of Mantua, to form a palace and has since undergone few changes. The Marriage Chamber contains a series of frescoes by Mantegna (1464–74). The palace also contains groups of miniature apartments and stairs built for the dwarfs of Duke Vicenzo, and visitors can also see the music room and workroom of Isabella d'Este.

    Among the other exhibits are paintings of the Mantegna School, medallions, tombs and inscriptions, and portrait busts.

Milan

Ambrosian Library Art Gallery

Pinacoteca Ambrosiana, Piazza Pio XI 2, I–20123
*   Milano*
*   ☎ 02 800146*
Sun–Fri 10–5. Closed Easter Sun & Mon, May 1,
*   Aug 15, 16, Dec 25, 26.*
C

The library, which is not open to the public, is in a palace built in 1609 for Cardinal Federico Borromeo. The Gallery is on the first floor. It contains Italian Renaissance works, the *Mouse with a Rose* by Jan Brueghel, low-reliefs from the tomb of Gaston de Foix (1523) and two outstanding portraits, one by Leonardo da Vinci of the musician Gaffurio, and the other of Beatrice d'Este by Ambrogio da Predis.

    Also on display are Raphael's cartoons for the frescoes in the School of Athens in the Vatican.

Female funeral stele, 7th-century.
Manfredonia Museum.

Manzoni's House, Milan.

Brera Art Gallery

*Pinacoteca di Brera, Via Brera 28, I–20121
    Milano* ☎ *02 800985*
Tues–Thurs 10–1, 2–5; Fri–Sun 10–1.

C ⓘ ☞ ⌂

The 17th century mansion which today houses
the museum once belonged to the Jesuits. The
complex of buildings includes the 14th-century
church of Santa Maria di Brera and the
Academy of Fine Arts, founded in 1776 by
Maria Theresa of Austria.

This collection, one of Italy's greatest, is
particularly strong in works by Lombard and
Venetian artists, and consists of 14th–20th
century paintings and sculpture, 15th–20th
century drawings, and modern prints and
engravings. Among the exhibits are Rubens'
Last Supper, two Madonnas and a Pietà by
Giovanni Bellini, *St Mark Preaching* by Gentile
and Giovanni Bellini, Raphael's *Betrothal of the
Virgin*, Andrea Mantegna's *Christ* and a
Madonna by Ambrogio Lorenzetti.

There are also works by El Greco, Goya,
Brueghel, Van Dyck and Rembrandt.

Castle of the Sforzas

Castello Sforzesco, I–20121 Milano
    ☎ *02 800146*
*Sun–Fri 10–5. Closed Easter, May 1, Aug 15, 16,
    Dec 25, 26.*

C

In the mid 15th century, the Sforza family took
over control of Milan after the death of the last
Visconti. Their enormous brick castle, the seat
of the Dukes of Milan, now houses the
municipal art collections. The Romanesque,
Gothic and Renaissance sculptures, mostly by
Lombard artists, include the tomb of Bernabò
Visconti, with his equestrian statue and an
unfinished Pietà by Michelangelo. The artists
represented in the picture gallery include
Mantegna, Giovanni Bellini, Tiepolo and
Guardi. There is also a decorative arts section
and an outstanding collection of musical
instruments.

Cathedral Museum

*Museo del Duomo, Piazza Duomo 14, I–20122
    Milano* ☎ *02 860358*
*Tues–Sun 10–5. Closed Easter, May 1,
    Christmas.*

C

The building of Milan's flamboyant white
marble Gothic cathedral was begun in 1386 and
continued in the 15th–16th centuries. The
façade was completed in 1805–1809 on the
orders of Napoleon. The Museum is in the
18th-century Royal Palace. It contains models
and documents explaining the different stages in
the building of the Cathedral and has
collections of sculptures, stained glass, tapestries
and vestments from the 14th century to the
20th.

Gallery of Modern Art

*Civica Galleria d'Arte Moderna, Via Palestro 16,
    I–20121 Milano* ☎ *02 702819*
*Wed–Mon 10–5. Closed Jan 1, Easter, May 1,
    Aug 15, Dec 25, 26.*

C

The gallery is in the former Villa Belgioioso,
built in 1790, which was at one time the
residence of Napoleon and of his stepson,
Eugène de Beauharnais. It now contains one of
the more important Italian art collections,
which is especially strong in works by 19th-
century artists from Lombardy. It has neo-
classical paintings by Canova and sculptures by
Medardo Rosso (1858–1928) and by Marino
Marini (1901–80). The Grassi collection of
19th–20th-century paintings includes works by
the French Impressionists.

La Scala Museum of Theatre History

*Museo Teatrale della Scala, Piazza della Scala,
    I–20121 Milano* ☎ *02 8053418*
*May–Oct, daily 10–1, 2–5. Nov–Apr, Mon–Sat
    10–1, 2–5. Closed Jan 1, Easter, May 1, Aug
    15, Dec 25, 26.*

C

La Scala, the most famous opera house in the
world, was built in 1776–8. It can accommodate
an audience of 2,000. The museum's collections
illustrate the development of the theatre from
classical times until our own and include a large
number of documents and mementoes relating
to the history of La Scala and to the singers and
musicians who have performed there. It is
possible to visit the auditorium from the
museum.

Leonardo da Vinci Museum of Science and Technology

*Museo Nazionale della Scienza e delle Technica
    Leonardo da Vinci, Via S. Vittore 21, I–20123
    Milano* ☎ *02 487034*
*Tues–Sun 10–1, 2–5. Open Mon only when public
    holiday. Closed Jan 1, Easter, May 1, Aug 15,
    Christmas.*

C

This large and important museum was opened in 1953. It occupies a former Benedictine monastery, built in the 16th–18th centuries. Its collections and displays cover all the branches of science, technology and transport and it organises an extensive teaching programme. The Leonardo da Vinci Gallery contains models based on drawings of machines by Leonardo.

Manzoni's House

Casa del Manzoni, Via Morone 1, I–20121 Milano
☎ *02 871019*
Tues–Fri 9-12, 2–4. Closed month of Aug and public holidays.
F

The poet and novelist, Alessandro Manzoni (1785–1873), the author of *I Promessi Sposi (The Betrothed)*, was born and died in Milan. His house has been preserved as a memorial to him, with his workroom and the bedroom in which he died preserved as they were in his lifetime, together with many of his personal possessions, portraits, manuscripts, his library and first editions of his works.

Museum of the Risorgimento

Museo del Risorgimento, Via Borgonuovo 23, I–20121 Milano   ☎ *02 8693549*
Tues–Sun 9.30–12.30, 2.30–5.30. Closed Jan 1, Easter Sun, May 1, Aug 15, Dec 25.
C ⚲

The museum was established in the castle of Milan in 1896, but suffered severe losses, especially of archive material, during the bombing raids on the city in 1943. After reconstruction, it was able to open again, on a more ambitious scale, in 1986.

The collections illustrate the history of Italy from the beginnings of the occupation by French troops under Napoleon Bonaparte in 1796 until the achievement of the unity of Italy. Among the specially interesting exhibits are a number of relics of Napoleon I, including his insignia as King of Italy, and a collection of portraits and historical paintings by 19th-century artists. There are also exhibits relating to the First and Second World Wars and to the Fascist period.

Poldi Pezzoli Museum

Museo Poldi Pezzoli, Via Manzoni 12, I–20121 Milano   ☎ *02 794889*
Apri–Sept, Tues–Sat 10–1, 2–5; Sun 10–1. Oct–Mar, Tues–Sun 10–1, 2–5. Thurs throughout year also 9–11 pm. Closed Jan 1, Easter, May 1, Aug 15, 16, Nov 1, Dec 25, 26. Also closed some public holidays pm.
C

In his will, Gian Giacomo Poldi left his splendid house and its contents to the city of Milan to be used for the benefit of the public and it was opened as a museum in 1881. It has a very active educational programme and contains rich and

well arranged collections of furniture, paintings, weapons, armour, textiles, clocks and small 16th–18th-century bronzes. The paintings include portraits of Martin Luther and his wife by Cranach, a remarkable *Descent from the Cross* and *Virgin and Child* by Botticelli, a *Dead Christ* by Bellini and the *View of the Lagoon* by Francesco Guardi.

Modena

Este Gallery

Galleria Estensi, Piazza S. Agostino 309, I–41100 Modena   ☎ *059 222145*
Tues, Wed, Sun 10–1; Thurs–Sat 10–5. Closed public holidays.
C

This State museum, opened in 1883, is in the mansion built in 1753 for Francesco III d'Este. It contains 14th–18th-century Italian paintings, mainly by artists from Emilia, Florence and Venice. The sculptures include one of Bernini's best works, a bust of Francesco I d'Este. The gallery also has a remarkable collection of 35,000 coins and medals, only about 100 of which are displayed at any one time.

Museum of Art and Archaeology

Museo Civico di Storia e Arte medioevale e moderna, e Museo Civico Archeologico Etnologico, Piazza Sant'Agostino 5, I–41100 Modena   ☎ *059 223892*
Tues, Wed, Thurs, 9–1, 3–7; Fri–Sun 9–1.
C 🖼 ⚲

The institutions which make up this major museum complex are housed in a large building commissioned by Francesco III d'Este in 1764–9 as a home for poor people. After 1788 it gradually became transformed into a school of crafts and finally, in 1871, it became the Palazzo dei Musei.

It has very rich collections of prehistoric, Greek and Roman archaeological material from excavations in the region, as well as Renaissance sculpture and architectural fragments. There are also ethnographical collections from New Guinea and Peru. The second part of the museum reflects the art and

Holy water stoup, 12th-century. Museum of Art and Archaeology, Modena.

life of Modena from medieval times until the 19th century, with exhibits of Romanesque sculpture, goldsmiths' work, 13th-century frescoes from churches in the region, 16th–19th century Italian paintings, musical instruments, faïence and leather wall-hangings.

A separate section of the museum is devoted to furniture made by craftsmen in Emilia from the 13th century to the present day.

Mondavio

Museum of the Re-creation of History

Museo di Rievocazione Storica, Piazza Matteotti 11/12, I–61040 Mondavio, Pesaro e Urbino
☎ 07211 97102
Daily 9–12, 3–7
C ⓘ 💺 ⌨

The museum occupies the armoury of the great fortress, the Rocca, which was designed by the Siennese architect, Francesco di Giorgio Martini and built between 1482 and 1492. Constructed to withstand the new explosive projectiles, it is considered to be one of the masterpieces of Italian military engineering. The collections include 14th–15th-century weapons and armour and there are displays which reflect domestic and military life in the castle.

Murano

Museum of Glass

Museo Vetrario, Palazzo Guistiniani, I–30121 Murano, Venezia   ☎ 041 739586
Mon, Tues, Thurs–Sat, from 12; Sun 10–1. Closed public holidays.
C

Murano, on an island in the Venetian Lagoon, has been an important glass-making centre since the 13th century. The museum, in the 17th-century Palazzo Guistiniani, contains a remarkable collection of glassware from the Roman period to modern times, including many examples of local products. The most notable exhibit is the 15th-century Barovier Marriage Cup.

Naples

Aquarium

Acquario di Napoli, Villa Comunale, I–80121 Napoli   ☎ 081 5833111
Mar–Oct, Tues–Sat 9–5; Sun 9–6. Nov–Feb, Tues–Sat 9–5; Sun 9–2. Closed Aug 15.
C

Founded in 1873 by the German naturalist, Anton Dohrn, this is believed to be the only surviving example of a 19th-century aquarium in the world. It forms part of an internationally famous Research Station and contains living collections of the vertebrates and invertebrates of the Gulf of Naples, including several rare species. There is also a herbarium of sea algae from the Naples area.

Armoury display. Archaeological Museum, Naples.

Archaeological Museum

Museo Archeologico Nazionale, Piazza Museo 19, I–80135 Napoli   ☎ 081 440166
Mon–Sat 9–2; Sun and public holidays 9–1.
C ⓘ ⌨

The 17th-century building was originally a riding school. It was then used to house the University and then, at a time when Naples was under Bourbon rule, the Royal Museum. The new museum attracted the Farnese collection, the Borgia collections, the frescoes, mosaics and other material discovered in the ancient towns overwhelmed by Vesuvius and during excavations at the necropolis at Cuma. There is also bronze and marble sculpture from the Papiri villa at Herculaneum.

Palazzo Capodimonte

Palazzo e Galleria Nazionale di Capodimonte, via Capodimonte, I–80136 Napoli
☎ 081 7410801
Tues–Sat 10–1
C 💺

The former royal estate of Capodimonte includes the palace, built between 1738 and 1838, a large park and what remains of the celebrated 18th-century porcelain factory. The porcelain museum is housed in five rooms of the Palace. An additional room contains the Chinese-style Porcelain Room from the royal summer residence at Portici, which has been reassembled here.

The Art Gallery, opened to the public in 1957, is among the most important in Europe. The collection of Italian primitives includes Simone Martini's *St Louis of Toulouse* and a *Crucifixion* by Masaccio. The Renaissance period is represented by works by Botticelli, Filippo Lippi, Raphael, Lorenzo Lotto, Vivarini, Mantegna and especially Giovanni Bellini, with his *Transfiguration*. There is an excellent collection of paintings by artists from Naples and rooms are devoted to Corregio, to El Greco, to Titian, including the family portrait of Pope Paul III with his nephews, and to portraits by Il Parmegiano.

The Royal Palace

Palazzo Reale di Napoli, Piazza del Plebiscito,
I–80132 Napoli   ☎ *081 413888*
May–Sept, daily 9–7. Oct–Apr, Mon–Fri 9–2;
Sat, Sun 9–1.30.
C ☕

The palace was built in stages between 1600 and
1664 for the Spanish viceroy and some changes
were made during the 18th century. After the
19th-century unification of Italy, the palace lost
its importance and a large part of the collections
were gradually dispersed to other buildings. In
recent years, there has been a determined policy
to restore as many as possible of the missing
items to their rightful homes.

The state rooms contain 16th–19th-century
Italian and foreign paintings, especially by
Neapolitan, Flemish and German artists. There
are also 16th-century tapestries from the Royal
Neapolitan Tapestry Galleries and French
furniture of the Napoleonic period.

San Martino Museum

Museo Nazionale di San Martino, Largo San
Martino 5, I–80100 Napoli
☎ *081 5781769*
Tues–Sat 9–2; Sun 9–1. Closed Jan 1, Easter
Mon; May 1, Aug 15, Dec 25.
C ☕ ☕

The museum is in the former Carthusian
Monastery of San Martino. There are exhibits
relating to the monastery and collections
illustrating the history of the Kingdom of
Naples, together with maps, plans, paintings
and watercolours of the city at different periods.
Other sections of the museum are devoted to
festivals and popular customs, cribs, costumes
and 14th–19th-century paintings, especially by
artists from the south of Italy. There are also
models of 17th–20th-century ships, 16th–19th-
century prints and drawings and 14th–18th-
century works by Italian sculptors.

Nizza Monferrato

Bersano Museum of Peasant Life

Museo Bersano delle Contadinerie e delle Stampe
sul Vino, Piazza Dante 21, I–14049 Nizza
Monferrato, Asti   ☎ *0141 721273*
Apr–July & Sept, Mon–Fri 9–11, 3–5; Sat, Sun
by appt. Closed Aug.
F ☕ ☕

The Bersano Winery (Bersano Antico Podere
Conti della Cremosina SpA) with 12 vineyards
on different sites, is one of the most important
in Piedmont. The museum and its collections
were established by Arturo Bersano, the founder
of the firm, and are adjacent to the Winery. The
exhibition is in two parts. The first consists of
16th–20th-century printed material relating to
agriculture and to the production of wine, and
the second of tools, implements and vehicles
once used in vineyards and on farms, together
with peasant furniture and domestic equipment.

Nove

Museum of Ceramics

Museo della Ceramica, Istituto Statale d'Arte
G. de Fabris, Via Giove 1, I–36055 Nove,
Vicenza   ☎ *0424 82022*
Mon–Sat 8–12. Other times by appt.
F ☕

The State Institute of Art in Nove was founded
in 1875 through the generosity of the local
sculptor, Giuseppe de Fabris (1790–1860),
whose name was given to the institute. The
institute included a 'School of Design and
Modelling as applied to Ceramics' and it was felt
that it would be useful to set up a Museum of
Ceramics in connection with this, so that
students could be brought into contact with
examples of the best work of the recent past and
of the present day.

The museum's collections consist mostly of
19th–20th-century majolica, porcelain and
earthenware from factories and workshops in
Nove and in the province of Vicenza, but there
are a number of contemporary and foreign
exhibits.

Novellara

Gonzaga Museum

Museo Gonzaga, P. le G. Marconi 1, I–42017
Novellara, Reggio Emilia   ☎ *0522 654242*
First Sun in month, 10–12.30, 3–6
F ☕

The Gonzagas' castle, which houses the
museum, dates from the 15th century. Some of
the rooms have preserved their original coffered
ceilings and marble fireplaces. The exhibits
include Faenza ceramics, among them 140 jars
from a 16th-century Jesuit pharmacy, which are
some of the finest in Italy, 13th-century
Byzantine frescoes and paintings by Lelio Orsi
(1511–87). There are also coins and medals of
the period of the Gonzagas.

Bersano Museum of Peasant Life, Nizza
Monferrato.

Portrait of a Youth by Giovanni Bellini, late 15th-century. Eremitani Museum, Padua.

Padua

Bottacin Museum

*Museo Bottacin, Piazza Eremitani 8, I–35138
    Padova*   ☎ 049 662512
*Mar–Sept, Tues–Sun 9–7. Oct–Feb, Tues–Sun
    9–5.30. Closed May 1, Aug 15, Dec 25, 26.*
Ⓒ 🖠

Nicola Bottacin (b. 1805) was a Trieste
merchant and an honorary citizen of Padua, and
in 1865–70 gave his rich collection of coins,
medals and objets d'art to that city. The
numismatics section is of world importance and
contains rare or unique specimens.

The 19th-century paintings and sculpture
and the silver, porcelain and miniatures on
ivory in the museum came from Bottacin. The
piece which Bottacin himself valued most was
the Statue of Flora, in Carrara marble, by
Vincenzo Vela (1820–91). There are two other
statues by Vela in Padua, one of Dante and the
other of Giotto.

Eremitani Museum

*Museo Civico Eremitani, Piazza Eremitani 8,
    I–35121 Padova*   ☎ 049 8750975
*Mar–Oct, Tues–Sun 9–7. Nov–Feb, Tues–Sun
    9–5.30.*
Ⓕ 🖼 ↩

In 1985 the city of Padua's municipal art
collection, one of the most important in Italy,
was transferred to new quarters in the Piazza
Eremitani. The 543 paintings by Italian artists,
the Emo Capodilista collection, covers the
15th–18th-centuries and emphasises the
achievements of the Venetian School. Other
sections of the museum are devoted to 5th–
18th-century sculpture, Neolithic archaeology,
the history of Padua during the Napoleonic
Wars, and the Risorgimento.

Paestum

Archaeological Museum

*Museo Archeologico Nazionale, Via Nazionale,
    I–84063 Paestum, Salerno*   ☎ 0828 811023
Tues–Sun 10–5
Ⓒ

Paestum is one of Italy's most important
archaeological sites. It was discovered
accidentally in the mid 18th century during
road-building activities. A Greek colony was
established here c. 600 BC. The city was
conquered by the Lucanians, a local tribe c. 400
BC and became Roman in 273 BC. Towards the
end of the Roman Empire, malaria forced all the
inhabitants to leave.

Visitors can see the extensive ruins, which
have been excavated and include those of the
Temple of Ceres, the Gymnasium, the
Amphitheatre, the Forum, the Curia, the
Temple of Neptune and the Temple of Hera
(Juno), as well as part of the 5 km city wall. The
exhibits in the museum include vases and other
ceramics, bronzes and numerous sculptures,
chief among which are the celebrated metopes,
6th-century BC low-relief sculptures from two
temples 6 km north of Paestum. There are also
some exceptional Greek tomb-paintings.

Palermo (Sicily)

Cathedral Treasury

*Tesoro della Cathedrale, Corso Vittorio Emanuele,
    I–90133 Palermo, Sicilia*   ☎ 091 24773
Mon, Wed–Sat 10–1, 2–5; Sun 10–1.
Ⓒ

In turn Phoenician, Roman, Byzantine and
Saracen, Palermo was conquered by the
Normans in 1072. The 12th-century cathedral
contains the tombs of the Norman kings and the
treasury displays objects found in these tombs. It
also has collections of vestments, illuminated
manuscripts, embroidery, enamels, breviaries
and goldsmiths' work, illustrating six centuries
of the cathedral's history. One of the treasury's
most important exhibits is the magnificent
imperial crown, which belonged to Constance
of Aragon.

Pitrè Museum of Sicilian Ethnography

*Museo Etnografico Siciliano Giuseppe Pitrè, Casina
    Cinese, Via Duca degli Abruzzi 1, I–90144
    Palermo, Sicilia*   ☎ 091 6711060
*Sat–Thurs 9–1. Closed Easter Sun and mid-week
    holidays.*
Ⓒ ↩

The origins of the museum are unusual.
Giuseppe Pitrè had published a series of volumes
called *The Library of the Popular Traditions of
Sicily.* In 1909 he established the museum as a
commentary on *The Library.* After being
temporarily accommodated in the corridors of
an old school building, which had previously
housed a monastery, the museum found a home
in part of the Chinese Palace, a remarkable

Carved and painted Sicilian carriage. Pitrè Museum of Sicilian Ethnography, Palermo.

structure commissioned by Venanzio Marvuglia in 1798, after taking refuge in Palermo following the invasion of Naples by the French.

The museum occupies 30 rooms of the palace, which has its original furnishings, its collections illustrating many aspects of the traditional life of Sicily. The exhibits include furniture, costumes, musical instruments, tools and equipment for spinning, weaving, hunting and agriculture, handicrafts and popular art.

The museum has generated its own folklore. It is now a local custom for couples to be photographed on their wedding day in front of a marble bust of Giuseppe Pitrè, which stands in the courtyard of the museum.

Vittorio Emanuele Museum of the Risorgimento

Museo del Risorgimento Vittorio Emanuele Orlando, Piazza San Domenico 1, I–90133 Palermo, Sicilia ☎ 091 582774
Mon, Wed, Fri 9–1
C

This is a museum which presents the events of the Risorgimento as they affected Sicily. It is financed and run by the Sicilian Society for Patriotic History and exists, in the words of the society and of Machiavelli, 'to give the people an opportunity to meditate on the lessons of the past, in order to be able to build a better future'.

There is a large collection of portraits, busts, battle and revolutionary scenes, medals, weapons, uniforms, newspapers of the day, items of clothing worn by Garibaldi and contemporary relics.

Parma

Bodoni Museum

Museo Bodoniano, Palazzo della Pilotta, I–43100 Parma ☎ 0521 22217
Tues–Sun 10–1
C

The great typographer and printer, Gian-Battista Bodoni (1740–1813), worked in Parma. The museum tells the story of his career and achievements and has a collection of 80,000 of his punches and matrices, together with a complete set of the books produced by him. The museum is in the Palatine Library, which forms part of the Palazzo della Pilotta and dates from 1769.

Glauco Lombardi Museum

Museo Glauco Lombardi, Via Garibaldi 15, I–43100 Parma ☎ 0521 33727
June–Sept, Tues–Sat 9.30–12.30, Sun 9.30–1. Oct–May, Tues–Sat 9.30–12.30, 3–5; Sun 9.30–1.
C 🖤

The museum occupies part of the mansion known as the Palazzetto di Riservo, built in the 17th century and reconstructed in the 18th. In 1816, after the death of Napoleon, it became the residence of his second wife, the Empress Marie-Louise, Duchess of Parma, whose son was the King of Rome. The Empress married, first, the Count of Neipperg and then the Count of Bombelles. She died in Parma in 1847.

The museum which was opened in 1961 contains collections relating to the history of Parma from the end of the 17th century to the beginning of the 19th, together with 18th- and 19th-century Italian and French paintings and sculpture, costumes and furniture. There are also mementoes of the Duchess of Parma.

Guatelli Collection

Raccolta Guatelli, Ozzano Taro, I–43046 Parma ☎ 0521 809100
Daily 10–5
F 🐴

This collection, formed and run as a museum since 1973 by Ettore Guatelli, is one of the most remarkable and significant in Italy. It represents the results of a lifetime of collecting the full range of objects relating to the old peasant culture of the Parma region. The total number of items on display is very large and the quality is impressive. They range from an enormous collection of craftsmen's tools to an equally wide selection of domestic equipment, and from agricultural implements to the toys made by poor people for their children. A special section is devoted to travelling entertainers, including musicians and the men who trained performing bears and monkeys.

National Gallery

Galleria Nazionale, Palazzo della Pilotta, I–43100 Parma ☎ 0521 33309
Tues–Sun 10–1. Closed Jan 1, Apr 25, May 1, Aug 15, Dec 25.
C

The Palazzo della Pilotta was built for the Farnese family between 1589 and 1622. It takes its name from the game of Pilotta, a kind of fives, which was played in its courtyards. The core-collection was formed by Philippe de Bourbon from 1752 onwards. It was greatly augmented between 1787 and 1816 by works of art taken from churches and monasteries which had been compulsorily closed as part of the Napoleonic anticlerical campaign.

Most of the exhibits are of 14th-, 15th- and 16th-century Emilian, Tuscan and Venetian paintings. The artists represented include two from Parma, Antonio Corregio (1489–1534) and Il Marmegiano (1503–40). There are also works by Leonardo, El Greco, Canaletto and Tiepolo. Several rooms are devoted to French painters who had a connection with Parma.

Visitors to the palazzo can also see the Farnese Theatre, built in wood in 1619 and what has become known as Corregio's Room, the former dining-room of the abbess of the Convent of St Paul. The ceiling was decorated by Corregio.

Toscanini's Birthplace

Museo 'Casa Natale Arturo Toscanini', Via Rodolfo Tanzi 13, I–43100 Parma
☎ *0521 285499*
Mon–Sat 10–1. Closed Jan 1, 6, 13, Easter, Apr 25, May 1, Aug 15, Nov 1, Dec 8, 25, 26.
[F]

Opened in 1967, the museum had to be closed for repair after the earthquake of 1983 and reopened in 1987. The conductor, Arturo Toscanini (1867–1957) was born here, the son of a tailor, but his parents moved soon afterwards to Genoa. In the museum there is a large collection of memorabilia and relics illustrating every stage of Toscanini's life and musical career. The exhibits include letters from D'Annunzio, Einstein and other famous people, musical scores, documents and photographs of Toscanini and his contemporaries.

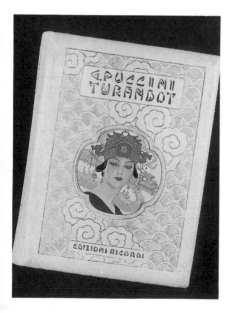

Pavia

Pavia Museums

Musei Civici, Castello Visconteo, I–27100 Pavia
☎ *0382 33853*
Jan, July, Aug, Dec, Tues–Sun 10–1. Other months Tues–Sat 10–1, 2–5. Closed Apr 4 and public holidays.
[C]

In the 14th century, under the Visconti, Pavia became one of the most important intellectual and artistic centres of Italy. The brick-built Visconti castle now houses the city's collections of archaeology, medieval and Renaissance sculpture, and 13th–17th-century paintings. The more remarkable paintings include an altarpiece by the Brescia artist, Vincenzo Foppa (1427–1515), the chief figure in Lombard painting until the arrival of Leonardo, a *Virgin and Child* by Giovanni Bellini and a *Christ Bearing the Cross*, by the late-15th-century Lombard artist, Ambrogio Borgognone. There are also separate museums of documents and relics relating to the Risorgimento and of material from the former Italian colonies.

Perticara

Museum of Minerals

Museo Storico Minerario, Via A. Orlani, I–61017 Perticara, Pesaro e Urbino   ☎ *0541 927267*
Tues–Thurs, Sat, Sun 10–12, 3–6
[C] 🛈 🖼 🍴

Sulphur in its crystalline form was until recently mined in Perticara over a period of many centuries. The museum tells the story of this important industry, of the techniques and equipment involved and of the life of the miners. There is also a representative collection of the minerals of the whole of Italy.

Perugia

Art Gallery of Umbria

Galleria Nazionale dell'Umbria, Palazzo dei Priori, Corso Vannucci, I–06100 Perugia
☎ *075 20316/64241*
Mon–Sat 9–1.30, 3–7; Sun and public holidays 9–1.30
[F] 🛈 🖼 ♿ 🍴

The gallery has 14th-century frescoes from churches in Perugia, Umbrian and Sienese primitives, and Tuscan paintings, including works by Fra Angelico and Piero della Francesca. There are also medieval and Renaissance sculptures in wood and stone, and 13th–14th-century French enamels and ivories.

Score of Puccini's *Turandot*. Toscanini's Birthplace, Parma.

Larian Boats Collection, Pianello del Lario.

Pesaro

Rossini's House

Casa di Rossini, Via Rossini 34, I–61100 Pesaro
Tues–Sun 10–1
C

Pesaro was the birthplace of the composer,
Gioacchino Rossini (1792–1868). The house
has recently been restored and contains exhibits
illustrating his life and work, with portraits,
manuscripts and some of his personal
possessions.

Pessione

Martini Museum of Wine-Making

Museo Martini di Storia dell'Enologia, Martini &
Rossi SpA, Piazza Rossi, I–10020 Pessione,
Torino   ☎ 011 57451
Daily 9–12.30, 2.30–5.30. Closed Jan 1, Easter
Sun, Aug, Dec 25, 26.
F ♿

The museum occupies 13 rooms in the cellars of
a 17th-century villa, the same cellars where the
production of Martini vermouth began in 1863.
The exhibits are arranged in such a way as to
give the visitor a detailed idea of the various
stages of wine-making, the different methods of
grape-pressing and the ancient ways of
transportation, storage, pouring and drinking
wine. Although it is a private museum
belonging to the company, the Martini Museum
is not used for publicity purposes, and only one
section is concerned with the company. It
contains equipment, stills, vats and laboratory
equipment used by Martini & Rossi during the
period 1860–70.

Piacenza

Palazzo Farnese

Museo di Palazzo Farnese, Piazza Citadella,
I–29100 Piacenza, Emilia Romagna
☎ 0523 20643
Tues, Thurs, Sun 10–1, 2–5; Wed, Fri, Sat 10–1.
Closed public holidays.
C

The Farnese Palace was begun by Margaret of
Austria (1480–1530), daughter of the Emperor
Maximilian, and never completed. The large
collection of paintings is mainly composed of
17th–18th-century works by artists from Emilia
and Romagna. Among the exhibits is a
remarkable series of paintings known as the
Farnesian Calendar (*Fasti farnesiani*), executed
between 1680 and 1720 by several painters of
repute, including the decorative artists,
Sebastiano Ricci (1659–1734), who did a great
deal of work in England and is well represented
in the Royal Collection.

Pianello del Lario

Larian Boats Collection

Raccolta della Barca Lariana, I–22010 Pianello del
Lario, Como   ☎ 0344 87267
Easter–June & Sept 16 – Nov 2, Sat 2.30–6.30,
Sun 10.30–12.30, 2.30–6.30. July 1 – Sept
15, daily 2.30–6.30. Guided tours. Other
times by appt.
C ♿ ♿

Established in 1982, the museum has a
collection of 160 boats, which are housed in a
former factory building, dating from the second
half of the 19th century. The boats, propelled
by oars, sails and motors, were originally used
for fishing, for freight and for sports purposes
and a number of them worked on Lake Como.
Each boat carries its autobiography and a note of
its special characteristics.

Pinerolo

Cavalry Museum

Museo Storico della Cavalleria, Viale Giolitti 5,
I–10064 Pinerolo, Torino   ☎ 0121 793139
Tues, Wed, Fri, Sat 9–11.15, 3–5.15. Closed Jan
1, Easter Sat, Sun, May 1, Aug 15, Oct 30,
Nov 1, Dec 8, 24–6, 31.
C ♿ ♿

Housed in a building which held the Cavalry
School from 1849 to 1943, the museum, opened
in 1968, illustrates the history of the Italian
cavalry regiments from the 16th century to the
1930s and during the period from then onwards
when horses gave way to tanks and armoured
cars. The collections include paintings,
uniforms, campaign relics, flags, weapons and
documents. A section is devoted to the service
of the cavalry regiments in the Italian colonies.

Pisa

Cathedral Museum

Museo dell'Opera del Duomo, Piazza
Arcivescovado, I–56100 Pisa ☎ 050 561820/
560547
Daily 9–4.30, 8–7.30 during summer months.
Closed some public holidays.
C ♿

The 13th-century cathedral contains, in its treasury, important collections of 14th–15th-century religious sculpture, 16th–17th-century paintings, church-hangings, silver ornaments and liturgical items, and examples of inlaid woodwork.

Mazzini's House

Domus Mazzini, Via Mazzini 71, C.P. 322,
   I–56125 Pisa   ☎ *050 24174*
Mon–Sat 8.30–1.30. Closed public holidays.
F

The Italian patriot, Giuseppe Mazzini (1805–72), died in the Casa Rosselli in Pisa. His house was destroyed by bombing in 1943, but was reconstructed after the war. The museum contains exhibits illustrating Mazzini's life and times, including a number of his personal possessions, portraits of his friends, manuscripts, documents and books belonging to him.

Museum of Frescoes

Museo delle Sinopie, Piazza Duomo 17, I–56126
   Pisa   ☎ *050 561820*
Apr–Sept, daily 9–12.45, 3–6.30. Oct–Mar, daily
   9–12.45, 3–4.30. Closed some public holidays.
C

The cathedral at Pisa contains one of the most important series of medieval frescoes in Europe. Painted in the 14th and 15th centuries, they are known as 'sinopie' in Italian, after the reddish-brown pigment, originally obtained from Sinope, in Paphlagonia, which was often used for underdrawing the painting.

Macaroni-sellers in Naples at the turn of the century. Pasta Museum, Pontedassio.

Pontedassio

Pasta Museum

Museo Storico degli Spaghetti, Collezione Agnesi,
   Via Garibaldi 96, I–18027 Pontedassio,
   Imperia   ☎ *0183 27091*
By appt.
F

Pasta may have been made in Italy in the 13th century, but it would have been a simple affair, compared with the 98 different types and shapes, each with its special name, which are known today. In 1824 Paolo Battista Agnesi bought the mill at Pontedassio and established there the pasta business which is now one of the largest and most celebrated in the world.

The museum illustrates the history of pasta and of the techniques for making it and tells the story of the Agnesi enterprise. The exhibits include pasta being prepared and eaten, historic machinery and equipment used in the industry, and models of machines. The pictures reveal that for a long time pasta was eaten with the fingers, not with a fork.

Portoferraio (Elba)

Napoleonic Museum

Museo Napoleonico, Palazzino dei Mulini,
   I–57037 Portoferaio, Elba   ☎ *0565 93846*
Tues–Sun 10–1
C

Following his abdication, Napoleon was exiled to the island of Elba. Between May 1814 and February 1815, he ruled over Elba and maintained a small court there. The museum is in a modest 18th-century house which he sometimes occupied. It contains his personal library and a collection of memorabilia.

Villa San Martino

*Museo Napoleonico, Villa San Martino, I–57037
    Portoferraio, Elba*   ☎ 0565 92688
*Tues–Sun 10–1. Closed Jan 1, Dec 25 and public
    holidays.*
C

The Villa San Martino, with its magnificent
views over the Bay of Portoferraio, was
Napoleon's summer residence during his exile
on Elba. The Emperor had it converted from an
old warehouse. Exhibits relating to Napoleon
are arranged in rooms which he and Marshall
Bertrand used to occupy.

Possagno

Canova's Birthplace

*Casa Natale del Canova, Via Canova, I–31054
    Possagno, Treviso*   ☎ 0423 54323
*Thurs–Sun 10–1, 2–5. Closed Jan 1, Dec 25,
    public holidays.*
C

Antonio Canova (1757–1822) was the most
successful and influential sculptor of the late-
18th-century neo-classical movement. He
worked a great deal for the Papal Court and
among his other clients were Napoleon, the
Duke of Wellington, and Catherine the Great.
In 1816 the pope created him Marchese d'Ischia
and he retired to his birthplace, Possagno,
where he built a studio, which now contains a
number of casts and plaster models of his works.
The Temple of Possagno, designed by Canova
himself, contains his tomb and his last
sculpture, a *Descent from the Cross.*

Prato

Pecci Museum of Modern Art

*Museo d'Arte Contemporanea Luigi Pecci, Viale
    della Repubblica, C.P. 1149, I–50047 Prato,
    Firenze*   ☎ 0574 570620
Wed–Mon 10–7
C 🛈 ⬛ ♿ ☕

Opened in 1988, the Pecci Centre for Modern
Art, which is a major international institution,
comprises the Museum, the Centre for
Information and Documentation of the Visual
Arts, and the Department of Education,

Pecci Museum of Modern Art, Prato.

Graphics and Events. In its exhibitions,
acquisitions and educational activities, the
centre concentrates on the artistic creations of
the past decade. There is a regular programme of
exhibitions and the policy is to form the
permanent collection by purchasing selected
items from each exhibition, so that the museum
is forming its own history.

Premana

Premana Museum

*Museo Etnografico Comunale, Via Roma, I–22050
    Premana, Como*   ☎ 0341 890175
*Apr–June & Sept–Oct, Sat, Sun, 3–6. July–Aug,
    Wed–Sun 3–6. Other times on request.*
C 🛈 ☕

The museum, established in 1974, has
collections of documents, tools and equipment
illustrating domestic life, handicrafts, the local
ironworking industry and traditional methods of
agriculture. There is also a section devoted to
costumes and accessories. Many of the objects
are displayed in room or workshop settings.

The museum has made itself responsible for
the restoration of a series of 15th-century
frescoes of high quality discovered recently in a
hay-loft.

Quartu S. Elena (Sardinia)

Sa Dome Farra Museum

*Casa Museo Sa Dome Farra, Via Eligio Porcu 143,
    I–09045 Quartu S. Elana, Sardegna*
    ☎ 070 812340
Daily 10–5
C

The museum, opened in 1978, has been created
within the buildings of a large farm, one of the
oldest in the district. The farmhouse, barn and
outbuildings are arranged around a courtyard.
The 35 rooms which constitute the museum
contain a remarkable private collection of
objects illustrating the traditional rural life of
Sardinia. There are room reconstructions
showing the living-styles of different social
classes and a wide range of domestic equipment,
farm implements and craftsmen's tools, with a
complete blacksmith's forge.

Ravenna

Dante Museum

*Museo Dantesco, Via Guido da Polenta, I–48100
    Ravenna*
*Tues–Sat 10–1, 2–5; Sun 10–1. Closed Jan 1,
    Dec 25, 26, public holidays.*
C

Dante Alighieri (1265–1321) was exiled from
Florence, his native city, in 1302 and eventually
settled in Ravenna, where he died. The classical
building which now contains his tomb was
erected in 1780. It is a short distance from the
museum, which was opened in 1921, on the

600th anniversary of the poet's death. Its collections illustrate Dante's turbulent life and his literary career, and include the urns which are reputed to have contained his remains from the 16th century to our own times.

Ravenna Art Gallery

Pinacoteca Comunale, Via di Roma 13, I-48100 Ravenna ☎ *0544 35625*
Tues–Sun 9–1, 2.30–5.30. Closed Jan 1, Nov 1, Dec 25.

F ⌂ ↝

In 1829 both the Academy of Fine Art and the Art Gallery were founded in Ravenna. The gallery was intended to help in the education and training of the students of the Academy. It acquired at the beginning the collections belonging to the religious orders, which were suppressed during the Napoleonic period, together with other items presented by the citizens of Ravenna. Considerable additions were made during the second half of the 19th century and the gallery is now able to provide a representative selection of the work of artists who have lived and worked in Romagna and the surrounding regions since the 14th century.

St Augustine by Romagnolo, 15th-century. Ravenna Art Gallery.

Recanati

Art Gallery and Beniamino Gigli Museum

Pinacoteca Comunale e Museo Beniamino Gigli, Palazzo Comunale, Piazza Leopardi, I-62019 Recanati, Macerata ☎ *071 982772*
Apri–Sept, Tues–Sun 10–1, 4–7. Oct–Mar, Tues–Sun 10–1, 3–6. Closed Jan 1, Easter, May 1, Aug 15, Dec 25.

C ↝

Recanati is known especially as the birthplace of the poet, Count Giacomo Leopardi (1798–1837) and the operatic tenor, Beniamino Gigli (1890–1957), both of whom have parts of the museum devoted to them. The Gigli section contains a reconstruction of his dressing-room, arranged according to the instructions of his servant. The art collections include several works by Lorenzo Lotto (c. 1480–1556). The works by contemporary artists mostly came to the Gallery as a result of a bequest by the sculptor, G. Birrond.

Redipuglia

Military Memorial of the First World War

Sacrario Militare della Prima Guerra Mondiale, Direzione Sacrario Militare di Redipuglia, I-34070 Redipuglia, Gorizia ☎ *0481 489024*
May 16 – Sept 30, daily 9–6.45. Oct 1 – May 15, daily 9–11.45, 2–4.45.

C ⌂ ▪ ↝

The Memorial Museum contains documents, photographs and mementoes of the First World War, and the nearby military cemetery contains the remains of nearly 100,000 members of the Italian forces who died in the War.

Reggio Emilia

Parmeggiani Gallery

Galleria Anne e Luigi Parmeggiani, Corso Cairoli 1, I-42100 Reggio Emilia ☎ *0522 37775*
Tues–Sat 9–12; Sun 9 12, 3–6.

F ↝

The gallery was opened in 1924, in a specially-designed building described as being in the Catalan-Gothic style. Luigi Parmeggiani, alias Louis Marcy, was an art forger and the gallery named after him contains examples of his work. The other exhibits are, however, entirely reputable and include European paintings and sculpture, especially Flemish, Central European and Spanish, with works by Tiepolo, Veronese, Van Dyck and El Greco. The decorative arts are also well represented, with collections of goldsmiths' work, textiles, crystal, ivories and weapons.

Reggio Emilia Museum

Civici Musei e Gallerie, Via Spallanzani 1, I-42100 Reggio Emilia ☎ *0522 37775*
Tues–Sat 9–12; Sun 9–12, 3–6.

F ⌂ ↝

The complex of five museums occupies a former Franciscan monastery, which was active from the 14th century until its dissolution at the end of the 18th. The archaeological collections emphasise the culture of Rome and especially goldsmiths' work of the Imperial period. There are also necklaces from the barbarian tribes and 5th-century gold coins from Ravenna and Constantinople, and prehistoric exhibits.

Display of coral. Natural history collection,
Reggio Emilia Museum.

The natural history section of the museum is
based on Lazzaroni Spallanzani's collection of
zoological, mineralogical and fossil material,
acquired by the city in 1799 and since
considerably augmented. Within the same
building, there is a separately organised Museum
of the Risorgimento, which tells the story of the
struggle for independence in the region from the
Napoleonic period until the First World War.
The collection of Risorgimento medals is an
important one. The museum also possesses
documents relating to the Liberation Movement
in 1943–5.

Rende

Rende Museum

*Museo Civico, Via Raffaele de Bartolo, I–87036
    Rende, Calabria*   ☎ 0984 443593
Mon–Sat 9–1
F

The museum, opened in 1985, is located in the
17th-century Palazzo Zagarese. The collections
are divided into two parts. The first contains
contemporary art, mostly Italian, and the
second is devoted to the traditional life and
customs of the region, arranged in nine sections
– the population of central and northern
Calabria; vernacular buildings; lighting, heating
and water supply; the kitchen; clothing;
domestic activities and agriculture; religious and
social life and popular music; and emigration to
Canada.

Rivoli Veronese

Napoleonic Museum

*Museo Napoleonico, Piazza Napoleone 14,
    I–37010 Rivoli Veronese, Verona*
    ☎ 045 7281023
Apr–Oct, daily 10–12, 3–5.30. Nov–Mar, by
    appt only. Closed Easter, May 1, Aug 15.
C ♟ ⚘

The museum commemorates Napoleon's
victory against the Austrians in 1797 at the
Battle of Rivoli and its effects on European
history. It is situated in the middle of the
battlefield, north of Verona and east of Lake
Garda, and illustrates the history of the
Napoleonic period in Italy. The exhibits include
paintings, documents, weapons and
memorabilia, with 12 autograph letters from
Napoleon and others from important
personalities of the period. One of the museum's
valued possessions is a bed which belonged to
the Empress Marie Louise.

Rome

Borghese Gallery

*Museo e Galleria Borghese, Villa Borghese, Via
    Pinciana, I–00198 Roma*   ☎ 06 858577
Tues–Sat 10–5; Sun, Mon 10–1. Closed some
    public holidays.
C ♟ ⚑

The villa which houses the museum was built in
the early 17th century on the orders of Cardinal
Scipione Borghese, the nephew of Paul V. His
intention was to illustrate patronage and
collecting in Rome in the 17th century. The
collections were robbed during the period of
Napoleonic rule and the museum became State
property in 1902. The exhibits include classical
and 17th-century sculpture, notably *Apollo and
Daphne*, commissioned by the Cardinal from the
young Bernini, and 16th–17th-century Italian
paintings.

Burcardo Library and Theatrical Collection

*Biblioteca e Raccolta Teatrale del Burcardo, Via del
    Sudario 44, I–00186 Roma*   ☎ 06 6540755
Mon–Sat 9–1.30. Closed public holidays and
    month of Aug.
F

Bishop Giovanni Burcardo (b. 1450) held the important post of Pontifical Master of Ceremonies for 23 years. The house which he built for himself in Rome has always been known as the Burcardo. In the centuries following his death, parts of it were demolished, but early in the present century the remainder was restored by the city, and the Italian Society of Authors and Publishers was granted a lease on it in order to store and display the important theatrical collection which it had been left in 1918 by Luigi Rasi, the director of a well-known school of acting. This has since been considerably augmented and now contains theatrical memorabilia, books and manuscripts relating to the history of the entertainment world in Italy and in a number of other countries. There are also collections of costumes and masks, together with 18th–19th-century marionettes.

Castel San'Angelo

Museo Nazionale di Castel San'Angelo,
Lungotevere Castello 50, I–00193 Roma
☎ 06 6875036
Mon 2–7.30; Tues–Sat 9–2; Sun 9–1. Closed
Jan 1, May 1.
F 🦽

The Emperor Hadrian, the adopted son of Trajan, whom he succeeded, was born in Rome in AD 76 and ruled as Emperor from 117 to 138. He designed his own tomb, on the model of that of the Emperor Augustus, and located it on the banks of the Tiber, in an area where there had already been many important burials. To withstand the rivers frequently disastrous floods, the tomb was built in the form of a strong, broad tower, with very deep foundations. The intention was that the members of the Imperial family should continue to be buried in the tomb and perhaps 15 of them were, the last being the Emperor Caracalla in AD 217.

From the end of the 3rd century the mausoleum began to be fortified and it played an important part in the defence of Rome against barbarian attacks. The popes sought its safety from time to time and a chapel dedicated to the

Archangel Gabriel was built at the top, surmounted by a statue to him, which replaced the previous figure of the Emperor Hadrian. The building became a papal possession in 1377. It was extensively altered and embellished by successive popes, but has remained virtually unaltered since 1734. A lift was installed by Leo X (1512–23), who was so gross that he found it difficult to climb the ramps to the upper floor.

To visit the interior of this complex building is to experience the history of Rome and is a satisfaction in itself, but, in addition, as museum attractions, there are displays of weapons and armour, frescoes, paintings and sculpture.

Museum of the Bersaglieri

Museo Storico dei Bersaglieri, Porta Pia 2, I–00198
Roma   ☎ 06 486723
Tues, Thurs 9–1. Groups at other times by appt.
Closed public holidays.
F

The Porta Pia, in the line of the wall built by the Emperor Aurelian to defend Rome in AD 271, was designed by Michelangelo. The building adjoining the gateway contains the museum. Facing the Porta Pia is the national monument to the Bersaglieri, who first appeared in Rome in 1849. The museum tells the story of the corps and has exhibits of weapons, equipment, uniforms and photographs.

Museum of the Carabinieri

Museo Storico dell'Arma dei Carabinieri, Piazza del
Risorgimento 46, I–00192 Roma
    ☎ 06 6896696
Tues–Sun 8.30–12.30. Closed Aug.
C 🦽

The Carabinieri, a form of gendarmerie, was, literally, 'the men armed with carbines'. The corps was set up in 1814 and the museum's collections of uniforms, weapons, relics, paintings, photographs and documents tells its story. Among the most cherished exhibits are the Act which created the corps and its first flag, which came surprisingly late, in 1894.

Museum of Ostia

Museo Ostiense, Scavi di Ostia Antica, I–00192
Roma   ☎ 06 6650022
Tues–Sun 10–1. Closed public holidays.
C

Founded in the 4th century BC, Ostia, at the mouth of the Tiber, was the port of Rome for 800 years. The harbour then gradually silted up and the ruins of the town soon became covered by mud deposited by the Tiber. The site was rediscovered in 1909 and since then excavations have revealed the extensive remains of this large and prosperous town. The museum displays the finds from the excavations – tools, sculptures, portrait busts, religious cult objects, domestic items and examples of the mosaics, paintings and frescoes used to decorate the interior of the buildings.

Museum of the Bersaglieri, Rome.

National Gallery of Ancient Art

*Galleria Nazionale d'Arte Antica, Via delle
    Quattro Fontane 13, I–00184 Roma*
    ☎ 06 4750184/4814591
Tues–Sat 9–2; Sun 9–1.
🅕 ♟ 💻 ⚘

In 1623 Cardinal Maffeo Barberini became Pope
and took the title of Urban VIII. He set about
building himself a suitable residence, the Palazzo
Barberini. Bernini and Borromini both worked
on it and Pietro de Cortona executed
magnificent ceilings.

The proposal to establish a National Gallery
of Ancient Art surfaced at the end of the 19th
century and its collections grew steadily, but
without finding a satisfactory home. The
proposal to take over the Palazzo Barberini for
the purpose was put forward. A large part of the
building has been occupied since 1934 by the
Armed Forces Club, which so far refuses to give
it up and in consequence the museum's
collections are divided between the Palazzo
Corsini, the Palazzo Barberini and the Villa
d'Este at Tivoli, the 13th–17th-century works
being in the Palazzo Barberini.

Among the most important works in the
museum are Raphael's *La Fornarina*,
Caravaggio's *Narcissus* and *Judith and Holofernes*,
and the 18th-century section of the decorative
arts collection.

National Museum of Popular Art

*Museo Nazionale delle Arte e Tradizioni Popolari,
    Piazza Marconi 10, I–00144 Roma*
    ☎ 06 5926148
*Daily 10–5. Closed Jan 1, May 1, Dec 25, public
    holidays.*
🅒

The museum's collections illustrate the
traditions and customs of the whole of Italy.
There are sections devoted to craftsmen's tools,
domestic equipment, furniture, costumes, rugs
and carpets, popular religious art, ex-votos,
majolica, masks used in the Commedia
dell'Arte, and household carvings and
sculpture. The museum also has a large
collection of photographs and prints relating to
traditional activities, occupations and buildings.

Pirandello's House

Casa di Pirandello, Via Bosio 15, I–00121 Roma
    ☎ 06 858047
*Daily 10–1. Closed Jan 1, May 1, Dec 25, public
    holidays.*
🅒

The house in which the poet, playwright, short-
story writer and novelist, Luigi Pirandello
(1867–1936) lived from 1913 until his death
became State property in 1962. It is now a
museum dedicated to him. His workroom and
library and the room in which he died have been
preserved as they were in his lifetime. The house
also serves as the headquarters of the Institute of
Contemporary Italian Theatre and Pirandello
Studies.

Mail delivery van from 1920. Postal Museum,
Rome.

Postal Museum

*Museo Storico PT, Sede Ministeriale, Viale
    Europa, CAP, I–00144 Roma*
    ☎ 06 54602092
*Mon–Sat 9–1. Closed public holidays and month of
    Aug.*
🅒 ♟

The museum first opened in 1959, on the
premises of the Roma Prati post office. In 1982
it moved to its present location, in the Roma
Eur building. It presents the history of the
postal, telegraph and telephone services in Italy,
as well as of radio and television. Among the
historic exhibits is the apparatus used by
Guglielmo Marconi during his 1901
experiments between Cornwall and
Newfoundland. There is also a major collection
of Italian and foreign postage stamps dating back
to the first half of the 19th century.

Vatican Museums

*Monumenti Musei e Gallerie Pontificie, I–00120
    Città del Vaticano   ☎ 06 6983332*
*Easter week and July–Sept, Mon–Sat 8.45–4.45.
    Rest of year, Mon–Sat 8.45–1.45. Last
    admission 3.45. Open last Sun in month.
    Closed religious holidays.*
🅒 ♟ 💻 ♿

There are 18 museums within the precincts of
the Vatican in Rome. All are accessible to the
public. The most important of them are the:

Art Gallery (Pinacoteca)
This was established by Pope Pius VI. It
contains Italian paintings from the Byzantine
period to the 18th century, with the
Renaissance and the Baroque particularly
strongly represented. There are also tapestries
woven to designs by Raphael.

Cabinet of Coins and Medals (Medagliere)
These collections were formed by the Vatican
during the 19th and 20th centuries. They
contain Roman and medieval coins with a
particular relevance to the Holy See.

Chiaramonti Museum (Museo Chairamonti)
The exhibits here reflect the special interests of
Pius VII Chiaramonti. They consist of Roman
statues of divinities, portrait statues and busts,
altars, architectural ornaments, sarcophagi and
funerary urns.

Collection of Contemporary Religious Art
(Collezione d'Arte Religiosa Contemporanea)
Here one finds works by contemporary artists
from a number of countries, the core of the
collection being items shown in an
international exhibition held in 1974.

Egyptian Museum (Museo Egizio)
The museum dates from 1839 and shows the
interests of Gregory XIV. The collections,
which cover a wide range of Egyptian
antiquities, have been added to continuously
since then. The displays include reconstructions
of Egyptian tombs.

Gallery of Tapestries (Galleria degli Arazzi)
The gallery displays 16th-century Brussels
tapestries, made from cartoons by Raphael,
16th-century tapestries from Vigevano and
17th-century tapestries from the workshops of
Barbernini di Roma.

Historical Museum (Museo Storico)
This was established by Paul VI. It contains
coaches and carriages belonging to the Popes
and other prelates, together with uniforms and
equipment of the Papal Guard.

Lapidary Gallery (Galleria Lapidaria)
This is an epigraphic collection, with 3,000
items, established by Pius VII in the early 19th
century, with the intention of setting Christian
inscriptions by the side of Roman examples.

The whole of the Vatican is, of course, one
huge museum and art gallery.

**Relief of Adam and Eve. Fantoni Museum,
Rovetta.**

Rovereto

Italian Museum of the History of War

*Museo Storico Italiano della Guerra, Via
Castelbarco 7, I–38068 Rovereto, Trento*
☎ 0464 438100
*Mar & Nov, daily 9–12, 2–5. Apr–June & Oct,
daily 9–12, 2.30–5.30. July–Sept, daily 9–7.*
Ⓕ ⚓

The castle of Rovereto was built in the early
15th century by Italian military engineers on the
site of much earlier fortifications. It suffered
siege and attack during the succeeding centuries
and served as an Austrian army base during the
First World War. Immediately after the war, the
decision was taken to restore the castle and to
install in it a large museum which would present
the history of weapons and battles through the
ages, emphasising the horrors and futility of war.
The approach is international and considerable
use is made of artists' interpretations of war. The
collections have been extended to include the
Second World War.

Rovetta

Fantoni Museum

*Museo della Fondazione Fantoni, Via A.
Fantoni 1, I–24020 Rovetta, Bergamo*
☎ 0346 72944
July–Sept, Tues–Sun 3–5. Guided tours.
Ⓒ ⚱

The Fantoni family were active as sculptors and
carvers in 15th-century Rovetta and continued
to distinguish themselves well into the 19th
century. The museum has been established in
the house which was formerly their home and
studio. The collections and displays illustrate
their life and work over the centuries, with
drawings, sketches, models and finished
sculpture.

San Benedetto Po

Polirone Museum

*Museo Civico Polironiano, I–46027 San Benedetto
Po, Mantova* ☎ 0376 615911
Mar 1 – Nov 14, Tues–Sun 9.30–12.30, 3–6
Ⓒ ⚱

The former Benedictine Abbey at Polirone was
one of the largest in Europe. Built between the
11th and 18th centuries and maintained in a
complete condition, it has a 12th-century
Romanesque church, three 15th-century
cloisters and a large refectory with frescoes by
Corregio. The monastery buildings can also be
visited.

The museum contains agricultural and
craftsmen's tools and equipment, fishermen's
and watermen's equipment from the River Po,
marionettes from the north of Italy, carved
woodwork from farm carts, and popular prints
and religious images.

San Leo

San Leo Museum

*Museo, Pinacoteca e Galleria d'Arte
    Contemporanea del Forte di San Leo, I–61018
    San Leo, Pesaro e Urbino*   ☎ *0541 916231*
*April–Oct, daily 9–12, 2–6. Aug, also 9–11 pm
Nov–Mar, daily 9–12, 2–5.*
Ⓒ 🛈 ↩

The spectacularly sited hill-town of San Leo has
its origins in the 8th century BC. The Romans
built a temple to Jupiter here and later a fortress.
St Francis of Assisi preached at San Leo in 1213
and Dante, who visited the town *c.* 1306, used
it as a model for the ruined keep of purgatory.
The castle in its present form dates from 1479.
During the Risorgimento, the fort was used as a
prison for those who fought for the reunification
of Italy. Among these patriots was Felice Orsini
(1819–58), who threw a bomb at the coach of
the Emperor Napoleon III and the Empress in
Paris in 1858 and was executed as a result.
    The museum is housed in the fort. It
contains a historical display of weapons,
including those of the Hunter Batallion of San
Leo (1860) in the Risorgimento. There are also
collections of 16th-century furniture, 15th–
16th-century paintings, including Corregio's
Dispute between the Doctors, and works by 19th-
and 20th-century Italian artists.

Sansepolcro

Sansepolcro Museum

*Museo Civico, Via Aggiunti 65, I–52037
    Sansepolcro, Arezzo*   ☎ *0575 732218*
*Daily 9.30–12, 2–6. Closed Jan 1, Aug 15,
    Dec 25.*
Ⓒ 🛈

The museum occupies a late 14th-century
mansion. It contains 15th–17th-century Tuscan
paintings, including some of the most famous
works of Piero della Francesca and the della
Robbias. There are also 13th–17th-century high
and low reliefs in stone and majolica and 16th–
17th-century engravings and prints. The
museum also has a collection of items from the
cathedral treasury, including 17th–19th-century
hangings, reliquaries and chalices.

Siena

Cathedral Museum

*Museo dell'Opera del Duomo, Piazza Duomo,
    I–53100 Siena*   ☎ *0577 283048*
*Mar 15 – Oct 31, daily 10–5. Nov 1 – Mar 14,
    daily 10–1. Closed Jan 1, Dec 25.*
Ⓒ

The museum is surrounded by the remains of a
huge cathedral, which was begun in 1339 and
never finished. The present cathedral was
planned as its transept. The museum contains
13th–16th-century paintings of the School of
Siena, illuminated manuscripts, and gold and

silver liturgical items and religious ornaments.
Also on display are the 13th-century statues by
Giovanni Pisano, which were originally on the
façade of the Cathedral and the *Maestà* (Virgin
in Majesty) altarpiece (1311) by Duccio, which
has a Virgin and Child on the front and 26
scenes from Christ's Passion on the back.

Siena Art Gallery

Pinacoteca, Via S. Pietro 29, I–53100 Siena
    ☎ *0577 281161*
*Tues–Sat 10–5; Sun 2–5. Closed Jan 1, May 1,
    Dec 25.*
Ⓒ

The gallery is in the former Buonsignori
mansion, which dates from the 15th century. It
is the largest collection of 13th–17th-century
Sienese paintings to be found in any museum.
Among the works displayed are Duccio's *Virgin
of the Franciscans*, the *Virgin and Child* by
Simone Martini, and a number of paintings by
the 14th-century artists, Pietro and Ambrogio
Lorenzetti, including a large altarpiece, the *Pala
del Carmine* by Pietro Lorenzetti.

Siena Museum

*Museo Civico, Piazza del Campo 1, I–53100
    Siena*   ☎ *0577 292111*
*Apr–Oct, Mon–Sat 9.30–7.30; Sun 9.30–1.30.
    Nov–Mar, daily 9.30–1.30. Closed Jan 1,
    Easter, May 1, Dec 25.*
Ⓒ 🛈

The town hall in Siena dates from the period
during which the culture of Siena had reached
its highest point, the second half of the 13th
century and the first half of the 14th and it was
then that Simone Martini, Duccio di
Buoninsegna and Ambrogio Lorenzetti executed
frescoes of such remarkable quality that the
town hall has gradually had to be made part of
the museum. Including these, the museum has
the most important collection of Sienese
paintings and sculpture from its beginnings to
the 18th century.

**The 15th-century fort of San Leo, now
housing the San Leo Museum.**

Painted ceiling of the town hall of Siena, which now houses the Siena Museum.

Sorrento

Correale di Terranova Museum

Museo Correale di Terranova, Via Correale 50, I–80067 Sorrento, Napoli ☎ *081 8781845 Tues–Sun 10–1*
Ⓒ

The museum occupies an 18th-century mansion and contains collections given to the town by Alfredo Correale and by other members of the family at the beginning of the present century, considerably augmented by subsequent gifts and bequests. The collection of 17th–18th-century Neapolitan furniture is outstanding and other exhibits include majolica from Sicily, Lombardy and Faenza; 17th-century Italian and foreign porcelain; 17th–18th-century Italian and foreign clocks; 18th–19th-century lace; and 15th–17th-century paintings by artists from Naples, Bologna and Rome, as well as a section devoted to prehistoric, Hellenistic and Roman archaeology. The poet, Torquato Tasso (1544–95) was born in Sorrento and the museum has material relating to him.

Syracuse (Sicily)

Orsi Archaeological Museum

Museo Archeologico Regionale P. Orsi, Viale Teocrito, I–96100 Siracusa, Sicilia ☎ *0931 66222 Tues–Sun 9–2*
Ⓒ

Paolo Orsi, who died in 1937, devoted his life to the discovery and study of prehistoric and historic Sicily and the new museum, opened in 1988 in a building designed for the purpose, is named after him. It has some of the most important archaeological collections in Europe, spread over an exceptionally long and continuous series of cultures, from Palaeolithic times onwards. Most of the material relates to the settlements of Eastern Sicily.

Terrasini (Sicily)

Terrasini Museum

Museo Civico, Via Cala Rossa 4, I–90049 Terrasini, Sicilia ☎ *091 8682652 July–Aug, daily 9–1, 6–11 pm. Jan–June, Sept, Nov–Dec, daily 9–1. Closed Oct.*
Ⓕ ⬦

The museum has three sections. The most spectacular is the one devoted to the celebrated Sicilian cart. Very strong and with brightly-painted pictures and designs, it was a form of folk art, as well as a method of transport which, with its large wheels and small body, was well suited to the very inadequate roads. The archaeological collection concentrates particularly on the Roman and Greek material found by underwater archaeologists. The natural history section is the result of the acquisition of four collections covering the geology, minerals, fossils, birds and mammals of Sicily.

Tolmezzo

Gortani Museum of Carnian Popular Art

Museo Carnico delle Arti Popolari Michele Gortani, Piazza Garibaldi 2, I–33028 Tolmezzo, Udine ☎ *0433 43233 Apr–Sept, Tues–Sun 9–12, 2–6. Oct–Mar, Tues–Sun 9–12, 1–5.*
Ⓒ ⬦ ⅋ ⬦

The Carnia is a mountainous region near the border with Austria. It suffered considerable damage during the First World War and during the early 1920s Professor Michele Gortani worked assiduously to discover and salvage what remained as evidence of the traditional way of life of the mountain community. The results are to be seen in the museum created in the Palazzo Campeis, a 16th-century mansion in the centre of Tolmezzo. The exhibits date from the 14th to the 19th centuries and are displayed in 30 rooms. They illustrate the occupations, the domestic and social life, the religious practices, and the costumes of the region. Many items are shown in room and workshop settings.

Torgiano

The Wine Museum

Museo del Vino, Corso Vittorio Emanuele II, I–06089 Torgiano, Perugia ☎ *075 982348 Apr–Sept, daily 9–1, 3–8. Oct–Mar, daily 9–1, 3–6.*
Ⓒ ⬦ ⬦

The museum, opened in 1974, occupies 14 rooms of the 16th-century Palazzo Baglioni. It is administered by the Lungarotti family, who have a winery in the town. The exhibits illustrate the history and techniques of wine-production since classical times and show how wine has been stored, served and drunk at different periods and in different countries. Sections are also devoted to wine in art and wine in mythology.

Gortani Museum of Carnian Popular Art, Tolmezzo.

Trieste

Museum of Natural History

Museo Civico di Storia Naturale, Piazza Hortis 4,
I–34123 Trieste   ☎ *040 301821*
Tues–Sun 9–1
C

This very old-established museum dates from
1846. Its collections illustrate the natural
history of the Adriatic, with sections devoted to
its rocks and minerals, plants, birds and fish,
animals and insects. There are also exhibits of
the fossils found in the caves of Venezia Giulia.

Museum of San Giusto

Civico Museo del Castello di San Giusto, Piazza
della Cattedrale 3, I–34121 Trieste
☎ *040 766956*
Tues–Sun 9–1. Closed Jan 1, Easter, Apr 25,
May 1, Aug 15, Dec 25.
F

The present castle of San Giusto was built by
the Hapsburgs at various times between 1470
and 1630, but there had been earlier
fortifications on the site, including a Roman fort
and a Venetian castle. Some of the rooms are
provided with 16th–18th-century furniture and
there are good collections of Italian and foreign
weapons and armour, as well as 16th-century
Flemish tapestries, wooden sculpture, Italian
paintings, and Venetian lamps and flags.

Museum of the Sea

Civico Museo del Mare, Via Campo Marzio 5,
I–34123 Trieste   ☎ *040 304987*
Tues–Sun 9–1
C

The building now occupied by the museum
dates from 1721. It was previously used as a
prison and as the Arsenal for the Artillery. Its
collections illustrate the maritime importance of
Trieste within the historical period. There are
models of ships used in the Adriatic,
navigational instruments, and models of ports
and port facilities. A section is also devoted to
the history, techniques and equipment of the
Adriatic fishing industry.

Sartorio Museum

Civico Museo Sartorio, Largo Papa Giovanni
XXIII 1/3, I–34123 Trieste   ☎ *040 301479*
Tues–Sun 9–1. Closed Jan 1, Easter, Apr 25,
May 1, Aug 15, Dec 25.
F 🖼

This late-18th-century house, subsequently
restored and modified, was the family home of
the Sartorio family. It was given to the City of
Trieste in 1944 by Baroness Anna Segrè
Sartorio, to be used as a 'museo di ambiente'
(museum of atmosphere and environment) and
for exhibitions of objects selected from the
Sartorio collections of 15th–19th-century
paintings, miniatures, silks, porcelain, clocks,
prints, tapestries and Murano glass. It has
preserved most of its original furnishings.

Trieste Museum of History and Art

Civico Museo di Storia ed Arte, Via della
Cattedrale 15, I–34121 Trieste
☎ *040 362531*
Tues–Sun 9–1. Closed Jan 1, Easter, Apr 25,
May 1, Aug 15, Dec 25.
F 🖼

The museum contains archaeological material
from prehistoric, Greek and Roman sites in the
Giulia region, including weapons, sculpture,
bronzes, glass, amber, tools, altars and ceramics.
There are also medieval collections. A lapidary
garden adjacent to the museum displays
architectural and archaeological material from
the old city of Trieste, from Roman times
onwards. In the same building are the museum's
photographic studios and restoration workshop
and the collections of prints and drawings.

Turin

Abruzzi Mountain Museum

Museo Nazionale della Montagna 'Duca degli
Abruzzi', Via G. Giardino 39, Monte dei
Cappuccini, I–10131 Torino ☎ *011 688737*
Tues–Fri 8.30–7.15; Sat–Mon 9–12.30, 2.45–
7.15.
C 🍴

In 1871 the municipality of Turin acquired the
former Capuchin Monastery, which occupied a
mountain site outside the city. With the help of
the Italian Alpine Club, and Luigi di Savoia,

Duke of Abruzzi, it established a look-out point, an observatory and, in 1874, a museum. As a result of structural weaknesses, considerable rebuilding had to be carried out during the 1930s. The museum was reopened in 1942 and seriously damaged by wartime bombing in the following year. A fully restored and enlarged museum was eventually opened to the public in 1981.

The exhibits illustrate the geology, mineralogy, wildlife and ethnography of the Alpine region, together with the history and techniques of mountaineering in the Alps and of the equipment used by its enthusiasts.

Biscaretti di Ruffia Automobile Museum

Museo dell'Automobile Carlo Biscaretti di Ruffia, Corso Unità d'Italia 40, I-10126 Torino
☎ 011 677666
Tues–Sun 9–12.30, 3–7. Closed Jan 1, Dec 25.
C ▮ ▟ ▰

Turin is the most important centre of Italy's automobile industry and the museum is one of the largest of its kind in the world. In 1960 it was transferred to the present distinguished group of buildings. What is on display is based on the collection of vehicles, memorabilia and archives built up over many years by Carlo Biscaretti. He was the museum's first president and it took his name on his death in 1959.

The collection of more than 400 items offers a panorama of the motorcar and its engines from the earliest days and includes a number of unique or very rare items. Among them are Bordino's steam-driven landau (1854), the Itala which won the Paris–Peking race in 1907, and several of the prestigious Isotha Fraschinis.

Museum of the Risorgimento

Museo Nazionale del Risorgimento Italiano, Via Accademia delle Scienze 5, I-10123 Torino
☎ 011 511147/513/19
Tues–Sat 9–7; Sun 9–1. Closed mid-week holidays.
C ▮

The Risorgimento, the movement to free the Italian states from domination by the French and the Austrians and to link them together into a single country, lasted in its acute and final form from 1859 to 1870. In 1878 Vittorio Emanuele II, the King of Piedmont and Sardinia, and subsequently the first King of the whole of Italy, died and the Common Council of Turin, the capital of Piedmont, decided to create a Museum of the Risorgimento in his memory. After a number of sojourns in temporary premises, the museum found its way to the Palazzo Carigno, in which Vittorio Emanuele II had been born.

The collections now illustrate the Italian struggle for independence from the early 18th century to the end of the Second World War. The process is linked in the displays with similar events elsewhere in Europe during the same period. The museum exhibits include the hall in which the first Italian Parliament met.

Sabauda Gallery

Galleria Sabauda, Via Accademia delle Scienze 6, I-10123 Torino
☎ 011 547440
Tues–Sun 10–1
C

This is one of Italy's principal art museums. It has five sections. The first has a comprehensive collection of works by 15th–17th-century artists from Piedmont. The second is devoted to the other leading Italian schools – Tuscany, Lombardy, Ferrara, Bologna, and Venice. The Dutch and Flemish collections, which form the third section of the gallery, are the finest in Italy and include *The Passion* by Hans Memling, *The Children of Charles I of England* by Van Dyck, and *An Old Man Asleep*, by Rembrandt. Section Four has the Gallery's French, Spanish and Italian paintings and Section Five is concerned with sculpture, furniture and gold and silversmiths' work, with some Renaissance paintings and 18th-century pastels.

Udine

Friuli Museum of Popular Art

Museo Friulano delle Arti e Tradizioni Popolari, Via Viola 3, I-33100 Udine
☎ 0432 290861
Tues–Sat 9.30–12.30, 3–6; Sun 9.30–12.30.
F

The 16th–18th-century building in which the museum is situated contains two frescoes of interest, *The Judgement of Paris* by Francesco Chiarottini (1748–96) and *The Triumph of Bacchus and Ceres*, by Jacopo Guarana (1720–1808).

The museum, opened in 1963, illustrates the traditional rural life of the Friuli area, with collections of costumes, 18th–19th-century furniture, craftsmen's tools and equipment, handicrafts, domestic equipment and farm implements. Sections are also devoted to religious life and to popular art.

Urbino

National Gallery of the Marches

Galleria Nazionale della Marche, Piazza Duca Federico, I-61029 Urbino, Pesaro e Urbino
☎ 0722 27604014
Daily 10–1
C

Construction of this great palace of the Dukes of Montefeltro began in 1444, on the orders of Duke Federico. The rooms have their original decorations. There are notable collections of Gobelins tapestries, inlaid furniture, porcelain, and 14th–16th-century paintings, especially by Venetian artists. The particularly important works include Paolo Uccello's *Profanation of the Host*, Piero della Francesca's *Flagellation* and Raphael's famous portrait of a woman, *The Mute*.

Raphael's Birthplace

Casa Natale di Raffaello, Via Raffaello Sanzio 51,
  I–61029 Urbino, Pesaro e Urbino
  ☎ *0722 320105*
Apr–Oct, Tues–Sun 10–1, 2–5. Nov–Mar, Tues–
  Sun 10–1.
C

Raphael, more properly, Raffaello Sanzio,
(1483–1520) lived in this 15th-century house
until he was 16. There is a library devoted to
him, together with copies of his works, 17th–
18th-century furniture, coins and documents.

Venice

Accademia Gallery

Gallerie dell'Accademia, Campo della Carità,
  Dorsoduro 1023, I–30123 Venezia
  ☎ *041 5222247*
Daily 9.30–1.30
C 🏛 💻

The gallery contains the most important and the
most comprehensive collection anywhere of
Venetian art from 1300 to 1700. It is housed in
an historic group of buildings, the Scuola
Grande della Carità, which can be visited. The
school was founded in 1260 and rebuilt in
1441–52. The Monastery of Lateran Canons
was designed by Andrea Palladio in 1561.

Correr Museum

Museo Correr, Piazza San Marco, I–30124
  Venezia   ☎ *041 5225625/5222185*
Mon, Wed–Sat 10–4; Sun 9–12.30. Closed
  Easter, May 1, Dec 25.
F 🏛

The museum takes its name from Teodoro
Correr (1750–1830), who belonged to an old
Venetian noble family. He was a passionate
collector and on his death left everything to the
city of Venice. The museum building is the
Procuratorie Nuove, designed by Vincenzo
Scamozzi (1552–1616). It was formerly the
offices of the Procurator of San Marco, one of
the most important posts in the Venetian
Republic.

The exhibits include views and plans
illustrating the development of Venice, 16th–
18th-century portraits of the Doges, documents
relating to the maritime history of Venice and to
its government and to the history of the
Risorgimento. There are also 13th–17th-
century Venetian, Flemish and German
paintings, 16th–17th-century engravings, 16th-
century Italian ivories, ceramics, and silks,
designs of Venetian ships and gondolas, and
Venetian coins.

The museum has, as a central exhibit, the
toga of the Doges.

Goldoni House

Casa di Goldoni, S. Tomà 2794, I–30125 Venezia
  ☎ *041 5236353*
Mon–Sat 8.30–1.30
C 📖 💻

The courtyard of the Goldoni House, Venice.

The dramatist, Carlo Goldoni (1707–93) was
born in Venice and lived here until 1762. His
former home dates from the 15th century and
has an outside staircase. It contains memorabilia
of Goldoni and a large library on all aspects of
the history of the theatre. The house is now an
important centre for theatre studies in general
and of Goldoni research in particular.

Museum of Jewish Art

Museo d'Arte Ebraica, Cannaregio 2902/B,
  I–30100 Venezia   ☎ *041 715359*
Mar 15 – June 30, Mon–Fri 10.30–1, 2.30–5;
  Sun 10.30–1. July–Oct, Mon–Fri 10.30–5;
  Sun 10.30–1. Nov–Mar, Mon–Fri, Sun 10–
  12.30. Closed Jewish holidays.
C 🏛

The museum building is part of the area of high
buildings, a very early example of a city's
vertical expansion, which made up the
Venetian ghetto where Jews were forced to live
from 1516 onwards.

The two rooms of the museum are the first
part of a larger project which represents the
whole of the ghetto as a museum area, with
guided tours that start from the museum. The
exhibition contains objects used in the
performing of religious ceremonies in both the
synagogue and the home. Most of them date
from the 17th–18th centuries and many of them
were used either to adorn the Scroll of the Law,
or to help in its reading. Many of the items on
display belonged to the synagogues that are
shown on the guided tours.

Museum of Naval History

Museo Storico Navale, Castello 2148, I–30122
  Venezia   ☎ *041 5200276*
Mon–Fri 9–1, Sat 9–12. Closed public holidays.
C 🏛

Opened in 1919, the museum is located near the
Arsenal in one of Venice's old granary
buildings. It has wide-ranging collections

relating to Italian naval history, a particular strength being its ship models. Those made in the days of the Venetian Republic were preserved in a special building, the Casa dei Modelli. Some of these are in the present museum, although most of them were destroyed during the sack of the Arsenal in 1797. Today's museum commemorates Venetian ships and boats, as well as those built in the Arsenal for the navies of the French and Austrian occupying powers (1797–1866), for the Kingdom of United Italy (1860–1946) and for the Italian Republic. The most spectacular model is that of the 'Bucintoro', the ceremonial barge of the Doge of Venice. The museum also has paintings, documents and relics illustrating Italian naval history.

Museum of the Risorgimento

Museo del Risorgimento e dell'Ottocento Veneziano, Piazza San Marco 52, I–30124 Venezia ☎ *041 5225625 Mon, Wed–Sat 10–4; Sun 9–12.30.*
F 🛈

The museum is in a 16th–17th-century building in St Mark's Square. It tells the story of Venice from the fall of the Republic in 1797 until its inclusion in the Kingdom of Italy in 1866, with separate sections relating to the periods of French and Austrian domination and to the reaction against foreign rule. Special exhibitions are devoted to Daniele Manin, one of the leaders of the Risorgimento in Venice, prominent in the 1848 Revolution, and to freemasonry in Venice as a liberalising and patriotic influence.

The museum's collections include weapons and uniforms, and 18th–19th-century paintings, prints and documents.

Querini Museum

Museo della Fondazione Scientifica Querini Stampalia, Castello 4778, I–30122 Venezia ☎ *041 5203433 Tues–Sun 10–12.30. Closed Jan 1, Easter, Apr 25, May 1, 1st Sun in June, Aug 15, 1st Sun in Nov, Dec 25.*
F 🛈

The Querini family was as old as Venice and was playing a leading part in the city's public life in the 12th century. In 1300 their nobility was enriched by the additional title of Stampalia, the name of a Greek island bought by the family. The Querinis were notable collectors and in 1868 Count Giovanni Querini left his estate, including his splendid library, to a new foundation.

The museum, like the library, is in the 16th-century Querini mansion, which has frescoes and furnishings of the 17th century. It contains furniture, tapestries and engravings, but its greatest strength lies in its collection of 14th–18th-century paintings by Venetian artists. Among those represented are Giovanni Bellini, Antonio Canova, Lorenzo di Credi, Giovanni Battista Tiepolo and, above all, Pietro Longhi.

Treasury of St Mark's

Tesoro di S. Marco e Museo della Basilica, Piazza San Marco, I–30124 Venezia ☎ *041 5225205 Mon–Sat 10–5; Sun 2–5. Closed Wed–Fri during Holy Week.*
C

The treasury, in the chancel of the cathedral, is distinguished especially by its collection of Late Antique and Byzantine religious art and liturgical objects brought to Venice after the pillage of Constantinople by the Crusaders in 1204. The Museum of the Basilica has the Greco-Roman bronze horses, which were once on the front of the cathedral. They were brought from Constantinople by Doge Dandolo in 1204 and remained in Venice until they were taken to Paris by Napoleon. They were returned after the fall of the French Empire.

Vercelli

Leone Museum

Museo Camillo Leone, Via Verdi 30, I–13100 Vercelli ☎ *0161 65604 Mar–Nov, Tues, Thurs, 3–5.30; Sun 10–12.*
C 🛈 💼 🔧

On his death in 1907, the Vercelli lawyer, Camillo Leone, left the greater part of his collections to the Institute of Fine Arts to be used as a museum. The museum was opened in 1910, but continues as a private institution, with some support from public funds. Its exhibits illustrate the history and culture of Vercelli and its region since prehistoric times, with sections devoted to archaeology, paintings by local artists, porcelain, glass, bronzes, coins and medals, weapons, jewellery and silver. Among the more important items on display are 4th–3rd century BC Apulian vases, medieval illuminated manuscripts, and ceramics.

Verona

Museum of Modern Art

Galleria Comunale d'Arte Moderna e Contemporanea, Palazzo Forti, Via A. Forti, I–37121 Verona ☎ *045 8001903/596371 July–Oct, daily 9 am–11 pm. Nov–June, Tues–Sun 9–7.30. Closed public holidays during winter period.*
C 🛈

The Palazzo Forti, which houses the gallery, has its origins in a 13th-century building which was rebuilt c. 1450 and again in the 16th century. The principal façade dates from the second half of the 17th century. In 1854 the palazzo was bought by Israele Forti, who restored it, and in 1937 it was left to the city of Verona by Achille Forti, who asked that it should be used as a museum of modern art and of the Risorgimento.

The gallery, entered from the Corso S. Anastasia, was opened in 1982. It contains Italian paintings, sculpture and graphics from the 18th century to the present day.

Vigevano

Bertolini Museum of Shoemaking

Museo della Calzatura Cavaliere Pietro Bertolini,
Corso Cavour 82, I–27029 Vigevano, Pavia
☎ *0381 70149*
Sat 2.30–6.30; Sun 10–12.30, 2.30–6.30. Other
times by appt. Closed month of Aug.
Ⓒ ▮

Vigevano is traditionally a shoemaking town
and in 1930 Pietro Bertolini, whose family was
prominent in the industry, began to make an
international collection of shoes and of
materials connected with their manufacture and
sale, with the aim of one day establishing a
museum.

The museum was eventually opened in
1972, in a 19th-century mansion. It is divided
into eight sections – Historical; Famous Persons;
Military; Ethnological (Europe); Ethnological
(America); Ethnological (Africa); Ethnological
(Asia); and Various – documentation,
miniatures, curiosities, tools. The earliest boot
or shoe in the historical collection is 1700 and
among the famous persons whose shoes are
presented here are Pope John XXIII and the
Emperor Haile Selassie of Ethiopia.

Villafranca Lunigiana

Lunigiana Ethnographic Museum

Museo Etnografico della Lunigiana, Via dei Mulini
71, I–54028 Villafranca Lunigiana, Massa
Carrara   ☎ 0187 493417/494400
Apr–Sept, Tues–Sun 9–1, 4–7 Oct–Mar, Tues–
Sun 9–1, 3–6.
Ⓒ ▮

The museum, opened in 1977, is in a restored
15th-century watermill. It was founded by the
Manfred Giuliani Society for Historical and
Ethnographical Studies, which was set up in
1969 in order to study and preserve the culture
and traditions of the Lunigiana area. The
museum, which reflects the aims of the society,
is divided into ten sections, devoted to tools and
equipment for processing and weaving hemp;
carpentry and joinery; traditional forms of
medicine; the kitchen; water-milling; the use of
chestnuts; tools and implements for growing,
threshing and winnowing wheat; basketmaking;
weights and measures; and the dairy.

Vinci

The Leonardiano Museum

Museo Leonardiano, Castello dei Conti Guidi,
I–50059 Vinci, Firenze   ☎ 0571 56055
Daily 9.20–12, 2.30–6. Closed Jan 1, Easter,
May 1, Aug 15, Dec 25.
Ⓕ ▩ ⚬

The castle at Vinci was built before 1000. Since
1953 it has contained an exhibition of 40
full-size reconstructions of machinery designed,
but never built, by Leonardo, who was, of

The Leonardiano Museum, Vinci.

course, born at Vinci. Each exhibit is
accompanied by a descriptive panel and by
Leonardo's notes and drawings. The machines
include a bicycle, a flying machine, a parachute
and diver's breathing apparatus.

Zogno

Zogno Regional Museum

Museo della Valle, Via Cardinale Furietti 1,
I–24019 Zogno, Bergamo   ☎ 0345 91473
Tues–Sun 9–12, 2–5
Ⓒ ▮ ⚬

The museum was founded in 1979, at a time
when it was becoming increasingly difficult to
find evidence of the old rural culture of the area.
The aim was to preserve such material before it
disappeared for ever. As a result of diligent
searching at the eleventh hour, large and
important collections have been accumulated
from the Brembana valley. They are displayed in
a 16th–17th-century house which once
belonged to Cardinal Furietti, consisting
principally of objects connected with popular
religion, furniture and domestic items,
handicrafts and craftsmen's tools and
agricultural equipment. There is also a section
containing archaeological material from local
excavations.

Loom in Zogno Regional Museum.

LIECHTENSTEIN

Triesenberg

Walserian Museum

*Walser Heimatmuseum, Verkehrsbüro, 9497
 Triesenberg* ☎ *21926/23535*
*Jan–May and Sept–Dec, Tues–Sat 1.30–5.30.
 June–Aug, Tues–Sat 1.30–5.30; Sun 2–5.*
Ⓒ

The museum is in the village of Triesenberg and
is concerned primarily with the history and
culture of the Walserians. The collections
illustrate their religious practices, domestic life
and handicrafts. Other sections of the museum
relate to the peasant traditions of the
Triesenberg region and to agriculture, milk
production, weaving, crafts, transport, weights
and measures and the distillation of schnapps.

Vaduz

Liechtenstein Museum

*Liechtensteinisches Landesmuseum, Städtle 43,
 Engländerbau, 9490 Vaduz* ☎ *22310*
*Jan–Apr and Oct–Dec, Tues–Sun 2–5.30. May–
 Sept, daily 10–12, 1.30–5.30.*
Ⓒ 👤

The museum's collections illustrate the geology
and cultural history of the principality of
Liechtenstein. There are sections dealing with
archaeology from the Neolithic to the
Alemannic periods, Medieval and Renaissance
weapons and religious art, coins and medals,
furniture, household equipment and agriculture.
Since 1972 the museum has occupied a 15th-
century tavern, restored and remodelled to
make it suitable for its new purpose.

Postal Museum

*Postmuseum, Städtle 37, Engländerbau, 9490
 Vaduz* ☎ *66258*
Daily 10–12, 2–6.
Ⓒ 👤

The museum is devoted to the postal history of
Liechtenstein, which has issued its own stamps
since 1912. The exhibits include a complete
collection of Liechtenstein stamps, together
with designs and proofs. Liechtenstein has
always taken great pains to produce stamps
which are attractive to collectors and for this
reason both the number and variety of the
principality's stamps are exceptionally large.
There are also exhibits of franking machines,
exhibition awards made to Liechtenstein in
acknowledgement of the quality of its stamps,
and rare philatelic items from all over the world.

State Art Gallery

*Staatliche Kunstsammlung, Städtle 43,
 Engländerbau, 9490 Vaduz* ☎ *22341*
*Jan–Mar and Nov–Dec, Tues–Sun 10–12,
 2–5.30. Apr–Oct, daily 10–12, 1.30–5.30.*
Ⓒ 👤

The princes of Liechtenstein have large and
important collections which are kept in the
castle at Vaduz. Changing exhibitions of items
from these collections are displayed in the new
State Gallery. They include 15th–19th-century
German paintings and sculpture, paintings by
Rubens, weapons, furniture and tapestries.

The village of Triesenberg.

LUXEMBOURG

Ehnen

Wine Museum

Musée du Vin, Ehnen, Luxembourg ☎ *76026*
Apr–Oct, Tues–Sun 9.30–11.30, 2–5. Nov–
  Mar, by appt. Closed Jan.

The museum has been created within the
premises of a former winemaking establishment,
facing the Moselle and at the foot of hillsides
bearing celebrated vineyards. The exhibits are
displayed in the former vat-room and illustrate
all the processes involved in growing grapes and
in making, storing and bottling wine. Visitors
are able to visit one of the surrounding vineyards
and to see current work in progress. The
demonstration vineyard is planted with the
principal varieties of grape grown in the
Luxembourg Moselle region and includes
Elbling, Rivaner, Auxerrois, Pinot blanc, Pinot
gris, Riesling and Traminer.

   Most of the objects in the museum have
been given or lent by local people. Tasting
Moselle wines is an important and appreciated
part of the visit.

**Luxembourg, 1936, by J. Kutter (1894–
1941). Luxembourg Museum.**

Luxembourg

Luxembourg Museum

Musee d'Histoire et d'Art, Musées de l'Etat,
  Marché-aux-Poissons, L–2345 Luxembourg
  ☎ *479330*
Tues–Sun 10–12, 2–6. Department of Decorative
  and Popular Art; 2–6. Department of National
  History and Collection of Weapons: Tues,
  Thurs, Fri 2–6. Nov–Mar, closed Sat am.

The museum has been created in order to
illustrate the many different cultural movements
to which the Grand Duchy has been exposed
during its turbulent history. It occupies a group
of historic buildings in the old city, which have
been linked, restored and remodelled to make
them suitable for their present purpose. The
exhibitions, arranged in more than 150 rooms,
are devoted to Gallo-Roman, Merovingian and
Medieval archaeology, fine art, coins and
medals, popular art, handicrafts and the natural
sciences. Special sections are devoted to
weapons and armour, uniforms and the history
of the fortress of Luxembourg.

**Rural living-room, 18th-century. Department
of Decorative and Popular Arts, Luxembourg
Museum.**

MALTA

Valletta

Museum of the Co-Cathedral of St John

St John's Street, Valletta   ☎ 220536
Mon–Sat 9.30–12.30, 3–5. Closed public
  holidays.
C 🛉

The cathedral was at one time one of the richest
in the Mediterranean countries, as a result of
the frequent gifts which it received from
members of the Order of St John. In 1798,
however, it was despoiled of most of its treasures
by the army of Napoleon, who issued orders to
have the silver melted down and reissued as
coinage. A number of outstanding items have
survived. They include the Gothic 'Reliquary of
St Peter', with its remarkable set of 13th-
century enamel plaques, and a set of 28 Flemish
tapestries woven from the cartoons of Peter Paul
Rubens. There are also two paintings by
Caravaggio and fine collections of choral books
and antiphonaries, 15th–18th-century
vestments, monstrances and other religious
ornaments.

National Museum of Fine Arts

South Street, Valletta   ☎ 225769
Daily 8.30–4.30. Closed public holidays
C

The mansion which houses the museum was
among the first to be built in Valletta after the
Order of St John officially moved to the new city
in 1571. It was radically restored in 1761–3.
After the capture of Malta by Napoleon, it had a
chequered history and in 1821 it was leased to
the naval authorities, who used it as the official
residence of the Admiral Commander-in-Chief,
when it became Admiralty House. Ownership
was transferred to the Maltese Government in
1961 and it opened as a museum in 1974.

There are a number of mainly 17th–18th-
century paintings connected with the history of
the Order of St John in Malta. They include a
number of Baroque paintings by Mattia Preti (d.
1699). Among the modern works are sculptures
by Antonio Sciortino (d. 1947).

Exposition throne. Museum of the Co-
Cathedral of St John, Valletta.

National Museum of Malta

Republic Street, Valletta   ☎ 227730
June 16 – Sept 30, daily 7.45–2. Oct 1 – June 15,
  Mon–Sat 8.15–5; Sun 8.15–4.15. Closed
  public holidays.
C

The museum contains important archaeological
material from Stone Age, Phoenician, Roman
and Arab sites on the island, together with
portraits and vestments of Grand Masters of the
Order of St John, topographical paintings and
prints showing the development of Malta, and
silver from the Hospital of the Holy Spirit.
There are also collections of Maltese coins,
Tarxian sculpture and iron anchors from the
galleys of the Knights of St John.

Zabbar

Wickman Maritime Collection

'La Capitana', Dwardu Ellul Street, Xghajra,
  Zabbar   ☎ 823655
By appt.
F 🖭 ⚓

The museum, opened in 1961, is on the
approaches to the Grand Harbour of Malta. Its
collections concentrate on the development of
Maltese maritime trade during the period of
British rule, 1800–1964. There are ship models
which illustrate the ties between Malta and the
various shipping companies trading in the
Mediterranean and paintings of Maltese-owned
sailing ships. Malta's links with the Royal Navy
are emphasised by portraits of British admirals
who commanded the Mediterreanean
Squadron, models of warships and a variety of
naval artefacts, including the binnacle of HMS
Magpie, donated by HRH the Duke of
Edinburgh.

Choral book. Museum of the Co-Cathedral of
St John, Valletta.

MONACO

Monaco-Ville

Museum of Napoleonic Relics and Palace of Monaco

Musée des Souvenirs Napoléoniens et des Archives du Palais de Monaco, Palais de Monaco, MC–98000 Monaco-Ville ☎ *93 251831*
Dec 16 – May 31, Tues–Sun 10–12.30, 2–5. June–Sept, daily 9.30–6.30. Oct 1–22, daily 10–5.
C

The museum, in a gallery designed for the purpose, forms part of the southern wing of the Princes' Palace. The Napoleonic collections were begun by Prince Louis II and augmented by Prince Rainier III. They contain portraits and busts of Napoleon Bonaparte, relics of his campaigns and of his exile on St Helena, the clothes he wore at his baptism and one of his legendary hats.

The upper floor of the gallery displays documents relating to the history of Monaco and to the House of Grimaldi, stamps and coins issued by Monaco, topographical paintings, engravings and postcards showing the development of Monaco and uniforms worn by the Palace guards at different periods.

Oceanographic Museum

Musée Océanographique de Monaco, Avenue St Martin, MC–98000 Monaco-Ville ☎ *93 301514*
Jan–Mar and Oct–Dec, daily 9.30–7. Apr–June and Sept, daily 9–7. July–Aug, daily 9–9. Closed Sun afternoon following Ascension Day.
C ⋔ ⬛ ⵜ ⌂

The museum, opened in 1910, is perched 80 metres above the sea on the Rock of Monaco. It owes its existence to the initiative of Prince Albert I, a pioneer of oceanography, and was originally planned to house the scientific collections accumulated by him in the course of his oceanographic researches.

The museum has a 90-tank aquarium, containing 350 species of fish from all over the world, displayed in settings similar to those of their native environment. There are also skeletons of whales, models and prepared specimens of marine fauna and a gallery devoted to products of the sea, such as sponges, mother-of-pearl, tortoiseshell and coral.

Among the other exhibits are models of Prince Albert l's four oceanographic vessels, especially the *Princesse Alice II*, from which, in 1909, the Prince trawled up fish from a depth of 6,035 metres, a record at the time. A reconstruction of a laboratory installed in 1911 in one of these ships shows the facilities available to research workers at that date.

Princes' Palace

Palais Princier, MC–98000 Monaco-Ville ☎ *93 251831*
June–Sept, daily 9.30–6.30. Oct 1–22, daily 10–5.
C

The palace of the Princes of Monaco has been developed from an early-13th-century Genoese fortress. The Grimaldi family began to control Monaco in the 15th century and from then onwards the building was gradually transformed into a palace. It suffered considerable damage and spoliation during the French Revolution, but during the present century it has recovered much of its former glory.

The State apartments are open to the public. They contain 17th–18th-century furniture and paintings and a series of portraits of members of the Grimaldi family. The Hercules Gallery, which can also be visited, has 17th-century frescoes representing the Labours of Hercules.

Surgeon-fish. Oceanographic Museum, Monaco-Ville.

NETHERLANDS

Alkmaar

Dutch Cheese Museum

Het Hollands Kaasmuseum, Waagplein 2,
1811 JP Alkmaar ☎ *072 114284*
Mon–Thurs, Sat 10–4; Fri 9–4.

Ⓒ 🛈 ⚬

Alkmaar has one of the principal cheese markets in the Netherlands. The museum is in the old weigh house, which is still regularly used. The displays illustrate the development of cheesemaking methods in the Netherlands. There are collections of cheese presses and of other equipment and instruments.

Sea-Dike Exhibition

De Dijk te Kijk, Zuiderhazedwarsdijk te Petten,
Postbus 22, 1800 AA Alkmaar
☎ *072 193636*
May, June and Sept, Sat, Sun 2–5. July– Aug,
Mon–Fri 10–5; Sat, Sun 2–5. Groups at other
times by appt.

Ⓕ 🛈 ⚬

A large part of the Netherlands, which has no natural protection in the form of dunes, would be regularly flooded if dikes had not been built to keep the water out. This is particularly true of North Holland, much of which is several metres below sea-level. Construction of the sea-dike here began in the 15th century. The present dike is 4.5 km long. The exhibitions show how it came into existence, how much maintenance is required and what has still to be done in order to provide a reliable defence against the worst gales and high seas.

Amersfoort

Flehite Museum

Museum Flehite, Westsingel 50,
3811 BL Amersfoort. Correspondence to:
Breestraat 80, 3811 BL Amersfoort
☎ *033 619987*
Tues–Fri 10–5; Sat, Sun 2–5. Closed public
holidays.

Ⓒ 🛈 ⚤

In 1878 a group of Amersfoort enthusiasts excavated a group of burial mounds on Leusden Heath in the eastern part of the province of Utrecht, known as Flehite. The finds from these excavations, together with other antiquities from Amersfoort and the surrounding area, formed the basis of the Flehite Museum, which was opened in 1880. It is now the historical museum of Amersfoort, with exhibits ranging from prehistoric times to the present day.

There is a special display relating to Johan van Oldenbarneveldt (1547–1619), who was a native of Amersfoort. He was beheaded in The Hague in 1619 and the museum has the cane on which he leant on his way to the scaffold. Other sections relate to the painter, Piet Mondrian, born in Amersfoort in 1872, and to the problems faced by Amersfoort during the First World War. There are also collections of fossils and archaeological material from the region.

Amsterdam

Anne Frank's House

Anne Frank Huis, Prinsengracht 263,
1016 GV Amsterdam. Correspondence to:
Keizersgracht 192, 1016 DW Amsterdam
☎ *020 264533*
June–Aug, Mon–Sat 9–7; Sun 10–7. Sept–May,
Mon–Sat 9–5; Sun 10–5. Closed Jan 1, Yom
Kippur, Dec 25.

Ⓒ 🛈 ⬛

Otto Frank and his family escaped from Germany in 1933, when the persecution of Jews was becoming intolerable. In 1940 he set up his business at 263 Prinsengracht. Early in 1942, when the Nazi occupation of the Netherlands was in its third year, Otto Frank prepared a secret hiding-place for the eight members of his family on the upper two floors and attic of the house. They lived here undetected for two years, but they were eventually betrayed and taken to extermination camps. During the whole period when they were in hiding, Anne Frank, who was 13 in 1942, kept a detailed diary of her experiences. Eventually published, it became one of the most celebrated documents of the war years.

The museum at 263 Prinsengracht was opened in 1960. The secret living quarters used by the Frank family and friends have been preserved and the original diary can be seen. Exhibitions tell the story of the Franks, and illustrate the history of the Netherlands and anti-Semitism during the Nazi period.

Dutch Cheese Museum, Alkmaar.

Buddhist manuscript in Khmer script. Dortmond Museum of Handwriting, Amsterdam.

Dortmond Museum of Handwriting

Schriftmuseum J. A. Dortmond, University Library Amsterdam, Singel 425, 1012 WP Amsterdam
☎ *020 5252476*
Mon–Fri 10–1, 2–4.30. Closed public holidays.
F ⬛

The museum, opened in 1976, is housed on the second floor of the 'Militia' building of the University Library, dating from 1610. The collections, formed by the Society for the Improvement of Handwriting, under the presidency of J. A. Dortmond, present a survey of the history of writing, by means of tablets, manuscripts and other media, from Mesopotamian times to the 20th century. The exhibits include cuneiform and hieroglyphic scripts, different forms of Arabic writing, medieval manuscripts and letters from famous people including Tolstoy, Goethe, William of Orange, Peter the Great, Napoleon Bonaparte and Adolf Hitler.

Electric Tramway Museum

Electrische Museumtramlÿn Amsterdam, Haarlemmermeerstation, Amstelveenseweg 264, 1075 XV Amsterdam ☎ *020 737538*
Late Mar–June and early Sept–late Oct, Sun and public holidays 10.30–5.30. July–early Sept, Tues–Thurs, Sat 1–4; Sun and public holidays 10.30–5.30.
C ⬛ ⬛ ⬛

Established in 1975, the museum has an international collection of electric trams, built between 1910 and 1950. They run over a 6 km section of track from Haarlemmermeer station to Amstelveen. The tramcars, which come from Amsterdam, The Hague, Rotterdam, Groningen, Kassel, Vienna, Graz, Prague and Budapest, have all been restored to their original condition.

Jewish Historical Museum

Joods Historisch Museum, Postbus 16737, 1001 RE Amsterdam ☎ *020 269945*
Daily 11–5. Closed on Yom Kippur.
C ⬛ ⬛ ⬛

The museum, opened in 1987, is located in the carefully-restored Ashkenazi synagogue complex, which consists of four 17th- and 18th-century synagogues, all of which were built for the Orthodox Jewish Congregation of Amsterdam. Its displays illustrate the culture and history of the Jewish communities in the Netherlands. In the three main departments of the museum, the visitor is introduced to the themes of Jewish identity, Jewish religion and the social history of the Jews in the Netherlands.

The buildings suffered severe damage during the Second World War, and since the neighbourhood, once the home of many of the Jews who attended these synagogues, had lost most of its population, the complex was sold in 1955 to the city of Amsterdam. The restoration programme and the installation of the new museum has been the responsibility of the Dutch Government, with the help of the Jewish communities in Amsterdam and other towns.

The museum has a large library and an archive of photographs, slides, videos, sound tapes and documents. The Kosher Coffee Shop serves Jewish specialities.

Museum of Amsterdam

Amsterdams Historisch Museum, Kalverstraat 92, Amsterdam. Correspondence to: Nieuwezijds Voorburgwal 359, 1012 RM Amsterdam
☎ *020 5231822*
Daily 11–5. Closed Jan 1.
C ⬛ ⬛ ⬛

In 1926 the city set up an Amsterdam Historical Museum in the former weigh house, built as St Anthony's Gate in 1488. In 1975, the 700th anniversary of the founding of Amsterdam, the museum, which had long outgrown the weigh house was opened in what had been the Civic Orphanage, after considerable building work had been carried out. The emphasis of the museum is on the economic development of Amsterdam from the 13th century to 1945.

The collections include paintings and other items from the town hall and from orphanages, almshouses and houses of correction. There are also former possessions of the Amsterdam guilds and the civic militia. Among the items which belonged to the militia are a series of large 16th- and 17th-century portraits of the Amsterdam civic guard, 16th-century Dutch silver and a number of embossed suits of armour, made in Italy in the 16th century. There are also many paintings, drawings and prints given by private individuals, including works by Leonardo da Vinci, Van Dyck, Rubens and Rembrandt. The museum has a major collection of playing-cards with examples of all the cards produced in Amsterdam. An important section is devoted to material discovered by archaeologists in the course of excavations in the city.

Netherlands Maritime Museum

Nederlands Scheepvaart Museum,
  Kattenburgerplein 1, 1018 KK Amsterdam
  ☎ 020 5232222
Tues–Sat 10–5; Sun 1–5. Closed Jan 1.
Ⓒ ♟ 🍴 ♿ ♨

The museum is housed in the former arsenal of
the Amsterdam Admiralty, built in 1656. Ships
constructed in the nearby dockyard were rigged
and fitted out here and supplied with clothing
and victuals for the crews. After the Royal
Dutch Navy had abandoned the arsenal in
1971, it was converted into a museum which
gives an overall picture of Dutch maritime
history.

The major themes – commerce, fishing, war
at sea, yachting and navigation – are
represented by ship models, paintings, charts,
instruments, weapons and other objects. The
museum also has a print room, a department of
plans and drawings, and a library. Three historic
ships are moored at the landing stage of the
museum.

Rembrandt's House

Museum het Rembrandthuis, Jodenbreestraat 4–6,
  1011 NK Amsterdam
  ☎ 020 249846
*Mon–Sat 10–5; Sun and public holidays 1–5. Dec
  2, 24, 31, 10–4. Closed Jan 1.*
Ⓒ ♟ ♨

Rembrandt lived here and worked in the house,
which was built in 1606, from 1639 until 1660.
In 1908–11 it was restored as nearly as possible
to its original condition and opened as a
museum.

The rooms are partly furnished in the style of
the 17th century. The collection includes 250
etchings by Rembrandt, almost the whole of his
graphic work. Some of his drawings are also on
display, together with paintings by his masters
and pupils.

Rijksmuseum

Rijksmuseum, Stadhouderskade 42,
  1007 DD Amsterdam
  ☎ 020 732121
Tues–Sat 10–5; Sun 1–5. Closed Jan 1.
Ⓒ ♟ 🍴 ♿

The museum was founded in 1817. It was
established in its present neo-Renaissance
building, designed for the purpose by P. J. H.
Cuypers, in 1885. Its particular strength lies in
its collections of Dutch and Flemish paintings,
but it has also sections devoted to works by
foreign artists and to sculpture, tapestries,
furniture, silver, liturgical objects, ecclesiastical
vestments, jewellery, tiles, pottery and
porcelain.

A separate department illustrates the
political and military history of the
Netherlands, with paintings, ship models,
weapons, flags, gold and silver objects, costumes
and documents. Other sections of the museum
are devoted to Asiatic art and to Dutch and
foreign prints and drawings.

Stedelijk Museum

Stedelijk Museum, Paulus Potterstraat 13,
  1071 CX Amsterdam. Correspondence to:
  Postbus 5082, 1007 AB Amsterdam
  ☎ 020 5732911
Daily 11–5. Closed Jan 1.
Ⓒ ♟ 🍴 ♿ ♨

This is Amsterdam's Museum of Modern Art.
The building dates from 1893–5 and was
designed for the purpose by the Municipal
Architect of Amsterdam, A. W. Weissman. It
has been extended and modified several times
since it was first opened.

The collections are of an international
character and include works from the late 19th
century onwards. From the 1960s, the visual arts
were joined by new media – photography, film,
video, music and the performing arts. When it
was set up in 1934, the collections of the
Decorative Arts Department consisted of
examples of Dutch craftsmanship, such as
ceramics, furniture, textiles and objects made of
wood, glass and metal. After 1945, typography,
posters and industrial design were added.

Van Loon Museum

Museum Van Loon, Keizersgracht 672,
  1017 ET Amsterdam   ☎ 020 245255
Mon 10–5
Ⓒ ♟

The house in which the museum is located was
built in 1671–2. It was bought by Hendrik Van
Loon in 1884 and now belongs to the Van Loon
Foundation, which has restored and furnished it
to its late-18th–early 19th-century condition.
The principal exhibits in the house are more
than 50 17th- and 18th-century portraits of
members of the Van Loon family, which was
one of the most powerful in the Netherlands,
both politically and commercially, between the
revolution of Amsterdam against the Spaniards
in 1578 and the French-inspired revolution in
1795, when Amsterdam came to be ruled by a
self-perpetuating oligarchy.

Willet-Holthuysen Museum

Museum Willet-Holthuysen, Herengracht 605,
  Amsterdam. Correspondence to: Nieuwezijds
  Voorburgwal 359, 1012 RM Amsterdam
  ☎ 020 5231870
Daily 11–5. Closed Jan 1.
Ⓒ

No. 605 Herengracht was built in 1689. In
1855, after several changes of ownership, it
passed into the hands of Pieter Gerard
Holthuysen. When he died in 1858, his
daughter, who married Abraham Willet in
1861, continued to live in the house. Willet had
a keen interest in art and built up large
collections of glass, ceramics, silver and
paintings, together with an important library on
the history of art. In her will, Mrs Willet left the
house and all its contents to the city of
Amsterdam, on condition that it was to be

opened to the public under the name of the 'Willet-Holthuysen Museum'.

The museum opened its doors to the public in 1896, but until the Art Historical Institute of the University established its headquarters in the building in 1932, there were so few visitors that it was said of the museum that it was one of the few places in Amsterdam where a gentleman could meet his mistress unobserved. Abraham Willet's collections were particularly strong in 18th-century Dutch porcelain, and visitors to the house can see important exhibits from the factories at Weesp, Loosdrecht, Amstel and The Hague.

Andijk

Het Grootslag Polder Museum

Poldermuseum 'Het Grootslag', Dijkweg 319,
*   1619 EG Andijk*   ☎ 02289 2227
May–Sept, Wed–Sun 2–5. Oct–Apr, Sun 2–5.
*   Other times by appt.*
Ⓒ ⌂

The museum is in the former 'Het Grootslag' pumping station, with steam-powered machinery dating from the 1820s which was used to control the water level before the West Frisian Ring Dike was completed after the Second World War and the polder, or reclaimed area greatly extended. The museum contains objects from the Stone Age period onwards which have been discovered during the work of reclaiming and resettling the area, together with an extensive collection of horticultural equipment and tools.

Favourable conditions led to the establishment of horticulture, bulb-growing and seed-production in the region and the museum complex also includes the National Seed and Herb Museum, which illustrates the development of vegetable and flower seeds in the Netherlands and of the seed trade.

Anjum

Anjum Mill

De Anjumer Molen, Molenbuurt 18,
*   9133 ZT Anjum*   ☎ 05193 1926
Mon–Sat 10–5. Closed Easter, Dec 25.
Ⓒ 🔔 ⌂

Built in 1889, this is one of the largest windmills in the region. It is still fully operational. It opened as a museum in 1973 and contains collections of scale models of different types of windmills, agricultural implements and farm equipment, as well as seashells.

Apeldoorn

Het Loo Palace

Paleis Het Loo, Koninklijk Park 1,
*   7315 HR Apeldoorn*   ☎ 055 212244
Tues–Sun 10–5. Closed 25.
Ⓒ 🔔 ⬛ ᚠ ⌂

Het Loo Palace, Apeldoorn.

This moated palace was built in 1685–6 for Prince William III of Orange, later William III of England, who had an addiction to hunting in the area. Considerable alterations were made both to the palace and its gardens during the late 17th, 18th and 19th centuries and by Queen Wilhelmina in 1911. Following her abdication in 1948, Queen Wilhelmina retired to Het Loo. She died in 1962 and Princess Margriet and her family lived in the palace from 1967 to 1972, when they moved to a new house in the park. The palace then became a national museum. The conversion involved the demolition of the 19th- and 20th-century additions, restoration of the exterior to its original condition, and the reconstruction of the gardens.

The furnishing of the central part of the house and the pavilions gives an impression of how the palace has been lived in at different periods by members of the House of Orange. In the east wing there are paintings, prints, medals, objets d'art and documents illustrating the lives of the reigning members of the House of Orange Nassau and their Court. The first floor of the west wing accommodates the Museum of the Chancery of the Netherlands Orders of Knighthood, with a large collection of Dutch and foreign orders and decorations, costumes and swords of honour. The stables display carriages, coaches, sledges and vintage cars.

Arnhem

Bronbeek Museum

Museum Bronbeek, Velpenweg 197,
*   6824 MB Arnhem*   ☎ 085 641538
Daily 9–12, 12.30–5
Ⓒ 🔔 ⬛ ᚠ ⌂

The present house, which forms the centre of the Bronbeek estate, was built in 1847. In 1857 it was bought by Willem III (1817–90) as a residence for his mother, Anna Paulowna (1795–1865). Two wings were added to the house at this time. After Anna Paulowna's death, the buildings were converted into a home for former soldiers of the Netherlands Colonial Army. Since 1963 they have contained a museum in two parts. The first has exhibits illustrating the customs and life of people in the former Netherlands East Indies and the second tells the story of the Colonial Army, with paintings, prints, photographs, weapons, equipment and uniforms relating to the soldiers who served in the Netherlands Indies, Surinam, New Guinea and the Antilles.

Museum of the Guards Regiment

Historisch Museum Grenadiers en Jagers, Onder de
*   Linden 101, 6800 HL Arnhem*
*   ☎ 085 531444*
Mon–Thurs 8.30–12, 1.30–4; Fri 8.30–12.
F

This is the oldest military museum in the Netherlands, the original collections having been opened to the public in 1884. As it is organised today, it illustrates the history of the Guards Regiments from 1829 to the present, with uniforms, weapons, equipment, medals, paintings, photographs and flags. The museum is maintained by the Foundation for the Preservation of the Traditions of the Guards Regiments.

Netherlands Open-Air Museum

Nederlands Openluchtmuseum, Schlemseweg 89,
*   6816 SJ Arnhem   ☎ 085 57611*
Mar 23–Oct 22, Mon–Fri 9–5; Sat, Sun 10–5.
C

In 1912 a group of private individuals decided to form an open-air museum in the Netherlands, similar to those which already existed in Scandinavia. Collecting began and in 1918 the museum was opened to the public on a 33-hectare site in Arnhem. Since then characteristic buildings from all over the Netherlands have been transferred to the museum site. During the Battle of Arnhem in 1944 considerable damage was done to the museum. Several buildings were destroyed and the entire costume collection was lost.

The aim of the museum is to give an historically reliable picture of the pattern of daily life in the past. More than 80 houses, farms, mills, workshops and other buildings have been rebuilt in the museum park. Wherever possible, they are located in suitable surroundings and fitted out with appropriate furniture and equipment.

Baarn

Groeneveld Castle

Kasteel Groeneveld, Groeneveld 2,
*   3744 ML Baarn   ☎ 02154 20446*
Tues–Fri 10–5; Sat, Sun 12–5. Closed Dec
*   15–Jan 10.*
C

This château-style house and its estate dates from the 17th century. The park was laid out in the English style. It has functioned as a museum since 1981, and has exhibits relating to wildlife and nature conservation and to forestry techniques today and in the past. There are also collections of paintings with nature-themes and of books printed on wood.

Barger Compascuum

National Peat-Moor Park

Nationaal Veenpark, Berkenrode 4,
*   7884 TR Barger Compascuum*
*   ☎ 05913 49631*
Mar 15–Oct 31, daily 9–6
C

Set in the middle of the extensive local peat-moors, this ecomuseum, covering 150 hectares, shows how the important peat-digging industry operates today and how it was carried on in the past. There are exhibits of tools and equipment and visitors can also see an ancient steam-engine used to drive the peat-extracting machinery, the steam-railway and barges for transporting the peat, together with the shops, school, houses and church of the local village community. There is a large collection of photographs, showing the traditional methods employed in digging the peat and the life of the people who worked in the industry. There is also an exhibition of the plants and wildlife of the peat-moors and of the farming methods employed in the district.

Best

De Platijn Museum of Wooden Shoes

Klompenmuseum 'De Platijn', Brockdijk 16,
*   5681 PG Best   ☎ 04998 71247*
Apr–Sept, daily 10–5
C

The area around Best contains large numbers of poplars and for generations the wood from these has been used for making wooden shoes. Until recently, these were made entirely by hand and, with the help of demonstrations, the museum shows all the processes involved, from the log to the finished shoe with a collection of the variety of tools involved. A factory next to the museum shows the continuation of the industry, using machines instead of hand-tools, and can be visited by the public.

Netherlands Open-Air Museum, Arnhem.

Boskoop

Nursery Museum

Boomwekerijmuseum, Reyerskoop 54,
2771 BF Boskoop   ☎ *01727 17756*
Mon–Sat 1–5
© ♿

Boskoop has been famous for its nursery gardens
and especially for its fruit trees and bushes for
more than 500 years. Nearly 1,000 nurseries are
still in existence, providing a living directly or
indirectly for more than half of the town's
14,000 inhabitants. On narrow strips of peaty
soil, surrounded by water, the old craft is still
carried on by people bearing the same names as
the pioneers. The museum, opened in 1975,
contains old tools and equipment used in the
gardens, many of the items dating from the 18th
century. There are also invoices and other
papers which illustrate the type and scale of the
business that was carried on.

An old nurseryman's house has been
restored and furnished in its original style. At
the back of it, a miniature nursery garden has
been established, planted with original
varieties.

Broek op Langedijk

Museum of the Broek Auction

Museum 'Broeker Veiling', Voorburggracht 20,
1721 CR Broek op Langedijk. Correspondence
to: Postbus 1, 1720 AA Broek op Langedikj
   ☎ *02260 13807*
May–Sept, Mon–Fri 10–5. Groups by appt only.
© ♿ 🖤 ♿ ♿

Broek is an area where market-gardening has
been carried on since the 16th century. The
crops are grown on 2,000 narrow rectangular
islands, separated by broad ditches, from which
the mud is regularly scooped out and spread over
the fields as a fertiliser. In 1887 the growers
began to auction their produce, which was then
sent on by barge to Amsterdam. This is claimed
to be the oldest vegetable auction in the world.

**Museum of the Broek Auction, Broek op
Langedijk.**

The bidding, which is now done electronically,
goes from high to low, the system of a 'Dutch'
auction.

Visitors are given boat trips around the
islands to see the system of cultivation and
transport and a museum, with both outdoor and
indoor sections, was established in 1974, to
explain the local economy and to preserve and
display traditional types of boats and barges and
a wide range of tools and equipment used by the
growers.

Buren

Museum of Farm Wagons

Boerenwagenmuseum, Acter Bonenburg 1,
4116 BD Buren   ☎ *03447 1431*
Apr 30–Oct 1, Tues–Sun 1–5. Groups at other
   times by appt.
© ♿ ♿

The museum occupies two adjacent 17th-
century buildings, the Culemborg and the
Muurhuizen. The collection consists of wagons
and their components, dating from 1850 to
1940 from the regions of Gelderland and South
Holland. They are skilfully decorated with
fanciful carving and with brightly-coloured
paintings of allegorical and Biblical scenes.

The museum has a complete cartwright's
workshop and a blacksmith's forge. A collection
of accurate models, built to the scale of 1:15
illustrates wagon-types from other parts of the
Netherlands.

Delft

Hoefer Army and Weapons Museum

Koninklijk Nederlands Leger en Wapenmuseum
   Generaal Hoefer Armamentarium, Korte Geer
   1, 2611 CA Delft   ☎ *015 150500*
Tues–Sat 10–5; Sun 1–5.
© ♿ 🖤 ♿

The museum of the Royal Netherlands Army
has recently been relocated in the town's
historic arsenal, built in 1662–9. It tells the
story of military forces in the Low Countries
since medieval times and of the campaigns in
which they took part. There are collections of
weapons of all types and sizes, armoured
vehicles, uniforms, military equipment,
decorations and flags, and displays showing the
use of canals for defensive purposes. The latest
methods of museum presentation are used
throughout.

The museum is named after General Hoefer,
who created the first army museum early in the
present century.

Meerten Museum of Ceramics

Museum Lambert van Meerten, Oude Delft 199,
   2611 HD Delft   ☎ *015 121858*
Tues–Sat 10–5; Sun and public holidays 1–5.
June–Aug, also Mon 10–5. Closed Jan 1, Dec
25.
© ♿ 🖤 ♿

The building which is now the museum was constructed in 1891–3 as the home of Lambert Anthony van Meerten, the director of the Delft Yeast and Spirit Factory and a noted collector of architectural fragments of demolished buildings, many of which are built into the interior of his house. In 1907, after the collector's death, the house became a national museum of arts and crafts and subsequently broadened its field to include Dutch tiles, Delft pottery, silver, copper and pewter objects and paintings.

Museum of Mineralogy and Geology

Mineralogisch-Geologisch Museum, Faculteit Mijnbouwkunde en Petroleumwinning, Mijnbouwstraat 120, 2628 RX Delft
☎ 015 786021
Mon–Fri 9–5. Sat, groups by appt only. Closed public holidays.
F ■ ⚲

This large and important collection has been created by the Faculty of Mining and Petroleum Engineering of the Technical High School in Delft. It contains examples of minerals, rocks, ores and fossils from all over the world. Among the exhibits are a fossilised skeleton of a dodo, a triceratops skull, meteorites and geological models of famous volcanoes.

Nusantara Ethnographic Museum

Volkenkundig Museum Nusantara, St Agathaplein 4, 2611 HR Delft ☎ 015 602375
Tues–Sat 10–5; Sun and public holidays 1–5. June–Aug, also Mon 10 5. Closed Jan 1, Dec 25.
C ⌂ ■ ⚲

The museum's basic collection of ethnographical objects was formed during the existence of the Netherlands Indies Institute (1864–1901) and was used for the instruction of officials who were to be posted to the former Netherlands Indies. Since the abolition of the Institute, other items have been added from time to time.

The museum provides a survey of the arts and crafts found in the variety of Indonesian cultures, from prehistory to the present day. The exhibits include textiles, copper and brassware and weapons. One gallery, which contains a gamelan, among other objects, is completely devoted to the culture of Java and is sometimes used as a concert room. The name, 'Nusantara', meaning 'many islands' was given to the museum in 1976.

Prinsenhof Museum

Stedelijk Museum Het Prinsenhof, St Agathaplein 1, 2611 HR Delft ☎ 015 602357
Tues–Sat 10–5; Sun and public holidays 1–5. June–Aug, also Mon 10–5. Closed Jan 1, Dec 25.
C ⌂ ■ ⚲

The Prinsenhof or Princes' Court, was formerly the Convent of St Agatha, established in 1400.

Portrait of Prince William of Orange, 1584. Prinsenhof Museum, Delft.

In the late 16th century, the building was used by Prince William of Orange as his court. He was murdered here in 1584. Visitors can see a number of the rooms including the chapter room, the library, the scriptorium, the spinning room, the dormitory and the infirmary. The one room in the convent which could be heated was the spinning room. The states and the court of Holland assembled here.

The ceiling and wall paintings in the refectory were executed in 1667–8 by Leonard Bramer, the fireplace being added at the same time. The ceiling, with the painting of the Ascension of Christ, has been preserved.

Tétar van Elven Museum

Museum Paul Tétar van Elven, Koornmarkt 67, 2611 EC Delft ☎ 015 124206
May–Oct, Tues–Sat 1–5
C ⌂

Paul Tétar van Elven (1823–96) was a painter and a teacher at Delft Academy. He left his 17th–18th-century house, at 67 Koornmarkt, and its valuable contents, to the town, on condition that it became a museum. It is the only private dwelling in Delft which is open to the public and has fine ceilings, some of them painted, panelling and a 17th-century newel staircase. The eight rooms contain Dutch furniture and paintings, some of them by Tétar himself, Chinese and Japanese export porcelain, together with Dutch Delft ware and tiles.

Dordrecht

Dordrecht Museum

Dordrechts Museum, Museumstraat 40, 3311 XP Dordrecht ☎ 078 134100
Tues–Sat 10–5; Sun and public holidays 1–5. Closed Jan 1, Dec 25.
C ⌂ ■ ♿

Dordrecht is the oldest city in the Netherlands. It was important as a trading centre and in the

16th–18th centuries painters were attracted to the city because the many wealthy merchants who lived there were anxious to commission portraits of themselves and their families. During the second half of the 19th century the Society for the Promotion of a Dordrecht Museum collected paintings and money for a future museum, including works by Ary Scheffer (1795–1858), who was born in Dordrecht. A museum was eventually opened in 1904, in a building which had been successively a convent, a home for the sick, an orphanage and a mental hospital, and it has remained there ever since.

The collections consist of Dutch paintings, drawings, graphic art and sculpture from the 17th century to the present day. Among the artists represented are Aelbert Cuyp, who was born in Dordrecht, and the Dordrecht pupils of Rembrandt, including Nicolaes Maes, Samuel van Hoogstraten and Aert de Gelder.

Drachten

Bleeker House

It Bleekerhûs, Moleneind 14, 9203 ZP Drachten
    ☎ *05120 15647*
Tues–Sat 10–5
Ⓒ 🛈 🍴

The building now containing Drachten's museum was formerly the home and practice of Dr H. W. Bleeker, well-known as a doctor in Drachten earlier in the present century. The museum's collections are concerned partly with the archaeology, history and traditional occupations of Drachten and its surroundings and partly with the work of artists connected in some way with Drachten, especially Pier Pander (1864–1919). Among the other artists represented are Ids Wiersma (1878–1965), Jan Planting (1893–1955), Sjoerd H. de Roos (1877–1971) and Sierd Geertsma (b. 1896).

Dronten

Flevohof

Flevohof, Spijkweg 30, 8250 AA Dronten
    ☎ *03211 1514*
Apr 1–Oct 20, daily 10–6
Ⓒ 💺 ♿ 🍴

Home-grown pineapples are amongst the produce of the Dutch agricultural industry, whose methods are on show at Flevohof, Dronten.

Dronten is one of the new communities created in the new province of Flevoland, which has resulted from the draining of the former Zuiderzee. Flevohof, an educational and recreational park, covers an area of 150 hectares and contains large exhibits explaining the methods and organisation of the agricultural and horticultural industries in the Netherlands and the processing and marketing of their products. There are also collections of horse-drawn vehicles, agricultural implements and tools and bakery equipment.

Egmond aan Zee

Egmond Museum

Museum van Egmond, Zuiderstraat 7,
    1931 GD Egmond aan Zee
June 1–Sept 15, Sun–Fri 2–4. Group visits at other
    times by appt.
Ⓒ 🛈

Egmond is 30 miles north-west of Amsterdam. Its museum is housed in a former Protestant church, dating from the early 19th century. It tells the story of the three Egmond villages, Egmond Binnen, Egmond aan den Hoef and Egmond aan Zee, the origin of which go back to the 10th century. After 1900, the old fishing village, Egmond aan Zee, became a popular seaside village. Until that time, the flat-bottomed fishing boats were kept on the beach. Ship models, old photographs, paintings and an authentic 'fisherman's room' help visitors to visualise the village as it was in its fishing days. The maritime past of Egmond is symbolised by the display in the museum of an 1895 rowed lifeboat.

The medieval period is represented in archaeological finds, excavated from the moat of Egmond Castle, once one of the largest in the Netherlands, which was destroyed in 1573.

Emmen

Noorder Zoo and Biochron

Noorder Dierenpark Zoo Biochron, Hoofdstraat 18,
    7801 BA Emmen   ☎ 05910 18800
Mar–May and Oct, daily 9–5. June–Aug, daily
    9–6. Nov–Feb, daily 9–4.30.
Ⓒ 🛈 💺 ♿ 🍴

The Noorder Dierenpark was established in 1935 as a conventional provincial zoo. More recently it has acquired an international reputation as a living museum, in which animals can be observed in environments which are very close to nature. The zoo is divided into continent areas. Animals which would live alongside one another in their natural habitat have, wherever possible, been allowed to do so in the zoo. Illustrated information boards, demonstrations and small exhibitions near the animals' quarters provide visitors with many opportunities to learn about the habits and characteristics of the many species in the zoo. The Asian section contains ten Indian elephants, acquired from the Burma Teak

The Lute Player, 17th-century, by Jan Steen. Twenthe Museum, Enschede.

Company. Keepers demonstrate them at work and explain the different commands.

Biochron is a large museum which deals with the history of life on earth. It has an aquarium complex which is unrivalled in Europe and a tropical butterfly garden. The Africanium includes not only the Africa House, with its tropical vegetation and African birds and reptiles, but also the Ethnological Museum, which shows how African people have created a way of life in close interaction with nature, and the Natural History Museum, which has changing exhibitions on topical themes.

Enkhuizen

Weigh House Museum

Stedelijk Weegmuseum, Kaasmarkt 8,
1600 AA Enkhuizen   ☎ 02280 15540
Apr–Oct and Christmas holidays, Tues–Sat
10–12, 2–5; Sun 2–5.
Ⓒ 🏯

The weigh house, an outstanding example of the Dutch Renaissance style, was built in 1559. It replaced a much smaller weigh house, dating from 1394. The change was made necessary by the great increase in local trade, the commodities to be weighed being mainly butter and cheese. In 1636 the first floor was placed at the disposal of the Guild of Surgeons, which panelled the walls and embellished it in other ways. The main room was used for the scientific and festive meetings of the guild and for the education and examination of prospective surgeons.

Nowadays the entire building is used as a museum. The collections include old medical instruments and equipment, the inventory of the weigh house and a range of pewter articles. There is also a dentist's surgery dating from 1925, a 1910 hospital room and a late-18th-century lying-in room.

Zuiderzee Museum

Rijksmuseum Zuiderzeemuseum, Wierdijk 18,
1601 LH Enkhuizen   ☎ 02280 10122
Late Mar–late Oct, daily 10–5
Ⓒ 🛈 🖭 ♿ 🏯

During the present century the size of the Zuiderzee has been greatly reduced by a drainage and reclamation policy which has created agricultural polders where there was previously water and fishing villages. The museum, opened in 1983, contains 120 houses and other buildings from the area and documents the life of the former fishing and shipping communities.

Enschede

Twenthe Museum

Rijksmuseum Twenthe, Lasondersingel 129–131,
7514 BP Enschede   ☎ 053 358675
Tues–Fri 10–5; Sat, Sun and public holidays 1–5.
Closed Jan 1.
Ⓒ 🛈 🖭 🏯

The museum was presented to the Dutch State by the Van Heek family, who were well-to-do mill owners and cotton manufacturers. It was officially opened in 1930. The collections are in three departments, pre-modern art, modern art and cultural history and crafts. The core of the pre-modern department consists of a large collection of 15th–19th-century European paintings, with the Middle Ages, religious art, 18th–19th-century landscapes, still-life paintings and portraits all well represented. The modern and contemporary art is almost all Dutch. The cultural history collections include archaeological material and exhibits reflecting the life of the nobility, the clergy and the peasantry. In the crafts section there is an extensive collection of 17th–19th-century Dutch tiles, together with 17th–18th-century Delftware and some large Brussels tapestries, displayed in a gallery specially built to house them.

Franeker

Eise Eisinga Planetarium

Eise Eisinga Planetarium, Eise Eisingastraat 3,
8801 KE Franeker   ☎ 05170 3070
May 1–Sept 15, Mon 10–12.30, 1.30–5; Tues–
Sat 10–12.30, 1.30–5; Sun 1–5. Sept 16–Apr
30, Tues–Sat 10–12.30, 1.30–5.
Ⓕ 🛈

Eise Eisinga (1744–1828) was, like his father, a woolcomber. His real interest, however, was in mathematics and astronomy and, as a young man, he published books on both subjects. On 8 May 1774, Mercury, Venus, Mars and Jupiter all appeared with the moon under the sign of Aries and this remarkable phenomenon induced Eisinga to build a moving planetarium, as a way of giving his contemporaries a better understanding of celestial affairs. He used the ceiling of his living room for the purpose, the movements of the planetary system being

Eise Eisinga Planetarium, Franeker.

achieved by clockwork. In 1825 King Willem I bought the ingenious and beautifully designed planetarium for the State, stipulating that Eisinga and his son Jacobus after him should be allowed to live in the house rent free and receive a stipend for its upkeep. In 1859 the State presented the planetarium to the community of Franeker. It is the oldest functioning planetarium in the world.

In addition to Eisinga's planetarium, the museum contains many other old astronomical instruments, including telescopes, sextants and orreries. The museum also has exhibits relating to modern space research.

Gouda

Catharina Hospital Museum

Museum 'Het Catharina Gasthuis', Oosthaven 10, 2801 PB Gouda   ☎ *01820 88211*
Mon–Sat 10–5; Sun and public holidays 12–5. Closed Jan 1, Dec 25.
Ⓒ 🛈 ☕

The oldest part of the hospital dates from the 14th century. Considerable additions and changes were made in 1665–6, giving the hospital substantially its present appearance. It was converted into a museum in 1939, with 19 of the rooms used for exhibition purposes. Three of them are presented as period rooms, to give an impression of how interiors were furnished in the 17th, 18th and 19th centuries and the surgeons' room has its original furnishings. In the remaining areas there are individual and group portraits, altarpieces, vestments and silver liturgical objects from local churches, and dolls, toys and children's games.

The hospital kitchen has been furnished and equipped in the style of the 18th century and the dispensary looks as it would have done later that century. There is a reconstruction of an 18th-century classroom and visitors can also see the only surviving example in the Netherlands

of a mad-room, in which the insane who became troublesome were locked up until they calmed down.

The museum also has an important collection of 19th- and 20th-century paintings, presented by the painter-collector, Paul Arntzenius (1883–1965).

The Moriaan Museum

Museum 'De Moriaan', Westhaven 29, 2801 PJ Gouda   ☎ *01820 88211*
Mon–Fri 10–5; Sat 10–12.30, 1.30–5; Sun and public holidays 12–5. Closed Jan 1, Dec 25.
Ⓒ 🛈 ☕

The Moriaan, a late medieval building, was given a new façade in 1617. Originally the premises contained a sugar refinery and in the 18th century the proprietors also started selling spices to the captains of barges passing through Gouda. The trade in pepper and cloves and particularly coffee, tea and tobacco became increasingly important, which is probably why the name of the company was changed to Moriaan (Blackamoor), because black people were supposed to smoke all day.

The Moriaan was opened as a museum in 1938. It contains an 18th-century tobacco shop with its cutting room, relics of the once flourishing Gouda clay-pipe industry, and a collection of 20th-century decorative Delftware and 17th–19th-century Gouda earthenware.

Groningen

Groningen Museum

Groninger Museum, Praediniussingel 59, 9711 AG Groningen   ☎ *050 183343*
Tues–Sat 10–5; Sun 1–5. Closed Jan 1, Aug 28, Dec 25.
Ⓒ 🛈 ☕ 🖼

The museum opened in 1874 and was later transferred to a 1904 building. It will move into new purpose-built premises in 1992. It has collections illustrating the history of Groningen, together with paintings, prints and drawings from the 16th century to the present day. The art gallery contains, among other Dutch 17th-century drawings, 17 by Rembrandt, and paintings by Rubens and Fabritius. There is also a collection of European and Oriental ceramics.

Niemeyer Tobacco Museum

Niemeyer Tabaksmuseum, Brugstraat 24–26, 9711 HZ Groningen   ☎ *050 122202*
Tues–Sat 10–5; Sun 1–5. Closed Jan 1, Aug 28, Dec 26.
Ⓒ 🛈 ☕

The museum of the history of tobacco and tobacco smoking established by the Niemeyer Company was opened in 1932. Its collections cover the use of tobacco by the American Indians, the history of smoking fashions in Europe, and present-day anti-smoking campaigns. There are also exhibits showing how use was made of materials such as crystal, ivory, porcelain, silver and meerschaum in a wide range of smoking and snuff requisites, including rasps, snuff-boxes, cuspidors and tobacco pipes.

Northern Museum of Shipping

Noordelijk Scheepvaartmuseum, Brugstraat 24–26, 9711 HZ Groningen   ☎ *050 122202*
Tues–Sat 10–5; Sun 1–5. Closed Jan 1, Aug 28, Dec 26.
ⓒ 👜 💻

The museum tells the story of the ships and their crews which operated from Friesian ports, of the voyages they made and of the trade in which they were engaged. The exhibits are also concerned with coastal shipping and with transport on the inland waterways. The collections include ship models, marine engines, ships' figureheads, navigational instruments, a reconstruction of a room in a sea-captain's house, to illustrate his standard of living and the contents of his seaman's chest.

Haarlem

Frans Hals Museum

Frans Halsmuseum – De Hallen, Groot Heiligland 62, 2001 DJ Haarlem   ☎ *023 319180*
Mon–Sat 11–5; Sun and public holidays 1–5. Closed Jan 1, Dec 25.
ⓒ 👜 💻 ♿ ♠

The museum occupies a former almshouse for old men, built in 1608. It houses a collection of 17th- and 18th-century paintings by artists who worked in Haarlem. Eight group portraits of Civic Guards and Regents by Frans Hals are the most important items in the collection, which also contains portraits, still lifes, genre scenes and landscapes. There is also a notable collection of Haarlem silver, an 18th-century dolls' house and a reconstructed pharmacy, with fine examples of 18th-century Delftware.

The Banquet of the Officers of the St George Militia Company, 1616, by Frans Hals. Frans Hals Museum, Haarlem.

The collection of modern and contemporary art consists of paintings, graphics, sculpture, objets d'art, textiles and ceramics. Besides work by artists from Haarlem and the surrounding area, it contains examples of Dutch Impressionism and Expressionism, Cobra and current trends.

Haastrecht

Bisdom van Vliet Museum

Museum van de Stichting Bisdom van Vliet, Hoogstraat 166, 2851 BE Haastrecht
☎ *01821 1354*
Apr 15–Oct 15, Tues–Thurs, Sat, Sun 10.30–4
ⓒ ♠

The Bisdom family came to live in Haastrecht in the 17th century. In 1755, they added van Vliet to their name having bought an estate at Vliet, between Hekendorp and Oudewater. In 1874–77 their old house in Hoogstraat was pulled down and the present mansion was constructed on the site. In 1923 Paulina Bisdom van Vliet bequeathed the house and its contents to a foundation formed for the purpose. The furnishings, decorations and family possessions provide an exceptional opportunity to see the standard at which the Dutch upper middle-class lived at the end of the 19th century and the beginning of the 20th.

The Hague

Netherlands Costume Museum

Nederlands Kostuummuseum, Stadhouderslaan 41, 2715 AC Den Haag   ☎ *070 514181*
Tues–Fri 10–5; Sat, Sun 12–5. Closed Jan 1.
ⓒ 👜 💻 ♿ ♠

This municipal museum was opened in 1957, in a new building. It displays items from its collections of fashionable costumes and accessories worn in the Netherlands from the 18th century to the present day. There are special sections devoted to lace and to fans. The library contains books relating to fashion and 16th–20th-century prints and photographs.

Sikkens Museum of Signs

Sikkens Schildersmuseum, Televisiestraat 3,
*   2525 KD Den Haag*   ☎ *070 889501*
Mon–Fri 10–4

Ⓕ 💺 🚗

The museum was opened by the Sikkens Paint
Company in 1981. The firm was founded by
Willem Sikkens in 1792. The collections
illustrate the tools, materials and techniques
used by signwriters and coach and house-
painters since 1700. There is a reconstruction of
a 1900 painter's workshop and exhibits of the
scaffolding, ladders and transport used by
painters, together with examples of stencilling,
sign-writing, lettering and etching on glass, and
the imitation of marble and wood-graining. A
display also demonstrates the techniques of
making paint by hand.

Heerlen

Roman Baths

Thermenmuseum, Coriovallumstraat 9,
*   6411 CA Heerlen*   ☎ *045 764581*
Tues–Fri 10–5; Sat, Sun and public holidays 2–5.
*   Closed Jan 1, Carnival, Easter Sun, Queen's*
*   birthday, Whit Sun, Dec 25.*

Ⓒ ⓘ 💺 ♿

Coriovallum, as Heerlen was called in Roman
times, was established at the point where the
Roman highway from Boulogne-sur-Mer to
Cologne crosses the one from Xanten to Trier
and Aachen. It was originally a civilian
settlement and market town, but in the 3rd
century AD it was fortified against raids by
Germanic tribes.

     The large bath-system was a centre of leisure
and recreation for the entire community and
played an important rôle in social life.
Adjoining the baths there was a sportsfield, a
swimming pool, shops and a restaurant. The
museum contains a wide range of objects
discovered during excavations on the site.

Metalworker, by Pieter de Josselin de Jong;
late 19th-century. Helmond Museum.

Den Helder

Dorus Rijkers Museum of Lifesaving

Nationaal Reddingmuseum 'Dorus Rijkers',
*   Bernhardplein 10, 1780 AH Den Helder*
*   ☎ 02230 18320*
Mon–Sat 10–5; Sun and public holidays 1–5.

Ⓒ ⓘ 💺 ♿ 🚗

The coastal waters of the Netherlands present
particular dangers, since storms cause the
sandbanks to shift and ships to run aground.
The museum illustrates the history of lifesaving
methods and organisations in the Netherlands,
especially since 1824, when the North and
South Holland Life-Saving Association
(NZHRM) was founded. There are models of
lifeboats, examples of equipment, details of
impressive rescue achievements and medals and
citations given to men, including Dorus Rijkers,
after whom the museum is named, who played a
notable part in rescues. There are also actual
examples of old lifeboats and the beach-wagons
that were used to launch them.

Naval Museum

Helders Marinemuseum, Hoofdgracht, 1780
*   CA Den Helder*   ☎ *02230 57137*
Tues–Fri 10–5; Sat, Sun 1–4.30. June–Aug, also
*   Mon 1–5. Closed Dec 1–3rd week in Jan.*

Ⓒ ⓘ 💺 🚗

Den Helder has an important naval dockyard.
Since 1966 the museum has been
accommodated in one of the dockyard
buildings, constructed in 1826. Its exhibits
include paintings, prints, ship models,
photographs, uniforms and equipment, and
illustrate the history of the Netherlands Royal
Navy from 1813 onwards. Attention is also paid
to the historical development of Den Helder
and of the dockyard.

Helmond

Helmond Museum

Gemeentemuseum, Kasteelplein 1,
*   5701 PP Helmond*   ☎ *04920 47475*
Mon–Fri 10–5; Sat, Sun and public holidays 2–5.
*   Closed Jan 1, and three days at Carnival.*

Ⓒ ⓘ 💺 🚗

The museum is housed in part of the town's
14th-century castle, some of the rooms of which
are accessible to visitors only by appointment.
Helmond is an industrial town, important for its
textile manufacturing, and the museum's
exhibits are concerned particularly with local
industrial and social history during the 19th and
20th centuries. There is also an important
collection of paintings by Dutch artists, which
are presented under the general title of 'Men
and Work'.

     The museum has a collection of modern
Dutch art, selections from which are presented
in temporary exhibitions held in another
building in the town, the Meyhuis.

Cruquius Museum, Hoofddorp.

's Hertogenbosch

Museum of North Brabant

Noordbrabants Museum, Verwersstraat 41,
*   5200 BA 's Hertogenbosch*   ☎ *073 139664*
Tues–Fri 10–5; Sat 11–5; Sun 1–5. Closed Jan 1,
*   Carnival, Dec 25.*
Ⓒ ▮ ◼ &

The museum, opened in 1987, is in the former
residence of the Governor of North Brabant
dating from 1768, with additional wings built in
1987. Its collections illustrate the history of
North Brabant and of works by artists living in
the province or which have subjects relating to
it. There are particularly important collections
of late medieval sculpture and of flower still-life
paintings.

Slager Museum

Museum Slager, Choorstraat 16, 5211 KZ
*   's Hertogenbosch*   ☎ *073 133216*
Tues–Fri 2–5; Sun 2–5. Groups at other times by
*   appt. Closed Jan 1, Easter Sun, Whit Sun,*
*   Dec 25.*
Ⓕ ▮ ◢

Established in 1976 by the P. M. Slager
Foundation, the museum presents the work of
eight members of three generations of painters
belonging to the gifted Slager family, who lived
and worked in 's Hertogenbosch. They were the
father, P.M. Slager (1841–1912), his sons, Piet
and Frans, his daughters, Jeannette and Corry,
his grandson, Tom and his daughters-in-law,
Suze Slager-Velsen and Marie Slager-Van Gilse.
    The collection consists of portraits, views of
's Hertogenbosch, landscapes, still-lifes, flowers,
drawings and etchings. Among the exhibits are

a painting, executed by P. M. Slager in 1875 on
the occasion of the 60th anniversary of the
Battle of Waterloo, of six veterans gathered
round the bust of their former commander,
Prince Willem, later King Willem II, and
Portrait of my father and teacher, made by Piet
Slager in 1904.

Hilvarenbeek

De Doornboom Museum

Museum De Doornboom, Doelenstraat 53,
*   5081 CK Hilvarenbeek*   ☎ *04255 4093*
May–Sept, Tues–Fri, 10–12, 2–5; Sat, Sun 2–5.
Ⓒ ▮ ◼ ◢

The museum, opened in 1986, illustrates all
aspects of the life of the country doctor in the
Netherlands from 1800 until the present
century. The collections contain medical and
surgical instruments and other equipment used
by the village doctor, together with
photographs, documents and memorabilia. The
museum takes its name from the adjoining
windmill, 'De Doornboom' (the Hawthorn
Tree).

Hoofddorp

Cruquius Museum

Museum 'De Cruquius', Cruquiusdijk 27,
*   Cruquius, Haarlemmermeer. Correspondence*
*   to: Postbus 250, 2130 AG Hoofddorp*
*   ☎ 023 285704*
Apr–Sept, Mon–Sat 10–5; Sun and public holidays
*   12–5. Oct–Nov, Mon–Sat 10–4; Sun and*
*   public holidays 12–4. Groups (up to 20) Mon–*
*   Fri by appt.*
Ⓒ ▮ ◼ & ◢

In 1838, the decision was taken to drain the
Haarlemmermeer, the large lake south-west of
Amsterdam. The task was carried out by three
steam pumping stations, named after three
important Dutch hydraulic engineers,
Leeghwater, Lijnden, and Cruquius, the last-
mentioned being the Latinised name of Jacobus
de Kruik, such names being a fashion at the
time. These three pumping stations worked
non-stop for three years and produced, instead
of a lake, a polder, 8,300 hectares of fertile land.
To maintain the polder, pumping had to
continue for ever, the water being delivered into
a specially dug ring-canal and from there into
the sea. The Lijnden and Leeghwater stations
were eventually equipped with modern
machinery and the steam engines were removed
but Cruquius continued to work until 1933 and
has been preserved as a technical monument.
    It was constructed on a foundation of 1,100
piles and contains eight beam engines, made by
Harvey's of Hayle, in Cornwall, England. They
are housed in a neo-Gothic building, designed
in what is known in the Netherlands as the
'public works style'. The former boiler-room
now contains an exhibition of models, old
machinery, maps and plans, showing how the
Netherlands are drained.

Hoogeveen

'Venendal' Hoogeveen Museum

Hoogeveens Museum Venendal, Hoofdstraat 3,
7902 EA Hoogeveen   ☎ *05280 91359*
Mon–Fri 10–12, 2–4.30; Sat 2–4.30. Closed
public holidays.
C ▯ ↝

In 1653 Jonkheer Johan van Echten, son of the
founder of Hoogeveen, built himself a mansion
called 'Venendal'. It was subsequently
considerably altered and rebuilt and its present
appearance dates from 1888. The museum has
occupied it since 1971. The museum's
collections illustrate the history of Hoogeveen
and the surrounding area. There are 18th–19th-
century period rooms, including a kitchen,
Dutch tiles, 17th–19th-century pottery, 17th–
18th-century Chinese and Japanese porcelain,
local costumes and 19th–early-20th-century
paintings by artists who lived in Hoogeveen,
including the celebrated 19th-century
watercolourist Albert Steenbergen.

Most important among the exhibits are a
collection of peat-digging tools and a model of
the site where that activity began. It started in
1625 and was the origin of Hoogeveen's
existence.

Hoorn

West Frisian Museum

Westfries Museum, Rode Steen 1, Hoorn.
  Correspondence to: Achterom 2–4,
  1621 KV Hoorn   ☎ *02290 15783*
Mon–Fri 11–5; Sat, Sun 2–5. Closed Jan 1,
  Lappendag (2nd or 3rd Mon in Aug), Dec 25.
C

The museum, founded in 1880, occupies the
former headquarters of the Regional
Government, a richly ornamented Renaissance
building dating from 1632. Its collections
illustrate the history of Hoorn and West
Friesland. There are 17th–19th-century period
rooms, painted wall-hangings, 17th-century
paintings of the Civic Guard, 19th-century
handicrafts and craftsmen's tools and a section
devoted to the Dutch East India Company.
Other exhibits are of Stone and Bronze Age
archaeology, weapons, banners, uniforms, coins

**Tile panel with tulips. West Frisian Museum,
Hoorn.**

and medals, ship models, navigational
instruments, furniture, pottery, porcelain,
silver, glass and pewter.

Katwijk aan Zee

Katwijk Museum

Katwijks Museum, Voorstraat 46,
  2225 ER Katwijk aan Zee   ☎ *01718 13047*
May–Sept, Tues–Sat 10–12, 2–5. Oct–Apr,
  Thurs–Sat 10–12, 2–5.
F ▯ ▆ ↝

Katwijk has a long history as a fishing port. The
museum, opened in 1983, is installed in an
early-20th-century shipowner's house and
illustrates the development of the port and the
way of life of its inhabitants during the 19th and
20th centuries with period rooms, ship models,
costumes, paintings and photographs. A fishing
boat, KW 88, is moored in front of the museum
and inside there is an example of the two-
wheeled carts used by the shellfish gatherers.
One room is devoted to paintings, etchings and
book illustrations by the local artist, Tjeerd
Bothema, who died in 1978, and by his wife and
two daughters.

Kerkrade

Mining Museum

Mijnmuseum, Heyendahllaan 80,
  6464 EP Kerkrade   ☎ *045 457138*
Tues–Fri 7–5; Sun 1–5. July–Aug, also Sat 1–5.
  Closed public holidays.
C ▯ ⅋ ↝

The museum was established in 1974, after
coalmining in the Netherlands had come to an
end, in the buildings of the former abbey of
Rolduc. Founded in 1104, this is the largest
complex of monastery buildings in the
Netherlands. Coal was being extracted on its
estates as early as the 12th century.

The museum tells the story of coal
production in Limburg. There are maps and
models of mines, exhibits of mining tools,
lamps, equipment and machinery and sections
devoted to safety in mines and to the social
history of the mining community.

Ketelhaven

Museum of Maritime Archaeology

Museum voor Scheepsarcheologie, Vossemeerdijk
  21, Ketelhaven, 8251 PM Dronten
  ☎ *03210 13287*
May–Sept, daily 10–5. Oct–Apr, daily 11–5.
  Closed Jan 1, Dec 25.
C ▯ ▆ ⅋ ↝

The draining of the Zuiderzee and the resulting
creation of Flevoland, an area of polders for
agriculture and new settlement has produced a
great deal of archaeological material, mostly
from wrecks of ships. A large proportion of what
has been discovered is displayed in the new

museum at Ketelhaven, which is situated on what was formerly the shore of the Zuiderzee, near the mouth of the River Ijssel. So far, more than 350 wrecks have been found and excavated, greatly increasing our knowledge of the history of shipbuilding, especially during the medieval period. When the Hanseatic trade developed in the late Middle Ages, the Zuiderzee became the starting and finishing point for voyages extending over the whole world.

One of the most impressive exhibits in the museum is the wreck of a merchant ship, 30 metres long, which sank in the middle of the 17th century. Whole families sailed aboard the small cargo ships and the museum has a very wide range of household equipment in consequence, as well as children's toys and the remains of clothing and shoes. There are also items from cargoes and equipment and materials used to operate and maintain the ships, including pulley-blocks, ropes, sails, tools, pitch and nails.

De Koog

EcoMare Centre

EcoMare Centrum voor Wadden en Noordzee,
  Ruyslaan 92, 1796 AZ De Koog
  ☎ *02220 17741*
Apr–Oct, daily 9–5. Nov–Mar, Mon–Sat 9–5.
  Closed Jan 1, Dec 25.
Ⓒ 🛆 ⚏ ⟵

The centre, established in 1975, provides an introduction to the natural history of the Wadden Sea and North Sea area and to the history and archaeology of Texel. The surrounding dune area contains interpretation panels explaining the landscape and its plants and wildlife, and forms part of EcoMare, a special type of ecomuseum, which draws attention to the relationship between man and the marine environment.

Lauwersoog

ExpoZee

ExpoZee, Strandweg 1, 9976 VS Lauwersoog
  ☎ *05193 9045*
Apr–Sept, Tues–Fri 10–5; Sat, Sun 2–5. Public
  holidays, including Mon 10–5.
Ⓒ 🛆 ⚏ ⟵

Lauwersoog lies in the middle of the Dutch section of the Wadden Sea, on the boundary between Groningen and Friesland. Pressure to drain the area in order to form polders has been resisted and the aim of the Dutch, Danish and German governments is now to preserve and protect it as a nature reserve, with an emphasis on its remarkable bird life.

ExpoZee has been set up by the Ministry of Transport and Public Works to illustrate the natural history of the Wadden Sea, to explain the damage which has been done to the environment in the past, especially by the discharge of sewage and industrial waste, and to explain what is being planned for the future.

Decorative arts display. Frisian Museum, Leeuwarden.

Leek

Museum of Coaches

Nationaal Rijtuigmuseum, 'Nienoord',
  9351 AC Leek   ☎ *05945 12260*
Apr–Sept, Mon–Sat 9–5; Sun 1–5.
Ⓒ 🛆 ⚏ ⅋ ⟵

'Nienoord', the large country house which has accommodated the museum since 1958, was built in 1885–6, to replace a 16th-century house that was destroyed by fire. It contains the collection of horse-drawn passenger vehicles and their accessories formed by the Netherlands Horse and Carriage Foundation, which administers the museum.

The exhibits include examples of the mail coach, berlin, hansom cab, coupé, brake, phaeton and omnibus. There are also royal carriages, sleighs and paintings, prints and watercolours with carriages as a subject.

Leeuwarden

Frisian Museum

Fries Museum, Turfmarkt 24,
  0911 KT Leeuwarden   ☎ *050 123001*
Tues–Sat 10–5; Sun 1–5.
Ⓒ 🛆 ⚏ ⅋ ⟵

The Frisian Society of History, Antiquity and Linguistics was founded in 1827. In 1877 it organised the Historic Exhibition of Friesland in the King's Palace at Leeuwarden, which was a great success and provided the society with the money to buy a large 18th-century house in the Koningstraat and establish a museum in it. Considerable additions have been made to the building since then and the museum is now one of the largest in the Netherlands outside Amsterdam.

Its collections cover the archaeology, history and art of the province of Friesland and include paintings, furniture, popular art, glass, porcelain, pottery and textiles. There are reconstructions of period rooms, old shops and a silversmith's workshop. The artist, Christoffel Bisschop (d. 1904), who was born at Leeuwarden, left the entire contents of his house at Scheveningen to his native town and four of the rooms have been reconstructed in the museum.

Museum of the Resistance in Friesland

Verzetsmuseum Friesland, Zuiderplein 9–13,
8911 AM Leeuwarden ☎ *058 133335*
Tues–Sat 10–5; Sun and public holidays 1–5.
Closed Jan 1, Apr 30.

Ⓒ ▮ ⌘

The museum aims to give an objective account of the causes and events of the Second World War and to present the story of Friesland during the years of the German occupation, with collections of photographs, models, documents and objects relating to the period. There are also dioramas and video presentations.

Leiden

De Lakenhal Museum

Stedelijk Museum de Lakenhal, Oude Singel
28–32, 2301 CA Leiden
☎ *0/1 120180/254620*
Tues–Sat 10–5; Sun and public holidays 1–5.
Closed Jan 1, Dec 25.

Ⓒ ▮ ⬛ ⓑ ⌘

The museum building dates from 1642. It was originally the Cloth Hall and the headquarters of the Drapers Guild. Its conversion to a museum took place in 1874. The collections cover the archaeology and history of the Leiden area and Dutch 16th–19th-century paintings and sculpture. The paintings include Lucas van Leyden's triptych of the Last Judgement and works by Jan Steen, Jan van Goyen and Rembrandt.

There are also sections devoted to Dutch furniture, glass and silver. Contemporary Dutch art is presented in temporary exhibitions.

'De Valk' Mill Museum

Stedelijk Molenmuseum 'De Valk',
2ᵉ Binnenvestgracht 1, 2312 BZ Leiden
☎ *071 254639*
Tues–Sat 10–5; Sun 1–5. Closed Jan 1, Oct 2, 3,
Dec 25.

Ⓒ ▮ ⬛ ⌘

The 'De Valk' (The Falcon) windmill dates from 1743. It is a tower-mill, built of brick, and is eight storeys high. After the death of the last miller, W. Van Rhijn, in 1964, the mill was extensively restored. The original machinery, with its wooden gearing, is complete and occupies the four upper floors. The Van Rhijn dwelling on the ground floor has been kept intact, the caretaker now lives on the first floor and the remaining space contains a museum of millwrights' tools, mill implements and mill parts.

University Museum

Academisch Historisch Museum, Academiegebouw,
Rapenburg 73, 2311 GJ Leiden
☎ *071 277242*
Wed–Fri 1–5. Closed public holidays.

Ⓕ ⌦ ⌘

Print of the anatomy theatre at Leiden University in 1610. University Museum, Leiden.

The University was inaugurated in 1575, in the middle of the Dutch revolt against Spain. In its early years it was housed in the former convent of St Barbara. In 1577 this particular convent was prepared for the accommodation of Prince William of Orange and then became known as the Prinsenhof. The University was temporarily transferred to another church – many churches and convents were available at this time, because the practice of the Catholic religion had been banned – and in 1581 the former Dominican Church of the White Nuns was made over to the University. Since then it has been much rebuilt and embellished and is nowadays used for lectures and ceremonial occasions.

It contains objects, documents and pictures relating to the history of the University and to student life. In 1865 Victor De Stuers decorated the walls of a spiral staircase, known as *Gradus ad Parnassum*, with a series of drawings depicting the career of a student at the University. A room called the Sweating Chamber, where students waited for the results of their examinations is also decorated with suitable drawings by De Stuers and by the celebrated political cartoonist, Louis Raemakers. The Senate Hall has a collection of the portraits of 18th-century professors.

Lelystad

New Land Information Centre

Informatiecentrum Nieuw Land, Postbus 600,
8200 AP Lelystad ☎ *03200 60799*
Apr–Oct, Tues–Sun 10–5. Nov–Mar, Tues–Fri
10–5. Open Easter Mon and Whit Mon.
Closed Jan 1, Dec 25.

Ⓒ ▮ ⬛ ⌘

Lelystad is one of the new towns established since the Second World War on the large area of land reclaimed as a result of the draining of the Zuiderzee and the creation of agricultural polders. The exhibits in the centre tell the story of the process by which water has been turned into land.

Castle Museum, Grosskirchheim (Austria).   *Stiglmaierplatz* by Wilhelm Heine. City Museum, Munich (Germany).

The sitting-room at The Béguine's House, Bruges (Belgium).

Residence Museum, Munich (Germany).

Maarsbergen

'De Weistaar' Museum of Cheesemaking

Kaas en Botermuseum De Weistaar,
Rottegatsteeg 6, 3953 MN Maarsbergen
☎ *03498 1943*
Mon–Sat 8–6
Ⓒ 🛈 💻 🚗

'De Weistaar' is a museum of cheesemaking,
situated in a cheesemaking farm. The Dutch
take cheese very seriously and eat 12 kilos per
head each year, compared with the British
achievement of only 6 kilos. The museum's
displays show how cheese is made today and
how the various processes were carried out in
the past. There is a collection of old
cheesemaking utensils and equipment and
visitors can watch regular demonstrations of
cheese being made.

Maassluis

Museum of Tugs and Towing

Nationaal Sleepvaartmuseum, Hoogstraat 1–3,
3140 Maassluis ☎ *01899 12474*
Wed 2–5; Sat 11–5; Sun 1–5. Closed Easter Sun,
Whit Sun, Dec 25.
Ⓒ 🛈 🚗

The Dutch are acknowledged to be world
experts in the specialised art of ocean towage.
The museum, established in 1979, in the former
17th-century town hall, presents a survey of the
history and development of the Dutch towage
industry, attention being paid both to deep-sea
towage and to towage on the Rhine and other
inland waterways. The exhibits consist of
photographs, ship models and equipment.
There is a particularly detailed model of the
Zwarte Zee, built in 1933, which was for a long
time the world's strongest tug.

Moddergat

The Fisherman's House

Museum 't Fiskershúske, Fiskerspaad 4–8A,
9142 VN Moddergat ☎ *05199 454*
Mar–Oct, Mon–Sat 10–5
Ⓒ 🐚 🚗

The museum consists of three former fishermen's
houses, the oldest dating from 1794, together
with a modern building which is used for
changing exhibitions. The houses, opposite the
sea-dike, are within a protected area. The
exhibits illustrate the history and techniques of
the local fishing industry and the life of the
fishermen and their families. There are
collections of ship models, popular art and
fishing equipment, as well as the complete
interiors of a fisherman's house as it was *c.*1900.

Naarden

Comenius Museum

Comenius Museum, Turfpoortstraat 27,
1411 ED Naarden ☎ *02159 43045*
Tues–Sun 2–5. Closed last two weeks of Dec and
first week of Jan.
Ⓕ 🛈 🚗

The museum building, known as the Spanish
House, dates from 1615. It was originally a
weigh-house, constructed from the ruins of the
town hall, destroyed by Spanish troops in 1572
during the Dutch Revolt. Since 1924, it has
been used as a memorial to the Czech
educational reformer and philosopher, Jan
Amos Comenius, or J. A. Komenský, who came
to Amsterdam as a refugee and lived there for 14
years until his death in 1670. He was buried in
Naarden. The museum contains material
illustrating the life and career of Comenius
including part of his library. Attention is also
given to the Kralice printing house, important
in the history of book production in
Czechoslovakia.

Oosterbeek

Airborne Museum

Airborne Museum 'Hartenstein', Utrechtseweg
232, 6862 AZ Oosterbeek ☎ *085 337710*
Mon–Sat 11–5; Sun 12–5. Closed Jan 1, Dec 25.
Ⓒ 🛈 💻 🚗

'Hartenstein', which has housed the museum
since 1978, was the headquarters of Major-
General R. E. Urquhart in 1944, who
commanded the British and Polish Divisions
during the unsuccessful Battle of Arnhem. The
exhibits in the museum illustrate the purpose
and course of the battle, by means of dioramas,
photographs, uniforms and a large collection of
weapons and equipment belonging to both
sides.

**Title-page of *Didactica Opera Omnia*, 1657, by
J. A. Comenius. Comenius Museum, Naarden.**

Otterlo

Netherlands Tile Museum

Nederlands Tegelmuseum, Eikenzoom 12,
6731 BH Otterlo   ☎ 08382 1519
Tues–Sat 10–12, 2–5; Sun and public holidays
2–4. Closed Jan 1, Dec 25.

Ⓒ ▯ ♿ ☕

In 1508 an Italian tile-maker moved to Antwerp and began to make decorated tiles there. The industry gradually moved north and by the 18th century there were 80 factories in what is now called the Netherlands. The tiles they made showed mainly Dutch landscapes and Biblical and pastoral scenes. Mauve was favoured, especially in Rotterdam, instead of the original blue. After 1800, the demand for tiles fell away and by 1900 only four tile factories remained.

The museum at Otterlo tells the story of decorated tiles in Europe from 1300 until the present day and explains the techniques of tile-making. The collection includes more than 8,000 old tiles.

Rijnsburg

Spinoza's House

Het Spinozahuis, Spinozalaan 29,
2231 SG Rijnsburg   ☎ 01718 29209
Mon–Fri 10–12, 2–4; Sun 2–4.

Ⓒ ▯ ☕

Soon after he was excommunicated by the Sephardic community of Amsterdam in 1654, the philosopher and scientist, Benedict de Spinoza (1632–66), moved to Ouderkerk and then to Rijnsburg, where he lived for a while before going to The Hague, where he died.

The museum contains portraits of Spinoza, models used by him in his scientific experiments and a bench used for grinding and polishing lenses, as a reminder that Spinoza earned his living in this way and was famous for the quality of his lenses.

The principal exhibit in the museum, however, is the reconstruction of his library, which contains all the books mentioned in the inventory drawn up after his death and arranged, in the 17th-century manner, according to their size.

During the Second World War, a Jewish lady and her daughter hid from the Germans for two years in the attic of Spinoza's small house.

Roermond

Roermond Museum

Gemeentemuseum Roermond, Andersonweg 8,
6041 JE Roermond   ☎ 04750 33496
Tues–Fri 11–5; Sat, Sun 2–5.

Ⓒ ▯ ▤ ☕

The museum is located in the former home and studios of the architect, Pierre J. H. de Cuypers (1827–1921) and in the adjacent house, built for the merchant F. Stolzenberg. Cuypers designed both houses himself in 1854 in the neo-Gothic style. The interior decorations and the extensions date from 1921, when the artist, Hendrik Luyten (1859–1945) donated his paintings and the museum was founded.

Cuypers and Stolzenberg founded an art workshop in Roermond which had a great influence on the development of the decorative arts in the Netherlands. By 1850 it employed 50 people. As an architect, Cuypers was responsible for the Rijksmuseum in Amsterdam (1885) and Amsterdam Central Station (1889), which caused him to be accused of fostering 'Roman Catholic' or 'monastery' architecture.

The museum contains memorabilia of Cuypers' works by Hendrik Luyten and collections illustrating the history, art and cultural activities of Roermond and the surrounding area.

Roosendaal

The Golden Rose Museum

Museum 'De Ghulden Roos', Molenstraat 2,
4701 JS Roosendaal   ☎ 01650 36916
Tues–Sun 2–5. Closed Shrove Tues, Easter, Lent
and Christmas.

Ⓒ ▯

The former presbytery of the parish church of St John the Baptist was built in 1762 on behalf of the abbey of Tongerlo, which as a result of subsequent political changes, is now in Belgium. The museum which now occupies the presbytery was founded in 1936 by the Historical and Antiquarian Society of the Golden Rose and transferred here in 1974. Its collections illustrate the history, handicrafts and industries of Roosendaal and its surrounding region and include weapons, pewter, porcelain, silver, stoneware from the Rhineland, toys and topographical drawings. There are also portraits and other material relating to the abbey of Tongerlo.

Portrait of the Empress Maria Theresa (1717–80). Roermond Museum.

Rotterdam

Rotterdam Museum: The Double Palmtree

Historisch Museum der Stad Rotterdam: De
Dubbelde Palmboom, Voorhaven 12,
Delfshaven, 3024 RM Rotterdam
    ☎ 010 4761533
Tues–Sat 10–5; Sun and public holidays 11–5.
Closed Jan 1, Apr 30.
© ▮

Rotterdam Museum occupies two buildings, the
Dubbelde Palmboom (Double Palmtree) and the
Schielandshuis.

The Double Palmtree was built in 1826 as a
granary, and subsequently became a gin
distillery and a furniture factory. The displays
are built around the theme of 'Life and Work in
the area of the Maas estuary from early times to
the present day'. There is archaeological
material from the prehistoric, Roman and
medieval periods, exhibits illustrating house-
styles and building techniques, handicrafts
before mechanisation and industrialisation,
agriculture, land-drainage, mills and peat-
digging. Other sections of the museum are
devoted to the maritime history of the port of
Rotterdam and to boatbuilding and the trades
associated with it.

Rotterdam Museum: Schielandshuis

Historisch Museum der Stad Rotterdam:
Schielandshuis, Korte Hoogstraat 31,
3011 GK Rotterdam   ☎ 010 4334188
Tues–Sat 10–5; Sun 1–5. Closed Jan 1, Apr 30.
© ▮ ▰

The Schielandshuis is the only 17th-century
building in the historic centre of Rotterdam to
have survived the German bombardment of
May 1940. After complete restoration, it was
opened in 1986 as the city's principal museum
building. It presents a picture of the history of
Rotterdam, of the daily activities of its
inhabitants and of its artistic life in the 17th and
18th centuries. The collections include 18th-,
19th- and 20th-century costumes and textiles,
paintings, porcelain, silver, scientific
instruments, sculpture, tiles, majolica and
ornaments from the façades of houses. There are
also period rooms and displays of household
equipment. The Schielandshuis houses the
Atlas Van Stolk, an important collection of
prints and drawings on the history of the
Netherlands.

National School Museum

Nationaal Schoolmuseum, Neiuwe Markt 1A,
3001 AM Rotterdam   ☎ 010 4045425
Tues–Sat 10–5; Sun 11–5.
© ▮ ▰ ⅗ ↩

The museum is in a former library, dating from
1923. It is one of the few buildings in central
Rotterdam that was not destroyed during the air
raids of the Second World War. Its collections
illustrate the history of schools and education in

The 17th-century Schielandshuis, which now
houses the Rotterdam Museum.

the Netherlands since medieval times. There
are reconstructions of classrooms from 1200 to
1950 and a wide range of equipment used at
different periods, including material used for the
education of the blind.

Prince Hendrik Maritime Museum

Maritiem Museum 'Prins Hendrik', Leuvehaven 1,
3000 AZ Rotterdam.   ☎ 010 4132680
Tues–Sat 10–5; Sun 11–5. Closed Jan 1, Apr 30.
© ▮ ▰ ⅗

Opened in 1986, in a building created for the
old harbour area of Rotterdam, the museum
presents the history of ships and voyages by
means of material drawn from Dutch sources.
The exhibits are arranged by themes, illustrating
the six purposes for which ships have been used,
the transport of people and goods; the wielding
of power; the gathering of food and raw
materials; geographical, ethnological and
oceanographical research; recreation; and
support – dredging, towing, piloting and
lifesaving.

The 19th-century warship, *Buffel*, is moored
outside the museum and is used as a museum-
annexe. It has been restored and reconstructed
to its original condition and illustrates the
methods of naval operations at the time, the life
of the officers and crew and the techniques
which were available. The *Buffel* is one of 20
ships which form part of the museum's floating
collection.

Scheveningen

Schevening Museum

Schevenings Museum, Neptunusstraat 92,
2586 GT Scheveningen   ☎ 070 500830
Tues–Sat 10–4.30. Open Mon during public
holidays.
© ▮ ▰ ⅗ ↩

Scheveningen is an old fishing port which
became a seaside resort during the 19th century.

The museum's exhibits illustrate both aspects of its history, with models of different types of fishing vessel, displays showing fishing techniques, fishing and navigational equipment and paintings, watercolours, photographs and picture postcards of Scheveningen and its fishing industry.

There is a reconstruction of the crew's quarters on a 1900 fishing boat and the museum also has sections relating to the harbour trades, fishermen's handicrafts and the history of sea-bathing since 1818.

Schiphol

Aviodrome

*Aviodrome, Nationaal Lucht- en Ruimtevaart
    Museum, Luchthaven Schiphol–C,
    1118 AA Schiphol*   ☎ *020 604521*
Ⓒ ⓘ 💻 🚗

The museum is housed in a geodesic dome at Schiphol Airport. Its collections consist of 40 civil and military aircraft used in the Netherlands since the beginning of the present century – 30 are on display at any given time – together with aero-engines and flying equipment. There are also exhibits devoted to space-flight and to satellites.

Sint-Annaland

De Meesthof Regional Museum

*'De Meesthof' Streekmuseum voor Tholen & St
    Philipsland, Bierensstraat 6, 4697 GE Sint-
    Annaland*   ☎ *01665 2649*
*Whit Sun–Oct 1, Tues–Sat 3–5. Groups at other
    times by appt.*
Ⓒ ⓘ 🚗

The museum is concerned with the history, occupations and traditions of the delta areas of St Philipsland and Tholen. It contains reconstructions of a shop, a schoolroom and a doctor's consulting room and collections of costumes and accessories, furniture, paintings, popular prints, pottery, coins and medals, shells

and maps. There are also sections devoted to household equipment and agricultural tools and equipment.

Among the specially featured exhibits are objects dredged up from the South Beveland area, which was submerged before 1531, a collection relating to the growing of madder and to the dye made from it, and pottery by the Dutch ceramicist, Charles Lanooy.

Sneek

Frisian Museum of Shipping and Local History

*Fries Scheepvaart Museum en Oudheidkamer,
    Kleinzand 12, 8600 AD Sneek*
    ☎ *05150 14057*
Mon–Sat 10–12, 1.30–5
Ⓒ ⓘ 🚗

The museum was established in 1938 and moved in 1947 into a patrician mansion, built in 1844. The section devoted to shipping is concerned with navigation on the sea from Frisian ports and with the use of inland waterways in the Province. There are 17th–19th-century paintings of maritime subjects, ship models, mementoes of the Frisian Admiralty, navigational instruments and shipbuilding tools, as well as exhibits relating to the local fishing industry and to pleasure-boating.

Period rooms illustrate the lifestyle of Sneek at different social levels in the past and there are also displays of Sneek silver, tiles and popular art. The archaeological section contains material found during excavations in Sneek and the surrounding district.

Soesterberg

Museum of Military Aviation

*Militaire Luchtvaart Museum, Postbus 160,
    3769 ZK Soesterberg*   ☎ *03463 35815*
*Apr–Dec, Tues–Fri 10-4.30, Sun 12-4.30.
    Closed Easter Sun, Whit Sun, Ascension,
    Dec 25.*
Ⓕ ⓘ 💻 ♿ 🚗

The collection of 30 historic aircraft, displayed in two halls, illustrates the history of military aviation in both the Netherlands and the Netherlands East Indies. The exhibition devoted to aircraft engines represents all generations of piston and jet propulsion from 1909 to the present day. The collections also include flying equipment and paintings, photographs and documents relating to military flying and to people linked with its history in the Netherlands.

Spakenburg

Museum of Costumes and Fishing

*Klederdracht- en Visserijmuseum, Kerkstraat 20,
    3751 AR Spakenburg*   ☎ *03499 81315*
May–Aug, Mon–Sat 10–5
Ⓒ 🚗

Aviodrome, Schipol.

Spakenburg is an old inland fishing village, the inhabitants of which lost their traditional source of income when the Zuiderzee and the Ijsselmeer were drained and agricultural polders created on the former fishing ground. The museum illustrates the local way of life in Spakenburg's fishing days, with ship models, fishing equipment, paintings and reconstructions of house-interiors. There is also a collection of large dolls, dressed in local costumes used on different occasions from 1780 onwards.

Staphorst

Farmhouse Museum

Gemeentelijke Museumboerderij, Binnenweg 26,
*   7950 AA Staphorst*   ☎ 05225 2844
Apr–Oct, Mon–Sat 10–5
Ⓒ ♿ ☕

The farmhouse and its outbuildings were built in the 1830s. The complex has been carefully restored and furnished to show how 19th-century farming families lived. In addition to the domestic exhibits, there is a handloom, dating from 1610 and a collection of clogmakers' tools. The vegetable garden attached to the house is planted out as it would have been in the 19th century.

Tilburg

Netherlands Textile Museum

Nederlands Textielmuseum, Goirkestraat 96,
*   5046 GN Tilburg*   ☎ 013 367475
Tues–Fri 10–5; Sat, Sun 12–5.
Ⓒ ♿ ☕ ♿ ☕

The museum is located in the restored buildings of a late-19th-century textile factory. Its collections illustrate the history of the Dutch textile industry from 1850 onwards and the development of Dutch textile design from 1880 to 1940. Visitors can see yarn being dyed, carpets and tapestries being woven and tufted, and cords, ribbons, braids and tassels being produced. Nearly every machine displayed is in working order and is used both for production and for educational purposes. Special departments are concerned with machine knitting and with the manufacture of linen.

Utrecht

Catharine Convent State Museum

Rijksmuseum Het Catharijneconvent,
*   Nieuwegracht 63, 3512 LG Utrecht*
*   ☎ 030 313835*
Tues–Fri 10–5; Sat, Sun and public holidays 11–5.
*   Closed Jan 1.*
Ⓒ ♿ ☕

The museum, winner of the 1980 European Museum of the Year Award, occupies the partly restored 16th-century monastery of the Knights of St John and an adjoining house dating from the 18th century.

Carving of St Ursula, *c.* 1530. Catherine Convent State Museum, Utrecht.

The exhibits illustrate the history of Christianity in the Netherlands from the 2nd century to the 1980s. The museum has one of the finest collections of medieval art in the Netherlands, especially of sculpture, textiles and manuscripts as well as gold- and silversmiths' work. There is also an interesting collection of 16th- and 17th-century paintings, including works of Rembrandt and Frans Hals.

Netherlands Railway Museum

Nederlands Spoorwegmuseum, Johan van
*   Oldenbarneveltlaan 6, 3501 XZ Utrecht*
*   ☎ 030 318514*
Tues–Sat 10–5; Sun and public holidays 1–5.
*   Closed Jan 1, Easter Sun, Whit Sun, Dec 25.*
Ⓒ ♿ ☕ ♿ ☕

The museum is at the former Maliebaan railway station, dating from 1874. Extensive reconstruction has recently taken place in order to make the building more suitable for museum purposes. There is a large collection of rolling stock and locomotives, including the oldest and the last steam locomotives in the Netherlands (1839 and 1958). Among the other exhibits are models, uniforms, documents, paintings and operating equipment of all kinds. There is a model railway system within the museum. Visitors can arrive at the museum by a special service from Utrecht Central Station.

Valkenburg aan de Geul

Valkenburg Mine

Steenkolenmijn Valkenburg, Daalhemerweg 31,
*   6300 AA Valkenburg aan de Geul*
*   ☎ 04406 12491*
Easter–Nov, daily 9–5. Dec–Easter, Tues–Sat,
*   guided tour at 2 pm.*
Ⓒ 🔒 💺 ⓑ ⚲

Coal has been extracted in the South Limburg
area of the Netherlands since Roman times, but
serious commercial exploitation did not begin
until the 18th century. The industry reached its
peak in 1958, when it employed 63,000 people.
A decline began in 1965 and the last pit closed
in 1975.

In 1917 a replica of a mine was built in a
marlpit. After the ending of mining in South
Limburg, this museum-mine, the Valkenburg,
was considerably developed. Modern machinery
was transferrd to it from recently closed pits and
the expanded museum tells the full story of
coalmining in the area in underground galleries
which reproduce the conditions under which
coal has been extracted at different periods.
Former miners are used as guides. The museum
has a section devoted to the fossils which are
found in the local coal and chalk deposits.

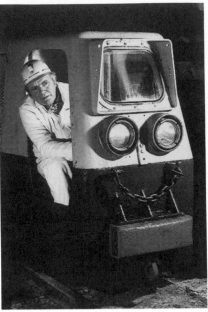

Underground diesel locomotive. Valkenburg
Mine, Valkenburg aan de Geul.

Vlaardingen

Fishery Museum

Visserijmuseum, Instituut voor de Nederlandse
*   Zeevisserij, Westhavenkade 53/54,*
*   3131 AG Vlaardingen   ☎ 010 4348722*
Mon–Sat 10–5; Sun and public holidays 2–5.
*   Closed Jan 1, Dec 25.*
Ⓒ 🔒 💺 ⚲

The museum occupies a house built in 1740,
which was the residence of the then mayor,
Abraham van den Linden, who had interests in
the fishing and whaling industries. The displays
illustrate the history and techniques of
commercial fishing in the Netherlands and the
life of the communities which have earned their
living from it. There is an aquarium,
information about fishing grounds and exhibits
showing the development of Dutch fishing craft.
The museum also contains reconstructions of
two rooms which show the living style of well-
to-do Vlaardingen residents in the 18th century,
and the living room of a fisherman's cottage and
the interior of shipowner's office in the early
years of the present century.

Vogelenzang

De Oranjekom Visitor Centre

Bezoekerscentrum 'De Oranjekom', le Lelyweg 4,
*   2114 BH Vogelenzang   ☎ 023 246781*
Tues–Thurs 9.20–4; Sat, Sun 9–5.
Ⓕ ⓑ ⚲

The centre has been established by the
Amsterdam Water Company. The first

waterworks to supply Amsterdam was built in
this dune area in 1853. There are exhibitions on
the history of the waterworks and on the plants
and wildlife of the dunes. The centre, which has
200,000 visitors a year, is the starting point of a
nature route through the dunes and for guided
excursions.

Wageningen

Museum of Agricultural Technology

Museum voor Historische Landbouwtechniek,
*   Droevendaalsesteeg 50, 6708 PB Wageningen*
*   ☎ 08370 15774*
Mon–Fri 9–12, 1–4. Closed public holidays.
Ⓒ 🔒 💺 ⓑ ⚲

The most important agricultural college in the
Netherlands is at Wageningen, making the
town a very suitable place for the museum. The
collections consist of agricultural tools,
machinery and equipment from the period
1800–1956. The museum also contains a
celebrated collection of exact models of 19th-
century agricultural machines and an archive of
more than 30,000 items, including catalogues.

Warffum

Het Hoogeland Open-Air Museum

Openluchtmuseum Het Hoogeland, Schoolstraat 2,
*   9989 AG Warffum   ☎ 05950 2233*
Apr–Oct, Tues–Sat 10–5; Sun and public holidays
*   1–5. Nov–Mar, groups and parties by appt.*
Ⓒ 🔒 💺 ⚲

The museum was established in 1959 by a
foundation which aims at preserving and

exhibiting examples of local rural architecture and the style of furniture and domestic equipment of ordinary people in the past. The eight buildings so far installed on the site include a home for poor and widowed women (1768, with furniture c.1850); a sailor's house (c. 1850); an inn and grocery shop (c. 1850, with furnishings of 1900); a single-room day-labourer's cottage of c. 1800; two semi-detached houses of 1909, furnished in Art Nouveau style; a barn for stray cattle (1850), a house of 1857, with period rooms of 1840 and 1875, and a kitchen of 1890, as well as a house of 1834, fitted up as a Jewish butchers' shop.

Wieringerwerf

Wieringermeer and Zuiderzee Exhibition

Wieringermeer en Zuiderzeewerken: Permanente Tentoonstelling, Loggersplein 1, 1771 CE Wieringerwerf ☎ 02272 2344
F ⬛ ♠

The drainage of the Zuiderzee and Wieringermeer and the conversion into agricultural land of what had previously been sheets of water rank among the greatest civic engineering achievements of the present century. The exhibition shows how the work was carried out and how the various technical problems were solved.

Zierikzee

Zierikzee Museum

Stadhuismuseum, Meelstraat 6–8, Gemeente Zierikzee, 4300 KA Zierikzee ☎ 01110 13151
May–Sept, Mon–Fri 10–12, 1–5. Closed public holidays.
C ♠

Zieke Man, 1972, by Co Westerik. Henriette Polak Museum, Zutphen.

The town of Zierikzee has owned a collection of paintings, prints, silver, glass, ship models and curiosities since the late Middle Ages. Since the 15th century it has been displayed to the public form time to time. Silver was assayed in Zierikzee from the 14th to the 18th century and the town was celebrated for the skill of its silversmiths. Sections of the museum are devoted to the siege of Zierikzee by the Spaniards, the local madder dye industry, 17th- and 18th-century toys, 18th-century wooden models of some of the town's bridges and cranes, and the flood disaster of 1953. Two 18th-century period rooms contain furniture, copperware, clothing and domestic equipment.

Zutphen

Henriette Polak Museum

Museum Henriette Polak, Zaadmarkt 88, 7201 DE Zutphen ☎ 05750 16878
Tues–Fri 11–5; Sat, Sun and public holidays 1.30–5. Apr 1 and Dec 31, 11–4. Closed Jan 1, Easter Sun, Apr 30, Whit Sun, Dec 25.
C ♠ ♠

The museum is housed in a large mansion called De Wildeman (The Wild Man), a name it has borne since the 17th century, when it was an inn. The museum is named after Mrs Henriette Polak (1893–1974) who presented the mansion and her collection of 20th-century Dutch figurative art to the town of Zutphen, her birthplace. The artists represented were all born between 1900 and 1920 and maintained contact with the Academy of Art in Amsterdam. The friendship between them is illustrated by the portraits they made of one another. According to Mrs Polak they were generally underrated, 'due to certain contemporary tendencies'. The collection has acquired national importance as a result of the growing interest in figurative art in recent years. The house also contains a concealed Catholic chapel built in 1628.

Zutphen Museum

Stedelijk Museum, Rozengracht 3,
  7201 JL Zutphen   ☎ *05750 16878*
Tues–Fri 11–5; Sat, Sun and public holidays
  1.30–5. Apr 1 and Dec 31, 11–4. Closed
  Jan 1, Easter Sun, Apr 30, Whit Sun, Dec 25.
C ✐ ▣ & ⚟

The museum is in a disused Dominican
monastery, founded in the 13th century. The
main room is the former refectory, which has
pointed windows and wooden barrel vaulting
and was built *c*.1500. It contains an early
15th-century altar chest, on which the
Crucifixion is painted. The museum's
collections present the history of Zutphen and
the surrounding region. There is a strong
medieval section, including murals of *c*.1300,
which were discovered in a house in Zutphen,
and a 14th-century town seal. Maps and views
of the town show how its appearance has
changed over the years and there are a number
of portraits of inhabitants of Zutphen.

  In the 17th and 18th centuries
silversmithing was an important craft in
Zutphen. The museum has a collection of silver
potpourri vases, which were a local speciality.
The Clock Room has some examples of work by
the Ruempols, a celebrated clockmaking family,

who used to live in the region. There are also
collections of costumes, 18th–20th-century
furniture and old toys. The Dutch artist and
illustrator, Jo Spier who was born in Zutphen in
1900, presented his entire collection to the
museum in 1975. Part of it is permanently on
view.

Zwolle

West Overijssel Natural History Museum

Natuurmuseum West Overijssel, Voorstraat 32,
  8011 ML Zwolle   ☎ *038 227180*
Tues–Sat 10–5; Sun 2–5. Closed public holidays.
C *(ex children)*

The exhibits in the museum, which was opened
in 1984, present the geology, botany and
wildlife of the region, using fossils to show how
the plants and living creatures to be found here
have changed over the ages. A particularly
prized possession is the complete fossil skeleton
of a woolly mammoth, the only example to have
been discovered in the Netherlands.

**Museum of Agricultural Technology,
Wageningen.**

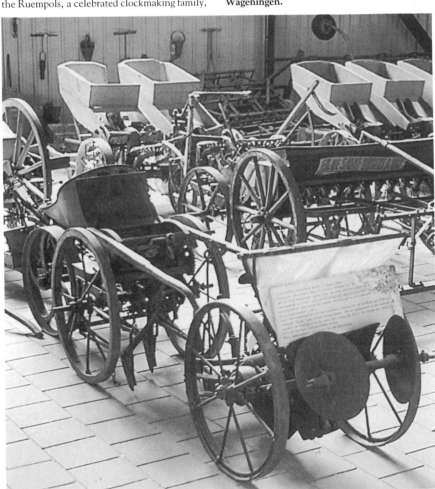

NORWAY

Ådalsbruk

Klevfos Industrial Museum

Klevfos Industrimuseum, N-2345 Ådalsbruk,
  Hedmark   ☎ 065 90505
May 15-Sept 15, daily 10-4. Other times by appt.
Ⓒ ✎ ☛ ↩

This is one of Norway's most historic industrial
sites, with an early pulp and paper mill, which
has been preserved intact as an industrial
monument, complete with its production halls,
dam, canals and workers' houses.

Åsgårdstrand

Munch's House

Munchhuset, Munchsgate, N-3155 Åsgårdstrand,
  Vestfold   ☎ 033 82330
May and Sept, Sat, Sun 1-7. June-Aug, Tues-
Sun 1-7.
Ⓒ ↩

In 1889, the artist, Edvard Munch (1863-
1944), spent the first of many working summers
in Åsgårdstrand. Eight years later, he bought a
late-17th-century fisherman's cottage here. He
called it 'Lykkehuset', the happy house, and
found inspiration for many of his paintings in
the area. After his death, the local authority
bought the cottage, together with some
adjoining land, which became a park. The
house and studio are now a museum, with the
interior preserved as they were in Munch's
lifetime.

Bergen

Bergen Aquarium

Akvariet i Bergen, Nordnesparken 2, N-5005
  Bergen, Hordaland   ☎ 05 327760
May-Sept, daily 9-8. Oct-Apr, daily 10-6.
  Closed Good Fri, Dec 24, 25.
Ⓒ ▮ ☛ & ↩

Nordnes Point, on which the aquarium and the
adjoining Institute of Marine Research are
situated, was at one time an important arsenal
and defence post. It was also the place where
witches were burnt. It is one of the very few
aquaria in the world with access to unlimited
supplies of clean seawater, which is pumped
from a depth of 140 metres, at which
temperature and salinity remain unchanged all
the year round.
    The 51 tanks contain an extensive
collection of marine fauna, especially from
Norwegian waters. They are scientifically
arranged to show their evolution. The breeding
groups of grey and harbour seals are a feature of
the exhibition and there is a large outdoor pond
for penguins and European sea-otters.

Bergen Art Gallery

Bergen Billedgalleri, Rasmus Meyers Allé 3,
  N-5016 Bergen, Hordaland   ☎ 05 311130
Mid May-mid Sept, Mon-Sat 11-6; Sun and
  public holidays 12-3. Mid Sept-mid May,
  Tues-Sun 12-3.
Ⓒ ▮ &

Originally opened in 1925, the gallery received
substantial additional collections in 1978. It has
international collections, but its particular
strength is in works by Norwegian artists,
including J. C. Dahl, Christian Krohg and
Edvard Munch, who are all well represented.

Bryggens Museum

Bryggens Museum, Bryggen, N-5003 Bergen,
  Hordaland   ☎ 05 816710
May-Aug, Mon, Wed, Fri 10-4; Tues, Thurs
  10-8; Sat, Sun 11-3. Sept-Apr, Mon-Fri
  11-3; Sat 12-3; Sun 12-4. Closed Easter
  Sun, May 1, 17, Whit Sun, Dec 25.
Ⓒ (ex children) ▮ ☛ &

The museum, opened in 1976, was built to
house archaeological material found in Bergen
and the central part of West Norway. It was
constructed around the remains of the
settlement around Bryggen (The Wharf), found
during the extensive excavations of 1955-69
and from further work carried out since then.
The exhibitions concentrate on life in Bergen in
the 12th and 13th centuries. By 1300 Bergen
was the largest town in Norway, a cosmopolitan
trading centre, with a wide range of crafts and a
rich cultural life. It was also the national capital
and the ecclesiastical centre for most of West
Norway. Both from the results of the
excavations and from written records, the
museum is able to present a picture of the life,
housing conditions, thoughts and beliefs of the
townspeople in Bergen during the Middle Ages.
Among the particularly interesting exhibits is
the largest collection of runic inscriptions in
Scandinavia and a section of a 13th-century
merchant ship.

Humboldt penguin. Bergen Aquarium.

Hanseatic Museum and 'Schøtstuene'

*Det Hanseatiske Museum og Schøtstuene,
Finnegårdsgate 1a, N–5003 Bergen,
Hordaland*　　☎ 05 314189
*May and Sept, daily 11–2. June–Aug, daily 10–4.
Oct–Apr, Hanseatic Museum: Mon, Wed,
Fri, Sun 11–2. Schøtstuene: Tues, Thurs, Sat,
Sun 11–2. Closed Easter holiday, May 1, 17,
Christmas holiday.*
C ▪

Bergen was one of the medieval group of
Hanseatic trading towns, others being Lübeck
and Hamburg. The museum, which occupies
one of the oldest and best preserved wooden
buildings in Bergen, gives a comprehensive
picture of the life of the merchant community
during the Hanseatic period, from the Middle
Ages until 1750. The Schøtstuene is the old
Assembly Rooms building. The collections in it
illustrate social life among Bergen's Hanseatic
merchants.

**Reconstructed wooden buildings which form
part of the open-air Museum of Old Bergen.**

Maritime Museum

*Bergens Sjøfartsmuseum, Nygårdshøyden, Bergen.
Correspondence to: Boks 2736, N–5026
Bergen-Møhlenpris, Hordaland* ☎ 05 327980
*Sun–Fri 11–2. Closed Jan 1, Good Fri, Easter
Sun, May 1, 17, Whit Sun, Dec 23–25, 31.*
C *(ex children)* ▪ ↩

The ability to make a living from the sea has
always been of great importance for the
Norwegians, possibly more than for any other
nation. The museum aims to provide a survey of
the development of Norwegian ships from
ancient times up to the present day. Extensive
use is made of models and the oldest find, the
Halsnøy boat, from c. 330 BC, is exhibited. The
Norwegian merchant fleet expanded from a
tonnage of 300,000 in 1850 to 1.5 million in
1870. The second half of the 19th century, the
golden age of sailing ships, is one of the best
represented in the museum. There are also
collections of paintings and photographs,
navigational instruments, shipbuilding tools,
equipment of all kinds, ships' figureheads and
sailors' personal possessions.

Museum of Old Bergen

*Gamle Bergen Museum, Elsesro, N–5035 Bergen-
Sandviken, Hordaland*　　☎ 05 256307
*Early May–mid June and late Aug–mid Sept, daily
12–6. Mid June–late Aug, daily 11–7. Guided
tours on the hour, every hour until 6. Closed
May 17. The museum houses are closed during
the winter but the museum area is open
throughout the year.*
C ▪ 🖳 ↩

This is an open-air museum of wooden buildings
representative of Bergen architecture in the
18th and 19th centuries. They have been re-
erected on the estate created by a master
shipbuilder and his son during the period 1785–
1822. The buildings forming the museum
include dwellings, shops and workshops. All of
them are fully furnished and equipped in the
style of their particular period. One or two are
inhabited. The 32 buildings include the houses
and workshops of a watchmaker, sea-captain,
baker, ropemaker, seamstress, glazier and
shoemaker.

Rasmus Meyer Collection

*Rasmus Meyers Samlinger, Rasmus Meyers Allé 7,
N–5016 Bergen, Hordaland. Correspondence
to Bergen Art Gallery*　　☎ 05 311130
*June–Aug, Mon–Sat 11–4; Sun 12–3. Sept–May,
Mon, Wed–Sun 12–3.*
C ♧

The museum has important collections of
Norwegian and Scandinavian paintings,
drawings, prints and furniture. All the main
18th-, 19th- and early-20th-century Norwegian
artists are represented, including Edvard
Munch. Nordic art of the 1880s is a special
feature of the museum. The paintings are
presented in room settings.

Theatre Museum

*Bergens Teatermuseum, Villavei 5, N–5007
Bergen, Hordaland*　　☎ 05 212963
*Sun 12–3. Also open during Bergen Festival (May/
June), daily 12–3. Groups at other times by
appt. Closed Easter, Whitsun, Christmas.*
C ▪ ↩

The museum has existed since 1919. It is
administered by the Institute of Drama Research
at the University of Bergen and is the oldest
theatre museum in Scandinavia, and one of the
oldest in the world. The exhibits illustrate the
history of the theatre in the city since the 18th
century and include costumes, masks, props,
models, posters and photographs. There is a
collection of Ibseniana, including a model of the
theatre in which Henrik Ibsen worked in the
1850s. The museum also has a model of a
theatre stage in 1886, with original work by the
Danish theatre painter, Carl Lund.

Bodø

Nordland Museum

Nordlandsmuseet, Prinsensgate 116, N–8000
    Bodø, Nordland   ☎ *081 21640*
Museum: Mon–Fri 9–3; Sat 10–3; Sun 12–3.
    Kjerringøy: Mid May–Sept 1.
ⓒ 🛈 💻 ☞ 🚌

Established in 1904, this is the regional museum
for Nordland. Its exhibits are concerned with
the history and culture of the province and
contain costumes, domestic equipment,
furniture, handicrafts and tools. Its collection of
Nordland boats is the best in Norway and there
are sections devoted to the local fishing industry
and to Lapp culture, with a Lapp house and
tools and equipment used by the Lapps.
    Kjerringøy Trading Centre, 25 miles north
of Bodø, forms part of Nordland Museum. It is
one of Norway's most important collections of
buildings preserved from the 19th century. The
centre was established at the end of the 18th
century, after the Bergen and Trondheim
monopoly over trade in Nordland was lifted.
There was a particularly important trade with
the Lofoten islands.

Brevik

Brevik Museum

Brevik Bymuseum, Postboks 103, N–3951 Brevik,
    Telemark   ☎ *03 570061*
Mid June–mid Aug, Mon–Sat 11–2. Other times
    by appt.
ⓒ 🛈 🚌

Brevik has some of the best preserved wooden
town architecture in Norway. The museum,
opened in 1975, is in the 1760 town hall. The
exhibits illustrate the history of the town. They
include Brevik's post office, which celebrated its

Reconstructed store from the last century.
Brevik Museum.

300th anniversary in 1989, a photographer's
studio dating from 1910, a dry goods store from
c. 1900, which is fully stocked with goods and
advertising posters, and the town's old chemist's
shop. A special section deals with events in the
district during the Second World War.

Dalen

Grimdalen Memorial Museum

Anne Grimdalens Minne, N–3880 Dalen,
    Telemark   ☎ *036 77797*
June 15–Aug 31, daily 10–5. Other times by appt.
ⓒ 🛈 🚌

The gallery, on the Grimdalen family mountain
farm, contains works by the sculptor, Anne
Grimdalen (1899–1961). There is an open-air
display of bronzes, and a farm-loft with elaborate
carvings. The farmstead itself has eleven old
buildings and is arranged as an open-air
museum.

Drammen

Drammen Museum

Drammens Museum, Fylkesmuseum for Buskerud,
    Konnerudgate 7, N–3045 Drammen, Buskerud
                    ☎ *03 838948*
June 15–Aug 31, Tues 11–7; Wed–Sat 11–4; Sun
    11 5. Remainder of year, Tues–Sun 11–3.
ⓒ 🛈 💻 🚌

This is the district museum for Buskerud. Its
exhibits illustrate the cultural history of the
region from the Middle Ages to the present day,
with an emphasis on domestic life and
handicrafts. There is an open-air section of rural
buildings, but the main part of the museum is in
a manor house of c. 1770, with period interiors
and collections of religious art, paintings and
sculpture by regional artists, weapons, flags,
uniforms and agricultural implements. There are
also exhibits relating to the maritime history of
the area.

Egersund

Dalane Folk Museum

Dalane Folkemuseum, Slettebö, Boks 338,
    N–4371 Egersund, Rogaland   ☎ *04 491479*
June 1–15 and Aug 15–Sept, Sun 2–6. June 16 –
    Aug 14, Mon–Sat 11–5; Sun 2–6. Oct–May,
    by appt only.
ⓒ ✐ 🚌

This is the regional museum for Dalane and
South Rogaland and was opened in 1910. Its
exhibits include period rooms and craftsmen's
workshops and there is a section devoted to the
traditional occupations of the area, expecially
fishing and farming. The museum occupies a
farm, with mid-19th-century buildings, formerly
used to provide an income for the district
magistrate.

Faïence Museum

Egersund Fayancemuseum, Elganeveien 1, Eie,
*   N–4371 Egersund, Rogaland* ☎ *04 491479*
Sun 2–5. Mid June–mid Aug, also Mon–Sat 11–5.
*   Other times by appt.*
C i ⬛ ⌂

The celebrated Egersund Faïence Factory was
established in 1867. The museum, opened in
1986 as a branch of Dalane Folk Museum, tells
the story of the factory and has an exhibition of
production equipment and an historical
collection of Egersund pottery and glazed
earthenware.

Eidsvoll Verk

Constitutional Memorial Museum

Eidsvollsminnet, Carsten Ankers vei, N–2074
*   Eidsvoll Verk, Akershus* ☎ *06 951304*
May–mid June and mid Aug–Sept, daily 10–3. Mid
*   June–mid Aug, daily 10–5. Oct–Apr, daily*
*   12–2. Closed Jan 1, Easter weekend, Dec 24,*
*   25, 31.*
C ⬥ ⬛ ⌂

This is one of the most important historic
monuments in Norway. It has been a museum
since 1858. In 1814, the Norwegian
Constitution was worked out and signed here; a
Danish prince, Christian Frederik, was elected
king; and Norway was declared independent of
Denmark, with which it had been united for 430
years. At that time the manor belonged,
together with its ironworks, to Carsten Anker, a
nobleman who was a member of one of the most
prominent families in Norway and a friend of
the Danish King. Prince Christian Frederik
often stayed in the house, which had 30 rooms
for a family of five. All the servants lived
upstairs and the kitchen was in the basement.
    Visitors can see the rooms used by the Anker
family, with their furnishings and portraits, the
rooms for the Constitutional Committee, and
the Financial Committee, the meeting room for
the National Assembly, planned as a ballroom,
the King's Room, and the library.

Elverum

Glomma Valley Museum

Glomdalsmuseet, N–2400 Elverum, Hedmark
*   ☎ 064 11800*
June 15–Aug 14, daily 10–6. Aug 15–June 14,
*   Mon–Fri 10–3; Sat, Sun 12–4. Closed Easter*
*   holidays, May 17 and Christmas holidays.*
C i ⬛ ⬥ ⌂

This open-air museum, the largest in Norway,
was founded in 1911. It is the museum for the
eleven rural districts along the Glomma Valley.
It has 88 buildings, brought from all parts of the
province of Hedmark, and contains appropriate
furnishings and equipment. The buildings have
been sited in woodland bordering the River
Glomma and its rapids at Prestfossen. They
include farmsteads of different types, mills,
saunas, forest workers' cabins, and a tannery. A

Glomma Valley Museum, Elverum.

purpose-built exhibition hall was opened in
1974. It contains three display sections, the
Farming Year, Handicrafts, and Transport and
Communication, as well as a large library and
archive. The Museum also has important
collections of folk art, traditional costumes and
music.

Norwegian Forestry Museum

Norsk Skogbruksmuseum, Boks 117, N–2400
*   Elverum, Hedmark*
*   ☎ 064 10299*
June–Sept, daily 10–6. Oct–May, daily 10–4.
*   Closed Jan 1, Dec 24–26, 31.*
C i ⬛ ⬥ ⌂

The museum's large collections illustrate the
history and techniques of forestry, hunting and
fishing in Norway, together with the natural
history of the country. There are specimens of
most Norwegian mammals and birds, an
aquarium for freshwater fish and an arboretum,
primarily of northern coniferous species. Special
sections are devoted to forestry tools, timber-
floating, social conditions in forestry, forest
products, sawmilling, hunting weapons – there
is a large collection of sheath knives – trapping,
big game, rodents, hunting in the Arctic, and
freshwater fishing.
    There is a large outdoor section, with cabins
used in forestry, hunting and fishing,
boathouses, trapping and hunting devices, and
exhibits relating to charcoal-burning, iron-
smelting and tar-production.

Fagernes

Valdres Folk Museum

Valdres Folkemuseum, Tyinvegen, N–2900
*   Fagernes, Oppland*
*   ☎ 063 60377*
June–Aug, daily 10.30–4. Sept–May, indoor
*   exhibitions only, Mon–Fri 8–3.*
C (ex children) i ⬛ ⌂

This open-air museum was founded in 1901,
only slightly later than the Norwegian Folk
Museum in Oslo and the Sandvig Collections at
Lillehammer. The first building was bought and
opened to the public in 1906. When the
original site became too small, the museum
moved to its present site, taking its buildings
with it. In 1950, the area was considerably
extended, making it possible to give a

comprehensive picture of the development of farming in the region.

There are now 62 farm buildings, the earliest being dated c. 1200 and the most recent 1903. All contain appropriate furnishings and equipment. They represent valley, mountain, forest and cotters' farms. Traditional folk costumes from different parts of Norway are on display in the exhibition buildings. There are also performances of folk music and folk dancing and regular demonstrations of traditional handicrafts.

Aulestad, Karoline and Bjørnstjerne Bjørnson's Home, Follebu.

Follebu

Aulestad: Karoline and Bjørnstjerne Bjørnson's Home

Aulestad, Karoline og Bjørnstjerne Bjørnsons Hjem, N–2620 Follebu, Oppland
☎ *062 20326*
May 18–31 and Sept 1–15, daily 11–2.30. June and Aug, daily 10–3.30. July, daily 10–5.30.
Ⓒ ⬛ ⬛ ⬛

Few Norwegians have played as important a part in their country's literature and history as Bjørnstjerne Bjørnson (1832–1910). He wrote the National Anthem and other much-loved songs, he breathed new life into Norwegian literature, he took an active part in politics and the peace movement and, with Henrik Ibsen, he created the modern naturalistic theatre in Norway. He was awarded the Nobel Prize for Literature in 1903.

Bjørnson bought the farm of Aulestad in Gausdal in 1874. It remained his home until his death in 1910 and after the death of his widow at the age of 99 in 1936, it became the property of the Norwegian people and a State Museum. Everything in the house, apart from two rooms, is as it was when Karoline Bjørnson lived there. The two exceptions are new exhibition rooms: one for objects given by members of the Bjørnson family in order to give the visitor a better idea of the personalities of Bjørnstjerne Bjørnson and his wife; the other for mementoes of his funeral.

Grimstad

Ibsen's House and Grimstad Museum

Ibsenhuset og Grimstad Bymuseum, Henrik Ibsensgate 14, N–4890 Grimstad, Aust-Agder
☎ *041 44653*
May 15–Sept 15, daily 10–3. Rest of the year, by appt only.
Ⓒ ⬛ ⬛

This is the 18th-century house where Henrik Ibsen (1828–1906) lived and worked as an apprentice in a pharmacy from 1843 until 1850. It has been a museum since 1916 and now possesses the world's largest collection of objects relating to Ibsen. In the part of the Museum which has no connections with him there are exhibits illustrating the social and maritime history of Grimstad, with collections of costumes, domestic equipment, furniture, handicrafts and paintings.

Hamar

Hedmark Museum and Cathedral Ruins

Hedmarksmuseet og Domkirkeodden, Strandveien 100, N–2301 Hamar, Hedmark
☎ *065 31166*
Mid May–mid Sept, daily 10–6.
Ⓒ ⬛ ⬛ ⬛

Hedmark Museum has several sections. The Medieval Museum comprises the ruins of the cathedral and the Bishop's Fortress and the foundations of a monastery, a cathedral school and a number of farm buildings belonging to the church, which still remain covered by the turf of the adjacent Storhamar park. The construction of the cathedral was begun in 1152, when the see was founded, and the Bishop's Manor was fortified in stone in the 14th century. Both the cathedral and the fortress were destroyed in 1567, during the Seven Years' War. The Storhamar Barn was built in the early 18th century directly on top of the ruins of the fortress and the present museum, displaying objects found during excavations of the medieval site, was formed within the barn in 1969–74.

There is a reconstruction of a monastery herb garden, with 150 cultivated and wild plants used for dyes, medicine and flavourings for food and drink. The open-air Folk Museum contains 18th- and 19th-century farm buildings brought to the museum site, together with objects relating to farming, alcohol production, transport and the marketing of goods. The Emigrant Museum illustrates the history of Norwegians who emigrated to America and other countries in the 19th and 20th centuries. It has large archives of 'American letters' and two emigrant houses, brought from Minnesota and North Dakota.

Open-air folk museum site at the Hedmark Museum, Hamar.

Kirsten Flagstad Collection

Kirsten Flagstads Minnesamling, Kirkegaten 11,
    N–2300 Hamar, Hedmark   ☎ 065 27660
June 10–Aug 20, daily 11–5. Other times by appt.
Ⓒ ⏸ ⇜

The museum presents the life and artistic career
of the celebrated opera singer, Kirsten Flagstad,
in 'Strandstuen', the oldest house in Hamar,
where she was born. There are collections of
costumes worn by her, photographs,
programmes and personal possessions. Visitors
can listen in a special studio to recordings made
by Kirsten Flagstad.

Museum of Norwegian State Railways

NSB Jernbanemuseet, Strandveien 132, N–2300
    Hamar, Hedmark   ☎ 065 21560 extn 218
May 21–Sept 30, daily 10–4
Ⓒ ⏸ 🚊 ⇜

This is the national railway museum. The
collections are displayed partly indoors and
partly on open-air tracks. They include
Norway's oldest station building, from Kløften,
and a number of locomotives, including some
made in England by Stephenson's company. In
addition, there are No. 16 and No. 17, from the
1860s and *Dovregubben*, Norway's biggest steam
locomotive. The rolling-stock includes coaches
used by members of the Royal family. There are
also displays of uniforms and operating
equipment and photographs and documents
illustrating engineering achievements on a
railway system which, because of the
mountainous terrain, was exceptionally difficult
and expensive to construct.

Holmestrand

Holmestrand Museum

Holmestrand Museum, Nils Kjaers gate 4, N–3080
    Holmestrand. Correspondence to:
    Solåsveien 27, N–3080 Holmestrand, Vestfold
    ☎ 033 53922/51380
June 15–Aug 15, Mon–Sat 11–3. Remainder of
    year, Sun 12–4.
Ⓒ ⬗

The museum building, Holst House, dates from
1756. The exhibits illustrate the history of the
Holmestrand and Botne area from 1650 to 1920,
featuring especially the way of life of the affluent
timber merchants and shipowners between 1700
and 1900 and the living conditions of the local
middle and seafaring classes. Holmestrand was a
popular summer resort *c.* 1900, much frequented
by artists. The museum has a section containing
paintings by artists connected with the town,
together with a number of their personal
possessions.

Hop

Troldhaugen

N–5043 Hop, Hordaland   ☎ 05 911791
May–Sept, daily 10.30–1.30, 2.30–5.30
Ⓒ ⏸

In 1885, the composer, Edvard Grieg (1843–
1907) and his wife, Nina, moved into their new
summer residence on the shore of
Nordåsvannet, outside Bergen. They called the
property Troldhaugen – Troll Hill. Nina Grieg
survived her husband by 28 years. In 1919 she
was forced to sell the house to the composer's
second cousin, Joachim Grieg, and the
furnishings were auctioned. Soon afterwards, he
offered it to the local council on condition that
it should be used 'for a purpose that would be in
the spirit of Edvard Grieg'. A committee began
the arduous task of hunting down and re-
acquiring the furnishings and by 1928
Troldhaugen could be opened as a museum.

The dining-room and the lounge are much
as they were during the last years of the
composer's life. The kitchen quarters now
contain a collection of Grieg memorabilia,
including original manuscripts and letters. One
wall is covered by Erik Werenskiold's portraits of
Grieg.

Hornindal

Anders Svor Museum

Anders Svor Museum, N–6790 Hornindal, Møre
    og Romsdal   ☎ 057 79407
June–Aug, daily 11–5
Ⓒ ⇜

Anders Svor (1864–1929) was born on the Svor
farm in Hornindal. He showed a precocious
talent for woodcarving and when he was 17 he
went to Christiania (Oslo), where he worked as
a woodcarver in a piano factory. Four years later
he became a student of sculpture at the
Copenhagen Academy of Art and, after working
for a while in Paris, established his studio in
Christiania. He lived alone and is buried in the
churchyard at Hornindal.

The museum was opened in 1953, as a joint
venture between the local community and the
Norwegian Government. Collected here are
450 of Svor's works, the major part of his
production.

**Ship's figurehead. Museum of the Navy,
Horten.**

Horten

Museum of the Navy

*Marinemuseet, Karl Johansvern, N–3191 Horten,
Vestfold*   ☎ *033 42081*
*June–Sept, Mon–Fri 10–3; Sat, Sun 12–4. Oct–
May, Mon–Fri 10–3; Sun 12–4. Closed Good
Fri-Easter Mon, May 1, 17, Whit Sun.*
🄵 ⓘ ﬩ ⚓

The museum was founded in 1853. It was
transferred to its present site ten years later,
where it occupied part of the largest brick
building in Norway, completed in 1863 as a
naval depot, on the main Navy base, which was
moved to Bergen in 1961. Most of the other
buildings on the base are 18th and 19th century.
The museum shows the history and
development of the Norwegian Navy since
Viking times. There are collections of ship
models, of which 104 are on display,
figureheads, uniforms, documents, paintings,
photographs and a wide range of equipment, as
well as a library of approximately 30,000 items.
The world's first torpedo boat, *Rap*, built in
Britain in 1872, is displayed outside the
museum, together with a large collection of
naval guns.

Høvikodden

Henie-Onstad Art Centre

*Henie-Onstad Kunstsenter, N–1311 Høvikodden,
Akershus*   ☎ *02 543050*
Tues–Fri 9–9; Sat–Mon 11–5. Closed Dec 23, 24.
🄲 ⓘ 🖻 ﬩ ⚓

In 1961 the Norwegian skating celebrity, Sonja
Henie, and her husband, Niels Onstad,
established the Foundations which bear their
names. Their donations included a large part of
their art collection and funds for the
construction and maintenance of an art centre.
A splendid site overlooking the Oslo Fjord was
made available and the centre opened in 1968.

The large collection consists of 20th-century
paintings, sculpture and graphics. The 'pioneers'
include Bonnard, Matisse, Gris, Villon,
Picasso, Léger and Miró. The French abstract
school of the 1920s is well represented and so
are the Expressionists, such as Appel and
Alechinsky. Works by a range of Norwegian
artists are also to be found at the centre.

Jaren

Hadeland Folk Museum

Hadeland Folkemuseum, N–2770 Jaren, Oppland
☎ *063 34012*
June–Aug, daily 12–5. Sept–May, Mon–Fri 9–3.
🄲 ⓘ 🖻 ⚓

This mainly open-air museum was founded in
1913 for the Hadeland region and serves the
communities of Jevnaker, Lunner and Gran. It
contains more than 20 old buildings from the
region, dating mostly from the 18th and 19th

Sogn Folk Museum, Kaupanger.

centuries. They are grouped around a Viking
burial mound, believed to be that of Halfdan the
Black. Most of them have appropriate furniture
and domestic equipment. There is also a large
display of farm tools and implements.

The museum is situated on the hill of
Tingelstad, near Tingelstad old church, which
was built in the 12th century and continued to
function as the parish church until 1866, when
it was superannuated as being too small. It is a
stone church, which is exceptional in Norway,
where the great majority of old churches were
constructed of wood. It claims to be the only
medieval church in Norway which has its 16th-
and 17th-century interior and furnishings
intact. Another building on the site shows
examples from 200 years of glass production at
Jevnaker.

Kaupanger

Heiberg Collection: Sogn Folk Museum

*De Heibergske Samlinger: Sogn Folkemuseum,
N–5880 Kaupanger, Sogn og Fjordane*
☎ *056 78206*
May–Sept, daily 9–6
🄲 ⓘ 🖻 ﬩ ⚓

The museum dates from 1909, but was reopened
in 1980 on another site. It is the district
museum for Sogn and for the communities along
the Sogn fjords. It has both permanent and
temporary exhibitions, with sections devoted to
agriculture, crafts, fishing, textile production
and leisure-time activities. Houses, barns, outbuildings, a mill and a school have been moved
from their original sites, restored and
appropriately furnished and equipped. The
collections of old tools and implements are
extensive and there are regular demonstrations
of farm work, performed in the old style, and of
handicrafts.

Kongsberg

Norwegian Mining Museum

*Norsk Bergverksmuseum, Hyttegate 3, N–3501
    Kongsberg, Buskerud*   ☎ *03 731275*
*May 18–Aug 31, daily 10–4. The mine train runs
    at fixed hours daily and by prior arrangement.*
© 🛈 🖼 ⚲

The museum, illustrating the history of silver-
mining in the area, is in two parts: a museum
mine with an underground railway 2,300 metres
below the surface, at Saggrenda, 7 km from the
town centre; and large mining collections,
dating back to the 17th century, in the centre of
the town. Production came to an end in 1957.

Lillehammer

Lillehammer Art Gallery

*Lillehammer Bys Malerisamling, Kirkegate 69,
    N–2600 Lillehammer, Oppland*
    ☎ *062 51944*
Tues–Fri 11–4; Sat 10–2; Sun 12–4.
© *(ex children)* ⚲

Established in 1927, the museum, the only art
gallery in the region, collects and displays
Norwegian paintings from 1820 to the present
day. Among the artists represented are J. C.
Dahl, Edvard Munch and J. Weidemann. A
special section is devoted to the works of
painters living in Lillehammer. There are
temporary exhibitions of both contemporary
and earlier paintings.

Maihaugen – The Sandvig Collections

*De Sandvigske Samlinger – Maihaugen,
    Maihaugveien 1, N–2600 Lillehammer,
    Oppland*   ☎ *062 50135*
*Open-Air Museum: June– Aug, daily 10–6. May
    and Sept, daily 10–4. Crafts gallery: open all
    year, Oct–Apr 11–2. Closed May 1, 17, Dec
    24, 31.*
© 🛈 🖼 ⚲

This is a museum for the Gudbrandsdal Valley, a
region of mountain and valley villages covering
6,000 square miles. The museum, of the
Skansen open-air type, was created from 1887
onwards by a Berlin-trained dentist, Anders
Sandvig (1862–1950), who was the son of a
poor fisherman and farmer from Romsdal. After
a serious illness, Sandvig settled in Lillehammer
for his health, at a time when the struggle to
establish a national identity was causing a new
interest in Norwegian rural culture. Sandvig was
also strongly influenced by Darwinism and
believed that buildings evolved in the same way
as living creatures.

The museum covers about 35 hectares,
which is large by Norwegian standards. The
open-air section contains more than 100
buildings from various parts of Gudbrandsdal
and there are plans for erecting a further 30. In
the main building, the Old Workshops, there is
a collection showing the history of handicraft

The open-air farm museum of Maihaugen (The
Sandvig Collections), Lillehammer.

techniques. This is made up of material from all
over Norway. The museum is divided into five
sections – the History of the Dwelling House,
the Old Farm, the Mountain Farm, the Old
Workshops and Urban Culture. The last section
is being developed at the moment.

Lysøen

Lysøen Museum

*Museet Lysøen, Lysøen, N–5215 Lysekloster,
    Hordaland*   ☎ *05 309077*
*May 15–Sept 30, Mon–Sat 12–4; Sun 11–5.
    Other times by appt. Parties by appt May–Oct.*
© 🛈 🖼 ⚲

In 1872 the celebrated violinist, Ole Bull
(1810–80) bought the island of Lysøen and built
a house there, designed by himself and the
architect, C.F. von der Lippe. With domes and
spires, it has an exotic appearance in the
environment of Lysøen. The museum's exhibits
illustrate Bull's life and career and contain many
of his personal possessions.

Modum

Cobalt Works

*Modums Blaafarvevaerk, Modum, N–3340 Åmot,
    Buskerud*   ☎ *03 784900*
Late May–Sept, daily 10–8
🅵 🛈 🖼 ⚲

The works was founded in 1772 by Christian VII
of Denmark and Norway to extract and process
cobalt from the Modum mine for the porcelain
and glass manufacturers of the world. Meissen,
Sèvres, Limoges, Wedgwood, Japan and China
were among the most important customers. The
works was at one time the largest industrial unit
in Norway. It closed in 1898 and is now a
museum. Visitors can see the buildings of the
mine estate, including the workers' village,
exhibition galleries showing how the cobalt was
mined and processed, and glass and porcelain
made with cobalt blue. An exhibition of works
by celebrated Norwegian painters is held each
summer.

Molde

Romsdal Museum

Romsdalsmuseet, Museumsvegen, N–6400 Molde, Møre og Romsdal ☎ *072 52534*
June 1–15 and Aug 16–30, Mon–Sat 10–2; Sun 12–3. June 16–Aug 15, Mon–Sat 10–6; Sun 12–6.

C

The museum, of the open-air type, served eight communities in the area. Its buildings and their contents illustrate the lives of the people who have earned a living from small farms along the fjords and from coastal fishing. There are regular demonstrations of handicrafts and domestic skills. The buildings on the museum site range in date from the Middle Ages onwards. They include a medieval chapel and all contain appropriate furnishings and equipment.

Mosjøen

Vefsn Museum

Vefsn Museum, Austerbygdveien 3, N–8650 Mosjøen, Nordland S ☎ *087 72000*
June 1–Sept 1, Mon–Fri 9–4; Sun 11–6. Parts of the museum are open at other times of the year by appt.

C *(ex children)*

The regional museum of the Vefsn, Grane and Hattfjelldal districts consists of an open-air farm section near Dolstad church and Sjøgata, a group of preserved waterfront buildings in the town centre, the most extensive area of preserved wooden buildings in Northern Norway. The display gallery contains collections of furniture, domestic equipment, handicrafts and costumes from the region.

Nesbyen

Hallingdal Folk Museum

Hallingdal Folkemuseum, Postboks 87, N–3540 Nesbyen, Buskerud ☎ *067 71485*
June 1–15 and Aug 20–31, daily 10–2. June 16–Aug 19, daily 10–4. These times may change.

C

Hallingdal is one of the oldest open-air museums in Norway. It was founded in 1899 by Gudbrand Tandberg, Director of Agriculture. The first buildings were transferred to the site without any attempt to create an appropriate environment for them. More recently, an attempt has been made to give an impression of the natural setting in which the buildings originally stood. The earliest exhibit dates from the early 14th century, but most of the others are 17th–early 20th century. They include houses of different types, a rural school, a mill, storehouse and a silver fox farm.

The exhibition building, constructed in 1914, was a gift from the founder of the museum. It houses most of the museum's collection of objects – textiles, household utensils, furniture, tools and handicrafts. There is also a large collection of weapons, photographic equipment and other articles used by members of the Norwegian Resistance Movement during the Second World War.

Oslo

Bogstad Manor

Bogstad Stiftelse, Bogstad Gård, N–0758 Oslo ☎ *02 504859*
Mid May–mid Sept, Sun 12–5. Guided tours every hour, last tour at 5. The park is open every day, mid May to mid Aug 10–9, mid Aug to mid Sept, 10–7. Guided tours at other times by appt.

C

Bogstad is administered by the Norwegian Folk Museum. It was the centre of one of the largest farms, forests and industrial enterprises in Southern Norway. It shows how a wealthy Norwegian family lived between the mid 17th century and the mid 20th. The Manor House dates from the second half of the 18th century and has interiors designed on a palace scale, with important collections of furniture, porcelain and paintings.

City Museum

Oslo Bymuseum, Frognerveien 67, N–0266 Oslo ☎ *02 430645*
June–Aug, Tues–Fri 10–6; Sat, Sun 11–5. Sept 1–Dec 15 and Jan 15–May 31, Tues–Fri 10–4; Sat, Sun 11–4. Closed Dec 15–Jan 15, Easter and public holidays.

C

The museum is in Frogner Manor (1790), the elegant country home of Bernt Anker (1745–1806), the richest man in Norway of his time. The exhibits illustrate the history of Christiania and, as it later became, Oslo, from medieval times to the present day. There is an extensive collection of models of buildings in the city, including the original model of the Royal Palace, as well as paintings and prints of Christiania and Oslo by artists associated with the city.

Reconstructed rural building. Hallingdal Folk Museum, Nesbyen.

Edvard Munch Museum

Munch-Museet, Tøyengata 53, Tøyen, N–0608
    Oslo   ☎ 02 673774
May–Sept, Mon–Sat 10–8; Sun 12–8. Oct–May,
    Tues, Thurs 10–8; Wed, Fri, Sat 10–4; Sun
    12–8.

C ♿ 💼 ♿

Edvard Munch (1863–1944) bequeathed all the
works in his possession to the city of Oslo. The
bequest comprised 1,200 paintings, 4,500
drawings, 18,000 prints and 6 sculptures, in
addition to lithographic stones, woodcut blocks,
etching plates and a large collection of notes,
books, newspaper cuttings and other
documents. His sister, Inger, subsequently
donated a number of other paintings and
drawings, as well as Munch's extensive
correspondence.

To ensure that the public should benefit
from this gift, a suitable building was
constructed in 1960–3. The building costs were
met from the profits of Oslo's municipal
cinemas.

Museum of Applied Art

Kunstindustrimuseet i Oslo, St Olavsgate 1,
    N–0165 Oslo   ☎ 02 203578
Tues–Fri 11–3; Sat, Sun 12–4. Late opening
    announced locally.

C ♿ 💼

The museum contains displays of applied art and
industrial designs from the Middle Ages to the
present day, with both Norwegian and
international collections. There are
reconstructed interiors of old city mansions,
18th-century glass and faïence from
Nöstetangen and Herreböe, goldsmiths' and
silversmiths' work, costumes and textiles.
Among the special attractions are the 13th-
century Baldishol tapestry, the gallery of Royal
costumes and the gallery of Scandinavian
design.

Museum of the Norwegian Resistance

Norges Hjemmefrontmuseum, Bygn 21, Akershus
    Festning, Oslo mil/Akershus, N–0015 Oslo
            ☎ 02 403135
May–Sept, Mon–Sat 10–4; Sun 11–4. Oct–Apr,
    Mon–Sat 10–3; Sun 11–4. Closed Jan 1,
    Good Fri-Easter Sun, Dec 24–26.

C ♿

Opened in 1970, the museum tells the story of
the Resistance Movement and of daily life in
Norway during the Second World War. The
exhibits include illegally-made weapons, radios,
documents, photographs, posters and an
original heavy water flask. The museum is in
two stone-built vaults at Akershus Castle,
constructed c. 1650 to accommodate cannons
and a powder magazine. They were used as a
military storehouse until 1962.

The museum adjoins the place where
Norwegian patriots were executed between 1940
and 1945.

National Gallery

Nasjonalgalleriet, Universitetsgaten 13, N–0033
    Oslo   ☎ 02 200404
Mon, Wed, Fri, Sat 10–4; Thurs 10–8; Sun 11–3.

F ♿ 💼 ♿ ♿

The gallery was established by Parliament in
1836. It houses the most important collections
of Norwegian and foreign art in Norway. The
collection of paintings contains about 4,000
items, of which 1,500 are by foreign artists. For
over 100 years, the chief aim has been to collect
important works by Norwegian artists.

The pictures shown include the main works
of Edvard Munch (1863–1944) from the 1880s
and 1890s. Among these are The Sick Child
(1885–6); Madonna (1894); and The Scream
(1894). There is also El Greco's St Peter
Repentant, a collection of Russian icons and
good collections of French Impressionists and
Post-Impressionists.

Still Life, c. 1888–90, by Paul Cézanne. National Gallery, Oslo.

National Museum of Contemporary Art

*Museet for Samtidskunst, Bankplassen 4, N–0034
    Oslo* ☎ 02 335820
Tues–Fri 11–3; Sat, Sun 12–4.
🅵 🛈 🚘

The museum building, which dates from 1902,
was formerly the head office of the Bank of
Norway and is a major architectural work of the
period. It has been the National Museum of
Contemporary Art since 1945, with works by
both Norwegian and foreign artists.

Norwegian Folk Museum

*Norsk Folkemuseum, Museumsveien. 10, Bygdøy,
    N–0287 Oslo* ☎ 02 437020
*May 15–Sept 30, Mon–Sat 10–6; Sun 11–6.
    Oct 1–May 14, Mon–Sat 11–4; Sun 12–3.
    Nov–Jan, the indoor collections are closed to the
    public but the park remains open. Closed Jan 1,
    Shrove Tues, Good Fri, Easter Sun, May 17,
    Dec 24, 25, 31.*
🅲 🛈 🚘 🛤

The Folk Museum, the largest in the country,
aims to show how the people of Norway, rich
and poor, have lived from the 16th century to
the present day. It was founded in 1894 by Hans
Aall, who was only 25 at the time and who
subsequently became its first director. The open-
air section covers 14 hectares and contains 170
buildings, from all over Norway. The rural
buildings are grouped together by region of
origin, while the urban houses have been laid
out to form an Old Town.
    The indoor section, which has 160,000
exhibits, contains furniture, household
equipment and utensils, examples of the
woodcarver's and 'rose-pointer's' art, clothing
tapestries and other textiles for decoration and
everyday use. Farm implements and logging
equipment illustrate the development of
agriculture and the forestry industries and a
collection of riding gear, harness and
conveyances provides a picture of transport in a
country whose roads for a long time presented a
challenge to wheeled vehicles.
    There are also music and ecclesiastical
sections, where recitals are held on the
museum's own instruments, and a section
devoted to the culture of the Lapps, who
depended on hunting, fishing and reindeer
herding. It has examples of Lappish art and
handicrafts.

Norwegian Maritime Museum

*Norsk Sjøfartsmuseum, Bygdøynesveien 37,
    N–0286 Oslo* ☎ 02 438240
*Apr 20–Sept 30, daily 10–8. Oct 1–Apr 19, Mon,
    Wed, Fri–Sun 10.30–4; Tues, Thurs
    10.30–7. Closed Jan 1, Good Fri, Easter Sun,
    May 17, Dec 25.*
🅲 🛈 🚘 🛤

The present building, opened in 1974, is
situated directly on the sea. It presents the
maritime history of Norway from the Viking age
to modern times and has collections illustrating

**Reconstructed stave church. Norwegian Folk
Museum, Oslo.**

the life of the coastal communities, fishing and
hunting. The Boat Hall contains a display of
Norwegian coastal vessels and other ships are
moored outside the Museum. They include the
Polar sloop, 6J6A, the first ship to sail the entire
North-West Passage, commanded by Roald
Amundsen in 1903–6. There are gallery displays
of a number of ship interiors, including the main
deck of a sailing ship and a midship section of
the three decks of the coastal express steamer,
Sandnaes.

Polar Ship *Fram*

Polarskipet Fram, Bygdøy, N–0286 Oslo
    ☎ 02 7438370
*Apr and Oct, daily 11–2.45. May 2–15 and Sept,
    daily 11–4.45. May 16–Aug 31, daily
    10–5.45. Nov, Sat, Sun 11–2.45.*
🅲 🛤

The Polar expedition vessel *Fram* was built in
1891–3 by Colin Archer in order to allow
Fridtjof Nansen to test his theories on the
currents of the Arctic Ocean. It was used by him
in 1893–6, and subsequently by Otto Neumann
Sverdrup in 1898–1902 and by Roald
Amundsen in 1910–14. In 1935 the ship was
taken to Oslo, where she was hauled ashore and
a building constructed over her. The museum
was opened by King Haakon VII in 1936.
    Fram is believed to be the strongest wooden
ship ever built, and the conventional ship
which has been the farthest north and the
farthest south. Visitors are allowed to go on
board and can see the cabins, the galley and
details of the strong construction. There is also
an exhibition relating to *Fram*'s voyages and to
activities in the Polar regions.

Ski Museum

Skimuseet i Holmenkollbakken, Kongeveien 5,
*　N–0390 Oslo*　　　☎ 02 141690
May and Sept, daily 10–5. June, daily 10–7. July,
*　daily 9 am – 10 pm. Aug, daily 9–8. Oct–Apr,*
*　Mon–Sat 10–3; Sun 11–4.*
🄲 🛈 💼 ♿

The museum is inside the celebrated
Holmenkollen Ski Jump, which has been rebuilt
more than once since it was first constructed in
1892. Its displays illustrate the history of skis
and skiing in Norway since prehistoric times.
The earliest skis shown date from c. 600 and
were found preserved in bogs. The collections
include a wide range of skis, ski poles and
bindings, made for different regions, purposes
and snow conditions. Special sections are
devoted to ski jumping, military skiing, Royal
family skiing, cross-country skiing, alpine
skiing, ski-making, ski-waxes and stamps
showing skiing. There are also exhibits of the
equipment used by members of Nansen's Polar
expedition of 1893–6 and Amundsen's of 1910–
12.

University Museum of National Antiquities

Universitets Oldsaksamling, Frederiks gate 2,
*　N–0164 Oslo*　　　☎ 02 416300
May 15–Sept 14, Tues–Sun 11–3. Sept 15– May
*　14, Tues–Sun 12–3. Closed Jan 1, Good*
*　Fri-Easter Sun, May 1, 17, Dec 24–26, 31.*
🄴

The collections illustrate the archaeology of
South Norway, with material ranging from the
Stone Age to the medieval period. Among the
special features are the Viking treasure from
Hon, in Buskerud and a large and important
collection of medieval art, including paintings
from Ål stave church.

Vigeland Museum and Park

Vigeland-Museet, Nobelsgate 32, N–0268 Oslo
*　☎ 02 442306*
May–Oct, Tues–Sun 12–7. Nov–Apr, Tues–Sun
*　1–7. Closed Jan 1, Good Fri, Easter Sun, Whit*
*　Sun, May 1, 17, Dec 24, 25, 31.*
🄴 🛈 💼 ♿

From 1902 until 1924, the sculptor, Gustav
Vigeland (1867–1943), worked in a dilapidated
studio lent to him by the municipality of Oslo.
In 1921, when it became necessary to demolish
the building, Vigeland, who by that time was
famous, entered into an agreement with the city
council to make over to the city all the
sculptures, drawings and woodcuts in his
possession, as well as the original models of all
future works. In return the city council agreed to
build him a studio which could be converted
into a museum after his death. Living quarters
for him were included in the bargain and in
1924 Vigeland moved in. As a result of this
arrangement, Vigeland was almost certainly
given better working conditions than any
sculptor before him and probably since. The
exhibition rooms of what is now the museum are

**Man and Woman, 1897 bronze by Gustav
Vigeland. Vigeland Museum and Park, Oslo.**

not large enough to show all the collection and
a drastic selection has had to be made. By his
own wish, Vigeland's ashes are kept in the
tower of the building.

The adjoining park, which can be visited
free of charge at any time, covers 30 hectares. It
contains 192 large sculptures in bronze, granite
and wrought-iron, and over 600 figures, all
modelled by Vigeland with no assistance from
pupils or other artists. The sculptor also
designed the architectural setting and layout of
the grounds. The project took 40 years and
Vigeland was still working on it at the time of
his death.

Viking Ship Museum

Vikingskipshuset, Huk Aveny 35, Bygdøy,
*　N–0287 Oslo*　　　☎ 02 438379
May and Nov, daily 11–3. Apr and Oct, daily
*　11–4. May–Aug, daily 11–6. Sept, daily*
*　11–5. Closed Jan 1, Good Fri, Easter Sun,*
*　May 1, 17, Dec 24–26, 31.*
🄲 🛈 ♿

The museum contains three large Viking ships
and their contents, excavated at sites along the
Oslo Fjord in the late 19th and early 20th
centuries. Known from the places where they
were found as the Oseberg, Gokstad and Tune
ships, they had been used for the burials of
important people and a wide range of objects
were placed inside them at the time, including
elaborately carved sledges and a wagon, small
boats, domestic utensils, tools, combs and
equipment for spinning, weaving and sewing.
All the ships and the other major items have
been fully restored.

Porsgrunn

Porsgrunn Museum

Porsgrunn Bymuseum, Storgaten 59, N–3900
  Porsgrunn, Telemark   ☎ *03 555797*
June–Aug, Mon–Fri 10–3; Sat 12–2; Sun 12–3.
  Other times by appt.
C 🛈 ♨

The museum consists of a group of historic
buildings, centred on a parsonage farm dating
from 1784, which has been preserved complete
with period interiors. The complex also includes
a number of other houses and shops, among
them those of an apothecary and a dairyman and
a 19th-century sea-captain. The 1780 Customs
House is used to display a collection of the
products of the celebrated Porsgrunn Porcelain
Factory, established in 1887. There is also a
19th-century school and, moored nearby, the
Kjell, a tug built of concrete in 1918.

Rjukan

Industrial Workers' Museum

Industriarbeidermuseet, Postboks 43, N–3661
  Rjukan, Telemark   ☎ *036 95153*
June–Aug, Mon–Fri 10–6; Sat, Sun 11–3. Sept–
  May, Mon–Fri 10–3; Sat, Sun 11–3. Closed
  Jan 1, Dec 25, 26.
C 🛈 🖵 ♨

At the beginning of the present century
Vemork, near Rjukan, was the site of what was
at the time the world's largest hydro-electric
plant. It later became linked to works for the
production of fertiliser and of heavy water. The
museum, in the plant's former machinery hall,
preserves much of the original equipment and
tells the story of hydro-electricity supply in
Norway and of the working and living
conditions of the men employed at Rjukan.
  A special Second World War section
describes life at Rjukan under the German
occupation and concentrates on the Allied
efforts to sabotage the production of heavy water
at the plant and the sinking of the ferry, *Hydro*,
which was attempting to take supplies of it to
Germany.

The Old Vicarage, Porsgrunn Museum.

Røros

Copper-Smelting Museum

'Smelthytta', Rørosmuseet, Malmplassen, N–7460
  Røros, Sør-Trøndelag   ☎ *074 10500*
Jan 2–May 20 and Sept 11–Dec 31, Mon–Fri
  10.30–4; Sat 10.30–2; Sun 12–2. May 21–
  June 19 and Aug 21–Sept 10, Mon–Sat
  10.30–4; Sun 12–4. June 20–Aug 20, Mon–
  Fri 10.30–6; Sat 10.30–4; Sun 12–4. Closed
  Jan 1, May 1, Dec 24, 25.
C 🛈 🖵 ♿ ♨

Røros is on the UNESCO list of World Heritage
Sites. The town grew up around its large copper-
smelting works and the associated copper mines
in the district. The first works was built in 1646
and production continued until 1953, when the
main building was badly damaged by fire. Since
then extensive reconstruction has taken place.
One part of the building is now devoted to a
museum of the copper industry, showing work in
the mines and the smelter, and the other deals
with the natural and social history of Røros and
with the culture of the Lapps.

Sandefjord

Commander Christian Christensen's Whaling Museum

Kommandør Christian Christensens
  Hvalfangstmuseum, Museumsgaten 39,
  N–3200 Sandefjord, Vestfold   ☎ *034 63251*
May–Sept, daily 11–4. Oct–Apr, Sun 12–4;
  Thurs 4–7.
C 🛈 🖵

The museum was founded in 1917 by Lars
Christensen, in memory of his father, the
whaling captain and shipowner, Commander
Christian Christensen. It tells the story of
whaling and of the part played by Norway in the
development of the modern whaling industry.
There are also sections on the geology,
geography, zoology and ethnography of the
Antarctic.

Maritime Museum

Sjøfartsmuseum, Prinsensgate 18, N–3300
  Sandefjord, Vestfold   ☎ *034 63251*
May–Sept, daily 11–4. Oct–Apr, Sun 12–4.
F ✏

The museum was founded in 1956 to present
Sandefjord's long association with the sea and
ships. The town has been an important
maritime centre for over 1,000 years. Among
the exhibits is one illustrating the celebrated
excavation of the Viking ship at Gokstad in
1880. Visitors can also see the reconstruction of
a sea-captain's home c. 1900 and of the poop
and galley of a sailing ship of the 1880s. There is
also a collection relating to Roald Amundsen,
formed by Helmer Hanssen, who served with
Amundsen on his Arctic and Antarctic
expeditions.

Sarpsborg

Borgarsyssel Museum

*Borgarsyssel Museum, Fylkesmuseum for Østfold,
    Gamlebygate 8, N–1701 Sarpsborg, Østfold*
    ☎ 09 155011
*May 18–Aug 31, Mon–Fri 10–3; Sun 12–5.
    Exhibitions open all year, Mon–Thurs 8–3.30;
    Fri 8–3.*
Ⓒ ✎ 🖷

Borgarsyssel comprises roughly the area of the
present county of Østfold – a 'syssel' is an
administrative region and this one used to be
ruled from the old city of Østfold. Since its
foundation in 1921, the museum has tried to
reflect the social and cultural history of Østfold.
There are prehistoric and ethnological
collections and a large open-air section, which
includes a farm, with its sawmill and tenants'
cottages, a rectory, a magistrate's house and a
ferry stage. The dwelling houses and their
contents illustrate the living style of both the
members of the farming community and the
well-to-do families of the region.

The joinery and restoration workshops are
an important part of the museum. They
undertake all types of woodworking for
Borgarsyssel and other museums in the county
and they also undertake private work.

Sellebakk

Roald Amundsen's Memorial Museum

*Roald Amundsens Minne, Kulturkontoret,
    N–1650 Sellebakk, Østfold   ☎ 09 348326
June 15–Aug 15, Mon, Wed, Fri 10–3.*
Ⓕ ✿

The museum is in 'Tomta', the birthplace and
childhood home of the Polar explorer, Roald
Amundsen. It contains memorabilia of
Amundsen and collections illustrating his career
and achievements.

Skien

Museum of Telemark and Grenland

*Fylkesmuseet for Telemark og Grenland, Øvregate
    41, N–3700 Skien, Telemark   ☎ 03 523594
May 15–Sept 1, Tues–Sat 12–4; Sun 12–6. Park
    open daily 11–8.*
Ⓒ 🖷 ♿ ✿

This is the county museum, with large
collections covering the history of both the
urban and rural regions of Telemark, with an
open-air section. It was established here in
1909, on the Brekke estate. The early-19th-
century manor house has been adapted for
museum purposes, with collections of 18th–
19th-century furniture, paintings and procelain.
There are also maritime, ecclesiastical and crafts
sections and reconstructions of Henrik Ibsen's
reading room, drawing room and bedroom in his
house in Oslo. In the bedroom, everything is
arranged as it was when Ibsen died in 1906. The
collection of Ibsen memorabilia includes letters,

medals and decorations, and silver wreaths
presented by the town of Skien and the
Norwegian Parliament. There is also a section
on the history of gardening, with 19th-century
tools and machinery, and exhibits of agricultural
and forestry equipment.

Venstøp Farm

*Venstøp, Fylkesmuseet for Telemark og Grenland,
    Øvregate 41, N–3700 Skien, Telemark*
    ☎ 03 523594
June 1–Aug 15, daily 12–4. Other months by appt.
Ⓒ *(ex children)* 🚹 ✿

The playwright, Henrik Ibsen (1828–1906)
spent his childhood at Venstøp, from his 7th to
his 15th year. The house and outbuildings have
been preserved as they were in the early 19th
century. Visitors can see the building in which
the young Ibsen produced puppet shows and the
attic which later featured in *The Wild Duck*. The
barn contains agricultural and beekeeping
exhibits.

Stavanger

Faste Gallery

*Stavanger Faste Galleri, Madlaveien 33, N–4001
    Stavanger, Rogaland   ☎ 04 530900
June 15–Aug, Mon–Fri 11–2; Sun 11–3. Sept–
    May, Mon–Fri 9–2, 6–8; Sat 12–3; Sun
    12–5. Closed Easter and Christmas.*
Ⓕ 🚹 ♿ ✿

The gallery was opened in 1966. It contains
Norwegian paintings, graphics and sculpture
from the mid 19th century to the present day.
An important feature is the large collection of
the paintings of Lars Hertervig (1830–1902),
who died in Stavanger and had long-standing
associations with the town. More than 500
artists are represented in the museum.

Ledaal

*Ledaal, Eiganes 75, N–4005 Stavanger.
    Correspondence to: Stavanger Museum, Muségate
    16, N–4005 Stavanger, Rogaland*
    ☎ 04 526035
*June–Sept, Tues–Sun 11–3. Other times by appt.
    Closed Dec.*
Ⓒ *(ex children)* 🚹

The manor house was built in 1800 by the
patrician Kielland family. It is now the Royal
family's residence when visiting Stavanger. It
has interiors furnished in the styles of 1800 and
1865. A room is dedicated to the social crusader
and novelist, playwright and short-story writer,
Alexander Kielland (1849–1906).

Maritime Museum

*Sjøfartsmuseet og Handelsmuseet, Muségate 16,
    N–4005 Stavanger, Rogaland ☎ 04 526035
Jan–May and Sept-Nov, Sun 11–4. June–Aug,
    Tues–Sun 11–3.*
Ⓒ 🚹 ♿ ✿

A traditional Lappish form of transport: the reindeer sledge. Sør-Varanger Museum, Svanvik.

The museum was set up in 1985 to tell the story of shipping, harbour management, maritime trade, shipbuilding and the development of the port of Stavanger during the past 200 years. The collections are displayed in a group of early-19th-century warehouses, the conversion of which earned the museum the Europa Nostra Diploma in 1986. The exhibits include shipbuilding tools, navigational instruments, sea-chests, a model of Stavanger harbour in 1890, ship models, reconstructions of a shipowner's office, a captain's cabin from the sailing-ship period, and the first-class lounge from a passenger steamer (1914). There is also an authentic sailmaker's loft. The museum owns the Larvik-built yacht *Wyvern* (1896) and the sloop, *Anna of Sand*, a cargo vessel built in Hardanger in 1848.

Svanvik

Sør-Varanger Museum

Sør-Varanger Museum, Strand, N–9925 Svanvik, Finnmark ☎ 085 95113
Apr 16–June 24 and Aug 16–Oct 15, Mon–Fri 9–2; Sun 11–3. June 25–Aug 15, daily 12–7.30. Oct 16–Apr 15, Mon–Fri 9–2.
Ⓒ 🛈 🍴 🚗

The museum is decentralised, comprising more than 20 buildings within a multi-cultural region, which includes Norwegian, East Sami (Lappish), Coast Sami and Finnish settlements. The main museum building, at Strand, on the Soviet border, is a former boarding school, built in 1905 for the purpose of teaching Norwegian to the many Finnish immigrants in the area. Following the discovery of magnetic iron-ore at the beginning of the present century, the population of Sør-Varanger grew rapidly from 3,000 to 10,000 and the town became a melting-pot of cultures.

The museums illustrate the natural history and social history of this very varied region. The policy has been to leave and preserve historic buildings on their original sites wherever possible.

Svartskog

Roald Amundsen's House

Roald Amundsens Hjem 'Uranienborg', Roald Amundsensvei 192, N–1420 Svartskog, Akershus ☎ 02 800105
May 15–Dec 15, Tues–Sun, guided tours on the hour between 11 and 4.
Ⓒ 🚗

The house, 'Uranienborg' which has been open to the public since 1935, is preserved as a national monument. It remains as it was when the Polar explorer left it in 1928.

Tønsberg

Vestfold Museum

Vestfold Fylkesmuseum, Farmannsveien 30, N–3100 Tønsberg, Vestfold ☎ 033 12919
May 17–Sept 15, Mon–Fri 10–5; Sat, Sun 1–5. Sept 16–May 16, Mon–Fri 10–3.
Ⓒ 🛈 🍴 🚗 🚗

This is the county museum of social history, with the displays and temporary exhibitions at the main gallery at Farmannsveien and an open-air section at various sites which extend along a footpath to Slottsfjell. The exhibits illustrate Vestfold urban and rural life in the 17th–19th centuries, agriculture, shipping and whaling. The museum has the biggest collection of whale skeletons in the world, including a blue whale skeleton 25 metres long.

Tromsø

Art Museum of Northern Norway

Nordnorsk Kunstmuseum, Muségaten 2, N–9000 Tromsø, Troms ☎ 083 80090
Tues–Sat 10–4; Sun 12–4.
Ⓒ 🛈 🚗

The museum is devoted to Norwegian art and applied art, with an emphasis on the art of northern Norway. The exhibits form part of the collections of the National Gallery and of the National Museum of Contemporary Art and include 19th–20th-century paintings, sculpture, etchings, photographs, textiles, ceramics, glass, wood and leatherwork.

Town Museum

Tromsø Bymuseum, Skansen, N–9000 Tromsø, Troms ☎ 083 83714
June–Aug, daily 11–3. Sept–May, Mon–Fri 11–3.
Ⓒ 🛈

The museum is in a former customs house, built in 1789. Its collections illustrate the political and cultural history of Tromsø and its region from the 18th century onwards and of the Skansen fortifications, where the museum building is located and which were constructed *c.* 1250, possibly as a defence against Karelian invaders from the White Sea.

Tromsø Museum

*Tromsø Museum, Folkeparken, N–9000 Tromsø,
    Troms*   ☎ 083 86080
*June–Aug, daily 9–6 (Aquarium 10–5). Sept–
May, Mon–Fri 9–3; Sat 12–3; Sun 10–3;
Wed also 7–10pm (Aquarium, Sun 11–2).
Closed Jan 1, Easter Sun, May 17, Dec 25.*
C 🖿 💻 🅰

The museum has sections devoted to the
geology, botany, zoology and archaeology of
northern Norway, together with departments of
modern social history and of the culture of the
Sami (Lapps). Among the special attractions of
the museum are an Enchanted Forest, a reptile
display and a birds' nesting cliff.

Trondheim

Archbishops' Palace

*Erkebispegården, Nidaros Domkirkes
    Restaureringsarbeider, Bispegt. 5, N–7013
    Trondheim, Sør-Trondelag   ☎ 07 521253
June 15–Aug 15, Mon–Fri 9–3; Sat 9–2; Sun
    12–3.*
C 🖿

The palace (c. 1160), which is the property of
the Norwegian State, is the oldest secular
building still standing in Scandinavia. It
displays sculpture and architectural fragments
from the cathedral. The armoury contains a
military museum, with 16th–20th-century
weapons, uniforms and equipment and
memorabilia of those who died during the
Second World War.

Museum of Applied Art

*Nordenfjeldske Kunstindustrimuseum,
    Munkegaten 5, N–7013 Trondheim,
    Sør-Trøndelag   ☎ 07 521311
Mon–Wed, Fri, Sat 10–3; Thurs 10–7; Sun 12–4.
    Closed Easter Sun and Mon, Whit Sun and
    Mon, Dec 24, 25.*
C 🖿 💻

The museum was established in 1893 and has
collections illustrating the development of
applied art and design from c. 1600 to the
present day, with large historical and
contemporary collections of furniture, textiles,
glass, ceramics and metalwork. The present
policy is to concentrate on acquiring
contemporary works.

Trøndelag Art Gallery

*Trøndelag Kunstgalleri, Bispegaten 7b, N–7000
    Trondheim, Sør-Trøndelag   ☎ 07 526671
June– Sept, daily 11–4. Oct–May, daily 12–4.*
C 🖿 💻

This is the art museum for the county of
Sør-Trøndelag. It specialises in Norwegian art of
the 19th and 20th centuries and has fine
collections of paintings, sculpture, watercolours
and graphics within this field, including an
Edvard Munch room, with 25 of his graphic
works. European artists are also represented and
there is a section devoted to negro sculpture.

Trøndelag Folk Museum

*Trøndelag Folkemuseum, Postboks 1107,
    Sverresborg, N–7002 Trondheim,
    Sør-Trøndelag   ☎ 07 522128/531490
May 20–Aug 31, daily 11–6. Special activities June
    23, July 29. Craft demonstrations daily in July
    and Aug. Closed Whit Sun.*
C 🖿 💻 🅰

The collections cover the social history of the
central Norwegian counties of Trøndelag and
Nordmøre. The open-air museum contains over
60 buildings from within this region. They
include a stave church and a Sami turf hut. The
collection gallery displays handicrafts, popular
art, woodcarving and objects illustrating daily
life. There is also a ski collection. The ruins of
the castle built by King Sverre of Norway in
1182–83 form part of the museum.

Utne

Hardanger Folk Museum

*Hardanger Folkemuseum, N–5797 Utne,
    Hordaland   ☎ 054 66900
May 18–Aug 31, Mon–Sat 11–4; Sun 12–4. July,
    open until 7. Sept 1–May 17, Mon–Fri 10–3.
    Guided tours at other times by appt.*
C (ex children) ⟨⟩ 💻 ♿ 🅰

This is the district museum of the inner
Hardanger area. It has collections of rural
costumes, handicrafts, embroidery, rose-
painting and Hardanger fiddles and an open-air
section with 16th–17th-century reconstructed
rural buildings, all fitted out as they would have
been when in use.

    The museum is responsible for two branch-
museums, created by private collectors. The one
at Lofthus has open-air and rural collections
formed by the artist, Bernhard Greve (1886–
1962) and Norwegian art collections of the
schoolmaster-author Jon Bleie (1905–81). At
Bu there is the local open-air and rural
collection of Aamund K. Bu (1872–1944),
which has as its special features two 18th-
century smoke-stove farmhouses, an armoury
and a collection of rural textiles and costumes,
including 600 embroidered bodices.

Verdal

Verdal Museum

*Verdal Museum, Stiklestad, N–7650 Verdal,
    Nord-Trøndelag   ☎ 076 71304
June–Aug, daily 11–8. Play by Hans Rotmo
    performed at weekends in June and July.*
C (guided tours only) 🖿 💻 🅰

The open-air museum has 25 buildings
illustrating rural architecture in the central
Norwegian counties of Trøndelag. They include
an operational watermill and Stiklestad Church,
which is believed to have the largest open-air
theatre in Scandinavia, where performances of
the Saga of St Olav take place. St Olav, the
patron saint of Norway, fell in battle near here
in 1030.

PORTUGAL

Alcobaça

Alcobaça Museum

Museu de Alcobaça, 2460 Alcobaça
☎ 062 43469
Apr–Sept, Tues–Sun 9–7. Oct–Mar, Tues–Sun
9–5. Closed Dec 25.
© ⬤ ⬧

The museum consists of the buildings and contents of the former Cistercian Abbey, founded in 1153. The monks played an important part in the settlement and development of the region and the kings made generous donations to the monastery, which eventually became one of the largest and most progressive landowners in Portugal.

During the French invasions at the end of the 18th century, the monastery was pillaged and great damage caused to its buildings, which were later restored. Sufficient of the original decorations remain, however, to give an idea of the monastery's former grandeur.

Visitors can see the church, with the magnificent 14th-century tombs of King Pedro I and King Inês, the old sacristy, the chapter house, the kitchen and refectory, the 17th-century reliquary, the cloister, the monks' dormitory and the King's Room. The monks were forced to leave in 1834, when the religious orders were suppressed.

Alpiarça

Dos Patudos House

Casa-Museu dos Patudos, Estrada Nacional (EN)
118, 2090 Alpiarça
☎ 043 54354/57390
Thurs, Sat, Sun and public holidays, 9–12.30,
2–5.30. Other days by appt.
© ⬧

'Dos Patudos' was the country home of the wealthy politician, farmer and connoisseur, José Relvas (1858–1929). Since 1968 it has been a museum, housing his great collections. These include Arraiolos rugs – the most remarkable collection in Portugal – 17th–19th-century tapestries, Indo-Portuguese silk carpets, Castelo Branco coverlets, and porcelain from Portugal, France, Germany and the Far East. The important collection of tiles includes Spanish-Arab work and an 18th-century series illustrating the life of St Francis of Assisi from the monastery of Santo António de Chamusca. There are paintings and watercolours by some of the most important Portuguese artists. Among the foreign painters represented are Reynolds, Pieter de Hooch and Delacroix.

Aveiro

Aveiro Museum

Museu do Aveiro, Rua de Sante Joane Princesa,
3800 Aveiro
☎ 034 23297/21749
Tues–Sun 10–5
©

The museum is in the former Dominican Convent of Jesus, founded in 1461 and closed in 1834. Between then and 1910 the buildings were used as a college and in the following year, after certain constructional work had been carried out, they became a museum of Portuguese religious art, with collections of 14th–20th-century paintings, sculpture, woodcarvings and textiles. Visitors can also see the church, refectory, cloisters and workrooms of the convent.

Batalha

Monastery of Santa Maria da Vitória

Museu do Mosteiro de Santa Maria da Vitória,
2440 Batalha
☎ 044 96497
May–Sept, daily 9–6.30. Oct–Apr, daily 9–5.
Closed Jan 1, Dec 25.
© ⬧

The Dominican monastery was founded in 1388 by King João I, in order to fulfil a vow made to Santa Maria that he would build it if he won the Battle of Aljubarrota. Construction continued until 1533 and it is considered to be the most important monument in Portugal, partly because of its size – it is the country's largest monastery – and also because of its architectural distinction and the quality of its sculpture and decoration. It was used as a training school for architects, sculptors and glassmakers.

The whole complex of buildings is now a State museum, noteworthy especially for its Gothic tombs, medieval glass and religious sculptures.

Tomb of King Pedro I. Alcobaça Museum.

Beja

Beja Museum

Museu Regional de Beja, Largo da Conceição,
*   7800 Beja*   ☎ 084 23351
Mar 1–Oct 14, Tues–Sun 10–1, 2–5.30.
*   Oct 15–Feb 28, Tues–Sat 10–1, 2–5; Sun*
*   10–1.30. Closed public holidays.*
Ⓒ ✑

The museum occupies the former Convent of
the Conception, which has a Baroque chapel
and, in the cloisters and some of the rooms, one
of the finest collections of 15th- and 16th-
century decorated tiles in Portugal. The
convent acquired notoriety after one of its nuns,
Mariana Alcoforado (1640–1723) was
suspected, wrongly, of having written the
famous *Lettres Portugaises*, published in France
in 1669, five passionate love-letters purporting
to have been written by a Portuguese nun to a
French nobleman. Immensely popular, they are
now considered to have been the invention of
the publisher. The museum has a substantial
library of books about Mariana Alcoforado,
together with collections of woodcarvings,
Visigothic sculptures, Christmas crib figures and
15th–17th-century paintings.

Braga

Biscainhos Museum

Museu dos Biscainhos, Rua dos Biscainhos, 4700
*   Braga*   ☎ 053 27645
Tues–Sun 10–12.30, 2–5.30. Closed public
*   holidays.*
Ⓒ ⚓

From the 17th century until 1963, the building
which now contains the museum was the home
of a noble family. It has 18th-century pictorial
tiles and ornamented and painted ceilings. The
gardens also date from the 18th century. The
collections illustrate the decorative arts of the
17th and 18th centuries, with exhibits of
furniture, porcelain, pottery, tapestries and
carpets. The house itself is an interesting
example of Portuguese domestic architecture of
the 17th century.

Caldas da Rainha

José Malhoa Museum

Museu de José Malhoa, Parque D. Carlos I, 2500
*   Caldas da Rainha*   ☎ 062 31984
Tues–Sun 10–12.30, 2–5. Closed public holidays.
Ⓒ ✑

The museum was opened in 1934. Its present
building, which dates from 1940, was the first in
Portugal to be designed specifically for museum
purposes. There is an important collection of
works by José Malhoa (1855–1933), and of
paintings, sculpture, drawings and medals by
contemporaries who followed his naturalistic
style. A section of the museum is devoted to
19th- and 20th-century ceramics from the local
pottery.

**Decorative flying-fish. Museum of Ceramics,
Caldas da Rainha.**

Museum of Ceramics

Museu de Ceramica, Quinta Visconde de Sacavém,
*   Rua Illidio Amado, 2500 Caldas da Rainha*
*   ☎ 062 23157*
Tues–Sun 10–12, 2–5. Closed public holidays.
Ⓒ ✑

Opened in 1984, the museum occupies a house
built in 1892 for the Viscount of Sacavém as a
summer residence. It is surrounded by gardens
characteristic of the Belle Epoque. A ceramics
workshop was erected in the grounds, with the
main purpose of decorating the house and
providing objets d'art, an activity which lasted
for four years, from 1902 to 1906.

The large collection displayed in the
museum comprises a wide range of ceramics,
from tableware to ornaments, mostly made at
Caldas da Rainha, but including pieces from
other areas of Portugal. There is also a section
devoted to Dutch glazed tiles.

Coimbra

Machado de Castro Museum

Museu Nacional de Machado de Castro, Largo
*   Dr José Rodrigues, 3000 Coimbra*
*   ☎ 039 23727*
Tues–Sun 10–12.30, 2–5.30. Closed public
*   holidays.*
Ⓒ ▮

Coimbra was the Roman town of *Aeminium*.
The museum, opened in 1913, occupies the
former Bishop's Palace, which was constructed
on the site of the gateway to the Roman forum.
The remarkable cellars of the gateway form part
of the museum.

The museum contains 15th–20th-century
Portuguese paintings, 12th–16th-century
sculpture in wood and stone, 16th-century red
clay vases, 12th–16th-century goldsmiths' work,
musical instruments and church plate. There are
also collections of stained glass from the Royal
Palace of Leiria, memorabilia of Queen Saint
Isabel and Roman archaeological material from
excavations in Coimbra. A section of the
museum is devoted to oriental art.

Estremoz

Agricultural Museum

*Alfaia Agrícola, Rua de Serpa Pinto 87, 7100
    Estremoz* ☎ *068 22711*
Tues–Sun 10–12, 2–6. Closed public holidays.
Ⓒ ⚭

The three-storey building which houses the
museum dates from the beginning of the present
century and was the first electrically-powered
mill in the region. There are more than 4,000
exhibits, covering all aspects of farming in the
days before mechanisation and including
equipment used in the dairy, bakehouse and
kitchen. There are also examples of carts used
for work and festivals and early machines used
on the farm.

A room on the ground floor is devoted to
miniature models carved in wood and cork with
the point of a penknife by two local artists,
Joaquim Velhinho and José Vinagre 'Santinha'.
They depict aspects of the rural life of the
district.

Estremoz Museum

Museu Municipal, Largo D. Dinis, 7100 Estremoz
    ☎ *068 22711*
Tues–Sun 10–12, 2–6. Closed public holidays.
Ⓒ ⚭

The large building which has housed the
museum since 1975 was formerly the Hospicio
de Caridade or Alms House. It contains
fragments of 16th-century architecture. The
museum's collections illustrate the history and
traditional life and occupations of the people of
Alentejo, with collections of costumes, regional
furniture, weapons and armour, handicrafts,
coins, tiles and religious art. One of the most
important sections of the museum is devoted to
ceramics produced in Estremoz. These include
multi-coloured 18th–19th-century clay figures
and the famous Estremoz red pottery, which
includes water jars, bottles and small drinking
cups, known throughout Europe in the 16th
century.

There is also a gallery of contemporary
Portuguese art, a permanent exhibition covering
the work of artists from the 1920s to the 1980s.

**Butcher preparing sausages, 19th-century clay
figure. Estremoz Museum.**

Rural Museum

*Museu Rural, Rossio Marquês de Pombal, 7100
    Estremoz* ☎ *068 22711*
Tues–Sun 10–1, 3–5. Closed public holidays.
Ⓒ ⚭

Established in the late 1940s, the museum
occupies an 18th-century building which
formerly belonged to a convent and is now the
property of the Misericórdia (National Charity
Organisation). Its collections, illustrating the
traditional life and occupations of the area,
have come from members of the Charity
Organisation. They consist mostly of
handicrafts which used clay, wood, rushes,
straw, cork, fibres and metals as their raw
material and aim to demonstrate the creativity
of country people and their awareness of the
practical and decorative aspects of the objects
they make.

Faro

Ramalho Ortigão Maritime Museum

*Museu Marítimo Almirante Ramalho Ortigão,
    Departamento Marítimo do Sul, 8000 Faro*
    ☎ *089 22001*
*Mon–Fri 9.30–12.30, 2–5.30; Sat 9.30–12.
    Closed public holidays.*
Ⓕ ⚭

The museum is in the headquarters of the
Maritime Department of Southern Portugal. It
gives a general picture of seafaring and fishing in
the Algarve. The exhibits include models of
ships, navigational instruments, fishing
equipment and illustrations of the marine fauna
to be found in the region.

Guarda

Guarda Museum

*Museu da Guarda, Rua General Alvares Roçadas
    30, 6300 Guarda* ☎ *071 23460*
*Mar 15–Sept 14, Tues–Sun 10–1, 2–6.
    Sept 15–Mar 14, Tues–Sun 10–1, 2–5.
    Closed public holidays.*
Ⓒ ⚑ ⚭

The museum was installed in 1940 in part of the
large building constructed in the early 17th
century as an episcopal seminary. Before being
used for museum purposes, it had served as a
barracks and a prison. Restoration work was
carried out in 1982. It contains exhibits which
illustrate the history of the town and the region
and which include archaeological material,
religious paintings and sculpture, weapons and
armour, costumes, handicrafts and craftsmen's
tools and equipment. There are also collections
of ceramics, furniture, coins and medals,
photographs, goldsmiths' work, 19th–20th-
century Portuguese paintings and the flora and
fauna of the region.

St Martin, St Sebastian and St Vincent, 16th-century, by Frei Carlos. Alberto Sampaio Museum, Guimarães.

Guimarães

Alberto Sampaio Museum

Museu de Alberto Sampaio, Rua Alfredo Guimarães, 4800 Guimarães
    ☎ 053 412465
Tues–Sun 10–12.30, 2–5.30. Closed public holidays.
Ⓒ 📱

The museum building was formerly the wealthy Collegiate Church of Nossa Senhora da Oliveira (Our Lady of the Olive Tree), which developed from a 10th-century monastery. Most of the museum's collections consist of fine and decorative arts from the Collegiate Church and the other churches of Guimarães. The exhibits include 14th–17th-century liturgical items and religious ornaments in silver or silver gilt, medieval religious sculptures, Portuguese and Delft ceramics, and 16th-century Portuguese paintings.

Martins Sarmento Museum

Sociedade Martins Sarmento, Rua Paio Galvão, 4800 Guimarães   ☎ 053 415969
Tues–Sun 9.30–12, 2–5. Closed public holidays.
Ⓕ

A society was founded in 1882, in honour of the Guimarães prehistorian and ethnologist, Dr Francisco Martins Sarmento. The museum dates from 1885. Its first collections consisted of objects found by Dr Martins Sarmento in the course of his excavations at the Briteiros Iron Age settlement during the 1870s and 1880s. It now contains the second most important collection of prehistoric and early historical material in Portugal and is responsible for the sites of the pre-Roman cities at Briteiros and Sabroso.

The museum also has sections devoted to the ethnology of the region and to paintings, sculptures and drawings by contemporary Portuguese artists.

Ilhavo

Ilhavo Museum

Museu Maritimo e Regional, 3830 Ilhavo
    ☎ 034 321797
Wed–Sat 9–12.30, 2–5.30; Sun, Tues 2–5.30. Closed public holidays.
Ⓕ 🚗

The history of Ilhavo is centred around its shipping, fishing and shipbuilding industries. The museum has collections relating to these and includes ship models, navigational instruments and paintings of regional and maritime scenes. There are also sections devoted to seashells, porcelain from the Vista Alegre factory and the customs and traditions of the region.

Lamego

Lamego Museum

Museu de Lamego, Largo de Camões, 5100 Lamego   ☎ 054 62008
Tues–Sun 10–12.30, 2–5
Ⓒ 📱 🚗

The museum is in the former Bishop's Palace, rebuilt in 1750–86. It has outstanding collections of 15th–20th-century Portuguese goldsmiths' and silversmiths' work and 16th-century Brussels tapestries. Other sections are devoted to 16th–18th-century Portuguese sculpture and paintings, and to furniture and religious art.

Lisbon

Calouste Gulbenkian Museum

Museu Calouste Gulbenkian, Avenida Berna 45, 1093 Lisboa   ☎ 01 735131/730585
July–Oct, Tues, Thurs, Fri, Sun 10–5; Wed, Sat 2–7.30. Nov–June, Tues–Sun 10–5. Closed public holidays.
Ⓒ 📱 💻 ♿ 🚗

Calouste Sarkis Gulbenkian (1869–1955), an Armenian who acquired British nationality, made a fortune as a pioneer of the oil industry in the Middle East. The Calouste Gulbenkian Foundation, set up in 1956, has a wide-ranging programme of educational and cultural activities, one of which is the museum in Lisbon, which displays and stores the 6,440 items of Calouste Gulbenkian's private art collections, previously assembled in Paris, London and Washington. Gulbenkian lived in Lisbon from 1942 until his death and gave his eclectic collection to Portugal in 1953. It is housed in a modern complex, opened in 1969.

It includes European paintings and sculpture, French furniture and porcelain, Mesopotamian, Egyptian and Islamic art, Greek and Roman coins and Far Eastern ceramics and prints.

Coach Museum

*Museu Nacional dos Coches, Praça Afonso de
    Albuquerque, 1300 Lisboa*
☎ 01 638164/638022
*June–Sept, Tues–Sun 10–1, 2.30–6.30. Oct–
    May, Tues–Sun 10–1, 2.30–5. Closed public
    holidays.*
Ⓒ ▲

The museum was founded in 1905 by Queen
Amélia. The building is an 18th-century riding
school and was part of the Royal Palace of
Belem. It is notable for its magnificent painted
ceilings. The museum has the finest collection
of horse-drawn vehicles in the world. It includes
17th–20th-century coaches, berlins, gala and
processional carriages, wheeled chaises,
cabriolets and litters. There are also collections
of harness, equipment for tournaments, races
and cortèges, coachmen's liveries and trumpets
and other instruments used by the Royal
musicians, together with portraits of the Royal
family.

Museum of Archaeology and Ethnology

*Museu Nacional de Arqueologia e Etnologia,
    Mosteiro dos Jerónimos, Praça do Império,
    1400 Lisboa*   ☎ 01 610100/616241
*Tues–Sun 10–12.30, 2–5.30. Closed public
    holidays.*
Ⓒ ▲ � ↝

The museum is located in the former monastery
of the Order of St Jeronimo, built in the 16th
century to commemorate the Portuguese
voyages of discovery. It contains the major
Portuguese archaeological collections, covering

the prehistoric, Roman and medieval periods.
Among the particularly interesting exhibits are
Roman statues, memorials, mosaics and
boundary stones and a number of inscriptions in
Iberian characters. There is a small Egyptian
collection, including mummies from Akhmin.

The ethnological collection contains
exhibits illustrating Portuguese crafts, among
them 16th–18th-century glazed tiles. There are
also examples of modern pottery from Alentejo
and the Algarve, and of African arts and crafts.

Museum of Art

*Museu Nacional de Arte Antiga, Rua Janelas
    Verdes, 1293 Lisboa*   ☎ 01 664151/672725
Tues–Sun 10-1, 2.30–5. Closed public holidays.
Ⓒ ▲ ▯

The museum, opened in 1884, occupies a
former palace, to which was added a new
building, constructed on the site of a Carmelite
convent. The beautiful chapel of the convent
has been preserved and is incorporated in the
museum.

The collections include 15th–19th-century
Portuguese paintings, sculpture, silver,
ceramics, furniture and textiles, together with
14th–19th-century European paintings and
silver. There are also sections devoted to the art
of countries visited by the Portuguese
navigators, especially Benin, India, China and
Japan.

**Royal coaches, 16th–18th-century. Coach
Museum, Lisbon.**

Museum of Contemporary Art

*Museu Nacional de Arte Contemporânea, Rua
    Serpa Pinto 6, 1200 Lisboa*
    ☎ *01 3468028/3463475*
*Tues–Sun 10–12.30, 2–5.30. Closed public
    holidays.*

Ⓒ 🔶

The museum building was formerly a Franciscan
monastery, founded in the 12th century. In
1836, after the suppression of the religious
houses, it became, on the order of Queen Maria
II, the first official Fine Arts School in Portugal,
the Academia de Belas Artes de Lisboa. It
contains collections of Portuguese art from 1850
to the present day, with displays of paintings,
portraits, sculpture, drawings and ceramics,
together with small exhibits of coins, tapestries
and furniture.

Museum of Costume

*Museu Nacional do Traje, Largo Júlio de Castilho,
    Lumiar, 1600 Lisboa   ☎ 01 7590318*
*Tues–Sun 10–1, 2.30–5. Closed public holidays.
    Park open 10–7 (May–Oct), 10–5 (Nov–
    Apr).*

Ⓒ ⓘ 🖼 🔶

The museum is located in an 18th-century
palace. It belonged to the Marquis of Anjeja
(1716–88) and to the Duke of Palmela (1818–
64), both of whom were Prime Ministers of
Portugal. In 1975 the palace was bought by the
State from the House of Palmela for conversion
to the museum. It has collections of period and
traditional costumes, dolls and toys, which, for
conservation reasons, are shown in temporary
exhibitions. There is also a gallery, with
permanent exhibitions showing how textiles
and clothes are made. There are in addition
regular displays of work by contemporary textile
and fashion designers and jewellery-makers.

Museum of Decorative Tiles, Lisbon.

Museum of Decorative Tiles

*Museu Nacional do Azulejo, Rua da Madre de
    Deus 4, 1900 Lisboa*
    ☎ *01 824132/8147747*
Tues–Sun 10–5. Closed public holidays.

Ⓒ ⓘ 🖼 🔶

The museum is in a former convent, dating from
the 16th century. The church, sacristy and
choir contain some of the finest baroque
decoration in Portugal, with decorated tiles,
paintings and carved and gilded woodwork of
high quality.

Among the large number and wide range of
15th–20th-century tiles on display in the
museum are Hispanic-Arabic tiles in a great
variety of Portuguese patterns and pictures, the
large tile-panel of Our Lady of Life (Nossa
Senhora da Vida), made *c.* 1580 and a huge
tile-panel, 35 metres long, dating from *c.* 1730
and depicting the Great Fire of Lisbon.

Museum of San Roque

*Museu de São Roque, Largo Trindade Coelho,
    1200 Lisboa   ☎ 01 3460361*
Tues–Sun 10–6. Closed public holidays.

Ⓒ ✎

John V of Portugal (1706–50) ordered the
furnishings, fittings and decorations of the
Chapel of St John in San Roque's Church from
Rome, where they were made by Italian artists,
including Luigi Vanvitelli, in 1741–7. They
include liturgical objects, religious ornaments,
paintings, sculptural groups and decorative
metalwork. There is also a collection of 16th–
18th-century Portuguese paintings.

National Pantheon

*Igreja de Santa Engrácia, Panteão Nacional,
    Campo de Santa Clara, 1100 Lisboa*
    ☎ *01 871529*
Tues–Sun 10–5. Closed public holidays.

Ⓒ ✎ 🔶

The church of St Engrácia, which contains the
National Pantheon, has had a chequered
history. There had been an earlier church on
the site, but after it had been broken into and
looted in 1630, further Christian worship was
forbidden in the building. A group of a hundred
noblemen, the Brotherhood of the Slaves of the
Most Holy Sacrament, was formed, sworn to
revenge the sacrilege. The building of a new
church began in 1632, but work was very slow
and in 1681 the main chapel collapsed in a
storm. A new start was made, but this building,
widely considered to be the most important
example of baroque architecture in Lisbon,
remained unfinished until 1966, when it was
quickly completed in order to allow a National
Pantheon to be installed there, as a celebration
of the 40th anniversary of the Salazar régime.

The cenotaphs in what is now a temple pay
tribute to distinguished figures in the history of
Portugal, including writers, Presidents of the
Republic and those, such as Vasco da Gama,
who made notable contributions in other fields.

Naval Museum

Museu da Marinha, Praça do Império, 1400 Lisboa
☎ 01 614741/616725
Tues–Sun 10–5. Closed public holidays.
Ⓒ ⓘ ⌂

The Naval Museum was opened in 1863. For
the first 85 years of its life it was housed in the
old Naval Academy. At the beginning the bulk
of the collections were objects which had been
brought together over the years by the Royal
Family and stored mainly at the Royal Palace of
the Ajuda. These were steadily added to, but in
1916 a large part of the contents of the museum,
including most of the ship models, was
destroyed by fire.

In 1947 Henrique Seixas, a great naval
enthusiast, died and left his remarkable
collection of ship models, contemporary
documents relating to the Navy and
photographs of naval events to the museum, on
condition that it was removed from his house
within three months of his death. This speeded
up the process of finding a new home for the
museum and it moved into the Palácio Farrobo
in 1948. The skilled model-makers and artists
who had worked for Mr Seixas were transferred
to the staff of the museum.

With its collections continuing to expand,
the museum moved again in 1962, to its present
home, the monastery of Jerónimos. Its displays
include Royal barges from the 18th century
onwards, local and traditional Portuguese boats,
charts, navigational instruments, including
16th–17th-century astrolabes, uniforms and the
Portuguese Navy seaplane used by Gago
Coutinho and Sacadura Cabral to cross the
South Atlantic in 1922. There is also a large
and important collection of models of
Portuguese ships from the 15th century to the
present day.

Ornate royal barge propelled by forty oarsmen.
Naval Museum, Lisbon.

Theatre Museum

Museu Nacional do Teatro, Estrada do Lumiar 10,
1600 Lisboa ☎ 01 7582594/7582547
Tues–Sat 10–1, 2.30–5; Sun 10–1, 2.30–6.
Closed public holidays.
Ⓒ ⓘ ⌨ ♿ ⌂

The museum's collections illustrate the history
of the theatre in Portugal. They are displayed in
an 18th-century building which was burnt out in
the 1960s. The interior was rebuilt in order to
make it suitable for museum purposes. The
collections include theatre costumes, sets and
costume designs, photographs, music sheets,
programmes, props, posters, sound and video
recordings, press cuttings and a wide range of
memorabilia related to stage shows.

Vasco da Gama Aquarium

Aquário Vasco da Gama, Dafundo, 1495 Lisboa
☎ 01 4196337
Daily 10–6
Ⓒ ⓘ ⌂

The aquarium was opened in 1989 as part of the
programme celebrating the 400th anniversary of
the discovery by the Portuguese navigator,
Vasco da Gama, of the sea-route to India by way
of the Cape of Good Hope. The exhibits include
200 species and 4,000 specimens of marine
fauna, displayed in 93 fresh and saltwater
aquaria. There are also preserved specimens
from the coasts of Portugal and its former
colonial territories, gathered during expeditions
organised by Carlos I between 1896 and 1903.

Nazaré

Manso Museum of Ethnography and Archaeology

*Museu Etnográfico e Arqueológico do Dr Joaquim
  Manso, Rua D. Fuas Roupinho, Sitio, 2450
  Nazaré*   ☎ 062 51346/51687
Tues–Sun 10–12.30, 2–5. Closed public holidays.
C ⚓

The museum, opened in 1976, occupies the
19th-century house which was formerly the
home of the distinguished journalist, Dr
Joaquim Manso, a prominent figure in the
cultural life of Portugal. Its collections include
Palaeolithic, Neolithic, Bronze Age, Roman
and Visigothic archaeological material from
local excavations. There are also displays of
traditional costumes, household equipment and
objects associated with popular beliefs and
superstitions, as well as equipment used by
fishermen. A section of the museum is devoted
to regional paintings, sculpture and ceramics.

Oporto

António Carneiro House

*Casa Oficina de António Carneiro, Rua António
  Carneiro 363, 4300 Porto*
☎ 02 579668
*Tues–Thurs 10–12.30, 2–5.30; Fri, Sat 10–
  12.30, 2–6; Sun 2–6. Closed public holidays.*
C ⚓

**Chinese polychrome sculptures, 17th–18th-
century. Guerra Junquerio House, Oporto.**

The museum is in the former studio of the
20th-century Oporto painter, António Carneiro
(b.1900), one of Portugal's most distinguished
contemporary artists. It contains a display of his
paintings, watercolours and drawings.

Guerra Junqueiro House

*Casa-Museo de Guerra Junqueiro, Rua D. Hugo
  32, 4000 Porto*
☎ 02 313644
*Tues–Thurs 10–12.30, 2–5.30; Fri, Sat 10–
  12.30, 2–6; Sun 2–6. Closed public holidays.*
C ⚓

The museum, housed in an 18th-century
mansion, contains the collections of 13th–19th-
century sculpture and decorative arts formed by
the poet, Abilio Guerra Junqueiro (1850–
1923). They include Portuguese furniture and
silver, Flemish sculpture and tapestries and
15th–16th-century Hispano-Arabic pottery.

Museum of the Romantic Era

*Museu Romântico da Quinta da Macieirinha, Rua
  Entre Quintas 220, 4000 Porto*
☎ 02 691131
*Tues–Thurs 10–12.30, 2–5.30; Fri, Sat 10–
  12.30, 2–6; Sun 2–6. Closed public holidays.*
C ⚓ ⚓

Carlo Alberto (1798–1849), the exiled King of
Sardinia and father of Vittorio Emmanuele II,
lived in this house for the last two months of his

life. In this short period he became for the
people of Oporto a martyr to the cause of liberty
and a symbol of the Romantic period. In the
1960s, the Municipality of Oporto bought and
restored the house and furnished it in a way
which would re-create the mid-19th-century
atmosphere. Patient and determined searching
tracked down many of the original furnishings
and objets d'art which were in the house in the
time of Carlo Alberto. The garden,
appropriately, is planted with camelias and
roses.

Soares dos Reis Museum

*Museu Nacional de Soares dos Reis, Palácio dos
  Carrancas, Rua de D. Manuel II, 4000 Porto*
☎ 02 27110
*Tues–Sun 10–5. Closed public holidays and June
  24.*
C ⚓

The Soares dos Reis Museum has developed
from the first publicly founded museum in
Portugal, established in 1833. Since 1942 it has
occupied the Palácio dos Carrancas, built in the
late 18th century for the Morais e Castro family
and acquired in 1861 by Pedro V, as the Royal
residence in the north of Portugal. It contains
collections of European and Portuguese
paintings and Portuguese ceramics, glass, silver,
jewellery and silver. A section of the museum is
devoted to works by the country's most notable
19th-century sculptor, Soares dos Reis (1847–
89).

Madonna by Vitale da Bologna, 14th-century, oil on panel.
Vatican Museum Art Gallery, Rome (Italy).

The Potato Diggers, 1870, by Paul Henry.
National Gallery, Dublin (Ireland).

Book of martyrs, 15th-century. Art Museum,
Gerona (Spain).

Portalegre

José Régio House

*Casa-Museu José Régio, Rua José Régio, 7300
    Portalegre*   ☎ *045 23625*
*Tues–Sun 9.30–12.30, 2–6. Closed public
    holidays.*
ⓒ

José Régio was the pseudonym of José Maria dos
Reis (1901–69). He was a distinguished poet,
playwright and novelist and taught Portuguese
and French in Portalegre for 34 years. During
that time he formed the collections which are
now displayed in his former home. They consist
mainly of religious and popular art, including
more than 300 figures of Christ, in wood,
terracotta and ivory. There are also many
examples of furniture, ornaments, household
equipment and other rural handicrafts.

Queluz

Palace of Queluz

*Palácio Nacional de Queluz, Largo do Palácio,
    2745 Queluz*   ☎ *01 4350039*
Wed–Mon 10–1, 2–5. Closed public holidays.
ⓒ 🍴 🚌 🚗

In 1747 work began on the transformation of
the 17th-century manor house of the Castelo
Rodrigo family into what was intended to be a
summer palace. The project lasted until 1807,
although most of the work was finished in 1786,
owing to the need to make Queluz the
permanent residence of the Royal family, their
Palace of Ajuda having been burnt down. In
1807 the King and Queen and their family fled
to Brazil, ahead of the French invasion, taking
most of the palace furniture with them. They
returned in 1821. In 1908 the last King of
Portugal gave the palace to the State.

**Virgin and Child, 16th-century, by Frei
Carlos. Soares dos Reis Museum, Oporto.**

It now houses a museum of decorative arts.
The collections, most of which belonged to the
Royal family, are displayed in their proper
period surroundings and illustrate the
development of style in Portugal from the mid
18th-century to the early 19th.

Sintra

Anjos Teixeira Museum

*Casa-Museu Anjos Teixeira, Rio do Porto, 2710
    Sintra*   ☎ *01 9233919*
Daily 10–5
ⓒ 🚗

The museum, in an old watermill restored for
the purpose, contains sculptures, plaster casts,
models and studies by Anjos Teixeira (1880–
1935) and his son, Pedro Anjos Teixeira (b.
1908), as well as works by people who were
friends of the Teixeira family.

Ferreira de Castro Museum

*Casa-Museu Ferreira de Castro, Rua Consiglieri
    Pedroso, 2710 Sintra*   ☎ *01 9231818*
Tues–Sun 10–5
ⓒ 🚗

The museum is devoted to the life and work of
the writer, José Maria Ferreira de Castro (1898–
1974), who is buried at Sintra, a town for which
he had a great affection. It contains
manuscripts, editions and translations of his
works, memorabilia, photographs, drawings and
paintings and an extensive collection of letters.

Pena Palace

Palácio Nacional da Pena, 2710 Sintra
    ☎ *01 9230227*
Wed–Mon 10–12, 2–6
ⓒ 🍴 🚗

Ferdinand of Saxe-Coburg-Gotha married
Queen Maria II of Portugal in 1836. In 1839 he
bought the ruins of the 14th-century monastery
which had once belonged to the Jeronimos friars
and here, high up in the Sintra mountains and
at the place where Our Lady of Pena was said to
have appeared, he built his romantic palace-
castle. It was completed in 1885, the year of his
death. The park which surrounded it is planted
with trees brought specially from Africa,
Australia and Brazil.
    Queen Maria died in 1853 and Ferdinand
succeeded as Regent until his son, later King
Pedro V, came of age. In 1865 he married Elisa
Hensler, a German opera singer. On her
husband's death, she inherited the palace, but
the public outcry was so great that the State
acquired the property by a special decree.
During the last years of the monarchy, the
palace was frequently visited by the Royal
family. In 1910, after the establishment of the
Republic, it became a museum, distinguished by
the remarkable design and decoration of the
buildings and by its collections of furniture,
paintings and ceramics.

Sintra Museum

*Museu Regional, Praça da República 23, 2710
    Sintra*   ☎ 01 9235079
Tues–Fri 9.30–12, 2–6; Sat, Sun 2–6.
F 🚶 🚍

The museum, opened in 1985, occupies the
building of the former Hotel Costa. It is mainly
concerned with archaeology, with collections
drawn from nearly a hundred sites in the
district, from the Neolithic period to the Middle
Ages. Separate sections are devoted to stone
inscriptions, and to pottery and displays of work
by modern and contemporary Portuguese artists.

Viseu

Grão Vasco Museum

Museu de Grão Vasco, Apartado 266, 3500 Viseu
    ☎ 032 26249
*Apr–Oct, Tues–Sun 9.30–12.30, 2–5. Nov–
    Mar, Tues–Sun 10–12.30, 2–5.*
C 🚶 ☕ 💺

The granite building now housing the museum
was constructed in the late 16th century to serve
as a seminary and as the Bishop's Palace. It
contains mainly collections of Portuguese fine
and decorative art, including 16th–20th-
century paintings, 15th–18th-century stone and
wood sculpture, furniture and gold- and
silversmiths' work. The ceramics collection
includes some foreign porcelain and pieces made
for the East India Company.

The ornate 18th-century interior of the Palace
of Queluz.

St Peter, c. 1535–40, by Vasco Fernandes.
Grão Vasco Museum, Viseu.

SPAIN

Antequera

Antequera Museum

Museo Municipal, Coso Viejo, 29200 Antequera,
  Málaga   ☎ 952 842180
Tues–Fri 10–1.30; Sat 10–1; Sun 11–1.
Ⓒ ♿

The museum, opened in 1970, is in an early-
18th-century mansion, which was built for an
aristocratic family and is still known as the
Palacio de Nájara. Its collections illustrate the
archaeology, mainly Roman, and the history,
traditional life and customs of the area. There
are also exhibits of 16th–18th-century religious
paintings and goldsmiths' work. Among the
more remarkable items on display is a
polychromed wooden statue of St Francis of
Assisi by the sculptor Pedro de Mena (1628–
88), who had a thriving workshop in Malaga
which sold sculptures, especially of saints, all
over Spain.

Barcelona

Catalan Museum of Art

Museu d'Art de Catalunya, Palau Nacional de
  Montjuïc, Parc de Montjuïc, 08004 Barcelona
  ☎ 93 4231824
Tues–Sun 9–2
Ⓒ ♿ 🍽 🅿

The museum is in the National Palace, built in
1929 for the international exhibition held in
Barcelona that year, and now perhaps the most
important building on the city skyline. It has
one of the largest halls in Europe, covering an
area of 5,000 square metres. The collections
include sculpture, woodcarvings, enamels and
16th–17th-century Spanish paintings, with
works by Velásquez, Ribera, Zurbarán and El
Greco. The museum also claims to have the best
collection of Romanesque mural paintings in
the world.

Cathedral Museum

Museo Catedrálico, Calle Obispo, 08002
  Barcelona   ☎ 93 3153555
Daily 11–1
Ⓒ ♿

Barcelona's Gothic cathedral was built between
1298 and the beginning of the present century
and contains frescoes, altarpieces, ceiling-
paintings, stained glass and stone-carving of
very high quality. The museum is in the richly-
decorated chapter hall, in a room above it and
in the Sala de la Cabrevación, formerly
occupied by the official responsible for surveying
the Royal properties. The exhibits consist
mainly of paintings from the cathedral and other

buildings in Barcelona, but there are also
notable sculptures in both stone and wood and a
number of textiles, including a series of altar
frontals of embroidered silk, depicting scenes
from the life of Christ.

The outstanding item in the museum is the
Pietà, signed and dated 1490, by Bartolomé
Bermejo. Painted on wood, this is one of the
earliest Spanish oil paintings and one of the
greatest creations of Spanish art of this period.

Ethnological Museum

Museu Etnològic, Avinguda Santa Madrona, Parc
  de Montjuïc, 08004 Barcelona
  ☎ 93 4246807
Mon 2–8.30; Tues–Sat 9–8.30; public holidays
  9–2. Closed Jan 1, Good Fri, Easter Sun and
  Mon, May 1, June 24, Dec 25, 26.
Ⓒ ♿ 🍽

This is one of Spain's major ethnological
museums. It was opened in 1948 in one of the
pavilions constructed for the World Exhibition
of 1929, but soon outgrew the space available
and a new building was completed in 1975. The
collections illustrate the traditions, customs and
popular art of Spain, Africa, Central and South
America, Australasia, the Far East and the
Pacific.

Among the exhibits of particular interest are
those of Japanese ceramics, objects used by the
Australian aborigines and by the natives of
Papua New Guinea, and pre-Columbian items
from Peru, Ecuador, Costa Rica, El Salvador
and Mexico.

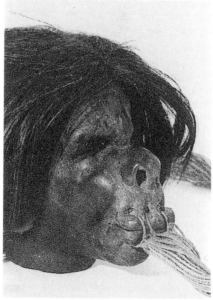

South American head trophy. Ethnological
Museum, Barcelona.

Frederic Marès Museum

Museu Frederic Marès, Plaça Sant Iu 5–6, 08004
Barcelona   ☎ 93 3105800
Tues–Sat 9–2, 4–7; Sun and public holidays 9–2.
Closed Jan 1, Good Fri, May 1, Dec 25, 26.
C &

The museum, opened in 1948, occupies part of
the former Royal Palace. Its large and very
important collections illustrate the development
of sculpture in Spain from the Greek, Roman
and early Christian periods to the 18th century.
There are also sections devoted to medieval
sculpture and religious art. The remainder of the
museum – 13 galleries – contains exhibits of the
popular arts and traditions of Spain, in the
period before industrialisation.

Joan Miró Foundation

Fundació Joan Miró, Parc de Montjuïc, 08004
Barcelona   ☎ 93 3291908
Tues, Wed, Fri, Sat 11–7; Thurs 11–9.30; Sun
and public holidays 10.30–4.30. Closed Mon
except when it is is a public holiday.
C ◷ ▆ & ▆

The Catalan painter, sculptor, graphic artist
and designer, Joan Miró (1893–1983),
established the Foundation bearing his name in
1971, and the building which forms the centre
of its activities was opened in 1975, in his native
city. The Foundation is at the same time a
centre for the study of Miró's work and an
agency for publicising and promoting
contemporary art in general. The collection of
works by Miró, donated by the artist, contains
217 paintings, 153 sculptures, 9 tapestries, his
complete graphics and 5,000 drawings, covering
the period from 1901 until close to his death.
The collection entitled 'To Joan Miró'
comprises contributions made by artists from
many countries to express their admiration for
him and as a token of friendship.

Maritime Museum

Museu Marítim Porta de la Pau 1, 08001
Barcelona   ☎ 93 3011831
Tues–Sat 10–2, 4–7; Sun 10–2.
C &

The building which houses the museum was
originally the Royal shipyard of Catalonia. The
collections illustrate the evolution of the
Spanish navy, with a special emphasis on
Catalonia. There are a number of full-size boats
and ships, both originals and reconstructions, of
which the most important example is the
reconstruction of the Royal Galley, the
captain's ship, of Don John of Austria at the
Battle of Lepanto (1571). The collection of ship
models is also extensive. An important section
of the museum is devoted to cartography and
navigation, with instruments, charts and
atlases. Among the exhibits there is a map made
in 1439 for Amerigo Vespucci.
    Other items in the collections include
paintings, drawings and engravings of ships,
ships' figureheads and other wooden sculptures,

votive offerings from sailors and their families,
fittings and equipment from ships, and
documents relating to shipbuilding and the
Navy.

Museum of Ceramics

Museu de Ceràmica, Palau Nacional de Montjuïc,
08004 Barcelona   ☎ 93 2051967
Tues–Sun 9–1.30. Closed Jan 1, Good Fri, Whit
Mon, May 1, June 24, Dec 25, 26.
F ▆ ▆ ▆

The museum is on the first floor of the National
Palace. Opened in 1977, it illustrates the history
of Spanish ceramics from the 13th century to
the 19th century. The extensive collections
include fragments of ceramics from medieval
archaeological sites, lustreware and polychrome
pottery.

Museum of Costume

Museu Textil i d'Indumentària de Barcelona,
Montcada 12–14, 08003 Barcelona
    ☎ 93 3197603
Tues–Sat 9–2, 4.30–7; Sun 9–2. Closed Jan 1,
Good Fri, Easter Mon, May 1, June 24, Dec
25, 26.
C &

The museum occupies the 13th-century town
mansion of the Marquis of Lió, which has been
considerably modified over the centuries.
Opened in 1969, it contains large and important
collections of 16th–20th-century fashions and
accessories, 16th–20th-century lace and 17th–
20th-century dolls. In recent years the
collections have been greatly enriched by gifts
from the principal Spanish designers and
couture houses. Sections of the museum are also
devoted to the machinery and equipment used
in the textile industries, to ecclesiastical
vestments and to ancient and medieval textiles.

18th-century Catalan pottery. Museum of
Ceramics, Barcelona.

The Wait (Margot), 1901, by Pablo Picasso.
Picasso Museum, Barcelona.

Museum of Performing Arts

Museu de les Arts de l'Espectacle – Palau Güell,
Nou da la Rambla 3–5, 08001 Barcelona
☎ 93 3173974
Mon–Sat 11–2, 5–8. Closed public holidays.
©

On the death of his father, Eusebi Güell (1846–
1918) inherited a large fortune and in 1886
decided to build a town house. He had become a
close friend of the architect. Antonio Gaudi
(1852–1926), and gave him the contract to
design the house. The result, the Palau Güell,
was designated a World Heritage Site by
UNESCO in 1985, due to the originality of the
concept and detailing and its architectural
importance. It was restored during the 1970s
and contains the Theatre Institute and Museum
of Performing Arts. The collections illustrate
the evolution of the theatre, especially in
Catalonia, with exhibits of posters, models and
drawings of stage sets, costumes and
memorabilia of theatre personalities.

Picasso Museum

Museu Picasso, Montcada 15, 08003 Barcelona
☎ 93 3196310
Tues–Sun 10–8. Closed Jan 1, Good Fri, Easter
Mon, May 1, June 24, Dec 25, 26.
© ✎

The museum is devoted to the works of Pablo
Ruiz Picasso (1881–1973). It was opened during
his lifetime, in 1963, and occupies the
Berenguer de Aguilar Palace, which dates from
the 12th–13th centuries. Many of the large
number of paintings, drawings, engravings and
ceramics on display were given to the museum
by Picasso in 1970. The exhibits cover the
artist's working life from 1917 onwards.

Verdaguer Museum

Museu Verdaguer, Villa Joana, Vallvidrera, 08017
Barcelona   ☎ 93 2047805
Tues–Sun 9–2. Closed Jan 1, Good Fri, Easter
Mon, May 1, June 24, Dec 25, 26.
© ♿ ☕

The priest and poet, Jacint Verdaguer (1845–
1902) was largely responsible for the 19th-
century Catalan literary renaissance. He was in
constant trouble with his bishop and was
suspended from parochial duties for a time. Of
peasant origin, his major contribution was his
renewal of the Catalan poetic language by
means of words and phrases used by the
peasantry in connection with nature and
country life.

The museum, set up in 1962 by the
municipality of Barcelona, is in the house where
the poet died. It contains original furnishings,
together with portraits of Verdaguer, objects
illustrating his life and career and early editions
of his works.

Bilbao

Museum of Fine Art

Museo de Bellas Artes de Bilbao, Parque de Da.
Casilda Iturriza, 48011 Bilbao, Vizcaya
☎ 94 4410154/4419536
Tues–Sat 10–1.30, 4–7.30; Sun 10–2. Closed
public holidays.
© ♿ ☕

Established in 1914, the museum's collections,
which are among the best in Spain, contain
Spanish and Basque paintings and sculpture
from the 12th to the 19th century. There are
also sections devoted to 15th–17th-century
Flemish and Dutch, 17th–18th-century Italian
and 18th–19th-century French paintings. The
Basque collections, which are displayed in 12
galleries, are the most important in the country,
with more than 40 artists represented.

There is also a growing international
collection of 19th–20th-century paintings,
sculpture and graphics.

Burgos

Monastery of Santa Maria la Real de las Huelgas

Monasterio de Santa María la Real de las Huelgas,
09001 Burgos   ☎ 947 201630
Tues–Sat 11–2, 4–6; Sun and public holidays
11–2.
© ♿ ☕ ♿

The monastery, a Cistercian house, was founded
by Alfonso VIII and his Queen, Eleanor of
Aquitaine, in 1187. It contains the tombs of the
Kings and Queens of Castille and León. There
are important collections of medieval costumes,
fabrics and jewellery, taken from the Royal
tombs, and among the other exhibits is a banner
captured from the Moors in 1212 at the Battle of
Las Navas de Tolosa.

Cathedral Museum

*Museo Diocesano-Catedrálico, Plaza Rey San
    Fernando y Santa María, 09001 Burgos*
☎ *947 204712*
Daily 9–1, 3–8
C

The great Gothic cathedral in Burgos, built
between 1221 and 1567, is one of Europe's most
important architectural monuments. Its
museum, opened in 1930, occupies the upper
cloister and the chapel leading off it. The
exhibits illustrate the former wealth and
importance of the church in Burgos. They
include tapestries, religious ornaments, and
liturgical objects, paintings and vestments.

Cáceres

Cáceres Museum

*Museo Provincial, Plaza de las Veletas 1, 10003
    Cáceres*   ☎ *927 247234*
*Tues–Sat 10–2.30; Sun 10.15–2.30. Closed
    public holidays.*
C 🛈

Cáceres is one of the most completely preserved
medieval walled towns in Europe. Its museum is
in a 16th-century mansion, with a Moorish
watertank, constructed on the foundations of an
earlier building. It contains very rich
archaeological collections from sites throughout
the province, from Palaeolithic times to the
period of the Visigoths. There are important
exhibits of 1st century BC – 4th century AD
bronzes, Roman funeral monuments and
Visigothic eagle-brooches, together with
sections devoted to the art and pre-industrial
culture of the province.

Cadiz

Cadiz Museum

Museo de Cádiz, Plaza de Mina, 11000 Cádiz
☎ *956 21430/212281*
*Mon–Sat 10–1.30, 3.30–5.30; Sun 11–1. Closed
    public holidays which do not fall on a Sun.*
C

This important State museum has two sections,
one devoted to art, the other to archaeology.
The first includes 15th–20th-century Spanish
paintings, including works by Zurbarán and
Murillo. There are also exhibits of tapestries,
jewellery and 18th-century sculpture. The
archaeological section includes material from
the Phoenician necropolis in Cadiz.

Cardedeu

Tomàs Balvey Museum and Archive

*Museu-Arxiu 'Tomàs Balvey', Plaça Sant Joan 1,
    08440 Cardedeu, Barcelona* ☎ *343 8461004*
Sun 12–4 or by appt.
F ✏

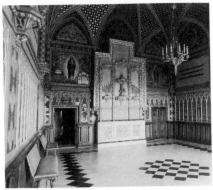

**The Gothic Chapel at the Ducal Palace,
Gandia.**

Tomàs Balvey (1865–1954) was a great
collector. He bequeathed his collections to his
native town, as the basis of a museum which
eventually opened in 1975. The large number of
exhibits includes 19th-century costumes,
weapons, ceramics, handicrafts and natural
history material, all linked to the history and
character of the town and its region. There is an
important collection of 11th–19th-century
parchment manuscripts illustrating the history
of the area, and the museum also has the
furnishings and equipment of the 17th–18th-
century Balvey family pharmacy, one of the
most complete and best preserved in Spain.

Cordoba

Calahorra Tower

Torre Calahorra, Puente Romano, 14009 Córdoba
☎ *957 293929*
Daily 10–8
C 🛈 🚗

The Calahorra was the place from which bread
was distributed in times of scarcity. The museum
is in the 10th-century Tower of the Caliph of
Cordoba, a former Moorish fortress. It contains
exhibits illustrating the history of Cordoba and
especially the contribution made to science and
technology during its Moslem period. Much use
is made of large models and audio-visual
demonstrations.

Palace of the Christian Kings

*Alcázar de los Reyes Cristianos, Campo de los
    Mártires, 14009 Córdoba*   ☎ *947 296392*
*May–Sept, daily 9.30–1.30, 5–8. Oct–Apr, daily
    9.30–1.30, 4–7.*
C

The Alcázar, dating from 1328, is a particularly
important example of 14th-century Spanish
public architecture. For more than 300 years
after 1490, it was the headquarters of the
Inquisition, and afterwards served as a prison. It
was then restored and opened to the public in
1860. Visitors can see the principal reception
room, the galleries and the tower. A collection
of Roman archaeology is exhibited in the
palace.

El Toboso

Dulcinea's House

Casa de Dulcinea del Toboso, Calle José Santonio,
    45820 El Toboso, Toledo
    ☎ 925 197288
Tues–Sat 10–2, 4–6.30; Sun 10–2. Closed Jan 1,
    May 1, Dec 25.
ⓒ (ex children) ▲

This typical La Mancha farmhouse has been
identified with the house of Don Quixote's
Dulcinea in Cervantes' novel. It was acquired by
the Spanish State in 1967. Its collections
illustrate the traditional life of the region and
include exhibits of ceramics, basketmaking,
ironwork and kitchen equipment. Visitors can
see the wine-cellar, with its large earthenware
storage jars, the mill, agricultural implements
and the stables. There is also a display of
cheesemaking equipment. The house has 17th-
century furniture, contemporary with the
publication of Don Quixote. Next to the
farmhouse is one of the largest oil-presses in the
province of Toledo, with a beam more than 15
metres long.

Figueras

Dali Theatre Museum

Plaça de Gala y Salvador Dalí, 17600 Figueras,
    Girona   ☎ 972 505697
Mon–Fri 11–12.30, 4.30–7.30; public holidays
    11–1.30, 4.30–7.30. Closed Good Fri, Dec
    25.
ⓒ ▲

The surrealist artist, Salvador Dali (1904–89)
was born in Figueras. In 1969, the municipality
decided to convert the former theatre, dating
from 1850, into a Dali museum. The building
had been badly damaged by fire during the Civil
War. It was restored for museum purposes and
embellished externally by Dali. It now contains
a large and representative collection of his works
in a number of media.

Fuendetodos

Goya's Birthplace

Casa Natal de Francisco de Goya, Plaza de Goya,
    50142 Fuendetodos, Zaragoza
    ☎ 976 143830
Apr–Sept, Tues–Sun 11–2, 4–7. Oct–Mar, Tues–
    Sun 11–2, 3–7. Closed public holidays
ⓒ ▲ ▉

Francisco de Goya (1746–1828) was the most
powerful and original European artist of his day.
The 18th-century house, in the village of
Fuendetodos where he was born, now belongs to
the municipality, which opened it in 1945 as a
museum to him. It contains furniture, ceramics
and domestic objects typical of the region,
together with 170 of Goya's engravings.

Evaristo Valle Museum, Gijón.

Gandia

Ducal Palace

Palacio del Santo Duque, Santo Duque 1, 46700
    Gandia, Valencia   ☎ 96 2871203
May–Sept, Mon–Sat guided tours at 11, 12, 6, 7.
    Oct–Apr, Mon–Sat guided tours at 10, 11, 5,
    6. Closed public holidays.
ⓒ ▲ ▟

The palace was the residence of the Borgia
family, Dukes of Gandia from the 15th to the
late 19th centuries. It is best known as the
birthplace of the Fourth Duke, Francisco, in
1510. After the death of his wife, Duke
Francisco entered the Society of Jesus, where he
reached the rank of Third General. He was
canonised after his death. In 1887 the Jesuits
bought the palace, which was in a ruinous
condition, at auction. They restored it and until
1968 it was a formation house for members of
the Order. It now houses a small community,
and many of the rooms can be visited. Much of
the Borgia family furniture and pictures remain,
together with mural and ceiling paintings and
objects recalling the life of St Francisco.

Gijón

Evaristo Valle Museum

Fundación Museo Evaristo Valle, 'La Redonda',
    Somió, Gijón, Asturias   ☎ 985 334000
June–Sept, Tues–Sat 5–8; Sun and public holidays
    12–2. Oct–May, Tues–Sat 4–6; Sun and
    public holidays 12–2. Groups by appt at other
    times.
ⓕ ▲ ▉ ▟

Evaristo Valle (1873–1951) was one of the most
important Spanish painters of the 20th century.
He was born in Gijón and in 1983 a museum
devoted to his life and work was opened at 'La
Redonda'. This is a 19th-century mansion,
surrounded by magnificent gardens, on the
outskirts of Gijón, which was made available by
Valle's niece, María Rodríguez del Valle. The
gardens are partly English, partly French, and
were created by William McAlister, the British
vice-consul in Gijón, who bought the estate in
1885, and by José María Rodríguez, who married

Evaristo Valle's niece and who lived in the
house from 1914 onwards.

The museum contains 120 paintings,
watercolours and drawings by Valle, together
with all the personal possessions which were in
his studio at the time of his death. There is also
a substantial collection of sketches and literary
manuscripts. A separate section of the museum
is devoted to the large collection of shells from
the China seas and the Caribbean, formed by
the painter's father and containing more than
2,500 items, of 700 species.

Gerona

Art Museum

Museu d'Art, Plaça Catedral 12, 17004 Girona
    ☎ 972 201958
Tues–Sun 10–1, 4.30–7. Public holidays, 10–1.
C ▮

The museum adjoins the cathedral, in the
former Bishop's Palace, a Romanesque building,
enlarged during the Renaissance and restored
and remodelled in 1979–83 to accommodate the
museum, which contains the art collections of
the diocesan and the provincial museums. Many
of the exhibits come from churches in the
diocese and include paintings, sculpture,
goldsmiths' work, textiles and illuminated
manuscripts. The collections date from the 4th
to the 20th century and among the items on
display are some celebrated and remarkable
pieces, such as the 10th-century portable altar of
San Pedro de Roda, the Virgin of Besalú (15th
century) and the Reredos of Sant Pere de Púbol.

Gerona Museum

Museu d'Historia de la Ciutat, Força 27, 17004
    Girona   ☎ 972 209160
Tues–Sat 10–2, 5–7; Sun and public holidays,
    10–2.
C ▮ ♿

**16th-century altarpiece of St Philip. Art
Museum, Gerona.**

The museum is in the old Jewish quarter of
Gerona, near the Cathedral. It occupies the
former monastery of St Anthony, founded in
1762 by the Capuchin friars. It had a burial
chamber in the basement, where bodies were
interred in a sitting position. After the
dissolution of the monasteries in 1835, the
buildings were taken over by a teachers' training
college, then opened as a museum in 1981. Its
collections cover the prehistory and history of
Gerona and the surrounding region. The
exhibits include material illustrating the first
occupation of European territory by people
coming from Africa. Other sections are devoted
to the Sardana, the traditional Catalan dance,
to the musical instruments which accompanied
it and to autographed scores of the music
composed for it.

One of the museum's most important
collections is concerned with early experiments
with electricity and telephonic communication
in Gerona, carried out by a local engineer,
Narcis Xifra i Masmitjá. On display is the first
telephone based on Alexander Graham Bell's
system to be used in the region and machinery,
plans, photographs and equipment relating to
Gerona's first power-station.

Granada

Archaeological Museum of Granada

Museo Arqueológico Provincial, Carrera de Darro
    41, 18010 Granada   ☎ 958 225603
Tues–Sat 10–2. Closed public holidays.
C

The beginnings of the museum go back to 1922,
when it was installed in the Casa de Castril, a
Renaissance mansion constructed in 1539 by
the heirs of Hernando de Zafra, Secretary to the
Catholic Kings, who had received the dominion
of Castril as a reward for his services in the
conquest of Granada.

The very rich collections illustrate the many
cultures which have formed the inheritance of
Granada since prehistoric times – Phoenician,
Greek, Iberian, Celtic, Roman, Visigothic,
Moslem, Mudéja and Moorish. Among the
exhibits are a Neanderthal frontal bone,
Neolithic pottery and idols, and Bronze Age
weapons. There is also pottery from the famous
Spanish centres of Manises and Fajalavza, and
glass from Castril and La Granja.

Manuel de Falla's House

Casa-Museo Manuel de Falla, Antegueruela 11,
    18010 Granada   ☎ 958 221544
May–Oct, Tues–Sun 10–1, 5–8. Nov–Apr,
    Tues–Sun 10–1, 4–6. Closed public holidays.
C

The museum was established by the
municipality in 1962 in the house in which
Manuel de Falla (1876–1946) lived from 1922
until the outbreak of the Second World War. It
contains collections illustrating the life and
work of the composer, including furniture,
personal possessions, portraits, manuscripts and
letters.

Bust of Ganymede. Archaeological Museum of Granada.

Museum of the Chapel Royal

Museo de la Capilla Real, Oficios 1, 18001 Granada   ☎ 958 229239
May–Sept, daily 10.30–1, 4–7. Oct–Apr, daily 10.30–1, 3.30–6. Closed Maundy Thurs pm and Good Fri.
C ▌

The museum has been established in the richly-decorated chapel and the adjoining sacristy. The chapel contains the marble tombs of what are known as 'the Catholic Kings' and their wives: Ferdinand (d.1516), Isabella (d. 1504), Philip the Handsome (d. 1506) and Joanna the Mad (d. 1555). Among the exhibits are memorabilia of the kings, paintings, including 15th-century panels by the Flemish artist, Rogier van der Weyden, and Hans Memling; religious ornaments, illuminated books and flags and ensigns.

Javier

Javier Castle

Castillo de Javier, Plaza del Santo Javier, Javier, Navarra   ☎ 948 884024
Daily 9–1, 4–7
F ⚓

This picturesque 14th-century castle is strategically situated on the frontier which divides Navarre and Aragon. It was the birthplace of St Francis Xavier (1506–52), the Jesuit who had a remarkable missionary success in Japan. Today, the castle is the property of the Jesuit Order. It is in good condition and contains 16th-century furniture, together with a number of medieval and Renaissance items, as well as an art gallery, containing works by 15th–20th-century Spanish painters. One of the most remarkable exhibits is a 15th-century alabaster reredos, with a painting of the Adoration of the Magi.

Jerez de la Frontera

Museum of the Art of Flamenco

Museo del Arte Flamenco, Calle Quintos, 11400 Jerez de la Frontera, Cádiz   ☎ 956 349702
Daily 10–2. Closed public holidays.
C

The museum was created in 1972 by the Department of Flamencology at the Athenaeum of Jerez. It has close connections with the Museum of Fine Art in Cadiz, which made relevant material available to the new museum. The collections illustrate the history and techniques of flamenco and include musical instruments, costumes and popular art. There are also a library of recordings of flamenco performances and an archive of documents and other printed material with a bearing on the subject.

La Losa

Riofrio Royal Palace and Museum of Hunting

Palacio Real y Museo de Caza de Riofrio, Bosque de Riofrio, 40420 La Losa, Segovia
☎ 911 480142
Mon, Wed–Sat 9.30–1.30, 3–5; Sun and public holidays 10–2.
F ▌ ☕ ⚓

In 1751 Isabella de Farnesio, the widow of Philip V, gave orders for the construction of a palace and estate which would be exclusively her own and where her son, Don Luis, could indulge his passion for hunting. Riofrio was, in effect, a small state, in which the Queen had full jurisdiction. She soon lost interest in the project and today only the palace remains, an almost square stone building, with sides 84 metres long. It was subsequently converted into a hunting pavilion. After the Civil War, General Franco, who greatly appreciated Riofrio, had the palace completely restored and suitably furnished. It is now open to the public.

The Hunting Museum which was opened in 1965 occupies part of the palace. Its collections, most of which formerly belonged to the Royal family, illustrate the history of hunting since prehistoric times and include 17th–19th-century paintings – among the artists are Velásquez and Rubens – 18th-century tapestries from the Royal factory of Santa Barbara, sculptures, furniture and weapons. There are also dioramas showing all the species of animals and birds hunted in Spain.

Las Palmas (Canary Islands)

Columbus Museum

Casa-Museo de Colón, Colón 1 DP, 35001 Las Palmas de Gran Canaria, Islas Canarias
☎ 28 312386
Mon–Fri 9.30–5; Sat, Sun 9.30–1.30. Closed Aug.
C ☕

The beautiful courtyard house which now contains the museum was at one time the residence of the governors of the Island and tradition has it that Christopher Columbus stayed there in the course of his voyages. The theme of the exhibition installed in it is the links between the Americas and the Canaries in the time of Columbus and afterwards. There are collections of maps and charts from the 13th century onwards, models showing the routes followed by Columbus during his four voyages to America and a group of 15th-century nautical instruments.

Néstor Museum

Museo Néstor, Parque de Doramas, Pueblo Canario, 35005 Las Palmas de Gran Canaria, Islas Canarias   ☎ 28 245135
Tues, Wed, Fri 10–1, 4–7; Thurs 10–1, 4–8; Sat 10–1; Sun 11–2. Closed public holidays.
Ⓒ 🛈 ♿

Néstor Martin Fernandez de la Torre (1887–1938), 'Néstor', was born in Las Palmas. He achieved an international reputation as a theatre and ballet designer and for his posters. In 1937 he painted a watercolour called *Canarian Village*, a fantasy design for a group of public buildings, based on the traditional local architecture. Using the watercolour as a guide, the village was constructed in 1939–40. It is used as an exhibition and conference centre and also houses a museum devoted to his life and his development as an artist. It contains many of his personal possessions and some of his furniture, as well as a number of his paintings. A separate gallery is devoted to temporary exhibitions of works by contemporary artists living in the Canary Islands.

Logroño

Museum of La Rioja

Museo de La Rioja, Plaza de San Agustín 23, 26001 Logroño, La Rioja   ☎ 941 222735
Tues–Sat 10–2, 4–7; Sun and public holidays 11.30–2. Closed Jan 1, Good Fri, Dec 25.
Ⓒ

The museum has been housed since 1971 in an 18th-century mansion, known as the Palacio de Espatéro, after General Espatéro, the Spanish Regent, who lived here in the 19th century. In 1884 it became the Bishop's Palace and the episcopal coat of arms can still be seen over the balcony. The collections were mostly created from two sources: works which were formerly in monasteries and churches in the diocese; and prizewinning paintings and sculpture from the National Fine Arts Exhibition held in Santander during the 19th century. The exhibits include works from the 14th century to the 20th, with a growing collection of contemporary works. There are also sections devoted to prehistoric, Celtic, Roman and medieval material from archaeological sites in the province. The recently established department of regional ethnography contains a notable collection of regional popular ceramics.

Painting of flamenco dancers by Néstor Martin Fernandez de la Torre. Néstor Museum, Las Palmas.

Los Palacios

Antonio Urquijo Museum of Bullfighting

Museo Taurino Antonio Urquijo, Cortijo 'Juan Gomez', Apartado 16, 41720 Los Palacios, Sevilla   ☎ 954 865000/865172
Daily, by appt, for groups only
Ⓒ 🖾 ♿

The museum was established in 1975 on a farm which has its private bullring, where visitors are welcome to try their skill and luck at bullfighting. The museum's collections illustrate the history and techniques of bullfighting, with displays of the equipment and clothing of picadors, toreadors and matadors, together with trophies, paintings, sculptures and photographs of famous bulls and bullfighters and bullfighting posters.

Luanco

Maritime Museum of the Asturias

Museo Marítimo de Asturias, Mariano Suárez Pola, 33440 Luanco, Asturias
☎ 985 880002
Tues–Sun 11–1, 4–6
Ⓕ ♿

Since medieval times, Luanco has had important fishing and fish-preserving industries. From the 13th century onwards, it was also much involved in whaling. The museum's collections illustrate the history of the town's maritime activities with exhibits of charts, maps, navigational instruments, ship models and fishing equipment.

Madrid

Army Museum

Museo del Ejercito, Mendez Nuñez 1, 28014
*   Madrid*   ☎ *1 5211285*
Tues–Sun 10–2

C 🛈 💼

Established in 1803, the museum is one of the
oldest in Spain. It occupies a palace constructed
in 1631–2 by Philip IV, which remained a royal
residence until 1788. The museum has been
considerably modernised in recent years and has
collections, arranged in 22 galleries, illustrating
the history of the Spanish Army from medieval
times until the present day, with exhibits of
uniforms, badges, weapons and equipment.
Sections are devoted to the activities of the
army in the former Spanish colonies.

Goya Museum

Museo-Panteón de Goya, Glorieta de San Antonio
*   de la Florida, 28008 Madrid*   ☎ *1 5420722*
Tues–Fri 9.30–3; Sat, Sun 10–2. Closed public
*   holidays.*

F 🛈

In 1776 it was decided, for town-planning
reasons, to demolish St Anthony's Hermitage
and eventually to find another site for its
successor. In 1792 Carlos IV acquired the palace
and garden, where the Hermitage was built and
in 1798 Francesco Goya (1746–1828) began
work on the frescoes which decorate it. They
constitute one of his major works. The building
suffered damage during the Civil War, but it was
carefully restored and in 1988 the municipality
of Madrid took over responsibility for
maintaining it and for running it as a museum.
It now contains engravings, drawings and
paintings connected with the life of the artist.
His granite tomb is under the dome which he
himself decorated.

Lope de Vega's House

Casa Museo Lope de Vega, Cervantes 11, 28014
*   Madrid*   ☎ *1 4299216*
Tues–Sun 11–2. Closed July 15–Sept 15.

C

The dramatist, poet and novelist, Lope de Vega
(1562–1635), claimed to have written more
than 1,800 plays, but the figure is undoubtedly
exaggerated. Even so, the range of his literary
work is enormous, and his religious lyrics and
sonnets are among the finest in Spanish. The
museum is in the house where he lived from
1610 until his death. It is furnished in the style
of the period and contains memorabilia and
personal possessions of the dramatist.

Museum of Decorative Arts

Museo Nacional de Artes Decorativas, Montalbán
*   12, 28014 Madrid*   ☎ *1 5221740*
Tues–Fri 9.30–3; Sat, Sun 10–2. Closed public
*   holidays.*

C *(ex children)*

The museum occupies a large mansion,
constructed in the late 19th century for the
Duchess of Santoña. It was bought by the State
in 1941 and in 1962 both the building and its
contents were classified as a national monument
of historic and artistic importance. The
collections are arranged in 60 galleries and
illustrate the decorative arts of Spain from the
13th century onwards, although in certain
cases, especially glass, the starting date is much
earlier, with material discovered during the
excavations of Roman sites. The collections of
furniture and ceramics are particularly
impressive, ranging from everyday peasant
pieces to the most elaborate and valuable items.

Museum of Madrid

Museo Municipal de Madrid, Fuencarral 78,
*   28004 Madrid*   ☎ *1 5225732*
Jan–June and Oct-Dec, Tues–Sat 10–2, 5–9; Sun
*   10–2.15. July and Sept, Tues–Fri 9–3; Sat*
*   9–2; Sun 10–2.15. Closed public holidays and*
*   month of Aug.*

F 🛈

The museum was installed in 1929 in the
early-18th-century buildings of the former poor
house of Madrid. Its collections illustrate the
history of Madrid since prehistoric times, with
an emphasis on developments in the 16th–20th
centuries. The story is told by means of
paintings, drawings, engravings and
photographs. There is a large model showing
Madrid as it was in 1830. Among the exhibits
are Goya's painting, *The Allegory of the Town of
Madrid*, and the *Virgin and Child* by Pedro
Berruguete. There are also collections of popular
arts and handicrafts, medals, insignia, sculpture
and coins from the local mint.

**Kitchen interior with decorative tiles, 18th-
century. Museum of Decorative Arts, Madrid.**

Museum of the Navy

*Museo Naval, Montalbán 2, (entrance in Paseo del
    Prado 1), 28014 Madrid*   ☎ *1 2210419*
*Tues–Sun 10.30–1. Closed Jan 1, Dec 25 and
    month of Aug.*
F ▪

The museum, which is on the first floor of the
Ministry of Marine building, illustrates the
history of navigation and of the Spanish Navy.
The collections are particularly strong in maps,
charts and globes and include the map of the
world made by Juan de la Cosa in 1500, and an
important group of 18th-century manuscript
maps. Sections of the museum are devoted to
astrolabes and other navigational instruments,
naval guns and equipment, uniforms, and
documents. Among the large collection of ship
models is one of a 16th-century Flemish galleon.

Museum of Popular Arts

*Museo de Artes y Tradiciones Populares, Canto
    Blanco, 28049 Madrid*   ☎ *1 3974270*
*Mon–Fri 11–2; Tues, Thurs also 5–8. Closed
    Aug.*
F ▣

The museum, opened in 1975, forms part of the
Independent University (Universidad
Autónoma) of Madrid. Its basis was the private
collection formed by its original Director,
Guadalupe Gonzalez-Hontoria, who spent many
years visiting Spanish villages in search of
material which illustrated rural life before the
coming of industrialisation. The museum has
sections illustrating customs associated with
birth, marriage and death, regional festivities,
handicrafts, popular art and religion and
domestic life. Other exhibits relate to hunting,
fishing, agriculture and cattle-breeding and
rearing.

National Museum of Ethnology

*Museo Nacional de Etnología, Alfonso XII No. 68
    & Paseo Infanta Isabel No. 11, 28014
    Madrid*   ☎ *1 2306418/2395995*
Tues–Sat 10–6; Sun 10–2. Closed public holidays.
C ▪

The neo-classical building which houses the
museum dates from 1875 and was constructed
on the private initiative of Dr González Velasco.
After his death, the building and all its contents
were acquired by the State. By a Royal Order of
1910 the section of Anthropology, Ethnography
and Prehistory was converted into the present
museum. It received its present title in 1940.

The bulk of the very rich collections relate
to Spain itself and to the former Spanish
colonies in Africa, Oceania, America and the
Philippines. The most important section
illustrates the culture of the Philippines. Its
contents, together with material from
Micronesia – the Mariana and Caroline Islands
– came from an important exhibition about
these one-time Spanish colonies, which was
held in Madrid in 1887.

Wooden sculpture from Equatorial Guinea.
National Museum of Ethnology, Madrid.

Palace of El Pardo

*Palacio Real de El Pardo, El Pardo, 28048
    Madrid*   ☎ *1 2164845*
*Tues–Sat 10–1, 3–6 (3.30–6.30 in winter); Sun
    10–1. Closed for official functions.*
C ▪ ◅

The origins of the palace lie in a medieval
hunting lodge, which Enrique III began to
convert into a palace in 1405. The work was
continued by his 15th- and 16th-century
successors. After a disastrous fire in 1604 it was
restored and remodelled. It suffered considerable
damage during the 1936–39 Civil War and was
then converted by General Francisco Franco
into his official residence. It is now used to lodge
visiting foreign heads of state.

It is noted especially for its frescoes and
ceiling paintings, its paintings by Spanish,
Italian and Flemish artists, and its remarkable
collection of tapestries, which include designs
by Goya.

The Prado Museum

*Museo Nacional del Prado, Paseo del Prado, 28014
    Madrid. 19th-century section at Casón del
    Buen Retiro, Calle de Felipe IV.*
*Paseo del Prado: June–Sept, daily 10–6. Feb–May
    and Sept 21–Oct 31, daily 10–5.30. Nov–Jan,
    daily 10–5.*   ☎ *1 4680950*
*Calle de Felipe IV: Mon–Sat 10–2, 5–9; Sun and
    public holidays 10–2*   ☎ *1 2309114*
*Both museums closed Jan 1, Good Fri, May 1,
    Nov 1, Dec 25. Free admission Sat.*
C ▪ ▣ ♿

The Prado National Museum was opened to the
public in 1819 under the title of Royal Museum
of Painting and Sculpture, in a building which
had been designed to house a museum of science

and natural history, but which had never been used for that purpose. In 1870 the collections of the Prado and the Museum of the Trinity were combined. The Museum of the Trinity contained large art collections from monasteries in Madrid, Avila, Segovia and Toledo, which had been suppressed in 1835.

The museum is largely based on the collections formed during three centuries by the Habsburg and Bourbon kings of Spain, who had shown themselves to be exceptionally lavish and discriminating patrons of art. The collections cover European art in a remarkably comprehensive way and include the world's largest and finest grouping of 12th–19th-century Spanish paintings, with El Greco, Velásquez and Goya very strongly represented. Artists of the Italian, Dutch, Flemish, German, French and English schools also have impressive sections devoted to them. The museum's collections of Hieronymus Bosch and the Dutch landscape painter, Joachim Patenier (d.1524) are unsurpassed. There are also large collections of drawings, engravings, coins and of sculpture, mainly Greek and Roman.

Malaga

Museum of Popular Arts

Museo de Arte y Tradiciones Populares, Pasillo de Santa Isabel No. 10, 29005 Málaga
☎ *952 217137*
Tues–Sat 10–1.30, 4–7; Sun 10–1.30. Closed Aug.
F 🛉

The museum building was constructed in 1632 for the Franciscan Friars of the Victoria monastery. Over the years, the various uses to which it was put caused serious dilapidation to the building, and when the Malaga Provincial Savings Bank bought it in the early 1970s, it was in a ruinous condition. It has now been fully restored and contains exhibits illustrating the traditional life and occupations of Malaga, particular attention being paid to domestic equipment and handicrafts.

Manises

Museum of Ceramics

Museu de Ceràmica, Sagrari 22, 46940 Manises, Valencia ☎ *96 1545116 extn 31*
Mon–Sat 11–2, 4–7. Closed public holidays.
C 🛥 🔂

Since the Middle Ages, Manises has been one of the principal Spanish centres for the production of ceramics. The museum, opened in 1967, occupies an 18th-century building which has been adapted for its new purpose and recently extended in order to provide better display facilities. The extensive collections illustrate the history of the local ceramics industry from the 14th century to the present day. There are also exhibits showing the development of the town during the same period.

Traditional fishing boat. Museum of Popular Arts, Madrid.

Merida

Museum of Roman Art

Museo Nacional de Arte Romano, José Ramón Mélida s/n, 06800 Merida, Badajoz
☎ *924 311690/311912*
May–Sept, Tues–Sat 10–2, 5–7; Sun and public holidays 10–2. Oct–Apr, Tues–Sat 10–2, 4–6; Sun and public holidays 10–2.
C 🛉

Opened in 1986, this large museum occupies what is probably the most architecturally distinguished new museum building of the past 50 years, and one which all students of brickwork should visit. Merida, the Roman colony of *Augusta Emerita*, was the capital of the province of Lusitania. The excavation of its extensive ruins has produced exceptionally rich archaeological material, which is displayed in the museum.

The exhibits are arranged on three floors, each floor having between 8 and 10 galleries. The lower floor is devoted to the buildings provided for public spectacles, religion, funeral rites, the Roman house and the Forum. The second floor displays ceramics, glass, lamps, the burial and cremation of the dead, coins, goldsmiths' work and handicrafts using bone as a material. The third-floor galleries contain exhibits relating to civic and provincial government, the professions, movements of population, portraits, cultural activities and the practice of Christianity in *Augusta Emerita* and Lusitania.

Pamplona

Diocesan Museum

Museo Diocesano, Catedral, Calle Dormitaleria, 31000 Pamplona, Navarra ☎ *948 214980*
May 15–Oct 15, Tues–Sun 9.30–1, 4–7
C

The cathedral was constructed in 1397–1525, on the site formerly occupied by the Roman

Capitol and by an earlier Romanesque cathedral, capitals from which are exhibited in the Navarre Museum. The museum, opened in 1960, occupies the 14th-century refectory and kitchen of the monastery which was attached to the cathedral. It contains material brought from churches and religious houses in the diocese, including medieval frescoes, vestments, statues, and silver and gold liturgical items and religious ornaments.

Ribadavia

Museum of Popular Arts

Museo de Artes y Costumbres Populares, Santiago 10, 32400 Ribadavia, Orense
☎ 988 471843
Tues–Sun 10–3. Closed public holidays.
🄵 ▌

The museum was set up in 1986 by the Ministry of Culture in a 17th-century house. Its collections illustrate the history and traditional life of the province of Orense, in north-west Spain and especially of the Ribeiro region, with exhibits of furniture, domestic objects, costumes, material relating to agriculture, festivities and superstitions, popular religious art and handicrafts. There is an outstanding collection of everyday ceramics made in Orense.

Santa Cruz de la Palma (Canary Islands)

Museum of the Island of La Palma

Museo Insular de la Palma, Plaza de San Francisco, 38700 Santa Cruz de la Palma, Islas Canarias
☎ 922 420558
Mon–Fri 10–1, 4–7; Sat 10–1.
🄵

The museum was created in 1987 by the amalgamation of the previously existing museums of natural sciences and archaeology, fine art and ethnography. Accommodation for the new museum was provided in a former Franciscan monastery, dating from the 16th century. The collections illustrate the history of the island since Neolithic times. There are displays on the natural history and traditional culture of the region, with a section devoted to 19th-century Spanish paintings.

Santander

Maritime Museum of Cantabria

Museo Marítimo del Cantábrico, San Martín de Bajamar, 39004 Santander, Cantabria
☎ 942 274962
June 16–Sept 15, Tues–Sat 11–1, 4–7; Sun and public holidays 11–2. Sept 16–June 15, Tues–Sat 10–1, 4–6; Sun and public holidays 11–2. Closed Jan 1, Good Fri, May 1, Dec 25.
🄵 ▌ ⟲

Established in a new building overlooking the sea in 1981, the museum illustrates the natural and maritime history of the Cantabrian region of northern Spain. The aquarium has a comprehensive collection of the fish and marine fauna of the local coastal waters and there are a number of skeletons of cetacea, the largest of them, of a whale, being 24.5 metres long. Sections are devoted to the story of the fishing industry and the shipyards, with collections of tools, fishing equipment and navigational instruments. There are also a number of ship models, some of which were made in the 18th and 19th centuries.

Santiago de Compostela

Museum of Galicia

Museo do Pobo Galego, Santo Domingo de Bonaval, 15704 Santiago de Compostela, La Coruña   ☎ 81 583620
Mon–Sat 10–1, 4–7
🄲 ▌ ⟲

The museum, opened in 1977, occupies the Monastery of Santo Domingo de Bonaval, which was founded in 1219. The present buildings date from the 17th and 18th centuries and are remarkable for their ingenious circulation system, based on a staircase constructed as a triple helix, with three separate ramps. The museum displays illustrate the trades and handicrafts of Galicia, showing in each case the raw materials, processes and tools, together with the finished product. The craftsmen concerned are the tinplate workers, the repairers of earthenware vessels, the knife-grinders and umbrella-repairers, the makers and repairers of shoes and clogs, the saddlers, the brick and tile makers, the sawyers and carpenters, the charcoal-burners, the blacksmiths, the quarrymen and masons, the weavers, the basketmakers, the potters and the lace-makers. Other sections of the museum are devoted to musical instruments and popular music, costume and vernacular architecture.

Museum of Ceramics, Manises.

Burial cave at Miento. Museum of the Island of La Palma, Santa Cruz de la Palma.

Sant Salvador del Vendrell

Pablo Casals' House

Casa-Museu Pau Casals, Avinguda Palfuriana 59–61, 43130 Sant Salvador del Vendrell, Tarragona   ☎ 977 680117
Apr–Oct, Tues–Sun 11–2, 2–8. Nov–Mar, Tues–Sun 11–2.
ⓒ ⌂ ⇗

The great cellist, Pablo Casals (1876–1973) was born in Sant Salvador del Vendrell and lived there until he was 12. The house which he subsequently bought was opened as a museum to him in 1975. Its collections illustrate his long career as a performer, composer and teacher, including his travels and concerts abroad and the period he spent in exile during the Civil War and the Franco régime. The exhibits include his furniture, musical instruments and a wide range of personal possessions, as well as photographs, concert programmes, portraits, letters, and awards relating to Casals and his friends.

Seville

Museum of the Alcazar of Seville

Museo del Alcázar de Sevilla, Plaza del Triunfo, 41000 Sevilla   ☎ 954 207099
May–Sept, Tues–Sun 9–12.45, 4.30–7. Oct–Apr, Tues–Sun 9–12.45, 3–5.30.
ⓒ

Construction of the great Moorish palace at Seville began in the 12th century and continued at intervals until the 16th. Substantial restoration work had to be carried out after the earthquake of 1755 and the fire of 1762. The appearance of the exterior was changed by 19th-century restorations. Now, as a State museum, it contains important collections of tapestries, paintings and mosaics. Among the exhibits is the 15th-century *Virgin of the Navigators*, by Alejo Fernández, the first European work of religious art connected with the discovery of the Indies.

Cathedral Museum

Museo Catedrálico, Plaza Virgen de los Reyes, 41000 Sevilla   ☎ 954 214971
May–Sept, Tues–Sun 10.30–1, 4–6.30. Oct–Apr, Tues–Sun 10.30–1, 3.30–5.30.
ⓒ

Seville's great Gothic cathedral was constructed in 1403–1506. It contains the comb and library of Columbus and is also celebrated for *La Giralda*, the bronze statue of Faith carrying the banner of Constantine, which revolves as a weather vane. It dates from 1558. The museum has important exhibits of church plate, paintings, sculpture and vestments, together with objects illustrating the history of the cathedral from the 15th century to the 20th.

Murillo's House

Casa-Museo Murillo, Santa Teresa 8, 41000 Sevilla   ☎ 954 221829
Tues–Sun 10–2
ⓒ

The painter, Bartolomé Esteban Murillo (1617–82) spent much of his life in this house. It became the property of the State in 1972 and is now the responsibility of the Museum of Fine Art in Seville. Its collections illustrate the life, work and times of the artist.

Museum of Fine Art

Museo de Bellas Artes, Plaza del Museo 9, 41000 Sevilla   ☎ 954 221829
Tues–Sun 10–2
ⓒ

After the Prado in Madrid, this is the second most important art museum in Spain. It was established in 1835 following the suppression of the religious houses. It is housed in a former Franciscan friary. Its larger collections are of 15th–20th-century Spanish artists, especially those living and working in Seville, including Murillo. There are also sections devoted to sculpture, drawings, ceramics, furniture and weapons.

Sitges

Museum of Cape Ferrat

Museu del Cau Ferrat, Calle Fonollar, 08780 Sitges, Barcelona   ☎ 93 8949364
Tues–Sat 10–4, 5–7 (4–6 in winter); Sun 10–2.
ⓒ

The Catalan painter and poet, Santiago Rusiñol (1861–1931), studied in Paris and was one of the main channels through which the influence of modern French painting was introduced into Spain. In 1891 he bought two adjoining fishermen's cottages at Sitges and had them converted into a museum. The exhibits include Rusiñol's large collection of European wrought ironwork, one of the most important in the world, Spanish and Italian ceramics, furniture and glass. There are also works by El Greco, Picasso and Rusiñol himself.

Museum of the Romantic Era

Museo Romántico: Casa Llopis, Sant Gaudenci,
08780 Sitges, Barcelona   ☎ 93 8942969
Tues–Sat 10–2, 5–7 (4–6 in winter); Sun 10–2.
Ⓒ

In the 1930s and 1940s, the city of Barcelona
was given two splendid late-18th-century
mansions and their contents, one at Sitges and
the other at Vilanova i la Geltru. It decided to
organise them as two sections of a museum of
the Romantic period.

The Llopis House, which forms this
museum, was the ancestral home of an old
Sitges family and contains, on the first floor, a
sumptuously decorated and furnished music
room, ballroom, card room and dining room.
On the ground floor, there are three series of
dioramas. The first shows the most important
stages in the life of a lady born in 1825, the
second illustrates different aspects of social life
in the region during the 19th century and the
third is concerned with Catalan popular
traditions and customs. The wine-cellars have
been restored, to show what was consumed in
the household and to remind visitors of the
famous Malmsey which the Llopis family
produced last century.

Terrassa

Textile Museum

Museu Textil, Salmeron 19–22, 08222 Terrassa,
Barcelona   ☎ 93 7857298
Tues–Sat 10–1, 5–8; Sun 10–2. Closed Jan 1, 6,
Good Fri, May 1, June 24, Aug 15, Sept 11,
Dec 6, 25, 26.
Ⓒ ♟ ⟲

Established in 1946, this important museum was
moved to a new building in 1970. It has large
collections of textiles and costumes dating from
the 3rd to the 20th century. The exhibits come
from Spain, from medieval and Renaissance
Europe as a whole, and from the Near and Far
East and South America. A section of the
museum is devoted to Spanish lace and there is
also a collection of 18th–19th-century Spanish
prints and engravings.

Toledo

El Greco Museum

Casa y Museo del Greco, Samuel Levi 3, 45002
Toledo   ☎ 925 224046
Tues–Sat 10–2, 4–6; Sun 10–2. Closed local
holidays.
Ⓒ *(ex children)* ♟ ⟲

Domenikos Theotocopoulos (1541–1614), the
painter, sculptor and architect, was born in
Crete, but eventually settled in Spain, where he
was known as El Greco, 'the Greek'. He worked
a good deal in Toledo, where two of his greatest
altarpieces are still to be seen, and in 1910 the
Ministry of Culture opened his former home as a
museum. It contains a number of paintings by
him and by other 15th–17th-century Spanish

artists. Among his works in the museum are a
view of Toledo and several portraits. There are
also photographs of all his other known works,
together with furniture and decorative material
made during his lifetime.

Museum of the Alcazar of Toledo

Museo del Alcázar de Toledo, General Moscardo 4,
45001 Toledo   ☎ 925 213961/221673
Tues–Sun 9.30–1.30, 3.30–6
Ⓒ ♟ ⚔ ⟲

'Alcazar' comes from two Arabic words,
meaning 'the castle' or 'the fortress' and the
great square Alcazar at Toledo, several times
destroyed and rebuilt, provides a summary of
Spanish history since the 3rd century AD. Its
last reconstruction followed a 90-day siege in
1936 during the Civil War. The museum
contains exhibits documenting the siege, which
has become one of the epics of Spanish history.
Several rooms, forming a separate museum, are
devoted to the history of the Army.

Museum of the Moorish Workshop

Museo Taller del Moro, Taller del Moro 4, 45002
Toledo   ☎ 925 227115
Tues–Sat 10–2, 4–6.30; Sun 10–2. Closed Jan 1,
May 1, Dec 25.
Ⓒ

This is the only early-14th-century civil
building to have survived in Toledo. Designed
in the Moorish style, its rooms recall those in
the Alhambra. The exhibits in the museum
illustrate Moorish craftsmanship in Toledo
during the 14th and 15th centuries and include
pottery, tiles, woodwork and architectural
sculpture. There is a tradition that in the
Middle Ages what is now the museum served as
a workshop for the building of the cathedral.

Museum of the Visigoths

Museo de los Concilios y de la Cultura Visigoda,
San Clemente 4, 45002 Toledo
☎ 925 227872
Tues–Sat 10–2, 4–6.30; Sun 10–2. Closed Jan 1,
May 1, Dec 25.
Ⓒ ♟

The Visigoths were the Western Goths and in
418 AD they invaded Gaul and moved down
into the Iberian peninsula, where they
established their capital in Toledo. During the
5th–8th centuries they developed a style of
architecture and ornament which combined
Byzantine influence with the local Roman
tradition. The museum, established in 1969,
displays elements from their buildings in
Toledo, together with inscriptions and items of
jewellery. The Church of San Román, which
was restored to accommodate the museum, is on
the highest site in Toledo. It is a notable
example of Toledan Moorish architecture and
has interesting 13th-century mural paintings
which show both Romanesque and Hispano-
Arab influence.

The Church of San Román, now restored as the home of the Museum of the Visigoths, Toledo.

Santa Cruz Museum

Museo de Santa Cruz, Miguel de Cervantes 3,
45001 Toledo ☎ 925 221402
Tues-Sat 10–6.30; Sun 10–2. Closed Jan 1, May 1, Dec 25.
Ⓒ *(ex children)* 🗼

The building, in the shape of a Greek cross, was originally a hospital, constructed in 1504–14 on the orders of Cardinal Pedro González de Mendoza. A regional museum, it has important archaeological material from the Roman, Visigothic, Arab and Moslem periods in Toledo, and extensive collections illustrating the customs, traditions and handicrafts of the area, including textiles, glassware, ceramics, gold- and silversmiths' work, and wrought iron. The paintings on display are mainly by 16th–17th-century artists belonging to or closely associated with Toledo, including El Greco (1541–1614), José de Ribera (1591–1652) and Bartolomé Murillo (1617–82).

Sephardic Museum

Museo Sefardí, Sinagoga de Samuel-La-Levi Abulafia, Alamillos del Transito, 45001 Toledo ☎ 925 223665
May–Sept, Mon–Sat 10–2, 3.30–7. Oct–Apr 10–2, 3.30–6. Closed pm public holidays.
Ⓒ

Toledo had for centuries an important Jewish community. The museum's collections illustrate the history and culture of the Jewish community in Spain. They are displayed in a 14th-century synagogue and in an adjoining monastery. The exhibits include Jewish tombstones, liturgical lamps, religious ornaments, manuscripts and documents relating to the Jewish community in Spain.

Valencia

Museum of Bullfighting

Museo Taurino, Pasaje del Doctor Serra 18, Junto a la Plaza de Toros, 46006 Valencia
☎ 96 3511850
Sun–Fri 10.30–1.30. Closed public holidays.
Ⓕ

The Valencia Bull Ring dates from 1851. The museum building, constructed in 1970, adjoins it. The original collection was formed by a Valencia bullfighting addict, Luis Moróder, who in 1929 opened Spain's first museum devoted to this national passion. Many other objects have since been added to the collection as a result of gifts and bequests. The exhibits include mounted bulls' heads, posters, bullfighters' costumes, cloaks, personal possessions of famous bullfighters and sculpture depicting personalities and aspects of the sport. There is an historical collection of the swords used by matadors at different periods. Rooms are devoted to celebrated bullfighters from both Valencia and elsewhere in Spain.

Museum of Ceramics and the Sumptuary Arts

Museo Nacional de Cerámica y de las Artes Suntuarias, Poeta Querol 2, 46002 Valencia
☎ 96 3516392
Tues–Sat 9–2, 4–6; Sun and public holidays 9–2. Closed Jan 1, Good Fri, Dec 25.
Ⓒ ✍

The museum is in the 15th-century palace of the Marquesses of Dos Aguas, which was substantially rebuilt in the 18th century and further modified c. 1875. There are important collections of 13th–19th-century Spanish tiles and ceramics, including three tiled floors brought from mansions in Valencia. Five pieces of pottery designed by Picasso were dedicated to the museum and they are on display. Five rooms in the museum contain contemporary ceramics and glassware and there are also a number of notable specialist collections, including fans, Valencia lace, jewellery – mostly designed to be worn with traditional Valencia costumes – furniture and graphic art.

Museum of Fine Art

Museo de Bellas Artes, San Pío V, 9, 46010 Valencia ☎ 96 3693088
Tues–Sat 10–2, 4–6; Sun and public holidays 10–2. Aug, 10–2 only. Closed Jan 1, Good Fri, Dec 25.
Ⓒ 🗼 ▆

This is one of Europe's major art museums. The building which it has occupied since 1946 dates from 1683. It has been successively a residence for missionaries and a theological college, a military academy, a poorhouse, a warehouse and a military hospital. The original collections were formed in the 18th century by the three Fine Arts Academies. Other works were added as a result of the suppression of the convents during the French Revolutionary period and of the dissolution of the monasteries in 1835 and of subsequent bequests and purchases.

The museum has two separate sections, archaeology and art. The first contains collections of Hispano-Roman altars, milestones, tombstones and mosaics. The art section has one of the best collections of 14th–16th-century paintings in Europe, including numerous reredos paintings. The 17th century is illustrated by works by Ribera and Van Dyck and by a self-portrait of Velásquez. The prolific and important Valencia School of the 18th century is well represented. The Goya Room has four outstanding portraits by him, as well as drawings made during his visit to Valencia. There are many works by the portraitist, Vincente Lopez (1772–1850) and his contemporaries and by the 19th-century Valencia Impressionists. There is also a growing collection of works by contemporary Valencia artists.

Valladolid

House of Cervantes

Casa de Cervantes, Calle del Rastro 7, 47000 Valladolid   ☎ 983 229505
Mon–Sat 10–6. Closed pm public holidays.
C

This was the house in which Miguel Cervantes lived from 1603 until 1606, and in which he probably wrote the first part of *Don Quixote*. The museum has been equipped with contemporary furnishings and there are exhibits illustrating the history of the house and the life and work of Cervantes.

Vilafranca del Penedès

Vilafranca Museum

Museu de Vilafranca, Plaça Jaume I no. 1, Vilafranca del Penedès, Barcelona
☎ 93 8900582
Tues–Sun 10–2, 4–7.
C ▮ ▆

More than half of the cultivated land in the Upper Penedès is devoted to growing grapes and Vilafranca is the capital of a great vineyard. It is therefore not surprising that a large part of its museum is devoted to the history and techniques of vine-growing and wine production, around which the life of the local people has revolved since classical times. Items in the displays include wine-glasses, gourds and other containers, corks and cork-making equipment, barrels, vats, bottles and labels. There are also sections devoted to the geology, natural history and archaeology of the region, and to the work of local artists.

Vilanova i la Geltru

Museum of the Romantic Era

Museo Romántico: Can Papiol, Calle Major 32, 08800 Vilanova i la Geltru, Barcelona
☎ 93 8930382
Tues–Sat 10–2, 4–7; Sun 10–2.
C

This is the second half of the Romantic Era Museum organised by the city of Barcelona, the first being at Sitges. The Papiol mansion, which houses the museum was built by Francesco Papiol at the end of the 18th century. In 1959 the city bought it from the family, together with its contents. The richly-decorated rooms on the first floor include the antechamber, the ballroom, the billiard room, with its magnificent 19th-century Barcelona-made billiard table, the drawing-room and the dining-room, with a splendid bronze lamp. The service areas, including the kitchen, bread-oven, oil-store, pantry, wine-cellar and stables, have been restored to their original condition.

Vitoria-Gasteiz

Museum of the Archaeology of Alava

Museo de Arqueología de Alava, Correría 116, 01001 Vitoria-Gasteiz, Alava
☎ 945 225773
Tues–Fri 11–2, 5–7; Sat, Sun and public holidays 11–2. Closed Jan 1, Good Fri.
F ▮

Alava is famous among archaeologists for its cave-dwellings, which were in use from Palaeolithic times until the Iron Age, and which have provided an exceptionally rich source of information about prehistoric cultures, in the form of artefacts, human and animal remains and rock-paintings. The museum holds regional archaeological material from sites ranging in date from the Stone Age to the medieval period, in the remarkable 16th-century building which it has occupied since 1975. The displays are attractively and imaginatively presented and make a point of relating the objects to the sites where they were found.

St Bruno, by Francisco Ribalta (1565–1628). Museum of Fine Art, Valencia.

SWEDEN

Borås

Borås Art Museum

P. A. Halls Terrass, Box 55015, S-500 05 Borås,
Älvasborgs län   ☎ 033 167672
Tues, Thurs 12–8; Wed, Fri 12–4; Sat 10–3; Sun
1–5.

[F] 🛉 💻 🚕

This municipal museum was established in 1975
to collect and display Swedish paintings,
sculpture, decorative and applied arts and
graphics, with an emphasis on works by
contemporary artists. A section of the museum
is devoted to works by the portrait miniaturist,
Peter Adolf Hall (1739–93), who went to Paris
in 1766 and soon made a reputation there, being
elected a member of the Academy in 1769.

Borlänge

Museum of the Future

Framtidsmuseet, Jussi Björlings väg 25,
S-781 50 Borlänge, Kopparbergs län
☎ 024 380185
Museum: Mon–Wed 10–5; Thurs 10–9; Fri 10–5;
Sat, Sun 12–5. Planetarium: Thurs 7 and 8;
Sat, Sun 2 and 3.

[F] 🛉 💻 🚕

Borlänge is a rapidly developing new town with
modern industries, the Silicon Valley of
Sweden. The museum forms part of a recently
constructed convention and leisure centre.
Under the same roof there is a hotel, restaurant,
café, dance-hall and complex of conference
rooms. The visitor to the museum is first given
an introduction to the broad themes of Swedish
history in the 19th and 20th centuries and then
encouraged, after being shown a series of
scientific exhibits, to ask questions about the
future.

The museum has both a normal type of
planetarium and a small portable one, which
can be packed into a car and taken out to
schools.

Bunge

Bunge Museum

Bungemuseet, Box 35, S-620 35 Fårösund,
Gotlands län   ☎ 0498 21018
Apr 1–30, May 15–31, Mon–Fri 10–2; Sat, Sun
12–4. June and Aug 1–2, daily 10–6. July,
daily 10–7. Aug 13–Sept 2, daily 10–4. Closed
June 11.

[C] 🛉 💻 🚕

The open-air museum at Bunge was created by a
local school-teacher, Th. Erlandsson (1869–
1953), who wanted to show how the peasants
lived in earlier times. The first buildings were
moved here in 1908 and 21 items are now on

the museum site. They include two farmsteads,
a fisherman's cottage, a charcoal-burner's hut, a
water-driven sawmill, fulling mill and cornmill
and a lime-kiln. There is also a burial ground
and a group of Viking pictorial stones. The
dwellings have appropriate furniture and
domestic equipment and show the style of life of
their former inhabitants.

School Museum

Bunge Skolmuseum, Box 35, S-620 35 Fårösund,
Gotlands län   ☎ 0498 21018
June 15–30 and Aug 1–15, daily 11.30–6. July,
daily 11.30–7.

[C] 🛉 💻

The school building dates from 1846 and
continued in use until the 1930s. It has been
preserved with all its furniture and equipment
and looks as it did when it was functioning as a
school. The apartment where the woman
teacher lived is on the first floor and is furnished
in 1930s style.

Eskiltuna

Rademacher Forges

Eskiltuna Museer, Faktoriholmarna,
S-631 86 Eskiltuna, Södermanlands län
☎ 016 102290
May–Sept, Mon–Fri 10–6. Oct–Apr, daily 10–4.
Closed Good Fri, Easter Sat, May 1, Whit Sat,
Midsummer Eve, Dec 31.

[F] 🛉 💻 🚕

Charles X invited Reinold Rademacher to
Sweden in 1658 and granted him letters patent
to build and operate a State manufactory here.
A complex of 120 forges was planned, but only
20 were actually built, of which six have
survived. Each is a combination of living
quarters and workshop. Today's celebrated
Eskiltuna metalworking industry developed from
the forges. They and the town attached to them
were designed by the Royal architect, Jean de la
Vallée and were together given the name of Carl
Gustafs Stad. The earliest products included
knives, needles, stirrups, spurs, candlesticks,
awls, and locks and fittings.

Falun

Dalarna Museum

Dalarnas Museum, Stigaregatan 2–5,
S-791 21 Falun, Kopparbergs län
☎ 023 18160
May–Aug, Mon–Sat 11–5; Sun 12–5. Sept–Apr,
Mon–Thurs 12–7; Fri–Sun 12–5.

[F] 🛉 💻 ♿

The museum has been created in order to present aspects of the traditional culture of Dalarna. It has collections of costumes, painted furniture, folk music and musical instruments, handicrafts using copper, domestic equipment and popular art.

The Bergslag Ecomuseum is also administered from Dalarna Museum. It comprises a large area of central Sweden, characterised by the remains of the ironmining and ironworking industries which were of great importance in the area during the 18th and 19th centuries.

Some of these sites include a small museum and the task of the Ecomuseum is to publicise places of special interest and to federate them into a cohesive unit.

Falun Copper Mine

Stora Museum, S-791 80 Falun, Kopparbergs län
☎ 023 80427
May–Aug, daily 10–4.30. Sept–Apr, daily 12.30–4.30. Closed Jan 1, Good Fri, Midsummer Eve and Day, Dec 24, 25.
C ♦ ▆ ♠

Coppermining was being carried on here from c.1080 and by the 17th century the extraction and smelting of ore from the Great Copper Mountain (Stora Kopparberg) had become the most important industrial enterprise. In 1687 the rock wall between two adjacent pits collapsed, producing a gigantic pit 100 m deep and 300 m wide which is a major attraction today.

Subsequently, other products from the mine became more important then the copper. They included the red paint which gives Swedish farm buildings their characteristic appearance, iron, zinc, lead, and gold. The older parts of the mine were opened up to tourists in 1970 and receive 50,000 visitors a year. Today, the Stora Kopparberg Company combines mining, electric power generation, steelmaking and forestry operations and is one of the most important in Sweden.

The museum is in the company's former administration building, which dates from 1771–85. Its exhibits illustrate the history of mining, especially at Falun. It has models of the mine, some from the 1740s and includes models of mining inventions by Christopher Polhem (1661–1751). There are also examples of coins made of copper from the mine, an 18th-century mineral cabinet and a company charter of 1347.

Gammelstad

Hägnan Open-Air Museum

Friluftsmuseet Hägnan, S-954 00 Gammelstad, Norbottens län   ☎ 0920 51280
June 15–Aug 20, daily 10–5. Other times by telephone appt.
F ▆ ♠

The museum, opened in 1973, contains buildings brought from a number of sites in

Scale model of mining machinery. Falun Copper Mine.

Norbotten. It illustrates the living conditions of country people in the area during the 18th and 19th centuries and includes various types of farmhouse, a stable, a bakehouse, a cowhouse and a fisherman's cottage. Most of the exhibits are built of timber and the houses contain the appropriate painted wooden furniture and domestic equipment. The museum adjoins Gammelstads Kyrksted (Old Church Town) which has a medieval church and town plan and over 500 small 'church cottages' – churchgoers' lodgings – together with a number of houses from the 17th, 18th and 19th centuries.

Gävle

Railway Museum

Sveriges Järnvägsmuseum, Rälsgatan 1, Sörby Urfjäll, S-801 08 Gävle, Gävleborgs län
☎ 026 144596
May and Sept, Tues–Sun 1–4. June–Aug, daily 10–4. Oct–Apr, Thurs, Sat, Sun 1–4. Closed some public holidays.
C ♦ ▆ ♠

The museum, financed and administered by Swedish State Railways, was established in 1915 in Stockholm and moved to Gävle in 1970. The collections, which illustrate the history of railways in Sweden, are housed in two locomotive roundhouses. The exhibits include about 40 locomotives and 50 carriages; 16 of the locomotives are 100 years old, or even older, and five of these are still in working order. There are also many models of locomotives, train-ferries, bridges, stations and other railway buildings and collections of tickets, uniforms, badges and signalling equipment.

Silvanum Museum of Forestry

Skogsmuseet Silvanum, Kungsbäcksvaägen 32,
S-801 31 Gävle, Gävleborgs län
Tues–Sun 10–4

F ▯ & ▯

As anyone looking down on Sweden from an
aeroplane soon realises, a large part of the
country is covered by forests. This gives the
museum a special significance. Opened in 1961,
it is situated in the Valls Hage Arboretum,
which contains about 250 varieties of trees
which grow in Sweden, 70 kinds of shrub and a
rose collection. The displays tell the story of
silviculture and forestry in Sweden, past and
present, and show the processing of timber from
felling to the finished product.

Gothenburg

Historical Museum

Göteborgs Historiska Museum, Norra Hamngatan
12, S-411 14 Göteborg ☎ *031 612770*
May–Aug, Mon–Sat 12–4; Sun 11–5. Sept–Apr,
Tues–Sat 12–4; Sun 11–5; Wed also 6–9.

C ▯ ▮

The museum occupies part of a distinguished
building which dates from c.1756 and which was
constructed as a store and auction house for the
Swedish East India Company. During the
upheavals of the Napoleonic Wars the company
ceased to exist. The building then became a
State warehouse until 1861, when it was
converted for museum purposes. In addition to
the Historical Museum it now houses the city's
Archaeological and Ethnographical Museums.

Its collections illustrate the history, life and
culture of Western Sweden, especially
Gothenburg. There are interiors from the homes
of peasants and from 16th-, 17th- and 18th-
century middle-class houses, with collections of
furniture, clothing, household utensils, coins
and medals and religious art. The Swedish East
India Company has a place of honour in the
museum. There are collections of porcelain and
other objects brought back from the Far East by
the company's ships and a large collection of
heraldic china, imported from China by
Swedish noble families.

Maritime Museum and Aquarium

Sjöfartsmuseet med Akvariet, Karl Johansgatan
1–3, S-414 59 Göteborg ☎ *031 611000*
May–Aug, Mon–Sat 12–4; Sun 11–5. Sept–Apr,
Tues–Sat 12–4; Sun 11–5; Wed also 6–9.
Closed Good Fri, May 1, Midsummer Eve,
Dec 24, 25, 31.

C ▯ ▮

The museum's collections relate to the maritime
history of Sweden, especially Gothenburg.
There are sections devoted to the merchant
marine, the Navy, fishing and shipbuilding.
Special subjects include ships' figureheads, sea
transport between 900 and 1600, the 18th-
century Swedish East India Company, sailors'
souvenirs, portraits of ships, 19th-century
sailing ships, oceanography, lighthouses and
pilotage, Gothenburg harbour, the shipbuilding
yards of Gothenburg, and Swedish naval history
from 1600 onwards. The aquarium contains
both Nordic and tropical species of fish.

Military Museum

Götesborgs Militärmuseum, Box 7135,
S-402 33 Göteborg ☎ *031 612770*
Wed 7–9; Sat 1–34; Sun 12–3.

F ✍ ▯

The Kronan Fortress which contains the
museum dates from 1687 and has display
accommodation on three levels. The exhibits
illustrate military history, mainly Swedish, and
include an almost complete collection of
Swedish army uniforms, together with field
guns, hand weapons and other equipment from
the 17th century until the Second World War.

Museum of Theatre History

Teaterhistoriska Museet, Berzeliigatan,
S-412 53 Göteborg ☎ *031 209215*
Tues–Sat 12–4; Sun 11–5.
C

The museum, opened in 1957 is in the early-
19th-century Lorenburg theatre which was in
use until 1937. Its collections illustrate the
history of the theatre in Gothenburg from 1780
until the present day and include paintings,
portraits, models of sets, stage designs, theatre
programmes and reviews.

Röhss Museum of Arts and Crafts

Röhsska Konstlöjdmuseet, Box 53178,
S-400 15 Göteborg ☎ *031 200605*
May–Aug, Mon–Sat 12–4; Sun 11–5. Sept–Apr,
Tues–Sat 12–4; Sun 11–5; Wed also 6–9.
C ▯ ▮ & ▯

The museum was founded as a result of a bequest
to the city of Gothenburg in 1901 by two
brothers, August and Wilhelm Röhss. The
building, designed in a national romantic style,

**The uses of timber: a log cabin with shingled
roof and a fence of coppiced poles. Silvanum
Museum of Forestry, Gävle.**

was erected in 1912–14 and the museum was opened in 1916. Additions to it were made in 1937 and in the early 1960s.

It is the only museum in Sweden specialising in arts and crafts and industrial design. The collections are international, but mainly European and with Sweden strongly represented. The exhibits range from the Renaissance to the industrial design of the 1980s and include furniture, pottery, textiles, pewter, ironwork, bookbinding, silver and glass. There are room interiors, showing changes in European style. The Oriental collection is mainly from China and Japan.

Gustavsberg

Ceramics Centre

Keramiskt Centrum, Box 310,
   S-134 00 Gustavsberg, Stockholms län
   ☎ 0766 35650
Mon–Fri 10–5; Sat 10–3; Sun 11–3. Closed
   Midsummer Day, Dec 24, 31.
🄵 🛆 ⬛ ♿

Porcelain has been made at Gustavsberg since 1825. From the 1860s the factory produced bone china, white porcelain figures and colour glazed majolica; from c. 1900 imitations of Wedgwood Jasper and tableware in Art Nouveau style. The museum contains examples of the factory's products from its beginnings until the present day and illustrates the techniques involved. There are reconstructions of old workshops and visitors can also see the housing provided by the company for its workers in the 19th century.

Ceramics Centre, Gustavsberg.

Halmstad

Halland Museum

Museet i Halmstad, Tollsgatan,
   S-302 31 Halmstad, Hallands län
   ☎ 035 109480
Mon–Fri 10–4; Sat, Sun 12–4; Wed also 7–9.
   Other times by appt.
🄲 🛆 ♿ ♿

The museum, founded in 1886, moved into its own purpose-built building in 1933. It is concerned with the history and traditions of the county of Halland, and has sections dealing with prehistory, the Middle Ages, the history of Halmstad, handicrafts, trade and navigation. There is a large collection of 18th–19th-century peasant paintings on fabric and paper, with themes taken from illustrated bibles and prayer-books, together with woodcuts and church paintings. The museum also has a large and growing collection of works by contemporary Halland artists.

Hallandsgården

Galgberget, S-302 31 Halmstad, Hallands län.
   Correspondence to: Museet i Halmstad,
   Tollsgatan, S-302 31 Halmstad
   ☎ 035 109480
May–Sept, area open daily 1–6. Some buildings
   open 1–6 between June 12 and Aug 13.
   Between June 29 and Aug 18, also Wed 1–9.
🄵 ⬙ ♿

This open-air museum was established in 1925. Its purpose was to preserve and display some of the earlier rural buildings in Halland – a wooden cottage with a hole in the roof instead of a chimney, a farmstead, a windmill, a watermill and several other small houses from different parts of Halland. The museum was also seen as a place where traditional customs and skills could be kept alive. Later additions include a waterdriven sawmill, a barn, a storehouse, and a school. The buildings are all appropriately furnished and equipped.

Härnösand

Murberget Museum

Länsmuseet Murberget, Box 2007,
   S-871 02 Härnösand, Västernorrlands län
   ☎ 0611 23240
June 28–Aug 6, daily 11–5. Other times by appt.
🄵 🛆 ⬛ ♿ ♿

The Västernorrlands Museum Society was founded in 1880, with the aim of building up a museum of antiquities and natural history. These collections were arranged in the Provincial Government building in Härnösand. In 1913 a beginning was made with an open-air museum outside the town at Murberget. This now has more than 80 buildings from the province, including farmhouses, a school, a fishing shed and the old town hall of Härnösand.

Examples of Sámi (Lapp) craftwork. Ájtte
Mountain and Lapp Museum, Jokkmokk.

Helsingborg

Frederiksdal Open-Air Museum

*Frederiksdals Friluftsmuseum och Botaniska
Trädgård, Box 1283, S-251 12 Helsingborg,
Malmöhus län*   ☎ 042 105959
May–Sept, daily 10–6
© 🛈 💷 🚶

Frederiksdal manor house was built in 1787 for
Frederik Wilhelm Cöster. In 1918 it was
donated to Helsingborg by Mrs Gisela Trapp in
memory of her husband, who had been one of
the founders of modern Helsingborg, with the
stipulation that the town should create an
open-air museum which would reflect the
culture of north-west Scania and that an
adjoining botanical garden should be established
containing all the wild plants of Scania. Both of
these wishes have been carried out.

The Open-Air Museum has a wide range of
both town and country buildings including a
section of central Helsingborg consisting of
buildings from different sites and farms and the
town's former rectory. The botanical gardens are
the only ones in Scandinavia which illustrate
the plants of a single country.

Vikingsberg Art Museum

*Vikingsbergs Konstmuseum, Vikingsbergsparken,
Box 1283, S-251 12 Helsingborg, Malmöhus
län*   ☎ 042 105988
*May–Aug, Mon–Sat 11–6; Sun 12–6. Sept–Apr,
Tues–Sat 11–4; Sun 12–4.*
© 🛈

Vikingsberg was built in 1875 in the classical
style as a private mansion. It was subsequently
acquired by the municipality and has served as
its art museum, since 1929. There are
collections of European paintings, sculpture and
furniture from the 17th century to the present
day, including portraits by Frans Hals (1581–
1666) and the Swedish artist, Alexander Roslin
(1718–93). There are also 19th–20th-century
Swedish paintings, including a number of
contemporary works by artists from north-west
Scania.

Höganäs

Höganäs Museum

*Höganäs Museum, Polhemsgatan 1,
S-263 37 Höganäs, Malmöhus län*
☎ 042 41335
Mar–Dec, Tues–Sun 1–5
© 🛈

The museum is run by the Manufacturing and
Craft Association of Höganäs. It occupies a
former industrial building, dating from 1814,
which contains a miner's flat from the same
period. The collections illustrate the history of
Höganäs, with special reference to its mining
and pottery industries. There are examples of
ceramics made by the local firm, Höganäs AB,
between 1830 and 1950 and regular exhibitions
of 20th-century ceramics from the Nordic
countries. Sections of the museum are devoted
to the work of the court photographer, Peter P.
Lundh, with a reconstruction of his studio, and
to the 19th-century ethnologist, Nils Månsson
Mandelgren.

Hudiksvall

Hälsingland Museum

*Hälsinglands Museum, Storgatan 31,
S-824 00 Hudiksvall, Gävleborgs län*
☎ 0650 19600
*May–Aug, Mon–Fri 9–7; Sat, Sun 10–4. Sept–
Apr, Mon–Fri 9–4; Sat, Sun 12–4.*
Ⓕ 🛈 ♿ 🚶

The museum was created in 1904 by the
Archaeological Society of Hälsingland and was
first housed in the old hospital and then, in
1937, in a former bank. In 1949 it was given to
the town. Sections of the museum are devoted
to medieval religious sculpture, local
shipbuilding and seafaring, the fishing industry,
the development of the town, handicrafts and
industries and peasant furniture and tapestries.
There are also collections of glass, ceramics and
pewter and paintings by John Sten (1879–1922)
and other Swedish artists.

Jokkmokk

Ájtte Mountain and Lapp Museum

*Ájtte Svenskt Fjäll- och Samemuseum, Kyrkogatan
3, S-960 40 Jokkmokk, Norbottens län
Correspondence to: Box 116,
S-960 40 Jokkmokk.*   ☎ 0971 17070
*June 15–Aug 15, Mon–Fri 9–7; Sat, Sun 11–7.
Aug 16–June 14, Mon–Fri 9–4; Sat, Sun
12–4.*
© 🛈 💷 ♿ 🚶

'Ájtte' is the Sámi (Lapp) word for storage shed.
The museum has taken this name because, as for
an *ájtte*, it collects and preserves objects,
knowledge, experience and traditions. It
specialises in the natural history and culture of
the Swedish mountain area and it is the
principal museum for the Sámi culture in
Sweden. The emphasis of the museum is on

ecology and the interplay of man and nature. The exhibits include silver spoons and cups, a magic drum, log houses and a *goatti* (nomadic family's tent), together with examples of modern Sámi handicrafts. The museum is the focus of an annual fair, which has been held in Jokkmokk for nearly 400 years.

Jönköping

Jönköping Museum

Jönköpings läns Museum, Box 2133,
   S-550 02 Jönköping, Jönköpings län
   ☎ 036 160010
Museum: Mon, Wed, Fri 11–4; Tues, Thurs
   11–8; Sat 11–3; Sun 1–5. Open-Air Museum;
   June-Aug, same times. Closed some public
   holidays.

Ⓕ 🛈 💻 👆 🚶

The museum's collections present the cultural history of the county of Jönköping. There are exhibits of medieval and later crafts, especially ironworking, native art, ceramics and Swedish art, with an emphasis on works produced at the turn of the century. There is also a large collection of works by John Bauer, the celebrated illustrator of fairytales.

Match Museum

Tändsticksmuseum, V. Storgatan 18a,
   S-551 89 Jönköping, Jönköpings län
   ☎ 036 105543
Jan–Mar and Nov–Dec, Tues 3–7; Thurs–Sun
   11–3. Apr 1–June 11 and Sept–Oct, Tues,
   Wed 1–5; Sat 1–7; Sun 11–3. June 12–Aug
   31, Mon–Fri 10–5; Sat 10–7; Sun 10–3.
   Closed public holidays.

Ⓒ 🛈 🚶

The museum is in Jönköping's first match factory. It was founded by J. E. Lundström in 1848 and achieved world renown for the production of safety matches from 1852 onwards. The exhibits illustrate the history of matchmaking and the factory, and show the living and working conditions of the employees. There are examples of matchmaking machinery and of the equipment used for fire-making before the invention of matches, as well as collections of matchboxes and labels.

Julita

Julita Agricultural Museum

Julita, Sveriges Landbruksmuseum, Nordiska
   Museet, Julita gård, S-640 25 Julita,
   Södermanlands län
Apr 29–June 4 and Aug 21–Sept 30, Sat, Sun and
   public holidays 11–5. June 5–Aug 20, daily
   11–5.

Ⓒ 🛈 💻 🚶

Julita is an estate of 2,400 hectares, with 350 buildings. It was bequeathed to the Nordic Museum in Stockholm in 1944 and is now run as an independent branch, comprising the manor house, a separate museum with furniture collections, a small open-air museum, a dairy

Fairy-tale illustration, 1912, by John Bauer. Jönköping Museum.

museum in the 1884 estate dairy and a fire-brigade museum. One of the three largest agricultural collections in the world is at Julita. It is at present stored, awaiting the construction of a building to display it. Julita also has a gene-bank for old varieties of apples and pears and has notable collections of rhubarb, hops and old varieties of cereals.

The manor house was rebuilt in the mid 18th century. It is shown to visitors as it looked c. 1900. A museum was built in the park in 1926–30, by Arthur Bäckström, the last private owner of the estate. It contains a number of room interiors and a section devoted to Henning Forsman (1870–1956), the estate cabinet-maker, who made much of the furniture for the manor house. The open-air museum, also created by Arthur Bäckström, has 10 buildings, mostly from the estate.

Karlskrona

Blekinge Museum

Blekinge läns Museum, Fisktorget 2,
   S-371 22 Karlskrona, Blekinge län
   ☎ 0455 80120
July–Aug, Mon–Fri 9–6; Sat, Sun 1–5. Sept–
   June, Mon–Fri 9–4; Sat, Sun 1–5.

Ⓕ 🛈 💻 👆

The Wachtmeister Palace, which houses the museum, was built in 1705 for Admiral Count Hans Wachtmeister. It has a Baroque garden. The property became a national monument in 1967 and has housed the Museum since 1977. The collections illustrate the cultural history of the province. An important section is devoted to fishing and the processing of fish – there is a fishball-making machine from the 1920s – and the museum is responsible for one of the largest collections of peasant boats in Sweden. There are also exhibits relating to prehistory, stone quarrying, boat and shipbuilding, navigation, medieval church art, textiles, 18th–19th-century embroidery and household enamelware.

The museum also has an open-air section at Vämö Park, which has 15 buildings from different parts of the Province.

Naval Museum

Marinmuseum, Amiralitetsslätten,
S-371 30 Karlskrona, Blekinge län
☎ 0455 84000
July, daily 12–8. Aug–June, daily 12–4.
Ⓒ ⓘ ⌂

Karlskrona has Sweden's most important naval dockyard and the town has developed around it. The Naval Museum, which dates from 1752, is one of the oldest in Sweden. Its present aim is to illustrate Swedish naval development in general and in particular to show the life and work of previous generations in the naval dockyard. There are sections devoted to the history of the town and the dockyard, to shipbuilding, cooperage, mast-making, rigging and tackle-making, rope-making, figureheads, uniforms, crime and punishment in the navy, weapons, naval technology, military music and food on board. A special exhibition deals with the achievements of the great 18th-century shipbuilder at Karlskrona, Fredrik Henrik af Chapman, who developed a method of series-construction for warships, by which the time for laying the keel to launching was reduced to 45 days.

Kungsgården

Rosenlöf Printing Works

Bröderna Rosenlöfs Tryckeri, Bruksgrafiskt
Museum, Rosenlöfs Tryckeri, Fack 46,
Korsikavägen 26, S-812 03 Kungsgården,
Gävleborgs län ☎ 029 037618
May, June and Sept, Sat, Sun 11–5. July–Aug,
daily 11–5. Groups throughout year by appt.
Ⓒ ⓘ ▣ ⌂

In 1880 the Rosenlöf brothers, Helmer and Ruben, founded their printing works in Kungsgården. They were jobbing printers and ran a book-bindery and a stationer's shop on the same premises. The business was at its peak in the 1920s and 1930s when it employed about 15 people. When it closed in 1974 it was bought by the municipality and preserved intact as a museum. The works underwent little change after the turn of the century and shows a working environment typical of the industry in

Display of fishing. Blekinge Museum, Karlskrona.

the years between the age of craftsmanship and the arrival of the computer. An attempt has been made to give the visitor the impression that work has just stopped for the weekend on a Friday evening.

Kyllaj

Strandridaregården

Strandridaregården Kyllaj, Hellvi, S-620
34 Lärbro, Gotlands län. Correspondence to:
Box 35, S-620 35 Fårösund, Götlands län
☎ 0498 21018
June 15–Aug 15, daily 1–5. Other times by
telephone appt.
Ⓒ ⓘ

The manor house was built in 1730 for the Customs officer and ex-cavalry officer, Johan Ahlbom, on his marriage at the age of 50 to the 15-year-old daughter of the richest man on the island. Ahlbom was the owner of several limekilns on the island. He was wealthy and, as the decorations and furnishings of the house show, he lived in considerable style. Since 1945 the house has been a museum and an outstation of the main museum at Bunge.

Lidingö

Carl Milles's House

Millesgården, Carl Milles väg 2, S-181 34 Lidingö,
Stockholms län ☎ 08 7315060
May–Sept, daily 10–5. Oct–Apr, Tues–Fri 11–3;
Sat, Sun 11–4.
Ⓒ ⓘ ⌂

Carl Milles (1875–1955), one of Sweden's most famous sculptors, bought a plot of land on the island of Lidingö and in 1908 he had a house and studio built there. He remained here at Millesgården until 1931, after which he spent 20 years in the United States. As time went on, he bought further land and expanded the estate in the form of terraces. The property was given to a foundation established in 1936 and is now one of Sweden's foremost tourist attractions.

Milles' collections of Greek and Roman antiquities, European paintings, Chinese statuettes and other works of art were bought by the Swedish State in 1948 and are displayed at Millesgården, together with many of his own works.

Lidköping

Museum of Handicrafts and Navigation

Lidköpings Hantverks och Sjöfartsmuseum,
Mellbygatan 9, Lidköping. Correspondence to:
Box 2097, S-231 02 Lidköping, Skaraborgs
län ☎ 0510 83065
Tues–Fri 12–4; Thurs also 4–7; Sat 10–2; Sun
12–6.
Ⓕ ⓘ ⌂

Lake Vänern, 100 miles long and 50 miles wide, is the largest lake in Sweden and has been an important inland transport route for centuries, with a number of important towns, including Lidköping, situated on its shores. The museum presents the history of shipping and navigation on Lake Vänern and has exhibits of the crafts connected with shipping. The museum building, which dates from 1877, was originally a girls' school and is significant as a school building of this period.

Linköping

Museum of Military Aviation

Flygvapenmuseum, Box 13300,
  S-580 13 Linköping, Östergötlands län
  ☎ *013 283567*
June–Sept, daily 12–4. Oct–May, daily 12–3.
  Other times on request. Closed Jan 1, Good
  Fri, Easter Sat, May 1, Midsummer Eve,
  Dec 24, 25 31.
F 🛈 💺 ♿

This State-owned musuem was opened to the public in 1984 and was doubled in size in 1989. It is close to a military air base. The exhibits illustrate the history of the Swedish Air Force and include some very rare aircraft, a Nieuport IV G, a Macchi M 7, and a Fokker CVE.

Old Linköping

Gamla Linköping, Kryddbodtorget 1,
  S-582 46 Linköping, Östergötlands län
  ☎ *013 206550*
May–Aug, daily 10–5, with guided tours and
  admission to house interiors. Sept–Apr, general
  area only open.
C 🛈 💺 ♿

This is not an ordinary open-air museum. During the 1940s the population of Linköping increased by 50 per cent, largely as a result of the expansion of the Saab factories. Because the traditional 18th- and 19th-century buildings were being replaced by modern shopping centres and housing, 80 of them, from the heart of the town, were moved out to form Old Linköping, placed in a street pattern which has been copied from the town centre. Old Linköping shows what a Swedish provincial town looked like in the second half of the 19th century. The street, lighting, fences, signs, trees, flowers and buildings reproduce the everyday urban environment of the day. Each building is fully documented. Over 50 people live in the houses, and craftsmen have their workshops here and sell their products.

Östergötland Museum

Östergötlands läns Museum, Vasavägen 16,
  S-581 02 Linköping, Östergötlands län
  ☎ *013 230300*
June–Aug, Tues 12–9; Wed–Sun 12–4. Sept–
  May, Tues–Thurs 12–9; Fri–Sun 12–4.
  Closed Good Fri, Easter, May 1, Whitsun,
  Midsummer Eve and Day, Dec 24, 25, 31.
F 🛈 💺 ♿

Gerda, Erik and Donatello, 1933, by Arvid Fougstedt. Östergötland Museum, Linköping.

The museum in Linköping was established early, in 1864. In 1939 it moved into a specially-designed building, architecturally interesting as a good example of late functionalism. An additional exhibition hall, also architecturally significant, was added in 1989. The collections are primarily concerned with the history and traditions of Östergötland and particularly with the agricultural and fishing communities. 17th–19th-century country furniture and regional costumes are well represented and there are sections which illustrate the more bourgeois culture of the town. There are also collections of 12th–20th-century European paintings and sculptures including medieval religious vestments and liturgical objects. Two of the museum's most valued possessions are a painting by Lucas Cranach the Elder, *The Fall of Man* (c. 1530) and a Romanesque crucifix of c. 1150.

Ljusdal

Ljusdal Museum of Rural Life

Ljusdalsbygdens Museum, Kyrkogatan 26,
  S-827 00 Ljusdal, Gävleborgs län
  ☎ *0651 11675*
Tues–Fri 11–4; Sat, Sun 1–4.
F 🛈 ♿

Opened in 1963, in a building created for the purpose, the museum belongs to and is run by a foundation. It is concerned with the traditional culture of the Hälsingland region, an area of farms and forests. There are collections of furniture and domestic equipment, especially objects made of wood, handicrafts, textiles and textile manufacturing equipment, costumes and farm and forestry tools and implements. There is also a large photographic archive, illustrating life and work in the region during the 19th and early 20th centuries.

Ludvika

Mining Museum

Ludvika Gruvmuseum, Ludvika Gammelgård,
*   S-771 03 Ludvika, Kopparbergs län*
*   ☎ 0240 10019*
Open-air section permanently open. June 15–Aug
*   15, guided tours daily. At other times by*
*   arrangement.*

Ⓒ ⓘ ⬛ ⬃

This open-air museum is in two parts, divided by
a railway, reflecting the fact that mining in
Sweden, which meant mining metallic ores, not
coal, was a rural activity, in which it was normal
for miners to be farmers as well. The first part of
the museum, through which visitors enter, is
arranged as a farm, with stable, cowshed and
barns. To reach the mining museum one has to
cross the railway. In the mining section there
are 21 buildings which have been brought to the
site from elsewhere. They include waterwheels,
a horse-windlass, a pump-house, the pithead
building, a crusher, a concentration mill, a
conveyor, a compressor house, various
storehouses and an office. There is also a typical
19th-century miner's dwelling, built of timber
and consisting of one room and a kitchen,
furnished and equipped as it would have been at
the turn of the century.

Lund

Kulturen Museum

Kulturen, Tegnérsplatsen, S-221 04 Lund,
*   Malmöhus län   ☎ 046 150480*
May–Sept, daily 11–5. Oct–Apr, daily 12–4.
*   Closed Good Fri, Easter Eve, Midsummer Eve,*
*   Dec 24, 25, 31.*

Ⓒ ⓘ ⬛ ⬃

Kulturen, 'The Culture', was founded in 1882
by one of the great Swedish museum pioneers,
George Karlin, to collect and preserve objects
illustrating the cultural history of southern
Sweden. Material from the Middle and Far East
was added for comparative purposes. In 1892,
the collections found a permanent home in the
centre of the medieval city, where a house and
its large garden were acquired and an open-air
museum begun. Its first four buildings illustrated
the lifestyle of the four estates of the realm, the
nobility, the burghers, the clergy and the
peasants. Karlin was the first person to bring a
town house to a museum. He further built up an
entire urban quarter here and in this he
anticipated Skansen in Stockholm, where a
similar area was not created until 1932.
    In 1926 the adjoining 'White House' was
purchased and is now the main museum
building. A Textile Hall was opened in 1961.
The museum has large collections of
Scandinavian folk costumes, uniforms,
furnishing fabrics and items which reflect the
various forms of peasant culture in Sweden –
farming, fishing, handicrafts and
communications. There are also reconstructed
house interiors.

Lycksele

Forestry Museum

Skogmuseet, Gammplatsen, S-921 00 Lycksele,
*   Västerbottens län   ☎ 0950 37945*
June and Aug, daily 10–6. July, daily 10–8.
*   Sept–May, Mon–Fri 11–5; Sat, Sun 12–4.*
*   Other times by appt.*

Ⓒ ⓘ ⬛ ⬥ ⬃

For Lycksele, as for Västerbotten as a whole,
forestry is of great importance. Three of the
major forest companies have their
administrative offices in Lycksele and a high
proportion of the town's inhabitants are directly
or indirectly employed in the industry. The
exhibitions and activities of the museum, which
was opened as a county and municipal enterprise
in 1984, aim at spreading and gathering
knowledge of the history of forestry, especially
in northern Sweden.
    There are sections devoted to forest
workers' smallholdings, grazing in the forests,
the huts in which forest workers lived, the old
techniques of tree felling, haulage roads, horse-
drawn timber-sledges, power-saws, reforestation
and trade unions.

Malmö

Maritime Museum

Malmö Sjöfartsmuseum, Malmöhusvägen 7,
*   S-201 24 Malmö, Malmöhus län*
*   ☎ 040 344453*
May–Aug, Mon–Wed, Fri, Sat 12–4; Thurs
*   12–9; Sun 12–4.30. Sept–Apr, Tues, Wed,*
*   Fri, Sat 12–4. Thurs 12–9; Sun 12–4.30.*
*   Closed public holidays and preceding day.*

Ⓒ ⓘ ⬛ ⬃

The museum deals with the history of seafaring,
shipping and navigation in southern Sweden.
There are sections devoted to the development
of harbours in the region from 1600 to the
present day, to the fishing industry, to
lighthouses and beacons, to ferries and to
pilotage. Visitors can also see the interior of the
U3 submarine, launched in 1943. There are
replicas of Viking and pirate ships for children
to climb aboard.

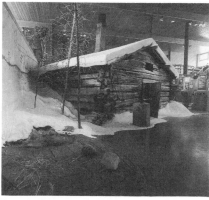

Forestry Museum, Lycksele.

Microscope, 18th-century, taken to Sweden from Britain by the scientist, Mårten Triewald. Technical Museum, Malmö.

Technical Museum

Malmö Tekniska Museum, Malmöhusvägen 7, S-201 24 Malmö, Malmöhus län
☎ 040 344438
May–Aug, Mon–Wed, Fri, Sat 12–4; Thurs 12–9; Sun 12–4.30. Sept–Apr, Tues, Wed, Fri, Sat 12–4; Thurs 12–9; Sun 12–4.30. Closed public holidays and preceding day.
Ⓒ ▯ ☕ ☞

The museum has a collection of 17th–18th-century scientific instruments, including the original of von Guericke's air-pump, made in the 1650s. There are historical scenes with wax figures of famous scientists and inventors, including Otto von Guericke (1602–86), Tycho Brahe (1546–1601) and Mårten Triewald. There are also exhibits of aviation history, steam-engine and automobile technology, horse-drawn trams, cars and motorcycles.

Norrköping

Dyers' Houses

Färgargården, St Persgatan 3, Norrköping. Correspondence to: Stadsmuseum, Västgötegatan 19–21, S-602 21 Norrköping, Östergötlands län ☎ 011 152640
May 1–Sept 15, daily 12–4
Ⓕ ▯ ☕ ☞

The Dyers' Houses constitute an open-air museum close to the Motala river, to the west of Norrköping. They show how the local dyers lived and worked in the mid 19th century. The buildings consist of a dwelling-house, a shop, a stable, a summer-house, a dyeing-house, a milling-house and a pressing-house. There is also a small garden, which grows herbs and plants used in dyeing. The museum has collections of the tools and equipment belonging to the dyers.

Norrköping Museum

Norrköpings Stadsmuseum, Västgötegatan 19–21, S-602 21 Norrköping, Östergötlands län
☎ 011 152620
Mon, Wed, Fri 10–4; Tues, Thurs 10–8; Sat, Sun 12–4. June 15–Aug 15, times as above, except Tues 10–4. Closed public holidays.
Ⓕ ▯ ☕ ☞

During the 19th century Norrköping developed as a major centre of the Swedish and European textile industry, originally as a result of the water-power provided by the river. In the 1860s it was the second largest industrial city in Sweden, but its reliance on the textile industry caused its economy to stagnate. The last large textile enterprise in Norrköping closed in 1970, leaving the city with a major planning problem, since many of the mills, factories and warehouses were of great architectural merit. To preserve the urban landscape, it was necessary to find new uses for these great industrial monuments and to create an informed public interest in the problems of conservation.

Norrköping Museum has played an important part in this. It occupies three old industrial buildings on the Motala river. Its exhibitions present the social and industrial history of Norrköping. There are sections dealing with the prehistoric and medieval periods, handicrafts, trades, the techniques and economic importance of the textile industry, labour conditions, domestic life and leisure activities.

The museum is also responsible for the care of the large number of Bronze Age rock-carvings found close to the city.

Örebro

Agricultural Museum

Landbruksmuseet, Karlslunds kvarn, S-700 00 Örebro, Örebro län   ☎ 019 272120
Jan–June and Aug 16–Dec 31, Mon–Fri 12–4.20; Sat, Sun 12–4. July 1–Aug 15, Mon–Fri 10–4.20; Sat, Sun 12–4. Closed public holidays.
Ⓒ ▯ ☕ ☞

The museum occupies a cornmill dating from 1881, which functioned commercially until 1975. For 50 years the machinery, which is still in place and in operating condition, was driven by a water-turbine, but in 1931 it was replaced by electric power. There is stabling for eight horses, which were used to haul corn from the railhead to the mill, and the premises also include a smithy, a storehouse, and sleeping accommodation for farmworkers who brought corn to the mill and took the meal and flour away.

The museum explains the techniques of milling and tells the story of the development of agricultural technology in the country of Örebro, by means of its comprehensive collection of tractors, farm machinery and equipment and vehicles.

Örebro Museum

Örebro läns Museum, Engelbrektsgatan 3, Örebro.
   Correspondence to: Box 314,
   S-701 46 Örebro, Örebro län
   ☎ 019 130095
Mon, Tues, Thurs–Sat 12–4; Wed 12–9; Sun
   12–5. Office hours 8–4 (including library and
   archives) Closed some public holidays.
F ♦ ⬛ ↩

The history of this large museum goes back to 1856. Until 1963, when a specially-designed building was opened, the collections were housed in the castle. The exhibits are now arranged in 21 galleries, with a courtyard garden used for sculpture exhibitions. The special areas are archaeology, arms and armour, coins and medals, musical instruments, toys, local history, religious art, ecclesiastical vestments, rural life, costumes, contemporary Swedish paintings and sculpture, and prints. Rooms are also devoted to Prince Eugène (1663–1736) and to Axel Borg.

Nearly all the old timber houses of Örebro have been replaced by modern buildings. Some of the best of the old houses have been re-erected on a pleasant site near the river to form a section of an 18th–19th-century provincial town, which has been given the imaginary name of Wadköping. Two of the houses have been converted into functioning workshops, one for a needle-maker and one for a shoemaker.

Technical Museum

Örebro läns Tekniska Museum, Hamnplan 1,
   S-702 12 Örebro, Örebro län
   ☎ 019 139920
Jan–June and Aug 16–Dec 31, Mon–Fri 12–4.20;
   Sat, Sun 12–4. July 1–Aug 15, Mon–Fri
   10–4.20; Sat, Sun 12–4. Other times by appt.
   Closed public holidays.
C ♦ ⬛ ↩

The museum, founded in 1967, is in an 1888 3-storey harbour warehouse. Örebro has been one of Sweden's principal industrial towns since the 17th century, when its gun factory was established. Örebro was also noted for its 80 shoe factories at the end of the 19th century and for its railway workshops and biscuit-making. It is now increasingly an educational centre. The museum has sections devoted to steam and electric power, gas and gas equipment, printing and bookbinding, automobile, marine and aircraft engines, shoemaking, woodworking, domestic equipment, mining, photography and medical equipment, all of which have played a rôle in the industrial development of Örebro and its region.

Örnsköldsvik

Örnsköldsvik Museum

Örnsköldsviks Museum, Läroverksgatan 1,
   S-891 33 Örnsköldsvik, Västernorrlands län
   ☎ 0660 88601
Tues, Wed 11–8; Thurs–Sun 11–4.
F ♦ ⬛ ↻ ↩

The museum presents regional cultural history from prehistoric times until the present day with about 14 temporary exhibitions a year in addition to its permanent displays. The collections include Stone Age tools found in the area, regional furniture from 1660 to 1800, agricultural implements, weaving and flax-processing equipment, and the tools and equipment of a shoemaker, joiner, watchmaker and dentist. There is also a notable collection of 17th–19th-century handicrafts, especially those using wood as a material, and reconstructions of a country kitchen and of the studio of the sculptor, Bror Marklund.

Oskarshamn

Döderhultar Museum

Döderhultarmuseet, Hantverksgatan 18,
   S-572 28 Oskarshamn, Kalmar län
   ☎ 0491 11725
June–Aug, Mon–Sat 9–6; Sun 11–4. Sept–May,
   Tues–Thurs 1–7; Fri–Sun 12–4. Groups daily
   9–7.
C ♦ ⬛ ↻ ↩

Axel Petersson, the woodcarver, was born in the parish of Döderhult and spent most of his adult life in Oskarshamn. He was nicknamed Döderhultar after he was discovered and his genius recognised at a caricature exhibition in Stockholm in 1908. He worked best in alder and succeeded in conveying the essential characteristics of poor peasants, especially their early ageing as a result of hard living conditions, and their submission to authority. His figures are painted in subdued colours, mostly black and ochre. They are usually 20–30 cm high and arranged in groups. It is in the combination of figures that he brings out the burlesque or tragic quality of the situation.

The museum, established in 1976, has Sweden's only permanent collection of Döderhultar's work. The collection includes more than 200 sculptures and sculptural groups.

Örnsköldsvik Museum.

Maritime Museum

*Oskarshamns Sjöfartsmuseum, Hantverksgatan
18–20, S-572 00 Oskarshamn, Kalmar län*
☎ 0491 11725
*June–Aug, Mon–Sat 9–6; Sun and public holidays
11–4. Sept–May, Tues–Thurs 1–7; Fri–Sun
12–4. Closed Jan 1, Good Fri, Easter Eve and
Day, Dec 24, 25, 31.*
ⓒ ⓘ ⓖ ⓐ

Fishing and seafaring were the main occupations
of the inhabitants of Oskarshamn for many
generations and in the 1930s an association was
formed to collect historical material relating to
these activities and eventually to display it in a
museum, which was opened in 1976. The
collections illustrate the history of shipping,
shipbuilding and fishing in the area since Viking
and medieval times. The exhibits include maps,
models and paintings of ships, navigational and
fishing equipment, sailmaking and shipbuilding
tools, material relating to the harbour at
Oskarshamn, the contents of seamen's chests,
medicaments used on board and the clothing
worn by seamen. There are also portraits of
noted local captains and shipowners.

Östersund

Jämtland Museum

*Jämtlands läns Museum, Box 650, Museiplan,
S-831 27 Östersund, Jämtlands län*
☎ 063 127125
*Mon–Fri 9–4; Sat, Sun 12–4; Tues also 4–9.
Closed Good Fri, Dec 24, 25.*
Ⓕ ⓘ ⓛ ⓖ ⓐ

The museum is concerned with rural life and
traditions in Jämtland. Its best-known exhibit is
the early-12th-century Överhogdal tapestry,
one of Sweden's great cultural treasures, with
designs illustrating the period of change from
heathen times to Christianity. There is also a
large collection of textiles from the region, for
everyday use and for festive occasions, and made
from flax, hemp, wool and other fibres. They are
accompanied by exhibitions of spinning and
weaving. A section is devoted to folk music in
the area. The prehistoric and early historic
displays show the development of Jämtland from
the Stone Age to the Middle Ages. The exhibits
show what a Stone Age dwelling looked like,
what prehistoric tools were used for, how iron
was made, what was used for currency in the
Iron Age and how the Vikings dressed. A
section is devoted to the Great Lake Monster of
Östersund.

Jamtli

*Jamtli Historieland, Jämtlands läns Museum, Box
650, Museiplan, S-831 27 Östersund,
Jämtlands län*   ☎ 063 127125
*June 23–Aug 13, daily 11–6. The museum area
and restaurant are open all year, but the houses
are only open during the summer. Also open
during special events and holidays.*
ⓒ ⓘ ⓛ ⓖ ⓐ

Jamtli is an open-air museum. The buildings
brought to the site include two complete groups
of farm buildings, one dating from 1785, the
other from 1895, a mountain shieling, a forest
hamlet, an inn (1820) and a general store,
complete with contents, of 1900. Other exhibits
include a watermill, an 18th-century gunsmiths'
shop, a sheep-barn, a cottage in which pilgrims
used to rest on their way to the grave of St Olaf
in Trondheim, and a forest-workers' hamlet,
with a lodge in which up to 20 foresters and
horse-drivers lived. The museum has its own
livestock and the houses are inhabited by
costumed employees, who cultivate the
farmland, look after the animals and
demonstrate their craft skills.

Ransäter

Geijer's House

*Geijersgården, Ransäter, Box 6680,
S-684 00 Munkfors, Uppsala län*
☎ 0552 30039
May 15–Sept 15, daily 9–6. Other times by appt.
ⓒ ⓘ ⓛ ⓖ ⓐ

The historian, poet and composer Erik Gustaf
Geijer (1783–1847) was born in the manor
house at Ransäter, now called Geijer's House
(Geijersgården), and spent most of his
childhood and youth there. He was professor of
history at the University of Uppsala and has a
very distinguished place in the cultural history
of Sweden. Since 1912 the house has been
owned by an association of members of the
Geijer family, who have restored it to its
original condition. The contents reflect Geijer's
many-facetted life as an historian, literary
figure, musician and politician.

Sigtuna

Sigtuna Museum

*Sigtuna Museet, Stora Gatan 55,
S-193 00 Sigtuna, Stockholms län*
☎ 0760 51018
*May 15–Sept 15, daily 12–4. Sept 16–May 14,
Tues–Sun 12–4.*
Ⓕ ⓘ ⓛ ⓐ

**Överhogdal tapestry. Jämtland Museum,
Östersund.**

The main museum building at Stora Gatan 55 contains exhibits of local archaeological material from the Viking and medieval periods. The museum is also responsible for Sigtuna's former town hall, a charming 18th-century wooden building, which has been preserved intact, with its portraits, coats of arms and 18th-century furnishings, and for what is known as the Lundström House. Carl August Lundström (1844–1904) was born in Sigtuna and spent his whole life there, as a merchant, municipal treasurer, assessor at auctions and legal adviser. The house remained in private ownership until 1958, when it was left, together with its contents, to the town of Sigtuna. It is now used as a guide to middle-class life in the 19th and early 20th centuries. An adjoining hardware shop, also with its contents from the 1950s, forms part of the property.

Simrishamn

Gislöv Blacksmith's Museum

Gislövs Smidesmuseum, Gislöv,
*   S-272 92 Simrishamn, Malmöhus län*
*   ☎ 0414 25050*
June–Aug, daily 1–5.
Ⓒ 🛈 🚗

Gislöv is a village south-west of Simrishamn. In the former village school, a building dating from 1846, and in a group of outbuildings, there is now a museum which shows how a village blacksmith operated in the days before rural electrification in the 1920s and the standard and range of work of which he was capable. The smithy at Gislöv functioned until the 1940s and all its tools and equipment are now in the museum, as a unit. The 500 exhibits include locally-made agricultural, industrial and domestic tools and equipment and a wide variety of artistic items.

Stockholm

Drottningholm Theatre Museum

Drottningholms Teatermuseum, Filmhuset, Borgvej
*   5, S-102 51 Stockholm   ☎ 08 7590406*
May–Sept, daily 12–5.
Ⓒ 🛈 🚗

The theatre and the pavilion containing the permanent exhibition are in the grounds of the palace at Drottningholm, where the Royal Family has its residence. The exhibits in the museum tell the story of the theatre and, with the help of pictures and documents, set it within the context of the court and of the 18th-century theatre in Sweden.

Museum of Maritime History

Sjöhistoriska Museet, Museivägen 3,
*   S-115 27 Stockholm   ☎ 08 6664900*
Daily 10–5. Spring and Autumn, also Tues 6–8.30
*   pm. Closed Jan 1, May 1, Dec 24, 25, 31.*
Ⓒ 🛈 🚆 🚗

The museum has three sections, shipbuilding, the Mercantile Marine and the Navy. Each deals in detail with the developments of the 17th–20th centuries but the collection of models carries the story of Swedish ships back to the 10th century. Shipbuilding techniques during the 17th–18th centuries can be studied with the help of a fine series of models from the Royal dockyards. Sections of the hulls of old wooden ships provide evidence of the complex skill of the shipbuilders and reconstructions of the crews' quarters at different periods show the conditions under which sailors lived. There are also exhibits relating to Swedish harbours and to navigational instruments and their use.

Museum of Medieval Stockholm

Stockholms Medeltidsmuseum, Strömparterren,
*   Norrbro, Stockholm. Correspondence to: Box*
*   350, S-100 12 Stockholm   ☎ 08 7000500*
Jan–May and Oct–Dec, Tues–Sun 11–5; Wed also
*   5–8. May–Sept, Tues–Sun 11–5; Tues–Thurs*
*   also 5–7. Closed some public holidays.*
Ⓒ 🛈 🚆 🚗

The museum, entirely underground, was opened in 1986, on the site of large-scale excavations which were carried out in 1978–80. The entrance area is in the vaults underneath Norrbro (Northern Bridge) and the exhibition halls are new constructions underneath the Parliament buildings. The museum contains stretches of the early-16th-century city wall and other ancient monuments, finds from 50 years of archaeological investigations in Stockholm's medieval layers, and reconstructions of houses and the urban environment, in a dramatic setting. The Building Site illustrates medieval building techniques. The origins of the city and its early development are shown by means of maps and models of the area, and there is a section devoted to the Harbour, with its wharves, jetties, boathouse, warehouses and weighing office.

The Great House is a fanciful composition of various features of some of the best-preserved medieval buildings of Stockholm. The warship, 22 metres long, was excavated, together with a number of cannon, in the waterway leading to the city in 1930.

The building site: an exhibition of medieval building techniques. Museum of Medieval Stockholm.

National Museum of Antiquities

Statens Historiska Museum, Narvavägen 13–17,
  S-114 84 Stockholm   ☎ 08 7839400
Tues–Sun 11–4. During winter, also Thurs 4–8.
  Closed some public holidays, including Easter,
  May 1, Midsummer, Chrismas and New Year.

Ⓒ ⓘ ⚑ ♿ ♨

The museum dates from 1647. It has occupied
its present building since 1943. It is a central
museum of Swedish cultural history from the
Stone Age to the Reformation and for church
art for the subsequent period also. The museum
contains the Royal Coin Cabinet and the
National Museum of Coins, Medals and
Monetary History, presenting the monetary
history of Sweden over a period of 1000 years.
The collection of coins is the largest in the
world and that of banknotes is the oldest in
Europe.

Among the exhibits are a reconstruction of
an Iron Age house, Gotlandic picture stones,
rich collections from churches and monasteries,
spoils from the Thirty Years War in Germany, a
reconstruction of a small Swedish church
c.1500, and a large collection of medieval
church textiles of major international
importance.

Nordic Museum

Nordiska Museet, Djurgårdsvägen 6–16,
  S-115 21 Stockholm   ☎ 08 6664600
June–Aug, Mon–Wed, Fri 10–4; Thurs 10–8;
  Sat, Sun 12–5. Sept–May, Mon–Wed 10–4;
  Thurs 10–8; Sat, Sun 12–5. Closed some
  public holidays.

Ⓒ ⓘ ⚑

The aim of the museum is to provide an
introduction to the life and work of the Swedish
people from the end of the Middle Ages down to
our own times. It was founded by Artur
Hazelius, who was also responsible for the
pioneering Skansen open-air museum (1891).
The collections were opened to the public for
the first time in 1873. The present specially-
designed building was inaugurated in 1891.

The collections illustrate traditional
costumes, the farmer's household economy,
hunting and trapping, Lapp culture, fishing, the
guilds, seasonal activities and family occasions,
village, farm and work, food and drink, Nordic
folk art, textiles, Swedish homes, Swedish
furniture and toys.

Skansen

Skansen, Djurgården, S-115 21 Stockholm
  ☎ 08 6630500
Park: May–Sept, daily 9 am–10 pm. Oct–Apr,
  daily 9–5. Buildings: May–Sept, daily 11–5.
  Oct–Apr (certain buildings only), daily 11–3.
  Closed Dec 24.

Ⓒ ⓘ ⚑

Opened in 1891, Skansen, the brainchild of
Artur Hazelius, is the oldest open-air museum
the world. It has about 150 buildings of
historical, architectural and cultural interest

Southern City Hall, 1660–85, the museum
building of Stockholm City Museum.

from various parts of Sweden, representing both
town and country and different periods and
social contexts from the Middle Ages to the
present century. Each building is appropriately
furnished and equipped.

Regular demonstrations are given of 18 old
trades and handicrafts. Skansen also presents a
picture of the Swedish countryside and its
wildlife and is Stockholm's foremost centre for
national festivals and traditional seasonal
activities.

Stockholm City Museum

Stockholms Stadmuseum, Peter Myndes backe 6,
  S-116 46 Stockholm   ☎ 08 7000500
Jan–May and Sept–Dec, daily 11–5; Tues–Thurs
  also 5–9. June–Aug, daily 11–5; Tues–Thurs
  also 5–7. Closed Jan 1, Good Fri, May 1,
  Midsummer Eve and Day, Dec 24, 25, 31.

Ⓒ ⓘ ⚑ ♿

The Italian baroque-style building now housing
the museum was completed in 1685 as the town
hall of the district of Södermalm. The museum
was established in 1933, with the task of
providing documentation and information on
the city of Stockholm. Its staff take a leading
part in archaeological work in the city, and the
museum also serves as Stockholm's Board of
Antiquities.

The exhibits illustrate the development of
Stockholm since prehistoric times. Sections are
devoted to trades and crafts during the 15th–
18th centuries with models of city buildings in
this period, and to the development of the
industrial city during the 19th and 20th
centuries. There are reconstructions of domestic
interiors and working places at this time. The
museum has a large photographic archive and a
collection of topographical paintings and prints
showing the development of the city.

One of the museum's most popular features
is its programme of evening and Sunday walks in
Stockholm and its suburbs, which provide on-
the-spot information on the history of the city.

Vasa Museum

Galärvarvet, Djurgården, Stockholm.
  Correspondence to: Museivägen 3,
  S-115 27 Stockholm   ☎ 08 6664900
Mid June–mid Aug, daily 9.30–7. Mid Aug–mid
  June, daily 10–5. Closed Jan 1, May 1, Dec
  24–6, 31.
🅲 ⓘ ☕ ♿

The 64-gun warship, *Vasa*, sank near
Stockholm on her maiden voyage in 1628 and
was raised in 1961, together with her contents,
which are a remarkable source of information of
social and naval history. After conservation
treatment, much of it of a pioneering nature,
the ship and the objects on board are now
displayed in a striking copper-clad building,
completed in 1990, which provides a precise
micro-climate for the ship. The *Vasa*, of 1,200
tonnes and 60 m long is a notable example of
early-17th-century shipbuilding.

Wine and Spirit Museum

Vin & Sprithistoriska Museet, Dalagatan 100,
  S-113 43 Stockholm   ☎ 08 333255
Tues 10–7; Wed–Fri 10–4; Sun 12–4.
🅲 ⓘ ☕

Sweden, like other Scandinavian countries, has
attempted to control alcoholism by making the
supply of alcohol a State monopoly. The
Swedish Wine and Spirit Corporation organised
a museum in Stockholm in 1967 and redesigned
it in 1989, in the form of a Stockholm wine-
shop at the beginning of the present century. It
is housed in a wine-store dating from 1923. It
deals with the history of the wine and spirit
trade in Sweden and with legislation concerning
alcohol from the Middle Ages onwards. There

are exhibits relating to the history of wine-
making and of Swedish aquavit. Among the
items on display are a 1930 bottling machine
and a mechanical sniffing cabinet for schnapps
essence.

Sundborn

Carl Larsson's House

Carl Larsson-Gården, S-790 15 Sundborn,
  Kopparbergs län   ☎ 023 60053
May–Sept, Mon–Sat 10–5; Sun 1–5.
🅲 ⓘ ♨

The painter, Carl Larsson (1853–1919), is well-
known for his large-scale murals in public
buildings, but is particularly associated with
watercolours of every corner of his own home in
Sundborn. These were very popular in colour
reproductions and have had a lasting influence
on the Swedish attitudes towards furnishing and
interior decoration.

The wooden house was built in 1835 and
given to Carl Larsson by his wife's father and
mother in 1888. It was then furnished, with
plain, solid furniture and decorated in bright
colours in a style quite different from what
prevailed in Sweden at the turn of the century.
After the death of Karin Larsson in 1928, a
family association was formed to preserve the
house and its contents unchanged. The
members of the association, now numbering
c. 150, stay in the house as often as they can and
do their best to make sure that it remains a
living home, not a dead museum.

The studio. Carl Larsson's House, Sundborn.

Sundsvall

Open-Air Museum

Hantverks- och Friluftsmuseum, Norra
  Stadsberget, S-852 50 Sundsvall,
  Västernorrlands län   ☎ 060 111748
June 13–Aug 19, Mon–Fri 9–12, 12.30–6; Sat
  12–6. Aug 20–June 12, Mon–Fri 9–12,
  12.30–4; Sat 12–3; Sun 11–3.
Ⓕ 🔥 💼 ♿

Established in 1906, this is an early example of
an open-air museum in Sweden, founded as a
result of the first wave of enthusiasm after the
creation of the mother-museum, Skansen, in
Stockholm. The collections consist of arts and
crafts from the Sundsvall region, displayed in 34
traditional timber buildings, including a house
dated 1310 and a 1502 tithe barn. The exhibits
inside the buildings include material relating to
Sámi (Lapp) culture. Among the objects
displayed are items of household equipment,
weapons and craftsmen's tools, with
reconstructed workshops.

Sundsvall Museum

Sundsvalls Museum, Kulturmagasinet,
  S-851 96 Sundsvall, Västernorrlands län
  ☎ 060 191803
Mon–Thurs 10–8; Fri 10–6; Sat, Sun 11–4.
Ⓕ 🔥 💼 ♿ ♿

In 1888 a fire destroyed most of the wooden
buildings in Sundsvall. The wealth of the
merchants, based mainly on the local
sawmilling industry, made it possible to employ
the best architects for their new warehouses
when the town was rebuilt in brick and stone in
the 1890s. Four of these large warehouses have
been adapted to form Sundsvall's Cultural
Centre, the buildings and the streets between
them being given an all-over glass roof. The
whole unit now contains the museum, which
has both historical and art sections, the
Municipal Library, the Provincial Archives, a

Sundsvall Museum.

large café and extensive heated strolling-spaces.
The museum, which won the European Museum
of the Year Award in 1989, presents the social
and industrial history of Sundsvall and the work
of contemporary artists.

Tanum

Rock-Carvings Museum

Hällristningsmuseet vid Vitlycke, Tanum,
  S-457 00 Tanumshede, Göteborgs och
  Bohuslän   ☎ 0525 20950
May–June and Aug 15–Sept 15, daily 10–5. July
  1–Aug 14, daily 10–8.
Ⓒ 🔥 💼 ♿

The celebrated Tanum pictures, mostly of ships,
date from the Bronze Age and are c. 3,000 years
old. They were incised in exposed slabs of
granite and the outlines emphasised with red
colouring matter. A large thatched Bronze Age
house has been reconstructed near the pictures
and there are demonstrations of contemporary
technology, including the dressing of animal
skins, bronze-casting and pottery-firing.

Tärnaby

Sámi House

Sámigården, Tärna Sámiförening,
  S-920 67 Tärnaby, Västerbottnes län
  ☎ 0954 10440
June–Aug, daily 11–6
Ⓒ 🔥 💼 ♿

This is an exhibition relating to the Sámi
(Lapp) culture of the region. It aims to show
how the Lapp people have adapted themselves
to the environment and the climatic conditions;
their traditional methods of hunting, fishing,
constructing dwellings and housing themselves.
There are collections of 18th–19th century
objects illustrating the Lapps' way of life and
sections devoted to their religion and to the
education provided for their children.

Umeå

Västerbotten Museum

Västerbottens Museum, Gammlia,
  S-902 34 Umeå, Västerbottens län
  ☎ 090 118635
June–Aug, Mon–Fri 9–6; Sat, Sun 11–6. Sept–
  May, Mon–Fri 9–4; Sat 12–4; Sun 12–5.
  Closed Easter Sun, Dec 25, 31.
Ⓕ 🔥 💼 ♿ ♿

Gammlia is Umeå's open-air museum and was
started in the 1920s. The present arrangement
of buildings dates from the 1950s. It includes
traditional houses of different types and sizes
from the Umeå region, a chapel, a one-roomed
school, several farm buildings, a windmill, a
watermill and a bakery. There are also
exhibitions on fishing, seal-hunting and
navigation, which include a boathouse, a
lighthouse and the tugboat, *Egil*. The open-air

museum is open only during the June–August
period, when regional handicrafts are
demonstrated and farm animals are kept on the
site.

The indoor section of the museum, open all
the year round, has three exhibitions, each of
which presents three themes relating to the
cultural history of this northern part of Sweden,
linked under the general title of 'Once in
Västerbotten'. All of them are regularly
changed. They cover the natural environment
of the area, the prehistory – it has been
inhabited for at least 800 years – reindeer
breeding, the new 17th-century settlers, the
19th-century development of the city of Umeå,
and of agriculture, industrialisation, fishing,
seal-hunting and seafaring.

The ski museum (Skidmuseet), which forms
part of the museum, is notable. Among its
exhibits it has the oldest ski ever found, 5,000
years old.

Uppsala

Linnaeus's House

Linnés Hammarby, S-755 98 Uppsala
☎ 018 326094
*Park: May 2–Oct 1, daily 8–8. Museum: May
2–Oct 1, Tues–Sun 12–4.*
Ⓒ ⓘ 💻 ᴀ

In 1758, the great Swedish naturalist, known as
Carolus Linnaeus (1707–78), bought a farm at
Hammarby, 15 km south-east of Uppsala, as a
summer residence. Linnaeus was elevated to the
nobility in 1761 and assumed the name of Carl
von Linné. The soil in his botanic garden in
Uppsala was difficult to cultivate and he moved
some of the plants to Hammarby, including a
collection of Siberian plants given to him by the
Empress Catherine. He also built a small
museum at Hammarby, where he kept his great
botanical collections. They were, however,
attacked by moths and mice and after his
father's death, Linnaeus's son moved the
herbarium back to Uppsala.

In 1879 Hammarby was opened as a State
museum. It contains some of Linnaeus's
furniture, including his bed, writing table, one
of the herbarium cupboards and many portraits,
as well as paintings of his favourite pets. Much
of the original wallpaper survives, including that
in his study, with a pattern composed of famous
botanical illustrations.

Uppland Museum

*Upplandsmuseet, St Eriks gränd 6,
S-752 20 Uppsala*   ☎ 018 102290
*May–Sept, Tues–Sat 11–4; Sun 11–5. Oct–Apr,
Mon–Fri 12–4; Sat 11–4; Sun 12–5.*
Ⓕ ⓘ 💻

The museum, founded in 1909, is a cultural-
historical museum for the province of Uppland.
Since 1959 it has occupied the University's old
millhouse, the Academy Mill, which dates from
the 1760s. The collections illustrate the history
of the province and of Uppsala since medieval

Linnaeus's House, Uppsala.

times, with sections devoted to the natural
history of Uppland, popular art, including 18th–
19th-century paintings, folk music and musical
instruments, the University and its students,
and regional handicrafts and industries.

Varberg

Varberg Museum

*Museet i Varberg, Fästningen, S-432 44 Varberg,
Hallands län*   ☎ 0340 18520
*June 15–Aug 15, daily 10–7. Sept–May, Mon–Fri
10–4; Sat, Sun 12–4. Closed some public
holidays.*
Ⓒ ⓘ 💻

Varberg has one of the two county museums in
Halland. The museum, in the 13th–17th-
century castle of Varberg, presents the cultural
history of the town and the province, with
collections illustrating regional traditions
occupations and styles of living. Among the
exhibits is what is known as the Bocksten find, a
complete 14th-century costume, the only one
from this period which is known to have
survived anywhere in the world. The museum
also has the assassin's bullet which killed
Charles XI (1688–1718), putting an end to his
grandiose plans for an international alliance.

Västerås

Vallby Open–Air Museum

*Friluftsmuseum, S-722 11 Västerås,
Västmanlands län*   ☎ 021 161830
*Daily 7 am–10 pm. Guided tours daily in summer
at 1 and 4.*
Ⓕ ⓘ 💻 ᴀ

Vallby, established in 1921, is one of the largest
open-air museums in Sweden. It aims at being
'Västmanland in miniature' and it now contains
40 buildings brought from different parts of the
province, which give an impression of life in
Västmanland in the days before mechanisation
and industrialisation. They include different
types of houses, farm buildings, the county
executioner's house, stables, a school and a
mission hall. The town section has workshops of
a silversmith, brushmaker, potter and batik-
printer.

Uppland folk music exhibition. Uppland Museum, Uppsala.

Västmanland Museum

Västmanlands läns Museum, Slottet, S-722 11 Västerås, Västmanlands län ☎ *021 125154 May–Aug, Mon–Sat 12–5; Sun 1–4. Sept–Apr, Mon–Fri 12–4; Sat, Sun 1–4.*

F ℹ 🖤 🚗

The museum, opened in 1966, is in the town's square, courtyard-like castle, which was begun in the 13th century and given its present form in the 16th. Part of the buildings, notably the State Apartments, were restored after a serious fire in 1736. A spinning mill made use of the premises as a store during the early part of the present century.

The exhibits tell the story of Västmanland from prehistoric times onwards. There are departments devoted to the Stone, Bronze and Iron Ages, to weights and measures and the measurement of time, textiles, Swedish porcelain, agriculture, mining, ironworking estates and the Middle Ages, medieval wooden sculpture and the town's Dominican monastery.

Visby

Gotland Art Museum

Gotlands Konstmuseum, St Hansgatan 21, S-621 02 Visby, Gotland ☎ *0498 47090 May 15–Aug 31, daily 11–6. Sept–May 14, Tues 12–4, 7–9; Wed–Sun 12–4. Closed Good Fri, Easter Sun, Midsummer Day, Dec 24.*

C ℹ ♿

Opened in 1988 the museum occupies a former school building, which dates from 1845 and was the first publicly-provided school in Gotland. The collections illustrate the development of art in Gotland during the past 100 years, from the fashion for open-air painting in the 1880s to the much more varied situation today. An outstanding feature of the museum is the large collection of paintings, ceramics, sculpture and arts-and-crafts objects by the artist and designer, Tyra Lundgren (1897–1979).

Gotland Historical Museum

Gotlands Fornsal, Strandgatan 14, S-621 02 Visby, Gotland ☎ *0498 47010 May 15–Aug 31, daily 11–6. Sept–May 14, Tues–Sun 12–4.*

C ℹ 🖤

Founded in 1875, the Historical Museum is the oldest part of Gotland's County Museum. The main part of the building was originally a distillery and dates from the 1770s. The 13th-century block in the south-west corner was built as a storehouse. The museum is concerned with life in the region during the Stone Age and Viking periods and in the Middle Ages, with the development of agriculture, with domestic life 1500–1900, with shipping and with clothes. Three important sections are devoted to ecclesiastical art from 1050 until 1800.

Painting of a Paris garden, 1923, by Tyra Lundgren. Gotland Art Museum, Visby.

SWITZERLAND

Aigle

Museum of Wine

*Château d'Aigle, Musée Vaudois de la Vigne et du
Vin, Association pour le Château d'Aigle,
CP 453, CH-1860 Aigle, Vaud*
☎ *025 26 21 30*
Apr–Oct, daily 9–12.30, 2–6
Ⓒ ▯ ▱

In the 13th and 14th centuries the Château
d'Aigle was one of the advance strongholds of
the Dukes of Savoy. In 1475 it was almost
completely destroyed by the people of Bern,
who later rebuilt it as their governor's residence
and as a challege to Savoy. In 1798, after the
Canton of Vaud declared its independence, the
castle became the property of the town of Aigle,
which used it as a prison until 1972, when it was
restored and converted into a museum, both of
the history of the castle and of vineyard
cultivation and wine production in the region.

The castle is surrounded by large vineyards.
The collections of the museum include bottles
and measures, wine presses, inn signs, barrels,
pumps and cellar utensils, and works of art with
wine as a theme. There is also a reconstruction
of the dwelling of a 19th-century vine-grower
and exhibits explaining seasonal work in the
vineyards and the organisation of the vine-
growers' guild. Wine-tasting is one of the forms
of refreshment available to visitors.

Alberswil-Willisau

Swiss Museum of Agriculture

*Schweizerisches Museum für Landwirtschaft und
Agrartechnik 'Burgrain', CH-6248 Alberswil-
Willisau, Luzern* ☎ *045 71 28 10/81 20 77*
*Apr–Oct, Tues–Sun 2–5. Groups at other times by
appt.*
Ⓒ ▯ ▱ ▰

The museum was established in 1974 at
Burgrain. The principal building dates from
1870 and contains historical collections
illustrating the techniques and equipment
employed in Swiss farming and forestry. The
exhibits include farm vehicles, agricultural tools
and implements, tractors, sledges and peasant
handicrafts. Sections are devoted to fruit and
vineyard cultivation, beekeeping, Swiss
farmhouses, rural domestic life, cattle-breeding,
Alpine cheesemaking, milling and forestry.

Ascona

Monte Verità Museum

*Museo Monte Verità, Casa Anatta/Casa Selma/
Chiaro Mondo dei Beati, CH-6612 Ascona,
Ticino* ☎ *093 35 01 81*
Apr–Oct, Thurs–Sun 2.30–6
Ⓒ ▯

The museum is in the Casa Anatta, the former
home of the founder of the Tolstoyan 'life
reform' group, mostly from Germany and the
Netherlands, which settled on the Monte Verità
c.1900. The colony which they established
attracted naturists, vegetarians, anarchists,
theosophists, writers and artists from all over
Europe for more than 40 years. The museum
tells its story and illustrates the philosophy and
lifestyle of the people who found the Monte
Verità a congenial place to live.

Aubonne

Museum of Wood

*Arborétum du Vallon de l'Aubonne, Musée du
Bois, En Plan, CH-1170 Aubonne Vaud*
☎ *021 808 51 83*
Apr–Oct, Sun 2–6. Weekdays by appt only.
Ⓕ ▯ ▱ ▰

In 1973 an association was formed in Aubonne
to create and manage an arboretum 'for
scientific, educational and recreational
purposes'. The association bought and restored
an 18th-century farmhouse to serve as its
headquarters, together with surrounding land
and in 1977 established, as part of its
educational programme, a museum of the forest
industries and of trades using wood as a raw
material. There are collections of wooden
household utensils and of tools and equipment
used in forestry, logging and charcoal-burning,
as well as reconstructions of the workshops of a
number of skilled tradesmen, including a
carpenter, joiner, turner, cabinet-maker,
stringed instrument maker, cooper, clogmaker
and wagon-builder.

**The pleasures of hedonism: painted panels at
the Monte Verità Museum, Ascona.**

Basle

Basle Historical Museum

Historisches Museum Basel, Barfüsserkirche, Steinenberg 4, CH-4051 Basel
☎ 061 22 05 05
Wed–Mon 10–5. Closed Jan 1, Good Fri, May 1, Dec 24, 25, 31. Free admission Sun.
C

Since 1894, the museum has occupied the former Franciscan church, built in the 14th century. Its collections illustrate the art and cultural history of Basle and the Upper Rhine area since Celtic times.

The exhibits include medieval paintings, tapestries, furniture, and sculptures in stone and wood, goldsmiths' work, 15th–17th-century period rooms, 17th–18th-century Basle guild silver and other objects, 16th–17th-century painted glass, including items by Holbein the Younger, and coins. Much of the treasury of the Minster in Basle has been dispersed over the centuries, but a substantial proportion still remains in the city and is now in the Historical Museum.

One of the museum's particular treasures is the Amerbach Cabinet, which had its origins in the collection bequeathed to Bonifacius Amerbach by Erasmus of Rotterdam, who died in Basle in 1536. It became modern Europe's first civic-owned public museum, when it was bought by the government and University of Basle in 1561. The Faesch Museum, founded by Renigius Faesch (1595–1667) and acquired by the University in 1823, represents a later stage of the collection.

Museum of Basle

Stadt- und Münstermuseum, Unterer Rheinweg 26, CH-4058 Basel
☎ 061 681 07 07
Tues–Sat 2–5; Sun 10–5. Closed Jan 1, Good Fri, Easter Day, Pentecost, May 1, Dec 24, 25, 31.
C

The convent of Dominican nuns in Basle was founded in 1274. After the Reformation it served as almshouses and a hospital. In 1860 the cloisters and the nuns' quarters were demolished, but the church, the refectory, the kitchen and certain other buildings survived and the museum has occupied them since 1939. It contains models, plans and drawings illustrating the architectural history of Basle.

There is also an important collection of 11th–15th-century sculptures, both original and as casts, from the Minster, as well as its medieval stalls.

Swiss Jewish Museum

Jüdisch Museum der Schweiz, Kornhausgasse 8, CH-4051 Basel
☎ 061 25 95 14
Mon, Wed 2–5; Sun 10–12, 2–5. Closed Jewish holidays.
F

Silver Hannukah lamp. Swiss Jewish Museum, Basle.

The Jewish community in Switzerland dates back to the early 13th century. The first Zionist Congress, organised by Theodor Herzl, was held in Basle in 1897. The Basle Programme, approved by delegates to the Congress, was destined to play an important part in the development of the Zionist Movement. The museum, founded in 1966, presents the history of the city's Jewish community and has exhibits illustrating Jewish teaching, religious observance, festivals and daily life.

Bern

Art Museum

Kunstmuseum Bern, Hodlerstraße 8–12, CH-3011 Bern ☎ 031 22 09 44
Tues 10–9, Wed–Sun 10–5. Closed public holidays.
C

In 1879, the museum was established in a classical gallery built for the purpose. An extension was added in 1983. The collections include 15th–20th-century Swiss paintings, with an emphasis on works by Bern artists; Italian paintings, especially of the 14th century; and 19th–20th-century European paintings, particularly French and German. The section devoted to Paul Klee contains a large part of the works left by him, including 40 paintings and 2,200 drawings.

Bern Museum

Bernisches Historisches Museum, Helvetiaplatz 5, CH-3000 Bern ☎ 031 43 18 11
Tues–Sun 10–5
C

Founded in 1840, the museum has been in its present building since 1894. Its extensive collections illustrate the cultural history of the city and canton of Bern from the medieval period to the 19th century. There is also important prehistoric material, mainly from local excavations. There are exhibits of textiles, wrought iron, religious art, furniture, porcelain, faïence, costumes and musical instruments. The department of coins and medals is a large one, with its particular strengths in material from the Roman Republic, Switzerland and the Far East.

The museum also has large ethnographical collections, with material from Africa, South America, India, China, Japan and the Pacific.

Einstein's House

*Albert Einstein Haus, Kramgasse 49, CH-3011
    Bern* ☎ *031 21 00 91
Feb-Nov, Tues–Fri 10–5; Sat 10–4.*
F ♿

The physicist and mathematician, Albert Einstein (1879–1955), lived at Kramgasse 49 from 1903 to 1905, the year in which he published four of his most important works, including the *Special Theory of Relativity*. The apartment which Einstein occupied has been restored to its original condition and the museum also contains photographs and other pictures illustrating his life and career, together with documents and a small number of memorabilia.

Swiss Alpine Museum

*Schweizerisches Alpines Museum, Helvetiaplatz 4,
    CH-3005 Bern* ☎ *031 43 04 34
May 15–Oct 15, Tues–Sun 10–5. Oct 16–May
    14, Tues–Sun 10–12, 2–5. Closed public
    holidays.*
C ♿

The British Alpine Club was founded in 1857 and the Swiss Alpine Club followed six years later, and on a broader basis. In 1963, its centenary year, the Swiss Club had 44,649 members, organised in 92 branches. The museum was established in 1905 on the initiative of the Swiss Club. Its displays present the history and techniques of Alpine climbing, with sections devoted to equipment, rescue methods, maps and map-making, geology, glaciology and meteorology, as well as to the plants and wildlife of the Alps and the costumes, tools, and dairying and household equipment of Swiss peasants in the mountain areas.

Swiss Postal Museum

*Schweizerisches PTT-Museum, Helvetiastraße 14,
    CH-3006 Bern 031 62 77 77
Mon 2–5; Tues–Sun 10–5.*
C ♿ ▄

In 1990 this ever-expanding museum moved to new premises. On two floors it now presents exhibits illustrating the history of Swiss postal services and telecommunications. It has a comprehensive collection of Swiss postage stamps since 1843, and a very large collection of stamps from other countries, forming together what is claimed to be 'the largest stamp collection in the world'. A separate section deals with the history of tourism, including timetables, travel literature and information about hotels and resorts. Among the items on display in the museum are letter-sorting and franking machines, vehicles used by the Post Office at different periods, uniforms worn by postmen, telephone exchange equipment, radio and television sets, Morse code apparatus and telephone receivers from the earliest days.

Boudry

Museum of Wine

*Musée de la Vigne et du Vin, Château de Boudry,
    CH-2017 Boudry, Neuchâtel
    ☎ 038 42 10 98
Tues, Thurs, Fri 2–5; Sat 10–2, 2–5.*
C ▄ ↩

The museum, in the 13th-century Château de Boudry, which was restored by the Cantonal government in 1955–8, was created by a specially formed society of people connected with the production of wine in the area. There have been vineyards in Neuchâtel for 2,000 years. The museum tells the story of the industry and displays collections of tools and equipment used in vineyard cultivation and in wine production. Among the exhibits are a collection of 19th-century wine labels, paintings of vineyard scenes by Gustave Jeanneret and a tapestry by Jean Lurçat.

Solitary drinker, 1902, by Picasso. Art Museum, Bern.

Cowherd with yoked cattle. Museum of the
Gruyère District, Bulle.

Bourg-St-Pierre

Museum of the Great St Bernard Pass

Musée du Grand-Saint-Bernard, CH-1946 Bourg-
    St-Pierre, Valais   ☎ 026 87 12 36
June 15–Oct 15 (when access is possible) 8–7
Ⓒ ♟ ↩

The museum, created and administered by the
Hospice of the Great St Bernard Pass, was
opened in 1987. It tells the story of the Pass, the
route between Switzerland and Italy since
prehistoric times, and of the Hospice, founded
in 1050 by Bernard de Menthon to help
travellers. The collections include minerals,
plants and wildlife of the Alps, Roman
antiquities found on the Pass, coins and
religious objects from the Treasury at the
Hospice. Visitors can also see live St Bernard
dogs.

Brienz

Swiss Open-Air Museum

Schweizerisches Freilichtmuseum für ländliche Bau-
    und Wohnkultur Ballenberg, CH-3855 Brienz,
    Bern   ☎ 036 51 11 23
Apr–Oct, daily 10–5
Ⓒ ♟ 🖷 ♿ ↩

The Association for the Creation of an Open-
Air Museum in Ballenberg was founded in 1962
and the museum was opened in one of the most
beautiful parts of Switzerland in 1978, on a
200-hectare site, of which 80 hectares are
occupied by paths and buildings. It is still
developing and at present contains over 60
buildings from 16 Cantons, dating from the
15th to the 19th century, all with appropriate
furniture and equipment. In addition to
preserving and displaying the buildings, the

museum has daily demonstrations of more than
20 old trades and handicrafts and shows how
agriculture has changed over the centuries. It
also has a collection of old and rare breeds of
farm animals.

Bulle

Museum of the Gruyère District

Musée gruérien, place du Cabalet, CH-1630 Bulle,
    Fribourg   ☎ 029 2 72 60
Tues–Sat 10–12, 2–5; Sun 2–5.
Ⓒ ♟ ↩

The museum was founded in 1917 by the writer
and editor, Victor Tissot (1845–1917). In 1978
it moved into its new building which it shares
with the town's public library. The exhibits
illustrate the natural environment of Bulle,
together with its history and traditional life and
occupations. There are collections of 15th–
19th-century furniture, household equipment,
musical instruments, popular religious objects,
18th–19th-century local costumes, craftsmen's
tools and paintings by Swiss, Italian and French
artists. Sections of the museum are devoted to
Gruyère cheesemaking and to memorabilia of
Victor Tissot and the Abbé Joseph Bovet
(1879–1951), who composed the
internationally known song, 'The Old Chalet
up on the Mountain'.

Bürglen

William Tell Museum

Tell-Museum Uri, Postplatz, CH-6463 Bürglen,
    Uri   ☎ 044 2 41 55/2 20 22
May, June, Sept, Oct, daily 10–11.30, 1.30–5.
    July, Aug, daily 10–5. Other times by appt.
    Nov–Apr, groups of at least 10 people, by appt
    only.
Ⓕ ♟ ↩

The museum is in one of Bürglen's 12th-century towers. It contains material relating to the legend of William Tell, who refused to show respect to the Austrian Emperor and was sentenced by the Austrian bailiff, Gessler, to shoot an apple from his son's head as a punishment. The collections include paintings, engravings, sculptures, coins and medals relating to the legend, together with what is claimed to be the oldest portrait of Tell (1577) and the original score of Rossini's opera, 'William Tell'.

Chur

Cathedral Museum

Dom-Museum der Kathedrale Chur, Hofplatz 18,
CH-7000 Chur, Graubünden
☎ *081 22 92 50*
Mon–Sat 10–12, 2–6. Groups by appt Sun pm.
Closed Dec 22–Jan 15, Holy Week and the
morning of public holidays.
Ⓒ 🛈 🕭

Chur is one of the oldest bishoprics north of the Alps. According to tradition, it was founded in the second half of the 4th century by St Luzius, the first bishop, and there is evidence of a cathedral in the 5th century. The treasury is exceptionally interesting, with examples of religious art dating from as early as the 3rd century. The exhibits include reliquaries, crosses, shrines, monstrances, wooden sculptures, carving and textiles. An unusual feature of the collections is a group of 14th–15th-century reliquaries in the form of portrait busts of saints.

Raetian Museum

Rätisches Museum, Hofstraße 1, Museumplatz,
CH-7000 Chur, Graubünden.
☎ *081 22 82 77*
Tues–Sun 10–12, 2–5. Open Easter Mon and Mon
after Whit Sun, 10–12, 2–5. Closed Jan 1,
Good Fri, Easter Sun, Ascension, Whit Sun,
3rd Sun in Sept, Dec 25. Also closed afternoons
of Thurs before Good Fri, Aug 1, Dec 24, 31.
Ⓒ 🛈

House Buol, in which the museum is located, is a former patrician residence built in 1675 for Baron von Buol zu Strass- und Rietberg. The roof construction is particularly interesting. It

can be seen from the upper floor of the museum. The archaeological, historical and ethnological exhibits illustrate the history of Canton Graubünden from prehistoric times to the early 20th century. There are large collections of coins, pewter, ceramics, textiles, furniture, agricultural implements and equipment and weapons made and used in Graubünden and, in addition, a gallery containing antiquities from the Mediterranean and ethnographical material from Asia, Africa and America.

Among the particularly interesting objects on display are a coach used on the Splügen and San Bernardino passes until 1920, spinning wheels and accessories, 16th–18th-century chests, and an early-16th-century canopied table organ.

Dübendorf

Museum of Military Aviation

Fliegermuseum, Überlandstraße, CH-8600
Dübendorf, Zürich ☎ *01 823 23 24*
Tues–Fri 1.30–5; Sat 9–5; Sun 1–5. Special
opening times in Dec (☎ 01 823 22 83).
Closed public holidays.
Ⓒ 🛈 🖳 🕭

The history of Swiss military aviation goes back to 1899, when a balloon unit for artillery observation was set up. In 1914, on the outbreak of war, all Swiss who were able to fly were ordered to report to the airfield at Dübendorf in their own aeroplanes, where possible. The museum, established in 1979, tells the story of Dübendorf and of military flying in Switzerland, on an airfield which is still operational.

There is a collection of historic aircraft, engines, components and equipment, dating from 1910 to 1971, together with balloons, armaments, uniforms, medals and insignia, photographs and models.

Ebnat-Kappel

Ebnat-Kappel Museum

Heimatmuseum Ebnat-Kappel, Ackerhusweg 16,
CH-9642 Ebnat-Kappel, St Gallen
☎ *074 3 19 05*
Tues–Fri 10–12, 2–5; 2nd and 4th Sun in month,
2–5. Sat by telephone appt only. Closed 1st and
3rd Sun in month.
Ⓒ 🛈

Albert Edelmann (1886–1963) was a teacher and a collector of folksongs from the Toggenburg region. On his retirement in 1952, he moved to a house, 'Acker', built in 1752, where he had room for the remarkable collection of Toggenburg antiquities, especially painted furniture, which he had been assembling for many years, and for his musical instruments, including house-organs, and examples of peasant art.

Museum of Military Aviation, Dübendorf.

Echallens

House of Wheat and Bread

La Maison du Blé et du Pain, place de l'Hôtel-de-
Ville, CH-1040 Echallens, Vaud
☎ *021 881 50 71*
Feb–mid Dec, Tues–Sun 9–6
Ⓒ ▮ ☕

The museum, opened in 1989, has already
established itself as a major attraction both for
local people and for tourists. It describes itself as
'a living museum of craftsmanship'. It has been
set up in a former farmhouse, on the initiative of
an association created for the purpose. In
addition to historical exhibits related to the
growing and milling of wheat and to the
processes involved in breadmaking, it contains a
bakery, making the range of bread for which
Switzerland is famous and which is sold on the
premises. Four ovens are in regular operation.
Two are modern and two of the types used by
previous generations of bakers. Visitors are
encouraged to try their hand at making bread
and are able to take their efforts away with them
after their visit to the museum.

The House of Wheat and Bread organises
regular demonstrations and other activities
connected with milling, and the training of
bakers as well as farm visits.

Frauenfeld

Thurgau Historical Museum

Historisches Museum des Kantons Thurgau,
Schloß, CH-8500 Frauenfeld, Thurgau
☎ *054 21 35 91*
Tues–Sun 2–5. Closed main religious holidays,
including Jan 1, Easter, Whitsun and
Christmas. Free admission Wed, Sat, Sun.
Ⓒ ▮

The earliest part of the castle, Schloss
Frauenfeld, in which the museum has been
located since 1960, dates from the early 13th
century. The collections illustrate the history of
Canton Thurgau from prehistoric times until
the 19th century, with archaeological material
from sites in the region. There are interesting
collections of religious art, several period rooms
including a court room, a farmhouse sitting-
room, a mid-18th-century bourgeois salon with
painted walls and ceiling, and an early-19th-
century section. Other sections of the museum
are devoted to ceramics, painted glass, clocks
and watches, astronomical instruments, coins
and weapons. There are also several tiled stoves
of outstanding quality.

Fribourg

Museum of Art and History

Musée d'Art et d'Histoire, rue de Morat 12,
CH-1700 Fribourg   ☎ *037 22 85 71*
Tues, Wed, Fri–Sun 10–5; Thurs 10–5, 8–10.
Ⓕ ▮ ☕ ♿ ■

The museum occupies an unusual complex of
buildings, the Hôtel Ratzé, a Renaissance
mansion and the municipal slaughterhouse,
constructed in 1834–6 and of remarkable
architectural quality. The exhibits of medieval
and Renaissance paintings, sculpture and
metalwork are outstanding. They include the
finest collection of late Gothic wooden
sculpture in Switzerland and carved stone groups
from Fribourg fountains. Other sections are
devoted to 15th–19th-century furniture,
pewter, faïence, porcelain, tapestries, 15th–
18th-century stained glass and coins and
medals. There is also a good collection of
18th–19th-century drawings by Fribourg artists.

Geneva

Jean-Jacques Rousseau Museum

Musée Jean-Jacques Rousseau, c/o Bibliothèque
publique et universitaire, promenade des
Bastions, CH-1211 Genève 4
☎ *022 20 82 66*
Mon–Fri 9–12, 2–5; Sat 9–12. Closed during New
Year, Easter and Christmas Holidays.
Ⓕ ▮

Rousseau (1712–78), the writer and
philosopher, was born in Geneva and died in
Paris. The museum, organised by the Jean-
Jacques Rousseau Society, has collections
owned partly by the society and partly by the
library in which they are displayed. They
illustrate Rousseau's life and work and include
manuscripts of his works or relating to him, first
editions of his publications, the death mask
made by Houdon, portraits, a miniature of his
father and old views of places where he lived at
one time or another. There are also a number of
his personal possessions.

**Painted glass, c. 1590. Thurgau Historical
Museum, Frauenfeld.**

Maison Tavel

*Maison Tavel, 6, rue du Puits-Saint-Pierre,
    CH-1204 Genève*   ☎ *022 28 29 00*
Tues–Sun 10–5
Ⓕ ⬙ ♿

The Maison Tavel is the oldest surviving private
house in Geneva. In the Middle Ages it
occupied a commanding position in the centre
of the upper town. In 1334 it was partially
destroyed by a disastrous fire which left half the
city in ruins. The present architecture of the
house dates from the reconstruction necessitated
by the fire. The sculptures on the exterior are of
remarkable quality and have retained their
original medieval colours. Restoration work was
carried out between 1972 and 1981.

The Maison Tavel was the property of
successive powerful Geneva families, beginning
with the Tavels, and continued in private
occupation until 1956. It was acquired by the
city in order to create a museum in 1963. The
collections now displayed in it illustrate the
cultural history of Geneva and include
paintings, drawings and prints, 16th–19th-
century pewter, for which Geneva was famous,
ceramics, silver, furniture and costumes. The
kitchen, which still has its original sink, water-
stove and chimney, is fitted with period
furniture and equipment and the drawing-room
has Geneva and French furniture of c.1750,
once the property of Geneva families, and
18th-century portraits by local artists.

Museum of Art and History

*Musée d'Art et d'Histoire, 2, rue Charles Galland,
    CH-1211 Genève 3*   ☎ *022 29 00 11*
Tues–Sun 10–5
Ⓕ ▮ 🖾

The museum's encyclopaedic character is
unique in Switzerland. The archaeological
section contains eight departments – Egypt (the
most important in Switzerland), origins of
writing, Near East, Greece, Etruria, Rome,
Byzantium, and coins and medals. The
historical galleries have three general themes –
woodwork, furniture, and arms and armour. The
Fine Art section contains two panels originally
in Geneva Cathedral, which were painted by

**Wax model of Voltaire, in the philosopher's
original costume. Voltaire Museum, Geneva.**

Conrad Witz in 1444. It is the first Geneva
landscape painting to have survived. The
museum also has 18th–20th-century paintings
by Geneva artists, sculptures, especially by
Rodin, 16th–20th-century Limoges and Geneva
miniatures, 16th–19th-century clocks and
watches, medieval art, weapons and armour,
and musical instruments. There are also models
and documents illustrating the history of
Geneva.

Voltaire Museum

*Institut et Musée Voltaire, 25, rue des Délices,
    CH-1203 Genève*   ☎ *022 44 71 33*
*Mon–Fri 2–5. Closed New Year and Christmas
    holidays.*
Ⓕ ▮

The French writer, François-Marie Arouet
(1694–1778), always known by his pen-name of
Voltaire, owned the building which is now
museum from 1755 to 1765. It was his chief
residence from the spring of 1755 to the autumn
of 1760. The exhibits illustrate his tempestuous
life and work and include manuscripts by him or
relating to him, first and other 18th-century
editions of his works, portraits of him and of his
friends and enemies, view of places where he
lived, and furniture and other objects which
belonged to him.

Heiden

Henri Dunant Museum

*Henri Dunant Museum, CH-9410 Heiden,
    Appenzell–Ausserrhoden*
Ⓕ ⬯

In 1901 Jean Henri Dunant (1828–1910) was
awarded the first Nobel Prize, jointly with
Frédéric Passy, after a lifetime of struggling,
protesting and writing against war. He was one
of the original promoters of the International
Red Cross. A memorial museum to him was
opened in 1969 in the house in Heiden where
he spent his last years. It contains photographs,
documents and memorabilia relating to his life
and work.

Hirzel

Johanna Spyri Museum

Johanna Spyri-Museum, CH-8816 Hirzel, Zürich
    ☎ *01 729 9267*
*Mon 3–5, 7–10; Sun 2–4. Other times by appt.
    Closed public and school holidays.*
Ⓕ ▮

Johanna Spyri (1827–1901), the author of the
Heidi stories, is one of the most translated and
widely-read children's authors in the world. The
museum to her, opened in 1981, is in the
original Hirzel school, which dates from 1660
and which was attended both by Johanna Spyri
and her mother. The exhibits illustrate her life
and work and her family background, together
with manuscripts, her complete printed works
and a number of her personal possessions.

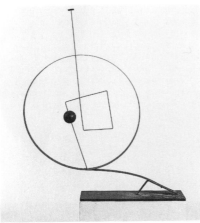

Window towards the Sky, 1958, by Walter
Linck. Museum of Art, La Chaux-de-Fonds.

Ittingen

Ittingen Museum

Ittinger Museum, Kartause Ittingen, CH-8532
Warth, Thurgau   ☎ *054 21 89 87*
Mon–Fri 2–5; Sat, Sun 11–5. Closed between
Christmas and New Year.
C ▲ ⬛

At some time after 1139 the Lords of Ittingen
founded an Augustinian priory within their
stronghold and became canons of St Augustine
themselves. In 1461, after poor harvests,
vagrancy and famine, the wholly impoverished
monastery was sold to the Carthusians. In 1524,
during the Reformation, it was set on fire and
practically destroyed. It was gradually rebuilt
and in the 17th century the economic situation
improved and in the 18th century the monastery
reached the peak of its prosperity. The
magnificently decorated buildings which one
sees today date from then. In 1848 the
monasteries in Canton Thurgau were dissolved
and their possessions transferred to public
ownership.

Carefully restored, the buildings became a
museum in 1983. There are, in fact, two
museums. One presents the history of the
monastery and the Carthusian order and the
other is devoted to contemporary international
naive art and to works by contemporary artists
living and working in Canton Thurgau. Visitors
can see the splendid Baroque church, which is
again in use for worship, the communal rooms
and the monks' cells, and gain an impression of
how the Charterhouse functioned and of the life
of the monks.

Kiesen

Swiss Dairy Museum

Milchwirtschaftliches Museum, Bernstraße,
CH-3317 Kiesen, Bern   ☎ *031 45 33 31*
Apr–Oct, daily 2–5
F ▲ 🚗

To begin with, Swiss cheese was produced in
quantity only in the Alps. In 1815 the hamlet of
Kiesen between Bern and Thun, set up a small
pioneering factory outside the mountain regions
and it was soon followed by others, giving
Switzerland a cheese industry on a commercial
scale. The little enterprise in Kiesen was in use
until the end of the 19th-century and in 1974
the Swiss Dairy Produce Association converted
it into a museum. The old cheesemaking room
has been restored to its original appearance and
the upper floor houses exhibitions on the history
and techniques of Swiss cheesemaking and on
its varieties.

La Chaux-de-Fonds

Museum of Art

Musée des Beaux-Arts, 33, rue des Musées,
CH-2300 La Chaux-de-Fonds, Neuchâtel
   ☎ *039 23 04 44*
Tues–Sun 10–12, 2–5. Wed, open until 8 and free
   admission.
C ▲

The museum building, opened in 1926, was
designed by R. Chapellat and Ch. L'Eplattenier,
who were the first teachers of Le Corbusier
(1887–1965). The collections contain works by
artists from La Chaux-de-Fonds, including Le
Corbusier, 19th–20th-century paintings and
sculpture by Neuchâtel and Swiss artists, and
international contemporary art since 1950.

Also in the museum is the R. and M. Junod
collection of 19th–20th-century European
paintings, including works by Constable,
Delacroix, Pissarro, Van Gogh, Matisse, Derain
and Rouault.

Museum of Watches and Clockmaking

Musée international d'horlogerie, 29, rue des
   Musées, CH-2300 La Chaux-de-Fonds
   Neuchâtel   ☎ *039 23 62 63*
Tues–Sun 10–12, 2–5
C ▲ ⬛

La Chaux-de-Fonds has a long tradition of
watch and clockmaking. The museum's
collections of more than 3,000 items illustrate
historical developments in the methods of
measuring time. They include sundials,
primitive clocks, 17th-century enamelled
watches, pendulum clocks, astronomical clocks
and modern timepieces. There are also displays
which explain manufacturing processes and
which give information on the clock and
watchmaking trades.

Langnau-Emmental

Chüchlihus Museum

Heimatmuseum 'Chüchlihus', Bärenplatz 2,
   CH-3350 Langnau-Emmental, Bern
   ☎ *035 2 18 19*
Feb–Nov, Tues–Sun 9–11.30, 1.30–6. Closed
   public holidays.
C ▲ 🚗

The museum, set up as a community enterprise in 1932, was reorganised in the early 1960s. The building which it occupies is the oldest in the district and is constructed entirely of wood. The collections include examples of Langnau ceramics, Flüeli glass and Schiff glass, and there are reconstructions of the workshops of a potter, organ-builder and woodturner, and of an Alpine cheesemaking diary. Other exhibits are devoted to craftsmen's tools and equipment especially for weaving, and to the local agricultural and milk industries. The museum has memorabilia of several local celebrities, including the miracle-working doctor, Micheli Schüppach.

Lausanne

Lausanne Museum

Musée Historique de Lausanne, place de la Cathédrale 4, CH-1005 Lausanne, Vaud
☎ 021 312 13 68
Tues, Wed, Fri–Sun 11–6; Thurs 11–8.

C ⬛

The building now housing the museum was the Bishop's Palace from the 11th to the 14th centuries. It was restored in 1987–89. Its collections illustrate the history of Lausanne, by means of both permanent and temporary exhibitions. There are exhibits of prehistoric, Roman and medieval archaeology, furniture, pewter, paintings and 18th–19th-century Lausanne silver. There are also several reconstructed room interiors, showing living styles in the 17th–19th centuries.

Le Locle

Col-des-Roches Underground Mills

Moulins Souterrains du Col-des-Roches, Confrérie des Meuniers du Col-des-Roches, Secrétariat des Musées, Hôtel de Ville, CH-2400 Le Locle, Neuchâtel   ☎ 039 31 62 62
May–June, Sat, Sun 10–12, 2–6. July–Sept, Mon–Fri 2–5; Sat, Sun 9–12, 1–6. Oct, Mon–Fri 2–5; Sat, Sun 10–12, 2–6. May–Oct, groups by appt.

C ⬛ ⬛ ⬛

A selection of pipes unearthed at the Col-des-Roches Underground Mills, Le Locle.

Near the Franco-Swiss border, the river has cut an underground channel more than 2 km long. In the 16th century mills were constructed on this stretch of the river. They were improved and added to in the course of time and abandoned in 1898. A section has now been restored by a group of volunteers helped by sponsors, and is in working order. They are believed to be the only underground mills in Europe.

Liestal

Old Arsenal Museum

Museum im alten Zeughaus, Zeughausplatz 28, CH-4410 Liestal, Basel
☎ 061 925 59 86/061 925 50 88
Tues 10–12, 2–5, 7–9. Wed–Fri 10–12, 2–5; Sat, Sun 10–5.

F ⬛ ⬛

The five-storey building which contains the museum dates from 1530. Over the centuries it served both as an arsenal and as a granary. It was partially rebuilt in 1834–5 and restored in 1879–81, and now accommodates concerts and theatrical performances, in addition to the museum. The museum began life in 1837 as a Cabinet of Natural Curiosities. Since reorganistion its collections have been divided into two sections. Local industries, especially the weaving of silk ribbons, occupy two floors and 'Traces of Civilization', that is, archaeology and ethnography, the third. The museum has important collections of Neolithic, Bronze Age, Hallstatt, La Tène, Roman and Alemmanic material from local sites.

Lottigna

Museum of the Blenio Valley

Museo di Blenio, Casa dei Landfogti, CH-6711 Lottigna, Ticino   ☎ 092 78 19 777
April (or Easter)–Nov 2, Tues–Fri 2–5; Sat, Sun and public holdays 10–12, 2–5. Groups at other times by appt.

C ⬛ ⬛

The Casa dei Landfogti, or House of the Governors, which contains the museum, dates mainly from the early 16th century, although parts are earlier. The collections illustrate the traditional life of the valley. Sections are devoted to agriculture, forestry and transport, vine-growing and wine-making, butter and cheesemaking, the manufacture of fabrics and of everyday articles in wood and iron, and artistic rural handicrafts. There are also displays of costumes, beekeeping equipment, religious art, and kitchen equipment, and of material relating to the local militia, to weapons and prisons and to emigration.

About 20 varieties of trees which grow in the valley have been planted in the grounds of the museum, with the intention of forming an attractive botanical record of the region.

Displays of pottery and glass at the Historical Museum, Lucerne.

Lucerne

Historical Museum

*Historisches Museum, Pfistergasse 24, Postfach
    164, CH-6000 Luzern   ☎ 041 24 54 24
Tues–Fri 10–12, 2–5; Sat, Sun 10–5.*
Ⓒ ▮

The museum is in Lucerne's former arsenal, which was built in 1567–8 and which served its original purpose until 1983. As early as the 18th century the equipment in the arsenal, especially captured weapons, was shown to interested members of the public. During the occupation of Lucerne by the French during the Napoleonic period, a large part of this collection was sold as scrap metal or given away to French officers. Exhibited in the 19th century and until 1970 in part of the town hall, the historical material relating to Lucerne has been redisplayed in the present building since 1986.

It includes costumes, products of the local glassworks, 15th–18th-century items relating to the trades and guilds, weights and measures, reconstructed rooms from two local hotels, coins and medals of Lucerne, goldsmiths' tools and equipment, stained glass, and 19th-century views of the city. There is also the Fountain of the Wine Market, carved c.1481 and one of the most important fountains in Switzerland. The museum has an interesting collection of armour, shields, war bugles and uniforms.

Museum of Costume and Folk Life

*Schweizerisches Trachten- und Heimatmuseum
    Utenberg, Dietschibergstraße, CH-6006
    Luzern   ☎ 041 36 80 58
Easter–Oct, daily 9–5*
Ⓒ ◇ ♨

The museum is in Utenberg Castle, built in the 18th century. It contains Swiss costumes and accessories and examples of needlework, together with country furniture, household equipment and toys. The archives of the Federal Yodelling Association are also in the museum, as well as a European collection of accordions.

Swiss Transport Museum

*Verkehrshaus der Schweiz, Lidostraße 5, CH-6006
    Luzern   ☎ 041 31 44 44
Mar–Oct, daily 9–6. Nov–Feb, Mon–Sat 10–4;
    Sun 10–5. Closed Dec 24, 25.*
Ⓒ ▮ ♨ ♿ ♨

The Swiss national transport museum was founded in 1959 as a private association. It is now one of the most comprehensive and successful transport museums in the world, with 12 buildings on an area of 40,000 square metres, of which 20,000 form the exhibition area, and continues to be run as a self-supporting enterprise. It illustrates the development of the Swiss transport system as a whole and in its social context, and includes postal services and telecommunications as well as tourism. There is also a section relating to space travel, with the Cosmorama, a multi-media show on the history of space flight, the Swissorama, a circular-screen cinema presenting Swiss landscape and customs, and Switzerland's only planetarium.

Montreux

Museum of Old Montreux

*Musée du Vieux-Montreux, 40, rue de la Gare,
    CH-1820 Montreux, Vaud
    ☎ 021 963 80 33
Easter–Oct, Tues–Sun 10–12, 2–5*
Ⓒ ♨

The museum belongs to a private society. It was opened in 1874 and transferred to its present home, a group of 14th–19th-century buildings, in 1919. The collections illustrate the history of Montreux and the surrounding region, from Neolithic times to the Golden Age of hotel-keeping in the town. The exhibits include household equipment, weights and measures, militaria, reconstructions of a joiner's workshop and of a bedroom in the Hotel Bristol, and cheese- and wine-making equipment.

Morges

Military Museum of the Vaud

*Musée militaire vaudois, Le Château, CH-1110
    Morges, Vaud   ☎ 021 801 26 15
Feb 1–Dec 15, Mon–Fri 10–12, 1.30–5; Sat, Sun
    and public holidays 1.30–5.*
Ⓒ ▮ ♨ ♨

The museum, opened in 1925, is in a 13th-century castle, built by the House of Savoy. It contains 15th–16th-century military material, with an emphasis on the 19th century, on local military units and on Swiss units in the service of France and the kingdom of Naples. The exhibits include weapons, armour, uniforms and flags. Four galleries are devoted to 50 dioramas, representing historical scenes from classical times to the 19th century and containing extremely accurate and realistic figurines.

The vaulted cellars of the castle are occupied by the Artillery Museum, which has 40 original pieces and a large number of models.

Môtiers

Jean-Jacques Rousseau Museum

Musée Jean-Jacques Rousseau, CH-2112 Môtiers,
Neuchâtel ☎ 038 61 28 22
Apr–Oct, Tues–Thurs, Sat 2–4. Nov–Mar, Tues–
Thurs 2–4. Other times by telephone appt.
C ♦ ⚘

Born in Geneva, the writer and philosopher,
Jean-Jacques Rousseau (1712–78) spent most of
his life in France, but was compelled to go into
exile, first in Switzerland and then in England,
after the publication of *Émile* and *On the Social
Contract*, both in 1762. The museum, opened in
1969, is in the rooms which Rousseau occupied
from 1762 to 1765, during his stay in Môtiers. It
contains portraits and statuettes of him, and
engravings and etchings relating to his life and
work, together with a number of memorabilia,
including a plate give by him as a prize in a
shooting competition at Môtiers.

Müstair

Convent Museum

Klostermuseum, Kloster St Johann, CH-7537
Müstair, Graubünden ☎ 082 8 52 65
Easter week, Whitsun, July–Oct, Mon–Sat 10–11;
Sun 3–5.
C ♦

A Benedictine monastery was founded here in
the late 8th century, reputedly by Charlemagne.
In the 12th century it became a convent of
Benedictine nuns and still has this function.
The buildings, several times restored and
extended, are distinguished, especially the
splendid church, parts of which date from the
time of Charlemagne. The museum was
established in 1938 and reorganised in 1978. It
contains Carolingian sculptures from the
monastery, Romanesque frescoes removed from
the church in 1947–52, Gothic and Baroque
painted sculptures, liturgical objects, 16th–
17th-century furniture, and reconstructions of
rooms from the convent.

**Detail of porcelain with scattered decoration of
flowers and insects. Historical and Porcelain
Museum, Nyon.**

Näfels

Glarus Museum

Museum des Landes Glarus, Freulerpalast, CH-
8752 Näfels, Glarus ☎ 058 34 13 78
Apr–Nov, Tues–Sun 10–12, 2–5.30
C ♦

The Freuler Palace which today houses the
museum, was built in 1642–8 by Colonel Kaspar
Freuler (1595–1651). It is one of the most
interesting secular buildings in Switzerland. The
mid-17th-century panelling, stoves and
decorations are of outstanding quality. The
museum contains material relating to Colonel
Freuler, who was Commander of the Regiment
of Swiss Guards in the French Army, and
information concerning notabilities from the
Glarus region in science and the arts. There are
also exhibits illustrating the history of the
Glarus textile-printing industry, 16th–19th-
century weapons, uniforms and flags, and
prehistoric and Roman finds from the area.

Neuchâtel

Museum of Art and History

Musée d'Art et d'Histoire, Quai Léopold Robert,
CH-2001 Neuchâtel ☎ 038 25 17 40
Tues–Sun 10–12, 2–5. During summer months,
10–5.
C ♦

The museum contains paintings, drawings,
sculptures and prints by Swiss artists, especially
from the Canton of Neuchâtel. There are also
collections of documents and other material
illustrating the history of Neuchâtel, 18th–
20th-century French paintings, coins, ceramics,
glass, portraits and weapons, especially of the
Napoleonic period. Other sections are devoted
to the Neuchâtel watch and clock industry, and
to automata made by members of the Jacquet-
Droz family.

Nyon

Historical and Porcelain Museum

Musée Historique et des Porcelaines, Château de
Nyon, CH-1260 Nyon, Vaud
☎ 022 61 58 88
Apr–Oct, daily 9–12, 2–6
C ♦

The earliest parts of the castle date from the
12th century. Considerable modifications and
extensions took place during the 13th–15th
centuries and the buildings were restored
between 1945 and 1977. The municipality
bought the castle at auction in 1801 and it
became a museum in 1888. The collections
illustrate the prehistory and history of Nyon and
the surrounding region, with collections of
Roman antiquities, material from Burgundian
graves and medieval pottery.
The museum's outstanding collections are of
porcelain and faïence made at Nyon between
1781 and 1831, and of 17th–20th-century
pharmacy jars.

Nautilus shell-cup, early 18th-century. Silver collection, Historical Museum, St Gallen.

Museum of Lake Geneva

*Musée du Leman, quai Louis Bonnard 8,
    CH-1260 Nyon, Vaud*   ☎ *022 61 09 49
Apr–Oct, daily 9–12, 2–6. Nov–Mar, Tues–Sun
    2–5.*
C ♿ ⚓

The museum, in an 18th-century house, has collections relating to the natural history, navigation and fishing of Lake Geneva, as well as a gallery containing paintings by Abraham Hermanjat (1862–1932). There is an exhibit relating to François-Alphonse Foret (1841–1912) and to his biological studies of the lake. Among the items displayed are Foret's plankton nets. The section devoted to navigation illustrates the history of transport on Lake Geneva by both sailing boat, steamer and motorboat, with the steam-engine of the saloon boat *Helvétie* and a complete freight sailing ship. There is also a collection of ship models and a 25,000-litre aquarium containing fish found in the lake.

Roman Museum

*Musée Romain, rue Maupertuis, CH-1260 Nyon,
    Vaud*   ☎ *022 61 75 91
Apr–Oct, daily 9–12, 2–6. Nov–Mar, Tues–Sun
    2–5.*
C

The important Roman colony of *Julia Equestris* was founded c.45 BC by Julius Caesar. It was spread out between the river Aubonne, Lake Geneva, the Rhône and the Jura mountain range. The centre of the chief town,

Noviodunum, the modern Nyon, was occupied by a rectangular forum with a temple, a basilica – the general meeting place and the law and commercial centre – porticoes and public baths. Towards the end of the 1st century AD a new basilica was built to replace the original one.

The museum, which dates from 1979, has been created in the middle of the ruins of the basilica. It contains Roman archaeological material from throughout *Julia Equestris* and includes sculptures, inscriptions and architectural elements from *Noviodunum*, ceramics, tools, jewellery, coins, religious items and objects in everyday use. There is also a model of the centre of the Roman city.

Sainte-Croix

Museum of Mechanical Art

*Musée du Centre International de la Mécanique
    d'Art, rue de l'Industrie 2, CH-1450 Sainte-
    Croix, Vaud*   ☎ *024 61 44 77
Tues–Sun 1.30–6.30. Last admission 5.15. Closed
    Dec 25.*
C ♿ ⚓ ♿

For generations, Sainte-Croix has been famous for its production of musical boxes and other mechanical musical instruments. At one time, Geneva and Sainte Croix shared the musical box market between them. The museum's collections illustrate the range and development of these objects. The industry died out in Geneva at the beginning of the present century, but it is still carried on in Sainte-Croix. The museum is in the factory of the former Paillard Company, which made musical boxes, Paillard radios, Hermes typewriters and another local speciality, Bolex film cameras.

St Gallen

Historical Museum

*Historisches Museum, Museumstraße 50,
    CH-9000 St Gallen*   ☎ *071 24 78 32
Tues–Sat 10–12, 2–5; Sun 10–5. Closed public
    holidays.*
C ♿ ⚓

The museum's collections illustrate the history of the town and Canton of St Gallen. There is archaeological material from the Stone Age to Roman times, together with maps and models showing the town at different stages in its development, religious paintings, sculptures and goldsmiths' work from the 14th century onwards and a series of 14th–18th-century period rooms, including the 1679 Council Chamber form the old town hall. Other sections are devoted to household equipment, inn signs, painted and carved furniture, portraits, Swiss porcelain and ceramics, uniforms of Swiss militiamen and cadets, banners and musical instruments. A special exhibition presents the history of the linen industry and trades of St Gallen, by means of documents, paintings, tools, equipment and products.

Schwyz

Archives of the Confederation

Bundesbriefarchiv, Bahnhofstraße 20, CH-6430
  Schwyz   ☎ *043 24 20 64*
Daily 9.30–11.30, 2–5. Closed Good Fri, Dec 25,
  26.
F ▮ ↝

The original Swiss Confederation, linking the
communities of Uri, Schwyz and Nidwalden,
was ratified in 1291. Other cantons joined the
Confederation subsequently. The museum
displays original documents relating to the
Confederation, including the Act of 1291. It
also has a collection of local and battle flags
from Schwyz, 1315–1802, and specially
commissioned sculptures illustrating aspects of
the Confederation.

Ital Reding House

Ital Reding-Haus, Rickenbachstraße 24, CH-6430
  Schwyz   ☎ *043 21 45 05/24 14 54*
May-Oct, Tues–Fri 2–5; Sat, Sun 10–12.
C ↝

The house was built in 1609 for the governor of
Schwyz, Ital Reding. In addition to the
governor's residence, the complex contains farm
buildings and another dwelling house, the
Bethlehem House, which is dated 1287 and is
the earliest surviving timber-framed building in
Switzerland and older than the Swiss
Confederation itself. The Ital Reding House has
painted period rooms, together with a gallery of
von Reding portraits and memorabilia of the
family.

Swiss musical box. Museum of Mechanical
Musical Instruments, Seewen.

Seewen

Museum of Mechanical Musical Instruments

Schweizerisches Musikautomaten Museum, Dr H.
  Weiss-Stauffacher Stiftung, Bollhübel, CH-
  4206 Seewen, Solothurn   ☎ *061 96 02 08*
Mar–Nov, Tues–Sat 2–5. Other times by appt.
C ▮ ♿ ↝

The museum was opened to the public in 1979.
Its collection was formed by Dr H. Weiss over a
period of 56 years and contains more than 600
exhibits, all restored to working condition. The
section devoted to Swiss musical boxes is
claimed to contain more examples than can be
found anywhere else. The exhibits were made in
the 18th, 19th and 20th centuries and include a
36-register concert organ, with 1,400 recorded
rolls for automatic playing and a Steinway
which has 1,200 pieces of music available, all
recorded by celebrated pianists between 1904
and 1933.

Sennwald

Textile Museum

Textil und Heimatmuseum, c/o Aebi Verwaltungs
  AG, CH-9466 Sennwald, St Gallen
  ☎ *085 7 54 54*
Mar–Oct, daily 10–12, 2–5
F ↝

The Industrial Revolution came late to
Switzerland. The first textile factories date from
the 1870s. In 1971 the Paul Aebi Foundation,
which has been set up by the Aebi cloth-
manufacturing concern, opened a museum in a
17th-century house which had belonged to a
family of peasants and weavers. The museum is
in two parts. The first illustrates the
development of the local textile industry and

the second the history of the district. There are exhibits relating to the traditional trades, including Alpine dairy and cheesemaking and reconstructed workshops of a blacksmith, cabinet-maker, weaver, spinner and embroiderer. A section of the museum is devoted to the noble family of Sax-Forstegg. The mummified body of Baron Johann Philipp von Sax-Forstegg, who died in 1596, is to be found in Sennwald Church.

Stans

Nidwalden Museum

Nidwaldner Museum, Höfli, CH-6370 Stans,
Nidwalden. Correspondence to: Marktgasse 3,
CH-6370 Stans   ☎ *041 61 77 11*
Wed–Mon 9–11, 2–5. Closed Good Fri, Easter
Sun, Dec 25.
Ⓒ ✍

The museum has recently been completely reorganised and the collections are now distributed among four historic buildings. The Höfli and the Winkelried House are both medieval in origin, but their present appearance is the result of remodelling in the 16th–18th centuries. The Salt Warehouse dates from 1700 and Fürigen Fortress was constructed during the Second World War. The divisions of the material roughly correspond to the way in which the four buildings have been used in the past. Fürigen Fortress, which has been preserved in its original form, has exhibits of weapons, flags and uniforms. The Höfli's collections illustrate the history of public life in Stans, and those shown in the Winkelried House are concerned with furniture, costumes, domestic equipment and handicrafts. The exhibitions in the Salt Warehouse are of 20th-century paintings and sculpture by local artists.

Teufen

Grubenmann Collection

Grubenmann-Sammlung, Dorf 7, CH-9053
Teufen, Appenzel-Ausserrhoden
☎ *071 33 24 42*
Mon, Wed, Sat 2–4; Fri 6–8 pm; 1st Sun of
month, 10–12. Closed Jan 1, Good Fri, Easter
Sun, Whit Sun, Aug 1, Dec 25, 31.
Ⓒ ♨ ⚒

The prosperity of the Canton's textile industry in the 18th century produced a great demand for new buildings of all kind. Three generations of the Grubenmann family of carpenters found ample opportunity for their exceptional talent. Their reputation spread throughout Switzerland and their work can be seen in the large number of wooden bridges, churches and important houses for which they were responsible. They introduced many innovatory constructional techniques, which are of great importance in the development of wooden structures. The museum explains these and provides an introduction to the range, quality and quantity of Grubenmann buildings which can still be

seen in Switzerland today.

Uli Grubenmann (1668–1736) had three sons, whose skill and achievements exceeded even his own. Hans Ulrich (1709–83) was known particularly for bridge construction – the one over the Rhine at Schaffhausen is particularly famous; Jakob (1694–1758) specialised in churches, and town and country mansions; and Johannes (1707–71) was renowned for clock and bell-towers, large houses and bridges.

Vallorbe

Museum of Iron

Musée du Fer, Office du Tourisme, Grandes Forges
II, CH-1337 Vallorbe, Vaud
☎ *021 843 25 83*
Palm Sun–May 31, Tues–Sun 9–12, 1.30–6.
June–Oct, daily 9–12, 1.30–6.
Ⓒ ♨

Iron has been worked here since prehistoric times. The museum was established in 1980, to tell the story of the origins of the local iron industry, and to illustrate its present products and markets. Production of cast-iron at Vallorbe came to an end in the late 17th century, when the inhabitants turned to the manufacture of files, tools and chains, which acquired an international reputation.

The museum occupies two buildings, an ironworks which dates from 1495 and which is driven by three waterwheels and, on the other side of the river, a forge, now called the Estoppey Forge, which is known to have existed in 1693, and which has a tilthammer, grindstone, drilling machine and hacksaw, all water-driven.

Museum of Iron, Vallorbe.

Vevey

Museum of Old Vevey

*Musée historique du Vieux-Vevey, rue du Château
2, CH-1800 Vevey, Vaud*
☎ 021 921 07 22
Tues–Sat 10–12, 2–5; Sun 11–12, 2–5.
F ✐

Founded in 1897, the museum was transferred in 1953 to the present building, 'Le Château', which dates from 1599 and which was the residence of the Bailiffs of Bern from 1733 to 1798. During the 19th century, it served as a hotel, which accommodated, among other celebrities, the writers, Lamartine, Sainte-Beuve, Zola and François Coppeé, the politician, Gambetta, and the painter, Courbet.

It contains archaeological material from local prehistoric and Roman sites, Egyptian, Greek and Roman antiquities, and collections of regional costumes, furniture and 15th–18th-century French and Italian ironwork. There are also reconstructions of a pewter-maker's workshop and of the printing works of the *Messager Boiteux*. A section of the museum contains 19th-century weapons and uniforms of Swiss soldiers in the French service.

Wildhaus

Zwingli's House

*Zwingli Geburtshaus, Lisighaus, CH-9658
Wildhaus, St Gallen* ☎ 074 5 21 78
*Tues–Sun 2–4. Groups at other times by appt.
Closed Apr 15–May 20 and Nov–Dec 26.*
F ✐

The Alpine house in which the religious reformer, Huldrych Zwingli (1484–1531) was born dates from the 15th century. The interior has been restored to something like its original appearance, with period furniture. There are exhibits illustrating Zwingli's life, including a number of memorabilia.

Winterthur

Lindengut Museum

*Museum Lindengut, Römerstraße 8, CH-8400
Winterthur, Zürich* ☎ 052 23 47 77
*Main building: Tues–Thurs, Sat 2–5; Sun 10–12,
2–5. Toy Museum: Wed, Sun 2–5. Closed 4
weeks during July/Aug and some public
holidays.*
C ▯

The museum occupies a late-18th-century house, built by a south German industrialist who had become wealthy as a result of his activities in the salt trade. The collections illustrate the cultural history of Winterthur in the 16th–19th centuries and include clocks, coats of arms, paintings on glass and toys. There are a number of 18th-century furnished rooms and a fine collection of tiled heating stoves.

First climbers of the Matterhorn, 1865. Alpine Museum, Zermatt.

Wohlen

Freiamt Straw Museum

*Freiämter Strohmuseum, Bankweg 1, CH-5610
Wohlen, Aargau*
☎ 057 22 60 26
*Wed 2–5; Fri 4–8; Sat 10–12; Sun 2–4. Closed
for 4 weeks during July/Aug.*
C ▯ ↩

Plaiting straw was probably introduced into Switzerland from Tuscany in the 12th century. It became an important local industry in the 18th century and during the 19th century workers produced some extremely fine straw plait designs, especially for hat trimmings. The museum illustrates the history of the industry, especially during the 18th and 19th centuries, displays a selection of its products and explains the techniques involved.

Zermatt

Alpine Museum

*Alpines Museum, Bahnhofstraße, CH-3920
Zermatt, Valais*
☎ 028 67 41 00
*May–Sept, Sun–Fri 10–12, 4–6. Oct, Dec
21–Apr, Sun–Fri 4.30–6.30. Closed Nov
1–Dec 20.*
C

The museum was opened, in a building designed for the purpose, in 1958. It has sections devoted to the geology, flowers, birds and animals of the Valley of Zermatt and to the history of Alpine climbing in the Zermatt area, especially of ascents of the Matterhorn. There are photographs and portraits of Zermatt guides and of their more celebrated clients, memorabilia of mountaineers, records of accidents and photographs of the annual festivities held by the guides at the end of each summer season.

Zürich

House for Art

Kunsthaus Zürich, Heimplatz 1, CH-8001 Zürich
    ☎ 01 251 67 65
Mon 2–5; Tues–Fri 10–9; Sat, Sun 10–5.
© ▮ ☕

When the Kunsthaus – House for Art – was
opened in 1910, the Swiss avoided calling it 'a
museum', a word which suggested the princely
temples dedicated to the Muses to be found
elsewhere, rather than their own restrained and
more intimate Jugendstil building. Since its
foundation, the Kunsthaus, which is maintained
by the Zürich Art Society, has received many
important gifts and legacies, which have given it
international status.

The collections are in four sections. The first
contains medieval, especially German,
sculpture and Dutch, Italian and German
paintings of the Baroque period. The second
section comprises works by Zürich arists from
the 15th century to the present day, and the
third, 19th- and 20th-century Swiss paintings.
The fourth section is international and is
concerned with movements since
Impressionism, with important works by Monet,
Nabis, Munch, Kokoschka, Picasso, Chagall,
Rodin and Alberto Giacometti.

Swiss National Museum

Schweizerisches Landesmuseum, Museumstraße 2,
    CH-8001 Zürich   ☎ 01 221 10 10
Tues–Sun 10–5
Ⓕ ▮ ☕

The National Museum, opened in 1898, is the
only museum in Switzerland to be funded
completely by the Confederation, all the others
being the responsibility of the Cantons in which

**Gold bowl, 7th–6th century BC. Swiss
National Museum, Zurich.**

they are located. The Federal Act of 1890 set
out the task of the museum as being to 'create a
complete up-to-date exhibition of Swiss culture
from its beginnings to the present day'. With
this in mind, it has acquired only objects which
were made in Switzerland or which have been
used in the territory of modern Switzerland.

The collections include archaeological
material illustrating the prehistory and early
history of the country, weapons from the former
Zürich armoury – one of the largest collections
in Europe – flags, uniforms, gold and silver
objects, pewter, ceramics, glass, textiles,
costumes, coins, seals, stained glass – one of the
most important collections in the world –
sculptures, paintings, prints, furniture,
including complete interiors, clocks, musical
instruments, toys, agricultural implements and
craftsmen's tools and equipment.

Parts of the collections of the National
Museum are displayed in other buildings,
porcelain and faïence at the Guildhall 'Zur
Meisen' and domestic culture in the Museum of
Living Styles in the Bärengasse.

**Swiss daggers, late 16th-century. Swiss
National Museum, Zurich.**

Index of subjects

Index of museum names

Index of museums associated with individuals

Acknowledgements

The illustrations in this book are reproduced by courtesy of the museums to which they relate. Acknowledgement is also due to the following (references are to page numbers):
6 (left), Linster Fotografie; 8, Fotostudio Gartler; 12, MM Verlag; 16, NÖ Landesregierung Bildstelle; 20, ACL Brussels; 37, English Life Publications; 61, British Waterways Board Photo Library; 75, Peter Nahum Ltd; 76, National Museums and Galleries on Merseyside; 89, Woodmansterne Ltd, Watford; 91, Marlborough Gallery, London; 117, York Archaeological Trust; 130, Helga Anchers Fond; 136, Iittala-Nuutajärvi Oy; 146, Turku Provincial Museum; 153, Photo Képi Blanc; 162, Patrick David, Musée de Normandie; 167, Editions Pierre Véricel; 179, J. Mayer, Grasse; 200, Patrick Jean, Musées du Château des Ducs de Bretagne; 201, CDRP de Nice; 207, L'Association du Spectacle, Paris; 208, Jim Purcell/Cliché Musées Nationaux; 213, Photo Padrig Sicard; 217, A. Allemand; 221, J. Bergeon; 222, Cliché Musées Nationaux; 224, Cliché Musées Nationaux; 227, Photo Contact; 250, Rheinisches Bildarchiv: 100632; 259, Fotostudio/Gerd Remmer; 265, Gebr. Metz, Tübingen; 273, VSE

Bildarchiv–Nr. 868432; 275, Landesbildstelle Baden; 285, Bildarchiv Foto Marburg; 287, Ruth Kaiser, Viersen; 291, Fotostudio/Gerd Remmer; 298, Vesper & Trost, Rottweil; 301, Ditmar Schädel, Hildesheim; 310, Kreis Borker; 326, Dr A.M. O'Sullivan; 330, Commissioners of Public Works, Ireland; 346, Servizio Beni Culturali; 348, Azienda Autonoma di Soggiorno e Turismo, Manfredonia; 357, Foto Alinari/Collezione Agnesi; 362, Amministrazione delle Poste e delle Telecomunicazioni; 365, Scala, Firenze; 371, Swiss National Tourist Office, London; 375, Capital Photo Service, Schipol; 391, S.G. Zwart, Bussum; 393, Foto Tom Kroeze, Rotterdam; 396, Airphoto Netten, Maastricht; 449, Karl-Johan Johannson, Lycksele; 471, Maja Zimmermann, Winterthur.

Colour illustrations:
The Béguine's House: AVM Oostende; The Mackintosh House: Pitkin Colour Slides; Iittala Glass Museum: Iittala Nuutajärvi Oy; Grobet-Labadié Museum: Yves Gallois Photographe; Residence Museum: Die Bayerische Verwaltung der staatlichen Schlösser, Garten und Seen Museumsabteilung.